Praise for *Frederick Douglass*

"A stunning achievement. Blight captures an icon in full humanity. From riveting drama in slavery and Civil War, his Douglass rises into clairvoyant genius on the blinkered centrality of race in our struggle for freedom."

> —Taylor Branch, Pulitzer Prize–winning author
> of *America in the King Years 1954–63*

"David Blight's incandescent *Frederick Douglass* is a monumental achievement of biographical empathy, historical context, and grim comprehensiveness, a much-awaited masterpiece of a life that emblematized slavery as the problem of the nineteenth century, as was race that of Du Bois's twentieth, and the legacy of both the problem of our twenty-first century."

> —David Levering Lewis, Pulitzer Prize–winning author
> of *W.E.B. Du Bois: Biography of a Race, 1868–1919*

"*Frederick Douglass: Prophet of Freedom* is a triumph—elegantly written, with much new material about one of the most famous and important men in modern history. David Blight has created a vibrant and convincing portrait of a towering figure who was also, Blight says, 'thoroughly and beautifully human.'"

> —Annette Gordon-Reed, Pulitzer Prize–winning author
> of *The Hemingses of Monticello: An American Family*

"A work not only of stunning scholarship but also of literary artistry. David Blight's—and Frederick Douglass's—achievements have immeasurably enriched our understanding of slavery, abolitionism, the Civil War, and Reconstruction."

> —James M. McPherson, Pulitzer Prize–winning author
> of *Battle Cry of Freedom: The Civil War Era*

"Magnificently expansive and detailed. . . . [A] sensitive, careful, learned, creative, soulful exploration of Douglass's grand life."

—Randall Kennedy, *The Atlantic*

"The most comprehensive biography of Douglass ever written. . . . Will likely stand as definitive for decades to come."

—Clayton Butler, *The Philadelphia Inquirer*

"David Blight brilliantly illustrates both the perils and possibilities of our national history through a rich and humane portrait of a man and his times. This is a remarkable book about a remarkable American and his enduring impact."

—Drew Gilpin Faust, former president, Harvard University, and author of *This Republic of Suffering: Death and the American Civil War*

"No American of his generation did more than Douglass, both in word and deed, to propel his people, and the nation, toward a reckoning with its original sin. Now he is brought vividly and delightfully to life once more in the flesh and bones of this masterful biography by one of our greatest historians. . . . A monumental achievement."

—Henry Louis Gates Jr., Alphonse Fletcher University Professor, Harvard University

"David Blight's magnificent book bares the radical fury and inner dilemmas that drove one of the greatest American lives. No scholar has known Frederick Douglass better, or written about him with such emotional as well as historical acuity. It is a biography truly worthy of its eloquent, conflicted, elusive, and heroic subject."

—Sean Wilentz, George Henry Davis 1886 Professor of American History, Princeton University, and author of *The Rise of American Democracy: Jefferson to Lincoln*

"David Blight's career-long fascination with Frederick Douglass has finally given historians the definitive biography of one of America's leading prophets of freedom. Blight's work not only humanizes Douglass but it also reframes our understanding of the nineteenth century through the lens of the life of Frederick Douglass."

—Lonnie G. Bunch III, Director, National Museum of African American History and Culture

"Good historians make the best biographers. David Blight, one of our finest historians, has skillfully placed Frederick Douglass into his time and place and given us a psychologically penetrating portrait enriched by new details grounded in thorough research. This is the best biography of Douglass ever written, the one Douglass has long deserved."

—James Oakes, author of *The Radical and the Republican: Frederick Douglass, Abraham Lincoln, and the Triumph of Antislavery Politics*

"Never before has Frederick Douglass's life been portrayed with such scope and authority. . . . David Blight's probing biography will be indispensable for anyone hoping to understand this towering figure in the central drama of American history."

—Andrew Delbanco, Alexander Hamilton Professor of American Studies, Columbia University, and author of *The War Before the War: Fugitive Slaves and the Struggle for America's Soul from the Revolution to the Civil War*

"Astonishing in its breadth and depth, and told with exceptional sensitivity, this account of an epic life that intersected with black freedom and violent white backlash is also a story of rage and forgiveness, loneliness and charisma, bitter discouragement and fervent faith. All the way through this soaring, page-turning book, the piercing wisdom of the extraordinary Douglass echoes and endures into our own troubled century."

—Martha Hodes, author of *Mourning Lincoln*

"David Blight's beautifully written *Frederick Douglass* uses previously unplumbed archives to give us the deepest portrait yet of one of America's greatest intellectuals. The radical thinker and revolutionary is revealed here in all his complexity by a gifted and learned historian with an ear for Douglass's oracular voice and an eye for the tragedies of nineteenth-century America. This is a biography worthy of the man."

—Wendy Warren, author of *New England Bound: Slavery and Colonization in Early America*

FREDERICK

DOUGLASS

PROPHET *of* FREEDOM

DAVID W. BLIGHT

Simon & Schuster Paperbacks

NEW YORK   LONDON   TORONTO   SYDNEY   NEW DELHI

Simon & Schuster Paperbacks
An Imprint of Simon & Schuster, Inc.
1230 Avenue of the Americas
New York, NY 10020

First Simon & Schuster trade paperback edition January 2020

SIMON & SCHUSTER PAPERBACKS and colophon are registered
trademarks of Simon & Schuster, Inc.

For information about special discounts for bulk purchases, please contact Simon
& Schuster Special Sales at 1-866-506-1949 or business@simonandschuster.com.

The Simon & Schuster Speakers Bureau can bring authors to your live event. For
more information or to book an event, contact the Simon & Schuster Speakers
Bureau at 1-866-248-3049 or visit our website at www.simonspeakers.com.

Interior design by Paul Dippolito

Manufactured in the United States of America

1   3   5   7   9   10   8   6   4   2

The Library of Congress has cataloged the hardcover edition as follows:

Names: Blight, David W., author.
Title: Frederick Douglass : prophet of freedom / David W. Blight.
Description: New York : Simon & Schuster, 2018. | Includes bibliographical
references and index.
Identifiers: LCCN 2018007511 | ISBN 9781416590316 (hardback) | ISBN
1416590315 (hardback)
Subjects: LCSH: Douglass, Frederick, 1818–1895. | Abolitionists—United
States—Biography. | African American abolitionists—United States—Biography.
| Slaves—United States—Biography. | Antislavery movements—United
States—History—19th century. | BISAC: BIOGRAPHY & AUTOBIOGRAPHY /
Historical. | HISTORY / United States / 19th Century.
Classification: LCC E449.D75 B557 2018 | DDC 973.8092 [B]—dc23
LC record available at https://lccn.loc.gov/2018007511

ISBN 978-1-4165-9031-6
ISBN 978-1-4165-9032-3 (pbk)
ISBN 978-1-4165-9388-1 (ebook)

Front endpaper: Frederick Douglass, February–April 1863, Westfield,
Massachusetts, Thomas Painter Collins photographer, *carte de visite*.
Rear endpaper: Frederick Douglass, May 10, 1894, Denis Bourdon photographer,
Notman Photograph Company, Boston, Massachusetts.

To Walter O. Evans and Linda J. Evans and
to Jeffrey Brown Ferguson, 1964–2018

There is a prophet within us, forever whispering that behind the seen lies the immeasurable unseen.

—FREDERICK DOUGLASS, 1862

CONTENTS

Introduction   xiii

1 First Things   1

2 A Childhood of Extremes   19

3 The Silver Trump of Knowledge   35

4 Baltimore Dreams   48

5 Now for Mischief!   67

6 Living a New Life   87

7 This Douglass!   102

8 Garrisonian in Mind and Body   116

9 The Thought of Writing for a Book!   138

10 Send Back the Money!   156

11 Demagogue in Black   178

12 My Faithful Friend Julia   202

13 By the Rivers of Babylon   228

14 My Voice, My Pen, or My Vote   252

15 John Brown Could Die for the Slave   280

16 Secession: Taught by Events   310

17 The Kindling Spirit of His Battle Cry   335

18 The Anthem of the Redeemed   355

19 Men of Color to Arms!   385

20 Abolition War, Abolition Peace   416

21 Sacred Efforts   440

22 Othello's Occupation Was Gone   464

23 All the Leeches That Feed on You   495

24 Ventures   520

25 What Will Peace Among the Whites Bring?   551

26 An Important and Lucrative Office   581

27 Joys and Sorrows at Cedar Hill   610

28 Watchman, What of the Night?   638

29 Born Traveler   665

30 Haiti: Servant Between Two Masters   691

31 If American Conscience Were Only Half-Alive   714

    Epilogue: Then Douglass Passed   745

    Acknowledgments   765

    Notes   771

    Illustration Credits   859

    Index   863

INTRODUCTION

Behold, I have put my words in your mouth . . .
to pluck up and to break down,
to destroy and to overthrow,
to build and to plant.

—JEREMIAH 1:9–10

In his speech at the dedication of the National Museum of African American History and Culture in Washington, DC, September 24, 2016, President Barack Obama delivered what he termed a "clear-eyed view" of a tragic and triumphant history of black Americans in the United States. He spoke of a history that is central to the larger American story, one that is both contradictory and extraordinary. He likened the African American experience to the infinite depths of Shakespeare and Scripture. The "embrace of truth as best we can know it," said the president, is "where real patriotism lies." Naming some of the major pivots of the country's past, Obama wrapped his central theme in a remarkable sentence about the Civil War era: "We've buttoned up our Union blues to join the fight for our freedom, we've railed against injustice for decade upon decade, a lifetime of struggle and progress and enlightenment that we see etched in Frederick Douglass's mighty leonine gaze."[1]

How Americans react to Douglass's gaze, indeed how we gaze back at his visage, and more important, how we read him, appropriate him, or engage his legacies, informs how we use our past to determine who we are. Douglass's life and writing emerge from nearly the full scope of the nineteenth century, representative of the best and the worst in the American spirit. Douglass constantly probed the ironies of America's contradictions over slavery and race; few Americans used Shakespeare and the Bible to comprehend his story and that of his people as much as Douglass; and there may be no better example of an American radical patriot than the slave who became a lyrical prophet of freedom, natural rights, and human equality. Obama channeled Douglass in his dedication speech; knowingly or not, so do many people today.

Born Frederick Augustus Washington Bailey, a slave, in Talbot County, Maryland, in February 1818, the future Frederick Douglass was the son of Harriet Bailey, one of five daughters of Betsy Bailey, and with some likelihood his mother's white owner. He saw his mother for the last time in 1825, though he hardly knew her. She died the following year. Douglass lived twenty years as a slave and nearly nine years as a fugitive slave subject to recapture. From the 1840s to his death in 1895 he attained international fame as an abolitionist, editor, orator of almost unparalleled stature, and the author of three autobiographies that are classics of the genre. As a public man he began his abolitionist career two decades before America would divide and fight a civil war over slavery that he openly welcomed. Douglass was born in a backwater of the slave society of the South just as steamboats appeared in bays and on American rivers, and before the telegraph, the railroad, and the rotary press changed human mobility and consciousness. He died after the emergence of electric lights, the telephone, and the invention of the phonograph. The renowned orator and traveler loved and used most of these elements of modernity and technology.

Douglass was the most photographed American of the nineteenth century, explained in this book and especially by the intrepid research of three other scholars I rely upon.[2] Although it can never really be measured, he may also have been, along with Mark Twain, the most widely traveled American public figure of his century. By the 1890s, in sheer miles and countless numbers of speeches, he had few rivals as a lecturer in the golden age of oratory. It is likely that more Americans heard Douglass speak than any other public figure of his times. Indeed, to see or hear Douglass became a kind of wonder of the American world. He struggled as well, with the pleasures and perils of fame as much as anyone else in his century, with the possible exceptions of General Ulysses S. Grant or P. T. Barnum. Douglass's dilemma with fame was a matter of decades, not merely of moments, and fraught with racism.

The orator and writer lived to see and interpret black emancipation, to work actively for women's rights long before they were achieved, to realize the civil rights triumphs and tragedies of Reconstruction, and to witness and contribute to America's economic and international expansion in the Gilded Age. He lived to the age of lynching and Jim Crow laws, when

America collapsed into retreat from the very victories and revolutions in race relations he had helped to win. He played a pivotal role in America's Second Founding out of the apocalypse of the Civil War, and he very much wished to see himself as a founder and a defender of the Second American Republic.

In one lifetime of antislavery, literary, and political activism Douglass was many things, and this set of apparent paradoxes make his story so attractive to biographers, as well as to so many constituencies today. He was a radical thinker and a proponent of classic nineteenth-century political liberalism; at different times he hated and loved his country; he was a ferocious critic of the United States and all of its hypocrisies, but also, after emancipation, became a government bureaucrat, a diplomat, and a voice for territorial expansion; he strongly believed in self-reliance and demanded an activist-interventionist government at all levels to free slaves, defeat the Confederacy, and protect black citizens against terror and discrimination. Douglass was a serious constitutional thinker, and few Americans have ever analyzed race with more poignancy and nuance than this mostly self-taught genius with words. He was a radical editor, writer, and activist, informed by a hard-earned pragmatism. Douglass was Jim-Crowed more times than he could count, but loved the Declaration of Independence, the natural-rights tradition, and especially the reinvented US Constitution fashioned in Reconstruction. He fought against mob violence, but believed in certain kinds of revolutionary violence. In his own career he heroically tried to forge a livelihood with his voice and pen, but fundamentally was not a self-made man, an image and symbol he touted in a famous speech, and through which modern conservatives have adopted him as a proponent of individualism. He truly believed women were equal and ought to have all fundamental rights, but he conducted his personal life sometimes as a patriarch in a difficult marriage and while overseeing a large, often dysfunctional extended family.

Context and timing are often all. As James Baldwin wrote in 1948, casting sentiment and celebration aside, "Frederick Douglass was first of all a man—honest within the limitations of his character and his time, quite frequently misguided, sometimes pompous, gifted but not always a hero, and no saint at all." Baldwin's unabashed bluntness is a good place for a biographer to begin to make judgments from the sources. But so are the interpretations of a very different writer, the former neoconservative turned neoliberal journalist and political theorist Michael Lind. In 1995 Lind rejected both a leftist multiculturalism and a conservative self-help individualism and called for a "new nationalism," which he termed a "multiracial/mixed race Trans-America," with Douglass as the model. Telescoping the orator though time, Lind called Douglass "the greatest American of all time."

Indeed the old fugitive slave has become in the early twenty-first century a malleable figure adopted by all elements in the political spectrum, not least by current Republicans, who have claimed Douglass—quite ahistorically—as their own by elevating a single feature of his thought, black self-reliance, at the expense of his enduring radicalism. At the unveiling ceremony of the statue of Douglass in the US Capitol in 2013, chosen by the District of Columbia as one of the two representatives to which each state, and the District, are entitled, congressional Republicans walked around proudly sporting large buttons that read FREDERICK DOUGLASS WAS A REPUBLICAN.[3] Douglass descendants present, as well as some of us scholars with, shall we say, different training and research, smiled and endured. Whose Douglass? is a modern question rife with meaning.

This book seeks Douglass's complexity in all its forms, but never sidesteps his essential radicalism in a search for heroes we can hold dear and in common. Douglass was and is a hero; he has been all but adopted as a national figure in Ireland, Scotland, and Britain. His *Narrative* is read all over the world. He has appeared in countless murals, satirical political cartoons, twenty-first-century works of fiction, in paintings, and in a great deal of poetry. The sheer complexity of his thought and life makes him an icon held in some degree of commonality. He was brilliant, courageous, and possessed a truly uncommon endurance. He wrote many words that will last forever. His literary genius ranks with that of many of America's greatest writers of his century. But he was also vain, arrogant at times, and hypersensitive to slights. He did not take well to rivals who challenged his position as the greatest spokesman of his race, although he also mentored many younger black writers and leaders. He liked being on a pedestal and did not intend to get knocked off. Douglass was thoroughly and beautifully human.

Above all, Douglass is remembered most for telling his personal story—the slave who willed his own freedom, mastered the master's language, saw to the core of the meaning of slavery, both for individuals and for the nation, and then captured the multiple meanings of freedom—as idea and reality, of mind and body—as perhaps no one else ever has in America.

This book exists because of my lifetime interest in Douglass. But I would not have written it had I not encountered the extraordinary private collection of Douglass material owned by Walter O. Evans of Savannah, Georgia. The Evans collection, cited so many times in my notes, makes possible many new insights into the final third of Douglass's life. The younger Douglass—the heroic escaped slave and emerging abolitionist—is better known, in part because of the author's first two autobiographies. The older Douglass, from Reconstruction to the end of his life in 1895, has never been so accessible or rendered so fascinating and complicated as in the Evans collection. This biography is, I hope, the fullest account ever written of the last third of Douglass's complex and epic life.

Several primary themes inform and give texture to my portrait of Douglass. Douglass was a man of *words*; spoken and written language was the only major weapon of protest, persuasion, or power that he ever possessed. Throughout I try to demonstrate the origins and growth of this man's amazing facility to find the words to explain America's racial condition as well as the human condition. In one way, this book is the biography of a *voice*.

The autobiographies are themselves a major theme of the book. Douglass wrote and rewrote his life in three remarkable autobiographies; all Douglass scholars are deeply dependent upon them. But the first major problem in writing Douglass's biography is that the subject himself is in the way. The three narratives, over twelve hundred pages in all, are infinitely rich as sources of his traumatic youth and his public life of more than fifty years. In the memoirs he is a self-made hero who leaves a great deal unsaid, hidden from his readers and his biographers. Douglass invited us into his life over and over, and it is a rich literary and historical feast to read the music of Douglass's words. But as he sits majestically at the head of the table, it is as if he slips out of the room right when we so wish to know more—anything—about his more private thoughts, motivations, and memories of the many conflicts in his personal life. Confronting the autobiographer in Douglass is both a pleasure and a peril as his biographer.

Another guiding theme is Douglass's deep grounding in the Bible, especially the Old Testament. From his earliest speeches on the abolition circuit, through his political emergence in the 1850s, in his stunning orations and editorials about the Civil War as an apocalyptic break in history somehow under God's intervention, to his nearly endless postwar lecture tours, Douglass rooted his own story and especially the story of African Americans in the oldest and most powerful stories of the Hebrew prophets. In America the people had turned from or never embraced their creeds or their God; the American Jerusalem, its temples and its horrid system of slavery, had to be destroyed; the nation had to face exile or extinction and bloody retribution; and only then could the people and the nation experience renewal, reinvention, and a possible new history. Douglass was a living prophet of an American destruction, exile, war for its existence, and redemption. Jeremiah and Isaiah, as well as other prophets, were his guides; they gave him story, metaphor, resolve, and ancient wisdom in order to deliver his ferocious critique of slavery and his country before emancipation, and then his strained but hopeful narrative of its future after 1865.

It is easy to call Douglass a prophet; this book attempts to show how he merits that lofty title. "The prophet is human," wrote the great Jewish theologian Abraham Heschel, "yet he employs notes one octave too high for our ears. He experiences moments that defy our understanding. He is neither 'a singing saint' nor 'a moralizing poet,' but an assaulter of the mind. Often his words begin to burn where conscience ends."[4] Careful readers of Douglass will at times stop on passages that make them shudder or melt in recognition, as their minds are assaulted or perhaps uplifted. This book attempts to demonstrate how Douglass came by his King James cadences, as well as how he used biblical story to break down and rebuild, as Jeremiah recollected his own charge, an American world. Douglass succeeded and failed, as did the prophets of old.

From the middle of his turbulent life on, a primary theme of the book is how Douglass moved along crooked paths from a radical outsider, through time and transcendent events, to a political insider. During the greatest pivot of American history—the Civil War era—this man of language reaped great change to transform from a radical abolitionist into a Republican Party functionary. These changes are historical, inextricably linked to events and time, not merely a matter of moral growth or decline; and they provide a model for many other leaders, particularly African American, who have undergone the same process in the 150 years since. The outsider-to-insider story especially animates the second half of the book, and it caused one of Douglass's most challenging psychic dilemmas. He repeatedly faced the question of how uncompromising radicalism could mix with a learned pragmatism to try to influence real power, to determine how to condemn the princes and their laws but also influence and eventually join them.

Another theme that drives this book is the turbulent relationship of Douglass's public and private lives. Throughout I try to keep a balance between these two registers of any person's story. In Douglass's case, he married twice, first to Anna Murray Douglass, a black woman born free in Maryland who remained largely illiterate but the center of his home life through many dislocations for forty-four years, and second to Helen Pitts Douglass, a highly educated white woman twenty years his junior and a remarkably compatible companion during his final decade. Douglass sustained important friendships with two white European women, Julia Griffiths from England and Ottilie Assing from Germany, both of whom became extremely important influences of differing kinds in his life. Most important, though, Douglass and Anna had five children, four of whom lived into adulthood. Among them they produced twenty-one grandchildren for the Douglasses. During the last quarter or so of the famous man's life, this extended family, which came to include even some fictive kin and a variety of protégés, became financially and often emotionally dependent on the patriarch of a clan often in conflict with itself. Douglass sustained backbreaking and health-threatening lecture tours in his older years in part to support this extended family and a big house on a hill in Washington, DC, near the centers of Gilded Age power that he could only partially penetrate. This story is at once Douglass's own unique saga and very modern. He experienced at least two emotional breakdowns in his life, and both can be explained in great part by the treacherous character of this public-private divide.

And finally, this book probes how Douglass was a many-sided intellectual, an editor, a writer in numerous genres—memoir, short-form editorials, extended speeches, and one work of fiction. He wrote and spoke millions of words; his trove of commentary contains beauty, brilliant storytelling, sermons, political stump speeches, and assaults on the mind that are his legacy and the essential reason we know him. In roughly the last forty years Douglass has more and more been treated by scholars as a political philosopher, a constitutional and legal analyst, an author capable of prose poetry, a proponent of the natural-rights tradition, a self-conscious voice of and about the nature of memory, a religious and theological thinker, a journalist, and an advocate of broader public education. Today Douglass is taught and examined in law schools, in history, English, art, political science, and philosophy departments, in high schools, graduate schools, and community reading groups. In this book I try at all times to balance as best I can the narrative of his life with analyses of his evolving mind, to give his ideas a central place in his unforgettable story.

It is Douglass's story, though, that lasts and gives and instructs. There is no greater voice of America's terrible transformation from slavery to freedom than Douglass's. For all who wish to escape from outward or inward captivity, they would do well to feel the pulses of this life, and to read the words of this voice. And then go act in the world. In the final lines of *My Bondage and My Freedom* in 1855, as the politics of the slavery crisis embroiled the nation, Douglass wrote that he would never forget his "own humble origins" nor cease "while Heaven lends me ability, to use my voice, my pen, or my vote, to advocate the great and primary work of the universal and unconditional emancipation of my entire race."[5] As we look upon Douglass's leonine gaze in our own time, we may recognize that such universal work continues.

Chapter 1

FIRST THINGS

Genealogical trees do not flourish among slaves.
—FREDERICK DOUGLASS, 1855

Throughout the spring morning of April 14, 1876, a huge crowd, largely African American, began to assemble in the vicinity of Seventh and K Streets in Washington, DC. It had been eleven Aprils since the end of the Civil War, and eleven years to the day since the assassination of Abraham Lincoln. A parade involving nearly every African American organization in the city was about to step off at noon en route to the unveiling of an extraordinary monument to Lincoln.[1] The city had witnessed many remarkable parades since the end of the war, but this one would be different.

The day was declared a public holiday in Washington, and flags above the Capitol as well as other government buildings flew at half-mast. At the head of the procession rode a contingent of twenty-seven mounted police, followed by three companies of black militia troops, headed by the Philharmonic Band of Georgetown. Numerous other cornet bands, marching drum corps, youth clubs in colorful uniforms, and fraternal orders from both Washington and Baltimore filled in the long line with pride and pomp. The Knights of St. Augustine carried a large banner with a painting of the martyred Lincoln. Horse-drawn carriages carried, among others, the black, Virginia freeborn professor, and dean of the Howard University law school, John Mercer Langston, who would perform as master of ceremonies, and the orator of the day, a newly arrived resident of Washington, the famed abolitionist and editor Frederick Douglass, who had grown up a slave across Chesapeake Bay on the Eastern Shore of Maryland.[2] Langston and Douglass were soon to become open political and personal rivals, but on this day they joined in one of the most important public events of their lives.

The procession moved westward along K Street to Seventeenth Street,

then south a few blocks and through the grounds of the Executive Mansion (the White House, which in those days was not walled off by security), and on to Pennsylvania Avenue. The parade traveled eastward directly
toward the Capitol, turning briefly right on First Street West, then around
the south Capitol grounds to First Street East, and finally on to East Capitol Street. For eleven more blocks the bands, marchers, and carriages passed
throngs of people until they reached Eleventh Street, at the edge of fields
and an emerging residential square. The setting was much better than on
the Washington Mall, which at that time was swampy and unhealthy, used
in places as a dump.[3]

A festive crowd awaited the parade, and a tall statue stood draped and
concealed in flags and bunting. Next to the monument a stage and large
speaker's stand awaited a distinguished array of guests. President Ulysses
S. Grant, now nearing the end of his second and final term in office, arrived before the parade reached the park and was accompanied by many
US senators—including Oliver P. Morton, George Boutwell, John Sherman,
and Blanche K. Bruce—members of the president's cabinet, the justices of
the US Supreme Court, many members of the House of Representatives,
and a large contingent of other government officials as well as some former Union generals. Near the platform, the Marine Band struck up "Hail,
Columbia" as the speakers walked from their carriages and the hundreds of
marchers found their places in the vast audience.[4]

As the ceremony began, Bishop John M. Brown of the AME Church delivered an invocation, and J. Henri Burch of Louisiana read the Emancipation Proclamation. At the conclusion of the reading, the band played "La
Marseillaise." Langston introduced James E. Yeatman, a St. Louis banker
and head of the Western Sanitary Commission, the organization that had
led the fund-raising among the former slaves and black Civil War veterans
of Missouri and elsewhere in the country who provided the nearly $20,000
that paid for the monument. Yeatman explained how a former slave woman,
Charlotte Scott, had donated the first $5, and how the commission had
sought the American sculptor Thomas Ball, who resided in Italy, to con-
ceive and create the statue.[5]

This remarkable monument, the Freedmen's Memorial, as it became
known, was many years in the making, the result of various designs and
changes in purpose and meaning. In Yeatman's lengthy remarks, he told
of Ball's "labor of love," his "tribute to American patriotism" through the
"gratitude of the freed people." In a triumphal narrative, Yeatman described
how Ball sent four photographs of his original model of a standing Lincoln

The Freedmen's Memorial (Emancipation Monument).
Unveiled April 1876, Washington, DC. It stands today
in the middle of Lincoln Park. Thomas Ball sculptor.

and a kneeling slave to the Sanitary Commission, which in turn sent him a photograph of a former fugitive slave named Archer Alexander, whom the sculptor then depicted, with muscular torso, looking upward, his fist clenched, and in part breaking his own chains under the president's guiding arm. Since Ball had been convinced by the commission and by the image of Alexander to alter his conception from a "kneeling slave . . . represented as perfectly passive" (freedom given), to an "emancipated slave [as] agent in his own deliverance" (freedom seized), Yeatman concluded that the monument was an "ideal group . . . converted into the literal truth of history."[6]

Such a ceremonial day in the spring sunshine, surrounded by the highest officials of the federal government, at a monument unveiling unlike any other that had occurred in America, was hardly an occasion for literal truth, whether in bronze or in words. But through all the pageantry would waft some powerful symbolic truths in unforgettable language. Langston stepped to the podium and asked President Grant to come forward to pull the cord and unveil the monument. As Grant stood still for a long moment, the entire crowd hushed in rapt silence. Not a good ceremonial speaker, the president delivered no remarks. As the flags and draperies fell away, the throng broke into loud applause and shouts, cannon were fired nearby in a field, and the band struck up "Hail to the Chief." Those up close could see on the base of the monument the word EMANCIPATION, cut in large letters. Langston next read two congratulatory letters from people who had played roles in bringing about the monument. A poem, "Lincoln," written by a young black Washington poet, Cordelia Ray, was recited. Then, as parts of the crowd had settled into chairs and others felt the spring breezes over their heads, Langston finally introduced Douglass, orator of the day.[7]

Along with Langston and many other black leaders, Douglass had strongly supported various efforts to build a major Lincoln and emancipation monument since at least September 1865. That month he had called for a humble memorial that "would express one of the holiest sentiments of the human heart." His remark came in the immediate post–Civil War period when many white sponsors of such a Lincoln monument openly called on blacks to demonstrate "gratitude" for their liberation. Douglass had never been one to believe he had to prove his gratitude or dignity or even his acumen to whites generally. He had long understood that a national monument to Lincoln would be a major civic undertaking as well as a statement about the place of black people in America. From his own visceral experience as a slave and fugitive slave who plotted his own escape, he fully understood just how much freedom for black Americans was both seized and given. Douglass had long favored what he called a "people's monument . . . without distinction of color," a tribute that would reflect the story of interracial abolitionism that he believed had helped bring Lincoln to the Emancipation Proclamation, as well as to the new, potentially reimagined nation of 1865, devoted to a future of "common rights and common equality before the law."[8]

But as Douglass rose to speak in April 1876 to finally dedicate such a monument, he, the recognized voice of black America, had prepared a speech of remarkable honesty, poignancy, and present-minded historical insight. "First things are always interesting," he declared, "and this is one of our first things. It is the first time that, in this form and manner, we have sought to do honor to an American great man." Douglass made it clear that he spoke, at least at first, only as an African American, for his race. The event was a first for a second reason that Douglass did not mention: black people had never before been represented on a national monument.[9] In this charged atmosphere of artistic and political *firsts*, on the eve of the nation's centennial and amid the deeply disturbing decline and violent overthrow of Reconstruction in the South, Douglass struck notes both majestic and som-

ber. His speech assumed the tone of a requiem, tempered by modest celebration, restrained nationalism, and redemptive hope.

African Americans had tenuously arrived finally and openly in the center of the country's highest affairs. Douglass made it clear that the unveiling
of this monument to Lincoln and emancipation was a "national act," performed by citizens in the place where "every pulsation of the national heart
can be heard, felt, and reciprocated." He insisted on an initial history lesson,
referring to the "vast and wonderful change in our condition" (black freedom and citizenship). No such open commemoration by blacks in Washington would have been tolerated before the Civil War's transformations,
without opening "flood-gates of wrath and violence." Douglass congratulated all, white and black, famous and ordinary, on this "contrast between
then and now." The orator conditioned his audience for the harder truths
and starker metaphors to come by letting them feel the "long and dark history" of slavery as a matter of the past, replaced now by "liberty, progress,
and enlightenment." [10]

No African American speaker had ever faced this kind of captive audience, composed of all the leadership of the federal government in one place;
and no such speaker would ever again until Barack Obama was inaugurated
president in January 2009. Douglass, a master ironist about America, did
not miss this moment of supreme symbolism. He named each contingent
of every branch of the government sitting before him, including President
Grant, Chief Justice Morrison Waite, senators and representatives, cabinet
officials, all acknowledged as "wise and patriotic." In this moment, the government was something sacred and enduring, newly remade from recent
near destruction, the protector of a reconsecrated freedom for whites and
blacks. The high officials may have smiled and felt their chests swell at the
former slave's patriotic language. Douglass struck chords of civil religion
as he described the "stately pillars and majestic dome of the Capitol" and
the District's springtime surroundings as "our church." In this new America, "all races, colors, and conditions of men" composed "our congregation."
"We the colored people," proclaimed Douglass, "rejoicing in our blood-
bought freedom," now brought the same experience and sentiment, like all
other Americans who lay in nearby Arlington Cemetery. "For the first time
in the history of our people," the orator proudly announced, "and in the
history of the whole American people, we join in this high worship." [11]

Then Douglass turned to the memory of Lincoln, and the speech assumed a different tone. While claiming a place for his people in honoring the martyred president, Douglass suddenly used words that may have

shocked some in his audience: "It must be admitted, truth compels me to admit, even here in the presence of the monument we have erected to his memory, Abraham Lincoln was not . . . either our man or our model. In his interests, in his associations, in his habits of thought, and in his prejudices, he was a white man." Douglass must have caused some squirming in the chairs as he injected race so forthrightly into his rhetorical tribute. Grant might have inwardly flinched. It was as though Douglass had decided to give voice to the kneeling slave on the statue, who would now say thank you as well as speak some bitter truths about a real history, and not merely allow the occasion to be one of proud, national self-congratulation. It was as though Douglass was saying—you gave me this unique platform today, and I will therefore teach these lessons about the jagged and tragic paths by which black people achieved freedom in the agony of war. "He [Lincoln] was preeminently the white man's president," Douglass continued in his forceful baritone, "entirely devoted to the welfare of the white man. He was ready and willing at any time during the first years of his administration to deny, postpone, and sacrifice the rights of humanity in the colored people to promote the welfare of the white people of the country." [12]

Douglass employed a stunning level of directness for such a ceremonial occasion. He did not merely turn his moment in the national sun into a reminiscence about a good war and glorious outcomes. Lincoln's growth to greatness and to the role of Emancipator, he insisted, must first be seen through the disappointments of his first year in office. Douglass would not consider the triumphal memory of 1865 without first pulling his audience through the pain of 1861. During the secession crisis and into 1862, he remembered, Lincoln had promised to support all constitutional protections of slavery in the Southern states. He "was willing to pursue, recapture, and send back the fugitive slave to his master," a position Douglass had utterly condemned during the crisis. The former abolitionist forgot nothing of Lincoln's record on race and slavery, especially the episode in 1862 when in a meeting with five black ministers at the White House, the president "strangely told us that we were to leave the land in which we were born," or when "he told us he would save the Union with slavery" and "refused to retaliate our murder and torture as colored soldiers." [13] The litany of Lincoln's sins against the cause of abolition was long and ugly, especially for this celebratory moment. But Douglass rejected empty politeness.

Then came the most striking and lasting words of the speech. "The race to which we belong were not the special objects of his [Lincoln's] consideration," Douglass declared to the ages. "My white fellow-citizens . . . you are the children of Abraham Lincoln. We are at best only his stepchildren; children by adoption, children by forces of circumstances and necessity." But one of those stepchildren was lecturing the nation and its leaders on that April day. "To you," he told whites in the audience, belonged the prime responsibility of honoring Lincoln. Then, he implored them to let the step-children have their place in the commemoration. "Despise not the humble offering we this day unveil," he pleaded, "for while Abraham Lincoln saved for you a country, he delivered us from a bondage, according to Jefferson, one hour of which was worse than ages of the oppression your fathers rose in rebellion to oppose." [14]

Although blacks' faith in Lincoln, who had "tarried long in the mountain," had been sorely tested, Douglass found a middle way, a historically balanced remembrance of Lincoln in this new moment of national trial. Through a "comprehensive view . . . in the stern logic of events, and in view of the divinity that shapes our ends," he said, blacks, despite grief and bewilderment at the president's slow actions, concluded "that the hour and the man of our redemption had somehow met in the person of Abraham Lincoln." In Douglass's analysis, historical circumstance had in the end made Lincoln the "head of a great movement." Most important, Douglass used a refrain that formed the argument of his speech. "Under his rule," he repeatedly declared, all manner of great change came about: slaves were lifted from bondage to self-aware liberty; black men exchanged rags for Union soldiers' uniforms; two hundred thousand marched in the cause; the black republic of Haiti received recognition; the domestic slave trade was abolished and a slave trader hanged as a pirate and murderer; and the "Confederate States, based upon the idea that our race must be slaves . . . [was] battered to pieces and scattered to the four winds." And "under his rule," the "immortal paper," the Emancipation Proclamation, emerged, "making slavery forever impossible in the United States." [15]

Douglass had named the pain and betrayal of ages. Now he entered the celebration. He remembered poignantly his own special experience of Emancipation night, January 1, 1863, in Boston. He acknowledged that Lincoln had had to work toward emancipation against virulently racist opposition and therefore had to find the delicate method and timing for such a revolution. He recognized how deeply intertwined Union and emancipation had become, not least because of Lincoln's brilliant political statesmanship. Hence, "viewed from the genuine abolition ground, Mr. Lincoln seemed tardy, cold, dull, and indifferent; but measuring him from the sentiment of his country, a sentiment he was bound as a statesman to consult, he was swift, zealous, radical, and determined." [16] As the mature political activist and writer, observer of world-historical transformations and betrayals, Douglass had learned much about both the burden and the uses of ambivalence.

In the rhetorical twists and turns of this complex speech, Douglass had one overriding target—the declension and betrayal of Reconstruction in the South by the federal government. "Under his rule and in due time" was Douglass's way of saying not simply that Lincoln had personally saved and reimagined the Union, as well as liberated the slaves, but that the entire nation had done so and carried the burden of responsibility. That black freedom and the fate of the Civil War constitutional amendments—the civic lives and personal survival of the freedpeople—were on the line in the South at that very moment, and that Grant and the government had to be called to action, formed Douglass's essential subject. But, it already seemed too late.

By 1876, a pivotal general election year and the nation's centennial celebration, only three Southern states remained "unredeemed" by the white counterrevolution against Reconstruction. Each of them—Louisiana, South Carolina, and Florida—had Republican-controlled regimes teetering on the brink of political extinction at the hands of terror, murder, and election fraud organized in the service of the Democratic Party and white supremacy. Indeed, the white South's revival and takeover of its political fate, and the systematic destruction of black civil and political rights as well as economic independence, had left a cloud of despair over what remained of any Reconstruction policy by the Grant administration. Worst of all, the experiment in racial democracy born of emancipation and the remaking of the US Constitution—the dream come true in 1865 and the legacy Douglass had for more than ten years trumpeted as the long-term hope of his people—not only lay in tatters; it had been crushed by widespread, unpunished violence. Many hundreds murdered trying to vote or establish livelihoods, thousands more tortured or intimidated away from voting, and ballot boxes stuffed or stolen: this was the sorrowful state of American democracy in that spring of 1876. [17] Each note of either cautionary woe or modest celebration in Douglass's dedication speech at the monument with Lincoln standing majestically over the kneeling, subservient former slave needs to be considered through this story of the impending fateful defeat of Reconstruction. At one and the same time, the speech was Douglass's careful statement of the great growth and change that Lincoln had presided over during the revolutionary war years and a lament over the apparent success of the counter-revolution against it.

As he concluded, Douglass gave his audience a thoroughly mythic Lincoln, a gift from freed slaves to the nation's best sense of itself, despite all the terror emanating from the South. He brought the Illinoisan into the community of freedmen—the president had been "a man of work, a son of toil . . . the plebeian . . . honest boatman" whose "moral training" came from labor. On this anniversary of the assassination, Douglass culled that national nightmare for all its redemptive symbolism as well as power in the politics of memory. Lincoln's murder, he declared, was not only the "hell-black . . . revenge" of Confederate agents, but "the crowning crime of slavery" itself. As Reconstruction fell to new hell-black actions by ex-Confederates, Douglass spoke to and for the black people who had planned and provided this event. This was a "good work for our race today," he announced, "fastening ourselves to a name . . . immortal," and "defending ourselves" against all who would "scourge us beyond the range of human brotherhood."[18] Douglass's Freedmen's Memorial Address was the tortured effort of a national stepchild to find the words that might still make the high and mighty of the United States hold the remaining lifeline to his people. It was an extraordinary "first thing" he dearly hoped would not be a last thing.

Douglass knew something of "toil" and "honest boatmen"; he was born a slave within yards of the Tuckahoe River on Maryland's Eastern Shore. He traveled in a sloop out the Wye and Miles Rivers and up the Chesapeake Bay to Baltimore as a youth, and he crossed the Susquehanna and the Hudson in his epic escape from slavery. He knew something of rivers.

When the shad or herring were running, Betsy Bailey, Douglass's grandmother, a master fisherwoman, would often spend half days waist deep in the beautiful, nearly one-hundred-yard-wide Tuckahoe, tending and pulling her seine nets. One of the greatest stories in American history began in February 1818 at the northwest corner of a horseshoe bend in the Tuckahoe, just above its muddy banks and layers of lush reeds, around a humble cabin managed by Betsy, a slave, and her husband, Isaac Bailey, a free man. Douglass lived most of his life believing that he had been born in 1817, but a handwritten inventory of slaves, kept by his owner at birth, Aaron Anthony, recorded "Frederick Augustus, son of Harriet, Feby. 1818." He may have been born in the grandparents' cabin, or in slave quarters near the tenant farmer's house not far away where his mother likely lived, or even in a field

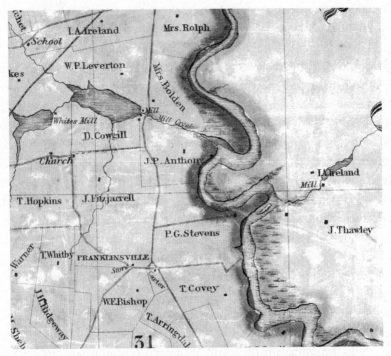

Map of Talbot County, Maryland, with farm limits, by William H.
Dilworth, 1858. It shows the Anthony farm on which Douglass
was born at the horseshoe bend in the Tuckahoe River.

nearby. The land and the extended families of slaves were part of the Holme Hill Farm, owned by Anthony, whom Douglass called "old master." Anthony owned some thirty people and adjoining farms of six hundred acres in all, although he did not live at Holme Hill; he was the managing overseer of a much larger operation, the Wye plantation, some twelve miles to the west.[19] By his brutal exercise of power, and possibly by blood, Anthony was, and still is, a crucial and mysterious figure in Douglass's story.

The district in which Douglass lived his first six years was known as Tuckahoe, in the northeast section of Talbot County, the whole of which was drained by the larger Choptank River as it meandered to Chesapeake Bay. Douglass later uncharitably described the area as "famine stricken" with a "worn-out, sandy, desert-like appearance of its soil." But he could also remember with a somber nostalgia the "stillness of Tuckahoe," and the "Kentucky Ravine," as it was locally known, which provided a path down to the river's edge. The nearest villages, and the first towns he ever saw, were Hillsboro just two miles upriver to the north of the Baileys' cabin, and Denton, due east across the river in Caroline County, some five miles away. The boy enjoyed many hours of watching the commercial bustle and the great wheel around Lee's Mill, just a mile north across fields of corn.[20]

Frederick Augustus Washington Bailey was the son of Harriet Bailey, one of Betsy and Isaac's five enslaved daughters. The second of the multiple names, most uncommon for a slave, can be attributed to his uncle Augustus, Harriet's brother, who had died two years before the boy's birth. Washington? Perhaps his mother, lonely and sexually abused, with so little to provide for her newborn, sought in a moment of anguished pride to link this child to the father of the country, rather than to a father he could never really know. Frederick only rarely saw his mother in the first years of his life; his tender and lyrical remembrances of her are almost pure invention. He never saw her at his grandmother's cabin, but recollected a handful of nighttime visits from his mother after he was transferred to the large Wye plantation at age six. Born in 1792, Harriet gave birth to seven children between 1813 and 1825. Year after year, she was hired out to other farms, often as much as twelve miles away; but she sometimes walked the distances to visit her children at night and trekked dusty paths back to meet the overseer's horn by morning. "My poor mother," Douglass wrote, "like many other slave women, had *many children*, but NO FAMILY!"[21]

Douglass's knowledge of his mother, he maintained, was "scanty, but very distinct. Her personal appearance and bearing are ineffaceably stamped upon my memory." As time passed in his autobiographical quest, Douglass's mother grew in stature, beauty, and influence. In 1845, he recollected that he had never seen her in daylight; but by 1855, she emerged from memory "tall and finely proportioned; of deep black glossy complexion; had regular features, and, among other slaves, was remarkably sedate in her manners." What the cruelty of slavery had stolen from him, he seized back in his empowering imagination. Douglass found a picture of an Egyptian king, Ramses, in James Cowles Prichard's *Natural History of Man*, "the features of which so resemble those of my mother, that I often recur to it with something of the feeling which I suppose others experience when looking upon the pictures of dear departed ones."[22] The mother he hardly knew became dignified, even regal, all but without gender, and one of many shields of protection he built around himself as a storyteller.

In a scene that became common in male slave narratives, Douglass told of the last time he saw his mother. In 1825 (perhaps February), not long after he had been taken to live with Anthony's family at the Wye House, and under the stern, abusive rule of the cook, Aunt Katy, Douglass remembered a wonderful visit from Harriet Bailey—at least while it lasted. Frederick had greatly annoyed Aunt Katy one day, and she promised as punishment to "starve the life out of me." When all the other children hanging around the kitchen received their warm corn bread, Katy purposely denied young Fred even a morsel. As he sat in a dark corner of the kitchen as the night wore on, hungry and stealing some Indian corn from a shelf, suddenly his mother appeared to save him. Harriet gave her boy a sweet ginger cake and "read Aunt Katy a lecture she never forgot." The cake was in the "shape of a heart, with a rich, dark ring glazed upon the edge of it," implying that it may have been Valentine's Day around the Anthony farms. Douglass called this a pivotal scene in his early life and converted it into both stinging anti-slavery propaganda, and an unforgettable expression of the personal pain and loss at the heart of his childhood. "That night I learned the fact," he remembered, "that I was not only a child, but somebody's child. . . . I was victorious . . . for the moment; prouder on my mother's knee than a king upon his throne." But the moment was brief. He dropped off to blissful sleep; in the morning his mother had gone back to her field hand's duty miles away. It was the last time he saw Harriet Bailey; she died sometime the next year in 1826, her illness and her grave unknown. Douglass implies that he was told of his mother's illness as she deteriorated out at the Holme Hill farm, but "was not allowed to visit her."[23]

As a world-famous abolitionist in 1855, Douglass knew well how this story would play on the emotions of his readers; but his words must also be read and interpreted as a child's screams transported by memory into the anguished heart of a lifelong orphan. "The heartless and ghastly form of slavery rises between mother and child, even at the bed of death," he offered to his sentimental readers. Then, he simply spoke for himself and millions of other former slaves, dead and living: "It has been a life-long, standing grief to me, that I knew so little of my mother; and that I was so early separated from her. The counsels of her love must have been beneficial to me. The side view of her face is imaged on my memory, and I take few steps in life, without feeling her presence; but the image is mute, and I have no striking words of her's treasured up." Douglass could see her only from a blurry side view, her voice muted, her very presence glimpsed from a picture of Egyptian majesty and physiognomy in a natural-history book. But he was not left silent. With great enthusiasm he said he later learned that his mother could read, and that she was the "only one of all the slaves and colored people in Tuckahoe" who could do so. Her "achievement . . . was very extraordinary," he proudly declared, and for his own love of letters he credited the "native genius of my sable, unprotected, and uncultivated mother—who belonged to a race whose mental endowments it is . . . fashionable to hold in disparagement and contempt."[24] For such a great orator and writer to make this claim says at the very least a good deal about how dearly he yearned to know and understand his genealogical and temporal roots in the people and soil of Maryland's Eastern Shore. It also may say that, even to Douglass himself, his extraordinary talent with language—his voice—remained something of a beautiful mystery.

The identity of his father was an equal, but hardly beautiful, mystery. This fact, Douglass wrote in 1855, "is shrouded in a mystery I have never been able to penetrate." For the rest of his life he searched in vain for the name of his true father. In his 1845 *Narrative*, Douglass stated, "My father was a white man . . . admitted to be such by all I ever heard speak of my parentage." Many in the neighborhood also "whispered that my master was my father; but of the correctness of this opinion I know nothing." By 1855, his father was still definitely a "white man, or nearly white." Now, however, Douglass said he was no longer giving credence to Aaron Anthony as his father; Douglass claimed that he had "reason to think he was not." By the 1881 writing of *Life and Times of Frederick Douglass*, the author's third autobiography, the paternity dilemma all but vanished with the simple statement "of my father I know nothing."[25] This was never the case for Douglass. The question was deeply important for him, and in 1855 he dwelled at great length on white fathers of slaves.

Indeed, he dwelled on Aaron Anthony. "I say nothing of *father*. . . . Slavery does away with fathers as it does away with families," he wrote. "The order of civilization is reversed here." Then he searched with intensity and descriptive detail for a sense of Anthony's character as the first father figure in his life. Anthony was fifty-one years old when Frederick Bailey was born, and he owned the adult daughters of Betsy Bailey. But as yet we have no smoking-gun evidence that Anthony is Douglass's natural father. Anthony had two surviving sons in 1818, Andrew and Richard, at ages twenty-one and eighteen; they are possible candidates, but with no evidence even of the hearsay variety that Douglass grew up with about the elder Anthony. Douglass carefully described the "old master" as essentially a cruel tyrant, capable of terrible physical and emotional violence, but a man victimized as much by the system of slavery as by his own nature, a theme Douglass repeated as a major part of his autobiographies. He also remembered occasional moments of distracted humanity in Anthony. Most of the time, Anthony paid little if any attention to the slave children around the

Wye plantation yards; he was a busy overseer of the overseers, managing the economic and labor demands of a huge agricultural and commercial enterprise. But on at least one occasion, Douglass remembered Old Master's "affectionate disposition . . . gently leading me by the hand—as he sometimes did—patting me on the head, speaking to me in soft, caressing tones, and calling me 'his little Indian boy.' " Douglass used this "almost fatherly" act as background for a withering portrait of a smoldering volcano, a "brittle . . . unhappy man . . . of haggard aspect . . . muttering to himself" as he "stormed about . . . cursing and gesticulating" at his "invisible foes." [26]

Born in 1767, Aaron Anthony was the seventh and final child of poor, illiterate farmers from the Tuckahoe Neck, the land immediately across the Tuckahoe River to the east in Caroline County. Douglass later described the poor whites such as Anthony who hailed from there as "the lowest order, indolent, and drunken to a proverb." Like Frederick Bailey, Anthony was an orphan (both parents died when he was a child) who made his own way in the world and became a self-made man from extremely humble roots. He loved and managed money well. Like many Eastern Shoremen he also handled boats well, became a seaman, and a captain eventually of the most prominent schooner on Chesapeake Bay, owned and operated by Edward Lloyd. Almost always upwardly mobile, Captain Anthony, as he was often called, married up to Ann Catherine Skinner in 1797 and soon took up residence in a rent-free house on the Lloyds' Wye plantation as head overseer of some thirteen farms, nearly ten thousand acres, and more than five hundred slaves. Since he owned Betsy Bailey, as a slaveholder Anthony likely did not need to buy more slaves of his own. Apart from the ten children Betsy herself bore, from 1799 to 1826, her five daughters gave birth to at least twenty more among them. By any measure, Anthony was a success story as the manager of the Lloyd slave empire and owner of three large farms of his own that he rented out, at least until after his wife died in 1818, the year Douglass was born. From then until his death in November 1826, Anthony may have descended into mental instability and increased sexual aggression. [27]

Douglass famously recorded an incident that gives credence to this image of Anthony as old and angry, lecherous and violent. Shortly after arriving at the Wye House at age six and joining the swarm of slave children there, Douglass was asleep early one morning in his normal place, "the floor of a rough closet, which opened into the kitchen." He was awakened by the "shrieks and piteous cries" of his fifteen-year-old aunt Hester. Anthony had dragged her into the kitchen at dawn, made her strip to the waist, forced her to stand on a bench on her toes as her wrists were tied to a wooden joist above her head. Old master stood behind Hester, her neck, shoulders, and back "entirely naked," an ugly cowskin switch (the lash) in his hand, shouting "d__d b__h" and other "epithets . . . too coarse and blasphemous" for readers to bear. Little Frederick looked on in horror through "cracks" in the boards as Anthony adjusted the whip in his hand, steadied his feet for leverage, and dealt one overhand blow after another to the young woman's bleeding neck and shoulder blades. The blood dripped on her clothes and down to the floor; the old man clenched his teeth, gripped the cowskin, and delivered his "torture," seemingly "delighted with the scene." [28]

Embedded in Douglass's rendering of this scene is his broader discussion of Anthony's motives for such a beating. Hester had been seeing a young slave teenager, Ned Roberts (also fifteen years old), and Douglass describes both of them as beautiful and attractive young people, falling in love. Hester had rejected Anthony's advances and paid dearly for it on that morning. Anthony, Douglass reported, wanted to "break up the growing intimacy" of the young lovers, but his efforts were to no avail. Douglass turned this episode of his childhood into a parable about the sexual corruption and the spirit-killing immorality at the center of the master-slave relationship. Hester lived with the "curse" of her "personal beauty," and Ned with his almost powerless desire to court and marry her. The jealous Anthony's intentions were "abhorrent" in every sense, his "methods . . . foolish." What slavery so lacked in sexual and familial relations, Douglass offered, was a sense of normalcy, of the peace in which to love freely. Hester should have been free to give her affections to the handsome young man she liked, and Ned free to become a husband. But "*who* or *what*," asked Douglass the autobiographer, "was this old master?" His answer? A tyrant with no bounds, a torturer, a man any civilized society would try and convict for his "awful criminality." But alas, Anthony, exhausted from the whipping, wiping off the "blood-clotted cowskin," ushered the mangled and weeping Hester out of the kitchen, not knowing that a little boy crouched in a closet peering in terror at the blood on the floor. [29] Douglass's crafting of the beating of his beautiful young aunt is a former slave's recitation of an overwhelmingly vivid, traumatic memory of a morning in a slave boy's terrible education. It took him many years to understand and find the language for the rage that old master's whip and Hester's blood had left in him.

If Anthony had been his father, Douglass dearly wanted to know the truth. But more important, he put him to use as a symbol, the sexual predator in the evil system that ruined all decency in humanity. Unforgivingly,

Douglass made Anthony into the father of fathers among slaveholders. He turned that haunting whisper of his youth ("master is your father") into a condemnation of the sexual abuse, and its spawn of hundreds of thousands of mulatto children, at the heart of slavery in America. The pain of not knowing with certainty the identity of his own father paled, he implied, next to the collective reality he witnessed. The slave status of a child was always that of the mother under American slave law. "This arrangement," Douglass declared, "admits of the greatest license to brutal slaveholders, and their profligate sons, brothers, relations and friends, and gives to the pleasure of sin, the additional attraction of profit. A whole volume might be written on this single feature of slavery, as I have observed it." [30]

Douglass experienced lasting individual trauma over his roots in this world of rural, lonely, familial, and violent sexual anguish. Few Americans ever more publicly and vividly remade themselves over and over quite like Douglass, and few had deeper reasons to try. Slavery meant to make him a "brute," Douglass wrote. "But what man has made, man can un-make." [31]

If indeed his twenty-year-old mother, still full of flowering beauty, youthful charm, and intelligence, had been raped by the power-besotted, sexually deranged fifty-year-old Anthony, Douglass had to find some story, or analysis, in which to comprehend it as he grew to adulthood. By retrieving his story from memory, he also had to try to dissolve it as he also created it. If he understood that he had not been conceived in love, then he could never know a father's love, although he would seek alternative fathers for much of his life. "A man who will enslave his own blood," he insisted, "may not be safely relied on for magnanimity. Men do not love those who remind them of their sins—unless they have a mind to repent—and the mulatto child's face is a standing accusation against him who is master and father to the child." Douglass wrote about his paternity with an acute and strategic sense of fatherlessness. Anthony, or whichever white man pursued Harriet Bailey into her quarters, or in the back of a kitchen in the dark, produced ultimately an angry Frederick Douglass, who would find the words to fight back. The extent of slavery's sexual assault on the idea of family, Douglass wryly claimed, was beyond the "design of my simple story." Hardly. So much racial mixture had emerged from American slavery, Douglass argued, that "if the lineal descendants of Ham are only to be enslaved, according to the scriptures, slavery in this country will soon become an unscriptural institution; for thousands are ushered into the world annually, who—like myself—owe their existence to white fathers, and, most frequently, to their masters, and masters' sons." Douglass knew this element of his story was old, complex, and, to most, salacious. He told it about as explicitly as he could. "The thoughtful," he said, "know the rest." [32]

In his abolitionist writings and his oratory, Douglass seldom missed an opportunity to convert his story into ways of defining slavery itself to his uninformed audiences. The orphan's anguished story of his roots in Tuckahoe, the parents unknown or vanished, provided the perfect chance to tear out his reader's heart as he bared his own: "There is not beneath the sky an enemy to filial affection so destructive as slavery. It had made my brothers and sisters strangers to me; it converted my mother who bore me into a myth; it shrouded my father in mystery, and left me without an intelligible beginning in the world." [33]

But in such cries in the night, he did tell us a good deal of what remained intelligible in his furtive memory. The "first things" Douglass did actually know and experience were boyhood memories of life at his grandmother's cabin, the trek to the Wye plantation (the "great house farm"), and his half-naked, half-starved time as a seven- and eight-year-old at Wye, scrounging for morsels of food and affection wherever he could find them. Even deeper, it was from in and around Grandma Betsy's "log hut . . . built of clay, wood, and straw" that Douglass, the adult writer, conjured his first memories. His memory flowed with images of the grandmother's majestic presence, her "freshly-ironed bandana," how "esteemed" she was on both sides of the Tuckahoe for her skills in planting and preserving "seedling sweet potatoes." As symbol and reality, Douglass gave us the first great yams in African American literature. Betsy perfected the art of placing the root of the potato at just the right depth and position so it would endure the winter's frosts, a talent for which she was recruited all over the region to assist others, slave and free. Among Douglass's first things was the well outside the cabin, where all the children (too many to count and almost all his cousins) would play, compete, and scheme. And then there was the simple, if magical, ladder inside the cabin. For Fred Bailey, the ladder up to a makeshift loft was one of those childhood objects or images that zipped in and out of his memory, "a really high invention, and possessed of a sort of charm." [34]

Eating his quick meals of cornmeal with an oyster shell, dashing to and fro and always craving his grandmother's attentions with deep seriousness against the bids of all the other urchins in the yard, and prancing across a cornfield to the busy mill up toward Hillsboro—these memories allowed Douglass to create a self-portrait of a boy in a state of nature. "Slave children *are* children," he instructed his romantic readers. In his earliest years, he could imagine, he had been a "genuine boy," running wild at times, "enacting, by turns, all the strange antics and freaks of horses, dogs, pigs, and barn-door fowls" without "incurring reproach." This little boy, protected by the seemingly powerful matriarch at that bend in the Tuckahoe, could "trot on . . . as happy as any little heathen under the palm trees of Africa." [35]

Or so the story demanded in his brilliant re-creation of childhood innocence peculiar to slavery, just before the fall, when befuddling rumors of old master's absolute power began to invade his euphoria. "Clouds and shadows" began to descend on him; he was told that Captain Anthony brought all the slave children at a certain age to his own homestead. Soon, Douglass kept hearing around Grandma Bailey's sanctuary, he would "*see sights* by and by." [36]

Chapter 2

A CHILDHOOD
OF EXTREMES

Extremes meet in mind as in matter.

—FREDERICK DOUGLASS, 1855

He remembered it as a "beautiful summer morning." Frederick Bailey's world turned upside down on such a morning in 1824. His time had come for removal from "the only home I ever had" (his grandmother Betsy's cabin), to the Wye plantation, and Aaron Anthony's homestead. It would be a day of momentary adventure, then fear and despair. First, out across fields to Tapper's Corner, and then on footpaths and through an extended stretch of dense trees called "Lloyds' long woods," Betsy Bailey led her grandson by the hand on a twelve-mile trek to his "introduction to the realities of slavery."[1]

In memory, Douglass used this turning point in his youth for several purposes. He paid tribute to the grandmother he loved (the only family member he could remember in any vivid way); she walked over the Talbot County landscape with the "solemnity of a priestess," her bandanna turban atop her "marvelously straight . . . figure, elastic, and muscular." When the boy tired on his short legs, she carried him on her shoulder like a bushel basket. With the customary writerly detail he had mastered by 1855, he remembered gripping his grandmother's hand tightly, as he imagined some logs and stumps in the dark forest as "wild beasts."[2]

Most strikingly, Douglass portrayed this childhood memory as an initiation into the separation and abandonment at the heart of slavery. For anyone who has ever watched a lone, shy child of six or seven join a band of other children on a playground, Douglass's poignant recollections of this episode ring true. As his grandmother prepared to leave him forever, she urged him to go play with a group consisting, he soon realized, of six of his cousins and his brother and two sisters, Perry, Sarah, and Eliza. Frederick had never met them. "Brothers and sisters we were in blood," he wrote, "but slavery had made us strangers." While Frederick stood alone against a wall in confusion, one of the children ran up and shouted, "Fed, Fed! grandmammy gone!" As he ran to look for her, he realized he had been dropped off in a new future—alone. Heartbroken, he remembered falling on the ground as he "wept a boy's bitter tears." In this world of children's logic and compensation, his siblings tried to give him peaches and pears, but Frederick "flung them away" in despair.[3]

As he widened his lens and found survival his only option, Douglass turned the childhood recollections of eighteen months on the Wye plantation into a stunning description of a *slave society* in microcosm. It was a place of jarring contrasts and brutal contradictions. The Lloyds' massive operation was at once a place "three hundred years behind the age, in all that relates to humanity and morals," but also a thriving business and agricultural enterprise. It was a place with all the sounds and wonders of nature, a "scene of almost Eden-like beauty." But also, Douglass said, a "dark domain," where "civilization is shut out," and the people with the power committed all manner of crimes with "as much impunity as upon the deck of a pirate ship."[4] In this world of fear and loneliness, but also of endless fascination for a child's boundless curiosity, Douglass burrowed into his interior imagination and found his own ways to be a boy.

Historians have made a distinction between "societies with slaves" and "slave societies." In the first, as Ira Berlin has argued, "slaves were marginal to the central productive processes," and the master-slave relationship was not the "exemplar" of life itself. But in a slave society, the master's authority over his bondmen defined all social relations, and all economic production depended intimately on the slaves' brawn, brains, and compliance. In a slave society, from dawn until dusk, everyone woke, labored, worried about money or hunger, ate, played, competed, loved, hated, married, worshipped God, sang, dreamed, and died in a world shaped at every turn by slavery, a system in America Douglass once defined succinctly as "the granting of that power by which one man exercises and enforces the right of property in the body and soul of another."[5]

The great Wye plantation was all about property. Douglass's memories of the place were one of the deepest roots of his evolving identity, and eventually of his abolitionism. His rich descriptions of the "Great House

Wye House farm, c. 1930.

Farm" depict a world of both absurdity and joy, of heroic human striving and of inhumane exploitation and violence. It had a marvel of a windmill to fan a child's imagination, as well as too many frustrated and depraved adults of both races wielding whips with impunity. The plantation seemed a place of permanence with no way out, but it also provided striking, constant views of a wide river with sloops and other sailing boats gliding by on the way to a bay called the Chesapeake and to a city called Baltimore. It had beautiful birds perched in the top of poplar trees and a scary, haunted graveyard that seemed ancient to the child's eyes.[6]

Although surrounded by people, animals, and bustling activity, Frederick was lonely and made no close friends among the younger slaves. He did, however, become close companions with twelve-year-old Daniel Lloyd, son of the patriarch of the plantation. Daniel apparently took a liking to Frederick's intelligence and precociousness. "Mas' Daniel" treated Frederick as both servant and playmate. They shared secrets and explored the estate together. They mimicked each other's dialects, and Douglass's testing of his wits and tongue against Daniel's was perhaps the slave boy's first imaginative experience with the wonders of language. He and Daniel may have also shared a good deal of knowledge. "The equality of nature is strongly asserted in childhood," Douglass maintained. Daniel "could not give his black playmates his company, without giving them his intelligence, as well." A full-time tutor from New England taught the Lloyd children in a special room to the left of the front portico of the mansion. That room had its own door opening outside, and some days Frederick waited in the front driveway, as inconspicuously as possible, for Daniel to finish his lessons. This may be where the future Frederick Douglass first sensed the power of what went on in the schoolrooms he could never enter.[7]

Throughout his life, especially in early adulthood, Douglass displayed a remarkable, hustler's ability to learn—to take and refashion useful knowledge to his own ends—from those around him. He began cultivating this survivor's skill at least as early as his romps about the Wye plantation with Daniel Lloyd. In afternoon competitive repartee, the future Douglass may have first experimented with the magic of words and unwittingly wielded the tools by which he would invent his life.

The Lloyds were perhaps the richest family in Maryland and a slave-holding dynasty. The Georgian Wye mansion that Douglass knew, and which still stands in full glory, was built by Edward Lloyd IV in about 1785. His son, Edward Lloyd V, long called Governor Lloyd, Douglass knew from a distance. By the 1820s the combined Lloyd operations had transformed into one of the largest producers of wheat in the United States, as well as a source of massive quantities of corn and pork. Huge flocks of sheep grazed the meadows, the stables were full of saddle and racing horses (a special passion of Lloyd's), and there was plenty of acreage for a private deer park. A beautiful eighty-five-foot-long French-provincial orangery, still standing today, with a gentlemen's billiards room on the second floor, graced the property a hundred yards or so behind the mansion. On the rear of that stunning structure were some attached slave apartments, likely for gardeners, their dark interiors today under archaeological investigation as they provide a sobering, eye-stopping contrast to the beautiful exterior surroundings. The long, regular slave-quarter buildings were a considerable distance from the main house and largely out of sight to any of the droves of visitors who came for the Lloyds' ostentatious midafternoon dinner soirees. Lloyd's wealth, said Douglass in his *Narrative*, was "almost equal to . . . the riches of Job."[8]

Edward Lloyd V was elected governor of Maryland three times and also served in the US Congress. He was as socially well connected as anyone in the Chesapeake region. Little Frederick would try to peer from a distance—or might hear tales from Daniel—when as many as two dozen overdressed guests would come for the feasts. Douglass described this "community" of whites and blacks and slaves and free people as a status-ridden universe. Essentially three families resided at the Wye plantation. He was part of the "kitchen family," consisting of some dozen black children under the tyrannical rule of Aunt Katy. The "house family" was Aaron Anthony's nuclear family, including his two sons and daughter, Lucretia, who married Thomas Auld, the captain of Colonel Lloyd's sloop. The Aulds would soon play a crucial role in Frederick's life. Finally, there were the "sacred precincts of the great house," including the Lloyds of course, who lived in splendor, groaning under the weight of their "blood-bought luxuries." But the great house also included the Lloyds' fifteen house servants, attired in fine clothing, selected for their faithfulness and personal appearance. This plantation "black aristocracy," as Douglass called them, were as remote from him as Colonel Lloyd himself. The house servants "resembled the fieldhands in nothing, except in color." It was as though they resided on another planet a few hundred yards away from overseer Captain Anthony's yard. Wearing fine "silks" and "fanning . . . breezes toward the over-heated brows of the alabaster ladies," these servants did not even know any of the "sorrow and hunger-smitten multitudes of the quarter and the field."[9]

Douglass later wrote about this childhood world of beauty and evil, of decadence and mass production, as both his playground and his "prison." He did so with astonishing detail, almost all the basics of which can be verified: overseers' names, and many of their terrible deeds of violence; how the field hands' basic food, the ashcake, was baked—"this peculiar bread . . . covered with ashes, to the depth of a sixteenth part of an inch"; and how a whip was made "entirely of untanned, but dried, ox hide" and "painted red, blue, and green," before being used on slaves' naked backs. Young Frederick loved horses and the stables, and when allowed, he would hang around them. The stables were run by the father and son pair of slaves Young Barney and Old Barney. Any given day might find the half-naked, barefoot boy in his sackcloth shirt dodging in and out of stalls, gazing at the huge thoroughbreds, admiring with awe the "splendid carriages, soft within and lustrous without." Here Frederick observed the fine functions of saddles and harnesses, and the "gigs, phaetons, barouches, sulkeys, and sleighs."[10]

Douglass possessed an extraordinary memory and cultivated it endlessly as a writer. By all accounts, and from the evidence of some of his special privileges, the youthful Frederick Bailey was remarkably bright, his powers of observation active and acute; he impressed those around him as smart and curious beyond his years. The detail of his autobiographies can to some extent be attributed to such sheer intelligence. But other factors were surely as important in his talent for recall. Eventually, the fugitive-slave Douglass of 1845 at age twenty-seven, as well as the more politically mature and famous Douglass of 1855 at age thirty-seven, knew he needed veracity for his story to be creditable in a world that doubted any literary acumen and, for that matter, basic intelligence in blacks. Even more, from his first moments as a speaker in his early twenties, a mere two or three years out of slavery, Douglass rehearsed over and over the stories he would eventually write up in the *Narrative* and revise in *Bondage and Freedom*. Memory is a mysterious and infinitely powerful human device, what Saint Augustine called "a deep and boundless manifoldness" and the "treasury" in the mind. With enough prompts and associations, a great deal of childhood memory, both difficult and pleasing, can be retrieved as it is refashioned. Douglass made as well as received his own story from memory; he summoned it with both private and public repetition for an audience he knew he had to persuade. "Self-making is, after all," writes the legal scholar of autobiography Jerome Bruner, "our principal means of establishing our own uniqueness."[11] And Douglass had the deepest of reasons to declare his uniqueness.

In *Bondage and Freedom* in 1855, Douglass disingenuously declares, "Let others philosophize; it is my province here to relate and describe; only allowing myself a word or two . . . to assist the reader in the proper understanding of the facts narrated."[12] Hardly. Douglass's representation of his early life as a slave is a thoroughgoing abolitionist manifesto, a penetrating portrait of the inner and exterior worlds of both slaves and slaveholders. And he may, indeed, have seen or certainly heard a good deal about all that he wrote. An ashcake may be an ashcake, but the blood that flows in what he called his "chapter of horrors" is full of philosophy as well as psychology.

Including the beating of his aunt Hester, Douglass had either witnessed or learned about from hearsay at least seven brutal whippings or murders by the time he was eight. This does not include the casual violence he saw from overseers, from the wretched Aunt Katy around the kitchen, or from his first instructor in religious devotions, a slave named Doctor Isaac Copper, whom Douglass turned into a "tragic and comic" character in his autobiography. Copper was a cripple, who with hickory switch in hand forced groups of children to learn the Lord's Prayer, as he also whacked them with his whip. "Everybody in the south," wrote Douglass, "wants the privilege of whipping somebody else. Uncle Isaac shared the common passion of his country." Shortly after memorizing "Our Father who are in heaven," Douglass quickly became a "truant" from Copper's devotions.[13] Details flowed in Douglass's recollections, emanating from pain and adventure tucked away in the secret garden of his memory. His great indictment of slavery came first and foremost from the accumulated injury of his own story.

Douglass made a careful study of the range of overseers he had known, from the sadistic to the reluctant to those who enacted violence as mere policy in the slave system. His master, Anthony, seemed to be the company man enforcing policy, except when sexually scorned; then he joined the darkest side. A James Hopkins seemed "as good as any man can be, and still be an overseer"; he whipped slaves with open discomfort. But under Anthony's general command were two other overseers, William Sevier (pronounced *Severe*) and Orson Gore (Douglass mistakenly identifies him as Austin Gore). These were not names invented by a novelist but real, hardened, paid accessories to slavery's crimes on the Wye plantation. One day near the slave quarters, Frederick heard noise and screaming. As he sauntered over to the scene, he witnessed Nelly Kellem, a tall, strong slave woman, being wrestled and dragged toward a tree by Sevier. Nelly gave as good as she got in this fight, clawing Sevier's face with her nails and hitting him as hard as he hit her. According to Douglass, three of Nelly's five children witnessed this bloody fracas, as Sevier finally subdued Nelly and roped her to a tree. As the children screamed, "Let my mammy go!," Sevier shouted foul curses and, like a "savage bulldog," beat Nelly to a bloody pulp, while the woman took the blows with fierce and indignant courage. As Douglass wrote of this event years later, he implied that the worst part for him was not Nelly's "back . . . covered with blood," but her screams "mingled with those of the children." [14]

Such was young Frederick's prolonged initiation into the world of human relationships, to notions of fairness and morality, of crime and punishment, of familial bonds and fissures. Overseers were the law enforcers and the courts. Nelly's offense that led to her bloody beating in front of her traumatized children was the ubiquitous slave crime of "impudence." The moral Douglass the abolitionist drew from the story was that Nelly—as a woman—had stood her ground as long as she could. She left the ugly Sevier scarred in his already deformed face. Her bravery, something Douglass would later claim for himself, proved the doctrine he invoked with excessive bravado: "He is whipped oftenest, who is whipped easiest." [15] That stirring statement, while manly and inspiring, has the air of smugness, offered from a safer position as author of his memoir many years after watching the slaves on the Wye estate live with the frightening daily grind of comprehending just who could muster such courage to resist and who could not. He could hardly offer us, or himself, any sense of what the bleeding Nelly told her sickened children that evening in the quarters. Fighting back was noble and possible; but Douglass also left the distinct impression that in the daily experience of Eastern Shore slavery even a child began to understand that sanity itself, as well as physical survival, might be at stake.

Douglass's litany of experiences with violence went even further; he analyzed the overseers as a "distinct class of southern society." Gore served as the prototype of the cold and calculated tyrant who could instill fear in slaves. He operated not with "disgusting swagger and noisy bravado," but with grave and "calm self-possession." Gore worked by reputation and action; his power was absolute and his method intimidation. He never allowed a slave even to answer back to his orders. Gore worked by the maxim, said Douglass, "that it is better that a dozen slaves suffer under the lash, without fault, than that the master or overseer should seem to have been wrong in the presence of the slave." Gore's words were few but shrill, and the result was "sensations of terror among the slaves." "I shunned him," wrote Douglass, "as I would have shunned a rattlesnake." He was still young enough to get away with such avoidance. In Douglass's portrayal, Gore seemed destined for his calling, the perfect creation of slavery itself, the ideal "chief of a band of pirates."[16] Gore seemed the perfect colonel in slavery's sick-minded, evil army patrolling the police state.

A twenty-year-old, robust slave named Bill Denby got into a scrape with Gore. In Douglass's telling of the episode, after a few lashes Denby ran and plunged into a creek, with the water up to his neck. Gore stood on the bank with a shotgun on his shoulder. He gave Denby to a count of three to come out of the water. The belligerent, heroic young man refused, and Gore shot him at point-blank range in the face. Although Douglass admittedly did not witness this killing, he heard about it all over the quarters and wrote about it in dramatic terms: "In an instant, poor Denby was numbered with the dead. His mangled body sank out of sight, and only his warm, red blood marked the place where he had stood."[17] Gore apparently made his case for a necessary killing to Colonel Lloyd, who gave his approval; no judicial inquiry occurred. Douglass used this case to show that the murder of slaves in Maryland not only remained legal and went unpunished, but that it stood as the terrifying symbol of a society of amoral lawlessness. At the heart of Douglass's autobiographies was the idea that slavery attempted to crush all semblance of natural rights for its victims. A society that sanctioned cold-blooded murder and fostered homicidal madness as necessary steps to social order could only be called by its names—piracy and tyranny. Douglass's later, prolific appeals to the natural-rights tradition, and even to the right of revolution, should be first considered in light of these compelling, damaging childhood memories of such cruelty.

Colonel Lloyd himself, the owner of the great pirate ship, employer of the "chief pirate" (Gore) in control of the captive deckhands, was hardly above employing the whip. At the stables at the Wye plantation, Douglass observed, "a horse was seldom brought out . . . to which no objection could be raised" by either Lloyd himself or by his sons and sons-in-law. Old Barney, the head groom and stableman, had to endure these barbs and humiliations. One day, Colonel Lloyd was especially displeased with the appearance of one of his riding horses and took it out on Old Barney. Lloyd ordered the "bald and toil-worn" man to kneel on the ground and laid "thirty lashes with a horse whip" on his bare shoulders. Barney "bore it patiently, to the last, answering each blow with a slight shrug of the shoulders, and a groan." This incident especially shocked Douglass, not it appears for the blood drawn, but for the unspeakable humiliation of an old man of dignity and talent by the master himself. The beating of Barney, said Douglass, revealed slavery in its "maturity of repulsive hatefulness."[18] In a child's eyes, and memories, something sick, frightful, or evil seemed to lurk around the corner of every building, in the sounds of every overseer's steps at the Wye enterprise. Long after he had left the Eastern Shore behind, such a prospect haunted Douglass.

"Such is the constitution of the human mind," Douglass wrote in 1855 while trying to capture his mentality as an eight- and nine-year-old on the Wye plantation, "that, when pressed to extremes, it often avails itself of the most opposite ends. Extremes meet in mind as in matter." With a probity unmatched by any other slave-narrative author, he remembered and analyzed a world of stark opposites, all but unalterable extremes that he had to learn to understand, navigate, and survive.[19] As his awareness of his predicament grew, Frederick became a thinking being trying desperately to preserve and protect his mind as well as his body from internal disintegration and external destruction. At every turn in his life as a slave, both mind and body were in constant danger. His mind, he learned, he could cultivate and protect more easily, with more self-control.

Douglass's experiences began to shape a disposition, a set of habits of mind, a personality that may have lasted all of his life. He was forever in search of a sense of "home," a concept he dwelled on at length in the autobiographies. He was capable of great love and compassion, but perhaps even more desperately in need of receiving love and compassion long into adulthood. He experienced great difficulty trusting other people, even those who seemed to be friends. With mixed results, he sought time and again to find parental figures in whom to invest his faith and from whom to garner emotional sustenance. And his was a childhood, he admitted, blessed with several turns of good fortune altogether uncommon to slaves, while at the same time we should not doubt that he carried with him from his youth a profound sense of rage against the violence and degradation he both witnessed and experienced. If a slave was thoughtful and dreamed of something better, Douglass believed, he must endure these extremes. As autobiographer, he ultimately imposed a rather romantic, individualistic self-made hero on his readers. But crafty and guarded as a writer, he nevertheless revealed a childhood laden with the traumas unique to slavery. Those traumas were a kind of emotional furniture in his psyche; he would forever try to control and rearrange them, but he could never fully expunge them. That emotional furniture may have darkened his outlook, but it also provided the wellspring of his great personal story. Douglass made "the nature and history of slavery" his youthful "inquiry," he maintained. We are led as his readers on the journey of an evolving, brilliant mind's bitter questioning of all around him. "Why am I a slave?" he asked so innocently in *Bondage and Freedom*. "Why are some people slaves, and others masters?" he demanded to know, as though representing a child's voice. This "subject of my study . . . was with me in the woods and fields; along the shore of the river, and wherever my boyish wanderings led me."[20]

Douglass was lucky to enjoy any boyish wanderings as a slave. As autobiographer, he sometimes portrayed himself as just out of the frame of the picture, observing, studying, accumulating the knowledge that might not only free him, but also persuade his audience of the merits of the antislavery cause.[21] Long before the age of psychology, Douglass provided a portrait of a young slave conducting psychological warfare against slavery, as that system conspired in every way to ensnare, weaken, and ultimately destroy him. His powers of recollection, fashioned beautifully into words, became his only available weapon. In words, Douglass always fought back not only to defeat slavery, but to make sense of its extremes and work through his pain. "Why am I slave?" is an existential question that reflects as well as anticipates many others like it in human history. Why am I poor? Why is he so rich, and she only his servant or chattel? Why am I hated for my religion, my race, my sexuality, the accident of my birth in this valley or on that side of the river or on this side of the railroad tracks? Why am I a refugee with no home? Why does my color define my life? Douglass's story represents so many others over the ages.

Douglass wanted us to believe that as a child he gained inner strength and self-knowledge from his sufferings. With caution because of his skilled literary invention, we ought not doubt most of what he claimed as an amateur child psychologist. Every student of Douglass tries to discern what in his memoirist's voice was real (factual?) and what was literary, often a false separation. But the two were almost always mixed for this gifted artist. As we consider the following remarkable passages, who would contest his comprehension of a child's understanding of justice and injustice? "As I grew older and more thoughtful," he wrote from the perspective of 1855, "I was more and more filled with a sense of my wretchedness." All the "cruelty . . . wrong and outrage" he witnessed or learned from others "led me," he said, "when yet but eight or nine years old, to wish I had never been born. I used to contrast my condition with the black-birds, in whose wild and sweet songs I fancied them so happy! Their apparent joy only deepened the shades of my sorrow." Then he tried to remember how a child's innocent imagination encounters the raw unfairness of the world and the essential venality of humankind. "There are thoughtful days," Douglass asserted, "in the lives of children—at least there were in mine—when they grapple with all the great, primary subjects of knowledge, and reach, in a moment, conclusions which no subsequent experience can shake. I was just as well aware of the unjust, unnatural and murderous character of slavery, when nine years old, as I am now. Without any appeal to books, to laws, or to authorities of any kind, it was enough to accept God as a father, to regard slavery as a crime."[22] There is no reason to doubt such an adult observation about a child's instincts. For this young slave the singing blackbirds did not lie.

Douglass's world of extremes flowed from his memory in sheer description as well as in metaphors of explanation. Most of the time he kept himself squarely within the frame of his canvas. He identified hunger and cold as his primary sufferings at the Wye plantation. He spent every day "almost in a state of nudity," wearing his "tow-linen" hanging down to his knees. He stayed on "the sunny side of the house" or in "the corner of the kitchen chimney" in winter to find warmth. At the Anthony house, the slave children, "like so many pigs," ate cornmeal mush out of a "large wooden tray, or trough," laid down on the floor of the kitchen or on the ground outdoors. An oyster shell was the only fork or spoon he knew until he moved to Bal-

Aerial view of the Wye House plantation, c. 1930.

timore. He slept in a closet, he tells us, and in extreme cold he would steal a bag used for carrying corn to the mill and, with "head in and feet out," fitfully sleep on January and February nights. There were no beds or blankets for the slave children.[23]

We must imagine Douglass the twenty-seven-year-old writer, sitting at a desk in his small, crowded apartment in Lynn, Massachusetts, in the winter of 1844–45, drafting his first autobiography. As he recollected these physical hardships of his childhood, his feet presumably warm enough, Douglass mingled past and present and announced his suffering and his literacy in one unforgettable metaphor: "My feet have been so cracked with the frost, that the pen with which I am writing might be laid in the gashes."[24] Memory is almost always a combination of retrieval and invention. The corn sack, a child's frozen feet, and the pen of an adult writer as a kind of medicinal weapon to cure the gashes in his feet and in his psyche helped Douglass explain the meaning of being a child slave.

Before he parted ways with Wye, Douglass did make what he referred to as "two friends." One was Daniel Lloyd, to whom he had been designated as playmate and companion. But more important, he was fortunate that Lucretia Auld took a liking to him. Around the Anthony household, with "so much that was harsh," Douglass characterized "Miss Lucretia" (Anthony's daughter and wife of Thomas Auld) as the first white woman who ever bestowed "the slightest word or look of kindness" upon him. She treated his wounds when he suffered a gash in his forehead in a fight with another boy. She took him "into the parlor," a room he had likely never entered, and quietly wiped the blood from his face and applied balsam and white linen to his head. That tender act is the first Douglass remembered from any white person. Lucretia may have "pitied me, if she did not love me," Douglass remembered. But he imagined and converted it into the love he so craved. She would occasionally give him extra bread, which led the boy to frequently linger, like the hungry dog or cat, beneath her backyard window. He transformed this tenderness into a formal sentence that speaks volumes about his deepest childhood needs: "When pretty severely pinched by hunger, I had the habit of singing, which the good lady very soon came to understand as a petition for a piece of bread. . . . I got well paid for my music." [25] Douglass does not recount what tunes or words he sang. But in these simple remembrances we see the boy who so yearned for love, for belonging, for an adult's embrace, even if it came only in the form of bread and a smile bought for the price of a child's song.

Douglass likely heard far more music than he ever sang at the Wye plantation, and on that subject he left some of his most compelling and complex remembrances. In so doing he exposed those extremes about which he could not stop thinking. On "allowance day" at the "Great House Farm," when designated slaves from all over the far-flung plantation came to the Wye House for their group's allotted monthly provisions, one might have witnessed a spectacle in which the "peculiarly excited and noisy" slaves gathered for social and musical communion. "While on their way," wrote Douglass, "they would make the dense old woods, for miles around, reverberate with their wild songs, revealing at once the highest joy and the deepest sadness." Douglass's recollection of these demonstrations of material need and slave culture was both festive and somber. In groups, the Wye slaves "would compose and sing as they went along, consulting neither time nor tune. The thought that came up came out—if not in word, in the sound. . . . They would sometimes sing the most pathetic sentiment in the most rapturous tone, and the most rapturous sentiment in the most pathetic tone." [26] Embedded in Douglass's memory was the slaves' mixed musical tradition of moans, rhythmic body movement, and improvised lyrics fashioned for specific moments as well as for their visions of eternity. For a long time, he remained both mystified and affected by that music, by the abiding stories he heard especially in their "tone."

Slaves on plantations could not own much of anything—land, tools, the clothes on their bodies, even their own children or their sense of a future. But they could at times and under certain circumstances own the sounds and rhythms, the melodies and lyrics, in the air as the great slave-driven machine of the Wye plantation refueled for the next month's production. In his vivid childhood memories Douglass felt both within and apart from the creation and the meaning of the songs. One gets the impression that the lonely boy may have been both scared by the collective power of the songs and strangely thrilled to be part of the community performing them. Douglass thought that hearing these songs might "do more to impress some minds with the horrible character of slavery, than the reading of whole volumes of philosophy on the subject." In the original *Narrative* of 1845 he fashioned a stunning memory of which he was so proud that he simply reprinted it in quotation marks with slight revision in the 1855 autobiography:

> I did not when a slave, understand the deep meaning of those rude and apparently incoherent songs. . . . They were tones loud, long, and deep; they breathed the prayer and complaint of souls boiling over with the bitterest anguish. The hearing of those wild notes always depressed my spirits, and filled me with ineffable sadness. The mere recurrence, even now, afflicts my spirit, and while I am writing these lines, my tears are falling. To those songs I trace my first glimmering conceptions of the dehumanizing character of slavery. . . . Those songs still follow me, to deepen my hatred of slavery, and quicken my sympathies for my brethren in bonds. If anyone wishes to be impressed with the soul-killing power of slavery, let him go to Col. Lloyd's plantation, and, on allowance day, place himself in the deep pine woods, and there let him, in silence, thoughtfully analyze the sounds that shall pass through the chambers of his soul.[27]

In this combination of childhood memory and antislavery propaganda, Douglass opened a wide window into his youth as a slave.

In his appeal to "analyze the sounds," it was as if Douglass left an invitation to modern historians of slavery, to anthropologists and folklorists, as well as to the readers of slave narratives in his own time, to try to time-travel with him to the pine woods around the great oval driveway of the Wye House to hear the true meaning of slavery. It was as though he believed that some part of the injustice of enslavement could not be fully described or explained and might only be grasped—felt—at the level of spirituality, in the "chambers" of the "soul." The songs still followed him into his adult, public life, he maintained, depressing but also quickening his spirit. Whether they sang about work and its rhythms, about the God welcomed into every aspect of daily life, about their masters or their intimate companions, or about animals through which they might imagine their own travail, slaves, Douglass argued, gave voice to their sorrow, not their contentment. "Sorrow and desolation have their songs," wrote Douglass, "as well as joy and peace. Slaves sing more to *make* themselves happy, than to express their happiness." [28] Absolution, redemption, survival? Slave songs were *made* out of the stuff of oppression, not merely found or anticipated in the hereafter. A boy could learn a lot on allowance day.

Whether in the form of moans or shouts, in spontaneous lyrics, or in the stanzas and refrains of a spiritual, slaves were always *making* their own balm in Gilead. But in Douglass's memory, as he represented his fellow slaves' prayer and complaint, it was as though, by then a deep reader of the Old Testament, he chose Jeremiah's original lament over the more famous spiritual's declaration of faithful certainty. In the song, "there *is* a balm in Gilead / to make the wounded whole." But Jeremiah had left an unanswered question: "*Is* there no balm in Gilead? Is there no physician there? Why then is there no healing for the wound of my people?" In song, as Douglass seemed to grasp, slaves fashioned some element of spiritual or psychological certainty in a temporal world that provided none for them. A slave child needed to believe in something. [29]

As an adult writer Douglass harbored much ambivalence about the sorrow and loss in those slave songs. When he would remember his days of plotting resistance and escape with his fellow band of disgruntled slaves as he grew toward adulthood, the songs somehow became more coherent, if still full of duality. The songs, Douglass said, "were mostly of a plaintive cast," but might also break into "all manner of joyful noises." And later, he seemed richly aware of an insight advanced by modern scholars of the slave songs: that the sacred and the secular mingled in a single worldview among American slaves. Douglass understood that the dehumanizing character of slavery had to be answered, tamed, and controlled by the weapon of words, in the music of song, or of oratory. [30] He struggled mightily to embrace confidence about language itself, whether in prose, or in the tone surrounding a song's revisiting of an Old Testament metaphor.

This Douglass came to grasp in remembrance of his later teenage years, and beyond. He used musical lyrics to capture the emotional meaning of his failed escape plans. He and his band of brothers, imagining their way out onto the Chesapeake and a watery liberation, could be "remarkably buoyant," he declared, "singing hymns and making joyous exclamations, almost as triumphant in their tone as if we had reached a land of freedom and safety." Then he remembered a specific song: "A keen observer might have detected in our repeated singing of 'O Canaan, sweet Canaan, / I am bound for the land of Canaan,' something more than a hope of reaching heaven. We meant to reach the *north*—and the north was our Canaan." Douglass recalled yet more lyrics in which to embed his story of determined, if unsuccessful, escape. A "favorite air" laced with "double meaning," went:

> *I thought I heard them say,*
> *There were lions in the way,*
> *I don't expect to stay*
>   *Much longer here.*
> *Run to Jesus—shun the danger—*
> *I don't expect to stay*
>   *Much longer here.*[31]

As a nine-year-old about to experience the first great lucky break of his life, Douglass did not yet understand how to analyze the sounds that had penetrated his boyhood soul. In Baltimore, he would learn a new kind of music, and a new kind of slavery.

Chapter 3

THE SILVER TRUMP
OF KNOWLEDGE

Education and Slavery were incompatible with each other.

—FREDERICK DOUGLASS, 1845

O n a spring day in March 1826, Lucretia Auld gave Frederick Bailey
the good news: he was to be sent to Baltimore in just three days to
live with the family of Hugh Auld, Thomas's brother, and to be the
boyhood companion for Tommy Auld, Hugh's son. Big changes were afoot
for all of Aaron Anthony's slaves. Old Master was ill and aging, his house
soon to be taken over by a new head overseer; the blacks had to be redistrib-
uted to other places in the Lloyd empire, hired out, or perhaps even sold.
Frederick was lucky, and Lucretia was happy for him; she promised him his
first pair of trousers if he would thoroughly clean himself before traveling
to the city. Douglass reports that he spent most of the next three days in
the creek scrubbing the "plantation scurf" and the "mange (as pig drovers
would call it)" off his body. The boy was sleepless with excitement, "working for the first time in the hope of reward." [1]

A boy might have been frightened by this prospect of such a drastic
change in his familiar surroundings. But not Frederick. He remembered no
dread and only exhilaration at seeing the Baltimore he had heard so much
about from an older cousin who worked on the *Sally Lloyd*, Colonel Lloyd's
sloop, and had come back with so many magical stories about ships, buildings, soldiers, and markets in the city. Frederick had no real family to leave
behind—no parents to miss, and his brother and sisters were but strangers
to him. He suddenly felt liberated from a future at the Wye plantation of
little more than "hardship, whipping, and nakedness." He remembered the
day as a Saturday, since he had no knowledge yet of months; with pride in

his new trousers, Douglass, sharing the deck with a flock of sheep, boarded the *Sally Lloyd* on what was likely March 18, 1826, for the journey to Baltimore. Ever giving his boyhood a narrative and a meaning, Douglass remembered himself the excited eight-year-old boy, stepping on the boat, as he "gave to Colonel Lloyd's plantation what I hoped would be the last look." Then he moved to the bow of the sloop and "spent the remainder of the day in looking ahead." This would not by any measure be the final time he would see the Wye plantation. He would come back again in both helpless fear and personal triumph. Talbot County and the Eastern Shore would forever be the deepest wellspring of his fertile memory. But at this juncture, no one could imagine how the history of the Chesapeake region, as well as that of the entire nation, would change in no small measure because this fresh-faced orphaned slave boy rode a boat to Baltimore that day in 1826.[2]

The sloop traversed Chesapeake Bay, which to Frederick, "opened like a shoreless ocean." It went into port first at Annapolis, where during a brief stay the boy was not allowed ashore; he did, however, see the dome of the statehouse of Maryland's capital. Since it was the first city he had ever seen, he remembered his youthful reaction as something like "travelers at the first view of Rome." Then on Sunday morning they arrived in Baltimore harbor. Frederick Bailey looked in awe as he saw two- and three-masted sailing ships, steamers, church spires, and four- and five-story buildings and warehouses. They landed at Smith's Wharf, near Gardiner's Shipyard, in Fell's Point, just southeast of the Inner Harbor. Since the 1760s, Fell's Point had been a hive of taverns and boardinghouses, as well as a growing center for the building and fitting out of oceangoing ships. In 1793, a French fleet overloaded with colonists escaping the slave rebellion in Saint Domingue (Haiti) arrived in the harbor. Among them was a ship's carpenter, Joseph Despeaux, and a contingent of Haitian slaves. With his workers, Despeaux founded Fell's Point's first shipyard, where soon they were constructing the famous Baltimore clipper ships, the fastest ocean crafts afloat.[3]

One of the sloop hands guided Frederick to the home of Hugh and Sophia Auld on Aliceanna Street (he remembered it as "Alliciana" Street), just a few blocks up from the harbor. He had arrived in one of most thriving and growing port cities in North America. It was one of the largest trading centers in the United States for tobacco, wheat, flour, and even coffee. Its shipbuilding industry was booming, and just a few months after his arrival, on July 4, 1826, the cornerstone was laid for the soon-to-be-famous Baltimore and Ohio Railroad (the B&O), which would link the Atlantic Ocean with the Mississippi River. The city had a population of nearly eighty thousand people, composed of approximately sixty thousand whites, four thousand black slaves, and more than fourteen thousand free blacks. Baltimore had the largest concentration of free persons of color in the United States, a demographic fact that would play a key role in Douglass's fate. The city proudly announced its civic consciousness in building major monuments; in October 1829, Frederick would have witnessed, at least from a distance, the unveiling of the massive Washington Monument, a 280-foot-high structure, with a 24-foot-high base and the first president's statue on top of the obelisk. The year of his arrival the first of three shot towers was erected, the massive stone structures in which shot was produced by dropping molten lead from the top to water tanks below.[4] This was a new visual, technological, and human universe for young Frederick. Here was a city with great churches, squares, and a skyline, and, to a boy from a plantation on the other side of the bay, an endless panorama for his senses and his imagination.

Douglass portrayed himself as the country bumpkin arriving in the big city. He felt the strange brick pavement under his feet, which would be so hot in summer heat, gazed at the buildings, and was especially struck at the noise, the "startling sounds reaching my ears from all directions." The boy felt "strange objects glaring upon me at every step" and raw fear. His chief trouble was the roving "troops of hostile boys ready to pounce upon me at every street corner." They chased him for sport and called him an "Eastern Shore Man." Thus facing a street hazing, a Fell's Point initiation that he called his "moral acclimation," Frederick learned that life had given him a break as it also thrust him into the unknown. He had arrived in an urban environment with slaves but not really a "slave city." Baltimore was undergoing a massive European immigration (130,000 arrived between 1820 and 1850), and those Fell's Point streets were full of Irish and German boys marking their territories. The port and the shipyards were booming; carpenters, caulkers, sailors, and dockworkers of all kinds competitively and jealously protected their livelihoods. The city broiled with volatile politics, sometimes led by firehouse organizations and their political clubs and gangs. Outbreaks of rioting and political violence were common. The ships continued to be built to make the future of a great seaport; the wheat trade boomed and a textile industry thrived in making clothing and ship's sails. But the labor for this great expansion was largely white, and the slave population was dwindling (from 4,357 in 1820 to 3,212 in 1840) as the free black community grew in numbers (from 10,326 in 1820 to 17,980 in 1840), if not in human rights.[5]

But Douglass, still numbered among the slaves, was someone's property with a mind and body growing almost beyond the system's capacity to contain him. Not long after Frederick's arrival, the Aulds moved a few blocks south, to a house on Philpot Street, as close as one could live to the shipyards, where Hugh was an aspiring shipbuilder. At the Aulds' house, Frederick met a white family who at first took him in like a relative. To his astonishment and joy, Sophia Auld—Hugh's wife—displayed "the kindliest emotions" in her face, and her tender demeanor toward the boy put him in a world he had never known from white people. And he hit it off immediately with "Little Tommy," of whom "his Freddy," as "Miss Sophia" put it, was to "take care." Surrounded by all this dreamlike affection, Frederick remembered his emotions: "I had already fallen in love with the dear boy; and with these little ceremonies I was initiated into my new home, and entered upon my peculiar duties." [6] Compared to all his previous experience it was a home and would remain so for several years; but it would also be a place for learning stern lessons for life, as well as to find and savor the one possession that might save his life.

For nearly his first two years with the Aulds, Sophia treated him "more akin to a mother than a slaveholding mistress." Indeed, as Douglass pointed out, Sophia Auld had never been a slaveholder before his arrival. She allowed him to feel like a "half-brother" to Tommy. She was pious, attended church regularly, and exuded kindness toward the black boy who was now turning ten or eleven years old. She was Douglass's humane "law-giver," he said, and such sweetness made him "more sensitive to good and ill treatment." Living on carpets, sleeping in a good straw bed, eating good bread, and wearing clean clothes did not hurt either. But the great gift she gave him was literacy. In 1845 Douglass recollected simply that Sophia had of her own accord taught him his ABCs as well as his first lessons in spelling. But by 1855 he remembered it a little differently. By then it was part of his "plan," and after repeatedly hearing her read aloud from the Bible, he frankly asked her to teach him to read. Either way, Sophia was proud of her pupil, and Frederick was an extraordinarily eager learner. [7]

In the sordid history of American slavery, few images are more powerfully ironic than that of Sophia Auld reading in what Douglass described as a "voice of tranquil music" while the slave boy lay asleep under a table near her feet. In a scene he retold in speeches, but not in the autobiographies, he remembered first hearing her read from the book of Job. She "waked me to sleep no more," Douglass declared in a speech in Belfast, Ireland, in January 1846. He often told of encountering the Bible by finding pages of it strewn on a Baltimore street a few years after first hearing it in Sophia's melodious voice. Ever awake to the power of a metaphor, he "raked leaves of the sacred volume" and, after washing and drying them, read the remnants. But from Sophia, a world had opened through, of all visions, that of the tragic, suffering, benighted Job![8]

Whether or not she read past the first chapter of Job to the boy, in his own later reading the adult writer and orator would have found countless resonances and uses of Job's voice. When Douglass was in the depths of despair, each of Job's uses of the question why fit Douglass's condition. "Why died I not from the womb? Why did I not give up the ghost when I came out of the belly?" Or even more poignant, as Douglass gained literacy, "Why is light given to a man whose way is hid, and whom God hath hedged in?" As Douglass came to see words as his holiest possession, he could share Job's deep frustration: "How forcible are right words! But what does your arguing reprove? Do ye imagine to reprove words, and the speeches of one who is desperate, which are as wind?" And surely, it was Job's declarative voice of complaint, defended directly to God over and again, that could teach Douglass a new tongue: "Therefore I will not refrain my mouth; I will speak in the anguish of my spirit; I will complain in the bitterness of my soul."[9] Could Sophia even have grasped what an instrument of power she had unleashed in Frederick?

If Sophia had not realized the potential danger of her actions, her husband soon informed her. When Frederick was about eleven years old, Hugh Auld suddenly forbade with stern anger any further instruction in reading for the young slave. Auld rebuked his wife; literacy was "unlawful" in Maryland for slaves, he claimed, and "learning would spoil the best nigger in the world." Douglass took great care to quote several lines he claimed he recalled his master speaking. They were to become a new kind of text for him in understanding and thwarting slavery's hold on his mind and body. If Douglass was taught to read the Bible, "there will be no keeping him," Auld reportedly said. It would "forever unfit him for the duties of a slave." And in full paternalistic gravity, the anxious slave owner maintained that "learning would do him no good, but probably, a great deal of harm—making him disconsolate and unhappy." Before long, the young slave would "want to know how to write," Auld warned. In retrospect, Douglass made the most of this traumatic juncture in his newfound life in Baltimore. He called master Hugh's chastisement of his wife in front of the slave the "first decidedly antislavery lecture to which it had been my lot to listen."[10]

As autobiographer, Douglass constantly portrayed especially his early life as a series of turning points, episodes of crisis, confrontation, and learning, where the hero is tested, sometimes brutally and beyond his will or strength. Most of the time, though, the hero endures and gains self-knowledge and some new ground in his personal war against his enslavers. None of these turning points or battles was ever more important than his ascent to literacy and knowledge.

Words would become Douglass's stock-in-trade; if Miss Sophia had provided the gift of literacy first, he now claimed, with no small amount of bravado, that master Hugh had also given him a gift. Auld's "iron sentences" became inspiration rather than denial. Douglass recollected himself awakening for the first time to the "white man's power to perpetuate the enslavement of the black man." If "knowledge unfits a child to be a slave," Douglass later wrote, then he had found the motive power of his path out, or at least inward, to freedom. Ever ready to employ biting irony to make his case, Douglass left this telling and honest description of the lesson learned: "That which he most loved I most hated; and the very determination which he expressed to keep me in ignorance, only rendered me the more resolute in seeking intelligence." Although still a child, Douglass nevertheless remembered the episode as a seismic shift in his conception of the world. "In learning to read, therefore," Douglass declared, "I am not sure that I do not owe quite as much to the opposition of my master, as to the kindly assistance of my amiable mistress." [11] Even as a child, Douglass learned to negotiate with and define himself by his opposition. This was a life lesson Douglass would invoke time and again in his later career, whether the enemy was a master, an overseer, a mob throwing brickbats, a stiflingly competitive fellow abolitionist, proslavery ideology, the Confederacy itself, Abraham Lincoln, or white supremacists who defined him out of the human family. Their opposition became his motive power, their arguments his own tools of counter-argument in the courts of moral justice.

In the case of the Aulds and reading, Douglass would steadily see to the center of one of slavery's mysteries, and into its evil heart. With his quest for literacy and the liberation of his mind, Douglass turned his own youth into one of the most profound meditations ever written on the character and meaning of slavery, of the slaveholders' mentality, and of human nature itself. In his first two autobiographies, Douglass seemed intuitively aware of Georg Hegel's famous insight about the mutual dependence of the master and the slave, of their inherent need for recognition from each other for the system to work. From experience, Douglass had his own ways of showing how the more perfect the slave, the more enslaved the master. And he showed how slavery, no matter how brutal its forms and conditions, was the meeting of two kinds of consciousness in a test of wills, and that total domination or absolute authority by the master was only rarely possible. He understood just how much the master's own identity as an independent, powerful person depended on the slave's recognition through his willing labor of that master's authority. But as Hegel put it, and Douglass lived it, in that labor, and the master's necessity of recognizing his humanity in performing it, "the bondsman becomes aware, through this rediscovery of himself by himself, of having and being a *mind* of his own." [12] The house on Philpot Street, as well as the entire teeming domain of Fell's Point, became for Douglass a kind of psychological and philosophical school in which he discovered that most precious thing— his mind. And he learned just how much his enslavers needed his mind as they struggled to suppress it. Emerging in the youthful slave was not only an intelligence and passion for survival and knowledge, but a political instinct as well.

According to Douglass, Sophia "lacked the depravity indispensable to shutting" her slave boy "up in mental darkness." She needed a great deal of "training," he wrote, to succeed in "forgetting my human nature," or in "treating me as a thing destitute of a moral and intellectual nature." But now, under her husband's orders, she surely tried to push against what Douglass called "nature" itself. "One cannot easily forget to love freedom," wrote the former slave, "and it is as hard to cease to respect that natural love in our fellow creatures." Sophia started out on her brief career as a slave master as a "tender-hearted woman," but under the new social strictures, her "lamb-like disposition gave way to one of tiger-like fierceness." By various clandestine "indirections," as he cleverly called it, the eager young reader smuggled newspapers and even books into the house, and even into his bed in a loft. Compellingly, Douglass observed the dark irony of Sophia's tragic learning curve. However hard she tried, it was all but impossible for her to see the black eleven- and twelve-year-old as mere chattel. "I was *more* than that," he asserted, "and she felt me to be more than that. I could talk and sing; I could laugh and weep; I could reason and remember; I could love and hate. I was human, and she, dear lady, knew and felt me to be so." [13]

Douglass later used his achievement of such self-awareness for numerous antislavery, as well as personal, purposes. But he also used it to demonstrate Miss Sophia's moral ruin, as he found his own moral ascent. "Conscience cannot stand much violence," Douglass philosophized. "In ceasing to instruct me, she must begin to justify herself to herself." Thus her anger when she saw Frederick in a corner "quietly reading a book or a newspaper." She came to treat him like a "traitor" launching a dangerous "plot." With Sophia constantly suspicious of Frederick's reading, and Frederick constantly wary of his mistress's policing of his habits and thoughts, together, as Douglass later phrased it, they reached the same conclusion: "education and slavery are incompatible with each other." [14] This master-slave relationship, having begun with motherly love and childlike adoration, became an all-out war for either total liberation or unconditional surrender. Outwitting his mistress and her angry husband, Frederick went out into the streets to recruit reinforcements for his little war.

For Frederick Bailey, reading was manna from heaven; but he was the one giving out the bread. Right on Philpot Street, near the Durgin and Bailey Shipyard, Frederick made friends with several white boys who lived in the same neighborhood. He would later claim this was all part of his "plan," cleverly "using my young white playmates" as teachers. But his recollections make clear that he developed a genuine bond with these struggling and hungry immigrant kids. Frederick carried his Webster's spelling book, and at every chance he would corner the white boys and, while "seated on a curbstone or a cellar door," solicit from them spelling lessons in return for his "tuition fee"—Sophia Auld's fresh warm bread. A "single biscuit" would also lead to animated discussions of why Frederick was a slave for life and why the white boys were free. The boys took him into their secret emotional havens and supported their enslaved friend. They told him slavery was unfair and that he would be free one day, especially when he turned twenty-one. Their words encouraged him, Douglass remembered. This convinced him that young boys were natural abolitionists, at least until they reached a certain age when they were no longer "unseared and unperverted" by slavery's material and moral logic. [15]

Douglass trusted the "consciences" of his young mates, whom he would not name in the early autobiographies to protect them from retribution in their adulthood. But by the time of writing *Life and Times* in 1881, he thanked four by name: Gustavus Dorgan, Joseph Bailey, Charles Farity, and William Cosdry. Here was Douglass's first comradeship with young Irishmen, his first trusted experience with humanism beyond race. As white boys condemned the hypocrisy and oppression of their parents toward one of their favorite fellow street urchins, perhaps Douglass found even ultimate experiential inspiration for his later speeches and writings. Whenever Douglass made arguments against slavery from the natural-rights tradition, which he did persistently after 1841, he could reflect upon this experience with the boys of Philpot Street, who often told him that "they believed *I* had as good a right to be free as *they* did," and that "they did not believe God ever made anyone to be a slave." [16]

As a slave in Baltimore, feeling more and more hemmed in as he grew in size and age, Douglass needed all the evidence he could muster to keep nature on his side. Then he found the book that changed his life. His white friends carried and studied a school reader, *The Columbian Orator*, by the compiler and teacher Caleb Bingham. On a day in 1830, Frederick took fifty cents he had earned on odd jobs around the shipyard, went to Nathaniel Knight's bookstore on Thames Street, and purchased a secondhand copy of the book he would later call his "rich treasure" and his "noble acquisition." [17] From that day forward in his life as a slave, *The Columbian Orator* became his constant companion, whether he was hiding in his loft reading space at the Aulds' Baltimore house, back on the Eastern Shore as a desperate teenager teaching some fellow slaves in a Sabbath school, or carrying it as almost his sole worldly possession when he escaped to freedom at age twenty.

The Columbian Orator went through twenty-three editions and many

The title page of the introduction and part of the table of contents of The Columbian Orator, *first published in 1797. Douglass carried his personal copy out of slavery with him.*

printings in at least ten cities from Vermont to Maryland over the more than sixty years it remained in print. With hardly any formal schooling, although a good deal of reading in his prairie farming background, the twenty-two-year-old Abraham Lincoln studied with relish the classical and Enlightenment-era oratory in *The Columbian Orator* during his first winter (1831–32) in New Salem, Illinois. That an urban slave youth living in Frederick Bailey's circumstances in Baltimore would, only a year earlier, discover this book through his white companions, who were in school, where there was an edition published in Maryland, is not surprising. That Douglass would embrace and later celebrate the language in this book is also not surprising. *The Columbian Orator* was much more than a stiff collection of Christian moralisms for America's youth. It was the creation of a man of decidedly antislavery sympathies, one determined to democratize education and instill in young people the heritage of the American Revolution, as well as the values of republicanism.[18]

Caleb Bingham's eighty-four entries were organized without regard for chronology or topic; such a lack of system was a pedagogical theory of the time designed to hold student interest. It held Frederick Bailey in rapt attention. The selections included prose, verse, plays, and especially political speeches by famous orators from antiquity and the Enlightenment. Cato, Cicero, Demosthenes, Socrates, John Milton, George Washington, Benjamin Franklin, William Pitt, Napoléon, Charles James Fox, and Daniel O'Connell (whom Bingham mistakenly identifies as O'Connor) all appear at least once, and some several times. Most of the pieces address themes of nationalism, individual liberty, religious faith, or the value of education. The reader as a whole reflected, as Bingham intended, New England's long transition from seventeenth-century Calvinism to nineteenth-century evangelical, freewill doctrine, from Puritan theocracy to the Revolutionary era's separation of church and state. As Douglass tackled the pages of *The Columbian Orator* in his early teens, whether he grasped the contexts or not, he would have repeatedly encountered irresistible words such as "freedom," "liberty," "tyranny," and the "rights of man."[19] Well before he read any serious history, he garnered and cherished a vocabulary of liberation.

Among the most striking features of the collection were eleven dialogues, most of them originally written for the book by David Everett, Bingham's associate in Boston. They were both serious and comical, aimed at the ethical imagination of young people and laced with moral tales about human nature, truth telling, and reversals of fate where underdogs outwit their oppressors. In "Dialogue Between the Ghosts of an English Duelist, a

North American Savage, and Mercury," the Englishman is revealed as the greater "savage," while the Mohawk Indian, respected for his cultural differences, achieves the higher virtue. With such stories about democratized education and ethnic pluralism, it was as if Frederick Bailey had landed in a modern multicultural classroom in the midst of a slave state. He read many speeches, and especially one dialogue, "repeatedly." "Dialogue Between a Master and a Slave" is to modern eyes a naïve and simplistic exchange between a slave owner and his bondman; but it profoundly affected Douglass as he read its improbable conclusion. If we can imagine our way into a thirteen- or fourteen-year-old's sensibility, what Douglass discovered in this story was that slavery was subject to "argument," even between a master and a slave. That the slave would convince the master to liberate him is improbable, but the teenager, psychologically imprisoned in his seemingly permanent fate, needed all the examples he could find of reason winning over power. The bondman even gets the last word in the dialogue, warning the slaveholder that despite his "kindness," he, the slave, is still "surrounded by implacable foes" bent on "revenge." [20]

On page after page of *The Columbian Orator*, Frederick found the reality of his condition, as well as dreams and justifications of his escape. His reading added not only to his "limited stock of language," he recalled, but it enabled him "to give tongue to many interesting thoughts which had frequently flashed through my soul." Young, angry, but exhilarated by the ferment and liberation in his mind, if not yet his body, Douglass felt his special book pouring "floods of light on the nature and character of slavery." He believed he had "now penetrated the secret of all slavery and oppression, and had ascertained their true foundation to be in the pride, the power and the avarice of man." [21] As an adult autobiographer, representing how a budding adolescent discovered knowledge of himself and of the human condition, Douglass left a transcendent record of the light emerging in his mind.

From *Slaves in Barbary: A Drama in Two Acts*, Douglass must have read aloud in solitude, which was his favorite habit, about a fascinating and motley collection of captives being sold as slaves. They include Turks, an Irishman, a black American slave named Sharp, and an American sea captain named Kidnap. In Douglass's imagination the story and the group may have felt a little like his gang of friends from the Baltimore streets. In a reversal of fortune, both Sharp and Kidnap are sold, but the white sea captain is put under Sharp's "instruction." Sharp has a thick slave dialect, which may have attracted the young Douglass, but he would surely have relished the eloquent speech of Teague (the Irish captive) in which he declares, "If men were made to be slaves and masters, why was not one man born with a whip in his hand and gold spoon in his mouth; and another with a chain on his arm, or a fetter to his heel?" And Douglass could not have missed the rousing ending, where Hamet, the "Bashaw of Tunis," frees a noble captive named Francisco, declaring, "Let it be remembered, there is no luxury so exquisite as the exercise of humanity, and no post so honourable as his, who defends THE RIGHTS OF MAN." [22] In his youth, Douglass had seen and learned so much about gold spoons, chains, and whips. He knew much about whites and blacks trapped in a system's fated destiny. But he never met a Bashaw he could trust.

From *The Columbian Orator* Douglass learned a great deal of motivation and confidence; but trust in the people around him, friend or foe, would be a long time coming. Above all, what Douglass found in this book was an elocution manual. Bingham's long introduction, "General Directions for Speaking," which drew upon the ancients to demonstrate a variety of practical techniques for effective oratory, may have been the most important thing Douglass ever read. The primary aim of oratory, said Bingham, was to create "action" between speaker and audience. "The perfection of art consists in its nearest resemblance to nature," the educator argued. True eloquence emerged when the orator could train his voice to "follow nature." [23] Bingham provided specific examples of such elements of speech making as cadence, pace, variety of tone, and especially gestures of the arms, hands, shoulders, and head. Young Frederick was enthralled, and though he could not yet know it, his life's vocation, his true calling, appeared as a saving grace.

Gaining knowledge—through experience, and now so importantly through reading, and slowly, through what he called the "art of writing"—became young Douglass's reason for living. It came with both joy and fear. In his first two autobiographies, Douglass wrote honest passages about his seizure of literacy that speak to the ages, to anyone who has ever found learning a pathway to genuine liberation. One can never know exactly how much Douglass imagined himself speaking to history, to millions of potential readers living behind walls of oppression. But he surely did here. "The increase of knowledge," he reported, "was attended with bitter, as well as sweet results. The more I read the more I was led to abhor and detest slavery, and my enslavers." More than overseers' beatings, fear of sale, or hunger and futurelessness, it was as if Douglass the writer of 1845 and the reviser of 1855 had found the existential core of his slave life: "As I read, behold! the very discontent so graphically predicted by master Hugh had already come upon me ... The revelation haunted me, stung me, and made me gloomy and miserable. As I writhed under the torment of this knowledge, I almost envied my fellow slaves their stupid contentment." Ten years earlier in the 1845 *Narrative*, Douglass had kept the point sharp and unforgettably eloquent:

I have often wished myself a beast. I preferred the condition of the meanest reptile to my own. Anything, no matter what to get rid of thinking! It was this everlasting thinking of my condition that tormented me. There was no getting rid of it. It pressed upon me by every object within sight or hearing, animate or inanimate. The silver trump of freedom had aroused my soul to eternal wakefulness. Freedom now appeared, to disappear no more forever. It was heard in every sound, and seen in every thing. It was ever present to torment me with a sense of my wretched condition. I saw nothing without seeing it, I heard nothing without hearing it, and felt nothing without feeling it. It looked from every star, it smiled in every calm, breathed in every wind, and moved in every storm.[24]

When Douglass's memory spoke within him, it often poured out in prose poetry. Remembering with all of his senses, did a twenty-seven-year-old writer ever express the craving for knowledge, life, and love, or the yearning for real freedom, any better?

Chapter 4

BALTIMORE DREAMS

Fear not . . . I am come for thy words.

—DANIEL 10:12

In the first seven years Douglass lived in the Auld household in Baltimore, he recollected, "As the almanac makers say of the weather—my condition was variable." He grew into his teenage years through a series of fateful encounters in Fell's Point on the harbor of Baltimore. From his enslavement he increasingly learned the meaning of his own humanity. Baltimore afforded him horizons to peer upon that the Eastern Shore closed off. With his "play fellows" along Philpot Street and around Durgin and Bailey Shipyard, he could test his wits and gain a sense of comradeship. In the Baltimore streets he also saw terrible cruelty and genuine humanity, "dark crimes without a name," as well as conditions that made a "city slave . . . almost a free citizen." He learned to assert himself mentally and physically, but that his "happiness was the sport of my masters." [1]

In October 1827, with Douglass still only nine years old, his owner, Aaron Anthony, died without a will. Frederick was forced to return to the Eastern Shore to be valued and divided up among twenty-eight other slaves as well as all of Anthony's other property. Anthony had three heirs, his sons Andrew and Richard, and daughter Lucretia (to whom Frederick had grown attached as a child). Unknown to the slave boy, Lucretia had died in the summer of 1827, and her portion of her father's property would go to her husband, Thomas Auld. Relatively delighted in his new life in Baltimore, the youth was about to receive a new lesson in the enormity of slavery's crimes against the human body and spirit. All of Frederick's slave kinfolk feared most falling into the hands of Andrew Anthony, a "cruel wretch," according to Douglass. Frightened and sorrowful, Sophia Auld and her son, Tommy, wept bitterly with Frederick as they delivered him to the docks and the schooner *Wildcat*, for the twenty-four-hour journey down the Chesapeake

Bay and back to the Eastern Shore. Sophia's hugs reflected a maternal bonding the boy desperately craved. He lounged on piles of tarpaulins aboard the slow tub of a boat and later recollected, "No one could tell among which pile of chattels I should be flung."[2]

The schooner circled up the Choptank River, then to the Tuckahoe, and dropped off Frederick near the Holme Hill Farm and his grandmother's cabin. He was a city boy now, and as Betsy Bailey greeted him, the other slave children looked on with strange gazes. Frederick felt an odd and sudden distance from this place of his birth. With excitement and anxiety, on October 18, 1827, twenty-nine slaves, almost all related by blood, some possibly the sons or daughters of the deceased master, representing three generations, lined up in a row and awaited their fate. Frederick's siblings were only vaguely familiar to him: his older brother, Perry, victim of a savage beating and kicking by Andrew Anthony only a short while before the day of division, was now fifteen and a field hand; his sisters, Sarah and Eliza, were thirteen and eleven. Following Maryland law and custom, the court-appointed appraisers, James Chambers and William Leonard, lined everyone up and did their assigned jobs. In most instances families were preserved and children remained with their mothers. In their heartless task, the appraisers divided the black people into three roughly equal lots. The total worth of the twenty-nine chattels was determined to be $2,800.[3] At a time when the cotton boom and the westward expansion of slavery surged into the Deep South and the Mississippi Valley, it is remarkable and against statistical odds that Frederick was given to Thomas Auld through his deceased wife. And apparently, Auld had already determined to send Frederick back to Baltimore to his brother Hugh's household.

Douglass spent one month on the Eastern Shore during this harrowing episode. Greatly relieved with a boy's self-interest, he seems not to have felt much attachment to his siblings, cousins, and aunts and uncles. He just wanted to be back in the atmosphere of Baltimore, where he could resume his urban adventure with literacy and somehow dream again. But as autobiographer, Douglass fashioned brilliant antislavery gems out of this darkest of slavery's evils. It "was the intensified degradation of the spectacle" that most lingered in the imagination. "What an assemblage!" he wrote. "Men and women, young and old, married and single; moral and intellectual beings, in open contempt of their humanity, leveled at a blow with horses, sheep, horned cattle and swine!" Douglass gave voice to the reality of *social death*. "Horses and men—cattle and women—pigs and children—all holding the same rank in the scale of social existence; and all subjected to the same narrow inspection, to ascertain their value in gold and silver. . . . How vividly, at that moment, did the brutalizing power of slavery flash before me! Personality swallowed up in the sordid idea of property! Manhood lost in chattelhood!"[4]

In his remembrance Douglass was a bit patronizing toward his fellow slaves and kinfolk. He claimed that in this frightful division of human beings that he likely "suffered more than most" because in Baltimore he had experienced more "tender treatment" than those left on the farm in Tuckahoe. He no longer faced the slaveholder's whip (for now), but they did. "The overseer had written his character on the living parchment of most of their backs, and left them callous." While a striking metaphor, this characterization is merely one in a long line of expressions by which Douglass beautifully represented the interior and exterior experience of slaves while also distancing himself from it on his self-styled path to fame. Assuredly, Frederick was thrilled to be back in Baltimore pitching pennies in the streets with his white buddies and learning to read from Sophia. His three sisters and one brother found a very different fate; all were allotted to Andrew Anthony, who drank himself into debt, selling off most of his slaves to the Deep South.[5] It would be decades and only through historic revolutions that Douglass would ever know most of his siblings again.

Frederick Bailey seized an education from the streets of Baltimore. From the city's young immigrant boys, from the laborers, smells, sounds, and dangers of the docks, from a mistress who tried to love him only to turn bitter foe, from a storefront preacher and a free black community that gave him hope, and from a book that made him dream, the future Douglass cultivated a furtive, lyrical imagination rooted in his discovery of language. From these days forward, that language forever churned inside him, ready to burst out on the page or in his voice. But his young life took shape from numerous twists of fortune that kept him back and forth to Baltimore instead of experiencing, as did many of his brothers, sisters, and cousins, a fate of obscurity in the booming slave markets.

Between the ages of ten and fourteen or so, Frederick grew stronger physically, but his falling-out with mistress Sophia over reading took a heavy emotional toll. The boy craved love and affection, and when he found it, he held on tight; when he lost it, he spun into despair. As he reached puberty and adolescence Frederick wanted some element of certainty, and now he seemed to find only confusion. Sophia's "abuse" fell upon him like a mother's sudden betrayal. "Nature had made us friends," he later wrote, "slavery made us enemies." Denied his joy in reading, unable to forge new forms of hope, Frederick descended into a "leaden, downcast" disposition. Sophia just could not understand his sorrow and chastised him for it. Her false smiles were met with an early teenager's rage. Douglass later claimed he was so despondent during this period of roughly 1830–33 that he "was even tempted to destroy my own life."[6] But as so often in his saga, in real time and in creative retrospect, he found emotional revival in words, and in yet another adult figure, this time a religious mentor.

Frederick overheard conversations in which master Hugh complained among his friends about the threat of "abolitionists." The boy smuggled newspapers, especially the *Baltimore American*, into the kitchen loft where he slept; in one article the paper reported the "incendiary information" that a "vast number of petitions and memorials had been presented to congress, praying for the abolition of slavery in the District of Columbia, and for the abolition of the slave trade between the states of the Union." These were, Douglass recalled, revelatory if mysterious words. With relish he found a dictionary and looked up the word *abolition*, only to find that it meant the "act of abolishing." Again he extracted his education from his white owners and oppressors. "There was HOPE in those words," Douglass wrote. Wielding adjectives like daggers, he named the "vindictive bitterness, the marked caution, the studied reserve, and the cumbrous ambiguity" of white folks expressing their fears of the word *abolition* as his evidence of things not seen. When one reads Douglass's autobiographies with modern eyes, these expressions can be dismissed as antislavery propaganda. But in his living situation in Baltimore, his intellectual curiosity exploding in the midst of the stultifying Auld household, gazing daily out on ships parting and arriving in the harbor, Douglass realized that slaveholders' fears of outside "denunciation" (which he increasingly found in his varied reading) provided him assurance that he "was not alone."[7]

In the late summer and fall of 1831, likely from overheard conversations at home and in the streets, but also perhaps from newspapers, Frederick learned that "the insurrection of Nathaniel Turner had been quelled, but the alarm and terror had not subsided." He does not tell us of any actual conversations in which he participated about the Turner rebellion; most slaves learned quickly to be silent and uninterested in such outbreaks of violence and resistance in front of white people who could wield absolute power over them. But he used the episode, which caused excitement around Fell's Point, to introduce the spiritual-religious awakening of his youth. He began to see, he wrote, that God's "judgments were abroad in the land" against "slaveholding wickedness." The idea of "abolition" gave him new hope, he said, because "I saw it supported by the Almighty, and armed with *Death*!"[8]

During the year of the Turner rebellion and its aftermath, Douglass found religion. He seems to have experienced a genuine conversion to faith in a personal Christian God. At thirteen and fourteen years old, Frederick had learned much already about survival and about the inner uses of solitude. But he was always nearly desperate to know he was "not alone." Young Frederick was enthralled with oratory and preaching, with words that could fill a room and stir an audience in mind and spirit. In his trusty companion, *The Columbian Orator*, Bingham's first selection, "An Extract from an Oration on Eloquence Pronounced at Harvard University, on Commencement Day, 1794," by William Perkins, Frederick found "eloquence" described with "great superiority over every other art." Powerful oratory, he learned, could "scatter the clouds of ignorance and error from the atmosphere of reason . . . irradiate the benighted mind with the cheering beams of truth." Inspired by such words, the teenager who felt emotionally and spiritually wretched was ready to discover the "business and glory of eloquence."[9] Preachers fascinated him, especially if they could wield words honestly and convincingly. He was drawn first to the performance, although the theology intrigued him as well.

At first, two white ministers influenced Frederick. Sophia Auld's pastor, Beverly Waugh, from the Wilk Street Methodist Church, would often visit Sophia in her own parlor to bolster her faith. Frederick listened, was impressed by the reverend's piety, as well as Sophia's open religious struggles, but not with anything Waugh said about the worlds beyond the walls of the house. He liked attending the sermons of another Baltimore Methodist reverend named Hanson because he preached that "all men, great and small, bond and free, were sinners in the sight of God; that they were by nature rebels against His government; and that they must repent of their sins, and be reconciled to God through Christ." "All men . . . bond and free?" Here was an early dose of theology and a modest nod to spiritual equality that would begin to condition Douglass for the moral persuasions of the abolitionists he would join some eight or nine years later. Is it possible that Frederick had heard the Reverend Hanson preach on Paul's letter to the Galatians? "There is neither Jew nor Gentile, there is neither bond nor free, there is neither male nor female: for ye are all one in Christ Jesus." Had Hanson possibly stumbled on 2 Corinthians' famous passage, with a young slave sitting in the back of the congregation? "But by an equality, that now at this time your abundance may be a supply for their want, that their abundance also may be a supply for your want: that there may be equality." Here, in a Baltimore church as a lonely teenager, young Frederick may have encountered his first textual lessons in the natural-rights tradition, the philosophy that would give him a voice.[10] In the future Douglass would always be drawn, as a believer and as a contrarian, to theological arguments and to the sheer power of biblical narratives and stories. But right now, with his Baltimore dreams lying dormant and cold, he needed personal faith.

Such an awakening also came from his contacts with black preachers. Many fundamental ideas, and especially the sermonic cadences of the language in Douglass's *Narrative* and in *My Bondage and My Freedom*, not to mention most of his early speeches, can be traced, in part, to the influences of a kind of black spiritual temperament and worldview that he soaked up from the African American religious community of Baltimore in his teenage years. Along with the stages of enslavement he experienced on the Eastern Shore, and from the knowledge he constantly *took* from all around him, this was Douglass's closest thing to schooling.

Frederick encountered a black lay preacher, Charles Johnson, who awakened the boy to prayer. Johnson spoke with him in "tones of holy affection," Douglass wrote. Through the "misery of doubts and fears," the desperate teenager underwent what he called a conversion to "faith in Jesus Christ, as the Redeemer, Friend and Savior of those who diligently seek him." With such language drawn from liturgy and confession, Frederick now cultivated his insatiable desire for knowledge by reading the Bible, Old and New Testaments. He might have even stumbled on the Sermon on the Mount. He now saw the world "in a new light," he recalled. He felt new impulses for living, "new hopes and desires." He even "loved all mankind—slaveholders not excepted; though I abhorred slavery more than ever. My great desire now was to have the world converted."[11] But his new faith was soon sorely tested.

In this state of mind, "religiously seeking knowledge," he met an old man, Charles Lawson, who quickly became his deepest influence. A drayman who worked for the owner of a ropewalk on Fell's Point, Lawson exuded a spirituality Frederick had never before encountered. Lawson lived only a short walk from Hugh Auld's house; the elder and the youth developed a cherished relationship. Douglass called Lawson alternately "uncle" and "Father." Above all, he was Frederick's teacher. To the young, despairing slave with a curious, if imprisoned, mind, Lawson was a holy man living in a hovel who prayed constantly, while walking the streets or even in the midst of conversations. Frederick listened to Lawson and loved him. They became spiritual companions, spending all available hours "singing, praying, and glorifying God." Lawson could read only a little, but he could interpret biblical metaphor, symbolism, and story as Frederick recited the words. For the young Douglass, slavery and life were his schools; but here he received a tutorial like no other at the feet of the tattered, prayerful old man. "I could teach him '*the letter*,' " wrote Douglass, "but he could teach me '*the spirit*.' " Perhaps in their readings and recitations, he and Lawson stopped in Paul's letter to the Romans, as Douglass learned that for believers "the law" (natural rights) was "written in their hearts." [12] Fred Bailey gained a lifelong fascination for Paul, the prisoner prophet.

Lawson gave Douglass two priceless gifts. One was faith; the other was the insatiable desire for knowledge through a love of words. Lawson instilled in the youth a belief about which Douglass wrote intensely. God "had a great work for me to do," he recalled as Lawson's charge, and the impressionable youth made a spiritual surrender to faith. His slavery was not permanent, Lawson helped him hope and believe. In thus nurturing Frederick's hope, Lawson prompted a craving for ideas, for books, for knowledge of the human morass in the Baltimore streets as well as in the wide world beyond. From Lawson, Douglass took the challenge that "I must go on reading and studying the scriptures." The praying drayman, like any of God's humble messengers in the Bible, had "fanned my already intense love of knowledge into a flame." Lawson was a Jesus figure of a kind for Douglass at a time when he desperately needed one. In 1855, he remembered Lawson as "my dear old father . . . the very counterpart of 'Uncle Tom.' The resemblance is so perfect, that he might have been the original of Mrs. Stowe's Christian hero." We can only guess at what biblical passages Lawson and Frederick dwelled on in their many days together. But what Lawson seems to have stressed most were the freedom from fear and the power of humility. The frightened teenager said he came to feel "under the guidance of a wisdom higher than my own." They may have read the startling visions in the book of Daniel. "Mourning" and "trembling" for many weeks, the prophet heard God speak to him: "Fear not Daniel; for from the first day thou didst set thine heart to understand, and to humble thyself before thy God, thy words were heard, and I am come for thy words." [13] Whatever they read, Douglass found hope in the presence of this spiritual father and was also beginning to find a calling.

Among Douglass's most powerful cravings now was to learn what he called the "art of writing." In his autobiographical memory, Douglass fashioned his emerging teenage literacy as his "means" of escape from slavery. It was his ultimate hunger, sometimes satisfied and sometimes not. In Baltimore, this early-nineteenth-century corner of a maritime world, full of immigrants, of the clash of languages and dialects, and of information that flowed in from the Atlantic Ocean and in front of his eyes via newspapers and books, Frederick observed the power of words. His job for a time at Durgin and Bailey Shipyard was to keep the fire burning under the steam box, and to watch the yard when the carpenters broke for dinner. In these intervals, Douglass would sit on a crate and study pieces of wood the carpenters were hewing into ships' timbers. They were labeled *S* for "starboard," *L* for "larboard," *S.F.* for "starboard forward," and so on. He memorized the letters and their uses. Moreover, Frederick loved it when the Aulds left him alone in the house; he had a "grand time," he reported, appropriating Tommy's copybooks and reworking them. He crammed a flour barrel and a chair up into his kitchen loft, and there, with minimal light, the future author copied words, sentences, and whole passages from a Webster spelling book, *The Columbian Orator*, the Bible, and a Methodist hymnbook. Out in the streets and at the docks, he created his own school tablets, even if he remembered it a bit romantically: "With playmates for my teachers, fences and pavements for my copybooks, and chalk for my pen and ink, I learned the art of writing." [14] This story alone should remind us why Douglass's autobiographies have sustained universal appeal. He knew that a slave stealing knowledge and the power of the word from the residue of urban maritime life, as well as from literary treasures no one could deny him, made a great story. By mining his memory for the details of his seizure of literacy, Douglass gave the world one of his greatest gifts. Words had become a reason to live.

In March 1833, Frederick Bailey, a literate, intellectually curious, spiritually awakened slave, found his Baltimore dreams brutally disrupted yet again. An ugly slaveholders' feud between the brothers Thomas and Hugh Auld, the one Frederick's owner and the other his current keeper, prompted his sudden forced departure back to the Eastern Shore. Thomas's wife, Lucretia (whom the child Douglass had adored), died in 1827, and he married Rowena Hamilton, the daughter of a wealthy Eastern Shore slaveholder, William Hamilton. Auld now lived in St. Michaels, the drab oyster-fishing town along the Miles River, only a few bends before it opened out to the Chesapeake Bay. According to Douglass, the dispute between the Aulds stemmed from how to treat Douglass's young cousin Henny Bailey, who

View of Baltimore harbor. 1850s. Photograph.

was among the brood of slaves Thomas Auld had inherited from Aaron Anthony. As a child, Henny had fallen into a fire and burned her hands, leaving
her with terrible disfigurement and incapable of most forms of labor. To
Auld, recalled Douglass, Henny was "of little more value than a horse with
a broken leg." So Thomas sent the girl to his brother's household in Baltimore. But Hugh and Sophia found her of no value either. They soon sent
her back to Thomas, who did not want her. This action led Thomas in a fit
of pique to conclude: "If he cannot keep 'Hen,' he shall not have 'Fred.'"[15]
Douglass's portrayal of this episode may represent his desire to keep himself always at the center of his autobiographical tale. But such were the small
destructive dramas in the daily life of American slavery. Were it not for the
fame and literary mastery of Douglass, we would never know about the
crippled Hennys of history.

Feeling a "shock to my nerves," the fifteen-year-old Frederick found
himself on a cold day aboard the sloop *Amanda*, again on his way back to
what would now seem the desolate, imprisoning landscape of his youth. As
he took his place in Auld's overcrowded house and general store at Cherry
and Talbot Streets (actually in a separate kitchen dwelling out back) in
St. Michaels, he was one of four town slaves, including his older sister Eliza,
his aunt Priscilla, and Henny. He wondered whether he would ever see Baltimore or feel its urban hopes and energies again. The seventeen-year-old

Eliza became Frederick's staunch ally; she was already considered married to a free black man named Peter Mitchell, to whom Auld would eventually sell her. She conspired with her angry younger brother in their day-to-day resistance to Auld's rule. Exceedingly depressed, Frederick not only missed his friends, the docks, his religious mentor, Lawson, his access to books and newspapers in Baltimore; he also now felt physical hunger.[16]

A growing teenager with likely an insatiable appetite, he scrounged for and stole extra food by almost any means necessary. Auld was "stingy," wrote Douglass of this dark time in his slave life, but his new wife, Rowena, was outright "cruel." Indian cornmeal was virtually the only food allowed the blacks at Auld's kitchen. Douglass's memory of this experience inspired in him one of his most elaborate philosophical defenses of natural-rights doctrine, as applied to slaves under the yoke of bondage. He had a perfect right to steal his master's food, or any other possession, Douglass later argued, because not only had Auld rendered him property, but the slave society had marked him "privileged plunder." Douglass believed he was, therefore, by birthright, "justified in plundering in turn." The hungry antebellum slave in an amoral system, the bored laborer with nearly crushed hopes of liberty, later spoke with a raw logic more powerful than the slaveholding revolutionaries of the late eighteenth century: "The morality of a free society can have no application to slave society. Slaveholders have made it almost impossible for the slave to commit any crime, known either to the laws of God or to the laws of man. If he steals, he takes his own; if he kills his master, he imitates only the heroes of the revolution."[17] In this brutal environment, Douglass became a student of human nature, of the slaveholder's mind, and of the fullest meanings of human rights. He was also becoming, by experience, a dangerous slave rebel. Frederick Bailey came to believe the plunderer shall in due time be plundered.

But he was still hungry. The gnawing stomach, boredom, rage, and a growing intelligence mixed to make Frederick a troublesome slave. He and Auld made a perfectly disastrous pair, symbolic of why slavery was not only evil but sometimes economically a dead end for both master and slave. By Douglass's account, Thomas Auld merited no respect as a person, much less as a slave owner. As an adult abolitionist, eight to ten years after his tormented years as a teenage slave, Douglass became the movement's most astute source on slaveholder mentality and character. Auld, he maintained, was not a "born" slaveholder; he was a "poor man," pilot of a Bay boat, and an inheritor of slaves by marriage. His main character trait was "meanness"; he lacked strength and consistency in his handling of slaves, and though he craved power, he seemed only weak and miserable in exercising it. Douglass lived to condemn Auld with words meant as daggers to the heart of all lordly masters: "He was cruel, but cowardly. He commanded without firmness." Auld tried to rule with the "fury of a demon," but he "might well be mistaken for an inquirer who had lost his way." He was, Douglass snidely said, "not even a good imitator." [18]

In August 1833, Frederick attained a special insight into Auld's character when his master allowed him to attend a religious revival at Bay Side, some eight miles from St. Michaels. This classic country Methodist camp meeting left indelible images in Douglass's fertile memory. People came from all over Talbot County; two steamboat loads of pilgrims also arrived from Baltimore. The gathering lasted a week, and slaves relieved of work for a few days could hardly resist the excitement of hundreds of campfires roasting meat, a veritable tent city with a preacher's stand in the middle and a "pen" marked off for "mourners" to enter and make their confessions, embrace the Lord, and be saved. A recent convert himself to Christian faith, although now struggling to understand whether God intended any justice on earth, Frederick witnessed the spectacle of master Thomas's wrenching, emotional breakdown and confession in that pen. Blacks were not allowed in the pen, nor in front of the preachers' performances, but Douglass tells us that he imposed his way close enough to hear Auld "groan," and to see his reddened face, his disheveled hair, and a "stray tear halting on his cheek." [19] Here festered the dark heart of the moral bankruptcy of slaveholders that the future abolitionist would make his central subject.

Douglass converted this memory into angry condemnations of the religious hypocrisy of the entire Christian slaveholding universe, especially the little microcosm of Auld's household, where the young slave now had to listen daily to loud praying and testifying by the white family, and to participate in hospitality extended to local preachers who were sometimes housed at Auld's home, all the while enduring the good Methodist's verbal and physical cruelty. For Douglass, the proof of any sincerity in Auld's "teardrop" manifested in his actions. In his deeds and his glances, wrote Douglass, it was as if the pathetic master had concluded, "I will teach you, young man, that, though I have parted with my sins, I have not parted with my sense. I shall hold my slaves, and go to heaven too." [20] Such a vow, imagined by Douglass from the memory of his owner's cowardly eyes, might serve as an unspoken motto of the Christian capitalists who ruled the antebellum South.

Amid this despairing situation, Frederick found what he called "something worth living for." A pious young St. Michaels white man named Wilson discovered that Fred Bailey was literate, with a Baltimore background, and asked him to help with a Sabbath school to be convened at the house of a free black man named James Mitchell. With a dozen old spelling books and a few Bibles, they began meeting with twenty pupils on Sundays. Frederick loved this chance to use his mind again. "I could not go to Baltimore," he reminisced, "but I could make a little Baltimore here." Before the second meeting finished, however, a mob led by Thomas Auld, and two other white slave owners Douglass named, stormed into Mitchell's house with sticks and epithets, driving the little band of eager learners back to their drab hovels. One of the "pious crew" in the mob accused Frederick of becoming "another Nat Turner," he recalled with ironic relish. By the 1840s, Douglass would become one of abolition's fiercest critics of proslavery religious and secular hypocrisy. But he did not need to learn that argument from William Lloyd Garrison nor any of the other Garrisonians, who made anticlericalism a major tenet of their crusade. Here in this isolated backwater of American slavery, Douglass had seen and felt on his body and in his soul the "blood-chilling blasphemy" at the heart of proslavery piety. The "professedly holy men" who owned his body and tried to own his mind had taught him virtually all he needed to know on that count.[21]

Douglass seems to have adopted a devil-may-care attitude of desperation toward Auld. Auld responded by beating Frederick for the first time; although as he recalled these whippings, the proud former slave portrayed his master's handling of the whip as that of a hapless amateur. Not so, however, when Auld tied up cousin Henny to a joist and took out his frustrations on the crippled girl. Auld would beat her mercilessly with a cowskin before breakfast, then leave her hanging by her strapped wrists for three to four hours, only to return later and beat her again. In Frederick's mind, Auld's piety dripped with Henny's blood. In this miserable circumstance, Frederick became essentially an unmanageable teenage slave. He verbally confronted Auld, refused to work, and repeatedly let the master's horse run away. Auld resolved to send Douglass "out . . . to be broken" by a local slave overseer who rented his time and humble farm for just such a service.[22] Auld's pious cruelty now transformed into an even darker hell.

On January 1, 1834, Douglass began a year of living in a kind of wilderness of horror at Edward Covey's dilapidated farmstead. With his few belongings wrapped in a bundle on a stick braced over his shoulder, Frederick walked seven cold miles westward from St. Michaels to a country setting overlooking the Chesapeake Bay. In the art of his autobiography, this place would be the "tyrant's home," the "dark night" of a strong young teenager broken and rendered a "brute" by a totalitarian regime ruled by one savage man.[23] Ishmael found his Ahab, the ultimate tyrant whose obsessions could never be tamed, and by whom the world could be wrecked and taken down; Douglass found his Covey, who would bludgeon and wreck the young slave, but against whom the sufferer would resurrect himself through violence and will and find another reason to live. Douglass's pivotal year as a sixteen-year-old under Covey's savagery is forever cloaked in some of his most beguiling and lyrical prose. The chapters on the time under Covey's brutal rule are the longest in Douglass's first two autobiographies. The experience is crafted so artfully that it is often discussed as little more than a literary creation, a brilliant text that lives beyond or above the barnyard, the fence posts, the oxen team, the silent corn and wheat fields, or the dense woods of that Eastern Shore landscape. But Covey was real, and Douglass left a good deal of blood in the soil of that archvillain's farm, while also extracting a story he would one day make almost as immortal as Herman Melville's whaling ship. Douglass's great gift, and the reason we know of him today, is that he found ways to convert the scars Covey left on his body into words that might change the world. His travail under Covey's yoke became Douglass's crucifixion and resurrection.

Although Douglass portrayed Covey as a professional slave breaker by trade, in 1834 he was actually a relatively poor twenty-eight-year-old farmer, with a wife and infant child, who hired slaves to work his rented farmstead. Covey paid Auld for one year's service of the strong young slave. Perhaps most disgusting to the young Christian Fred Bailey were Covey's and his wife's religious devotions, acted out in their house every morning and night. At night Covey would have his small family, which included a cousin employed as a worker, as well as the three slaves gather for hymns. Since Covey was a bad singer and Frederick had a fine voice, the master would order the slave to lead with the hymn. Douglass found such flaunting of religious hypocrisy nauseating; sometimes, he reports, he would lamely sing, other times he would simply refuse and dare his "brother in the church" to beat him. The daily problem was that Frederick was for the first time forced to be a "fieldhand," working from first light to sunset, performing tasks for which he had no experience. By any measure, Covey was a sadistic taskmaster, and for all those who simply refused to believe that the lash was a vivid part of the everyday lives of American slaves, Douglass demonstrated otherwise. On his third day at Covey's farm, the brute viciously beat him with a switch, making the blood flow and leaving painful "wales" on his back that would fester and hurt under his coarse wool shirt.[24] Those physical scars on his back would remain an occasional piece of Douglass's abolitionist repertoire the rest of his life. Rarely would he whip off his shirt and show them, but they were always there as a physical and rhetorical device to shock the complacent audience.

Within the first month Covey purposely sent Frederick out with a wagon and a largely unbroken team of oxen to retrieve wood. With no training in how to handle the massive animals and the reins, he lost control, crashing the wagon twice, once in the dense woods, and once into a gatepost. Douglass later gave an account of this episode with elaborate detail and converted it into a rich antislavery metaphor as he also converted Covey himself into the worst creature slavery could produce. "There I was, all alone," Douglass wrote, "in a thick wood, to which I was a stranger; my cart upset and shattered; my oxen entangled, wild and enraged; and I, poor soul . . . I knew no more of oxen, that the ox driver is supposed to know of wisdom." With an ax (at least he had chopped wood before) Frederick managed to disentangle the oxen and get his cart back to the farmyard to face the consequences of his disaster. In the memory of this episode, as with so many others, he taught his readers the meaning of slavery: "I now saw, in my situation, several points of similarity with that of the oxen. They were property, so was I; they were to be broken, so was I. Covey was to break me, I was to break them; break and be broken—such is life."[25]

He had become the beast, as Douglass remembered his mental and physical faculties during this period of despair. He anticipated future totalitarian systems and leaders as he remembered Covey's methods of terror and control. Sometimes the wordless farmer, with "the fierceness of a wolf," would grunt and lunge at Frederick with "sticks or cowskins" and slash his head and back over and over, leaving the laborer bleeding and all but resigned to these expected assaults. But Covey also possessed a cunning like no other slaveholder Douglass ever encountered. He and his two fellow unlucky slave workers on this isolated farm called Covey the "snake." The scoundrel would "crawl in ditches and gullies" or "hide behind stumps and bushes" to spy on his slaves and startle them into hard work. Covey, said Douglass, could make him "feel as though he was always present." To a lonely, despondent, brutalized, but literate sixteen-year-old slave who had seen the city and read of an even wider, wondrous world, Covey embodied the "system" that now imprisoned Fred Bailey in a desolate corner of the Eastern Shore, a wilderness of unseen, untold violence from which he might never have returned. By midsummer, in this daily hell, Covey achieved what Douglass claimed was the overseer's motive: "I was broken in body, soul and spirit. My natural elasticity was crushed, my intellect languished, the disposition to read departed . . . behold a man transformed into a brute." [26]

Sundays provided Frederick his only downtime. Lonely, with no one to confide in, he tells us he would lie down under a shade tree and spend many hours in "a sort of beast-like stupor, between sleep and wake." [27] Sometimes he would stroll over toward the Chesapeake Bay, which was only a short distance from Covey's depressing farmstead, and the people, black and white, with whom the tall, brainy boy found no conversation. There he would allow himself an occasional burst of imagination, a daydream he would ten years later capture in a beautiful and haunting metaphor of freedom. Sitting in a small room at a spare desk in Lynn, Massachusetts, in the winter of 1844–45, Douglass peered back into his memory and wrote a passage for the ages.

"Our house stood within a few rods of the Chesapeake Bay," he remembered, "whose broad bosom was ever white with sails from every quarter of the habitable globe." Douglass then captured slavery and freedom with artistry unparalleled in the genre of slave narratives:

> Those beautiful vessels, robed in purest white, so delightful to the eye of freemen, were to me so many shrouded ghosts, to terrify and torment me with thoughts of my wretched condition. I have often, in the deep stillness of a summer's Sabbath, stood all alone upon the lofty banks of that noble bay, and traced, with saddened heart and tearful eye, the countless number of sails moving off to the mighty ocean. The sight of these always affected me powerfully. My thoughts would compel utterance; and there, with no audience but the Almighty, I would pour out my soul's complaint, in my rude way, with an apostrophe to the moving multitude of ships.

Then, perhaps gazing through the wintry window in Lynn, Douglass shifts and speaks directly to the ships, trying to reenter a teenager's imagination:

> You are loosed from your moorings and are free; I am fast in my chains, and am a slave! You move merrily before the gentle gale, and I sadly before the bloody whip! You are freedom's swift-winged angels, that fly around the world; I am confined in bands of iron! O that I were free! O that I were on one of your gallant decks and

under your protecting wing! Alas, betwixt me and you, the turbid waters roll.[28]

In such a prose poem, Douglass wrote a psalmlike prayer of deliverance in his *Narrative*, rendering in the music of words the meaning of slavery's potential to destroy the human spirit, but at the same time transcending his remembered misery to declare at the end of the lament, in language reminiscent of the slave spirituals, that "there is a better day coming." Before ending this meditation, as though bracing his face and body to a sudden wind off the Bay, he declared that he would one day "take to the water" and bravely steer "a north-east course."[29] He would indeed one day toss his tears upon that sea and dream his way back to and out of Baltimore. And in the decade before the Civil War, as today, his readers could and can still stand with Douglass in the dark night of his soul along their own Chesapeakes and sense the deepest of human yearnings in their own souls.

One day in the terrible heat of August, Frederick broke down physically while threshing wheat in the hot sun with other slaves. He fell into a delirious stupor, experiencing what modern medicine would call heat exhaustion or stroke. With terrible head pain, his limbs trembling, and likely a dangerous fever from lack of water, the clammy-skinned youngster crawled to a post and rail fence for shade. The wheat fanning stopped, and Covey came out to the scene, demanding that Frederick stand up. Douglass remembers that he could not speak and that Covey kicked him savagely in the ribs. Then he beat the youngster about the head with a hickory stick, leaving a bleeding gash. As Covey joined the work crew, replacing Frederick, the stumbling slave regained his feet and fled into the woods. There, in fear and exhaustion, he resolved to walk through the nighttime forest back to St. Michaels to plead his case before his owner, Thomas Auld.[30]

Barefoot through "bogs and briers," staying off the roads so as to avoid Covey if he pursued him, Frederick made it to Auld's store that night. With blood clotted on his head and his torn shirt bloodstained, the ragged supplicant begged for Auld's protection. Auld paced the floor, refused to believe most of Frederick's horror story, and ridiculed him as the perpetrator of his own travail. The master ordered his slave to go back to serve out the remaining months of his term, lest Auld "lose the whole year's wages." With this lesson in slaveholders' avarice, Douglass stayed the night and, without food the next morning, made the seven-mile trek back to Covey's dreaded lair. "Broken in spirit," what did Douglass ponder as he stumbled back to a fate of more abuse? Did he think of Father Lawson and wonder if any God existed? Did he feel a loneliness in his bones far greater than the pains in his injured body? Did he imagine with near-homicidal scorn a picture of Auld and Covey in their Methodist pews, praying for good crops, healthy families, and the warrant of their own salvation? Was his mind simply lost in contemplations of the sheer scale and weight of injustice? Did he try to pray, with only tearful false starts and wasted sentence fragments for his efforts? All this and more, he implied, his bludgeoned mind thought and his body felt as he walked.[31] For now, he could not even see the sailing ships if they leaped off the ocean waves.

As soon as Covey saw Frederick step over a fence rail, the tyrant pursued him with a whip and a rope. The young man fled again into a field of tall corn, where he hid. The "ferocious hound," as Douglass called Covey, could not find him, likely expecting that his slave would ultimately return again out of hunger. Frederick found temporary safety in the woods, where the weary fugitive lay down on a bed of leaves, "shut in with nature, and nature's God." Confused and frightened during the night, he encountered a fellow slave, Sandy Jenkins, who was walking several miles to visit his wife, a free black woman. Jenkins too had been hired out for the year, and he took pity on the desperate younger man and, at considerable risk, ushered him to his humble home. Sandy's wife helped Frederick to wash his scarred and bloody body and fed him a freshly baked ashcake. Douglass remembered this human touch, "relieving a brother bondman," as a saving grace in the midst of his torment. In 1855 he called this moment at Sandy's cabin "the meal, of all my life, most sweet to my taste, and now most vivid in my memory." Before departing the next morning, Sandy, who fashioned himself a spiritual adviser and, to anguished Frederick, seemed "a genuine African," gave the runaway a special "root" to wear only on his right side for protection as he returned to Covey's domain. Unmoved by the logic of Sandy's "magical powers," Douglass nevertheless decided he had nothing to lose and wore the talisman as instructed.[32]

More in line with his own self-understanding and portrayal, though, Douglass attributed much of Jenkins's kindness toward him to the neighborhood knowledge of his literacy. Claiming he was the only slave in the region who could read and write, Douglass preferred to wear his learning rather than a conjurer's herbs from the forest floor. "Although I was hated by Covey and by my master," Douglass maintained, "I was loved by the colored people, because they thought I was hated for my knowledge, and persecuted because I was feared." Always ready to offer himself as a symbol of the power of the word and of the will, he nevertheless admitted that in this desperate summer night, his Good Samaritan had a strong case. "My book learning," he remembered Sandy telling him, "had not kept Covey off me, (a powerful argument just then)."[33]

It was a Sunday morning as Frederick once again came into Covey's yard, and the pious slave driver said good morning on his way to church services. Covey did not beat slaves on the Sabbath. Monday morning was another matter; what ensued was the most celebrated fight between a master and a slave in all of antislavery literature. For the elaborate details of this rumble in a stable and a farmyard, which Douglass claimed lasted for two hours, the autobiographer is our only source. He wrote of it with an odd formality, as though he were the observer cleaning up a deadly blood sport for sentimental readers. Whatever the duration and nature of this violent melee, for Douglass it grew into the pivotal turning point in his life as a slave. Slaves who resisted and fought their masters sometimes did not live to tell about it, or at least found themselves in transit to a worse fate farther south. Covey caught Douglass by surprise coming down from a hayloft and tried to tie his legs. In language that became melodramatic and moralistic, even if blow by blow and full of bravado, Douglass nevertheless admitted that he did not at first know from "whence came the daring spirit" and his "fighting madness." Douglass claimed to have fought "strictly on the defensive," which does not ring true. Covey became flustered, even "frightened," with much "puffing and blowing." He called on two other slaves to help him grab and hold Frederick; but the rebel kicked one of them into agonized submission and the other simply refused and comically said he just wished to work. The two grunting fighters grappled and threw each other on the ground. Douglass says he strangled Covey by the throat, drawing blood with his nails, and his tormentor simply gave up.[34]

As one scholar has suggested, Douglass wrote of this fight as though it were "a performance, a staged and ritualized battle" in this master-slave drama. Another historian has called the fight a stylized "death dance." It also later served the former slave's story as the establishment of his manhood by ritualized violence. "I was *nothing* before," he wrote, "I was a MAN NOW." As he told of it over and over in public forums later, he portrayed his victory over Covey as the demonstration of the physical force necessary for male dignity and power. He had bested the tyrant; he now possessed an inner freedom and an outward pride. "It was a resurrection from the dark and pestiferous tomb of slavery," Douglass said, "to the heaven of comparative freedom." He convinced himself, not without reason, that Covey exacted no public or legal retribution (Frederick could have been arrested, tried, and hanged for such resistance) because of a coward's shame and fear for his reputation. The wounded boy was now a man who could lift his head high and tell the world that old Covey never again laid a hand on him in his remaining months in that country prison. Most of all, embedded in all the talk of manhood, he admitted that his spirit, all but lost in the woods those despairing nights, could now revive; the defeat of Covey, he said, "rekindled . . . my Baltimore dreams." [35]

Chapter 5

NOW FOR MISCHIEF!

No man can tell the intense agony which is felt by the slave, when wavering on the point of making his escape. All that he has is at stake. . . . The life which he has may be lost, and the liberty which he seeks may not be gained.

—FREDERICK DOUGLASS, 1845

D ouglass likely never forgot the sensation of his hands gripping Covey's throat, his fingernails drawing blood, as he strangled the slave master. Whether it happened or not as Douglass later described it, the feeling became real in memory. By January 1, 1835, after spending the annual holiday week watching, and imbibing, with the rest of the slaves in the St. Michaels region as they frolicked, danced, and drank their days away with their masters' approvals, Frederick Bailey was ready for more "rational" sensations.[1] He was once again hired out by Auld for a year to another local farmer, William Freeland, whose land fronted on the Miles River.

As Douglass endlessly explained the nature of slavery to public audiences later in the 1840s, a major theme of his writing and speeches was the slaveholders' mentality, their quest not only for control of the bondman's body, but more important, "to destroy his thinking powers." By temperament and apparently strategy, Freeland, who did not even attend church and practiced leniency about food, labor routines, and general emotional autonomy among his slaves, allowed Frederick more space and time to think, read, and, as it turned out, to clandestinely teach. Freeland did not beat his slaves; though his soil was worn-out from too much tobacco husbandry, his tools were much better than most, and he was a fair broker with his slaves' need for rest. Frederick liked Freeland, especially in contrast to his previous year of suffering under Covey. Douglass's mind, he recollected, gained "increased sensibility." In *Bondage and Freedom*, he drew beautifully upon 1 Corinthians to say that the "natural" and "temporal" in human needs come first, and "afterward that which is spiritual." He later mused in memoirs and speeches about how his time with Freeland taught him that when a slave gets a "good" master, it makes him only wish "to become his *own* master."[2]

Frederick had gained a reputation in the region because of the fight with Covey; and his literacy made him a special seventeen-year-old among a mostly older group of male slaves who became his beloved "band of brothers" on Freeland's place. Douglass "loved" (a word he sparingly used in remembering his slavery years) especially four young men: brothers Henry Harris and John Harris, Handy Caldwell, and Sandy Jenkins (the root man), now working on the same farmstead with Frederick. As Douglass set up this scene of mental liberation amid a group of trusted comrades, he delivered a clever jolt of foreshadowing. "Now for Mischief!" he declared. "I had not been long at Freeland's before I was up to my old tricks."[3]

Quickly that winter and into summer, Frederick gathered eventually more than thirty male slaves on Sundays, and sometimes even on weeknights, in a Sabbath literacy school. He may have constructed the Covey fight as his resurrection from a living death into "manhood," but Douglass's real manhood, his real vocation, emerged here in his leadership among a cherished group of eager learners and fellow dreamers. Here on the farm of a "just" slaveholder, in downtime from working as a field hand, the future Frederick Douglass found his first abolitionist flock. Here "in the woods, behind the barn, and in the shade of trees," Frederick discovered his charisma and burnished his love of words. "The fact is, here I began my public speaking," he later wrote. With *The Columbian Orator* in his hands, which he had somehow kept hidden from the Coveys and Aulds in his life, and with a Webster's spelling book and a copy of the Bible, Frederick, now tall and with an adult's deeper voice, stood before these young men and preached the power of literacy as the means to freedom. Under an old live oak on the Eastern Shore on summer Sabbaths, practicing gestures with his arms and shoulders, and modulating the sounds and cadences of his words as *The Columbian Orator* instructed, the greatest antislavery orator of the nineteenth century first found his voice.[4] One wonders if before any of his thousands of speeches and appearances later in life, as he listened to someone drone on introducing him, or as he stepped to a lectern, a fleeting memory of his oak-tree congregations danced in his mind.

Sherwood Forest (Freeland Farm). Douglass lived and worked in these fields, 1835–36. Aerial view, c. 1930.

Douglass loved his days and nights teaching his fellow slaves. "I have had various employments during my short life," he wrote in 1855, "but I look back to none with more satisfaction, than to that afforded by my Sunday school." Douglass's autobiographical writing is often extremely self-centered, drawing hard boundaries around his sole character—himself as the melodramatic self-made hero. But his remembrance of the Sabbath school is one time when he expressed an abiding love, an "attachment deep and lasting," for his supporting cast. Frederick was the leader now of a local brotherhood, unlike anything he had known before, a gang of word lovers and emerging readers. They were "brave and . . . fine looking" as a group. He had never known other such friends in his life to the age of thirty-seven, as he rhapsodized in 1855. "No band of brothers could have been more loving." They had secret passwords for group protection in their risky business; and what they especially possessed was a sense of a male-bonded *home* in their wilderness of work and hopelessness. For Frederick's bursting spirit, "these were great days to my soul." [5]

In the midst of these clandestine adventures in literacy and comradeship, Frederick and his four closest friends launched an escape plot. At the beginning of 1836, Freeland rented Frederick for yet one more year of labor. Douglass later portrayed himself as glad to stay on Freeland's place; he could continue his teaching and building of his band of readers as he turned eighteen years old. But he also, perhaps quite honestly, remembered himself as "not only ashamed to be contented, but ashamed to *seem* contented." Frederick felt a new level of despondency, the kind born of the same increased liberty to think, speak, and create the "intense desire . . . to be free" in his devoted compatriots as he had felt at a younger age in Baltimore. He left many haunting expressions of this longing in the mind of a slave reaching adulthood with an imprisoned mind. "The grim visage of slavery," he wrote on behalf of all slaves, "can assume no smiles which can fascinate the partially enlightened slave into a forgetfulness of his bondage." [6]

In a combination of providential, psychological, and even military language, Douglass told of his escape plot that nearly ended his abolitionist career before it started. "The prophecies of my childhood were still unfulfilled," he claimed in retrospect. As he remembered Father Lawson's words (predicting God's purposes in Douglass's rise in the world), Frederick believed that at eighteen he had grown "too big for my chains." His group of five conspirators plotted their backwater rebellion like a tiny military company, with Frederick as their captain, always watching his own "deportment, lest the enemy should get the better of me." Just before the Easter holiday in the spring of 1836, they planned to steal away into Chesapeake Bay in a large canoe owned by William Hambleton, whose large estate bordered Freeland's farm (Douglass mistakenly calls him Hamilton in the autobiographies), rowing their way north some seventy miles to the head of the Bay, and then trekking by foot overland to the free state of Pennsylvania. Wildly ambitious and based on inadequate geographic knowledge, the plot had little hope of success, although they could visualize themselves out on the Bay claiming either to be fishermen working for their masters, or slaves allowed the holiday week off from labor. Frederick employed his literacy now to a political end for the first time—he wrote a "pass" for each member of the band, authorizing him to spend the Easter holiday in Baltimore, and signed *W.H.*[7] These desperate young men decided to steel their nerves in group solidarity, in songs, in their secret meetings and handshakes, and in their faith in their youthful leader, who stood erect over their battlements and strove for the right words of resolve.

Their bravado, however, had to coexist with fear. Frederick and his team met by night around their quarters and on Sundays out in arbors. The eighteen-year-old played the commanding officer of the platoon preparing for war; he argued for the plan against all its admittedly logical obstacles— what he called "phantoms of trouble." He cajoled, instilled spirit when they needed it, drew mental pictures of hope when they all felt desperation, and tried "to instill all with firmness." But Frederick's pep talks did not suffice. In his autobiography, Douglass later presented this episode brilliantly as a journey into the psychology of the runaway slave. Fred Bailey may have enjoyed his role as the band's leader by words and personality, but he shared their sense of psychological terror about betrayal and capture.[8]

As they "rehearsed" for their fateful day of flight out of "Egypt," Douglass remembered, they could preen and swagger for one another one moment, and the next, the Harris brothers might just stare in silent dread into Frederick's eyes, awaiting his next direction. "We were confident, bold and determined at times," wrote Douglass; "and, again, doubting, timid and wavering; whistling like the boy in the graveyard, to keep away the spirits." When they sang to steady their nerves, a favorite hymn rang out:

> *O Canaan, sweet Canaan.*
> *I am bound for the land of Canaan,*
> *I thought I heard them say,*
> *There were lions in the way,*
> *I don't expect to stay*
> *Much longer here.*
> *Run to Jesus—shun the danger—*
> *I don't expect to stay*
> *Much longer here.*

Douglass hastened to point out that for his band of runaways, it was not heaven they sought just then; "the north was our Canaan."[9]

But what about those lions? They could not sing them away. Nine years later, Douglass left a probing statement of the recurring dream/nightmare of the runaway slave, as though he wanted to tear apart the romance of the Underground Railroad and replace it with a vision of the fugitive slave's real psychic hell. "At every gate through which we were to pass," he wrote on behalf of his comrades and every other bold runaway, "we saw a watchman— at every ferry a guard—on every bridge a sentinel—and in every wood a patrol." The options faced by the runaway came from deep in historical time, from the ancient circumstance of the oppressed choosing life or death against the overwhelming weapons of the powerful. "On the one hand, there stood slavery, a stern reality, glaring frightfully upon us," wrote Douglass as dramatist of the macabre, "its robes already crimsoned with the blood of millions, and even now feasting itself greedily upon our own flesh. On the other hand, away back in the dim distance, under the flickering light of the north star, behind some craggy hill or snow-covered mountain, stood a doubtful freedom—half frozen—beckoning us to come and share its hospitality." Why tempt such a "monster" infesting their thoughts? On every side, they saw "grim death" in "horrid shapes." They saw themselves drowned in the ocean, their bodies torn by bloodhounds. After thus characterizing the mind of the fugitive slave, Douglass went to Shakespeare's *Hamlet* and allowed his comrades the moment to "rather bear those ills we had, than to fly to others, that we knew not of." But they could still somehow see that distant hill. Then Douglass invoked Patrick Henry's famous "Give Me Liberty or Give Me Death" speech from the American Revolution and claimed that the American slave rebel's right to this bold resolution was "more sublime" than any by one of the founding fathers. The "lash and chain" had bought that privilege.[10]

So, brave but terrified, Frederick and his small band awoke on their prospective day of deliverance, Saturday, April 2, 1836. They had packed little bags and gone to the field to do their early-morning work—spreading manure. Their plot fell into disaster almost immediately. They had been betrayed (Douglass later thought probably by Sandy Jenkins, who had withdrawn from the plot in tortured anxiety). As they gathered at the kitchen near Freeland's house, Frederick spied four white men on horseback, and two blacks walking with them, coming down the long lane into the property. Then came the aging and rotund William Hambleton riding at a gallop. After a brief consultation between Freeland and Hambleton, within seconds the constables seized Frederick and tied his arms with rope. Then they moved to the Harrises; John was subdued and tied, but Henry physically resisted, refusing to allow his hands to be tied by these men, who were armed. One constable drew his pistol, cocked it, and aimed it point-blank at Henry's breast. "Shoot me! Shoot me!" shouted Henry in defiance. "You can't kill me but once. Shoot!—shoot! and be d__d. I won't be tied." Then the whole group assaulted Henry, drove him to the ground, and subdued him in ropes. While all were distracted, Frederick threw his pass into the kitchen fire; later he instructed the others to eat theirs.[11]

In Freeland's front yard, the four bound young men were fastened with ropes to three horses, guarded by the mounted constables, and prodded off on a fifteen-mile forced march to the county jail in Easton. Before departure, Mrs. Betsey Freeland, the landowner's mother and Hambleton's sister, who had long-standing affection for the Harris brothers, railed at Frederick as the corrupter of the innocent. "You devil!" she screamed at him. "It was you who put into the heads of Henry and John to run away. But for you, you long legged yellow devil, Henry and John would never have thought of running away!" Douglass, the bound prisoner, met her gaze, he says, with a look that matched her wrath. After three miles the coffle stopped in St. Michaels at Thomas Auld's store, where Frederick's owner interrogated and berated him. But Douglass tells us that he defied and responded to Auld in kind with a lawyerlike argument that no crime had been committed, no evidence existed, and logically no one had any case against him, except for the words of a betrayer. Then the journey resumed on the dusty road to Easton.[12]

All along the roadway, through little hamlets called Spencer's Cove, Royal Oak, Kirkham, and Miles Ferry, crowds of what Douglass called "moral vultures" gathered to jeer, shout epithets, and indulge in "ribaldry" at the expense of the slave prisoners. Some yelled that Frederick should be hanged or burned. Such an event in rural slave country made for a spectacular break in routines and a feast for lurid rumors. Some slaves in fields, said Douglass, "cautiously glanced at us through the post-and-rail fences." Fear spread like the fastest wind when slave rebellions or runaways were thwarted; the eye contact Frederick may have managed with his fellow slaves only made the mutual dread more contagious. Upon arrival after hours of travel, the coffle was untied and interrogated. Frederick had urged the others to deny everything, like the fledgling revolutionaries they had tried to be. "Own nothing!" had been their leader's command while on the march.

They were placed in the stone jailhouse on the rear of the Talbot County courthouse, which still stands today. Behind heavy locks, bars, and iron latticework on the windows, for the first week of captivity the prisoners bonded again in their assumed fate—sale separately to the Deep South. They peered through the windows, wishing they could speak to one of the white-coated black waiters across the street at Solomon Lowe's Hotel. Like a "pack of fiends, fresh from perdition," slave traders, eager for new flesh for the Southern markets, lurked about the jail, taunting the prisoners and feeling their arms, legs, and shoulders to judge their fitness. This constituted the Eastern Shore's active domestic slave trade, about to feed four new pieces of property down its trough greased with filthy lucre. Later, Douglass did not miss a beat in using these daily encounters with slave traders to show that, however much detested by polite society in the slave South, these "whiskey-bloated gamblers in human flesh" were necessary to the master

*The Talbot County courthouse. In the rear of this building
Douglass was held in jail for two weeks after his aborted
escape plan in 1836. Today his statue stands out front,
unveiled in 2011. Postcard by Marian L. Covey, c. 1910.*

class's profit and expansion. The slave owner and the slave trader, declared Douglass, were partners in "blasphemy and blood."[13]

At the end of that first week in jail, Freeland and Hambleton arrived to extract the other three young men and take them back to their farms without any punishment. In this dreaded separation from his friends, Fred Bailey felt a "solitary . . . desolation." As ringleader, he now felt certain Auld would at any time arrive to sell him to Alabama or Georgia. For seven more lonely days Frederick fended off the probing hands and the insults of the traders and felt a volcano of rage and a numbing loneliness rising in him. When his tense and indecisive owner finally showed up, to Frederick's great surprise Auld had decided not to sell his slave, but to send him back to Baltimore with the promise that for good behavior, and learning a trade, Auld would free him on his twenty-fifth birthday. This moment may easily have been the greatest stroke of good luck in Douglass's life, and he seems to have known it. Auld could have sent him "into the very everglades of Florida," wrote Douglass of this turning point, "beyond the remotest hope of emancipation; and his refusal to exercise that power must be set down to his credit."[14] After many weeks of deadly mischief, of hope sublime and fear unbearable, the wretched imprisonment and humiliation, Fred Bailey must have found a little skip in his step as he realized he would once again see those clipper ships in Baltimore harbor.

Why did Thomas Auld send Frederick back to Baltimore at age eighteen? How or why did he resist the $800 or more he might have pocketed on the sale of his slave to the cotton kingdom? Certainly his wife, Rowena, who detested Frederick, would have craved the money from the young rebel's sale. The Freelands could now view Frederick only as dangerous and would have wanted him out of the neighborhood. And William Hambleton, Auld's own father-in-law, apparently told Auld in no uncertain terms that he would shoot the young man if he was not sold out of Talbot County. Douglass later learned from his cousin Tom Bailey that Auld fretted a great deal over his decision and "walked the floor nearly all night" before going to the Easton jail to retrieve Frederick. Perhaps his Christian conversion and a personal disdain for the vulturelike slave traders at the Easton jail played some role as well in Auld's choice. According to Douglass, Auld blustered for a day or two back in St. Michaels that he had an "Alabama friend" to whom he planned to sell Frederick. But the fictitious Alabamian never showed up. Auld may have hoped that as Frederick learned a trade, profits might be made from his labor in Baltimore. But it also appears that emotionally, Auld, whether because of extended family blood ties or out of watching this brilliant young rascal grow up for eighteen years, just could not bring himself to sell Frederick to a doomed fate. Auld had done Fred Bailey an extraordinarily good turn; it would be a long time before Frederick Douglass would fairly recognize the deed.[15]

Frederick had left Baltimore three years earlier as an awkward, despondent, long-legged boy; he returned in 1836 an approximately six-feet-one-inch, well-built young man, firm and strengthened by more than two years as a field hand, and, above all, more confident in mind and body. To Frederick, Baltimore was warmly familiar at first, but also greatly changed. The turbulent, increasingly violent city teemed with huge numbers of new Irish immigrant laborers. The free black population had rapidly risen to more than fifteen thousand, with an active community of churches and associations, while slaves numbered only just under four thousand. The Aulds had moved to Fells Street, just past the Shakespeare Alley, but still near the burgeoning docks and shipyards. Hugh's fortunes had eroded; he lost his own shipbuilding firm and was now working as a foreman in another yard. Grown to near manhood, Tommy Auld had gone to sea as a sailor aboard a brig called the *Tweed*, never to be seen again.[16]

To bring in wages for himself, and to teach the slave a trade as a caulker, Hugh Auld hired out Frederick to William Gardiner's shipyard, where the big builder employed at least one hundred men on breakneck schedules to fulfill a contract to construct two men-of-war for the Mexican government. The Gardiner yard was an exciting, and dangerous, place. Most of the carpenters were white, some were free blacks, and among the apprentices running about frantically at the beck and call of the older workers, Frederick may have been the only black. With all manner of racist taunts, white carpenters barked orders at Frederick: "Fred, come carry this timber yonder"; "Fred, bring that roller here"; "Fred! Run and bring me a cold chisel." All day long the young man tried to answer to "Halloo nigger," and "Say darkey," while doing every nasty job at an impossible pace. For eight months, wrote Douglass, this provided the "school" in which he learned the trade of caulker.[17]

In this ugly racial atmosphere, and with Frederick now hardly willing to back down to anyone, the young white apprentices turned on him. "The niggers," they said within his hearing, were taking white men's jobs and should be banished. One day Frederick snapped after being cursed at by a large white fellow named Edward North; Frederick grabbed the white worker, wrestled him to a dock, and threw him in the water. Now a street fighter of necessity and perhaps some relish, Douglass later claimed he could handle any of these toughs "singly." But he also found more mischief than he had bargained for. While pounding bolts into the hold of a ship, one bent, and a white worker named Ned immediately next to him shouted that it was Fred's fault; Fred took offense and blamed the white man. The two of them each grabbed weapons, Ned an adze (an arc-bladed hand ax), and Fred a maul, and after lunging at each other with vicious intent, they suddenly stopped before one of them ended up dead. One day four of the white apprentices, whom Douglass later named—Ned North, Ned Hays, Bill Stewart, and Tom Humphreys—pounced on him with a brick and a "heavy hand-spike." They beat him to the ground, and one of them landed a savage kick to his face, smashing his left eye, "which for a time, seemed to have burst my eyeball." With Frederick bloodied all over, his eye swollen closed, the group seemed satisfied; but he staggered to his feet, and waving a handspike, ran after them as they fled.[18]

When Frederick limped home to the Aulds' house, they met him with sympathy and outrage at his accidents. Sophia cried and tenderly nursed his wounds. The following day the enraged Hugh took Frederick to a justice of the peace to seek redress and arrests of the young men who had beaten his slave. But "Esquire Watson" could do nothing, he reported, without white witnesses; by law in Maryland, no black person could testify against a white person. Auld tended to follow the strictures of the slave codes, but in this case he fruitlessly protested. Douglass placed his memory of this event in a larger story of the new "murderous . . . spirit" of Baltimore; the city no longer provided a place of cosmopolitan dreams for a slave, especially since at least fifty white men had watched his beating, lifting no hand to stop it, as they shouted, "Kill the nigger!"[19] When, less than six years later, we find Douglass tilting under the weighted strictures of his fellow abolitionists' pacifism, we need only remember these bloody Baltimore fights and his experience in the proslavery criminal justice system to understand his ambivalence. A brawler of necessity, he would ultimately find philosophical nonviolence untenable.

Hugh removed Frederick from Gardiner's for his safety and got him work at Price's shipyard, where Auld was himself a foreman. There Frederick would learn well the craft of caulker and begin to take in from $6 to $9 per week. In this hothouse atmosphere of violence, racism, and embittered economic competition among an insecure working class, Frederick Bailey learned even deeper lessons about the natural struggle between labor and capital. In *Bondage and Freedom*, Douglass gave the economics of urban slavery and Southern race relations an astute analysis. Despite that thuggish white dockworkers had beaten and nearly killed him, Douglass keenly grasped the plight of the white poor. In their "craftiness," wrote Douglass, urban slaveholders and shipyard owners forged an "enmity of the poor, laboring white man against the blacks," forcing an embittered scramble for diminished wages, and rendering the white worker "as much a slave as the black slave himself." Both were "plundered, and by the same plunderer." The "white slave" and the "black slave" were both robbed, one by a single master, and the other by the entire slave system. The slaveholding class exploited the lethal tools of racism to convince the burgeoning immigrant poor, said Douglass, that "slavery is the only power that can prevent the laboring white man from falling to the level of the slave's poverty and degradation." Douglass imagined a time when white and black carpenters had worked peacefully side by side in the Fell's Point shipyards. He wrongly predicted that all these "injurious consequences" sowed by the master class would one day inspire the white non-slaveholding poor to rise in solidarity with slaves.[20] As later in his career, Douglass's economic analysis could alternate between astute and naïve, but he certainly understood class consciousness.

With historical distance, Douglass found sincere sympathy for those poor white workers who had pummeled and kicked him. But back in 1837–38, trying to garner wages as a hired slave, he kept his fists clinched. His stories have become so iconic today that the scene has even appeared in a major work of literature, *Sea of Poppies* (2008), by Amitav Ghosh. Ghosh tells an epic tale of a ship, the *Ibis*, built originally in Gardiner's shipyard in Baltimore and used in the illegal slave trade, heading out around the Horn of Africa for a voyage into the Indian Ocean. Aboard is a young seaman, a mulatto American freedman named Zachery Reid. After months at sea and much sickness and death among the crew, Zachery's mind "travels aback across the oceans to his last day at Gardiner's shipyard in Baltimore." He sees again "a face with a burst eyeball, the scalp torn open where a hand-spike had landed, the dark skin slick with blood." In his vision, Zachery sees "the encirclement of Freddy Douglass, set upon by four white carpenters; he remembered the howls, 'kill him, kill the damned nigger!'" He recalled how he and the other free black workers had "held back, their hands stayed by fear." Zachery hears "Freddy's voice" in his head, "not reproaching them [his fellow black workers] for not coming to his defense, but urging them to leave, scatter: 'It's about jobs; the whites won't work with you, freeman or slave: keeping you out is their way of saving their bread.'" It was then, says Ghosh, that Zachery quit the shipyard and went to sea.[21] In 1837 "Freddy" was still yearning to get out of those shipyards himself.

In the relative safety of Price's shipyard, Frederick found better days in 1837 and 1838; he began to read again, and most important, he joined in the life of the large free black community of Baltimore, especially a debating and social organization, the East Baltimore Mental Improvement Society. Here Frederick could let down his guard and employ his favorite weapons—words, and the growing charisma he cultivated while using them. He "was living among freemen," he recollected, and resented every aspect of his slave status against the lives of his free friends, especially the necessity of depositing most of his wages with Hugh Auld every Saturday night. Frederick chafed under such brutal contradictions. At nineteen and soon twenty years old, his future made no sense to him: "Why should I be a slave?" he recalled thinking. "There was no reason why I should be in the thrall of any man." Frederick made fast friends among a new band of brothers, especially five—James Mingo, William E. Lloyd, William Chester, Joseph Lewis, and Henry Rolles. Sometimes they met in Mingo's "old frame house in Happy Alley" and debated racial, religious, and political issues. One of them, Lloyd, wrote to Douglass in 1870, remembering that one night Frederick waxed so excited with his oratory that "you told me you never meant to stop until you got into the United States Senate."[22] Fred Bailey's speaking career began first on Freeland's farm and then in Happy Alley in Baltimore.

At one of the social gatherings of the debating society, or perhaps as likely at the Sharp Street AME Church, which Frederick joined, he met a young, dark-skinned free woman who liked music named Anna Murray. Anna was born in or around 1813, near Denton, in Caroline County, Maryland, on the Eastern Shore, within three miles or so of where Frederick was born. Their childhoods may have overlapped for a year or so in this region known as the Tuckahoe Neck; they knew each other's families, although Anna's had been more intact, and they had played at the same mill and wandered as kids in and out of Hillsborough. Anna was the seventh of twelve children born to Bambarra and Mary Murray, both slaves; but because of the manumission of her mother, Anna was the first born free. At age seventeen, likely in 1830 or 1831, while Fred Bailey was twelve or thirteen and living with Hugh and Sophia Auld, reading the Bible with Father Lawson, and combing through his *Columbian Orator*, Anna, with three siblings, Elizabeth, Philip, and Charlotte, moved to Baltimore to find work and a better life than what the right bank of the Tuckahoe offered. For two years Anna found employment as a housekeeper for a French family named Montell. Then, perhaps for as long as five years, she served the family of Mr. Wells, the postmaster of Baltimore, who lived on S. Caroline Street, only a half dozen or so blocks straight above Philpot and Thames, where Frederick lived during his years in the city.[23]

Dressed likely in a drab white or gray calico dress and apron by day, Anna may have donned a special head scarf and a prettier dress on whatever day or evening she met the strapping nineteen- or twenty-year-old brainy slave from the Eastern Shore. They may have known each other simply from passing in the streets, but when they met, they must have fallen into a long, smiling conversation about where they were from, the people they knew (each other's cousins), and stories of growing up along the Tuckahoe. Finding Frederick was not the only reason Anna had moved to Baltimore as a teenager, but she surely must have thought so now. And Bailey, perhaps still a bit awkward around young women, must have craved Anna's admiration, emotional support, and adoring eye contact. She was older, had lived in this free black community for years, and perhaps gave the young slave some credibility among his new friends. She may have even provided caring advice on how to take care of his injuries and scars from the rumbles down on the docks. Somewhere between Caroline and Thames Streets the two fell in love and discovered they needed each other. Douglass had found a woman who would help him imagine a new life.

Anna worked for her meager wages for the Wells family and as part of a burgeoning group of free black women struggling for domestic-service positions in white people's homes. Anna did manage to save some money and owned two feather beds and other household goods when she became engaged to Frederick; but her daily life was a battle against poverty, paying rent for her lodging, buying firewood, always striving to be the efficient and prim housekeeper the Wells family expected. In her twenties, she was one lonely worker who, as historian Seth Rockman aptly wrote, "scraped by on the 'economy of makeshift.' "[24] Frederick needed a helpmeet with whom to dream and plan his way out of Maryland, and Anna needed a future that might not include carrying white people's chamber pots every morning.

Frederick absolutely hated Hugh Auld's "right of the robber" in taking the slave's earnings. Here Frederick was again, now twenty years old, treated as a boy serving the ends of white people who still owned his body and his labor. His troubles, he maintained, as ever, were "less physical than mental." Remembering these last months of his time in Baltimore, Douglass penned another gem about the psychology of slave and master: "To make a contented slave, you must make a thoughtless one. It is necessary to darken his moral and mental vision, and as far as possible, to annihilate his power of reason. . . . The slave must know no Higher Law than his master's will . . . if there be one crevice through which a single drop can fall, it will certainly rust off the slave's chains." Frederick's chains had long since rusted into powder, and a mental and pecuniary tug-of-war now ensued between Auld and his slave that forced the young man to a desperate flight for freedom. In the spring of 1838, Frederick and Hugh made a deal, allowing the slave to take his own lodgings, hire his own time, and keep any wages above $3 per week. From May until August 1838, Frederick worked hard, bought his own caulking tools, and forged more personal time to, perhaps under Anna's influence, take up music at church. Above all, work itself now seemed to equate with liberty.[25]

Until Frederick went to a camp meeting one Saturday night some twelve miles from Baltimore and, having a grand time, stayed until Monday, thus missing his payment time (Saturday night) by forty-eight hours. Upon his return, Auld was furious, threatened to whip the grown man, and accused him of plotting to run away. The owner rescinded Frederick's "partial freedom"; he could no longer hire himself and keep part of his wages. Sulking for at least a week, Frederick refused to go to work at all; Auld, in his fury, verbally abused the lad, threatened beatings, and even sale. With genuine fear that Hugh and Thomas Auld might indeed finally sell him south, Frederick and Anna, with the assistance of other free black friends, hatched his escape plot.[26]

Over the next three weeks, Frederick worked hard down at the yards so as to dispel Auld's suspicion of a scheme. On one Saturday, the spiteful master took Frederick's $9 and gave him back a puny twenty-five cents. Between the two of them, Frederick and Anna pooled resources to buy him a real train ticket, as well as the symbolic "fare," as he wrote, "on the underground railroad." His plan required cunning, courage, and luck, not to mention Anna's own devil-may-care bravery and material support. According to family lore, Anna sold one of her feather beds to raise cash for Frederick's journey. With a terrible sense of "internal excitement and anxiety," the pain of separation from the only friends he possessed, and memories welling up from the Freeland-farm debacle of two years earlier, Frederick searched for someone's "free papers" to use at various checkpoints. A friend from Fell's Point, a retired black sailor named Stanley, provided the young man with his "sailor's protection," a remarkable document never to be forgotten with an American eagle at the top of the page. Nothing was fail-safe, and a cautious person would never have attempted this plot. Frederick obtained clothing to present himself in full "sailor style . . . red shirt and a tarpaulin hat and black cravat, tied in sailor fashion, carelessly and loosely about my neck." It would be quite a performance; he knew the language of ships and sea and declared himself ready to "talk sailor like an 'old salt.' "[27]

On the appointed day, Monday, September 3, 1838, Frederick went to work early, then met Anna on the way to the Wilmington and Baltimore train station just a few blocks above the City Dock. With tears and an embrace Anna sent her sailor boy pacing back and forth near the waiting train. So that he would not have to face the scrutiny of a ticket window, Frederick had arranged for his friend and drayman Isaac Rolles to bring Frederick's baggage along just as the train started moving; the boy from the bend in the Tuckahoe jumped on the crowded Negro car and began the most famous escape in the annals of American slavery.[28]

With excited fear, Anna retreated to a workday at the Wells house and to several days of anguished waiting for some sign of the good word. What could she have thought? He will make it to a place far north called New York? He will go all the way to Canada, to worlds way beyond the horizons of Chesapeake Bay? I too will ride that train to join him somewhere? I will never see him again? He will be returned within the day in ropes and chains, bloodied, soon to be shipped south and out of my life? She too had her bags packed; controlling her outward emotions, even eating and sleeping, must have seemed impossible. She probably prayed in all her quiet moments.

As the train churned toward Havre de Grace, Maryland, a distance of thirty-seven miles to where the Susquehanna River empties into the top of Chesapeake Bay, Frederick encountered his first danger; the gruff conductor meandered through the car checking tickets and documents (the sailor Stanley was much darker in complexion than the mulatto Fred Bailey), but softened in the face of such a young sailor, for whom Douglass maintained there was widespread social respect. The conductor barely glanced at that eagle on his document, and the fugitive's sudden terror subsided. At Havre de Grace passengers boarded a ferry to cross the Susquehanna; Frederick had to do his nervous best to shake a young black boat worker who kept up a steady questioning of the well-attired sailor's origins and destinations. Now, for approximately another thirty-seven miles, half through Maryland and half through Delaware, slave states, the train trudged on. "Minutes were hours, and hours were days," Douglass recalled of his drama. "The heart of no fox or deer, with hungry hounds on his trail," said the autobiographer, had ever beat "more anxiously or noisily." At a stop, Frederick looked out his window and immediately next to him in the opposite window of a train heading in the other direction was a ship's captain named McGowan, on whose revenue cutter the young caulker had just worked the week before. He knew McGowan would recognize him, but the captain never turned his head or made eye contact. Then Douglass encountered a German blacksmith he knew from the Baltimore shipyards, who looked him over knowingly but thankfully "had no heart to betray me." [29]

At Wilmington, Delaware, Frederick coyly, if rapidly, walked through town from the train station to the wharf, where he boarded a steamboat that soon set out into the "broad and beautiful Delaware" River. Arriving in Philadelphia in late afternoon after thirty unmolested miles on the steamer, Frederick walked off the gangplank onto free soil for the first time. He wasted no time in relishing the moment and asked the first safe-looking black man he saw how to find the train to New York. Directed to the Willow Street station, Edward Covey's broken bondsman paid the fare and took the night train up through New Jersey to the Hudson River landing and railroad terminus in Hoboken. There, around sunrise on Tuesday, September 4, Frederick boarded a ferry that chugged southeasterly across the mighty Hudson River to a dock at the end of Chambers Street. [30] On a bright September morning, with the sounds of snapping waves and the shouts of men's voices along the wharves, Harriet Bailey's lost orphan stepped into the busy streets of New York, wide-eyed, thrilled, and frightened.

Douglass later struggled for those magical words to describe his feelings that special morning. "Walking amid the hurrying throng, and gazing upon the dazzling wonders of Broadway," he felt the sensation of a "free state around me, and a free earth under my feet! What a moment was this to me! A whole year was pressed into a single day. A new world burst upon my agitated vision." But these sensations stymied this eventual word master, he admitted. They were "too intense and too rapid for words." He later managed a little poetry nonetheless. "Anguish and grief, like darkness and rain, may be described, but joy and gladness, like the rainbow of promise, defy alike the pen and pencil." Although he was careful about whom to speak to in those dangerous streets, he remembered words from inside his soul like a shout: "I was a FREEMAN, and the voice of peace and joy thrilled my heart!"[31] On that morning the words swirling in his head would have been the frightened fragments of a fugitive, eyes darting this way and that, wondering which impulse to trust. It took some years in the development of his genius with language for Douglass to shape this, and many other parts of his story, into the tale of the ascendant barefoot slave boy who would go forth and change the world.

Hungry and friendless, Frederick soon realized he still stood in "an enemy's land" and had no time for odes to joy. In reality, Fred Bailey had escaped Maryland slavery with extraordinary bravery, but now he was a disoriented fugitive without any real plan. Numbed by loneliness, he trusted no one; every white man appeared as a potential kidnapper, and every black man a possible betrayer. He felt like everyone's "prey" in the great metropolis. Later in his career as he portrayed over and over for abolitionist audiences the experience of the "panting fugitive," he knew exactly of what he spoke. For at least one and possibly two nights, Frederick slept among the barrels at the wharf. By day he encountered a fellow fugitive he recognized from Baltimore, known in slavery as Allender's Jake. Jake warned Frederick at length about ever-present slave catchers. Then he met a black sailor named Stewart, to whom he entrusted his story, and by whom he was directed to the house of David Ruggles, on 36 Lispenard Street at the corner of Church Street, a mere four or five blocks from the wharves.[32] This was good fortune to rank along side the day Thomas Auld decided to send his slave back to Baltimore at age eighteen.

Ruggles was a free black grocer, abolitionist, newspaper editor, and especially the leader of the New York Vigilance Committee, the organization that openly and clandestinely aided fugitive slaves within and through New York City. From his house, Ruggles edited the *Mirror of Liberty*, America's first black-owned and operated magazine, which printed reports of the Vigilance Committee's legal and illegal work on behalf of runaway slaves. In his house he also maintained an essentially public reading room, with antislavery books and newspapers aplenty. Ruggles, who was just then in and out of court, and for a time under arrest, for his role in advocating for a Virginia fugitive, Thomas Hughes, who had accompanied his owner, John P. Darg, to New York, found time to take the ragged Frederick under his roof and guidance. Here in Ruggles's reading room, amid the roiling controversy over the life and future of a fellow fugitive, and even at the courtroom where Frederick attended and witnessed his host's testimony, the Maryland slave first encountered the exciting and dangerous daily world of abolitionism.[33]

Frederick spent at least a full week sheltered at Ruggles's house. In some idle moment, his host suggested a speedy name change, and like so many other runaways seeking anonymity, Frederick decided to become Frederick Johnson. That name would last only for several days until his later arrival in New Bedford, Massachusetts, where he would take the name Douglass. Most important, as quickly as possible, Frederick wrote a letter to Anna in Baltimore, which Ruggles mailed for him. The letter, in a prearrangement, was likely addressed to one of the good friends Frederick had made in the debating society, who quickly, on or about September 10, rushed to Anna, who could not read, with the news that she was to take the train as soon as possible to New York. No one ever recorded or told the story of Anna's brave train and steamer journey, also done in twenty-four hours, leaving the only environments she had ever known, abandoning her paying job, to join her lonely, directionless fiancé, to attempt to make a life somewhere up north. But away she went, and according to her daughter Rosetta, among the household goods she carried in a trunk was a "plum colored silk dress" that, three days after her arrival, on September 15, she wore to be married to Frederick Johnson in the small parlor of Ruggles's home.[34]

To conduct the wedding, Ruggles invited the Reverend James W. C. Pennington, who had himself escaped from slavery near Rockland, Maryland, in 1827 when, like Frederick, he was twenty years old. Born James Pembroke, he had run overland and found shelter with Quakers in Adams County, Pennsylvania, before moving on to New York and Connecticut. Like other fugitives, he had changed his name, and after working as a blacksmith, he became a minister, pastoring both Congregational and Presbyterian churches in New Haven, Connecticut, and Brooklyn, New York. Like

*James W. C. Pennington. Pennington
escaped from slavery in Queen Anne's
County, Maryland. Engraving on paper.*

Frederick, his residence as a city slave had led to his desire to seek learning and freedom. Pennington had vigorously sought admission to classes at the Yale Divinity School, only to be rejected. James and Frederick had much to discuss, although it was wedding day, but Douglass left no account of conversations between the two fugitive slaves. Pennington left Mr. and Mrs. Johnson with a short certificate of their marriage, the text of which Douglass reprinted in the *Narrative*, as though he needed to display an official declaration of such a human and liberating act as marriage on free soil.[35]

Sensing that Frederick had no plan other than some vague idea of going to Canada, Ruggles firmly urged the newlyweds to move up the New England coast, to New Bedford, Massachusetts, a whaling port, where Frederick could find work as a caulker, and the couple would find a welcoming fugitive-slave and free-black community. Ruggles gave Frederick a $5 bill, and with no further ceremony, Douglass tells us he lifted the larger part of their luggage (which contained his beloved *Columbian Orator* and three song booklets) on his shoulder, while Anna carried the smaller bags, and they strode across lower Manhattan to the docks to embark on the steamer *John W. Richmond.* Full of gratitude for David Ruggles, that "whole-souled man, fully imbued with a love of his afflicted and hunted people," Frederick had quickly and happily gone from teacher to pupil.[36] Two strong and courageous black abolitionists had shown him the way. Holding his intrepid bride's hand, Frederick stepped beyond three years of bloody and beautiful mischief into freedom.

Chapter 6

LIVING A NEW LIFE

Yes, the world's a ship on its passage out, and not a voyage complete; and the pulpit is its prow.

—HERMAN MELVILLE, *MOBY-DICK*, 1851

Frederick Bailey had found his passage out, and Frederick Douglass now searched for a pulpit. By mid-September 1838, when Frederick and Anna arrived in New Bedford, Massachusetts, they had wrenchingly experienced what Douglass would later call the "upper-ground railroad," and what the world came to call the Underground Railroad. They had escaped slave territory to free soil by their own remarkable bravery, but they had also benefited immensely from the clandestine efforts of David Ruggles and a small network of people to whom Ruggles had referred the newlyweds. Still trusting nearly no one, the anxious fugitives were now armed with at least one letter of introduction as well as other names. After taking the steamer to Newport, Rhode Island, Frederick and Anna rode a stage up the coast into Massachusetts and arrived exhausted and penniless in the whaling port.[1]

In New Bedford they were directed immediately to the home of the free blacks Nathan and Mary Johnson at 21 Seventh Street. The Johnsons took them into their three-story, wood-framed house for the night, paid their stage fare, and welcomed Frederick and Anna as they had many such fugitives before. Nathan Johnson's origins are not fully known, but he had been involved in creating the growing black community in New Bedford, and in assisting fugitive slaves, since at least 1822. At breakfast on the morning after Frederick and Anna's arrival, Johnson urged the Marylanders to choose a new name. Too many Johnsons resided among the fugitive slaves of New Bedford, as well as in the broader North, said Nathan. Indeed, of the twenty-three Johnsons listed as head of households in the New Bedford town directory for 1839, twelve were labeled *c* for "colored." In his remembrances, Douglass gives no role to Anna in this decision. He tells us that he gave his host the privilege of choosing his new last name, but that he dearly wanted to retain *Frederick.* "I must hold on to that to preserve a sense of my identity," wrote Douglass in 1845. Johnson had just been reading Sir Walter Scott's *Lady of the Lake,* the classic and popular romantic Scottish poem of 1810. From the Highlander clan named Douglas, Johnson suggested a new name. Frederick liked the name's sound and strength as a word, and he quickly accepted, adding an *s* for distinction.[2] Thus began the long process of the most famous self-creation of an African American identity in American history.

In both its simplicity and its literary gravitas (Scott was wildly popular in America) Douglass wore his new name with increasing pride. Remembering this choice of new name in *Bondage and Freedom,* he referred to his two original middle names (Augustus Washington), given by his mother, as "pretentious." As the literary historian Robert Stepto has remarked, Douglass's sloughing off of his two middle names and the choice of the new surname provided him a kind of "ritual cleansing" of some of his slave "baggage" at this special moment in his new beginning. With retrospect, Douglass sighed that any fugitive slave had to adopt various names during his escape to survive because "among honest men an honest man may well be content with one name, but toward fugitives, Americans are not honest." And by 1855, he had long since read *Lady of the Lake* and was glad to be associated with the "great Scottish chief," although he acknowledged that his New Bedford benefactor, Nathan Johnson, might better represent the military "virtues" of Scott's Highlander hero. "Had any slave-catcher entered his [Johnson's] domicile," wrote Douglass, "with a view to molest any one of his household, he would have shown himself like him of the 'stalwart hand.'" This passage is really about Douglass himself, who had learned and practiced repeatedly by the mid-1850s the virtues and perils of protecting and transporting fugitive slaves. He does not tell us just how he incorporated his new name into his sense of self during his first years of relative obscurity in New Bedford. But with time he had clearly breathed some of Scott's language into his soul. He wanted to be viewed by his many audiences "Till whispers rose among the throng, / That heart so free, and hand so strong, / Must to the Douglas blood belong."[3] Douglass eventually developed above all a literary identity, a man of words spoken and written.

The New Bedford in which Douglass landed in 1838 had a population of nearly twelve thousand, perhaps as many as three hundred of whom were fugitive slaves among a free black population approaching one thousand. It was as open and thriving a refuge for runaways as anywhere in the North. And it was a booming whaling center, with some 170 ships making it their main port and employing as many as four thousand hands. In the year just before Douglass arrived, the town had some seventeen candle houses and oil manufactories. Of the 181,724 barrels of sperm oil and 219,138 of whale oil imported into the United States in 1837, more than 40 percent of the totals came in at New Bedford's docks. Within the ensuing decade down to 1849, whaling became the first international industry dominated by the United States, with New Bedford as its capital. By 1840, in New Bedford, with a population of 12,087, the whaling business grossed $7,230,000.[4]

Douglass himself would never go to sea as a whaler, although the crews of so many ill-fated ships were one place where blacks and Indians and all manner of young boys and men could find work. Like Baltimore, the sea at New Bedford brought the world into Douglass's vision, and the whale as a product made an economy in which he would find wage labor of all kinds for three years. As Herman Melville put it in *Moby-Dick*, the crews with whom he served and fought and mutinied on whale ships came from "all the isles of the sea, and all the ends of the earth." From his residence in New Bedford at the very time Douglass also lived there, Melville left unforgettable descriptions of the town. New Bedford, he wrote, "is a queer place," full of an almost infinite eccentricity of types and behaviors among the young mates of the whale fishery, of a variety of "wild specimens" from the hills of New England and the farthest isles of distant oceans.[5]

In his own way, Douglass was another wild specimen come to join this teeming seaport, and now he needed a job. From his years in Baltimore, Douglass knew much of the world of ships, seaports, the maritime trades, and especially of the men and women who lived by the wealth of the sea. But the body of the whale had for several decades built New Bedford and forged jobs for a young fugitive slave. Until the discovery of petroleum in Pennsylvania in 1859, which rapidly killed off the whaling business, the whale helped launch the modern industrial revolution, its oil used for all manner of lighting, its hairy bristles made into brooms, its bones transformed into everything from canes to umbrellas, its pearly spermaceti made into

The whaling ship Eliza Adams *in port with casks of whale oil, New Bedford, Massachusetts, c. 1850.*

the best candles, and even a foul black liquid from its gut somehow converted into perfume.[6]

Douglass's autobiographical writing about New Bedford served different ends than Melville's; it took its place in his antislavery polemic, drawing sharp distinctions between a Southern slave society and a Northern free-labor society. Yet, it was often no less lyrical than Melville's descriptions of the town. Many have speculated, though no one knows, whether Melville and Douglass somehow met or observed each other in New Bedford; they were both there in late 1840 and early 1841. The sailor-adventurer was preparing for his long voyage to the South Seas on a whaler, while the fugitive slave worked as a day laborer. Douglass admitted that the "wealth and grandeur" of New Bedford surprised him. He had been conditioned to consider slavery as the basis of wealth. Not in the whaling port. Working white men and black men alike owned homes and lived with dignity. Douglass seemed genuinely stunned at Yankee enterprise and apparent prosperity. Contrasting the "poverty and degradation" of poor whites in Baltimore and St. Michaels with the "superior mental character" of Northern workers, he used as his example Nathan Johnson. Douglass's host, though a workingman, lived in "a better house—dined at a richer board—was the owner of more books—the reader of more newspapers—was more conversant with the social and political condition of this nation and the world—than nine-tenths of all the slaveholders of Talbot County, Maryland." Johnson, Douglass contended, labored with his hands in New Bedford, was the worker-citizen, even an intellectual in this seaside free-labor community.[7]

Douglass also remembered that he felt safe in New Bedford, in part because the town contained so many Quakers, with their egalitarian and enterprising traditions. During his residence in the town, whaling seemed to be a commerce with an endless future. At the wharves, he insisted, were "industry without bustle, labor without noise, and heavy toil without the whip." For the young Douglass, all things before his eyes were in stark contrast to the slavery-ridden world from which he had fled. In the town's many whale-related enterprises, he maintained, "everything went on as smoothly as the works of a well-adjusted machine." The excited man in his early twenties was impressed with all the modern conveniences he encountered: "wood houses, indoor pumps, sinks, drains, self-shutting gates, washing machines, pounding barrels." Such observations vary widely from Melville's characterizations of the hard-drinking harpooners and other lost souls at the Spouter Inn and other stops along the streets of New Bedford. That "wise prudence" guided the sensibilities of this town would have seemed strange news to many of the young men seeking adventure and fortune on those whalers in the 1840s.[8] But Douglass was aiming for different places.

Within three days of arrival in New Bedford, Frederick found paid work loading oil casks onto a sloop bound for New York. He soon sought to use his trade as a caulker, but the white caulkers of the docks threatened to walk off their jobs if the young black man was hired. All was not so prudent or liberating after all. But in this case Douglass swallowed his pride and anger, put away his caulking mallet for now, and took every kind of job he found. One day he walked up to a prosperous house, knocked on the door, and asked the lady if he might put away her load of coal. As she dropped two silver dollars in his hand at the end of his dirty work, Douglass remembered, it "swelled my heart as I clasped this money, realizing that I had no master . . . *that my hands were my own.*" For three years, and for "honest" money, he said, he "sawed wood—dug cellars—shoveled coal—swept chimneys . . . rolled oil casks to the wharves—helped to load and unload vessels—worked in Richetson's candle works—in Richmond's brass foundry, and elsewhere." He also worked as a waiter for a prominent attorney, and did all manner of odd jobs for a local minister, Ephraim Peabody. A reminiscence later by a Peabody family member described how Douglass became a man-of-all-work at the minister's house, though much more inclined, it is said, to sit on the kitchen table and read than to work with his hands. The Peabody descendant reported that Douglass defended his "inactivity by affirming that he occupied his leisure hours by pursuing the study of French." At the foundry, Douglass characteristically tried to read while he did the hot and dirty job of working the bellows. "With little time for mental improvement," he recalled in 1851, "I often nailed a newspaper to the post near my bellows, and read while I was performing my up and down motion of the heavy beam by which the bellows was inflated and discharged." In old age he marveled that he could have been so earnest in pursuing knowledge as a young man, while having to struggle to feed his family.[9]

Anna gave birth to their daughter Rosetta on June 24, 1839, and their first son, Lewis, on October 9, 1840. Douglass does not tell us in the autobiographies about the circumstances or joys of these births; he only indicates how he worked with his callused hands to support his wife, "who was unable to work," and a growing family in two rented rooms. They lived first at the rear of 157 Elm Street, on the west edge of the main town, and after Lewis was born at 111 Ray Street, only a few blocks from the wharves. Frustratingly, Douglass wrote next to nothing of his domestic life throughout his long experience as an autobiographer. In these three years in New Bedford, what we do know is that he found work and stayed out of debt. In "rapturous excitement" at working freely for wages, and gaining some independence, Douglass believed he "was now living in a new world."[10]

Soon the day laborer looked for a church. Perhaps he was thinking of his children's spiritual welfare, or even Anna's lack of community. But as always, in the autobiographies, the story was only about himself. At this juncture of 1839–40, he admitted, he "had never given up, in reality, his religious faith." He considered himself in a "backslidden state" in his early twenties. The young man was looking for a pulpit, one he could listen to, and perhaps one he could step into. Father Lawson's faith still tugged at Douglass's spirit, and the stories and cadences of the Bible slumbered fitfully in his memory. He had grown up around Methodists on the Eastern Shore, many of them the hypocritical masters he used as a foil for resistance. Out of familiarity, he felt a duty to try to join the Elm Street Methodist church. Douglass attended the primarily white church, but found himself "proscribed" and not allowed to sit in the main pews. A dozen or so blacks attended and sat in a gallery. Staying for Holy Communion, he witnessed the ritual with "mortification"; as the Reverend Bonney finished serving all the white members, he called the blacks forward with a "voice to an unnatural pitch." His "black sheep," said Douglass, seemed "penned . . . slavish souls." Douglass walked out the back door of this humiliating scene.[11]

Douglass quickly found his way to the welcoming arms of the small black congregation of the African Methodist Episcopal Zion Church, pastored first by the Reverend William Serrington and then by the Reverend Thomas James, who had himself been born a slave in 1804 in upstate New York. In 1839, Douglass served as "sexton, steward, class leader, clerk, and local preacher" in this humble congregation that met in a little schoolhouse on Second Street, only three blocks uphill from the wharves. He also performed weekly duties as the church's Sunday school superintendent, responsible for the education of members. The Reverend James later claimed that Douglass, who was "right out of slavery," had been "given authority to act as an exhorter" at the church just before James's arrival. The reverend said he then licensed Douglass to preach, which Douglass later confirmed. Douglass remembered his deep associations with what he always called "Little Zion" as "precious," and "among the happiest days of my life." He expressed firm opinions on which of the church's ministers were most effective or possessed education. He said he "occupied the pulpit," when the minister asked, and dozens of times Douglass held forth on Sunday mornings or at evening gatherings. In a letter near the end of his life, written in December 1894, Douglass reminisced with joy about how the little AMEZ Church in New Bedford had offered his first chance to "exercise my gifts" and launched him in his "new vocation." In the 1841 town directory, Douglass's occupation had changed from "laborer" to "Rev."[12]

No recorded remarks survive from Douglass's sermons to the small church of fugitive slaves and free blacks. By at least the summer of 1840, though, earlier than scholars have previously known, Douglass was discovered by white abolitionists. In August of that year the Boston antislavery lawyer Ellis Gray Loring wrote to a friend in Toronto, the Reverend Hiram Wilson, excitedly telling of a "coloured man . . . we are anxious to employ as a lecturer." His name was "Fred" and he had been owned by "Thomas Auld of Talbot County, Maryland." This stunning young fugitive had escaped "two years ago"; he was a "light mulatto, tall, well-formed, of an open countenance & speaks very good English." Loring enlisted Wilson to be an agent to Auld to try to buy Douglass's freedom. "Fred is poor & a labourer," Loring wrote, but his speaking skills could "produce great effect."[13]

Nothing came of this early initiative to purchase Douglass's freedom. But the day laborer did not hide from view, especially on Sundays. The young father with his wife at home caring for two babies must have frequently taken time in his workaday life to consult his Bible, his *Columbian Orator*, and his vivid memory of the band of brothers at the Freeland farm as he prepared for his mornings in the pulpit.

The former Sabbath school leader among slaves seized upon his liberty and his new calling like a miner finding gold. At least by 1840, and perhaps as early as 1839, he registered to vote by paying his $1.50 poll tax. In Massachusetts in the late 1830s, men, including blacks, registered to vote by paying this small annual tax. In the sweep of America's racist and discriminatory history with voting rights, it is remarkable that the most famous black man of the nineteenth century, shortly after escaping from slavery, while living with a new, assumed name, with no other identification and certainly no proof of birth in the United States, and while still "illegal" as a fugitive from Southern justice and the property rights of his owner, could instantly become a voter by paying $1.50 and having his name placed on the tax rolls.[14]

Approximately four months after his arrival in New Bedford, Douglass also encountered an agent for William Lloyd Garrison's abolitionist newspaper, the *Liberator*. The paper and its editor changed Douglass's life forever. The young fugitive was too poor to pay for a subscription at first, but the agent nevertheless had the weekly sent to him. In the *Liberator* Douglass started reading an antislavery voice like no other. Garrison seemed prophetic, revelatory, like a "Moses, raised up by God, to deliver his modern Israel from bondage." So clear, radical, and uncompromising, Garrison's words seemed to Douglass like a "gospel . . . full of holy fire." The paper, Douglass wrote in 1855, "took its place with me next to the Bible." Here he found *moral suasion*, the appeal to reform the hearts of people before changing the laws of a society. For the young reader, so drawn to the mystery of writing and speaking, this was abolitionism through the power of language, words as weapons against evil and powerful institutions, truth spread by preaching.[15] Here was a new level of public hope, reinforcing and containing the fires of anger burning in his private heart.

In those initial issues of the *Liberator* that Douglass read in 1839, he encountered an inspiring world of antislavery activity and debate. He discovered that abolitionism had spread all over the North. He learned a new word, *immediatism*, for Garrison's theory that slaveholding was an individual and national *sin*, that all antislavery forces should make no compromise with slavery in any form—in church, legislature, or the public square—and should work now to destroy the institution, root and branch, in their own lifetimes. Douglass read about huge petition campaigns by abolitionists aimed at persuading the US Congress to end slavery in the District of Columbia and in the western territories. He now knew about "gag rules" practiced in Congress to suppress the voices of that body's few antislavery members. He found colonization schemes to send blacks out of the country, to Africa or elsewhere, roundly condemned over and over by Garrisonians, and especially by free blacks. He saw Garrison himself condemned in correspondence as everything from "dangerous" and "vile" to "seditious," and the leader of a "miscreant band . . . of demented fanatics." [16] All of this Douglass found thrilling; the waves of rhetorical and violent resistance to abolitionists seemed to the young fugitive one of their greatest recommendations.

Douglass further learned from the *Liberator* that women were involved in the movement, organizing fund-raising abolition "fairs," recruiting new members, stepping out of their assigned sphere and inviting great scorn. In many issues Douglass found news of both escaped as well as captured fugitive slaves in Northern states. In every issue, he saw confirmations of one of his own most vehement complaints—hypocritical Christian slave-holding and Northern clerical complicity. By April, he might have been bemused as he read about the Baltimore Annual Conference of the Methodist Episcopal Church (with some of his Maryland tormentors perhaps in attendance) turning down an antislavery resolution by an almost unanimous vote. He likely laughed out loud when he read about the black man in Cambridge, Massachusetts, working for a white merchant who prodded him into a practical joke. The employer offered to fill out a ballot for his employee (who was illiterate) and carry it for him to a polling place. But the black laborer got the last laugh; on his own initiative, he walked to the office of the *Liberator* and asked for a ballot; given the current copy of the newspaper, he promptly marched to the polling site and stuffed Garrison's weekly in the box. [17]

In some issues, Douglass could study the names and careers of a generation of black abolitionists. In April 1839 for the first time on paper he likely met James McCune Smith, with whom Douglass would develop a crucial friendship. Above all, Douglass must have fingered the words of Garrison himself, who so often all but shouted from the page. The "real abolitionists," declared the editor in March 1839, "know neither caste, country, nor color. The cause of suffering humanity is not with them a political question,

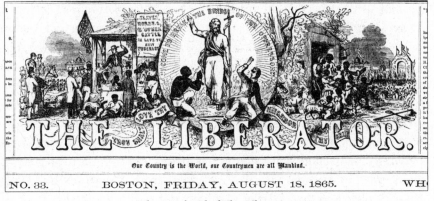

The masthead of The Liberator.

concerning only a certain class or community . . . it is their business, and it ought to be the business of every son and daughter of Adam." [18] To Douglass's impressionable spirit and hungry mind, this was abolitionism clear and pure; he wanted to join up.

To Douglass, Garrison was a hero exciting "love and reverence" before the two ever met. Thus began, in almost mythic terms, one of the most important and turbulent relationships of Douglass's long life. For Douglass, Garrison represented a *moral* voice—from a white person—against slavery, the likes of which he had only dreamed. He could now truly find out what "abolition" meant, perhaps even imagine a purpose or a vocation in its sacred circles. In April 1839, Garrison came to New Bedford to speak. Douglass sat in the extreme rear of the Old Congregational Meeting House and listened wide-eyed, with rapt joy. In *Life and Times*, he crafted a lyrical remembrance of this special moment. Whatever exactly Garrison said that night, Douglass recalled it as a classic litany of all the great editor's "heresies." Forgetting his many painful personal battles with Garrison for the time being, the memoirist of 1881 remembered the essentials of a Garrisonian: "His Bible was his textbook. He believed in sinless perfection . . . literal subjection to the injunction if smitten 'on one cheek to turn the other also.' " As though remembering the admonitions of a New Testament Christ delivering an abolitionist version of the Sermon on the Mount, Douglass continued, "Not only was Sunday a Sabbath, but all days were Sabbaths, and to be kept holy. All sectarianism was false and mischievous. . . . Prejudice against color was rebellion against God. Of all men beneath the sky, the slaves . . . were nearest and dearest to His great heart. Those ministers who defended slavery from the Bible were of their 'father the devil,' and those churches which fellowshipped slaveholders as Christians, were synagogues of Satan, and our nation was a nation of liars."[19]

That night in the back pew of a New Bedford church, on countless days in the pages of the *Liberator*, which Douglass carried to his jobs, and soon under Garrison's own guidance, Douglass found a text and a calling. Here was an antislavery morality he had lived and that all but screamed from within his own soul. He was not yet ready in 1839–40 to become a "public advocate," he tells us. For the moment, it was enough to "receive and applaud the great words of others, and only whisper in private, among the white laborers on the wharves, and elsewhere, the truths which burned in my breast."[20] But it would not be enough for long; Douglass was no whisperer.

During that winter of 1839, Douglass began to speak regularly at the AME Zion Church on Second Street. It is sometimes claimed that Douglass was a self-taught orator, but given his experience for at least two years in and around the pulpit at "Little Zion," this is only partially true. In a real sense, he was trained not only by the precepts he read in Bingham's *Columbian Orator*, but by the Reverends Serrington and James, as well as other visiting preachers from Boston and Providence, who taught him that the "ideal sermon" must appeal to the intellect, to emotion, and to the human will. It is easy for us to say that Douglass would have instinctively understood such homiletic techniques; but he still needed practice. Some weeks he would have preached on the liturgy and honed his biblical interpretation as well as storytelling; and what a compelling performer of Scripture readings the young Douglass must have made in front of the congregants in the simple room on Second Street.[21] Douglass had indeed found his first pulpit, and he did so in a distinctively African American church.

Outside the windows of the little schoolhouse church, the issue that seems to have brought Douglass to his feet as an orator was colonization. He had no patience with the idea that people such as himself, born on American soil, escaped from slavery to a tenuous free-labor life in a relatively safe environment such as New Bedford, ought to voluntarily take his family on a ship bound for Africa, a Caribbean island, or any other foreign place. The American Colonization Society, founded in 1816 and by the late 1830s falling on hard times, launched schemes of black expatriation that violated most free African Americans' sense of their natural rights. In the first publicly recorded instance of Douglass speaking at an antislavery meeting, held March 12, 1839, he was among ten New Bedford blacks who "ably sustained" several resolutions against colonization. The group invoked verbatim the opening lines of the Declaration of Independence, called colonization a form of tyranny, and declared with special emphasis, "We are *American citizens*, born with natural, inherent, just and inalienable rights." They announced themselves especially outraged by the way colonization made "impressions . . . on the public mind" about their "moral and intellectual abilities." That late-winter evening of 1839 was his first rehearsal for what would become a sustained, twenty-five-year condemnation of colonizationist ideas, whether they emanated from racist and profit-minded whites, or blacks themselves.[22]

By 1841, Douglass had delivered many sermons at AME Zion, presided over numerous meetings convened to oppose colonization, and delivered at least three addresses to white people at the Bristol County Anti-Slavery Society in New Bedford. He had further attended addresses by prominent abolitionists such as one delivered May 30, 1841, by the Reverend Henry Highland Garnet, himself another former slave from Maryland, and later an ideological rival. Douglass long remembered the Garnet speech as a special inspiration on his young abolitionist mind. Douglass was so effective as a speaker, even in his early twenties, that his local reputation spread in the streets, as well as beyond New Bedford. One or more of his performances impressed a white abolitionist in attendance, William C. Coffin, a local bookseller, Garrisonian devotee, and member of a prominent antislavery family. In August 1841, Coffin invited the black preacher to join a delegation of the Massachusetts Anti-Slavery Society for what Douglass would later describe as a "grand . . . convention" on the island of Nantucket.[23]

On August 9, 1841, the Bristol County Anti-Slavery Society held a meeting with many distinguished speakers in Liberty Hall in New Bedford. Garrison himself attended, along with other leading Massachusetts abolitionists such as Parker Pillsbury, George Bradburn, John A. Collins, and Edmund Quincy. By the evening session, several "col'd individuals" addressed the meeting, particularly about the issue of racial exclusion from public transportation and from some churches. Douglass, most likely, was one of those speakers. Although his speeches on Nantucket on the following days are more celebrated, Douglass may have spoken to a prominent group of white abolitionists for the first time on this August night in New Bedford. Garrison reported that among the "talented" blacks who spoke that night, one of them was "formerly a slave."[24]

The following day, Douglass and Anna boarded the steamer *Telegraph* for the trip out to Nantucket. Anna's presence is remarkable; after Douglass's speaking career took off in the 1840s, she rarely if ever accompanied him on the road. The racially mixed delegation on the steamboat numbered approximately forty, and as they boarded, the ship's captain, named Phinney, forced the blacks to a segregated area on the upper deck. The white abolitionists joined them for the sixty-mile journey, holding an impromptu antislavery meeting in which they passed resolutions of protest against the steamship company's discriminatory policy, as all the while, according to Parker Pillsbury, they "suffered from both sun and rain."[25]

On the second day of the convention, which met in the Nantucket Atheneum Hall and was attended by as many as a thousand abolitionists, Garrison offered a poignant resolution about prejudice against blacks, accusing discriminatory white Northerners of "putting arguments into the mouths of southern task-masters, and acting as the body-guard of slavery." Until that moment a spectator on what he later described as, in part, a "holiday," Douglass broke his silence and rose to be one of five men supporting the resolution. What followed was what Douglass called his "first" speech, delivered in three segments. That evening, August 11, he spoke haltingly and only briefly before adjournment.[26] But the next morning, the podium was his and the audience was rested and receptive.

No record exists of what he actually said on August 12 at Nantucket, but over time, as Douglass's fame grew, many witnesses competed to describe and take credit for his "discovery." Samuel J. May recollected that Douglass was "called upon," and after "much hesitation" and "embarrassment" at speaking before such an august gathering of white people, "he gave evidence of such intellectual power—wisdom as well as wit—that all present were astonished." Pillsbury too remembered Douglass's initial "embarrassment," but that he "gained self-possession" and rose to the "dignity of his theme." Douglass apparently held his auditors entranced with a personalized version of a slave's travail. Whichever stories from his youth he used to bare his heart, he held the hearts of the convention audience in his gesturing hands; the crowd, caught in the beauty and agony of the performance, could hardly have known that this young man had been practicing his new craft for some years. Douglass "spoke with great power," wrote one witness. "Flinty hearts were pierced, and cold ones melted by his eloquence. Our best pleaders for the slave held their breath for fear of interrupting him."[27]

Garrison may have left the most telling testimony of all about Douglass's sudden emergence those two days on Nantucket. In his endorsement of Douglass's *Narrative* in 1845, Garrison described a singular moment in abolition history: "I shall never forget his first speech at the convention—the extraordinary emotion it excited in my own mind—the powerful impression it created upon a crowded auditory....I think I never hated slavery so intensely as at that moment." Garrison was so moved by Douglass's debut that he saw it with biblical resonance as well as within the tradition of American civil religion. Drawing from Psalms 8:5, Garrison believed they had found "one in intellect richly endowed—in natural eloquence a prodigy—in soul manifestly 'created but a little lower than the angels.'" Then he compared Douglass's effort to "Patrick Henry, of revolutionary fame," and described the fugitive slave's speech as "more eloquent" in the "cause of liberty" than any by the founders.[28]

According to Douglass's own account, his theme was simply his "feelings" inspired by the occasion at the Atheneum, and the "fresh recollection of the scenes through which I had passed as a slave." He remembered "stammering" at the beginning of his sudden moment on the podium in front of such a crowd and claimed that he "trembled in every limb." Douglass clearly experienced an initial awkwardness and anxiety. But after gaining some poise, seeing the vivid attentiveness of people in the front rows, he stunned the audience with something most never forgot. They also never forgot Garrison's follow-up use of the young former slave's personal autobiographical remarks. A star was born in three days on Nantucket, and Garrison plucked the star out of the sky. Under Douglass's inspiration, Samuel May thought Garrison delivered "one of his sublimest speeches." Pillsbury observed a Garrison who "never before or afterwards felt more profoundly the sacredness of his mission." Garrison recalled asking the enthralled audience whether they would ever allow such a young fugitive to be "carried back into slavery," to which they answered "in thunder-tones—NO!" Garrison made Douglass "his text," recalled the fugitive slave. The Liberator's editor held forth with a "power, sweeping down, like a very tornado."[29] Before the delegation boarded the steamer for the return to New Bedford, a plan emerged, much to Douglass's astonishment and delight, to take this individual act as well as transcendent collaboration on the road. A new vocation beckoned.

Within one week of Nantucket, Douglass found himself whisked out on the railroads and into churches and halls of eastern Massachusetts and southern New Hampshire, telling his stories from the Eastern Shore, making witness against slavery, attacking racial prejudice and proslavery churches in the North. Douglass made a deal with John Collins, the "general agent" of the Massachusetts Anti-Slavery Society, to go out on the abolitionist speaking circuit for a three-month trial. Collins served as the young man's manager and traveling companion. Douglass said he worried that such publicity would expose him to capture and a return to slavery in Maryland. No doubt, Anna, with two babies in their crowded apartment on Ray Street in New Bedford, worried even more. But out her husband went, starting again, he later wrote, "a new life" with his "whole heart in the holy cause." Douglass was more than ready to change, he said, from a life sustained by the "hardness of my hands, as a means of supporting myself and rearing my children," to a life of the mind, one rooted in "reading and thinking," and sustained by nothing more material than the power of "the word."[30] For the next five decades the mastery of words became Douglass's life's work.

Such a path may seem but Frederick Douglass's destiny in retrospect, and he certainly portrayed it that way; but in the fall of 1841, nothing was certain—except that he would be paid to speak and face hatred, resistance, and violence, as he launched his more than fifty-year career as an orator. Taking enormous risks in proslavery America, Douglass eventually made untold thousands hold their breath as they listened to a voice like no other. Like Melville, he had found his "passage out," with no idea of just where the voyage might take him.[31] Only five and a half years after his Sabbath school sermons to his band of enslaved brothers on Freeland's farm, Douglass now had friends who would give him a pulpit to the whole country, even the world.

Chapter 7

THIS DOUGLASS!

I will not detain you long for I stand here a slave—a slave at least in the eyes of the Constitution. It is a slave by the laws of the South who now addresses you. My back is scarred by the lash—that I could show you—I would I could make visible the wounds of this system upon my soul.

—FREDERICK DOUGLASS, FANEUIL HALL,
BOSTON, FEBRUARY 4, 1842

The abolition movement had never seen anything quite like him. Tall, six feet one, brown skinned, careful of his physical appearance and the growth and part in his hair, handsome, with a sonorous voice he could modulate up or down but generally settled into a pleasing baritone, and with an astonishingly wide knowledge of both slavery itself and of antislavery strategies, Douglass took the abolitionists' traveling circuit by storm in the early 1840s. "I ran away from the South seven years ago," he said in a speech in New York in May 1845, "passing through this city in no little hurry. . . . Since then I have been engaged for three years in telling the people what I know of it."[1] Indeed he had been, all across the Northern states from Maine to Michigan, to small and large audiences, amid great adulation as well as vicious attacks.

Douglass found the vocation for which he believed he was fit at least since practicing speech-making with his *Columbian Orator* in hand. Although still only in his early to midtwenties, to see or hear this young Frederick Douglass became an American cultural phenomenon. Many of his auditors, friends and foes alike, left stunning descriptions of Douglass in action; none more remarkably than the abolitionist editor in Concord, New Hampshire, Nathaniel Rogers, who after witnessing a Douglass address in February 1844 could hardly contain himself. Typical of many abolitionist gatherings, especially on a Sunday, Douglass spoke to an afternoon meeting as well as an even larger one in the courthouse in the evening. Because of the Garrisonians' hostility to the clergy, as well as their persistent attacks on religious hypocrisy, no church in Concord opened its doors to the abolitionists. Douglass did not disappoint. In the "inconvenient, uncomfortable" space of the courthouse town hall, Douglass held forth in the afternoon on how he was "not a fugitive from slavery, but a fugitive slave." That he was still "in slavery" was due to the American churches' sanctifying and justifying the tyranny of slaveholding. Looking his audience in the eyes, he declared, "You are yourselves our enslavers."[2]

In the evening, the crowd was even larger; according to Rogers, Douglass delivered an unforgettable performance. Beginning slowly, with a "calm, deliberate . . . narrative of his life," the young man, who had just turned twenty-six years old, told of gaining his literacy from Sophia Auld—until her husband, Hugh, forbade it—as well as learning from his playmates and workmates in the streets and on the docks of Baltimore. This, Rogers observed, Douglass accomplished in a "hesitating way," reciting the facts, almost "dullish in manner." Then came "symptoms of a brewing storm" that took hold of the audience like nothing Rogers had ever seen. Douglass "gradually let out the outraged humanity that was laboring in him, in indignant and terrible speech." It was not so much eloquence, said the New Hampshire editor, but something "sterner, darker, deeper." Writing as though still breathing heavily while listening to Douglass, Rogers described a "volcanic outbreak of human nature . . . at last bursting its imprisonment." As Douglass now "stalked to and fro on the platform," Rogers saw an angry young man rise up "like the Numidian lion" and imagined "how that terrible voice of his would ring through the pine glades of the South, in the day of her visitation, calling the insurgents to battle, and striking terror to the hearts of the . . . despairing master." Rogers felt most impressed with the sheer "dignity" and "earnestness" of Douglass's effort. The speaker was not merely performing, said the local host. "He was the insurgent slave, taking hold of the right of speech, and charging on his tyrants the bondage of his race." Someone in the audience, as often occurred, objected to some aspect of Douglass's vehemence. Rogers enjoyed the result: "He better have run upon a lion. It was fearful but magnificent, to see how magnanimously and lion-like the royal fellow tore him to pieces, and left his untouched fragments scattered around him."[3]

In this great age of oratory, Rogers provided only one among many such recorded responses to Douglass the young lecturer. His power rested in part in his sheer talent with words on the platform. But it also emanated from his role, one he could almost never avoid, as symbol, as an exhibit of the black man, the slave with a stunningly informed, active, and brilliant mind. He was the Negro with intellect, a most unusual character to the imaginations of white-supremacist America. He was the ornament, the object, a former piece of property who could speak and write, who could match wits and logic with even his most determined critics, a youthful, beautiful brown man who made people think.[4] But he was also the preacher condemning sin and calling the fallen to repent, the analyst educating an ignorant populace that preferred comfortable stereotypes and shallow shibboleths to deeper knowledge of the realities of slavery, and the prosecutor trying to bring the nation and its citizens to a bar of public opinion if not justice.

When Douglass joined the abolition movement, 1841–44, the crusade was ascendant, but also riven with ideological, tactical, and personal disputes. At the heart of most of the internecine warfare among abolitionists was Garrison, a moral lightning rod who had inspired both deeply devoted followers and ferocious critics. Still only maturing as a sensitive fugitive slave desperately in search of community, security, and guidance, Douglass "loved" Garrison and held him in genuine reverence, as he often said. Once pressed on where he had achieved his advanced education, the former slave responded, "From Massachusetts University, Mr. Garrison, president." Douglass quickly knew he had joined a religious movement, what many historians have come to call a campaign of "Bible politics"; and its spiritual father was William Lloyd Garrison. One of Garrison's long-term admirers, Thomas Wentworth Higginson, recollected that the founder of the *Liberator* always sounded "like a newly discovered chapter of Ezekiel." But Garrison eagerly made many enemies. One found his style so harsh that he compared him to "the pert loquacity of a blue-jay." Even one among his own flock declared that it was all but impossible "to swallow Garrison whole."[5]

In the early 1840s, Douglass did swallow whole the cluster of ideas and strategies the prophetic Garrison had honed into rigid orthodoxy. To the doctrines of immediatism, moral suasion, anticlericalism, nonresistance (pacifism), and racial equality that Douglass had relished reading about in the *Liberator*, Garrison had now advanced perhaps his most controversial tenets of all: disunionism (urging abolitionists to withdraw from any complicity with the proslavery US Constitution); antipolitics (denunciation of political parties and of voting itself in a system so corrupted by slavery); and women's equality (demanding women's political and economic rights). These three doctrines did more than anything else to tear asunder by 1840 whatever unity remained in the American Anti-Slavery Society (AASS), the organization Garrison had done so much to build. Garrison took abolitionism into the realm of Christian anarchy, human moral perfectionism, and rejection of virtually all governmental authority.[6] Many devoted abolitionists, especially African Americans, stayed with him; his charisma and devotion alone could carry a crowd a long way. But many others, particularly evangelicals who did not believe all churches worth condemning, and especially those who saw antislavery potential in the Constitution and who believed it foolhardy to think that slavery could ever be eradicated outside the American political system, openly split with Garrison and his brand of ideological purity.

By fall 1841, as Douglass joined a stable of loyal lecturers, Garrison expressed great confidence about the movement. "Our antislavery struggle is constantly increasing in vigor and potency," he wrote to an English friend, "and never were our spirits better or our blows more effective.... Our fall and winter campaign will be carried on with unwonted energy." Invitations to speak came to Garrison himself and to his troops from "all parts of the free states." He relished the attacks on his methods and arguments from outside and from within abolitionism. The coffers of the American Anti-Slavery Society had grown and made possible the hiring of Douglass as well as other speakers. "The many base attempts . . . to cripple my influence, and render me odious in the eyes of the people," Garrison claimed, "have only served to awaken sympathy . . . and to open a wide door for usefulness." Portraying himself as undergoing a Job-like onslaught, Garrison exploited his enemies' wrath, a tactic Douglass soon mastered himself: "Thus has the Lord taken the cunning in their own craftiness, and carried the counsels of the froward headlong."[7]

But Garrison no longer spoke for the entire antislavery movement. By 1840 the American Anti-Slavery Society broke apart forever in a schism. In response to the near collapse of moral suasion as a guiding strategy, Garrison, if anything, took it to an even higher intensity. He argued that the whole of American society, especially the North, needed a "moral revolution" in values, a transformation from a nation of sin and infamy to the goal of human perfection. Garrison was a great organizer, an intrepid newspaper editor, and sometimes a magical platform speaker. But he could also demand absolutist doctrines of his followers, as in the biblical injunction he fondly employed: "Be ye perfect, even as your heavenly Father is perfect."[8] Garrisonians increasingly gained a reputation for extreme radicalism, of being either dangerous or irrelevant cranks. Sometimes they earned such an image, even among other abolitionists, and sometimes it was merely the by-product of embittered factionalism.

Led by Arthur and Lewis Tappan, wealthy abolitionist merchants in New York, a growing cadre of more politically minded reformers came to believe that far more Americans could be reached by antislavery beliefs if immediatism, a radical temperament and the strategy that sought abolition of slavery without delay, did not appear so militant. Garrison outorganized the Tappanites at the 1840 annual convention of the American Anti-Slavery Society, managed adoption of many of his doctrines by narrow margins, and elected the radical feminist Abby Kelley to the executive committee by a tally of 557 to 451. The Tappans and many of their adherents especially opposed women's equality in reform movements; they bolted the older organization and formed the new American and Foreign Anti-Slavery Society, based in New York City and devoted especially to a broader political and legal movement against slavery. That group had also been deeply instrumental in forming the Liberty Party, the first antislavery political organization to gain genuine traction in America.[9]

As Douglass found himself and his talents warmly embraced within the Garrisonian fold, he quickly discerned the ways of a swirling and contentious world of friends and enemies, devotees and apostates. For now, partly out of agreement, and partly because he knew where his bread was buttered, Douglass remained devoted to his mentor, who was thirteen years his senior and a man of prophetic qualities to the young romantic fugitive slave. Although only an upstart, Douglass joined up with the "old organization" men and their growing number of women activists, and he was more than eager to earn approval from his father figure, Garrison, by denouncing the heresies of the "new organization" men such as the Tappans, and the emerging political abolitionists in the Liberty Party.[10]

As Douglass remembered setting out on his three-month trial on the speaking circuit, he stressed his fears of capture as a fugitive; but he relished the opportunity. His handler, John A. Collins, was a thirty-one-year-old, Vermont-born radical Garrisonian and former theology student with a powerful reputation as an effective organizer. In town after town, Collins made things happen for groups of agents and speakers. Later in the autobiographies, Douglass would write with some contempt about Collins's efforts to control the younger man's message and style. Collins would introduce Douglass with quite some fanfare as a "graduate of the peculiar institution," and then on cue Frederick would tell his stories from the Eastern Shore. They became an effective tag team, and although Douglass undoubtedly tired of the same routine and his personalized rhetoric, Collins was without question a devoted companion and adviser. As a fellow abolitionist remarked, no one in the Garrisonian ranks could "plan and execute a campaign on the largest scale" as well as Collins.[11]

With a high forehead and a strong chin, Collins was no slouch himself on the platform. Garrison so trusted him that he sent Collins to England in 1840–41 to raise money and to spread the Garrisonian gospels among British abolitionists. Just before returning from England, Collins published a pamphlet, *Right and Wrong Among the Abolitionists*, in which he defended Garrisonian doctrines against the "misrepresentations" and "mean-minded malice" of other abolitionists. The *Liberator* sold Collins's manifesto at the same time it began to chart Douglass's tours in the fall of 1841.[12]

By the end of his trial period in late 1841, Douglass had spoken in at least twenty towns in Massachusetts, Rhode Island, and New Hampshire, sometimes at organized conventions and sometimes at little gatherings promoted on the spot. On many of these occasions he delivered multiple speeches or statements in support of resolutions. Douglass was often among a group of at least a half dozen speakers; a typical town's event would last at least two days and would include both daytime and evening meetings. The small troupes of abolitionists traveled by horse, in wagons, by stagecoach, and increasingly where possible by railroad. They stayed in private homes wherever friends could provide beds. The abolitionist gatherings occurred in churches, town halls, public meetinghouses, and outdoors on town greens. On some occasions, Douglass and colleagues would walk the streets or roads of a village passing out handbills announcing that evening's antislavery speeches. At Grafton, Massachusetts, in early 1842, while working solo, Douglass was met by mob hostility in addition to an unwelcoming clergy. So he went to a hotel and borrowed a "dinner-bell, with which in hand I passed through the principal streets," he recalled, "ringing the bell and crying out, 'Notice! Frederick Douglass, recently a slave, will lecture on American Slavery, on Grafton Common, this evening at 7 o'clock."[13]

The young Douglass had not only found his calling, but he quickly emerged as a rising star in the first great reform movement of American history. At this stage of his speaking career, his youth protected him from many of the physical ravages and bone-numbing challenges of the road. But this was only the beginning of a more than fifty-year career for this incomparable itinerant orator, of strained vocal cords and lost voice, but an intrepid heart, oratorical brilliance, and a vanity to match.

While touring under Collins's tutelage in the fall of 1841, and after he

Frederick Douglass, first known photograph, c. 1841. Daguerreotype.

was hired full-time as a lecturer in early 1842, Douglass shared platforms, meals, lecturing techniques, and ideas with all the leading Garrisonians: Garrison himself, Wendell Phillips, Stephen Foster, Edmund Quincy, Samuel J. May, Charles Lenox Remond, the leading black moral suasionist, and Abby Kelley, the stunning Quaker woman and radical whose talent as a speaker and whose controversial feminism had made her even more of a sensation than the celebrated fugitive slave. He also spoke out on virtually all the leading issues from proslavery churches to Northern racial prejudice, the virtues of moral suasion and the dangers of political parties, disunionism and nonresistance, and the psychological and physical character of slavery.

Douglass learned much from his road-savvy older colleagues; but whatever resolutions they addressed, only he brought the living story of the scarred and surviving slave to pulpits and lecterns. At his first outing, only one week after his debut on Nantucket in August, in the small town of Millbury, Massachusetts (Abby Kelley's hometown), southeast of Worcester, a witness reported that Douglass "called forth pity and horror at his story" from the Eastern Shore. The Garrisonians now trumpeted their new agent as the "fresh impulse" on the circuit, and his voice as something unprecedented in a movement entering its second decade. At Lynn, Massachusetts, in early October, in the first of Douglass's speeches recorded and published by a local journalist, the orator demonstrated the techniques that so captured audiences. After declaring how "embarrassed" he was to speak before white people (a ruse he employed for years), he announced his subject: "something about slavery—what I *know* of it, as I have *felt* it." Here, in Christian New England, among romantics who yearned for the intellectual and emotional knowledge of what slavery was like, and what race and its mixtures produced in human capacity, they could hear from a true witness.[14]

Douglass made the most of his authenticity. At Lynn, he honored his white abolitionist colleagues for their deep knowledge and passion. "But they cannot speak as I can from experience," he said directly; "they cannot refer you to a back covered with scars, as I can, for I have felt these wounds." Douglass grabbed the feelings of his audiences and made them clay in his hands as he drew such distinctions with his fellow white abolitionists. He offered audiences the "blood . . . sprung out as the lash embedded in my flesh." Before the Lynn address ended, Douglass introduced those gathered to the rigid religious hypocrisies of Thomas Auld, "class leader in the Methodist church," stories of the separation of families in his slave background, the dreams slaves entertained of emancipation, and even the ways Northern racism hung around his "neck like a heavy weight."[15] This became Douglass's stock-in-trade: stories drawn from his life, laid on with force and powerful indignation, penetrating the hearts of his auditors.

Rarely at home now in New Bedford, where Anna nursed and raised two babies, Douglass traveled incessantly from town to town. Their daughter, Rosetta, was just over two years old, and their son, Lewis, had been born on October 9, 1840. By the time Douglass had spoken in Lynn in 1841 just before Lewis's first birthday, that town had become an important marker in both his life and that of the movement.

The distances between the young abolitionist's private and public lives were thrown into stark contrast, which would only grow with time. Twice in September Douglass was insulted, accosted, or thrown off the Eastern Railroad, the second instance occurring at the Lynn depot. On September 8, Collins and Douglass had purchased train tickets in Newburyport to travel north to Dover, New Hampshire, to speak at the Strafford County Anti-Slavery Society. The two were sitting in one double seat as the gruff conductor ordered Douglass to immediately move forward to the Jim Crow car. For Douglass such constant practices of segregation were always about dignity, as much as the "mean, dirty, and uncomfortable" space of Jim Crow cars. Collins vehemently objected on behalf of his black companion, whom he described to Garrison in a long account, as only "one or two shades darker than Daniel Webster." With the conductor's "little fist flourished about my head," Collins reported, he too was ordered to leave the car. "If you haul him out, it will be over my person, as I do not intend to leave this seat," proclaimed Collins. The conductor brought in several of the railroad's hired thugs to do the deed. With Collins loudly protesting this was "no less than lynch law," five men dragged the strong Douglass over Collins's unmoved body, "like so many bloodhounds," and "thrust him into the 'negro car.'" In the fracas, Douglass's clothes were torn and Collins described himself as "considerably injured in the affray." Not missing an opportunity to make a Garrisonian doctrinal point, Collins told of a second conductor who went into the Negro car to console Douglass with the intelligence that the railroad's policy was not so bad after all, since so many churches "have their 'negro pews.'" [16]

On September 28 an even worse incident happened in this corner of the free North. Collins boarded the train in Boston heading north for an antislavery meeting in Newburyport. At the Lynn depot Douglass, along with fellow abolitionist James Buffum and an unidentified woman abolitionist, got on board. They had only assumed their seats when the same conductor grabbed Douglass by the collar and ordered him to the Jim Crow car. The group of four demanded the reason, and Buffum even asked that the passengers hold a vote. In what became a kind of standard performative response at these endless confrontations in his early career, Douglass pronounced, "If you will give me any good reason why I should leave this car, I will go willingly; but without such reason, I do not feel at liberty to leave, though you can do with me as you please, I shall not resist." [17] For now, Douglass responded to such racism with disciplined nonresistance. In a short time, however, his response would drastically change. His rage would be contained by other people's principles for only so long.

Collins fashioned this second Jim Crow railroad incident as a kind of theater. In a scene of great drama, other passengers in the car chimed in with a chorus of "Give him the reason!" As the surrounded, hapless conductor struggled for words, in a "half-suppressed, half-audible voice" he looked up at Douglass's face and said, "Because you are black," which "stuck in his throat, like Macbeth's *Amen.*" But the conductor was surrounded for only a short while. Soon a half dozen company bullies arrived and began to beat both Douglass and Collins. As Douglass held fast to the seat with all his arm strength and with Collins still holding on firm as well, the floor bolts gave way and the troupe of enforcers threw the men and the seat out the door and onto the ground with a great thud. Douglass's luggage was next thrown out on him as well.[18]

If Douglass had not already realized it, he surely did now: he was a key actor in a public drama, the survivor of slavery as abolitionist exhibit and the victim-symbol of Yankee racism. In the days immediately after the September 28 incident in Lynn, the town held large meetings of protest and indignation, and the Garrisonians made robust use of the event by launching a widespread protest campaign, threatening boycotts against such discriminatory railroads across New England. At least one of the town's newspapers, the *Lynn Record*, also expressed strong support of Douglass and the abolitionists. It may have been precisely because of these episodes of racial embarrassment brought on by the Eastern Railroad Company, and the public sympathies that flooded his way, that Douglass now planned to move his family to Lynn late in the fall of 1841. Lightning would not strike twice, and the prosperous shoe-manufacturing town had to make itself welcoming to the young black family, with the bruised and aggrieved celebrity at its head. Moreover, Garrison's AASS office appears to have either purchased a house for the Douglasses or financially helped him build one in Lynn, a town judged safer for a runaway than in the bigger port of Boston itself, where a fugitive slave might be more easily seized.[19]

We know little of what Anna thought of the move, but likely in November or early December, during a lull in his speaking schedule, Douglass began to move his family to the town on the north side of Massachusetts Bay. They took up residence near the center in what his daughter Rosetta remembered as a "cottage," and what his son Charles recalled as a small frame dwelling built by his father's own hands, on Union Street, which intersected with the railroad at Exchange Street in the heart of town. The house was a short walk from the depot where countless times over the next three years Douglass would embark and disembark on his speaking tours. That same depot where he was thrown on the ground in a tumbling train seat became the revolving door for American reform's most prominent traveling man. Unlike in New Bedford, he did not have to find jobs with his hands in Lynn; his vocation now was that of the public lecturer in perpetual motion, bringing home a modest salary. Douglass would never again lift a barrel of whale oil.[20]

Anna may have set up a house in Lynn that winter, but she was pregnant again, and she returned to New Bedford for the birth of Frederick Jr. on March 3, 1842, perhaps seeking out friends and the aid of a midwife. Douglass had a speaking engagement in Hubbardston, Massachusetts, on February 16, but was likely at his wife's side for the birth of his namesake. With three babies now at home by the summer of 1842 (Rosetta was almost three, Lewis a year and a half old), Anna eventually garnered some income for the struggling young family by working as a shoe binder, a common occupation for women in that industry. Occasionally, she would meet her husband at the depot with clean shirts and underwear as he sped off to the next anti-slavery meeting beyond her horizon. We know Douglass as the great public voice, the source of words that explain the nation's predicament with slavery and racism. Anna knew him through a hundred other kinds of images; but too often, the most common would be that of her well-dressed husband kissing and hugging good-bye as a whistle blows at the train station, she thrusting clean clothes and a bit of food into his outstretched hand, while holding a toddler in one hand and a baby on her shoulder.[21]

The sounds and smells of the railroad depot, the backaches and the stiff necks from so many fitful naps on the cars, the rhythm of the wheels rolling on the iron rails, the weight of his duffel bags as well as the romance of train travel, were Douglass's constant companions. So were an occasional sympathetic friend, a voyeuristic onlooker, or a racist heckler. Douglass took up residence in Lynn in late 1841 and early 1842, but most of the time over the next three years he lived on trains, on horseback, in carriages, and in other people's houses. Forty years later in *Life and Times*, he acknowledged some fifteen families by name in Rhode Island alone who took him into their "homes and hearths," although he possessed "few of the graces derived from free and refined society."[22] Reformers, like artists, need patrons, often perpetually.

Lynn was an address as much as a residence for Douglass. But the thriving industrial center produced 3 million pairs of shoes annually by the 1840s. Some nine miles north of Boston and five miles south of Salem, Lynn had 9,375 inhabitants in 1840. With a strong contingent of Quakers, the town had supported an antislavery society since 1832, and by 1838 when the Eastern Railroad was completed along its southern edge by the harbor, it sported three newspapers, almost 130 manufactories employing nearly three thousand workers, a dozen churches, nine schools, and ten hotels. In the year the Douglasses arrived, Lynn opened the new Lyceum Hall on Market Street, and it supported a thriving musical culture. John, Asa, Judson, and Abby Hutchinson, soon to be the famous abolitionist Hutchinson Family Singers, had just taken up residence in town and would soon be good friends and occasional traveling partners with Douglass.[23]

These were heady and inspiring months for the twenty-three-year-old

Douglass as he found his voice and individual style. As superlative reactions to Douglass's oratory began to follow nearly every appearance, it is easy to neglect his startling youth. Abolitionist Edmund Quincy wrote privately in October 1841 that some in the audience at one of Douglass's speeches thought that he (Quincy) had written the address for the young black man. So remarkable was the "favorable impression," said Quincy wryly, that "some of the people were amazed that a nigger could talk so well." This is where responses to Douglass's voice began in the 1840s: How could this bright and eloquent brown-hued man be the slave he claimed to be? A local newspaper editor, at a speech in Hingham, Massachusetts, in November, gushed, "As this Douglass stood there in manly attitude, with erect form, and glistening eye, and deep-toned voice, telling us that he had been secretly devising means to effect his release from bondage, we could not help thinking of Spartacus, the Gladiator." The auditor made the most of his manly metaphors. Douglass was the "daring insurgent . . . a man of . . . shrewdness, and . . . power both intellectually and physically." Stunned at Douglass's fluency with language, the editor described him as "forcible, keen and very sarcastic . . . a remarkable man." [24] Such masculine, almost erotic descriptions of Douglass became commonplace throughout his speaking career, even into old age.

"This Douglass" was a performer. A Lynn resident, David N. Johnson, in a book of reminiscences, recalled Douglass as though from a series of theatrical events. He was "more than six feet in height, and his majestic form . . . straight as an arrow, muscular, yet lithe and graceful," seemed like nothing else Johnson had ever witnessed in all the lectures he attended at Lynn's Lyceum Hall. Douglass's "flashing eye, and more than all, his voice, that rivaled [Daniel] Webster's in its richness, and in the depth and sonorousness of its cadences, made up such an ideal of an orator as the listeners never forgot." Even more, the young abolitionist's "burning words, his pathos . . . [and] the rich play of his humor" left greater impressions. Douglass already possessed the skills of a trained actor; his voice was musical in the fullest sense. "His eyes would flash with defiance, and now grow dim with emotions he could not control; and the roll of his splendid voice . . . would pass to the minor key whose notes trembled on his tongue." Douglass's performative fame spread so widely and quickly that notices about this "black rascal" appeared even in Southern newspapers. [25]

Who would not have wanted to see and hear this Douglass in a golden age of oratory? The great activist Elizabeth Cady Stanton, who later tangled bitterly with Douglass over the priority of women's or black male suffrage during Reconstruction, first saw Douglass speak in Boston in 1842 and left an unforgettable remembrance. "He stood there like an African prince," wrote Stanton in 1895, "conscious of his dignity and power, grand in his physical proportions, majestic in his wrath, as with keen wit, satire, and indignation he portrayed the bitterness of slavery." According to Stanton, Douglass rendered the large Faneuil Hall audience "completely magnetized with his eloquence, laughing and crying by turns." She also recalled that especially in the 1840s, Douglass's most popular topic was his "Slaveholder's Sermon," his famous mimicry of a Methodist preacher's appeals to slaves, based on the biblical text "Servants, obey your masters." She claimed that even after Douglass had held forth on other topics for an hour, audiences would shout and demand, "Douglass, give us the sermon."[26] And he rarely failed to entertain as he also blistered his listeners with abolitionist fervor.

In the winter and spring of 1842, Douglass was on the road almost constantly, preaching about clerical hypocrisy, exalting moral suasion, and assaulting the political methods of the Liberty Party, even putting his shoulder, if not his heart, into the utopian Garrisonian notion of disunionism. The "Slaveholder's Sermon" quickly became the standard of his repertoire. "Douglass gave it to the church with much vim," wrote one Garrisonian devotee to her sister approvingly after attending his speech in Weymouth, Massachusetts, in April 1842.[27]

That he delivered this performance so often and effectively is due to its humor, to its constant use of parallelism and antithesis, and to its resonance in Christian New England. Garrisonianism was above all a religious-social crusade against the conscience and sloth of the faithful. But the "sermon" was also funny, and its author could alter the tone, scene, or length to fit the occasion. Douglass often began by reciting the story of the Reverend Isaac Bonney in New Bedford separating blacks from whites for Communion. But one Sunday Bonney blundered. After a baptism in which several white and one black woman had been anointed "in the same water," the Communion cup was passed. A foolish, abolitionist-leaning deacon saw the black woman step in line between the whites, so he handed her the cup. But when "the precious blood which had been shed for all" reached the next white woman, "she rose in disdain and walked out of the church." Brimming for the sarcastic kill, the orator did not stop there. "Another young lady fell into a trance," barked Douglass. "When she awoke, she declared she had been to Heaven; her friends were all anxious to know what and whom she had seen there." One "good old lady" especially needed to know "if she saw any black folks in Heaven?" Then came the punch line: "Oh! I didn't go in the kitchen!"[28] Douglass paced to another position on the platform awaiting the howling laughter to subside.

Rooted in memories of watching Thomas Auld weep during his confessions in the ring at the Methodist camp meeting on the Eastern Shore, in Edward Covey's prayer sessions, and in his New Bedford preaching experience, Douglass saved his best for the Christian hypocrisy of the South. If he spoke in a church or hall with a gallery, he made special use of the setting, as he did in 1842 at Faneuil Hall in Boston. Peering up into the horseshoe balcony of that great arena before four thousand people, and spreading his arms out widely, he appealed as though to the slaves set apart in the gallery of a Southern church. With a mocking Southern accent, he called out, "And you too my friends have souls of infinite value—souls that will live through endless happiness or misery in eternity. Oh, labor diligently to make your calling and election sure. Oh, receive into your souls these words of the holy apostle—'Servants, be obedient to your masters." Amid "shouts of laughter and applause," Douglass pranced on the stage and drove his point home. "Oh, consider the wonderful goodness of God! Look at your hard, horny hands, your strong muscular frames, and see how mercifully he has adapted you to the duties you are to fulfill . . . while to your masters, who have slender frames and long delicate fingers, he has given brilliant intellects, that they may do the *thinking*, while you do the *working*."[29]

Douglass eventually boiled down these tales into a compelling assertion of contrasts that he used throughout the 1840s. By 1845 he could rip it off at a moment's notice, often right after reciting the Golden Rule: "In America Bibles and slaveholders go hand in hand. The church and the slave prison stand together, and while you hear the chanting of psalms in one, you hear the clanking of chains in the other. The man who wields the cowhide during the week, fills the pulpit on Sunday. . . . The man who whipped me in the week used to . . . show me the way of life on the Sabbath."[30]

A star had been born; a youthful, brilliant black voice of a fugitive slave had entered the fray of abolitionism. At a mere twenty-four years old Douglass stepped out now on countless platforms to preach a Garrisonian ideological mixture of radicalism and personal testimony. Soon, he carried abolitionist fervor and rhetoric, as well as the Frederick Douglass story, across the Northern states in a crusade he increasingly made his own.

Chapter 8

GARRISONIAN IN
MIND AND BODY

These hands—are they not mine? This body—is it not mine? I am your brother, white as you are. I'm your blood kin. You don't get rid of me so easily. . . . If I go to Lexington or Bunker Hill, there I'm a slave, chained in perpetual servitude. I may go to your deepest valley, to your highest mountain, I'm still a slave, and the bloodhound may chase me down.

—FREDERICK DOUGLASS, AN ADDRESS
IN NEW YORK CITY, MARCH 6, 1845

From 1842 to 1845, Douglass took his flourishing mind, his increasingly confident voice, and his Garrisonian body to the open road. His travel and speaking itineraries almost defy belief, and his devotion to Garrisonian ideology remained steadfast. From late March to early May 1842 he did an intensive tour of eastern and central Massachusetts. On this, his first solo tour, he spoke in at least forty-two different towns or small villages, often visiting two towns in a single day and lecturing twice in the same place in a single day. Immediately upon ending the Massachusetts tour, Douglass caught the train for New York, where he participated along with three thousand fellow abolitionists in the annual meeting of the American Anti-Slavery Society (AASS) at the Broadway Tabernacle.

At this New York meeting he likely first met James McCune Smith, a physician and intellectual, and the most educated African American in the United States. Their relationship would be long and enduring, although it would take time to develop; the young fugitive slave and gifted orator, soon to be a sterling writer without a day of formal schooling, and the New York–born man of learning with three advanced degrees from the University of

James McCune Smith, 1840s.
Engraving by Patrick H. Reason.

Glasgow in Scotland would become within a decade an extraordinary story of creative alter egos. No record survives of their first conversations, but they did speak up for the same resolution supporting an appeal to the US Supreme Court testing whether blacks possessed the "privileges and immunities of citizens."[1]

In the early 1840s, as abolitionism underwent the bitter schisms between moral suasionists and the advocates of political action, Smith remained ideologically a partial Garrisonian, a member of the AASS, but one who chose his allegiances pragmatically. Only five years older than Douglass, Smith was born a slave, but freed in the 1827 New York emancipation law. He had a thriving medical practice in lower Manhattan by the 1840s and already flourished as an essayist on many subjects; he was never the itinerant lecturer that his younger friend became. Douglass, however, took to the antislavery circuit constantly, performing as a loyal disciple of his mentor. For a week in June 1842, Douglass toured for the first time with Garrison as they barnstormed through meetings in six towns on Cape Cod. This tour also included George Bradburn, a Unitarian minister from Attleboro, Massachusetts, who never fully embraced Garrisonianism, but was a frequent companion of Douglass's on the circuit. Bradburn never adhered to the doctrine of antipolitics since he was the Whig Party representative from Nantucket in the Massachusetts legislature. The primary theme of the Cape Cod tour was nonresistance, the strict adherence to pacifism that Garrison advanced.[2]

Antislavery meetings that trumpeted nonresistance gave Garrison yet another opportunity to *use* Douglass, as Garrison also vigorously promoted Douglass's career. After Garrison spoke at length in support of moral suasion and nonresistance at the Barnstable meeting, Douglass took the platform and did his job with apparent fervor. Garrison's description of Douglass's speech is a stunning example of the mentor's unending effort to employ every element of the former slave's persona, his words, his very body, in the service of the cause. Douglass "stood there as a slave," announced Garrison, "a runaway from the southern house of bondage—not safe for even one hour, even on the soil of Massachusetts—with his back all horribly scarred by the lash." One cannot help wondering, in these years when the two men became close associates, and with Garrison so often referring to Douglass's physical scars, whether the young star orator ever actually showed his naked back to his mentor. Whether he did so or not, Garrison claimed Douglass had every right to be the "fierce outlaw and the stern avenger." Instead, Garrison pointed to his prime exhibit as the "genius of Christianity." That Douglass could rise on such occasions not to advocate retaliation, nor to "wade through blood to liberty" no matter how justified, but to preach with "forgiveness in his heart," made him a model for the potential "overthrow of every form of oppression on earth."[3] One wonders how much the youthful Douglass, inspired and proud to be on platforms next to Garrison, really believed in such utopian sensibilities. Not forever could his personal rage against slavery be contained in a pacifist ideological package.

At one of the Cape Cod meetings the three abolitionists spoke to a resolution: "Resolved, that a Christian cannot fight, with weapons, against his enemies, or the enemies of others; nor take the life of his fellow-man, nor assist or empower others to take it, either in self-defense or as a penalty for crime."[4] Douglass had many times violated this maxim during his life as a slave. For now he was all but swallowed up in an antislavery theology, and he managed to preach its creeds with anyone, as long as he was free to tell his own story, to pillory the proslavery clergy, and begin to expose Northern racism in his own style.

In his portrayals of Douglass, Garrison could be exultant in one sentence and condescending in the next. When Douglass spoke in support of the nonresistance resolution, Garrison saw the "power of an unsophisticated mind and the glow of an earnest heart." Douglass's words left a "visible impression" on the audience. In other words, Garrison got everything he wanted from his star pupil. At yet another Cape Cod stop, Centerville, Garrison said Douglass spoke "experimentally" in unmasking the "abominable hypocrisy" of Southern religion. Here, Garrison found his own awkward way to praise Douglass's emerging craft of mimicry. Perhaps white leader and black follower both rolled their eyes about each other in private. As an observer in North Dennis remarked, the young black man "gave us a good proof of the freedom of his mind . . . his wit and power of sarcasm."[5] He was at once Garrison's experiment and his own, emerging self-invention. Amid all the moral earnestness of an abolitionist meeting, Douglass had learned how to leave them laughing.

At the Hyannis meeting on June 20, in a Baptist church, Douglass experimented in yet another way. Giving testimony of "what his own eyes had seen," he "read a large amount of evidence . . . given by southern men . . . proving the entire slave system to be diabolical." Here Douglass likely read detailed descriptions from Theodore Weld's *American Slavery as It Is*, a technique he would use frequently in the 1840s. Published in 1839, Weld's moral-suasionist classic, an unprecedented compilation of the horrors of slave treatment and punishment drawn from travelers' accounts, newspapers, and slaveholders' own writings, was a storehouse of slavery's inhumanity. Douglass would often read at length a litany of statements about the numbers of lashes applied to slaves for certain offenses, and the physical brutalities and scars left on slaves' bodies as reported in runaway advertisements. What a compelling scene it must have been for an audience listening to Douglass, in his pounding baritone, referencing his own scars, then performing from Weld's lists of mutilations, burnings, shootings, and images of "ears cut off," hands "cut with an axe," chains around a slave's neck, and the like.[6] Douglass found his own ways to make moral suasion penetrate the heart by more than mere assertion; he learned how to leave them weeping.

In the early 1840s Garrisonian abolitionists caused a violent response around New England and the Northeast. Douglass continued his backbreaking travel in the late summer of 1842, returning to abolitionist conventions in New Bedford and on Nantucket (on the first anniversary of his original public appearance). Anti-abolition mobs attacked both gatherings. In New Bedford the mob seems to have been content with shouting down the speakers, but on Nantucket on August 11, ruffians disrupted the gathering, with Garrison, Collins, Douglass, and Stephen Foster all on the platform, by "hooting, screeching, throwing brick-bats and other missiles" through windows. On the following day, trying again to assemble, the meeting heard Douglass attack racism in the North as the cause of "exciting mobs against the colored people—preventing them from taking their places in society as equal members." And the mob was ready to enact their part of this dangerous ritual. This time the mob's numbers and weapons, including a "shower of rotten eggs," were such that the meeting finally adjourned in chaos.[7]

In one full year on the antislavery circuit Douglass had now collected many such badges of honor—well-publicized instances of being thrown off railcars, bricks hurled at his head, hooligans shouting "nigger" and bringing greater attention to abolitionist ideas as well as free speech. Even clearer now was that for a twenty-four-year-old black man with growing fame and an astonishing new voice, abolitionism was a dangerous business. But in this romantic age, the radical reformer who did not trouble the waters and stir the ire of his foes might be ignored. Ideas, spiritual passion, personal witness, and brazen effrontery were all part of the tactical repertoire. A fast learner, Douglass threw himself avidly into this fray, even as he traveled with a Garrisonian ideological cloak.

During a mere week's respite at home in Lynn in August, Douglass spoke at a large nonresistance meeting at the Lyceum Hall. Growing in confidence and boldness, he spoke about the nature of prayer. As reported by Nathaniel Rogers, Douglass argued that the "most effectual sort of prayer" was "DOING!" and not *"saying."* In what likely seemed the voice of an angry young man to his Christian neighbors, he said his prayers in "words" had never been answered as a slave. Only his own action by running away to freedom achieved a prayer answered. Rogers found Douglass "especially eloquent and powerful."[8] No brickbats flew in Lynn.

Douglass had hardly been home at all during that first full summer on the circuit. Now, sponsored by Garrison's office in Boston, and after hasty hellos and good-byes to Anna and the three small children, he headed out on a two-month crusade through New York State with seven other agents employed by the AASS, including Abby Kelley, the female sensation of the movement. Seven years older than Douglass, Kelley was born to a Quaker farm family in the rural hills of western Massachusetts, worked as a schoolteacher in Lynn, and eventually lived near Worcester. By 1840 she had emerged as one of the most tireless and militant speakers among the Garrisonians. Kelley was pretty, wore plain gray dresses, and at least in these early years skillfully argued the moral-suasionist case against slavery and for women's equality. She bought in fully to Garrison's form of perfectionism, was a staunch nonresistant, and for now denounced political parties. Soon she would marry Stephen Foster, an abolitionist from New Hampshire, and they would form a radical married couple like few others. She was sharp-tongued, and as adept as any of her male counterparts at abolitionist factional infighting. She wowed audiences even as they detested her very presence in public forums as a woman. Many a church sanctuary or town hall was closed to the troupe because of her leading role in antislavery tours, but they pressed on nonetheless, holding meetings in groves, meadows, and on town greens.[9]

Douglass was at first awed by Kelley and understood that he was the second billing on this grueling New York crusade, much of which Kelley had planned, in concert with Collins, the physician Erasmus D. Hudson, and the AASS executive committee, as a grand effort to revitalize local antislavery societies. In a promotional letter detailing the dates of "conventions" in twenty-four counties, Collins touted Kelley and Douglass as the headliners, declaring it "well worth a journey of forty miles to listen to the eloquent pleadings of FREDERICK DOUGLASS, the fugitive from our '*Peculiar Institutions.*'" Garrison eventually dubbed Kelley the "moral Joan of Arc of the world," and Douglass, so young and inexperienced with ideas about women's equality and with learned women, likely gained his first feminist education from the Quaker woman whom he watched facing all manner of vicious repression.[10] He was part of something new—an angry, radical beloved community, a salvation show traveling through the Burned-Over District.

Douglass joined Kelley, Hudson, Collins, and others in Rochester on August 26, more than two weeks into the tour. Hudson was an especially passionate, doctrinaire Garrisonian who kept a remarkable journal along the way. On this first visit to his future home, Douglass found Rochester hospitable. On the second night of the meetings, Douglass joined other abolitionists at the home of Amy and Isaac Post, local Quaker abolitionists; their meeting was the beginning of a long and abiding friendship. The abolitionists tried to convene meetings at a Presbyterian church, only to have the minister throw them out due to Kelley's presence. Gathering in yet a different church, Collins and Hudson were verbally attacked by a heckler for their claims against religious hypocrisy. Rising to defend his colleagues,

Abby Kelley Foster, 1850s. Daguerreotype.

Douglass, reported Hudson, chastised the assailant by using Christ's warnings to "scribes, Pharisees, and hypocrites, vipers, lawyers, whited sepulchers and making *Congregational* prayers." Douglass would have drawn from Matthew, Isaiah, or other parts of God's denunciations of the appearances of the good—"ye blind guides"—among those who do evil. Furious over church doors slammed in abolitionists' faces, Douglass commanded everyone's attention with such biblical ridicule as "Woe unto you, scribes and Pharisees, hypocrites! For ye are like unto whited sepulchers, which indeed appear beautiful outward, but are within full of dead men's bones." [11] Ever ready with God's voice from the King James text when he needed it, one imagines Douglass rebuking the heckler, Bible in hand.

Holding meetings in some nineteen towns, the intrepid abolitionist band trekked on, staying wherever they could find friendly accommodations. They traveled in farm wagons, in carriages and commercial stagecoaches, on the Erie Canal, and where possible on railroads. In the decade or so after the completion of the Erie Canal in 1825, the new commercial waterway connecting western New York, and therefore the Midwest, with the port of New York, frontier settlements along the route transformed into the thriving market and manufacturing towns of Albany, Utica, Syracuse, Rochester, and Buffalo. From 1820 to 1850 Rochester alone grew from a population of 1,502 to 36,403. Waves of religious revivalists, spiritualists, utopian socialists, millers, small-scale merchants, as well as droves of hard-drinking, tobacco-chewing immigrant laborers settled in these booming cities. [12]

Abolitionists such as the Kelley-Douglass band of 1842 across New York sought to harness the anxieties and hopes of this emerging middle class undergoing social and economic transformations. Radical abolitionists were a religious and political threat to this new social order. Their task was far from simple; some towns turned out large audiences, but in others they were met with shuttered church buildings or violently hostile mobs. At Vienna, Hudson recorded, a mob "pelted" the speakers with "a shower of brick bats & stones, and threw a little pig up into our hall." With the meeting broken up, the abolitionists retreated to the railroad depot. At Port Byron, Kelley spoke to an overflow crowd of four hundred at the National Hotel, amid "continual hissing and murmuring." When the Baptist meetinghouse in Ithaca threw the band of lecturers out of its evening session, they "adjourned into God's house—the open air"—and held their impromptu meeting in the courthouse square. Some in the mob eventually climbed to the tower and rang the courthouse bell to break up the meeting. Sometimes, when they could not secure a venue, they held an antislavery meeting in a tavern, as they did in late September in Trumansburg, on Cayuga Lake. Itinerant antislavery activism was a lonely, dangerous, and frustrating vocation. As Hudson put it, they were out to morally assault the conscience of every community, so many of which they found "full of slavery, war & all evil." Rejection became their badge of honor, one brickbat and epithet at a time. They were the suffering servants in Isaiah, and happy to remind all who would listen, "He is despised and rejected of men . . . he was wounded for our transgressions, he was bruised for our iniquities . . . and with his stripes we are healed." [13]

By the early 1840s, a decade of major railroad expansion, the New York Central Railway was completed along most of the route of the Erie Canal. Yet many of the towns and villages on the 1842 AASS tour, as well as countless more to follow in the coming years for Douglass, were not on railroad lines. Abolitionists were masters of the new technologies of printing and mass dissemination of newspapers and information, as well as eager adherents of the transportation revolution of the era. But for a troupe of four to eight antislavery lecturers, one of them a courageous independent, unmarried woman, travel was a saga of daily hardship as well as adventure. Broken braces underneath a stagecoach led to countless accidents and injuries. Famous English travelers such as Charles Dickens and Harriet Martineau left compelling and witty remembrances of their experiences on American railroads, canals, and in stagecoaches. From his journeys through New England and out to Ohio and the upper Mississippi Valley in 1842, Dickens made unforgettable observations about the travails of stagecoach travel. He rode the entire south-to-north length of Ohio in both the large twelve-seat mail coach and a four-horse, four-passenger "extra" stage that in some areas one could rent exclusively. Corduroy roads, made by "throwing tree trunks into a marsh," nearly "dislocated all the bones in the human body," wrote Dickens. On an especially bad road on a stormy night the passengers at one point were "all flung together in a heap at the bottom of the coach, and at another we were crushing our heads against the roof." Dickens saved most of his sarcasm for the "dirty, sullen, and taciturn" coachman who spoke only in monosyllables and cared far more for his horses than his passengers.[14]

Martineau and Dickens were both enthralled by the railroads and by the beauty and scale of American landscapes. Martineau, however, found American "travelling manners . . . anything but amiable." But she was entranced with the engineering achievement of the Erie Canal during her mid-1830s journeys, and she thought railroads a revolution without end for America. Like Alexis de Tocqueville just before her, Martineau left an indelible impression of a society constantly on the move, advancing the communication and transportation revolutions. All this she gushed over before writing the longest chapter of her *Society in America*, "Morals of Slavery," a penetrating, compassionate, but outraged examination of slavery's threat to all that America promised. Dickens too stopped to observe that "as a black man never travels with a white one, there is also a negro car, which is a great, blundering, clumsy chest, such as Gulliver put to sea in, from the kingdom of Brobdingnag." In such conveyances, under such conditions, day in and day out, Douglass, Kelley, and their companions spread the antislavery gospel across the hills and dales of the Northern landscapes—at four miles per hour on canals, six to eight on stagecoaches, and perhaps twenty or thirty on the iron horse. Since most of them were teetotalers, at least they did not have to share Dickens's disgust at being forced to drink bad tea and coffee at a "Temperance Hotel" where a glass of brandy was "not to be had for love or money."[15]

The New York tour ended in Cooperstown on October 25, and as the company disbanded, Douglass returned to Lynn. But he was quickly caught up in the cause célèbre of a fugitive slave named George Latimer, a case that would preoccupy New England abolitionism for many months to come. Douglass could not have been home with his family more than three days when he hurried to Boston to speak to a crowd of four thousand people on a subject dear to his heart.

The streets of Boston swarmed with competing crowds either resisting or supporting the arrest of Latimer on October 19. Early that month, Latimer, a light-skinned slave from Norfolk, Virginia, and his pregnant wife, Rebecca, had fled aboard a ship to Boston; because he had long worked around the maritime businesses of Norfolk and passed for white, he bought passage for two, and his wife traveled as his servant. Within their first week in Boston they were identified by a James Gray, a former employee of Latimer's owner in Virginia. Gray's slave-catcher agents had George arrested; quickly the news spread to the black community on Beacon Hill in Boston, and antislavery friends secretly hid Rebecca. As a crowd of at least three hundred mostly black protesters kept up a tense and loud vigil outside the jailhouse for several nights, demanding Latimer's release under a writ of habeas corpus, Massachusetts chief justice Lemuel Shaw ruled that Gray had a right to retrieve the jailed man under the federal fugitive slave law of 1793. As abolitionist lawyers obtained a continuance for Latimer, he was kept in jail under an agreement between Gray and the jailor. But as the captor and jailor became unnerved by the increasingly aggressive abolitionist protests, Gray, rather than allow police to take Latimer back and forth to the courthouse for his trial, offered to sell the fugitive, first for $800, then settling under pressure for $400 in late November.[16]

Latimer was freed to abolitionist Boston's jubilation, but not before a wave of rowdy "Latimer meetings" and rallies spread across New England, a new journal was founded in his name, and a massive petition drive began demanding repeal of the federal fugitive slave law. At a Faneuil Hall meeting, a crowd packed to the rafters became so noisy and disruptive that the speakers, including Garrison, Wendell Phillips, Charles Lenox Remond, and Douglass could hardly be heard. Despite the turmoil, Douglass, according to press reports, shouted and "gesticulated" for about twenty minutes and "tried to tell them he was a slave, and what were his fears for himself and hundreds of his brethren." With the Northern, freeborn African American Remond as companion, Douglass then took to the road for many days using the Latimer crisis to spread the antislavery word until his voice gave out and he fell sick.[17]

At home in Lynn, allowing Anna to nurse his ailing throat, Douglass wrote his first of many public letters to Garrison, and thereby to the *Liberator*'s readers. In quite formal language, Douglass reported as a good disciple about the New Bedford Latimer meetings. He described large crowds that "needed no bells to remind them of their duty to bleeding humanity." Under the urgency of the Latimer fugitive case, Douglass reported the Garrisonian machine in well-oiled form: "Not a word was lost; it was good seed, sown in good ground, by a careful hand; it must, it will bring forth fruit." He spoke an hour himself on "the question as to whether a man is better than a sheep," then sat down "seized with a violent pain" in his chest and short-ness of breath. That winter and into the spring of 1843, Douglass celebrated the sixty-five thousand signatures on the "monster petition" delivered to the Massachusetts legislature and applauded the personal-liberty law passed in March that forbade state officers from participating in the arrest of fugitive slaves. On a few occasions he appeared with Latimer himself, with Doug-lass doing most of the speaking about the plight of fugitives. As he turned twenty-five years old, Douglass now knew his calling, and something of the physical, personal, and intellectual demands of working in the ideological world of the Garrison church.[18]

Into the spring and summer of 1843 Douglass rarely escaped the speak-ing circuit of Massachusetts and Rhode Island for more than one week at a time. One can only guess at how Anna coped, binding shoes and nursing children in Lynn. How many sharp-tongued rebukes did she give her hus-band, or were they simply long sighs, as he told her a day or so after arriv-ing at home that he would be in Worcester or Providence or some other town for the next several days? Or did he tell her the itineraries at all? One might imagine that Anna lived vicariously through the travels of her peri-patetic, increasingly famous husband. But she might just as likely have been too worried about a child's winter cough or taking in a neighbor's washing for extra money to wish to know where all those countless towns existed on a map. Certainly she worried about Frederick's safety and health out on the road, facing anti-abolition mobs.

By any measure, the Garrisonians were uncompromising in their goals and tactics. Theirs was a biblically driven approach to the social and per-sonal sin of slaveholding. Slavery in America was a national sin with many complicitous institutions, none more so than churches and the clergy, but also political parties and governments themselves at both state and fed-eral levels. In his 1843 tours Douglass spoke in favor of one resolution after another advocating the dissolution of the Union and against "politi-cal action" as corrupt and inadequate. He supported abolitionists' disrup-tion of church worship services to condemn ministers and congregants to their faces, while saving most of his energy for his popular "Slaveholder's

Sermon" performances. Eventually their quest for purity of motive and strategy would drive the Garrisonians into a self-destructive isolation. Neither uncertainty nor ambivalence troubled this band of holy warriors, and Douglass appeared for now as one of their firmest voices. He proposed resolutions of his own, such as the one he announced at a Worcester County Anti-Slavery Society gathering on February 2: "Resolved, that the hands of the American church are full of blood, and that she is not, while she continues thus, what she assumes to be, the heaven-appointed instrumentality for reforming the world." Douglass disturbed as he also inspired audiences, accusing proslavery churches of refusing to see the "pit of slavery" they helped create. "On their way to . . . the mountain to discuss some new topic," he declared, ministers and their deacons "spread over this pit" the priest's "pontifical robe." [19] He performed this part of the Garrisonian repertoire better than anyone else.

But Douglass also played in season and out in his most expected role—as personal witness to the slaves' trauma. In March 1843, Anne Weston wrote to her sister Maria, who ran Garrison's headquarters in Boston, telling of seeing Douglass speak to a full house and feeling somewhat disappointed that he dwelled on his slave past. "He was more in the narrative and familiar vein & kept the audience laughing all the time. . . . He was eloquent occasionally, but as he was telling his own experience, there was not so much chance for flowers of rhetoric as might be." Such were now the burdens of expectation on the young abolitionist's shoulders, even among his friends. At a meeting in Lowell, Massachusetts, in April, appearing again with Latimer, Douglass made a typical pronouncement: "I am one of the *things* of the South!" "Drawing himself up to his full height, and spreading his arms wide," wrote an observer, Douglass declared, "Behold the thing!" With such performances, wrote his auditors, Douglass could "move the audience at will"; they "would hang upon his lips with staring eyes and open mouths." [20] Still tethered to the organization's ideological prescriptions, Douglass nevertheless made his mind and body into a story that his thousands of listeners would never forget.

Douglass spoke at the tenth annual meeting of the AASS in New York City, and then at a raucous, mob-disrupted gathering in Hartford, Connecticut, in the second and third weeks of May 1843. At the Hartford meeting Douglass was taunted with shouts of "nigger" and, with several abolitionist comrades, was thrown out of a hall, pelted with stones and eggs, and forced to speak on a makeshift box on the street, where the group made the right of free speech as much their subject as moral suasion.[21] Douglass then retreated to Lynn for a respite and to prepare for the biggest tour the Garrisonians had ever mounted—the One Hundred Conventions campaign throughout the remainder of 1843.

From July to December the board of managers of the AASS sponsored an ambitious tour, projected to be one hundred meetings in at least five Northern states (Vermont, New York, Ohio, Indiana, Pennsylvania) and with a goal of spreading the "truth before from three to five hundred thousand people." The six primary lecturers were Douglass, George Bradburn, Charles Lenox Remond, James Monroe, John Collins, and Jacob Ferris. Occasionally they would be joined by Abby Kelley, William A. White of Massachusetts, and Sydney Howard Gay of New York City. The troupes of speakers were to live off the land, so to speak, relying on abolitionist friends in every city or rural town. In the weeks before the first official convention, in Middlebury, Vermont, Douglass threw himself into fund-raising meetings in New Hampshire and Massachusetts. As he later remembered, he "never entered upon any work with more heart and hope." It would take a great deal of both, as well as sheer stamina and physical courage, to survive. By now Douglass knew how tumultuous abolitionist meetings and personalities could be. In June he wrote to Abby Kelley, describing a meeting he had just attended in Concord, New Hampshire, as "disgraceful, alarming, divided, united, glorious, and most effective."[22] In the coming tour he would need deep reserves of this sense of wit and irony. As a broad movement abolitionists were not united.

Embroiled now in a bitter rivalry with the emerging abolitionist Liberty Party, founded in part by the writer and activist Alvan Stewart of upstate New York, the Garrisonians attacked the political abolitionists as they were also confronted and pilloried by them nearly everywhere they went. Libertyites urged their followers to either boycott or disrupt the Hundred Conventions campaign. In the college town of Middlebury, Vermont, students, Douglass said, "placarded the town with violent aspersions" against the lecturers, accusing Douglass of being an "escaped convict from the state prison."[23] Bracing for such hostility, the activists headed into New York State, and after a poorly attended meeting in Utica, they moved on to Syracuse, where Douglass in particular ignited some useful and compelling fireworks.

Temporarily the sole lecturer trying to evangelize Syracuse, Douglass found no venue to welcome him for a meeting. So he held forth in a park under a tree before an audience of five people. Before the day ended, he had churned up a crowd of five hundred, and a Congregational church offered him and his colleagues an old abandoned building, where they met for three more days of speeches. Collins, Kelley, and Remond soon arrived to help create a full-fledged convention. But Collins, a recent convert to communitarianism, turned an entire morning gathering over to the question of abolishing private property. After listening to Collins's long speech against property and the abolitionists' alleged obsession with "chattel slavery," Douglass stood and openly objected. A fierce row ensued with many heated personal exchanges and eventually letters written back and forth with the AASS board headquarters in Boston. Douglass received a public "reprimand" for what he remembered as "insubordination to my superiors." Douglass believed Collins had hijacked antislavery with an extraneous cause—especially, claimed the former slave, when he argued that "property in the soil is worse than to enslave man." [24]

The dispute spread so widely that both men wrote self-defensive letters to Maria Weston Chapman at the AASS board. Collins accused Kelley of instigating the entire affair because she was "intolerant beyond degree" and reported that Douglass had audibly "groaned" during the property speech, while Remond called the very subject "humbug and moonshine." Douglass defended his public objection. Collins had a perfect right to oppose property, said the black orator, but not by assisting the "destruction" of the slave's cause. This was ugly; even Collins's wife got involved, snidely informing Chapman that Douglass and Remond had engaged in a "most ungenerous . . . assault." This seemingly ludicrous dustup was typical of others to follow on this and other tours; these earnest radicals, like those in virtually all such movements before and since, turned on each other, playing out jealousies, fatigue, ego wars, personality conflicts, and ideological differences. The AASS ignored Douglass's offer to resign as an agent. Tellingly, he added a quiet PS to his letter to Chapman. A message had arrived from Anna back home, asking for help to keep the household solvent. "I have none to send her," he informed Chapman. "Will you please see that she is provided with $25 or $30." [25] In a simple line begging for money from his benefactors, with whom he was now at odds, we have a small window into Douglass's personal and professional travail at this early juncture in his career. He awoke every day worrying about how to feed his family as well as how to best use his voice to free his fellow slaves. He struggled mightily in trying to do both.

Despite these internecine battles, the crusade surged on to Rochester and Buffalo, where Douglass and Remond would spend all of August

1843, achieving new successes and audiences. In a four-day convention at Rochester, Douglass played the central role, advocating the pure Garrisonian resolution that "the press and the living speaker" were the "only means by which to advance the cause of abolition." He later recalled how many Rochester-area abolitionists who had pledged support of the Liberty Party still allowed the troupe access to churches and their own homes. The battle among antislavery organizations seemed all-consuming at the time, a struggle Douglass summed up thus: the beliefs that slavery was either a "creature of law" or a "creature of public opinion." Reminiscing from the perspective of nearly forty years, he reflected on "how small the difference appears as I look back on it . . . yet at the time of it this difference was immense." Here in 1843, Douglass likely already saw Rochester as a welcoming potential home; he again stayed with the Quakers Amy and Isaac Post. Rochester made the young fugitive feel comfortable and it made him sing; on August 5, Douglass entertained a congregation with an abolition song before delivering his speech.[26]

At Buffalo, the only meeting space the lecturers could secure was, according to Douglass, "an old dilapidated and deserted . . . post office." Discouraged by the turnout of assorted street people and a mere handful of hackmen with whips in hand in such a bleak venue, Bradburn abandoned Douglass and went to Cleveland to visit relatives. For nearly a week, Douglass held forth alone in this forsaken dwelling, his audiences "constantly increasing in numbers and respectability," until a church opened its doors to an abolition meeting. The Baptist chapel soon proved too small, and Douglass moved on a Sunday into a park, where, he claimed, a throng of "four or five thousand" heard his "Slaveholder's Sermon."[27] Douglass played well in Buffalo, and again made a mark with his courage and endurance.

One extraordinary eyewitness account survives of Douglass's daily performances at the abandoned, windowless post office. A young woman, the daughter of Myron Holley, one of the founders of the Liberty Party in New York, attended every day with her little girl in tow. She had the "happiness to hear Frederick Douglass make a speech," she remembered, at a "poor little meeting—the odds and ends of the city—not a soul there I had ever seen." She had been so excited to hear a fugitive slave speak:

> He rose, and I soon perceived he was all alive. His soul poured out with rare pathos and power. Among other things, he told how a slaveholder would preach to an audience of slaves and take the text:

"Servants, be obedient to your masters," and then proceed to say, "the Lord in his providence sent pious souls over to Africa—dark, heathen, benighted Africa—to bring you into this Christian land, where you can sit beneath the droppings of the sanctuary and hear about Jesus! The Lord has so established things that only through the channel of obedience can happiness flow."

Douglass apparently completed this soliloquy with a story about a slave named Sam, who given a task by his master, refused, dropped his hoe, and fell into a summer's nap on the ground. As the master discovered his bondman's disobedience, the slaveholder announced from Scripture, "He that knoweth his master's will, and doeth it not, shall be beaten with many stripes." Sam was whipped and thus could "happiness flow." [28] With his use of these passages from Ephesians and Luke, Douglass pulled his audiences into his web of sarcasm and righteous indignation.

Fortuitously for Douglass and Remond, the Conventions tour had arrived in Buffalo just before the scheduled gathering of the 1843 Colored Convention of national black leaders. Here for the first time, Douglass joined as a delegate in this thirteen-year-old tradition. Of the seventy-three delegates, Douglass and Remond were the only ones from Massachusetts among the ten states represented. Most were from New York and members of the American and Foreign Anti-Slavery Society as well as of the Liberty Party. The tone of the convention was certainly not Garrisonian; the opening address by Samuel Davis of Buffalo asserted African Americans' citizenship and "equal rights" under the US Constitution. [29] Soon the convention was embroiled in one of the most famous disputes in the history of antebellum black leadership—over what manner of resistance to tyranny black people should adopt.

Henry Highland Garnet, born a slave on a plantation near New Market, Maryland, in 1815 (only a little more than two years before Douglass), now a Presbyterian minister, superb orator, and leading black proponent of the Liberty Party, electrified the convention with "An Address to the Slaves of the United States." Through a network of Quaker accomplices, Garnet had escaped slavery along with ten other mostly family members at the age of nine, landing safely in New York City, where by 1826 his father saw that he was educated at the African Free School. By the time of the Buffalo convention, Garnet had risen in black national leadership like few others and broken with Garrison and moral suasion; he now advo-

Henry Highland Garnet, 1860s. Engraving.

cated militant political action and potential revolutionary violence on the part of slaves.[30]

As the audience in Buffalo sat entranced, Garnet threw nonresistance out the window with a flourish; he invoked the memory of slave rebels Denmark Vesey, Joseph Cinqué, Madison Washington, and especially the "patriotic Nathaniel Turner." He changed the tone and object of such convention gatherings, black or white, and demanded that they address the slaves themselves. In terms with which Douglass would have agreed at first, Garnet drew everyone into the "streams of blood" that marked slavery's history: "Slavery had stretched its dark wings of death over the land, the church stood silently by—the priests prophesied falsely, and the people loved to have it so." He named the Declaration of Independence, the natural-rights tradition, and Patrick Henry's famous demand for "LIBERTY OR DEATH!" Garnet called slaves to their "DUTY TO USE EVERY MEANS, BOTH MORAL, INTELLECTUAL AND PHYSICAL" to attack their condition and their oppressors. Then came appeals to blood and retribution. Garnet urged African Americans to confront their masters and argued they had "far better all die—*die immediately*, than live slaves." How this message was actually to reach the slaves Garnet never indicated. He chastised them for inaction, but he assured them, and presumably their instigators, that the "fallen" would have "their names . . . surrounded by a halo of glory." "Let your motto be RESISTANCE! RESISTANCE! RESISTANCE!" he famously proclaimed.[31]

Douglass apparently squirmed and protested. An intense argument ensued as the convention debated the merits of Garnet's address; the author himself took nearly an hour and a half defending himself. Garnet did not want his words amended by an appointed committee and said blacks, slave or free, had waited long enough, and that the time had come to "take higher ground and other steps." As he finished, according to the minutes, the audience "was literally infused with tears." In this swirl of emotions and high-flown rhetoric, Douglass, partly from fledgling Garrisonian principle, but also from an emerging pragmatic and situational view of violence, objected: Garnet had called for "too much physical force," and Douglass preferred "moral means a little longer." To advocate "insurrection," Douglass held, would be irresponsible and result in disaster. Garnet rose to reply and urged slaves to tell their masters they wanted their liberty; if denied, "we shall take it." Just who "we" meant was unclear. Just how this was to be done was even less clear. Douglass soon had the full rhetorical support of editors and managers back at the *Liberator*'s offices in Boston. Two more times in the coming two days Douglass spoke vehemently against issuing Garnet's "Address" officially from the convention and helped carry the vote against doing so, once by 19–18 and another time by 14–9. Douglass also voted against a resolution declaring the delegates' "duty . . . to vote the Liberty ticket," but lost that one decisively. This tangle between the two former Maryland slaves over the nature and use of violence would endure forever in the history of black leadership. It would not be the last time Douglass disagreed publicly with Garnet, but within half a decade they would largely agree on the uses of violence.[32]

Having now missed several planned events on the Hundred Conventions tour in Ohio, Douglass and Remond hit the road again. They worked only a short time in Ohio, speaking at one large event "held in a great shed built for this special purpose by abolitionists," Douglass remembered, with an estimated crowd of a thousand in Clinton County, southeast of Dayton. Soon they crossed into Indiana, an anti-abolition terrain the abolitionists had rarely encountered. In approximately a week and a half in central Indiana, Douglass and his companions, who now included Bradburn and William A. White, entered the belly of the Northern proslavery beast. In five towns along their route, settled by migrants from the South, they met mobs nearly everywhere. Rotten eggs and stones and drunken hooligans were as usual in abundance. But at Pendleton, a short distance northeast of Indianapolis, an intoxicated gaggle of thirty or so men sought blood. Bradburn called them "savage looking loafers" making "murderous threats." The lecturers had tried to hold their meetings in a Baptist church, but the mob confronted them outside. Gathering on the steps of the church in the evening of September 15, Douglass, White, and Bradburn waded into the threatening band in what White called a "conversational way." It worked on the first night and they managed to make speeches about the "rights of northern working men." [33]

But the following day, banned from the church grounds, the abolitionists, with their 130 local friends, set up a meeting with benches "in the woods." Led by a man in a coonskin cap, the mob marched on the meeting and surrounded the gathering, and a few jumped on the speakers' platform and began smashing it to pieces. In the melee that followed, Douglass forgot all about nonresistance, grabbed a club, and waded into the crowd. He tried to give as he took and was beaten badly to the ground. His life may have been saved when White, seeing his comrade fleeing from "hell-hounds" shouting "kill the nigger!" like a "fearfully true picture of the flight of the fugitive slave," threw himself on Douglass's assailant. According to Douglass's own remembrances, he was clubbed "prostrate on the ground under a torrent of blows . . . my right hand broken, and in a state of unconsciousness." White lost teeth and suffered gashes in his head. Douglass was taken in a wagon to the farm of Neal Hardy, a local Quaker, whose wife helped the young orator recover his equilibrium. Along with his wounded compatriots, he was back on a makeshift platform speaking the next day. Douglass had experienced much violence before, but never on the abolitionist platform. His right hand was not properly set and, as he recalled many years later, "never recovered its natural strength and dexterity." [34]

The violence in Indiana remained forever a pivotal experience for Douglass. Within a few years he would date the end of his adherence to nonresistance to the Pendleton melee. And he would later tell William White how much he loved him for his bravery in defending him, and for how they "like two very brothers were ready to dare—do, and even die for each other." [35] One wonders how many times in his ensuing life, as a writer, the man who had escaped Covey's clutches, Thomas Auld's whip, Hugh Auld's epithets, the bloody rumbles on the docks in Baltimore, and hundreds of besotted white men calling him "nigger" would think of that old broken hand gripping the pen as he crafted some of the most magical phrases in American letters. The Pendleton mob may have put zeal in the pen held by the wounded hand.

In Indiana, the nerves as well as the bodies of the traveling band of abolitionists all but disintegrated. A mere week after the Pendleton attacks, the eastern reformers joined the Indiana State Anti-Slavery Society meeting in

Jonesboro. Relationships were frayed to say only the least, especially among Bradburn, Douglass, and Remond. These abolitionists were anything but unified. Douglass interrupted Bradburn during a long speech about why people objected to abolitionism and tried to direct discussion to other topics. The chair sustained Bradburn. An angry Remond came to Douglass's defense, and soon a personality-driven free-for-all of name-calling ensued, with words such as "colored men" and "monkeeism" spit out by Bradburn, and Remond accusing someone of being a "jackass." All this ugliness played out in front of public audiences. An Ohio abolitionist, Abraham Brooke, took sides and wrote to Chapman in Boston, suggesting the two black men were at fault; they were "still . . . unregenerate men," he claimed, and always desired to be the "lions of the party." By now Douglass may indeed have wanted to play the lone lion in these shows.[36] In the previous two months he had often worked alone, forging an independent voice and his own arguments. He was young, wounded, proud, and growing impatient with some moral-suasionist abstractions, as well as perhaps some of his companions. He did not take direction well anymore, and the leadership back in Boston again took note.

Douglass appears to have spent all of October 1843 in Ohio, some of it resting with antislavery friends in Clinton County, and largely lecturing on his own, his fame as a lone attraction growing as he moved eastward. Ohio newspapers raved about Douglass's oratory, one saying he left an audience "laughing and weeping at will," and another concluding that "Mr. D gave proof positive, intellectual proof that . . . he is MAN . . . of very extraordinary mental powers." Even Bradburn admitted "the people wanted to hear Douglass."[37]

By early November Douglass joined with other lecturers on the Hundred Conventions tour and, on horseback and an occasional steamboat, moved into Pennsylvania. On one of those boats, the *Michigan*, riding between New Brighton and Pittsburgh, Douglass "was driven from a table as if he were a dog," wrote a sympathetic observer. In his support, "two young ladies . . . rebuked this devilish spirit by leaving the table also." By now, these Jim Crow episodes, though wounding, only seemed to put more steel in the young reformer's soul. He regained his stride and voice, and at many stops, especially a weeklong meeting in Pittsburgh, Douglass stole the show over and over with his "Sermon," this time with a popular political twist, drawing Henry Clay, Daniel Webster, and John C. Calhoun into his repertoire of impersonations. Here one can see that Douglass, though still a Garrisonian who could skewer political parties and their most famous leaders with withering sarcasm, only pointed to how important they nonetheless were in the great debate over slavery's future. Moreover, everywhere he went, he was the enslaved body and mind breaking out. "DOUGLASS a SLAVE!" wrote an admiring Pittsburgh observer. "Who that heard it, did not feel his heart leap, as he [Douglass] exclaimed, 'NO! I am no SLAVE! Your law may manacle my limbs, but it cannot enslave my spirit—GOD made it free!" [38]

Across Pennsylvania the tour surged, with its second or third wind, culminating in a big meeting in Philadelphia on December 4–7. By the final stirring day of the three-thousand-mile western journey, Douglass had clearly emerged as not only a star attraction, but as an enormously skilled speaker. A Philadelphia paper described him as "graceful, winning, fluent, argumentative, logical and convincing." He could "transport his hearers," wrote the witness, "to the regions of rapture, or of *comus*, and lower them into the deepest feeling for suffering humanity." [39] Oratorically, Frederick Douglass had arrived as a great abolitionist voice, as well as a heroic, scarred veteran of the mob's fury.

Douglass resumed a home life with his family for most of two months until late January 1844. From February through early May he was once again hired to join an even-larger group of lecturers on what the AASS fashioned as the Massachusetts Hundred Conventions tour. This time he would travel with numerous speakers, including Parker Pillsbury and William White, and under the leadership of Wendell Phillips, the organization's new general agent. At some locations Douglass also performed next to the Hutchinson Family Singers, as well as Abby Kelley. Douglass respected Phillips enormously, but was not shy about asking that the speakers' wages be clearly determined ahead of time. He had a family to feed, and for fairness, he demanded that each agent be paid equally, which was $7 or $8 per week. Douglass also objected, as he had been asked, to making the Liberty Party "a special object of attack." He seemed still willing to preach Garrisonian disunionism, but had begun to abandon the antipolitics position. In at least thirty-one towns all over Massachusetts, some of them as tiny as Athol or Hubbardston, and larger ones such as Northampton or Pittsfield, Douglass spoke many dozens of times. At some sites, as in Groton in March, Douglass reported to Garrison a discouraging declension of the antislavery cause, with mostly empty seats, and those who did fill pews attending "merely to hear the singing." At Concord, home to Emerson and Thoreau, he reported a drunken mob threating the lecturers, and ministers aggressively closing their churches.[40]

Throughout 1844 Douglass continued to tour and speak, although he began to spend more time in Lynn. He still performed his "Slaveholder's Sermon" on demand. And he still gave full-throated, public fealty to moral suasion and Garrison, declaring in November that "the real, and only-to-be-relied-on movement for the abolition of slavery . . . is a great moral and religious movement . . . quickening and enlightening of the dead conscience of the nation into life." But during 1844 he also began to tell more thoroughly the tales of his slave youth. August of that year included an extensive speaking itinerary in eastern Pennsylvania as he continued to appear in Rhode Island, New Hampshire, and Maine as well. By the end of that year almost any town that merited a name in Massachusetts, and so many others across New England, the Northeast, and parts of the Midwest, had seen the face or heard the voice of Frederick Douglass.[41] His body and mind, as inspiration or threat, were now part of the mental imaginations of hundreds of thousands of Americans.

On October 21, 1844, Anna gave birth to her fourth child, Charles. Frederick stayed closer to home for now, helping Anna, but also because he had begun to write his first book. Now he would be a *writer*. "By my own table," he declared, "in the enjoyment of freedom, and the happiness of home," Douglass wrote his story. During at least seventeen to eighteen weeks that he remained at home in Lynn, writing in his small house on Union Street between December 1844 and May 1845, Douglass crafted the soon-to-be internationally famous autobiography *Narrative of the Life of Frederick Douglass, an American Slave, Written by Himself.* Since at least his teenage years, Douglass had understood the power of words; he had rehearsed over and over in oral form the tales of the slave who had descended into psychic despair, been beaten to his knees, risked all to find freedom, dreamed his way onto the decks of Chesapeake ships, fought with his hands and his brains to survive, and found in literacy his own way to breathe, dream, speak, and write his path to liberty. Now the twenty-seven-year-old wielded this weapon of words into a book for the ages.[42]

Chapter 9

THE THOUGHT
OF WRITING
FOR A BOOK!

He would not become soft. It was exhaustion he wanted—it helped him write. He needed each of his words to appreciate the weight they bore. He felt like he was lifting them and then letting them drop to the end of his fingers, dragging his muscle to work, carving his mind open with idea.

—COLUM MCCANN, *TRANSATLANTIC*, 2013,
IMAGINING DOUGLASS MEDITATING IN PRIVATE,
JUST AFTER HIS ARRIVAL IN IRELAND, FALL 1845

The publication of Douglass's *Narrative* made him in time the most famous black person in the world. Fame had its uses; but he possessed deeper aims both as an abolitionist and as a thinker. He continued to all but mystify himself, much less the audiences he addressed. In late 1844, in a note accompanying the draft of his first article for publication other than in a newspaper, Douglass mused with wonder, "I looked exceedingly strange in my own eyes as I sat writing. The thought of writing for a book!—and only six years since a fugitive from a Southern cornfield— caused a singular jingle in my mind."[1] The *Narrative* soon caused an extraordinary literary jingle in the United States; words had now become for him a source of magic, truth, influence, and power.

The May 9, 1845, issue of the *Liberator* carried news of the publication of Douglass's *Narrative*. It also contained verbatim the preface written for the book by Garrison, as well as a note about Wendell Phillips's letter of endorsement, also published with the volume. Both Garrison and Phillips prominently mentioned Douglass's marvelous white "sailing ships" metaphor, his teenage vision of freedom while gazing at Chesapeake Bay, from the text. They both seemed to realize they had just read something quite unprecedented in slave narratives, and in American literature more broadly. They had encountered a *writer*, although they could not resist portraying him as the necessary exhibit of the cause. Garrison wrote about Douglass with great admiration and a mentor's pride; Garrison also left him saddled with the highest symbolic expectations: to continue to be "an ornament to society and a blessing to his race." Phillips openly worried for Douglass's safety as a fugitive, since he had now revealed so completely his identity to the world. The Boston Brahmin radical, though, also placed Douglass in high company. Referring to Aesop's fable of "The Man and the Lion," Phillips asked Douglass to remember when "the lion complained that he should not be so misrepresented 'when the lions write history.' I am glad the time has come when the 'lions write history.' We have been left long enough to gather the character of slavery from the involuntary evidence of the masters."[2]

Soon the young lion, with armloads of his history, would be off to Britain and Ireland telling his story. The book became an instant success, selling five thousand copies in the first four months. By the end of 1847, after Douglass's twenty-month tour of the British Isles, the bestseller had gone through nine editions and sold eleven thousand copies. And by 1860, it had sold thirty thousand and been translated into French and German. As Douglass prepared for his journey to England, his book came out in a paper edition, sold at twenty-five cents apiece, or $2.75 per dozen.[3]

On Friday evening, August 15, 1845, at the large Lyceum Hall in Lynn, a "Great gathering" assembled to bid farewell to Douglass, to local abolitionist James Buffum, who was to be the black activist's traveling companion, and to Lynn's own Hutchinson Family Singers. Asa, John, Judson, and Abby Hutchinson sang to the throng in "their inimitable strains," an observer reported. Douglass spoke words of farewell, as he had also done two days earlier in his first Northern hometown of New Bedford. The meeting passed resolutions, especially a favorite-son message to Douglass of deep respect and best wishes in his journey to "the shores of the Old World." Buffum was a Lynn neighbor, a former Quaker who had become a militant Garrisonian radical, who now used his considerable fortune gained as a carpenter, house contractor, and financier to aid the abolitionist cause.[4]

The press did not report whether Anna and the three children attended, but they must have been at the young departing hero's side for this meeting. Rosetta was six years old, Lewis almost five, and Frederick Jr. almost three and a half as they watched their father depart now to travel across the sea. These countless leave-takings were now vivid childhood memories; over time they likely had felt, consciously or not, like abandonments, even as the children would convert the story into respectful honor toward their famous father and his cause. The ten-month-old Charles would not remember this one, but would recollect many more leavings and comings later in life. For Anna the farewell celebration of her husband must have resurrected the fears she harbored on the day Frederick fled Baltimore as she agonizingly awaited word of his safety and the message to join him after his escape. But this time he would be gone a year or more, she would not be joining him, and she was left to fend for herself, to care for the brood of little Douglasses, and to rely on their white abolitionist friends for financial assistance. We can only imagine Anna's stoic courage, when they embraced good-bye, and when he lifted each child in his arms—what future could the young hero promise them? Could he truly write and speak his way into an international antislavery universe in such a way as to provide for *their* future, as well as change the world? Was it possible that a *voice* was enough to build a family, a career, and some part of a new history? Anna had likely already reached a stage in their difficult but powerful bond where it simply was hers to do and not to ask why.

The day after the Lynn gathering, Douglass, Buffum, and the Hutchinsons boarded the *Cambria*, the great new 219-foot, wooden side-wheeler steamship of 1,422 tons on the Cunard Line, and were off on their eleven-day voyage to England. On that Saturday afternoon, a crowd of abolitionist well-wishers gathered on the Boston docks. The Hutchinsons "sang a song at parting in the time of 'Cranbambuli,'" wrote Asa in his journal, "in which we bid farewell to New England." The crowd onshore "bid adieu" by swinging hats and handkerchiefs, to which all the passengers responded with shouts and "copious gushing tears." The *Cambria* sailed first to Halifax, Nova Scotia, where they were met by the firing of cannons, then crossed the Atlantic to the port of Liverpool, encountering en route many three-masted ships as well as ominous icebergs. Douglass had experienced the waves of the Chesapeake, but this first encounter with the rhythms of the open North Atlantic may have even included a game of billiards or shuffle-board with the Hutchinsons. The *Cambria*, which had made its maiden Atlantic voyage only a year earlier and was the fastest commercial passenger steamer afloat, rode the waves like "a wild sea gull," reported Asa Hutchinson. Within a few days most of the passengers suffered from seasickness.[5]

Despite Buffum's attempt to buy first-class-cabin accommodations, the ship's captain, Charles Judkins, assigned the two abolitionists to steerage belowdecks. Douglass had faced Jim Crow's ugly ways more times than he could count, but now, on his first ocean voyage and after such a joyous send-off among friends, this episode probably stung more than he let on, even as it also became so publicly useful. Douglass was content in steerage, he recollected, because the Hutchinsons came to visit frequently, singing at his "rude forecastle-deck," keeping it alive with "music . . . and with spirited conversation."[6] Somewhere in relatively calm seas, a day or so before the arrival at Liverpool, though, another kind of storm brewed when Douglass and his abolitionist friends tried to stage an antislavery meeting at the saloon on the main deck.

The passengers of the *Cambria* were a multinational, multiracial, multireligious lot, a veritable sampling of the world and of America strewn together and sifted in the confined spaces of a ship at sea. Like the crew of Melville's *Pequod* in *Moby-Dick*, what Andrew Delbanco called "a dazzling array of human types . . . taking turns in a stage play," Douglass wrote in similar terms about his shipmates in a public letter back to Garrison. Ever the storyteller, Douglass described the *Cambria* as a "theater" with "all sorts of people, from different countries, of the most opposite modes of thinking on all subjects." Flung together, some of the *Cambria*'s diverse human cargo mixed well and some did not. She mingled the "scheming Connecticut wooden clock-maker, the large, surly, New York lion-tamer, the solemn Roman Catholic bishop, and the Orthodox Quaker." Also shipping to Liverpool were a "minister of the Free Church of Scotland, and a minister of the Church of England—the established Christian and the wandering Jew, the Whig and the Democrat, the white and the black." This cast could have become a comedy or a tragedy in the right hands. The "dark-visaged Spaniard and the light-visaged Englishman—the man from Montreal and the man from Mexico" had also boarded at New York or Boston. But if politics and religion might at least be somehow bridged for eleven days, a larger problem emerged because of the "slaveholders from Cuba, and slaveholders from Georgia." Douglass warmed to the irony. "We had antislavery singing," he wrote, "and proslavery grumbling, and at the same time that Governor Hammond's Letters [James Henry Hammond, governor of South Carolina] were being read, my *Narrative* was being circulated."[7] Here was America's greatest problem—slavery—festering on board a steamship about to land in Britain's former largest slave-trading port.

In this volatile mix Douglass accepted the invitation of the captain himself to deliver a speech. Before he had uttered a few sentences, what he called the "salt water mobocrats," led by a Mr. Hazzard of Connecticut, shouted him down with fists clenched in the air. "That's a lie!" bellowed his opponents as Douglass attempted a discourse on the conditions of slaves in America. Douglass kept trying to be heard over the hecklers, finally resorting to "reading a few extracts from slave laws." But the gathering deteriorated into near violence, as a Cuban shouted, "I wish I had you in Cuba!," and the Georgian, "I wish I had him in Savannah! We would use him up!" With these men rushing toward Douglass and threatening to throw him overboard, an Irishman as well as Captain Judkins came to Douglass's defense. The captain ended the melee by threatening to put the mob leaders "in irons." The proslavery thugs, with brandy cups in hand, scattered to other corners of the ship, and as Douglass remembered, "conducted themselves very decorously" for the remainder of the voyage.[8]

But they had performed their service to the cause, and after landing in Liverpool, did so even more. The Georgian and the Cuban, and perhaps other allies from aboard the *Cambria*, went to the British press to defend themselves and, in so doing, Douglass maintained, provided the black abolitionist "a sort of national announcement of my arrival in England."[9] Much sympathy came Douglass's way as news of his discriminatory treatment spread through reformist England and Ireland.

Douglass had attempted his speech on the main deck, with the Irish highlands within view. The next day, August 28, the *Cambria* steamed into the river Mersey and to the great quays of Liverpool. Douglass and Buffum spent a mere two days or so with their feet on the ground in the city, then were off on the ferry to Dublin across the Irish Sea. They took up residence at the home of Irishman James A. Webb, brother of the printer Richard D. Webb, both staunch supporters of abolition and temperance. At first the Webbs, especially Richard and his wife, Hannah, were generously hospitable hosts, although that relationship would sour over time. Bald and bespectacled, with a full white beard in Quaker style, Richard Webb was an astute businessman and a loyal Garrisonian with strong ties to Maria Weston Chapman; together with her at the helm in Boston, Webb took on a role as Douglass's manager. By mid-September Douglass reported that he had delivered numerous lectures to overflow crowds, at the Royal Exchange (now City Hall), at a Friends' meetinghouse, the Music Hall, and even one to the inmates at a local prison. Undergoing a personal awakening, he seemed especially astonished that he encountered no "manifestations of prejudice." He traveled on all conveyances and "was not treated as a color, but as a man." [10]

Douglass quickly found comfort on Irish soil, except with Webb himself. His host simply did not like Douglass's personality, calling him "absurdly haughty, self-possessed, and prone to take offense." Webb thought Douglass mistreated his white traveling companion, Buffum, and found Douglass too "willing . . . to magnify the smallest causes of discomfort or wounded self esteem into . . . insurmountable hills of offense." Webb accused Douglass of selfishness and "unreasonableness . . . when he thinks himself hurt." Their relationship stumbled on with much private grumbling by both men. Webb was thirteen years older than the star orator, who was indeed insecure and hypersensitive in his first foreign sojourn; Douglass did not take well to constant mentorship and oversight. They did share, however, the publication of the Irish edition of the autobiography, although its author found it unsatisfying. By late September, Webb's print shop on Great Brunswick Street had published the first Irish edition of Douglass's *Narrative* with a print run of two thousand copies. Thus, the young American abolitionist could stay stocked for a while on what now became a busy speaking schedule around the Emerald Isle. Douglass received as many invitations to speak at temperance meetings as at (his preference) those about international abolitionism. Before he left Dublin, after seeing both its great halls as well as its desperate poverty, Douglass had the special experience of witnessing a speech by Daniel O'Connell and then meeting the "Great Liberator." [11]

Legendary champion of all reforms, including the controversial repeal of the union of Ireland and England, O'Connell deeply moved Douglass, who was ever the student of oratory and still learning his craft. He had never heard a speech, Douglass wrote home, at which he "was more completely captivated." The address was "skillfully delivered, powerful in its logic, majestic in its rhetoric, biting in its sarcasm, melting in its pathos, and burning in its rebukes"—all the same oratorical elements Douglass had tried to master. By early October, Douglass and Buffum were off to speaking engagements in Wexford and Waterford, then traveled the difficult roads by stagecoach down the east coast to Cork. [12]

In Cork, on the southern coast of Ireland, Douglass may have felt safer. Here for a month in the fall of 1845, Douglass experienced a kind of sanctuary, living with the Jennings family in their sprawling house on Brown

Street, only steps down from Coal Quay on the River Lee. Thomas and Ann Jennings, with their eight curious and educated children, were religious dissenters in a city of Roman Catholics in a country ruled by the bishops of the Church of England. Jennings was a successful merchant who sold mineral oil, vinegar, and other farm goods from Cork's ocean port. Full of quirks and fascinations for universal reforms, and lovers of music and literature, the Jennings family extended to Douglass a kind of humane racial equality he had never quite known. None of them sought to control Douglass in any way. He seemed to relish talking with the Jennings children, especially the young daughters, Isabel, Charlotte, Helen, and Jane, who were enthralled with their American guest. Her large family was not easily impressed, reported Jane Jennings, but no speaker had ever "excited such general interest as Frederick," and he had "won the affection of everyone of us." [13]

Isabel Jennings in particular, who was secretary of the Cork Ladies Anti-Slavery Society, and who worked assiduously to collect funds and material goods for antislavery fairs in America, became Douglass's admirer and advocate. "He feels like a friend whom we had long known," she wrote to Chapman in the fall of 1845, "and I think before he goes we will quite understand one another. He is so free in acknowledging when he has been too hasty in judging." Isabel gushed over the stunning man making news in her town and her house. "There is an expression of great suffering at times on his countenance which only renders him more interesting." Chapman might have been even further intrigued by Douglass's impact on young Isabel when the Irish girl wrote, "There never was a person who made a greater sensation in Cork amongst all the religious bodies . . . in private he is greatly to be liked—he has gained friends everywhere he has been—he is indeed a wonderful man." [14]

Such a private, welcoming kind of comfort nourished the weary traveler so far from home; and Douglass relished all the adoration from young women, a pattern he would repeat many times in his life, finding emotional support from women of all ages. But the orator-writer was on a public mission and very much on display. Douglass was now the perpetual guest of honor with bookings to speak nearly everywhere people might gather. In nearly every waking hour, if with people, he provided the object for their curiosity and gaze: he had to be the black man who was really a pleasing brown and partly white, the slave who was also so eloquent, the genius that bondage could not destroy, the embodiment of a story that kept on giving. A press report of his first speech in Cork, given at Lloyd's Hotel, demonstrated the exoticized scrutiny Douglass faced with his Irish and British audiences. Enthralled with his mixed parentage, the reporter declared the orator's "appearance . . . singularly pleasing and agreeable. The hue of his face and hands is rather yellow brown or bronze, while there is little, if anything, in his features of that peculiar prominence of lower face, thickness of lips, and flatness of nose, which peculiarly characterize the true Negro type. His voice is well toned and musical." Exasperated by these racial characterizations, which he encountered almost everywhere, Douglass sometimes snapped back, declaring in a Cork newspaper that they "looked like a good advertisement from a slave trader."[15] Such racialized descriptions are hardly surprising in the middle of the nineteenth century; but such ideas and expectations were part of Douglass's daily encounters, even among friends and admirers.

Douglass was not sui generis for the Irish of Cork or other provincial towns; Charles Lenox Remond had visited before him. But a black American former slave with such mastery of language and physical attractiveness had never landed in their midst before. Men listened to Douglass with intensity, as did women, some of whom swooned. In his numerous lectures in Cork, Douglass was an instant celebrity. The "ladies" especially turned out in droves to see and hear him, the Cork press observed. They did so as well in Belfast a couple of months later, where one Irishwoman abolitionist observed after seeing Douglass, "I am convinced that there is scarcely a lady in Belfast who would not be anxious to join in any means calculated to promote the enfranchisement of the deeply injured Africans."[16] But all this attention, getting his *Narrative* published, and his own deep personal sensitivities to racial slights, and to all those in the Garrisonian orbit who tried to control him, embroiled the star itinerant in turbulent personality conflicts.

First there was Buffum, the ever-present companion and watchdog. Eleven years older than Douglass, Buffum possessed superb radical credentials and was a devout Garrisonian. He had worked to desegregate New England railroads and served as an officer in both antislavery societies and in a Fourierist utopian organization. But he was the American Anti-Slavery Society's (the "old organization's") appointed guardian of the volatile young Douglass. He reported directly to the power behind Garrison's throne, Maria Weston Chapman, who managed the office of the Massachusetts Anti-Slavery Society in Boston and especially the personal habits and ideological commitments of Garrisonian lecturers. At meetings Buffum would usually speak first and only briefly and anecdotally as a setup man for a Douglass performance. He played Sancho Panza to

Douglass's Don Quixote in some ways. Though certainly not of any peasant background or wisdom, Buffum did come across as the self-sacrificing Christian, necessarily a bit awestruck with his young charge, perhaps at times exhibiting racial paternalism. Booking agent, monitor of Douglass's arguments and behavior, Buffum became the friend from whom the orator needed to escape. Not unlike the Hundred Conventions tour of two years earlier, these two abolitionists were constantly in each other's company, and the nerves rubbed thin, especially as Douglass became aware of how much Chapman, and therefore Garrison, was trying to shape his image, his rhetoric, even his every movement. Douglass began to champ at the bit as his sponsors tried to rein him in.

This arrangement could only lead to conflict. The farther they traveled through Ireland and on to Scotland, Buffum repeatedly informed Chapman or one of her sisters about the "great applause" Douglass received at every event and the "great good" he did for the cause. But problems erupted in early 1846 when Douglass learned that Chapman had charged Buffum and Richard Webb with keeping their eyes on Frederick's ambitions, his ideological straying, and especially his desire for money gained from sales of his book. In an understatement, Buffum warned Chapman that Douglass was "quite sensitive" about such accusations. Webb went even further, writing to Chapman about his personal disdain for Douglass. Douglass, said Webb, had engaged in "offensive and ungrateful behavior" toward Buffum. The Dubliner thought the former slave the "least loveable and least easy of all the abolitionists with whom" he had associated. Webb unloaded bile on the young American, considering him all but incapable of kindness, and "extremely jealous and suspicious."[17] A psychological dance between an ever-rising star and his rivals in Ireland—the one a smothering travelmate and the other the publisher who could not provide books to his writer fast enough—became open emotional warfare, with the prompter of the nastiness, Chapman, improbably sitting in a Boston office. Douglass did not hide his wounded soul, born of his slave past and stoked in his celebrity present.

During his more than four months in Ireland, Douglass tried to sustain a cordial correspondence with Webb. Douglass frequently made aggressive demands for more books. He also used his new patron as a sounding board for the frustrations of constant travel and the demands of the overly curious public. "Everyone . . . seems to think he has a special claim on my time to listen to his opinion of me," Douglass complained to Webb, illustrating the self-importance that so annoyed the Irishman. Douglass detested the frontispiece image Webb used for the second Irish edition of the *Narrative*, which came out in early 1846, and told him so in no uncertain terms. To Webb, if we put it in modern terms, the young black man was uppity and never satisfied by his own recognition. Douglass also inveighed against expectations that he should speak on disunionism, nonresistance, or other Garrisonian doctrines, preferring to sustain his mission as "purely an Antislavery one." Douglass wanted to prescribe his own agenda, and as Webb complained to Chapman behind Douglass's back, he would not listen to his handlers.[18]

Douglass had, after all, escaped from slavery; he owed so much to his allies in the extended house of Garrison, including to Buffum, who had personally paid for the young man's passage on the *Cambria*. Douglass's wife and children were dependent on white abolitionists' charity and goodwill. He was trapped in a deal that both offered him the world and stifled the kind of freedom he perhaps cherished most—the freedom of mind and of the words he would choose to express himself. Without doubt, Douglass *was* hypersensitive to personal slights, especially if he sensed they were racial, and he moved through the social and intellectual circles of his foreign admirers with a natural distrust that put the burden of social intercourse on others. During the previous frenetic four to five years when the antislavery orator was in constant motion, Douglass had tried to forge a new sense of self—as a public man of intellect, of courageous activism, and now as a writer. He was ferociously competitive; he desperately needed friends, but would forever find forging close bonds, especially with men, difficult. The young adult Douglass always knew—and constantly rehearsed in front of audiences—that he was still that fugitive slave from an Eastern Shore cornfield, the pain of his whippings festering in his memory. In a sense he was forever hurt, and he did not take well to new hurts, even if only perceived or imagined. From under those crisp white shirts worn under the frock coat, the hair on his head growing high and parted neatly, Frederick fashioned an elegance that usually kept his rage against slavery submerged in social settings. But it would burst out in his platform rhetoric, and sometimes privately at his closest companions.

When he stepped onto and off platforms before hundreds of auditors, then personally sold them copies of his book as he shook their hands, how could this twenty-eight-year-old phenomenon, who had discovered just how much power he wielded over his audiences with his story, not have a high estimation of himself? He desperately wanted Irish and British abolitionists to *like* him; but if the Webbs, Buffums, or Chapmans could not loosen their clutches and dissolve their own prejudices, then he could keep running from their shadows, and sometimes telling them just what he thought. Plenty of welcoming eyes and temporary friends were in the audience at the next speech.

In March 1846, in a letter labeled "private," Douglass wrote to Chapman, openly challenging her efforts to manage him. He tried to remain respectful when he found out the extent of her efforts to stifle his liberties, but he could not stanch his anger. Webb had read portions of Chapman's letter to him, especially the accusations that Douglass would seek to enrich himself and that he might defect to the anti-Garrisonian British and Foreign Anti-Slavery Society, known in shorthand as the London Committee. Douglass barely controlled his rage, informing Chapman that he had sailed to England with $350 earned from the first American sales of his book, and that he now sustained himself largely from sale of the Irish edition. Douglass felt bitterly betrayed by Chapman's request to Webb to "watch over" him. No "love of money" nor "hate of poverty" could drive him from the "sacred cause," he declared. He found the insinuations "embarrassing" and "disappointing." He had resisted the Liberty Party in America, so "why should I not withstand the London Committee?" [19]

Then he became very personal. "If I am to be watched over for evel [sic] rather than for good, by my professed friends I can say with propriety save me from my friends and I will take care of my enemies!" He returned his own acid for Chapman's whispered betrayals. "If you wish to drive me

Maria Weston Chapman,
c. 1846. Daguerreotype.

from the Antislavery Society, put me under overseer ship and the work is done. Set someone to watch over me—for evil and let them be so simple minded as to inform me of their office, and the last blow is struck." Douglass kept declaring himself an old organizationist, but this exchange might be the beginning of the end of his ideological and personal loyalty to Garrisonianism. Perhaps the fugitive from the Eastern Shore cornfield could be "bought," but never, he insisted, for the wrong reasons. He would continue to sell his book, and he made no apologies.[20]

The Irish tour surged on. After six major events in Cork, with bands playing as part of the show, Douglass and Buffum trekked by stagecoach and carriage over difficult roads due north to Limerick in November 1845. At Limerick, Douglass openly criticized a local actor who performed a Jim Crow character in a minstrel show. He delivered many versions of his "Slaveholder's Sermon" as well as stories from the *Narrative* as he hawked copies at the end of each speech. Douglass also began to address openly political topics such as the annexation of Texas, and what he called "America's bastard republicanism." Then it was on to Belfast in the north, where Douglass spent more than a month at the Victoria Hotel, paid for by local abolitionists.[21]

In Belfast in late 1845 and early 1846, Douglass gave some extraordinary speeches, especially on the old theme of religious hypocrisy and the proslavery complicity of the churches. He also told riveting tales of his youth, of his brutal religion-professing masters, and of his struggle for literacy. He analyzed the nature of race and of proslavery claims of Negro inferiority. Moreover, the American orator aggressively thwarted claims for what might be called the Irish analogy—that the oppression and poverty of the Irish was equivalent to American slavery. Since beginning his tour he had felt "accosted," Douglass claimed, with the idea that many of the Irish lived as "slaves." He acknowledged the tyranny of British rule, but asked for careful distinctions about "what slavery really is." Mincing no words, Douglass argued that "slavery was not what took away any one right or property in man: it took man himself," and "from himself, dooms him a degraded thing, ranks him with the bridled horse and muzzled ox, makes him a chattel personal, a marketable commodity." With some in the crowd shouting, "Hear, hear," Douglass asked, "Had they anything like this in Ireland?" "Ah no!" he shouted, not waiting for his audience's reply. With time Douglass became ever more aggressive in denouncing such an equivalence between conditions in Ireland and America. By 1850 back in the United States, he was quite direct: "There is no analogy between the two cases. The Irishman is poor, but he is *not* a slave. He *may* be in rags, but he is *not* a slave."[22] Not all Irishmen agreed with him.

Everywhere he went, Douglass knew he had to continue "working wonders" and serving, as one Irish observer put it, as the "living example of the capabilities of the slave." But to the "whispers" that he was an "imposter," which surfaced, Douglass said in Belfast, he responded with both anger and humor. Dubliners, he said, had not needed so much as "a letter of introduction," nor had anyone else at his dozens of speeches around Ireland. But with biting sarcasm, he declared of his new hosts, "What sensible people you are in Belfast! How cautious lest they should make a mistake!"[23]

On December 23, 1845, Douglass delivered a bravura effort about slavery and religious corruption to a mixed Belfast audience of Catholics and Protestants. In an oration that included at least ten direct uses or paraphrases of scriptural passages and parables, Douglass turned Christian principles into weapons against proslavery religion—in his own country and in the British Isles. This forceful performance offended some of his auditors, while others all but fell over laughing and cheering. Caustic and sneering, Douglass demolished the very idea of a Christian slaveholder. They could "not serve God and Mammon," and they blasphemed in claiming any "fellowship with the meek and lowly Jesus." He lifted Matthew 23:15 to condemn Christian "man-stealers" and "cradle-plunderers" as "Christ denounced the Scribes and Pharisees, when he said that they would compass sea and land to make one proselyte, and after they had made him, he was ten times the Child of Hell." And he challenged the antislavery consciences of his audience. Would they be the "priest" who would not even see the suffering man by the side of the road, the "Levite" who looked and felt sympathy but chose a "middle course" and moved on, or would they be the "Samaritan" of compassion who bound the wounds of the victim? Or would they make Daniel's choice to break the law, never worship an earthly king's false gods, and risk death in the lions' den? With his memory still swirling with revenge against Thomas Auld, Douglass assured his well-churched Irish crowds that "a man becomes the more cruel the more the religious element is perverted in him. It was so with my master."[24] Douglass had learned to seamlessly weave biblical stories into his oratory with compelling effect.

During Douglass's months in Ireland the potato crop began to fail, and the greatest catastrophe in Irish history took hold in the countryside. A new fungal disease was first detected in Dublin in late August 1845, just as Douglass arrived on Irish shores. Its worst effects did not set in until a second wave of the potato blight in 1846. Within the next four years approximately 1 million Irish would die, first of epidemic infections, then of horrible dietary-deficiency diseases, and finally of outright starvation. Another 2 million would emigrate to the United States and Canada over the ensuing decade. The social, demographic, and political legacies of the Great Irish Famine still reverberate to this day. In the 1840s, two-thirds of the Irish population of 8.2 million made its living from subsistence agriculture, and most of them were fully dependent on the nutritious potato. When the crop began to show the brown splotches, then putrefy on the ground, huge numbers of people had nowhere to turn; they were soon caught up in the strained political entanglements at the heart of Ireland's links to Great Britain. As a leading historian of the Great Famine, Christine Kinealy, has said, with Ireland's "quasi-colonial status" within the British empire, "the United Kingdom was far from united."[25] No legacy of the famine is more embittered than the role of British policies, and imperial attitudes toward the Irish people in their time of greatest travail.

Douglass observed the horrors of Irish poverty, as well as the beginnings of the famine, although he could not have fully comprehended its causes and consequences at the time. As he barnstormed through Ireland, lecturing his hosts to reject the analogy of Irish suffering with American slavery, and demanding they open their Christian hearts as they fought with their own racial hypocrisies, a vast tragedy of mass death from hunger had begun its sweep through the Irish peasantry. The modern Irish writer Colm Tóibín remarked that contemporary literate observers of the ravages of the famine tended to write with a "mixture of flat description" while "desperately trying to describe the indescribable." He quotes one withering firsthand account from 1846 of the dead at an Irish hut: "Near the hole that serves as a doorway is the last resting place of two or three children; in fact, this hut is surrounded by a rampart of human bones, which have accumulated to such a height in the threshold . . . the ground is now two feet beneath it." These people had not been shot in a civil war, but had simply dropped dead from starvation. "In this horrible den," the account continues, "in the midst of a mass of human putrefaction, six individuals, males and females, laboring under most malignant fever, were huddled together, as closely as were the dead in the graves around." Douglass did not see this kind of death scene. But he saw the "extreme poverty and wretchedness" of the Irish "huts."[26] He was awed by them, and his prose was both inspired and stymied by them.

In a public letter to Garrison in February 1846, after he had moved on to Scotland, Douglass took time to reflect on what he had seen of Ireland. As the American abroad, he felt compelled to expose "other evils" than slavery. "I am not only an American slave," he wrote, "but a man, and as such, am bound to use my powers for the welfare of the whole human brotherhood. I am not going through this land with my eyes shut, ears stopped, or heart steeled." For the moment he put aside his disdain for the analogy between Irish misery and American slavery. Too many self-styled "philanthropists," maintained Douglass, "care no more about Irishmen . . . than they care about the whipped, gagged, and thumb-screwed slave. They would as willingly sell on the auction block an Irishman, if it were popular to do so, as an African." Now it was he making the equivalences between two kinds of suffering and evil. Although Douglass only glimpsed the famine's beginnings, he did seem to comprehend what Christine Kinealy observes: "One of the most lethal subsistence crises in modern history occurred within the jurisdiction of, and in close proximity to, the epicenter of what was the richest empire in the world."[27]

In his six weeks of wandering around the Dublin region, Douglass witnessed so many "painful exhibitions of human misery" that the fugitive slave from the sandy soil of the Eastern Shore could only "blush." The streets everywhere were "literally alive with beggars," many only "stumps of men . . . without feet, without legs, without hands, without arms." Douglass recounted being surrounded by "more than a dozen . . . at one time . . . all telling a tale of woe." The "little children in the street at a late hour of night . . . leaning against brick walls, fast asleep," parents nowhere to be seen, especially shocked him. He bothered with no abstractions nor made any distinctions here between the slave boy scrambling for food at a trough and the homeless, starving child of famine. Douglass viscerally understood abandonment from his own childhood. One can read such an impulse in his descriptions of the Irish children "with none to look upon them, none to care for them. If they have parents, they have become vicious, and have abandoned them. Poor creatures! They are left without help, to find their way through a frowning world."[28] The Fred Bailey who had waited at Miss Lucretia's window for morsels of food as he sang for attention stood awestruck at the starving Irish.

Douglass saw many of the Irish peasant huts. "Of all places to witness human misery, ignorance, degradation, filth and wretchedness," wrote Douglass, "an Irish hut is pre-eminent." After a long description of their dark bleakness and suffocating space, he could not resist his Garrisonian abolitionist's sense of irony at the presence of a "picture representing the crucifixion of Christ pasted on the most conspicuous place on the wall." Demonstrating that he did not yet grasp the nature and scale of the famine as it unfolded, as yet unaware of the draconian "poor laws" that would evict huge numbers of Irish farmers from land and force them into workhouses, Douglass the reformer argued that the immediate cause of such widespread poverty in Ireland was intemperance. In the faces of the most wretched of all, he claimed he could see the evidence that "drunkenness was still rife in Ireland." As Tóibín suggested about other writers contemporary with the famine, Douglass's own prose may have suffered a flattening, his thinking itself may have fallen lame, in the face of the "indescribable." [29] A brilliantly descriptive piece of travel journalism about extreme human suffering stumbled in the end over what seemed an obligatory nod to temperance propaganda.

Douglass had been deeply affected, even changed, by Ireland and her people. He had learned from and fought ideological and personal battles with them. He had found yet a new range of his powerful voice, and he relished the new throngs of admirers. In *Bondage and Freedom*, written nine years after he left Belfast, while remembering nostalgically the "almost constant singing" among slaves in the South as they worked, the "deep melancholy" of the "wild notes," his memory quickly leaped back to Ireland. "I have never heard any songs like those anywhere since I left slavery, except when in Ireland. There I heard the same *wailing notes*, and was much affected by them. It was during the famine of 1845–6." It seemed that only Irish starvation allowed him, through memory, to share the agony of Anthony's lash, Auld's kitchen, the Easton jail, and Covey's farmstead. Just which Irish songs he heard he does not tell us. But from his travels, like so many before and after him, Douglass brought away both a real and a mythic sense of the Irish people and their beautiful and terrible land. Maybe he even heard some versions of the longing and loss in "The Green Fields of Americay." [30]

As he prepared to leave Ireland, Douglass crafted one of his public letters to Garrison on January 1, 1846. The letter exhibits homesickness on New Year's Day, as he sat alone in a hotel in Belfast. But he also used his more than four months in Ireland as a springboard for one of the most embittered critiques he ever wrote about his own homeland. "I have spent some of the happiest moments of my life since landing in this country," Douglass assured his readers. "I seem to have undergone a transformation. I live a new life." He had been stunned by the lack of racial prejudice, the cordiality of his Irish friends. They had "flocked" to hear his words by the "thousands." In literary terms he made the utmost of national contrasts: "Instead of the bright blue sky of America, I am covered with the soft grey fog of the Emerald Isle." And yet, "I breathe, and lo! The chattel becomes a man." Douglass drifted into a remarkable statement about patriotism full of pain and longing. Did any American exile in the long history of this story of the scorned expatriate ever express such feelings of a man without a country any better? "I have . . . no creed to uphold, no government to defend; and as a nation, I belong to none . . . The land of my birth welcomes me to her shores only as a slave." [31] It was as if the deep sadness of Irish songs had entered his bones.

Then Douglass turned, as he so often did in his writing, to metaphors of nature to find the beauty and the agony in his story. "In thinking of America, I sometimes find myself admiring her bright blue sky," he rhapsodized, "her grand old woods—her fertile fields—her beautiful rivers . . . her star-crowned mountains." We can read him anticipating Walt Whitman, Langston Hughes, or Woody Guthrie. "But my rapture is soon checked, my joy is soon turned to mourning. When I remember that all is cursed with the infernal spirit of slaveholding . . . when I remember that with the waters of her noblest rivers, the tears of my brethren are borne to the ocean . . . and that her most fertile fields drink daily of the warm blood of my outraged sisters, I am filled with unutterable loathing." Douglass displays here what he would express repeatedly in his public life. He desperately wanted to belong in his own country, to make its stated creeds his own, but as he concluded, "America will not allow her children to love her." Hatred and love of country, impossible condition mixed with plausible hope, brutally racist law met with resistance born of secular and religious faith—these were forever the literary and intellectual wellsprings of this great ironist's work. He converted the remainder of his extraordinary last letter from Ireland into a litany of the ways he had faced Jim Crow's ugliest rebukes back home, ending each of seven examples with the refrain, *"We don't allow n___ers in here!"*[32] He had not heard that Americanism in Ireland, and no mob had taken brickbats and clubs to drive him from a lectern.

Shortly after arriving in Scotland, Douglass wrote his preface for the second Irish edition of his *Narrative*, the one he would now hope to sell to finance his tour of Britain. He gave four reasons for his tour of the British Isles, all reasonable and revealing. First, he wanted to "be out of the way" as his full identity as a fugitive slave emerged more widely in the United States. Second, he sought a new "stock of information" and "opportunities for self-improvement" in the "land of my paternal ancestors," a comment that kept many white Englishmen and Americans talking about his mixed blood for a long time. Third, he wished to spread the abolitionist crusade as far and wide as possible, to shame America before the wider world out of "her adhesion to a system so abhorrent to Christianity and to her republican institutions." And fourth, he wanted auditors for his lectures and especially readers for his book. His campaign sought to prove that he was a *writer* in a land that honored and celebrated people of the word. In an appendix he chose to include several "critical notices" about the *Narrative*. Two of them came from Belfast ministers who raved about the book's merits. Thomas Drew, a Church of Christ divine, wove Douglass's achievement into praise of God, but not without admitting that when reading the *Narrative* "the details of the writer absorbs all attention," and that the author was "a mind bursting all bounds." Even more, the Presbyterian minister Isaac Nelson called Douglass a "literary wonder . . . such an intellectual phenomenon as only appears at times in the republic of letters." [33] Douglass had indeed accomplished that most wondrous of things for a slave: he had written a book the world would read!

Chapter 10

SEND BACK
THE MONEY!

Your country is desolate, your cities *are* burned with fire: your land, strangers devour it in your presence, and *it is* desolate, as overthrown by strangers.

—ISAIAH 1:7

Frederick Douglass was fascinated with the theologically disputatious Presbyterians, and especially with the romantic and warlike history of the Scots. Historically, nothing had been more conflicted in Scotland than church history, and the black American abolitionist had arrived in the midst of the region's most embittered religious and institutional dispute of the nineteenth century. No people or country likes to be told by an outsider that their "whole head is sick, and the whole heart faint," or that their "hands are full of blood." Some of the Scots, though, in the 1840s, mired in one of their periodic internecine clerical struggles, seemed to welcome a stranger's jeremiads.[1] And that stranger now would garner a great deal of practice for arguments he would employ in his own country.

Political life in Scotland took place in or because of its churches. In 1843, led by the middle-class evangelical reformer Thomas Chalmers, a large group of ministers and their supporters bolted from the General Assembly of the national Church of Scotland and formed the Free Church of Scotland. More than one-third of the twelve hundred or so ministers in Scotland and perhaps as many as one-half of laypeople joined the new movement. To pay ministers and build churches the new organization desperately needed money. As part of its fund-raising campaign a delegation sailed to America in 1844 and collected several thousand dollars, largely in the South from slaveholding Presbyterians. As Douglass and a small band of American abolitionists began to draw large crowds in early 1846 in Glasgow, Edinburgh, and many smaller towns across Scotland, the region was aflame with controversy over slavery, and especially over the allegedly tainted lucre gathered from American slaveowners.[2]

In his first speeches in Scotland, Douglass had stuck to the nature of slavery and racial prejudice in the United States. Scottish audiences applauded and laughed vigorously as Douglass entertained them with tales of his youth and with ever more details of the incident aboard the *Cambria.* The Scots cheered wildly at some of his satire and mimicry of masters and preachers. He portrayed himself as the voice of the slave with dangerous enemies arrayed against him. Most of his crowds were glad to urge a self-appointed David to fight on against Goliath. And Douglass felt freer than ever in Scotland. "The spirit of British law," he maintained at the Glasgow City Hall on January 15, 1846, "makes liberty commensurate with the British soil, and which proclaims to the stranger and to the sojourner that the ground on which he treads is holy, and is consecrated to the genius of universal freedom." Thus appealing to Scottish pride and patriotism, he relished being the outsider who could draw his hosts into his struggle. He "wished to encircle America about with a cordon of Anti-slavery feeling—bounding it by Canada on the north, Mexico on the west, and England, Scotland and Ireland on the east," all joined in the cause of telling a slaveholder, wherever he goes, that he is "a man-stealing, cradle-robbing, and woman-whipping monster."[3] (An applause line if ever there was one.) Still the moral suasionist by method, Douglass dove into the local political fray.

At Dundee, on January 30, the Free Church debate became a cudgel in Douglass's hand as he leaned on an Old Testament prophet for support. He began by reading verses 4 to 20 from chapter 1 of Isaiah. Douglass's baritone rang out in cadences he first learned sitting with Father Lawson in Baltimore: "Ah sinful nation . . . Hear the word of the Lord, ye rulers of Sodom; give ear unto the law of our God, ye people of Gomorrah . . . your hands are full of blood." Douglass loved the language of the King James Bible, especially the Psalms and the Old Testament prophets. Their warnings about God's retribution for sin and evil, their poetry and storytelling, seemed to ring in his head like the lyrics of favorite old songs and hymns. Early in his career he mastered the oratorical art of the jeremiad, the rhetorical device made famous in America by the Puritans, but appropriated effectively by African Americans and many others. The jeremiad was the sermon that called the flock back from their declension, from their waning zeal to a renewed faith and activism. Douglass mastered the jeremiadic tradition, and Isaiah, Jeremiah, and other prophets provided an infinite storehouse of wisdom and argument. As Douglass began to seize their words and their stories, he found in the prophets his inspiration, a sense of wrath, mystery, pathos, history, and justice.[4]

Douglass and his traveling companions—including Buffum, the American utopian and ultraradical Henry C. Wright, and the British abolitionist George Thompson—had caught the wave of this Scottish controversy at just the right time. Douglass had "never seen a people more deeply moved than were the people of Scotland," he wrote, on the question of Southern money and the Free Church. "Public meeting succeeded public meeting," he later remembered. "Speech after speech, pamphlet after pamphlet, editorial after editorial, sermon after sermon, soon lashed the conscientious Scotch people into a perfect *furore.* 'SEND BACK THE MONEY!' " rang out the call, "from Greenock to Edinburgh, and from Edinburgh to Aberdeen."[5] Still trying to sell his *Narrative* at every venue, Douglass became the featured attraction. As his popularity soared, his Scottish speeches were one part moral indictment of both American and Scottish hypocrisy, one part jeremiadic sermon, one part his continued self-revelations, and one part comic entertainment.

At one of his Dundee addresses in March, Douglass left a crowd of twelve hundred people leaning over with laughter as well as understanding. Leveling charges against the Free Church, especially their "sophistry" of calling themselves "free" instead of labeling their real purpose—representing the "slave church"—Douglass told a "pig's foot" joke. He claimed that slaves in his area of Maryland referred to the idea of freedom as "pig's foot" so that whites would not know what they were talking about. Then he invented a dialogue between himself and Thomas Chalmers, leader of the Free Church, as well as with the Reverend George Lewis, a native of Dundee and the head of the delegation that had raised the money across the American South. Douglass takes his listeners back to the Eastern Shore and imagines "brother Lewis" arriving on his fund-raising tour at Thomas Auld's house. Young Frederick answers the door and witnesses the exchange. Mimicking voices, both Scottish and Southern American, Douglass has brother Lewis make his pitch: "My object in making this call this morning is to see if you would do something for the cause of religious freedom in Scotland." Auld ("my master") replies, "Brother Lewis, I deeply sympathize with your efforts; and as I see the cause recommended by Deacon such-a-one, I would like to have my name down with his. I'll tell you what I will do. I have a fine young negro who is to be sold, and I will sell him tomorrow and give you the contribution to the cause of freedom."[6]

Auld invited Lewis to come back in the morning, take breakfast, and ride with him to the county seat in Easton, Maryland. Here, whether his audience realized it or not, Douglass remembered real events. In the morning, Auld and Lewis read from the Bible together: "Blessed are the poor in spirit—Blessed are they that give to the poor." Lewis partakes of food "produced by the blood of the slave." Then they all get into a carriage, with young Frederick "tied behind." Looking out on his rapt audience, Douglass continues, "I am on the auction block and the auctioneer is crying, 'Who bids for this comely stout young negro. . . . Well, five hundred dollars are bid.' Oh, how brother Lewis's eyes twinkle! The auctioneer continues—'This is not half the value of the negro. . . . His master has no desire to get rid of him, but only wants to get a little money to aid the cause of religious freedom in Scotland.' Once, twice, thrice . . . and I am sold for six hundred dollars." Amid "great cheering," Douglass ended his performance with a crescendo. "When the Free Church says—did not Abraham hold slaves? The reply should be, Send back the money! When they ask did not Paul send back Onesimus? I answer, Send back the money!" Douglass concluded that the Free Church was less church and more a "manufacturing corporation." "Disgorge the plunder!" he proclaimed. "Disgorge the plunder!" Arms waving in air, he shouted, "Send back the money! There is music in that sound."[7]

A woman in the audience that day was so moved that she wrote an anonymous letter to Chalmers. She seemed especially stunned when a slave collar and whip were displayed on the stage as props. Douglass somehow used them to solicit laughter. "Oh it is too serious a matter," the woman wrote, "to make sport of." But "Fre. Douglass did make me laugh when he preached the boys in Dundee send back the money."[8]

All through winter and spring 1846, the Send Back the Money campaign kept Scotland in ferment, and "a blaze of anti-slavery agitation," Douglass proudly reported. The slogan appeared on flags and placards wherever the abolitionists rallied and became the subject of what Douglass called "popular street songs." Children shouted about the controversy from street corners. Douglass's voice and his image popped up in the lyrics of some songs, such as the one that captured the conflict between the black abolitionist and the Free Church's Chalmers:

> *Chalmy and Blackie ran a race,*
> *Chalmy fell and broke his face,*
> *Quo' Blackie I have won the race,*
> *And the sow's tail till him yet,*
> *And the sow's tail till him yet,*
> *And the sow's tail to Chalmy.*

In the turf on Arthur's Seat, the giant hill that overlooks Edinburgh, some industrious Scots carved SEND BACK THE MONEY! in huge letters visible all over the city. The controversy over the Free Church, Douglass told Webb, hurt his book sales, but he felt inspired nonetheless to be part of a public debate of such "grandeur and gravity."[9]

Douglass was effective on the platform for many reasons—charisma, passion, rhetorical skill, his authenticity as a former slave, his persuasive powers. But Vernon Loggins, in 1931, one of the earliest modern literary critics of Douglass's abilities, may have captured it best. Douglass, wrote Loggins, possessed a unique "gracefulness" in mingling "argument with in-

Sir Walter Scott monument, unveiled just two years before Douglass's first visit to Scotland in 1846, with Edinburgh Castle in the background, Edinburgh, Scotland.

cident." He could "bring out his sermon without destroying his story."[10] This storyteller thrived in Scotland, the land of sermons, song, and poetry.

It helped to be attacked in the press and in the lecture halls. Douglass relished the role of villain to proslavery forces. As he later recalled, "It has happened to me . . . often to be more indebted to my enemies than to my own skill." In the fall of 1845, after publication of Douglass's *Narrative*, an A. C. C. Thompson of Wilmington, Delaware, a man who had grown up on a farm near St. Michaels, Maryland, and who knew Thomas Auld and Edward Covey, challenged the veracity of the autobiography in the *Delaware Republican.* Thompson accused Douglass of writing a "budget of falsehoods," defended the characters of Colonel Edward Lloyd, of Auld, and of Covey as practicing Methodists; as "good Christian" men, they were incapable of the violence and abuse Douglass had claimed. Unwittingly, Thompson played right into the young abolitionist's hands. In a public letter to the *Liberator* in January 1846, Douglass sarcastically thanked Thompson for confirming his identity. The former Talbot County native had remembered the young slave as Fred Bailey. No one could now sustain a claim that he was an impostor, Douglass said, as he reminded Thompson of his inadvertent good deed: "You have done a piece of anti-slavery work, which no anti-slavery man could do." Thompson called Douglass a "recreant slave" and said he knew Douglass the year he lived with Covey. "Edward Covey is not a creature of my imagination," Douglass rejoiced.[11]

Thompson also asserted that Fred Bailey could not have written the book in question. One can feel the glee in Douglass's response, as writer, to this charge. "You must not judge me now by what I then was," he told Thompson. "Frederick Douglass the *freeman* is a very different person from Frederick Bailey, *the slave.*" Then he addressed Thompson personally: "You remember when I used to meet you on the road to St. Michael's, or near Covey's lane gate, I hardly dared lift my head, and look up at you. If I should meet you now, amid the free hills of old Scotland, where the ancient 'black Douglass' once met his foes, I suppose I might summon sufficient fortitude to look you full in the face; and were you to attempt to make a slave of me . . . you might find me almost as disagreeable a subject as was the Douglass to whom I just referred."[12]

Douglass had books to sell, a career to promote, and his liberty to protect. In the second Irish edition of the *Narrative*, he published his full exchange with Thompson and wrote about it in the preface. Thompson was the perfect representative of the slaveholders' mentality. "I am an American slave," wrote Douglass proudly, "who has given my tyrant the slip. . . . He

[Thompson] agrees with me in at least the important fact, that I am what I proclaim myself to be, an ungrateful fugitive from the patriarchal institution of the slave states." It was as if the fugitive had found Thompson sitting at one of Douglass's performances of the "Slaveholder's Sermon," chained him to a pew up front, acted out a dialogue with the squirming, sweating former Marylander, and could now summon him to stand and verify all that the orator had just preached.[13]

Douglass endured the clandestine innuendo and sniping of Webb and other Garrisonians behind his back; but he also had to face public attacks on his character. While he was in Belfast, not only had "Send Back the Nigger!" leaflets been distributed in the streets, but a Reverend Thomas Smyth, a Belfast-born emigrant to Charleston, South Carolina, had worked with other anti-abolitionist supporters of the Free Church to circulate a rumor that Douglass had been seen leaving a house of ill repute in Manchester, England. Smyth, a pillar of the Presbyterian synod of South Carolina, had played a primary role in raising slaveholders' contributions to the Free Church of Scotland. A glance at Douglass's speaking itineraries during his first half year in the British Isles indicates that he had not yet set foot in Manchester when Smyth launched the rumors. Such a scurrilous effort to discredit the black abolitionist blew up in the perpetrators' faces; Douglass publicly threatened to sue Smyth for defamation of character, forcing the South Carolinian to issue an apology through lawyers.[14]

Racist and proslavery forces provided Douglass with these opportunities to remake his story for yet wider audiences. In an April 1846 letter from Glasgow to Horace Greeley, Douglass publicly enlisted the famous editor of the New York Tribune in defending himself against all the enemies who would "break a bruised reed." The editors of the conservative New York Herald and New York Express had condemned Douglass's criticisms of America while on his tour of England. One called him a "glib-tongued scoundrel" for "running amuck in greedy-eared Britain against America, its people, its institutions, and even against its peace." In effect, Douglass used Greeley's paper to thank such enemies for their "vulgar epithets," and to shame his country for its brutal contradictions. He showed off by using a line from Othello to make his point: "The head and front of my offending hath this extent, no more." Then he defined patriotism: "The best friend of a nation is he who most faithfully rebukes her for her sins—and he her worst enemy who, under the specious . . . garb of patriotism seeks to excuse, palliate or defend them." Still a moral suasionist, he hoped to bring slaveholders themselves, and all their abettors among New York editors, to "repent and purify themselves" through a realization of their country's "monstrous anomaly."[15] He was grateful to become so notorious back home while working the antislavery stages of foreign lands. It made the strain and isolation of so many long days and nights in small Scottish and English towns worth it.

This kind of rhetorical or journalistic jousting animated Douglass, morally and psychologically. And during the Scotland-England sojourn of 1846–47, he needed frequent spiritual boosts. Douglass was often homesick. "I am enjoying myself as well as anyone can be expected," Douglass told Garrison in April, "when separated from home by three thousand miles of deep blue ocean. I long to be at home—'home, sweet, sweet, sweet home! Be it ever so humble, there is no place like home.'" He missed his family and mentioned that some new friends had urged him to stay and make Britain his permanent home. "But this I cannot do, unless it shall be absolutely necessary for my personal freedom." He also missed trusted old friends. In July, back in Edinburgh, he wrote a personal letter to William White, who had saved Douglass's life from the mob in Pendleton, Indiana. Douglass said he had just had a dream about White, how they had fought "like two very brothers," and how his friend "looked bleeding." Douglass assured White that he still loved him and wished White could come join him in Edinburgh, "one of the most beautiful cities" Douglass had ever seen. In a letter full of longing for comradeship, Douglass wondered openly whether White thought it safe for him to return home now that the Aulds knew so much of his whereabouts and might try to "take me from the Old Bay State."[16] There is evidence that Douglass felt tempted to try to transport Anna and their four small children to a new home in England. But such a move was never a genuine option.

Douglass betrayed an even deeper homesickness and loneliness to a fictive sister, Ruth Cox, who after her escape from Eastern Shore slavery adopted the name Harriet Bailey. She and Douglass first met in 1844 while he was on a speaking tour in Pennsylvania. Ruth Cox was born a slave sometime between 1818 and 1822 in Talbot County, Maryland. Her mother, Ebby Cox, had been a slave in the Easton home of US representative and senator John Leeds Kerr (1780–1844). Her father was a free black laborer who at some point relocated to Baltimore. Douglass may at first have mistaken Ruth for his sister Eliza, who had been named for their mother, and whom he had not seen since 1836. Facing imminent sale upon the death of her owner in 1844, Ruth escaped through Delaware and then to West Ches-

*Ruth Cox Adams, Douglass's
adopted sister, c. 1870. Tintype.*

ter, Pennsylvania, where she found refuge among the large Quaker community. The mistaken identities could not have lasted long; Douglass invited
Ruth, under the assumed role of the abolitionist's sister, to join his family
in Lynn, Massachusetts. As a fugitive slave in danger, Ruth, like her putative
brother, needed protection and a new name. In background, age, and experience, the two Eastern Shore natives had much in common. In 1836, when
the eighteen-year-old Frederick Bailey had been dragged in chains to the
Easton jail, Ruth lived only a few blocks up the street.[17] They eagerly shared
memories of people and events, and of the horrible as well as comic circumstances of slavery.

Ruth was literate, a crucial fact in the Douglasses' household. Ruth/
Harriet could read and interpret letters from the wandering Frederick to
the homebound Anna. For a few crucial years, especially during Frederick's long sojourn in England, the newly renamed Harriet became confidant, economic aide, babysitter, and sister to Anna. Harriet may for a
time have been the mediator in the Douglasses' difficult marriage. Douglass clearly looked to Harriet for sympathy and understanding. To her he
wrote the most intimate letters of any we have from this early part of his
career, in a down-home, insider dialect that he almost never otherwise
used. In May 1846, a lonely, discouraged Douglass, having "fits of melancholy," sent "a few loving words to my own Dear Sister Harriet." He
made it "very plain" so that she could read it "without much trouble." His
health was "tolerable," but he often had "real low spirits." Then the language seems to come from a slave quarters in Talbot Country, or perhaps

a kitchen conversation in the Lynn cottage. Douglass described himself as "down at the mouth. I felt worse than 'get out.'" The weary American traveler said his "under lip hung like that of a motherless colt. I looked so ugly that I hated to see myself in a glass. There was no living for me. I was snappish. I would have kicked my grand 'dadda'! . . . 'dats a fac! ole missus—is you got any ting for poor nigger to eat!!!' Oh Harriet could I have seen you then. How soon would I have been relieved from that Horrible feeling." Douglass needed a "Sisterly hand" stroking his "feverish forehead . . . to make me forget my sadness." [18] He needed anything that would emotionally take him home.

Douglass told Harriet that he had recently overcome his depression by buying an "old fiddle" he discovered in a store window near his London hotel. Thus demonstrating how early he had taken up playing the violin (self-taught), he said that making music cured him, as he struck up the tune "Camels a coming!" a song likely based on Genesis 24, the story of how Rebekah brought water from the well for the men and camels and became the wife of Abraham's son Isaac. "They say music is good for insane people," Douglass revealed to Harriet, "and I believe everybody are more or less insane—at times I feel very foolish when I come out of my fits of insanity." This was a dour and psychologically struggling Douglass, desperate for a woman's sympathy and not mere admiration. After all that brilliance and adulation in public arenas, he needed a private outlet, a person to whom he could complain and pour out his woes. Douglass enclosed a letter to Anna and instructed Harriet to read it "over and over again until she can fully understand its contents." He then profusely thanked Harriet for her devotion to his young sons, her attention to Anna, and for her "loving letters" sent to him in England. In return he promised Harriet "a brother's love and a father's care." [19]

Harriet received more of such care than she ultimately wanted. That summer she wrote to Frederick telling him of her intention to marry, but apparently without indicating the man's name or background, and certainly without asking her supposed brother's blessing. "Shocked and surprised," Douglass exploded with paternalistic anger. Not knowing Harriet's "lover," Douglass oddly worried that she might be "on the brink of distruction." "You don't honor me so much as to ask my advice," complained the wounded brother. Harriet had asked him for a "light silk dress" for her wedding. Douglass then lectured a woman three thousand miles away about marriage: "Marriage is one act of our lives—once performed it cannot be undone." He warned Harriet, who had lived through many struggles, not to

make a mistake that "may lead to a life of misery and wretchedness." Douglass may have revealed more here about himself than he intended. Pathetically, he tried to let go, but at least in this letter from isolated London, he
could only offer that he would "rejoice" to see her married, as long as the
groom was not "some ignorant—idle worthless person." "It will be a soar
trial," he moped, "for me to part with you."[20]

In November 1847 in Lynn, Harriet did indeed marry a free black laborer, also from Talbot County, Maryland, living in Springfield, Massachusetts, named Perry Frank Adams. Douglass stood at her wedding. Although
she remained a fugitive slave, she eventually took back her original name
and became Ruth Cox Adams. But during his British sojourn Douglass was
hurt by her news, losing control over a woman he clearly needed—for his
family's cohesion and welfare (of which at this point he provided little)
and for himself. As historian Leigh Fought has argued, Douglass had never
known a nuclear family until he and Anna created one in New Bedford and
Lynn. But Frederick had been gone on the lecture circuit for months and
now for nearly two years. Harriet may have been not only his best way to
communicate with his wife and family, but a link that made that family possible.[21] At times, Douglass, staying in other people's homes, in nice if ster-
ile hotels in beautiful European cities where he could only feel out of place,
may not have fully grasped which roles he wanted to assume toward Harriet Bailey. They shared so much; they were Eastern Shore Negroes, fugitive
slaves seeking refuge, confidants. Harriet was Anna's helpmate, companion to the growing Rosetta, the aunt who could help nurture three small
boys without their father, and perhaps even the image of the literate black
woman Douglass may at times have wished he had brought out of Baltimore with him.

Before leaving Scotland, Douglass became a tourist in search of the land's
romantic military history and especially of Robert Burns. While traveling to the north from Edinburgh, Douglass wrote to his friend in Boston
Francis Jackson about the landscape and its bloody past: "Almost every
hill, river, mountain, or lake has been made classic by the heroic deeds of
her noble sons. Scarcely a stream but has been poured into song, or a hill
that is not associated with some fierce and bloody conflict between liberty
and slavery." How Douglass seemed to love trying out his own version of
the epic story of the Highlands! He had seen the "Grampion mountains,"

he reported, where "ancient crown heads use to . . . struggle in deadly conflict for supremacy, causing those grand old hills to run blood." Suddenly the young romantic wrote as though he were the author of a popular Scottish history or even a tourist guidebook. Or perhaps he suddenly felt the burden of the namesake he had borrowed from Sir Walter Scott. Trying still to be a good nonresistant, he claimed his "soul now sickens" at this violent past, but admitted to seeing in himself "all those elements of character which were I to yield to their promptings might lead me to deeds as bloody as those." He could not yet know just how true that impulse would be about his own soul over the coming decades when he would abandon pacifism forever.[22]

In April, Douglass visited Ayr, birthplace of Burns, on the west coast of Scotland. Springtime found the young man's romanticism in full bloom. Informing his friend Abigail Mott of Albany that he was an "enthusiastic admirer of Burns," Douglass laced a letter with the names and lyrics of the love poet's most famous works. Douglass seems to have loved "Tam O'Shanter" and told Abigail so, despite that long poem's drunken and sexual ribaldry. To the proper Miss Mott, to whom the Douglasses sent their daughter Rosetta to live and study from 1845 to 1848, Frederick sent the two full verses of the tamer poem "The Banks o' Doon," a classic expression of nature, beauty, and lost love. He gushed over the Burns Monument, "the finest thing of the kind I ever saw." And he was especially drawn to a glass case containing a Bible given to Burns by "Sweet Highland Mary," accompanied by a lock of her hair. Mary had died, and Douglass admitted his reverence for the "deep melancholy" all around, even for the very sounds of the river Doon. He met the surviving sister of the great bard, Mrs. Beggs, who lived on the property. Her two daughters merited detailed description as "truly fine looking women." The sublime autobiographer seized the chance to try his hand at what he called "that broad Scottish tongue." Douglass adored Burns because he had stood against the "bigotry" of the clergy and the "shallow-brained aristocracy" of his own time. Burns remained heroic because he "broke loose from the moorings which society had thrown around him." Douglass admitted that Burns's famous sexual escapades meant that he had done "much good and much evil." But "brilliant genius" must be forgiven, Douglass said. "Let us take the good and leave the evil—let us adopt his virtues but avoid his vices." Here were precepts that Douglass would need in his own tangled life. And if Burns had lived and written with a unique "performative intensity," as

Robert Burns. Lantern slide.
Warren S. Parker photographer.

one of his modern biographers suggests, then Douglass had a model in
life and on the page.[23]

Between May 1846, when Douglass made his first appearance in London,
and April 1847, when he finally returned to the United States, he delivered
scores of formal speeches all over the towns and cities of England. It was a
year of great adventure and discontent. By August, Garrison sailed to England and now joined Douglass on platforms in many venues from London to Edinburgh. With Garrison and without, Douglass met many English
reformers and members of Parliament, dined with luminaries, and even,
movingly, met the great abolitionist Thomas Clarkson. Garrison arranged
the meeting at Clarkson's home in Ipswich on August 21, 1846. Douglass
felt completely awed by meeting the great British abolitionist, blind and
only one month from death, the living link to the crusades that had led to
the abolition of both the slave trade and slavery in the British empire. With
Garrison and famed British abolitionist George Thompson, Douglass entered Clarkson's parlor. Douglass remembered the meeting as an encounter with a world-historical figure, with the history Douglass himself now
hoped he had entered. "It was a meeting of two centuries," Douglass recollected; the young man with a sense of history had never quite felt its intensity so profoundly before. He never forgot how Clarkson "took one of my

hands in both of his, and in a tremulous voice, said, 'God bless you Frederick Douglass! I have given sixty years of my life to the emancipation of your people, and if I had sixty years more they should all be given to the same cause.'"[24] In his old age, when Douglass himself encountered people who just wanted to say they had touched his hand, he could say that he had touched the hands of Thomas Clarkson, whose intrepid travel, collecting, and advocacy had done so much to end slavery in the British empire.

Douglass continued to tangle with Richard Webb about the availability and layout of new copies of the *Narrative*, as well as over his financial accounts with the publisher. Webb continued to view the author with contempt in private letters. By September and October he snidely wrote to Chapman, describing a new "steadiness" in Frederick that he attributed to Garrison's presence. Douglass was a "sharp man," Webb reported, but he needed the "ballast" that his senior mentor supplied. Even nastier, Webb suggested that all the lionizing Douglass experienced in Scotland and England would cause him great disappointment when he returned to the harsh racial climate as well as his personal situation in America. "From what I hear of her, I wonder how he will be able to bear the sight of his wife," Webb remarked, "after all the petting he gets from beautiful, elegant, and accomplished women in a country where prejudice against colour . . . is laughed at." Douglass remained annoyed at best with Chapman's continued snooping into his every move. When challenged for attending a meeting of the British and Foreign Anti-Slavery Society (the Garrisonians' ideological rival), Douglass wrote to Chapman and told her to mind her own business. He did not attend out of "money temptations," he declared, assuring the conniving Chapman that he would "speak in any meeting where free speech is allowed."[25] We should not wonder why Douglass often found it difficult to trust people; in his dangerous world, friends and enemies were sometimes indistinguishable.

During his final year in Britain, Douglass contemplated returning home to America. But he was still a slave and needed to make money from book sales to pay his bills. He remained lonely and cantankerous, although he sustained a firm public face. In July he experienced some sort of falling-out with his special friend in Cork, Isabel Jennings. On the same day that he wrote the letter full of yearning and nostalgia to William White, Douglass apologized to "Dear Isa" for his "naughty letter" that made her so angry, as well as for an embittered exchange he had experienced with an Irish minister. "I cannot be always upon the mountain top," he remarked, asking for indulgence of his darker side. "You told me nothing new," he said to Isabel, "when you told me that I was imperfect. . . . I am indeed a very imperfect being." Even Garrison, who often sent brief remarks back to his wife about how Douglass was "doing a great work," admitted in September that "the poor fellow is—naturally enough—sighing to see his wife and children."[26]

In the summer of 1846 Douglass seems to have seriously entertained relocating his family to Britain, an issue that weighed heavily on his mind. In July he wrote to "my own dear sister Harriet," enclosing a special letter to Anna and one to a New Bedford friend, Jeremiah Burke Sanderson. As before, he implored Harriet to read them "over and over again until Dear Anna shall fully understand." He states that the "Boys must wait for presents till I come home, or until they come to this country." He further asks his adopted sister to speak frankly of "what you think of coming to this country."[27] This prospect would fade in coming months, but it is telling how seriously Douglass seems to have considered a permanent rejection of the United States. He did have some British friends he trusted; and he had countless times reminded audiences that he was still property under the laws of Maryland.

But the road beckoned, the speaking circuit demanded him, and Garrison was once again leading the way. Many of those adoring British supporters really did want to help. A consortium of Douglass's British friends, led by a Quaker, Ellen Richardson of Newcastle, and her sister-in-law, Anna Richardson, began working assiduously in 1846 to contact the Aulds in Maryland and arrange the purchase of Frederick's freedom. By at least May Douglass had learned that Thomas Auld had transferred ownership of his long-lost slave to his brother Hugh, and that the Baltimore merchant who had once tried to stop the boy from reading now publicly had stated his desire, at any cost, to return him to slavery. This claim of Auld's desire to exact revenge has never been documented and may have emerged as useful abolitionist lore. In a public letter to Garrison, Douglass enjoyed taunting Hugh Auld, calling him the "hungry blood hound." "Possess your soul in patience, *dear* master Hugh, and regale yourself on the golden dreams afforded by the prospect—'First catch your rabbit, &c. &c.'"[28]

Sometime that summer of 1846, on a visit to Ellen Richardson and her brother in Newcastle, Douglass's hosts took him out to the seaside for a holiday of a sort. According to an extraordinary interview conducted by Ida B. Wells in April 1894 with the eighty-five-year-old Ellen, the elderly Quaker remembered sitting on the sand talking at length with Douglass and, after "observing his sadness," hatching their plan to buy his freedom.[29] On one of those visits to Newcastle he also met Julia Griffiths, an unmarried English abolitionist, who would soon become an extremely important friend and coworker in Douglass's life.

Douglass underwent much confusion about when and how to return to his family in Massachusetts. As of late August he was determined to sail home in early November. To Anna Richardson, then already involved in negotiations with Hugh Auld, Douglass declared that "my Anna says 'Come home' and I have now resolved upon going home—the day is fixed and my dear Anna will be informed of it in a few days. I shall sail for America on the fourth November—and hope to meet the beloved one of my heart by the 20th of that month." He urged Mrs. Richardson to continue corresponding with Auld. But one month later, he wrote to Isabel Jennings, concerned that she would think him "the most fickle of men" because he had decided to "stay in this country six months longer." He claimed the strong advice of Garrison and George Thompson had led to such a choice—they deemed him more essential to the antislavery movement in Britain just then than in America. Indeed, now touring England with Douglass, Garrison acted a bit like the ship captain, and his young black orator was merely a member of the crew obeying orders. Garrison acknowledged Douglass's homesickness in mid-September, but wrote that "Frederick . . . will not return till next May" in time for "our New England Convention." If they took the black star off the British circuit, they would "lose a great deal of what otherwise will be permanently secured to us."[30]

Garrison's "us" did not include a financially struggling black family back in Lynn, Massachusetts. But Douglass was now also eagerly hoping for a deal with Auld and his manumission papers, although he was clearly troubled that he must once again disappoint Anna. "It will cause her some pain," he remarked to Isabel.[31] The pain of longing and separation were by then a way of life for the Douglasses. Douglass's choice left him holding a cleft stick: return to American soil a yet more famous and vulnerable fugitive slave in the midst of the Mexican War crisis, or wait until the possible purchase of his freedom.

By November–December the Richardsons succeeded in raising the money and securing Auld's agreement to manumit Douglass for £150 sterling, or $711.66. Likely with the help of Douglass's old friend William White, the Richardsons had contacted the wealthy and well-connected member of the AASS Ellis Gray Loring of Boston, who engaged a New York lawyer, Walter Lowrie, who then found a Baltimore attorney who became the intermediary with Hugh Auld. Through this set of actors, Auld had named his price in an exchange of letters directly with Anna Richardson from August to October 1846. From Auld came the words: "manumission of my slave Frederick Bailey, alias Douglass . . . in other words the papers will render him entirely and legally free." Rather than a cause for celebration, the purchase of a slave's freedom as property was an extraordinarily sensitive issue among some abolitionists, especially Garrisonians. Douglass received celebratory sentiments from friends, but also many objections to his "ransom" deal.[32] In response to the critics, he turned the purchase of his freedom into antislavery propaganda; and this time, it was not about sending back the blood money, but sending abolitionist lucre to America to own his body and life.

Douglass freely admitted his gratitude that the sale made it possible for him to return to his wife and family with security, whatever principle might be at stake for hard-line moralists. But in a private letter to fellow American, Garrisonian, and frequent traveling companion in Britain Henry C. Wright (who condemned the purchase), as well as in a public letter to a Durham, England, newspaper editor, Douglass elevated the issue to what he thought was even more radical high ground.

The objection was that no man had the "right of property" in another man and, therefore, paying for the freedom of a fugitive slave reinforced the evils so condemned by abolitionists. But the absolutists be damned; Douglass was happy to end his "present exile," he declared, on a basic human and familial level. He also argued that his liberty was of more value than "paltry gold." Then he converted the act into a fierce condemnation of the "brazen hypocrisy" of his country. Practicing arguments he would master later in the 1850s, he asserted that "Hugh Auld had no power over me but what was conferred by the United States government." To the "violation of correct principle," as one Ohio abolitionist paper put it, of "the redemption of one slave, when millions are in a condition equally bad," Douglass sighed impatiently and concluded with the weak claim that his friends had "denied" Auld's "right to receive" the money in their offer letter. Douglass said he was personally trapped like an unprotected merchant giving his "purse to a bloody pirate: take my purse, but spare my life." In this case, the pirate was a slaveholder with the power of "commander-in-chief of the army and navy." And to Wright's objection that Douglass would lose his symbolic power as a fugitive slave, Douglass scoffed, "I shall be Frederick Douglass still; and once a slave still. I shall neither be made to forget, nor cease to feel the wrongs of my fellow countrymen, who are yet in chains." Above all, Douglass relished now the chance to wave his manumission papers as the "brand of infamy" on his "nation of plunderers."[33] Despite some of the logic of his defense, Douglass had nevertheless been handed a new sword— his legal freedom purchased by blood money—with which to slay anew the dragons of American hypocrisy.

During his final six months in England in 1846–47, Douglass remained out on the antislavery stump all over the country, especially in the north, speaking to many issues, old and new. His British sojourn became a true flowering of personal independence, but also of intellectual challenge and growth. He and Garrison were uniquely confronted by the Chartist movement, the decade-old crusade for workers' rights, especially suffrage. By the time Douglass faced the question of the rights of British workers and their resistance to aristocratic rule in England, he had already both resisted and sometimes warmed to the analogy of Irish extreme poverty to American slavery. But now he encountered a large political working-class movement, part of which advocated peaceful parliamentary reform, based on the famous "People's Charter," forged in 1838 by the London Working Men's Association, part of which demanded tactics of "physical force" and revolution against the Poor Laws. The charter that gave the movement its name had originally been drafted at the Crown and Anchor Tavern in 1838 on the Strand in London, where Douglass and Garrison would themselves meet with Chartists in August 1846. The founding document contained several demands, but primarily they were universal male suffrage, annual elections, and other reforms meant to make Parliament more responsive to ordinary people. Garrisonians had been well aware of the Chartists since at least 1840, when Garrison himself partially embraced their cause on his visit to England.[34]

Douglass tended to follow Garrison's lead on the delicate issue of the Chartists and British workers. Here was a great opportunity for cooperative transatlantic reform. But the dream of the black-slaves/white-workers alliance around their mutual forms of oppression rarely advanced beyond rhetoric; a flourishing 1840s solidarity remained elusive. During Garrison's tour in England and Scotland in late summer and fall of 1846, accompanied most places by Douglass and George Thompson, the Bostonian openly embraced what he called the "moral suasionist Chartists," and their leaders, William Lovett and Henry Vincent. At a September 2 gathering of Chartists in London, Garrison reported speaking not in any "official capacity" as an abolitionist, but as a private citizen endorsing the "unpopular reformatory movements in this country." Thunderous applause rocked the hall in response to Garrison's personal support of the workingmen's quest for equal political rights. Douglass too could talk the talk of the moral-suasionist wing of Chartism. Writing publicly to Garrison, Douglass reported speaking at an earlier London meeting of the "complete Suffrage Association," the group of Chartists opposed to using physical force. He called "complete suffrage" the next reform movement. "Aristocratic rule must end," Douglass told his mentor in a flourish, "class legislation must cease," and "people, not property shall govern." [35] Douglass had heard and read the Chartists carefully, even if he never quite shouldered their cause fully.

Douglass enjoyed personal friendships with some Chartist leaders. Lovett recalled in his autobiography a social evening with Douglass, Garrison, Thompson, and Wright among others. Lovett wrote that after some speech-making of a kind, "our friend Douglass, who had a fine voice, sang a number of negro melodies. Mr. Garrison sang several antislavery pieces, and our grave friend, H. C. Wright, sang an old Indian war song." The group concluded with a rousing rendition of "La Marseillaise." [36] Douglass loved music but seemed to have too few opportunities to demonstrate it.

Such conviviality and mutual support was quite real. But what ultimately made Douglass pull back on the public platform was the frequent analogy between black American slaves and the alleged "white slaves" of the British wage system, a claim made inside and outside Chartism. As a man of words, Douglass faced many tensions and contradictions on this issue. He could claim over and over, as he had back in Ireland, that his mission was "purely an antislavery one," but write frequently how he was learning to "enter into the wrongs of others" as the only "true foundation for his antislavery faith." In a speech in Bristol in late August 1846, Douglass seemed to acknowledge "political slavery in England" and gave a nod to the virtual slavery of men in the British army and navy. He proclaimed his hatred for all forms of tyranny and oppression, but then stated firmly that "there was no similarity between slavery, as existing in the United States, and any institution in this country, than there was between lightness and darkness." A week later in Bridgwater, England, Douglass felt challenged by the analogy again. After reciting his litany of the evils of American slavery wreaked upon both body and mind, he concluded unequivocally, "Were there any such in this country? There was not one! The humblest man in the realm could resist the proudest aristocrat, backed up by the shield of the British law! Not so the slave." Douglass thus parted ways with those Chartists who still clung to slogans such as "Death to aristocrats!" and even with the moral-suasionist crusaders for workers' rights who knew something about just how much the laboring poor in England could ultimately resist the aristocrats whose boots crushed their necks.[37]

Douglass's heart, indeed his pride as a radical reformer, remained attached to the millions of his fellow bondmen back in republican America. He was surely inspired by the workers' plight and their movement culture in Britain, but pride of place in the worldwide argument over enslavement, he insisted, dwelt not with wage slaves but with those who possessed no wage and often no hope. Although he could often draw laughs with a favorite line such as "In the absence of the cash, there must be the lash," as he did in Sheffield in March 1847, the joke was dead serious.[38]

During Douglass's British tour he continued to hammer away at the hypocrisy of the churches. He spoke in chapels and churches of all sizes, in city halls and public rooms of all kinds, in the music halls of Leeds or Newcastle, or the Corn Exchange of Manchester. Douglass was everywhere (London one day and by the new train lines four hundred miles north in Edinburgh two days later). No wonder he could reflect so joyously on how he and his "trunk" had traveled with "electric speed" through all parts of the country. He lectured on behalf of temperance, against a favorite target (the hypocrisy of the international Evangelical Alliance and its refusal to reject slaveholders), and especially to promote the British Garrisonian organization, the Anti-Slavery League. Douglass addressed twenty-five hundred to three thousand at Finsbury Chapel in London in May 1846, an estimated four thousand at the Free Trade Hall in Manchester, and twenty-five hundred at the Concert Hall in Liverpool in October, among many other similar throngs. One intrepid twenty-first-century researcher has estimated that Douglass delivered 184 speeches during his British sojourn.[39] For a young former slave devoting his life to the brutally uncertain vocation of radical reformer, these cheering, laughing, and sometimes abusive audiences were his wellspring of hope.

On Douglass's nonstop farewell tour in winter and spring 1847, he blasted his own country and its entanglement in the great evil of slavery. The big theme he left ringing in the ears of thousands was the plight of the American slave, the deep contradictions of American professions and practices, and the nature of slavery itself, often embodied poignantly in his personal story. As he prepared to finally sail home with his freedom, his own country was his primary subject. On March 30, to an elegant and prominent audience, gathered to honor him by invitation only, estimated at four hundred to seven hundred (Charles Dickens sent a letter of regret), in the

London Tavern on Bishopsgate Street, Douglass delivered what he called his "Farewell Address to the British People." He quickly put ceremonial talk behind him and delivered a blistering critique of the American Constitution and the United States as a corrupted, wholly complicit slave society. His central theme, pronounced with humor, withering satire, and painful personal imagery, was his country as a "nation of inconsistencies, completely made up of inconsistencies."[40]

Douglass had been speaking almost nightly for as much as two hours each. But this was a bravura performance. He drew tremendous cheering with repeated claims that he had "no patriotic applause for America or her institutions." Here were his rehearsals for one of the great themes of his public rhetoric to come in the 1850s. Douglass dragged his overdressed auditors, sipping elegant drinks, through one "blood" metaphor after another. The "history," he declared, of "the sons and daughters of Africa . . . is nothing but blood! Blood!—blood in the morning, blood at noon, blood at night!" The symbol of America's history might be "gold dripping with gore from the plantations." His own country had become, he insisted, "one vast hunting ground for men." Slavery was ensconced in American society, "interwoven with the very texture—with the whole network" of institutions. Douglass entertained with voices, accents, and mimicry of slaveholding preachers and defenders of the Evangelical Alliance; the crowd roared with hilarity.[41]

But possibly what such a crowd would remember most was how Douglass wove his indictments of his own land and of slavery through his own personality, offering himself as the representative of all slaves. The twenty-nine-year-old had long employed this method, but so confident was he in front of British audiences that he offered himself as specimen—mind, body, and soul. "I scarcely know what to say in America," he said, "when I hear men get up and deliberately assert a right to property in my limbs—my very body and soul; that they have a right to me! That I am in their hands . . . a thing to be bought and sold!" Douglass made it more personal yet, describing how Thomas Auld, whom in this rare instance he called his "father," had given him away to his "brother" Hugh. "Thus was I transferred by my father to my uncle," he announced, in a statement that must have astonished some close readers of his *Narrative*, where his paternity had been left ambiguous. "I have as much right to sell Hugh Auld as Hugh Auld has to sell me," he shouted as some in the room bent over in laughter. Douglass effusively thanked his British compatriots for all their friendship, their financial help, and their inspirations during his nineteen months among them. With bravado, he vowed to return to "glory in the conflict" at home in America. He did his utmost to return their love, which he felt "daguerre-otyped on my heart" by their "sea of upturned faces." They had laughed and cried with him for more than an hour, and as the American sat down on the stage, "long-continued cheering" enveloped the London Tavern.[42]

Four days later on a quay in Liverpool, Douglass lifted his trunk onto the *Cambria* once again for the return voyage to America. He was a changed man, an experienced orator-writer and professional abolitionist with an international reputation, an "illustrious transatlantic," as a Sheffield newspaper had called him. He would never again be a good follower; from this day forward he did not take direction well from abolitionist handlers, although he would remain a constant learner and seeker of new strategies, new methods of mingling the power of the word with the power of politics. Douglass boarded the ship, again under humiliating conditions of segregated quarters, which became a cause célèbre in the British and American antislavery press. But now he was no longer a fugitive slave, and he held more than $2,000 from his British friends, intended as a support for his family but especially for his publicly declared intention to create his own newspaper.[43]

After a voyage of fifteen days in the North Atlantic, Douglass arrived in Boston Harbor on April 20, 1847. A delegation of friends gathered at the docks to meet him. But so anxious was Douglass to see his family, he all but ran to the train that took him to Lynn within a half hour. His detailed description of the homecoming in a letter back to Anna Richardson in England is one for the ages: "As soon as it was possible to land . . . from the steamer, I leaped on shore, without stopping a moment to look after luggage, and ran through a crowd of friends who had assembled on the wharf to meet me, simply bowing as I passed." With heart pumping, he looked out the train window, "from which I saw all my family five minutes before getting home, as I had to get out of the station. When within about fifty yards of our house, I was met by my two bright-eyed boys, Lewis and Frederick, running and dancing with very joy to meet me. Taking one in my arms and the other by the hand, I hastened into the house. Here imagination must fill up the picture." Stunningly, Douglass ended his letter to Anna Richardson with effusive gratitude, of how "all England is dear to me." Then he used two lines from Burns: "Kings may be blest, but I was glorious, / O'er all the ills of life victorious." Then followed a simple line of his own: "It is good to be at home."[44]

Chapter 11

DEMAGOGUE
IN BLACK

If I speak harshly, my excuse is that I speak in fetters of your own forging. Remember that oppression hath the power to make even a wise man mad.

—FREDERICK DOUGLASS, *NORTH STAR*,
NOVEMBER 17, 1848

For a week and a half in late April 1847, Douglass felt thrilled to immerse himself, as he wrote to Scottish Quaker friends, in the "warm bosom" of family. He rejoiced especially that his two oldest sons remembered him well, a wistful comment on the nature of their father's place in this home that Anna made. "For once," Douglass declared, "all cares of a public nature were cast aside, and my whole heart absorbed in grateful rapture."[1] But such joy among his children would not last long. Just where Douglass's whole heart could ever rest, and just how he might ever find balance between the public and the private demands of his chosen paths, emerged now as the defining feature of his life.

Invitations to speak poured into Lynn. Not everyone among his friends was entirely enamored with their protégé's new persona. Only three days after Douglass's arrival in Boston, Wendell Phillips wrote privately, "Douglass is here, the same old sixpence, fatter, with a tinge of English precise pronunciation, the same that Redmond [Remond] and Garrison infallibly bring home and which, though good in itself, is still so foreign to our slipshod manner that I hope he will get rid of it soon." Whether spouting some clipped English accent or not, soon the traveling man was back on the road, and this time with a confident and angrier voice. Stored in his soul, and his oratorical repertoire, were not only his life-changing triumphs in the British Isles, but also the segregated "loneliness" he had endured on the return voyage on the *Cambria*. Douglass processed this insult in his normal way: he poured it into his well of wounded but fierce pride and felt fortunate that he did not have to associate with the proslavery "band of wild, uproarious, gambling tipplers, whose foul-mouthed utterances interposed an impassable gulf between us." He tried to turn his foes' ugly ways to advantage, publicly exposing their absurd claims of superiority.[2]

But what to do with the anger? Douglass turned it on his own country in language that even some of his friends found troubling. In the coming year he would know precious little calm time in Lynn. After welcome-home meetings in Lynn and Boston and a trip to Albany, accompanied by Anna, to visit Rosetta, who resided there with her governesses, Abigail and Lydia Mott, Douglass was in New York on May 11 to speak at the thirteenth-anniversary meeting of the American Anti-Slavery Society. This was no ordinary occasion; a crowd of nearly four thousand, the largest ever at an AASS gathering, filled the Broadway Tabernacle. Implying that he was still working on his speech, Douglass entered the hall carrying a portable writing desk. Virtually all major American abolitionists were in attendance, as were many curious newspaper reporters. After Wendell Phillips spoke, Garrison introduced Douglass with a prolonged speech of his own about the former fugitive slave's successful sojourn in England. Garrison read from chapters 2 and 18 of Jeremiah, then long excerpts of press accounts of Douglass's farewell address in London as well as of his travail with discrimination aboard the *Cambria*. Garrison finally cut short his introduction as the crowd began to shout, "Douglass! Douglass!," thus forcing the mentor to make way for his star pupil.[3]

Douglass spoke not only as a returning hero from his foreign travels, but primarily as an angry young black American ready for a new kind of attack on his native land. He let it be known that, especially after his British experience, "home" and "country" were now ambivalent concepts. Douglass was excited to be back in the midst of this abolitionist community of comrades, but America was another matter. "I have no love for America, as such," he jarringly announced. "I have no patriotism. I have no country." Douglass let his righteous anger flow in metaphors of degradation, chains, and blood. "The institutions of this country do not know me, do not recognize me as a man, except as a piece of property." The only thing attaching him to his native land was his family, and his deeply felt ties to the "three millions of my fellow creatures groaning beneath the iron rod . . . with . . . stripes upon their backs." Only their "clanking . . . chains" and their "warm blood . . . making fat the soil of Maryland and of Alabama" drew him back to America. Such a country, Douglass said, he could not love. "I desire to see its overthrow as speedily as possible, and its Constitution shivered in a thousand fragments."[4] With loud cheers as well as hisses engulfing the entranced audience, Douglass stalked his prey.

Already a master of the rhetorical device of the jeremiad—calling the fallen nation back to its lost principles—but also now portraying himself as the victim of proslavery scorn, Douglass enjoyed being the aggressor. Claiming he was constantly accused of irritating Americans, rather than appealing to their better instincts, Douglass happily pled guilty: "I admit that we have irritated them," he declared. "They deserve to be irritated. As it is in physics, so in morals, there are cases that demand irritation, and counter irritation. The conscience of the American public needs this irritation. And I would *blister it all over, from centre to circumference,* until it gives signs of a purer . . . life than it is now manifesting to the world." Douglass named the demons and stalked his prey. As the latter-day Jeremiah he spoke as did the ancient prophet, calling the nation to judgment for its mendacity, its wanton violation of its own covenants, and warning of its imminent ruin.[5]

Saddled with the burden of having condemned his own country while abroad, Douglass reversed the charge. "Ministers of the Gospel from Christian America," he maintained, were "pouring their leprous proslavery distilment into the ears" of foreigners and were themselves the true traitors. The British public had needed its eyes and ears opened to "the secrets of the prison house of bondage in America." No place was safe in America for the nearly hopeless slave, nor for free blacks. "Slavery is everywhere. Slavery goes everywhere." And nowhere could moral power alone overthrow slavery. Not in political "parties," nor in the "press," nor in the "pulpit." Slavery had built its "ramparts" so strong and so high, it could thus far resist all critics. This angry and bleak portrait of the woes of his people and his country ended as only it could for a moral suasionist in the last stages of its ideological grip. Douglass turned to sentimental appeals to natural rights, argued that proslavery forces, however impregnable, could ultimately not resist the truth, then steadfastly declared himself still a man of peace and that he had never "stirred up warlike feelings while abroad," as his accusers had claimed. Just as he seemed to demonstrate a new degree of radicalism and authenticity, Douglass retreated into an earnest Garrisonianism. He had skipped over Jeremiah's chastisement of those who had declared, "Peace, Peace, where there is no peace."[6] Douglass had not quite yet achieved his full prophetic voice.

All of these ideas and arguments, while not new, were now a swirling set of conflicts in Douglass's mind, packaged in an angry voice that made him, as he wished, the target of a backlash. Some responses to his Broadway Tabernacle performance were positive, but many were hostile. The poet John Greenleaf Whittier thought Douglass had been too harsh, but considered the speech a "noble refutation of the charge of the natural inferiority urged against the colored man." But anti-abolition papers such as the *New York Sun* condemned the speech as "unmitigated abuse heaped on our country by the colored man Douglass." A group of Baltimore slaveholders published Douglass's speech in a pamphlet, distributed as a means of demonstrating the dangers of abolitionism. And a letter writer in the *Boston Post* reacted by labeling Douglass the new "demagogue in black."[7] Douglass was delighted to have caused such fear among his enemies, and especially to be reprinted in Baltimore! The angry young man who had stepped off the ship from Britain was ready for battle.

Notoriety, however, was a double-edged sword. Within a week of the New York speech, Douglass shot back at the *Sun*'s racist editor in a public letter to Thomas Van Rensselaer, editor of the black paper the *Ram's Horn*, published in New York. Announcing that he sought "a little . . . sport" at the expense of the *Sun*'s editor, Douglass thanked him for calling him "colored" and not "nigger," a "man" and not for once a "monkey." Then he returned the ridicule with palpable glee. To the accusation that one ought not enjoy an invitation "into a gentleman's house, accept his hospitality, yet ABUSE his fare," nor "abuse a country under whose government" one is "securely protected," Douglass reveled in the irony. As a black man in this American house he found an unsavory bill of fare: "He asks the cook for soup, he gets dish water. For salmon he gets a serpent; for beef, he gets bull frogs; for ducks, he gets gall." Leaving those metaphors to fester, Douglass called the nation's "Bill of Rights . . . towards us a bill of wrongs. Its self-evident truths are self-evident lies." Douglass announced that he would not provide peace where there was no peace: "The harmony of this country is discord with the ALMIGHTY."[8]

But he had an even more difficult accusation to thwart. While traveling with one of the Mott sisters on a steamer down the Hudson River from Albany to New York (after he and Anna had visited Rosetta) for the AASS meeting, Douglass slept overnight in a stateroom that adjoined his traveling companion's room by a common door. When the captain discovered the arrangement, he threatened Douglass with racist epithets and worse. Two newspapers, one called the *Switch* in Albany, and another called the *Sub-*

terranean in New York, exploited the story, forcing Douglass into a public explanation. The two papers entertained their readers with vile and lurid descriptions. Douglass was the "offensive creature" and the "Sambo" who walked "cheek by jowl" with Miss Mott when they visited the New York State Assembly chamber in Albany. He was the "soot head" and the "wool head," and white New Yorkers had been "gratifying their morbid tastes in lionizing a disgusting, impertinent negro who styles himself Frederick Douglass." Based on such stories, rumors spread, even among abolitionists, that Douglass and Miss Mott were "caught in bed together." On June 7 Douglass finally wrote a public letter to Garrison. His version of the story, a credible one, was that he faced two choices: to sleep out on the deck with the "dogs" since the steamer would not allow him as a black man to purchase a proper cabin, or to have Miss Mott book the room next to hers. Suffering, he said, from a "severe cold and hoarseness," a condition he frequently confronted, Douglass chose the indoor accommodation. His statement that "a thought of its propriety or impropriety never crossed my mind" seems less believable.[9]

In the "free, full and open explanation" he offered in the letter, Douglass denied any improper behavior, denouncing the scandal sheets. Then, as usual, whatever the truth about his flaunting of appearances, he converted the racist packaging of the charges into a fierce abolitionist argument against the worst elements of mid-nineteenth-century racism, some of which has never ceased in some American precincts. If he was "disgusting," then he made the most of it. "The buzzard and the condor," Douglass wrote, "are utterly disgusted with sound meat," and "a dog afflicted with hydrophobia is utterly disgusted with the sight and scent of pure cold water." Similarly, "a white man afflicted with colorphobia will invariably manifest . . . disgust at the sight of a respectable colored man. Colorphobia and buzzards—mad dogs and condors—think of these things!" He reminded his readers of the vicious subtlety of racism as well. His attackers had condemned his "sauciness." Really? he asked. "How, when, where and to whom? Not as a coachman, dressed in tinseled livery, driving some delicate white ladies through . . . Broadway . . . Not as a footman, on some gilded carriage. Not as a waiter in some fashionable hotel. Not as a servant, a barber, a cook, or a steward. No I am never disgusting to the most refined Americans in any of these capacities!" Douglass turned the tide on his attackers. White people's disgust commences "just when the colored man's inequality is dropped, and his equality is assumed."[10] This would not be the last time Douglass used stinging analysis of racism to explain allegations about his private life. Nor was it the last time that white-male fears of his sexuality would burst into the press.

In the summer of 1847 Douglass struggled to find his feet personally and professionally. He spent considerable time in Lynn and suffered at least two weeks with what he called a "severe illness" and a friend described as scarlet fever. He pondered whether to launch his own newspaper, and whether to move his family to western New York, or possibly to Cleveland. In late June Douglass managed a public explanation for why, reluctantly, he had "given up my intention of publishing a paper for the present." Oddly, he claimed he did not want to appear "superannuated" (older and out of touch). Appearances mattered; he worried that British philanthropy supporting his personal enterprise during the Irish famine might also be unacceptable on both sides of the ocean. But with such equivocations, it was amply clear that Douglass saw the printing press, should he buy it, as a "gift to my race." While Garrison and his "Boston Board" of leadership discouraged their protégé from launching a competitive newspaper, some readers of the *Liberator* were supportive of the idea, one of them even accusing the Garrisonians of "selfish considerations" in their hostility.[11] Douglass's desire to become a *black* newspaperman could not be restrained.

To keep emotional stress and the future at bay, Douglass sought out the one place he knew best—the lecture circuit. By mid-July, he assured Garrison privately that he did not feel "hemmed in on every side . . . subjected to the Boston Board," a statement at best only half true.[12] Soon he eagerly joined a group of black abolitionists, including Remond, Samuel Ringgold Ward, and Henry Highland Garnet, touring across upstate New York. He spoke especially at a West Indian emancipation celebration on August 2, in Canandaigua, which included well over a thousand blacks in an outdoor setting.

After local bands and choirs performed, Douglass was the first orator of the day; he delivered an extraordinary lecture on the ancient history of slavery, on the Atlantic slave trade, and especially on the British antislavery movement. For an outdoor festival with thousands seeking shade on a hot summer day, the speech was quite a learned effort. He named at least twenty-three British abolitionists and paid warm tributes especially to William Wilberforce and Thomas Clarkson. He reminded auditors that all civilizations had enslaved other peoples throughout history. Using Revelation 13:10, he cautioned, "He that leadeth into captivity, shall go into captivity."

Douglass offered a compelling narration of the capture of African slaves by European traders, the complicity of the African "Prince" in the sale, and the "grim death and desolation" of the slave ships. He gave instruction on the meaning of the *Somerset* case of 1772, which made Britain free soil for slaves arriving from abroad, and ended with a prolonged argument for human progress marked by British emancipation, for God as the ultimate arbiter of history, and for the eternal need for "fanatical dreamers" to push history to higher moral ground.[13] Douglass thus demonstrated that he was hardly the one-topic preacher of the "Slaveholder's Sermon." He was a *reader*. And by naming all those British abolitionists, he claimed their lineage.

Within the following week, with no visit to the family in Lynn, Douglass met up with Garrison for a "far West" speaking tour that would be the last great effort these two radicals would make together. They started in Philadelphia with refurbished energy and high hopes. They soon found inspired audiences as well as reinvigorated mobs determined to disrupt or destroy them. These were exuberant times for abolitionism. Garrison's organization needed money, the American population was spreading westward in leaps and bounds, and Ohio especially had emerged as the new antislavery battleground. The AASS had established a fledgling newspaper in Salem, Ohio, the *Bugle*, and the indefatigable Abby Kelley, along with her husband, Stephen Foster, and others, had laid the moral-suasionist groundwork in the booming Midwest.[14]

The nation strained under a war in Mexico that most abolitionists condemned as proslavery aggression, and over which the political parties be-

Frederick Douglass, May 1848. Daguerreotype. Edward White Gallery, New York.

gan to fray at their seams. Debate also raged over the Wilmot Proviso, a welcome resolution even to nonpolitical abolitionists (although it never passed Congress), which would have denied slavery any foothold in new states gained from the Mexican War. Manifest Destiny, war against a foreign "race," boundless expansion, and a renewed national debate over the future of slavery seemed to offer propitious prospects for radical reformers about to barnstorm into the thriving farming and market towns of the Old Northwest.[15]

Garrison established at least two strategic themes for the tour—"comeouterism" and "disunion." The first was the appeal that all right-thinking abolitionists should disavow any allegiances to proslavery churches. Comeouters, or denominational dissenters, had for years appealed to Revelation 18:4, to "come out" and seek a purer, more exalted Christianity. The second theme, disunion, was a more complicated, beguilingly anarchistic plea for a dissolution of the American Union as the only means to end Northern complicity with slavery. Douglass always tried his best with this Garrisonian tenet by talking the talk even when he, like many other blacks, never comprehended how to walk the walk. Disunionism was above all a test of ideological loyalty among Garrisonians. In one of his three speeches in Philadelphia, Douglass took heart from John C. Calhoun's increasingly steadfast rejection of any Southern compromises about slavery's expansion into the West, suggesting that this might force the North to a "separation from the slave power." "I welcome the bolt whether it come from Heaven or from Hell, that shall sever this Union," Douglass proclaimed as a crowd-pleaser.[16] But other issues now attracted him more, especially with black audiences.

In what became a common occurrence in many places with sizable free-black populations, the famous Mother Bethel African Methodist Episcopal Church of Philadelphia held a special event in Douglass's honor on August 6, 1847. Douglass donned his black leader's hat and reveled in the moment. He called his role as black representative a "religious duty" of the "sweetest enjoyment." Ideological purity hardly mattered here in the packed pews of Mother Bethel. What did matter was community survival, solidarity, and uplift. "I am one with you," the orator assured the flock, "one in position—one in the estimate of the whites—one in the effort to gain our rights and true social condition. I feel entitled from this oneness to be heard as to what you and I should do to secure the rights which have been robbed from us." Then he called them to greater unity and community self-help. According to press reports, Douglass left the Mother Bethel congregation in "tears" and "laughter." [17] Some nights, as he fell with weariness on a stranger's spare bed or sofa, or if lucky in a private room of an inn, Douglass must have felt special pride in these encounters with so many former fugitive slaves and free-black compatriots. He had, after all, begun his orator's career in front of an AME congregation.

But such joys were always short-lived. Before leaving Pennsylvania, Douglass and Garrison faced vicious mobs reminiscent of the early 1840s on the One Hundred Conventions tour. Radical abolitionists were generally widely feared and hated, but Douglass, his fame now spreading in advance of every appearance, was a special target. As they moved west, Garrison and Douglass held a gathering in the courthouse at Harrisburg, Pennsylvania. Garrison made it through a one-hour speech undisturbed, but only minutes after Douglass took the floor a mob began hurling rotten eggs and all manner of stones and brickbats through the windows and the door while shouting their practiced refrain, "Throw out the nigger!" Douglass tried to carry on, but as eggs smashed into Garrison's head and a stone grazed Douglass's own face, the meeting broke up in chaos. With the mob screaming, "Let the damned nigger have it!," and the room filling up with what he called "slavery's choice incense," Douglass locked arms with a small group of black men who provided a protective escort out of the building. [18]

The fearless reformers stayed on two more days in Harrisburg, where they addressed the local Colored Methodist Church. "A more interesting array of faces I have seldom looked upon," Douglass warmly reported. He was especially moved by the women of the congregation, who were so well turned out and in charge of a benevolent society for self-improvement they had named the Douglass Union. But after the train stopped in Chambersburg to switch the passengers to a stagecoach for the long journey over the Allegheny Mountains to Pittsburgh, Garrison's ticket had to be reissued for the following day as Douglass traveled on alone. For the next two days and nights through mountain passes and small villages, Douglass encountered what he called "brutal insults and outrages." He was denied food along the journey, spending forty-eight hours without a meal. Discouraged and hungry, he arrived in Pittsburgh to a welcome by a local brass band and handshakes from the local black lawyer John Vashon. These kinds of pitiful ironies—a hero in small black communities one day and the object of racist attacks and humiliations the next—now formed a way of life for this young symbol of abolitionism. Before leaving the Pittsburgh area, Douglass rejoiced that among the black delegation he met the enormously talented "noble specimen of a man" Martin R. Delany. [19] Within four months the two men would collaborate to create a newspaper. Douglass's ambitions were as expansive as his courage.

By mid-August, via steamboats, canal barges, coaches, and the occasional slow train, the western tour surged into Ohio, attracting growing outdoor gatherings unlike any other American abolition had ever seen. Douglass mustered a sense of humor about the hardships of travel in this crusade of retail radicalism: "We are carried by horses, fed by corn instead of fire—bone instead of iron." People came in wagons and on horseback from many miles around to festival-like meetings from Ashtabula to Youngstown, Massillon to Leesburg, Salem to Munson. They had tapped into the grass roots of the free-labor militancy and Christian idealism of the Western Reserve. Many of these revivalist assemblages grew to between three thousand and six thousand people. As Douglass announced to a colleague, "It was pleasant to see our cause *look* popular for once." Douglass was especially impressed with the women who played such key roles in organizing these events and with those such as Lucretia Mott and Abby Kelley who took to the rostrum as speakers.[20]

As the salvation show moved across the Midwestern farmland, some of these meetings took place in the great Oberlin Tent. A thousand feet in diameter, the tent could hold up to five thousand people. This structure, spread out on a rural Midwestern landscape, surrounded by booths, covered wagons by the hundreds, and the "auctioneering," as Douglass put it, of a grand antislavery fair, was a sight never to be forgotten. The Boston abolitionists called the great tent, constructed at the abolitionist college town in northern Ohio, the portable Faneuil Hall. After local choirs sang an audience into joyous expectations, Douglass and Garrison would step up on a platform and try to project to the outer edges of the tent flaps. They preached about the usual topics, as well as the dreams of the fugitives passing through northeastern Ohio. They inveighed against Ohio's notorious "black laws," the many discriminatory statutes still on the books that prescribed the political, civil, and educational lives of free African Americans. Douglass especially continued his embittered critique of an American promise gone wrong, stymied and poisoned by slavery, racism, and complacency even out on these fertile prairies where immigrants and New Englanders had gone for renewal. Sometimes, as the Garrisonian Samuel May reported, audiences "winced" at Douglass's ridicule of the nation's religious and political life.[21]

But it was not easy performing the role of twenty-nine-year-old hero-prophet. Both men became worn-out and ill. Douglass repeatedly suffered from his "old throat complaint," and often could "hardly make himself heard." By the time they reached Youngstown, as Garrison reported, Douglass was "entirely exhausted and voiceless." He would sometimes appear with a damp cloth tied around his throat. After rising on a makeshift platform to tremendous cheers, his voice would creak and crack. Garrison fared even worse under the punishing schedule. By September he fell extremely ill, leaving the tour and remaining debilitated and at times in delirium in Cleveland with what may have been typhoid fever. Douglass surged on without him. Garrison eventually recovered and returned to Boston in autumn, but not before the entire antislavery community wondered if the western tour might be the death of him.[22]

Douglass continued the tour back into western New York, holding meetings across the state from Buffalo to Rochester to Syracuse. He repeatedly visited post offices trying to get some word of Garrison's health. This issue became one among many matters of strain and dispute later, with Garrison claiming that his protégé had left him behind and had not even inquired about his well-being. The slow but certain parting of ways of the two abolitionists soon reached an acute stage as Douglass reversed himself and decided to found his own newspaper. Still in Cleveland in late October 1847, but finally recovering from his illness, Garrison wrote a long letter to his wife, Helen, ending with an embittered PS: "Is it not strange that Douglass has not written a single line to me, or to any one, inquiring after my health, since he left me on a bed of illness?" But worse, the weakened mentor felt silently rebuked and betrayed about the newspaper: "He never opened to me his lips on the subject," wrote Garrison, "nor asked my advice in any particular whatsoever. Such conduct grieves me to the heart." The *Liberator*'s founder had opposed Douglass's independent venture, which the young editor called the *North Star*, from the very inception of the idea; Garrison vowed that it "must be met with firmness," and he intended to determine who was "at the bottom of all of this."[23] Douglass had challenged the house of Garrison, which had formed and nurtured him, but could no longer fully contain his ambitions.

On the western tour, Douglass had laid the groundwork for the venture, especially by enlisting Martin Delany as a coeditor and connecting once again with his friends Amy and Isaac Post in Rochester. He also enlisted the black Garrisonian William Cooper Nell to join him as publisher, and John Dick, an Englishman who would relocate to Rochester to be Douglass's printer. Before returning home finally to Lynn in October, Douglass spent four days in Albany and Troy, New York, where he participated among the

William Lloyd Garrison, c. 1851.
Daguerreotype. Albert Sands Southworth
and Josiah John Hawes photographers.

sixty-six delegates at a National Colored Convention. Albany was a rough town, where Douglass yet again endured racist attacks, much of which he attributed to the "flood of immorality and disgusting brutality" arriving via the Erie Canal. Among the resolutions passed at the convention was one to create a "national press" for blacks. Tellingly, Douglass abstained on the resolution, knowing that he was about to announce his own paper, and holding his cards close to his chest.[24]

From the day he launched the idea of becoming an independent journalist, so much depended on his British benefactors. Some of them, especially Englishwomen who wrote to Maria Weston Chapman at the AASS office regaling her with how much they "loved," were "inspired by," or felt "deeply attached to" Frederick, had spilled the beans about the newspaper at the very headquarters of Garrisonianism. Nothing fired Chapman's ready suspicion about Douglass's evolving apostasy more than those adoring messages from British women. Chapman was, after all, trying to raise money for the *Liberator* from these same women. Douglass did not tell Garrison himself about his new intentions, a problem common in strained father-and-son-like relationships. The AASS had made it possible for Douglass to write his regular letters and columns in the *National Anti-Slavery Standard*, hoping that this would satisfy his desires in journalism.[25] But nothing could stop Douglass's quest to launch this new chapter in the making of his voice.

Douglass repeatedly said that he wanted to have his own enterprise as a mouthpiece for his race. But in a letter to his English friend Julia Griffiths, he revealed the deeper well of his ambition. With the help of numerous British comrades, many of whom Douglass named, Julia had sent Frederick a large "collection of books, pamphlets, tracts, and pictures," all to aid him on his journey to journalism. Griffiths's father, Thomas, a printer and publisher, had been one of the organizers of the farewell soiree for Douglass in London, an event Julia had attended with her sister, Eliza. Douglass was deeply moved by the gift, but even in this tender note of gratitude he remained the autobiographer watching his own life: "You will the more readily understand my pleasure at receiving such a gift when I tell you that but a few years ago, the fingers now penning this note of thanks, were used in fishing from the muddy street gutters in Baltimore, scattered pages of the Bible." Douglass conducted his public quest to destroy slavery and to be somebody with an eye almost always squinting in a backward glance to the Eastern Shore. "What a contrast is my present with my former condition. Then a slave, now a free man; then degraded, now respected; then ignorant . . . my name unheard of beyond the limits of a republican slave plantation; now my friends and benefactors, people of both hemispheres, to heaven the praise belongs!"[26] Within a year and a half Julia herself would join Douglass's newspaper enterprise.

By late October Douglass was "buying type and all the little &c.s of a printing establishment," as he informed Amy Post. British money kept flowing into Lynn in a timely fashion; he acknowledged a generous draft for £445 from Jonathan D. Carr, a successful Quaker biscuit manufacturer in Carlisle, who served as a treasurer among the Douglass fund-raising network in England. Douglass named the paper the North Star and in November moved to Rochester, a thriving city of fifty thousand, a hub on the Erie Canal, and a significant haven for fugitive slaves on their way to Canada. He rented an office in the Talman Building at 25 Buffalo Street, in the heart of the business district. Until February 1848, he boarded with Charles Joiner, a local black clothes cleaner, leaving his family back in Lynn. Once again, Anna and the children waited for the next disruption in their lives. Douglass plowed all of his money into the North Star, buying a printing press, which proved faulty. He repeatedly took on debt to keep the paper afloat during its first uncertain year. But the first issue came out on December 3, 1847, and Douglass made it clear that he was a political abolitionist in the making. In an open letter to the Whig Party leader, Henry Clay, Douglass unleashed a fierce attack on the Kentuckian's alleged moderation as a slaveholder. Clay, according to the new editor, was the worst of all things—a well-meaning slaveholder—and his alleged "benevolence" merely "so much of Satan dressed in the livery of Heaven." [27]

Douglass launched the *North Star* with great exuberance, and though it spoke for "Liberty, Humanity, and Progress," as he stated in the opening prospectus, the paper was to be a proud black enterprise. It would do what "it would be wholly impossible for our white friends to do for us." The four earlier black-edited papers had all been short-lived. "Our race must be vindicated from the embarrassing implications resulting from former non-success," Douglass announced. In a separate plea written directly to black readers, he promised to attack slavery in the South and racism in the North with equal fervor. He would offer himself as their voice assailing the "ramparts of Slavery and Prejudice." He further promised to advocate for rights, but also to chastise his fellow blacks when necessary about their obligations and failures. Above all he offered himself as model, "one with you," having "writhed beneath the bloody lash" and "under the slander of inferiority." He would vehemently promote learning in all its forms, but "accord most merit to those who have labored hardest, and overcome most in . . . pursuit of knowledge." [28] This was a black paper edited by a former slave! Irony was often Douglass's principal rhetorical weapon; now he boldly offered himself as its very embodiment.

He had taken a great risk. Douglass did not yet know how to edit a newspaper. Delany had some experience, sporadically editing his own *Mystery* (which ended in early 1847) in Pittsburgh, but his role was to go on the road all over the North to solicit subscriptions in black communities. When the printing press proved ineffective, Douglass had to hire out the printing to William Clough, one floor above the *North Star*'s office, for approximately $20 weekly. This fledgling operation stumbled along into 1848; subscriptions grew to approximately seven hundred by mid-January, with papers eventually sent before year's end to Britain, Canada, Mexico, Australia, and even parts of the South. In December, Douglass received a warm letter of support from Gerrit Smith, the wealthy upstate New York abolitionist, containing $5 for a two-year subscription, and signaling the beginning of an important long-term relationship with the rich political activist. Frustratingly, however, only handfuls of blacks took the paper, although Douglass did receive accolades from some fellow black abolitionists and friends. One of them, William Cooper Nell, worked hard for the *North Star*, but he struggled with his conflicted loyalties to Garrison and the *Liberator*. [29]

Delany, on the other hand, traveled widely on a "western tour" of free black communities during 1848, soliciting readers and subscriptions as well as writing a remarkable array of travel letters published in the paper. It has often been assumed that the Douglass-Delany partnership, because they soon severed ties and eventually became ideological rivals, crippled the *North Star* in its first years. But Delany's literary output for Douglass's paper left an important mark. Frustrations abounded, however, between the two men. In mid-January 1848, Douglass seemed frantic to know Delany's whereabouts, complaining about $55-per-week expenses, slow growth in subscriptions, and going to press yet "again much to my regret without a single line from your pen." A week later Douglass did receive the first of twenty-three public letters Delany would produce over the next thirteen months from such "western" cities as Pittsburgh, Columbus, Cincinnati, Cleveland, and Detroit. As Douglass wrote every week for the paper, while constantly running around upstate New York to lecture for fees that helped pay bills, Delany visited schools, churches, fraternal orders, and courtrooms in small communities across the Midwest, reporting back a kind of ethnography about the needs for "elevation" among the very people he and Douglass were trying to attract into their readership. Still, few bought subscriptions, leaving Douglass discouraged about the "uphill" task before them as he did "all I can by lectures and letters to keep our heads above the water." [30]

Whether Douglass and Delany were ever really "co-editors," as the masthead claimed, is doubtful. The two men hailed from quite different backgrounds. Born free in western Virginia, educated at the Harvard Medical School, Delany was six years older than Douglass and did not fit well as a subordinate partner. They had lived different lives; Delany was much darker than the lead editor and knew that all of his grandparents were African. But for a while they sustained an effective collaboration. In the spring and summer of 1848, Delany's letters from Pennsylvania and Ohio maintained a steady drumbeat for black self-improvement, a theme Douglass himself championed. They saw themselves as preceptors of black uplift within a rigidly racist society.

"Colored People!" Delany proclaimed, "we want more businessmen among us; farmers, mechanics and tradesmen. . . . Let our people put their children—first to school, next to trades." All over growing Ohio he spotted "respectable and praiseworthy" black families and was especially taken with the "cleanliness" of the cottages in the town of Hamilton. Douglass wrote a stinging editorial in July, "What Are the Colored People Doing for Themselves," in which he prodded blacks to higher attainments of "being

Martin R. Delany, 1860s.

honest, industrious, sober and intelligent," as he also berated them for not
subscribing to his newspaper. A hectoring Douglass complained that free
blacks might attend an Odd Fellows or a Freemason convention by the
thousands but could not stoop to read his paper. He bashed black preachers
and churches for filling their pews on Sundays but not "meddling with abolitionism" on weekdays. He wanted his people to "read . . . speak and write,"
and then to act. "What is the use of standing a man on his feet," declared
the discouraged editor, "if when we let him go, his head is again brought
to the pavement?" In what served as a motto of his own early life, Douglass
shouted from the page, "For the want of knowledge we are killed all day!"
With equally potent zeal, Delany preached from the same text in Midwestern depots such as Chillicothe and Cyrus Settlement.[31]

But both men too kept up a constant exposure of the racist mob violence that Delany encountered on the road, and which Douglass knew
all too well. They also levied an embittered critique of the black laws that
barred free blacks from courts of law, civic life, or the ballot box. As it
limped from week to week, the *North Star* became both a repository and a
trumpet for the great dual cause of black abolitionism—internal commu-

nity self-improvement and the external quest for citizenship. And it was a presidential election year; Douglass made sure the *North Star* kept one eye on the broiling issue of slavery expansion animating national politics.[32] Despite his financial worries, that editor's desk forced Douglass to think more broadly about the power and limits of words, and the nature of antislavery activism.

In this frenzied time, Douglass went back to Lynn and moved his family to Rochester in February 1848. The move was difficult for Anna; she had made a life for herself in Lynn, as a mother, a shoe binder, and seamstress who had lived more months without her husband than with him over the past six years. What she knew and understood of Frederick's world of ideas, friends, travels, and experiences she had processed through protective psychological barriers. This talented domestic woman, who remained illiterate next to the man made and sustained by words, packed up her three boys (Rosetta remained in Albany with her governesses, the Mott sisters) and trekked across Massachusetts and upstate New York to a small tenement in downtown Rochester. Isaac Post helped to secure the apartment. But no wonder Douglass wrote to the Mott sisters just after the family's move complaining of his "gloomy" circumstances. He was a "most unhappy man," he confessed. His "house hunting" floundered and Anna had "not been well—or very good humored since we came here." Douglass often unloaded his personal woes in letters to his best women friends, many of whom seemed thoroughly willing to perform as his sounding board. He missed those "words of love and sympathy" the Motts might provide him. He missed Rosetta and wished she would write to him more so he could "see her hand writing." And the travails of his lecturing travels weighed on him. "This riding all night is killing me," he moaned.[33]

In April the Douglasses purchased a house from a local abolitionist at 4 Alexander Street. The two-story, nine-room brick dwelling had a front porch where Anna could put a rocker and a yard for a garden as spring arrived. Upstairs, Douglass had a study with a table, books, and a "list of the words he found it hard to spell," as a neighbor reported. The children entered schools and Anna likely made some connections with the small black community of some 162 households in Rochester. All was not sour in the Douglasses' marriage; that summer they conceived their fifth child. In a personal reminiscence written in 1917, the youngest son, Charles, recalled a rosy, sentimental homestead at Alexander Street, where he and his brothers attended common schools but were increasingly "taken from school one day in each week to deliver the paper to local subscribers," or to learn type-setting. Charles believed the *North Star* survived as a collective family enter-prise: "To maintain this paper, every effort was put forth by every member of the family to keep it alive."[34]

But life on Alexander Street and getting out the paper on Buffalo Street were much more complex matters. Douglass never had enough money in these years and would soon have to mortgage his house again to pay his staff at the newspaper. In late April he wrote to Julia Griffiths that he was struggling to "find the bright side of the future." He worried openly that he might have "undertaken more than I have the ability to perform." He feared he had "miscalculated . . . the amount of support which would be extended to my enterprise." In this cry for help Douglass complained that Delany had not done enough to raise subscriptions, leaving the editor alone doing everything. He confessed that he had "expended more than the some [*sic*] sent me from England, and shall require sixty dollars per week for six months to come in order to keep my paper a float."[35] Douglass dearly needed help. Griffiths, who wrote to him frequently and sent him leading British newspapers, heard his cry. She visited him in Rochester for a short time later that fall, steadied his spirits, and a year later, in May 1849, making an extraordinary commitment, relocated to America and helped the *North Star*, and Frederick himself, survive into the 1850s.

Douglass's maintenance of an equilibrium amid all these pressures of home and his own ambition defied the odds. In part, he managed from month to month because of Anna's steadfast care for the children and the hearth; she was his ultimate "helpmeet," as he admitted many times. The family stood waiting there on each of his homecomings, and the *North Star* was theirs as well. Douglass sustained his inner psychological standing in part by the sheer force of will and what he called his "pen and tongue." That he managed to keep the *North Star* alive through those first years is a testament to his stamina and his growing felicity with the short essay. He had established himself as a world-class orator. But the newspaper now be-came his reason to be. The *North Star* "shall live" or "must be sustained," he would often say, not as a mere expression of business enterprise, but for his own sheer existence. The paper became, as he later recalled, the "motive power" of his life. Douglass tested his ideas and began to grasp the land-scape of politics through the lens of the *North Star*. "It was the best school possible for me," he wrote. "It obliged me to think and read, it taught me to express my thoughts clearly." He had to produce the words that were both burden and liberation. "I had an audience to speak to every week, and must say something worth their hearing or cease to speak altogether." Douglass relished what he called his editor's "sting of necessity," and his evolving voice became both more pragmatic and more radical as it became more political.[36]

That summer of 1848, Douglass made one of his big strides into the politics of reform by supporting women's rights and participating at the Seneca Falls convention on July 19–20. The idea for such a convention had longed brewed among feminists and women's rights advocates. Elizabeth Cady Stanton, who lived in Seneca Falls, and a group of Quaker women gathered around Mary Ann M'Clintock and her two daughters, Mary Ann and Elizabeth, in Waterloo, New York, along with the skillful aid of Lucretia Mott, put out a call for a convention in the *Seneca County Courier* on July 11. Douglass responded immediately by running the appeal in the *North Star* on July 14. Some three hundred people attended the two-day historic assembly in the Wesleyan Methodist Chapel of Seneca Falls. Douglass eagerly joined his Rochester friend Amy Post at the convention. The gathering was largely local with attendees coming mainly from the upstate region. Some husbands of these women reformers, as well as other male abolitionists, attended, but most did not. Issues of women's place, much less equal rights, had long been lightning rods in the antislavery movement in Britain and the United States.[37]

But Douglass never exhibited any ambiguity or caution. His many women friends had taught him much. The convention famously produced a "Declaration of Sentiments," modeled directly on the Declaration of Independence. With the word *women* inserted ("all men and women are created equal") where appropriate, the more than a dozen resolutions accompanying the document covered all manner of demands for equality in jobs, in courts of law, in family relations, religion, and education. All resolutions passed unanimously except the controversial claim for the elective franchise. So contested was the issue of voting that many women leaders, such as Lucretia Mott, refused to support it, fearing they would lose the ultimate hope of gaining any rights because of this demand. But during the afternoon debate of the second day's meeting, Douglass forcefully endorsed full women's suffrage, which may have helped win the day in a divided vote. In his *North Star* report about Seneca Falls, Douglass expressed great pride at participating and called the demands "simple justice." He freely admitted that all in favor of women's equality courted "ridicule . . . fury and bigotry." But he did not equivocate. Civil society had been deprived too long of the labor and talent of half the human family, he said. "There can be no reason in the world for denying to woman the exercise of the elective franchise." Douglass was the only black person attending the Seneca Falls convention, and it remained a matter of lifetime pride that he was among the thirty-two men and sixty-eight women who signed the "Declaration of Sentiments." He would always be delighted to be called "a women's rights man." The motto on the masthead of the *North Star*, "Right is of No Color and No Sex," had been no mere sentiment.[38]

Throughout 1848, Douglass took an ever-keener interest in national politics, even as he managed still to denounce the corruptions of parties. One Douglass biographer sees the editor's overall *North Star* prose style as "rather solemnly polemical," while another points to his love of "irony, humor and ambiguity" and therefore a prose that "sounded more genteel."[39] Neither is wrong, but it is hard to miss how Douglass's journalistic as well as oratorical voice in these years sounded furious and militant as he became more political. His rhetoric carried more Old Testament pain and rage; Jeremiah caught a second wind. He took up the editor's pen to provoke his readers into action. The humor and entertainment of the lecture hall gave way to opinion and the persuasiveness of the editorial. To that person who had called him the "demagogue in black," it was as if Douglass responded by saying something like *Thank you; if you want a demagogue, I will give you a demagogue.* His model journalist, after all, was William Lloyd Garrison.

Douglass read widely in the national and the British press about the republican revolutions breaking out all over Europe, especially in France in February and March 1848. He took heart as monarchy and slavery in the French empire came under assault from a movement of universal egalitarianism. "We live in stirring times and amid thrilling events," he told an audience at a West Indian emancipation celebration in Rochester on August 1. Brandishing historical detail, he turned a shared identity with the French proletariat back onto the "atrocious wickedness" of American slavery. While Europeans strove to free themselves from centuries of tyranny, Americans could only mouth awkward half-truths of support, and voters could only choose between "tyrants and men-stealers to rule over us."[40]

In revolutionary times, Douglass concluded, "some lives may indeed be lost." In public he frequently invoked the memory of Nat Turner as a noble slave rebel to compare to the French, Germans, and Italians at their barricades, gunned down in the streets. Douglass now mixed this early embrace of violent means with one of his favorite tactics—heaping blame on white Northerners for their complicity with slavery. In a speech in Faneuil Hall in

Boston, he told his friendly auditors, "You are the enslavers of my southern brethren and sisters." By their participation under the US Constitution, he similarly charged the Rochester throng on August 1 with bringing the "bristling bayonets of the whole military power of the nation" down on the lives of slaves. Had not Nat Turner, Douglass intoned, only acted with the "self-same means which the Revolutionary fathers employed?" Those Rochester journalists who remarked about the "sarcastic tones" and the "bitterness" of Douglass's public rhetoric had heard him loud and clear.[41]

Douglass also pulled the story back within the human heart. On September 3, 1848, the tenth anniversary of his escape from slavery, he published a public letter to his former master, Thomas Auld. The letter is a masterpiece of antislavery propaganda as well as an expression of personal rage. Although the missive contained some inaccuracies—especially the accusation that Auld had abandoned Betsy Bailey out to fields to fend for herself or die—which Douglass later had to recant, Auld's former property boldly put his old master to *his* service. With Auld as his model, Douglass flayed every slaveholder who had ever lifted a lash or sold a human being. This was Douglass's personal symbolic whipping of Auld and an indictment in front of a jury of history. The chosen tool of punishment was the pen.[42]

Douglass had many times used Auld as the "slaveholder" in speeches, especially when exposing the religious hypocrisy of Southern Methodists. Now, Douglass addressed him directly by name and dared him not to listen. The letter is funny, falsely and formally delicate, and at times quite moving. A Douglass biographer has contended that the letter is "one of the strangest pieces in the literature of American slavery" because of its "peculiar distortions." But accuracy is not the best measure of the letter. Douglass sought new recruits for the abolition cause and readers for the *North Star.* He hit some new notes as he settled some old scores. He played with Auld, offering a justification for invading the "proprieties of private life" in his former owner's quiet corner of the Eastern Shore. "I will not manifest ill temper by calling you hard names," he assured Auld. But he also made his intent explicit: "I intend to make use of you as a weapon with which to assail the system of slavery." Douglass did flail about a bit; but he landed many reverberating blows. He prompted angry responses to the humiliation of Auld from as far away as a slaveholder in Georgia who wrote, "As emancipationists you colored fellows are the worst. . . . As well may the dog claim to be a man, as the negro a free man and equal among those that God designed to be his superior. The order of nature can be as soon reverted to any good in the one case as in the other."[43]

In addressing Auld, Douglass lectured him about the natural right to self-ownership: "I am myself; you are yourself; we are two distinct persons, equal persons. What you are I am. . . . God created both, and made us separate beings. I am not by nature bound to you, or you to me. Nature does not make your existence depend upon me, or mine to depend upon yours." Douglass especially used Auld to demonstrate how far his slave had risen, how he had created a family, how he had made the successful "transition from degradation to respectability." He pointed to his comfortable house, his "industrious and neat" wife, his "four dear children," three of whom were in school. Then, by contrast, in the most moving lines of the letter, he wrenched his readers into slavery's domestic heart of darkness: "They [the children] are all in comfortable beds, and are sound asleep, perfectly secure under my roof. There are no slaveholders here to rend my heart by snatching them from my arms, or blast a mother's dearest hopes by tearing them from her bosom." Here, Douglass's rage against slavery found its outlet: "Oh! Sir, a slaveholder never appears to me so completely an agent of hell, as when I think of and look upon my dear children. It is then that my feelings rise above my control."[44]

Mercilessly, Douglass dragged Auld back into their shared history, with the tides turned: "Say not that this is a picture of fancy. You well know that I wear stripes on my back inflicted by your direction; and that you, while we were brothers in the same church, caused this right hand, with which I am now penning this letter, to be closely tied to my left, and my person dragged at the pistol's mouth, fifteen miles, from the Bay side to Easton to be sold like a beast in the market."[45] Douglass avoids how Auld did not sell him south, but sent him back to Baltimore. In 1848 the facts were aligned thus for a reason. A liberated Douglass, man of letters, must still be seen through the lens of the manacled Fred Bailey. He loved the reversal and reworked his story on Auld's back.

The letter to Auld was a public humiliation, a symbolic indictment of all the thousands of white slaveholding "fathers" through the years. Douglass demands to know from Auld whether he had sold his sisters. He even insists that his former owner imagine Douglass invading Auld's St. Michaels house, kidnapping his own daughter, Amanda, and selling her to the "brutal lust of fiendish overseers." Although there was no evidence that Auld had ever broken up families or sold away Frederick's female kin,

Douglass used the letter as a defense of the virtue of black womanhood.[46] In Douglass's innuendo about the rape of his mother, and in trading on slavery's sexual nightmares, as well as the mystery of his own paternity, he gave to antislavery literature this barely controlled eruption of human rage.

The *North Star* had to get written, edited, and printed every week. The nation's evolving crisis over slavery's expansion in the wake of the Mexican War, and especially the presidential election that fall, had to be explained. Douglass often blurred the lines between his private and public alienation. The demands of succinctness in the columns of the newspaper provided a disciplined retreat for this man of words, barely holding on to an equipoise he only half comprehended. Venting on Auld and blasting the slaveholding nation became one and the same task. In the election of 1848, Douglass supported the new Free Soil Party and its candidate, former president Martin Van Buren; Douglass even attended its convention in Buffalo in September. But he was deeply disappointed by the election of the slaveholder war hero General Zachary Taylor. In a postelection editorial, "The Blood of the Slave on the Skirts of the Northern People," Douglass wryly apologized if he "should seem severe" or "speak harshly." But he felt "a thousand poisonous stings" in his heart as he reflected on the state of the Union. Douglass told white Northern voters that the "blood of the slave is on your garments. . . . You have said that slavery is better than freedom—that war is better than peace, and that cruelty is better than humanity."[47]

Douglass kept Jeremiah's sword sharpened, addressing the nation as his audience: "What mean ye that ye bruise and bind my people? Will justice sleep forever? . . . Repent of this wickedness . . . by delivering the despoiled out of the hands of the despoiler." He refused to extend peace where there was no peace. Douglass signaled hope with the only weapon in his arsenal. Abolition would spring forth, he contended, "from the press and on the voice of the living speaker, words of burning truth, to alarm the guilty, to unmask the hypocrite, to expose the frauds of political parties, and rebuke the spirit of a corrupt and sin-sustaining church." Douglass announced, without fully knowing it, the theme of his and the country's life for the next decade: "Slavery will be attacked in its stronghold—the compromises of the Constitution, and the cry of disunion shall be more fearlessly proclaimed, till slavery be abolished, the Union dissolved, or the sun of this guilty nation must go down in blood."[48]

Words that burn—Douglass's stock-in-trade. He borrowed a page from Nat Turner as he also strove to honor the principles of Garrison. Ultimately he could not do both. Soon, Julia Griffiths arrived from England to help him navigate these troubled waters.

Chapter 12

MY FAITHFUL
FRIEND JULIA

Miss Griffiths . . . is industriously wielding her pen at another desk.

—FREDERICK DOUGLASS, MAY 21, 1851

By the early 1850s Frederick Douglass underwent a terrible estrangement from William Lloyd Garrison, experienced an ideological transformation in his view of antislavery strategy under the influence of Gerrit Smith, and to a great extent survived personally and professionally because of his friendship with Julia Griffiths. It was a time of loss and new imaginings, private despair, and a new public-political purpose for his life. As usual, although with new extremes, he was under attack. "Let no man hope to succeed in insulting me," Douglass announced on May 7, 1850, in his speech at the annual meeting of the American Anti-Slavery Society in New York.[1] This most turbulent gathering the old organization had ever held occurred during the intense debate in Washington, DC, over the Compromise of 1850 and its notorious Fugitive Slave Act. Fear for the Union and social order, as well as racist resistance to black assertions of civil liberty and to abolitionism, flowed into the Broadway Tabernacle where the activists met.

Some New York papers, especially the Democratic Party organ, the *Herald*, had ginned up great hostility and suggested violence against the AASS in advance of the meetings. As Garrison attempted to deliver the opening address, a mob stormed the platform, "yelling, cheering, swearing." They were led by Isaiah Rynders, a notorious gang leader and Tammany Hall boss of the Sixth Ward and the Five Points district. Profanely violent and racist, Rynders, born of Irish and German parents in upstate New York, was at the height of his powers in lower Manhattan's streets and faced no resistance from the hapless New York police who also attended the gathering. Rynders's gangs, known by names such as Plug Uglies or Dead Rabbits, were particularly adept at using clubs, knives, and guns to foment riots on behalf of some Irish interests. Notorious as a "sporting man" involved in gambling, horse racing, and boxing, Rynders was, according to one historian, "the nation's foremost political thug." But the Bible-quoting Rynders also possessed rhetorical skill at repartee and insult. Oddly, in the spirit of free speech, Garrison and the abolitionists invited the mob to have their say in what became a theater of the absurd.[2]

A "Mr. Grant," the orator designated by Rynders to speak for the mob, argued that blacks were not human but part of the monkey species and that the mixing of blacks and whites at this assembly violated "nature . . . and nature's God." Many among the disoriented, pacifist abolitionists began to shout for Douglass to speak. Douglass rose to the call and held forth, although bizarrely with "Captain Rynders at his elbow," as the press reported. At first Douglass walked into Rynders's trap by making himself and racial identity the subject. He complained about Grant's inhumane claims about blacks and appealed to the audience to look him [Douglass] in the face and at his "woolly head" and asked, "Am I not a man?" Rynders then made one of his frequent interruptions while standing at Douglass's side. "You are not a black man; you are only half a nigger," fumed the ward boss. To which Douglass replied, causing roars of laughter, "He is correct; I am, indeed, only half a negro, a half brother to Mr. Rynders."[3]

Douglass gave as he took in this dangerous situation, turning humiliation into humor. Declaring himself "from the South" and a "son of a slaveholder," Douglass suggested that if Rynders wished to "preach against amalgamation," he should aim at white men who wrote the laws so they could exploit their female slaves. Speaking as a black man, Douglass dared to challenge "my half brother Rynders" and all Irish immigrants, who "recently landed on these shores," enjoying greater privileges than African Americans. Amidst epithets of "mongrels all," Douglass made the case for blacks as older immigrants who had "watered the soil with our tears, and fertilized it with our blood." Their labor had "raised the cotton for the shirts on your backs" and "produced the sugar that sweetens your coffee." Douglass had long preferred associations with a different sort of Irish, the middle-class reformers and Quakers who had nurtured and adored him in Cork or Dublin. Here, in this grotesque sport of raw American racism and antebellum identity wars, he felt empowered to exhibit his own mind and body in contrast to those of his vicious opponents. "We only want our rights," Douglass pleaded in conclusion. "I care not whether I am descended from a man or a monkey. . . . I have a head to think, and I know God meant I should exercise the right to think. . . . I have a heart to feel, and a tongue to speak . . . and God meant that I should use that tongue in behalf of humanity and justice for every man." [4]

But Rynders's thugs had not come for a history lecture; they had no stamina to hear a black man's eloquent complaints. Remarkably, the two hours of disruption and confusion ended without violence; Rynders and his mob left the hall with apparent satisfaction that they had lampooned the hated abolitionists and their favored black orator. Douglass, as long as he survived to tell it, seemed to enjoy having Rynders as his foil. And for his part, Rynders later admitted that Douglass's response to him at the anti-slavery meeting was "as good a shot as I ever had in my life." [5]

Douglass, however, had one more violent humiliation to endure in New York. He attended the AASS meetings in the company of Julia Griffiths and her younger sister, Eliza. Julia had arrived in Rochester in May 1849 for what may have been planned as a permanent stay. For part of a year already she had been working as the business manager, fund-raiser, and assistant editor on the *North Star*. She lived in Douglass's home, and under her management the paper had increased in subscriptions and editorial quality. Eliza and John Dick, the printer in the *North Star* office, also boarded in the Douglasses' house. Eliza and John were about to be married and would emigrate to Canada in June 1850. [6]

The day after the AASS meetings ended, while awaiting his ferry for an engagement in Philadelphia, Douglass strolled in Battery Park at the lower tip of Manhattan with the Griffiths sisters. Reports conflict about whether they were "arm in arm," but according to Douglass, his presence on this fashionable promenade with two white ladies prompted a mob of a half dozen to assault them. Using "coarse and filthy language," several of the thugs struck the sisters on the head while one of them assaulted Douglass. The abolitionist fended them off with his umbrella, and they seemed to disperse, although as the Douglass party neared the steamer dock, one assailant jumped Douglass again and slugged him in the face. The attack soon appeared all over the press, including in London, where the *Times* reprinted articles from the *New York Globe* that argued Douglass deserved the attacks not only for his "audacious and disgraceful" violation of racial-sexual propriety, but for his "abusing" his "country, its patriots and constitution" in recent speeches. According to these versions of the incident, an "indignant gentleman" had graciously "separated" Douglass from the white women and given the black man a "dressing" he deserved.[7]

As before, Douglass used this attack for its fullest propaganda value, while revealing a good deal about himself and his relationship with Julia. In his account of the incident he declared the abuse in New York the most "demoniacal" he had ever endured. He felt as though he lived in "an enemy's land—surrounded on all sides." And he happily pled guilty to all charges, "glorying in having committed them," if it meant that the crime was "to be a man, entitled to all rights, privileges and dignity." He claimed the right to associate with anyone, including his white female friends, in public places. In editorials he admitted that his attackers were vicious people, but maintained they served as the appointed "bloodhounds of American slavery."[8]

Douglass turned the affair into an incisive analysis of racism. His offense, he argued, had never been the companionship with white women, but the assumption of equality with them. America's "aristocracy of skin" could not tolerate such behavior. He drew deep from nine years of lecturing and travel, declaring that he "could not remember to have made a single antislavery tour" when he had "not been assailed by this mean spirit of caste." Douglass argued that the term "prejudice" was simply too weak and "innocent" to capture what blacks endured. A more "savage" language was required to match the beliefs of all the Rynderses inside and outside of power. "Properly speaking," Douglass contended, "prejudice against color does not exist in this country. The feeling (or whatever it is) which we call prejudice, is no less than a *murderous, hell-born hatred* of every virtue which may adorn the character of a black man." Black men were acceptable when "appendages," he said. While "riding down Broadway in company with ladies," Douglass wrote, they observed "several white ladies riding with black servants." Those well-dressed carriage drivers did not offend the hooligans who attacked Douglass and his companions. Douglass relished his "impudence"; equality, not color, offended.[9] He had given definition and texture to the idea of racism. And he and Griffiths, daily colleagues in a struggle of head and heart, now had a bold public experience of violence that cemented their bond.

The abiding friendship of Frederick and Julia must be understood within this world of raw, belligerent racism. The handsome and most famous black man in the United States simply would not give in to its power. And he dearly needed the powers and skills that Griffiths brought to his work and life. Unmarried, seven years older than her host, and raised with deep reform commitments, Griffiths adored both Douglass and his cause. Little is known about Griffiths's early education, but she brought a knowledge of grammar, business acumen, and even political savvy to Douglass's office. Indeed, Douglass gave Griffiths not only acknowledgment for her talents, but for several years he gave her the *career* this Victorian woman had never achieved. Soon after her arrival in Rochester in May 1849, she wielded a "blue pencil" on the editor's copy, as she chastised the printers and their boss alike for the *North Star*'s misspellings and errors. Whether their connection had ever been love at first sight, as some have suggested, is speculation. She did write a song in honor of Douglass's departure from England, "Farewell to Frederick Douglass," which was published in London in 1847. But Griffiths was no mere starry-eyed devotee. She was a manager of business affairs, as well as of people. She was a voracious reader and learner; her devotion to radical abolitionism provided what the movement often desperately needed—astute organization, financial foundation, and an apparently pure commitment to help Douglass go out and be Douglass. She soon composed a regular column for the newspaper, "Literary Notices," signaling new books and magazines available at a local bookstore. She possessed a wide knowledge of literature, classical and popular. Griffiths also had a hand in some editorials and many times helped get the weekly paper out in the editor's absence.[10] No matter how awkward things became for Anna and the children at the house in Rochester, the *North Star*'s editor was all too glad to have Julia as a daily colleague.

This extraordinary and ultimately untenable situation of an educated white Englishwoman living in the Douglass home and laboring daily with him on his life's work, while Anna Douglass raised five children in its midst, leads us to wonder whether the relationship was ever sexual. We do not know for sure, and perhaps it does not matter. The tenderness of their associations and correspondence, and the intimacy with which Julia seems to have nurtured her younger hero, might lead us moderns to assume that of course they slept with each other. But right under the watchful eyes and immediate presence of Anna? Not likely. They already violated norms of appearance, whether they shared a bed or not. Griffiths's intelligence and deep caring were surely attractive to Frederick. Their mutual affection did not need to be sexual to be fulfilling, at least for Frederick. When Isaac Post met Julia, he described her as older than he expected. Samuel J. May called her "an ordinary looking white woman," although the famed British abolitionist George Thompson, upon his visit and fete with fifty guests at Douglass's house in 1851, made no notice of Anna while observing that he "had a pleasant evening irradiated by the mild splendor of a certain Julia." [11]

Frederick and Julia's quite public acknowledgment of a close working relationship implies that they kept things as proper as possible. Julia played many roles at the homestead, including unsuccessful attempts at tutoring Anna in literacy, and some care of the younger children. Julia provided many things Anna did not—intellectual companionship and challenge, a female face toward the public when he needed it, and a nurturing that the struggling thirty- to thirty-five-year-old Douglass desperately needed. Julia served a practical end as well—she raised a good deal of money that fed his family and kept the newspaper afloat. Indeed, in August 1849, during the full year that both Julia and Eliza boarded with the Douglasses on Alexander Street, they purchased with their own money the mortgage on the house, relieving Frederick and Anna of a huge worry. By 1850, like it or not, Anna and the family depended on Julia's presence. [12]

Douglass had already struck up a strong relationship with Gerrit Smith, the wealthy upstate New York abolitionist, before Julia arrived on the scene. But she helped cultivate that crucial connection, both financially and ideologically. In the summer of 1850, in one of her letters to Smith about the dire straits of the *North Star*, Griffiths reminded the philanthropist of her key role. "Remember dear sir, I am the Banker for the paper—& know always precisely how the accounts stand." [13] That is far more than Douglass could ever say on his own. Julia helped to polish a raw genius into a gem and, for a time, managed his emotional health as well as his bank accounts.

Gerrit Smith was a man of enormous emotional complexity, religious fervor, antislavery commitment, and wealth. By 1850 he had put aside long-standing ties to old colonizationists, then to Garrisonian moral suasion, as well as the temperance movement, and embraced political abolitionism. Along the way he was even a Millerite for a while, adopting the millennialist William Miller's predictions of Christ's second coming in 1843. Smith had been raised in the "mansion house" of his father, Peter Smith, in Peterboro, New York. Peter, an uneducated man and cold father, had amassed great wealth as a land baron in upstate New York, traded with Indian tribes such as the Oneida, and held numerous slaves, with whom his sons worked side by side until the Panic of 1819. As a young intellectual, Gerrit sought an education at Hamilton College in Clinton, New York, and fashioned himself a romantic Byronic hero who would become a man of letters. Smith never gave up entirely on his literary aspirations even after he inherited and reluctantly took over his father's huge estate.

Always susceptible to wild mood swings, Smith underwent a variety of religious conversions, first after the death of his beloved mother and his first wife, named Wealtha, within a year of their marriage in 1819, and again in the 1820s and 1830s as religious revivals spread through the region. By the time Douglass and Smith connected after the orator's move to Rochester, the Sage of Peterboro had established a "circle" of followers who would use political institutions, the Constitution, and the vote to try to crush the Slave Power in the United States.[14] Douglass, long chafing under Garrisonian strictures and open to new ideas, found Smith's overtures—toward political action, the Liberty Party, and an antislavery interpretation of the Constitution—irresistible.

From the beginning, Douglass and Smith engaged in an increasingly intense correspondence. Julia's interventions now enhanced the two distinct dimensions of this friendship, the one practical and pecuniary and the other intellectual and strategic. Smith was an early supporter of the *North Star.* But as Douglass struggled to keep the paper alive in the spring of 1849, he groused about being broke to the man with deep pockets. "My money is now all gone," the editor reported; he was at least $200 in debt. Douglass declared himself out on a limb. His "best friends" (Garrisonians) thought his venture unnecessary and "useless"; he had started the paper against their wishes. Douglass eagerly courted the donor. As Smith responded by sending small checks, he also aggressively recruited Douglass to the cause of political abolition.[15] Smith's new protégé would take most of a year to fully give in to the new ideology. All the while Griffiths revved up the fund-raising and saved Douglass from bankruptcy and psychological collapse.

The neighborhood and most of reform Rochester was all astir over the fascinating Englishwomen living in Douglass's home. The "spinsters of means and culture" caused endless curiosity in the city, according to a chronicler of Rochester. A reminiscence published in 1941 quaintly captures the way the locals observed the situation. "The appearance on the Main Street," wrote Howard Coles, "of Frederick Douglass with one of these ladies on either arm seriously threatened the order of the town for a while, and threats were openly made of what would be done if such aggressive demonstrations of race-mixture were persisted in. Frederick Douglass kept his head high as ever, the ladies filling the role of possible martyrs unflinchingly."[16] In reality,

Julia simply went to work, although she and Frederick understood the order they challenged.

Along with antislavery, Douglass became Griffiths's cause. The best windows we have into their relationship, as well as into Douglass's mental and physical health, are the remarkable letters Julia wrote to Gerrit Smith. She frequently depicted Frederick as psychologically distraught over the plight of the paper and the financial situation of his family, as well as physically incapacitated not only by constant throat ailments but by what she called "inflammatory rheumatism." At the age of thirty-two to thirty-three, Douglass was sometimes confined to bed for days at a time, his joints locked up, limbs swollen, unable to walk. In the summer of 1850 Julia reported him "quite sick" with a "grave attack" of this debilitating condition. "In the course of the last fortnight he has had three severe falls," Julia confided to Smith. The reports were remarkably intimate: "He has a good man who comes twice a day to wash him." By autumn, Julia asked Smith to keep all this knowledge "strictly private" as she described Douglass's "bad cough" and "light headedness." Julia proudly announced that she wrote the editorials as her comrade dictated. Then, "at night he was seized with . . . a fit & has been laid up with his throat ever since." [17]

Already by the 1850s, Douglass's public image was of a virile man of the world, holding audiences in rapt control with words as well as charisma. His baritone voice alone, coupled with authentic slave roots, mesmerized his audiences. Increasingly he sat for, as well as manipulated, many photographers who captured his unforgettable visage frontally and in profile—erect, with starched shirts, exuding intelligence and greatness. The fiery eyes, prominent nose, striking features, goatee surrounding prominent lips seemingly about to burst into eloquence, and that lion's mane of hair, carefully brushed and parted, all provided an image of a *man* for a heroic age. But this was not the man undergoing some sort of paralysis and nervous breakdown by 1851. The reports of Douglass's illnesses were so common that Smith wrote back to Griffiths in July, "Much grieved to hear of the continued sickness of our dear Douglass." That same month in the paper she publicly announced that the editor underwent a "severe relapse" of his illness and was "wholly unable to write for the present number." A week later, Douglass himself described his condition, verifying what had appeared in Griffiths's letters. He "suffered from a succession of attacks," he declared, for a full month. "First bilious fever, sharp, sudden and severe (brought on no doubt by over-exertion and in-

Frederick Douglass, August 1852. Daguerreotype.
Samuel T. Miller photographer.

cautious exposure) prostrated my energies and confined me to my room."
For five years, he admitted, these maladies, lodged in his "throat difficulty," had plagued him. When back on his feet Douglass rushed out on
speaking tours to raise money for the newspaper. He was frantically trying to make ends meet, feed his family, and, as he said in the paper, "keep
heads above water."[18]

Julia's most disturbing reports indicated that Douglass floated in and
out of mental collapse. In late July 1851 he was "quite unwell," one day able
to work at the office and the next two "unfit for it." "Although the seat of
the disease is the throat," she said, "I am inclined to think that serious anxiety for his paper has much to do with it." By late August, the great man
was "extremely depressed" because little money flowed into the coffers, a
dire circumstance especially since Frederick possessed a "perfect horror of
being in debt." Julia tried to "inspire him with hope," but often to no avail.
The alarm in her letters came embedded in constant appeals for money
from Smith. Indeed, without Smith's donations, $100 here and $200 there,
Douglass's paper would have folded. Anna kept an excellent vegetable garden, but Smith's largesse not only paid for the *North Star*'s printing, ink,
and paper bills, but it provided food for five growing children. And the
stress in the household was enormous. "We have not had sickness out of
the house for a single day since the end of June," Julia reported in August.

"All this naturally tends to depress our friend greatly—added to which he has recently had a considerable increase of those house trials about which I spoke to you and dear Mrs. Smith when at Peterboro." [19] Julia, not Anna, had accompanied Douglass on a social visit to the Smiths' mansion earlier that month.

"House trials"? Julia did not offer a definition, but we can surmise that this meant not only money stresses, and the demands of children needing their father's attention. It surely meant quarrels with Anna, whose considerable homemaking powers were held hostage to the success or failure of the enterprise Julia ran for her husband, day and night. Douglass was a women's rights man. But privately he struggled mightily with his sense of manliness in these years; he had never known a father who took care of him. But he was failing; he could go out and thrill an audience, but at home he was the patriarch who could not provide for his family. In the myth of the Self-Made Man, burgeoning all over the culture in antebellum America, and of which Douglass became a famous proponent, this archetype had to publicly prove, as the sociologist Michael Kimmel argues, that he mastered his "life, liberty, and property." In the psyche of every Self-Made Man roiled a nightmare of chronic insecurity in the volatile marketplace. "Manhood" required mobility and independence, as it also courted catastrophe. Griffiths remembered Douglass saying that soon, if his financial situation did not improve, he would be "digging potatoes." So embarrassed was Douglass that Griffiths's frequent appeals to Smith for money were something he would simultaneously deny he needed as he also begged for more. He wrote many direct appeals in his newspaper to delinquent subscribers to "pay up," and demonstrate their pride in an enterprise owned and edited by a former fugitive slave. Douglass felt the double-edged sword of denial; sometimes he pushed through its confusions and admitted it. In September 1851 he wrote to Smith, regretting "that you should be so soon called upon for a helping hand." The calls that year never stopped. "Necessity my friend, would listen to no regrets," Douglass admitted. "I was under the hammer and my friend Julia seeing it cried out in my behalf. You came to my help and I am on my feet again." [20]

Well, not really. In November, in another letter labeled "<u>Private</u>," Julia communicated her "frightful apprehension" about Douglass's psychological state. He suffered "immense anxiety (pecuniary & family)," and one evening "seemed . . . to lose his balance of mind," wandering around murmuring about "going crazy." She sat up late at night with him singing and reciting "repeated hymns and psalms," and an old favorite Robert Burns poem, "The Cotter's Saturday Night." The melancholy love poem contains this verse:

> O happy love! where love like this is found:
> O heart-felt raptures! bliss beyond compare!
> I've paced much this weary, mortal round,
> And sage experience bids me this declare,
> "If Heaven a draught of heavenly pleasure spare
> One cordial in this melancholy vale,
> 'Tis when a youthful, loving, modest pair
> In other's arms, breathe out the tender tale,
> Beneath the milk-white thorn that scents the evening gale.

Performing as a bonny lass in a Burns poem, Julia concluded, "I shall do all in my power to tranquilize him—and shall not feather my fears to anyone." But that hardly mattered. Douglass pronounced for all his readers by December 1851 that he was again "extremely unwell." He did travel to Providence to deliver one unusual lecture in which he bared his spiritual soul: "I have been for the past year under a cloud." He called for abolitionists to "pray" and "meditate" and foster "love." He openly worried that by so long lambasting the clergy in his "Slaveholder's Sermon," he had "destroyed in myself that very reverence for God and for religion." His illnesses had been so disabling, he declared, that for "compiling my paper the credit is due to my friend Miss Griffiths."[21] Douglass was at risk of total psychological collapse.

Anna and Julia were two different kinds of companions. As Rosetta remembered, Anna possessed "no knowledge of books" and did not participate in Douglass's frenzied activism. A Rochester local history laden with reminiscences deemed Anna a "model housekeeper" with "severe notions of the proprieties and duties of life." Her "greatest discontent," said the Rochesterite, was when admirers of her husband "persisted in dragging her into notice . . . to receive visitors."[22] Calling Julia the business manager and special friend, however, is not enough. It was as though Douglass had a conjugal and a companionate mate, and they were not the same person. Exactly how he justified or explained this to himself, or to Anna, he never tells us. One woman provided him a home and a family; the other helped him forge his professional life and calling. He loved both.

Douglass commonly signed off a letter to Gerrit Smith in the manner he did in May 1851: "I write from the office or I am sure that my wife would unite with Miss Griffiths (who is industriously wielding her pen at another desk) in sending love to you and your dear lady." Douglass constantly called attention to Griffiths's assiduous labors at his side. As the plans solidified by June 1851 to combine Smith's fledging Liberty Party paper with the *North Star* in a new venture renamed *Frederick Douglass' Paper*, the editor let his benefactor know that he was not working alone. "Julia Griffiths,—my faithful friend, and co worker," he assured Smith, "(to whom I am greatly indebted for many lessons of wisdom) is all zeal in our new enterprize." Repeatedly, Douglass acknowledged his dependence on Griffiths's energy and ideas. As they planned the launch of the new paper, the editor said "money matters" should be "left to the care of my industrious and vigilant friend and co-worker Julia Griffiths. With her eye on the subscription list—I think very little would go wrong in that quarter." Douglass openly worried about Julia as he exalted her to Smith, implying that her situation living in such proximity to Anna and his family caused her great strain. "To her the credit belongs that the 'Star' is now out of debts," he wrote. "She ought to have this credit for you need not be told that she has much to annoy—and at times weigh down her spirit. She feels happy at the prospect now before her and will doubtless enter upon her duties with much spirit." Douglass thus admitted the tensions among the women in his own household, as well as his own dire needs. Few statements survive from this period in which he expresses similar concern for Anna's emotional well-being. Douglass cherished the "co-worker" at his side in the office and the nursemaid in the depths of his depressions and illnesses—she gave him confidence and psychic ballast.[23]

Julia Griffiths was not the invisible other woman, neither in Rochester nor in the wider world of abolitionism. As Douglass made his ideological turn to political antislavery and underwent a bitter breakup with Garrison and his organization, she became part of the target of retribution. The split reached a full-blown stage in 1851 as Douglass openly embraced Smith's version of an antislavery interpretation of the Constitution, of voting, and political activism. As Smith mentored Douglass through this transformation, Julia tempered her colleague's anger and guided and prodded him through the bloodletting he encountered from and delivered to the Garrisonians.

Douglass's course was typical of that of the many abolitionists who came to see political action as essential to their cause. Although he had long expressed gratitude for Garrison's tutelage and patronage, the great Bostonian had become the father to leave behind. Douglass had long since headed out for his own new territory; the rigid doctrines of disunionism, nonvoting, and moral suasion no longer sufficed in the political climate of the 1850s, especially in the wake of the Fugitive Slave Act, and the violent unfolding of the crisis over slavery's western expansion.

Nonvoting and disunionism were the easiest of Garrisonian tenets for Douglass to discard. The meaning of slavery in relation to federal law proved more problematic. The Smith circle's view held that the Constitution empowered—even required—Congress to abolish slavery in the Southern states by direct legislation. Pioneered by the New York abolitionist Alvan Stewart, this argument gained wider adherence from the writings of William Goodell and Lysander Spooner in the 1840s. Douglass read these authors and slowly came under their sway. The Garrisonians would claim that Douglass turncoated only for Smith's donations and out of selfish ambition. But he was drawn to new ideas that offered him hope in killing the power of slavery. Goodell and Spooner pointed to constitutional guarantees of habeas corpus and a "republican form of government" for every state, the preamble's call for a "more perfect union" and promise to "secure the blessings of liberty," the enabling clause, and especially the Fifth Amendment's declaration that no person could "be deprived of life, liberty, or property without due process of law" as proof that the federal government was obligated to abolish slavery everywhere.[24] Especially as an editor, Douglass had always engaged with national politics. Now the *federal* authority at the base of slavery's stranglehold on America became his intensive focus.

The Goodell-Spooner antislavery constitutional theory differed markedly from that championed by the Ohioan Salmon P. Chase. From the early 1840s, Chase argued that the "intentions" of the founding fathers were for a speedy abolition of slavery. He believed that slavery was a creature of state law and therefore merely "local" in America. The federal government had the power, Chase maintained, to end slavery in all places where it had exclusive jurisdiction (the District of Columbia and the territories). Hence, the duty of abolitionists was to restrict, to cordon off, slavery, and to try with pressure over time to convince the Southern states to emancipate their slaves by state action. In the 1850s Chase's view became the basis of the Republican Party's doctrine of free soil and nonextensionism.[25]

Thus Douglass caught the scent of a potent idea—that constitutional principle could be elevated above constitutional practice and affect real power. He learned a new cast of mind—political philosophy as well as action—and he took to it eagerly. By 1849 he had already stepped beyond Garrison's notion of the Constitution as a "covenant with evil." He announced himself "satisfied that if strictly construed according to its reading," the Constitution was "not a proslavery instrument," although the original intent of the founders had made it so. Actual provisions of the document, coupled with natural law, made the Constitution a source of antislavery principles; history, Douglass believed, had made it proslavery in practice.[26]

By April 1850 Douglass still felt perplexed by parts of the Constitution question. "Liberty and Slavery—opposite as heaven and hell—are both in the Constitution," he wrote in an editorial. But this was precisely its "radical defect": it offered no resolution for the "war of elements which is now rocking the land." Douglass gave his "sympathies" to those who envisioned the Constitution as a source of freedom and justice, but not his "judgment." He concluded that, for the moment, the Constitution was "at war with itself," an apt description as well of his own mind. Douglass was an elastic thinker, especially about political ideology. As James Oakes has argued, Douglass's political thought is laced with a "series of reversals"; he would waver in response to events and to his own learning.[27]

January 1851 still found Douglass teetering between the imperatives of legal and moral logic, but much more impressed with Smith's reasoning. Confessing to Smith that their relationship had greatly affected his thinking, Douglass declared that he had "about decided to let slaveholders and their Northern abettors have the laboring oar in putting a proslavery interpretation on the Constitution." He still had some reservations as he swallowed the theory whole. "I am sick and tired of arguing on the slaveholders' side of this question," he complained, "although they are doubtless right so far as the intentions of the framers of the Constitution." Smith's arbitrary determination that because slavery was such a moral outrage it could never achieve legal status troubled Douglass, who still wondered about the confusion between moral perceptions and "American legal authority." Sheer power, he knew, still held the trump cards. Despite all his intellectual hand-wringing, Douglass assured his mentor that he had "ceased to affirm the proslavery character of the Constitution."[28]

Gerrit Smith, c. 1855. Daguerreotype.

Douglass had argued his way to this new position, rather than merely imbibing it. Smith wrote to his pupil in June 1851 with "much joy" that Douglass had accepted this interpretation. "I have observed for years that you were coming to this conclusion," Smith accurately said. But "far more joyful" was the student's realization that "slavery is incapable of legalization," and that "law is for the protection, not for the destruction of rights." They had found common ground in another kind of logic, explained by Smith tellingly: "Every man is an abolitionist; every man is selfish enough to be an abolitionist for himself, but every man is not unselfish enough to be an abolitionist for others."[29] In that logic one finds both the necessity for law, but also the reason why sometimes laws must be broken.

Douglass had found a new and more potent form of radicalism, but by mid-1851 he came under attack by the Garrisonians for his disloyalty to their principles. "There is roguery somewhere!" cried Garrison in an outburst at the May 1851 annual meeting of the AASS in Syracuse. He laid the charge on Douglass, who, in response to a resolution declaring that the society would endorse no newspaper that did not support a pro-slavery conception of the Constitution, announced his "firm conviction" that the national charter should be "wielded in behalf of emancipation." He had conducted "careful study," Douglass told all his old colleagues, and from now on he planned to advance the antislavery interpretation of the Constitution in his paper. In an uproar the convention promptly voted to exclude the *North Star* from the list of favored journals.[30] Orthodoxy held the Garrisonian church together, and Douglass was about to be excommunicated.

As Douglass now merged his journal, newly named *Frederick Douglass' Paper*, with the Liberty Party, which had a firm base in western New York, his perfidy only deepened in Garrisonian eyes; some accused him of selling out for Gerrit Smith's lucre, while others pointed to the arrogance of the new title. Douglass expected now, he told Smith, "to be made . . . an object of special attack. . . . I know too well the temper of my old companions to hope to escape the penalty which all others have paid who have ventured to differ from them." Douglass expressed relief at no longer feeling "glued to the non-voting theory," but admitted to being "pained" by the controversy. "The war will be waged," he predicted, "not against opinions, but *motives.*" He needed money badly and appealed to Smith constantly in 1851. He felt "anxious," Douglass told Smith. But Douglass was determined this time to "set an example of ability to take care of myself." Inadvertently, Douglass also quietly demonstrated the other reason his old friends resented and even condemned him, as he frequently signed off letters with personal acknowledgments to "Julia Griffiths, my faithful friend and co-worker." [31]

Griffiths had become not only Frederick's business manager but his gatekeeper. Charges of ingratitude against Douglass only intensified as some abolitionists complained of their old mate's inaccessibility and arrogance. Isabel Jennings in Ireland complained in 1851 that she had "heard only once" from Douglass since Julia had taken over his office, otherwise receiving only requests for money from "Miss J.G." Jennings worried that the situation would hurt the cause as well as Douglass's life. "Miss G. reads all F.D.'s letters," Jennings complained, as she snidely remarked, "I am sure he thinks antislavery zeal is the strongest emotion she is capable of." Abby Kelley Foster, who had come to despise Douglass, took it out privately on Julia. In 1852 she snarled about "that Julia Griffiths, making people think we're infidels," as her boss enjoyed "slandering all our English and American friends." As lulls occurred in the open conflict between Garrison and Douglass, tongues wagged in private and gossip letters flowed among the abolitionist elite, some reporting how Julia often walked the streets of Rochester in fashionable dresses and an abundance of fine jewelry.[32] She was not a Quaker in appearance or habits, unlike many in that antislavery community.

In May 1852 the AASS gathered for its annual meeting in Rochester, but home ground hardly protected Douglass from new assaults on his apostasy.

Numerous distinguished abolitionists, all his former traveling companions and friends, spent inordinate time and energy denouncing Douglass. They included Wendell Phillips, Stephen and Abby Kelley Foster, Oliver Johnson, and the black Garrisonians Charles Lenox Remond and Robert Purvis. Douglass had histories with all of these former comrades; he had forged his career with them on countless overnight train rides, and against many a racist mob. Now they treated him, as he said, only "as an enemy." Foster called Douglass a "cat in the meal," and Remond insisted the abolitionists should stop "handling Douglass with kid gloves." The marked man now felt certain that his old black colleagues in particular, Purvis and Remond, wanted to destroy his newspaper.[33] Remond had been the first black Garrisonian on the circuit and never accommodated to being displaced.

This public humiliation hurt Douglass to the bone. Phillips and Abby Foster especially let him know that the society had not rejected him; he stood "self-exiled" due to his changed strategic views of abolition. His motives assailed at every level with what Douglass called "vile insinuations," Stephen Foster made a bad situation worse. Douglass faced a choice: either he was "with us," or "we'll crush you, as we have the Liberty Party." It was one thing to fight rhetorical battles over tactics, and quite another to attack a colleague's personal character. Samuel May Jr. came forth to try to acknowledge Douglass's "genius" and indispensable role in the movement, stressing that he remained "calm, cool, collected," even as he withstood this withering attack. But Purvis joined Remond in announcing that he had canceled his subscription to Douglass's paper, accused the editor of taking a "bribe" of $20 from a colonization supporter, and, worst of all, declared it "no longer safe to trust the interests of colored people with Douglass." Garrison himself stooped low into the pettiness, suggesting that Douglass had allowed himself to be lauded by avowed AASS enemies at a Liberty Party convention.[34]

These were anxious times for members of the AASS; they steadily lost adherents as they came under attack from the rising tide of political abolitionism, the new Free Soil Party, and the unprecedented whirlwind created by Harriet Beecher Stowe's bestselling novel *Uncle Tom's Cabin*. Douglass reported in late June that Stowe's work had just sold its eighty thousandth copy.[35] The book had been published in the spring of 1852 and was taking the country by storm as no other book ever had while the old-organization abolitionists vied with one another publicly to discredit one of their own for his ideas.

How Douglass mustered what he called "rectitude" to withstand this public barrage from old friends is as remarkable as it is bewildering. On a personal level the breakup with the Garrisonians devastated Douglass even as he himself fueled the fires. Douglass cultivated the image of the strong individual, always questing for the next turn in the crusade to destroy slavery. And he was an intense watcher of his own life. As necessary, he would fly as the eagle, the lone bird soaring to the new horizon of ideas, rhetoric, and action. In his own slave-born ways Douglass imagined a kind of Whitmanesque "Song of Myself" at the heart of his journey. In so many lines of that great poem Whitman could have been imagining the struggling but determined Douglass of the early 1850s:

> *The past and present wilt. . . . I have filled them and emptied*
>   *Them,*
> *And proceed to fill my next fold of the future.*[36]

Douglass had long known that he could not stay within the Garrisonian fold. Even at age thirty-five he was still the angry young man finding and testing the limits of his own voice. But as we have seen, he never flew entirely alone.

Douglass nearly ran out of labels for the Garrisonian assault as he experienced it. The day after the Rochester convention ended, he wrote to Smith trying to characterize what he had endured. Treated as a "deserter from the fold," he nevertheless, or so he claimed, let his colleagues "search me and probe me to the bottom." Facing what he considered outright lies, he stood firm against the hailstorm of "side blows, innuendo, dark suspicions, such as avarice, faithlessness, treachery, ingratitude and what not." Whistling in the graveyard, he assured Smith proudly that he felt "strengthened to bear it without perturbation." Such was not the case a few days later as he wrote his long response for his paper. There he exposed his "grief" that "men engaged in a great and holy cause should fall out by the way" in such ugly form. Such differences could not be hidden, Douglass maintained, by "seeming to be at peace when there is no peace." So he took up the pen and fought back. Jeremiah and Isaiah had fought best against their own kind; their roles as brokenhearted, suffering servants calling people to grief, awareness, exile, and redemption gave Douglass models for finding his own prophetic voice, for turning affliction into hope, however many friends he might lose.[37]

In a long rejoinder to his critics he defended his right to change his views. "Denunciation, coldness, and unkindness" were not arguments, he contended, and hardly the way to "reclaim an erring brother." Putting several lines in capital letters, Douglass tried for high ground and struck his claim for freedom of thought and association: "I CONTEND THAT I HAVE A RIGHT TO CO-OPERATE WITH ANYBODY, WITH EVERYBODY, FOR THE OVERTHROW OF SLAVERY IN THIS COUNTRY, whether auxiliary or not auxiliary to the American Society." Here was a political conscious-ness at work. Douglass wielded daggers of his own, couched in Shakespear-ean metaphor. Drawing from Iago's contempt for Othello's unbounded jealousy, Douglass left no doubt of what he thought Remond and Purvis especially were up to. "Trifles, light as air / Are to the jealous, confirmations strong. / As proofs of Holy Writ." He had long dismissed Remond as his "old jealous friend," then twisted the knife deeper into both of the two for their "false witness" against a fellow black abolitionist, and, worse, for personally seeking to destroy "the last press remaining in the United States, wielded by a sable hand." There is no fight like a fight between the closest of comrades over notions of betrayal. Douglass could be ugly too; he accused Remond

Charles Lenox Remond, c. 1851–56. Daguerreotype.
Samuel S. Broadbent photographer.

and Purvis of joining with every "negro-hater in all the land" who would delight in liquidating Douglass and his newspaper.[38]

But Douglass's brilliant rejoinder only masked his loneliness and insecurity. He could be petty, even self-destructive, as he also found new inspirations. By July 1852, he revealed to Smith that "you not only keep life in my paper but keep spirit in me. I owe you much every way for my people and for myself." The paper still teetered on financial extinction as Griffiths continued to labor to get subscribers to pay up. Frederick remained uncomfortable about the constant appeals to his rich benefactor. Failure seemed always to be just around the corner on Douglass's open road, where lecturing and trying to sell copies of those lectures remained his primary "method or . . . means of living and traveling." With the bravado of a rather desperate man, he told Smith he did not want "one cent more" from his generosity. If the paper died "when that sum is exhausted, I will submit with resignation to its death," he wrote, despite saying in the next breath that he had "nursed" the paper so long, had loved it, and given it "half my worldly goods and the whole of my time for five years."[39] Cries for help continued to burst from under those starched collars and through the eloquent rhetoric.

In late 1852, allegedly because Anna "ordered" it, Julia moved out of Douglass's home and became a boarder with John and Mary Porter, friends in the Rochester antislavery community. Early the next year, Samuel D. Porter, a wealthy neighbor and friend, wrote to Douglass informing him that "scandalous reports" were rampant in Rochester about Frederick and Julia having an affair in his home under the eyes of his own wife and children. Douglass asked that the accusers make their claims more "definite" about "Miss G. and me," and then he might answer them. In vague terms he defended himself as a "husband and a father—and withal a citizen," declaring that he performed all the roles "honorably." He also aggressively defended Julia as a "free woman" who had moved out and simply "preferred to board in another family." Porter's letter does not survive, but the rumors were scurrilous by the measure of Douglass's response. "I am in no way responsible for her words, her deeds or her dress," the embarrassed editor said, "nor indeed, for her thinking me a 'God.'" But he firmly declared his "gratitude, respect and friendship" for his "clerk" and, awkwardly, described how they now spent only "business hours for business purposes" in each other's company.[40]

By summer and fall of 1853, the alleged illicit relationship exploded at the heart of a wider war of character assassination between Douglass and the Garrisonians. In the wake of the AASS annual meeting in May, Douglass suggested that Parker Pillsbury, Henry C. Wright, and Stephen Foster, prominent Garrisonians all, had stayed away "because their presence might give new force to the charge of infidelity" against them. Douglass had previously questioned the Christian sincerity of fellow AASS members. The charge simmered until a West Indian emancipation celebration in Framingham, Massachusetts, on August 1, at which Wendell Phillips publicly dressed down Douglass in front of six hundred people for the slur upon his friends and the organization, wondering how his fellow orator could even show his face among old comrades. Later that month Douglass wrote an editorial and delivered a speech at the heart of black Garrisonianism, the Belknap Street Church in Boston. He stepped up his attack on Garrisonian disbelief in the Bible, as well as viciously attacking his black rivals.[41]

To an extent, a vengeful Douglass now seemed out of control. In print and in an open meeting, he called Remond, Purvis, and William Cooper Nell (his old friend and former editorial assistant) "practical enemies of the colored people" for their loyalty to Garrison. Douglass threw some low blows. He associated Purvis, a mulatto whose white father had attained some wealth, with tainted "blood-stained riches." He considered Remond "selectively" rich because he had married into money. Worst, he labeled Nell, who now worked in Garrison's office, a "pitiful fool" and a "contemptible tool" of the Boston hierarchy. From September through November, the entire Garrisonian press fired back with pent-up rage. Douglass had long exposed his persecution complex, his self-portrayal as a lone rebel, the purveyor of new truths against all the ossified doctrines of the eastern "bishop" and his orthodox priests. In writing privately to Gerrit Smith in late August, Douglass claimed, disingenuously, that he was "greatly desirous of keeping out of quarrels with Boston." But they deserved a "going over" because of their "downright bigotry and pride of position." As though baring his teeth, he continued, "They talk down there, just as if the Antislavery Cause belonged to them . . . that no man has a right to 'peep or mutter' on the subject, who does not hold letters of patent from them."[42]

Douglass could neither hold his fire nor forget a slight. It was as though a part of his soul had forever been forged in the fight on Covey's farm, in the bloody rumbles on the docks of Baltimore, and against the countless white mobs who had assaulted him. Language replaced fists in this battle over personalities, status, and claims to righteousness. Douglass's hypersensitivity to criticism and rivalry had long been part of the personality his friends tolerated. Throughout the 1850s Douglass publicly disputed fiercely with other black leaders over both ideology and personal matters. He fought tooth and nail with Henry Highland Garnet and Martin Delany over emigration and colonization strategies, especially after the *Dred Scott* case. Their differences could not have been more fundamental. And he conducted an ugly spat with William Wells Brown in 1855 over whether Douglass had expressed derogatory estimations of Brown to mutual acquaintances in England. Their dustup got caught in the crosshairs of the editor's prolonged battles with Garrisonians. Douglass accused Brown of attacking his integrity ad hominem merely to demonstrate his "faithfulness to the American Anti-slavery Society." But Brown had accused Douglass of trying to ruin his prospects as a speaker in Britain with a secret, "underhanded . . . sneaking fling at me." Both charged each other with "dishonor," although the two men later found ways to make up. They shared so much—both were former fugitive slaves who had escaped at age twenty and achieved fame as writers.[43]

As friendships collapsed, and old memories crashed into new ones, Garrison complained of "how extremely sensitive he [Douglass] is to reproof—how readily he construes it into personal hostility." The founder of the *Liberator* had tried to remain largely silent in this fight, but now he unloaded a wail of bile. In September 1853 he reprinted a Douglass editorial in his regular feature column, Refuge of Oppression, a place normally devoted to articles about the brutalities of slavery itself. Garrison said he had always done everything in his power for Douglass's "welfare and advancement" and had helped to lift him to "his most eventful life." But now he found Douglass "intoxicated" by his fame and "cursed by selfish ambition." Garrison wasted no adjectives. Douglass's attacks on Phillips were "exceedingly base," and his treatment of his fellow black abolitionists would be "disgraceful to a barbarian."[44] The student had overstepped his bounds.

Garrison tried to take the high ground, claiming that the dispute was not about ideological change, but about Douglass's "alienated . . . temper and spirit." But then Garrison attacked Julia Griffiths and accused Douglass of the worst immorality. Garrison called Julia "a prejudiced sectarian Delilah," endorsing the storehouse of rumors. "For several years past, he [Douglass] has had one of the worst advisors in his printing office whose influence over him has not only caused much unhappiness in his own household, but perniciously biased his own judgment." The youthful black wonder of abolitionism could never have altered his worldview without a conniving white woman at his ear. When Douglass answered in defense that Julia had opened his eyes to many ideas, and that Garrison's handpicked "runners and whisperers" had all along sought to stifle him, things only got worse. Like a Shakespearean court intrigue, defamations and insinuations flew like autumn leaves in the fall of 1853. Oliver Johnson, editor of the AASS newspaper and a newly contemptuous critic of Douglass, called Julia "a Jezebel whose capacity for making mischief between friends would be difficult to match." As Douglass issued lengthy denials and refutations of the charge of marital infidelity, Johnson could only wreak more damage. He saw Douglass merely as "an exhibition of moral perversity, blindness and malice." [45]

No one involved remained untouched or unembarrassed by the scandal. Anna Douglass produced, or dictated, a short letter to Garrison, which the editor published: "Sir: It is not true that the presence of a certain person in the office of Frederick Douglass causes unhappiness in his family. Please insert this in your next paper." Garrison was unimpressed by the brief denial, calling it "evasive," although he soon openly regretted that he had ever raised the marital question. For her part, Julia hardly sat on her hands or went into seclusion over the scandal in which her name was a constant byword for intrigue and adultery. We do not know for sure what she or Anna might have said to Frederick. We do not know who may have confronted whom, nor if anyone did. But we do know that Julia worked hard to create the Ladies' Anti-Slavery Society of Rochester, of which she served as secretary and guiding force. Even more extraordinarily, Julia produced and edited two remarkable volumes under the title *Autographs for Freedom*, the first published in 1853 and the second in 1854. These stunning collections of short essays, poetry, and letters, which included Douglass's own sixty-five-page novella, "The Heroic Slave," all written by celebrity abolitionist authors, were not only unique in antislavery literature but became yet another moneymaker for her comrade's cause. These volumes required enormous correspondence and editorial labor to bring to fruition; they included some thirty-six authors in the first volume and forty-nine in the second, almost all of whom were squarely in the camp of political abolitionism. [46] Those authors also demonstrate that Douglass had another and even wider circle of friends, thinkers, and coworkers apart from the Garrisonians.

The scandal did not die out in 1853 without sufficient public and private recrimination to fill a year's worth of script for a modern soap opera. Purvis wrote a letter published in the *Liberator* in which he dismissed Douglass as a "shameless ingrate and base slanderer." Wounded badly, Nell, a sensitive and loquacious man, frequently wrote privately about his pain over Douglass's statements. "I cannot easily imagine the circumstances that would result in my speaking to him," he lamented. "I can remember the Sunny Side—and only wish I could forget the shady side of his Character." Nell remained shocked at Douglass's "venom" in his attacks on Garrisonians, especially on himself in "battle axe stile [*sic*]." "Where will he stop?" Nell moaned. After reading Douglass's long defense in December, Nell said he couldn't help saying, "Whom the Gods would destroy, they first make mad." By January 1854, the Garrison loyalist, happy in his day job, criticized *Autographs for Freedom* as an "anti-Garrison" creation by the "F.D. with J.G. contingent," but then secretly confessed to a "slight wish I could have contributed."[47]

Douglass left his mark on the scandal as though he strove for the last word. He crafted a long, alternately turgid and eloquent defense in his paper on December 9, 1853. He also reprinted many columns of the articles that had appeared over the months in the three primary Garrisonian papers: *Liberator*, *National Anti-Slavery Standard* (*NASS*), and the *Pennsylvania Freeman*. Writing at times like a lawyer with a veiled threat of a lawsuit, and then like a wounded, lonely warrior defending himself against his enemies' "hatchet of fratricidal war," Douglass did not provide his finest hour. He could not resist venting his spleen. The Garrisonians' aim, he said, was to drive him from the field, to send him back to caulking "ships in New Bedford." They sought nothing less, he claimed, than the "moral extermination of one humble, solitary individual." The line-by-line attempts at rebuttal gave the whole effort a sanctimonious tone. Not without some reason, the editor of the *Pennsylvania Freeman*, Rush Plumbly, called Douglass's tone a "whine of persecution."[48]

Douglass claimed that he had tried to sustain "honorable silence," but the "assaults" had become unbearable, especially about his private affairs. Garrison had seen fit, wrote Douglass, "to invade my household, despise the sacredness of my home . . . to blast me in the name of my family." His denial of any affair with Julia took the form of a defense of Julia's "eminent services" as his coworker, and a prolonged eight-part declaration that the "happiness or unhappiness" of his household was nobody's business but his own. He denied the affair as he continued to contend that he was under no obligation to do so.[49]

With thousands of highly charged words wielded as daggers to the heart in this sordid affair, inevitably it became racialized. With paternalistic pique, Garrison had argued that Douglass, as a former slave, could perhaps no longer comprehend the full demands of abolitionist leadership. "The antislavery cause," said the founder, "both religiously and politically, has transcended the ability of the sufferers from American slavery and prejudice as a class, to keep pace with it or to perceive what are its demands or to understand its philosophy."[50] "Philosophy"? From the first days that

Douglass's early Garrisonian colleagues had tried to monitor and manage his thinking and his actions, here was the attitude that Douglass had spent a decade resisting. He pulled the arrow out of his chest and fired it right back at Garrison's heart.

Is it their own liberty that black people will next be told they do not comprehend? he asked. This was an old subject for the former slave, but now he gave it new sting. For black folk, said Douglass, "every day and hour is crowded with lessons to them on the subject, to which the whites as a class are strangers." In effect he was saying to his old dear friend, if you want *this* fight, I will destroy you. Personal insults and judgments about morality were one thing, but an intellectual insult cut even deeper. "Who will doubt hereafter," Douglass anguished, "the natural inferiority of the Negro, when the great champion of the Negroes' rights, thus broadly concedes all that is claimed respecting the Negroes' inferiority by the bitterest despisers of the Negro race." Douglass's demolition of some of the Garrisonians' accusations would have left an open-minded reader wondering just who were the "egotists" or the "alienated spirits" in this row.[51]

The tragic dimension of this mutual self-destruction is manifest in such exchanges between two men who had loved and served each other, who had learned so much from each other, the one a father figure and the other a prodigal son in a life-affirming cause. But words can kill, and sometimes love and hate ride together. It is an ancient story, fated and repeated down through the ages in variations on Abraham and Isaac or Cain and Abel. Both Douglass and Garrison lived to see their travail redeemed a decade later in the freedom of the slaves, even if they fundamentally never made up.

In November–December 1853 as the Garrison-Douglass war came to its baroque conclusions, both protagonists paid separate visits to Harriet Beecher Stowe, newly ascendant to extraordinary literary fame. Although political crises and broader events overtook the petty inhumanities of the breakup, Stowe took it upon herself to call a truce. In November, Garrison had exchanged long letters with Stowe over her objections to the tone and theological outlook of the *Liberator* and some of its agents. She had worried that the unrelenting criticism of churches, ministers, and proslavery religion carried on by Garrisonians would "take from poor Uncle Tom his Bible." Stowe wanted peace in the ranks. On December 19 she wrote to Garrison of her recent face-to-face meeting with Douglass. She admitted to earlier contributing to gossip about Douglass's personal life. She now found Douglass most impressive; he did not seem "malignant or revengeful" and had only been caught up in a "temporary excitement." Douglass must have charmed the observant author. Poignantly, she described Douglass's ideas as the "growth from the soil of his own mind . . . and not a twig broken off other men's thoughts." She thought him no more to blame than his accusers. "Where is this work of excommunication to end?" Stowe demanded. She found all "allusion to his family concerns" "unjustifiable." She pleaded with Garrison for silence and suggested tellingly that "what Douglass *is* really, time will show." Presciently, Stowe scolded Garrison: what he had "cast aside as worthless" would one day "be a treasure."[52] Stowe seemed to be telling Garrison what he ought to know—that genius often makes superhuman demands on tolerance.

In this wrenching period of his bitterly public split with Garrison, Douglass had thrown himself into the worlds of political abolitionism. Through physical and emotional collapses, and through the ever-invigorating and debilitating lecturing tours, he found the time and repose to assist numerous fugitive slaves toward their liberty, to begin a sustained and brilliant critique of the Slave Power in national affairs, to write his first work of fiction for Griffiths's *Autographs for Freedom,* and to now craft the greatest speech of his life at the invitation of her Ladies' Anti-Slavery Society of Rochester.

Chapter 13

BY THE RIVERS
OF BABYLON

I have this day set thee over the nations and over the kingdoms,
to root out, and to pull down . . . to build, and to plant.

—JEREMIAH 1:10

Frederick Douglass had learned the hard way that oppression, loss, and anger had to be controlled and braced with knowledge if a former slave with an extraordinary mind was to survive in the United States. He was a man of the nineteenth century, a thoroughgoing inheritor of Enlightenment ideas, but for justification, and for the story in which to embed the experience of American slaves, he reached for the Old Testament Hebrew prophets of the sixth to eighth centuries BC. Isaiah, Jeremiah, and Ezekiel were his companions, a confounding but inspiring source of intellectual and emotional control. Their great and terrible stories provided Douglass the deepest well of metaphor and meaning for his increasingly ferocious critique of his own country. Their Jerusalem, their temple, their Israelites transported in the Babylonian Captivity, their oracles to the nation of the woe to be inflicted upon them by a vengeful God for their crimes, were his American "republic," his "bleeding children of sorrow," his warnings of desolations soon to visit his own guilty land.[1] Their story was ancient and modern; it gave the weight of the ages to his cause. Their awesome narratives of destruction and apocalyptical renewal, exile and return, provided scriptural basis for his mission to convince Americans they must undergo the same. The Old Testament prophets helped make Douglass a great ironist and a great storyteller; they fueled his growing militancy and brought pathos and thunder to his voice as they also shaped his view of history itself. Douglass not only used the Hebrew prophets; he joined them.

The Hebrew prophets delivered their sayings and poems orally in public gatherings. Whether Douglass understood this or not, it makes his oratorical use of the jeremiadic tradition all the more poignant. As Isaiah "came . . . and said," and Jeremiah followed God's call to "go and cry in the ears of Jerusalem," so Douglass proclaimed antislavery oracles to vast public audiences in proslavery America. God had visited Jeremiah and instructed him, "Behold, I have put My words in your mouth," and given him his calling. Beginning with the black churches he attended in Baltimore, where he would have first heard preaching on the Exodus story, Douglass had reached that moment as well. He was an American Jeremiah chastising the flock as he also called them back to their covenants and creeds. Moreover, Douglass, like other American writers and orators from the Puritans to modern times, found his own way to comprehend as well as rewrite Old Testament narratives, in the words of biblical scholar Robert Alter, as both "sacred history" and "prose fiction," as models of literary style and a national story. And as the Jewish theologian Abraham Heschel wrote, "Prophets must have been shattered by some cataclysmic experience in order to be able to shatter others."[2] By this standard, Douglass qualified.

In early summer 1852, surrounded by rumors about his relationship with Julia Griffiths, suffering periodically with ill health, and embroiled in his fight with the Garrisonians, Douglass was invited by the Rochester Ladies' Anti-Slavery Society to deliver a Fourth of July address in the majestic Corinthian Hall, only a few blocks from the *North Star*'s office. Maria G. Porter was president and Griffiths the secretary of the society, which in late March had raised $233 at a festival to support Douglass's newspaper. The society sponsored a regular series of antislavery lectures in Corinthian Hall, announced by Griffiths in Douglass's paper. In accepting the invitation, he insisted on delivering the speech on July 5, which had long been a practice among New York State African American communities. In the South, moreover, slave auctions had often been conducted on July 4, further sullying the date in African American memory. The Fourth fell on a Sunday, and for that reason also the Rochesterites moved it to Monday. For at least three weeks in advance of the event Douglass worked hard on the text, as well as personally promoting the event in his paper. He clearly aimed the speech not only at his local audience but beyond the hall to the nation at large. Immediately after the oration he had it printed in bulk and sold it in his paper as well as out on the lecture circuit at fifty cents per copy, or $6 per hundred.[3] What Douglass crafted and delivered on July 5 was nothing less than the rhetorical masterpiece of American abolitionism.

Nearly six hundred people packed Corinthian Hall on that warm July day; a "grand dinner" was prepared by the Ladies' Society for after the speech. The beautiful edifice, which took its name from four Corinthian columns adorning the high front wall, had just opened in 1849 and was Rochester's most prestigious venue for concerts, lectures, balls, and fairs. Four great chandeliers hung from the high ceiling, and tall windows on both sides admitted plentiful natural light. The buzz of mass conversation quickly fell silent as local abolitionist James Sperry called the meeting to order. The Reverend S. Ottman of Rush, New York, delivered a prayer, then the Reverend Robert R. Raymond of Syracuse performed a reading of the Declaration of Independence. Without introduction, sporting his high white collar, vested suit, and large mane of hair carefully parted, Frederick Douglass stepped forward, his hands slightly trembling with the thirty-page text he held.[4]

In a conventional apologia audiences came to expect, he began quietly with a disclaimer of his ability to address such an august assembly: he had never appeared more "shrinkingly" before an audience. He knew such dis-

Corinthian Hall, Rochester, New York, 1850s. Lithograph.

claimers were taken by his auditors as "flat and unmeaning," but he begged their indulgence of his awareness that this was something special; he knew he spoke in the house of his friends, whom he now used as stand-ins for the nation. In an old move of false self-deprecation, he said the "distance between this platform and the slave plantation, from which I escaped, is considerable" and left him with a "quailing sensation." Wishing he had had time for more "elaborate preparation" and more formal "learning," Douglass finally reached his subject.[5] Invited to participate in a celebration of American independence, Douglass delivered a political sermon, steeped in the Jeremiah tradition.

Douglass's Fourth of July speech came in the midst of many turbulent contexts. Douglass faced the personal crises of his own life just discussed, and *Uncle Tom's Cabin* had become an instant phenomenon. For nearly two years free blacks and their allies had defied the hated Fugitive Slave Act. Massive protest meetings condemned a law that denied the right of habeas corpus and trial by jury to alleged fugitive slaves, as well as threatened the kidnapping of free people of color into slavery. Douglass himself had stepped up his assistance to runaway slaves in Rochester and participated in recent months in some of the clandestine rescues of fugitives across the North. Now, under the American flag, observed Douglass, so deep was the fear in Northern black communities that hundreds had fled to Canada like "a dark train going out of the land, as if fleeing from death." In virtually every issue of his paper, Douglass and his staff ran articles and reports about kidnappings or escapes of "refugee" slaves in the North or into Canada.[6] And as abolitionists turned more toward violent means of resistance, and political parties began to tear themselves asunder, the country faced another general election in the coming fall.

Douglass channeled all of this tension into a kind of music; his speech was like a symphony in three movements. In the first movement, Douglass set his audience at ease by honoring the genius of the founding fathers. He called the Fourth of July an American "Passover" and placed hope in the youthful nation, "still impressible" and open to change. "Three score years and ten is the allotted time for individual men," said the calm Douglass, "but nations number their years by thousands." As he began a historical tribute to the bravery of the American revolutionaries of 1776, subtly referencing Thomas Paine's times that "tried men's souls," he dropped hints of foreboding, of "dark clouds ... above the horizon ... portending disastrous times." He began with hope, though: "There is consolation in the thought that America is young. Great streams are not easily turned from channels, worn deep in the course of ages." Douglass called the Declaration of Independence the "RINGBOLT to the chain of your nation's destiny," and the preamble the nation's "saving principles." With active, gleaming metaphors landing on his listeners in every spoken paragraph, the music became louder. "From the round top of your ship of state, dark and threatening clouds may be seen," Douglass sang. "Heavy billows, like mountains in the distance, disclose to the leeward huge forms of flinty rocks! That bolt drawn, that chain broken, and all is lost. *Cling to this day—cling to it*, and to its principles, with the grasp of a storm-tossed mariner to a spar at midnight."[7]

His baritone voice now projecting to the rear of the hall, Douglass had laid the groundwork of prophetic irony in the first movement for the main argument to come. The scene-setting beauty of the string instruments soon gave way to full-throated horns and kettledrums. The warnings already lay in the politicized possessive pronouns: "your fathers," "your national independence." America's story of its founding in the Revolution and its aftermath was taught, Douglass intoned, in "your common schools, narrated at your firesides, unfolded from your pulpits . . . as household words . . . the staple of your national poetry and eloquence."[8] A voice truly free and independent had arrived.

Then, as though slamming his fist down on the lectern, Douglass announced the shift to the second and longer movement of the symphony—a new version of that national poetry. Quoting Longfellow's poem "A Psalm of Life," he announced that his concern was the present: "Trust no future however pleasant, / Let the dead past bury its dead; Act, act in the living present, / Heart within, and God overhead." As Douglass reminded his largely white audience of their national and personal declension, the speech found its theme—the hypocrisy of slavery and racism in a republic. He harkened to Genesis and Exodus and the twelve children of Jacob boasting of Abraham's paternity but losing Abraham's faith. This great human folly was both "ancient and modern," Douglass proclaimed. The children of Israel "contented themselves under the shadow of Abraham's great name, while they repudiated the deeds which made his name great." For Americans, said Douglass, George Washington was the Abraham of their new Israel; and though Washington had freed his slaves in his will, "his monument is built up by the price of human blood, and the traders in the bodies and souls of men."[9] Complicit in the oldest stories in their spiritual and national lives, the audience sat primed for the onslaught to follow. The oracle turned wrathful.

Now Douglass brought his hammer down even harder, and for approximately fourteen pages, the second and longest movement rained down like a hailstorm. He pulled no punches, making the good abolitionists and the Ladies' Anti-Slavery Society squirm as he dragged them through a litany of America's contradictions. Second-person pronouns crashed into his singular "I." "Fellow-citizens," he firmly stated, "pardon me, allow me to ask, why am I called upon to speak here today? What have I, or those I represent, to do with your national independence?" Douglass personified all slaves, past and present. "I am not included within the pale of this glorious anniversary! This Fourth of July is *yours*, not *mine*. You may rejoice, I must mourn. To drag a man in fetters into the grand illuminated temple of liberty, and call upon him to join you in joyous anthems, were inhuman mockery and sacrilegious irony. Do you mean, citizens, to mock me by asking me to speak today?" Then, in the most beautiful move in the speech, he warns that "there is a parallel" as he flows unannounced back to the captivity of the ancient Jews in Psalm 137:

> By the Rivers of Babylon, there we sat down. Yea! we wept when we remembered Zion. We hanged our harps upon the willows in the midst thereof. For there, they that carried us away captive, required of us a song; and they who wasted us required of us mirth, saying, Sing us one of the songs of Zion. How can we sing the Lord's song in a strange land? If I forget thee, O Jerusalem, let my right hand forget her cunning. If I do not remember thee, let my tongue cleave to the roof of my mouth.

Douglass's answer to the summons? He would not sing any praise songs on the nation's birthday. Instead, he recrafted Jeremiah's tales of God's wrath and the people's mourning as he proclaimed, "Above your national, tumultuous joy, I hear the mournful wail of millions! whose chains, heavy and grievous yesterday, are today, rendered more intolerable by the jubilee shouts that reach them." [10]

Douglass loved the Declaration of Independence, but since its principles were *natural* rights, like the precious ores of the earth, he refused to argue for their existence or their righteousness against the claims of pro-slavery ideologues. "What point in the antislavery creed would you have me argue?" he asked. Why must he prove that the slave is human? Rather, Douglass claimed his authority from two great scriptures, "the Constitution and the Bible," and announced that "the time for argument is passed." Instead, the American condition demanded "scorching irony." Douglass had not come to Corinthian Hall for polite discourse. "O! had I the ability, and could I reach the nation's ear, I would today pour out a fiery stream of biting ridicule, blasting reproach, withering sarcasm, and stern rebuke. For it is not light that is needed, but fire; it is not the gentle shower, but thunder. We need the storm, the whirlwind, and the earthquake. The feeling of the nation must be quickened . . . the hypocrisy of the nation must be exposed."[11] And so for twenty-five minutes—the second movement—he did just that.

Douglass poured out a litany of historical and contemporary evils caused by American slavery. He did not merely call Americans hypocrites; he showed them and made them feel, see, and hear their "revolting barbarity" in aggressive language. First, he delivered a thoroughgoing condemnation of the domestic slave trade. As lyrical as it was terrible, Douglass made his audience look at the "human flesh-jobbers" who operated the slave markets, hear their "savage yells and . . . blood-chilling oaths . . . the fetters clank . . . and the crack . . . sound of the slave-whip" and indeed "see" the slave mother's "briny tears falling on the brow of the babe in her arms." He forced them to "attend the auction" and look on the "shocking gaze of American slave-buyers." No one could do this quite like Douglass, who personified the terror by telling of his own memories of hearing the "rattle of chains and the heart-rending cries" from the slave coffles along the docks of Baltimore.[12]

Douglass next blasted the Fugitive Slave Act and the proslavery stances of American churches. The new law demanding complicity by Northerners in the retrieval of fugitive slaves, he told his countrymen, transformed "your broad republican domain" into a "hunting ground for men." Everyone must now practice "this hellish sport," including "your President, your Secretary of State, your lords, nobles, and ecclesiastics . . . as a duty you owe to your free and glorious country." Withering sarcasm indeed. The sheer corruption of the Fugitive Slave Act, which mandated paying commissioners double the money for consigning a runaway back into slavery as opposed to allowing his freedom, could only be matched, said the orator, by the "flagrantly inconsistent" practices of the churches who willingly served as the "bodyguards of the tyrants of Virginia and Carolina." In Douglass's unrelenting staccato labeling, the "tyrant-killing, king-hating, people-loving, democratic Christian defenders" of the Fugitive Slave Act were no better than the pious "scribes, Pharisees, hypocrites who pay tithe of mint, anise, and cumin" at the temple rather than act with "mercy and faith." Far too many clergymen, said Douglass, mouthed the words of the Declaration of Independence but in their religious practice only abetted the "tyrants, man-stealers and thugs." [13]

So he pulled Isaiah from his arsenal and delivered what he believed the churches deserved: "Bring no more vain oblations; incense is an abomination unto me; the new moons and Sabbaths, the calling of assemblies, I cannot away with; it is iniquity . . . I am weary to bear them; and when ye spread forth your hands I will hide mine eyes from you. Yea! When you make many prayers, I will not hear, YOUR HANDS ARE FULL OF BLOOD; . . . cease to do evil, learn to do well; seek judgment; relieve the oppressed." [14] Douglass bore the news that the nation's crimes stood condemned by the prophets of old in the people's own sacred texts.

Douglass brought the second movement to a close in classic, frightening jeremiadic style. After one final long list of the ways slavery "brands your republicanism as a sham, your humanity as a base pretense, and your Christianity a lie," he begged his audience and the nation to break loose from their doom before it was too late. "Oh! be warned! be warned!" he shouted. "A horrible reptile is coiled up in your nation's bosom; the venomous creature is nursing at the tender breast of your youthful republic; for the love of God, tear away, and fling from you the hideous monster, and let the weight of twenty millions crush and destroy it forever!" [15] With such urgency and terrifying imagery Douglass took a breath and paused.

The short and final third movement began calmly with a firm embrace of the antislavery interpretation of the Constitution. That charter, though full of potential double meanings, was in Douglass's view "a GLORIOUS LIBERTY DOCUMENT" full of "principles and purposes, entirely hostile to the existence of slavery." There was still time to act, and legal and moral tools aplenty for his countrymen to save themselves. In a move common in the American jeremiad, Douglass ended with visions of hope. He counseled faith in three elements that had now taken root in his thought. First was the antislavery interpretation of the Constitution. Second was his oft-expressed belief in Divine Providence, in the idea that a moral force would in the end govern human affairs. Seeking again his justification in Isaiah, he confidently asserted, "There are forces in operation, which must inevitably work the downfall of slavery. *'The arm of the Lord is not shortened,'* and the doom of slavery is certain." And third, he appealed to the "tendencies of the age" to modernity. "Change has now come over the affairs of mankind. The arm of commerce has borne away the gates of the strong city. Intelligence is penetrating the darkest corners of the globe. . . . Wind, steam, and lightning are its chartered agents. Oceans no longer divide, but link nations together. . . .

Space is comparatively annihilated. Thoughts expressed on one side of the Atlantic are distinctly heard on the other." Keep faith, he urged Rochester and the nation at large, slavery could not hide from "light" itself.[16]

Having paid a kind of homage to Gerrit Smith with the fulsome statement on the Constitution, Douglass breathed one more famous passage from the Psalms into his own rhythms and on behalf of his race: "Ethiopia shall stretch out her hand unto God." Then, remarkably, he paid an even fuller homage to Garrison and ended the speech with four verses of the abolitionist's poem "The Triumph of Freedom," a testimony of radical biblical devotion to cause:

> God speed the year of Jubilee
>   The wide world o'er! . . .
> Until that year, day, hour arrive . . .
> With head, and heart, and hand I'll strive.

In both secular and sacred terms, prescient in its vision and powerful in its unforgettable language, Douglass had delivered one of the greatest speeches of American history. He had transcended his audience as well as Corinthian Hall, into a realm inhabited by great art that would last long after he and this history were gone. He had explained the nation's historical condition and, through the pain of his indictment and the force of his altar call, illuminated a path to a better day. Douglass the ironist had never been in better form as he converted collective suffering into something like national hope. As Douglass lifted his text from the podium and took his seat, nearly six hundred white Northerners stood and roared with "a universal burst of applause."[17]

Douglass's Fourth of July Address, and his political thought generally in the 1850s, are often remembered and interpreted for their "nearly always hopeful" character, as August Meier once put it. But this assessment hardly captures either the ideological transformations Douglass underwent or the tone, method, and spiritual resolve of his major speeches and writings. The making of Douglass as a political abolitionist in the 1850s should be grounded in the prophetic tradition in which he came to see himself. His was a kind of radical hope in the theory of natural rights, and in a Christian millennialist view of history as humankind's grand story, punctuated by terrible ruptures followed by potential regenerations.[18]

The idea of prophecy is unsettling to the modern secular imagination. But the rhetorical, spiritual, and historical traditions on which Douglass drew so deeply envisioned the prophet as a messenger of God's warnings and wisdom. The poetic oracles of Isaiah or Jeremiah, however bleak or foreboding, were prophetic speech, and therefore God's voice. Douglass, a man of words, needed a language and a story in which to find himself and his enslaved people. Although he never portrayed himself as literally a messenger of God, he found such a language in the Hebrew prophets in whose words, as the theologian Abraham Heschel writes, "the invisible God becomes audible." The "words the prophet utters are not offered as souvenirs," wrote Heschel. "He undertakes to stop a mighty stream with mere words." In Old Testament tradition the prophets were reluctant messengers; God chose them and not the other way around. God spoke through the burdened Jeremiah, who wrote hauntingly, "But his word was in mine heart as burning fire shut up in my bones, and I was weary with forbearing, and I could not *stay*." Douglass felt this same fire of the words in his bones that must get out, although he was never so good at playing the reluctant visionary. The Old Testament prophets fit with Douglass's temperament and his predicament. As James Darsey argues, "It is precisely because the prophet engages his society over its most central and fundamental values that he is radical." Thus prophets are rarely welcome friends; they are always trouble to other people's consciences. They are companions, but not easy companions. They are not "reasonable," says Darsey; they do not abide "compromise," and their role in the world is that of a sacred "extremist." [19] In the 1850s, Douglass relished and tried to perform just such a role.

American Jeremiahs wove the secular and sacred together in their repeated warnings and appeals for higher strivings. As a rhetorical device and as a conception of America, the jeremiad was as flexible as it was pervasive. America's "prophets of doom" thwarted despair and alienation in the temporal vastness and redemptive destiny of their New Israel. Yet this was never the result of a mere temperamental optimism, a flimsy substitute for the kind of hope Douglass forged through enslavement, despair, violence, and his favorite biblical prophets. The land of Judah, after all, lay in utter ruin before God saw fit to redeem Jacob, to offer answers to whether there was "a balm in Gilead," or finally a promise that "there is hope in thine end . . . that thine children shall come again to their own border." For a man who frequently reinvented himself, Douglass saw America in dire need of the same transformation. He had read those prophets as he came to see himself, in some ways, as their descendant exiled in a new Babylon. And his people needed a story to believe in, one with the "radical hope," as Michael Walzer has argued, contained in the Exodus story. "Exodus is a model for messianic and millenarian thought," writes Walzer, "and it is also a standing alternative to it—a secular and historical account of 'redemption' . . . that does not require the miraculous transformation of the material world but sets God's people marching through the world toward a better place in it." [20] For black Americans, Exodus is always contemporary, history always past and present.

Douglass was no formal theologian, but his political hope was hard earned, and he relished the ancient stories in which to find purpose. He did not sit back awaiting God's entry into history; he argued for it in endless variations on the Exodus story. By the early to mid-1850s, he forged a worldview from these biblical roots, from Enlightenment doctrine, especially natural rights, and in the face of several issues and events through which he defined himself. First was the never-ending question of colonization— whether black people could be induced to voluntarily leave the United States and return to Africa—a matter thrust back into the faces of abolitionists in 1849 by Henry Clay and the American Colonization Society's renewed embrace of the strategy.

From December 1850 into February 1851, Douglass delivered a series of formal Sunday lectures in Corinthian Hall. The furor over the passage of the Fugitive Slave Act as well as other issues compelled him to try his hand at such a series, which he intended, as he told Gerrit Smith, to "publish . . . in book form." The hall was nearly packed on at least nine Sundays in these winter months, and Douglass approached his subjects—the nature of slavery itself, fugitive slaves and resistance, the "Slave Power" in the federal government, and colonization—with his usual rhetorical flare and humor, but also now with research. Douglass eagerly used his neighbors, friends, and curiosity seekers to try out his chops as the political commentator he had already become in the pages of his newspaper. "We are in the midst of a great struggle," he announced in the opening lecture. "The public mind is widely and deeply agitated; and bubbling up from its perturbed waters . . . whose poisonous miasma demands a constant antidote." [21]

By late January of 1851 his topic was colonization because Congress, the press, and Clay himself had "breathed upon the dry bones" of the scheme and given it another life. Since his earliest days of reading the *Liberator*, Douglass had encountered the colonization issue. Almost nothing prompted his ire quite like the recurring machinations of colonizationists, who could only imagine an American future through the impulse, as he put it, of "out with the Negroes." When Clay and the American Colonization

Society (ACS) announced a plan for voluntary removal to Africa by free blacks, by a line of steamers financed by the federal government, Douglass turned anger into opportunity. He hated all versions of colonization because it cut to the heart of American racism—the assumptions about African Americans' inferiority, and their inability to cope and compete in a white-dominated society. Douglass saw everything at stake in the colonization debate. It did not matter to him whether the advocacy of colonizing blacks outside of America came from the great moderate slaveholding Whig Clay; the crusading antislavery journalist and editor of the *New York Tribune* Horace Greeley; Douglass's former friend and coworker Martin Delany, who by 1852 launched a campaign for American blacks to emigrate to Central Africa or the Caribbean; or from Abraham Lincoln in 1861–62. Douglass considered it all "diabolical" at its core. He spared no words in his condemnations. The ACS had existed since 1816 as the "offender . . . and slanderer of the colored people," its schemes only a plot to remove blacks from society. To Douglass colonization was never anything but "Satan" with the "power to transform himself into an angel of light—to assume the beautiful garments of innocence." Even to a friend of abolition such as Greeley, Douglass declared in 1852 that colonization in any guise meant "ultimate extermination" for his people.[22]

On this grievance and others Douglass demonstrated that he would not merely denounce the issue but analyze it. He would mix his Old Testament rebukes with argument, wit, and exposition. In a February 1851 speech, "Colonization Cant," Douglass made his aims explicit as a political critic. He had two choices for how to wield his pen and voice: "One is to denounce, in strong and burning words, such theories and practices." This would be the "easiest and commonest." But the other was to "illustrate and expose, by careful analysis." Even when he may have felt weak against such powers as the largest-circulation newspaper in America (Greeley's *Tribune*) or the longtime standard-bearer of the Whig Party (Clay), Douglass loved this kind of rhetorical contest. He expanded his reading, followed congressional debates closely, and laid down a brilliant testimony about both the injustice and the absurdity of colonization. He marshaled statistics about the growth and stability of the free black population in the Northern states and recommended Clay and his "pious" associates consult Exodus 1:10–12. As the children of Israel were made captive, their oppressors were called "to deal wisely with them lest they multiply . . . therefore they did set over them taskmasters, to afflict them with their burdens. . . . But the more they afflicted them, the more they multiplied, and grew."[23]

When Clay argued in Congress that removing blacks from the country *"with their own consent"* was the "great project" of the age, Douglass assaulted Clay's logic by suggesting that the republican revolutions of 1848 in Europe, building a transcontinental railroad across North America, land reform to end poverty the world over, and the effort to establish international arbitration to settle and end wars might rank higher. He shattered Clay's notion of expecting black folks' "consent" for removal. In the Kentuckian's apparent regard for black people rested the real evil, as Douglass summoned Shakespeare's *Henry VIII* to make his point: "My Lord, my Lord, I am much . . . too weak / To oppose your cunning; you are meek and humble-mouthed; / You sign your place and calling in full seeming, / With meekness and humility; but your heart / Is crammed with arrogancy, spleen and pride." Oh, that history might have given us a public debate between Douglass and Clay. The black abolitionist was unrelenting: "If a highway-robber should at the pistol's mouth demand my purse, it is possible that I should 'consent' to give it up. If a midnight incendiary should fire my dwelling, I doubt not I should readily 'consent' to leave it." In such an imagined debate we can see the warring assumptions that were tearing America apart. "The highway-robber has his method," Douglass declared, "the torturous and wily politician has his." [24]

A second, and even more ascendant, issue around which Douglass forged his political consciousness was resistance to the Fugitive Slave Act and the uses of violence. Deep in his soul, Douglass had never relinquished his belief in the right of physical resistance. But nothing had ever forced him to clarify his principles like the reality of the Fugitive Slave law. From his home in western New York, and so close to the northern border, Douglass remembered watching countless fugitives "suddenly alarmed and compelled to flee to Canada." This "dismal march," as he called it, was a large exodus: an estimated twenty thousand blacks may have moved to Canada in the 1850s. In the fall of 1850, Douglass even reported that a "party of manhunters" had come to Rochester intending to seize him and wrest him back to slavery. He admitted to worrying whether his bill of sale and freedom letter from Hugh Auld would withstand legal challenge if he was seized. In speeches Douglass made great use of this threat. For a time, he said, he held up in a "loft, or garret" in his house, having alerted local friends to be watchful. The confrontation never happened, but Douglass made it clear, whether with firearms or other lethal weapons, he was prepared to "greet them . . . with

PRACTICAL ILLUSTRATION OF THE FUGITIVE SLAVE LAW.

*"Practical Illustration of the Fugitive Slave Law," Currier & Ives cartoon, 1852. Note
Douglass's presence in the cartoon as part of the violent resistance with Garrison.*

a hospitality befitting the place and occasion." To a cheering audience in
Boston on October 14, 1850, he urged all Northern blacks to be "resolved
rather to die than to go back." If a slave catcher sought to take the slave
back, shouted Douglass, he "will be murdered in your streets." This was a
new rhetoric born of a new reality; the man of words now found himself at
the center of a crisis in which there were "blows to take as well as blows to
give."[25]

In a speech in Syracuse in early 1851, "Resistance to Blood-Houndism,"
Douglass heightened the rhetoric. At a convention where Garrisonians attacked Douglass's violent language as the "blood and murder" approach, he
found allies among the few Liberty Party loyalists attending. "I am a peace
man," Douglass announced somewhat disingenuously. "But this convention
ought to say to slaveholders that they are in danger of bodily harm if they
come here, and attempt to carry men off to bondage." He pleaded with his
fellow abolitionists, most of them moral suasionists who had long preferred
to "frown slaveholders down," that they should seek "nothing short of the
blood" of any slave catcher in their midst. The slaveholder who chooses the

role of "bloodhound," he continued, had "no right to live." With bravado, Douglass spoke words that would stick to his changing reputation forever: "I do believe that two or three dead slaveholders will make this law a dead letter." Such language had always been latent in the storehouse of Douglass's personal memory; now it burst out with stunning furor, although he provided little advice on just how such a response was to be organized.[26]

Douglass had learned much from the Hebrew prophets, but in pro-slavery America he felt torn between their mixed messages on violence and war. He loved Isaiah's brilliant condemnations of war; beating "swords into plowshares" is one of the most profound pleas in world literature. But he also harkened to the truth in Jeremiah's injunction that in Babylon God's "golden cup" of woe had made the nations "drunk" and "mad."[27] Just when was righteous violence a necessary evil, or even a good? The American Babylon now challenged the radical reformer to decide when vengeance was not only the best strategy, but right.

Many blacks and their white abolitionist allies did not need Douglass's provocations to take to the streets to resist the law or rescue fugitives. Indeed, since the 1830s blacks in Northern cities and towns, from Boston to Pittsburgh and Philadelphia to Detroit, had organized in Vigilance Committees to protect fugitive slaves. Their leaders, such as David Ruggles in New York, who was so instrumental in Douglass's own escape in 1838, had fought in the courts to secure former slaves' freedom, as well as organized clandestine rescues of runaways seized by captors. Douglass paid tribute to these brave pioneers of resistance in an 1851 speech, naming some and honoring their courage to act as long as "a single slave clanked his chain in the land." And in an October 1851 column in his paper, Douglass called the Fugitive Slave Act the "hydra . . . begotten in the spirit of compromise," which assumed the "cowardly negro" who would not fight. But on the contrary, such "legalized piracy" had made the "government . . . their enemy." He predicted that "the land will be filled with violence and blood till this law is repealed."[28] From late 1850 to 1854 numerous attempts were made to rescue former slaves from the grips of police powers, some violent, and with mixed success.

All across the North in black communities people held meetings and passed resolutions vowing resistance to slave catchers with "the most deadly weapons." A new spirit of defiance fed on actual rescues of fugitives. Douglass cheered the news of the successful action in Boston in February 1851 when a Virginia fugitive, Shadrack Minkins, was rescued and spirited off to Canada. The outcome for Thomas Sims in April was not as good. A fugitive from Georgia, Sims was jailed and quickly convicted as white Massachusetts abolitionists worked unsuccessfully either to rescue or bribe him out of custody in Boston. He was returned to slavery even as hung juries refused to convict the many rescuers put on trial for the Minkins rescue. A rescue Douglass celebrated widely was that of Jerry Henry in Syracuse, New York, on October 1, 1851, where a mob born of a Liberty Party convention occurring in that city stormed a jailhouse and broke the fugitive out and took him to Canada. A large police dragnet and investigation led to some twenty-six indictments; no one was convicted, however, by local juries, and of those charged, among the twelve blacks, nine escaped to Canada and were never tried. Because it occurred closer to his own terrain in upstate New York, Douglass made the "Jerry Rescue" a staple of editorials and platform rhetoric as he built the case for the natural right of violent resistance to a law so at odds with human liberty.[29]

Just before the Jerry Henry rescue, in September 1851, Douglass got his own opportunity to directly aid fugitives escaping after violent resistance. At the "Christiana Riot," which occurred in Lancaster County, Pennsylvania, on September 11, a slaveowner, Edward Gorsuch, of Baltimore County, Maryland, attempted at gunpoint to retrieve several of his escaped slaves. In and around an isolated farmhouse, William Parker, a twenty-nine-year-old local black activist and himself a former fugitive slave from Maryland, led a crowd, some with pitchforks and some with guns, to defend the runaways. Parker had for several years led a self-protection society in Lancaster County that fought to rescue fugitive slaves from their pursuers. Gorsuch was shot dead in the melee in Christiana and his son badly wounded. Parker, astute and knowledgeable of Douglass's work in helping fugitives into Canada, quickly led two of the desperate slaves, named Alexander Pinckney and Abraham Johnson, on a two-day, five-hundred-mile journey by foot, horse-drawn carriage, and train to Rochester.[30]

Fugitive slaves running through western New York frequently ended up on Douglass's doorstep. Just as Parker and his charges arrived, and Anna fed and arranged sleeping quarters for them in the house, the news of the Christiana bloodshed arrived in Douglass's hands via the telegraph and the New York newspapers. Great anxiety overtook the household, Douglass recalled. He wrote a short note to his neighbor Samuel Porter asking for help: "There are three men now at my house—who are in great peril. I am unwell. I need your advice. Please come at once." Julia Griffiths too had been sick, she wrote on September 24 in a letter to Gerrit Smith, reporting recent "great excitement in our house" about the Christiana fugitives. Douglass and his small team acted decisively in this little corner of what was already widely called the Underground Railroad. "I dispatched my friend Miss Julia Griffiths to the landing three miles away on the Genesee River," he wrote in *Life and Times*, "to ascertain if a steamer would leave that night for any port in Canada." Douglass drove the three men in his "Democrat carriage" (a small three-seat buggy) to the landing, which is where he feared trouble from officers hot on their trail. He arrived with fifteen minutes to spare before departure. Douglass always remembered this episode with special pride and drama. "I remained on board till the order to haul in the gangplank," wrote Douglass. "I shook hands with my friends, received from Parker the revolver that fell from the hand of Gorsuch when he died, presented now as a token of gratitude and a memento of the battle for liberty at Christiana, and I returned to my home with a sense of relief."[31] That gun remained a sacred talisman in the Douglass family.

When Parker and his small troupe reached Kingston and Toronto, they found black communities rather reticent to embrace them because news had spread of their deeds and that lawmen were in hot pursuit. Parker contrasted such self-protective fear among Canadian blacks, also largely fugitives, to the "self-sacrificing spirit of our Rochester colored brother [Douglass], who made haste to welcome us to his ample home."[32] In their brief encounter, brothers in arms, Douglass and Parker forged a bond of experience.

In Douglass's own early account of the Christiana event, published in his paper on September 25, it was as if he had found the African American equivalent of the Battle of Lexington and Concord in the American Revolution. In Parker and Christiana he had a new character and event to exalt. His "Freedom's Battle at Christiana" is at once a brilliant piece of propaganda, astute reporting, and a mythic testament designed to give the resistance movement bold inspiration. Douglass mocked the proslavery public that seemed shocked that "hunted men should fight with the biped bloodhounds" and kill them out of self-defense. "Didn't they know that slavery, not freedom, is their natural condition? Didn't they know that their legs, arms, eyes, hands, and heads were the rightful property of the white men who claimed them?" He portrayed Christiana and the whole universe of dread and violence caused by the Fugitive Slave Act as a kind of theater of the absurd. Americans did not hunt "fox, wolf, and the bear" anymore. Hunting men, said Douglass, had become the official "choice-game, the peculiar game of this free and Christian country." Such hunters had stepped out of the natural "orbit" of humanity and therefore had "no right to live."

In his re-creation of the Christiana affair, based apparently on his brief interviews with Parker and the other two fugitives, Douglass fashioned a dramatic dialogue between Gorsuch and Parker in their lengthy "parley" at the farmhouse. Gorsuch demanded his "property," and Parker spoke as from a natural-rights treatise saying, "There is no property here but what belongs to me. . . . I own every trunk chair or article of furniture." Parker lectures Gorsuch about how "it is a sin to own men," as Gorsuch's son fires the first shot, which misses Parker.[33]

Douglass converted the entire story into an argument for natural rights, especially after the news came that some thirty blacks and two whites were captured and to be indicted for "treason" in the case. "The basis of allegiance is protection," wrote Douglass. The only law a slave could acknowledge was the "law of nature." "In the light of the law, a slave can no more commit treason than a horse or an ox can commit treason." Then he all but thanked the legal authorities of Pennsylvania for the charge of treason against the Christiana rioters because, he said, "it admits our manhood."[34] Douglass always knew when he had irony, if not the law, on his side.

A relative lull ensued in anti–Fugitive Slave Act rescues during 1852 and 1853. But the furor resumed with new intensity in the spring of 1854 in Boston with the seizure, trial, and return to Virginia of a fugitive named Anthony Burns. The Franklin Pierce administration in Washington, as well as Massachusetts state officials, especially Democrats, made a test case of Burns as they determined to enforce the Act of 1850. Before Burns was finally marched down Boston streets that were draped in mourning by the black community and guarded by several thousand federal troops, a major effort was made to rescue him, resulting in the death of one deputy US marshal, James Batchelder, a local truckman hired as a guard. Although the Burns case was a short-term failure for abolitionism, it became a cause célèbre across the country. During 1852–53 Douglass had kept up a steady drumbeat of attacks on the Fugitive Slave Act. At the Free Soil Party convention in August 1852 he called for "half a dozen or more dead kidnappers carried down South" to keep slaveholders' "rapacity in check." He wanted body counts, and lest the "lines of eternal justice" be "obliterated," he called for "deepening their traces with the blood of tyrants." America had become polarized by the fugitive-slave crisis; even some Garrisonians began to talk of violence. "The line between freedom and slavery in this country is tightly drawn," Douglass argued by early 1852, "and the combatants on either side

. . . fight hand to hand. . . . There is no neutral ground here for any man." [35] He became his own kind of self-styled war propagandist long before 1861.

In the wake of the Burns case Douglass penned a much-discussed editorial, "Is It Right and Wise to Kill a Kidnapper?" He had been answering this question affirmatively for years, but here he claimed the high ground of "moral philosophy." The natural law of self-defense against aggressors or kidnappers, Douglass argued, carried the same power as the "law of gravitation." But this was about human actions and not gravitational pull. So when "monsters" deliberately violate the liberty of a fellow human, other men are justified in killing them if necessary. Further, he contended, if government failed to protect the "just rights of an individual man," then "his friends" may exercise "any right" to defend him. [36]

Douglass dove foursquare into American racial reality. He felt no sympathy for the slain Boston man who got in the way, nor even for his widow. By becoming the hired "bloodhound" Batchelder made "himself the common enemy of mankind, and his slaughter was as innocent, in the sight of God, as would be the slaughter of a ravenous wolf in the act of throttling an infant. We hold that he had forfeited his right to live, and that his death was necessary." But Douglass went even further. This was a public death and was not done as a last resort; rather, it emerges in Douglass's logic as a first resort, an aggressive use of violence to make a political statement. He argued that the killing in defense of Burns would lift the label of "submission" from the heads of black people. They needed this deed for their self-respect. An image in the American mind, Douglass asserted, had to be destroyed—that of fugitives who "quietly cross their hands, adjust their ankles to be chained, and march off unhesitatingly to the hell of slavery." In the public mind, he said, such behavior was judged "their normal condition." But no longer. "This reproach must be wiped out, and nothing short of resistance on the part of colored men, can wipe it out. Every slaveholder who meets a bloody death . . . is an argument in favor of the manhood of our race. Resistance is, therefore, wise as well as just." [37] Douglass harbored no moral ambivalence about violence now; he demanded dead slave catchers as recognition and revitalization of black humanity.

Douglass's harsh, masculine case became both primal and philosophical, bursting from his embittered heart. In the fugitive-slave crisis, Douglass counseled killing kidnappers, and slaveholders generally, because it enhanced the self-respect and "manhood" of his people. His was a position of a gendered moral quicksand, but also astute, political revolutionary violence. He had once fought Covey in a last resort for self-respect. Now he advocated a much larger violence, with greater political meaning, and as a first resort. Douglass now believed in killing slave catchers and slaveholders; the means to such an end were the strategic and moral challenge. He had long laid out deeper and older justifications for such violence than he offered in the 1854 editorial. In many speeches he had limned the old prophets as his steady keel in these troubled waters. Over and over again in 1853 and 1854, Douglass used Isaiah 57:20–21 to make his case: "But the wicked are like the troubled sea, when it cannot rest, whose waters cast up mire and dirt. There is no peace, said my God, to the wicked." Douglass made this holy writ his own kind of oracle in New York in May 1853, in a speech entitled "No Peace for the Slaveholder." The machinations of the Slave Power, he contended, were "done to give peace to slavery. That cannot be done. Peace to the slave-holder! He can have no peace. 'No peace to the wicked, saith my God.'" For Douglass this was a matter of faith and political motivation. The nation may act so "our southern brethren may have peace," he told a Manchester, New Hampshire, audience in January 1854. But "they have undertaken to do what God Almighty has declared cannot be done."[38] The violent imag-ination desperately needed authority and precedent. And a new prophet dearly needed the old ones.

Sometime in February 1853 Douglass paid a visit to Andover, Massachu-setts, at the home of Harriet Beecher Stowe. In an extraordinary column, "A Day and a Night in 'Uncle Tom's Cabin,'" the editor wrote of the en-counter as a magical experience. Not yet a year in circulation, Stowe's book had reached "the universal soul of humanity," Douglass said. He crafted an extraordinary portrait of Stowe. She was at first impression an "ordinary" woman, but in conversation she exhibited a "splendid genius," a "keen and quiet wit," and an "exalted sense of justice." Douglass had many models as a writer and orator; but he may have found a new one. With Stowe, he ob-served, "the words are . . . subordinate to the thought—not the thought to the words. You listen to her rather than to her language." As she talked, he remembered her eyes flashing with "especial brilliance." The inspiration, Douglass said, was "not unlike that experienced when contemplating the ocean waves upon the velvet strand." As though practicing his own fictional chops, the editor continued, "You see them silently forming—rising—rolling and increasing in speed, till, all at once they are gloriously capped in sparkling beauty." Douglass could hardly contain his "reverence," com-paring Stowe to Burns and Shakespeare, "the favored ones of earth." He left

Harriet Beecher Stowe, 1850s.
Photograph, albumen print.

feeling assured that Mrs. Stowe was his "friend and benefactress." He had visited, in part, to discuss her possible support for the "elevation" of free blacks.[39]

Douglass sat down at his desk in early spring 1853 to write a work of short fiction, "The Heroic Slave," which reflected his personal state of mind, his evolving ideas on violence, and the national crisis he sought to influence. The story, first published in his newspaper in March, re-created a five-year period in the life of Madison Washington, the slave who led a successful revolt aboard the domestic slave-trading ship *Creole* in 1841 and sailed it into Nassau harbor, a British port, resulting in the liberation of the more than three dozen slaves.

Douglass had long addressed the story of Washington and the *Creole* mutiny in speeches in the late 1840s in Britain and America. He had kept its memory alive as a historical precedent for slave rebellion and as a rhetorical weapon. He did so especially in New York in April 1849 to twelve hundred blacks at the Shiloh Presbyterian Church, where he told Washington's tale in imaginative terms to the delight and laughter of his audience. In such speeches Douglass tried out some scenes that ended up in the novella, although much of the 1849 effort was devoted to the irony of monarchial Britain freeing self-liberated slaves from "free, democratic" America; he especially relished the image of the former bondmen escorted off the ship in Nassau by "a platoon of black soldiers." He reserved a special sarcasm for how this American "property" emerged as human beings from the clutches of outraged US senators such as Henry Clay and John C. Calhoun, and the secretary of state, Daniel Webster, who issued formal protests to the British. Unmistakably, Douglass left those public audiences with a dire warning: "There are more Madison Washingtons in the South, and the time may not be distant when the whole South will present again a scene something similar to the deck of the *Creole.*"[40]

Literary scholars have suggested many reasons why Douglass turned to fiction, although any explanation begins with his obligation to produce something original for Julia Griffiths's book, *Autographs for Freedom.* The turn to fiction to expose the full danger of the fugitive-slave crisis was also a logical progression in Douglass's evolution as a man of words; he had mastered oratory, achieved fame with autobiography, and now independently engaged the world of journalism. Fiction was the next form, and it offered him some artistic range that even his most creative oratory had not. As critics Shelley Fisher Fishkin and Carla Peterson have shown, Douglass could drop his ever-present *I* pronoun and adopt the more versatile third-person narrator as the voice of his polemic. He gave a profound voice to the slave rebel, in the person of Madison Washington, for an audience that could see such figures only as a dangerous lot. Robert Stepto effectively points to how fiction enhanced Douglass's brilliance in using contradiction and irony. Douglass also found in Washington's story a striking means to give another "salute" to British abolitionists, and especially to declare in storytelling just how much he had broken with Garrisonian moral suasion and pacifism.[41]

Literary historian Robert Levine, moreover, argues that "The Heroic Slave," with its depictions of a noble, stunningly intelligent, yet violent slave rebel, was Douglass's critique of *Uncle Tom's Cabin* (only a year into its enormous success), as well as a potential allegory about the abolitionist's relationship with Harriet Beecher Stowe herself. Washington prays effusively in the novella for his liberation, yet in the end does not rely only on God for freedom. He is beaten savagely like Uncle Tom, but is no Jesus figure. He is the militant, praying rebel, willing to use a "temperate revolutionary" violence, a mixture perhaps of Uncle Tom and George Harris. Douglass did express ambivalence about Stowe's novel in turning to fiction, although he never stopped honoring Stowe herself.[42] He admired her deeply and loved the impact of her book, even as he invented alternative characters.

Douglass's increasingly strident advocacy of violent resistance against the terror practiced against fugitive slaves found an interesting outlet in Washington's story. "The Heroic Slave" allowed Douglass, as one critic has argued, to create "a new edition of himself." He had always portrayed himself as a reluctant fighter, a rebel in self-defense only, the means directed to the end of natural, God-given liberty and self-possession. Douglass was primarily a man of intellect, not brawn, words, not military action. But in Washington he created a character who was a noble combination of all those elements. The plot of the story breaks down at times, and some lame transitions mar its literary quality. Douglass relies, not surprisingly, on a narrator, on speech-making in long soliloquies rather than sustained character development. But within the sentimental literary conventions of the time, it is not difficult to see why many readers, especially if they had read Douglass's and other slave narratives, would have found the story moving and well paced.[43]

When Mr. Listwell, a traveling Ohioan, happens upon the desperate Madison out in the woods, praying and contemplating escape as he also fears leaving his wife and children, we encounter a description of a fabulously heroic figure who represents every element of nineteenth-century manliness, except that of freedom and self-possession. Madison is a "manly form." He is "tall, symmetrical, round, and strong." He combined the "strength of a lion" and a "lion's elasticity." His "torn sleeves" exposed "arms like polished iron." Douglass's Madison was a man of transformative eloquence as well as action. His "heart-touching narrations of his own personal sufferings" to the silent forest, overheard by Listwell, convert the Ohioan immediately to radical abolitionism. And in Listwell ("listens—well") Douglass created a striking character, a stand-in for all the Yankee white abolitionists he had known who had, in their best instincts, helped slaves such as himself to freedom, knowledge, and self-realization.[44] In Mr. Listwell he was trying to tell the Garrisonians something about the role he [Douglass] preferred for them, instead of the one he had come to expect from them.

"The Heroic Slave" contains some striking dialogue and effective narration, a story of how the Underground Railroad did sometimes work for fugitives heading to Canada, and especially of a dilapidated, gothic Virginia tavern, occupied largely by drunken "loafers," where Listwell once again encounters Madison trapped in a slave coffle trudging in chains to Richmond for sale. That tavern, its foreboding, decaying setting, and the dialogues between the loafer and Listwell about slave trading, are Douglass's metaphors for the South and for the nation's predicament with slavery. We never actually see the blood and killing on the deck of the ship, a consideration for the white readers, but witness Madison's magnanimity in saving the first mate's life, as he also converts him to the realization that with this slave rebel he is "in the presence of a superior man."[45] Madison Washington conquers his foes with courage, character, and with the power of the word. He also conquers with the sword as he must. But more restrained than in his speeches and editorials about the need for dead slaveholders or slave catchers, Douglass spares his readers the pools of blood on the deck of the *Creole*. Fiction seems to have allowed for artistic control over the rage within.

Would that Douglass had attempted more works of fiction; he possessed a stunning ability with narrative. By the force of his will, from constant discipline, and from the help of friends, especially Julia Griffiths, he had emerged by the mid-1850s as a versatile and accomplished writer, one deserving a place eventually in that era's literary American renaissance. By late 1854 and early 1855 he took to his desk for even longer stints of time to revise his original *Narrative*, to remake himself once again in print, and produced *My Bondage and My Freedom*, arguably the greatest of all slave narratives. This second autobiography would be at once more revealing and more revolutionary than the first because more political. Douglass was a great storyteller; but now he courted yet new dimensions of personal and public conflict as he plunged into the art of politics. It was one thing to try to be the prophet in Babylon, but quite another thing to be a prophet in party politics.

Chapter 14

MY VOICE, MY PEN, OR MY VOTE

His were not mere words of eloquence ... that delight the ear
and then pass away. No! They were work-able, do-able words
that brought forth fruits in the revolution.

—JAMES MCCUNE SMITH, 1855

By the mid-1850s Frederick Douglass had become a thoroughgoing
political abolitionist. As an outspoken supporter of Gerrit Smith
and the Liberty Party, he rejoiced in Smith's election to Congress
as a radical abolitionist in 1852. "The cup of my joy is full," he told Smith.
"You are now ... within sight and hearing of this guilty nation."[1] Just what
kind of political abolitionist Douglass would be remained a roller-coaster
ride of changing allegiances between principles and politics, between radical fringe political parties and the emerging, powerful Republican Party,
founded in 1854. Clearly, though, his break with Garrisonianism was nowhere more evident than in his embrace of political action, and in his newly
adopted faith that *votes* could one day weaken and destroy slavery. The story
of Douglass's politics in the decade before the Civil War is about the complex education of a pragmatist who never gave up his radicalism.

In a speech to the Ladies' Anti-Slavery Society of Rochester, in January
1855, Douglass delivered an address on the "nature, character, and history
of the antislavery movement." In this deliberative but revealing discussion
of his evolving philosophy of reform, he left no doubt about his independence from Garrisonians. Their doctrines had become "plainly absurd";
they hated slavery sufficiently, but strict moral suasion and disunionism
possessed "no intelligible principle of action." His former Boston friends
represented to Douglass a dying "theory which can never be made intel-

ligible to common sense." As he announced himself a Liberty Party man, embracing the antislavery conception of the Constitution, and not a Republican willing merely to stop the expansion of slavery, Douglass nevertheless seemed to hold his options open. "I would unite with anybody to do right," he said, "and with nobody to do wrong."[2] Douglass's crooked path into the art of politics would be just as troubled as his earlier battles within abolitionism. Since childhood he had understood a great deal about the power slaveholders wielded over their chattel. Now he would try to leverage and destroy that power at its highest levels. As Douglass so often remade himself, so too he reimagined his politics.

Late in 1854, and especially during the first half of 1855, Douglass spent many weeks at his desk writing his ultimate declaration of independence, *My Bondage and My Freedom*, his second, more thorough and revealing autobiography. In long form, it was the masterpiece of his writing life, a work that modern scholars have given a prominent place in the literary American renaissance. *Bondage and Freedom* is not a mere updating of the *Narrative* of 1845; rather, it is an extensive revision of that one great tale Douglass believed he must tell—the story of himself.

A quite different person—a much more mature, politicized writer—crafted *Bondage and Freedom*, as opposed to the twenty-seven-year-old orator of 1845 who needed to establish his identity through literacy. The 1855 book of 464 pages (four times longer than the *Narrative*) came from, as Douglass reminded readers in the first three chapter titles, an "Author" already free and ready to use literacy to engage in an epic argument with his country. Julia Griffiths still resided in Rochester and served as Douglass's coeditor of his newspaper right up until her departure back to England in midsummer 1855. Her labors in the printing office in order to free his time to write certainly testify to her support, if not also her editorial hand in helping make the book possible. Douglass published it in August with Miller, Orton and Mulligan of Auburn, New York, at the price of $1.25. The sales were spectacular—five thousand copies in the first two days and fifteen thousand within three months. Douglass helped market the book by serializing parts of it in his paper, and in the next few years he sometimes took one or more of his sons out on the road with him to sell the book for $1 apiece at his public lectures. Only two years after publication, the same printing house issued a new edition with a banner, "Eighteen Thousand," inscribed on the title page, indicating the number then in print.[3]

Bondage and Freedom achieved what Douglass most wanted: readers and public impact. He could feel buttressed in his belief that words could shape and change history. But he wrote the book for many reasons. In a prefatory letter to his editor, Douglass claimed, with awkward falseness, that he had always possessed a "repugnance" to writing or speaking about himself, and to the "imputation of seeking personal notoriety for its own sake." This odd disclaimer was a convention of the literary apologetics of that era, although ironic in a book that ended with a brilliant argument that human dignity depended directly upon public recognition. But what is most interesting about Douglass's preface is that he turns the disavowal of "vanity and egotism" into a larger purpose. He must write this book, he says, because he is "exceptional" in a world that denies black equality. Douglass portrays himself as the reluctant prophet who must tell his story with a principle at stake for the "whole human family." Slavery was "at the bar of public opinion" now as never before. The "whole civilized world" had to render "judgment," especially because of the growing power of proslavery forces. Moreover, Douglass argued, he wrote for the same reason he founded his own newspaper. The humanity of his people must be demonstrated before a racist world.[4] Such a claim for the public duty of writing a second autobiography reflects just how much this new literary self-creation was a political act.

Douglass further felt compelled to write *Bondage and Freedom* because he had so much to say about the transformations, losses, and gains of his life since the summer he boarded a ship for England. He had many tales to tell about his flowering in the British Isles and about the independence he had sought since returning to America. He was now a more reflective and analytical thinker, and the new autobiography demonstrated this in his embrace of reading and "study," his advocacy of the natural-rights tradition, and his conceptions of violence. Douglass was now truly a *black* leader, a widely acknowledged proponent of the self-reliance and elevation of blacks and their communities. In 1855, Douglass fully emerged as the black Jeremiah.[5]

Over the years dozens of literary critics and historians have interpreted Douglass's autobiographies. Perhaps none has done so more incisively than the first, James McCune Smith, Douglass's good friend, ideological soul mate, and the man he asked to introduce *Bondage and Freedom*. Smith was born a slave in New York City in 1813 and freed by the Emancipation Act of the State of New York in 1827. His mother was a self-emancipated black woman, and like Douglass, his father was presumed white, although Smith

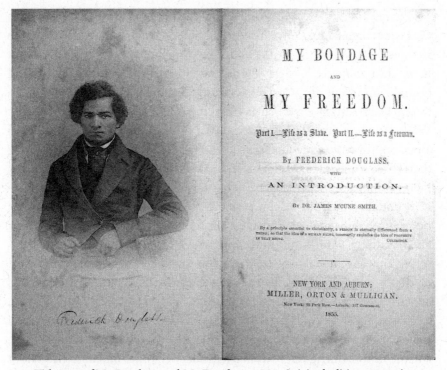

Title page of My Bondage and My Freedom, *1855. Original edition, engraving
from a lost daguerreotype of Douglass. Daniel Vierra photographer.*

seems to have never known his identity. A star student at the African Free
School no. 2 in New York, Smith became an intellectual prodigy. He studied
Latin and Greek and applied to the medical schools at Columbia College
and in Geneva, New York, but was denied admission. With financial help
from New York City black friends, Smith journeyed to Glasgow, Scotland,
at age nineteen, where between 1832 and 1837 he achieved the BA, MA, and
MD degrees.[6]

Upon his return to New York, Smith opened a medical practice and a
pharmacy in lower Manhattan in the year Douglass escaped through the
city as a fugitive. In his spare time, Smith launched his remarkable career
as an abolitionist, a polymath writer and intellectual. He wrote on all manner of subjects, from abolitionist strategies to moral philosophy, from natural sciences to ethnology and chess, from American and world history to
literature. After he met Douglass in the late 1840s, they struck up an extraordinary friendship, perhaps as each other's alter ego. Douglass could learn
so much from Smith, who became a kind of older brother for the former

field hand and caulker. And Smith too learned so much from Douglass's genius with language and from his force of will. Steeped in the classics and the
romantics, Smith found in the younger former runaway a special kind of
hero. The two shared a worldview and abolitionist strategies. Smith too had
become an ardent anti-Garrisonian and shared Douglass's fierce opposition to black emigration schemes emerging from Martin Delany and others.
When the Garrisonian *NASS* tried to trump up a "feud" between them in
1855, Smith wrote in Douglass's paper that no "gnashing of teeth" among
their rivals could sever this "open and avowed friendship between two black
men." Perhaps they also talked about their separate times in Glasgow. They
had combined their mutual prestige in trying to persuade the black convention movement to adopt a plan for an industrial school for young blacks
and a National Council of leadership in 1853. Lack of funding and the pe-
rennial internecine ideological warfare among black leaders doomed most
of their educational and institutional endeavors. Nevertheless, Douglass
and Smith became frequent collaborators.[7]

In addition to his masterful essays, Smith became an experimental
writer, with works often appearing under the pseudonym Communipaw,
a name he took intriguingly from a legendary colonial Indian settlement in
what became Jersey City, New Jersey, a place where an interracial community of blacks, Indians, and Dutch settlers had resisted the English crown.
Smith also penned satires and vignettes under the series title "Heads of the
Colored People" in Douglass's newspaper from 1852 to 1854. These pieces
were depictions of working-class black New Yorkers, giving dignity to the
bootblack, washerwoman, whitewasher, steward, sexton, schoolmaster, and
others. In the term "Heads," Smith brilliantly parodied reigning racial theories of the time, such as phrenology, which argued that the alleged racial
superiority of whites stemmed from larger craniums. Douglass admired
Smith's wit and wordplay and was delighted to publish such forms of literary resistance to the daily racism blacks endured in cities such as New
York. But Douglass confessed to a different taste and criticized some of his
friend's experimentation, preferring instead to portray their race as respectable seekers of the middle class rather than poor, noble laborers. Douglass
considered some of Smith's "Heads" essays too close to "faithful pictures of
contented degradation." The editor warned his friend to watch out for "a rap
or two over his head with a broom-stick," or for the washerwoman throwing "a few drops of moderately hot suds upon his neatly attired person."
In a response to Smith's series in 1853, written after his own recent visit to
New York, Douglass maintained that blacks were better observed not in the

streets but "at their homes." He preferred images of indoor respectability to ironic outdoor subversion, stressing black involvement in churches, literary societies, and especially noting the "watches, clocks, gold pens, pencils, and all sorts of jewelry" he saw in black homes.[8] Douglass seemed to keep his shirts more starched than the good doctor, but such disagreements about class and race only enriched, rather than harmed, the relationship between these two intellectuals.

Smith and Douglass constantly sought out each other about writing and shared a mutual respect for a life of the mind for black men. They shared a brotherhood of experiences of racism, outside and inside the antislavery movement. Douglass judged Smith "without rivals" among black leaders for his "talents and learning" and for his "known devotion to the cause of the oppressed people." Smith's views of Douglass could wax even more effusive. Back in 1848, when the *North Star* appeared, McCune Smith wrote to Gerrit Smith with special praise: "I love Frederick Douglass for his whole souled *outness*, that is the secret of his noble thoughts and far-reaching sympathies. You will be surprised to hear me say that only since his Editorial career has he begun to become a colored man! I have read his paper very carefully and find phrase after phrase develop itself as regularly as in one newly born among us."[9]

In the introduction to *Bondage and Freedom*, McCune Smith imposed a great burden on Douglass, declaring the former slave the embodiment of the cause of human equality, leader among the "living exemplars of the practicability of the most radical abolitionism." When Smith described Douglass's "sacred thirst for liberty and learning," Smith was writing about himself as well.[10] The introduction is not only an intellectual's tribute to another intellectual, but the most formally educated black man of the nineteenth century telling the world what it means that a Frederick Douglass exists at all in slaveholding America.

Smith took special care to show readers that this autobiography was in the end *literature*. Douglass's techniques, according to Smith, were manifold. "Memory, logic, wit, sarcasm, invective, pathos, and bold imagery of rare structural beauty," he argued, "well up as from a copious fountain, yet each in its proper place, and contributing to form a whole, grand in itself, yet complete in the minutest proportions." Douglass's ability with language, Smith maintained, was not in fashioning "mere words of eloquence," but "*work*-able, *do*-able words" that might forge a "revolution" in the world. Douglass wrote *persuasive* prose. In this public use of his personal story as a "Representative American man," Smith believed that Douglass had written an "American book, for Americans in the fullest sense of the idea." [11] In other words, what could be more American at this juncture in history than a brilliantly rendered, lyrical, and terrible story of a man's journey through hell from slavery to freedom? Surely Douglass was moved by his friend's political description of the purpose and power of words doing the work of "revolution."

Nothing seems to have impressed McCune Smith quite like Douglass's uncanny personal memory fashioned seamlessly into an abolitionist polemic. As an intellectual and scientist, Smith was stunned at the extensive probing Douglass gave to his own childhood, of how the autobiography provided a model for just "when positive and persistent memory begins in the human being." Long before neuroscience, Smith pointed to universal psychological and moral insights as well as to features distinctive to an American slave experience. Smith admired his friend's "rare alliance between passion and intellect" as a biographer, his "energy of character" and sheer will, whether working to be "king among caulkers" or craving after language as reader and orator. The scientist was deeply intrigued by Douglass's capacity for recollection. According to Smith, it was Douglass's "wonderful memory" that made his autobiographical writing so powerful. Smith felt moved not by Douglass's mere recall of facts, but by the literary act "when the memory of them [facts] went seething through his brain, breeding a fiery indignation at his injured selfhood," then bursting out in story and characters. [12]

The physician's introduction is one of the early meditations on the art of memory, with a former slave as the subject. Smith knew Douglass well enough to understand how much his younger comrade's persona was now entwined with his identity as a writer. Hence Smith acknowledged Douglass's "descriptive and declamatory powers" and his "logical force." But above all the author of *Bondage and Freedom*, as well as of so many great orations, possessed "style." [13]

Smith took an excursion on the "intellectual puzzle" of Douglass's literary style, wondering whether it stemmed from his white ancestry or from his "negro blood." Here he followed Douglass down the romantic but blind lane of his mother's literacy as the source of the writer's skill. But for Douglass's style, Smith should have looked no further than the rhetoric itself, its cadences, diction, word choices, and indeed its storytelling. The rhythms of Douglass's language were oratorical, and they were deeply indebted, consciously or not, to his life of reading and using the King James Bible. As the literary scholar Robert Alter writes, it was the Old Testament prophets who spoke so compellingly to the "American situation" of the nineteenth century and gave the essence of "style" to its best writers. Style, says Alter, is not "merely a constellation of aesthetic properties," but the "vehicle of a particular vision of reality." Style is not the mere drapery hung on the more important ideology and politics driving the best writing; it is the very life-blood of any prose that persuades about its politics. The Bible gave texture to American prose, and the "King James translation," according to Alter, be-came the "wellspring of eloquence" and the "national book of the Ameri-can people."[14] That is where any "puzzle" about Douglass's source of style should be solved.

That style is on display all over *Bondage and Freedom*. In his brilliant de-piction of slaveholders' psychic unease about the evil system they practiced on the Wye plantation, we can feel Douglass's cadences even as he names his text. "This immense wealth," he wrote, "this gilded splendor; this profusion of luxury; this exemption from toil; this life of ease; this sea of plenty; aye, what of it all?" Douglass loved repetition. Then he begins to throw down his warnings of future reckoning. "Lurking beneath all their dishes are invisible spirits of evil, ready to feed the self-deluded gormandizers with aches, pains, fierce temper . . . lombago and gout." Their souls cannot rest. "To the pam-pered love of ease," Douglass intones with his trademark contrasts, "there is no resting place. What is pleasant today, is repulsive tomorrow; what is soft now, is hard at another time; what is sweet in the morning, is bitter in the evening." Then he simply gives Isaiah and Jeremiah the last word in this or-acle about the woe in history's plan for slaveholders. "Neither to the wicked, nor to the idler, is there any solid peace: '*Troubled like the restless sea.*'"[15] Thus for Douglass style and argument flowed together in the same torrent of words.

All great autobiography is about loss, about the hopeless but necessary quest to retrieve and control a past that forever slips away. Memory is both inspiration and burden, method and subject, the thing one cannot live with or without. Smith grasped just how true this was for a former slave who seized literacy. Douglass's past was a dangerous place to go, but as he re-turned to it over and over, he made memory into art, brilliantly and mis-chievously employing its authority, its elusiveness, its truths, and its charms. Douglass's memory was fraught with conflicted images; sometimes he flat-tened them out to control his tale of self-made ascension, but other times he just described the brutal contrasts and reached for truth. He often hid as much as he revealed, especially about his family and personal life. But what he did reveal in *Bondage and Freedom* is one man's deeply personal indictment of the past and present of his country, and a risky, bold vision of a different future. Smith understood the power of such a symbol. He stressed Douglass's essentially "American . . . *mixed race*" identity. Here, Americans could see their future, Smith contended. Douglass was one of the "Romuluses and Remuses who are to inaugurate the new birth of our republic."[16] Neither man yet knew the prescience of that claim.

Hence, in part via Smith's guidance, we can see the political character of Douglass's second autobiography. If a "stranger" landed in the United States, Smith maintained, and sought out America's most prominent men from the sheer volume of attention in newspapers and on the telegraphs, he would discover Douglass. "During the past winter—1854–5— very frequent mention of Frederick Douglass was made," said Smith. Douglass had emerged as one of those people to whom others say, " 'Tell me your thought!' And somehow or other, revolution seemed to follow in his wake." Indeed, in 1854 the orator's name started to appear frequently in the press in comparison to the other Douglas—Stephen, senator from Illinois. The *New York Tribune* published a poem the former slave must have enjoyed: "Let slavery now stop her mouth, / And quiet be henceforth: / We've got Fred Douglass from the South - / She's got Steve from the North!" The two men nearly encountered each other in Illinois in October that same year. Douglass dogged Douglas as the latter barnstormed, selling the Kansas-Nebraska Act; once they even rode the same railcar, but the senator feigned illness to avoid a confrontation. On the floor of Congress by 1856 a Democrat and a Republican squared off over the principles of their respective parties. The Republican said his adversaries "blindly follow and worship Mr. Douglas." But the Illinois Democrat retorted that while "we worship Stephen A. Douglas," the Republicans "worship Fred Douglass."[17] Smith grasped Douglass's desperate ambition as well as his genuine fame.

Douglass divided *Bondage and Freedom* into two sections, "Life as a Slave" and "Life as a Freeman." Especially in the second section, but even in the first, in some of his enhanced portrayals of his Maryland origins, he wrote as the political abolitionist. In *Bondage and Freedom*, Douglass revised many moments in his story to show himself as a young leader among his fellow slaves, even as the potentially violent black rebel. When Thomas Auld and his fellow Methodists broke up Douglass's first effort at a Sabbath school in St. Michaels, using clubs, one of "the pious crew," recalled Douglass, "told me that as for my part [as leader] I wanted to be another Nat Turner; and if I did not look out, I should get as many balls into me, as Nat did into him." In 1845, Douglass wrote that master Auld found him merely "unsuitable" due to his urban Baltimore experiences. But by 1855, this changed to the tale of a much more aggressive, rebellious slave invoking the bloodcurdling image of slave rebellion.[18]

In the *Narrative* Douglass gave approximately eleven pages to the story of his travail with Edward Covey, while in 1855 he devoted approximately thirty-two pages to this pivotal experience in the grip of the "tyrant's vise." In 1845 Douglass did not seem to hold back in showing how Covey beat him mercilessly when he had fallen to the ground weak with sunstroke; his "blood ran freely." But in *Bondage and Freedom* this episode, which precipitates his delirious flight through the woods to St. Michaels to seek Auld's protection, gets much bloodier still. A half dozen uses of the words "blood" or "bleeding" turn in the revision to fifteen expressions of the same words in two pages. The language becomes biblical, Douglass's sufferings all but a slow crucifixion. His body is mangled by "briers and thorns," his hair "clotted with dust and blood," his feet and legs "scarred" with "blood marks." In the end Auld does not protect him; this would-be Jesus must face near death before he can find redemption. Auld forsakes his wounded slave, saying he "deserved the flogging" because of laziness. He rejects Frederick's appeal for help with the cowardly and revealing statement that, as a hired hand to Covey, he (Auld as owner) could not lose his slave's "wages for the entire year." By 1855 Douglass knew just which biblical story in which to place this moment. He threw the charge of laziness right back at Auld. Slaveholders, he wrote, using Matthew 23:4, "bind heavy burdens, grievous to be borne, and lay them on men's shoulders; but they, themselves, will not move them with one of their fingers." The passage comes just before Jesus demands "woe unto you scribes, Pharisees, hypocrites!"[19]

The much deeper texture of the 1855 work reveals a writer who would now "sound the profounder depths of slave life," to set up his ultimate "disenthrallment." Douglass became "a fish in a net, allowed to play for a time," but was "soon drawn rapidly to the shore." He was now rendered "a wild young working animal," not merely learning to drive the oxen, but becoming the oxen. "I now saw . . . several points of similarity with that of the oxen. They were property, so was I; they were to be broken, so was I. Covey was to break me, I was to break them; break and be broken—such is life." All these metaphors set up the necessity that it is Covey who must be broken in violent resistance. The psychological and physical tyranny portrayed on Covey's farm in *Bondage and Freedom* is the kind that can only result in

Frederick Douglass, c. 1855–58.
Daguerreotype.

not merely individual but collective revolution. As Douglass got the best of Covey in their barnyard rumble, the desperate slaveowner called out to his slave named Caroline (a "powerful woman") to come to his aid. But Caroline, who does not appear in the 1845 version of the scene, steadfastly refuses to answer her master's command, leading the autobiographer to wryly conclude, "We were all in open rebellion that morning." [20]

Thus "goaded almost to madness," and savagely brutalized, Douglass created a vision in which only violence could result, a condition in which he soon argued the entire nation would find itself. In *Bondage and Freedom*, Douglass still claimed he fought Covey only from a defensive posture. But this time he attacked with a "fighting madness" and left no doubt that Covey deserved to be bloodied or even killed. This violence was for the good of the slave's own soul, not merely a matter of natural right. "I was a changed being after that fight," said Douglass the completely recovered Garrisonian. "I was nothing before; I was a MAN NOW. It recalled to life my crushed self-respect . . . A man without force is without the essential dignity of humanity." Similarly, his defense of the escape plot among his fellow slaves on the Freeland farm no longer stood merely as an act of natural right. In *Bondage and Freedom* it stemmed from the right of revolutionary violence. "The slaveholder, kind or cruel . . . is . . . every hour silently whetting the knife of vengeance for his own throat," wrote the autobiographer who was also now the rescuer of the Christiana-riot fugitives. A slaveholder "never lisps a syllable in commendation of the fathers of this republic . . . without . . . asserting the rights of rebellion for his own slaves." [21] A leitmotif in *Bondage and Freedom* is an expectation of violence.

Examples abound in *Bondage and Freedom* of Douglass's more assertive, political brand of autobiography. He captures his burgeoning independence from the Garrisonians in a voice that needed new terrain, new horizons. Walt Whitman could have had a former slave like Douglass in mind in "Poets to Come":

> *Poets to come! orators, singers, musicians to come!*
> *Not to-day is to justify me and answer what I am for,*
> *But you, a new brood, native, athletic, continental, greater*
> *than before known,*
> *Arouse! for you must justify me.*

We do not know if Whitman ever read Douglass. Whitman would have found a new prose poet remembering his "reading and thinking," the orator who "was growing and needed room," now looking steadfastly to "speak just the word that seemed to me the word to be spoken by me." "I myself but write one or two indicative words for the future," said Whitman, "but advance a moment only to wheel and hurry back in the darkness." [22] Douglass wrote in 1855 in depth about his past of darkness so as to chart a much wider future. The reason we remember Douglass is because he found "the word."

Douglass portrayed his sojourn in the British Isles as in part an education in self-realization and political action. The ways that racial prejudice aboard the *Cambria* helped him as a "stranger to get fairly before the British public" read as a primer for his later role as independent editor and activist. The ways Douglass learned to court public scorn, to relish being "unpopular" and "notorious," his defense against the accusation that his speeches attacking America in Britain and upon his return to his native country had been "harsh in spirit," read like the preparation of the Jeremiah of 1852. Like the Old Testament prophets, Douglass knew that he had to lay down the story of grievance and suffering as well as national betrayal before imagining historical renewal. *Bondage and Freedom* contained many elements of the prophetic tradition—warnings, destruction, and reinvention. His splendid apostasy against the Garrisonians led him to a "radical change" in his opinions, and a new platform of political action. [23]

When describing his last years struggling as a moral suasionist, Douglass said he had performed with "pen and tongue." But on the last page of *Bondage and Freedom* he announced his new "disposition." His book added his story to a long "blood-written history," and clouds full of "wrathful thunder and lightning" hovered over the land. But Douglass gave a full-throated statement that "progress is still possible." Then in the final sentence of the book he promised that while "Heaven" lent him "ability," he would strive to "use my voice, my pen, or my vote." [24] Whether the temple could be destroyed by votes remained to be seen.

Douglass spent the decade from 1841 to 1851 trying to denounce voting as a mechanism of black freedom. In the 1850s, however, to secure and cast that vote, along with a recurring struggle with the beast of violence, became the central questions of his public life. Douglass saw slavery as an all-encompassing evil but also as a threat to national existence, and therefore an immensely political problem. Writing much later in *Life and Times*, Douglass described his outlook during these crisis years before the Civil War: "I confess to a feeling allied to satisfaction at the prospect of conflict between North and South. Standing outside the pale of American humanity, denied citizenship, unable to call the land of my birth my country . . . I was ready for any political upheaval which would bring about a change in the existing condition of things." [25] Beneath these remembered yearnings lay the tormented experience of a black abolitionist desperate for political strife that could forge revolutionary change. But in real time, how could a radical with a pen, a voice, and an individual vote ever bring this about? Did he simply await the moral logic and force of history? Or did he act to try to force a cataclysm?

In the years 1854 to 1857, such an upheaval arrived with the passage of the Kansas-Nebraska Act, which potentially opened all western territory to the expansion of slavery. Moreover, a border vigilante war known as Bleeding Kansas broke out and helped to cause the birth of the Republican Party. Douglass threw himself into this new political fray. He launched new lecture tours, with *Bondage and Freedom* in tow. But the "home trials," frequent illnesses, and financial insecurity dogged his life. Having just returned from yet another grueling lecture trip in March 1855, Douglass offered a rare glimpse of his personal moods. His anxiety over the turmoil roiling in the country masked a similar tension in his domestic world in

Rochester. He seemed a weary man reaching out publicly for solace. "Words of cheer in a gloomy moment," he said, "have an inspiring tendency. They brush away the cloud, and let in the sunlight. They cause a smile to nestle in the countenance, once distorted with sorrowful emotions." Was this Douglass's personal cry for help? "This is a cold, bleak world," he concluded, "but not without its oases."[26]

Douglass returned in yet another homecoming to the house out on the edge of Rochester, surrounded by Anna Douglass's ever-enlarging garden. Julia Griffiths still lived with the Porters down the road and labored daily in town at the newspaper office. His five children, all still at home, ranged in age from six to sixteen. Despite the lecture fees, and soon the sales of the second memoir, the newspaper was still in dire straits. In the coming year Douglass was once again beholden to Gerrit Smith's largess to keep *Frederick Douglass' Paper* alive. "I am almost convinced that my paper cannot be sustained," wrote a discouraged Douglass as he told Smith of his $1,500 debt. "I have failed, at least for the moment. The prospect is dark." His explanation was that he was not partisan enough, refusing to join up as a Republican Party organ, but also, as he had long complained, "The colored people do very little to support it." Douglass was privately desperate as he once again begged for money from his benefactor. "I am sick at the thought of the failure of my paper. But when a man cannot stand up he must fall down." His children were "growing up and increasing their demands upon me," Douglass told Smith; he felt a father's "humiliation." He whistled positively as he also pled for help, calling himself "quite well off . . . having health and heart, a good house and lot." *Bondage and Freedom* would sell, he hoped, "as long as I can lecture."[27]

Douglass seemed a man who did not know, once again, quite where to turn. His trusted confidant and coworker Griffiths returned to England in June 1855, her welcome worn-out around the Douglass household. Before leaving, in a partly illegible letter to Gerrit Smith dated September 9 (likely 1854), Julia discussed her plans to return to England. An unnamed "leader" thought it "expedient for me to re-cross the Atlantic," she remarked, although "many others doubtless, (& they weigh greatly with me) . . . seem to indicate this to be my post—I like my occupation exceedingly when I have health & strength to go through my duties to my satisfaction; but that has not been the case of late." Before concluding, Julia left a cryptic Old Testament inspiration: "Pharaoh's Chariot Wheels have dragged heavily."

Frederick Douglass with daughter Annie
Douglass, c. 1854. Daguerreotype.

Drawn from Exodus 14:25, she referred to God opening the waters of the Red Sea for the children of Israel to cross to freedom as pharaoh's soldiers retreated, their chariot wheels breaking and falling off.[28]

Julia would never return to America, despite a claim that her voyage back to England was only a temporary absence. But she would remain a vigorous supporter of Douglass's paper, a loyal correspondent and antislavery organizer in Britain as long as the two lived. Indeed, upon her return to England she began a series of more than eighty public letters, published in Douglass's paper, providing coverage of British antislavery as well as a kind of travel diary of a literary Victorian woman. The first of those letters, in a series entitled "Letters from the Old World," provided a gem of travel writing, complete with portraiture of people she met, of conversations, and the power and beauty of nature. As her ship sighted land on the return voyage, she "beheld the Welsh mountains, clothed with verdure, and irradiated by the soft sunshine of early morning." However burdened, Douglass could escape into Julia's frequent travelogues, especially when she reached the Scotland he so loved. She was a beautiful, if florid, writer, especially in the land where "Walter Scott is echoed everywhere," in "every wind that blows, every breeze that sighs, every bird that sings, every flower that blooms."[29] Julia knew how to make her friend miss her.

Within a year of Griffiths's departure from Rochester, another white woman stepped into Douglass's life and caused even more private complication, even as she too became an assiduous participant in the reformer's intellectual life. Ottilie Assing, a German Jewish radical Forty-Eighter, moved to America to pursue a new career as a journalist in 1852, taking up residence in Hoboken, New Jersey. She traveled, met many reformers, and wrote numerous essays for the German journal *Morgenblatt*. Well educated, freethinking, and nonreligious, steeped in the German romantics, she read *Bondage and Freedom* in 1855 and determined to translate it into German, which she did by 1860, with her own introduction replacing that of McCune Smith. She came to Rochester to meet Douglass in 1856 and, for the next twenty-four years, almost never left. Douglass's relationship with Assing would be tempestuous to say the least, but oddly with little controversy—except at home.[30]

Douglass's marriage was greatly strained in the 1850s. He and Anna rarely shared the same friends, nor an intellectual companionship. The meaning of his life's calling and ambition drew them apart even as Frederick greatly depended on Anna's skill and devotion as homemaker and mother. Douglass left few open comments about Anna and their marriage, but he did sometimes complain to friends. In 1857, after returning from the speaking circuit, Douglass wrote harshly of his wife: "I am sad to say that she is by no means well, and if I should write down all her complaints there could be no room to put my name at the bottom, although the world would have it that I am actually at the bottom of it all." Then his anger turned ugly in a comment about Anna's use of language: "She still seems able to use with great ease and fluency her powers of speech, and by the time I am home a week or two longer, I shall have pretty fully learned in how many points there is need of improvement in my temper and disposition as a husband and father, the head of the family!" This rare glimpse into Douglass's domestic situation adds meaning to the fear of failure he had expressed to Gerrit Smith. As husband and father, he also had much to ponder. That their marriage survived is a testament not only to the rarity of divorce in the nineteenth century, but especially to Anna's utter lack of options and to Douglass's own lifelong craving for a sense of "home," about which he wrote so compellingly in *Bondage and Freedom*.[31] In the mid-1850s, as be-

Anna Murray Douglass, 1840s.

fore, Douglass plowed his private woes into great public activism. He and Anna sustained a home under trying circumstances that for moderns might have driven them apart.

In the 1852 political campaign Douglass established a pattern of shifting party allegiances and endorsements; in that year he remained ostensibly a member of Gerrit Smith's fledgling Liberty Party while openly supporting the new Free Soil presidential ticket of John P. Hale and George Julian. The Free Soil Party drew its energy and electoral strategy from the crisis over the Mexican War in the late 1840s and the Fugitive Slave Act of 1850. At the Free Soil convention in Pittsburgh in August, Douglass announced himself proudly a "disciple" of Gerrit Smith and especially of the doctrine that any government legally sanctioning slavery was a "foul and blasting conspiracy."[32] But from that radical high ground Douglass stepped down to continually learn that politics and perfectionism did not easily mix.

That summer and fall, Douglass all but surrendered the editorship of his paper and allowed Julia Griffiths and his assistant, John Thomas, to take the reins. He went on the road constantly all over New York State and for a two-week tour of Ohio in September. Douglass felt for the first time politically "called to the field," he told his readers. Julia asked subscribers to be patient, since "the summons for him [the editor] seems to come simultaneously from almost every county in the state of New York." Wherever the train lines or a carriage could carry him, Douglass stumped for the Free Democracy (Free Soilers) and against both the Whig and Democratic Parties. He delivered some fifteen lectures in and around Dryden and McGrawville, New York. On October 1 he announced appearances in at least eleven towns in Tompkins County alone. The schedule was backbreaking, but on an earlier stop in Ithaca in late July, Douglass described a little break before the evening speech. He hiked a "mile or two" along the east bank of Cayuga Lake until he found "a suitable place to renew my acquaintance with the art of swimming." He told of his sheer joy in a kind of diary for the paper: "Here all my boyish pranks in the front basin of Baltimore were renewed. I had a glorious swim." [33]

On his Ohio tour, which included a convention in Salem, Douglass was Jim-Crowed twice. Going west on a boat on Lake Erie between Buffalo and Cleveland, the captain forced him to sleep on wood planks on the deck. On the return eastward, a captain "assaulted" Douglass at a dinner table. He "pulled the chair from under us and brought us down upon the cabin floor," wrote the traveler. In Buffalo, Douglass consulted a lawyer, only to be told that the law was clearly on his side, but that no local judge would convict someone in such a case. "There is something canine in the bark and growl of a genuine negro-hater," concluded the weary traveler, who could still smile. "But a truce to puppies!" He loved his Ohio audiences of abolitionists. He felt inspired by the throngs "composed . . . mainly of hard-handed farmers, their industrious wives, daughters, and sisters." Back home in New York surging in and out of small towns and villages, Douglass spoke twice a day, he said, for a week in Oneida and Herkimer Counties. In mid-October he spoke in ten towns in seven days, and at the end of the campaign he reported a total of eighty lectures in some forty days on the road. [34]

Everywhere Douglass went, he denounced the Fugitive Slave Act, argued that slavery could never be legal, demanded his auditors enter the civic and political fray, and acknowledged that the characters in *Uncle Tom's Cabin* danced in the heads of voters in this season of politics. Abolitionist principles, he believed, had never had such a political airing as now. At a speech in Ithaca in October he boiled down his decadelong career to a personal statement of his politics: "I have one great political idea. That idea is an old one . . . widely and generally assented to; nevertheless . . . generally tramped upon and disregarded." The best expressions of his views, he said, were "found in the Bible." From Proverbs, he declared, "RIGHTEOUSNESS

EXALTETH A NATION—SIN IS A REPROACH TO ANY PEOPLE." Such a moral declaration, he concluded, "constitutes . . . the whole of my politics." Such a choice of Scripture is interesting for a recovering moral suasionist. In all the maxims about wisdom and folly in Proverbs, though, Douglass would also have read many passages about how the prudent gain knowledge and understanding, and the deceitful fall in folly.[35] His politics was anything but settled; like his sense of abolitionist strategy, it grew into a mixture of righteousness and pragmatism.

In his paper, Douglass delivered a ringing endorsement of Hale and the Free Soilers, despite that Hale had refused to declare slavery a form of "piracy," as demanded by the Liberty Party. The bulk of Douglass's endorsement reveals a mind torn between moral principle and political action. He urged Liberty men to remember that a vote could seldom represent all of one's moral convictions. Sounding like a veteran politician, he offered a "rule" for action: "The voter ought to see to it that his vote shall secure the highest good possible, at the same time that it does no harm."[36] Once converted to political abolitionism, Douglass characteristically gave it his heart, mind, and soul; but he demanded more of it than it could deliver. Demonstrating his political fickleness, just before the November 1852 elections, Douglass withdrew his support of the Free Soilers and instead rejoiced in Gerrit Smith's election to the US Congress.

Within a year and a half everything seemed to change. Douglass's initial reaction to the Kansas-Nebraska Act in early 1854 was a combination of outrage and refurbished hope. In his view, the repeal of the Missouri Compromise (the geographical guarantee against slavery north of the 36°30' parallel) resulted from the "villainy of the slave power" and the "pusillanimity of the North." "The Republic swings clear from all her ancient moorings," he rejoiced from the isolation of Rochester, "and moves off upon a tempestuous and perilous sea. Woe! Woe! Woe to slavery! Her mightiest shield is broken . . . and for one, we now say . . . let the battle come." He felt encouraged by the increasing severity of the various drafts of the Kansas-Nebraska bill. "If we must have the repeal of the Missouri restriction," Douglass wrote privately, "let nothing be done to soften the measure." With good reason he anticipated a political awakening in the North, a rise in antislavery sentiment, and the splintering of political parties along sectional lines. Here was the anticipated political upheaval beyond anyone's control. "Let the old parties go to destruction," Douglass gleefully urged, "and henceforth let there be only a free party, and a slave party."[37] A whole new front of attack seemed now to have opened, the ironic result of the Slave Power's insatiable quests for dominion.

The social furor and the rapid political realignment that gave birth to the Republican Party in 1854 provided the kind of revolutionary circumstance Douglass sought. He exploited every opportunity to expose the growing hostility between North and South, employing the concept of "irrepressible conflict" considerably before the Republican William H. Seward made it famous in 1858. Douglass strove not to assuage fears of the impending crisis but to hasten its coming. By 1855 he proclaimed, "The hour which shall witness the final struggle is on the wing. Already we hear the booming of the bell which shall yet toll the death knell of human slavery." As the old prophets had foretold for their own decadent and lost age, a vengeful and just God, and Douglass would add natural law, made this American conflict a certainty. His message was—people, get ready. "As a nation," Douglass exhorted, "if we are wise, we will prepare for the last conflict . . . in which the enemy of Freedom must capitulate." His fondest hope was that the new politics would bring an age of "Truth and Error, Liberty and Slavery, in a hand-to-hand conflict." In the old stories, Douglass told his readers, they would find the vision to end all compromises. He performed in editorials as a prophet with an ultimate duty of hope. "The disintegration of the once powerful political parties," he announced, "is a cheering and significant sign of the times. The throne of the despot is trembling to its deep foundations. There is a good time coming."[38]

The imprecision of such rhetoric required at least a clarified enemy. The abstract evil of slavery was never sufficient. But in the concept of the Slave Power Douglass found a means to convert the enemy of black people into the enemy of all Americans. The idea of a Slave Power conspiracy was at least as old as the 1820s, but in the 1850s it became the staple of antislavery rhetoric. Douglass had plied these waters before the Republicans made it their own. In May 1853 he gave the Slave Power clear definition. It was "a purely slavery party" in national affairs, and its branches reached "far and wide in church and state." The conspiracy's chief objectives were suppression of abolitionist speech, removal of free blacks from the United States, guarantees for slavery in the West, the "nationalization" of slavery in every state of the Union, and the expansion of slavery to Mexico and South America. If not stopped, the Slave Power would "drive the Almighty from the councils of the nation" as it "shot its leprous distilment through the lifeblood" of the people. Slavery was no longer merely a moral wrong committed against black people in the South, but a widening threat to the liberties of white people. "One end of the slave's chain must be fastened to a padlock in the lips of northern freemen," Douglass wrote, "else the slave will himself become free." [39]

Here now was an enemy of all mankind. Everything was at stake. "Slavery aims at absolute sway," Douglass argued in 1854. "It would drive out the schoolmaster and install the slave-driver, burn the schoolhouse and install the whipping post, prohibit the Holy Bible and establish the bloody slave code, dishonor free labor with its hope of reward, and establish slave labor with its dread of the lash." This evil heart of the political system had to be surrounded, stopped, and killed. By 1855, as the Kansas crisis deepened, Douglass saw the Slave Power as an all-encompassing national plague with a "natural craving after human flesh and blood." It was an onslaught upon the rights of all Americans to sustain the claims of a few. Most poignantly, the Slave Power delivered its "Decalogue of slavery . . . written all over the country, in its highways and its hedges, its villages and towns, and cities." It had to expend "every energy in expanding the area of despotism" to feed its survival. Citizen Douglass, imagining the unknown revolution to come, demanded war upon this monster. "Show the enemy no quarter," he pleaded. "Annihilation, not restriction, this is the motto to be inscribed upon our banners. Off with his head and his heart will cease to beat forever." [40] He put prudence aside; the politics of fear exploded from the pages of the radical journalist in Rochester.

Like several other abolitionists, Douglass later became a kind of historian of the Slave Power, devoting an entire chapter, "The Increasing Demands of the Slave Power," to the topic in his 1881 autobiography, *Life and Times*. Searching for a central theme of the 1850s, Douglass honored his fellow abolitionists, but gave greater credit to the "aggressive character of slavery itself." In Douglass's telling, antislavery agitators merely reaped the political results of the slavocracy's innate aggression to dominate the nation's future. In *Life and Times* he quoted the long section of his 1853 New York speech in which he analyzed the character of the Slave Power. He chose an excerpt probing the slaveholders' anxious obsession with "security." But again, he summoned Isaiah to his aid: "There can be no peace, saith my God, to the wicked." Even if "every antislavery tongue . . . were silent— every antislavery organization dissolved," Douglass said, "still the slaveholder could have no peace." In 1881, as in the 1850s, Douglass still needed to declare God, nature, history, and psychology on the side of abolition. "In every pulsation of his [the slaveholder's] heart, in every throb of his life, in every glance of his eye . . . would still be waked an accuser, whose cause is, 'thou art verily guilty concerning thy brother.' " [41]

As the accuser Douglass found a new arena in politics. But the struggle demanded a new kind of will and persuasion. Douglass wanted the controversy to cause Americans to look inward and not simply to the West or to Washington. Confrontation with the Slave Power, the editor hoped, would force an even deeper confrontation with race. Black humanity, or whether blacks had rights exceeding those of a horse, Douglass claimed in 1856, formed "the grand hinge of American politics." He did not want the Slave Power frenzy at election time to deflect attention from a deeper enemy—racism itself. He remained on guard against the tendency in anti-slavery politics of "opposing slavery but hating its victims." Hence, Douglass's bitter chastisements of Horace Greeley on the issue of black suffrage. The famed editor of the *New York Tribune* advised blacks to lie low, be patient about the right to vote, and concentrate rather on their own "moral debasement." They should stop "jawing about their rights," Greeley wrote with what Douglass called "condescension." Such counsel of patience appalled Douglass, and he fought back, insisting upon complete equality at the polls, vowing never to keep "out of sight," and invoking Byron: "They who would be free, themselves must strike the blow." Greeley's comments remained useful as a recruiting device. To draw blacks to a national convention in the fall of 1855, Douglass said, "The eye of the world is upon us." Urged to "keep out of sight," he wryly announced, "our counselors should be aware that black bodies appear to better advantage in the sunlight." [42]

As Douglass made the Slave Power rhetoric his own, he also worried about the potential for compromise. Seeking consensus with the Slave Power, Douglass maintained, would be "thawing a deadly viper instead of killing it." A radical pragmatist had many fences to straddle now; all he could do was to keep faith in the "monster's" inherent tendency to overreach and destroy itself. Coining a new label in 1855, Douglass called the slavocracy the "Black Power," arguing that it would go the way of all absolute despotisms. "While crushing its millions," he said, "it is also crushing itself." It had "made such a frightful noise" with the "Fugitive Slave Act . . . the Nebraska Bill, the recent marauding movements of the oligarchy in Kansas," that it now performed as the abolitionists' "most potent ally." Douglass detected a great change in Northern public opinion. Instead of regarding the abolitionists as mere fanatics "crying wolf," the masses now perceived the evil in their midst and themselves cried "kill the wolf." [43]

. . .

More than from any other single issue before the war, Douglass derived his sense of political pragmatism from coming to grips with the Republican Party, the odd assemblage of former Whigs, antislavery Democrats, Liberty Party men, and even nativists who all coalesced around stopping the expansion of slavery. His reactions ranged from vehement opposition to cautious support. Two contradictory themes run through all of Douglass's rhetoric regarding the Republicans. He demanded adherence to abolitionist principles; the free-soil position, therefore, offered him little immediate satisfaction, even as it provided hope of thwarting slavery's future. But simultaneously, he found it impossible to resist the appeal of a broad coalition that could discredit slavery.

From 1854 to the Civil War, Douglass found much to attack in Republican ideology. At times he condemned "free soilism" and the Slave Power with almost the same ire. "Free soilism is lame, halt, and blind," wrote Douglass in 1855, "while it battles against the spread of slavery, and admits its right to exist anywhere." His editorials occasionally burned with bitterness over the nonextension argument. Drawing a boundary around slavery, though a departure, seemed so limited to one who had grown up on immediatism. "Instead of walking straight up to the giant wrong and demanding its utter overthrow," he complained, "we are talking of limiting it, circumscribing it, surrounding it with free states, and leaving it to die of inward decay." To Douglass in 1855–56, the Republican vision seemed a hollow promise leaving millions doomed to bondage.[44]

By the presidential election year of 1856, Douglass refused to formally join the Republican Party and tried to steadfastly adhere to abolitionist principles. The Republicans, he asserted in April, possessed "not a single warm and living position . . . except freedom in Kansas" and represented only a "sinuous political philosophy, which is the grand corrupter of all reforms." As the title of an editorial indicated, Douglass intended to do his "duty as an antislavery voter." That duty meant emphasis on the "sin" of slavery and the impossibility of property in man; it meant, at least at this juncture, the preservation of his "antislavery integrity."[45] But another potent force drew Douglass to the duty of hope, to the agonizing awareness that slavery had to be met in the shadow lands of politics.

Douglass's denunciations of the Kansas-Nebraska Act led almost inevitably to tacit support of the emerging Republican Party, formed in the law's turbulent wake. The Kansas controversy had become the "great question of the age," he said by fall 1854, and it prompted him to devise his own strangely naïve scheme for making Kansas a free state. Douglass proposed an ambitious emigration plan by which one thousand free black families from Northern cities would be resettled in Kansas territory. His "army of One Thousand families" was to be organized and financed by Northern philanthropy. But fervor is about all Douglass could give his own idea. "The true antidote . . . for black slaves," he argued, "is an enlightened body of black freemen." Suddenly, Douglass was an impractical emigrationist dreamer. Douglass's plan conveniently ignored, for an interlude, that the "free labor" ideology around which the Republicans had formed meant for many free *white* labor.[46] Douglass soon abandoned what he admitted was an "imperfectly presented" scheme.

From such a combination of confusion, idealism, and frustration, Douglass approached the election of 1856. The "purity" and "high anti-slavery ground" he had demanded in spring gave way slowly over the summer. He continued to proclaim himself a devotee of Gerrit Smith and his new Radical Abolition Party, which pushed the doctrine that the federal government had the duty to abolish slavery everywhere. In a June 1856 endorsement of the Radical Party, he kept faith with his mentor that "Policy is controlled by Principle, and not Principle by Policy." Using a strict antislavery conception of the Constitution, Douglass stayed on high ground: "Whatever is right is practicable." But by August Douglass did an about-face, shocking some of his friends, and enthusiastically endorsed for president the Republican John C. Frémont, famous western explorer and former California senator. Suddenly, Douglass preached expediency like an old ward boss. His "heart and judgment" still clung to Gerrit Smith's principles, he insisted, like "ivy to the oak." But the "time has passed," Douglass now believed, "for an honest man to attempt any defense of a right to change his opinion as to political methods of opposing slavery." He justified his flip-flop by claiming a desire to affect power by any means possible. "Antislavery consistency itself requires of the antislavery voter that disposition of his vote . . . which, in all the circumstances . . . tend[s] most to the triumph of Free Principles. . . . Right antislavery action is that which deals the . . . deadliest blow upon slavery that can be given at that particular time. Such action is always consistent, however different may be the forms through which it expresses itself."[47] He thus offered a capacious definition to political pragmatism.

Douglass further defended his turnabout by arguing that he would do his best to uphold the Radical Abolition platform within the ranks of the Republicans. Moreover, all the depredations of the Slave Power demanded a forceful response. He wanted abolition politics to be the "aggressor" at the ballot box, instead of always on the fringe. With "slavery extension," Douglass argued, slaveholders had given abolitionists an invitation to battle, and he understood just how much Republicans, with their capacity to win high offices, threatened the South. Douglass urged his radical friends to "take them [Republicans] . . . not merely for what they are but for what we have good reason to believe they will become." Republicans were millions strong, while Radical Abolitionists operated like "dwellers in the mountain peaks of the moral world." Douglass urged a vote for Frémont as the path to do "a possible good thing" while larger aims could wait. Stop seeking purity, he told his critics among radicals, and start with what is possible. "The Ethiopian can change his opinion," he wrote during the fall campaign, "if not his color, and yet be perfectly true to the great cause of his life." [48]

Douglass's 1856 endorsement of the Republican Party conformed to a pattern he had established in 1848 and 1852 when he supported the Free Soil Party. In the Liberty Party and its doctrinal successor, the Radical Abolitionists, Douglass always had a party for his principles, but in the Republicans, as with the Free Soilers before, he found a party for his hopes. In late August 1856 he wrote to Gerrit Smith, hoping his mentor would understand if not approve: "I support Fremont as the best thing I can do now, but without losing sight of the great doctrines and measures, inseparable from your great name and character." It would hardly be the last time Douglass cast his vote for hope in general elections, then in off-year contests retreated to his principles among the radicals. By the fall of 1857, in the wake of Frémont's defeat by James Buchanan, Douglass changed his tune markedly about the Republicans, charging them with "culpable imbecility" and "narrow, contracted conservatism." Because it had not embraced any form of black equality and sought only power in numbers, the Republican Party had become "rotten," Douglass maintained, and did not "deserve success." [49]

But for the rest of his life Douglass voted for a Republican for president. Frémont did extremely well against the Democrat James Buchanan, known widely as a Northern man with Southern sympathies. Although defeated, the Republicans, as a sectional antislavery party, loomed as a powerful threat to Southern interests, despite their not even being on the ballot in most slave states. Buchanan was elected with only 45 percent of the vote, while Frémont drew 33 percent and the Know-Nothing party (nativist) candidate, Millard Fillmore, garnered 21 percent. The election settled little in the slavery crisis, except that the Slave Power, in the view of most antislavery Northerners, now had a willing advocate in the White House and the Republicans had the potential to divide American politics.

Within two days of Buchanan's inauguration in March 1857, the US Supreme Court announced the *Dred Scott* decision, and once again, everything seemed to change. Dred Scott's legal quest for his freedom because of a nearly five-year residence on the free soil of the state of Illinois and the free territory of Minnesota had wound its way through lower courts for years in Missouri and finally reached the docket of the Supreme Court in 1854. Chief Justice Roger B. Taney, a Marylander and former slaveowner, and his 7–2 majority on the Court first ruled on jurisdiction, declaring Scott not a citizen due to his race and therefore without any right to sue in federal court. Under pressure to somehow "settle" the vexing problem of slavery expansion once and for all, Taney and his majority went further and declared the Missouri Compromise line of 1820 unconstitutional. They upheld a slaveholder's right to use and transport his private property in slaves under the due process clause of the Fifth Amendment. Congressional authority over slave property, said Taney resoundingly, extended only to "guarding and protecting the owner in his rights." But then Taney went further yet and made infamous history with an opinion proclaiming that blacks "had for more than a century been regarded as beings of an inferior order . . . so far inferior that they had no rights which the white man was bound to respect."[50]

To antislavery Northerners the idea of a Slave Power conspiracy had never seemed so evident. In the wake of *Dred Scott v. Sandford* shock waves spread across American society like nothing before it in the long story of the slavery debate. Most white Southerners could not have been more delighted by a decision of the High Court confirming their long-argued claim of state sovereignty—the right of slave ownership everywhere. The message to the North was that legally, slavery could indeed not be prevented in any western territory, and perhaps even in the free states themselves. Some Republicans openly anticipated now a second *Dred Scott* decision doing just that—making slave property inviolable in the entire United States.[51] On the day after Taney's announcement African Americans, free or enslaved, lived in the land of the *Dred Scott* decision, in the country that now declared from its highest councils that black people had no future as citizens in the United States.

In the wake of *Dred Scott*, the operative emotion in Northern black communities and among abolitionists was either despair or revolutionary outrage. It quickly caused a revival of emigrationist fervor and divisive debate among black leaders trying to imagine a secure future. And it revived open contemplation of violent resistance. In May 1857, Douglass delivered a major address, "The Dred Scott Decision," in New York as well as other venues in the coming summer. The long speech is a remarkably tortured illustration of his efforts to perform his self-styled duty of hope in the face of the thunderous rejection handed down by the American nation. The court's decision, said Douglass, was a "vile and shocking abomination." Though it seemed that "the omens are all against us," and ultimate emancipation merely a "wild, delusive idea," he promised to signal "signs of encouragement."[52]

Douglass drew from his most fundamental sources of history, spirit, and philosophy, from the natural-rights tradition and a biblical sense of long-term faith that Providence would still guide their cause toward justice. This was, however, a tough sell in 1857. He first had to lay down the status of woe and gloom by embodying the despair: "I own myself not insensible to the many difficulties and discouragements that beset us on every hand. They fling their broad and gloomy shadows across the pathway of every thoughtful colored man in this country." Douglass captured the horrible uncertainties of the moment. "I see them clearly, and feel them sadly. With an earnest, aching heart, I have long looked for the realization of the hope of my people . . . and looking out upon the boundless sea of the future, I have sought in my humble way, to penetrate the intervening mists and clouds, and perchance, to descry in the dim and shadowy distance the white flag of freedom, the precise speck of time at which the . . . long entombed millions rise from the foul grave of slavery and death." Personal and group pain had to be named and expressed before any new resolve could be imagined; Douglass thus gave Taney and the nation an answer as lyrical as it was terrible: "But of that time, I can know nothing, and you can know nothing. All is uncertain at this point."[53]

As usual, Douglass then shifted key and appealed to God and nature, to the old stories and old faiths. Where else could he go? "David, you know," pleaded Douglass, "looked small and insignificant when going to meet Goliath, but looked larger when he had slain his foe." He took heart that antislavery had transformed into its new political mode. He reminded his auditors that every compromise on slavery extension had purported to "settle" the question, but had never succeeded. "The fact is, the more the question has been settled, the more it has needed settling." Above all, Douglass turned to "higher law" doctrine. "The Supreme Court of the United States is not the only power in the world," Douglass fervently declared, "but the Supreme Court of the Almighty is greater." Taney "could not change the essential nature of things, making evil good, and good evil." Repeatedly Douglass invoked the "law of nature" and of God's imminent actions. The speech became a kind of political prayer delivered by a prophet summoning God to the aid of history.[54]

In Douglass's view, God and history were merely "keeping the nation awake," as the Slave Power advanced too far, "poisoning, corrupting . . . the institutions of the country," readying the people for "the lightning, whirlwind, and earthquake" to come. He grasped hope from a dreadful narrative of cataclysm and woe. Douglass's speech fell at times into a frustrating vagueness, with appeals to keep faith in the "tendencies of the age." But stunningly, he ended the address with open advocacy of violence, an entreaty for all to remember that the slaves might at any time rise in insurrection. Most strikingly, he recited two verses of his own poem "The Tyrant's Jubilee," a long, remarkable work he had published in his paper in January 1857:

> *The fire thus kindled, may be revived again;*
> *The flames are extinguished, but the embers remain;*
> *One terrible blast may produce an ignition,*
> *Which shall wrap the whole South in wild conflagration.*
>
> *The pathway of tyrants lies over volcanoes;*
> *The very air they breathe is heavy with sorrows;*
> *Agonizing heart-throbs convulse them while sleeping,*
> *And the wind whispers Death as over them sweeping.*

Slavery was doomed, Douglass assured his audiences; of that he was "morally certain." But he stood ready to expect emancipation by "fair means or foul means, in quiet or in tumult, in peace or in blood."[55] Prophets must say what they see, however dreadful and uncertain. Within eight months of his *Dred Scott* speech, Douglass and his family hosted for three weeks at their Rochester house a guest who would fulfill and trouble Douglass's prophecy.

Chapter 15

JOHN BROWN COULD
DIE FOR THE SLAVE

John Brown's raid upon Harpers Ferry was all his own. . . . His zeal in the cause of freedom was infinitely superior to mine. Mine was as the taper light, his was as the burning sun. I could speak for the slave. John Brown could fight for the slave. I could live for the slave, John Brown could die for the slave.

—FREDERICK DOUGLASS, HARPERS FERRY, 1881

John Brown was charismatic, inspiring, confounding, courageous, mysterious, intimidating, given to religious zealotry, and even at times a bit boring. But he and his deeds were unforgettable. Before Frederick Douglass first met Brown in 1847, or possibly early 1848, in Springfield, Massachusetts, Douglass had heard about him, especially from other black abolitionists, who "when speaking of him, their voices would lower to a whisper."[1] A touch of legend, creatively crafted in *Life and Times*, infused Douglass's extraordinary remembrance of his relationship with the leader of the Harpers Ferry raid.

In real time, Douglass's first recorded description of Brown, written in the *North Star* in February 1848 after returning from a lecture tour, conforms to later remembrances. Brown was among the key people Douglass met in Springfield after delivering a lecture that the local paper deemed objectionable because the former fugitive had "stigmatized the whole country" as a "slave hunting community." Whether Brown attended the lecture is not clear, but in what Douglass called a "private interview" Brown left a lasting impression on Douglass. "Mr. Brown is one of the most earnest and interesting men that I have met," said the orator. Although white, Brown came across in "sympathy a black man, and is deeply interested in our cause, as though his own soul had been pierced with the iron of slavery."[2]

Brown ran a wool business in Springfield out of a large store and warehouse, one of many such enterprises as a merchant, a tanner, and a farmer that he launched over three decades, almost all of which failed and left his huge family poor. During this first encounter, Douglass spent the night with Brown's family in what Douglass remembered as their "Spartan" house. So large and controversial had Brown grown in national memory, that in his recollection in *Life and Times* Douglass strove for unusual detail. He remembered the simple ingredients served at dinner, the walls "innocent of paint," the table "unmistakably of pine and of the plainest workmanship." Everything about John Brown and his house reflected, said Douglass, the "stern truth, solid purpose, and rigid economy" of the man. Brown "fulfilled St. Paul's idea of the head of the family," Douglass observed, his wife and children treating him "with reverence." As though fashioning the precise characteristics of a fictional character, Douglass described Brown's facial features, his hair, his height and weight, even the color of his eyes, which in "conversation . . . were full of light and fire." Brown walked with "a long, springing race-horse step, absorbed by his own reflections." Here, rising out from the "whispers," Douglass announced was "Captain John Brown . . . one of the most marked characters and greatest heroes known to American fame."[3]

But a great deal of troubled reality lay beneath Douglass's literary reinvention of 1881. The twelve-year relationship between Douglass and Brown is one good lens through which to view both men. During the 1850s, as Douglass moved toward at least open support of violent means, the two abolitionists spent many hours and days in each other's company. As Douglass came within John Brown's orbit of religious fervor and theories of violent resistance, Douglass listened even as he was sometimes repelled.

Born in Torrington, Connecticut, in 1800, Brown grew up primarily on the Western Reserve in Hudson, Ohio. His father, Owen, bestowed a staunch Calvinism in his son. Brown's memories of childhood were layered with dislocation and loss, especially that of his mother, who died when the boy was only eight. His father married three times and sired sixteen children, a pattern John eventually more than matched with two wives and twenty children, many of whom did not reach adulthood. In John's youth, the Browns' household in Ohio funneled fugitive slaves on to liberty in the region or in Canada; Owen was a devout Christian abolitionist. By the time

Douglass and John Brown met, and for the duration of their relationship, among the sensibilities and experiences that they shared were a relative lack of formal education, the humiliations and necessities of begging for money, an Atlantic crossing to Liverpool on the *Cambria* (at separate times), a Bible-inspired sense that history could undergo apocalyptic change, and a passionate hatred of slavery as a system at war with humanity.[4]

At that first meeting in Springfield, Brown and Douglass conversed long into the night at a table in candlelight. Brown unfolded a large map of the United States and pointed to the Alleghenies. "These mountains," Douglass recalled Brown asserting, "are the basis of my plan. God has given the strength of the hills to freedom; they were placed here for the emancipation of the Negro race." For many years to come, decoding just what the elements of Brown's "plan" were became a beguiling preoccupation for Douglass and others. On that night in Springfield, he was enthralled but skeptical; he never claimed to know with any certainty the purpose of the Virginia mountains, morally or geologically. Brown, however, imagined them "full of natural forts" and "good hiding places." Beginning with only twenty-five trained men, he would "run off the slaves in large numbers" in at least one Virginia county. Somehow in these mountain hideaways they would fight off the inevitable force that would assemble in counterattack, and many of the local slaves would join their force. The "true object," Douglass gleaned, seemed to be destroying "the money value of slave property." That aim Douglass understood. But then he pushed back with questions Brown could answer only in moralistic, not strategic, terms. How would he "support" his men? Douglass asked. What would Brown do when surrounded by the "bloodhounds" of the Slave Power's police state when roused? Brown thought he could whip them, but if he could not and was killed in such guerrilla action, "he had no better use for his life than to lay it down in the cause of the slave."[5] In this reinvented conversation, Douglass expressed a harsh truth about Brown. The old warrior worked passionately for years on a plan that in the end may have represented a personal desire to sacrifice for the slaves more than a genuine strategy for revolution.

In these years Douglass looked anxiously for a logic in violence. The problem with Brown was that he could never be completely squared with rationality. But as we have seen, in the wake of the Fugitive Slave Act or *Dred Scott*, logic was no longer the weapon of choice for a radical abolitionist. Douglass admitted that the more contact he had with Brown, "my utterances became more and more tinged by the color of this man's strong impressions." Douglass and Brown continued to correspond through the early 1850s, and they eventually met on many more occasions. At least as early as 1851 the two exchanged letters making sure Brown received Douglass's paper. And in 1854, after Brown had moved to Akron, Ohio, he wrote an extraordinary epistle to Douglass in the voice of an Old Testament prophet chastising the evils of American leaders and their poisoned institutions. It was as though Brown wanted to join Douglass in condemning the Slave Power, but to do so with even more biblical rage. Worried about the fate of the American republic, Brown had no doubt about what stood in its path: the proslavery "extreme wickedness" of political and religious leadership at all levels, even the "marshals, sheriffs, constables and policemen."[6]

We do not have Douglass's direct response to this letter, but what he read in Brown's condemnations of American perfidy was a denunciation, even beyond higher-law doctrine, that left only violence as an option. American leadership was taking the country into "anarchy in all its horrid forms," Brown argued. Therefore, he had a ready answer: "What punishment ever inflicted by man or even threated by God, can be too severe for those whose influence is a thousand times more malignant than the atmosphere of the deadly Upas—for those who hate the right and the Most High." To Brown, God governed the universe and its man-made nations. Hence, the only alternative for the righteous was to destroy such "fiends clothed in human form." Brown trusted Douglass's knowledge of Scripture as he poured forth passages from the Old and New Testaments. To a degree Brown and Douglass shared a biblical grounding. The real laws of the United States for Brown were God's commands. "Thou shalt not deliver unto his master the servant which is escaped. . . . Thou shalt not oppress him," he recited from Deuteronomy in his letter to Douglass. From Matthew, Brown revisited the famous command "Therefore all things whatsoever ye would that men should do to you, do ye even so to them; for this is the law and the prophets." And in Nehemiah he found his indictment of rulers who had forsaken God's law: "Remember them, O my God, because they have defiled the priesthood." Nehemiah had "smote" and "cleansed" when necessary the wayward Israelites. As Brown wrote to Douglass in early 1854, even before the Kansas-Nebraska Act, Brown seemed lonely and mired in a deep Christian despair over the "abominably wicked . . . laws" of the country. But he fully expected a reckoning to come. "I am too destitute of words to express the tithe of what I feel," Brown concluded, as he begged Douglass to convey his appeal in "suitable language" to a larger world.[7]

By and large, Douglass did just that. He admired and used the Hebrew prophets, and Brown not only looked and talked like one, he seemed willing to challenge or destroy the wicked Jerusalem. In *Life and Times*, Douglass confessed that he never felt in the "presence of a stronger religious influence" than in the company of John Brown. Although Douglass honored human law more, perhaps the sensibility that he and Brown shared most in the long run was a millennial and apocalyptic sense of history, drawn from the old stories of the prophets and from the zeitgeist of antebellum America. In that era millennialist thought was a cluster of religious and secular ideas forged into a kind of national creed. In its more hopeful mode, it held that Christ would have a Second Coming in the "new Israel" of America, or at least that the country possessed a mission as a "redeemer nation" destined to perform a special role in history. Millennialism was an outlook on history, a disposition about human nature, a belief that America was a place where mankind had been given a second chance; and above all, that God governed history and chose the moments of transformation. A nation of Protestants could interpret events as steps in its providential destiny. The darker side of millennialism exposed the burden of chosenness; an eschatological expectation of God's wrath and destruction meant that people must constantly prepare for a break in time and new beginnings.[8]

Both Douglass and Brown shared this vision. Sterner and bleaker, Brown's millennialism manifested in daily devotions and instructions to his children. Brown's son Salmon remembered his father's strict Sabbath observance: "Sunday evenings he would gather the family and hired help . . . and have the Ten Commandments and the Catechism repeated. Sometimes he would preach a regular sermon. . . . Besides we had prayers morning and night of every day, with Bible reading, all standing during prayer, father himself leaning on a chair, upreared on the forward legs, the old-fashioned Presbyterian way." Brown's faith was rooted in a deeply personal concern about sin, his own and that of others, especially his children. "He constantly expostulated with us," said Salmon, "and in letters when away. His expressed hope was 'that ye sin not, that you form no foolish attachments, that you be not a 'companion to fools.' "[9]

Brown was often hardest on himself, on his own profound need for atonement. His record of business failures, his struggle to provide meager sustenance to his brood as he lost more than one farm, and his imprisonment for debt in the wake of the panic of 1837 left him many inner demons. Writing to all his children in late 1852, he worried that they had lost the faith he had instilled in them, even as he blamed himself. He admitted to "*little*, very *little* to cheer" and hoped that his "family may understand that this world is not the *Home* of man." He urged his sons and daughters not to reflect on how their father had "wandered from the Road," but to pray to God for their own "thorough conversion from sin" and to stay "steadfast in his ways through the very short season of trial you will have to pass." In the midst of such religious affliction, Brown ended the letter worried about whether the family could afford to "pay for Douglas paper." In a remarkable letter to his eldest son, John Jr., in 1853, Brown expressed "pain and sorrow" at the young man's loss of faith. Then John Sr. drew upon passages from the first five books of the Old Testament to warn his erring son with the words of Moses, Joshua, Judges, Ruth, and Samuel not to fall into the "same disposition in Israel to backslide." Brown's sons were devoted abolitionists; they followed their father for their own reasons, perhaps least of all because he had used Joshua to instruct them. John Jr. later experienced a mental breakdown in Kansas in 1856, captured, beaten, and imprisoned after fighting as a guerrilla warrior at his father's side. Another son, Frederick, was killed in the Kansas war. John Brown's personal holy war on slavery became an extended family disaster.[10]

Douglass, on the other hand, was a father deeply concerned with his children's literacy and education, but we do not know as much about his concern for their religious temperaments. He seems to have worried more about their writing skills than their faith. "I know this is not as good writing as you would like to see," wrote his fifteen-year-old son Charles in 1860, "but I am in haste so good night."[11]

In these years, Douglass's millennialism and his religious faith were a set of root values layered throughout his oratory and his writing. He arrived at his spiritual understanding of history through his lifelong informal theological means—reading the Bible and a good deal of history, and especially by his years of rhetorical engagement on abolitionist platforms, listening to and arguing with Garrison, Phillips, Gerrit Smith, McCune Smith, Remond, Delany, Abby Kelley, and others. Douglass's millennialism was forward-looking and activist. Waiting for the "jubilee" of black emancipation and the fulfillment of America's national destiny required patience, but also struggle; it demanded faith, and suffering.

Douglass played the prophetic role of the "suffering servant" with zeal. His famous statement about agitation, delivered in a speech in 1857, has stood the test of time and numerous protest ideologies: "If there is no struggle there is no progress. Those who profess to favor freedom and yet deprecate agitation, are men who want crops without plowing up the ground, they want rain without thunder and lightning. This struggle may be a moral one, or it may be a physical one, and it may be both moral and physical, but it must be a struggle. Power concedes nothing without a demand. It never did and it never will." Those were what McCune Smith had called Douglass's "work-able, do-able words" for the ages.[12]

In his analysis of the Slave Power, Douglass accepted political and moral loss as the price of an inevitable progress. Sometimes his rhetoric could seem driven by a vague moral determinism. The enemies, slavery and freedom, were irreconcilable, he wrote in 1855, but freedom must triumph because it had the "laws which govern the moral universe" on its side. A collision between these two enemy forces "must come," Douglass maintained, "as sure as the laws of God cannot be trampled upon with impunity."[13] Millennialists had a peculiarly persistent need for that word "must." It kept them moving through the thickets of uncertainty.

But for Douglass millennial symbolism was not merely a rhetorical device to sustain collective hope; it was a real source of faith. He wanted his thousand black listeners to see "a celebration of the American jubilee," Douglass declared in Canandaigua, New York, in 1857. "That jubilee will come. You and I may not live to see it; but . . . God reigns, and slavery *must* yet fall; unless the devil is more potent than the Almighty; unless sin is stronger than righteousness, slavery *must* perish." History possessed a trajectory, not easily discerned. "There was something God-like" in the British decree of emancipation in the West Indies in the 1830s, Douglass proclaimed. He knew that British emancipation was more complex than spiritual imagery alone could convey, but he could not resist calling the event a "wondrous transformation" and a "bolt from the moral sky." He called on African Americans to see West Indian emancipation as "a city upon a hill" to light the way toward their own new history.[14] Such faith was difficult to sustain after the *Dred Scott* decision.

In a letter to a Scottish antislavery society, with which Julia Griffiths now worked to raise money for Douglass's paper, the editor acknowledged dark portents hanging over the abolitionist cause. Then he gave his correspondent a good dose of millennial medicine: "I am now at work less under the influences or inspiration of hope, than the settled assurances of faith in God—and the ultimate triumph of Righteousness in the world. The cause of the slaves is a righteous and humane one. . . . Though long delayed, it will triumph at last."[15] Torn at times between warring options, Douglass knew he *must* travel by faith as much as by sight.

But he would also have his fellow blacks see and act as well as believe in their path to liberation, and thus perhaps his sustained interest in Brown's revolutionary schemes. Emancipation in the British empire gave Douglass a grand historical precedent and a reason to issue a call to arms in his own country. Americans were good at "fast days and fourth of Julys," Douglass said, but their "sequel" never showed anything but "men whose hearts are crammed with arrogancy, pride, and hate." Then, characteristically, Douglass found his firm footing and his story in Isaiah 58: "We have bowed down our heads as a bulrush, and have spread sackcloth and ashes under us." Isaiah had warned so poignantly against false fasting. The House of Jacob fasted, but in the end "seest not" and "takest no knowledge." In his own best King James language, Douglass argued just the same for Americans who could not or would not learn from the past. British emancipation had been an act, he believed, not about "commerce, but conscience," a "spiritual triumph," and a "product of the soul." Rewriting Isaiah nearly word for word for a new century and place, Douglass declared his countrymen incapable of what the British had created: "a chosen fast of the Living God . . . a day in which the bands of wickedness were loosed; the heavy burdens undone; the oppressed let go free; every yoke broken; the poor that were cast out of the house brought in; and men no longer hiding themselves from their own flesh." [16] Instead, Americans were just so many marsh plants sagging over silently in the swamp.

To Douglass, though, history was both warning and inspiration. He also used the model of West Indian emancipation to remind audiences that Jamaican slaves had rebelled many times on their road to a parliamentary edict of their freedom. He reminded his black audience in upstate New York of McCune Smith's overt plea in 1856 that they [blacks] not wait for liberty to be given, as in the British empire, and instead celebrate their own heroes such as Denmark Vesey and Nat Turner. As he so often did in the 1850s, Douglass quoted the passage from Byron's *Childe Harold's Pilgrimage*, "Who would be free, themselves must strike the first blow." Then, rather stunningly, he reminded his auditors of the black heroes who had risked death rather than endure slavery—Margaret Garner's infanticide, Madison Washington of the *Creole* shipboard rebellion, Parker and the Christiana rioters, Joseph Cinqué of the *Amistad* mutiny. Douglass stressed how much insurrection had ultimately influenced British colonial planters to accept abolition and awakened the guilty fears of white Southerners when "General [Nat] Turner kindled the fires of insurrection in Southampton." Douglass was ready to probe the dark "rebellious disposition of the slaves" if only he could find someone with a plan he could trust. [17]

. . .

During the decade before Harpers Ferry, Douglass sustained an abiding interest in aiding Brown's crusade, less perhaps on strategic grounds than because of the white radical's demonstrable commitment to racial equality. Although their temperaments differed markedly, their face-to-face encounters, correspondence, and shared interest in the possibilities of violence sustained a friendship. Many black abolitionists would eventually honor Brown's racial openness after he died a martyr's death; at the heart of his immediate legacy, after all, was the idea that he was the white man who died to set black people free.[18]

In 1848, shortly after his first meeting with Douglass, Brown published a satirical essay, "Sambo's Mistakes," in the black newspaper *Ram's Horn*. Written in the voice of a black man who needs to confess his misdeeds of apathy, materialism, and sloth, the piece invoked many stereotypes about Northern free blacks. Instead of taking advantage of education, this Sambo spent his time "devouring silly novels & other miserable trash." Instead of saving money to buy a good farm, he preferred "chewing & smoking tobacco." Rather than attaining "character & influence among men," this ne'er-do-well was "obliged to travel about in search of employment as a hostler shoe black & fiddler." He could never practice self-denial and loved his "Chains, Finger rings, Breast Pins." And worst, he confessed to failing as "a citizen, a husband, a father, a brother, a neighbour."[19] Witty but bizarre, this awkwardly written essay demonstrated not only a Puritanical obsession with the foibles of others, but a direct attack on the lack of self-reliance among blacks. It could be read as misguided racial paternalism, as ironic self-revelatory guilt, or as a righteous chastisement of a disorganized black community that needed upbraiding.

With McCune Smith, Douglass had long demanded greater black self-improvement initiatives and felt frustrated by an apathy he found among free blacks. He could "stand the insults . . . and slanders of the known haters" of his people. He welcomed them as a "natural incident of the war." But what exasperated him was the "listless indifference" hanging over so many struggling blacks "who should be all on fire." Hence, not only was Douglass impressed with Brown's egalitarianism, but with his direct efforts to help raise black aspirations. In 1846 Gerrit Smith purchased a huge tract of 120,000 acres of land in upstate New York with the intent of granting it to urban free blacks so they could become independent landowning farmers and thus qualify to vote under that state's suffrage law. Although the environment was harsh, some blacks took advantage of the utopian plan; and in the spring of 1849 Brown, with his wife, Mary, and five children, joined them in North Elba. There Brown for a while devoted himself to living among "these poor despised Africans," as he put it, in settlements known as Timbucto. Brown employed a free black man named Thomas Jefferson as well as a fugitive slave from Florida named Cyrus. Blacks often took meals with the Browns at their farmhouse. Though as poor as the winters were cold, Brown dispensed occasional barrels of pork and flour to his neighbors as well as a good deal of advice about religion, personal conduct, and resistance to the Fugitive Slave Act.[20]

Douglass was amply aware of Brown's antiracist venture in North Elba; Gerrit Smith had granted the Rochesterite a piece of land (which he never occupied) and did the same for most other black abolitionists. This kind of pioneering agricultural activism was never Douglass's sphere, but he eagerly welcomed Smith's uplift philanthropy among blacks. The sentiments of "Sambo's Mistakes" appeared in many of Douglass's editorials and speeches, some of which Brown read in the former slave's paper. Whether from the backbreaking exertions of farmers on that mountain terrain of North Elba, or the literary and organizational leadership of black intellectuals, Douglass believed, as he stated in 1855, that "every day brings evidence . . . THAT OUR ELEVATION AS A RACE IS ALMOST WHOLLY DEPENDENT UPON OUR OWN EXERTIONS. If we are ever elevated, our elevation will be accomplished through our own instrumentality." He eagerly wanted blacks to take their fate into their own hands. "Nothing is more humiliating," Douglass smugly declared in 1857, than his own people's apathy.[21] He could only be moved and glad that a Gerrit Smith and a John Brown wished so sincerely to lend their lives to the quest for equality. But blacks could not wait for their white patrons.

To black audiences Douglass could preach as stern a brand of conservative self-improvement as any black voice of his era. In rhetorical moves representative of a brand of black nationalism, Douglass often turned attacks on white racism into angry rebukes of black lethargy. In an 1855 speech at Shiloh Presbyterian Church in New York to a mixed audience, Douglass, with McCune Smith chairing the meeting, wondered aloud about how difficult it was to address certain sensitive issues among blacks in front of whites. Blacks, Douglass said, too often provided a "spectacle" for all the world to watch in its desire to measure the "heights of civilization." Douglass admitted that the larger world constantly asked, are blacks "like other men?" Could the "negro do without a master," can he rise from "ignorance to intelligence," or "disorder to order?" These questions could not "be answered by the white race." They were "peculiarly the duties of the colored people." And blacks' "doubt among ourselves" stood in the way and caused Douglass, he confessed, to "blush" and fall into "gloomy thoughts." His people must "show them" (whites) by becoming "skillful architects, profound thinkers, originators and discoverers of ideas." They must produce their own Webster, Clay, and Calhoun.[22]

Then, as Douglass marched through this stern message, a group of "colored gals" walked into the sanctuary, distracting and annoying the orator, who stopped to upbraid them for not being "punctual." Regaining his composure, Douglass gave a vigorous appeal for violent resistance to slave catchers. "Fear inculcates respect," he proclaimed. "I would rather see insurrection for the next six months in the South than that slavery should exist there for [the] next six years." He left his Shiloh audience laughing with jokes about how whites automatically think of blacks as drunk or lazy and ended by singing an abolition ballad to the tune of "I'll Never Get Drunk Again."[23] Brown would have wholeheartedly agreed with every gesture, except possibly the jokes.

Similarly, three years later, at the same church, but to a largely black audience gathered to protest historic discrimination on the Sixth Avenue Railroad in New York, Douglass blasted the "spirit of caste" that robbed his people of every kind of civil right. But worst of all, now one year in the wake of *Dred Scott*, he feared that the "emancipated colored man" risked having "burned into his very soul the brand of inferiority." He openly worried in front of his fellow blacks that an impression had settled upon them implying that "we ourselves are unconcerned and even contented with our condition." Douglass confronted his auditors harshly: "I detest the slaveholder, and almost equally detest a contented slave. They are both enemies of freedom." With no jokes to soothe the message, he left the 1858 protest rally with the warning that "oppression . . . deadens sensibility in its victims." The only recourse was to sustain faith not in law but in "ourselves."[24] Such fierce appeals for self-reliance, mixed with demands for violent resistance, in the late 1850s made for a potent if toxic brew of confusion, rage, and bloodlust.

As Douglass tried to find firm footing with these issues and with his emerging relationship with Brown, another kind of confusion walked forthrightly into his life. Seeking permission to translate and publish *My*

Bondage and My Freedom in German, Ottilie Assing first came to visit Douglass in Rochester in the summer of 1856. Born in 1819 in Hamburg to a physician-poet father and a mother who was a teacher and Romantic poet, Assing had veered from one kind of idealistic and romantic cause to another until, in personal frustration and desperate for independence, she moved to America in 1852 to pursue a new career as a journalist. Emotionally volatile (the survivor of at least one suicide attempt with a dagger she took to her chest when she was twenty-three), a freethinking atheist, and a devotee of Alexander von Humboldt's ideas about human equality, Assing soon saw that the most compelling issues in her adopted America were race and slavery. As a German romantic she was always in search of the hero in history, the maker of new nations, new ideas, and new times. By attending antislavery meetings in New York after she took up residence among other German émigrés across the Hudson River in New Jersey, Assing began to discover candidates for her ideal hero. First there was Wendell Phillips, whom she saw speak and found enthralling at the annual gathering of the American Anti-Slavery Society in 1854. Then for a while she became fascinated with James Pennington, the minister of Shiloh Presbyterian Church in New York; Assing wrote a long, unwieldy essay on the black preacher and translated some of his narrative, *The Fugitive Blacksmith*, until she lost interest, possibly because of a fundamental distaste for religion and the black church.[25]

The only account we have of Assing and Douglass's first meeting is Assing's own, which, in her breathless style, she self-servingly included in her introduction to the German edition of *Bondage and Freedom*. She must have come to Rochester all but unannounced since she first stopped at the office of the *North Star* only to discover that the editor was still at home. As a fellow journalist, she had come to interview Douglass. So as directed, Assing walked the more than two miles to South Avenue to find the editor's homestead. She found a "handsome villa, surrounded by a large garden . . . situated on a hill overlooking a charming landscape." But she reserved most of her *Vorrede* to *Sclaverei und Freiheit* (the German title of Douglass's book) for sensuous physical descriptions of Douglass as well as a spectacular tribute to his skills as an orator. Employing the words "brilliant" or "brilliance" three times in two sentences, Assing's Douglass possessed "perfect mastery of language," and the most "mellifluous, sonorous, flexible . . . voice speaking to the heart as I have ever heard." His very name filled American halls to overflowing, she maintained, "as if a new apostle had revealed to them for the first time a truth that had lain unspoken in everyone's heart."[26]

Assing identified Douglass as a "light mulatto of unusually tall, slender, and powerful stature." "His features are striking," she gushed: "the prominently domed forehead with a peculiarly deep cleft at the base of the nose, an aquiline nose, and the narrow, beautifully carved lips betray more of his white than his black origin. The thick hair, here and there with touches of gray, is frizzy and unruly but not wooly." Having dispensed with these common nineteenth-century racialized depictions, Assing made it clear she had found a romantic hero for the age: Douglass's "whole appearance, stamped by past storms and struggles, bespeaks great energy and will power that shuns no obstacle . . . in the face of all odds." She observed briefly their wide-ranging conversation, then, in a telling non sequitur, acknowledged bluntly that she met the family: "Douglass's wife is completely black, and his five children, therefore, have more of the traits of the Negro than he." The family, especially the children, would get to know Assing as friend, intruder, and benefactor. The German journalist, with her powers of observation, had found her Siegfried ready to go slay the American dragons.[27] Assing's attraction to Douglass was permanent, and she would do her best as a propagandist, at least for German audiences, to shape the Rochester editor's reputation in relation to John Brown.

Frederick Douglass, c. 1858.
Print from a lost daguerreotype.

• • •

The saga of how Douglass and Brown forged an important, if tragic, alliance publicly commenced at the inaugural convention of the Radical Abolition Party in Syracuse, New York, June 26–28, 1855. By then, five of Brown's sons, led by John Jr., whose farm in Ohio was failing from drought and debt, had moved to Kansas. That territory had become the feverish test case of the doctrine of "popular sovereignty" laid out in the fateful Kansas-Nebraska Act of 1854. Flocks of proslavery and Free Soil settlers were moving into the land west of Missouri, and the region teetered on the brink of guerrilla war. Brown praised his sons for their commitment to go to Kansas "with a view to help defeat SATAN and his legions." The father was still committed to his work among blacks in North Elba, but by the spring of 1855, John Jr. wrote from his farm near Osawatomie that "every slaveholding state is furnishing men and money to fasten Slavery upon this glorious land, by means no matter how foul." When his father trekked over hill and dale for 150 miles to get to Syracuse for the convention of the only political party Brown may have ever joined, Kansas not only fired his imagination, but that of the nearly three hundred delegates as well.[28]

The Radical Abolition Party lasted a mere five years. At the 1855 gathering, McCune Smith chaired the proceedings, which Douglass especially celebrated as something to which black people could "ever proudly refer." Gerrit Smith was in his glory as the primary host and funder of the proceeding; and the convention spent a great deal of time debating and justifying what Douglass referred to as the "iron-linked logic" of the antislavery interpretation of the Constitution. Most important, the convention's delegates from ten states and Canada passed a resolution affirming the use of violence to overthrow slavery. Brown was exhilarated by the convention. According to Douglass, Brown presented the case for his own decision and that of his sons to go to Kansas and fight for the free-state cause. Brown quoted from Hebrews as he also appealed for money: "Without the shedding of blood there is no remission of sin." Gerrit Smith read two letters aloud to the assembled body from Brown's sons to their father, which only the proud patriarch could have provided. In one letter they advised the abolitionists to "thoroughly arm and organize themselves" as they begged for revolvers, rifles, and bowie knives, which they needed "more than . . . bread."[29]

This gathering exuded a radical, biblical militancy not yet seen in formal political abolitionism. McCune Smith used the term "Bible politics" to describe the party's point of view and called its platform a "Jubilee doctrine . . . more important than the diffusion of the principle of science." The biracial throng of abolitionists, the physician announced, would "go hence to proclaim the gospel of liberty—for it is the good news, glad tidings of great joy, that we have to tell." Douglass seems to have left Syracuse inspired as well. In his paper he especially reported on the "sweet" abolition songs at the Radicals' convention, as well as that one delegate had been a fugitive slave who had "been obliged to avail himself of the underground railroad" in order to participate and was now safely residing in Canada. But above all, Douglass said that he and his comrades at Syracuse were fed up with the idea of limiting slavery and hoping that it "may die out." He said he now belonged to a party that would lay "the axe to the tree" with a single demand: that it was "THE RIGHT, THE POWER, AND THE DUTY OF THE FEDERAL GOVERNMENT TO ABOLISH SLAVERY IN EVERY STATE IN THE AMERICAN UNION." [30] Behind the scenes in Syracuse he had conversations with Brown and helped raise money for his cause. The two would not meet again until late 1856, after the intriguing radical had carved out a bloody history in Kansas and launched a conspiracy to attack slavery in the South with which Douglass became deeply entwined.

No one who knew John Brown ever doubted his bravery, his passion, or that he believed he was living and dying as an agent in God's plan. He went to Kansas in the fall of 1855 to make war on slavery. As Douglass published and promoted *Bondage and Freedom* that autumn, Brown, accompanied by his teenage son Oliver and a son-in-law, Henry Thompson, traveled west to eastern Kansas primarily by walking, but also with a horse and a wagon full of weapons. There, with parts of his extended family, including women and children, living in tents and shanties, the fifty-five-year-old, soon called Captain Brown, led a band of warriors among the free-state forces in what soon became "Bleeding Kansas." [31]

Kansas was a brutal physical and political environment. Members of Brown's clan suffered frostbite and near starvation during the winter of 1855–56, and by that spring, the numerous murders and depredations by proslavery "border ruffians" from Missouri signaled the wider bloodshed to follow. In May 1856, after proslavery bands attacked and burned Lawrence, Kansas, the Free Soil bastion of the territory, Brown snapped with rage. In retaliation, and against the wishes of some of his sons, Brown orchestrated a bloody middle-of-the-night raid on three proslavery dwellings along Pottawatomie Creek, resulting in the savage murder of five men. The victims, all non-slaveholders but supporters of the slave-state cause, were seized from the clutches of their families, taken a couple hundred yards from their cabins, and slashed to death and mutilated with broadswords. At least two were also shot in the face or chest, likely after they were already dead. The "Pottawatomie massacre" would forever be part of John Brown's legacy, an uncomfortable challenge to his sympathetic biographers, but ample evidence to those who take a clear-eyed look at how Old Brown understood the uses and meaning of terror. Brown planned and ordered the murders, and though he may not have actually committed the slashings, he may have fired the gun. Back east, among his abolitionist supporters and funders, the facts about Pottawatomie remained for the ensuing three years a matter of willful mystery and avoidance, as well as part of a legend that the "Old warrior" now cultivated about himself in the service of broader schemes.[32]

In December 1856, as Brown was traveling eastward to raise money and men, he stopped in Rochester and took dinner at Douglass's house. Little is known of what they discussed that evening, but in the next two years their collaboration deepened as Brown repeatedly tried to recruit Douglass to the cause of fomenting a slave uprising in Virginia. Possibly they discussed Brown's long-standing interest in military history, slave revolts, and Maroon colonies, as well as some details of the Kansas bloodshed. Whether Brown divulged the reality of Pottawatomie is doubtful, although the idea of slaveholders' blood on Brown's coat, whether fresh from the Battle of Osawatomie or from a preemptive, primal killing in the dark of the night, would only have inspired Douglass. But by the time he wrote about Brown with long retrospect in 1881, Douglass knew and approved of what had happened in Kansas. By then Brown was the mythic hero whose "hour had come." Old "Osawatomie Brown" had merely "met persecution with persecution, and house-burning with signal and terrible retaliation." In *Life and Times* Douglass harbored no hesitation in defending Brown's deeds and methods, and likewise, in 1857 it is not likely he did either. "The horrors wrought by his iron hand," Douglass wrote, "cannot be contemplated without a shudder, but it is the shudder which one feels at the execution of a murderer . . . necessity is the full justification of it to reason."[33] His problem with the Old Man was strategic, not ethical, although Douglass continually struggled to square killing with reason.

Above all, Brown needed money. Throughout most of 1857, he traveled across the North, fashioning Kansas as a moral crusade and enlisting some of the most prominent abolitionists in his effort. In March in Worcester, Massachusetts, Brown was a platform guest as Douglass gave a speech. But Brown's fund-raising efforts floundered as the economic panic of 1857 swept across the country. Staying with abolitionist allies, Brown wrote numerous letters in which he appealed to the New England antislavery conscience as well as for his destitute family and band of soldiers. He made many important connections with abolitionists who were convinced that the Kansas free-state cause demanded their moral and financial support. Gradually, Brown managed a tempestuous alliance with a "secret six" group of activists including Samuel Gridley Howe, Thomas Wentworth Higginson, Franklin Sanborn, Theodore Parker, Gerrit Smith, and especially George Luther Stearns, a self-made magnate enriched by linseed oil and lead-pipe manufacturing, who, after his wife received Brown's appeal, pledged thousands of dollars. All in their own ways were attracted to Brown as a romantic warrior-hero who would take the antislavery cause to the field of battle as none of them could.[34]

Like many of his fellow abolitionists, Douglass no longer had to imagine or invent a John Brown; he showed up at Douglass's doorstep, hat in hand, but also again with maps, plans, and half-told tales. In the last week of January 1858, Brown arrived in Rochester and became a boarder with Douglass's family at $3 per week for three weeks. From this and other encounters, Douglass became as well informed of Brown's ultimate aims as any abolitionist or accomplice outside of his small personal band. From upstairs at Douglass's house, and in secrecy using the alias N. (Nelson) Hawkins, Brown carried on a near-daily correspondence with his family and with potential supporters and donors. To Higginson, Gerrit Smith, Sanborn, and Stearns he wrote cryptically of his "Rail Road business of a somewhat extended scale" as he asked for money to accomplish his clandestine work. As the letters flowed in and out of the house, with thirteen-year-old Charles Douglass as the carrier to and from the post office, Douglass learned intimately of Brown's "plan of running off slaves" by establishing safe locations in the mountains of Virginia. Such a scheme for "rendering slave property in Maryland and Virginia valueless [and] insecure" intrigued Douglass, who recalled his own desperation for "any new mode of attack" on slavery.[35]

Also while staying with the Douglasses, and eating at Anna's table, Brown drafted his "Provisional Constitution," which he intended to put in place as an interim government in Virginia if his invasion succeeded. Just how much Brown and Douglass debated political philosophy and constitutionalism is unknown, but Douglass kept a personal copy of the constitution with its forty-eight articles, which together provided a bold, if redundant, blueprint first for revolution and then for order to control anarchy and chaos in wartime. Above all, Douglass surely agreed wholeheartedly with Brown's pre-

John Brown, c. 1857. Cameo portrait.

amble, much of which could have been lifted from editorials and speeches written by the host. The provisional government would be established in the name of the "proscribed, oppressed, and enslaved citizens . . . of the United States." Slavery, proclaimed the document's first line, "is none other than a most barbarous, unprovoked, and unjustifiable war of one portion of its citizens upon another portion—the only conditions of which are perpetual imprisonment and hopeless servitude or absolute extermination." Brown wrote the document to present to a convention in Chatham, Canada, that he would convene in May 1858 as a means of recruiting among the substantial free-black and fugitive community in that region of western Ontario. That convention did eventually attract thirty-four black and twelve white delegates, but the only noted black abolitionist was Martin Delany, then living in Canada; the whites were primarily members of Brown's Kansas band of soldiers. Notably, neither Douglass nor any of the New England backers of Brown's crusade attended.[36]

Philosophizing about the nature of slavery and how it poisoned American institutions was one thing; fomenting an abolitionist revolution and creating a government in the midst of a slave state were quite another. Douglass described Brown as obsessed with his constitution during the winter days in Rochester. "It was the first thing in the morning, and the last thing at night," Douglass recalled, "till I confess it began to be something of a bore to me." This remarkable comment reflected Douglass's response to the bizarre character of the constitution, and an admission that Brown's personality, as well as his combination of zeal and lack of clarity, could wear down a busy, discerning person such as Douglass. The autobiographer remembered the Old Man mentioning the possibility of attacking the federal arsenal at Harpers Ferry to seize weapons. Douglass soon realized the gravity of such a turn in the warrior's vision. Brown asked Douglass to put out two planed boards, on which Brown diagrammed "forts" and "secret passages" in the mountains where he would stage his revolution. Douglass began to listen with caution. He admitted that he was less interested in the drawings and board gaming than his children were. Brown even used a set of blocks to illustrate his plans to the assembled children, who surely never forgot those wintry evenings. What Anna Douglass thought of this austere man with the long white beard whom she was feeding each day is not known. On February 4 he wrote to his eldest son that Douglass had promised him $50, but "what I value vastly more he seems to appreciate my theories & my labors."[37]

Perhaps, but Douglass's wry remembrances of those "theories," as well as his actions, remind us of the most basic fact in this union of awkward allies. As long as Brown bravely advanced the idea of funneling fugitive slaves out of the upper South and thereby politically threatened the slave system generally, Douglass was on board despite the risks. But when assaulting a large US arsenal emerged in the scheme, the writer parted ways with the warrior.

Douglass also performed as a conduit, even a kind of banker, for Brown with other black leaders; they sent modest drafts of money to Rochester for the editor to pass on to the revolutionary. In mid-March in Philadelphia, Brown and John Jr. met with Douglass, Henry Highland Garnet, and the famed Underground Railroad activist William Still. They gathered at the home of Stephen Smith, a successful black lumber dealer and protector of runaway slaves in that city. What Brown or Douglass might have divulged about invasion or insurrectionary plans is not known; these and other meetings like them were essentially to prime the pump of a constant fund-raising campaign. But through most of 1857–58 Brown's clandestine enterprise was broke. He established a training base in Tabor, Iowa, for his diminishing band of men. He then squandered an exorbitant amount of money hiring a soldier of fortune, Hugh Forbes, an English fencing teacher Brown had met in New York City who had fought in the Italian Revolution with Giuseppe Garibaldi and promised to write a training manual and serve as the drill instructor. Unfortunately, Forbes was a scoundrel who sought to enrich himself off New England humanitarians as he betrayed the invasion plan to high American officials when he did not receive his promised compensation.[38]

In late March 1858, Brown paid a ten-day visit to his home, his wife, Mary, and their small children in North Elba, New York. This may have been a kind of leave-taking since he planned to launch the Virginia adventure later that spring or early summer. Surely Brown sought emotional solace in what was left of his devastated family. Six of Brown's sons and one son-in-law had fought in Kansas. By that spring, one was dead, two badly wounded, and two others had undergone imprisonment, torture, and severe mental breakdowns. In letters Brown wrote from his retreat at Douglass's home in February, he had counseled Mary and the family, "Courage, courage, courage!—the great work of my life (the unseen Hand that 'guided me, and who has indeed holden my right hand, may hold it still') . . . I may yet see accomplished."[39] Kansas and ultimately Harpers Ferry were a gruesome disaster that Brown brought upon his own family; in the face of such poverty and loss, he, not to mention his wife and surviving children, needed a profound faith in that helping hand.

On April 4 Brown once again arrived in Rochester, where he spent a night with Douglass. Accompanied by the former fugitive slave Jermain Loguen, and still preparing and recruiting for his convention in Chatham the next month, he then traveled to St. Catharines, Canada, to visit and try to enlist Harriet Tubman in his cause. The legendary Tubman, with her years of experience rescuing slaves in Maryland, Virginia, and Delaware, now lived in St. Catharines. Although she encouraged and advised Brown and left the Old Man in awe, she never made any promises to join him. If he could muster enough men, money, and guns, Brown had planned to launch his raid in 1858 soon after the Chatham gathering. But the knave Hugh Forbes, claiming lack of payment, informed three US senators, as well as the editor of the *New York Tribune*, Horace Greeley, of the operation. The entire scheme was therefore postponed for at least a year. Although Douglass met with and paid the hotel bill for Forbes when he visited Rochester seeking personal funds in late 1857, the editor exaggerated his own role in exposing the Englishman's betrayals to Brown (claiming to have first broken the news). Douglass had embarrassing tracks to cover on this count; through his friend Ottilie Assing he had introduced Forbes to a series of New York acquaintances as potential donors, all of which only added to the danger of blown secrecy.[40]

The "Forbes postponement," as participants and scholars came to call it, forced Brown to return to Kansas and lie relatively low until 1859. The fifty-eight-year-old with the flowing white Moses-like beard fell ill for weeks with malarial fevers. He chose yet another new alias, Shubel Morgan, the first name meaning "captive of God." Hatred and violence over the slavery question still roiled in Kansas. In December 1858, a slave named Jim Daniels crossed over from Missouri, found Brown, and summoned his assistance in protecting him and his young family from their owner, who intended to sell them away southward. Physically recovered, Brown strapped on his guns and led eighteen guerrillas into Missouri; they liberated Daniels's family as well as one other group of slaves from two farms, resulting in the death of one slaveholder, and spirited the eleven rescued people back into Kansas. Here finally—Brown had liberated slaves from under the noses of their owners.[41] Then what ensued was possibly the most heroic and admirable feat of Brown's troubled career.

After hiding in makeshift quarters and among antislavery settlers in Kansas for a month, Brown led an epic eighty-two-day, thousand-mile midwinter trek, on foot and horseback, as well as with an oxen-driven wagon, across Nebraska, Iowa, Illinois, and Michigan. With the aid especially of abolitionist activists in Grinnell, Iowa, Brown and his liberated entourage eventually rode in a special boxcar by train to Chicago and on to Detroit. On a blustery March 12, 1859, Brown bid a tearful farewell to the now twelve liberated blacks as they were spirited to freedom across the Detroit River at Windsor, Ontario. Back in Kansas, Jim Daniels's wife had given birth to a baby boy christened John Brown Daniels. When Brown's daughter Ruth asked him later about his feelings during that scene on the Detroit River, her father merely answered with Scripture: "Lord, now lettest thou thy servant depart in peace, according to thy word: For mine eyes have seen thy salvation."[42]

That night in Detroit, Brown returned to earthly matters as he met with Douglass, who was on an extended western speaking tour. Brown had written ahead when he heard of Douglass's presence and urged him to wait for a rendezvous. Douglass heard Brown's latest plans among a group of black Detroiters, led by George DeBaptiste, the militant leader of that city's Colored Vigilance Committee, which worked to direct fugitive slaves into Canada. Despite the success of the Missouri rescue, Douglass had gone cold on Brown's scheme, especially if it included Harpers Ferry. The Old Man's heroic image was now thoroughly compelling; he was the revolutionary that abolitionists such as Douglass had yearned for. Or was he? That winter, during the rescue journey, Douglass's daughter Rosetta wrote to her father demonstrating how the warrior had become an intimate part of their family lore: "Old Brown will have to keep out of sight for a while. The governor of Missouri has a reward of $3000 offered for his capture." In Brown's travels eastward in mid-April for more money raising, he stopped by Douglass's printing office for an afternoon to make yet another appeal to the most famous black activist. Brown believed, dubiously, that Douglass's presence would attract other courageous blacks to the cause of violent action. Douglass provided a serious conversation, but no promises. He reported in his paper, though, very publicly, that "a hero . . . 'Old Brown' of Kansas memory" had just visited Rochester and made an appearance to speak at City Hall. His host was angry at local Republicans for their disappointing or cowardly turnout.[43]

Later that summer Brown rented a farmhouse (the Kennedy farm) in western Maryland, a mere five miles north of Harpers Ferry, as his secret staging base for the attack on the federal arsenal across the Virginia border. Douglass was certainly informed of the location and now of its purpose. He and Brown kept up a correspondence through that fateful summer, and on August 10 Douglass met with John Brown Jr. in Rochester. Soon after that encounter, the editor answered the Old Man's summons to come meet him in a stone quarry near Chambersburg, Pennsylvania, just across from the Maryland line.[44] Douglass recorded a detailed recollection of this fateful final meeting between the two men. In autobiographical time Douglass could control the narrative; but in real time on August 19–20, when he met the revolutionary, who was disguised as a fisherman and camped among bleak large stones, an agonized emotional tension enveloped their friendship.

Douglass brought a $20 contribution given him on a stop in New York City by a black couple, the Reverend James Glocester and his wife, as well as one significant recruit, a fugitive slave named Shields Green, who had escaped from slavery in Charleston, South Carolina. Green was a man of few words but steel nerves and had met Brown on one of his visits to Douglass in Rochester. As Douglass arrived in Chambersburg, a town with a sizable free-black population, he was immediately recognized and asked to deliver a speech. Not wishing to blow his cover, he responded as asked in a local black church. Then for two days Brown and Douglass, along with John Kagi, one of Brown's most trusted aides-de-camp (with Green present as well), debated the Harpers Ferry scheme. Douglass did not exaggerate when he remembered feeling that he "was on a dangerous mission." Indeed, at the confluence of the Potomac and Shenandoah Rivers, and only sixty-five miles from Washington, DC, the federal arsenal at Harpers Ferry housed the largest stash of munitions in the United States. Brown begged Douglass to join him for the raid, as Douglass listened but resisted and then vehemently strove to dissuade the Old Man from the attack. Brown looked bedraggled, "storm-beaten . . . his clothing . . . about the color of the stone quarry itself." But the final realization of his imminent invasion of Virginia put fire in the Old Man's eyes. Possibly Douglass still did not know fully of the intent to attack the arsenal until he arrived in Chambersburg, although he had heard it "hinted" at several times before.[45]

That Douglass made such an extremely risky trip to southern Pennsylvania at this late date may indicate that he knew a great deal, but perhaps not quite enough. It also reflected a kind of desperate loyalty he had always demonstrated toward Brown—showing up with money and a recruit, the two things the warrior had always sought. Still gravely in search of that logic of violence that he could embrace in the mind, not merely the heart, Douglass stepped away from Brown's bleak, death-defying heroism. The writer-orator looked reality in the face and said a resounding no. At age forty-one, Douglass was not prepared to die in such futility.

Douglass told Brown that the raid would prove fatal to all earlier plans for running off slaves and the creation in the mountains of a militarized Underground Railroad, the one aspect of Brown's schemes that attracted Douglass. Brown threw his arms around Douglass at their campfire and begged him to lend his life and reputation to the cause. "Come with me, Douglass," Brown pled, "I will defend you with my life. I want you for a special purpose. When I strike the bees will begin to swarm, and I shall want you to help hive them." But the former slave knew far too much about the instinctive suspicions of slaves toward their would-be liberators as well as about the bloodshed surely to follow any slave insurrection. Above all, Douglass looked Brown in the eye and told him that, despite his apparent aim of "rousing the nation," he was attacking the federal government, which would marshal all its military might against him. He was "going into a perfect steel trap," Douglass told Brown in no uncertain terms, and warned that "Virginia would blow him and his hostages sky-high, rather than that he should hold Harpers Ferry an hour." The conversation deteriorated into a grim, if noble, despair. Douglass knew he had encountered a tragedy he could not stop. He let Shields Green make his own choice, and the young man's response was simple: "I b'leve I'll go wid de ole man." Green would be captured at Harpers Ferry along with Brown and hanged on December 16, two weeks after the Old Man; his body was given for dissection to a Virginia medical school.[46]

Autobiography allows for an ordering of time and motives. In the clear-minded moment of August 20, 1859, Douglass made one of the great rational decisions of his life. Soon, though, the man who had expended so much rhetoric advocating violence in the 1850s would have to explain himself as an exile in a doubting world.

In the first nine months of 1859, before Harpers Ferry changed everything, Douglass had hardly sat on his hands waiting for Brown to strike his blows. From February 1 to March 12, Douglass launched one of his exhausting lecture tours across the Midwest in the states of Illinois, Wisconsin, and Michigan. He delivered some fifty speeches in six weeks. Douglass encountered no mobs and only a little hostility (he was viciously Jim-Crowed in a hotel in Janesville, Wisconsin). He found the tour debilitating but "soul-cheering"; as a black voice he served as an "excellent thermometer" of the political climate. The slavery question seemed uppermost in everyone's mind among his huge audiences that spring. In the heartland where the Republican Party found its deepest allegiances, Douglass kept up steady criticism of the party's moderate policies, especially its tendency to support "exclusion" laws to deny settlement by blacks in western territories. He attacked Republicans' Free-Soilism as never enough, calling it "an inconsistent, vacillating, crooked and compromising advocacy of a good cause." During his absence from the *Douglass' Monthly* (the name was newly changed), he gave over the editor's chair to McCune Smith, who dazzled the paper's readers with essays on black education, self-reliance, suffrage, and politics. The orator might have also given himself over to full-time lecturing for a while as a fund-raiser; he repeatedly appealed to his subscribers to pay up and keep his paper afloat.[47]

While John Brown plotted, Douglass kept up a steady and fierce debate with fellow black leaders such as Henry Highland Garnet over emigration schemes. Douglass respected Garnet and the right to emigrate, but attacked the idea of willful African American removal from the United States. Douglass loathed the notion that some of the best black leaders would abandon the American ship at this pivotal hour in history. Garnet's mission was to extend "civilization and Christianity" to the heathen of Africa, and to end slave trading, but Douglass, who referred to West African rulers who sold slaves as "savage," angrily insisted that American slaves must be freed first.[48]

In January 1859 Garnet and Douglass exchanged honest missives, disagreeing vehemently. Garnet accused his "dear brother" of enjoying the "comforts of the editorial chair" rather than venturing to Africa to make a new civilization for their people. Garnet even accused the editor of a "toil-fearing spirit." Douglass reacted with grace but firmly condemned once again all forms of colonization as false prophecy and a historical dead end. Although he sometimes expressed modest interest in possible migrations to Haiti, to Douglass, removal, even in the wake of *Dred Scott*, only fueled the idea that black people could never be equal in America. The best way to defeat racism, said the editor, was to stop "with wandering eyes and open mouths, looking out for some mighty revolution in our affairs here, which is to remove us from this country." Douglass and Garnet wanted different revolutions. "*You* go there, *we* stay here, is just the difference between us," Douglass told the minister.[49]

Douglass sustained as well his radical critique of Republicans, demanding that abolitionists "return to your principles" and reject appeals on "behalf of free white labor." Energized by the public lectern, throughout 1859 Douglass kept up his drumbeat against racial segregation and about uses of force. With special urgency, by summer he blasted the limits of Republican "non-extension," calling the slave system "a fiery dragon" sweeping across the South. "While the monster lives," Douglass characteristically declared, "he will hunger and thirst, breathe and expand. The true way is to put the knife into its quivering heart."[50] Rhetorically, Douglass had long been ready for violence.

Among the final editorials Douglass wrote before Harpers Ferry was one entitled "The Ballot and the Bullet." The piece is a measure of Douglass's frustrations as well as his passions. Reacting ostensibly to a Garrisonian challenge that abolitionists should employ only the "sword of the spirit" and abandon all appeals to the ballot or the bullet, Douglass reflexively declared such a debate "nonsense." "Hearts and consciences" were crucial, he admitted, but "truth to be efficient must be uttered in action as well as in speech." If speech could end slavery, Douglass said, it "would have been done long ago." He demanded an "anti-slavery Government," but the political system seemed to offer only "can't," and he was "sick of it." Hence, the "ballot is needed, and if this will not be heard and heeded, then the bullet." "Law" was necessary, but so was "physical force."[51] As an exclamation point on the bankruptcy of moral suasion, Douglass also unwittingly exhibited that an expectation, even a justification, for violence could leave a gaping, unbearable chasm between words and actions.

When news broke about the raid on Harpers Ferry on October 17–18, Douglass was in Philadelphia, where he gave a speech at National Hall. Late on the night of October 16, Brown and his eighteen men had seized the arsenal. Within thirty-six hours the raid was over; ten of Brown's men were killed in the raid, some captured, including the badly wounded Brown himself. While five escaped, three of whom would die fighting in the Civil War, the captives were hanged in the coming months by the state of Virginia. Three slaves temporarily liberated by Brown's band died in the raid or its aftermath. Five town residents or workers, including the Harpers Ferry mayor, were killed, and nine militiamen or US marines were wounded in the day of street battles. The raid was a strategic disaster, yet with time emerged as the most catalytic and successful symbolic event in the history of the antislavery cause. Newspapers screamed with shocking and confused headlines such as the litany on the cover of the *New York Herald* for October 18: "Fearful and Exciting Intelligence"; "Extensive Negro Conspiracy"; "Seizure of United States Arsenal by the Insurrectionists." Within a day of Brown's capture and arrest Douglass's name appeared in newspapers across the country as one of the conspirators identified in a large collection of papers confiscated from a trunk left at the Kennedy farm in Maryland. Wild rumors mixed with some facts as many newspapers gave over their entire sheets for days to telegraphic reports about Harpers Ferry. By October 29 *Frank Leslie's Illustrated Newspaper* began its extraordinary pictorial coverage of Brown, the raid, the trials, and the executions, giving the country a feast of images well into 1860. There had never been an event like this in American history; Douglass recalled it as news with "the startling effect of an earthquake . . . something to make the boldest hold his breath." [52]

Douglass quickly realized he was in dire trouble. He delivered his Philadelphia lecture in which he openly referred to Brown's raid approvingly. But soon afterward he was informed by friends that John Hurn, the city's sympathetic antislavery telegraph operator, had received a dispatch from government authorities to the local sheriff ordering that Douglass be arrested and detained as a conspirator. Hurn delayed its delivery for three hours as long as friends "agreed to get Mr. Douglass out of the state." (Hurn became a prominent photographer, and Douglass sat no fewer than eight times for him in the 1860s and 1870s, a measure of the bond the two men developed.[53])

Douglass swiftly departed from the Walnut Street wharf over to Camden, New Jersey, a route he remembered well from his escape to freedom in 1838. Now he was a fugitive again of another kind. Hurrying northward, he took the train to New York, and late on the night of October 19 he caught the ferry to Hoboken, to the home of Mrs. Marks, where Ottilie Assing lived as a boarder. There Douglass spent the night as he made a risky decision to use the railroads to continue his flight home to Rochester. Worried about "sundry letters and a constitution written by John Brown" locked in his desk in Rochester, he dictated a telegram to Assing to be sent the next morning to Douglass's eldest son, Lewis. Addressed to the telegraph operator in Rochester, whom the editor knew well, it read, "B. F. Blackall, Esq: Tell Lewis (my oldest son) to secure all the important papers in my high desk." To keep secrecy, he did not sign his name. In the *Life and Times* reminiscence, Douglass observed that in the 1880s the "mark of the chisel" still remained on the old desk, where Lewis had pried it open, one of the family "traces of the John Brown raid." Both John Hurn and Assing eventually staked claims to having saved Douglass's life.[54]

On October 20, Assing and another neighbor took Douglass in the dark of night in a private carriage to Paterson, New Jersey, so that he could take the Erie Railroad to Rochester, not the train he might normally be expected to occupy. He arrived safely, but immediately was informed by his neighbor Samuel Porter that the New York lieutenant governor was prepared to arrest Douglass if Governor Henry Wise of Virginia, now in charge of the investigation, issued such an order. Indeed, Wise was especially determined to capture Douglass, who eventually reprinted the Virginia governor's remarkable letter to President James Buchanan, requesting his assistance in finding and apprehending "the person of Frederick Douglass, a negro man . . . charged with murder, robbery, and inciting servile insurrection." In emotional desperation, with hardly time for a serious reckoning with Anna and his children, Douglass packed a bag, and by what was likely October 22, Amy and Isaac Post drove him to the docks and a ferry across Lake Ontario into Canada. It was widely reported that Douglass escaped from Rochester a mere six hours before federal marshals arrived at his home seeking his arrest.[55]

Anna's despair and his children's fears can only be imagined. They had by then lost count of the times when they felt abandoned by their beloved husband and father; but this time it may have felt as if their world had ended. The countless earlier appeals for the blood of slaveholders had found an astounding result fraught with horrible uncertainty.

In Canada, Douglass first stayed in a tavern in Clifton, which is today Niagara Falls. He was due west of Rochester, although soon it became clear that he could not go home anytime soon. Not only was Henry Wise searching for him, but he soon learned of severe criticism from one of Brown's captured men, John Cook, as well as from some black leaders claiming that the abolitionist had promised to join the raid and betrayed the cause. Douglass may have let the sound and awe of the falls soothe his psyche; he certainly did not fall on his sword with guilt and affliction, although the accusations put him painfully on the defensive. On October 27 he wrote to Amy Post in Rochester implying that he would return to the New York side of the border soon, admitting however that it "will take many months to blow this heavy cloud from my sky." He hated his current exile and worried about the possible confiscation of his property if his indictment held. But he whistled with false confidence: "It cannot be lost unless I am convicted. I cannot be convicted if I am not tried. . . . I cannot be arrested unless caught; I cannot be caught if I keep out of the way—and just this thing it is my purpose to do." [56]

On October 31 Douglass responded the only way he could—with his pen in a public letter to a Rochester newspaper that was in turn reprinted all over the country. To Cook's jailhouse accusation of "cowardice" against him, Douglass first blamed the hothouse of "terror-stricken slaveholders" surrounding the sensational situation in Virginia. Then, with a degree of comic irony he may have regretted, he answered the personal charge: "I have not one word to say in defense or vindication of my character for courage. I have always been more distinguished for running than fighting—and tried by the Harpers Ferry insurrection test, I am most miserably deficient in courage." Soon he would have to endure an extraordinary cartoon that appeared in *Frank Leslie's Illustrated Newspaper*, depicting Douglass leaping through the air in sheer fright with a trunk on his shoulder, his shoes and hat flying off. To his side is the small signpost TO CANADA; the title reads, "The Way in Which Fred. Douglass Fights Wise of Virginia," and the caption below, "I have always been more distinguished for running than fighting." [57]

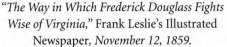

THE WAY IN WHICH FRED. DOUGLASS FIGHTS WISE OF VIRGINIA.

" I have always been more distinguished for running than fighting."—Fred. Douglass' Letter to the Rochester Papers.

"The Way in Which Frederick Douglass Fights Wise of Virginia," Frank Leslie's Illustrated Newspaper, *November 12, 1859.*

Douglass unequivocally denied ever promising to join Brown's band at Harpers Ferry. Whether from wisdom or cowardice, Douglass said, his "field of labor for the abolition of slavery has not extended to an attack upon the United States arsenal." He did not fear being "made an accomplice in the general *conspiracy* against slavery." Then he succinctly stated his long-term dilemma with violence: "I am ever ready to write, speak, publish, organize, combine, and even to conspire against slavery, when there is a reasonable hope for success." Such had been the gaping hole in his quest for the logic of violence, as in the earlier Chambersburg moment of truth. As to why he had not joined Brown in Virginia, Douglass gave an honest answer: "The tools to those that can use them." [58] There was a time for every purpose—for the war makers, and for the war propagandists. Douglass knew his tools.

Also while sitting in Clifton, Canada, and reading wire dispatches and newspapers, Douglass followed Brown's celebrated trial in Charles Town, Virginia, which began on October 25. He penned an extraordinary column for his paper, "Capt. John Brown Not Insane," which was not only a vintage, sharp-edged piece of abolitionism, but also Douglass's earliest effort to help build the majestic cross of John Brown's martyrdom. To allow a charge of insanity for Brown soiled "this glorious martyr of liberty." Had Americans "forgotten their own heroic age?" Douglass wondered, as he quickly marched Brown into line next to the "heroes of Lexington, Concord, and Bunker Hill." Brown was already "Gideon" of "self-forgetful heroism." All the bad strategy and exasperatingly mysterious plans evaporated in the preparation for the gallows. John Brown had never made it easy to love him, until he found what one scholar has called his "creative vocation" of seeking martyrdom.[59]

Within two weeks of his capture, the bearded prophetlike hero had suddenly offered the nation a new history. Douglass was already writing a first chapter, almost a prose equivalent of the song "John Brown's Body." "This age is too gross and sensual to appreciate his deeds, and so calls him mad," Douglass wrote, "but the future will write his epitaph upon the hearts of a people freed from slavery, because he struck the first effectual blow." Douglass realized in mythic terms his logic of violence; Brown had used the "weapons precisely adapted" to destroy slavery. As poems, songs, and editorials flowed forth in American and European journals, Douglass made his own mark. "Like Samson," said a lonely Douglass in Canada, Brown "has laid his hands upon the pillars of this great national temple of cruelty and blood, and when he falls, the temple will speedily crumble to its final doom." Brown would have loved the metaphor since Samson was one of his own oft-repeated self-comparisons. "I expect to effect a mighty conquest," Brown had written with customary grandiosity in 1858, "even though it will be like the last victory of Samson."[60] Douglass and Brown could both claim old biblical stories that each man had expected their America to reenact.

In the second week of November, Douglass passed through Toronto, took a steamer across Lake Ontario and down the Saint Lawrence River to Quebec, where on the twelfth he departed on the ship *Nova Scotia* for Liverpool. He feared, as he remembered many years later, that he "was going into exile, perhaps for life." On the bitterly cold decks of a ship in the North Atlantic, Douglass felt deeply troubled. In two sittings aboard the ship on its ten-day voyage to Liverpool, the lonely exile crafted a long letter. He amused himself and settled his nerves with comments on the Frenchness of Montreal, the majesties of the ocean, and the sturdiness of the steamer. "My head is hardly less confused than the waves," he admitted, "and my hand not more steady than the ship."[61] As John Brown eagerly charted his plan to die from his jail cell in Virginia, Douglass now had to plot a plan to live.

Chapter 16

SECESSION: TAUGHT BY EVENTS

I am for a dissolution of the Union—decidedly for a dissolution
of the Union! Under an abolition President, who would wield
the army and the navy of the Government for the abolition of
slavery, I should be for the Union of these States.

—FREDERICK DOUGLASS, BOSTON, DECEMBER 1860

Among the most driving compulsions of Frederick Douglass's
public life was his quest to alter, shape, or change history. He
craved those moments and opportunities to gain access to real
political power, to bend wills, and to be a creator of events and not merely
their interpreter. Over and again he learned the limits and frustrations of
such a quest. During the Civil War era Douglass spent great energy trying to
discern and then affect what he frequently called the "stern logic of events."
In *Life and Times*, he reflected poignantly on how during America's final
road to disunion in 1859–61, he had done all in his power to convince his
readers and listeners that the fate of the country depended on the "liberation of the slave." From the safety of retrospect, Douglass expressed a certain hard-won wisdom about the nature of history: "In every way possible,
in the columns of my paper and on the platform, by letters to friends at
home and abroad, I did all that I could to impress this conviction upon the
country. But nations seldom listen to advice from individuals, however reasonable. They are taught less by theories than by facts and events." [1]

John Brown's raid on Harpers Ferry, as well as the election of 1860 and
the secession crisis that flowed in its wake, were just such seismic breaks in
time when people were taught by events. Douglass could only react to and
flee from the John Brown revolutionary moment; with time, however, he

had a great deal to say about its political, moral, and religious meanings. Harpers Ferry became one of the markers of his life's story. Ten months before the raid, in January 1859, with palpable despair, Douglass had yearned for hope and a historical clarity he could not find. "Would that this might prove the year of the jubilee to those now toiling millions!" he proclaimed in his paper. "Would that this were the day of release. But no wavering shadow of this coming event falls upon our vision. We walk by faith, not by sight." Bleakly, Douglass admitted that his well was dry. "How long! How long! O Lord God of Sabbath! shall the crushed and bleeding bondsman wait. . . . O! who can answer—who can tell the end we long to know?" [2]

But exactly a year later, Douglass was living in exile in Halifax, England, in northwest Yorkshire, at the home of his old friend Julia Griffiths Crofts, and her husband, the Reverend Dr. Henry O. Crofts. On December 19, the *New York Times* reported Douglass safely in England, where he defended John Brown and the raid. "John Brown has not failed," said the new exile. "He has dropped an *idea*, equal to a thousand bombshells into the very Bastille of slavery. That idea will live and grow, and one day will unless slavery is otherwise abolished, cover Virginia with sorrow and blood." By then, Douglass must have read Brown's pre-gallows dark eloquence about a land "purged with blood." By January 1860, the orator was once again back on the British antislavery speaking circuit, delivering tributes to Brown and historical lectures on the slavery issue in America. At Bradford on January 6, an upbeat Douglass argued that American abolitionism had undergone "continual progress" since the first campaign of James Birney as the Liberty Party candidate for president in 1840; now some seventeen Northern states had become politically antislavery, and John Brown's raid had enhanced the cause like nothing before. [3]

In his speeches during a six-month exile, he appropriated Brown's raid to a new variation of a prophetic tradition Douglass had long practiced. At Edinburgh, Scotland, on January 30, Douglass used Brown's story to entertain as well as instruct his audience, garnering "loud and prolonged cheering" with the argument that American slaveholders were the real "insurrectionists." The huge Queen Street Hall crowd thrilled to Douglass's radical interpretation of Harpers Ferry: "The 350,000 slaveholders, with the American Government so-called at their back, were but an armed band of insurgents against the just rights and liberties of their fellow-men. John Brown merely stepped in to interrupt and arrest this insurrection against the rights and liberties of mankind; and he did right!" The next night in Glasgow at a reception in his honor in the City Hall, Douglass heard loud applause as he delivered a similar speech in which Isaiah's "no peace to the wicked" formed his theme. He garnered laughs with his claim against any implication on his part in Brown's raid as he also played with double meanings for "peace." He was "thus for peace," Douglass maintained, but "there could be no peace between one man standing on the neck of his brother and the man who was under his heel." The American announced that the "slave would be free, whether by peace or by war." Douglass told his Glasgow comrades that Brown had "succeeded much better . . . by failure than he would have . . . if he had held out till this time." Martyrdom on the gallows gave the war propagandist an unbounded way to make the old story new.[4]

Just before leaving Canada Douglass had written a farewell message to "My American Readers and Friends." He betrayed great anxiety and sadness in his forced exile. "Neither the long experience of partings and meetings, nor the calmness borrowed from philosophy," eased his fears. But he took heart in making the most of "the stern old hero" awaiting execution and martyrdom. "The Christian blood of Old John Brown," he declared, "will not cease to cry from the ground long after the clamors of alarm and consternation" from slaveholders had ceased. Douglass announced himself "glad to use the event at Harpers Ferry" to assault with yet new fervor the "benumbed conscience of the nation." He may have fled for his life to a temporary asylum in England, but he now had a great new story and adoring audiences that allowed him to walk by sight.[5] Having saved himself from death on a gallows in a Virginia field, a living Douglass had work to do.

Douglass's exile had landed him among friends. In March 1859, Julia Griffiths had married Henry O. Crofts, a Methodist minister and missionary who had served from 1839 to 1851 in Canada and whom she had met in 1857. They provided a welcome landing for the newly fugitive Frederick. When Douglass came ashore in Liverpool on November 24, he traveled immediately to Halifax where he "found my old friend Julia quite glad . . . to see me—and what was of equal importance, her husband too." Douglass had earlier described the Reverend Crofts as an "excellent antislavery man" who had worked among fugitive slaves in Canada. They all had much in common, not least of which was still coping with the residue of Garrisonian scandalmongering about Frederick and Julia. After Griffiths's return to England in 1855, the Garrisonians (namely Parker Pillsbury while touring) had tried to monitor her activities, believing absurdly that Douglass had dispatched Julia to raise money not only for his paper and his mortgage but to forge rival abolition groups in Britain. Pillsbury wrote in 1856 that the two alleged lovers had "been mortgaged to each other and both to the devil."[6] Garrisonian orthodoxy reached far beyond US borders.

But no such rumors deterred Griffiths in the least from her new career of organizing women's antislavery societies in England and Scotland, nor from writing her extraordinary public letters to Douglass's paper. By February 1859 she reported that she had succeeded in organizing twenty new antislavery groups among her British sisters, and in reorganizing many older ones. Griffiths was a brilliant publicist and activist who, as a woman alone, crisscrossed England, Scotland, and Ireland raising consciousness and money for Douglass's paper, as well as for the Rochester ladies' antislavery fairs and for supporting fugitive slaves in New York State. She was the driving force behind the Edinburgh Ladies New Anti-Slavery Association and reported memberships of thirty-one in Wakefield and forty-one in her own town of Halifax. Such heroic efforts did not go unnoticed publicly by her friend; in April 1858 Douglass wrote to the Halifax women, "I wish your society could have seen the twenty fugitives we have helped on their way to Canada during the past week. . . . Every example leaves the system weaker." Griffiths's women even sent $10 for John Brown's widow in late 1859. As Douglass hit the circuit in England and Scotland, Julia stepped in seamlessly as his manager. Her friend's presence had fostered a "highly successful" fund-raising campaign, she reported in March 1860. Invitations poured in from all over England and Scotland, and Julia served as agent. "It has been a great pleasure to his friends," she said, "to see him once again safe in Old England, and to welcome him to their . . . firesides."[7]

During his second British sojourn, and well beyond, Douglass had many other rumors and accusations to face as well. The tales of his alleged betrayal of promises to Brown and his men refused to die, and a US Senate committee spent six months engaged in a somewhat hapless investigation of the Harpers Ferry conspiracy. The stories about Douglass's abandonment of Brown referred back to an unconfirmed rumor that at their Detroit meeting in March 1859, Brown had accused Douglass of cowardice to his face because of his refusal to enlist in the Harpers Ferry scheme. But over time the complaints about Douglass's role emanated largely from Brown's surviving children, Anne, Salmon, Ruth, and John Jr. In the summer of 1859, some of Brown's men, especially John Kagi, apparently felt convinced Douglass would personally join them in Maryland. In June, Kagi wrote to Douglass to congratulate him on his decision to join and told the editor that his name was magic in recruiting other black men. According to Franklin

Sanborn, a group of Philadelphia blacks wrote a letter to Douglass pledging support for his family in Rochester should he not return from the invasion of Virginia. Yet another unsubstantiated rumor had it that Douglass had escorted Shields Green to Chambersburg to join Brown's band as his own "paid substitute." An interview conducted in 1909 by Katherine Mayo, Oswald Garrison Villard's research assistant on his biography of John Brown, turned up a reminiscence from a Mrs. Russell, a Bostonian who had visited Brown in his jail cell before the execution. She claimed that Brown "had no fondness for Fred Douglass" and stated that his "defeated plan . . . we owe to the famous Mr. Frederick Douglass!" [8]

Such claims were always much more ex post facto bitterness than reality. Someone had to be blamed for the Old Hero's folly, especially after he walked so gracefully to the hangman's noose to die for the nation's sins. It is a rather pointless speculation to suggest, as one scholar has done, that Douglass's opposition was "detrimental" to the raid. Brown himself seemed fully aware that his own faulty strategy and indecision had led to defeat. In famous letters from jail while awaiting the gallows, he wrote to his brother Jeremiah: "I am worth inconceivably more to hang than for any other purpose." And to his wife, Mary, Brown offered this agonizing self-epitaph: "I have been *whipped* as the saying is; but am sure I can recover all the lost capital occasioned by that disaster; by only hanging a few moments by the neck; & feel quite determined to make the utmost possible out of a defeat." With a culture of martyrdom emerging around "John Brown's Body," blaming Douglass for the defeat at Harpers Ferry seems strange in retrospect.[9] This Jesus and his glorious cross needed no Judas, and soon his cause grew vaster than even the Old Man might have imagined.

From England, Douglass monitored the investigation conducted in the Senate by a committee chaired by James Mason of Virginia. The Mason Committee met with regularity from December 16, 1859, to June 14, 1860. Consisting of Senators Mason, Jefferson Davis of Mississippi, and G. N. Fitch of Indiana for the majority Democrats, and Senators Jacob Collamer of Vermont and James R. Doolittle of Wisconsin for the Republican minority, the hearings, with Davis serving as chief inquisitor, interrogated many witnesses to ascertain whether any "subversive organizations" had been involved in Brown's exploits. But during this volatile election year, the Mason Committee turned into more of a political exercise, with the Democrats seeking to identify and blame Republican congressmen as culprits and with most Republicans striving to keep distance between themselves and Brown's radicalism. The committee interviewed Republican luminar-

ies William H. Seward, the presumptive Republican presidential nominee, Henry Wilson and John Andrew of Massachusetts, and Representative
Joshua Giddings of Ohio. Correspondence from Giddings had been found
in Brown's trunks after the raid. The hearings also included the questioning
of two members of the group of Brown supporters known as the Secret Six,
George Luther Stearns and Samuel Gridley Howe, but the Mason Committee seemed less interested in proving a legal conspiracy than in eventually
putting the whole affair behind the nation before the election. Since Douglass was out of the country, the indictment against him, as well as nearly all
others, was abandoned. Only four arrest warrants were issued, and those
because they had refused to testify: John Brown Jr., James Redpath, Franklin
B. Sanborn, and Thaddeus Hyatt. Only Hyatt was jailed—for three months
in Washington, DC, before being released when the committee issued its
reports.[10]

In the end the Mason Committee, despite Jefferson Davis's personal
ire for Seward, Giddings, and all abolitionists, chose not to delve into the
reality of Brown's conspiracy. Its legal work seemed dictated more by the
much-anticipated Democratic Party nominating convention to be held in
Charleston, South Carolina, in April and the Republican convention in Chicago early that summer. The Mason Committee's majority report delivered
special censure for all the New England financial and military support for
Brown's Kansas crusade, as well as for abolitionists' belief in "higher law"
doctrines. But it seemed convinced that Brown's invasion was the work of
a relatively lone, deranged outlaw striving to incite "servile insurrection."
Hovering over the Mason Committee's deliberations was that Virginia had
already created one martyr, the consequences of which had produced a
toxic political environment, and it had no wish to create any more.[11]

Too much was at stake politically for all concerned in 1860 for the committee to seek anything resembling the deeper truth. Douglass was one beneficiary of an incompetent congressional inquiry into America's deepest
dilemma; he never had to face the future president of the Confederacy in a
Senate hearing. It would not be the last time Douglass found himself first
trapped by and then offered the open opportunity to exploit his country's
refusal to face its past or present. Soon, he could return to the United States,
relatively comfortable knowing that he did not face arrest or execution for
the crime of conspiracy in which he now declared great pride.

While in England, Douglass, as usual, buried his personal anxieties
in travel and lecturing. He remained on the defensive about his flight to
Canada and Britain, as well as his family's fate. Douglass felt under scru-

tiny about his choices, as he wrote to an old Irish friend, Maria Webb. He had to escape arrest and trial in Virginia. "I could never hope to get out of that state alive," he told Webb. "If they did not kill me for being concerned with Dear old Brown they would have done so—for my being Frederick Douglass." [12] *Being Frederick Douglass* is what he did in England to overflow crowds and with the stirrings of controversy.

Douglass appealed to the religious and national pride of his Scottish audiences. "The Christianity of Scotland," he said, "had no sanction for chains or slavery," whereas in the American South "the clank of the fetter might be heard along with the chime of the bell that called to prayer. Men might be seen going to prayer on one side of the street, and chain gangs on the other side." In Scotland he sang the old songs about Christian hypocrisy with new urgency. In Glasgow in February 1860, Douglass delivered a remarkable historical lecture on how America had descended from two distinct societies, one born among the Bible-inspired believers in the Magna Carta aboard the *Mayflower* in 1620, and the other aboard a "Dutch galley" slave ship landing in Virginia in 1619. One society led to "light" and the other "darkness"; the first brought "Christ" and the other "Belial," or the Old Testament conception for evil and Satan. This dichotomous simplicity gave way to a narrative of how the country had collapsed into the "most trying crisis in her history," bounded by the enactments of the Fugitive Slave Act and the *Dred Scott* decision, which Douglass called the "moral assassination" of his "whole race." [13]

At the same time, in Glasgow, Newcastle, and other cities, Douglass got into a nasty scrap with British Garrisonians, especially the famed George Thompson, over disunionism and the antislavery interpretation of the Constitution. Douglass plied old waters, but he seemed eager for another go at his old nemeses. Thompson responded with public rebuttals and specially published addresses denouncing Douglass's views and his harsh style. The Glasgow Emancipation Society reported that an April 3 address in the City Hall by Thompson had been a "refutation . . . lucid and triumphant" against "the charges that F. Douglass had brought against the lecturer." [14]

But Douglass loved these public squabbles, and his well of resentments and supply of sarcasm against Garrisonians seemed bottomless. He even made a vigorous case for the potential antislavery power of the Republican Party in America, appropriating it to his natural-rights conception of the Constitution. Although he gladly engaged in a personalized fight with Thompson over their respective readings of the Constitution, Douglass believed the time had passed for arcane argument. His Scottish audiences liked a vaguer kind of eloquence. "Slavery is essentially a dark system," he declared in Glasgow in March 1860; "all it wants is to be excluded and shut out from the light. If it can only be boxed in where there is not a single breath to fall upon it. . . . It dreads the influence of truth."[15] By his own circuitous route, Douglass may have landed on the central truth of why the Republican Party posed such a threat to Southern slavery. Such a political force could use parts of the Constitution, should it gain power, to bring slavery to an ultimate destruction.

Douglass also faced new issues in England as he found traction with older arguments. His own large audiences and Griffiths's extraordinary labors to revive antislavery societies notwithstanding, the British abolition movement appeared in decline. Many in the British public had soured on the question of West Indian emancipation, arguing that it had failed and that Africans and their descendants were proving incapable of free labor. Worse, increasingly American forms of racism that Douglass had not seen in 1846–47 appeared now on British streets, in theaters, and even in social discourse. A new roiling of racism in Britain disturbed him immensely. In his speech "British Racial Attitudes" in Newcastle, Douglass reminisced about encountering "not the slightest ill feeling toward me because of my complexion" in 1846. But now, "American prejudice might be found in the streets of Liverpool and in nearly all our commercial towns." He especially blamed "that pestiferous nuisance, Ethiopian minstrels," who "brought here the slang phrases, the contemptuous sneers all originating in the spirit of slavery." He made it clear that he hated seeing "the negro represented in all manner of extravagances, contented and happy as a slave." Groups of touring minstrels were indeed common in England by 1860, entertaining large audiences with exaggerated dialects and grotesque caricature. A Newcastle paper reported that Douglass experienced personal "hostility to his color" as never before, and that in a speech he condemned both American ministers as well as the minstrels alike for pouring "the leprous distilment of their proslavery poison into the ears and hearts of the British people."[16] British abolition dearly needed a revival; for at least a brief time, Douglass gave it his voice and energy.

In January 1860, while Douglass was in England, Ottilie Assing's German translation of *My Bondage and My Freedom* appeared. According to her biographer, Maria Diedrich, Assing sought to "invent a Douglass that was all hers." Indeed, that was the case, although with only the slimmest evidence via a third-party source, Diedrich maintains that Assing planned to join Douglass for a secret romantic holiday in France. Douglass did seek to travel to France by his own account, but could not go because the American government denied him a passport. Douglass openly blamed the racism of the Democratic Party's minister to the Court of St. James's, George Dallas.[17]

Assing may have dreamed of joining Douglass on his new "European career," as Diedrich suggests, but nothing from Douglass's hand or voice ever indicated such intentions. Assing's designs on Douglass's heart and career come to us entirely by her own telling of the tale. All he later admitted to was a "long-cherished desire to visit France." That he and Assing conducted an on-and-off intimate and important relationship seems certain from Assing's letters. It appears that Douglass had begun to study German at Assing's behest. Assing was utterly infatuated with Douglass and saw him as a romantic hero as well as, according to Diedrich, the "legitimate heir" of John Brown to lead the antislavery revolution. Assing's breathless hagiography of Brown and Douglass in the wake of Harpers Ferry knew no bounds. Diedrich rightly declares that Assing "feared neither contradiction nor inconsistency" in her writing. Her hopes and grandiosity halted abruptly, however, as did Douglass's second British sojourn, when news arrived in early spring while he was visiting Glasgow that his daughter Annie, just short of her eleventh birthday, had died in Rochester on March 13, 1860, of an extended illness.[18]

Ottilie Assing, c. 1871.

A grief- and guilt-stricken Douglass made haste to sail home to the United States despite lingering concerns over his legal fate. He may have received the news of Annie's death from Rosetta, who was now an occasional correspondent with her father. Annie herself had written the faraway parent in December 1859, telling of her joys and successes in school, especially her "German lessons." "I am the first reader and I can read," she told the exiled Douglass. Assing had taken a sincere interest in the education of Douglass's daughters. Anna Douglass was devastated by the loss of her namesake and final child of her marriage to the peripatetic world citizen she had once known as the lonely and ambitious boy from the Baltimore docks. A letter from Rosetta to Douglass's adopted sister, Harriet (Ruth Adams), opens a small window into Anna's bleak but courageous bereavement. "I have just asked Mother what I should say for her," said Rosetta to Harriet. "She sends her love to you and thanks you as heartily as myself for your sympathizing letter, and as she is unable to write will allow my letter to be in answer for both. . . . She is not very well now being quite feeble though about the house." Then Anna asked her daughter to tell Anna's sister-in-law to, politely, "if you desire," write to her famous brother and tell him to come home to Rochester. Along with her adult daughter and teenage sons, Anna would have seen to the burial of Annie. How horribly conspicuous Douglass must have seemed to all of them by his absence. Thirty-five carriages rolled along Rochester streets and roads to Annie's burial, according to a report in *Douglass' Monthly*. The "disease was one of the brain" that had baffled the doctors. During the funeral observances, wrote the observer, "frequent allusions were made to the father of little Annie, so far away, who would be so sad to be present, and yet more sad to be absent." [19]

Douglass wrote few public words about his daughter's death. He later called Annie "the light and life of my house." As he rode the trains from Glasgow to Halifax, said good-bye to Julia and Henry Crofts, then hurried on to Liverpool, his lonely burden numbed him. The cheering had stopped; those huge and engaging audiences in the ornate halls of Edinburgh and Glasgow were suddenly a world away from his personal reality. The helpless self-made man headed home to face events he could not control. In one of Rosetta's letters to Harriet she told of receiving letters from her father (which do not survive) indicating that "his grief was great" and hoping for another message with "more composure of mind." Douglass took a steamer to Portland, Maine, remaining inconspicuous as he returned to Rochester via Canada. After a seventeen-day voyage he was home by late April, where he would remain off the lecture circuit for nearly four months, still wary of the Senate investigation and doing his best to help Anna grieve and to provide a father's presence for Annie's four siblings. The youngest son, Charles, reminiscing many years later, said this sequence of events left them all a "dismembered family." "Thus at the age of 16," he wrote, "I left my father's house never to return again only as a visitor."[20]

They needed him; in a public letter to his "British Anti-Slavery Friends" of May 26, 1860, Douglass told of his "sorrow-stricken family" and how his presence felt "sacredly beneficial." But then he all but politicized Annie's death, thanking his English friends for their sympathy and suggesting that her demise resulted "from overanxiety for the safety of her father, and deep sorrow for the death of dear old John Brown, upon whose knee she had often sat only a few months before." All of this tenderness of sentiment and memory presaged Douglass's appeal about the never-ending problem of "receipts" and "expenses" of his newspaper. The *Douglass' Monthly* was broke again, political antislavery desperately needed his voice, and he enticed his British network with the news that ten more fugitive slaves had passed under his own roof in the mere month he had resided back in Rochester.[21] The public letter was a common genre in this era, but rarely had Douglass or anyone else in his abolitionist orbit mixed such private sorrow with fund-raising.

In July of 1860 Ottilie Assing came for a somewhat extended visit to Rochester, where among other activities she took an oath of allegiance to the United States and became an American citizen. According to her biographer she tried hard during this time to persuade Douglass away from his religious faith and biblical literary voice, but to no avail. Assing often had exquisitely bad timing and judgment. Whatever else they shared in affection and ideas, her atheism and his Christian worldview and millennial sense of history clashed, ultimately fatally. Douglass had planned a return visit to Britain that September to resume his effort to revive British abolitionism, but called it off because of the American presidential election campaign and his desire to affect it. "He who speaks now," he wrote in the *Monthly*, "may have an audience. We wish . . . to strike while the iron is hot." He further expressed great confidence in his "ever faithful friend and coadjutor, Mrs. Dr. Crofts" in forging a new antislavery sentiment in Great Britain.[22]

Moreover, Douglass continued to clash openly with Garrisonians, exchanging nasty counteraccusations in October and November over whether

he sought the demise of the American Anti-Slavery Society, which he vehemently denied. During this season of intense public furor in the land, he
and Garrison made sure not to appear in the same physical space. Douglass also found time in late September to attend a "Seventh Annual Clam
Bake," a large social gathering of free African Americans, held that year in
Fort Lee, New Jersey, on the Hudson River. Conceived by the New Yorker
Peter A. Williams in 1853, this "grand rural banquet" drew people to days of
entertainment and reunion from Boston, Newport, Providence, New York,
Philadelphia, Hartford, and other towns. After a feast at Fort Lee, speeches
were made, and Douglass, as usual, was front and center. The *Anglo-African*
reported that as guests found their places, "a form arises towering head and
shoulders over the whole company, it is Frederick Douglass, thenceforth as
ever the lion of the occasion." Douglass knew how to work a crowd. In his
own report on the occasion he maintained that his people should never lose
their "heart for amusement. . . . We like to study our people at play as well
as at prayer." [23] Soon they were back to work that needed their prayers.

That summer and fall of 1860, Douglass threw himself back into his
journalism and into the most transformative election in the nation's history. Hope and principles were at war, and even serving each other, as never
before. Since the Democrats tore themselves into two sectionalized parts,
one supporting Stephen A. Douglas for president and the other John C.
Breckinridge of Kentucky, and since the Republicans' nomination of Abraham Lincoln, who despite being apparently more moderate than his chief
rival, William H. Seward, threatened the South in unprecedented ways,
Douglass felt inspired by the pending election campaign. Assuming his
election-year pose, he girded up for another walk along the thin line between endorsement and denunciation of Republicans. "The Republican
party," he told his British friends, "is . . . only negatively antislavery. It is opposed to the political power of slavery, rather than to slavery itself." But it
possessed what no previous political force had because it could "humble the
slave power and defeat all plans for giving slavery any further guarantees of
permanence." [24]

Douglass promised to work for the Republicans even as he expressed
contradictory cautions. Despite being disappointed by the Chicago platform, in a June 1860 editorial he praised Lincoln. "Untried" and without
claim to "any literary culture beyond the circle of his practical duties," the
Illinois lawyer was nevertheless "honest," possessed a "well balanced head,"
and "great firmness of will." Douglass decided the Republicans really did

nominate, in Lincoln, a "radical . . . fully committed to the doctrine of the 'irrepressible conflict.'" Although Douglass regretted the Republicans' lack of moral abolitionism and would have preferred the "brave and inspiring march of a storming party," in its absence he would settle for "the slow processes of a cautious siege."[25] It was the political season indeed, and Douglass had never known a political persuasion that he could not both cheer and attack depending on the audience and purpose. His observations about Lincoln proved astute in the long run; at this tense juncture, however, Douglass tilted in political crosswinds.

On July 2, he wrote in a confused tone to Gerrit Smith, who struggled with a mental breakdown in the wake of Harpers Ferry. "I cannot support Lincoln," Douglass asserted, "but whether there is life enough in the Abolitionists [Radical Abolition Party] to name a candidate, I cannot say. I shall look to your letter for light on the pathway of duty." Then in August Douglass wrote in the *Monthly* that the "vital element" of the Republican Party was its "antislavery sentiment." "Nothing is plainer," Douglass argued, "than that the Republican party has its source in the old Liberty party." It would live or die, he contended, "as the abolition sentiment of the country flourishes or fades." Vexed by his commitments to moral principle and political action, Douglass announced that he would vote for what historian Richard Sewell rightly called the remnant of Gerrit Smith's "miniscule" radical party, while assiduously working for Lincoln's election.[26]

Douglass's political fluctuations in 1860 were hardly unique; his public editorials were the searching efforts of a black leader to comprehend an amalgam of political interests and a party that seemed to both despise and champion his people. The American party system was undergoing a revolution, and the nation now teetered on the brink of a potential disunion that both worried and thrilled Douglass. His political positions in 1860, as in 1856, reflected a personality trait historian James Oakes has called "impulsive and voluble," a tendency to "sharp reversals" as he rushed his ideas into print each month in his paper. But Douglass's critiques of Lincoln and the Republicans were less rushed than representative of his lack of leverage and his isolation outside of the party's inner circles. The only prominent Republican with whom Douglass had any regular correspondence was Massachusetts senator Charles Sumner, whom Douglass deeply admired as a radical, the "Wilberforce of America" with the daring and nerve to denounce the "barbarism of slavery" on the floor of the Senate.[27]

Sumner was what Douglass wished the Republican Party would become—a force that would "grapple with the hell-born monster itself."

But he knew it was a coalition of interests, and he found an uncomfortable foothold among some of its guiding ideas, especially the "denationalization" of slavery, a theory advanced most prominently by Salmon P. Chase that sought to turn slavery in upon itself, where it would suffocate and die. Wherever federal jurisdiction existed—the District of Columbia, the territories, foreign and interstate commerce, the postal service, the Fugitive Slave Act—Republicans would either deny slavery protection or attack it. Douglass saw this variation on nonextensionism as merely the first step in a constitutional plan to restrict slavery geographically and then ultimately to eradicate it by federal action. He absolutely disagreed with Lincoln's and the Republicans' idea that they could not constitutionally end slavery in the states where it already legally existed; Douglass had been arguing the opposite for nearly a decade. "It will be a great work accomplished," a newly encouraged Douglass wrote in June, "when this Government is divorced from the active support of the inhuman slave system." He wanted to "turn the tide of the National Administration against the man-stealers of this country."[28] Thus Douglass found his own way to fold radical rhetoric into moderate methods and, at least most of the time, sing hosannas to the Republicans.

Excited and wary, Douglass did not merely await election returns in the fall of 1860. In the thirty-two hundred words of editorials and the seven thousand words of a major speech on the West Indian emancipation anniversary in August alone, Douglass delivered a remarkably astute political analysis of the 1860 election, a journalist's first draft of history if ever there was one. With informed precision and a propagandist's zeal, Douglass depicted the Republican coalition's diverse attitudes toward slavery in five parts: one, because it was an expensive and wasteful "system of labor"; two, because it created an "aristocratic class who despise labor," which in turn led to a broader "contempt" for all others who "work for an honest living"; three, because a small Southern oligarchy had become "masters of the United States" and the "governing class" of the nation's institutions; four, because it led some whites with an "aversion to blacks" to deny them all rights and liberties and to exclude them from new territories; and five, because the genuine "abolition element" saw slavery as the "most atrocious and revolting crime against nature and nature's God," a system of inhumanity to be destroyed out of a "mighty conviction." The only group missing from Douglass's characterization of the Republican coalition were the nativists, the former Know-Nothing, anti-immigrant Protestant white Northerners who had made huge inroads into American politics in the early 1850s.[29] By 1860, they too found a place under the Republicans' broad tent.

Douglass gloated over the splitting of the Democrats into Northern and Southern factions. The Democrats, argued Douglass, had historically surpassed all others in "heartless cruelty" toward blacks; their division now opened a floodgate for the Republican waters to rush through, and he sent up "a jubilee shout over the fact that the wisdom of the crafty had been confounded . . . the counsels of the wicked . . . brought to nought." But in a different mood in the same brief period, the enthusiastic political junkie turned into a dark moral philosopher. Douglass knew the political calculus indicated that Lincoln and the Republicans would win in November, but the previous decade had taught him not to trust the American "national character." For his people slavery had always been experienced as "grim and bloody tragedies . . . rehearsed day by day." But most Americans, including Northerners about to vote Republican, were but "spectators in a theatre" watching the slavery crisis "as a grand operatic performance." [30]

Americans, Douglass believed, instinctively and culturally watched history and preferred not to act in it. Douglass summed up his bitter complaint as "this terrible paradox of passing history" rooted in a distinctively American selfishness. "Whoever levies a tax upon our Bohea or Young Hyson [two forms of Chinese tea], will find the whole land blazing with patriotism and bristling with bayonets." If some foreign power tried to "impress a few Yankee sailors," Americans would go "fight like heroes." Douglass fashioned a withering chastisement of American self-centeredness that would match any modern complaint about the culture's hyperindividualism. "Millions of a foreign race may be stolen from their homes, and reduced to hopeless and inhuman bondage among us," he complained, "and we either approve the deed, or protest as gently as 'sucking doves.' " His "wickedly selfish" Americans loved to celebrate their "own heritage, and on this condition are content to see others crushed in our midst." They lived by the "philosophy of Cain," ready with their bluntly evil answer to the famous question "Am I my brother's keeper?" Douglass's use of the Cain and Abel parable is all the more telling if we remember that, unlike the more sentimental ways the "brother's keeper" language is often employed today, Cain had just killed his brother, and to God's query as to Abel's fate, Cain replies in effect, why should I care? Douglass wanted the indifferent Americans, with blood on their hands as well, to read on further in Genesis and know Cain's fate as "a fugitive and a vagabond in the earth." [31]

On the eve of such a new and encouraging election, Douglass's gloom seems odd at first glance. But this radical was still trying to comprehend just how to be a Republican; his writings were the reflections of a hardened abolitionist not certain whether the impending political collisions augured the liberation or the sacrificial doom of his people. The cynic in Douglass left him saying, "Heaven help the poor slave, whose only hope for freedom is in the selfish hearts of such a people." [32] But the radical pragmatist kept one eye trained on just how to apply that American self-interestedness to the cause of abolition.

That fall Douglass never found peace on either side of his self-imposed divide between pure abolition and antislavery politics. Personally, he threw his vote away in 1860; then as a social reformer he prepared to help push the new anti-Southern, antislavery politics along the course of abolition. In an August 1860 speech, he tried to clarify his position: "I would gladly have a party openly combined to put down slavery at the South. In the absence of such a party, I am glad to see a party in the field against which all that is slaveholding, malignant and Negro-hating, both in the North and the South, is combined." Whatever aroused the ire of the Slave Power was the friend of the slave. "The slaveholders know that the day of their power is over," Douglass declared, "when a Republican president is elected." At the very least, Southern fears of Lincoln's potential victory served as "tolerable endorsements of the antislavery tendencies of the Republican Party." [33] More than anything else, the editor wanted to hasten a decisive conflict, a rupture in the body politic that would force everyone to be taught by the events.

On Election Day, November 6, 1860, Douglass was in Rochester, working from morning until night at the polls. His most immediate concern was a proposal on the New York State ballot to abolish the $250 property requirement for black voters (no such requirement existed for whites). This movement for equal suffrage had attracted the racist scorn of Democrats and only limited endorsement from Republicans, but for black leaders it was the object of a vigorous campaign. Coordinated from Albany by the black lobbyist and Underground Railroad activist Stephen A. Myers, and from New York City by McCune Smith—Douglass managed western New York efforts—the campaign distributed thousands of copies of a tract, *The Suffrage Question in Relation to Colored Voters in the State of New York*. The effort also created dozens of local suffrage clubs and auxiliaries of their New York State Suffrage Association (with some fifty-six in New York City and Brooklyn alone). In the two months before the election, Douglass barnstormed western New York and distributed twenty-five thousand copies of the tract. [34]

A constitutional amendment providing equal suffrage had passed the

New York legislature in 1857 but was never brought to a referendum. In 1860 the measure reemerged with almost unanimous Republican support and solid Democratic opposition. In the campaign, however, most Republican newspapers and speakers quietly ignored or opposed the referendum, fearing that it might hurt Lincoln's chances of winning the state. In October, Douglass wrote a brilliant editorial lambasting Democratic papers such as the *New York World* that denounced equal suffrage on the grounds that it caused blacks and whites to be "intermingled in the same community." This position was not merely "mean and base," and a "gross injustice," but ultimately lacked "saneness," said the wry editor. The *World* was at least largely honest with its racism. But in a passage that would fit perfectly into an early-twenty-first-century American debate over voter-suppression measures, Douglass forcefully asked, "What is *The World* afraid of? Does it fear that with equal protection Negro blood would prove more than a match for Anglo-Saxon blood in the race of improvement? Does it apprehend the departure of the reins of Government out of the hands of the white race, and for this reason is in favor of continuing extra weight and an additional disability upon the Negro?"[35]

Douglass worked exhaustively for equal voting rights that autumn; but the result left him bitter and disillusioned. While Lincoln carried New York by 50,000 votes, the suffrage measure met a resounding defeat, 337,985 to 197,503. What Republican legislators had enacted they treated with disdain at the polls. Here was proof of Douglass's August reflections on American selfish individualism in the face of basic human rights. A large number of Republican voters had simply abstained on black suffrage as they voted for Lincoln. Douglass felt betrayed by Republican silence on the suffrage issue: "The blow is a heavy and damaging one. Every intelligent colored man must feel it keenly." The defeat cut to the bone with its message of black political powerlessness. "We do not even wring from this vote the poor consolation that anybody was afraid of our influence or power," Douglass lamented. "The victory over us is simply one of blind ignorance and prejudice."[36] The man who believed he could somehow change history by his pen, his voice, and now his vote felt inaudible.

But as before, Douglass converted the election of Lincoln, and the threats of secession from the Deep South, into a performance of his duty of hope, albeit a hope tinged with anger and exhausted cynicism. By December, from his Rochester desk, an ambivalent Douglass gave his best interpretation of the meaning of the election. Despite carrying only approximately 40 percent of the total vote, Lincoln's victory in the four-way, sectionalized contest had altered the balance of power in America. But to what end no one could yet know, especially a black editor in his western New York outpost. The Republicans' rise to federal power might discredit the Fugitive Slave Act as well as extinguish the South's efforts to revive the foreign slave trade, Douglass posited. Abolitionist ideas had been thoroughly disseminated by the campaign, he reasoned, and therefore the "chief benefit" may simply have been the "canvass itself." Lincoln's election had at least broken the "enchantment" too many Northern politicians had felt toward the Slave Power; a new political force had finally ended the "perpetual bondage to an ignoble fear." [37] But these were hardly celebratory words for the victors of 1860. In the immediate wake of the election Douglass hedged all of his bets.

On the eve of South Carolina's secession, Douglass was not convinced that enough radical disposition existed on either side to cause an open split, especially one that would lead to war. He reprinted nearly three full pages of reactions from Southern newspapers, what he called "Southern Thunder," but interpreted it as largely bluster. Despite all the secessionist rhetoric, he contended that the South had overreacted to Lincoln's threat and misinterpreted his intentions. Because of his high office and essential moderation, Douglass argued, Lincoln could even become the abolition movement's most powerful enemy. Disappointingly, Douglass saw "no sufficient cause for the dissolution of the Union"; indeed, he feared that the Union might now be saved—through compromises—for all the wrong reasons, thus blunting if not destroying the abolitionists' voice and leverage. Although slaveholders might not realize it, Douglass predicted that slavery would be "as safe, and safer, in the Union under such a President [Lincoln] than it can be under any President of a Southern Confederacy." Under the stress and strain of just what secession would mean, amid days and weeks of great confusion over what a silent Lincoln would do, Douglass argued that the election had taught the country the "possibility of electing if not an Abolitionist, at least an antislavery reputation to the Presidency of the United States." While the editor possessed the "pen, voice and influence of only one man," he would stay his course and "join in no cry . . . less than the complete and universal *abolition* of the whole slave system." [38] Douglass took solace from simply wielding his pen in the service of the old cause as he awoke every day for the news in a crisis like no other.

Douglass found little encouragement in the behavior of the Northern public during the secession crisis. The bulk of white Northerners had always viewed abolitionists with suspicion or contempt, and with the threat of disunion in the air, hostility to antislavery agitators rose to new levels of violence. By December 1860, Northern workingmen, along with merchants, shipowners, and cotton manufacturers, were deeply worried about the impact of potential disunion, while bankers and industrialists squirmed as the prices of stocks declined markedly. The specter of financial ruin caused the spirit of political reconciliation to revive, and the conservative and the Democratic press teemed with pro-compromise sentiment as well as incendiary attacks on abolitionists. While Southern state conventions debated secession, mob violence against antislavery speakers raged in several Northern cities in the first two months of 1861. A revolution was afoot, but no one quite knew its course or consequences. Abolitionists provided ready scapegoats for mobs engulfed by economic and political panic.[39]

Douglass and many of his comrades faced just such a mob in force on December 3, 1860, at a gathering in Tremont Temple in Boston, called to commemorate the first anniversary of the execution of John Brown. Freed from the remoteness of his editor's desk, Douglass seemed to welcome a fight, verbal or otherwise. That is exactly what he got. As the abolitionists gathered to address the broad topic of "How can American slavery be abolished?," a well-dressed crowd, what Douglass called "a gentlemen's mob," quickly outnumbered them and physically overtook the platform. For three hours this daytime meeting was nothing less than a shouting, chaotic melee complete with insults and epithets of all kinds, fisticuffs, chairs smashed and thrown, a swaying battle for control of the hall by the two competing sides. Eventually the Boston police took over and forced a clearing of the building. At the center of the fight for the abolitionists was Douglass, coat removed, sleeves rolled up, and in full angry voice returning nearly every insult with one of his own. First James Redpath and then Franklin Sanborn tried to exercise control as chairmen, but they were shouted away by what Boston and New York reporters called the "Unionists," who hijacked the meeting. Amid "great confusion and noise," Douglass, invited as a featured speaker, "frequently interrupted" the mob's chairman, a Richard S. Fay. When Fay complained that he could not make himself heard over the tumult, Douglass warmed to the game by shouting, "When thine enemy thirst give him drink!" to "applause and hisses."

The Unionists put forward a series of anti–John Brown resolutions, to which Douglass again led the resistance, with some of the abolitionists now standing on their chairs, fists raised and calling on their champion, Douglass, to speak. Shouts of "Douglass! Douglass!" rang out around the Temple.[40]

The orator, who had both endured and enjoyed these violent rituals before, demanded the floor with a voice all apparently could hear, prompting Fay's partisans to yet-louder screams of "Nigger!" . . . "Knock him down!" and "Treason!" For a few minutes Douglass managed some coherent statements, as he shouted down his opponents with "You are in the service of the slaveholders of the United States. . . . It is said the best way to abolish slavery is to obey the law. Shall we obey the blood-hounds of the law who do the dirty work of the slave catchers?"[41]

Douglass gave as he took. With disturbances breaking out all over the hall throughout this bizarre struggle, Douglass fought for the podium, at one point pushing his way through a line of men and fighting, said one Boston reporter, "like a trained pugilist." He even fought with one man for possession of a chair in which to sit. But Douglass fought most the battle of words. He asked the gathering to "cast aside with indignation the wild and guilty fantasy that man owns property in man, even in that stout, big-fisted fellow down there, who has just insulted me." As someone shouted, "Go on, nigger!," Douglass answered from Exodus, "The freedom of all mankind was written on the heart by the finger of God!" Then from the sublime to the ridiculous, he screamed at another heckler, "If I was a slave driver, and had hold of that man for five minutes, I would let more daylight through his skin than ever got there before." These hateful exchanges, however relished by the combatants, ended in pushing, shoving, and fists thrown wildly, coats torn off. One group dragged Douglass down by his hair (or his "wool" as reported), until a group of his friends rescued and protected him. Only the police could end such madness, but not before Douglass, who so defended his dignity and pride from even the smallest of slights, proclaimed that he felt "no more embarrassment by this uproar than if I had been kicked by a jackass." As the police took over the stage and the hall, Douglass shouted, "Three cheers for liberty!," as the opponents shouted, "Three cheers for Governor Wise!"[42]

Later that night, the abolitionists reassembled at a black church on Joy Street in Beacon Hill to remember John Brown and honor free speech. Perhaps with a clean shirt, Douglass again was a key speaker. For the first time in nearly eight years by his own count, he appeared on the same platform with old Garrisonian comrade Wendell Phillips. Douglass announced hearty agreement with Phillips that "all methods of proceeding against slavery" should be used, including the "John Brown way." With John Brown Jr. in attendance at the small church, and with a large crowd outside trying to get in, Douglass preached in favor of violence and war. They needed to keep all slaveholders in "fear of personal danger," Douglass pronounced. "I rejoice in every uprising at the South" among slaves. Douglass even drew from Old Man Brown's crowd-pleasing poetic, if faulty, military idea: "There is liberty in yonder mountains . . . in the Alleghenies . . . a thousand men scattered in those hills, and slavery is dead." Feeling the spirit after that day's mob attack, Douglass called for an American Garibaldi to march into the South and "summon to his standard sixty thousand, if necessary, to accomplish the freedom of the slave." Unfortunately, in the little war already breaking out in Boston, white mobs dogged Wendell Phillips on his path home, threatening his life. Several blacks while leaving the church around 10:15 p.m. were assaulted and some seriously injured.[43] Douglass, the war propagandist wishing for blood and disunion, retreated from the former antislavery citadel of Boston unharmed.

In late December 1860, Douglass welcomed the news of South Carolina's secession from the Union. Heaping scorn upon the Palmetto State's rash act, as well as relishing it as an opportunity, Douglass all but thanked the secessionists for "preferring to be a large piece of nothing, to being any longer a small piece of something." Secessionists had resharpened his wit. They provided what he initially hoped would be the long-awaited opening for his cause—disunion, political crisis, and some form of sanctioned military action against the South and therefore against slavery. He would get his wish, but only through the confusion and fear of the secession winter of 1860–61. "Her people [South Carolina's]," Douglass declared with anxious glee, "(except those of them held in slavery, which are more than half her population) have hailed the event as another and far more glorious Fourth of July, and are celebrating it with plenty of gunpowder, bad brandy, but as yet no balls, except those where perfumed ladies and gentlemen move their feet to the inspiring notes of the fiddle." With no veiled intent, Douglass wished for a fight: "Other balls may yet come, and unless

South Carolina shall retreat, or the Federal Government shall abdicate its functions, they must come."[44]

Douglass had dreamed of this kind of moment, events that could dislodge history from its worn paths and move it in new directions. In editorials he lampooned what South Carolinians imagined as "peaceful secession," celebrated by "bonfires, pyrotechnics . . . music and dancing." He cautioned Carolinians over their confidence about "a thing as easily done," so he maintained they believed, "as the leaving of a society of Odd Fellows, or bidding good night to a spiritual circle." Excitement over secession, in South and North, according to the editor, tilted from an "undercurrent of doubt, uncertainty, distrust and foreboding." Then he delivered a historical and constitutional analysis of secession. South Carolina was out of the Union, argued Douglass, only "on paper," and in "resolutions and telegrams." Governments "rest not upon paper, but upon power. They do not solicit obedience as a favor, but compel it as a duty." Douglass, the sudden American nationalist, acknowledged the "right of revolution" for a state or a political group, but no constitutional "right of secession." A state could not secede; it could revolt. "Revolution in this country is rebellion, and rebellion is treason, and treason is levying war against the United States, with something more than paper resolutions. . . . There must be swords, guns, powder, balls, and men behind them to use them." Secession was no abstract debate over federalism or states' rights, no issue resolved merely by ordinances, but a matter of power and guns. "The right of South Carolina to secede," declared the angry but thrilled abolitionist, "depends upon her ability to do so, and to stay so."[45]

Twenty years of pent-up personal travail and abolitionist struggle now flowed through Douglass's pen in Rochester. He believed, as many reasonable Americans have ever since, that the significance of any exercise of states' rights doctrine is in the issue for which it is employed. To Douglass, civil war was frightful, but by January and February 1861, he cast the prospect in positive and apocalyptic language. The "God in history everywhere pronouncing the doom of those nations which frame mischief by law," he declared, had caused a "concussion . . . against slavery which would now rock the land, and sends us staggering about as if shaken by an earthquake." National will and institutions had not solved the problem. "If there is not wisdom and virtue enough in the land to rid the country of slavery, then the next best thing is to let the South go . . . and be made to drink the wine cup of wrath and fire, which her long career . . . [of] barbarism and blood shall call down upon her guilty head."[46]

Frederick Douglass, Pittsburgh,
Pennsylvania, c. 1861.

Highly polemical, not always attuned to the nuances and divisions among the Republicans nor to the scale of unionism in parts of the divided South, and filling his own cups of wrath, Douglass wanted the clarity of polarized conflict. He wanted war. Perhaps his greatest fear as the secession crisis unfolded was the potential for concession and compromise. For a former slave and then an orator and an editor whose political consciousness had awakened with the Mexican War and the Compromise of 1850, who had seen the fate of the slaves bandied about in one political crisis after another, and who had struggled to sustain hope in the face of the *Dred Scott* decision's egregious denials, a resolute stand by the North against secession and the Slave Power was hardly a sure thing. The best hopes of blacks, Douglass said that winter, had always been dashed by the "old medicine of compromise." As he observed resolutions and conventions intended to settle the crisis, he complained that secession's enablers, North and South, had "filled the air with whines of compromise." [47]

Compromise proposals came into Washington from all quarters of the North. Some were resolutions passed at pro-compromise Union meetings, and some were the petitions of committees of industrialists eager to sustain their Southern commercial ties. All politicians were wary of the wrath and fears of their constituents and fervent to preserve the Union. On December 18, 1860, John J. Crittenden of Kentucky introduced the most comprehensive of the compromise initiatives, a series of constitutional amendments that blanketed the range of conciliatory measures. The debate over the Crittenden Compromise and others like it paralyzed Congress during the entire interregnum and secession winter.[48]

Douglass feared compromise for good reason. Thirty years of antislavery agitation and its meager gains, as well as the very meaning of the Republican Party, were at stake. Attended by delegates from twenty-one states (although none from the Deep South) and sponsored by the Virginia legislature, a peace conference convened in Washington on February 4, 1861. After three weeks of confusion and negotiation, the uninspired gathering reported a compromise proposal nearly identical to that of Crittenden. No compromise measures ever passed the divided Congress; week after week of wrangling gave evidence that most Democrats but only a handful of Republicans were willing to appease the South and extend the life of slavery in order to save the Union. As six more of the cotton states joined South Carolina and bolted the Union by early February, most Republicans across the North had resolved to prevent any conciliation. Most Northern state legislatures also refused to support compromise; only New Jersey formally endorsed the Crittenden plan, which was a set of one-sided concessions to the South.[49]

Douglass observed the secession crisis with a combination of excitement and dismay. At least until late February he believed the prospect for a major compromise to be real. He simply did not yet trust the will of the Republican Party and its president-elect, Lincoln. Discouraged, he complained that the state of the abolitionist cause was "somewhat gloomy and dark." Abolitionists had "plied the national heart and conscience with sound doctrine," but they seemed "as far from accomplishment of their work as during the proslavery mobs of twenty-five years ago." Plenty of new mobs raged in the present. In January in Rochester, a convention of abolitionists meeting in Corinthian Hall was attacked by a violent crowd. The abolitionists reconvened at the Spring Street AME Zion Church to complete their meeting, out of which developed a series of weekly Sunday lectures organized by Douglass that lasted throughout the secession crisis.[50]

Uncertain of whom to trust or on whom to turn his anger, Douglass felt an acute sense of powerlessness as the Union dissolved. He feared that secession would become a struggle only over the survival of the Union and not over slavery. "What disturbs, divides, and threatens to bring on civil war . . . and ruin this country," he pled in February, "but slavery?" Only the "morally blind," he argued, could fail to see it.[51] What Douglass dreaded most was that a great opportunity to strike a lasting blow for black freedom might forever be lost through peaceful reconciliation. So he braced for the worst and anxiously awaited the inauguration of Abraham Lincoln.

By March, Douglass seemed well aware that his fondest hopes were at the mercy of events. He knew the secession crisis was a test of power; whether it resulted in war depended upon the reaction of the incoming Lincoln administration, which to him represented the "one ray of hope amid the darkness of the passing hour and the reign of doubt and distraction." But by early April Douglass was anything but confident that "coercion" against the South would ever truly come. He could only feel despair. "All talk of putting down treason and rebellion by force, by our demoralized Government and people," he agonized, "are as impotent and worthless as the words of a drunken woman in a ditch." He still expected "schemers" to reach a deal.[52] And so he imagined a future where abolitionists would have to attack slavery in a separate, independent country, and their work would take revolutionary turns. Then, as of old, he reached for desperate hope in a logic of violence. Faith strained against unpredictable daily events and a volatile politics he could only dimly discern. These were the sentiments of a man observing a revolution, the directions of which he could not control. But then the startling turn of events caused by the bombardment of one island fort in Charleston Harbor changed everything.

By April, in Rochester, lecturing at the Spring Street AME Zion Church, where he had done so nearly every week during the past two months, Douglass spoke for his community: "I have never spent days so restless and anxious. Our mornings and evenings have continually oscillated between the dim light of hope and the gloomy shadow of despair. We have opened our papers, new and damp from the press, tremblingly, lest the first line of the lightning should tell us that our National Capital has fallen into the hands of traitors and murderers."[53] The secession crisis took an enormous emotional toll on Americans of every persuasion. The only thing foggier than war itself can be the path to its frightening, if too often exciting, outbreak. Douglass ached for the event that would relieve the emotional tension and teach the world a new history.

Chapter 17

THE KINDLING SPIRIT
OF HIS BATTLE CRY

The human heart is a seat of constant war.

—FREDERICK DOUGLASS, JUNE 1861

More than a century and a half after Appomattox, surveying the landscape of horror and mass destruction that modern war has wreaked upon the human species, reasonable people pause in examining those leaders in the past who have been bold advocates of war, as well as the creators of hated enemies targeted for attack and elimination. The willingness to kill and the desire to urge others in organized armies to kill for a cause are both primal and historical, personal and ideological. By the spring of 1861, Frederick Douglass yearned for war; his long rehearsal as a war propagandist had reached its final stages.

As the poet Paul Laurence Dunbar suggested in a eulogy in 1897, Douglass, as much as any Northern partisan in the Civil War, kindled a "battle cry" of freedom:

> He dared the lightning in the lightning's track,
> And answered thunder with his thunder back. . . .
>
> We weep for him, but we have touched his hand,
> And felt the presence of his magic nigh,
>
> The current that he sent thro'out the land,
> The kindling spirit of his battle-cry.

Douglass welcomed the outbreak of the Civil War in April 1861 with a combined spirit of relief and rage. He was not a warrior himself, as he had discovered in his struggle with John Brown. But he was more than ready to wield his pen and voice to send millions to destroy slavery, slaveholders, and anyone shouldering arms in their defense. "The contest must now be decided, and decided forever," Douglass demanded in March 1861, "which of the two, Freedom or Slavery, shall give law to this republic. Let the conflict come, and God speed the right." In May, after war had begun, he rejoiced, "For this consummation we have watched and wished with fear and trembling. God be praised! that it has come at last."[1]

For Douglass the road to war had been emotionally and intellectually crooked. With great anticipation he awaited President Lincoln's inaugural address, a historical moment dominated, said Douglass, by fear that the Government had been allowed by the previous Buchanan administration to "float to the very verge of destruction." On February 18, Douglass joined a throng of fifteen thousand people who gathered at the Rochester train station to get a glimpse of Lincoln as the president-elect passed through on his storied, whistle-stop journey to Washington, DC, for the inauguration. Douglass did not record whether he waved and cheered the Illinoisan as he stepped out on the rear balcony of the presidential train, or whether Douglass merely reflected with anxiety on the festive occasion. Under threat of assassination and with military preparations minimal and unstable, Lincoln entered Washington in secrecy and in the dark of the night only a few days before the March 4 inauguration. Douglass exploited the ironies for all they were worth, writing, "Mr. Lincoln entered the Capital as the poor, hunted fugitive slave reaches the North, in disguise, seeking concealment, evading pursuers, by the underground railroad . . . not during the sunlight, but crawling and dodging under the sable wing of night." Douglass welcomed Lincoln to the status of fugitive slave.[2]

Lincoln's speech, however, was a disappointment to the abolitionist. Lincoln's olive branches for the South were to Douglass so much "weakness, timidity, and conciliation." He judged the address a "double-tongued document" for its declarations of support for the right of property in slaves in the existing slave states, and especially for Lincoln's quoting of the original fugitive-slave clause in the Constitution and his promise to enforce all lawful efforts to return fugitive slaves to their owners. To Lincoln's cautious rhetorical and legal gestures to the South, Douglass responded with outrage and as a former fugitive slave. Instead of meeting the South's revolution with "honest rebuke," charged Douglass, the president served up "palliations and apologies." As harsh as he could get, Douglass accused Lincoln of telling "the slaveholders what an excellent slave hound he is, and how he regards the right to recapture fugitive slaves a constitutional duty." Douglass did grudgingly acknowledge the president's vehement rejection of secession as the "essence of anarchy" and assertion of the Union as "perpetual." Douglass demanded, however, that Lincoln not argue with secessionists or "parley with traitors" but fight them; he denounced the new president as "the most dangerous advocate of slave-hunting and slave-catching in the land."[3] Such was the beginning of the difficult, if eventually historic, relationship between Frederick Douglass and Abraham Lincoln.

A discouraged, even floundering Douglass all but reversed one of his long-standing positions by the spring of 1861. He considered emigrating from America. The Scottish-born abolitionist, former supporter of John Brown, and peripatetic radical James Redpath had been leading a campaign for African American emigration to Haiti since early 1860. Douglass not only ran frequent advertisements for the company, but warmed to the idea himself by early 1861. In January he declared that he could "raise no objection" to the Haitian emigration movement, his opposition to earlier schemes of relocation to West Africa notwithstanding. The Republic of Haiti was in the Western Hemisphere, closer for black Americans to their cousins enslaved in the United States, and officially welcoming immigrants. For once, Douglass maintained, the Haitian alternative might provide a means for some of emigrating without "appealing to our enemies for the means of getting out of the way of their hatred." Further, it meant that blacks were not "conceding that Africa is our only home, and that we have no right to remain in America." Douglass despised the idea of emigration when it merely confirmed the racist notion that blacks and whites could never live together in equality. For a time, Haiti seemed to provide him a means of still detesting colonization as fashioned by white enemies, while acknowledging a basic human right to leave for brighter climes. That winter he gave his best wishes to twelve Rochester African American families who followed their Baptist minister in moving to Haiti.[4]

By March, Douglass accepted emigration if driven by the human motives for better "food, clothing, property, education, manhood, and material prosperity" and not by the "charms of a Colored Nationality." With his own brand of romance about the history of the Haitian republic born in black revolution, Douglass became a qualified emigrationist in the troubled secession winter. He was deeply worried for the safety of Northern free blacks, and even more about the new insurrectionary rumors and tensions emanating from the South. "The United States is in great trouble," he announced. "Slavery, vengeance, and settled hate frown and threaten the free colored people." He warned that no one could any longer tell where pro-slavery mobs would strike next. They had become "contagious" since his violent encounter in Boston in December. "The disorder has travelled like the cholera from East to West."[5]

In the *Monthly*, Douglass announced that, with his daughter Rosetta, now twenty-two years old, he had booked a steamer for April 25, embarking from New Haven, Connecticut, and at the invitation and largesse of the Haitian consulate in Philadelphia, to visit the island nation. Redpath had brokered the arrangements. What Douglass did not say is that he might have been traveling as a threesome; Ottilie Assing announced in her own column in *Morgenblatt* that she too "was making plans to take a trip to Haiti, in order to learn by direct encounter about the conditions in this Negro republic." Whether Douglass and his German friend made these travel plans "together" for romantic reasons, as her biographer suggests, is dubious. Why would he invite Rosetta to join them? Possibly Douglass entertained the fantasy of escape in this tense political atmosphere. Asking his smart but volatile and restless adult daughter, however, to share the trip seems incongruent at best. Douglass was surely capable of embodying and living such contradictions, perhaps even quite publicly at times. Assing and Rosetta knew each other well by then from the lady's summer visits to Rochester. But as always, Assing is our only source for these plans and motives.

Rosetta Sprague Douglass, late 1850s.

Whatever alternative futures Assing may have imagined, what we do know is that she and Douglass frequently wrote about the same issues, often in similar tone and language.[6]

Douglass described his mission to Haiti as reflecting a citizen's need for study and travel and a journalist's desire to report on and "do justice to Haiti, to paint her as she is." He was going as well with a black man's pride in showing that Haiti was "free, orderly and independent," admitting also that he had always longed to stand on the "soil of San Domingo, the theater of many stirring events and heroic achievements, the work of a people, bone of our bone, and flesh of our flesh." He came close to recommending what he had earlier denounced: the "charms of a colored nationality." He waxed exuberant about escaping Rochester's wintry cold for Haiti's tropical warmth. Politically, his trip was to observe whether the Haitian republic might be "an asylum from the apprehended storm which is about to beat pitilessly upon African Americans."[7] Douglass could not have known that overnight he would be writing about a very different storm.

On April 12, before Douglass went to press with his paper, Confederate insurgents fired on Fort Sumter in Charleston Harbor, and the Civil War commenced. Douglass appended a brief postscript to his editorial "A Trip to Haiti." The editor tried to capture the nation's as well as his own sense of the drama of that moment: "Since this article . . . was put in type, we find ourselves in circumstances which induce us to forego our much desired trip to Haiti." War fever surged through Northern communities and turned a divided and anxious populace into a swarm of excited unity. In her columns, Assing joined the journalistic fray, sometimes clearly modeling Douglass's writings in the *Monthly*, which came out before she took up her pen. She described the news of Fort Sumter hitting New York City "like a bolt of lightning," citizens so enthused as though "walking on a volcano." She observed militia drilling in the streets, huge lines of men of all ethnicities volunteering for the army. At times she modeled Douglass's columns, but in other moments wrote with her own distinctive gusto. She witnessed Jefferson Davis depicted in a "life-size effigy of straw and wood" hanging from a banner over a street, flags waving everywhere on buildings, on carriages, and even on horses' heads. Douglass likely never read her columns, since they were written in German, although he was surely delighted to have some of his own ideas disseminated among German progressives. A world-changing event had occurred, and Douglass never missed a chance to instruct with events. "The last ten days have made a tremendous revolution in all things pertaining to the possible future of the colored people of the

United States." Northerners, he said, had experienced some of the "savage barbarism of slavery," and he would now do his part to teach them "to make war upon it."[8]

"I hated slavery, slaveholders, and all pertaining to them," Douglass wrote in *Bondage and Freedom* in 1855; "and I did not fail to inspire others with the same feeling, wherever and whenever opportunity was presented." He crafted that passage, one of many in his autobiographies about his enduring rage against his oppressors, to capture the perceived danger and power of his newfound literacy among his fellow slaves. That literacy, he said, had made him "a marked lad among the slaves, and a suspected one among the slaveholders."[9] To say the least, Douglass had always cherished this power to hurl words, and when necessary hatred, against slavery and slaveholders. History had seemingly opened a broad door to a new opportunity to inspire a vast nation as he had once done on Freeland's farm in Talbot County, Maryland, for a tiny band of brothers.

But in the spring of 1861 Douglass complained that words and their meanings had been debased in the crisis of disunion: "The strangest feature of this eventful drama is the complete inversion of the sense of . . . words." "Treason" and "Armed Rebellion" were "now simply the sovereign right of Secession, and the execution of the Laws is now called 'Coercion.'" To Douglass, the secessionists were the mortal enemies of the government as they inspired resistance among abolitionists. Traitors merited no quarter; President James Buchanan was no mere benign lame duck but the "chief of sinners," and Douglass insisted over and again on his own label for the Deep South's revolution—the "treasonable Slaveholding Confederacy."[10] Douglass had been practicing this kind of rhetoric for a long time; by 1861, it was as if the secessionists, as well as truckling Yankees, had flipped his switch into overdrive.

Douglass seized the moment with a fervor as great as any other in his career. To him the central meaning of secession and the coming of the war was that it raised at least the possibility of "armed abolition," of mingling the cause of the slave and the rights of free black people with the life of the nation. "At last our proud Republic is overtaken," he enthused in April 1861, after Fort Sumter. Although he predicted that the nation would suffer untold destruction, the moment felt "propitious," and the war welcome. "Now is the time to change the cry of vengeance long sent up from the . . . toiling bondman into a grateful prayer for the peace and safety of the Government." He had rarely spoken of the United States government in such warm tones. This was only possible because he beheld a crisis that "bound up the fate of the Republic and that of the slave in the same bundle." Douglass put the fears of the secession winter aside now and rejoiced in the crisis. The nation, he said, "has put one end of the chain upon the ankle of the bondman, and the other end about its own neck." In a land that must "now . . . weep and howl amid ten thousand desolations brought on by the sins of two centuries," he turned again to the old prophets for his own cry to the nation: *"Repent, Break Every Yoke, let the Oppressed Go Free for Herein alone is deliverance and safety!"*[11] For the next four years, Douglass's Civil War became his very own cry of vengeance.

In a struggle Douglass and many others on both sides saw increasingly as a "holy war" over slavery and freedom, blame had to be precisely assigned to foment sufficient fervor and bloodlust to fight it. In a homespun set of metaphors Douglass provided clear images about responsibility for the war. And he thus unveiled his apocalyptic sense of history—a belief in the occasional cosmic collision of forces, necessary rendings and bloodlettings when God chose to enter history and overturn it for the creation of a new age. In an April 1861 editorial, "Who Killed the American Eagle?," Douglass seemed confident at least that the old Union was dead. "By an old agreement . . . between Mr. South and Mr. North, the eagle was to be raffled off between the contracting parties every four years, and whichever got the highest number, was to take the bird for the next four years. For many years Mr. South had regularly won the eagle, and enjoyed its services. He had trained it to hunt slaves, to protect slave-traders . . . to steal from Mexico, to tear the flesh of offensive strangers, to guard, protect and extend slavery." Mr. North had always coveted this bird of prey, and he "determined that if he should ever get possession of the eagle, he would teach him better manners, and train him to better habits." At last, in 1860, Mr. North won the eagle, but "before handing it over, as in honor bound, the treacherous Mr. South filled the unsuspecting bird with a heavy dose of secession powder so that our once majestic bird was as good as dead."[12]

In this revealing vignette, Douglass shows his conception of the Union, a once powerful republic hopelessly corrupted by slavery. Why had the eagle died? "The bird must die," Douglass argued, "and the verdict of the inquest must be that it died of poison, treacherously administered at the instigation of Mr. South by one James Buchanan."[13] Douglass used the word "must" to demonstrate his vision not only of secession but of history itself. Slaveholders, in association with their Northern accomplices, had killed the old

Union. They *must* kill it, he reasoned, and it *must* die, for otherwise a new Union—a new nation with a new future—was not possible. Such metaphors only confirmed Douglass's deep desire for an overturning and remaking of America and of his faith in apocalyptic change.

In 1861 Douglass's quest to fashion the enemy and to define the nature of the Union cause took many forms. His newspaper was never more important as a mouthpiece for his activism than in the first two years of the Civil War. Although he stayed closer to Rochester in 1861 than normal, Douglass held forth publicly nearly every Sunday afternoon from winter to late summer at the AME Zion Church. Some of the gatherings became so large that they relocated to the Rochester City Hall. As wartime so often necessitates, these were community-solidarity gatherings, attended by blacks and whites, and crucial to sustaining morale in abnormally tense times. Douglass treated that pulpit at the corner of Spring and Havor Streets—a black church—as a place to conduct his own kind of war rallies. "Like the rod of Moses," he declared on May 5, "which swallowed up all the petty creations of the Eastern magicians, the awful and sublime crisis in our national affairs, swallows up all other subjects." Just two days before, some twenty thousand Rochesterites had gathered in the city center to watch and cheer as eight companies of soldiers paraded to the train station and off to war to become the Thirteenth New York Volunteers. Douglass celebrated the "solemn departure of the troops . . . composed of the sons, brothers, husbands and fathers of some . . . of those who hear me." Although he had already argued a week earlier for the recruitment of "colored regiments," no black men were part of that first Rochester war parade. Nevertheless, Douglass described the scene as a "thrilling spectacle" and admitted to witnessing it "with feelings I cannot describe." [14] But describe his feelings about the war is just what he did in the coming months.

In those Sunday talks Douglass also tried to represent the feelings of his audiences, especially blacks. That "rod of Moses" worked for them. "We cannot see the end from the beginning," he announced only two weeks into the war. "We live but today, and the measureless shores of the future are wisely hid from us. . . . There is a general feeling amongst us, that the control of events has been taken out of our hands, that we have fallen into the mighty current . . . of invisible forces." As war fever swept over the land, conceptions of time and sensibility had changed, the world suddenly appeared both more dangerous and more exhilarating, and individuals felt a part of a larger whole even as anxiety prevailed. For Douglass the outbreak of war easily incited his practiced zeal to assault slavery in all its manifestations at a moment of special vulnerability. But the war also prompted untypical expressions of patriotism and American nationalism. He spoke for the "oppressed and enslaved," Douglass said, but now he could "also speak as an American. All that I have and am are bound up with the destiny of this country." Douglass may never have completely stopped believing such sentiments, but they had rarely formed the key lines in speeches. Of the American republic, he told his Rochester neighbors, "I still feel that she is my country, and that I must fall or flourish with her." [15] For the man who had often claimed he had "no country," the events of April made him feel his patriotism. Fort Sumter and Lincoln's call for seventy-five thousand volunteers to put down the rebellion had changed nearly everything, especially on Sunday afternoons.

Before any major battles were fought, Douglass called for a long and merciless war that would not only root out and destroy secession but the "monster" of slavery itself. He continued to grouse about the potential for compromises that might still be struck between cowed Northern politicians and Confederate leaders. "The spirit of compromise is still abroad here," he wrote in a June column. Fear seemed to rule most people in the North, who, he contended, "cherish no deeper feeling against slavery than that which arises from a sense of mischief it does to the white race, and the troubles and dangers it brings upon the country." From England, Julia Crofts agreed and wrote for the *Monthly* of her own struggles to explain the reactions to secession in the North to her English friends: "The Southerners, of the two, are far better understood by us all. They act more . . . straightforward in their course—bad as it is." But Northern reactions to potential war puzzled her, as she wielded adjectives as floridly as her Rochester colleague. "For the poor, timid, cowardly, servile, dishonest North, I can find no words to express the contempt I feel. They cannot be made to see the power they . . . might wield in the sacred cause of human freedom." Northerners did not yet grasp that they had been visited, as Douglass contended, with a "glorious opportunity" at destruction and reinvention. [16]

At first Douglass could hardly contain his combination of enthusiasm and rage. In the first month of the war, he prepared three full pages of articles and letters in his paper, detailing a litany of brutality, violence, rape, and other crimes in the South. He offered such a display as his "chapter of horrors" about the enemy, "an illustration of the peculiar manners, temper, and morals of our slaveholding society." Gleaned from papers North and South, the collection of brutalities, an old antislavery technique, included lynchings of Northerners, jailings of people with abolitionist sentiment, and all manner of beatings and duels, one fought over a mulatto girl. For clarity Douglass boiled the notion of enemy down to three big ideas. Slavery, treason, and rebellion, he argued, were the "trio of social monsters" that must be crushed. Stridently, he called for a war that "must go on until one of the parties to it is ground to powder." The Union could only win a war to destroy slavery "the longer it lasts." In the summer of 1861 the fire-breathing Douglass wanted "slaveholding rebels . . . starved out, broken down, overpowered, and totally exhausted, before they can consent, after their high sounding threat, to sue for peace." He stoked war fever with unabashed fervor, especially urging black men in his audiences to "drink as deeply in the martial spirit of the times as possible," and to brandish their manliness so that they might never again be "despised as cowards." Above all, he prayed for a long war that would subject the South to devastation. "I should regret the sudden and peaceful termination of this conflict," Douglass proclaimed. "Now, the next best thing, if we cannot make them [Southerners] love us, is to make them fear us." [17]

With these high, sanguinary aims Douglass could only find disappointment in the short run. But in the war's first summer he expressed a clamorous certainty about its meaning and purpose. The South's cause was an evil, growing, misbegotten element of "nature" itself that had to be wiped out. Slavery and its advocates, manifested in huge armies, were the "foul and red-mouthed dragon" against which Northern men must now learn war in order to slay it.[18] In the dark art of war propaganda, thumping out from press and pulpit all over America that summer, Douglass set the pace for the abolitionist North.

If his audiences needed moral and religious justification, he was ready. "Men have their choice in the world," Douglass pronounced in June. "They can be angels, or they may be demons. In the apocalyptic vision, John describes a war in heaven. You have only to strip that vision of its gorgeous Oriental drapery, divest it of its shining and celestial ornaments, clothe it in the simple and familiar language of common sense, and you will have . . . the eternal conflict between right and wrong, good and evil, liberty and slavery, truth and falsehood." Then he tried to blend ancient biblical apocalypticism with the Union war effort. "Michael and his angels are still contending against the infernal host of bad passions, and excitement will last while the fight continues . . . till one or the other is subdued. . . . Such is the struggle now going on in the United States. The slaveholders had rather reign in hell than serve in heaven." [19] Thus did Douglass give the Civil War a cosmic definition on the eve of the Battle of First Bull Run. In the slaughter to come, he would provide as much bloodthirsty passion as he could for the side of the angels.

Douglass's quest in 1861 to create the hated enemy of the Union cause was both personal and political. The outbreak of the war allowed him to cultivate a long-standing psychological need to find a real-world outlet for an inner vengeance against slavery and slaveholders. He had spent the first twenty-eight years of his life as a slave or a fugitive slave; his sense of self-definition took its departure from his slave origins as a child of a black mother and her white master. Douglass always had to begin to understand himself in the sordid but defining story of the sexual exploitation of slave women by white men. He was both a reflection of the system into which he was born—a chattel formed of both races—and therefore, especially with his rise to intellectual fame, the most prominent contradiction of that system. Douglass had never resolved his anger toward his masters and overseers, toward their physical abuse, but perhaps especially about the mental oppression at the heart of slavery. He knew slavery as a potentially total system rooted in dehumanization and violence.[20] He knew slaveholders had hearts and souls; but he had also seen and experienced their dark depravity. His body had been possessed, manipulated, and bludgeoned by a man named Covey, and his future had once been owned and calculated by men named Auld and Anthony. Douglass understood the primal loathing, the soul-destroying elements of inhumanity, and the lethal force slavery required in order to survive. Slavery had also taught him a great deal about the uses of violence, and it had taught him how to hate.

Once the bit of war propaganda lodged in his mouth, Douglass was relentless in pursuit of the enemy. He fits well into the writer Barbara Ehrenreich's characterization of how the war urge, once commenced, takes on a life of its own. "However and wherever war begins," wrote Ehrenreich, "it persists, it spreads, it propagates itself through time and across space with the terrifying tenacity of a beast attached to the neck of living prey." In June at Spring Street Church, philosophizing as though he entertained a modern notion of innate aggression, Douglass dropped this telling line into the middle of his invocation of the apocalyptic vision from Revelation: "The human heart is a seat of constant war." The rage at the heart of the war propaganda Douglass produced so profusely in the Civil War stemmed less, though, from biological instinct than from emotion rooted in experience and ideas.[21] He had his own war to pursue as he also primed the pump of Northern morale.

Douglass's inner war stemmed from his desire to possess the power, the sense of belonging, indeed the realization of nationhood and citizenship, that white men enjoyed. And it stemmed from fantasies of revenge, the deep desire to finally thwart and then destroy the physical, mental, and political worlds slavery had made. One world had to end before a new one could be created. Douglass engaged in a lifelong autobiographical quest for a coherent story of ascendance and familial identity.[22] Douglass did carry a "seat of constant war" in his heart, as he himself implied. But that story was much more than the desire to comprehend his paternity, his bloodlines, and his kinfolk in Maryland. He needed revenge and redemption in blood for himself and for the afflicted generations of the people he represented. Douglass wanted slaveholders humiliated, then eliminated, and in their wake he might find his place in a dominion of human equality. To get to that distant shore, to a new America, he probed the darkest ranges of human wrath.

Douglass reveled in the war psychology exploding across the North in the summer of 1861; he did his best to cultivate the violent imagination of his readers and convert the older notion of the Slave Power, the object of abstract fear, into a hatred of slaveholders themselves. He wanted the "high looks of the lordly Assyrians . . . brought low." Echoing the war poems of Walt Whitman, but with blunter edges, Douglass beat his chest for war. "Drums are beating, men are enlisting," he wrote, "companies forming, regiments marching, banners are flying." He imagined a united North: "People, press, and pulpit . . . are knitted together like the iron links of a coat of mail." He held nothing back: "The cry is now for war, vigorous war, war to the bitter end, and war till the traitors are effectually and permanently put down." In his view no awful fate was quite enough for the slaveholding rebels. "Let the ports of the South be blockaded," Douglass preached; "let business there be arrested; let provisions, arms and ammunition be no longer sent there; let the grim visage of a Northern army confront them from one direction, a furious slave insurrection meet them at another, and starvation threaten them from still another." In this early vision of total war, Douglass joyously imagined a horrendous end for slaveholders. They were "only on the outer wave of the whirlpool of treason; every circle they now make will bring them nearer the centre that is certain to swallow them up, and hurl them to the bottom of its howling waters."[23] In such a tempest Douglass, trying to see an unknowable end from the beginning, fashioned the apocalyptic fate of the Confederacy.

Frederick Douglass's pen with inkwell, date unknown.

As the war ensued, Douglass did his utmost to keep the character of slaveholders before the eyes and ears of his audiences. In an assault that ran counter to most Republican propaganda, Douglass portrayed non-slaveholding whites as mere "tools of the slaveholders." They were "ignorant, besotted, and servile," possessing "no opinions of their own in political affairs." The power of the master class was absolute. "The slaveholders are the South," argued Douglass. "The six million of free nonslaveholding whites are but freight cars full of cattle, attached to the three hundred and fifty thousand slaveholding locomotives. Where the locomotives go, the train must follow." In peace, the Slave Power was to be feared and opposed; in war, it was the "barbarous and bloody" culture that must be liquidated.[24]

In June at one of his Spring Street Church lectures, Douglass demonstrated that he believed he had found the perfect enemy. "What is a slaveholder but a rebel and a traitor?" he queried. Douglass portrayed slaveholders as inherently depraved, natural criminals; he wanted his listeners to equate treason with slaveowning and therefore fight to destroy both. "Southern men," Douglass assured the assembled Rochesterites, "are all of the same species" and could understand "no law but the law of force." Douglass's speeches were deeply personal illustrations of his vision of the conflict. "I want the monster destroyed!" he shouted from the AME pulpit, fist clenched, fire in his eyes.[25]

Douglass envisioned the "revolution" the country now faced as "an excellent instructor," especially about the nature of the enemy. He saw an America experiencing an epic upheaval. The drama needed a plot and direction, heroes and villains, and Douglass possessed a ready-made narrative. The slaveholders, and their insatiable desires for more expansion, profits, power, and therefore more human chattel to achieve their aims, had overreached and brought down divine wrath and a political revolution to resist them. Douglass was fond of the Greek proverb that he employed in one of his Sunday lectures: "Whom the Gods would destroy they first make mad." In editorials later in the summer he would put it other ways: "The slaveholder must be master of society, otherwise he cannot long be master of his slaves." [26] Douglass's greatest hope was that a sufficiently outraged Northern people would fight to defeat this mortal enemy of humankind.

By the end of the first summer of the war, though, Douglass was deeply frustrated with Northern public opinion, the government's policy toward slavery, and military defeat. He was especially angry with federal insistence on returning fugitive slaves who had escaped to Union lines, and he hoped that the Union debacle at Bull Run in late July would teach the North harsh lessons. This salutary reaction to Bull Run was common among abolitionists and conservative intellectuals alike. In defeat, Douglass wanted the North to learn the necessity of "effectively putting down the whole class of pestiferous slaveholders, so that the nation shall know them no more, except in history, to be execrated and loathed, with all other robbers and tyrants which have cursed and ruined human society." [27]

Throughout the first two years of the conflict, such a quest to make Yankees *hate* slaveholders was a constant theme of Douglass's war of words. In his conception, Northerners did not comprehend the "exterminating vigor of a settled and deadly hate" with which Southerners prosecuted the war; only when Northerners felt the same "quenchless fire of a deadly hate," he wrote in August 1861, would they find the "secret" to military success.[28] The South was in earnest and understood its cause, Douglass maintained, while the North did not. He equated Northern resolve with the willingness to kill slaveholders and all that they stood for.

Douglass would have to wait a long and discouraging year before he would see the war turn decisively against slavery as well as the Confederacy. But by the autumn of 1861, he seemed certain of his own duty. This time the duty of hope was not merely to prescribe political faith in the face of proslavery laws and institutions. It entailed bloodlust, and looking long and hard at a dark reality neither he nor any other Americans had ever quite seen: savage, prolonged, all-out civil war. Everything was at stake. "The dangerous and demonical character of slavery . . . we have been endeavoring to expose," he wrote in October, "and to teach the nation they must hate and abolish, or be hated and abolished by it." As massive mobilization ensued in late 1861, and as Union and Confederate armies arrayed in Virginia, Kentucky, Tennessee, and many other places, Douglass predicted a "long, revengeful, and desolating" war. Only in an unlimited war, he believed, would slavery crumble by "iron necessity," if not from moral idealism. Responding to a disheartened correspondent who challenged his optimism, he defended his sense of hope as he warned that Northerners had "not yet been sufficiently deluged with slaveholding contempt . . . not drunk deep enough of the poisoned cup of slaveholding malignity."[29] They had not yet learned to hate the foe, and Douglass saw himself as their educator.

Douglass made the most of every opportunity to instill contempt for the South. When allegations were made of atrocities by Confederate soldiers, he printed and exploited the stories. In August he recycled the story that Confederates at Bull Run had "amused themselves in sticking their bayonets in the dead, and setting the wounded up against stumps, and shooting at them as targets." In December 1861, under the heading "Signs of Barbarism," he reported the claim that Virginia rebels had produced candles made of the tallow from dead Yankee soldiers. He also reprinted an account from the *New York Post* reporting the "distribution of the skin of Old John Brown's son," who had been killed in battle. According to Douglass, these episodes demonstrated that if "left to themselves, the Southerners would wholly barbarize under the influence of slavery." What moral sense they did possess, he maintained, was due only to their "connection with the superior civilization of the North." By 1862, Douglass portrayed slaveholders as barbarians. "Digging up the bones of our dead soldiers slain in battle, making drinking vessels out of their skulls, drumsticks out of their arm bones, slaying our wounded soldiers on the field of carnage" were only some of the wild accusations Douglass flung at Southerners. For Union military success a "deadly hatred" of all things born of a slaveholding society would have to be engendered in the hearts and minds of Northerners.[30]

Although they seem vicious and even simplistic, Douglass's appeals for hatred of the South fit his apocalyptic conception of the war. God's retribution was at the heart of millennial expectations in the nineteenth century. Evil was to be eradicated through great calamity; a new age of peace and justice might then follow. But millennialism was an activist faith; the overturning of a society depended greatly on human action. Douglass's own sense of revenge against slaveholders came unleashed; as he passionately vented a long-pent-up desire for righteous violence in the cause of abolition, he felt freed to advocate the death of every Edward Covey in the South. Thus hatred provided a creative force. Douglass envisioned a war that might be enduring and tragic, but also cleansing. Hatred of slaveholders, therefore, had great purgative power—for one human heart or for millions—and an appointed role in America's Armageddon.[31]

By late summer and into the fall of 1861, Douglass found himself frustrated as the Union armies and the Lincoln administration seemed determined not to make war on slavery, nor to liberate slaves who sought refuge behind Union lines, and especially not to accept black men into military service. Without knowing yet just what large armies could do to each other, nor the character of the destruction that rifled muskets and cannon could exact en masse on human bodies, Douglass ached in July for real war to begin. "We know that rebellion cannot be talked down, written down, or coaxed down," he asserted with relish. "It has got to be beaten down. . . . There is no whipping the traitors without hurting them. War was made to hurt, and those who provoke it ought to be hurt; and the only conceivable good which can come out of war, comes because it hurts."[32]

But Douglass had left his keenly interested British correspondent Julia Crofts in a lurch of inadequate information. "It was in the railway carriage," she reported, "while coming from Edinburgh, that the sounds, *'Defeat of the Federals,' 'Bull Run,' 'Manassas Junction,'* first met my ears." Julia felt "shame" in hearing the gentlemen on her train express joy that the Union "cowards had been defeated," as she beseeched Douglass to provide the "numbers *really killed.*" She could only send her heartfelt wish that "every colored family" in the Northern states would cross into Canada and live "sheltered beneath the British flag." Desperate, Julia then broke into a typically religious exhortation: "God reigns in Eternity. We know and feel that He will overrule all this confusion, this wrath of men and clang of arms, for the final deliverance of the poor bondsmen . . . out of the prison-houses surely as He brought the children of Israel out of Egypt."[33] Julia had read her Douglass and knew something of her friend's views on how such assurances marched with confusion, wrath, and war. And he surely took reassurance from her words.

Before the war reached its second month, some slaves found their way into Union lines around the rim of Southern war fronts and were famously labeled "contrabands of war" at Fortress Monroe, Virginia, by Union general Benjamin Butler. The idea of escaped slaves as confiscated enemy property caught on in the Northern imagination, and a new word entered the national lexicon. For most of 1861, federal military policy about slavery, however, evolved in an incoherent, topsy-turvy manner, sometimes ordering Union officers to return fugitive slaves to their owners and sometimes protecting and liberating the growing waves of runaways. In his paper, Douglass reprinted the leaked correspondence from Secretary of War Simon Cameron to Butler, informing the general that his bold order was "approved," although the actual "final determination" of the freedmen's legal status would be left for the future. Officially, the Lincoln administration avoided measures that might lead to any wholesale emancipation, fearing that the four border slave states, especially Kentucky, might join the Confederacy otherwise, and therefore sought to restore the Union without enlisting black soldiers or making a revolutionary assault on slavery itself.[34]

Throughout the war's first year, these two profound issues—the status of fugitive slaves and the prospect of black enlistment in the military—dominated Douglass's mind and, therefore, his journalism. He was hardly alone. It seemed that everyone across the Northern press and in political circles was talking about the "contrabands"; even poets and songwriters appropriated the new concept. From the opening months of the war Douglass argued vehemently for the recruitment of black troops. Borrowing language from Old Brown, he demanded a "liberating army" of "slaves and free colored people . . . carrying the war into Africa." His war fever surging, Douglass proclaimed that symbolically "one black regiment alone would be, in such a war, the full equal of two white ones" and teach the slaves themselves "more . . . than a thousand preachers."[35]

Earlier in the war than most scholars may realize, Northern journalists and buck privates alike began to ponder how emancipation might become a "military necessity" for the Union cause. On June 15, 1861, the *Chicago Tribune* spoke for many mainstream newspapers in concluding, "If the war continues one year or more, 'what will we do with the slaves?' will . . . become the question of the day." Douglass agreed entirely, but hardly with the patience and dispatch of a reporter. His was the moral zeal of militant activism, although he put his faith in events as much as people. "Though it is generally true," he wrote in August, "that governments move only as they are moved upon by the people, they do sometimes find themselves moved by events which they cannot control." [36] In this instance, Douglass was painfully prophetic in naming the problem at the heart of the strife engulfing the country.

From the beginning of secession Douglass had called the crisis the "slaveholders' rebellion." Since Fort Sumter he had called for an "abolition war," and nothing short of it. When we consider his impatience with the Lincoln administration's halting, and sometimes hostile, approach to emancipation, it is worth contemplating the lens through which Douglass judged the war's purpose. In August, Douglass righteously claimed that "everyone knows that this is the slaveholders' rebellion and nothing else." The war, he said, was the work of a "privileged class of irresponsible despots, authorized tyrants and blood-suckers, who fasten upon the Negro's flesh, and draw political power and consequence from their legalized crimes." It is against that rhetorical background that we should understand Douglass's response to the most controversial issue of late 1861 in the Northern war effort. On August 30, General John C. Frémont, commanding Union forces in Missouri, then racked with chaos and outbreaks of guerrilla war, declared martial law, ordering the summary executions of rebels, confiscation of their property, and most important, emancipation of the slaves of Confederates. Frémont acted without authorization from Lincoln or any higher military command, although with tumultuous approval among abolitionists. President Lincoln, to sustain civilian control of the military and especially sensitive to keeping Kentucky securely in the Union, promptly revoked Frémont's declaration and eventually removed him from command.[37]

Infuriated, Douglass struck with rhetorical vengeance against Lincoln's revocation of Frémont's emancipation edict. Throughout the autumn, joining a chorus of abolitionists, he made a heroic figure out of the inept Frémont, and a symbol of the emancipation edict. He argued that the general had been sacrificed to appease the proslavery sentiment of the border states and because of Lincoln's constitutional conservatism. Not without reason, historian James Oakes portrays Douglass's reactions to the Frémont affair as an example of the abolitionist's "sourest invective" against Lincoln's caution. Oakes calls Douglass "myopic" in his impatience with federal policy, and a "flexible dogmatist" who simply refused to grasp the burdens and imperatives of a president conducting a civil war. Fair enough. But Douglass's priorities and aims were not the same as Lincoln's. And Douglass's impatience drew upon the blood of untold millions of the enslaved, not on the question of constitutional authority. Lincoln had to consider public opinion at every turn in the story of emancipation; Douglass's goal, as it had always been, was to bend and shape that opinion toward just the kind of revolution and conflict Frémont had touched off in Missouri. Douglass's scornfulness and disdain for legalism were a duty, just as Lincoln possessed a profound duty to try to navigate uncharted constitutional waters. Lincoln had to worry about voters; Douglass wanted slaveholders' "rights" and their armies crushed in order to educate a new generation of antislavery voters.[38]

If the conflict was ever to truly be an abolition war, and if slavery was, as Douglass frequently claimed, the "stomach of the rebellion," then in his view the border states, rather than being crucial and sensitive allies, were the "millstone around the neck of the government." Who needs "such friendship," Douglass argued, when it only serves as a "shield to the treason of the cotton states?" He engaged in faulty strategic thinking, but good abolitionist politics. Douglass spewed even more scorn on Lincoln's constitutional restraint about property rights: "As if this were a time to talk of constitutional power!" Douglass exhorted. He wanted Lincoln to seize the "war power" and use it as a "moral" weapon. Douglass's invective became ugly in October. He characterized Lincoln's thwarting of Frémont as a sign of "weakness, imbecility, and absurdity." Douglass had hoped Frémont's order might be "the hinge . . . upon which the character of the war was to turn." Instead, the "cunning technicalities of the crafty lawyer" won out over "the cannon and courage of the determined warrior."[39]

No one knew the future in this terrible war. Timing mattered, but no one should have expected patience from Douglass or any other radical abolitionist. He could not have known about the remarkable private remark Lincoln made that fall about the attitudes of the radicals. Abolitionists, said Lincoln, "would upset our applecart" if they "had their way." "We'll fetch 'em [slaves]," the president is reported to have said, "just give us a little time. We didn't go into this war to put down slavery, but to put the flag back . . . for I never should have had votes enough to send me here if the people had supposed I would use my power to upset slavery. . . . We must wait until every other means have been exhausted. This thunderbolt will wait." Likewise in December, Lincoln and his aides probably did not read the passage embedded in one of Douglass's editorials on the Frémont affair. After saying that the general's proclamation would never be forgotten, and declaring the war part of a design that would ultimately succeed, Douglass, liberally wielding italics, dropped this prediction into the mix: "In *three years more* the people will sanction the death of slavery *in the man of their choice*. And too, this unnatural war will render its death constitutional."[40] From their own peculiar dispositions, both men saw the thunder coming in 1862 and beyond.

But Douglass could not yet hear the thunder. Lincoln had moved in quiet and small ways to authorize emancipation and even the beginnings of black military service in 1861, but Douglass did not know it. The president had grudgingly supported the First Confiscation Act, passed by Congress in August, which included slaves in the property that Union troops could seize from Confederates. The freedom of such persons was not yet legally determined, but this was an important beginning.[41]

In his first annual message to Congress, submitted December 3, 1861, Lincoln, with rigid caution, reiterated his pledge to protect the slave property of "loyal" Southerners. He expressed solicitude toward the four border states to keep them in the Union. Most important in Douglass's mind, Lincoln discouragingly began to lay out a "plan of colonization" for any slaves liberated in the growing war, an issue the editor would take up with great vehemence in the coming year. He could not have been surprised to see Lincoln declare once again "the integrity of the Union" to be the primary goal of the war. But perhaps nothing sank Douglass's heart as much as when he read the president's famous statement of how "anxious and careful" he had been that the war "shall not degenerate into a violent and remorseless revolutionary struggle." Lincoln received heavy criticism for the caution in his annual message from parts of the North. The Illinois senator Lyman Trumbull, a close friend of the president's, received many constituent letters protesting that Lincoln's address contained no battle cry for the Union war effort. Douglass wanted precisely the revolutionary struggle that Lincoln did not at this stage want, and Douglass was more than ready to provide the battle cry roaring in the ears of all who would listen. To one of his own readers, eager for hope, Douglass pointed to the "higher law" at work overturning constitutional restraint, and to the "mighty current" moving the war toward radical ends. "Keep pounding on the rock," Douglass prescribed, and listen for the thunder.[42]

Chapter 18

THE ANTHEM OF
THE REDEEMED

It is difficult for us who have toiled so long and hard, to believe that this event, so stupendous, so far reaching and glorious is even at the door.

—FREDERICK DOUGLASS, ROCHESTER,
DECEMBER 28, 1862

On Sunday, December 28, 1862, after hundreds of thousands of words, nearly as many backbreaking miles traveled, and twenty-one months of bloody civil war, Frederick Douglass stepped to the familiar pulpit of Spring Street AME Zion Church in Rochester and uttered a remarkable paragraph. In words and sentiments he had dreamed of saying for most of his nearly forty-three years, the striking, well-attired orator with the graying streak swooshed over the right side of his hair began almost plaintively, declaring it "scarcely a day for prose." Offering no apologetics for garnering the congregation's time and attention, Douglass summoned the old dream into the church sanctuary and invested his audience in a moment they might never forget. "It is a day for poetry and song, a new song," said the preacher. Then he delivered a piece of prose poetry he had stored up inside since his first time in an AME Zion pulpit twenty-three years earlier in New Bedford. "These cloudless skies, this balmy air, this brilliant sunshine (making December as pleasant as May), are in harmony with the glorious morning of liberty about to dawn upon us."[1]

Eyes must have welled up in the pews among black and white abolitionist Rochester, as Douglass captured their feelings. "Out of a full heart and sacred emotion, I congratulate you my friends, and fellow citizens, on the high and hopeful condition, of the cause of human freedom and the cause of our common country, for these two causes are now one and inseparable and must stand or fall together." It had not yet officially happened, but Douglass offered his own kind of prayer of assurance, as the faithful kept watch for the day of Jubilee. "This sacred Sunday in all the likelihoods of the case, is the last which will witness the existence of legal slavery in all the Rebel slaveholding States of America." Then he folded some Lincoln-esque legal phrasing into an old abolitionist standby drawn from John Wesley, while landing a direct blow on Roger B. Taney of *Dred Scott* case infamy: "Henceforth and forever, slavery in those States is to be recognized, by all the departments of the American government, under its appropriate character, as an unmitigated robber and pirate, branded as the sum of all villainy, an outlaw having no rights which any man white or colored is bound to respect." Taking a breath, and perhaps choking down his own emotion, Douglass finished the opening of his praise song: "It is difficult for us who have toiled so long and hard, to believe that this event, so stupendous, so far reaching and glorious is even now at the door. It surpasses our most enthusiastic hopes that we live at such a time and are likely to witness the down-

Frederick Douglass, Philadelphia, Pennsylvania, January 14, 1862. John White Hurn photographer, carte de visite.

fall, at least the legal downfall, of slavery in America." As the congregation nodded with recognition, he concluded, "It is a moment for joy, thanksgiving, and Praise."[2] The following day Douglass boarded a train for Boston to join in a special gathering that would keep watch for the word.

The road to such anticipated joy about emancipation was crooked, bloody, and at times laden with blind curves. In mid-November 1861 in Syracuse, New York, Douglass encountered threats of a lynch mob. Before his scheduled two-speech billing, potential assassins had flooded the town with handbills announcing, "NIGGER FRED COMING," calling the orator among other epithets "a reviler of the Constitution . . . a Thief! Rascal! and Traitor!" The handbills called on people to "rally" and give Douglass a "warm reception." Due to the quick work of the mayor and local sheriff, who called on seventy police and some forty-five young troops from the nearby army camp, no violence occurred, and Douglass, guarded by soldiers with loaded muskets, spoke for well over an hour on the causes of the rebellion before eight hundred people. Douglass thanked his protectors as he acknowledged a historical moment when "the mob howls, and slavery with bloody hands is throttling the liberties of the nation."[3]

Violence dominated everyone's mind. In the year and nine months leading up to Abraham Lincoln's signing the Emancipation Proclamation on January 1, 1863, approximately 270,000 Union soldiers and sailors and 212,000 Confederates had died or were wounded in the Civil War at heretofore unknown places called Fort Donelson, Shiloh, Seven Pines, Malvern Hill, Cedar Mountain, Manassas Junction, Antietam, or Marye's Heights at Fredericksburg. Such scale of sacrifice had been unthinkable in 1860, but now it occupied the daily consciousness of most Americans. The long war Douglass desired was under way. By spring 1862, he declared the conflict "no longer a short war either in fact or in imagination, but one the end of which is away off in the dark and misty future." Written in blood, the very nature of the war transformed. A rising tide of African American slaves kept testing every battlefront, waterway, or Union army outpost to seek their freedom. Douglass scoured newspapers for news, and in December 1861 he reprinted more than a dozen accounts of daring escapes by "contrabands" in war zones. Far from docile, slaves were alert and aggressive. "The Negroes at the South," he wrote, "are shown to be as keenly alive to the events going on about them as the majority of their masters, and quite ready to take their freedom in any way that is presented to them." *Any way* indeed. Uncounted numbers of freedpeople were dying or suffering with disease in contraband camps all around the perimeter of the South. The Jubilee had arrived, forged by bravery and through fear and loss, well before it was signed into law.[4]

From 1861 to 1863, Douglass devoted his daily labors to fomenting an "abolition war." Along with other abolitionists, Douglass passed through many valleys of fear and confusion before they ever found a "sacred Sunday" such as the one he described in December 1862. Indeed, one year earlier, he and Gerrit Smith had exchanged depressing letters. Douglass despaired "of finding any sound place upon which to build a hope of national salvation. I am bewildered by the spectacle of moral blindness . . . and helpless imbecility which the Government of Lincoln presents. Is there hope?" Three days later, Smith replied by sending $10 to "sustain your paper," but remarking in somber tones, "I cannot get rid of the impression that our country is lost."[5] The two men felt especially discouraged by the Lincoln administration's embroilment in the *Trent* Affair, a diplomatic standoff between Great Britain and the United States.

The primary aim of Confederate diplomacy was to secure European and especially British recognition and, if possible, intervention on their behalf. In September, the Confederate government appointed James Mason of Virginia and John Slidell of Louisiana as ministers plenipotentiary to Britain and France respectively. The two slipped through the Union blockade. But when they stopped in the harbor of Havana, Cuba, to switch to a British ship, the *Trent*, they were seized as "contraband of war." The capture quickly became a diplomatic crisis. The London government cried foul, and Prime Minister Palmerston ordered troops to Canada, strengthened the British Atlantic fleet, and sent an ultimatum to the Lincoln administration demanding an apology and the release of the Confederate envoys. After much saber rattling on both sides, the United States saved face on December 25, 1861, by allowing Mason and Slidell to continue on to the foreign capitals.[6]

In the midst of this crisis, Julia Crofts wrote from England in a state of great fear over her native country's "probable war with America." Everyone but the "cotton party," she wrote, "shudders at the thought." If war with Britain happened, she urged Douglass to "cross the frontier with all your household & edit your paper at Toronto." After many weeks of these tensions, Douglass complained of "confusion and contradiction" in Washington. He thought the *Trent* Affair another measure of the "hesitating, doubting, shrinking" approach of Lincoln's government to the real issue of fighting slavery. "Our honor cannot require England's dishonor," wrote

Douglass the Anglophile.[7] Above all, Douglass wanted to prevent British intervention and to enlist English abolitionists in the crusade to end slavery.

Wartime heightens anxiety as it also alters conceptions of time itself, not only for combatants but for civilians, who must follow its every desperate surge or drought of news. In particular, 1862 was just such a year; little would ever be the same again. War possesses an awful logic and causes a psychic drama like few other human experiences. The direction and tide of the Civil War could change with any military success or failure. As Douglass said at the beginning of the year, "But a single day, but a single event may change the whole prospect. Let us, therefore, hope for that day, and continue to labor for that event."[8] His mood swings in 1862 were like recurring earthquakes, some destructive and others reordering the landscape with astonishing new hope.

Douglass did not find it easy to follow his friend Julia Crofts's prescription for their mutual frustration about the war: "While we labor for the redemption of the bondman, we must learn also to wait." They shared a faith in an activist Divine Providence, but not in Christian fatalism. During a midwinter lull in fighting, he complained bitterly of the many months the Army of the Potomac under the command of General George B. McClellan lay "idle" around Washington, DC. Six months of reading every morning that it was "all quiet on the Potomac" was enough, said the angry editor, "to exhaust the patience of Job." Douglass vigorously protested against McClellan's dismissal of the Hutchinson Family Singers from his camps for singing abolitionist songs. Douglass expressed defeatism in February 1862. The "stand-still, do-nothing policy" of Lincoln's government led Douglass to accuse the administration and its military team of "treason or . . . utter incompetency." Only a robust effort to defeat slaveholders, he believed, could prevent the rebels from winning their independence once the armies moved in the spring.[9]

Douglass delivered two major speeches that winter, one in Philadelphia in January and the other a month later in Boston. Both laid out his apocalyptic vision of the war. In both speeches, as well as in many editorials in the first half of 1862, Douglass asserted the case for black loyalty, for the recruitment of black troops, as he also vigorously denounced all colonization schemes emerging from the Lincoln administration. Exasperated by the slow pace of the war, Douglass offered many ideas about how to make the bloodletting meaningful and holy.

"I am to speak to you tonight of the civil war," Douglass announced to his Philadelphia audience in National Hall, "by which this vast country—this continent is convulsed." Nations, like individuals, the orator maintained, receive divine warnings that they must either heed or face destruction. Americans were being "taught" in this war "as with the emphasis of an earthquake." Their warning arrived "not in comets blazing through the troubled sky, but in the terrible calamity of a widespread rebellion enacted before our eyes." Douglass spoke glowingly at first of the American republic as a "young nation," giving it personal qualities—"great in mental, moral and physical resources." But any nation, like a person, must suffer, fall, and reform. Drawing on Hamlet's lament, Douglass observed that "the face of every loyal citizen is sicklied over with the pale cast of thought. Every pillar in the national temple is shaken. The nation itself has fallen asunder in the centre." Douglass himself pulled with all his might now to make those pillars fall. Slavery's poisoning of the national character, he contended, threatened destruction more than the Confederate armies. Lacing his narrative with Scripture, Douglass proclaimed, "We have faithfully copied all the cunning of the serpent without any of the harmlessness of the dove, or the boldness of the lion." Drawing deep from his favorite well, Douglass observed, "It would seem in the language of Isaiah that the whole head is sick, and the whole heart is faint, that there is no soundness in it."[10] With the old prophets as guides, Douglass watched the American temple destroyed so that it might be reinvented.

Frederick Douglass's Bible.

Glimmers of hope emerged from the Congress and the White House that spring. But first Douglass had to make the argument for why this was a black American's war. In 1862, Douglass proffered a wide-ranging discussion of the *loyalty* of his people. He made effective use of the idea of black loyalty, whether speaking in his role as an abolitionist or that of a war propagandist. "I believe up to this time," Douglass said in February, "no man . . . has been able to cast a shadow of a doubt upon the loyalty and patriotism of the free colored people in this the hour of the nation's trial and danger." But he was bitter that the federal government had spurned the service of black loyalists. "The Washington Government wants men for its army, but thus far, it has not had the boldness to recognize the manhood of the race to which I belong."[11] The orator wanted black patriotism acknowledged in all its forms.

Douglass believed American history and character were essentially the embodiment of contradiction. "He is the best friend of this country," said Douglass in early 1862, "who, at this tremendous crisis, dares tell his countrymen the truth, however disagreeable that truth may be; and such a friend I will aim to be." He had taken such a position on patriotism since his days as a Garrisonian. "I will hold up America to the lightning scorn of moral indignation," he said in an 1847 speech. "In doing this I shall feel myself discharging the duty of a true patriot; for he is the lover of his country who rebukes and does not excuse its sins." Douglass could be included among those Americans the modern theologian Donald W. Shriver Jr. has called "honest patriots," those who manifest an ironic-tragic love of country by learning, narrating, and working through its past of contradiction and evil, and not by evading it.[12]

Upon this philosophical basis Douglass built his case for black patriotism as well as for revolutionary change. He had more confidence in "Southern villainy" than in "Northern virtue." He believed the Union side had two classes of loyalists. The two "talk alike," he told his Boston audience in February. But "one class is for putting down the rebellion . . . by force and force alone, and without abolishing slavery, and the other is for putting down the rebellion by putting down slavery on every rod of earth which shall be made sacred by the footprints of a single loyal soldier. . . . One class would strike down the effect, the other would strike at the cause." Unmistakably, Douglass equated true loyalty and patriotism with abolitionism, an ironic, if vexing, notion among a white population that increasingly believed slavery had to be killed of "necessity" to win the war.[13]

Douglass constantly professed his own loyalty. "I allow no man to exceed me in the desire for the safety and welfare of this country," he pronounced in Boston. He called the Union the "shield" protecting Americans from "treason, rebellion and anarchy." He asserted his sense of birthright: "I am an American citizen. In birth, in sentiment, in ideas, in hopes, in aspirations, and responsibilities, I am an American citizen." Then he stated the collective case for free blacks, linking loyalty with military service. Blacks had demonstrated the "most ardent desire to serve the cause," only to be met with rejection at recruiting stations. "Colored men were good enough to fight under Washington," Douglass wrote. "They are not good enough to fight under McClellan." [14] Against all odds, Douglass staked his case on the loyalty of potential black soldiers.

But Douglass was equally fond of demonstrating the perseverance of loyalty among black civilians. "The Negro is the veritable Mark Tapley of this country," he wrote in July, referring to the amiable character in Charles Dickens's savagely comic *Martin Chuzzlewit*. "That most obliging good tempered character . . . was not more determined to be jolly under severely unfavorable circumstances, than the Negro is to 'come out strong' in patriotism under every possible discouragement." Douglass's reference to Dickens's Mark Tapley is particularly intriguing. It reflects more than his affinity for Dickens; Tapley is the "jolly" but serious voice of the downtrodden, as well as a critic of his own country's hypocrisies and faults, especially slavery. [15]

For Douglass, who himself became a master of sarcasm and irony in the face of the absurdity of slavery and racism, Dickens was a vivid model. *Martin Chuzzlewit* is Dickens's novel written after his disappointing visit to the United States in 1843, in which he spared America none of its pretensions and evils, especially the lies at the root of slaveholding. It is the jovial Tapley who captures the meaning of the selling of the daughter of an elderly black man named Cicero: "Lord, love you sir, they're so fond of liberty in this part of the globe, that they buy her and sell her and carry her to market with 'em. They've such a passion for Liberty, that they can't help taking liberties with her." Bitingly, Tapley cries: "Liberty forever. Hurrah! Hail Columbia!" Ten years before emancipation, a Dickens-inspired attitude toward absurdity may have fueled Douglass's famous call in his greatest speech for "scorching irony . . . biting ridicule . . . [and] withering sarcasm" after asking: "Would you have me argue that man is entitled to liberty?" [16]

Loyalty and patriotism are tortured concepts in time of war. For Douglass in 1862–63, loyalty was both an aspiration and a pragmatic device for the war propagandist. A yearning to belong might yet be combined with the right to fight in a cause blacks could view as their own.

From the beginning of the war, Abraham Lincoln faced the increasingly dominant question of slavery. The Republican-controlled Congress began to act with, and sometimes before, the president in 1862. Lincoln had always hated slavery and wished it somehow destroyed. But he was very much a constitutionalist working within what he viewed as the restraints of his legal power as commander in chief. Moreover, Lincoln had always been a Henry Clay Whig. His instinctive and ideological approach to slavery's ultimate demise derived from three ideas: that emancipation ought to be gradual, compensated, and ultimately result in the colonization of as many blacks as possible outside the United States.[17]

Lincoln's temperament, as well as this set of deeply honed political instincts, racial views, and strategies, collided head-on in historic proportions with increasingly all-out war. Lincoln began to think constantly about slavery by early 1862, and in March he began to act. Until then, Lincoln's approach to slavery had emerged as an assortment of floating ideas and incoherent policies. But he possessed a remarkable capacity to adapt, grow, and change on this most crucial question. On March 6, the president sent a message to Congress recommending that it authorize funding for gradual and compensated emancipation for the border slave states still in the Union. He stressed that this would merely be an initiation of a "gradual and not sudden" process and stated that he would not threaten slave property "within state limits," meaning in the Confederacy. The message was subject to the "free choice" of those northernmost border states, who might, if they accepted, send a signal to the seceded states to the south that they would never join them. In unveiled language, Lincoln declared it "impossible to foresee" what further consequences the war would bring for slavery and the South if it continued.[18]

Abolitionists responded with surprise and enthusiasm to Lincoln's message. Wendell Phillips called it "unexpected as a thunderbolt in a clear sky." And Douglass breathed a new tone. "It is really wonderful," he said by April 1862, "how all efforts to evade, postpone, and prevent its [emancipation] coming have been mocked and defied by the stupendous sweep of events." Douglass rejoiced that he had lived to "see the President of the United States deliberately advocating emancipation." Above all, Douglass captured the future irony of Lincoln's move: "Time and practice will improve the President as they improve other men. He is tall and strong, but he is not done growing; he grows as the nation grows." In a flourish of hope in a Rochester speech, Douglass warmed up to Lincoln for the moment; the president was now "an honest patriot endeavoring to save his country in its day of peril." The March message, however nuanced, fell as "the brick knocked down at the end of the row by which the whole line is prostrate." [19]

Lincoln tried assiduously to convince border-state congressmen and special delegations to accept his offer of gradual, compensated emancipation, but to no avail. Maryland, Kentucky, Missouri, and even Delaware, with its small number of slaves, officially resisted abolition. The most telling response Lincoln and his administration received to these overtures was that virtually all border-state officials strongly supported colonization. If the war by its force and logic did cause the liberation of some slaves, border politicians wanted the government to provide for removal of free blacks from the country. [20] A huge fight on that issue loomed on the immediate horizon, as in April another brick was about to fall.

From mid-March to early April, Congress fiercely debated a measure to emancipate the thirty-two hundred slaves in the District of Columbia, where the federal government held jurisdiction. The roiling debate in both houses centered on the capacities of black people to cope with freedom, and what was to be done with them after emancipation. In the end, all Republicans voted for the bill, and all but four Northern Democrats voted against it, a prelude to many further fights to come. The measure provided $300 per slave in compensation to slaveholders, as well as $100,000 for schemes of colonization in the wake of abolition in the District. After much consternation, Lincoln signed the bill on April 16. Douglass rejoiced, although he hated the colonization provisions in the emancipation bill. Even before passage, he wrote to Charles Sumner, who had gained close access to the president, thanking him for his efforts. "I trust I am not dreaming," Douglass said, "but the events taking place seem like a dream." [21] As each brick in a row fell, some more easily than others, Douglass measured progress as he tempered his own emotions.

The federal treasury paid out approximately $900,000 to slaveholders in the District, who lined up to receive their checks. To assess the value of slaves, the government employed a Baltimore slave trader for advice. Despite all these acknowledgments of slaves as "property," and the white supremacy expressed in so much of the legislative debate, for the first time in history a federal statute gave freedom to slaves. In June, in yet another thoroughly partisan enactment, Congress ended slavery in all western territories. Few slaves actually lived there, but the measure possessed great symbolic significance given the issue's centrality to so much of American political history. Finally, by July, after protracted, embittered debate over unprecedented constitutional questions about the authority to liberate slaves or employ black soldiers, Congress passed and then Lincoln signed the Second Confiscation Act. On July 12, Lincoln made one last-ditch effort to persuade a large delegation of border-state representatives to initiate gradual, compensated emancipation in their states. The president lectured the delegates gathered at the White House, arguing that the war would in time erode and eliminate slavery by "mere friction and abrasion." But the border representatives' steadfast rejections once again pushed Lincoln to more radical action.[22]

For many months, pressure had precipitously risen for action against slavery as a "military necessity," a phrase used widely all over the North. Douglass applauded this change in Northern sentiment. "Tens of thousands" were "now having the scales torn from their eyes," he said. "The result will be nearly the same to the slave, if from motives of necessity or any other motives the nation shall be led to the extinction of slavery."[23] Attacking slavery became increasingly popular to large numbers of Northerners as a means of defeating the Confederacy. Lincoln's conception of his war powers changed as he faced the potential of General McClellan's colossal defeat in the Peninsula Campaign in Virginia. The general's ambitious plan to take Richmond from the east ended disastrously at the Battle of the Seven Days in late June and early July. Lincoln faced a Confederate invasion of Northern soil by midsummer 1862. The war had escalated into a bloody multifront crusade on both sides; the pillars of the temple were falling, as Douglass wished, but the Union cause required revolutionary measures in order to win.

The Confiscation Act was just such a measure; it freed all slaves of disloyal owners in Confederate territory occupied by Union forces, as well as any slaves escaping to Union lines. The law further authorized the president to employ blacks as he deemed "necessary and proper for the suppression of the rebellion." It also suggested that as many blacks as were willing should be colonized "in some tropical country." Fraught with contradiction, the Second Confiscation Act nevertheless meant, as the antislavery *Springfield Republican* put it, that "every victory [by Union forces] is a victory for emancipation."[24]

Douglass worried as he watched and alternately cheered or denounced this historic process. In March 1862 he reported on a lecture tour just completed of more than a thousand miles, speaking to "tens of thousands of people," through many towns in the states of Massachusetts, New York, and New Jersey. He described himself as encouraged by his audiences, and by conversations along the way. "The popular ear is open, and the popular heart is everywhere sensitive to impression," he announced. The same month, Douglass wrote a long piece, "The Situation of the War," in which he listed every military engagement in the first year of the war, celebrated the recent Union victories at Forts Henry and Donelson in Tennessee, and prematurely declared "failure . . . plainly written on the rebellion as a military power." Douglass did not yet fully grasp military campaigns, their logistics and results on the ground, thus leading him to rash statements sometimes laced with confused political sentiments. He accurately predicted worse fighting to come as spring offensives commenced. He still feared political compromise with slavery that might yet arise from the Lincoln administration, as well as "weak and treacherous magnanimity" on the part of some Union generals who refused to fight a relentless war. In awkwardly chosen words, Douglass wrote, "The North has been angry with the South only as a child is angry with a pet, and that anger soon passes away when the pet has been well kicked." After the horrifyingly bloody battle of Shiloh in southwest Tennessee on April 6–7, with its twenty thousand killed and wounded on both sides, he needed more chastened and graceful language to describe the Union war effort.[25]

As the bloody summer of 1862 dragged on, Douglass followed every development from Rochester and from the speakers' circuit. He was at first thrilled with the Second Confiscation Act, reprinting its primary emancipation provisions, but then declared it "significant or insignificant only as the President himself shall determine." He also reprinted in full Lincoln's formal exchange from July with the border-state congressmen. Douglass's heart sank as he read the president's forthright final appeal for gradual and compensated abolition in the four states to be followed by some degree of black removal. Such an appeal was especially unnerving given the historical precedent of Indian removal accomplished a quarter century earlier. "How much better to do it while we can," Lincoln had said, "lest the war ere long render us pecuniarily unable to do it. How much better for you, as seller, and the nation as buyer, to sell out and buy out that without which the war could never have been, than to sink both the thing to be sold and the price of it in cutting one another's throats." After this business advice about how and when to profit from their slaves, Lincoln appealed to the one issue that would animate and anger Douglass the most. "Room in South America for colonization can be obtained cheaply and in abundance," the chief executive lectured his recalcitrant guests, "and when numbers shall be large enough . . . the freed people will not be so reluctant to go."[26] Douglass would soon be lecturing the president about just how much he should presume to know the intentions and spirits of black people for leaving their own country to satisfy the demands of white supremacy.

On June 18, 1862, Julia Crofts wrote to Douglass from London, parroting back some striking sentiments she had just read in her old friend's voice in the current issue of his paper: "Oh! why will the Government trumpet give an uncertain sound?" Overcome by tears after hearing for the first time the singing of the "John Brown" song in England, she wished that the next Fourth of July, in her former coeditor's words, "might witness a glorious declaration of Liberty to the captive, and the opening of the prison to them that are bound!"[27] By the time Douglass printed that letter, he had indeed crafted another major July Fourth address.

Early on the morning of July 4, Douglass took the Elmira and Canandaigua Railroad from Rochester southeast approximately sixty miles to a tiny town called Himrods Corners, New York. Arriving at the sleepy village located between Keuka and Seneca Lakes, some eight miles south of Penn Yan, Douglass stepped off the cars and "found no one to receive" him. So he simply started walking until he encountered someone who could take him to his hosts. Soon this little settlement of "two taverns, one church, six neat little cottages, one store," and a "pile of sawed wood" began to transform for celebration. By late morning, Douglass saw the Star-Spangled Banner flying from many a liberty pole, and before long, by rail and in farm wagons, a throng estimated at two thousand arrived and assembled in "a grove of noble pines, under a bright blue sky." They had not gathered, said their orator, "for fun and frolic, not for mirth or senseless parade," but to listen to Douglass consider "the perilous condition of the country." Under a canopy of trees, to a throng of western New York and Finger Lakes region farmers and townspeople, many of whom had sons, brothers, or fathers in the army in Virginia, Douglass delivered a carefully prepared address he called "The Slaveholder's Rebellion."[28]

Most of his arguments had been well rehearsed in editorials and speeches that spring and summer. With reports of the shocking bloodshed all around the eastern perimeter of Richmond, and the retreat of

McClellan's army to the James River in defeat just trickling in, Douglass acknowledged a "midnight blackness" intruding on their beautiful day. The country was undergoing a "social earthquake," the national "house" was "on fire." Douglass addressed big subjects: the origin of the war, its "tap root, and its sap, its trunk and its branches," all born of slavery; the Confederacy's quest to forge in revolution an eternal slaveholders' republic; a history of the litany of compromises with slavery over time; the many perversions of the Declaration of Independence in the service of satisfying the demands of the Slave Power; the inevitability of the war; and McClellan's alleged disastrous incompetence as well as the duplicity within the Lincoln administration. The war had now reached such scale of bloodshed that it was no longer about constitutional authority, but about which side had the will to fight to win.[29]

In this sobering critique of the Union war effort, one new and important element emerged. In the shade of a beautiful grove, the floor of the natural arena strewn with pine needles, Douglass's deep baritone called out an honest abolitionist's patriotism. Contrary to his magnificent jeremiad for the Fourth of July in 1852, where the orator rang down a hailstorm separating himself and "your fathers," "your" Declaration of Independence, and "your" Fourth of July, this time at Himrods Corners, ten years later and in the midst of a war that now showed vivid signs of becoming a struggle against slavery, Douglass suddenly altered the pronouns: "The claims of *our* fathers upon *our* memory, admiration and gratitude are founded in the fact that they wisely, and bravely, and successfully met the crisis of their day." This time he took ownership in the special day and gave it new meaning. "If the men of this generation would deserve well of posterity, they must like their fathers, discharge the duties and responsibilities of their age." It was now his age, his duty, and especially *his* country. They had gathered this time, said the black Jeremiah in softer tones, to draw a new meaning "around the birth of *our* national independence." Douglass linked past to present as he instructed the throng sitting on wagons and leaning on trees. "We are only continuing the tremendous struggle, which your fathers and *my* fathers began eighty six years ago" (italics added). Douglass had never before called the American founders his "fathers."[30] For him, a second American revolution was under way—more bloody, but perhaps more enduring and important than the first. He claimed his place among the founders of the second republic.

For Douglass, emotionally and ideologically, the remainder of 1862 was as turbulent as any period in his life. The path to emancipation, despite the triumphal meanings we retrospectively give it, was never linear or certain.

Douglass now witnessed and interpreted the greatest changes as well as some of the most discouraging challenges he ever faced. At stake were the character and the future of black freedom. Douglass plowed every ounce of his millennial and apocalyptic sensibility into his vision of events. Keeping faith in the jubilee to come out of this epic struggle required a belief that God could enter human affairs, that history could undergo sudden and radical change. The escalating war, however dark, made such a faith fathomable. Douglass frequently used such terms as the "laws of God" or "laws of nature" to describe the engines of history. "The world," he announced, in an early-1863 speech, "like fish preached to in the stream, moves on in obedience to the laws of its being, bearing away all excrescences and imperfections in its progress. It has its periods of illumination as well as of darkness, and often bounds forward a greater distance in a single year than in an age before." [31] With this apocalyptic mentality, Douglass watched, lived, and interpreted the history enveloping him.

In September 1862, in the wake of the terrible Union defeat at Second Manassas in late August, and as Robert E. Lee's Confederate army invaded Maryland in the most threatening moment of the war to date, Douglass called for "stern, vigorous, unrelenting war with rebels." Divine messages lay in "sufferings, disasters, defeats." In language strikingly similar to that used by Julia Ward Howe in her "Battle Hymn of the Republic," first published as lyrics earlier that year in the *Atlantic Monthly*, Douglass measured progress now in blood. A "fiery sword of justice" waved over the land, Douglass wrote. "We are to be saved as by fire." His message was about a brutal chastening from a vengeful God. He acknowledged the need to "grieve with the sorrow-stricken families all over the North, but their terrible afflictions and heavy sorrows are their educators." [32] With this harsh outlook the steely-eyed editor confronted as well the most frustrating issue of all—colonization.

Colonization had deep and complex origins in the early American republic. What some historians call the phase of "benevolent colonization," especially from roughly 1816 to the 1840s, stemmed from a complicated set of motives on the part of some white Americans. They advocated emigration as an ancient right of peoples to seek new beginnings so that blacks (like other migrants) could develop their own independent societies unburdened by white racism, in a quest for equality apart from a stronger or dominant race, and as an abiding part of the biblical Exodus narrative. The story of Exodus has long driven the attraction of emigration schemes, especially in times of crisis, among black Americans. [33]

But for Douglass, colonization was an old and agonizing question. With only some exceptions—some plans led by blacks themselves aimed at staying in the western hemisphere—he had always hated the premises of colonization. He did honor and report about Martin Delany's journeys during the war to West Africa in search of sites for colonies. Douglass gave qualified endorsement to the spirit of Delany's quest, if not to his theories about racial purity, his "hyperbole" about finding a land of "the pure black uncorrupted by Caucasian blood." As early as 1849 Douglass had warned against "slaveholding charmers," in any guise, who had always "conjured up their old familiar spirits of colonization." He despised its aims, as he said in 1856, because of its capacity to "confirm existing prejudice as a thing natural and unsurmountable." Douglass always saw colonization as a debate over human dignity, not over improving race relations by separating blacks from whites; he never viewed it merely as a policy or a strategy. However well intentioned, or packaged in liberal aims, it was removal, never reform. By wartime, as the Lincoln administration launched various schemes of colonization, Douglass called it the "bugbear . . . that has so troubled the American people," and the "singularly pleasing dream" of white supremacists.[34]

Lincoln, a longtime sympathizer with colonization, set in motion a multilayered effort to expatriate blacks from the country. As early as March 1861, Lincoln had instructed Elisha Oscar Crosby, the newly appointed minister-resident to Guatemala, to seek a place for black colonists in Central America. Crosby organized his mission throughout 1861, despite opposition from both the Guatemalan and Honduran governments. An ill-fated colonization scheme in Panama also emerged in the first year of the war.[35]

From April to August 1862, Lincoln received a great deal of advice regarding colonization. The president's cabinet remained quite divided on the issue, while strong support still existed in many quarters of the administration and Congress for sending freed blacks to the nation of Liberia in West Africa. For a while Lincoln also entertained a scheme that would have sent ten thousand black troops into Florida to defeat Confederates, thereby seizing back the state for the Union and forming the basis of a large migration to reconstruct that state. Serious interest in black emigration also took hold in Brazil, the British West Indies, and the Danish island of St. Croix. By the end of August 1862, agents from several West Indian colonies were on their way to Washington. But due to the delicate diplomatic relationship between the United States and Britain, as well as American abolitionist resistance, the West Indian initiatives never came to fruition.[36]

At this crucial juncture, Lincoln decided on August 14 to meet with a small delegation of black ministers at the White House to discuss colonization. This infamous meeting, Lincoln's worst racial moment, was anything but a discussion; a nearly desperate president gave a one-way lecture looking for self-sacrificing black men to volunteer to leave their country to assuage the fears of white people who now had to imagine the end of slavery. The delegation, all from the Washington, DC, area, was led by Edward M. Thomas, president of an organization called the Anglo-African Institute for the Encouragement of Industry and Art. This hastily assembled meeting did not include the more prominent Douglass, nor even the black emigrationists the Reverend Henry Highland Garnet or Martin Delany.[37]

After shaking hands with his guests at this first-ever meeting of a president with black leaders, and with one or more members of the press invited to listen and record, Lincoln read a formal statement to the stunned ministers. Lincoln could not have been more forthright: "You and we are different races. We have between us a broader difference than exists between almost any other two races. Whether it is right or wrong I need not discuss, but this physical difference is a great disadvantage to us both." Blacks and whites mutually "suffer" from each other's presence in the same land, argued the president. For this reason, Lincoln concluded, "We should be separated."[38]

Lincoln shockingly blamed the war on the presence of blacks. "But for your race among us there could not be war, although many men engaged on either side do not care for you one way or another." The host acknowledged that blacks, slave or free, were enduring "the greatest wrong inflicted on any people," but racial equality of any kind, in his view, could never be possible in America. "On this broad continent," said Lincoln, "not a single man of your race is made the equal of a single man of ours." He did not wish to debate this inequality, since it was "a fact, about which we all feel and think alike, I and you." With one astonishing presumption after another, he argued that slavery had "evil effects on the white race" as well. "See our present condition—the country engaged in war!—our white men cutting one another's throats." Lincoln beseeched the five black representatives, who must have felt more than a little bewildered, to swallow their wishes for a future in the land of their birth and lead their people to a foreign colony. He did not wish to seem "unkind," but for them to reject his plea to lead in voluntary repatriation would be "an extremely selfish view of the case" and not in the best interest of their race. "It is exceedingly important that we have men at the beginning capable of thinking as white men," he bluntly continued, "and not those who have been systematically oppressed."[39]

Did the president really invite these men to the executive mansion to insult them? Perhaps not. But in conceiving the audience as the wider nation, he surely understood whose prejudices he stoked, and at whose expense. Lincoln concluded by putting the best possible face on Central America as the site of his colonization project. He employed the old racist canard that blacks could thrive in a "similarity of climate with your native land." He promoted the prospect of employment in the coal mines. He suggested, against his own diplomatic intelligence, that the countries of Central America would warmly welcome them, and as president, he pledged personally that he "would endeavor to have you made equals." He wanted "a hundred" to start the colony, but almost like an auctioneer, he said he would take "fifty," or even "twenty-five able-bodied men, with a mixture of women and children" to "make a successful commencement." This wretched encounter ended with Edward Thomas saying they would get back to Lincoln with an answer.[40] As before and after, this discussion of colonization turned on two fundamentally different conceptions of the future of black Americans. To Lincoln, a biracial democracy in America would never be possible. Most black leaders, however, were flushed with new hopes about a future precisely opposite from that outlined in Lincoln's appeal.

Douglass was outraged at Lincoln's address to the black delegation. In September he reprinted Lincoln's remarks in full in his paper, then penned the harshest criticism he ever leveled at the president: "Mr. Lincoln assumes the language and arguments of an itinerant Colonization lecturer," charged Douglass, showing all his inconsistencies, his pride of race and blood, his contempt for Negroes and his canting hypocrisy. How an honest man could creep into such a character as that implied by this address we are not required to show." The editor lambasted Lincoln's claim that the mere presence of blacks had caused the war. Dissolving his anger in sarcasm, Douglass likened Lincoln's logic to "a horse thief pleading that the existence of the horse is the apology for his theft or a highway man contending that the money in the traveler's pocket is the sole first cause of his robbery."[41] In this tragic humor, Douglass did Lincoln, the famous storyteller, one better.

The war, contended Douglass, emerged from the "cruel and brutal cupidity of those who wish to possess horses, money, and Negroes by means of theft, robbery, and rebellion." Douglass slammed Lincoln's affirmation of white supremacy, calling him "a genuine representative of American prejudice and Negro hatred." Douglass had no interest in acknowledging Lincoln's need to assuage white fears or to appeal to border-state sensitivities. Douglass felt betrayed by Lincoln's stark appeal to blacks to leave the country for white people's reasons. The tenor of Lincoln's address especially hurt: "The tone of frankness and benevolence which he assumes in his speech to the colored committee is too thin a mask not to be seen through. The genuine spark of humanity is missing in it. . . . It expresses merely the desire to get rid of them [blacks] and reminds one of the politeness with which a man might try to bow out of his house some troublesome creditor or the witness of some old guilt." [42] An embittered Douglass laid bare the fullest meaning in colonization schemes.

Blacks generally exploded with ire at Lincoln's colonization address. Protest meetings were held across the North. In language rich with patriotism and resolve, a Queens County, New York, gathering lectured Lincoln: "This is our native country, we have as strong attachment naturally to our native hills, valleys, plains, luxuriant forests . . . mighty rivers, and lofty mountains as any other people." An African American group in Philadelphia pointed to its social progress as evidence that white supremacy could be thwarted. "Shall we sacrifice this, leave our homes, forsake our birthplace, and flee to a strange land," they asked, "to appease the . . . prejudice of the traitors now in arms against the Government?" An A. P. Smith of New Jersey replied to Lincoln by writing to Douglass's paper. Even if racism was impregnable, as the president believed, "must I crush out my cherished hopes and aspirations, abandon my home, and become a pauper to the mean and selfish spirit that oppresses me?" A white radical abolitionist, Beriah Green, accused Lincoln of "braying—babbling . . . enough to turn the stomach of an ostrich." [43] The debate over colonization always came back, as in these testimonies, to its root: the American struggle over white supremacy.

Some blacks, although a diminishing minority, responded favorably to the Lincoln administration colonization proposals. By October 1862, Kansas senator Samuel Pomeroy, the administration's chief promoter of colonization schemes, claimed he had received 13,700 applications from potential black emigrants, two of whom were Douglass's frustrated sons Lewis and Charles, who, now as young adults, broke with their father's wishes and decided to consider moving to Panama. Two months earlier, Pomeroy had issued a widely published call, "The Appeal to Free Colored People of the United States," describing the advantages and noble purposes of the Central American scheme. Lewis Douglass was just shy of twenty-two years old and Charles of eighteen. Douglass had written to Pomeroy a letter of introduction for at least one son, likely Lewis, whom Douglass described as "of age, forms his own opinions, pursues his own plans and agrees with me, and differs from me in the exercise of that liberty as American young men generally, who have their own way to make in the world." We can know little about the intensity of these father-son disagreements or of the surges of youthful independence of black males with limited options living at home in Rochester. Within half a year those prospects, however, markedly changed; the Central American initiative crumbled nearly as fast as it emerged in the face of its proprietor's corruption and new historical imperatives.[44]

The president's intentions with colonization have long been the subject of rigorous debate in Lincoln scholarship. One recent biographer has called his August 14 White House meeting the "puzzling . . . low point" in Lincoln's race relations, while another has analyzed it as part of the president's larger "strategic racism." Yet another writer has oddly complimented Lincoln for his "remarkable racial candor" and stressed that his brand of colonization only asked for volunteers, as opposed to the expulsion of blacks advocated by the harsher members of the administration. Still another biographer, while thoroughly quoting the most racially insensitive lines of Lincoln's address, concludes that it should be seen as the chief executive "trotting out colonization to smooth the way for emancipation." Some Lincoln scholars have long chosen to believe that the president was never truly serious about colonization and used it as a trial balloon to condition public opinion for his larger rendezvous with history—the Emancipation Proclamation. Over time, many have chosen to see their Lincoln as morally whole, from 1865, rather than back in the volatile, revolutionary moments of 1861–62. Still other scholars have forcefully argued that Lincoln was a true believer in colonization and never relinquished it as a policy option until he had to. As Eric Foner has written, "there is no reason to doubt the sincerity of Lincoln's" ten years of public support for colonization; it had always been one part of a larger vision of how slavery might end.[45]

To Douglass, Lincoln's colonization appeal on August 14 was not merely a personal insult to his or any African American's integrity; it was a denigration of humane values, a vile dashing of newfound hope. "To these colored people," said Douglass, "without power and without influence the President is direct, undisguised and unhesitating. He says to the colored people: I don't like you, you must clear out of the country."[46] Racism is sometimes a political maneuver, a strategic position in the face of vicious opposition, a habit of mind entailed upon one's soul, or a structural or institutional force beyond the grasp of individuals. But sometimes it must be comprehended, indeed felt first, in the heart of the insulted. Candor is ultimately judged by its recipient.

In September 1862, Douglass launched a counterattack, insisting that Negro-hating mobs and colonization agents were united by what he called the "satanic spirit of colonization." He sought to refute the racial determinism at the heart of colonizationism and took dead aim at its central assumptions: that white prejudice was unconquerable; that blacks naturally gravitated toward tropical climates; that color was a natural barrier to interracial marriage; that race fixed physical and intellectual aptitude; and that the "character" of blacks and whites required social separation. United by these lethal theories, mobs provided the "brickbats and pistols," Douglass said, while colonizationists furnished the "arguments and piety." Douglass felt driven to resist what he called a "miserable philosophy." To claims about the black man's "nature" inclining him to servility, Douglass charged that it was "color" and not his nature that so troubled the proponents of removal. He reaffirmed his belief in "a common human nature of all men" and called racial prejudice just "another proof of man's perverse proclivity to create the causes of his own misery." Douglass all but enjoyed dismissing the absurdity of climatic racial theory by suggesting that if colonizationists considered climatic distribution of the races their mission, he would demand that Caucasians who had emigrated to every continent on earth be sent back to Europe. To the belief that a "ban of nature" prevented intermarriage between the races, he simply pointed to the large mulatto population in America, and therefore to himself.[47]

Douglass's modern and absurdist critique of the racism at the heart of colonization schemes seems driven by both outrage and amusement. It came through a brilliant critique of racist psychology. To him the fear of miscegenation always reflected a larger purpose: "Whenever any new villainy is to be perpetrated, or any old one against the Negro perpetuated, the popular prejudice is rallied by a denunciation of amalgamation." Ridicule was his only alternative. Douglass cast the denial of racial equality in global terms: "If men may not live peaceably together . . . in the same land, they cannot so live on the same continent, and ultimately in the same world." If heterogeneity could not work in America, where could it? "If the black man cannot find peace from the aggressions of the white race on this continent," he reasoned, "he will not be likely to find it permanently on any part of the habitable globe." Douglass never wavered, as he had said as early as his famous address on ethnology in 1854, from the cardinal belief in "the instinctive consciousness of the common brotherhood of man."[48]

In the fall of 1862, through Postmaster General Montgomery Blair, the Lincoln administration tried to officially enlist Douglass to help lead their colonization schemes. Responding to Douglass's letter of protest to Senator Pomeroy (which does not survive), Blair sought to assure Douglass that there was "no question of superiority or inferiority involved in the proposed removal." Blair invoked the reputation of Thomas Jefferson to underscore the necessity of racial separation. The minority race, argued Blair, must go elsewhere to imitate the civilization established by the majority race ("thinking as white men," as Lincoln put it); the propriety of colonization stemmed from "the differences between them . . . and it seems as obvious to me as it was to . . . the mind of Jefferson that the opinion against which you protest, is the necessary result of indelible differences thus made by the Almighty."[49] Here it was again: colonization theory, gilded by the image of Jefferson, determined by God, driven by white supremacy while claiming otherwise, and callously argued by a member of Lincoln's cabinet. No ancient Exodus story or impulse for the natural right of emigration motivated Blair's appeal to racism.

In Douglass's public reply, one of the most extraordinary letters in American history from a black leader to a high-ranking government official about race, Douglass thanked Blair for the opportunity to assess the colonization issue. Then, writing on September 16, on a day between the surrender of huge numbers of Union troops to Confederate general Stonewall Jackson at Harpers Ferry (on the fifteenth), and the battle of Antietam in Maryland on the seventeenth (the bloodiest day in American history), Douglass lambasted Blair's theory and purpose. As evidence to refute climatic theory, Douglass pointed to nearly 250 years of black residence on American soil: "If ever any people can be acclimatized, I think the Negro can claim to be so in this country." Perhaps Douglass was wryly smiling about all the winters he had spent in the snow belt of Rochester, New York. The idea of racial climate zones had gained wide acceptance in antebellum America, especially due to the work of the Harvard biologist Louis Agassiz, who had applied the notion of "zoological provinces" for animal and plant life to the races of man. Douglass refused to see "scientific" racial theory as anything but ideology; he considered all discussion of "confining different varieties of men to different belts of the earth's surface" to be "chimerical in the extreme."[50]

Refusing any longer to be lectured to, Douglass did the lecturing. He bluntly rejected Blair's white nationalism, insisting that blacks and whites could live "under the same government." "We have readily adapted ourselves to your civilization," he continued. "We are Americans by birth and education, and have a preference for American institutions as against those of any other country." In direct language that might apply to any xenophobic panic or racial-exclusion impulse down through American history, Douglass put Blair on notice: "That we should wish to remain here is natural to us and creditable to you."[51] Douglass and the Republicans came to a similar view of the future of slavery in America. But on the future racial character of an American nation, they were as yet far apart. As a final objection to Blair's entreaty, Douglass once again addressed the pernicious effects of colonization, which he saw as proslavery theory in disguise. Douglass insisted that slavery, racism, and future black equality be discussed as a single question, to be settled on American soil within American institutions.

Douglass ended his letter to Blair with an appeal for national regeneration born of the cruel war, declaring confidently that out of "this terrible baptism of blood and fire through which our nation is passing . . . not as has been most cruelly affirmed, because of the presence of men of color in the land, but by malignant . . . vices, nursed into power . . . at the poisoned breast of slavery, it will come at last . . . purified in its spirit freed from slavery, vastly greater . . . than it ever was before in all the elements of advancing civilization."[52] The angry orator's demolition of Blair is one for the ages, and one of the great documents of his writing life.

Douglass's best answer to this personal challenge from colonizationists was to assert his people's claim to American nationality. For forty years African Americans had faced colonization as both threat and opportunity. But in 1862 the debate took place in an urgent, wartime atmosphere. In the midst of the war, with emancipation on the horizon, Douglass led this struggle against a last hurrah of colonization. As Douglass parried with Blair over the consequences of freeing black people, President Lincoln was preoccupied with whether, when, and how to do it.

On September 15, 1862, President Lincoln received dispatches from General McClellan about his somewhat exaggerated sense of victory that day at South Mountain and Crampton's Gap in Maryland. As Robert E. Lee's army reorganized along Antietam Creek, Lincoln wrote back a quick message: "God bless you, and all with you. Destroy the rebel army, if possible." Just two days earlier at the White House, Lincoln had met with a delegation of clergy from Chicago who delivered to him a direct appeal for a proclamation by the president of "general emancipation" of the slaves. They believed that such a decree was God's "Divine will," and that "marvelous conversions to the wisdom of emancipation" had recently swept across the North. Lincoln engaged the ministers in an open exchange over the timing and consequences of an emancipation edict. He had abandoned constitutional qualms about freeing slaves as commander in chief; he viewed it, he said, as "a practical war measure." In these tense weeks, Lincoln seemed almost at war with himself about just what to do about slavery. He seemed worried about his actual power on the ground. How could he stop, for example, rebel troops from kidnapping blacks from Maryland back to Virginia and selling them into slavery, when the Union army could not seem to stop Lee's invasion? How could his "word" free slaves when, he admitted, "I cannot even enforce the Constitution in the rebel states?" Lincoln feared doing only what would appear as "inoperative." A proclamation might only be "like the Pope's bull against the comet!" the president half joked. After this parley about ending slavery, Lincoln assured the ministers that "the subject is on my mind, by day and night, more than any other." [53]

Lincoln had prepared a draft of his Preliminary Emancipation Proclamation at least as early as July 22, 1862, when he announced to a cabinet meeting his intention to issue such a document. Timing in the end was all. In the wake of the battle of Antietam and Lee's retreat across the Potomac River into Virginia, the president had victory enough on the battlefield so as not to worry that emancipation by executive order would be ineffective. Likely on Sunday, September 21, Lincoln redrafted in hand his Proclamation. The document put the South and the world on notice that on January 1, 1863, unless the Confederacy ceased the war, Lincoln would free all the slaves in the states "in rebellion." Again, he urged gradualism as well as colonization of freed blacks by their "consent . . . on this continent or elsewhere." [54]

Demonstrating his haste to get the document before his cabinet and proclaimed on September 22, the president used scissors to cut out sections of both Congress's "Article of War" from March ordering the army and the navy to receive all fugitive slaves into their lines, and the Second Confiscation Act of July 17, reinforcing even more forcefully the same principle. He then pasted these sections into this original draft. In the document's third paragraph, in language never to be forgotten in American civil religion, and which Douglass seized upon with renewed hope, Lincoln said that "all persons held as slaves" in the designated states and regions, as of January 1, "shall be then, thenceforward, and forever free." All members of the armed forces of the United States were commanded to do "no act or acts" impeding the freedpeople from exercising "their actual freedom." [55]

In Lincoln's cabinet, Douglass's colonization nemesis, Montgomery Blair, was the sole member to oppose the Preliminary Proclamation. Response in the border states was generally hostile as well. The stock market declined, and across the North and at the battlefronts, some Union soldiers initially declared their hostility to fighting to free black people; the Proclamation was openly ridiculed among McClellan's officers. But overall, the Northern reaction to this revolutionary shift in the purpose of the war was positive. Democratic Party papers mocked the Proclamation as mere "paper thunder" or as "radical fanaticism," "social revolution," and "gross unconstitutionality." Republican papers, however, rejoiced, declaring it "the beginning of the end of the rebellion; the beginning of the new life of the nation." Among Republican politicians, enthusiasm soared, although some wished for a more unconditional assault on slavery. Massachusetts governor John Andrew wanted more, but distinguished between the text and its ultimate meaning in a telling observation: "It is a poor document, but a mighty act; slow, somewhat halting, wrong in its delay till January, but grand and sublime after all." At the front lines, many Union soldiers now saw some kind of reality beneath their endless campfire conversations about the "military necessity" of emancipation.[56]

In Rochester, Douglass sat at his editor's desk, as he did so often, looked out on the war, and tried to speak for 4 million slaves, converting despair into hope: "We shout for joy that we live to record this righteous decree." Acknowledging Lincoln's "cautious, forbearing, and hesitating way," he seized on the words "forever free" and urged all to join the "long enslaved millions" in honoring and celebrating "this hour of . . . deliverance." Douglass expressed new confidence in Lincoln in words very different from a month earlier. "Abraham Lincoln may be slow, Abraham Lincoln may desire peace even at the price of leaving our terrible sore untouched . . . but Abraham Lincoln is not the man to reconsider, retract and contradict words and purposes solemnly proclaimed over his official signature." The duty of hope soared with new energy. "Confide in his word," Douglass advised about Lincoln, all the while falling back, as before, on faith in "events greater than the President, events which have slowly wrung this proclamation from him." Douglass also placed new faith in the document's "implied" meanings, especially Lincoln's apparent decision to put aside "border state influence" as well as "half-loyal" Democrats who claimed to be Unionists. And if some

Union enlisted men and officers threw down their arms and refused to fight to free the slaves, Douglass concluded, so be it: "Let the army be cleansed from all such proslavery vermin." The editor allowed himself to believe that the war he had advocated was now at hand, especially if Northerners would let "the black man have an arm as well as a heart in this war." Gird your loins, Douglass urged, for the "last struggle with the monster slavery."[57]

In the fall congressional elections of 1862, the Democrats made sweeping gains; Republicans suffered at the polls because of emancipation, and a "depressed" Lincoln, as numerous biographers have suggested, did not know quite where to turn. Northern voters were also prompted by a drumbeat in the press over fears of slave insurrection, by resistance to Lincoln's suspension of habeas corpus and to arrests of newspaper editors, as well as by virulently racist Democratic Party rhetoric about emancipation leading to "scenes of lust and rapine" in the South and a "swarthy inundation" of black workers into the North. In the anxious hundred days between the Preliminary and final Emancipation Proclamations, jubilation gave way to confusion in abolitionist and free-black communities. Above all, the news never abated about Lincoln and his men still planning for colonization. In late-September cabinet meetings Lincoln pushed his ministers to continue the effort for voluntary removal and by November he still hoped privately to make colonization in Central America a reality.[58]

Douglass exhibited a strikingly new mood in the fall of 1862, even about the dreaded bugbear of colonization. By November, he published contradictory reports about the state of colonization schemes still percolating from Washington. In one brief column he said that Pomeroy's expedition to Panama was soon to depart, and that some black monitors should accompany the emigrants. But in an adjoining, longer piece, he claimed that his contacts in "high authority" had informed him that the Central American expedition had been cancelled. Douglass editorialized, as though still trying to convince his own sons not to leave, that colonization made no sense economically. In America, said the editor, blacks are the workers; they had built the nation's wealth, and it was "wasteful and ruinous" to deport them now.[59]

For Douglass, his family, and the entire abolitionist community, the fall of 1862 was a sleepless watch night that lasted three months. "The next two months," Douglass wrote in November, "must be regarded as more critical and dangerous than any similar period during the slaveholders' rebellion." The "apprehension," he said, felt "far more political than military." Douglass threw himself into the election fray as a partisan Republican. The biggest enemy at that moment, he argued, were Northern Democrats. Douglass asserted that a vote for Democrats in the congressional elections was a vote for "Jefferson Davis and his rebel government." Instinctively impatient, Douglass urged Lincoln to abandon the grace period for Confederate "repentance" and proclaim immediate emancipation. Lincoln's Proclamation had given Douglass a new political voice as an American nationalist. "Liberty and country first," he wrote, "everything else afterward."[60] He had indeed found the new politics he had sought for a decade.

Douglass further took heart from reports he received about liberated slaves swarming into contraband camps established by the War Department around the rim of the South. A correspondent, H. Oscar, wrote to Douglass from Cairo, Illinois, located at the confluence of the Ohio and Mississippi Rivers, rejoicing that "it begins to look as though the jubilee sure enough had come in this country." The "old barracks" of the town were full of black refugees, yet "still they come." Every morning, a new contingent of freedpeople, men and women of all ages and all colors, appeared on the levee seeking shelter and asking about jobs and wages. The contrabands faced considerable white hostility, however, in the surrounding community; Oscar reported a rape of a black woman by three white men.[61]

Douglass also kept up a fervent correspondence about emancipation and a fund-raising campaign with his British friends. Constantly, his paper needed money to survive, and he received numerous small contributions throughout 1862 from Julia Crofts's network of supporters. In October Douglass wrote a public letter to his British and Irish friends, in which he gushed with new hope for the cause, gratitude for past financial and moral resources, and made an aggressive appeal for more money. Douglass became a one-man political-action committee for emancipation. He expressed special thanks for all the support over the years for the Underground Railroad, but as of September 22, he remarked, its "agents" were "out of employment." With Lincoln's Proclamation, Douglass assured his foreign readers, America had started the "first chapter of a new history." Now was the time for continued aid, said the editor with bills to pay and a thrilling new revolution to lead. "The end is not yet," he cautioned. "We are at best only at the beginning of the end." The following month, Douglass the cheerleader proclaimed the Preliminary Proclamation the nation's "moral bombshell" shaking everything into new forms. Rumors of slave insurrections in Virginia, he maintained, terrified the Confederate leadership and "would well nigh paralyze Lee and Cornwall Jackson" (Stonewall Jackson) in ensuing campaigns. The war propagandist had found a new argument, even a new sense of humor. Douglass falsely said he would "regret" such insurrections, even as he hoped they would be "formidable" if they must occur.[62]

The wait for January 1 was almost unbearable, especially when Douglass read Lincoln's annual message in December, in which he forthrightly appealed yet again for colonization to accompany emancipation, reminding the nation that he could not "make it better known than it already is that I strongly favor colonization." But so long conditioned for less than full measures of change from history or from Providence, Douglass journeyed to Boston for New Year's Day and a planned celebration like no other. A highbrow event took place at Boston's Music Hall, with many of New England's most famous literati in attendance, including Henry Wadsworth Longfellow, Oliver Wendell Holmes, Charles Eliot Norton, John Greenleaf Whittier, Edward Everett Hale, Francis Parkman, and Ralph Waldo Emerson. Harriet Beecher Stowe sat prominently in the balcony. Emerson read some original verses for the occasion; in a transcendent moment the throng of hundreds rhythmically called for Mrs. Stowe to stand and bow, to resounding cheers. Then an orchestra played Mendelssohn's *Hymn of Praise*, followed by a rousing rendition of Beethoven's Fifth Symphony. A day for "poetry and song" indeed, as Douglass had anticipated.[63]

But beginning at 10:00 a.m., a largely black-organized meeting assembled throughout the day, reaching approximately three thousand people, at the magnificent Tremont Temple. Presided over in the early hours by black Garrisonians William Cooper Nell and Charles Lenox Remond, the speeches, poetry, and singing were confidently joyous. Garrison himself attended the upper-crust event at the Music Hall, perhaps letting his old enemy from Rochester have that Tremont platform to himself. William Wells Brown, yet another old rival of Douglass's, delivered a rousing autobiographical tribute to the enterprise and self-reliance of former slaves all over the country. Douglass was the final speaker at the afternoon session. He alluded with irony to two years earlier when he and others had been driven from that same stage by a mob prepared to kill abolitionists. He honored the slaves of the South for their forbearance in not rising in insurrection and appealed for what he hoped would be the imminent enlistment of black men in the Union armies. On behalf of abolitionists he boasted that their warning delivered for decades was now coming to fruition in the "blood" of the moment, as he also predicted much more blood to come. Douglass soared, assuring the audience they had lived through a "period of darkness" into the "dawn of light." His final refrains were constantly punctuated by shouts of "Amen!" and "Bless the Lord!"[64]

After a break, the huge crowd grew even larger for the nighttime celebration and the anticipated news of Lincoln's signing the Final Proclamation. But a mood of anxiety and doubt set in throughout the hall as the evening hours crept by without the word. The organizers maintained a group of runners to and from the telegraph office in downtown Boston. They all awaited, as Douglass remembered, "the first flash of the electric wires." Their emotions danced between hope and fear. Would Lincoln indeed sign the wonderful decree? Would it be altered? Would there be some last-minute compromise in Washington or even with the Confederacy? Rumor and experience pushed back constantly against analysis and biblical expectation of the Jubilee. Amid all the restlessness Wells Brown and Douglass both got control of the audience and kept up a hopeful but strained rhetoric. "Every moment of waiting chilled our hopes," Douglass recalled years later. "Eight, nine, ten o'clock came and went, and still no word." With a "visible shadow" falling over the crowd, Douglass said, a man finally stepped hastily through the crowd and shouted, "It is coming! It is on the wires!" He was immediately followed by someone who tried to read some portion of the text of the Emancipation Proclamation, but was quickly drowned out by shouting and a "scene . . . wild and grand." In the next hour Douglass hugged perhaps more people than he had before in his entire life, some of whom were old enemies. That night there were no Garrisonian or anti-Garrisonian tears. An old preacher named Rue stood front and center with Douglass as they led the assembled in the anthem "Blow Ye the Trumpet, Blow" and repeated the verse "Sound the loud timbrel o'er Egypt's dark sea, / Jehovah hath triumphed, his people are free." According to witnesses, Douglass's baritone had never been in better form.[65]

Tremont Temple had been hired only until midnight. But at that hour most of the celebrants decided to reassemble at the Twelfth Baptist Church on Phillips Street in Beacon Hill, the black section of Boston, a twenty-minute walk away. Douglass and the revelers, singing, humming, shouting, walked out onto Tremont Street into a gentle, glistening snowfall to march to what all called the "Fugitive Slave's Church." What swirling memories transported them along only they could tell. At the church they were welcomed by its minister of many years, Leonard A. Grimes, who oversaw an all-night celebration of music and refreshments. "At Grimes's church," said Douglass, "we got into such a state of enthusiasm that almost everything seemed to be witty and appropriate to the occasion." Sometime near dawn, in exhausted jubilation, Douglass walked out of the church amid the quiet snowflakes and headed, bleary-eyed, to the train station. In *Life and Times* he remembered the meaning of that night with his own poetry: "It was not logic, but the trump of jubilee, which everybody wanted to hear. We were waiting and listening as for a bolt from the sky, which would rend the fetters of four millions of slaves; we were watching, as it were, by the dim light of the stars, for the dawn of a new day; we were longing for the answer to the agonizing prayers of centuries. Remembering those in bonds as bound with them, we wanted to join in the shout for freedom, and in the anthem of the redeemed." [66] At that moment, and for its duration, the cruel and apocalyptic war had become holy.

Chapter 19

MEN OF COLOR
TO ARMS!

During times of peace, the sons bury their fathers, but in war it is
the fathers who send their sons to the grave.

—HERODOTUS, *THE HISTORY*

In 1863, more than ever, the Civil War became a family affair for Frederick Douglass and his household with four unmarried adult children. Lewis and Charles Douglass, at the ages of twenty-two and eighteen, enlisted in the Fifty-Fourth Massachusetts Regiment in March, recruited personally by their father. "Charley, my youngest son was the first to put his name down as one of the company," Douglass wrote to Gerrit Smith with exuberance. By later that summer, Frederick Jr., age twenty-one, also at his father's behest, went to Mississippi, not as a soldier, but as a recruiter of black troops. There is no evidence that any of the sons had ever shouldered as much as a hunting rifle when growing up in western New York. But off to the war they went, and apparently willingly, abandoning earlier interests in emigration from the United States. Their father spoke and wrote proudly of their service and their bravery. "I have implored the imperiled nation to unchain against her foes, her powerful black hand," Douglass wrote forcefully on March 21, 1863, in his famous recruiting broadside, "Men of Color to Arms!" "Words are now useful only as they stimulate to blows." But Douglass's effusive public words urging young black men "to fly to arms, and smite with death the power that would bury the government and your liberty in the same hopeless grave," may have masked the private family anguish of a father recruiting his sons to go to war for their reasons as well as his own. It remained to be seen whose "manhood" was at stake in this family drama, the father's or the sons'.[1] We know precious little of what Anna

Douglass thought of seeing her sons march off to war where they might easily be enslaved or killed.

For Lewis and Charles in particular, their lives were forever altered by their military experience. Sending the middle son, Frederick, to the Deep South, though far more thrilling for him than staying at home, could only have been fraught with anguish as well.[2] Moreover, for most of 1862 and early 1863, the Douglasses' daughter, a disgruntled twenty-three-year-old Rosetta, sought independence by boarding in other cities with relatives and abolitionist families, seeking more education and teaching school.

All of Anna's children were getting out of the house; the Douglass family in its own way went to war. "I have been launched among strange people during the last six months," Rosetta wrote to her father in August 1862 from Salem, New Jersey, while living with Anna Douglass's brother Perry. Earlier, she had stayed in Philadelphia with the Dorsey family, where she said she felt "in bondage." Homesick and "gloomy," Rosetta seems to have hated Mrs. Dorsey's accusations that Douglass had sent her away to keep her from pursuing young men. In Salem, Rosetta complained of the same treatment: Uncle Perry and Aunt Lizzy both claimed she was "sassy and unruly," and that she became their boarder to cure her of "growing intimacy with men." Rosetta did find a teaching job, which she relished, reporting that her fifty students "all . . . appear to love me." By October she took extra odd jobs at knitting and embroidery.[3]

Rosetta's letters to her father exhibit a deep tenderness, a desperate desire to please, and the tensions in the Douglass household. She repeatedly thanked her father for the money he sent her and craved his affection, writing about their mutual loneliness: "I often think of your loneliness, for I well perceive the necessity of congenial companions. . . . I flatter myself if I were at home I might in a measure contribute to your happiness as well as to mother's." Then she observed the problem of the separate worlds of her parents through an impulse of family love: "I wish to be all you would have me be, and I wish also to do something to make mother happy and if both were interested in the same pursuits—it would be much easier for me to be just what I wish to be—a comfort to both parents." According to his daughter, Douglass had tried to instruct all his children in "uprightness and character." In apologetic tones, Rosetta admitted she had learned so much from her father. "Though I never said much when our table talks were going on, I made resolutions to follow your lessons." Rosetta did remain informed about war news; she also reported on visits from her restless brother Lewis, who was pursuing business. A business card survives, dated as early as 1860, labeled "L. H. & F. Douglass Jr., 'Groceries and Provisions,'" on 151 Buffalo Street, Rochester. Rosetta counseled her father not to "grow despondent" in waiting for emancipation day; she was always eager to receive the *Monthly*, read the editor's extraordinary exchange with Postmaster Blair about colonization with keen interest, and by December 28, 1862, longingly wished to read the newspaper reports of the big meeting in Boston on January 1.[4]

One additional part-time guest in the Douglass home did not leave as often as Anna Douglass might have wished. For many summers between the late 1850s and 1872, Ottilie Assing came to Rochester and stayed in the house as Frederick's intellectual and emotional companion. She lived most of the year in Hoboken, New Jersey, and corresponded with her friend regularly. Assing tried futilely to reshape Douglass's views on various subjects, especially religion, even as she parroted so much of his own rhetoric in essays for her German readers. How this ménage à trois functioned for so long still remains, in part, a mystery. Assing lived in Rochester for several months at a time, assisting Douglass with the newspaper and writing her own columns for *Morgenblatt.* He was on the road lecturing for long periods when Assing may have gone back to New Jersey.

Assing's biographer suggests that the two women reached some kind of "truce" by which the arrangement endured. Although Assing sipped tea occasionally with Mrs. Douglass, she held Anna in utter contempt, disrespecting her lack of education, and even at times privately denigrating her role as homemaker. As Leigh Fought has written, Assing's annual visits were intrusions on the household, to say the least. In letters to Douglass, Assing referred to Anna as "border state," as the misfitted wife and unnatural impediment in the way of the German woman's designs and alternative views of love and marriage. Assing hoped that once the war ended, a separation or divorce might finally happen and she might be able to walk tall as the rightful "Mrs. Douglass."[5] Assing and her host were probably lovers, and his response was surely as responsible as her pursuit. But she would be sorely disappointed on the notion of severing the marriage.

"Perhaps no other home received under its roof a more varied class of people than did our home," wrote Rosetta in an understatement while reminiscing about her mother. Rosetta honored her mother for being frugal, for her great skill as a housekeeper. But as Rosetta pursued a world beyond Rochester, Anna Douglass retreated into her own largely closed world and took charge at home. Anna rebelled in her own way. If a visitor expressed something disagreeable about the house or about Anna herself, that person might be "vigorously repelled," remembered the daughter, "in a manner more forceful than the said party would deem her capable of." How often this may have happened to the righteously opinionated Assing, her mind and demeanor preoccupied by literary imagination and with Anna's husband, we can only guess. Anna lived daily life with extreme "reserve," said Rosetta. "She could not be known all at once, she had to be studied."[6] Such a study repelled Assing, and Douglass enabled the intruder.

Despite all these exciting changes and domestic troubles in the Douglass household, kept entirely hidden in the writer's autobiographies, the winter and spring of 1863 was a time for public glory, a time to reap all the possibilities of what Douglass called "the greatest event of the century"—the Emancipation Proclamation and the sacred history that flowed from it. The Final Proclamation included two significant changes from the Preliminary: it contained no provisions for colonization, and it called for the recruitment of black men into the Union armed forces. The "destiny" of the American nation had changed forever, Douglass argued. On January 1, the "national ship" would now "swing round, her towering sails . . . swelled by the trade winds of the Almighty and she will either be wafted off gloriously to the open sea . . . or furiously driven by rebellious gales upon the sharp and flinty rocks only to mark the place of danger to . . . aftercoming voyages."[7] Douglass bet on the glorious open sea and an Almighty on the side of freedom.

In January and much of February 1863 Douglass traveled more than two thousand miles from Boston to Chicago and many places in between, attending Jubilee meetings, cautiously anticipating the new war, the new history made possible by the emancipation. His new standard speech was a tour de force of apocalypticism, moral philosophy, and a thunderous appeal for the enlistment of blacks in the army with equal status. The Proclamation, even with its limitations (freeing slaves only in the Confederate states or in occupied areas), brought about a world-historical moment, "a complete revolution in the position of a nation." The republic was undergoing a second founding, and Douglass felt more than ready to be one of its fathers. An amazing change was under way, argued Douglass, not only for blacks and for the nation, but for "justice throughout the world." "We are all liberated by this Proclamation," declared the unusually joyous orator. "Everybody is liberated. The white man is liberated, the black man is liberated, the brave men now fighting the battles . . . are now liberated."[8] The old nation might now be bludgeoned into ruin, and a new one imagined.

Emancipation prompted from Douglass an effusion of millennial faith and expressions of the doctrine of progress. As Michael Walzer has argued, the Jewish and Christian sense of Exodus, of a possible liberation through and after affliction and slavery, has been so compelling over time because it is based essentially on a promise. The Exodus story is both so powerful and so adaptable because it is not an account of miracles, of merely waiting for God's intercessions. God will choose moments to intervene, but the great Exodus narrative gets "God's people marching," writes Walzer, "through the world to a better place in it." Hence, the Old Testament story can be such a source of "radical hope" if people possess sufficient faith; they can march off with expectation that "the world is not all Egypt." Douglass believed events gave evidence that a "moral chemistry" and an interventionist God now drove history forward. He had rehearsed for this moment for more than twenty years; a prophet issues the warnings and must be ready to reap history's results. Words, faith, inspiration, and an abiding pathos, argues Abraham Heschel, are the prophetic stock-in-trade. A prophet spares no piety; he is an "assaulter of the mind." The words of a true prophet, says Heschel, are "a scream in the night" rooted in a sense of history.[9] And timing may be all. With a reasoned scream, Douglass discerned that Babylon might now be falling.

"I believe in the millennium, the final perfection of the race," declared Douglass in his post–January 1 speech, "and hail this Proclamation, though rung out under the goading lash of a stern military necessity." He counseled his large crowds not to dwell on the pronouncement's imperfections. "Men may see in it only as a military necessity. To me it has a higher significance. It is a grand moral necessity." Both moralist and humorist, he entertained as he preached. The mixture of God and history should startle or shock, he argued. "A great truth breaks upon the vision of some early riser," said Douglass, "and straightaway he wakes up the drowsy world with the announcement of the day and the work. Sleepy people don't like to be disturbed. They hate the troubler . . . draw their curtains . . . turn their backs to the light." A century later, James Baldwin may have been channeling Douglass as he observed a new crisis over race and freedom. When Americans reflect on history, Baldwin wrote, "words are mostly used to cover the sleeper, not to wake him up." Emancipation in the midst of all-out war was the kind of history that awakened all sleepers. Proof of progress now seemed palpable everywhere. Douglass kept a New York Cooper Institute audience laughing about signs of progress. Only a hundred years ago, some Irish, he said, exploiting common prejudices, "thought that the proper way

Frederick Douglass, Hillsdale, Michigan, January 21, 1863. Edwin Burke Ives and Reuben L. Andrews photographers, carte de visite.

to attach a horse to a plow was by the tail. It seemed to them that was what the tail was made for." Two hundred years back in time some Christians in the West Indies "thought it a sin to baptize persons of color who were slaves" because they were property. More recently, he said, right in New England, an older woman who might be a "little eccentric" and especially "gifted . . . stood a smart chance of being hanged as a witch." And just the last few years demonstrated the recent progress that all knew well. "Good old John Brown was a mad man at Harpers Ferry," pronounced Douglass. "Two years pass away, and the nation is as mad as he is." [10]

Measuring progress now became a daily affair. The most revolutionary sign of all was the impending enlistment of black soldiers in the Union army. The "paper Proclamation" would thus "be made iron, lead, and fire." Douglass demanded "fair play" for black troops, equality in provisions, ranks, and respect. He insisted that they would not only fight, but "fight with vengeance." He chided whites to "stop calling them 'n__rs,' and call them soldiers." "Give them a chance!" he shouted, then led the audience in repeating the chant with vigor: "Give them a chance!" The black soldier would be the redemptive agent of the apocalyptic war. "You have wronged us long and wronged us greatly," Douglass said as though speaking to the nation, "but it is not yet too late to retrieve the past. We still stand ready to serve you, and will do it with a will, at the first sound of your war trumpet." [11] In 1863, Douglass did not wait to hear anyone else's trumpet.

Massachusetts led the way in the cause of black enlistment. Its governor, John Andrew, was a staunch antislavery Republican and worked vigorously to convince the Lincoln administration to allow him to mobilize black troops. In January 1863, he received authorization from Secretary of War Edwin Stanton to recruit a regiment. Stanton promised equal pay and treatment for black soldiers but denied Andrew's request for black commissioned officers. Although Stanton did not keep all his promises, and the denial of officer's rank caused deep resentments, the recruiting began for the famous Fifty-Fourth Massachusetts Infantry Regiment. The Massachusetts legislature paid for recruiters and to transport troops, and Andrew called on the wealthy Boston abolitionist George Luther Stearns to direct the recruiting. For the remainder of the war Stearns devoted himself and a fair portion of his fortune to the cause of black enlistment. Stearns quickly established recruiting posts all across the North and enlisted as agents a who's who of black abolitionists: Douglass, Charles Lenox Remond, John Mercer Langston, William Wells Brown, Henry Highland Garnet, and Martin Delany (friends, but mostly Douglass's rivals). Stearns paid Douglass's expenses at $10 per week, less than what the editor thought his services were worth; although he uttered no public objection, he did complain privately about his compensation. Douglass threw himself into recruiting with electric energy; Massachusetts, he declared, was "not only the most direct way to the heart of our slaveholding rebellion, but she is the colored man's way to . . . political and civil liberty." The historic link between soldiering and citizenship had never before been given such an open door; Douglass's task was to convince black men to march through it. [12]

And march they did. The Fifty-Fourth Massachusetts was a national black regiment, with members from fifteen Northern states, all four border states, five Confederate states, and some from Canada and the West Indies. They were overwhelmingly freeborn blacks, although at least thirty men in the regiment's ranks were former slaves. The men of the Fifty-Fourth formed a remarkable cross section of working-class black life in America. Fifty-one barbers, thirty-eight seamen, thirty-four waiters, twenty-seven boatmen, twenty-four teamsters, and two peddlers signed up. The ranks included one cabinetmaker, a dentist, and a druggist. Five called themselves students, and only one preacher enlisted among the original one thousand

and seven. Twenty-seven strong joined in New Bedford, Massachusetts; one of their number, a bright and literate twenty-six-year-old seaman named James H. Gooding, would write a series of weekly letters to the hometown newspaper, providing that community a rich record of the regiment's story, until his death after five months at Andersonville prison in Georgia in July 1864. James Caldwell, the grandson of Sojourner Truth, enlisted from Battle Creek, Michigan. Thirty-eight men over forty years old served in the regiment, the oldest of whom, at forty-six, was Peter Vogelsang, a clerk from Brooklyn, New York. The recruits underwent a rigorous medical examination, and doctors rejected nearly one out of three men.[13]

Douglass first met with Stearns in late February; they launched their frantic crusade together. Within days, Douglass issued his broadside, "Men of Color to Arms!" Stearns's correspondence with Douglass took on a breathless quality as he (Stearns) tallied the numbers by town and region and gave instructions about the price to pay for transport ("can send in second class cars at $3 each"), which railroads were cooperating with free fares and which were hostile. At some junctions they had constant "fear of disturbance." No one in America, even in modestly antislavery upstate New York, had ever seen anything like this: groups of boisterous black men, often singing, riding the cars and strutting through train stations on their way to take up arms for their country. Charles Douglass proudly remembered having "the honor of being the first to enroll at Rochester for the 54 Mass. Inf. Feb. 9, 1863." Soldiers never forget those dates. Similarly, his older brother Lewis wrote with equal pride to his sweetheart, Amelia Loguen, in late March that he had been appointed a noncommissioned sergeant major. He described the seventeen recruits with whom he left Syracuse as *his men*. They rode the "first class cars," and "on the way to Binghamton my men amused themselves by singing John Brown." Lewis's chest swelled as he wrote from camp, wearing his new uniform. He felt respected and a sense of honor as never before. "I have enlisted for three years or during the war," he told Amelia. "I am thought a good deal of here."[14]

By mid-April Douglass had sent more than one hundred men off to Readville, Massachusetts, just outside Boston, the training site of the Fifty-Fourth. He barnstormed the cities and towns of western New York and the Hudson valley, as well as made special trips to New York City and Philadelphia to address large recruiting meetings. It is a telling scene to imagine Douglass standing before gatherings of blacks, exhorting his people to grasp the opportunity to get guns and uniforms and go fight. Many of these people had heard Douglass before in a church or a hall, but never on this subject.

Douglass's listeners were wary and sometimes openly distrustful. Would black soldiers really be treated fairly in the Union army? What would happen if they got sick or were captured? Who would lead them? Men born free in the North had never been in the slave states of the South. For people who had lived lives of skepticism or outright contempt for the federal government, why should they trust Douglass's promises? At times, though, the great orator's appeals to patriotism, flag, and self-interest must have been irresistible. At the end of some of his recruiting speeches he broke into song and led the assembled in "John Brown's Body," the early versions of which contained the lyrics: "He's gone to be a soldier in the army of the Lord . . . / His soul's marching on / John Brown's knapsack is strapped upon his back / His soul's marching on!" Douglass invited his audiences to participate, dream, and sing in a story now both old and new. Douglass recruited twenty-five men in Syracuse, and twenty-three more followed him away from Glens Falls, Little Falls, and Canajoharie; the orator personally escorted some of the volunteers all the way to the Fifty-Fourth's encampment in Readville. One company, unable to secure rail transport, walked 360 miles from Elmira, New York, to Boston. In such small black communities this recruitment comprised a relative exodus of men and left emotions sizzling as well as troubled. In some places Douglass was less successful— the war had caused near full employment, even among blacks. Privately, Douglass admitted to some hesitation about black enlistment due to the denial of officer's status, but for the moment, he told Gerrit Smith, blacks "should hail the opportunity of getting on the United States uniform as a very great advance." [15]

Publicly, Douglass counseled, "Action! Action! not criticism . . . words are now useful only as they stimulate to blows." "Men of Color to Arms!" was mass-produced across the North. Published in a different version as an editorial in the March 1863 issue of the *Monthly*, the broadside was distinctively Douglass's own. Despite his call to martial action, rhetoric, as always, remained his weapon. He called black men to service almost as an archangel, a Gabriel with trumpet, delivering an oracle, calling men to step forward and join this epic of their own liberation. Douglass crafted the broadside in terse pronouncements: "TO ARMS! TO ARMS! NOW OR NEVER. This is our golden moment!" A model of other such broadsides, the recruiting poster was a manifesto of martial spirit and manliness. He

"Men of Color to Arms!" Broadside by Frederick Douglass,
March 1863, widely mass-produced in many sizes, including a
giant banner that hung over a street in Philadelphia.

employed the word "manhood" four times and made the case for enlistment as one of bravery versus cowardice. Douglass asked black men to offer their selfless blood for country, family, and their future "Citizenship and Equality." Although Douglass would never lead the volunteers on actual battlefields (his son Lewis did), it was as if the recruiting speeches allowed him to deliver his own brand of a St. Crispin's Day speech: "This story shall the good man teach his son," declares Henry V. ". . . We few, we happy few, we band of brothers; / For he today that sheds his blood with me / Shall be my brother." In the broadside and in recruiting speeches, Douglass addressed his audiences as "Brothers and Fathers"; the war had become a special affair of black fraternity and manhood.[16]

In his more discursive editorial, Douglass personalized the appeal, asking directly for the potential soldiers' trust in his promises of equal "wages . . . rations . . . equipments" due to his "twenty years of unswerving devotion" to the cause of abolition. "This is your hour and mine." He invoked not only the history of Massachusetts' antislavery activism, but especially the great black heroes. "Remember Denmark Vesey of Charleston; remember Nathaniel Turner of Southampton; remember Shields Green and Copeland, who followed noble John Brown, and fell as glorious martyrs." He reached for their hearts. "The day dawns; the morning star is bright upon the horizon!" sang the messenger. "The iron gate of our prison stands half open. One gallant rush from the North will fling it wide open, while four millions of our brothers and sisters shall march out into liberty." [17] Here was a biblical vision of a Jubilee, and a prison metaphor as powerful as any others in his writing.

At every stop on the recruiting tour Douglass offered volunteers an elaborate list of reasons to enlist, both practical and emotionally stirring. The practical ends included self-defense through learning the "use of arms"; self-respect by demonstrating the courage and manhood of blacks; self-involvement by making their own history and destiny; and finally, the ultimate act of self-interest—retribution against slaveholders on behalf of their race. Recruiting provided Douglass an enhanced opportunity to vent his own rage against slaveholders; he could now invite young men to do the work of slaying them. The long-awaited chance had arrived: "Now the government has given authority to . . . black men to shoulder a musket and go down and kill white rebels." [18] For so long he had yearned for such sanctioned killing of slaveholders. Like any clever propagandist, though, he kept his image of the enemy simple, never bothering to acknowledge that most Southern soldiers were non-slaveholders.

Finally, Douglass demanded that black men strike the blow for citizenship rights. "To fight for the Government in this tremendous war," Douglass claimed, "is . . . to fight for nationality and for a place with all other classes of our fellow citizens." He tried to sow the deepest seeds of nationalism in his recruits by linking black patriots of the Civil War with their white counterparts in the American Revolution: "The white man's soul was tried in 1776," wrote Douglass, "the black man's is tried in 1863. The first stood the test, and is received as genuine—so may the last." Douglass boldly promised great dividends from sacrifice. He contended that once a black man could "get upon his person the brass letters U.S. . . . , an eagle on his button, and a musket on his shoulder, and bullets in his pocket, there is no power on earth . . . which can deny that he has earned the right of citizenship in the United States." [19] Douglass advocated a gallant rush of black men into uniform; they were now shining symbols, liberating warriors who alone made suffering meaningful. Transforming this conflict into a black peoples' war demanded such great leaps of faith, even as sober history in retrospect tells us that sweet reason, moral truth, and blood sacrifice by themselves have never defeated racism.

Lewis and Charles certainly caught the spirit their father preached. Lewis wrote with pride from Camp Meigs about how the men of the Fifty-Fourth were becoming "proficient in the manual of arms." With an older brother's protective condescension, he observed that "Charley," in charge of a company, needed to learn how "to boss his men around." Lewis also celebrated how the men were "kicking up their heels" as "cullud persons . . . laughing in 'our' peculiar style." For good reason, though, Lewis was worried about his brother. In early May the youthful Charles got into an altercation with another soldier and had to be restrained. Worse, Charles was sick in the hospital within a week of the regiment's departure for the South and would be left behind in camp. This began a long pattern of illness, disappointment, and complaint by Charles. On July 6, with his regiment at the front in the sea islands of South Carolina, Charles wrote to his father about yet another altercation he'd experienced with an Irishman who called him a "black nigger" on a street in Boston. "I felt as though I could whip a dozen Irish," said the immature eighteen-year-old soldier boy who felt lost and abused in his troubled adventure.[20]

The Douglass boys' father came for day visits at Camp Meigs during two consecutive weeks in May and was "much pleased" at Lewis's appearance. According to one observer, during a visit Douglass gave "one of his . . . soul-stirring addresses" to the assembled troops. Anna and Rosetta also visited for at least a week in May, staying with a friend in Boston, and coming out to the camp to watch the troops train every day. This was an extraordinary trip for Anna; it must have been a special, if bittersweet, joy for her to join in the festival of gawking tourists who went to watch the black men march and perform with rifles. Above all, Lewis fed his beloved Amelia Loguen a steady diet of patriotism and florid soldierly devotion. He had read his father's prose: "Remember that if I fall that it is in the cause of humanity," he told his girl in waiting, "that I am striking a blow for the welfare of the most abused and despised race on the face of the earth." Lewis dwelt on his possible death, but with a wide-eyed bravado. "Do not think of me enduring hardships, do not think of me grappling with that non-respecter of persons Death! Think of me as aiding the glorious work of bursting loose those chains which keep the husbands, wives, children, lovers and friends, of millions asunder, as aiding to overthrow a system . . . which degrades millions of human beings." Eager to go South, Lewis sent Amelia his photograph, showing him in his blue uniform, and begged her "never to be ashamed of it."[21] The Union army had no more devoted soldier, especially before seeing combat.

For two and a half months in the spring of 1863, the Fifty-Fourth Regiment slowly but surely assembled at Camp Meigs. As their commander, Governor Andrew personally selected Robert Gould Shaw, the twenty-five-year-old son of a wealthy New York–Boston family. His parents, Francis George and Sarah Blake Shaw, were radical abolitionists. A child of fortune, Shaw had traveled to Europe for education as a teenager and attended Harvard from 1856 to 1859, but quit before graduating. In his time abroad the youthful Shaw had been a profligate, indulgent party boy and, contrary to his parents, indifferent to if not contemptuous of abolitionism. At the outbreak of the war, bored in a job given him by an uncle in a mercantile business, Shaw enlisted in the Seventh New York militia, and then in the Second Massachusetts, in which he served as a first lieutenant and fought in the battles of Winchester, Cedar Mountain, and Antietam in 1862. At first Shaw turned down the command of the Fifty-Fourth Massachusetts; but war and leadership had matured him and he quickly changed his mind and accepted the challenge. In one of his long letters to his father from the front, Shaw described the scene around him on the night after the horror at Antietam: "At last, night came on . . . all was quiet. The crickets chirped, and the frogs croaked, just as if nothing unusual had happened all day long, and presently the stars came out bright, and we lay down among the dead, and slept soundly until daylight. There were twenty dead bodies within a rod of me." Once promoted to colonel, Shaw took to his new appointment commanding the black regiment with genuine zeal; when he barked out orders, his matured voice carried the grim weight of those scenes at Antietam. The training at Readville was at times notoriously tough and the discipline rigid.[22]

By the middle of May the regiment's ranks were full. On May 18, several special train cars carried a host of dignitaries on the Providence and Boston line down to Readville for the Fifty-Fourth's presentation of colors. Douglass joined his old disaffected mentors William Lloyd Garrison and Wendell Phillips, among numerous Boston abolitionists. Whether the two rival editors actually had much conversation is not recorded; Garrison had now become a robust supporter of the war effort and Lincoln's Proclamation, an irony Douglass enjoyed. With the entire regiment drawn up in ranks and a large crowd watching, Governor Andrew delivered a long, deeply Christian speech. As he presented to Shaw the regimental and American flags, Andrew instructed the men in their "sacred charge." The whole world would be watching them vindicate their race. They were to fight not merely for state and country, but for humanity and for "the religion of our Lord itself." Their mission would only "fail when the last patriot, the last philanthropist, and the last Christian shall have tasted death." In words oft quoted since in melodramatic depictions of this famous regiment's destiny, the governor declared the highest stakes: "I know not, Mr. Commander, where, in all human history, to any given thousand men in arms there has been committed a work at once so proud, so precious, so full of hope and glory as the work committed to you." The stakes were high; in camp, Lewis Douglass wondered again after the ceremony about whether he would ever come home alive, adding tersely that the governor would never "have reason to regret the steps he has taken in raising the regiment." [23] War stories begin but rarely end with flag ceremonies.

On May 28, the regiment arrived early in the morning in Boston for their public departure for South Carolina. Led by a spritely band and with Shaw on horseback at their lead, the men of the Fifty-Fourth marched a circuitous route of Boston streets. Thousands lined the route, cheering and waving flags. As the regiment passed the house of Wendell Phillips, Garrison stood on its balcony, his hand resting on a bust of John Brown. As they passed 44 Beacon Street, with its balcony graced by Shaw's mother, four sisters, and newly married wife, Annie, Shaw halted and kissed his sword. He had learned theater and romance as well as war. The troops turned left into Boston Common at Charles Street and formally paraded for nearly an hour in front of a viewing stand. As huge crowds of people roared huzzahs on all sides, some waving handkerchiefs and others a souvenir containing the Byron quote "Those who would be free, themselves must strike the first blow," the Fifty-Fourth exited the Common and marched to the Battery Wharf, with the band playing "John Brown's Body." [24]

No one who witnessed this event would ever forget what they saw that day: a thousand smartly stepping black men with Enfield rifles, leaning forward gracefully, moving as one body toward history, heroism, and death to prove to their slaveholding country that they were indeed truly men. The witnesses were privileged to see not only what would become an iconic moment of American military history, but a spectacular, if genuinely tragic, illustration of both the agony and the potential transcendence of this Second

Revolution. Some family members and friends mingled with the soldiers at the dock as they prepared to board the big new steamer *De Molay.* Douglass himself joined the state's adjutant general, William Schouler, and a few others on board the ship and rode with the men out until it had almost cleared Boston Harbor. At nearly dusk, the father-civilian could go no farther, said his emotional farewells to his son Lewis, as well as to many other men he had recruited, and was assisted down onto a tugboat that returned him to shore.[25] Each man on that ship had his own private joys and fears to ponder. As Frederick and Lewis Douglass watched each other fade into the harbor's dimming light, their minds and hearts swelled with the unspeakable love and dreadful anxiety that war creates in fathers and sons. The great man of words left us no statement of his thoughts that memorable night.

On June 3, the *De Molay* arrived in the vicinity of Hilton Head Island and made its way up the Port Royal inlet. Early on the morning of June 4, the regiment came ashore in Beaufort, South Carolina, a beautiful town now occupied by Union forces and officials. The men of the Fifty-Fourth spent several days bivouacked at Beaufort, now a teeming depot of war, working essentially as laborers. Lewis reveled that in this hub of military activity he met not only Robert Smalls, the famous former slave who had stolen and piloted a Confederate boat out of Charleston to freedom, but Harriet Tubman herself, who, as Lewis put it, "is a captain of a group of men who pilot the Union forces into the enemy's country." Soon the regiment was dispatched to St. Simons Island on the Georgia coast, where they became embroiled in a brutal and controversial attack on the town of Darien. The Fifty-Fourth, against Shaw's vehement protests, were ordered to destroy and burn houses and resources in the town. Lewis tried to write soberly about such duty but failed. They "could discover no enemy," he reported, and lifted a fortune in goods from private houses. "The women we left after burning every building or shelter in the place to the ground. I felt a little sympathy for the feminines." Southern newspapers called the Fifty-Fourth Massachusetts "accursed Yankee vandals" and "cowardly . . . negro thieves."[26]

The Fifty-Fourth's young commander chafed to get his men into combat next to white troops to prove their skill and bravery. The regiment spent at least three weeks encamped on St. Simons, with rations dwindling, and morale damaged by bizarre rumors that the government was going to take their rifles away and arm them only with pikes. Finally, on July 9–11, they were transported to James Island at Charleston Harbor. Union forces under General Quincy A. Gillmore began a constant bombardment of Fort Wag-

ner, which guarded the entrance to the harbor and therefore to the prize itself, Charleston. While on picket duty at dawn on July 16, the Fifty-Fourth
was frontally attacked by approximately nine hundred Confederates. They
had to retreat, but ultimately held their ground valiantly in this their first
combat action. On that day they lost fourteen killed, eighteen wounded,
and thirteen missing. Lewis survived unhurt. Shaw was ordered to bring
his men as quickly as possible across mudflats and swamps for an impending infantry assault on Battery Wagner, an impregnable, well-armed fortress built of palmetto logs, stone, sand dunes, and abatis near the northern
tip of Morris Island, with Fort Sumter and the mouth of the great harbor
looming behind it.[27]

Marching for eight hours overnight, often in a relentless thunderstorm,
on wooden planks and in swamp water to their knees, the regiment reached
a safe open beach where they rested. By the night of the seventeenth a
steamer ferried them across an inlet onto Morris Island, where they could
see their challenge. Asked if he wanted his men to lead the assault Shaw
gladly assented. One of Gillmore's generals was heard to say, "Put those
d__d negroes from Massachusetts in advance, we may as well get rid of
them, one time or another." Shaw looked at his exhausted, hungry, but determined men and, in the early evening of July 18, at about six hundred
yards from the fort, ordered the black soldiers to form two lines of battle,
fix bayonets, and lie on the sand. With the sound of the ocean waves lap-
ping up just to their right, the men scratched notes and letters, told one
another where and to whom to send them if they died, and prepared for
their hour of truth. Shaw said to his second-in-command, Ned Hallowell,
"I shall go in advance of the men with the National Flag. . . . It will give the
men something to rally round. We shall take the fort or die there." Shaw
stepped out front at about 7:45 p.m. and gave an order with a firm voice:
"Move in quick time until within a hundred yards of the fort, then double
quick and charge!" His men shouted a war cry and rose to their feet as Shaw
turned, drew his sword, and cried, "Forward!" Many white soldiers in the
other thirteen regiments that had assembled for the attack, as well as some
Northern journalists standing off on a sand dune, cheered with respect as
the black men led the way.[28]

As darkness fell and Shaw and the first members of the unit came close
to the fort's guns, Confederates opened a horrifyingly destructive fire.
Men screamed, spun, and fell dead and wounded all around into potholes
caused by earlier artillery fire, and into the seawater of a moat immedi-

ately beneath the parapet. Somehow Shaw and some men trailing him, including Lewis Douglass (survivors remembered hearing his booming voice urging his fellows on), clambered up onto the parapet. Men saw Shaw wildly waving his sword and exhorting them on; he was hit as he leaped into the fort. Nearly half the regiment made it into the fort, fought hand to hand with Confederates, stabbing and smashing one another with rifle butts and bayonets. The Fifty-Fourth held the fort's southeast salient for a short, thrilling time before being driven out and back into the darkness and carnage of the beach and ocean waves. It was all over in a little more than one frightful hour. "Our men fell like grass before a sickle," one surviving officer recounted. But they had performed the immortal "one gallant rush" Douglass had called them to deliver. Of the 600 members of the regiment who stormed across the beach, 272 were officially killed, wounded, or captured among the more than 1,500 Union troops who fell that night.[29]

Miraculously, Lewis made it out of the fight alive. Less than forty-eight hours later, still on Morris Island, he wrote to Amelia with a chastened but remarkable spirit: "Not a man flinched. Men fell all around me. A shell would explode and clear a space twenty feet, our men would close up again." Shocked but determined, Lewis offered a common sentiment of soldiers down through the ages who had seen the hell of war. "How I got out of that fight I cannot tell, but I am here. . . . Remember if I die I die in a good cause. I wish we had a hundred thousand colored troops we would put an end to this war." That same night, Lewis wrote to his parents to assure them he was among the lucky. "I cannot write in full," he reported, still expecting counterattacks and listening to shells fly overhead. "We made the most desperate charge of the war on Fort Wagner," he said, Douglass likely reading the letter aloud to Anna, "losing in killed, wounded and missing three hundred of our men. The splendid Fifty-Fourth is cut to pieces." Lewis reported the desperate camp myth that Shaw was only wounded and a prisoner, and that all other officers except eight were lost. "I had my sword sheath blown away while on the parapet of the Fort. The grape and canister shell . . . swept us down like chaff, still our men went on and on, and had we been properly supported we would have held the fort, but the white troops could not be made to come up." Lewis signed off in a terrible, withering expression of why he had followed his father's call to go to war: "Good bye to all. If I die tonight I will not die a coward. Good bye." The elder Douglass printed the letter in the August *Monthly* without comment.[30] Sometimes

Lewis H. Douglass, Fifty-Fourth
Massachusetts Infantry Regiment, c. 1863.

the great man's silence, though frustrating, possessed its own eloquence. The profound heroism of Fort Wagner was best left to an eyewitness Douglass, the fortunate son still alive in the marshes and blistering heat of Morris Island.

Soon Lewis, like multitudes all across the North, would know that Shaw had been thrown with some of his men into a mass grave in the sand in front of Fort Wagner. Shaw became an instantaneous patrician martyr for the cause of black freedom; over time, in poetry, music, and bronze, he emerged as an iconic symbol of the emancipationist memory of the Civil War.[31] The siege of Charleston would continue for another year and a half. Survival from wounds was only one crisis the men of the Fifty-Fourth and all other black soldiers faced that summer. They now fought, suffered from disease, and died under the weight of brutal discriminations.

In June 1863, the War Department added insult to injury in its treatment of black soldiers. To the denial of commissions, it added the policy of unequal pay. White privates were paid $13 per month, while blacks were to receive $10, from which $3 would be deducted to cover the expense of clothing.

Such a policy was shabbily justified on the grounds that the Militia Act of 1862 had empowered the president to enlist black troops at a standard of $10; previous solemn pledges of equality by Secretary of War Stanton, Governor Andrew, and numerous generals and recruiting agents such as Douglass were simply disregarded.[32]

As black enlistment moved into the border states and the Deep South, resistance to unequal pay swelled. Whole units of black troops began to refuse pay altogether while it remained unequal; some regiments, including the Fifty-Fourth Massachusetts, accepted no wages at all well into 1864. This bitter reality caused desperate problems for impoverished black families back home in Northern communities and in freedmen's camps. Noncommissioned officers were especially angered when they realized that the highest-ranking black sergeant (such as Lewis Douglass) earned less than a white private. Letters and petitions from outraged black soldiers poured into the offices of Stanton, Lincoln, and state governors (especially Andrew). James Gooding, a corporal in the Fifty-Fourth, wrote an especially eloquent appeal to the president in September. Gooding told Lincoln that he and his comrades had been "obedient . . . , patient, and solid as a wall." "Now your Excellency," he wrote with the sacrifice at Fort Wagner in mind, "we have done a Soldier's Duty, Why can't we have a Soldier's pay?" Sergeant George E. Stephens, a Philadelphian, became a kind of official spokesman for the men of the Fifty-Fourth in his regular letters to the weekly *Anglo-African*. In early August 1863, he denounced unequal pay as the "Lincoln despotism." Anger erupted into violent confrontations between officers and enlisted men, insubordination, and genuine mutiny in the Fifty-Fourth and many other regiments by early 1864. Indeed, some protests ended in courts-martial in some units and executions by firing squads for refusal to perform duty without equal pay.[33]

These direct appeals to the highest power spoke of the anguish of betrayal and deprivation, as well as the spirit of citizenship. The situation caused Douglass "deep sadness and discouragement." In a pattern so old and agonizing, history once again giveth profound change while racism waited in the wings and taketh it back. Douglass eventually found the words to express such agony: "It really seems that nothing of justice, liberty or humanity can come to us except through tears and blood."[34]

Prior to the government's enactment of the unequal-pay policy, Douglass had steadfastly maintained that blacks should enlist despite the denial of commissions. Although ambivalent, he was ready to reconcile the inequality with the old argument that blacks faced two enemies—Southern slavery and Northern racism. "We shall be fighting a double battle," he said repeatedly, "against slavery at the South and against prejudice and prescription at the North." Blacks should not let one enemy prevent them from thwarting or destroying the other. They should "expect annoyance, but let no man hold back on this account. . . . A half loaf is better than no loaf."[35] But by midsummer 1863, the struggle was no longer a mere annoyance and the word-master recruiter knew it.

The idea of a "double battle" formed a constant theme in Douglass's wartime thought. George Stearns employed the same notion, persistently arguing to young volunteers, "You must fight . . . to obtain the right to fight on terms of equality." But for men who bought into the argument initially, the bold-faced, flagrant character of the inequality they faced at the front made it impossible to abide while risking their lives for a vague hope of justice later. Douglass had admitted in April speeches that black enlistment had come about by a "tardy, back-door manner" and that his own "blood boiled at the discriminations," even as he urged black men to join up.[36]

On July 6, in Philadelphia, at a rally where he made a last attempt to reconcile enlistment with discrimination, Douglass tried to chart a pragmatic course. But he found tiptoeing around the inequality issue no longer tenable; few men came forward from the huge crowd of five thousand in National Hall. The appalling casualty numbers from the Battle of Gettysburg, fought only ninety miles west of Philadelphia, had reached the audience by the time Douglass addressed them. Only a week later, draft riots broke out in New York City, in which at least a dozen blacks were murdered and many more injured. Douglass was still in Philadelphia, working among black troops at the huge Camp William Penn, when the New York violence began. He managed, with the aid of a friend, probably Ottilie Assing, to travel by train through Newark and New York to the Hudson River Railroad and on to Rochester, narrowly escaping rampaging mobs. Douglass had faced many violent mobs before, but these, he recollected, were "something more and something worse. . . . They were the fire of the enemy opened in the rear of the loyal army." These were mobs not merely throwing brickbats; they were intent on lynching black people. Perhaps most disheartening of all, the Confederate secretary of war, James A. Seddon, had ordered the death penalty for black soldiers taken as prisoners, followed by the Confederate Congress's authorization for treating captured blacks and their white officers as insurrectionists,

*Camp William Penn, Philadelphia, Pennsylvania, late 1863, Eighty-
Eighth Pennsylvania Regiment. Douglass spoke and recruited here;
the camp was a rendezvous for United States Colored Troops units,
near the North Pennsylvania Railroad. Stereo photograph.*

thus subject to death.[37] Thus 1863 was indeed a year of revolution and
counterrevolution.

The Union government's lack of response to these inhumane policies
angered Douglass even further. Sometime in late July, after the news from
Fort Wagner, he penned two editorials in which he attacked Lincoln's silence on the killings of black prisoners and the threats of their enslavement.
He now had to square his own son's heroism and that of his comrades, dead
and alive, with Confederate, and apparently federal, disregard for their very
humanity. "The slaughter of blacks taken as captives," wrote an outraged
Douglass, "seems to affect him [Lincoln] as little as the slaughter of beeves
for the use of his army." The editor-recruiter-father wanted an eye for an
eye—one Confederate put to death for every black soldier killed as a prisoner of war. Like most Northern leaders, Lincoln had little stomach for this
kind of retaliation, but the appeal did not go unanswered. Three days after
Fort Wagner, the president issued a retaliatory order that contained a one-
for-one policy, one rebel soldier put to death for each "soldier of the United

States" executed, and one put to hard labor for every Union soldier sold into slavery.[38] The cruel war had escalated to a new scale of savagery.

By August 1, not yet aware of the retaliatory order, a furious Douglass in protest quit recruiting and weighed his options. In an official letter to Stearns, he declared a duty to his people, especially those he had enlisted, "to expose their wrongs and plead their cause." Douglass abruptly switched hats, temporarily ceasing his role as a war propagandist and recruiting agent while returning to the role of black leader. His faith in national leadership was "nearly gone." "When I plead for recruits," he told Stearns, "I want to do it with all my heart, without qualification. I cannot do that now." Douglass atoned for his promises of equal treatment in the army and admitted to helping foster a "false estimate" of the Union government's generosity. He seemed not only discouraged, but even exhausted and confused. His zigzag on the inequality issue no doubt reflected the strain of constant travel and recruiting before increasingly reluctant audiences. Moreover, the presence of his sons at the war front may have curbed his enthusiasm. In a letter to a white friend, Martha Greene, Douglass described his sons as fighting "with halters about their necks." Greene, whose own son had been wounded in the war, wrote back expressing her sympathy for the orator as a black parent. "The white mothers and fathers think it hard to send our sons to fight, with every assurance of their protection," said Mrs. Greene, "how little we know the depth of earnestness it must require in you to send yours." Such depths had been a constant tension now for many months in Douglass's family. Fort Wagner now loomed large in Douglass's conscience, which he made movingly clear to Stearns: "How many 54ths must be cut to pieces, its mutilated prisoners killed, and its living sold into slavery, before Mr. Lincoln shall say: 'Hold, enough!' "[39]

Stearns did not allow his most prominent recruiter to step aside easily with such cries in the night. He sent Douglass the news of Lincoln's retaliatory proclamation and urged Douglass to go to Washington and present the black soldiers' grievances directly to the president. On August 9–10, Douglass took the B&O train south through Baltimore to the nation's capital. Although he never left the cars, traveling alone, it marked the first time he had returned to a slave state and to the city from which he had escaped in 1838. Poignant memories surely flowed in his weary mind on the overnight train. As he stepped out in Washington only a few blocks from the Capitol, the city gave the impression of one large wartime hospital. The streets swarmed with troops and military vehicles, while thousands of escaped slaves trying to forge secure lives without adequate housing and food appeared all around as the well-attired, forty-five-year-old Douglass strode up

Pennsylvania Avenue toward the Executive Mansion.[40] The Revolution was both ugly and thrilling.

Douglass had no invitation from the White House, but he did have contacts, especially Senator Samuel Pomeroy of Kansas, who had agreed to help. They first went to the War Department, where Douglass and his portly senatorial guide were promptly admitted in the early morning to see Secretary Edwin Stanton. With his wire glasses and his long beard hanging down on his chest, Stanton was all business and no small talk. "Politeness was not one of his weaknesses," Douglass recollected of Stanton. His "brusqueness" seemed to fill the air of the office, as if "he might turn his back on me as a bore at any moment." The visitor got right to the point, and Stanton engaged in a full thirty-minute discussion about the plight of black soldiers. Douglass instructed Stanton about the "Negro character." Too many people think blacks are either "angel" or "demon," Douglass said, but they ought not be viewed in extremes. Some are "brave and others cowardly," some "ambitious" and "another part quite otherwise." Douglass protested in no uncertain terms the unequal "pay and place" for black troops, putting the secretary on the defensive to the extent that he confessed full verbal support for equality. Douglass backed off for comity's sake, saying that blacks should still fight because they "had a cause quite independent of pay or place." Before leaving, Stanton surprised Douglass by declaring that he wanted the orator to go to the Mississippi River valley and join General Lorenzo Thomas as an adjutant in recruiting and organizing black troops. "Sufficient papers" (an appointment as a commissioned officer) would soon be forthcoming. No smiles, and only quick handshakes, were necessary as the flattered Douglass, with Pomeroy in tow, exited the War Department.[41]

At Stanton's instruction they next visited Secretary of the Interior John Usher to receive Douglass's "pass" to go south through army lines. Usher signed it in a beautiful hand, after which Pomeroy also added his signature boldly just below. The pass read, "Frederick Douglass is known to us as a loyal, free man, and is, hence, entitled to travel unmolested. We trust he will be recognized everywhere as a free man and a gentleman." As the men departed the Interior Department, they had a chance encounter with Postmaster General Montgomery Blair, who also wanted in on the special identity document for the former slave. He too signed his name to the bottom of the letter with the inscription "Pass this bearer, Frederick Douglass, who is known to be a free man."[42] No one ever wrote Douglass a pass to get out of slavery. Now the government's highest officials were signing on to pronounce this black man free. One wonders if Douglass could hardly contain laughter at the irony of

Blair, the nemesis of less than a year ago who had insultingly tried to enlist Douglass to oversee the administration's colonization schemes, now falling all over himself in a government hallway to endorse the same man to go find former slaves to put in uniform. At times Douglass's life must have seemed to him like a hundred rickety bridges held together with wire made of irony. He could not know for sure if those signatures were sincere or merely a means to keep him moving through hallways and out of Washington. Keep the black man running is an old mantra in America.

But Douglass had one more conversation to have and one more signature to secure. He and Pomeroy walked to the White House and joined the daily line of patronage seekers. The editor gave his card to an attendant and sat down on the stairs expecting a long wait. To his great surprise, Douglass was quickly ushered past the chagrined crowd of white men in front of him, at least one of whom muttered something about a "nigger." Time and events would soften and sentimentalize Douglass's memory of this signal moment: "I shall never forget my first interview with this great man." In the coming months, Douglass turned a remembrance of the interview into a classic performance. In December 1863, he entertained an audience of prominent abolitionists with a rather flatulent telling of his presidential visit. He spoke jokingly about how he had always been warned about traveling too near to the slave border states. "I can go down there now," said Douglass, garnering applause. "I have been down there to see the President." He knew his listeners could not resist hearing how a president "received a black man at the White House." As though he were converting this deeply symbolic historic moment into instant folklore, Douglass made his audience laugh as well as feel lumps in their throats. The meeting was "just as you have seen one gentleman receive another; with a hand and a voice well-balanced between a kind cordiality and a respectful reserve. I tell you I felt big there!" [43]

"Big" indeed. In reality, Douglass was awed by Lincoln. But the story had only begun; a lifetime of making himself into a character now blossomed because Douglass had found the ultimate counterpart actor—at least in the power the other character represented. Douglass had finally made it to the inner sanctum of American power, to the headquarters where this apocalyptic war was conducted, to "the head man," as he put it, "of a great nation." Here was the authority he had spent so much energy and time attacking and trying to influence. He relished telling the tale of "getting to him," of "elbowing" his way up the stairway past all the angry white office seekers, as "the only dark spot among them." Douglass had his audience gasping with laughter as he related, with a lightness of being, the scene in the messy office full of papers and hustling aides. "The President was sitting in his usual position, with his feet in different parts of the room, taking it easy." Douglass then shouted to a reporter, milking laughs into a roar, "Don't put this down, I pray you. I am going down there again tomorrow!" Then Douglass reached the punch line of the tale. As the two men approached, the president "began to rise, and he continued rising until he stood over me," Douglass declared while shrinking under the imaginary hulking Lincoln. The two shook hands firmly as Lincoln uttered, "Mr. Douglass, I know you; I have read about you, and Mr. Seward has told me about you." With the visitor feeling "at ease," the two men got down to business with Lincoln listening intently as Douglass entered his grievances.[44]

Douglass's later recollections of this meeting, though romanticized and vainglorious, square with his immediate report. Only two days after the visit, he told Stearns that he fully understood why Lincoln was called "Honest" Abraham, and that he had "never seen a more transparent countenance." Douglass thanked the president for his retaliatory order while also pushing for equal pay and commissions. Lincoln had responded frankly to "vindicate his policy respecting the whole slavery question and especially that in reference to employing colored troops." The chief executive did not equivocate and firmly defended himself against the charge of "tardiness, hesitation," and "vacillation," of which Douglass had personally accused him. Douglass quoted Lincoln, "I think the charge cannot be sustained. No man can say that having once taken the position I have contradicted it or retreated from it." Lincoln argued that with the retaliatory order, as with emancipation itself, he always had to weigh "public popular prejudice" first, and that his paramount job was the "necessary preparation of the public mind" for such enactment.[45]

Lincoln further told Douglass that the bitter inequality black troops faced was "a necessary concession" for them to serve at all. These were not the sentiments Douglass had hoped to hear; he swallowed the painful reminder that policy had been the handmaiden of racism. But he told Stearns that he found Lincoln's decency and forthrightness gratifying and that he left the meeting feeling assured that the melancholy man in charge would "stand firm," that "slavery would not survive the war and that the country would survive both slavery and the war." In this stunning encounter, Douglass had been disarmed to an extent by his host's unpretentiousness and received a political education of a kind; Lincoln too had perhaps learned something of how a black leader felt about the war for their future and the inhumanities they endured to fight it. The president might also have sensed for future reference how this brilliant radical pragmatist sitting with him that morning might be useful to the nation's survival. It is equally possible that the burdened and wily Lincoln could have played Douglass to get rid of an immediate problem. As Lincoln lounged in his chair in familiar surroundings, though, amid the terrible anxiety of the war, the son of an Indiana dirt farmer surely understood in some fleeting moment that he had helped the most famous former slave and free black man in America feel "big" in the president's mansion. Would that Lincoln had lived to tell of it in his own performative way in a memoir. As he was leaving, Douglass told Lincoln of Stanton's invitation for him to go south as a recruiter and showed his pass. Lincoln read the document with the signatures, turned it in his hand, and wrote on its side, "I concur. A. Lincoln. Aug. 10, 1863." [46]

Douglass ended his "flying visit," as he called it, and took the afternoon train out of Washington. He left believing he had a promise of a commission in the US army from Stanton, who may have been more adept at getting the abolitionist visitor out of his office than at sincerity. With a new excitement Douglass returned to Rochester and quickly decided to cease publication of his newspaper, rushing a final "Valedictory" issue into print. Ending the paper that had been a center to his life for sixteen years involved emotions he could hardly express. His new prospect of going South (he thought, with an officer's rank) felt daunting. His decision was not "dictated by love of change or adventure. My stability is quite equal to that of most men. My paper ends its existence in the same room on the same street where it began." Along with his ubiquitous oratory and his autobiographical writings, editor was the only professional vocation he had ever known. He did hear from Stanton, receiving orders to report to General Thomas in Vicksburg, Mississippi; Douglass's transportation would come at government expense. But to his great disappointment, the commission never arrived. Apparently Stanton (and perhaps Lincoln as well) had second thoughts about commissioning a black man. On August 14 Douglass wrote to the War Department, inquiring as to the "conditions" of his service. The reply one week later discussed only his remuneration and again instructed him to report to Mississippi, where he would be expected to exercise "influence" among the freedmen. [47]

So long practiced at weathering or resisting racial slights, this was one he could not abide. Without the commission Douglass did not go south. Why did he not budge from Rochester without the commission, and further, why had he not already enlisted in active service? Certainly his recruiting campaign, paid for by government and private funds (Stearns), had been a form of service. Earlier in the year, the Ohio black abolitionist

H. Ford Douglas, who had also lived in Canada and Illinois and supported Delany's plans for emigration, wrote to Douglass urging him to take the symbolic lead and enlist in the army. H. Ford Douglas had himself enlisted in an Illinois regiment, and now he called on the famous orator to "finish the crowning work of your life, you are the one of all others." Douglass disagreed with his colleague, who was a mixed-race former fugitive slave from Virginia, self-educated, and thirteen years younger. Douglass understood the call to "put down the quill and take up the sword," he said. "But we have no very high opinion of our fighting qualities, and have no military knowledge but we suppose we could fight if cornered." [48] He had fought when cornered many times, but he was no warrior; with voice and pen, the writer-orator preferred to recruit younger men.

In *Life and Times*, Douglass's explanation of why he did not go to Mississippi without the commission is lame: "I knew too much of camp life and the value of shoulder straps in the army to go into the service without some visible mark of my rank." Yet this is exactly what he had urged thousands of younger blacks, including his sons, to do. His reaction to Stanton's initial offer was no doubt sincere; he did end his beloved *Douglass' Monthly*. But he may also have simply been highly stressed and confused about his priorities. As late as August 19, Douglass told a correspondent of his disappointment that no commission had arrived; "I shall obey, however, hoping that all will be well in the end." [49] Douglass may have felt as much flattered by his Washington interviews and the invitation to a commission as he was ever inspired about venturing into the Mississippi River valley.

Before the end of the month Douglass decided not to obey his "orders" from the War Department. His best reasons were likely deeply personal. Two sons were in the daily peril of war, and Frederick Jr. was already in Mississippi laboring as a recruiter (he would soon be back in Rochester, ill and convalescing). Douglass had to be a father as well as the Union war effort's fiercest propagandist. Those dual, contradictory roles now collided and forced a reckoning. He often referred to his sons that summer with swelling pride, as if they were his surrogates at war. They must have felt that way too. He corresponded with them often, sending them money and loving encouragement. In July 1863, a correspondent to the *Anglo-African* called him to task for sending his sons to a war he would not fight himself. Douglass bristled and called the charge "malicious." He again disclaimed any ability as a soldier. "When came this . . . confidence in me as a warrior? When have I been heard as a military man?" He felt no compulsion to enlist until his fellow blacks found someone "to fill my place at the North." Irked by the claim that he let his sons do his fighting for him, he simply replied, "I am proud to refer to my two sons." [50]

But the sons were in dire need of help. Charles was still in Boston in August and September, alternately sick or complaining bitterly of hunger, ill-treatment, and the general anguish of army life. Under a regimen of working in an army hospital, he craved an officer's praise for his labors, but also alarmed his parents by noting that he was losing weight: "I fell away like a skeleton." A lonely Charles promised that he "never brought any disgrace upon the family," but he insisted that the remnants of the Fifty-Fourth were "treated worse than dogs" since the full regiment had deployed to the South. He had heard news that Lewis was "highly spoken of" and might get a commission, but also that he had fallen sick on Morris Island. By December, Charles was embroiled in a lawsuit against someone he alleged had mistreated him. [51]

Lewis had been more badly injured at Fort Wagner than he had initially let on. On August 15, he wrote to Amelia complaining of terrible headaches. As artillery shells were "flying and whizzing in our front," Lewis moved to the "Sick and Wounded Hospital No 6" in Beaufort, directed by the "irrepressible" Harriet Tubman. By August 27 he reported that he felt a little

Charles Remond Douglass, member of the Fifty-Fourth Massachusetts Infantry Regiment, c. 1863.

better, but writing from a "water soaked tent," he was still ill. As Union artillery sustained a daily bombardment of Forts Wagner and Gregg on the marshy island and Sumter in the harbor, the Fifty-Fourth were part of the troops who continued to dig ditches and trenches up the beach, right to the face of Wagner. Again, Lewis reflected on death with austere fatalism: "Death must be dealt out and must be received. Some of us will live to see rebellion crushed and some of us will die crushing it. Either is glorious." On September 6–7, Fort Wagner was finally evacuated after weeks of bombardment and much loss of life on both sides. Given his bad health, Lewis likely was not part of the victorious group that occupied the huge heap of destruction. Henry Gooding of the Fifty-Fourth was appalled by what he found: "The smell in Wagner was sickening, dead men and mules are profuse, some exposed to the rays of the sun, and others being half buried by earth thrown over them by our shot and shell during the bombardment." The men of the Fifty-Fourth had now seen many weeks of the horror and the refuse of mangled humanity that war wrought.[52]

George Stephens also reported the glorious fall of Fort Wagner and noted that some furloughs had been granted for the first time for the Fifty-Fourth. Among those heading north on a steamer by the second week of September was Lewis Douglass, who had become very sick. While Lewis suffered at an army hospital in New York in September and early October, his father arranged for his dear friend and doctor James McCune Smith to examine him. Whether due to battle wounds or general camp exposure, Smith diagnosed Lewis on October 6 with "gangrene of left half of Scrotum," and for the time being, unfit for service. With Ottilie Assing possibly at his side, Douglass hurried to New York, and as he reported to Gerrit Smith he spent "the last three weeks bending over the sick bed" of his ailing son. The father was proud that the son's furlough was granted for "good conduct in the field." Lewis recovered later at home in Rochester in his mother's care and would be discharged from the army in February 1864. He eventually married Amelia Loguen in 1869, but the war-ravaged romantic recruit of spring 1863, who also nurtured a lifetime pride in his service, never conceived children.[53] Other than expressing fierce pride, Douglass never betrayed any of his feelings from those weeks of hovering over Lewis's bedside, nor from any visits to other wounded men in that hospital. Douglass kept his fears, as well as any guilt in his heart, private.

• • •

Douglass was a reformer, not a soldier. As an adjutant, recruiting refugee freedmen from cotton plantations in Mississippi, he may have envisioned himself a fish out of water or stultified under a general's orders—since leaving the Garrisonians, he had never operated under anyone else's direction. How could he continue to reach the widest possible audiences and touch the highest levels of power in Washington if he relocated to Vicksburg? Douglass received a great deal of reinforcement for his self-image as black symbol and spokesman. No doubt, if given a voice, Anna would have opposed the move south. Certainly Ottilie Assing did not want the object of her obsessive concern journeying off to the war fronts of Dixie either. Most of all, Douglass heard forcefully from his British friends, especially Julia Crofts, as he also continued to receive their financial support. Crofts vehemently discouraged his plans to give up the paper and especially pleaded with him not to join the army. Douglass had written earlier in the year about an interest in enlisting if the State of New York would guarantee equal rights. "By everything dear to you my friend," Crofts responded, "*do not take any commission* that leads you personally into the fighting ranks . . . never go South—or killed you most assuredly will be . . . you are a *marked man.*" Julia's wise advice may have weighed on him as he rejected the assignment in the South. She had left this ringing plea in his ears: "The pen is ever greater than the sword—the head is greater than the hand—your work is with your pen and tongue." By December, his dearest English friend wrote of her relief that "the dangerous task of recruiting in the South is given up," but she lamented the newspaper, and wondered how he would carry on his mission without it.[54]

In November, President Lincoln went to the ravaged town of Gettysburg to dedicate a cemetery for the unprecedented numbers of dead on that battlefield. A staggering nearly six thousand had been killed between July 1 and 3 on the two sides, with over twenty-seven thousand wounded and almost twelve thousand missing. Lincoln too gave a new speech; he had long worked on or conjured the central themes he would address in his short masterpiece delivered on November 19. In but three paragraphs, he attempted an explanation of the war. As a superb student of Lincoln's rhetoric, Douglas Wilson, has put it, the president answered a huge and terrible question: What was the war *about*? With astonishing succinctness, Lincoln told his countrymen that the old republic had died on that battlefield; it was being buried in all the unfinished graves. Out of the bloodletting, the American people, indeed the nation, could experience a "new birth of freedom." Popular government as an idea might yet be saved, human freedom forged in new definitions, and even that most vexing Enlightenment idea of all, "equality," launched on a new history. The first republic was dying before their eyes; at horrible cost, a new one could yet be achieved.[55]

That breathtaking metaphor of *rebirth* in many versions had long been Douglass's favorite metaphor as well. He had himself delivered variations of the Gettysburg Address throughout the war. Now, with resounding implications, by the end of that terrible year of 1863, Lincoln and Douglass spoke from virtually the same script, one of them with the elegance and restraint of a statesman, the other, the fiery tones of a prophet. One spoke with an eye on legality and public opinion, while also listening to his evolving moral self; the other as though he were the national evangelist.

In his annual message of December 8, 1863, Lincoln declared that "the policy of emancipation ... gave to the future a new aspect." This "new reckoning" might now remake America into "the home of freedom disenthralled, regenerated, enlarged." Douglass could not have said it better, but came close. Embarking on a new speaking tour in fall 1863 and winter 1864, he honed one of his greatest speeches. In "The Mission of the War," the black leader declared that however long the "shadow of death" cast over the land, Americans should not forget the moral "grandeur" of the struggle. The shuddering scale of death in this war had to be rendered sacred, Douglass contended in this signature oration, or the slaughter could not be defended. "The mission of this war," Douglass pronounced, "is National Regeneration."[56] Together, Lincoln and Douglass, rarely in purposeful tandem and against overwhelming odds, had provided the subjunctive and declarative voices of the Second American Revolution—and by the last year of the war, they were nearly the same.

Chapter 20

ABOLITION WAR, ABOLITION PEACE

The most hopeful fact of the hour is that we are now in a salutary school—the school of affliction. If sharp and signal retribution, long protracted . . . and overwhelming, can teach a great nation . . . respect for justice, surely we will be taught now and for all time to come.

—FREDERICK DOUGLASS, FEBRUARY 1864

In Frederick Douglass's view, during the final year and a half of the Civil War one America died a violent, necessary death; out of its ashes a second, redefined America came into being amid destruction and explosions of hope. At war's end, Douglass could almost fashion himself as one of the unusual founders of this emerging second American republic, born in a revolution even bigger than the first. As 1864 dragged on, Douglass contemplated the war's revolutionary and prophetic meaning for himself, his family, his people, and his nation. The issues of Reconstruction also captured his attention. Douglass sought to convince everyone of what he believed: the American nation, and history itself, had taken a rare, fundamentally *moral* turn.

Douglass took to the lecture circuit with "The Mission of the War," his fullest expression of the war's meaning. In Philadelphia on December 4, 1863, at the thirtieth-anniversary meeting of the American Anti-Slavery Society, Douglass offered a refutation (in the presence of his old mentor) of William Lloyd Garrison's declaration that this might be the final meeting of the organization, now that emancipation had dawned. Announcing that "our work is not done," Douglass warned of the deep racism within Northern society and in the Democratic Party. He especially called for black male suffrage. Casting the argument in humor, Douglass reminded his auditors that the American "body politic" had never been healthy. He had many times seen "Ignorance" trying to vote alongside a swerving man from the street with a "black eye." And as he was long fond of saying, he had seen drunken "Pat, fresh from the Emerald Isle," stepping up to the poll, "leaning upon the arms of two of his friends, unable to stand." The franchise would protect blacks in the South, Douglass argued to rousing laughter and applause, from "the jaws of the wolf." His people ought to be "members of Congress," he asserted. "You may as well make up your minds that you have got to see something dark down that way. There is no way to get rid of it. I am a candidate already!" His Irish jokes notwithstanding, he left the abolitionists cheering as he demanded that they join his plea for an "Abolition war" and an "Abolition peace."[1]

Douglass's new speaking tour, like so many before, took on the character of a traveling crusade. Within two days he was in Washington, DC, where over consecutive nights, December 7–8, he delivered the "Mission" speech to overflow crowds at the African American Fifteenth Street Presbyterian Church. More than a thousand people, according to a journalist, thronged the church, "jumping over the fence, some crawling over someone's back," jamming the sanctuary, filling the aisles, and sitting on the floor. With hats and bonnets falling off all around, the "glorious conglomeration" anticipated the arrival of the "African lion of the antislavery platform," said the *Christian Recorder*. Amid shouting and applause Douglass slowly made his way down the crammed central aisle as the organ played "The Star-Spangled Banner." He took the pulpit, told tales of his emotions while passing through Baltimore on his journey, and made his appeal for "Abolition war" to the finish, a struggle of conquest between "slavery and Liberty."[2]

No one went home disappointed, since the following evening an equally packed and raucous crowd gathered to hear Douglass make his appeal for access to political rights, to the ballot box alongside the "drunken Irishman" and the "ignorant Dutchman." Douglass soared rhetorically, calling on the nation to allow black men to "swell the body politic" as they helped win the war. The racially mixed audience all seemed pleased, said the correspondent: "They had seen the great Douglass." As the celebrity orator held forth at Fifteenth Street Presbyterian with his vision of the apocalyptic revolution under way, some dozen blocks directly south, President Lincoln, on that same day of December 8, issued his annual message to Congress, in which he reflected on how the policy of emancipation had given "to the future a new aspect" and launched "a total revolution of labor" throughout the South. Within the same hours, both men, Lincoln with his pen, Douglass with his voice, imagined a nation "regenerated" through bloodshed on battlefields and the social misery in the streets surrounding them.[3]

In the crowd that swarmed around the church where Douglass appeared were many former slaves from the surrounding Virginia and Maryland countryside. Washington had become a massive military base, a series of hospitals functioning in churches, schools, and government buildings, and a massive street-based refugee camp. In 1862–63, a freedmen's exodus had rolled into the capital, with thousands of refugees taking up residence in tar-paper shanties, and former soldiers' barracks, such as Camp Barker, an old military residence and sometime prison converted into a tent city at Q and Twelfth Streets, near the current-day Logan Circle. By war's end the black population of the District swelled to forty thousand.[4] Douglass saw and likely visited Camp Barker since it was only four blocks east of the Fifteenth Street Church. Indeed, he made his "Mission" speaking tour, in part, a fund-raising campaign for contraband relief organizations.

During his stay in Washington, Douglass visited the burgeoning Freedmen's Village contraband camp on Arlington Heights across the Potomac River, on the former estate of Robert E. Lee. His fellow slave-narrative author and former Rochester neighbor Harriet Jacobs worked in that camp and in others around the city. The "misery" she witnessed there had to "be seen to be believed," she wrote. Refugees arrived daily from the war fronts of Virginia, and despite their destitution as well as the mistreatment many experienced from Union troops, she found these people "quick, intelligent, and full of the spirit of freedom." "What but the love of freedom could bring these old people thither?" Jacobs unforgettably asked. During Douglass's brief visit among the freedpeople in Arlington, as he strode for the first time on Virginia's soil, a small ceremony was arranged at which a group of children sang for him. Only three days later, his close Rochester friend Amy Post visited the freedmen's camps in Washington. Post left a detailed description of the Arlington site, met numerous former slaves of the Lee family, and observed "at the school room . . . Frederick Douglass's autograph, which was the first intimation that he had visited any of the camps."[5]

We do not have Douglass's account of his own emotions, but he did write to friends describing the episode. In January 1864 he wrote to Julia Crofts in England; she felt thrilled to know that Douglass felt so moved by his "visit to Washington and Arlington Heights—how I should liked to have been an eyewitness of your visiting those dear . . . little children! & to have heard the singing!" "My eyes would not have been dry!" she continued, marveling at Douglass's news of the "slaveholder's smokehouse being converted into a school house for his freed slave children!" So eager were some of Douglass's British friends for news of the war and his activities that Julia took his letters out on the circuit to local antislavery societies and tried to bolster support and raise money by reading "extracts of your letters relative to the contrabands." Moreover, Douglass's voice, in a manner, migrated into Germany in 1864 through the columns of Ottilie Assing in *Morgenblatt*. Partly by projecting Douglass's ideas about the war, as well as with her own keen, radical observations, Assing told her readers in January that American abolitionists, despite their divisions, represented the "spirit of the nineteenth century" and of "civilized progress." They represented the "vanguard of the present revolution, as Montesquieu, Voltaire, and Rousseau were the vanguard of the French Revolution." By March, she considered black regiments marching south the best representation of "a great revolution."[6] In her passionate essays, Assing echoed her hero's mission and emancipation as a world-historical event.

Close friends wrote to Douglass wondering when "your mission" would bring the orator to their town. From England, by April, the intrepid Julia Crofts sent £33 in contributions to contraband aid, as well as for "F. D.'s Mission," from antislavery societies in Edinburgh, Liverpool, Coventry, and Aberdeen. Another old British friend, Mary Carpenter, joined Crofts in scolding Douglass for ceasing the publication of his paper, upon which British abolitionists depended so much for news of the cause. She wondered about the fate of the mission and where their hero traveled. "We know you live," she said, "to promote that cause, but others ask what is F. D. doing now that his paper is given up." Carpenter sent a check for £5 and felt resigned to "sympathize affectionately with you . . . in the painfully exciting life you must now be living."[7]

Painful and exciting indeed. Sponsored by the Women's Loyal League, an organization advocating a constitutional amendment abolishing slavery, Douglass delivered the "Mission" speech to a packed house at the Cooper Institute in New York on January 13. He led with his millennial vision of the war, filling the hall with a tone of high moral certainty and with arguments both shuddering and hopeful. To Douglass the war in all its destruction was like a terrible, necessary gift from history and from Providence. The South's rebellion was the "rapid educator" by which the Union leadership moved from "slave-hunting" on behalf of their enemies to now equipping the Negro with a Springfield rifle. Ever the earnest war propagandist, now in need more than ever, he believed, Douglass minced no words in describing the Confederacy as "a solitary and ghastly horror, without a parallel in the history of any nation," a political crusade of "naked barbarism" in its attempt to give slavery an eternal foundation. He drew on Psalm 91 to make clear the character of the enemy: the Confederates and their cause "rivaled the earthquake, the whirlwind and the pestilence that walketh in darkness, and wasteth at noonday." Confederates had to be met and slaughtered, no matter how "long and sanguinary" the struggle. The ferocity of Douglass's language knew no limit; acknowledging that he had been accused of prolonging the war, his angry answer was "the longer the better if it must be so." An audience that may have been a majority of women stood on their feet, waved their hats, and shouted approval.[8]

In thus sacralizing the killing of Southern soldiers and of the Confederacy itself, Douglass found the war's meaning. The orator believed he described only stark facts: time and events, and fierce Southern resistance, had made the contest an "Abolition war." Northern Democrats and white Southerners denounced "abolition war" as the inhumane path to sanguinary race war. Both sides felt something deeply sacred at stake, and no one more than Douglass. Yes, he acknowledged, the war was for Union and for the Constitution, but it must be a wholly new Union, and a new Constitution to replace the old one now torn and tattered. The country must not "put old wine in new bottles," he argued, nor make "new cloth into old garments." Douglass warned that liberal and open-minded people such as abolitionists themselves were rarely as unified as the forces of reaction and darkness. But in this historic moment, they had to be. "That old union," he shouted, "whose canonized bones we saw hearsed in death and inurned under the frowning battlements of Sumter, we shall never see again while the world standeth." Stop fighting for a "dead past," Douglass urged his auditors, and instead fight "for the living present."[9] Here flowed a set of rebirth metaphors flaming, bloody, and much bolder than the succinct, if beautiful, suggestion in Lincoln's Gettysburg Address. "Mission of the War" stood as Douglass's radical abolitionist Gettysburg Address, a rhetorical sword into the Confederacy's heart, and a statement of the war's meaning as ancient as the Old Testament. Above all it was Douglass's vision of the new founding of an American republic.

Douglass ultimately appropriated a common American language to capture the meaning of the war: "We have heard much in other days of manifest destiny. I don't go all the lengths to which such theories are pressed, but I do believe that it is the manifest destiny of this war to unify and reorganize the institutions of this country—and that herein is the secret of the strength, the fortitude, the persistent energy, in a word the sacred significance of this war." In a line that challenges us still in our moral imagination, Douglass said that without the destruction of slavery, the world might view the Civil War as only "little better than a gigantic enterprise for shedding human blood."[10]

Not only had the war delivered the nation a "broken Constitution," requiring a legal refounding, but history itself had been broken and had to be made anew. Douglass volunteered to lead a generation of new founders. "Events are mightier than our rulers," Douglass asserted, and "Divine forces" had decided the mission of the war. The people had to line up, sacrifice, send forth their sons, and perform the sacred duty of holy war. Douglass left his rapt audiences that winter of 1864 with a clear, if harsh, message: "I end where I began—no war but an Abolition war; no peace but an Abolition peace; liberty for all, chains for none; the black man a soldier in war, a laborer in peace; a voter at the South as well as at the North; America his permanent home, and all Americans his fellow-countrymen." In a finale that anticipates Martin Luther King Jr.'s "I Have a Dream" speech a century later, Douglass invoked Isaiah once again: "Such, fellow-citizens, is my idea of the mission of the war. If accomplished, our glory as a nation will be complete, our peace will flow like a river, and our foundations will be the everlasting rocks."[11] Thousands heard Douglass deliver this speech; those drawn into his voice and his story were present at the new creation.

Dreams by definition, though, are always unfinished; this was certainly the case for Douglass's blood-soaked vision of 1864. Imagining a new, reinvented country brought one challenge; but the war remained a very personal affair for Douglass and his family. In the fall of 1863 Rosetta Douglass gave up on her faltering teaching career and her formal education and took a husband. On Christmas Eve in Rochester, she married Nathan Sprague, a handsome former fugitive slave from Maryland who had been working as a gardener at the Douglass home. Rosetta very much resembled her mother, including her darker skin. Although unlike her mother, and very much modeling her father, she seemed to embrace having her photograph taken, especially in elegant earrings. Sprague was lighter and, in family lore, may have been descended from a Maryland governor, Samuel Sprigg. Over the next eleven years Rosetta and Nathan would have five daughters and one son. In this tempestuous marriage, Sprague never developed a gainful career and eventually caused financial and legal troubles for his father-in-law. Steadiness and talent were not his forte. Like her mother, though, Rosetta seems to have almost always stood by her husband. Douglass recruited Sprague into the Fifty-Fourth Massachusetts before the wedding, and after living with Rosetta in the Douglass house on the hill on South Street in the winter months, he joined the regiment in the spring of 1864.[12]

After recovery from his wounds, Lewis Douglass tried to rejoin his regiment but was discharged formally on February 29, 1864. By that summer, Lewis traveled on army transports back to South Carolina, though not as an active-duty soldier. He witnessed the continual bombardment of Fort Sumter from Morris Island and, in August, wrote to his father, wishing the "state of New York would give me an appointment to recruit for them I could get a great many men." In the sea islands Lewis saw the rich harvest of possible black soldiers for the Union army. His brother Frederick Jr. was at that very time in Vicksburg, Mississippi, recruiting among former slaves, witnessing the human and natural ravages of war as he tried to enlist men from cotton plantations. For the twenty-two-year-old namesake of his famous father, the world of the cotton kingdom under siege and devastation represented the revolution the elder Douglass had imagined. Nothing was more revolutionary than ushering former Cotton Belt slaves into Union blue. Details are elusive about just how Frederick Jr. functioned as a recruiter. Lewis, on the other hand, always had an eye out for how to make money from any circumstance, telling his father of "offers of partnership in business as a sutler" for the army.[13]

Charles Douglass, despite his recurring sickness, stayed in the army as long as he could, still trying to prove his courage and worthiness as a warrior. He was discharged from the Fifty-Fourth and transferred to the Fifth Massachusetts Cavalry, where he served as a noncommissioned first sergeant. Through the awful summer of 1864, the delicate Charles served in Virginia during the early siege of Petersburg and at Point Lookout in Maryland, located at the southernmost tip of the peninsula on the Western Shore, where it meets the mouth of the Potomac River. Charles was now a soldier in the ranks of his dismounted unit, and he found his own real war. Black units of the United States Colored Troops were some of the first to occupy the City Point position where the James and Appomattox Rivers meet.[14] City Point soon grew into the biggest military depot and headquarters of the war. His regiment had mercifully missed the horrific battles of the Wilderness and Spotsylvania Court House in May, and they remained at City Point during the disastrous slaughter at Cold Harbor, fought just east of Richmond, June 1–3.

On May 31, in a letter to his father, Charles expected "to be called into line of battle every moment," as he anticipated what became the beginnings of the siege of the city of Petersburg. With a soldier's trembling bravado, he told his father that "our boys" are "anxious for a fight. . . . As for myself, I am not over anxious, but willing to meet the devils at any moment and take no prisoners." Luck was Charles's companion; his unit was kept largely in reserve on guard, picket, and logistical duties. Charles felt especially proud to report capturing a rebel prisoner while on picket duty. He also joyfully announced that they had brought in a large group of contrabands. He further reported an ugly tragedy—their commanding officer "had to shoot one of the men for being drunk and misbehaving, but the bullet hit the wrong man." Charles dropped this pitiful irony almost as fast as he told it.[15] All the Douglasses learned that this great revolution had an underside of horror, terror, and futility.

Later in the summer Charles's health failed yet again, and he was transferred to the huge prison and hospital complex at Point Lookout. While stationed along the Chesapeake, Charles apparently took a brief leave, crossed the Bay, and went to St. Michaels, where he became the first member of the Douglass family to connect with some Bailey cousins. The war crushed one world and reconnected another. What Charles may or may not have known is that his father, who had now developed a relationship with Abraham Lincoln, had written to the president in late August asking him to intercede and formally discharge his son from the army. "I hope I shall not presume too much upon your kindness," wrote the abolitionist to the commander in chief, "but I have a very great favor to ask. It is . . . that you will cause my son Charles R. Douglass . . . to be discharged." On September 1, the president sent the letter to the War Department with the endorsement "Let this boy be discharged, A Lincoln." On September 15 Charles wrote to both of his parents informing them that he was "honorably discharged [from] the service of the United States" and would be home within two weeks.[16] Douglass had asked his sons to hear and follow his trumpet, to risk all for the cause of black freedom; now, he also reversed course, and with emotions he never fully described, did whatever he could to save one of them.

The summer and fall of 1864 were thus harrowing as well as hopeful months for the Douglass household in Rochester. They found great cause for personal relief, as both Lewis and Charles were out of the army, at least for the time being, and not in danger. Nathan Sprague still served with the Fifty-Fourth Massachusetts, but Rosetta, pregnant with her first child, resided at home under her mother's watch and care. Rosetta's daughter, named Anna Rosine Sprague (called Annie for Rosetta's deceased sister as well as her own mother) was born on November 27, giving the Douglasses their first of what would be twenty-one grandchildren.[17] Although she probably retreated more and more now to her kitchen and garden, Anna Douglass happily had a new baby Annie in her house, as her husband, with no editor's desk to retreat to, pondered and wandered the new political landscapes of a nation at war.

At the beginning of that bloody year, all three Douglass sons and one son-in-law had served at the war front in some capacity, while the patriarch himself rode the rails across the North on his mission to convince multitudes to fight the cruel war to its bitter end. All of Douglass's children had to imagine their own new homes in this time of all-out war and revolutionary change as their father tried with the words and deeds of a self-styled prophet to influence history and power in the highest places.

In practical terms, what Douglass meant in his "Mission" speech by "abolition war" was a military conquest of the South, complete emancipation, continued enlistment of black soldiers without discrimination, and legal guarantees of black freedom and equal rights. An "abolition peace" would mean the subjugation of the Confederacy's slaveholding and treasonous leadership, full black citizenship and enfranchisement, and a strong role for the federal government in protecting the freedpeople and in reconstructing Southern society. The war, this divine "school of affliction," in Douglass's words, provided the "signal and the necessity for a new order of social and political relations among the whole people." Preserving the old Union was but a "miserable dream"; what Douglass the visionary wanted was a fundamentally new republic.[18] Hence, as early as any Northern politician, he pondered the nature of the potential postwar Reconstruction.

As early as 1862 Douglass counseled his readers to hold no illusions about the difficulties blacks would face when emancipated. Indeed, the problems of peace suddenly seemed much greater than the problems of war. If emancipation was accomplished, Douglass surmised, it would happen in great violence, and its aftermath might prompt even greater backlashes of violence. "The sea of thought and feeling lashed into rage and fury by the war" might foment a frenzied wrath among the defeated. After the fighting, Douglass suggested, "will come the time for the exercise of the highest of all human faculties. A profounder wisdom, a holier zeal, than belongs to the prosecution of war will be required." He wondered about uncharted constitutional terrain, about the use of federal authority in reconstructing state governments. Although he was no more prescient than the next person, Douglass envisioned Reconstruction as a long ideological struggle. "The work before us is nothing but a radical revolution," he declared in an editorial, "in all the modes of thought which have flourished under the . . . slave system." A new order could not happen overnight. "There is no such thing as immediate Emancipation either for the master or for the slave," he asserted. The "invisible chains of slavery" might take generations to break, Douglass predicted with an uncanny, tragic foresight.[19]

Naturally, Douglass's wartime concern with Reconstruction centered upon the welfare of the freedmen, and he laid out a paradoxical prescription combining classic self-help with outside philanthropy and activist government intervention. His early answer to the question of what was to be done with the emancipated slaves was, to "do nothing with them." "Your doing with them is their greatest misfortune," he lectured his fellow countrymen; "just let them alone." Slavery, he implied, had always been a measure of avaricious, powerful people "doing" too much with and to black people. In language modern antigovernment conservatives, including Supreme Court justice Clarence Thomas, have loved to appropriate and rip out of historical context, Douglass gave his prescription: "If the Negro cannot stand on his own legs, let him fall. . . . Your interference is doing him positive injury." In 1862, Douglass expressed doubts about the freedmen's relief efforts, although within a year he went on the lecture circuit to raise money for just such organizations and even donated his speaking fees to the cause. Wishing for a world of fairness and merit early in the struggle, however, Douglass denounced what he oddly called the "old clothes system of benevolence." He did not want the freed slaves to "depend for their bread and raiment upon the benevolence of the North," arguing, naïvely in retrospect, that the freedmen would make it on their own if left alone.[20]

Emancipated slaves undergoing terrible hardships dearly needed to gain self-respect. But their need for food, clothing, medical care, and protection quickly became even more necessary. Douglass's insensitive remarks about Northern benevolence were shortsighted and misplaced at best. Later, in the 1870s, Douglass would preach a black self-reliance and a laissez-faire individualism that echoed the reigning Social Darwinism of the day, and which may always have roiled under the mental surfaces of this proud, putative self-made man. Such contradictions emanated from deep in the psycho-

logical well of a man who had so long himself relied on the financial benevolence, as well as the emotional support, of influential and wealthy white
reformers as well as the fund-raising campaigns of his devoted British female friends. No one ever worked harder, nor at greater risk, for the liberation of American slaves than Douglass. But he had processed hard psychic
lessons for years about loving and hating the hands that feed one's family,
buy one's freedom, help educate one's children, and keep the printing press
rolling.[21] During the slaughter and displacement of the war, however, he
soon found that the fate of the freedmen was a much more complex problem than the "do nothing" rhetoric had implied.

The tension between the doctrine of self-reliance and the necessity of
government support for the freedmen produced a working paradox in
Douglass's thought throughout the war and postbellum period. He never
stopped arguing that the legacy of slavery would require federal aid to the
freedpeople, but he also never surrendered his commitment to a fierce individualism. As both belief and strategy, he advanced both doctrines at once,
a position of stark contradiction after the war in an age decreasingly receptive to humanitarian reform. While expecting a rugged self-reliance from
his people, so many of whom emerged from slavery with little or no human
or physical capital, he also demanded justice and fairness from the nation.
In 1862 Douglass warmly called the government the "shield . . . from the
fury and vengeance of treason, rebellion and anarchy." In every discussion
of the welfare of the freedmen during the war, Douglass insisted that the
government "deal justly" with blacks.[22] Douglass assiduously advocated for
both bootstraps and aid, all the while learning that among the many casualties of the total war were impulses of humane fairness.

What Douglass meant, in large part, by "do nothing" was "do justice."
Coupled with his calls for black self-help were his demands for education,
wages, protection in the workplace, civil rights, and suffrage. All of these
aims would require extraordinary use of federal power, new laws, military
enforcement, and fundamental changes in social attitudes. He expected a
great deal from revolution wrought by the war; in millennialist historical
thinking, the limits of change are in God's imagination as much as in mankind's. "We would not for a moment check . . . the benevolent concern for
the future welfare of the colored race in America," wrote Douglass in 1862,
"but . . . we earnestly plead for justice above all else."[23] But by 1863, "justice"
was a many-headed, bloody dream as it underwent rebirth.

From Northerners, Douglass wanted less pity and more ballots, less benevolence and more black land ownership. He would never be comfortable

with any widespread confiscation or redistribution of Confederate lands in the wake of the war. Instead, he wanted freedmen to obtain land by means consistent with the sanctity of private property, although in his view the government ought to have a primary role in securing and arranging the sale of such land. With time, Douglass applauded every function of the Freedmen's Bureau, the unprecedented federal agency created in early 1865 to try to provide massive social welfare to the millions of black and white displaced people in the South. But when emancipation itself was still a revolutionary policy in the making, he seems to have concluded that white audiences needed strategic preparation that would feel consistent with their worldviews. "What shall be done with the four million emancipated slaves if emancipated?" Douglass asked. "Pay them honest wages for honest work; dispense with the biting lash, and pay the ready cash; awaken a new class of motives in them; remove those old motives of shriveling fear of punishment which benumb and degrade the soul, and supplant them by the higher motives of . . . self-respect . . . and personal responsibility." Then Douglass shifted the point of view decisively; "They [blacks] have been compelled hitherto to regard the white man as a cruel, selfish, remorseless tyrant. . . . Now let him see that the white man has a nobler and better side to his character."[24] This was thoroughgoing political liberalism sprinkled with twists of old-fashioned moral suasion. It was not economic radicalism. The substance of Douglass's message to white Americans, therefore, was *morally change yourselves.* The new order was as much for whites to give as it was for blacks to take.

Douglass knew that the prospect of emancipation had always needed sweetening in Northern ears, just as it had in numerous other nations and empires. The "do nothing" dictum might allay white fears; he portrayed blacks as hardworking people who only needed simple justice and a fair chance. Land ownership would make each of them a "better producer and a better consumer." Northerners need not fear massive migrations, vagrancy, or criminality, Douglass contended, if blacks were given equality before the law. Douglass believed blacks had been perceived as an "exception" too long, and he wanted to prevent their becoming permanent social pariahs.[25] What do nothing meant, in part, was to free the slaves without colonizing or subjugating them as a racial caste; then give them equality and allow them to learn, work, and vote. Douglass demanded governmental action, not merely letting the freedmen live or die by their own pluck.

Douglass feared a "vindictive spirit sure to be roused against the whole colored race" in an imagined postwar South. He repeatedly called on Northern reformers to improve the condition of the former slaves. Whenever the shooting stopped, "the whole South," Douglass declared, "as it never was before the abolition of slavery will become missionary ground." Capturing the spirit of freedmen's aid societies, Douglass urged reformers and teachers to "walk among these slavery-smitten columns of humanity and lift their forms towards Heaven." The freedmen's needs would require what the orator called "all the elevating and civilizing institutions of the country." [26] Modern Republicans, eager to find a black spokesman for personal responsibility, have not bothered to read deeper into Douglass.

As Douglass addressed during wartime the question of Reconstruction, he more and more stressed black suffrage. With the war nearing its end in April 1865, he gave an address to abolitionists in Boston entitled "What the Black Man Wants," in which he outlined at length the reasons why his people needed the vote. He contended that "women, as well as men, have the right to vote," but in the moment, women must wait for "another basis" to gain suffrage, a position that would ultimately land him in a bitter feud with many women reformers. The ballot, he believed, would serve as protection from white racism, a means of education, and a source of self-worth. Douglass treated suffrage with special urgency at the war's end; the opportunity might never come again in anyone's lifetime: "This is the hour, our streets are in mourning . . . and under the chastisement of this rebellion we have almost come up to the point of conceding this great, this all-important right of suffrage." Hence, with prophetic insight, Douglass urged abolitionists to harness for all time the extraordinary forces the war had unleashed. "Judgments terrible . . . overwhelming, are abroad in the land," he counseled. "I fear if we fail to do it now . . . we may not see, for centuries to come, the same disposition that exists at this moment." [27]

Whether an abolition war could ever be waged to its conclusion was very much still in doubt in the bloody summer of 1864. The revolution could still be lost. In the election campaign of that year Douglass continued to be troubled by the ambiguous policies of the Lincoln administration. Conflicting factions within the Republican Party vied to influence and control the evolving emancipation as well as Reconstruction policies. Postmaster General Montgomery Blair, the old leader of colonization, would accept emancipation of slaves in reconstructed Southern states, but opposed any political or civil rights for freedmen. He did so in fearmongering, Negro-phobic public speeches, claiming without authority to speak for the president as Blair warned against racial "amalgamation." He traveled the North with a message as antiblack as it was antislavery. He called the abolitionists' advocacy of equality "a fundamental change in the laws of nature . . . blending different species of the human race." He continued to advocate for the colonization of liberated blacks to their own natural "climes" and "hemispheres." The other wing of Republicans, the more ascendant Radicals, led by Congressman Henry Winter Davis of Maryland and Senator Charles Sumner of Massachusetts and others, wanted immediate emancipation followed by the beginnings of equality, including black suffrage. Lincoln sought above all to sustain party unity, to make emancipation a certainty, although by gradual and orderly means if possible. In late 1863, Lincoln had responded to a Michigan Republican who had urged him to move faster against the conservatives by saying that he hoped "to stand firm enough not to go backward, and yet not go forward fast enough to wreck the country's cause."[28] This was the Lincoln who had exasperated Douglass in 1861–62, and as the war collapsed into horrible stalemate in 1864, Douglass lost faith for a time in whether he and Lincoln had ever worked from the same script.

One of Lincoln's greatest concerns was chaos or even guerrilla race war in the South as the war ended. Douglass insisted that secure land ownership and especially the right of the freed slaves to vote would be essential buttresses against that very disorder. Lincoln feared potential white violent resistance to blacks voting; Douglass believed black Southerners would need to be armed with the vote to protect themselves. Both men would in the long run be proven right; but in what order and by what pace ought this revolution take place? On that question, they greatly disagreed; Douglass possessed his own vengeful spirit to work through, and Republicans struggled for consensus.

As the presidential election campaign of 1864 approached, Douglass found himself attracted to a dump-Lincoln movement among Radicals in the Republican Party. The most contentious question that divided Republicans against themselves was Reconstruction policy, as well as perceptions of Lincoln's indecisiveness and conservatism. A good deal of scurrilous political ambition drove passions for a new candidate as well, especially that practiced by the treasury secretary, Salmon Chase. Chase's desire to unseat Lincoln was a wide-open secret among the political class. Lincoln had long needed Chase for his skill as an administrator and his antislavery credentials, but fully understood that he was infected with "the White House fever." Chase had allies, but primarily he relied on a somewhat broad discontent among Radicals with what they variously considered the president's "temporizing" approach to slavery and the prosecution of the war. Widespread contempt also simmered under the surface because of Lincoln's frequent "joking" habits and character. Chase, in persistent efforts to damage Lincoln, had openly complained that cabinet sessions were merely "meetings for jokes." On policy, many Radicals objected to Lincoln's lenient approach to reconstructing Southern states and rendering justice to Confederates. Lincoln, however, was popular outside Washington, DC, and across the North. Moreover, Chase faded from the picture by the spring and early summer of 1864 due to his own embarrassing overreach; after numerous offers by Chase to resign his cabinet position, Lincoln finally accepted the fifth time.[29]

A more serious challenge to Lincoln's nomination came from a group of Radicals who touted John C. Frémont for the head of the Republican ticket. Frémont, who had been the Republican standard-bearer in 1856, collected many abolitionist supporters, including some old Garrisonians. Garrison himself, however, broke with his friends and steadfastly stayed in Lincoln's camp. Wendell Phillips called Lincoln a "half-converted, honest Western Whig trying to be an abolitionist." Garrison, however, believed that despite his caution Lincoln had "at one blow, severed the chains of three millions three hundred thousand slaves." Douglass walked a fence in this politically dangerous terrain. He endorsed the call for the Frémont movement's convention, but did not attend when it met in Cleveland on May 31 to nominate the Californian for president and John Cochrane, the nephew of Gerrit Smith, as his running mate.[30]

Disgruntled and painfully impatient with Lincoln administration ideas about black equality and Reconstruction, Douglass decided to join the attack. The unequal-pay controversy in the Union army burned among black troops and their communities until midsummer, and the federal government showed no disposition to grant black suffrage in such occupied Southern states as Louisiana. Even before announcing his "Proclamation of Amnesty and Reconstruction" in December 1863, Lincoln had communicated forcefully to his commanding general in Louisiana, Nathaniel P. Banks, that he desired a "tangible nucleus" of Unionist leaders of whatever number, "which the remainder of the state may rally around." This was the kernel of Lincoln's vision of Reconstruction—a fluid, experimental process, a part of military policy, run by the president and not by Congress, and heavily dependent on his faith in an inherent Unionism within the Confederate states. A local, loyal white elite, therefore, must not be threatened off by the prospect of black suffrage. The president's evolving Reconstruction policies made him appear passive, or even obstructionist, to Radicals. Certainly Banks looked so as he conducted elections in early 1864 with the vote restricted exclusively to white men, and as he instituted a plan to force black freedmen to work for wages capped by the government at $10 per month. Banks's system also included prescriptions that freedmen remain on their old masters' plantations, in "perfect subordination," disciplined often in the old methods of slavery.[31]

White and black Radicals, within Louisiana and across the North, were outraged. Some abolitionists, stationed with the army in Louisiana, condemned the Banks measures as the "reestablishment of slavery," or the substitution of "serfdom for slavery." As Lincoln, by and large, supported the Banks system, Douglass joined the chorus of anger and frustration. Asked to explain in May why he supported the Frémont movement, the orator laid it on the line as an uncompromising Radical. Douglass demanded "complete abolition of every vestige, form and modification of Slavery in every part of the United States." Leaving no room for experimentation and gradualism, he insisted on "perfect equality for the black man in every state before the law, in the jury box, at the ballot box and on the battlefield." He wanted nothing short of full equality for blacks in access to "offices and honors" in the military and the government.[32]

After emancipation in 1863, Douglass had hoped he would never again have to attack Lincoln. But in June 1864, he wrote a stinging public rebuke of the president. It was now a "swindle" that the federal government asked "the respect of mankind for abolishing slavery," all the while "practically re-establishing the hateful system in Louisiana." Douglass had tried to believe in Lincoln's steadfastness, but now his "patience and faith" dwindled. The president had "virtually laid down this as the rule of his statesmanship," Douglass boldly stated: *"Do evil by choice, right from necessity."* He chastised Lincoln for not signing Congress's Wade-Davis Bill, which was the Radicals' Reconstruction plan, requiring a majority of voters in a Confederate state, as opposed to only 10 percent in Lincoln's plan, to renounce secession and declare a loyalty oath before returning to the Union. Douglass called Lincoln's Ten Per-Cent plan an "entire contradiction of the constitutional idea of the republican Government." Especially incensed with Republican hostility to black voting rights, Douglass slashed away at his old targets of hypocrisy and racism. "We invest with the elective franchise those who with bloody blades and bloody hands have sought the life of the nation, but sternly refuse to invest those who have done what they could to save the nation's life." Most demoralizing of all, he argued, was what government policy implied for the freedman once peace arrived: "to hand him back to the political power of his master, without a single element of strength to shield himself from the vindictive spirit sure to be roused against the whole colored race."[33]

From the Democrats, who were about to nominate former general George B. McClellan as their candidate, and from the Frémont third-party effort, Lincoln's reelection was in dire trouble that summer. War weariness had never been so debilitating across the North; abolitionists remained split over whether to support Lincoln's reelection as the casualty reports from Virginia and Georgia drove Northern morale into despair. The situation was "never so gloomy," wrote Sydney Gay, editor of the *National Anti-Slavery Standard*. He feared that the people would vote for any compromise or follow a "party for peace at any price, even disunion."[34] A war that might not be won for union surely could not secure the emancipation of slaves. Douglass followed Lincoln's public utterances in these months, but he surely could not know the beleaguered president's personal thoughts. On one compelling matter, however, they unknowingly shared a great deal—the effort to discern and explain, if possible, the place of God's will in this horrible, unending conflict.

With differing style and scope, Lincoln and Douglass shared an outlook of millennial nationalism—America as a nation with a special destiny, fraught with contradictions, and living out a historical trajectory under some kind of providential judgment. Lincoln's "house divided against itself" and "last best hope of earth" had long been Douglass's nation of "shameless hypocrisy," its "hands . . . full of blood," but also the nation "so young," its original "great principles" so old and profound, that it could yet be redeemed. Both men possessed pliable, deeply curious minds; and they were intellectual brooders. Both expressed ambivalence about theological orthodoxy. But neither could imagine human affairs, history itself, without the idea of an active God shaping its direction and outcomes. Both kept watch over history and worried intensely about a vengeful God's interest in the American republic. Their individual paths to the dark crisis of 1864 were both riddled with expressions of such a religious-historical worldview. Lincoln, writes the biographer Ronald White, typically "thinks his way into a problem," looking at all sides, and "working through the logic of a syllogism." Douglass too loved to logically weigh two sides of an issue, and like Lincoln he possessed a well-earned respect for mystery and uncertainty. Through irony he often gave the impression that he knew precisely where he would land with a typically thunderous argument. Douglass could logically and pragmatically think his way to his truths as much as the quieter Lincoln. By 1864, both men were intellectual self-reinventions of earlier selves, and both envisioned the nation in biblical terms, undergoing transformation by fire. In late 1862, Lincoln had warned the nation, "We cannot escape history . . . the fiery trial through which we pass, will light us down, in honor or dishonor, to the latest generation." Two months earlier, Douglass, had in his own way said the same: "We are saved as by fire, we grieve with sorrow-stricken families all over the North, but their terrible afflictions and heavy sorrows are their educators." [35]

As another biographer, Richard Carwardine, has demonstrated, the withering demands of Lincoln's cruel presidency "swept [him] along to a new religious understanding." His wartime language increasingly included claims of his "firm reliance on the Divine arm," that he sought "light from above," was acting with "responsibility to my God," and that he hoped to discern God's wishes in "the signs of the times." Lincoln, very possibly in 1864, famously scratched on a fragment of paper what his secretaries and future historians would call his "Meditation on the Divine Will." No better example exists, except for his Second Inaugural Address, for which this statement provides a foretaste, of Lincoln's austere, biblically informed sense of tragedy:

> The will of God prevails. In great contests each party claims to act in accordance with the will of God. Both may be, and one must be wrong. God cannot be for, and against the same thing at the same time. In the present civil war it is possible that God's purpose is something different from the purpose of either party. . . . I am almost ready to say this is probably true—that God wills this contest, and wills that it shall not end yet. . . . He could have either saved or destroyed the Union without a human contest. Yet the contest began. And having begun He could give the final victory to either side any day. Yet the contest proceeds.

Lincoln's private reflection invokes a profound sense of the costs and the tragedy at the heart of this "human contest." [36]

Characteristically, Lincoln couched his emerging sense of a frightening truth in words such as "almost" and "probably." Douglass, while sharing the same ideas, was rhetorically beyond qualifiers. Ever since his first autobiographical writing, he had conducted his own meditation on divine will.

He protected his own uncertainty perhaps more rigidly by rooting it explicitly in the rhetoric of Isaiah and the Hebrew prophets. Douglass's wartime apocalypticism breathed with Old Testament fire and justification. He frequently employed phrasing such as "the laws of God," the "stern logic of events," or the "tradewinds of the almighty" to give both tone and substance to his explanation of the war's meaning. Douglass's subject was less the shaping of policy than it was to persuade a people to rise, make holy war, and answer God's call to repent and sacrifice. "The land is now to weep and howl amid ten thousand desolations," he cried early in the war. "Repent, Break Every Yoke, let the Oppressed Go Free for Herein alone is deliverance and safety!" Douglass repeated his great wartime theme over and over. The "Mission" speech was his jeremiadic, prosecutorial summation. A chosen but guilty people had to suffer and reform or lose their destiny altogether. Douglass decided that his best options were to stand with Isaiah and Jeremiah and issue the warnings about God's intentions; His people might be listening at this moment as never before.[37] We do not know just how or whether Lincoln or Douglass prayed. But by late summer of 1864, both men, facing this existential predicament from different positions, solemnly pondered what course God might have in mind for this terrible war.

*Frederick Douglass, Chicago,
February 1864. Samuel Montegue
Fassett photographer.*

• • •

Lincoln's famous public letters and addresses where he showed his commitment to emancipation may or may not have had a role in softening Douglass's ire toward the president in 1864. But in August, Lincoln stunned Douglass by inviting him to the White House for an urgent meeting that in the view of the black leader would change almost everything once again. Lincoln's notion to invite Douglass to Washington emerged out of his meetings during the week of August 10–17 with John Eaton Jr., a New Hampshire–born, Dartmouth-educated chaplain of an Ohio regiment in the Union army. General Ulysses Grant had appointed Eaton superintendent of freedmen in 1862, and by 1864 the minister had established a large number of contraband camps in the lower Mississippi valley. On his way to Washington that month to brief the president and the War Department, Eaton had heard Douglass deliver the "Mission" speech in Toledo, Ohio, and had conversed with him about it afterward.[38]

Few people understood the plight of the freedpeople on the ground in the South quite like the devoted abolitionist Eaton. In reminiscences of his meetings with Lincoln, Eaton found the chief executive's interest in the situation of freed slaves "astonishing." Worried about the military stalemate and the process of emancipation, Lincoln, according to Eaton, "alluded to John Brown's raid," openly suggesting that "every possible means" ought to be considered to maximize the liberation of slaves. The president asked about a "grapevine telegraph" that might be "utilized to call upon the Negroes of the interior peacefully to leave the plantations and seek the protection of our armies." Here was some version of Brown's old militarized underground railroad, the idea that almost drew Douglass to Brown's band of ill-fated warriors. Eaton informed the president of some of Douglass's criticisms voiced in Toledo, especially about the leniency of the Reconstruction plan, the lack of action on black suffrage, and "retaliation against cruelty to Negro soldiers." Lincoln abruptly arose, went to a private desk, drew from a drawer, and read aloud a copy of his March 13 letter to Governor Michael Hahn of Louisiana, in which Lincoln suggested that the "elective franchise" might be extended to "some colored people . . . the very intelligent, and especially those who have fought gallantly in our ranks." Defensively, Lincoln beseeched Eaton, did Douglass know about this letter? Further, could "Douglass be induced to come see him" at the White House? Arrangements were quickly made, and the Rochester orator, on the road constantly that summer, was on a train through Maryland to the Baltimore and Ohio station at New Jersey Avenue and C Street in the capital.[39]

As Douglass sat in the reception room at the White House awaiting his interview with the president on August 19, Douglass had a chance encounter with Judge Joseph T. Mills of Wisconsin, who was also awaiting an appointment. In his diary, Mills recorded telling the president the story of how dark it felt in the reception area. So dark that "there in the corner," said Mills, "I saw a man quietly reading who possessed a remarkable physiognomy. I was riveted to the spot. I stood & stared at him. He raised his flashing eyes & caught me in the act. I was compelled to speak. Said I, Are you the President? No, replied the stranger, I am Frederick Douglass." Douglass had been stared at in countless such situations before, and we can only imagine the stern eyes and proud if indignant voice with which Douglass responded to this kind of encounter. Mills found the episode so humorous that in his conversations later with Lincoln, while sitting next to him on a sofa, he told of seeing Douglass: "Mr P, are you in favor of miscegenation?" Mills recorded. "That's a democratic mode of producing good Union men, & I don't propose to infringe on the patent."[40] In such an exchange of stares, between an educated white jurist who supported the Union war effort, and a smartly dressed black man, reading as he waited to speak with the president of the United States, we can discern an old and enduring form of American racism still alive in parlor talk: What *is* that black man doing in the White House? How did he get there? We can hope Lincoln ignored the joke.

In Douglass's second meeting with Lincoln, this time at the president's invitation, the two had a longer and remarkably frank exchange. Douglass had not minced words out on the circuit about Lincoln, accusing him in the "Mission" speech of "heartless sentiments" and an absence of "all moral feeling" on too many questions. "Policy, policy, everlasting policy," Douglass complained in an unveiled swipe at Lincoln, "has robbed our statesmanship of all soul-moving utterances." Lincoln seemed aware that he now sat face-to-face with a fierce but useful critic, a situation this politician had managed many times before. Twice during their interview, a secretary interrupted to tell the president that Governor William Buckingham of Connecticut was waiting at the door, but in Douglass's memory, Lincoln kept dismissing the intrusion and said, tell the Governor to wait, "for I want to have a long talk with my friend Frederick Douglass."[41] Forever proud of this highlight moment in his career, Douglass relished retelling it.

Lincoln quickly cut to the chase and unburdened his fears that he would not be reelected, that the war could collapse into a negotiated peace, and that, especially, emancipation would grind to a halt. Lincoln, recollected Douglass, was deeply troubled by all the attacks he received from fellow Republicans. The president looked much older than the last time they met, and he "spoke with great earnestness and much solicitude." Lincoln, who later that day swapped a Sambo story with Mills (according to the judge), looked Douglass in the eye and asked the former slave to help him devise "the means most desirable to be employed outside the army to induce the slaves in the rebel states to come within the federal lines." Lincoln sought Douglass's advice on how he should answer his critics, and especially on how to usher as many slaves as possible out of the border states into freedom and security before the election and the president's potential defeat. As Lincoln talked, Douglass must have leaned forward with a stunned visage; he saw in the president "a deeper moral conviction against slavery," he later said, than he had ever imagined. In Douglass's retelling, Lincoln asked the former coconspirator of 1859 who had fled America for his life, "to undertake the organizing of a band of scouts, composed of colored men, whose business should be somewhat after the original plan of John Brown, to go into the rebel states, beyond the lines of our armies, and carry the news of emancipation, and urge the slaves to come within our boundaries." Douglass listened with "profoundest satisfaction," and perhaps even disbelief.[42]

Overnight, it seemed, Douglass had gone from frustrated outsider and fierce critic to special presidential adviser and organizer of a radical military mission, the purpose of which was to destroy as much of slavery as possible before political fortunes changed. We cannot know what Douglass felt in his heart that morning as he looked into Lincoln's eyes, nor can we know fully how the old prairie lawyer processed this irony-laden moment. For those hours at least the former slave from the Tuckahoe and the Indiana dirt farmer's son were making a revolution together.

After leaving the White House, Douglass returned to the home of a black friend with whom he stayed while in Washington. Eaton met him there and found the black leader pacing in a parlor in "a state of extreme agitation." Douglass was both thrilled and troubled. The plan he had just agreed to help Lincoln and the army implement was inchoate and daunting. It also meant that the legitimacy of the Emancipation Proclamation was utterly dependent on military success, and therefore on the election. Douglass felt exhilarated to have been "treated . . . as a man," and with no thought of the "color of our skins" by Lincoln. But frankly, he had little idea of just how to lead the plan to infiltrate the South, inform slaves, and funnel them north to safety. Suddenly, the man of supreme eloquence and hard rhetoric had to think about policy, organization, and clandestine logistics. Eaton said Douglass already had pen and paper on a table nearby, preparing to draft a memorandum to the president. A day or so later, before leaving the capital, Douglass received a White House messenger, accompanied with a carriage, inviting him to join Lincoln for tea out at the Soldiers' Home, the presidential summer retreat within the District of Columbia. The orator had a speaking engagement and had to turn down the invitation, something he would always regret, especially after the terrible events of the following April.[43] We do not know what Lincoln had in mind for discussion at that tea.

On the very day Douglass met with Lincoln at the White House, Julia Crofts wrote from England, full of anxiety over "all the wretchedness & misery & blood-shedding" of the war, and begging her old friend to "not go toward Washington during this time. . . . Your life is one that would be sacrificed at once if you ever reached the hands of those southern tyrants." By the time Douglass read that letter, however, he had already drafted an outline of a plan for the president. On August 29, the old editor sent his four-part proposal for a general agent (himself presumably); subagents, selected by Douglass, stationed in various densely populated slave areas of rebel states conducting "squads of slaves" into the North; close ties and clear orders between commanding Union generals and subagents; and finally, proper provisions of food and shelter for all freedmen swept up in the liberation scheme. For himself, he wanted a "roving commission," giving him full legitimacy amid the army officers throughout war zones. This was Douglass's best effort at a formal proposal for the militarized underground railroad in the midst of all-out war. He told Lincoln that he had consulted several other black leaders in the mere week since their parley; all believed in the wisdom of the idea, he reported, but only some thought it practicable. Although willing to lead such an operation, it is unlikely Douglass felt much practical enthusiasm for it. Just how he would coordinate his "band of scouts," as he later called the idea, he never made clear.[44] Soon, events rendered the entire scheme unnecessary.

On September 2, the day the Democratic National Convention in Chicago nominated George McClellan for president, news flashed across the country of the fall of Atlanta to General William Tecumseh Sherman after a long siege. Just as the Democrats met to declare the war a failure and crafted a platform that would lead to a negotiated Confederate independence of some kind, Sherman famously sent a telegram to Washington: "Atlanta is ours and fairly won." Confederates' rising hopes plummeted, and many war-weary Northerners, represented by the famous New York diarist George Templeton Strong, saw victory now on the immediate horizon: "Glorious news this morning—Atlanta taken at last!!! It is . . . the greatest event of the war."[45] The Democrats' peace platform put Lincoln's apparent moderation in a different light; and Douglass had seen a devotion in the president's heart and mind.

By late September, Frémont withdrew from the race and the choice simplified. "When there was any shadow of a hope that a man of a more decided antislavery conviction . . . could be elected, I was not for Mr. Lincoln," Douglass wrote to fellow abolitionist Theodore Tilton. "But as soon as the Chicago [Democratic] convention, my mind was made up, and it is made still. All dates changed with the nomination of Mr. McClellan." Like other abolitionists, Douglass wanted to actively campaign for Lincoln's reelection. But sensing the clear Republican desire not to be identified as the "N-r party," he stayed away from the political stump. Some things had greatly changed and some had not. "The Negro is the deformed child," Douglass complained to Tilton in September, "put out of the room when company comes."[46] The orator still had to find his own psychic balance between the high of the Lincoln interview in late August and the low caused by the subtle and blunt indignities of Republican cold shoulders in September. For now those racist stares were not as important as winning the war and achieving universal emancipation and the right to vote.

But the school of affliction was hardly over. As Douglass had learned so many times, in the election campaign and its historic aftermath down to the end of the war and beyond, he had to keep rethinking the tragic wisdom in Job. The Lord not only giveth and taketh away, but history itself, even in its most convulsive leaps forward, giveth and taketh away.[47]

Chapter 21

SACRED EFFORTS

And the dove came in to him in the evening; and, lo, in her mouth was an olive leaf plucked off: so Noah knew that the waters were abated from off the earth.

—GENESIS 8:11

During the final months of the Civil War, Frederick Douglass's emotions and ideas careened from fear to exhilaration, from hope to despair, and in and out of Old Testament–style tribulation and redemption. In a special address to a black convention in Syracuse in October 1864, Douglass tackled many of the war's personal and existential meanings. This national gathering, the first such convention to be held in nine years, attracted approximately 150 representatives from eighteen states, including small delegations from Mississippi, Missouri, Florida, Virginia, and North Carolina. The delegates collectively denounced colonization and explicitly demanded "equality before the law." [1]

Possibly no previous convention had drawn a list of African American luminaries of such diverse backgrounds and talents. Virtually every major black religious, political, literary, or community leader attended. For nearly four days, all manner of rivalries were largely checked at the door while such men as Henry Highland Garnet, William Wells Brown, George T. Downing, John Mercer Langston, Jermain Loguen, and others matched wits over the great issues of the war: equality in the army for black soldiers; the dire necessity of complete abolition as the war's aim; equal civil and political rights in the aftermath of emancipation. These men were both former slaves and freeborn; some were longtime "friends" of Douglass's, and others had already spent much energy as his rival, a trend that would only increase in the postwar era. Douglass's closest black comrade, James McCune Smith, ill with the beginnings of congestive heart failure, did not join the fifty-three-member New York delegation. [2]

The delegates elected Douglass as their president; he was ushered with "great applause" to the stage by the younger, Oberlin-educated Langston. Douglass swiftly announced in his sonorous voice that "the cause which we come here to promote is sacred." He envisioned the "wide, wide world" watching them as they promoted no less than the "freedom, progress, elevation, and perfect enfranchisement of the entire colored people." On the following mornings or evenings the convention would begin with prayers by the Reverend Garnet or others, and strikingly, with song, including "John Brown's Body," "Blow Ye the Trumpet, Blow," and on the final day, Julia Ward Howe's recently composed "Battle Hymn of the Republic." How moving it must have been to hear full-throated renditions of such paeans to the emancipationist vision of the war and of the old Exodus story. At least one woman, Edmonia Highgate of Syracuse, addressed the convention, introduced by Douglass. The minutes do not record her speech, except to say that Highgate urged the men to steadfastness in the cause until the "glorious day of jubilee shall come." Most poignant of all, at the afternoon session of the second day, Garnet took the lead in unfurling across the platform the battle flag of the First Louisiana Colored Troops, a unit that had achieved fame for its bravery at the battle of Port Hudson in July 1863.[3]

Delivered on the final day of the convention, Douglass's speech was both celebration and warning. Since the Republicans did not want him out on the stump campaigning, he delivered his own political accounting to his fellow African Americans on this election eve. He addressed the question of history itself, bounding forward it seemed, to illuminate new barriers and obstacles to progress. In eloquence tinged with anger and anxiety, Douglass appealed to his own people, but especially to the generic "you" of white Northerners about to go to the polls. Nations could "learn righteousness" from supreme crises, he argued, and this was a moment when "mourning mingles everywhere with the national shout of victory." Douglass asserted that the opportunity to crush slavery, throw back racism, and reinvent the American republic around principles of racial equality "may not come again in a century."[4]

Everything was at stake in defeating the Democrats and finishing the war. Douglass provided a litany of the horrors that would result if the Democrats, allied with Confederates, managed a negotiated peace settlement, resulting in the reestablishment of "the white man's country," and the obliteration of "all the lessons taught by these four years of fire and sword." Douglass portrayed the Democrats as the enemies of mankind, and of history itself. They were the "fiendish . . . hellhounds" ready to pounce on black people and their allies at their first grasp of power. They had cleverly cultivated the political landscape with what the next century would call Orwellian language. Avoiding the words *slavery* or *slaves* or *slaveholders*, Douglass maintained, Democratic doublespeak sought the "perpetuation" of slavery in their platform under the guise of such "verbiage" as *private rights* or the *basis of Federal Union* or *the Constitution.*[5]

Douglass took up the meaning of friends and enemies, claiming to be as worried about the Republicans' hostility to black voting rights as to the Democrats' darkest aims. "It is . . . not the malignity of enemies alone we have to fear," he announced, "but the deflection from the straight line of principle by those who are known throughout the world as our special friends." Douglass worried about possible peace plans that might get consummated before slavery legally ended. As though directly addressing Congress and a reelected President Lincoln, he employed a moving refrain four times in a single paragraph calling for the Thirteenth Amendment: "We implore you to abolish slavery," he sang out over and over. Only then, he believed, would slavery's destruction and the "national welfare" achieve "everlasting foundations."[6]

Then Douglass signaled what would be for him a primary argument throughout the postwar era—he demanded in the classic terms of political liberalism the franchise as the greatest of all rights. Arguing from natural-rights moral doctrine, Douglass contended that in a republic all elements of liberty—"personal freedom; the right to testify in courts of law; the right to own, buy and sell real estate; the right to sue and be sued"— depended for protection on suffrage. The vote, said Douglass, was the "keystone to the arch of human liberty." But he also accurately anticipated that the black male vote would bring great practical value to Republicans in the postwar era. The only guarantee about a postemancipation order in the South, he said, was the "sullen hatred towards the National Government" and the freedmen on the part of ex-Confederates. Theirs would be a "sacred animosity" toward their conquerors, black and white. "We may conquer Southern armies," proclaimed Douglass, "but it is another thing to conquer Southern hate." The only weapon available was the votes of 4 million new "friends."[7] With these astute strokes of war propaganda and moral philosophy, Douglass awaited the election results.

The convention delegates in Syracuse had good reason for anxiety over the presidential election of 1864. They had keenly observed events for months, as the Thirteenth Amendment abolishing slavery, supported by Lincoln, had passed in the Senate but failed of the two-thirds majority in the House of Representatives. With the war in terrible military stalemate in Virginia and Georgia, Lincoln and his administration fell into turmoil over its own emancipation policy. "Peace Democrats" relentlessly attacked Lincoln and emancipation as the obstacles to ending the bloodshed. His reelection in danger, the president authorized an ill-advised, informal peace mission to meet with Confederate representatives. But the effort backfired on Lincoln. He allowed the nettlesome Horace Greeley to go to Niagara Falls, Canada, in July and meet with what turned out to be bogus Confederate representatives. Lincoln crafted a brief letter addressed infamously "To Whom It May Concern," declaring that "any proposition" for peace would be received from Confederates as long as it included reunion of the states and the "abandonment of slavery." The Niagara letter was a public-relations disaster. Confederate sympathizers in the North (known to their foes as Copperheads) and the Democratic Party newspapers seized on this news and pilloried Lincoln as the bloodthirsty war maker standing in the way of peace in order to free slaves. The *Cincinnati Enquirer* declared Lincoln's clandestine actions "a finality, which . . . will preclude any conference for a settlement. Every soldier . . . that is killed, will lose his life not for the Union, the Stars and Stripes, but for the Negro."[8] From here, the Democratic campaign of 1864 descended into ever-more-savage racism, driving many Republicans into obfuscation on the emancipation amendment.

From where Douglass and other black leaders sat, the Republicans only added fuel to the Democrats' racist fires. No less than Secretary of State William Seward and Secretary of the Interior John Usher suddenly denied that emancipation would be a condition of reunion if Lincoln was reelected. They asserted, confusingly, that abolition would be left "to the arbitrament of the courts of law." Douglass called out Seward by name and quoted him at length in the Syracuse speech. The secretary's "studied words" at this crucial time could only mean that the federal government was about to "not only . . . make peace with the Rebels, but to make peace with slavery." Like a prophet in despair, Douglass felt betrayed, thrown back into 1861–62 and onto his apocalyptic imagination. The "surest . . . ground of hope" now, he said, was in the "madness" of the Confederates to continue their war until "destitute . . . and . . . divested of their slaves."[9] This was hardly the prescription for the "abolition war" in which he had placed confidence in 1863. But betting on his enemy's actions had become an old habit.

Most dismaying of all was the Democrats' racist rampage in using the label of "miscegenation" on Lincoln and the Republicans. The very term was first employed in early 1864 in a pamphlet, *Miscegenation: The Theory of the Blending of the Races*, written by two reporters, David Croly and George Wakeman (although published anonymously), at the Democratic *New York World*. The pernicious pamphlet purported to be crafted by Republicans touting the values of interbreeding blacks and whites to improve both. Most people detected the hoax, but the idea exploded as a political weapon more lethal than any impending constitutional amendment. Congressmen picked up the term and used it to attack Republican measures such as early efforts to establish the Freedmen's Bureau. Demonstrating white men's fears about racial purity as well as gender disorder, the tactic also exposed the depth of white supremacy abolitionists confronted.[10]

Democrats labeled Lincoln "Abraham Africanus I" and the "original ourangoutang," suggesting he had African ancestors. Democratic campaign handbills, lithographs, and songs about race mixing as the "Republican solution" for the war flooded the North. "All the painful woes that wreck our lovely land," moaned one ditty, "Are due the Abolitionists, the Miscegenation Band." A widely distributed print from the *New York World* showed the scurrilous caricature of "The Miscegenation Ball," a fake dance held at the "Central Lincoln Club" for "colored belles" and white Republican men pining with "love sick glances" for the "octoroons."[11] Frightening and disheartening to African Americans, this kind of race-baiting politics knew no bounds; at the polls, however, it did not work with enough white voters, especially after Union military successes in Georgia, the Shenandoah Valley, and Mobile Bay turned the tide in Lincoln's favor.

In this extraordinary wartime election, in which nineteen states allowed soldiers to vote at the front, the incumbent president carried the popular vote by 2,206,938 to McClellan's 1,803,787. In the electoral college Lincoln won 212–21. Despite fears that a good deal of the Union army might still be loyal to one of its former generals, Lincoln carried a stunning 78 percent of the soldier vote. Those thousands of men in blue who stood at ballot boxes in Virginia, Georgia, Tennessee, or Mississippi knew they were casting their vote for emancipation as well as saving the Union. Few black soldiers could vote in their states, but that did not stop their own officers at the front from letting them express themselves. Christian Fleetwood, a free black man from Baltimore and twenty-four-year-old noncommissioned sergeant major in the Fourth US Colored Troops, left this simple line in his diary: "Nov. 8, 1864—polled the regiment. 300 majority for Lincoln." Fleetwood, who could not yet vote in Maryland, earned the Congressional

Medal of Honor for extraordinary heroism at the Battle of Chaffin's Farm, near Petersburg, Virginia, September 29, 1864.[12]

On Election Day, November 8, Douglass voted in Rochester. A local citizen later reminisced about working at the poll and tallying the famous orator's ballot for Lincoln. That night the two men were walking back into downtown Rochester to follow the nationwide returns at the telegraph office. Four drunken white men blocked the street and challenged Douglass by shouting, "Nigger." According to this witness, "Douglass stepped right out in front of them" and with fists raised challenged them in return. "Come on I am ready to settle this thing with you right here and now." The drunken cowards "slunk out of the way and into the darkness," wrote the former poll worker. He asked Douglass if he was hurt, to which the former editor replied, "Oh, no, I am not hurt in the least; the boys were probably not pleased with the news they had heard and wanted to give vent to their disappointment." That night, asserted this witness, Douglass owned a "physical victory as well as a great political triumph."[13] The tortured election season of fear and racism had ended in relief and reasons to believe the war had made a profound turn toward Union and abolitionist victory.

On the Sunday after the election a celebration took place at Spring Street AME in Rochester. Douglass took to the pulpit to praise the reelection of Lincoln and to announce that he was about to embark on a special journey to Baltimore, his first-ever public return to the city where he had escaped from slavery. In the comfort of this hometown congregation, he drew on metaphors from Genesis and Noah's Ark. The "waters of the flood were retiring," he rejoiced, and he saw a "sign that the billows of slavery are rolling back to leave the land blooming again." In the ancient story, Noah had sent a dove flying out the window of the ark to determine if the waters of the great flood had receded; the bird returned the first time with an "olive leaf" in its bill. The second time the dove did not return, and Noah "removed the covering of the ark and looked, and behold, the face of the ground was dry." We cannot know for certain how Douglass prepared for such speeches or sermons, but that he consulted the first book of his Old Testament to grapple with the meaning of the Republican victory and the new prospects for emancipation is profoundly telling. He was not merely trying to connect with his black church audience; he reached, as he had so many times before, for ancient wisdom and metaphor, for a sense of sacred transformation amid the profane violence of war and the sordid practices of politics. He mixed the prophetic voices of the Hebrew prophets with his own. Something higher than the human capacity for folly to thwart good had just occurred. The election, said Douglass, had been "one to determine . . . life or death to the nation." It had wrought "changes . . . vast and wonderful." He linked the afflicted present to the oldest rebirth story in his culture.[14]

Douglass believed the fate of black folk in America now depended on a new order of power, law, and rights that would rise from the war. He told the packed pews of Spring Street AME that he discerned signs in the election, a "redeemed and purified nation," not unlike Noah, had seen green land, the world reviving anew. He offered faith that the country, despite its worst elements, could now save "republican government," pass the constitutional amendment, and "not return the sword to the scabbard" until the Confederacy and slavery were destroyed. So sanguine was Douglass that he even claimed victory over "all the negro minstrels, all the low clowns of the circus . . . all the rowdies of the street" who had fought so hard "in favor of the vile slaveholding traitors."[15] When he challenged those four thugs on the street in Rochester on election night, Douglass was the political analyst ready to fight with all the weapons he possessed—words, fists, and votes.

By November 1 the state of Maryland had adopted a new "free Constitution," abolishing slavery in a referendum by the narrow margin of 30,174 to 29,799. Douglass made his dramatic return to Baltimore on the sixteenth, and the next day, he addressed a primarily black standing-room-only gathering at the Bethel AME Church in Fell's Point, the place where he may have met Anna Murray. Reporters covering the event deemed Douglass the "illustrious exile." A "perfect torrent of rapturous applause" echoed in the church as Douglass strode down the main aisle arm in arm with his older sister, Eliza Bailey Mitchell. Eliza was fifty-two years old and had traveled sixty miles from Talbot County for the reunion with her famous brother. They had not seen each other since 1836, when Fred Bailey had last departed from the Eastern Shore. Eliza had been free since 1844, when after years of difficult labor, she and her husband, Peter Mitchell, managed to purchase her liberty from the Aulds. She had never learned to read or write, but had nonetheless followed keenly her brother's career and, in 1856, named one of her daughters Mary Douglass Mitchell. Variations on this reunion of siblings, free and former slaves, occurred all over the South in the coming year; indeed Douglass experienced more of them himself. The contrasts at the church that day were both happy and achingly poignant. Eliza had raised nine children, and all labored in various menial jobs to live, while Frederick had become a citizen of the world conquering lecture halls from Boston and New York to London and Edinburgh.[16]

The press reported that Douglass spoke for three hours that night, from a pulpit surrounded by American flags. He wished to rise above "egotism" for this homecoming, but that was not possible: "The fact that I am where I am, is really the subject, and the whole subject . . . for this evening." As in Rochester a few days earlier, he harkened to Noah and Genesis. This time he was himself the "sign" on the dark clouds; he embodied Noah's dove from the ark. "The return of the dove to the ark, with a leaf," declared Douglass, "was no surer sign that the flood had subsided from the mountains of the east, than my coming among you is a sign that the bitter waters of slavery have subsided from the majestic hills, and fertile valleys of Maryland." [17]

Douglass reminisced about each preacher he had heard in that church in the 1830s, about fighting with the "town boys" on the docks, and especially how it was in Baltimore where he first became a "thoughtful boy" cultivating a "faculty of the mind." He declared himself a proud member of the "children of Maryland." All of his kinfolk, black and white, were rooted in the soil and blood of Maryland. Douglass described a family romance with the state and region, reversing metaphors he had prominently used in his *Narrative* to represent the hopelessness of his bondage. "Then I left [his escape in 1838], shaking the dust from my feet," he rhapsodized, "as leaving a doomed city, now I return to greet with an affectionate kiss, the humblest pebble from the shores of your glorious Chesapeake." Freedom could change everything, especially in a tear-filled church of memory where he had hatched his "Baltimore dreams." It was as if he announced that one of the "swift-winged angels," the sailing ships of the Bay on which he had yearned to fly while imprisoned by Covey, had brought the "exiled son" home. [18]

Douglass took the Baltimore speech out with a brilliant political analysis of the right of "self-ownership," the absurdity of "property in man," and of America's dilemma over race. "Liberty is logical, as well as slavery," he proclaimed; "the one demands the restoration of all rights, as sternly as the other demands the destruction of all rights." Above all others the right to vote was the "solid rock" on which to build the foundation of a new American state. [19] He ended by calling whites and blacks to exercise a new psychological logic, to look into their hearts and minds to cross the racial divide of centuries.

Douglass addressed white people directly. What are you afraid of? he asked. He reminded them that in the race of "civilization" and history, their "Anglo-Saxon branch" possessed all the advantages. "Knowledge is power, and you have knowledge: Wealth is influence, and you have wealth. Majorities rule under our form of government, and you are the majority." In phrasing and arguments so modern, that might fit any twenty-first-century discussion of racism and privilege, Douglass demanded to know why thinking white people so feared competition with their fellow black humans. Too many whites, he said, were "haunted with the idea, that to invest the colored race with equal rights is dangerous to the rights of white men." Such a "mischievous heresy" had for far too long paralyzed history. In no uncertain terms Douglass concluded, "I deny that the black man's degradation is essential to the white man's elevation." To believe otherwise, was to "pay a sorry compliment to the white race." [20]

Then Douglass turned to his fellow blacks and delivered a stern prescription of hard work and self-reliance, one that would ride in tandem with his political liberalism throughout Reconstruction and beyond. The joyous and tearful homecoming ended with the plea to his people not to misinterpret freedom as release from labor. "You must be industrious," he lectured his fellow former slaves, as he also urged those from the lower, rural counties of Maryland to "stick to their agricultural pursuits." Nothing ambiguous or metaphorical here. "I believe $150 in the country is better than $400 in the city. . . . All men are equal naturally, but not practically." He urged blacks to save money, "buy land," "educate their children," and forge a new generation "capable of thinking as well as digging." He promised them that the "more intelligent and refined" they became, the more white people will "respect you." [21] These were complex dreams even for a jubilee meeting. Just where and how Douglass himself fit on this spectrum of striving he soon had to decide.

Douglass did not yet understand just how grim the prospects were for such self-help dictates in the daily lives of freedmen in places such as the Eastern Shore. His son Lewis visited Eliza Mitchell's struggling family in June 1865. The war was over, blacks were free, but Lewis called St. Michaels "one of the worst places in the South." No matter how hard they worked, Lewis observed Eastern Shore blacks stymied economically at every turn. "The white people will do everything they can," he wrote to his father, "to keep the blacks from buying land. Large tracts of woods that the whites will neither use nor sell to the blacks lie idle and wasting." Wages were pitifully meager for black farmhands, and even those who worked in "oystering" could not use their savings to buy land. In the neighborhood in which his father had grown up, Lewis saw the social results of the protection of white status the elder Douglass had warned about in Baltimore. [22]

In all, over the next twelve days, Douglass gave some six lectures at five different black and white churches in Baltimore and Washington, DC, including a version of his "Mission of the War" address. But apart from all the public oratory, and revealing his private desire to connect with his former owners, he called on Sophia Auld, the former mistress who had taught him his first letters and who now lived on Ann Street. But she refused to see him; at the door Douglass was rejected by Benjamin Auld, Sophia's son and younger brother of Tommy, for whom Fred Bailey had originally been sent to Baltimore as the slave companion. Benjamin, now a Baltimore policeman, had read Douglass's autobiography and let him know in no uncertain terms that his family resented the author's treatment of them in the portrayal of his slave youth. In *Bondage and Freedom*, in the public "Letter to My Old Master," and in many early speeches in Britain and America, Douglass had indeed assailed the Aulds as quintessential models of evil slaveholders. He would have to wait many years for the genuine reconciliations he sought with the Aulds and their descendants.[23]

For Douglass, his family, and his closest friends, the final months of the Civil War provided days of rejoicing and days of mourning. For Douglass, constantly on the road lecturing, these months were frenzied and exhausting. After his grueling tour to Maryland in November, he was speaking in Portland, Maine, to benefit a soldiers' home by December 16. By January 2, 1865, he was one of many speakers—including Garrison and William Wells Brown—at the second annual celebration of the Emancipation Proclamation in Tremont Temple in Boston. Two sessions occurred, one morning and one evening; Douglass and Garrison did not have to share a platform. During an especially brutal Northern winter, in January and February, the Rochester orator held forth at all kinds of "jubilee" meetings and benefits from Troy and Albany, New York, to Boston, to Wilmington, Delaware, and stops in between in Hoboken, New Jersey, New York City, Philadelphia, and again in Baltimore. In Douglass's standard stump performance that winter he exulted in the "events" that now seemed to happen with such "velocity" as to "dazzle us." The Proclamation was the "mountain rock amid the dashing waves of a troubled ocean." Lincoln's reelection and black soldiers in the field were causes for jubilation. But nothing was secure or lasting until black men attained the right to vote. Douglass warned that the freedpeople must not be "citizens in war and aliens in peace."[24] Real victory was far from won.

In Rochester, Anna, as always, kept the home fires burning in these winters as her husband rode the rails up and down the country. Her children all now grown and struggling to be independent, Anna had few companions other than whoever in the Spring Street church may have looked in on her. Rosetta and her new baby were nearby, and no doubt Anna was indispensable to the young mother. The lonely "reserve" and "acrid" personality that Rosetta recalled about her mother only deepened in these winters, despite all the hopeful political and war news. Rosetta admiringly said her mother "strived to live a Christian life instead of talking it." But by 1865, Anna must have missed the older family "custom," as her daughter recalled it, "to read a chapter in the Bible around the table, each reading a verse in turn until the chapter was completed." [25] Douglass himself, no doubt, chose those passages in the children's youth, giving Anna, as listener, her own personalized Bible study.

Frederick Jr. never served as a combat soldier, but remained proud throughout his life of having helped recruit especially members of the Fifty-Fifth Massachusetts black regiment. He would not marry until 1870 and lived only to be fifty-one, dying in 1892. He must have taken hard the news in December of the bloody Battle of Honey Hill, on Hilton Head, South Carolina, where the Fifty-Fifth regiment lost nearly one hundred men. Charles and Frederick Jr., as the youngest Douglass sons, wrote frequently to each other in that last year of the war. Charles worked at the freedmen's hospital in Washington, DC, but as the war wound down, he felt adrift, financially stunted, even desperate to find new employment. He wrote to his father in February 1865 of his frustrations, thinking of relocating at war's end to Nashville or Savannah, where he had heard rumors of business opportunities. "I mean to have some money," Charles wrote, "and I want to go off . . . on my own hook as every young man does. I see nothing ahead for me unless I have money." He still asked for his father's "consent," but insisted on a "bold start." Such a sentiment reflected a long pattern of Charles's desperation for the elder Douglass's approval. "If I fail I will not return home a beggar," he said. "I will stay and strive until I am worth something. I am in earnest and mean to go ahead." [26] To the father who preached a stern self-reliance to gatherings of black former slaves, these words must have been painful to read from his youngest boy, who had just turned twenty. To the son the father's fame and achievement was one part inspiration and one part albatross.

Meanwhile, Lewis Douglass, recovering from his war wounds in late 1864 and early 1865, kept up his long, frustrating courtship of Amelia Loguen (they did not finally marry until 1869). He wrote to Amelia of his desire to be "more self-reliant, more independent." He promised to labor at "making life," and especially at getting "money, for without that we would be like a ship without a helm, soon to go wreck on the rock of poverty." In September 1864, Lewis wished he had already proposed marriage to Amelia; but he could only conclude that the war had left him "so unsettled," without any clear "identity." Feeling too old to go back and live under his mother's roof, he declared, "I do not know where my home is." Amelia apparently stopped responding. By March 1865, Lewis wrote of the many weeks of "anxiety" over her silence. "What's de matter," he scrawled in dialect. He described terrible spring floods in Rochester damaging "stone and brick buildings," and the Main Street bridge "knocked and bruised fearfully," as though they symbolized his own temperament. He did seem gleeful at least that the Confederacy was collapsing, "their vision of an empire founded on the unpaid toil of black millions fading away from their longing sight."[27] Lewis could craft prose almost like his father; he simply was not having luck with love or with making a living. His model for achievement, much less greatness, was a mountain too high.

The elder Douglass, however, managed a complicated romantic and emotional life. Ottilie Assing remained very much in love with Douglass through the end of the turbulent war years and beyond. Their relationship greatly frustrated her at times, and at other times was richly fulfilling. Exactly what it meant to him is not clear. He needed Ottilie for intellectual stimulation, emotional support, and perhaps physical intimacy; he continued to cultivate their long-term relationship by stopping at her boardinghouse in Hoboken on his travels whenever he could, often for only one day and sometimes for as long as a week. Assing introduced Douglass to her circle of Hoboken German émigrés, some of whom became his close friends, especially Sylvester Rosa Koehler, a much younger curator and art historian who took a deep interest in the American abolitionist. Astonishingly, Assing spent as many as three to four months in Rochester during the summers, living upstairs in the Douglass home, especially after 1865. How she and Mrs. Douglass coexisted in Anna's house endures as an intriguing mystery, although by the frenzied war years and their aftermath, short- and long-term guests, especially women, were hardly a new thing at the Douglass homestead.[28]

Much of what we know about Assing and of her connection with Douglass comes from Ottilie's letters to her sister, Ludmilla, who lived in Italy. Particularly as the war ended, and Douglass searched for a new career, Assing dreamed and schemed assiduously from 1865 into the early 1870s to convince her special companion to join her on a long-term, if not permanent, journey to Europe. He probably never seriously considered it, although he appears to have listened. A common refrain in Ottilie's letters was that she stood "ready and willing" to travel back to Europe, "but could not convince Douglass and could not make up my mind to go by myself and to, on top of things, rob him of the only time of year [summer] that he looks forward to with joy and anticipation." When in Rochester, Ottilie often appeared contentedly at home "on the green marvel island," the homestead surrounded by a large garden and orchard with well-kept walking paths. She constantly wrote of her pleasure in introducing books to Douglass and reading them with him, from Dickens to German and French works. In August 1868, a forty-nine-year-old Ottilie wrote from the hill on South Avenue that she was so "completely content with the kind of garden life I am living here that I have no desire for anything else." If the domestic situation was awkward or disappointing, which she would later say in embittered language, the "garden" itself had "a world to offer. . . . It constitutes a great pleasure for me to collect fruit from under the trees every morning, which given the great size of the garden as well as the number of fruit trees can involve a rather long journey." She seems to have thrilled to the sheer "activity . . . the different views, the lighting and the constellation of clouds." Her closest companion was Fox, her "civilized and most faithful cat." [29]

Assing may have expunged loneliness at the same time she lived it in a different way while in Rochester. Her secret garden was no secret at all to anyone looking. Ottilie never wrote of Douglass taking long strolls with her in the garden paths. That garden and orchard had been the product of Anna's labor, imagination, and desire. But this poetic, deeply literary woman somehow established for a time her own place near, if not truly with, Douglass, and somehow in the middle of Anna's world. Assing never mentioned whether she peeled any of the pears she picked to help prepare a meal for all the mouths that were fed from the Douglass kitchen, where Anna ruled.

Assing remained a frequent, astute commentator on the war, emancipation, and many other issues in its aftermath as long as *Morgenblatt* maintained publication. She wrote at length and with acuity about the election of 1864. The months of the campaign brought a "fever pitch" and passed with "brooding anxiety." Echoing Douglass's speeches, she thought the election would determine the "fate . . . of the entire country." She effectively exposed some of the "sophistries" of Democrats and Copperheads, but held little enthusiasm for Lincoln, whom she considered a political creature without a genuine antislavery core. She preferred the alternative candidacy of the more radical Frémont, but as a political analyst, she delivered an astute explanation of his failure, especially in the wake of Union military successes. Assing voraciously read newspapers and walked in the circles of radical German émigrés such as Carl Schurz. Never lacking for confidence in her own judgments, she drew class and ethnic lines indelibly across American politics. Chief among supporters of the Copperheads, peace Democrats were the "crude, brutal, ignorant" Irish, "given to drink and full of hatred for the Negro." Leading the way for the enlightened Republicans were "radical, educated Germans," immigrants such as herself and her Hoboken circle, who brought the "German mind" to the contest in their adopted country. Assing told a poignant story of attending an election-eve speech by Schurz at the Cooper Institute in New York, crowds spilling into the hallways. The stage was decorated with "red, white, and blue" flags, and for a lectern, "they had piled up cannonballs" from which the orator delivered a brilliant endorsement of Lincoln's reelection.[30] Assing appreciated political symbolism as long as it did not embrace religion.

Although Assing continually misapprehended Lincoln, her interpretation of the election results was perceptive. Northerners had voted for "the complete suppression of the rebellion" and for emancipation. She saw the importance of the soldier vote, and by the beginning of 1865, much as Douglass had many times said, she put as much faith in the "suicidal blindness and rigidity" of Confederate leadership, insisting on their "independence," as in the "firmness" of the Lincoln administration. Assing had become not only an American citizen, but a talented political commentator on the "revolution" in her new country.[31] Whether Douglass read her columns is unknown. But their encounters provided crucial occasions for the flow of ideas from which both of them benefited.

She was "intoxicated with joy," she reported on February 3, 1865, "about the adoption of the constitutional amendment in Congress" abolishing slavery. Working especially hard on a list of retiring Democrats and relying on eight others who absented themselves from the chamber, the Lincoln administration and Republican House leadership managed a decisive roll call of 119–56 in favor of passage of the enactment; they had only two votes to spare to rally the required two-thirds. Some states immediately ratified the Thirteenth Amendment, but full ratification by three-fourths of the states would not come until December 1865. There had never been a legislative moment quite like this when the simple but resounding language entered law: "Neither slavery nor involuntary servitude, except as a punishment for crime, whereof the party shall have been duly convicted, shall exist within the United States, or any place subject to their jurisdiction." Emotionally, Assing almost choked on her astonishment: "Reality, at times, does go beyond anything the powers of imagination can draw up."[32]

Douglass lectured in Boston on January 27 and Troy, New York, on February 1. Hence, he could not be in Washington on January 31 to witness the unprecedented jubilation that engulfed the congressional chamber the moment the amendment was adopted. Republican Congressmen wept and shouted like revelers; they knew they had done something special, a historic act for the ages. Many blacks attended the session, sitting and standing in the galleries above with electric anticipation. Among them was Charles Douglass. Shortly afterward, he wrote to his father, "I wish that you could have been here the day that the constitutional amendment was passed forever abolishing slavery in the United States, such rejoicing I never before witnessed, cannons firing, people hugging and shaking hands, white people I mean, flags flying all over the city." Charles would never forget that day, nor did his father ever forget his son's depiction of it: "I tell you things are progressing finely, and if they will only give us the elective franchise and shoulder straps (which is only simple justice) that will be all I ask. . . . It is a big thing for me to see all this."[33]

That tender son-to-father letter echoed some of the themes the elder Douglass proffered now out on the lecture circuit. From January to May 1865, throughout the Northeast and mid-Atlantic states, from Massachusetts to Delaware and Maryland, Douglass vehemently demanded the right to vote for black men guaranteed at the federal level. He warned of the poverty and lack of education of the liberated freedpeople as well as the hostility and potential violence to come from the white South in the wake of their defeat. He also articulated an evolving vision of Reconstruction. Everywhere he appeared, Douglass celebrated victory as well as delivered warnings of the unprecedented struggles ahead. To two thousand people in Cooper Institute in New York he announced that they were "living at a glorious moment" in the nation's history. But the Republican Party had to learn now to be as "logical" as the Democratic Party, by which he meant that antislavery and pro-black-rights efforts had to overcome decades of proslavery demands in law and morality.[34]

At every stop Douglass preached the moral value and the practical meaning of the right to vote. He called the prospect of the vote his "one idea." Everything else—blacks' demonstrated ability to work, to fight, to serve faithfully in the face of all manner of racism—depended on "the immediate, unconditional, and universal enfranchisement of the black man." The vote had been earned in blood, it embodied citizenship, and it would be the freedpeople's protector against the "treason" and "deadly hate" of the defeated Confederates. In a world where African Americans had never been taken seriously as a voting bloc, the franchise would lift the "stigma of inferiority" from their heads.[35]

Here was Douglass's political liberalism at its most hopeful. But he almost never recited his litany of reasons for the franchise without trotting out his drunken Irishman joke, especially among New England Yankees. He could easily garner laughter and applause, as he did in Boston on January 26, with "If we know enough to be hung, we know enough to vote. If the negro knows enough to pay taxes . . . he knows enough to vote. . . . If he knows enough to shoulder a musket and fight for the flag . . . he knows enough to vote. If he knows as much when he is sober as an Irishman knows when drunk, he knows enough to vote." He was eager to counter the Uncle Tom image of the quiescent black man, the "perfect lamb" exuding Christian piety but not standing up, demanding and fighting, while exploiting the "picture of the Irishman, drunk and good humored." Moreover, he asserted African Americans' claims to "a state of civilization" by contrasting them with "the Indians," who may "die out." "The Indian, to be sure," said Douglass, "is a stout man; he is proud and dignified; he is too stiff to bend, and breaks. He sees the plowshare of civilization casting up the bones of his venerated fathers, and he retires from the lakes to the mountains. . . . He will not even imitate your wearing apparel, but clings to his blanket, lives in hollow trees, and finally, dies."[36]

To these brutal racial images, Douglass compared "the negro," who "likes to be in the midst of civilization," in the "city . . . where he can hear the finest music, and where he can see all that is going on in the world." A black man, declared Douglass with some obvious personal reference, "wears a coat after the latest European pattern. . . . If you see him go down town and not see his face, you would think that it was a [white] man going along. They are not going to die out."[37] Such egregious racial characterizations fit nineteenth-century popular attitudes as much as they clang painfully on our ears today. But for a man who spent so much of his life trying to thwart America's endemic racism, it is troubling to observe his use of racial and ethnic stereotypes to exalt the capacities and claims of his own people. So desperate was America's scramble for rights and resources among its marginalized peoples that even Douglass employed ugly language for comparative advantage.

In the spring of 1865, however, Douglass tended to end his speeches on a high scriptural note, the parable of Lazarus and the rich man in Luke 16. Douglass believed that with emancipation and the defeat of Southern slaveholders, Americans witnessed the "fulfillment" of the tale of "a certain poor man who laid at the gate of a rich man." In the ancient story that has inspired a black spiritual and a famous modern folk song ("Rock My Soul in the Bosom of Abraham"), a rich man "was clothed in purple and fine linen, and fared sumptuously every day." A poor beggar named Lazarus, "full of sores" from leprosy, lay at the rich man's gate, "desiring to be fed crumbs which fell from the rich man's table." Dogs lick the poor man's wounds. Both men die; the beggar is "carried by the angels into Abraham's bosom," while the rich man is buried and descends into hell. As he begins to burn, the tormented rich man sees Lazarus "afar off" resting in the comfort and security of Abraham's embrace. He cries out, "Father Abraham, have mercy upon me, and send Lazarus that he may dip the tip of his finger in water, and cool my tongue." As the rich man is slowly engulfed in flames, Abraham (God) answers that the tables have turned and it is too late; he scolds the rich man for never listening to "Moses and the prophets." [38]

Douglass brilliantly employed the parable, and his auditors seemed to love it. "Everybody is calling for Lazarus now at the North and the South," he announced. "We all know who the rich man is in this country, and who the poor man is, or has been." "The slaves" were the "Lazaruses of the South, lying at the rich slaveholder's gates; but it has come to pass," said Douglass in his best King James paraphrases, "that the poor man and the rich man are dead, for both have been in a dying condition for some time." Eliciting great laughter and applause from a New York audience in January, he concluded that the "poor man is said to be very near in Abraham's bosom. And the rich man is crying out, 'Father Abraham, send Lazarus.'" By April in Boston, Douglass confidently applied the story to Lincoln and the end of the war. Richmond had just fallen, the haughty slaveholding Confederates were in flight, those "arrayed in purple . . . in silk and satin," with "breast sparkling with diamonds," were defeated and pleading to have their Lazaruses back. "Send Lazarus back," cried the rump of Jefferson Davis's revolution and Robert E. Lee's army. Douglass provided the new answers: "But Father Abraham says, 'If they hear not Grant nor Sherman, neither will they be persuaded though I send Lazarus unto them.'" With an arm gesture to the sky, Douglass shouted the transformation: "I say we are way up yonder now, no mistake!" With his audience shouting approval and in "great merriment," Douglass had recrafted a piece of Scripture to fit the moment of impending victory—for the federal Union and for black freedom.[39] Just how much the mortal Father Abraham's bosom (the United States) could hold and comfort the freedpeople as they came back to life was to be determined. And very soon that mortal Abraham was gone.

Eager for a place at the center of American politics, especially among Republicans, as well as yearning to see, feel, and shape historic events, Douglass traveled to Washington, DC, in early March for Lincoln's second inauguration. Douglass arrived a couple of days earlier than the Saturday, March 4, ceremony, on a crowded train at the B&O depot, where he listened to a band playing "The Battle Cry of Freedom." The city was a rain-soaked mess, many streets mere troughs of mud. Every hotel was jammed to capacity, with cots assembled in hallways for the throngs of visitors. Although the end of the war was in sight, Washington was anything but a festive national capital. Almost every available building had become a hospital for the wounded and dying soldiers of the Union armies—some merely large makeshift sheds, others in churches and armories, while still others were government buildings such as the Patent Office, and the Capitol itself. Amputees hobbling on crutches and standing on corners with empty shirtsleeves could be spotted everywhere. By spring 1865 nearly forty thousand liberated slaves had migrated into Washington, some living in freedmen's villages and others always in search of housing and work. Well over a thousand visible Confederate deserters had also swelled the ranks of the military and civilian homeless by March, causing no shortage of fear about violence and disorder.[40] Lazarus, it turns out, had come to Washington and was lying at the gates.

Douglass remembered the scene in dramatic, novelistic language. He felt "danger" everywhere, he said, and "murder in the air." The "rebellion" of the Confederacy, though almost spent, "had reached the verge of madness," and its vengeful agents lurked in the District's muddy alleys. The day before the inaugural, Douglass took tea at the home of chief justice of the Supreme Court, Salmon Chase. The abolitionist wrote about the visit, and much else, as a series of steps in his own rising status. Chase had known Douglass from "early antislavery days," but having the black leader for tea with "dignity and grandeur" at his own table was in the guest's view a public tribute. Douglass remembered fondly assisting Chase's daughter, Kate, as she helped her father try on his new robe for the inauguration.[41] The former slave surely felt like an insider in such private settings that he could justifiably make into racial triumphs.

Douglass observed the parade on March 4, accompanied by Mrs. Thomas J. Dorsey, the former Louise Tobias and wife of a successful Philadelphia caterer, real estate entrepreneur, and former slave. Douglass had known the Dorseys a long time as family friends; his daughter Rosetta had once boarded with them in Philadelphia. He did not say why Mrs. Dorsey was his companion on such a special day; perhaps her status as part of the Philadelphia black elite helped him secure introductions and housing in Washington. As many as thirty thousand gathered for the ceremony on the East Portico of the Capitol. Douglass and Mrs. Dorsey secured a place in the crowd, standing in the center up front. After a morning of gale winds and hard rain, the skies cleared at the appointed hour. The sea of umbrellas disappeared, but Douglass still remembered the scene as one of "leaden stillness." While awaiting Chase's administering of the oath, Douglass remembered seeing the sitting Lincoln tap Vice President Andrew Johnson and point to the famous black orator up front in the crowd. The president "pointed me out to him." Johnson's initial reaction, wrote Douglass, as "the true index of his heart, was one of bitter contempt and aversion." Then, recovering his poise, the "frown" changed to a "bland and sickly smile." The autobiographer used this recollection to draw a sharp distinction between the martyred Lincoln and the villainous Johnson. As Douglass later learned, Johnson had been inebriated, having indulged in whiskey due to an illness, for his rambling formal speech inside the Capitol only a short time before taking his place for the outdoor ceremony.[42] For Douglass, such a memory, crafted in 1881, was infused with the experience of confronting Johnson's white supremacy firsthand, as well as having battled the seventeenth president's bitter obstructions of Reconstruction.

Lincoln's magnificent speech that day left Douglass breathless and clapping his hands "in gladness and thanksgiving." He said it "sounded more like a sermon than a state paper." He was stunned by its biblical foundations, moved by the forthright statement of slavery as "cause" and emancipation as "result" of "this mighty scourge of war." Douglass observed the lack of vindictive celebration, but felt thrilled by the sentiment of retribution, as Lincoln promised that "every drop of blood drawn by the lash, shall be paid by another drawn with the sword." In Lincoln's "woe due to those by whom the offence came," Douglass heard echoes of his own jeremiads and his relentless war propaganda. He tried to read the emotions of those around him in the audience, but found them "widely different." He would quote from the third paragraph of the Second Inaugural countless times in the coming years. Douglass believed he had never heard such "vital substance . . . compressed in a space so narrow" as in the 703 words of Lincoln's greatest speech. "There seemed at the time to be in the man's soul," Douglass declared in an 1893 speech, "the united souls of all Hebrew prophets." For four long years of war, Douglass had dreamed of writing that speech for Lincoln, to place such words in the president's mouth as "all knew that this interest [slavery] was, somehow, the cause of the war." [43] That Lincoln himself wrote those words in the tragic but exhilarating spring of 1865 was the far more important fact. It was a tribute to the power of events, to Lincoln's own moral fiber and growth, as well as to the political and rhetorical bond the former slave now felt with the president.

On the evening of the inaugural, accompanied again by Mrs. Dorsey, Douglass stepped out and joined the "grand procession" entering the White House reception. He later complained that many other blacks had refused to join him, complaining that they would be rejected. Douglass used the event as a source of personal pride and distinction: "I had for some time looked upon myself as a man, but now in this multitude of the elite of the land, I felt myself a man among men." [44] Douglass stood tall and confronted the White House guards.

As the abolitionist and his black female companion approached the door of the executive mansion, two guards "took me rudely by the arm and ordered me to stand back," Douglass recalled, saying they could "admit no persons of color." After a lifetime of such rejections, Douglass rebelled and demanded entry. The guards acquiesced deceptively by ushering the two African Americans into a hallway where they found themselves "walking some planks out of a window" arranged as a temporary exit. Then Douglass, in raised voice, insisted someone inform the president, "Frederick Douglass is detained by officers at the door." Soon he and Mrs. Dorsey were allowed into the elegant East Room gala. "Like a mountain pine high above all others," wrote Douglass, "Mr. Lincoln stood, in his grand simplicity and homely beauty." [45]

Then followed a scene for the ages as Douglass tells it. "Here comes my friend Douglass," announced the president for all to hear. Lincoln said he had seen the orator in the crowd that afternoon listening to the speech and was eager to know his reaction. Douglass demurred, urging the president to attend to his guests. But focused fully on the unmistakable black man with the large mane of graying hair, Lincoln insisted, "There is no man in the country whose opinion I value more than yours." "Mr. Lincoln," replied the former slave from Tuckahoe, "that was a sacred effort."[46] We do not know what small or deeper talk ensued as other guests crowded into this special meeting of two parts of America. We can only guess at the thrill in Douglass's heart, knowing that the cause he had so long pleaded—a sanctioned war to destroy slavery and potentially to reinvent the American republic around the principle of racial equality—might now come to fruition. Standing in the White House East Room, the Chesapeake Bay no great distance out of the windows to the east, Douglass could fairly entertain the belief that he and Lincoln, the slaves and the nation, were walking that night into a new history.

On the night of April 14, 1865, Good Friday, when the crack from John Wilkes Booth's pistol rang out in Ford's Theatre, mortally wounding Abraham Lincoln in the back of the head, Douglass had just returned to Rochester from speaking engagements in the East, where he had witnessed whole towns in great joy over the Confederate surrender and the end of the war. He, like millions, would never forget the moment he heard the news. Of the "many shocks" endured in four years of war by Americans, Douglass said in a speech some eight months later, the assassination of Lincoln was "heaviest of all." Douglass called it a "grand convulsion," as if the "solid earth opened and swallowed up one of our chief towns or cities." The event instantly became an eternal marker in personal human memory. "A hush fell upon the land," said Douglass, "as though each man in it heard a voice from heaven, an uninterpreted sound from the sky and had paused to learn its meaning." The extremes of feeling were all but impossible to bear, and as the historian Martha Hodes writes, in North and South, among blacks and whites, "irreconcilable personal responses to Lincoln's assassination" would always be "intertwined with different understandings of the war that had just ended." Such it would be for Douglass, who over time fashioned several different kinds of eulogies and symbols of the martyred Lincoln. Douglass never let his audiences forget that though Booth and his conspirators were individual assassins and fierce Confederate partisans, it was "slavery" itself, the "insolent, aggressive, and malignant oligarchy," in a last spasm of madness, that had murdered the president.[47]

In Rochester, as in hundreds of other towns and cities across the North, as well as in a thousand places in the South among former slaves, a springtime of relief turned overnight into horror and mourning. On the fifteenth a huge throng of people gathered at Rochester's City Hall at 3:00 p.m., "not knowing what else to do in the agony of the hour," as Douglass put it. Much of the crowd could not even fit into the space, as Mayor Daniel Moore presided. Several clergymen spoke, including Ezekiel Robinson. Douglass was sitting at the rear of the hall as a loud chant began to ring out: "Douglass! Douglass! Douglass!" The mass of people parted for a pathway as the orator walked to the platform. He recalled feeling "stunned and overwhelmed." In his remarks, he declared it a "day for silence and meditation; for grief and tears."[48] He tried to wrest hope from all the despair, and he was hardly silent.

Less than twenty-four hours after the assassination, on that Easter weekend, Douglass insisted on seeing in the president's sacrifice the nation's new life: "Though Abraham Lincoln dies, the Republic lives." In Lincoln's "blood," they would find the "salvation of our country." Douglass tried to mute his partisanship in this time of grief, but he could not suppress it. The subdued audience began to cheer, even laugh, as the orator complained that it was only yesterday that too many people "were manifesting almost as much gratitude to General Lee for surrendering as to General Grant for compelling him to surrender." Douglass insisted on Appomattox as victory, not a story of mutual honor. "Crimes of treason and slavery," he demanded, ought not be met with "amnesty and oblivion in behalf of men whose hands are red with the best blood of the land." He pleaded that people not be too ready to "do the work of restoration," not make "haste to nurse the spirit that gave birth to Booth."[49]

Douglass must have been carrying a copy of the Second Inaugural in his pocket, or perhaps by then he had memorized key passages. After telling of shaking Lincoln's hand on inauguration day a month earlier, the speaker deftly floated into the president's poetry: "Fondly do we hope, fervently do we pray that this mighty scourge of war may speedily pass away." If Douglass did this from memory or not, many in the crowd choked back gasps and tears. "Yet if God will that it continue until all the wealth piled by the bondman's two hundred and fifty years of unrequited toil shall be sunk, and until every drop of blood drawn by the lash shall be paid by another, drawn with the sword, as was said three thousand years ago, so still must it be said, that the judgments of the Lord are righteous altogether." For so long Douglass wanted to write such words for Lincoln to speak; now, he could indeed speak them for the president, in a shared "sacred effort." Before he ended,

Abraham Lincoln, Washington, DC, February 5, 1865. Alexander Gardner photographer.

the former slave put it all in a simple paraphrase of Lincoln's own argument: "Let us not forget that justice to the negro is safety to the nation." [50]

Much later, in *Life and Times*, Douglass gave this moment a special personal meaning: "I had resided long in Rochester and had made many speeches there which had more or less touched the hearts of my hearers, but never to this day was I brought into such close accord with them. We shared in common a terrible calamity, and this touch of nature made us more than countrymen, it made us Kin." His use of the words *countrymen* and *kin* is revealing. So much of the war's meaning, of his own life, were caught up in those words. In common grief with his mostly white fellow citizens, the black orator felt a sense of belonging. The war had provided a common sense of nationhood, Lincoln's death virtually a common sense of family. Douglass had often used his own story as the embodiment of America's representative exiled son. Out of a common search for meaning in Lincoln's violent death at the dawning of peace, Douglass felt a unity with other Americans. His sense of birthright may have felt more complete that afternoon than ever before. The exiled son who had returned to the free state of Maryland in late 1864 as Noah's "sign" that the flood (slavery and the war) was almost over, was the same exiled son returning to Rochester in April 1865 to announce national redemption through Lincoln's blood. Both were homecomings, one to Douglass's native Maryland, and the other to his adopted western New York. His two lives, two homes, two sides of the Chesapeake, slavery and freedom, were no longer divided. At least for now, Douglass could weep tears of kinship with his countrymen.[51]

Chapter 22

OTHELLO'S OCCUPATION WAS GONE

But where should I go, and what should I do? . . . A man in the situation in which I found myself has not only to divest himself of the old, which is never easily done, but adjust himself to the new, which is still more difficult.

—FREDERICK DOUGLASS, 1881

On the eve of the war, Douglass was a frustrated leader of an enslaved people, considering emigration, and entirely closed out from Republican Party power brokers. Four years later, slaves, with joy and hardship, had experienced varying degrees of emancipation, and black soldiers were stationed across the South. President Lincoln and other Republicans had sought Douglass's counsel. By any definition a revolution had rolled over America. A new era in the nation's racial history had begun, though few could envision the nature of its struggles.

The future of that revolution left Douglass facing enormous personal and intellectual dilemmas. Just what did emancipation mean? Where was the stricken, devastated nation headed? Where in history, philosophy, or prophecy could he find guideposts to help shape a new national order? Would the freed slaves achieve civil and political rights, and would they be protected by the government that had helped to free them? What's more, how would the drumbeating war propagandist, visionary of an apocalyptic struggle for black freedom and the destruction of white slaveholders' civilization, convert overnight into new roles and vocations? What would he do *after* abolition? What would his soldier-veteran sons do with their lives?

How would he, the family patriarch, support his extended and growing network of kinfolk? What would become of a troubled marriage now that all of Anna and Frederick's children were adults starting their own families?

Douglass had ceased editing his newspaper in August 1863—that professional-emotional stem of his life for sixteen years as a radical abolitionist. Although many others had earned the label, no African American had taken on the mantle of "leader" quite like Douglass. That leadership had been rooted in the power of words. How would he now employ his incomparable voice? Who would be listening? If you have been the scorned outsider, what do you do if the door opens and they let you take the first steps inside? What does a radical reformer do if his cause triumphs?

In *Life and Times* in 1881, while reflecting back on the immediate aftermath of the war, Douglass admitted that "a strange and, perhaps, perverse feeling came over me." Great "joy" over the ending of slavery was at times "tinged with a feeling of sadness. I felt that I had reached the end of the noblest and best part of my life; my school was broken up, my church disbanded, and the beloved congregation dispersed, never to come together again." Antislavery had "performed its work," its leaders no longer had the society's attention. The huge audiences might never come back; the endless calls to lecture might cease. So Douglass drew from a scene in a Shakespeare tragedy to express his memory of that moment: "Othello's occupation was gone."[1] For a few years he would struggle with this sense of personal displacement and fear of irrelevance.

Othello was the "moor of Venice" who was in love with a white woman and a powerful man losing his bearings. Douglass surely read the text of the play and felt an affinity for its sense of lost authority and professional purpose. He was amply aware that in comparing himself to Othello he invoked one of the most potent symbols of racial and sexual mores in Western culture. Shakespeare's original Othello was of noble royal origin, a former general of great battlefield achievement, and black. He marries the beautiful young Venetian woman Desdemona. Iago, who has been to the wars with Othello, is his trusted friend. The central drama, however, is how Iago in reality is the coy, vile villain, hates Othello, and slowly renders him distressed and confused, then finally poisoned by jealousy and murderous revenge because of Desdemona's alleged infidelity with Cassio. Unaware of Desdemona's innocence and Iago's perfidy, the fated Othello kills his wife on her bed and, after the horrible, twisted discovery of the truth, kills himself as the confessed "fool" and is cursed by others as the "damned slave."[2]

"*Othello*"

Ira Aldridge, famed Shakespearean actor, as Othello, c. 1870, postcard.

In the eighteenth and early nineteenth centuries, moral questions about the passion of jealousy, betrayal, or a woman's alluring nature informed American reactions to *Othello*. But by the antebellum era, the Moor's color and the matter of interracial marriage dominated the meaning of the play. From the 1820s, Othello was still widely staged, including in the South, but the lead character was increasingly lightened, even whitened or portrayed as tan or as a slightly swarthy American Indian. The "sooty Moor" would no longer play for racist American audiences, even in the North. If Othello appeared as a mulatto or an octoroon, as he quite often did in these highly racialized times, the lesson most Americans took was that whites and blacks ought never to mix.[3]

In May 1869, at the brand-new Edwin Booth Theatre in New York, Douglass attended a performance of *Othello* with Ottilie Assing and a group of her German friends (with the famous Booth, the assassin's brother, in the lead role). We do not have Douglass's reaction to the night at the theater, but Assing called it a "magnificent evening . . . where we saw an amazingly beautiful performance of *Othello*." She thought Booth a "splendid Othello." Booth recrafted and produced his own *Othello*, published that year and premiered in his splendid new theater, complete with frescoed ceiling and statuary, at Twenty-Third Street and Sixth Avenue. The play Frederick and Ottilie saw was Booth's own. He had performed Othello for two decades by then, with his character wearing glittering Persian gowns, a purple-and-gold turban, speaking in a genteel, formal manner, and thoroughly purged of any taint of blackness. He was exotic and charismatic but certainly no longer the African with a violent warlike history, craving and possessing the white aristocrat's daughter. Some lines that explicitly invoked race were even expunged from Booth's text.[4]

Whatever endured in Douglass's mind and memory from that 1869 evening of seeing Booth's *Othello*, all we know is that he turned to the noble Moor's anguished soliloquy about lost masculine dignity and mental collapse as Douglass remembered his own professional and personal displacement in the wake of the Civil War:

> *What sense had I of her stol'n hours of lust?*
> *I saw't not, thought it not, it harm'd not me. . . .*
> *He that is robb'd, not wanting what is stol'n,*
> *Let him not know't, and he's not robb'd at all. . . .*
> *I had been happy, if the general camp,*
> *Pioneers and all, had tasted her sweet body,*
> *So I had nothing known. O, now for ever*
> *Farewell the tranquil mind! Farewell content!*
> *Farewell the plumed troop and the big wars*
> *That make ambition virtue! O, farewell,*
> *Farewell the neighing steed and the shrill trump,*
> *The spirit-stirring drum, the ear-piercing fife,*
> *The royal banner and all quality,*
> *Pride, pomp and circumstance of glorious war! . . .*
> *Farewell! Othello's occupation is gone!*

It is possible that, like many other Americans, Douglass loved Shakespeare as much for the rhetoric and oratory as for the literature.[5] But he could not have read *Othello* without reflecting on its deep probings of the ideas of trust, fate, status inside or out of the state, human evil, and interracial relationships. Douglass may have been saying "farewell" to his "big wars" in the late 1860s as well, but endless smaller ones, in his public and private life, had only begun.

• • •

In the early Reconstruction years, Douglass did consider a variety of career and personal options. In 1865–66, feeling in flux, he may at least briefly have contemplated an old urge to retreat to a life of farming if he could secure the right land. It is doubtful that he entertained such an idea for long. In Rochester, among Amy Post's correspondence, emerged the rumor that Douglass was planning to move to New Jersey (to be with Assing?). Salmon Chase, among others, invited Douglass to relocate to Alexandria, Virginia, to edit a new paper, to which he responded that he had no desire to "court violence or martyrdom" by going to the former slave state. He did apparently have new "Baltimore dreams" and gave some thought to moving to the town from which he had escaped from slavery. As the war ended in spring of 1865, Douglass confided as much to Julia Crofts in England, who still devotedly raised money and sent it to her old friend for freedmen's aid. In other letters he admitted his desire to meet Thomas Auld again, and more important, he had already experienced a hero's welcome in Baltimore and would again in September.[6] Along with his sons, he may have imagined business opportunities in the postwar port city with a large black population.

So worried was Crofts about Douglass's plans that she begged him not to move: "Pray very dear friend, stay in the northern states & leave Baltimore an untried field of labor—do not throw your valuable life away venturing near the old house—think of realities & let those romantic visions remain in abeyance." She believed Douglass would be a "marked man" in Baltimore or anywhere in the South and pleaded with him not to even visit for lectures in the city of his slave youth. Indeed, Julia had reason to worry. In the wake of Douglass's speeches in Baltimore in late 1864 or early 1865, an Augusta, Georgia, newspaper reported on his performance: "This saucy negro, one of the 'representative men' of the North, delivered the subjoined address at Baltimore. Poor old Maryland! She has had bitter pills enough, but here is something in the way of a black draught." So constant was Douglass's advocacy for black suffrage, and so eager was he for some kind of foothold inside power, that any withdrawal to a quiet life, or a long-term adventure in Europe with Assing, was never his desire.[7] After the war Douglass still wanted to affect history and not be merely one of its symbols.

In May 1865, the "black draught" joined his old friends and rivals at the thirty-second-anniversary meeting of the American Anti-Slavery Society in New York. The society engaged in an intense dispute over whether to disband in the wake of emancipation—to declare victory and fold its tent. Garrison, backed by a few loyalists, led the effort for dismemberment, declaring it "an absurdity to maintain an antislavery society after slavery is dead." But Wendell Phillips led a larger faction, outvoting Garrison 118–48, and urging the society to work for black civil and political rights. Called on to speak, Douglass reflected with nostalgia on his first years out on the circuit with the old Garrisonians, but committed himself to the much "good antislavery work" yet to be done. He made an especially forceful case for the right to vote. "Slavery is not abolished until the black man has the ballot," Douglass asserted. As long as the word *white* could be inserted or even implied in new Southern state constitutions, abolitionists had not lost their occupation. Stay the course of faith and devotion, Douglass counseled, quoting Exodus when Moses pleads with the people to believe that God will yet save them from the Egyptians: "Stand still and see the salvation of God." With Moses in the original Exodus, Douglass asked his audience for an almost unattainable faith. Believe, he exhorted, God's promise: "The Egyptians whom ye have seen today ye shall see them no more forever." But he urged against any naïve trust of their former enemies in the proslavery South. "Think you that because they are for a moment in the talons and the beak of our glorious eagle, instead of the slave being there, as formerly, that they are converted?" Abolitionists, Douglass argued, "had better wait and see what new form this old monster will assume."[8]

By September, Douglass was back in Baltimore for a special occasion, the dedication of a "Douglass Institute," a cultural-educational enterprise founded in a building of the former Newton University. The structure, on East Lexington Street, occupied by eight hundred people at Douglass's address, had been appropriated by the US army as a hospital during the war.[9] For this yet another extraordinary homecoming to Baltimore, Douglass crafted a beautiful address about the nature of education, civilization, and lives characterized by pursuits of the mind and soul and not merely by laborer's brawn. From a man with no formal schooling it was a moving embrace of intellect as well as an astute analysis of the history of racism.

In an effort both sobering and hopeful, Douglass rejoiced in having his name associated with such a "first." That blacks had rallied with some white benefactors to create an educational effort such as this was a "first sign of rain after a famine . . . the first sign of peace after ten thousand calamities." Douglass spoke in personal as well as collective terms of learning and overcoming the "chains of ignorance" imposed by centuries of slavery. That black people had been "shut out for ages from the arts, from science, and from all the more elevating forms of industry, [or] the higher wants and aspirations of the human soul," was, Douglass believed, "a great fact" of their history. Hence, this new beginning was a sacred act of human striving. Douglass wished that separate black schools and associations were not necessary. But he accepted their reality and used them as the source of a brilliant critique of racism.[10]

Black "representative . . . distinguished men" were always considered "exceptions," Douglass complained. Claims of black racial inferiority had over time been met with historical arguments about the achievements of ancient African civilizations in Ethiopia and Egypt or in the modern revolution in Haiti. Moreover, even pointing to the three centuries in which "Christendom" had "summoned heaven and hell" in forcing African peoples through the cruel filter of the slave trade had not converted the growing ranks of racial theorists. "Our history has been but a track of blood," said Douglass, and "mankind lost sight of our human nature in the idea of being property." He then lamented as he celebrated that black soldiers in the Civil War had proven "at least one element of civilization . . . manly courage, that we love our country, and that we will fight for an Idea." White civilization, Douglass argued, had for too long denied black people the fundamental element separating humans from all other animals—"consciousness," the capacity to discern, write, and transmit history. Douglass asserted for his people the same powers of all other men: "He learns from the past, improves upon the past, looks back upon the past, and hands down his knowledge of the past to after-coming generations." The former slave with no degrees wanted any such school as the Douglass Institute to be a place from which enlightenment and refinement in all their forms "shall flow as a river, enriching, ennobling, strengthening, and purifying all who will lave in its waters."[11] In such an assessment of what it meant to be human, Douglass sang out a kind of freedmen's dream, as he also showed that he had found at least a piece of Othello's postwar occupation.

In the early years of Reconstruction, Douglass did settle into what he called "a new vocation . . . full of advantages mentally and pecuniarily." He was still very much sought after as a lecturer, usually accruing $100 per night. His most common speech was "Self-Made Men," crafted first before the war and now in frequent demand after the conflict.[12] But Douglass's subjects were also very much about Reconstruction, the nature of "the races," freedmen's rights, especially suffrage, and the increasing violence against blacks in the South. He also sought and received invitations to speak in Washington, DC, at the center of the political tempest over Reconstruction. He missed his newspaper, but he now had easy access as a writer to several national journals such as the *Atlantic*, the *North American Review*, and the *Independent*. Douglass saw Reconstruction and its unprecedented challenges as a continuation of the purpose of the war, a sacred responsibility to the Union dead and to 4 million freed slaves. He also began to take a particular interest in American foreign affairs, especially in how a new United States—his nation now—might export its emancipationist vision to the Caribbean and elsewhere. The old abolitionist was now a nationalist, and an emerging internationalist.

Douglass's vision of Reconstruction fell squarely into the Radical Republican camp. Especially after congressional Republicans locked horns in political and ideological warfare by 1866 with President Andrew Johnson for control of policy, Douglass grasped how "radicalism, far from being odious, is now the popular passport to power." He believed the establishment of a new order in the South, especially the protection of the freedmen's rights, had to be done by activist, interventionist federal power. Douglass advocated what he called "something like a despotic central government" to vanquish, as much as possible, the tradition of states' rights. In a statement that went to the heart of the eternal American dilemma with federalism, the new doctrine of "human rights," he maintained, could not prevail "while there remains such an idea as the right of each state to control its own local affairs." [13] This old radical had found his own passport to power.

Douglass believed slavery itself still lurked everywhere in the South, and like an incipient disease, it would infest all aspects of life if not once and for all killed. He saw Reconstruction, as he had the war, through an apocalyptic historical lens. The "fiery conflict" had made possible the "national regeneration and entire purification" of the country, he wrote in 1866. But only if "authority and power" were exercised on the defeated South to render the "deadly upas, root and branch, leaf and fibre, body and sap . . . utterly destroyed." Douglass wanted the former Confederacy occupied and remade, with the former slaves as the central agents of a political and social revolution. In the early stage of the process, he nurtured the liberal faith that the franchise could protect the freedpeople from the coming retribution of the white South. His was a vision of the war and Reconstruction as redemptive tragedy, not unlike Herman Melville's 1866 plea: "Let us pray that the terrible historic tragedy of our time may not have been enacted without instructing our whole beloved country through pity and terror." While Melville wrote with bereaved wonderment about the scale of the tragedy and the harrowing tasks of Reconstruction, Douglass exuded a millennial hope.

To him the war had been an "impressive teacher . . . an instructor," and in the end "society is instructed."[14]

But this moral sense of history had to be enacted in policy and against formidable foes. Douglass learned this quickly about the new president, Andrew Johnson, and the ex-Confederates the Tennessean enabled. From humble origins, Johnson was a successful stump politician from east Tennessee. He had held nearly every level of political office by the late 1850s: alderman, state representative, congressman, two terms as governor, and US senator. Johnson was the only Southern senator from a seceded state who refused to follow his state out of the Union in 1861. In 1862 Lincoln appointed him war governor of Tennessee; hence, his symbolic place on the ticket in the president's bid for reelection in 1864. Although he opposed secession, Johnson was, nevertheless, an ardent states' rightist. He shared none of the Radical Republicans' expansive conception of federal power, and he was a staunch white supremacist who accepted the end of slavery but could not abide the idea of black civil and political rights. His philosophy toward Reconstruction rested in a slogan: "The Constitution as it is, and the Union as it was."[15]

Congress had recessed shortly after Johnson was sworn in after Lincoln's death. So during virtually all of the rest of 1865, the new president's lenient, rapid, presidential, and largely pro-Southern approach dominated what historian John Hope Franklin once called "Reconstruction, Confederate style." By September, when Douglass gave his speech in Baltimore about humane education and the nature of racism, Johnson had initiated a generous policy of pardons to ex-Confederates. Johnson also returned a good deal of confiscated and abandoned lands to their former white owners in the South, while he also did his best to thwart the work of the Freedmen's Bureau, the agency established to provide rations to hundreds of thousands of black and white war refugees as well as adjudicate new labor contracts for freedmen. In December, as Congress reconvened, Johnson declared Reconstruction complete eight months after Appomattox. The former states of the Confederacy had all drafted new constitutions and passed a wide array of "black codes," restricting freedmen's lives. It seemed to many, Douglass certainly, that blacks were being returned to servility, and no one would be held responsible for the war as many former Confederates were elected to serve in Congress. Hence, his fears stated back in May that if left to their own devices, white Southerners, "by unfriendly legislation, could make our liberty . . . a delusion, a mockery." At Baltimore in September he warned about "the persistent determination of the present Executive of the nation . . . to hold and treat us in a degraded relation."[16]

Douglass saw Confederate Reconstruction coming, but was still shocked by its brazen effrontery. Congressional Republicans called an immediate halt to presidential Reconstruction in late 1865 and early 1866. Congress devised the Joint Committee on Reconstruction, with fifteen members, twelve of whom were Republicans, which in January and February conducted extraordinary public hearings to investigate the conditions on the ground in the South. These unprecedented hearings heard the testimony of 144 witnesses, including Union army officers and Freedmen's Bureau agents; the ex-Confederates included none other than Robert E. Lee himself and former vice president Alexander H. Stephens, who offered a defense of secession and states' rights. The overwhelming message of the hearings, especially from federal military and civilian personnel, was that martial law, Union troops, and the Freedmen's Bureau were all dire necessities to quell violence and restore social order.[17]

Freedmen's Bureau agents reported over and again about violence against ex-slaves, including whippings, ritualistic torture, and murders. One described huge problems negotiating wage contracts with unwilling planters, and a "general hatred of the freedmen." Typical of Union officers' testimony was that of General Clinton B. Fisk, who had spent the war and its aftermath in Tennessee and Kentucky. He traveled incognito from plantation to plantation, talking to planters and "negroes in their quarters." Fisk had seen "slaveholders and returned rebel soldiers . . . persecute" the freedmen, "pursue them with vengeance . . . and burn down their dwellings and schoolhouses." The Joint Committee concluded that allowing ex-Confederates to rule in their former states had been a policy of "madness and folly," and it called for major legislation that would provide "adequate safeguards" for social order and freedmen's rights.[18] Later that spring and early summer, this seismic shift in Reconstruction policy and politics led to passage of a new Freedmen's Bureau bill, the first Civil Rights Act of American history, and the Fourteenth Amendment.

In the midst of the hearings, and the standoff between president and Congress, various groups of black men came to Washington to lobby the legislature for their rights. Some were denied entry to the galleries, much less the halls of lobbying. In a letter to Senator Charles Sumner, signed by Douglass and his son Lewis, among many other black leaders, they declared that out of "self-respect" they would not "consent to be colonized" in the US

Capitol. Douglass led a delegation of thirteen men (twelve black, including Lewis, and one white) to the White House for an extraordinary meeting with Johnson. They were not invited, but inspired by the Republican resurgence in the capital they insisted on an audience with the chief executive. George T. Downing of Washington, DC, shared the leadership and presentation with Douglass; the two had planned this effort to confront Johnson since mid-January, although Lewis played a key role as well in corresponding with the various members. Downing, a former successful hotel owner and caterer, current manager of the House of Representatives dining room, led off with a prepared statement in which the group declared the Thirteenth Amendment insufficient. Speaking for all black Americans, they demanded "their rights as citizens" and "equality before law." Above all, they insisted on being "fully enfranchised . . . throughout the land." Then Douglass stepped forward with formal deference. But unmistakably, he invoked Johnson's "noble and humane predecessor" as he demanded the "ballot with which to save ourselves." Whether he fully knew it or not, by his choice of words Douglass stoked Johnson's anger and deepest prejudices, baiting him with what had to seem false respect: "In the order of Divine Providence you [Johnson] are placed in a position where you have the power to save or destroy us; to bless or blast us." [19]

Johnson's rambling replies stand as perhaps the worst exchange an American president ever conducted in person with African American leaders. The president took the bait in his forty-five-minute speech. Johnson self-righteously declared himself ready to be the "Moses" of the freedpeople. One can only imagine Douglass's thoughts as he sat across the room from the president, less than a year after Appomattox, and heard him declare "the feelings of my own heart . . . have been for the colored man. I have owned slaves and bought slaves, but I never sold one." For the moment Douglass and his colleagues suppressed both laughter and outrage. Then Johnson complained that in his relationship to blacks "I have been their slave instead of their being mine. Some even followed me here, while others are occupying . . . my property with my consent." If the sanctimonious Tennessean had not offended his guests enough, he then threw a jab right at Douglass. He did "not like being arraigned," Johnson spouted, "by some who can get up handsomely rounded periods and deal in rhetoric, and talk about abstract ideas of liberty." The president brandished his fear of race war if his guests pursued their goals, coldly rebuked Douglass's advocacy of black suffrage, and suggested that colonization was still the best option for the freedpeople. [20] Douglass felt thrown back in time as though history had stopped somewhere before 1861.

Douglass tried to respectfully interrupt the host's obfuscating rejection of voting rights, but Johnson quickly stopped him with "I am not quite through." The president urged Douglass to consider the plight of poor, non-slaveholding whites, arguing that during slavery "the colored man and his master combined to keep him [the poor white] in slavery." Addressing Douglass directly, Johnson asked, "Have you ever lived on a plantation?" "I have, Your Excellency," replied the former slave. As Douglass tried to engage in a colloquy, Johnson pursued him with a nearly nonstop barrage. The guest had to listen as the president declared the abolition of slavery merely an "incident to the suppression of the rebellion" and predicted a "war of the races" if blacks got access to the ballot. Worse, Johnson insisted that nothing could ever be forced upon the majority of a community "without their consent." When Douglass objected to this defense of states' rights doctrine, remarking, "That was said before the war," Johnson shot back angrily, "I am now talking about a principle . . . a fundamental tenet in my creed that the people must be obeyed." Then, the leader of the country asked the former slave, "Is there anything wrong or unfair in that?" To which Douglass, according to the stenographer, "smiled" and replied, "A great deal wrong, Mr. President, with all respect." With derision in each man's demeanor, Douglass and Johnson then continued a tense, fruitless give-and-take for several minutes longer, the president making it clear he intended to have no debate and Douglass equally clear that he would not back down.[21]

Before leading the delegation out of the room, Douglass staked out a position. He reminded Johnson that if black life and liberty were left to the whims of Southern whites, the freedmen would be "divested of all political power." Douglass summed up their impasse to Johnson's face: "The very thing Your Excellency would avoid in the Southern states can only be avoided by the very measure that we propose." The meeting could hardly have ended in a worse manner. If the black delegation felt disgusted, Johnson was livid. According to Johnson's private secretary, "The President no more expected that darkey delegation yesterday, than he did the cholera." As the secretary reported to the *New York World*, after the black delegation left the room at the White House, Johnson declared, "Those d__d sons of b__s thought they had me in a trap. I know that d__d Douglass; he's just like any nigger, & he would sooner cut a white man's throat than not."[22] Douglass met many presidents; sobering as it was, he may have perversely held Johnson's epithets as a badge of honor.

Before the day was over, the delegation met with a group of Republican congressmen for a debriefing and signed a public response to Johnson. Drafted by the elder Douglass, dictated to Lewis, the statement did not mince words. It called Johnson's "elaborate speech . . . entirely unsound and prejudicial." The group rejected the president's stance against black enfranchisement on the grounds of old hatreds between poor whites and former slaves. Blame for such animosity lay with white masters, argued the black leaders. "They divided both to conquer each." They told Johnson they would not back down under any circumstances, reminding him, in one of Douglass's old abolitionist maxims, that "men are whipped oftenest who are whipped easiest." Finally, they unequivocally denounced Johnson's embrace of colonization as a discredited, proslavery "theory" of human degradation.[23]

As Douglass looked about for that "new vocation" in the wake of the war, he quickly realized that the revolution of emancipation had only begun. In the epic contest over Reconstruction policy in Washington, he discovered his new raison d'être. It was not unlike his career as he had always known it. "I . . . soon found," he later wrote in an understatement, "that the Negro had still a cause, and that he needed my voice and pen . . . to plead for it." Before the end of the year and into 1867, Douglass took a remarkable speech on the road, "Sources of Danger to the Republic." In cities from Brooklyn to St. Louis, Douglass skewered Johnson as an "unmitigated calamity," and a "disgrace" the country must "stagger under." So fearful of the situation was the orator that he went so far as to recommend a major constitutional revision, eliminating the president's veto and pardon powers, as well as the vice presidency itself. These measures reflect as much his visceral hatred for Johnson as prudent constitutional thinking. But Douglass did leave a timeless maxim for republics: "Our government may at some time be in the hands of a bad man. When in the hands of a good man it is all well enough. . . . We ought to have our government so shaped that even when in the hands of a bad man we shall be safe." [24]

A full twenty-five years into his public life, Douglass seemed to have realized yet again the nature of his only true weapon—*words*, spoken and written. Increasingly now, he wanted to get to the center of American political life, Washington, DC, and if possible, inside the circle of Republican Party leaders. He sought more lecture opportunities in the capital, spoke on political subjects, especially stressing the all-important matter of black suffrage. He cultivated growing friendships with congressmen and senators such as Charles Sumner, as well as with Chief Justice Salmon Chase. As a matter of livelihood, Douglass still conducted long, backbreaking lecture tours all over the country. Reconstruction was for Douglass the new cause not unlike the old abolition crusade; the revolution of Union victory and black emancipation could still be lost or won.

Douglass made no real distinction between Johnson's white supremacy and slavery itself. A constant refrain in his postwar rhetoric was his assertion that "slavery is not abolished until the black man has the ballot." In this reasoning, as long as Johnson controlled Reconstruction, the war was not over. The Slave Power endured, Douglass believed, in the handful of conservative Republicans and the droves of Democrats who supported Johnson's efforts to thwart the crucial legislation brewing up from Radical Republicans in Congress. In a private letter to Sumner, Douglass drew his line clearly. Former slaveholders should never be "trusted to legislate" about black rights. "Until Redeemers come from the pit instead of paradise, until the temperance cause can be left to rumsellers, until the morals of society can be safely committed to the care of those who habitually outrage all the decencies of life, the freedmen cannot be safely left to the care of their former masters."[25] The revolution was unfinished.

Douglass's grueling travel and lecture schedule in 1866 may not have allowed him to follow as closely as he might have the great debates in Congress over passage of the Civil Rights Act in April and the Fourteenth Amendment in June. Invitations poured in to speak all over the North. Douglass's son Charles, and daughter Rosetta, living in Rochester, tried frustratingly to keep up with their father's whereabouts as they processed his correspondence during 1866–67. Itineraries indicate that on the two days after the White House meeting with President Johnson, Douglass spoke in Philadelphia and Baltimore respectively. Four days after that, February 13, he was back in Washington lecturing, followed by five consecutive days in Pittsburgh, and then immediately by a full week of engagements out in Illinois, where he spoke in the State House in Springfield. Through bone-numbing travel by railroad, he was again speaking back in Washington, DC, and its environs on March 6–10.[26] The orator had hardly lost his occupation; he emerged in 1866 and 1867 as one of the most prominent itinerant spokesmen of freedmen's rights and the Radical Republican effort to shape Reconstruction.

Douglass's newly achieved enemies were well aware of the former abolitionist's effective voice in the national political arena. It would have pleased Douglass to know how much correspondence arrived at the White House condemning him for his well-publicized confrontation with Johnson. A for-

mer Democratic Party cabinet official, William L. Hodge, applauded Johnson's resistance to Douglass's "impudence" and "attempt to cram the negro
wool & all down our throats." Another Democrat, James H. Embry, monitored the black orator's speech in Philadelphia on February 9. Referring to
him only as "Fred Douglass," Embry said the speaker was "grossly insulting
and abusive" and "gave loose rein to satire, anger and slander." Comment-
ing especially on how blacks and whites had shared the same platform in
proximity, Embry nevertheless told Johnson not to worry. The speech was
only important as being the utterance of his friends in Washington, and he
merely the Mask behind which they strike." Douglass would not have been
flattered by the racist accusation sent to Johnson by a more humble Michigan supporter, complimenting the president: "You was more than a match
for the great *Fred* Douglass. . . . Many fanatics think their Pet Douglass is
far a head of Your Excellency in profound wisdom." By March administration friends wrote to warn the president and his aides that Douglass was
coming back to Washington to "excite the negroes to rebel." By May, some
Democrats called Johnson's argument that black suffrage would stimulate
race war (put forth to the February black delegation) "your Douglass argument."[27] These letters provide a glimpse into a kind of nineteenth-century
parlor racism. If the old abolitionist needed a new occupation, he surely
had one now—the frightening black man with brains who had penetrated
the racist psyches of powerful people with words and his physical presence.

Although none had dispatched him to the hustings as their mask and
he felt like no one's pet, Douglass had more allies among Republicans than
he realized. Lyman Trumbull, a moderate Republican senator from Illinois,
had been a principal author of the Confiscation Acts and the Thirteenth
Amendment. Now, Trumbull crafted the new Freedmen's Bureau bill, and
the Civil Rights Act of 1866. Douglass never developed a close relationship with Trumbull, whose political allegiances varied over time. Although
both measures contained elements that disappointed Radicals, Douglass
saw their enormous potential to his cause. The renewal of the Freedmen's
Bureau over Johnson's veto brought hope to insecure former slaves in the
South. The Civil Rights Act, which passed by a two-thirds vote in Congress
on April 9, overriding the president's veto, was a remarkable departure in
federal power and in central-government state relations. It did not include
political rights, to Douglass's chagrin, but it created national citizenship
for all persons (except Indians) born in the United States, and it identified
some "fundamental rights," as Trumbull put it, newly guaranteed to "every
man as a free man." Those rights included elements of contract law and

protection of free labor. The law also stipulated that cases of discrimination were to be heard in federal and not state courts, although it lacked precision on how such a process would be adjudicated. Moreover, the law was vague in that it largely addressed public and not private acts of injustice. The Civil Rights Act of 1866 was above all the first effort to breathe meaning and enforcement into the Thirteenth Amendment.[28]

Johnson's strident veto message, laced with a staunch states' rights position against all manner of "centralization" of power in the federal government, as well as with blatant white supremacy, invoking fears of racial intermarriage, caused a permanent break between the executive and the legislature, and set the stage for two years of constitutional crisis. Johnson even claimed that to extend the rights of blacks would discriminate against whites. He considered such expansion of civil rights "fraught with evil" and "made to operate in favor of the colored and against the white race," a set of notions some white Americans still cling to in the twenty-first century.[29] When Douglass lampooned Johnson out on the stump, he did so with good reasons.

Douglass did not develop strong ties with John Bingham or Thaddeus Stevens in the House of Representatives. Bingham was the principal author of section one of the Fourteenth Amendment, and Stevens the most Radical among the Republican architects of Reconstruction policy, and often its House floor manager. Bingham was a Christian abolitionist and Ohio congressman who had served as a judge advocate in the Union army, as well as on the commission that tried the conspirators in the Lincoln assassination in 1865. He had entered Congress in 1854; his political career was a deep reflection of the antislavery history of the Republican Party. He believed the liberation of the slaves had forced the United States to federalize the Bill of Rights and apply it to all Americans. Bingham considered the "rights of citizenship" the same as the "sacred rights of human nature." Stevens too embraced equality. The Pennsylvanian, already seventy-four years old and soon to die, in 1868, imagined Reconstruction as a movement to "rebuild a shattered empire . . . to plant deep and solid the corner-stone of eternal Justice, and to erect thereon a superstructure of perfect equality of every human being before the law."[30]

Inadvertently, Bingham and Douglass agreed on all the basics of Reconstruction. They employed similar apocalyptic rhetoric as well as the antislavery interpretation of the Constitution honed in abolitionist circles during the 1850s. The new cast-iron dome of the US Capitol was now completed to full majesty when Bingham stood in the House chamber on January 25, 1866, and introduced the Fourteenth Amendment. He insisted that the war had made the amendment necessary, though "not without sorrow, not without martyrdom . . . not without storm and tempest . . . and fire running along the ground." He insisted that the federal government enforce "equality" not merely as an abstraction but "in the states."[31] *In the states.*

Douglass closely followed the congressional debates and the Joint Committee's hearings and its report in the press that winter. In language so similar to that Douglass had used ever since Appomattox, he observed Johnson's "anti-coercive policy" characterized as "matchless wickedness," and tantamount to the "surrender by Grant to Lee." Douglass applauded Bingham's forceful denunciations of states' rights doctrines and his assertion of the "national authority" to enforce equality before law. Had Douglass attended congressional sessions, he would have relished Bingham's condemnation of opponents of the amendment as "conspirators" and "prodigal rebels," their Northern allies as "traitors whose hands are red with the blood of murder and assassination, who for four years struck at the life of its [the government's] defenders."[32] Such words were political music in Douglass's ears.

During the first six months of 1866 Republicans faced several great challenges. Three of them they met straight on in settled terms: defining citizenship; repudiation of Confederate war debts, including any claims to compensation for loss of slave property; and disqualification of ex-Confederates from officeholding. But three others remained historically unresolved and made the Fourteenth Amendment limited and controversial, though revolutionary. They did not settle the extent of the right to vote for black men and left women out of suffrage altogether; they did not give precision to the extent of civil rights made equal before law; and they struggled to reapportion representation of the "slave seats" given the Southern states under the "three-fifths clause."[33]

But Bingham's section one of the Fourteenth Amendment was something Douglass could embrace as a talisman; it was emancipation etched in parchment, enduring to this day as the most influential and far-reaching constitutional result of the Civil War. It attempted, on the matter of individual civil rights, to make the United States one body of people equal before law and not subject to local or state practice. At least in law, after embittered debate, when the amendment passed the Senate on June 8 by 33–11, and the House by 138–36, a second Constitution in America was born. Despite the myriad uses and abuses of the Fourteenth Amendment over time, and endless conservative attempts to thwart its egalitarianism, it is always worth remembering the enactment's immediate roots. Without the liberation of

4 million slaves, section one could never have been enshrined into America's legal DNA in the nineteenth century. Its two careful sentences are a resounding answer to the ghostlike language of Roger Taney in the *Dred Scott* case:

> All persons born or naturalized in the United States, and subject to the jurisdiction thereof, are citizens of the United States and of the State wherein they reside. No state shall make or enforce any law which shall abridge the privileges and immunities of citizens of the United States; nor shall any state deprive any person of life, liberty, or property, without due process of law, nor deny to any person within its jurisdiction the equal protection of the laws.[34]

Section one was a dream come true for old abolitionists. But as an adamant advocate of universal black male suffrage, Douglass found elements in section two of the Fourteenth Amendment that led him to oppose it during the coming year.

Black suffrage was still the greatest obstacle, even for Radical Republicans. Indeed, the Fourteenth Amendment contained sufficient ambiguity, especially about voting rights, that some Radicals opposed its ratification. Section two addressed suffrage, but extended the right to vote directly to no one. It stipulated that for whatever number of males denied the right to vote in a given state, that state's representation in Congress would be "reduced in proportion."[35] The measure represented one of the hard-won but awkward compromises that made passage of the amendment possible in the ideological hurricane of 1866.

As Douglass barnstormed across the country from Rochester to Washington, and out to Illinois prairie towns and back again, from February until April 1866, he ferociously attacked Johnson and the conservatives. His ridicule of the president was so aggressive that occasionally a venue would refuse to allow his speech, and some groups protested his appearances. He wished that the status of blacks might be "settled" by Reconstruction legislation. But the nation, he feared, would now "leave in the soil some root or fibre out of which may spring other rebellions and other assassinations [like Lincoln's]." If he were a "minister of the Gospel," Douglass told a Washington audience, he would "preach . . . for six months from one text. . . . Remember Lot's wife."[36]

The story in Genesis 18–19 is about God's awesome power to cause hopeful beginnings as well as dreadful endings by retributive justice. For their many sins, Sodom and Gomorrah are destroyed by God raining "brimstone and fire" down on them. But Lot and his family are alerted to flee, then rescued and saved in the mountains, excepting Lot's wife, who, warned not to look backward at the devastation, disobeys and is instantly "consumed" into a "pillar of salt." On the morning after, Abraham, patriarch of the whole biblical tradition, stands on the mountain and surveys the "plain" smoldering below in utter ruin. But Lot and his daughters are saved because "God remembered Abraham," as he had also remembered Noah after the flood. For Douglass the Old Testament was a template of pliant stories and historical lessons. In this case, the orator used the image of Abraham looking down upon the destroyed landscape to demand that Americans look down upon their own recent self-destruction, and all but unjustified survival, and *remember.* Desperately, Douglass announced, he "would show that nations should have memories." As the biblical scholar Walter Brueggemann contends, this story makes us "see" the destruction we have ourselves caused, to know it, feel it, and remember it. "With Abraham," we can then "know something urgent about God's call to us." [37] In 1866–67 Douglass demanded resistance to Johnson and his minions; repeatedly, he urged the victorious North to hear the call of remembrance.

"FREDERICK DOUGLASS ON THE PRESIDENT'S POLICY!" shouted a broadside announcing the orator's speech at the "Assembly Rooms" on Louisiana Avenue in Washington on March 10. Here Douglass faced an audience he relished; it included the Radical Pennsylvania congressman William D. Kelley, Senators Richard Yates of Illinois and Henry Wilson of Massachusetts, and especially General Oliver O. Howard, the director of the Freedmen's Bureau. This was the kind of political power center he sought. Douglass delivered a fierce defense of the integrity of "the Negro." Contrary to predictions, they would never "die out," despite ubiquitous images of them for white eyes at the mercy of "the lash, the bloodhound, and the auction-block." Blacks had risen from the depths of generations of enslavement to the heights of respectability, and hence the nation was "honor bound" to give them the franchise. Only the vote could provide self-protection. With "considerable humor and a good deal of sarcasm," wrote a reporter, Douglass pilloried Johnson for his racist contradictions expressed in their White House meeting. The chief executive's anxieties about race mixing, said the former slave, ought to be assuaged since "the white man and the negro agreed well" within his (Douglass's) own blood.

"What shall be said of Andrew Johnson?" Douglass asked. Better, he concluded, to "leave Mr. Johnson speak for himself as being the most damaging thing he can do." The president had "promised to be the Moses of the colored race," but was readily becoming "their Pharaoh." Then, Douglass tested the limits of propriety, saying that Johnson need not fear "physical assassination" from blacks. That would add nothing to the "refinements" of society; instead they only intended his "moral assassination." [38]

Over the summer of 1866, Douglass joined forces with old abolitionist friends Gerrit Smith and Wendell Phillips and openly opposed the Fourteenth Amendment on the grounds that it did not explicitly provide black suffrage. As the pivotal fall congressional elections loomed, the Republicans were deeply divided on the question of black voting rights. Thaddeus Stevens, who was a complex mixture of idealism and pragmatic politics, urged caution on suffrage, knowing that the vast majority of white Northerners, even Republicans, would not welcome political equality for blacks any more than they would social equality. Northern votes and control of Congress against Johnson's conservative coalition were at stake. But in this instance Douglass's own hard-earned sense of political pragmatism dissipated. He simply could not countenance citizenship without the right to vote. In July, he made the case in the *National Anti-Slavery Standard* that he had made on so many platforms. "Equal" citizenship, he said, without the franchise was "but an empty name. . . . To say that I am a citizen to pay taxes . . . obey laws . . . and fight the battles of the country, but in all that respects voting and representation, I am but as so much inert matter, is to insult my manhood." [39] In 1866–67, Douglass's political sensibilities careened between exhilaration and outrage.

Douglass also grew discouraged at the constant news of mob violence emanating from the South. Nothing tarnished the theory at the heart of political liberalism—that the vote could protect people—quite like the horrific riots/massacres in Memphis, May 1–13, and in New Orleans, July 30–31. The black population of Memphis had quadrupled during the year since the war. Hundreds of freedmen and black soldiers were now a very visible part of the city's life. When two horse-drawn hacks collided, one driven by a white man and the other a black, and black troops intervened, violence exploded for three days. White mobs attacked black communities; when the smoke cleared, forty-eight people were dead, all but two black. Five black women were raped, and African American houses and churches, as well as Freedmen's Bureau schools, torched. In the Crescent City, a new radical legislature, and a public procession of some two hundred black supporters, many of whom were former Union soldiers, tried to assemble. But city police, led by Confederate veterans, attacked the gathering, and gun battles broke out in the streets. Delegates and allies were shot down as they attempted to leave the convention hall under cover of white flags. The New Orleans bloodbath left thirty-four blacks and three white Radicals dead, and at least a hundred more wounded. The recalcitrant white South had risen with the vengeance Douglass had predicted.[40]

In August, the National Union Convention met in Philadelphia to rally around Johnson's policies. As a symbol of the sectional reunion that Johnson wanted to declare accomplished, the South Carolina ex–Confederate senator and current governor, James L. Orr, and former Union general Darius N. Couch walked into the convention arm in arm. Appalled by this display of obeisance to the former Confederate states, and against the backdrop of broad public awareness of antiblack violence, Republicans decided to convene their own counterconvention of "Southern Loyalists" in Philadelphia. Hundreds of Northern Republicans attended as honorary delegates, including Douglass, who was unexpectedly elected by fellow party members in Rochester. Demonstrating the depth of Republican squeamishness about black suffrage and the delicacy of the fall elections, none other than Thaddeus Stevens had urged Rochesterites not to send Douglass. Flouting Stevens or anyone else arguing that a black leader should remain invisible at this juncture, Douglass departed Rochester with a public statement: "If this convention will receive me, the event will certainly be somewhat significant progress. If they reject me, they will only identify themselves with another convention," Johnson's.[41] Douglass knew there was more than one way to wave a bloody shirt.

Douglass's presence at the convention was the subject of controversy even before he arrived in Philadelphia. Aboard a train somewhere between Harrisburg and Lancaster, Pennsylvania, a group of fellow delegates from western and Southern states approached him, expressed their "very high respect," and then urged him not to attend the convention. The scene on that train car was one among many Douglass remembered as an autobiographer. It told something revealing about both his life and the country. He felt like "the Jonah of the Republican ship," he recalled, "and responsible for the contrary winds and misbehaving weather." Among the group waiting upon him was the widely esteemed governor of Indiana, Oliver P. Morton. The chief spokesman making the awkward appeal was a New Orleanian with a "very French name" that Douglass could not recall. The "undesirableness" of a black man's presence, the group argued, was dictated by Northern racial prejudice. In the fall elections, these Republicans believed they must dodge the "cry of social and political equality" sure to be raised against them. In *Life and Times*, Douglass purported to remember verbatim his reply to the polite visitors: "Gentlemen, with all respect, you might as well ask me to put a loaded pistol to my head and blow my brains out, as to ask me to keep out of this convention." He remembered, gleefully, warning his detractors that should they persist in excluding him, they would themselves be "branded . . . as dastardly hypocrites." Not to have participated, he said, "would contradict the principle and purpose of my life."[42] Douglass had lived as a public symbol in America and abroad, but rarely had his physical presence caused such a stir in the house of his friends. Embarrassed, the Republican politicians returned to their railcars for the ride into Philadelphia.

On September 3, nearly three hundred delegates gathered in Independence Hall for a grand procession, two abreast, through the historic streets of Philadelphia. Having failed to exclude Douglass, most Republicans resolved to ignore him. Awkward and conspicuous, he stood alone as the lines formed; the delegates, he recalled, "seemed to be ashamed or afraid of me." The tall brown man with the recognizable silver-streaked mane of hair stood out like the black sheep in the flock. To his rescue came Theodore Tilton, a friend and the editor of the *New York Independent*. During the parade, Douglass and Tilton's arm-in-arm march garnered tumultuous cheers from the crowds, as well as scowls from some tense Republicans. At Ninth and Chesnutt Streets, Douglass spied a familiar face in the front line of the crowd. Amanda Sears, daughter of Thomas and Lucretia Auld, Douglass's second owners, stood waving with her two children. Douglass had nothing but fond memories of Amanda's mother. He broke ranks in the march and ran to Amanda, asking "what brought her to Philadelphia?" With "animated voice," said the autobiographer, the former slaveholder's daughter replied, "I heard you were to be here, and I came to see you walk in this procession."[43] The simpatico between the two childhood acquaintances, possible siblings, was apparent for all to see.

The Republicans' procession became the subject of ridicule in the Democratic Party and pro-Johnson press. Moreover, Thaddeus Stevens did not attend the convention, but was sufficiently irked at what he called the "arm-in-arm performance of Douglass and Tilton" to complain about it privately. He called the image a "practical exhibition of social equality" and worried that it would "lose us some votes."[44] When he got his chance on the platform in Philadelphia, Douglass took dead aim at any such sentiments that would bar him from political life.

For three days Southern and Northern delegates met separately and attacked Johnson and the Democrats. Douglass delivered at least three speeches in the packed Union League hall. Such constant speaking in this pyrotechnic political atmosphere rendered him hoarse by the fourth day. Douglass addressed many familiar themes with raucous humor: the all-important role of the ballot in solidifying black freedom; bitter ridicule of Johnson and even scorn for allies such as Stevens; Douglass's defense of the patriotism and assimilation of blacks to American culture contrasted with, again, the alleged retreat and decline of Indians.[45]

Douglass delivered a lengthy comparative, racialized rant about Native Americans. Blacks had achieved the "character of a civilized man," and Indians had not. The Indian, said Douglass by one invidious distinction after another, is "too stiff to bend" and "looks upon your cities . . . your steamboats, and your canals and railways and electric wires, and he regards them with aversion." The Indian "retreats," said Douglass, while the black man "rejoices" in modernity. Brutally ignoring so much history, Douglass claimed that against his people "there is a prejudice; against the Indian none." He complained that Indians faced only "romantic reverence," while blacks were "despised." It is astounding that Douglass would use race this way just as American Indians were fighting, and losing, so many western battles over their lands, and especially as the federal government, in alliance with Christian and philanthropic reformers, launched the reservation system, as well as the long effort to detribalize Native peoples. The prolonged effort of Bureau of Indian Affairs agents to achieve the forced deculturalization—"to destroy the Indian and save the man"—of Native Americans on a vast scale was a history very different from the one Douglass used to assert the cause of black rights.[46] The marketplace for racism was diverse and terrifying in Reconstruction America. Even its most visible and eloquent homegrown opponent could fall to its seductions in his fierce quest to be accepted by American "civilization."

The political context prompted from Douglass a folksy style in which he made himself the central subject. He garnered roars of laughter and applause by announcing that he had brought along "an individual that has been associated with me for . . . the last fifty years—the negro." To which someone in the audience shouted, "Bring your friend with you!" He was, he said, the "representative" of the "black race." He scored points far too easily with the scurrilous racial argument that blacks would never "die out like the Indian." Douglass could be very funny on his feet. "We ask a right to all the different boxes," he shouted, by which he clarified, the "witness-box, the jury-box, and the ballot box." Without these rights, said the orator, his people would remain in a "bad box." Style trumped substance in some of these performances. He even employed a new variation on his Irish joke about voting. If "a negro sober knows as much as a white man drunk," he surely "knows as much sober as Andy Johnson in any condition you may name." His hosts even picked up on Douglass's manner; Theodore Tilton and William Kelley introduced him on September 5 as a "runaway slave" in the house, who had been apprehended and brought before the meeting as "the prisoner at the bar," tried for his crime of "wonderful genius." Douglass had become the living exhibit, as well as the ironic relief, for some Republicans in Philadelphia. He thought his hosts' introduction a bit "jocular," he said, but had himself set the tone.[47]

Not everyone enjoyed the joke. Trouble began on the fourth day when Douglass, Tilton, and Anna Dickinson, a young Quaker orator, entered the hall of the Southern loyalists. Border-state delegates opposed black suffrage and tried to force adjournment, whereas delegates from the former Confederate states, directly dependent on black votes, held out for a suffrage resolution. The decisive moments came when Douglass and Dickinson were called upon to speak. Dickinson, a mere twenty-three years old and already heralded as the Joan of Arc of the abolitionist platform, urged the franchise for blacks as a major step in human progress. Answering the familiar cries from the audience of "Douglass! Douglass! Douglass!," the wordmaster stepped to the platform and caused a ruckus. "I responded with all the energy of my soul," Douglass later wrote, "for I looked upon suffrage for the Negro as the only measure which would prevent him from being thrust back into slavery." Some border-state delegates bolted the convention; meanwhile, the mass of Southern delegates reconvened the next morning, expressed thanks to Douglass and Dickinson, and endorsed black male suffrage.[48]

The Fifteenth Amendment was still three years away, but its momentum swung into motion at Philadelphia in 1866. Douglass reveled in the irony, as he put it, of how "the ugly and deformed child of the family" had won a "victory" over fear and expediency. He loved how his presence at this center of American politics still seemed to terrify white editors. A New Orleans reporter worried in the wake of Philadelphia that "as soon as Republicans could get President Johnson out of the way," they would "secure a Fred. Douglass or Sumner" in the presidency. And a Pennsylvania editor announced that soon "Fred. Douglass would be president," with "negro governments in every southern state, negro Senators and Representatives in Congress, and no bar raised against the perfect equality in society and in politics."[49] The former slave was delighted to infest the dreams of anxious whites worried about equality.

The leaders of the women's suffrage movement also had anxious dreams in the late 1860s. Elizabeth Cady Stanton and Susan B. Anthony increasingly demanded that the crusade for black male suffrage would now sweep women into the franchise as well. Douglass remained their old ally, dating back to Seneca Falls, throughout 1866. He wrote to Stanton in February thanking her for "the launching of the good ship 'Equal Rights Association,'" a new organization, of which Douglass became a vice president, devoted to achievement of universal suffrage. The two pledged mutual support of each other's cause in voting rights. He tried to soften Stanton's potentially volatile sensitivities by telling her there had been "no vessel like her . . . since Noah's Ark" and without the women the ark would have sunk.[50]

But signs of the schism to come emerged everywhere in the wake of the Fourteenth Amendment's inclusion of the word "male." In November 1866, Douglass spoke at the convention of the Equal Rights Association in Albany, a meeting called to advocate for equal suffrage provisions for blacks and women in the impending revision of the New York State constitution. For the audience, which included Stanton, Anthony, Lucy Stone, and a variety of old Garrisonians who supported women's suffrage, Douglass left mixed messages. "By every fact to which man can appeal as a justification of his own right to a ballot," he declared, "a woman can appeal with equal force." But then he drew historical distinctions. Women should realize the dire "urgency" faced by blacks, he argued, and wait. "With them it is a desirable matter; with us it is important; a question of life and death. With us disfranchisement means New Orleans, it means Memphis." If woman achieved the vote, Douglass maintained, she could only do so by "lifting the negro with her."[51]

As their suspicions grew, Stanton and Anthony wanted to know just where Douglass stood. Anthony wrote to Douglass in December 1866, de-

Frederick Douglass, February–March 1867. Samuel Root photographer, carte de visite.

siring to know if he would join her in the presentation to the state legislature in January. She urged him to "sacredly devote the last of the old and the first of the new year to the work." Similarly, Stanton wrote in January with the same query about whether they would make their case to the state government "together." Douglass did not show up at the January 23, 1867, hearing in Albany where the state Senate voted down the women's suffrage resolutions.[52] Soon, an ugly and prolonged breach developed over whether women's suffrage and black male suffrage coexisted on the same agenda.

With decreasing numbers of allies, Stanton and Anthony were no longer willing to play second fiddle in the race for suffrage. In their arguments they aimed both high and low. Their case for women's suffrage stemmed from deep grievances, and from a sophisticated argument about the vote as "protector" of economic, educational, and even personal security in a world that otherwise prescribed a women's sphere. Above all they demanded equality, not merely in the abstract, but in reality. Their demands became increasingly absolutist, uncompromising. Douglass too had often viewed the vote as protector of the safety and aspirations of blacks. But Stanton, in particular, resorted to indefensibly racist rhetoric in advancing the case for women over uneducated men of any race. In 1868, she took a stand against a "man's government," citing a history of "war, violence, conquest, acquisition . . . slavery, slaughter, and sacrifice" under male leadership. She believed a "man's government" is worse than a "white man's government" by the strange reasoning that it would only "multiply the tyrants." [53]

Then Stanton aimed at racial comparisons and forced Douglass and others to react. By denying American women the vote, politicians, Stanton contended, degraded their own "mothers, wives and daughters . . . below unwashed and unlettered ditch-diggers, boot-blacks, hostlers, butchers and barbers." But she did not stop there with her invidious class and racial-ethnic slurs. She asked her readers to imagine "Patrick and Sambo and Hans and Yung Tung who do not know the difference between a monarchy and a republic, who never read the Declaration of Independence . . . making laws" for refined, educated Anglo-Saxon women reformers. Douglass too had used his "drunken Patrick" jokes to argue for black suffrage. But Stanton and Anthony had crossed some lines. Many in the women's rights movement were also disgusted when Stanton and Anthony denounced the Republicans and allied with white-supremacist Democrats in 1868. They did so by welcoming the support of wealthy racist merchant George Francis Train, who funded the new journal *Revolution*, Stanton's ideological mouthpiece. [54]

Throughout this ugly debate over suffrage, Douglass maintained a remarkable grace and even friendship with Stanton, although not so with Anthony. A good deal of romance has evolved in popular memory about Douglass and Anthony, since they both resided in Rochester for so long, and in modern times a touching monument was erected of the two, depicting them having tea together. At the May 1869 meeting of the Equal Rights Association in New York, Anthony blew up and forced Douglass into an impromptu debate. Ninety percent of the large and raucous audience were women. Women had to stop stepping aside for the black vote, Anthony insisted. "Men cannot understand us women," she shouted. "They think of us as some of the slaveholders used to think of their slaves, all love and compassion, with no malice in their hearts." But watch out, she warned. Women were fed up with being "dependent" and demanded to earn their own "bread." She chastised Douglass for arguing that black men needed the vote because their situation was more "perilous" than that of women. [55]

Anthony slashed away, challenging whether Douglass would ever "exchange his sex & color . . . with Elizabeth Cady Stanton." Douglass tried to answer, but Anthony drowned him out with the assertion that votes for men but not women would send "fugitive wives" on the "loose" just as "fugitive slaves" traversed the landscape before the war. Declaring "we are in for a fight today," Anthony declared for "the most intelligent first" in voting and, therefore, "let . . . woman be first . . . and the negro last." The Fifteenth Amendment had severed the women's rights movement for the foreseeable future, with Stanton and Anthony fighting in isolation for their absolute principle. Douglass gave as he took. He objected to Stanton's use of such words as "Sambo," although he tried to do so with humor. He fiercely resisted the equivalence of women's plight with that of the freedpeople. "When women, because they are women, are hunted down in the cities of New York and New Orleans; when they are dragged from their houses and are hung from lamp-posts; when their children are torn from their arms, and their brains bashed out upon the pavement . . . when they are in danger of having their homes burnt down over their heads . . . then they will have an urgency to obtain the ballot equal to our own."[56]

Things only got worse as the Fifteenth Amendment passed Congress in February 1869 and became the template of disagreement. Stanton predicted that equipping black men in the South with the franchise would "culminate in fearful outrages on womanhood." The imagined demon of the black rapist crawled into the suffrage debate, courtesy of the leader of the women's rights crusade. As her biographer contends, Stanton was an "absolutist" more than a "strategist." Unrepentantly, she preferred die-hard principle to political maneuver. She even came out against black men's votes if women were denied, which is what the Fifteenth Amendment did. She proclaimed black women better off in slavery than in freedom: "Their emancipation is but another form of slavery. It is better to be the slave of an educated white man, than a degraded, ignorant black one." In her opening address at the May 1869 convention, she envisioned the nation heading toward "national suicide and woman's destruction" under "manhood" suffrage. The Fifteenth Amendment would create government where "clowns make laws for queens." Stanton's racial and social hierarchies allowed no concern for the complex logic of Reconstruction politics. Her racial and class code language cut to the bones of those who had spent their lives fighting for black freedom. The utter insecurity of black communities in the South simply did not interest her; she demanded the individual woman's right to vote regardless of social context or violence.[57]

*Elizabeth Cady Stanton and
Susan B. Anthony, c. 1870.
Albumen print. Napoleon
Sarony photographer.*

Trying to sustain civility, Douglass, who attended most of the women's rights meetings, pushed back. Countless times Douglass gave his full support to women's equal right to suffrage. By modern standards, he could seem rather patriarchal in his language, contending that white women had always been advantaged because their "husbands, fathers, and brothers are voters" and could protect women's interests. His humor at women's rights gatherings may sometimes have fallen flat, as in Rhode Island in 1868, when he remarked, "I cannot say much about woman's wrongs. The men love them too much to wrong them." He claimed as well that in every debate with a woman, he had "got the worst of it." He thought women had an "inside track" to the vote over black men because "you [white women] are beautiful and we are not." [58] Douglass abhorred, however, Stanton's and Anthony's embrace of Train and the Democrats. He was disgusted by their racist rhetoric. Most important, he had learned an abiding pragmatism from two decades of radical activism, war, and revolution in proslavery America. He wished the Fifteenth Amendment had gone further in outlawing qualification tests and in extending the vote to women. But this was hardly the first time Douglass accepted half measures from his fellow Republicans while working for a longer revolution. He knew that political rights derived from politics and had learned it the hard way.

In March 1869, Douglass had a chance encounter on a train in Ohio with Stanton and Anthony. It was still two months before the bitter breakup. They managed a friendly ride as well as an "earnest debate." Anthony extended her hand, although it would be one of the last times for many years to the man Stanton described in "a great circular cape of wolf skins." Stanton's remembrance was respectful but foreboding. She observed that Douglass had "a most formidable and ferocious aspect." In correspondence, Stanton wrote with sharp wit. "I trembled in my shoes and was almost as paralyzed as Red Riding Hood in a similar encounter." Douglass left her feeling "reassured" by a "gracious smile" and "hearty words." [59]

The black orator seeking new vocations never truly reconciled with Anthony, who remained embittered. But he did maintain friendly professional relations with Stanton in the coming two decades. Douglass attended many women's rights conventions in the years to come, and in 1870–71 he wholly endorsed the effort for a Sixteenth Amendment for women's suffrage as a robust "natural" right to govern themselves in every way a man could. At the same time he counseled women to have "the patience of truth while they advocate the truth." [60] The Big Bad Wolf remained obsessed with political rights, chalked up at best a partial victory, and moved on to new crises, national and personal.

Douglass's personal life was now fraught with many conflicting pressures. Throughout the Reconstruction years, the patriarch found himself over and again adjudicating rivalries and feuds among his children and their spouses. Everyone in his extended family struggled with money and livelihood, and Anna, still the center of the home everyone returned to in one way or another, suffered from recurring illnesses. The itinerant lecturer, needing to make a living on which all around him depended, sustained what his son Charles called the "hard and killing tours." A long-lost sibling from slavery days on the Eastern Shore was about to arrive wondrously in the Douglasses' lap in Rochester with his own family of former slaves in tow. Julia Crofts and the old editor sustained their transatlantic correspondence, full of nostalgia for past dreams and labors, assurances of their mutual deep "trust," and Julia's worries over Frederick's occasional "despondency." Clearly, Douglass could still confide in his old comrade, whatever the distance or subject. And Ottilie Assing, the adoring, opinionated, voluble, hidebound salon host in Hoboken, remained a presence in his life. She sustained strong views about how her occasional companion conducted his career, his family, his finances, and his political and religious ideas. Repeatedly, she also informed her sister in Italy of her desire to return to or visit Europe, but could not imagine "how I'm supposed to manage to untie myself from Douglass."[61] If anything, Othello had too many occupations.

Chapter 23

ALL THE LEECHES
THAT FEED ON YOU

Though I am not rich, I am not absolutely poor....I am
working now less for myself than for those around me.

—FREDERICK DOUGLASS, MAY 6, 1868

In midsummer 1867, Douglass experienced another reunion with a slave sibling. His brother Perry Downs (formerly Perry Bailey), born in 1813, the oldest son of Harriet Bailey, arrived in Rochester with his wife, Maria, and four children, to reconnect with his famous kinsman. During the forty years of separation, Frederick had only heard that Perry had been sold south to Louisiana. In a letter sent to Douglass the previous February, written by an intermediary, Perry reached his brother with the amazing story that Perry's wife had been sold to east Texas, and that he had gone to find her. Perry had labored as a field hand in cotton and sugar; in the wake of emancipation, he and his family, somehow surviving as a unit, made it to New Orleans, where a Reverend T. W. Conway supplied them a note of introduction to J. J. Spelman of New York City. Through Spelman's aid, Perry's family found their way to the hill in Rochester and the Douglass household.[1] An emotional, if strained, reunion took place there for the next two years.

Perry's family was illiterate, their habits and values bred in decades of slavery in some of its worst precincts. Nonetheless, Douglass was initially deeply moved by his brother's arrival, although the house now overflowed with needy guests. In September, Douglass wrote to Theodore Tilton, saying that he (and thereby Anna) had "been keeping a kind of hotel all summer!" His "poor brother Perry, after a bondage of fifty-six years, deeply marked by the hardships and sorrows of that hateful condition; and after a separation from me during forty years," suddenly appeared "as if he had lived on another planet." Douglass spent much of the summer working with Perry to build for his family "a snug little cottage" on the property. Douglass wanted his "long-lost brother" to spend the remainder of his days "in peace." Douglass wished Perry's old masters could see their former slave now, "strong and hopeful . . . taking care of himself." The younger brother and author pondered the possibility of writing Perry's story in a narrative, or perhaps even a novella. But "if slavery were not dead," said Douglass, "and I did not in some sort wish to forget its terrible hardships . . . and horrors, I would try to write the narrative of my brother's bondage." Douglass's life was likely too hectic and his travels too frenetic to write that book. Such a past was not easy for him to retrieve and he admitted so in a widely reprinted statement: "Let the old system go! I would not call its guilty ghost from the depths into which its crimes have cast it. I turn gladly from the darkness of the past to the new better dispensation now dawning." Douglass was never good at forgetting the past; but looking closely at what slavery had done to the bodies and minds of Perry and his family made Douglass yearn for release from its clutches. Shortly after Perry's arrival in Rochester, Douglass took him on the road to an August First celebration in Watkins, New York, at the base of Seneca Lake. No record survives of Douglass's speech that day; but he no doubt introduced his brother and told his story.[2] Perhaps Douglass could speak what he did not choose to write.

Tilton published Douglass's letter and called the episode a "beautiful and romantic chapter" in a great man's life, and "proof that truth is stranger than fiction." The problem, though, was that Douglass's kinfolk were truly strangers, especially to his own grown children, who had been born in the free North. With time the reunion in Rochester became anything but romantic. From his new post in Washington, Charles wrote to his father in confusion and resentment, grumbling, "I don't understand in what way those people you have at home are related to you; is it that Mr. Downs is your half brother? From what I have heard of their conduct, I should be afraid even to have them in the same neighborhood, and more especially when you are away in the winter months." What Charles "heard" likely came via his sister Rosetta, who lived with her family nearby in Rochester. When the cold months arrived, a frustrated Rosetta wrote to her traveling father about the struggles of Perry's family in surviving their first Rochester winter, and that they might soon be moving back south.[3]

So widespread was the story of Douglass's taking in his brother's brood that when British friends sent money, he promised to use it to support the new additions to his burgeoning household. The homestead on South Avenue also had another adopted stray. In Washington, at the end of the war, among the thousands of freedmen who trekked into the city as refugees was a thirteen-year-old former slave from Georgia, Henry Strothers, who had the good fortune of meeting and befriending Charles Douglass. Obtaining his father's approval, Charles sent Strothers to Rochester, where he would be employed as a gardener among other tasks and, most important, treated as a fictive son. An English friend wrote in January 1868 of how Julia Crofts had kept a network in Britain informed about Douglass's extended family. "Your life," wrote Mary Carpenter, "has been full of strange adversities, sad partings, wonderful meetings, bitter work, and thrilling joys such as *we* scarcely know anything of except in books of fiction." It all did seem rather romantic from outside the circle of reality. Douglass wrote to another English friend in May 1868 about his financial situation with at least partial honesty: "So far as my own circumstances are concerned, I am successful—far more so than I ever ventured to hope—and though I am not rich, I am not absolutely poor." Then came a genteel understatement: "I may say that I am working now less for myself than for those around me."[4]

Indeed Douglass labored, especially through his lecture tours, to financially sustain a growing clan of struggling, discontented, feuding siblings and their families. A bitter and enduring dispute grew in 1867 and lasted for many years among Charles, Rosetta, and her husband, Nathan Sprague, with Ottilie Assing piping in with toxic opinions. To say the least, Douglass himself was caught in the middle of some ugly cross fire. In these years, Lewis attempted without much success to run a school in Maryland. With his brother Frederick Jr., he moved out to Denver, Colorado, in 1866 and 1867 and tried his hand in a variety of businesses, including a laundry, and a "lunch room." The two brothers also spent a stint working for a mining company. Douglass's old friend H. O. Wagoner, who lived in Denver, assisted the brothers in getting started. He wrote to the father a revealing observation: "Lewis I take to be a young man of strong, clear good sense. He seems to drive right ahead at the object aimed at. Frederick, however, seems to be more cautious, reflecting, hesitative, and as you say, 'practical.' "[5] The financial and professional strug-

Frederick Douglass Jr., c. 1862.

gles of his sons were a constant worry for the elder Douglass, who for much of the rest of his life frequently extended them loans.

Back in Rochester in the winter of 1867, Charles tried to manage the patriarch's endless correspondence and speaking commitments. In February, Charles wrote to his father, who was on tour in Michigan, at length of the cost "to gravel the road in front of the house." Charles was desperate for a secure job that would allow him to provide for his pregnant wife (he had married the eighteen-year-old Mary Elizabeth "Libbie" Murphy, September 21, 1866). Meanwhile Rosetta, her husband, and their two babies had tried to make a go of it by buying a farm near Rochester. The venture failed quickly, and they sold the farm in spring 1867 and moved back into the city. Nathan wrote to his father-in-law of his desperate financial straits. Rosetta too wrote of the travail of moving and complained about anxiety over their dangerous Irish neighbors. Douglass gave Rosetta and Nathan a loan of what had to be several hundreds of dollars, with which the son-in-law bought a hack and a "handsome span of greys." For $640—$200 down and a payment plan of eighteen months—Nathan and his hack, Rosetta proudly if awkwardly announced, were "on the stand every day." But white hackmen insulted and threatened Nathan as a competitor; the business, like everything else the hapless Nathan attempted, did not pan out. By April 24, Rosetta reported an "outrage on Nathan's hack."[6] Nathan could not overcome Yankee racism or his own demons.

A young mother with a husband who could not effectively provide, Rosetta shouldered many burdens. She seemed to resent managing her father's letters. But in a mixed tone of embarrassment and gratitude she wrote Douglass obligatory notes: "Father, I cannot thank you too much for your kindness to Nathan and myself, and I can assure you Nathan is grateful and proud of your good opinion of him." Such opinions would not last for long. Worse yet, Rosetta monitored the "spirits" and physical health of her mother. "Ran up to the house" and mother was "not well" was a common report to the traveling orator, from whom she had just received letters from his stops in West Virginia and Pennsylvania. Receiving letters at hotels or post offices, Douglass learned in late April that Anna was "sick" with neurological attacks and had "collapsed at the sink" with "vomiting spells," after which "she seemed stupid." Rosetta summoned a doctor and the malady was pronounced a "bilious attack."[7] Out on the hustings where Douglass addressed audiences in town after town about the memory of the war, the character of republicanism, the right to vote, and the virtues of self-made men came a steady stream of difficult domestic news and demands for financial assistance. Often exhausted, the "self-made man" soldiered on.

That spring in 1867, Charles left his wife, Libbie, living with Anna in Rochester and moved to Washington to take a job as a clerk at the Freedmen's Bureau, a position his father's connections made possible. Charles worked as a personal assistant to Oliver O. Howard, the director, writing his correspondence. The son was especially proud to tell his father that Charles was only the "second colored man" to be given a "first class clerkship." Charles seemed happy about his employment—his white coworkers were "perfect gentlemen." He was, as always though, worried about money; the boardinghouse rent was high, and he boldly asked his father for an $1,800 loan to buy a house. The elder Douglass rejected the request, beginning an exchange lasting for years over the financial dependency of his youngest son. Then came the news that Libbie had delivered her baby on June 21, a boy named Charles Frederick, who would always be known as Freddie. Writing as the stressed and absent father of his firstborn, Charles said he had "no fears" because Libbie and the baby were "in good hands." His mother had a great deal of experience by now with these joyous new additions to the Douglass family. Oddly, though, Charles said he was "very well satisfied with the name you have given the boy." Apparently, as father, he had not participated in the choice; the women had taken care of that task. And though he addressed his letter to his father, on June 21 Douglass the elder was in Indianapolis, Indiana, speaking at Morrison's Opera Hall.[8]

That same summer of 1867, and for a decade to follow, the feud between Douglass's sons and his son-in-law, Nathan Sprague, festered and exploded. The quarrel began over money and loans between Frederick Jr., Charles, and Nathan, but eventually it descended into accusations of betrayal, lying, theft, and competing claims on the elder Douglass's property. Rosetta inevitably was caught between her brothers and her eventually estranged husband. Where Anna stood in all of this family warfare is hard to discern, but she likely defended her daughter, who remained her steady companion and nearby protector. Douglass himself tried to negotiate these treacherous waters and gave out some loans that he regretted as he traveled thousands of miles to make the livelihood necessary for these familial demands. In some letters to English friends, safely beyond the fray, he often told of recuperating from "hard travelling & speaking; ten thousand miles and a hundred speeches" in a three-month stretch.[9]

Like his three brothers-in-law, Sprague could not make a gainful living in Rochester. Repeatedly, he seemed to wear out his welcome at the Douglass household. Charles complained to his father of Nathan's alleged skulduggery. "I don't wish to trouble your mind about this affair between Nathan, Fred, and myself," Charles wrote in November 1867. "I know your mind and time are better occupied." But nothing stopped the flow of invective toward Nathan and Rosetta. "You may know the cause of the difficulty, but I know you don't know the whole truth, and it is hard to find it out under the circumstances." The mutual loathing between the brothers and Rosetta's husband and their feud were clearly over money and the elder Douglass's loyalty and largess. Nathan too went west in search of a livelihood in 1868, leaving his wife and two children, ages five and two, behind. From Omaha, Nebraska, he wrote directly to Douglass of his desperation for money and employment. Although racism lurked in his path at various junctures, one scheme after another of his failed. "I think I can make money here," wrote Nathan to his exasperated father-in-law, claiming he might open a "boarding house" for blacks.[10] But soon he was back in Rochester, a ward of the old man's bank accounts and an embarrassment to his wife.

From upper New England to the far Midwest, the road was undoubtedly a refuge for Douglass from all this family turmoil. But he could not escape it. Rosetta wrote to her father in Akron, Ohio, in early 1868 reporting that Nathan had left home for his western venture. This was the first of more than one marital separation for the Spragues. But Rosetta kept a stiff upper lip and pleaded her husband's case. She remained formally "appreciative" of all her father's "kindness" to Nathan and herself. But she confessed to being "sorry you have been obliged to form any unfavorable opinion and hope you will not lose any of the confidence you have been pleased to keep in him [Nathan] for I believe & know it is Nathan's desire to act honorably." [11] Those would turn out to be painfully unprophetic words.

Sprague returned to Rochester within a year, but the situation only got worse. In February 1869, Rosetta told her father that his letters "filled" her with "sadness." He had apparently drawn the line and declared that Nathan could no longer live "on the hill" (the Douglass house). Exasperation seemed to rule on both ends. Douglass was free "to choose," said Rosetta, "who you shall have around you and I could stand all the grumbling and fault finding that might arise by our remaining here." But she defended her husband's manly pride against Douglass's allegation that the unemployed son-in-law could not "exist" without the father's help. "He took exception," complained Rosetta, "to what you said . . . that it was 'all mouths and no hands,' that you included him with the rest—as being a burden." Douglass's cup of frustrations runneth over. The couple would move somewhere that Nathan could get employment as a "gardener," she painfully wrote, if her husband could overcome his "despondency." Pathetically, she said they did not wish to be any further "indebted" because of "the many demands for money from you by all of the family." [12]

A month later, Rosetta wrote what had to be one of the most depressing letters Douglass ever received from his dysfunctional family. When he thought back to what his grandmother Betsy and his mother, Harriet Bailey (for whom Rosetta's second child was named), had endured and survived, he surely felt a parent's despair. He could also vividly remember his own desperate experience of the early 1850s when he was dependent on the largess of Gerrit Smith and the fund-raising of Julia Griffiths. Nathan still needed Douglass's "approbation," Rosetta said. He needed to "float free" and escape "all kinds of unkind remarks" from the brothers. But the daughter desperately needed her father's compassionate heart. She felt cut off by her brothers, and she and Nathan could no longer tolerate their "taunts." She tried to tell her father how much she loved and needed him while at the same time she had to support her spouse. "You say to me husbands first and fathers second," Rosetta wrote. "I know it but I cannot help it— my affection for you is of the warmest kind and your words whether of censure or praise remain with me always and affect me accordingly." [13] She was a twenty-nine-year-old woman in the middle of the nineteenth century, pregnant with her third child, married to a man who could not make a living, begging her father, a world-famous, heroic achiever who had conquered slavery, to stop, listen, and love her unconditionally. Rosetta was an intelligent, highly literate woman trapped in a cluster of gendered values she could never escape. And she had to feed her children; she needed material support. Between 1864 and 1877 Rosetta gave birth to seven children with Sprague (six of them daughters), in a marriage that did manage to survive. Douglass deeply loved his daughter and had earlier cultivated her intellectual sensibilities, but now he did not hide his disappointments at her life choices.

Rosetta became very personal in a way both tender and sadly self-pitying. A picture emerges from her perception of a father so consumed by his work and his cause that he could never see her dilemmas, nor hear her cry. "You say you are a lonely man," she said to Douglass with uncustomary directness, "no one knows it better than myself. . . . I felt it for years for I have been in a measure lonely myself but would not allow myself to analyze my feelings as I was the daughter and had duties to fulfill in that relation." These are remarkable expressions in the era before psychology. Here was an adult woman saying, I did my duty as the daughter in our difficult home, as the oldest child and the go-between in the marriage made so troublesome by illiteracy and the frequently absent father and husband. "I knew where my sympathies were," she informed Douglass. "I do not know whether you thought much about it—having so many things to occupy your mind, but my position at home was anything but pleasant." Rosetta seemed to have stored up many feelings, and a good deal of anger, that she finally let fly at her father. "You used often to say that we were all glad when you left," she continued, "something that was so far from what was true as far as I was concerned. I never dared to show much zeal about anything where you were concerned, as I could never bear ridicule and as jealousy is one of the leading traits in our family I could very readily bring a storm about my ears if I endorsed any of your sentiments about matters pertaining to the household." [14]

Such a statement about Rosetta's youth at home reveals many realities: Anna Douglass's fierce grip on domestic affairs; Douglass's contradictory roles as both patriarch-guest and absent father; the daughter's long emotional need to feel engaged with her father's public world; and a young woman's resentment as well as fascination for the two brilliant European women who had left such a mark on that household. Perhaps Rosetta's lament implied that she had become more of her mother than her father and often wished it otherwise. She ended the letter with an agonizing admission: "I do not wish to pain you but I must say I have no pleasant remembrances of my brothers. I had my faults no doubt, but none so great that their feelings of dislike should follow me to this day." [15] As Douglass traveled the railroads of America speaking to thousands about the great issues of Reconstruction and plotted his career move to Washington, he awoke many days to the news that the "home" in Rochester festered with family conflict he simply could not resolve. And he was surely aware of his daughter's desperation for his love.

While worshipping their father, the sons carried their own burdens of being Douglass's offspring. Each eagerly sought a father's love and approval. None of the Douglass sons achieved any further education after the war, nor did their father push them. Lewis, with some assistance from his brothers, began keeping scrapbooks about the elder Douglass, as well as about themselves. These scrapbooks eventually grew to at least nine thick volumes collected over more than three decades. Their contents demonstrate that the brothers all shared great affection and solidarity among themselves. They even named their children for each other. As collectors of the details of their father's public life, they amassed newspaper clippings by the thousands; eventually, in the 1880s, the family hired a clipping service, the American Bureau, which collected material from nearly everywhere the elder Douglass traveled. The scrapbooks were intended to be a record of fame and achievement, but sometimes they revealed more than the brothers may have intended. [16]

Lewis began collecting when he was in Denver in 1866–67. He was an aspiring journalist and printer, as well as an activist, like his father. Everywhere he (his brothers as well) went, comparisons to the famous father emerged, sometimes with blunt openness. Lewis helped organize a Denver meeting of blacks in 1867 celebrating the advent of the "right of suffrage." He was recognized as a leader, but primarily as "son of the Old Champion." He made a "good chairman," said a reporter. "His face bears clear marks of resemblance to that of his father. . . . We think he will never take the proportions of the old warrior, but a survey of his face tells you, that the son, like the sire, will grapple terribly with conflict. You feel he is a 'Foeman worthy of his steal.'" The article then veered off into a litany of all the "struggles and self-denials . . . tears and heart pangs," and the words hurled like "avenging thunderbolts" from Douglass himself, that could somehow be seen in Lewis's "face." Lewis wore his alleged attributes as a proud burden, at least most of the time. In 1869 he finally convinced his longtime sweetheart, Amelia Loguen of Syracuse, to marry him. Their union was a long time coming, but tender. In December 1870, while living in Washington, Lewis jotted down a quick note to his beloved that he had to help Fred Jr. with an errand, then was "going over to Charley's," and hence, it was "the first meal I have missed with you since we were married."[17] The Douglass brothers were family men.

Lewis was a proud army veteran and aspired in every way for his father's kind of dignity and self-assertion. But jobs and respect were not easily achieved for a young black man in post–Civil War America. While staying in Philadelphia in February 1868, Lewis joined a small group of a "half dozen ladies and one gentlemen" on an ice-skating excursion to Camden, New Jersey. He soon found himself "surrounded by a number of white boys" who objected to the "good clothes" worn by the young women and shouted racial insults. Lewis removed his skates and took on the white thugs with the blades, "splitting [one's] head with the skates" and severing another's "thumb nearly off." He told the story to his fiancée, Amelia, with considerable bravado and assured her that he had "the praise of great coolness" from his companions, especially the ladies. But coming at a peak in mob violence across the South by the Ku Klux Klan and other groups, this incident showed that a Douglass always had to be on guard. Lewis, like his father, was a brawler if he had to be.[18]

While in Colorado in 1867 Lewis published letters in the press asserting his, and by extension all blacks', loyalty and patriotism born of the war experience. There, and by 1869–70, after they moved to Washington, Lewis and Frederick Jr. got into an ugly conflict over membership in a printers' union. Since they could find no one in the all-white printers' union to sponsor them, they took work where they could get it. The federal government had greatly expanded since the war, and it made good sense to try to find employment in its bureaucracy. Frederick Jr. wrote to a Simon Wolf of the Register of Deeds asking to be hired. He described himself as part of "that despised class" that had never before sought government positions. He had served his "country during the War under the colors of Massachusetts," and he noted that he was the "son of a man (Frederick Douglass) who was once held in a bondage protected by the laws of the nation . . . the perpetuity of which" he and many of his race had "struggled to maintain." Wolf responded with encouragement, since he too was from "a race equally maligned" (Jews).[19] Fred Jr. did not receive the job.

In the summer of 1869, Lewis faced public accusation as a "rat" and working for "unfair prices." He was denied membership in the Washington branch of the Columbia Typographical Union on account of his race. He protested, the dispute became a cause célèbre, and the elder Douglass forcefully defended his son in the national press as the representative of "our whole people rising up from degradation to respectability." For the elder Douglass, the issue was "clearly personal." He publicly denounced the "shams" and "excuses" used to deny Lewis membership—that his "card" had been improperly issued and that he had willfully worked for lower wages. Douglass employed old abolitionist metaphors to skewer the scoundrels: "They virtually say for the criminal that having cut off the ears of his victim, he has also the right to pluck out his eyes." Lewis was condemned for not joining a union whose racism prohibited his membership.

Whether overt or covert, racism hurt to the soul, and Douglass let his friends and enemies know it. He brought the story home to Rochester. His "goodly city" had always welcomed him personally; few other Northern cities were as "liberal and friendly to the colored race." But then he revealed a painful family tale to make the public argument. When Lewis returned from the war, wounded at the famous fight on "the walls of Fort Wagner," and "somewhat broken in health," the veteran was denied "work at his trade" week after week. Watching his son's demoralization made the elder Douglass feel the "iron of Negro hate" in his own soul. He especially felt wronged because for sixteen years on his own newspaper he had hired white apprentices to the tune, by his count, of $100,000.[20] That Douglass put a dollar figure on this particular kind of racism reflected the larger economic pain among his sons. He was telling whites that perhaps he was owed some interest on his investment in them.

The problem of employment and financial rivalry continued unabated as well between Charles and Nathan and Rosetta. So eager was Charles to own a home in Washington that he audaciously asked his father to "invest" and help him "buy a lot." Douglass sternly rebuked these overtures and urged his youngest to save his money, which only stimulated an aggrieved defensiveness on the part of the son. Charles outdistanced his sister for self-pity. "I had rather not have you lay out one cent in my behalf," Charles unconvincingly wrote to his father in 1868, "if you think that I am trifling with you and my money." He was doing his "best" and only hoped to benefit like the "other clerks . . . who have parents or friends to aid them." By fall 1868, Douglass had given Charles a new loan of at least $800, but the young man asked for $300 more to finish the roof on a house in a new black section of the District called Uniontown. Frederick Jr. too had moved to the area and opened a store. Charles craved being "wholly independent." His letters ached with such declarations as "I will prove to you that my word will be kept, all I desire is to get into my house." [21]

Charles's money woes were more and more encased in nasty diatribes at Nathan. Douglass must have sighed and rolled his eyes in frustration as Charles carped about how he would never pay the money he owed to Nathan until Rosetta's husband paid up what he owed to Frederick Jr. The Douglass family exploded in sibling rivalry, poisoned by matters of money, status, and personality. In September 1868, Charles accused his father of "bolstering up" Nathan more than the brothers, moaning that the hated brother-in-law "used to bring up his being better off than any of us boys, and acted as though he could get along and we could not." The racism of the outer world was bad enough; the elder Douglass agonized over the obnoxious drafts of human nature flowing from his kin, a situation suffused with both tragedy and farce. "I used to take it then," Charles whined, "but when I think over how he used to talk to me about Lew and Fred it makes me angry." [22]

In 1869–70, exchanges between Douglass and Charles became private family warfare over integrity and inheritance. They even teemed with

Nathan Sprague, Douglass's son-in-law, Union army veteran, 1860s.

threats and conspiracy theories about the house on "the hill" in Rochester. Charles judged Nathan little more than an incompetent farmer who had let the Douglass family cow die. Worse, Charles thought Nathan an unfaithful husband and a thief with designs on Douglass's estate. "I have no friendship for Sprague," Charles declared in February 1869. Sprague's "misrepresentations" had forced "me and the other boys" to be "sent away." This may have struck Douglass as absurd. But the despairing Charles, who lost his job at the Freedmen's Bureau in March and occasionally received a $100 draft from his father to keep him afloat, complained bitterly of being, in his view, closed out of the family: "Sprague has the advantage of mother, and if mother wants a letter written she has to go to Rosetta, and there it goes, and you only get one side of what transpires." This was no news to Douglass about the ways communications to and from Anna were accomplished. But it was depressing to read these missives from his dependent adult son. Moreover, in Washington, the employment of the Douglass brothers became increasingly a matter of public debate. Charles eventually landed a job as a clerk in the Treasury Department. "Such pets are the Douglass family," said one complaint in the press, "that they seem to think themselves entitled to the lion's share of choice offices." Therefore, "the honor and respect of the white people are bruised and outraged hereby." [23]

Charles and his brothers were Douglass's eyes in Washington. The youngest son was an astute observer of congressional and presidential politics. In February 1870, Charles attended the swearing in of Hiram Revels of Mississippi, the first African American member of the US Senate. Charles informed his father that he "heard it whispered several times in the galleries" that people wished it were Douglass himself being sworn in. Charles urged the orator to take aim at the Congress and cease the "killing tours through the west," one of which was under way that very moment in Indiana, Illinois, Iowa, Michigan, and Ohio. [24]

Charles's life in Washington was not all consumed in seeking government jobs and observing politics. During the five years after the war, he was directly involved in organizing two black baseball teams, the Alert and the Mutual Base Ball Clubs. Charles's embrace of baseball likely began in the army during the war. He also played second base for a Rochester team, the Excelsior Club, as early as summer 1865. For a while in 1867 he played for the Union Baseball Club and reported to his father in August that the team had played an out-of-town game against the Philadelphia Pythians. The elder Douglass invested in and attended some games, but did not participate. In the wake of the Civil War, baseball boomed in popularity in the capital, as well as in many other cities, especially in the North. All the rules of the American pastime were by no means settled in the 1860s. It was played with a bat, a ball, no gloves, and four bases. Foul lines were still evolving, but teams played with nine men. In this offense-favored game, a winning team's scoring a hundred runs on a weaker opponent was not uncommon. Baseball boomed in Philadelphia, New York, Chicago, and in Richmond, where teams of ex-Confederates played teams of ex-Union soldiers with the theme of sectional reunion already awkwardly in the air even as early as 1866–67.[25]

For Charles, and for so many of the other young government workers, black and white, baseball was a personal and community outlet. The war was over, and despite the tremendous political conflicts of Reconstruction, Washington was a burgeoning new city, with nearly forty thousand black residents and over eighty-eight thousand whites. Black baseball clubs, not unlike fraternal orders and churches in black communities, took on a social-political function. In these years the goal was never to gain full integration into white teams and leagues, but to achieve full access to the best playing grounds and to book matches with the best clubs, such as the famed Washington Nationals. In Washington, that meant getting to play official games on the "White Lot," the huge space eventually laid out in baseball fields between the White House and the Washington Monument. Charles, and occasionally his brothers, spent many a late afternoon hurrying from their jobs to the field to play a game. Black ballplayers of the late 1860s played with or against white players and clubs, a small part of the great experiment in racial democracy that Reconstruction wrought. It did not last, however; by 1876, the first formal "National League" was formed by white entrepreneurs, players, and coaches determined to keep the game segregated, a goal they by and large accomplished for the next seventy-five years. Charles Douglass was part of a huge throng of former slaves, Union soldiers, and black men born free who created a game forever embedded in the fabric of American democracy.[26]

The Douglasses needed sport and amusement. By spring and summer 1870, as Douglass planned a move to Washington to buy and edit a newspaper, the family feuds reached a new fever pitch. Nathan had brought a number of his own kinfolk to live at the Douglass homestead. Douglass had apparently acquiesced in allowing Nathan back on the premises, with his own siblings and cousins in tow. As always, Rosetta's growing family needed a home and Anna's skilled help. Douglass was the self-made patriarch-grandfather who tried to say no and take stands for self-reliance, but usually said yes.

Charles felt betrayed and took it out on his father via Nathan. "Sprague is making out a course . . . that will be a trap for his own destruction," Charles claimed in May 1870. He thought him as "ungrateful as a bear." Then Charles wrote lines he regretted: "None of us lie buried as deep in your pockets as he [Nathan] does, and if we had not a penny from you we would be the same to you as we are now, ready at all times to abide by your decision, and unspeakably grateful to you for all we have, and all the favors shown us by others." Such sad remarks by the unsuccessful son of a famous man descended deeper yet into a desperate jealousy: "I don't feel you are safe in your own home while such a conspiracy is going on." Sprague was the "prime mover in this dirty plot." He had placed "a whole generation of his relatives in and around you . . . and by trickery and lying he will get you to turn out all others, and then comes the stealings." Property and the quest for filial approval can make people crazy. "Us boys have an interest in that house," moaned Charles, "though we may never see it or be in it again . . . for the best part of our days were spent there, and the place grew with us." [27] Anna never saw these letters; how painful it would have been for her to hear such exchanges. But Charles was not altogether wrong about Sprague's intentions and character.

Douglass's response came immediately, and Charles felt "very bad." The father vehemently objected to the way Charles made demands on the elder's "possessions." Charles claimed many a misunderstood "inference." He did not mean to suggest that his father was a "dupe of Nathan." "I do not think you weak in mind." Self-pity turned to self-loathing. "I never had such a thought enter my head with regard to anything belonging to you," Charles wrote disingenuously. "I don't even feel the place I live in now to be mine. I look upon it as yours, because if it was not for your aid, I should not have gotten it." "Sprague and his wife" were "against me and mine." Over and again, Charles apologized for having "offended" his father. A month later, in June, Lewis and Fred Jr. were both boarding with Charles, their wives all back home in upstate New York. Charles developed a martyr complex. His clothes were "seedy," he had lost weight, and he experienced "sharp stinging pains" all down his side, a problem he attributed to "exposure during the war." And he was broke. With the latest check from his father Charles calculated his total indebtedness at $1,000.[28] The elder Douglass needed to make a career move, not merely for himself. And he had no lack of advice.

• • •

In each year of the postwar era through 1871, Ottilie Assing continued to spend as much of her summers as possible in Rochester, enjoying the garden and tiptoeing around the family strife. She usually arrived in late June or early July and stayed into September. She cherished whatever time and attention she could garner from the man of the house and did her part to contain as she also caused the cold war with Anna Douglass. We have no testimony from Anna about the nature of these summer visits. One current poet, M. Nzadi Keita, has tried through literary imagination to give Anna a voice for her seething resentments, to tell her side of this mysterious, anguished story. In one of several dozen poems, many of which try to suggest what "letters" and "words" meant in the ways Anna might have used them, Keita offers a version of Mrs. Douglass's estimation of Ottilie Assing. In "Attic Window," she calls Assing "a blue-eyed weed my husband found," a woman who was "no guest" and spoke with a "foreign mouth" and wondered "how could a mammy be a match for such a princely man."[29] Such poetry is not a historical source of Anna's interior world. But it does provide us a language by which we can gaze into it. Art provides a means to elusive truths, if not the truth itself. What we do know from Assing herself is that, at least in her own blunt letters, she exercised little restraint in judging the personalities, rivalries, and financial woes in Douglass's family. And Anna certainly knew a good deal of the educated German lady's opinions.

Assing felt disgust at Perry's family after their arrival in the summer of 1867. In a letter to Sylvester Koehler, one of her "gang" of German émigré intellectuals in New Jersey, she expressed gladness that the "dear family from Texas" had moved into their hastily constructed house on the grounds and no longer lived "in close proximity before our eyes and noses anymore." She thought them "incorrigible . . . especially the dear wife, who smokes her pipe" and "whips her children with a riding crop." Assing particularly objected that the former slaves understood neither the "concept of gratitude" nor the "concept of cleanliness." The sophisticated lady with the books on her lap in the garden hardly knew what to do when confronted with the raw, brutal legacies of slavery. This was high-German radical culture meets the American black peasantry, the dull, remote plantations of east Texas and Louisiana meets the literary salon of European freethinkers. Assing's abolitionism melted into contempt. But Ottilie melted herself one day a year later as a two-year-old "coffee-brown girl" (Perry's granddaughter) followed her and her cat around in the garden. Assing admitted to an urge to adopt this "child of Douglass's niece." Then in 1870, after a brief visit from Douglass, she summed up his "impressions from home" as a situation of "screaming children, people who are constantly at the verge of armed peace with one another." And eight years after that, when on one of his returns to the Eastern Shore, Douglass sought to retrieve an infirm Perry and bring him to live with him in Washington for his declining years, Ottilie snidely remarked, "That you should pick up Perry is just like you and natural enough. . . . Among all the leeches that feed on you he is one of the most harmless and least expensive."[30] Often, Assing's irony was simply out of place in Douglass's necessary but nearly impossible effort to bridge slavery and freedom in his family. He managed to live in and communicate with both worlds—Ottilie's intellectual salon and a black family, roiling with irreconcilable experiences.

In the postwar years Assing herself became one of Douglass's dependents, although she could never quite admit it. When she lost her place writing for *Morgenblatt* and relinquished the literary life, she became what her biographer calls "Douglass's auxiliary." Her dependency was primarily emotional; she cobbled together a living as a teacher-tutor in and around New York. She even began to refer to herself as Douglass's "pigtail" in letters, an appendage wishing to follow him if possible on his travels.[31]

Sustaining her ties to Douglass, even claiming to be his real wifely companion, became essential to Assing's identity as she aged. To her sister, Assing continually wrote about an internal bond she possessed with Douglass that transcended "all external circumstances"—meaning that he was married, had a large extended family, and maintained a widespread public reputation. She expressed lasting gratitude for her connection to Douglass, "even if," she wrote in 1872, "the external situation remains less than perfect." Grandiosity leaped from her letters. Assing believed she had been tested and had proved her mettle in romance. "Seventeen years, in defiance of all external circumstances, with people and prejudices of all kinds against us," she boldly asserted with self-delusion, "can legitimately be referred as a kind of trial by fire." A year later when her sister had troubles with her husband, Ottilie offered herself as a model: "When one stands in such intimate relation with one man, as is the case with me in relation to Douglass, one gets to know the whole world, men as well as women, from angles that would otherwise be closed off to one, especially in cases where the man has seen so much of the world and has been loved by so many women." Assing's fantasy—as the deeper spiritual wife of the world-historical man—prompted her to increasingly ugly denigrations of Anna, the real wife.

Ottilie and Frederick were "kept from one another," she wrote in 1874, by a "veritable beast" (could be translated "monster") who "neither has love to give nor knows how to appreciate it." Assing's "plight," she concluded with nods to German romanticism, meant that a "kind of fatality inheres in my name," a reference to the character Ottilie, who finds a tragic fate due to a form of spiritual adultery, in Goethe's *Die Wahlverwandtshaften*.[32]

Ottilie almost never gave up on her quest of drawing Douglass off to a new life in Europe; like spring itself, it was her annual recurring fantasy. She ruminated in letters to her sister about her desires to see Europe again. In 1869 she said she would "be ready with a thousand joys" if her man would give in and go. "Without Douglass," Ottilie concluded, she could not "implement my plan to visit France, Switzerland and several places in Germany, since travelling all by yourself is a rather sad pleasure." Sometimes she found a certain contentedness in asking her sister for photographs of their parents that she could give to Douglass, as though he were part of their German family. The American would have had "a close enough relationship" with her mother, Assing maintained, "if matters were the way they are supposed to be." She finally gave up in 1876 and made her journey to Europe after ten years of waiting out Douglass, although not without imagining in her grandiose way that he would still join her after the presidential election. Douglass may have at least encouraged the fantasy in some of his correspondence. By winter 1877, while in Rome, Assing wrote to Douglass wondering about his "schemes." "May I hope yet to see you in spring?" she wistfully asked. "If you only let me know exactly the time when you expect to touch this continent, I shall be ready to . . . receive you at the landing." Her dream remained unfulfilled and her letters became ever more forlorn.[33]

There is little evidence that Douglass had any intention of following Assing on such an impossible sojourn; rather, it was she who submitted to the schedules, behaviors, and encounters that he determined. She wanted to go to Germany and Switzerland and read Goethe with her companion on long summer evenings in village gasthauses; he had to take the sooty, lonely trains thousands of miles to lecture in Ohio and Indiana in the dark cold of January as a primary source of his livelihood. The trajectories of these two lives could never fully intersect. Around all the Douglasses, she was "Miss Assing," father's special family friend and intellectual confidant. Ottilie was hardly the first to occupy this role; many others had auditioned; one (Julia Griffiths) had laid all the groundwork. In some periods of their more than twenty-year relationship, Douglass needed Assing almost as much as she needed him. He did not need a pigtail bobbing in his busy wake; but he did benefit greatly from Assing's patient listening as a sounding board for his emotional and mental life. He likely cherished her unconditional admiration and devotion, as long as he could control its contours. Most important, she provided a unique intellectual stimulation from her circle of literary and political radicals among whom he was made welcome during his Hoboken stay-overs. Ottilie had a point as well in calling attention during the Reconstruction years to Douglass's occasional "guilelessness" with money, as well as with her claim that he might have achieved financial independence had it not been for "all the hangers-on and parasites" who abused his hospitality. But she was ultimately one of those hangers-on, albeit in a category all her own.[34]

Assing's judgments about the Douglass family disputes were no less rigid and morally certain than her political and ideological views. Presumably he listened, since she was in the middle of some of the dramas. She liked all three sons, even claiming a certain maternal connection with them by showing them off to her friends when they traveled through New Jersey and stopped to see her. Lewis once spent two weeks staying with Assing and her circle. In June 1868, Charles and Libbie Douglass gave Assing a tour of Washington, DC. She felt the romantic rush of seeing for the first time this center of republicanism and now grasped fully why Douglass wanted to be there. When they crossed over into Arlington, Virginia, she gushed, "What a triumph it is to enter the former slave states as free soil." Then the three companions took an excursion to George Washington's Mount Vernon estate. "Miss Assing treated us to a visit to Mt. Vernon yesterday," Charles wrote to his father, "and we had a very nice time." Ottilie was taken with the "minstrel" singers on the boat ride down the Potomac, as well as with an old black gardener at the estate who claimed to have been Washington's slave. Assing proudly announced for other tourists to hear that she was glad to shake hands with the old former slave, since they were meeting on free soil. Always self-serving, she felt especially proud as the white woman traveling with a well-dressed young black couple.[35] The earnest radical flaunted her egalitarianism on this border so steeped in history.

Ottilie was never afraid to say, though, that she thought Douglass sometimes spoiled his sons, even the oldest. In 1874 she gossiped that Lewis was back in Rochester being "fed like a little boy," along with "his terrible wife from Syracuse." At times, Assing seemed to believe, and said so, that no one was good enough for the great Douglass except her and the friends she would choose for him from within her circle of educated companions. Sprague was in her estimation a "disgraced villain" who suffered from

"mental inferiority." In letters to Douglass, she knew she could simply unload from her gut, and he let her do it. "A thousand times rather would
I undertake to teach a cat or even Border States [Anna] grammar," she
pronounced, "than to impress him [Nathan] with a sense of truthfulness
and honesty." Such was Ottilie's private way of laughing at Anna and telling Frederick that his own family members were stealing his shirt through
"littleness and trickery." [36] Her jealousy toward anyone who came between
her and her special friend was as palpable as her will to survive was strong.

Assing was ultimately on a fool's errand, but while it lasted, the relationship
brought her enormous satisfaction. Her "summer tour to Douglass," and his
coming to her intermittently in Hoboken on his speaking tours, provided an
emotional center to their lives that neither could otherwise attain. Douglass
tells us nothing explicitly about what his detours to Hoboken meant to him.
As autobiographer, the public man maintained a profound silence about
his private life. But we can glimpse his emotional life through Assing's portrayals of his visits and of her own pretensions and dreams. If only briefly,
he managed to relax in Hoboken. Douglass loved cigars, and Assing gave
them to him as gifts; their "fragrance" lingering at her boardinghouse was
a pleasant prod to memory for Ottilie. In Assing, Douglass had an adoring
and astute critic-reader. Much of what he wrote in the Reconstruction years
passed before her eyes. In late 1870 she wrote a formal paper about Douglass that she delivered to a literary society in New Jersey, a piece that once
again added to the mythos of her subject. She would also sometimes translate one of her essays into English "in order to read it to Douglass," when
he arrived for a stay-over. Ottilie reveled in garnering personal time with
Douglass to introduce him to high-German literary culture. One August,
she told her sister, Ludmilla, she was "so happy to have found a volume of
Goethe in good English translation here [Rochester], Faust, Egmont, Tasso,
Iphigenie and Goetz von Berlichingen, and you can imagine what a pleasure it is for me to introduce Douglass to all this." [37] We do not know just
how much of German literature Assing's companion digested; there is little
evidence of his ever quoting from it.

But Assing worked assiduously on Douglass's views about religion, trying to convert him to atheism via the writings of Ludwig Feuerbach. Assing
gloried in believing that she persuaded her friend to abandon all elements
of Christianity, a dubious claim at best and one Douglass never openly confirmed. In 1859, Assing bought an English version of Feuerbach's famous

1841 philosophical work, *The Essence of Christianity*, translated by George Eliot. She gave this manifesto of atheism to Douglass, accompanied by a bust of Feuerbach, which eventually resided among many other portraits and images in his study at Cedar Hill. She even wrote an extraordinary letter to Feuerbach thanking him for helping her convert the American reformer. Just how closely Douglass read Feuerbach is not clear. Religious hypocrisy about slavery and racism had sparked his thought and rhetoric throughout his public life. He had mastered the craft of the jeremiad, indeed *with* the core values of Christianity and its central stories, not *against* them. Condemnation of religious contradiction is not itself an antireligious prescription. In so much Christian, especially Protestant, tradition, it is precisely the opposite. As a freethinking, stern, self-contained individualist incapable of mustering the pragmatic open mind by which Douglass had matured into consciousness and activism, Assing seems never to have comprehended this element of her hero's character.[38]

With beguiling logic, Feuerbach made a layered case for God as the invention of man out of man's own consciousness and will. Religion, Feuerbach contended, was better understood as anthropology, a fascinating creation of man's need for culture. Feuerbach's atheism could add up to a blinding hubris or self-love. But parts of it might also have been liberating to Douglass's spongelike, evolving mind in the harrowing Civil War and Reconstruction years. He might have valued Feuerbach's notion that the end of love was "love," and the end of free will was to "be free."[39] An apocalyptic historical view of God's interventions in history might coexist well with such a call for humans to act when the time has come. Assing had somehow missed one of the essential arguments in Douglass's life's work: that without the Old Testament's bracing narrative of declension, destruction, exile, renewal, and return, African American slaves, their vanguard in the black regiments during the war, and their most famous prophetic voice might never have imagined their freedom in the Babylon of America.

Douglass's personal faith no doubt changed over time; the early influence of Father Lawson in the streets of Baltimore, Douglass's early years preaching from biblical texts in the AME Zion Church, gave way to a widely read, politicized mind and advocate of the natural-rights tradition. But as he employed the Declaration of Independence, the Constitution, and the new creeds of the nation's second founding against his own country, he never gave up on the Exodus story nor the majesty of Isaiah's wisdom nor Jeremiah's warnings. Much can be made of Douglass's endless critique of religious hypocrisy, and no greater example exists in his torrent of words than in the Fourth of July speech of 1852. In that lecture's brilliant middle section, the orator bludgeoned false prophets and slaveholding "scribes and Pharisees, hypocrites." Douglass showered his targets with hailstorms of their own sins: "For my part, welcome infidelity! welcome atheism! Welcome anything! in preference to the gospel, as preached by those Divines!" Assing's biographer quotes that passage as evidence of the author's early proclivity to atheism. But such an interpretation makes no sense when one turns the page and sees Douglass declare his embrace of a genuine Christianity by using the words of James 1:27: a "pure and undefiled religion," which is "first pure, then peaceable, easy to be entreated, full of mercy and good fruits, without partiality, and without hypocrisy." Then he deftly employed Isaiah, demanding that Americans exalt the poor over the rich, the slave over the tyrant, and bring "no more vain oblations" to their defiled Sabbaths. His was always a religion of action and faith. He demanded, when young and old, that Americans "cease to do evil, learn to do well . . . relieve the oppressed; judge for the fatherless; plead for the widow."[40] Douglass knew he had never invented Isaiah. If pressed, he might have admitted that it was the other way around.

Without a doubt, Douglass enjoyed the admiration and intellectual stimulation he received from Assing's salon of radical thinkers. Almost every time Douglass came to town, her friends would gather for conversation. It was especially important to Ottilie that her friends—the Koehlers; Dr. Gustav Frauensein, a physician; Karl Heinzen of Boston and Dr. E. J. Lowenthal, both German Forty-Eighters; Dr. Johannes Lange, an attorney; and C. N. Riotte, a German American diplomat—accepted Douglass. Assing preferred the conversation of the men and frankly despised most of their wives, whom she called "stupid" and "uneducated." A typical Douglass visit was often, whether he wished it or not, a "festive occasion." Ottilie had Frederick as guest for New Year's Eve 1870. They shared some time "beautifully undisturbed" until all of her neighbors and fellow boardinghouse mates assembled and began discussions, thoroughly "lionizing" her guest, which, according to Assing, he enjoyed as much as they.[41] All this undivided attention and respect gave Douglass something special in his life, and wholly different from "the hill" in Rochester. He no doubt tried out many political ideas on the members of Ottilie's group; she no doubt managed a fascinating discussion among the men. Nowhere else in Douglass's life did he find such a life of the mind.

For the former slave, these occasional visits among such a group allowed him the recognition that he had indeed risen into the thinking classes. Above all, Douglass *learned* from Assing; her arrogance and his less blustering conceits about his own self-created life of the mind made a strange but useful match. On his frenzied travels out on the western lecture circuit, or whenever he felt the dull, sandy soil of Talbot County and the Tuckahoe falling in around him, he knew he had such a retreat. Assing's circle gave him recurring evidence that he had crossed his Chesapeake to a refuge on a safe shore. Sometimes Ottilie's meddling in Douglass's work life prompted from him a strong response. When she spilled to Horace Greeley that he might be planning a trip to speak in Georgia, hoping by exposure to cause him to cancel, Douglass wrote to Koehler, whom Ottilie had enlisted in her scheme: "My good friend—Miss Assing, is wise in many things, but is sometimes disposed to look at 'Mole Hills' as Mountains." Carefully but firmly, Douglass let it be known that he did not want his plans "trumpeted to the world." His was a controlled anger. "I must be a little more careful how I whisper my thoughts to my dear Miss Assing. The vehemence of her opposition sometimes makes necessary a just sense of Independence to go straight forward."[42] But in Assing, Douglass had the intellectual companion, if not always a fully trustworthy one, that he had first known in Julia Griffiths. When he moved to Washington to edit a new paper, Assing would often be there with him at the editorial desk, or as a regular correspondent from New Jersey. The hero was his own unique creation, and he would increasingly draw that line of independence with Ottilie, but his story still evolved and he had much more to tell. He had always needed help, especially from skilled, loving, educated women.

To understand how Douglass could sustain both his marriage and his friendship with Assing, it is worth returning to elements of his early youth. The only real family attachment that Douglass remembered in his autobiographies was his grandmother, and though idealized and beloved, she always remained shrouded in the images of the day even she abandoned him. From the day Betsy Bailey, by slavery's evil logic, left him forever at the Wye plantation at the age of six, Douglass said he carried a "wounded soul" that "affected me so deeply." In lyrical language, Douglass made plain why he could never forgive slavery and his owners for robbing him of familial attachments. "I never think of this terrible interference of slavery with my infantile affections," he wrote in *Bondage and Freedom*, "and its diverting them from its natural course, without feelings to which I can give no adequate expression." Here, and in the *Narrative* before, he had signaled his lifelong quest for an idealized mother's care, and a home that might provide it. In his fleeting, invented memories of his actual mother, he imagined "a bright gleam of a mother's love." But that was memory acting as desire for love and some claim to a child's normal safety. Slavery, he maintained, had stolen from him all "filial affection," the most basic elements of parental love. Douglass was trying to tell us that he had never found it easy to love, while always seeking love as much as anything else in life. To grasp how he later coped with the deep complexities of his family and emotional life, we do well to remember his critique of slavery not merely as abolitionist propaganda, but as his cry for the healing of his own wounds: slavery "had made my brothers and sisters strangers to me; it converted the mother that bore me into a myth; it shrouded my father in mystery, and left me without an intelligible beginning in the world." [43]

Perhaps the thing in life he needed most was all but forever beyond his grasp, and certainly not achievable in one woman. Douglass might cling to some of the female relationships in his life at the same time any profoundly deep love may have been an unbearable intensity. Denied any family attachment in his youth, he fiercely sought and protected a sense of "home" once he and Anna could create one, from New Bedford to Rochester, and Washington, DC. Precisely how he justified to his entire family the blatant insensitivity of having Assing in his household is not altogether knowable. But he lived with that daily insensitivity and worked his brain and body to the bone to provide for them all. What Douglass sustained, sometimes under one roof, was the comforting presence—for him—of both Anna (the mother and grandmother who would never abandon him), and the equally comforting and stimulating presence of adoring intellectual women (Julia and Ottilie) who not only fulfilled realms of his ego that Anna could not, but may even have been idealized versions of that literate mother he created in the autobiographies. Douglass somehow possessed the stamina and mental stability to sustain all these contradictions into his fifties and sixties. [44] He was surely a willing, if at times humbled, patriarch. He was absolutely devoted to his children even as he expressed a parent's natural frustrations. Slavery had denied him a father; he would never let that happen to his children.

How this all affected Anna Douglass back in her domestic domain is ours to speculate. The poet Nzadi Keita can help again. In "History," we hear Anna beg to be heard: "When the writer turns to me, what shape will fill his mouth?" Anna wonders. "Will it be said that I could speak?" She painfully asks, "Who will remember bread and stew that set those bound for Canada on their feet?" Above all, she hopes no one will "paint across my truth." [45] No one should paint across Anna Douglass's truth nor forget her bread and stew. She was a good deal more than what we think we know, and far more than her husband ever told us.

Anna's life was long and often, no doubt, fulfilling. The loss of Annie in 1860 was surely unbearable, and seeing her boys off to war terrifying. Her husband's thousand long absences were at first fearful, but in time routine. The grandchildren came along eventually in bunches, although their lives were eventually fraught with disease and tragedy. Anna was likely a woman who knew fully what she could control and a good deal about what she could not. She had to fight for respect as a quiet, never cleverly verbal woman in an environment with too many comparisons, in a household defined at least in part by the literary genius and heroic activist who ruled it. Words were not her forte; her Maryland biscuits served up in her stolid manner left her mark. When Rosetta described her mother as her father's "faithful ally, guarding as best she could every interest connected with . . . his life-work," she captured something compelling.[46]

Anna came from a huge family in Denton, Maryland, on the far side of the Tuckahoe River. Both parents were enslaved, as were her seven older siblings. Anna was the first in her family born free. She left such a struggling, enormous clan of kin at age seventeen and went to Baltimore. We know her because of forty-four years of marriage to Douglass. The heart of her story, though, is not only that she was crucial in his liberation from slavery, but that she too, perhaps even more than he, understood the meaning of holding together and protecting a black family in racist, hostile America. Her garden for self-sufficiency, mothering skills, and stern personality made "the hill" on South Avenue possible as much as her husband's speaking fees and book royalties. Perhaps her acceptance of Assing's summers usurping her house by the late 1860s and beyond was simply out of fatigue and a sense of security; Anna acquiesced in what Douglass needed as long as nothing terrible happened to threaten the family any more than its own internal battles already did. She may even have developed sympathy for the lonely German lady who showed up every summer among the throng, as the irises gave way to daylilies in the garden.

Anna knew so much, and she too had the mental stability, as long as her health endured, to live with the arrangement. But on June 2, 1872, the world the Douglasses had made at the end of South Avenue in Rochester was destroyed. After nearly twenty-five years, Anna and Frederick would be packing again, in great sorrow, to go live in a place that would value his words and where she would spend her last decade as the "wife of an important man."

Chapter 24

VENTURES

There is for men and women no happiness without venture.

—FREDERICK DOUGLASS, SEPTEMBER 1, 1874

A round midnight on June 2, 1872, a fire broke out in the barn just
a short distance from the Douglass house on the hill in Rochester.
Within hours the wood-frame structures were all destroyed. Most
of the huge book collection was saved. Someone knew that was a priority.
Douglass's sets of the complete works of Shakespeare, Dickens, and Burns,
as well as many volumes about biblical exegesis, were strewn in safe piles
around the yard by the next morning. Rosetta and Nathan Sprague, the
men from a fire company, as well as other neighbors, helped save the books,
some furniture, and even a piano from the burning house. But much was
also lost. Twenty-one years of labor and of family memories lay in smoldering ashes.[1]

The fire company came up South Avenue as fast as it could behind its
horses but lacked enough water to stop the blaze. As though depicting a
fireworks display, a local paper described a macabre scene: "The flames lit
up the horizon for miles and cast lurid shadows on the surrounding trees,
rendering their foliage intensely beautiful." Anna, Rosetta, and Nathan all
rushed to save the couple's four small children—Annie, Harriet, Allie, and
Stella. One press report gave Nathan credit for a heroic dash back into a
bedroom in flames to save the less than two-year-old Stella. He also saved
the horses from an outlying stable a hundred feet from the house. Everything in the main barn, however, was lost. The *Rochester Democrat and
Chronicle* especially lamented the "beautiful grove" surrounding the Douglass homestead. It "was entirely destroyed, and with its well-kept walks, neat
out houses and picturesque situation was an ornament to our city." Rosetta
was pregnant at the time of the fire and within two months of delivering
her fifth child. Reports immediately indicated arson, or "undoubtedly the

work of an incendiary." Nathan told the press that "no light or fire" had been "used about the barn since last winter." No press coverage reported Anna Douglass's personal sense of loss.[2]

When the fire occurred, Douglass had taken up a second residence in Washington as he and his sons edited the *New National Era*, a paper he had purchased in 1870. He had spent the spring as far away as New Orleans lecturing, as well as up and down the East Coast. A telegram on June 3 informed him of the horrible news, but that his family was unharmed. Within twenty-four hours he arrived in Rochester at 1:00 a.m. in a torrential rainstorm. He did not know where his family would be so he tried to check into a hotel. Two hotels, the Congress Hall and the Waverly House, both denied him a room because they were full. A circus company was in town, although Douglass would not quite accept that explanation of his rejection. From the local police he learned that the Post and the Porter families had taken in Anna and the family. In the morning daylight Douglass walked through the mud out South Avenue to see the devastation. In his personal account, published a week later, he said it was "almost like going home to a funeral." Painfully, he described "twenty years of industry and economy" lost in a few hours. "Scarcely a trace of the building, except brick walls and stone foundations" remained to be seen on that awful morning.[3]

Douglass calculated his losses at "$4,000 to $5,000," especially stressing the additional full run of sixteen volumes of his newspapers, and "eleven thousand dollars worth of government securities."[4] The government bonds remained a serious contention in his family and marriage. Ottilie Assing had an interest in those bonds and, as usual, strong opinions about why they were lost. Her reaction to the news of the fire was one small part shock and a large part self-interest.

A week after the event Assing informed her sister that the house fire had "pulled the rug from under my feet." Her summer plans were ruined. She expressed not a word about the well-being of Douglass family members, but was quick to blame Anna for the potential loss of the government securities. Each bond had a corresponding number, and they had all been placed in a "light tin box" kept in Anna's bedroom. In the panic of the fire, Anna had allegedly forgotten the box. Assing's story was that "eleven thousand dollars . . . were burned, probably because the stupid old woman totally lost her head, as is usually the case with uneducated people, for she would have had sufficient time to save them . . . and she had been instructed a hundred times to save said tin box in case of a misfortune." The utterly self-certain Ottilie did not stop there: "No other explanation is possible. She [Anna] probably thought more of her wig and a dozen silver spoons." But Assing believed she had saved the day, since she herself had recorded all the numbers: "Thanks to my prudence, the numbers were safe." Above all, Assing felt "desperation" about what to do with her summer now. She had always considered the "beautiful residence" in Rochester "to be my home . . . deeply intertwined with my past and present." *Her* home had been destroyed. She worried that without the green gardens at South Avenue in Rochester as her retreat, she would "grow worn down and peeved."[5] One doubts that Assing ever expressed such a desecration of a family's grief to Douglass himself about the fire. If she did, all we can hope is that he denounced her.

Douglass had no doubts as to the origin of the fire and whose home had been torched. He assumed his house had been burned by a racially motivated arsonist. Rochester was one of the most liberal of Northern cities, he admitted. But it had "its full share of that Ku Klux spirit which makes anything owned by a colored man a little less respected and secure than when owned by a white citizen." No one was ever arrested for the arson. One local paper even printed the unfounded rumor that blacks had committed the crime. However, Douglass publicly placed his personal loss at the feet not only of Rochester, but of the entire nation's recent history of deadly racial violence. He knew a great deal about the nature of bone-deep racism. He and his kin had been attacked, he firmly believed, by "the spirit of hate, the spirit of murder, the spirit that would burn a family out of their beds."[6]

For the past five years that "spirit" had murdered and burned thousands of African Americans out of their beds. Douglass's explanation of what had happened to him in Rochester was a logical extension of the frequent reporting he had done about the Ku Klux Klan in the *New National Era*. The Klan had served as a primary weapon of the white Southern Democratic Party's counterrevolution against Reconstruction since the 1868 elections. Their attacks were campaigns to thwart and destroy black and Republican Party political activity. Their intimidation, torture, rape, arson, and murders had primarily been targeted at blacks who were either political leaders or people of economic independence. Douglass now felt that he and his family were among the victims.[7]

This sordid history of domestic terrorism makes Douglass's claim of a "Ku Klux spirit" in western New York plausible. Just as lynchings two decades later knew no North-South border, racial mob violence was a national practice. In 1870–71, Douglass had vigorously applauded the Grant administration's efforts by law and by prosecution to wipe out the Klan. In editorials, Douglass likened mob violence to prewar proslavery ideology and to the same white supremacy that animated the Confederacy. "A rebellion is upon our hands today far more difficult to deal with than that suppressed but not annihilated in 1865," he said in April 1871. "Ku Kluxism . . . now moves over the South like the pestilence that walketh in darkness and wasteth at noon-day." Douglass despised any conciliations to the white South. In November, he declared himself disgusted with "this cry of peace! peace! where there is no peace." Just one week before the fire in Rochester, Douglass published a column, "Shall We Surrender to the Ku Klux?," in which he linked Democrats with the "ex-rebel Klan's" efforts to "kill loyal men and women . . . to burn down school houses for the education of the Negro." The Klan and all the mobs inspired by them had put the whole country, he said, in an "attitude of war." [8] When he saw his house in ruin and his grove of trees scorched, Douglass observed the hill at the end of South Avenue as one small outpost in a vast and violent civil war that had never ended.

Rochester friends tried to convince Douglass to rebuild in the city. For as much as a year he may have considered staying, but in June 1873, he wrote to his close friend Samuel Porter and asked him to "advertise and sell that property for me." He also engaged a lawyer, Horatio Gates Warner, to whom he wrote, "I would prefer to sell outright and shall feel obliged if you will find me a purchaser." [9] Douglass would never cut all ties to Rochester, although he did sell the property. In the wake of the fire, he quickly determined to remove Anna and as much of the extended family as possible to Washington, where he purchased a town house at 316 A Street, only a few blocks east of the Capitol. While he certainly expressed his rage at the burning of his house, of his personal grief he said as usual very little. Of what it felt like to hug Anna, Rosetta, and the grandchildren while standing in front of the smoldering ruins of their homestead, the place that had once housed John Brown and at least a hundred runaway slaves, we learn next to nothing. What we do know is that Douglass eagerly relocated to the center of American power.

Douglass often portrayed himself as lacking faith in his political aptitude. But he learned fast and had honed such instincts during the great political struggles of the 1850s and the war years. Although he had spent much of his career as a radical outsider, now he aimed at offices and appointments that brought him inside circles of influence in the brave new world of Reconstruction Washington. His voice would still be that of a radical; but much more work emerged now for the pragmatist, the party man, and the racial symbol. "Variance between great men finds no healing influence in the atmosphere of Washington," Douglass wrote in *Life and Times.* "Interested parties are ever ready to fan the flame of animosity and magnify the grounds of hostility in order to gain the favor of one or the other." All communities did thus, he argued presciently, but nowhere more than in the capital, where "a large class of people" were "dependent for their daily bread upon the influence and favor of powerful public men." [10] Douglass, with his sons, joined that class full of hope born of the revolution of emancipation.

As early as 1867, President Johnson had tried to co-opt Douglass into replacing General Oliver Howard as director of the Freedmen's Bureau. Through the White House steward, William Slade, a message was conveyed to Charles Douglass that the job could be his father's if he so wished. A letter followed, in effect offering the elder Douglass the job. But Douglass smelled the rat and turned it down. He had seen this trick before—a presidential or cabinet initiative to co-opt him to make an agency less relevant. His reply to Slade, though careful and politic, included a wry swipe at the president he loathed. Douglass said he would "always be glad" to hear anything from the insider Slade on the "direction of events" from within the White House. Douglass was especially delighted to know that since Johnson wanted to "place a colored man at the head of the Bureau," he was well on the way to fulfilling his "purpose of being the Moses of the colored man in the United States." [11] Douglass wanted a federal appointment, but he would never do Andrew Johnson's bidding.

After campaigning vigorously for Grant in 1868, the first election in American history when blacks voted in significant numbers, Douglass entertained hope for some kind of presidential appointment. That took time. His first offer came not from government but from a former slave and Presbyterian minister in Washington, John Sella Martin. In 1869, Martin and a small group of black men, including George T. Downing, wanted to launch a black-owned-and-operated newspaper; they invited Douglass to be its editor in chief. Martin wanted Douglass and others to take on the paper as a matter of racial pride. "Its chief feature," Martin said, "is to manifest our interest in Reconstruction and our grasp of its problems." Martin asked for $5,000 from Douglass to start the paper; the former editor drew on experience and argued that it would need much more financial backing to succeed and further balked because he would be working without a salary. But on January 13, 1870, in the growing black community of Uniontown, a first issue of the weekly *New Era* was published, with Martin as editor, Douglass as corresponding editor, and Lewis Douglass as printer. The paper collapsed financially within six months. By September, it reemerged as the *New National Era*, with Douglass now as part owner and its editor. He shortly became its sole proprietor with an investment of at least $10,000. Douglass had told Martin earlier that he was not prepared to "venture upon this voyage of journalism upon so slender a bark as five thousand dollars."[12] But Douglass loved journalism and saw the opportunity not only to employ all his sons, but to establish an African American voice in the political center of Reconstruction.

During the three years that Douglass and his team—which included Lewis, Frederick Jr., and Ottilie Assing—published the *New National Era*, he made the paper into a personal organ with large ambitions. The issues were both new and old; they included social uplift and the role of religion in African American life, black and women's suffrage, foreign expansion, new postemancipation dilemmas over labor and capital, and especially electoral politics and Douglass's unique quest for control of the public memory of the Civil War. Once again Douglass demonstrated that he was one of the great activist journalists of American history. His family and friends hoped, futilely, that the role of editor would allow Douglass to cease the grueling speaking tours. Assing repeatedly pled with him to stop "those abhorrent winter lecturing tours to the west." Charles wrote with even more urgency in January 1873 about just how far westward Douglass had to venture: "I hope you will get home before the first of March. It seems to me that you might let your Nebraska appointments go. . . . Thirty years on railroads and steamboats, aside from lecturing night after night, would kill most any ordinary man."[13] But Douglass could not stop; he never abandoned the call of the platform or the necessity of lecture fees.

The passage by Congress of the Fifteenth Amendment in 1869 and its ratification by March 1870, guaranteeing the right to vote for black men, drew Douglass yet more to the lecture circuit even as he began editing the newspaper. Douglass was one of the leading voices in the chorus of celebration among former abolitionists. Although he would have preferred a broader amendment that would have prohibited qualification tests for suffrage, and he quickly became embroiled in controversy over the exclusion of women, he nevertheless rejoiced in its passage. In the spring of 1870 Douglass spoke at ratification rallies all over the North. At the meeting of the American Anti-Slavery Society in New York in April, after which it went out of business, Douglass spoke of his amazement at the historic changes of the past decade: "I seem myself to be living in a new world. The sun does not shine as it used to."[14]

One of the largest celebrations of the Fifteenth Amendment took place in Baltimore in mid-May. Twenty thousand blacks marched in a parade with brass bands, and an audience of six thousand listened to a series of speeches. The occasion reminded Douglass of his poignant first return to his old hometown in November 1864, when he had summoned Genesis—Noah's ark and the flood—to capture the meaning of Maryland as a free state. But five years and three great constitutional amendments later made him now look forward. In his remarks Douglass pointed to three great symbols of black progress: the "cartridge box," the "ballot box," and the "jury box." In this compelling moment, the former Fred Bailey stood in the central square of Baltimore, where he could feel if not almost see his slave roots down in Fell's Point, and addressed a cheering throng of his people claiming their birthright as citizens. "We have a future!" Douglass shouted as he concluded, "Everything is possible to us!" Despite the uncertainties over whether the Fifteenth Amendment could truly protect black suffrage against white subterfuge, the celebration was one for the heart more than the head. The gathering did not adjourn until it passed—or shouted—several resolutions, one of which recognized Douglass as the "foremost man of color in the times" and appealed to him to lead blacks "to a higher, broader, and nobler manhood."[15] Douglass had lived so much of his life, and written so many words, to imagine the sense of *future* in the air that day in Baltimore.

Soon, Douglass had little choice but to take a more sober approach to the meaning of the Fifteenth Amendment. A growing indifference toward the freedpeople among Northern whites, the reign of terror by the Klan in the South, the resurgence of the Democratic Party, and the readmission to the Union of the former Confederate states all put black rights under a cloud of uncertainty. Back at his editor's desk, Douglass entered the 1870s urging blacks to distinguish between what was "seeming" and what was "real" in their prospects; he cautioned people not to be absorbed by a "delirium of enthusiasm." The struggle to secure black equality had only begun. Citing the Declaration of Independence and the Bill of Rights, he urged his readers to remember America's historical contradictions between law and practice. "The settled habits of a nation," Douglass asserted, are "mightier than a statute." The editor's pen brought the soaring rhetoric of Baltimore back to earth. The nation must be vigilant fighting the "hardships and wrongs which continue to be the lot of the colored people," Douglass wrote by fall 1870, "because they wear a complexion which two hundred and fifty years of slavery taught the great mass of American people to hate, and which the Fifteenth Amendment has not yet taught the American people to love." [16]

In 1868–70, Douglass's lecturing, despite his receiving more invitations than ever, had gone a bit stale. His speaking itineraries in those two years were almost superhuman. From September 22, 1868, when he spoke at the tomb of Abraham Lincoln in Springfield, Illinois, on the sixth anniversary of the Preliminary Emancipation Proclamation, to late March 1869, he delivered at least forty-five lectures in ten states all across the North and back again. The schedule from fall 1869 to spring 1870, which included Fifteenth Amendment addresses, was even more arduous, totaling at least seventy-two lectures. He spoke on every day of December except one, including Christmas, in towns from Vermont and New Hampshire through Massachusetts to Rhode Island. From January through March 1870 Douglass barnstormed from Connecticut through Massachusetts and New York, to Washington, DC, and then west through Pennsylvania, Ohio, Indiana, Illinois, Iowa, Michigan, and back again to western New York. [17]

In the election year of 1872, his speaking schedule was nothing short of breathtaking, as he steamed across the American map. In a train station in Iowa in the cold of January, a *Milwaukee Sentinel* reporter cornered an exhausted Douglass for an impromptu interview. Having just witnessed the orator's speech, the journalist suggested that the audience had expected to see him "more active and fiery." Douglass's answers were playful but revealing: "I am getting about over my fiery days. I used to saw the air and split the ears of the groundlings; but I care more for reasoning out my point now." The correspondent wondered why Douglass appeared "less voluble." "I am older," admitted the white-maned sojourner. He no longer plied his trade in "torrents of words," Douglass declared. "Besides, if I warm up and speak rapidly, I am in danger of throwing my teeth out. They're false, you know." Douglass assured the nosy reporter, in a sentiment known to every celebrity in modern times, that among the most trying aspects of being on the road endlessly were the "friends" who persisted in desiring to "look at me . . . and question me all the time . . . leaving me half-exhausted." In November, Douglass wrote to Rosetta as a weary grandfather, worn-out from travel. He worried that his next lecture topic would not succeed and desperately sought relief in "the coming winter from labors, perils and fatigues of a lecturing campaign." [18]

Not only did the physical burden of travel wear him out, but he tried out a new speech that flopped. In late August 1868, Douglass told Gerrit Smith that he had spent that summer "endeavouring to make myself a little more familiar with history." Among the histories he was reading was the multivolume and widely popular *Rise of the Dutch Republic* (1856) by John Lothrop Motley, a Massachusetts-born and Harvard-educated historian. Just why Douglass took up Motley and the story of the sixteenth-century Dutch revolt against the Spanish empire is not altogether clear. Motley's triumphalist, muscular narrative may have been one draw. His repeated stress on how the Dutch republic ought to be the great model for all of the "Anglo-Saxon race" in finding the roots of its "master passion—the love of liberty," apparently did not bother this former slave reader. He assumed that he needed a new, carefully written address each year. Although fully aware that his personal story was why people still flocked and paid to see his performances, Douglass became weary of reciting the same tale over and over. In 1871, he admitted serious anxiety that he might never "get beyond Fredk. Douglass the self educated fugitive slave." On a lonely winter day in March 1873, he wrote to Amy Post from a "queer named place," Damariscotta, Maine, about a recent lecture in Philadelphia that was not a success. The story of my escape, he said, "was clumsily told because I had no heart in telling it. There is really nothing exciting in it." [19] Douglass wanted respect as a serious Emerson-like lyceum speaker. Sometimes he achieved such regard, sometimes not.

Douglass had good fortune on the circuit with speeches such as his "Self-Made Men" and "Composite Nation," an address about the idea of a multiracial society in America that he first delivered in 1867. But his effort in "William the Silent" was not his best work. Relying on Motley, Douglass tried to fashion an analogy between the Dutch rebellions against the Spanish with the American Revolution against the British, and even the winning of the Civil War against the Confederacy. In surviving texts of the speech, Douglass made a case for war as the "school" that "develops great characters, great deeds, great qualities." Liberty, he said, is "valued . . . for what it costs" and gained respect only when "marked in blood." In January 1869, he delivered the speech in Gettysburg, America's bloodiest battleground. To a full house in an agricultural hall, he spoke for an hour and three-quarters and garnered two opposite reactions. The local Republican paper thought the effort "*the* lecture of the season," and one of "impassioned eloquence." But the Democratic paper lampooned Douglass as the "pet . . . negro" of the Radicals, called him "Fred," and chastised him for his anti-Catholic comments. To the racist Democrats, the "ebony idol" victimized white people with his "impertinent and rancorous tirade." In many venues, race and politics mattered far more than any historical subject.[20]

At some performances the address seemed so anti-Catholic in its celebration of the achievement of Protestant religious liberty that some Catholic priests let Douglass know their objections. One Ohio priest pilloried the orator for his "very ugly insinuation against Catholics," calling the "repetitions of 'Pope,' and 'Bishops,' and 'Inquisition'" a "senseless tirade of a mob-lecturer." The address further included odd asides about Douglass's "peculiar acquaintance with women" and their "latent powers" as fighters. A strange defense of Mary Todd Lincoln against her critics also seemed out of place. The orator also entertained his audience with a self-reflective use of "nigger." The irony and humor may have worked in Cincinnati, but it had nothing to do with the subject at hand.[21]

This venture into history fell especially flat when Douglass asserted one final analogy he knew to be false: "A hundred battles might be lost, the nation never could lose confidence in Lincoln." Ottilie Assing was among those who found this use of Lincoln especially annoying. "I absolutely cannot stand things like that," she told Koehler, "and even if history is making a mistake with regard to Lincoln by passing on an inappropriately rosy picture of him to posterity . . . all of us should be all the more intent on not making said picture look even rosier." That season Douglass had assumed a low common denominator in his auditors' sense of history. Some apparently felt his condescension and objected. On one occasion, Douglass actually apologized for his lack of enthusiasm, saying that since "the death of slavery," he had no one or thing to "pitch into."[22] Sometimes Othello did lose his voice and his verve floundered.

Happily, the editor's pen beckoned. Douglass got his voice back in the *New National Era.* He loved the rush and excitement of getting the paper out every Thursday; he even liked setting type, although he left that now to Lewis's more dexterous fingers. Douglass especially thrived on having his own say on Reconstruction policy and national events. He wanted to be the mouthpiece for black people, but he very much spoke, as he had in the 1850s, for himself. And in the newly complex world of Reconstruction and beyond, a new generation of black editors and writers stood ready to challenge his leadership at every turn.

Douglass needed all the help he could assemble. In the first months of the paper, Assing reported, "Douglass is demanding a new article [from her] for the 'Era' almost every week." In August 1872, two months after the Rochester fire, she told her sister, Ludmilla, that Douglass had called her to Washington to assist in editing the paper. She moved into a room in the town house with the Douglasses and seemed thrilled "to have a hand in all these things as a journalist myself." Puffed up over her new post, Ottilie gushed about her professional partner: "Douglass is one of the most influential and magnificent leaders on the part of the Republicans." And the "Era has become a powerhouse all of a sudden."[23] Douglass did not quite feel those same sentiments himself; the paper always teetered on the verge of bankruptcy, and his influence was largely symbolic.

In the three years that he and his sons edited the *New National Era*, the Reconstruction policies of the Radical Republicans rose and then began to fall. As the survival of Reconstruction hung in the balance in successive elections, Douglass made the memory of emancipation his major preoccupation, pushing his readers to never forget what the war had been about. In the fall of 1870 he warned that Americans were by habit "destitute of political memory." As a partisan Republican and black advocate, Douglass resisted the efforts of Democrats and all other white supremacists to "bury dead issues." "The people cannot and will not forget the issues of the rebellion," he declared. Democrats "must continue to face the music of the past as well as of the present."[24] Douglass believed the political struggle over Reconstruction depended on winning the fight over the memory of the war.

The energized editor realized the power of the "Lost Cause" as both a historical argument and a racial ideology. The Lost Cause was in these early years essentially an explanation of defeat and a set of beliefs in search of a history—ex-Confederates' contentions that they had never been defeated on battlefields but by the Northern leviathan of industrial might; that they had never fought for slavery but for state sovereignty and homeland; that the South's racially ordered civilization had been tragically crushed by Yankee invasion; and that "just" causes can lose militarily but with time regain the moral and political high ground. Douglass vehemently resisted the rapid emergence in national political circles of these ideas. He was appalled at the national veneration of Robert E. Lee when he died in 1870. Disgusted at what he called the "bombastic laudation" and the "nauseating flatteries" of the "rebel chief," Douglass attacked the Lost Cause as a betrayal of the verdicts of the war. "It would seem," he wrote in a biting editorial, "that the soldier who kills the most men in battle, even in a bad cause, is the greatest Christian, and entitled to the highest place in heaven." By early 1871, after so much romance about Lee's death and the sentiment that he had "died of a broken heart," Douglass expressed a precise verdict: "He was a traitor and can be made nothing else."[25]

By intellectual predilection and by experience, Douglass embodied the idea that history mattered. The Douglass who endures as an unending subject of literary and historical inquiry—because of the autobiographies—is and was the creature of memory. The very nature of memory provided a subject of obsessive interest. His place as citizen Douglass, his own humanity, were products of his ability to create and record experience, to narrate his own story. Moreover, he knew that peoples and nations, like individuals, are shaped and defined by their pasts. Douglass was acutely aware that history was both burden and inspiration, something to be cherished and overcome. He also understood that although all people crave stories, some narratives are more honest than others. He knew that all groups desire a usable past, none more than blacks in America. "It is not well to forget the past," Douglass warned in a speech later in the 1880s. "Memory was given to man for some wise purpose. The past is . . . the mirror in which we may discern the dim outlines of the future and by which we may make them more symmetrical." Douglass thus knew that history and memory are never truly symmetrical, but that he could still try to make them so.[26]

The old abolitionist wrote and spoke so often about the fight over the memory of the war that some critics accused him of living in the past. American politics would "leave Mr. Douglass behind . . . ," declared one newspaper editor in 1872, "vociferating the old platitudes as though the world had stopped eight years ago." But to such critics, Douglass had ready answers: he would not forgive the South and he would never forget the meaning of the war as he saw it. At the first version of a tomb of the unknown soldier in Arlington Cemetery, on an early official observance of Memorial Day (1871), Douglass declared where he stood in a speech that became a template for countless such memory addresses over the next two decades. In the presence of President Grant, Douglass performed a moving and thoroughly nationalistic eulogy over the graves of some eleven hundred Union dead from the Bull Run battlefields of 1861 and 1862. The unknown dead were themselves "a silent, subtle, and an all-pervading eloquence." They had resisted slavery and disunion, and Douglass infused their meaning with a transcendent refrain: "They died for their country!" Borrowing then from Psalm 137, he stated his unequivocal case on the heights of Arlington: "We are sometimes asked in the name of patriotism to forget the merits of this fearful struggle, and to remember with equal admiration those who struck at the nation's life, and those who struck to save it—those who fought for slavery and those who fought for liberty and justice." Douglass spoke across time and place to our enduring national condition. "I am no minister of malice," he said, "I would not repel the repentant, but . . . may my tongue cleave to the roof of my mouth if I forget the difference between the parties to that . . . bloody conflict. . . . I may say if this war is to be forgotten, I ask in the name of all things sacred what shall men remember?" Unlike the Fourth of July speech in 1852, Douglass could now sing a song of Zion because he spoke not of a lost home in ruin, but for a new Jerusalem. His people, he reasoned, had passed out of Babylon.[27]

Douglass's harsh reactions to the emerging Confederate memory were a revealing measure of his enduring attitudes toward the South as well as toward the resurgent Democratic Party. He licked his chops as a propagandist on one of his favorite subjects. The defeated white South felt only "bitter hatred to the government of the North," Douglass said in 1870. They had lost "the labor of their slaves and the right to control their actions." Douglass not only showed no interest yet in any kind of sectional reconciliation, which Democratic Party papers already demanded, he denounced Southerners as depraved and unworthy of national inclusion. Douglass enthusiastically waved the bloody shirt for his party. To him, Democrats were "the party of treason," and in the midst of Klan violence in 1871, he said he was "entitled to call the Democratic party a party of murder, robbery, treason, dishonesty, and fraud." When he was accused of fanaticism against Southern Democrats, he said in effect thank you very much and argued that they did not deserve even "toleration." "The South has a past not to be contemplated with pleasure," wrote Douglass, "but with a shudder. She has been selling agony, trading in blood and the souls of men." He even wrote articles ridiculing the villages of Southern "poor white trash," where people "cling" to "ignorance . . . many centuries behind every other civilized country." Whenever reconciliationist political gestures appeared, Douglass derided them as the "hand-clasping across the bloody chasm business."[28]

The New National Era provided Douglass a partisan sheet in which to venture into the sectional and political fray. Just as he saw Reconstruction policy as a direct extension of the war's basic issues, Douglass viewed party conflict in the same way. To him, the Republican Party had been the author of emancipation, the embodiment of Union victory, and the custodian of black citizenship. Douglass considered the Republicans the only conceivable political home for black voters. He looked upon elections as referenda on his party's diligence in sustaining black rights. In 1871, Douglass simplified American politics to a contest between good and evil: "There are but two parties in the country. One is the party loyal to liberty, justice, and good order, and the other is the party in sympathy with the defeated rebellion. . . . Between these two parties we have no option."[29] Thus, Douglass embraced the tension of maintaining the radical-humanitarian vision of the Republican Party at the very time it was beginning to wane.

Douglass's loyalty to the Republican Party during Reconstruction was undoubtedly at times motivated by personal ambition and sustained by faulty analysis. He was a paid stump speaker for Grant in 1872, and he sought office and influence. In this age of "spoilsmen" Douglass expected some return on his efforts. The *New York Tribune* attacked him for allegedly receiving large sums of money for his pro-Grant speeches. Douglass responded that he had received only $500 from the Republican Party and $3,700 from literary societies during the lecture season of that past winter. His political work too was a venture; he labored hard for Grant. In August, Douglass informed one of his sons that he had just delivered seven speeches for the campaign in one week in Maine.[30]

Douglass's rhetoric on behalf of Grant's reelection and throughout the 1870s reflected a deeply held set of beliefs about recent history. He was fond of reviving the passions of the war, putting them to the ends of justice. In 1870, he provided in his paper a list of "great truths" that the nation should never forget: that the "Copperhead Democracy" had started the war "for the purpose of extending and rendering perpetual the foul curse of slavery"; that in the war "these rebel Democrats slaughtered a quarter of a million brave loyal men"; that "they wounded and disabled a quarter of a million more"; that "they made full a million of widows or orphans"; and that "these same rebel Democrats" now demanded that they be restored to power. By invoking these stark images, Douglass demonstrated that for him the bloody shirt appealed for more than votes; it meant that he was ready to play the role of grand master of Northern and national memory, offering an explicit refutation of the Confederate Lost Cause tradition. Democrats, Douglass warned with characteristic harshness, "are the apostles of forgetfulness . . . and no wonder, for their pathway has been strewn with the whitened bones of their countrymen."[31]

In the 1870s Douglass promoted and defended the Republican Party with persistent zeal. In his newspaper, he pledged fidelity to the Republicans. When necessary, he idealized the party's recent history. With his sons Lewis and Charles, Douglass traveled the four hundred miles back to Rochester from Washington to vote in November 1870. Speaking to a turn-away

Frederick Douglass, April 26, 1870. George Francis Schreiber photographer, carte de visite.

crowd in City Hall, he entertained his hometown fans. Race was useful, as ever, for humor at such political events: "I am called here to give color to the occasion, and to prevent the whole thing from having the appearance of being 'faded out.'" He reminded his black listeners and readers that Republicans were their party of hope. They might sometimes be "slighted" by Republicans, he cautioned, but they were "murdered" by Democrats. To the disappointed, he insisted that the aims of blacks could be "more easily accomplished inside than anywhere outside the Republican party."[32] The old "antislavery tendency" of Republicans had been enough to gain his hope and allegiance back in the 1850s. Now in the 1870s, as Radical Republicanism showed signs of decline, a pragmatic Douglass clung to his only political home as the party of memory.

In the turbulent election of 1872, Douglass steadfastly supported Grant and vehemently denounced Horace Greeley and the Liberal Republican movement. What he most objected to in the Liberals' revolt was their hostility to Grant's Southern policy, especially their desire for prompt sectional reconciliation. The Liberal Republicans were a motley coalition driven by a complexity of motives, but especially after their candidate—Greeley—joined hands with the Democratic Party in the summer of 1872, Douglass viewed them as the worst of enemies. Their "chief topic," Douglass argued in September, "is the clasping of hands across the bloody chasm, the great love feast of reconciliation cooked by Mr. Greeley, on which occasion our southern brethren are indirectly promised the first seats at the common table." The welfare of the freedpeople, black equality, and the very meaning of the war were at risk in Douglass's conception of the Liberal Republicans and their devil's bargain with Democrats. "The fruits of ten years of labor, suffering and loss are at stake," Douglass declared in a campaign editorial. Loyal Republicans, he believed, should not be thrown off guard by "the deceitful cry that all the questions raised by the war . . . are now settled." He warned his readers about the fragility of past victories: "The slave demon still rides the southern gale and breathes out fire and wrath. . . . The smoldering embers of the Lost Cause show themselves in shouts for . . . Horace Greeley." [33]

Douglass brooked no caution in attacking Greeley and the Liberal Republicans. He likened them to the secessionists of 1861, calling them "sorehead bolters," who schemed politically for personal ends. When Greeley's *New York Tribune* called Douglass out for what they termed the "brutish ingratitude" and "malignant blackguardism" of his rhetoric, he shot back. Greeley's odd political coalition would leave the Republicans "stabbed and slain . . . from behind." The *New York Times* seemed to enjoy seeing these old allies slashing each other to pieces in the 1872 campaign. Douglass, the *Times* said, wrote with "sharp, vigorous sentences . . . the kind which at once take hold upon the memory and appeal to the understanding." [34] Douglass enjoyed becoming a star partisan journalist in 1872.

The resurgent editor even expressed scorn for the Liberals' condemnation of corruption in the Grant administration and lampooned their appeals for civil service reform. He found these issues increasingly difficult to explain away, however, especially in the wake of the election when the Crédit Mobilier scandal (as part of the building of the transcontinental railroad) rocked the administration. By 1874 Douglass wrote to Gerrit Smith describing the "moral atmosphere" in Washington as "rotten," full of "avarice, duplicity . . . corruption . . . fawning and trickery of all kinds." By then he divided Washington politicians into two groups, "the class used" and the "class that uses them," and cynically declared himself one of the "used." Douglass understood the system from personal experience. In 1873, he received a begging letter from a desperate woman with a small child, asking his help in getting her a job in the Treasury Department. "Oh! Mr. Douglass if you could!" wrote a Julia Foster Sagendorf. "If you only could . . . I will teach my child to worship you." But in the heat of the 1872 campaign, Douglass defended Grant in language he surely regretted: there had "never been an administration since the government existed . . . which could better endure the most searching scrutiny" on corruption.[35]

To Douglass, Grant represented the only hope of continuity with Union victory, emancipation, and the work of Reconstruction. "The Republican party cannot be broken up at this juncture," Douglass wrote to Cassius M. Clay, "without . . . putting in peril not only the freedmen of the South, but the honor and safety of the country." So certain was Douglass that Republican disunity would lead to the doom of black freedom and equality that he declared it "better to put a pistol to my head and blow my brains out, than to lend myself in any wise to the destruction or defeat of the Republican party." Douglass never knew Grant well and could hardly claim a place for Grant in the abolitionist tradition, but Douglass could still attempt to do so for the president's party. It caused him no little pain to see the heroically antislavery Charles Sumner come out in support of the Liberals due to personal hatred of Grant. Douglass greatly admired Sumner but took umbrage at the senator's personal attacks on the president. "Personally, he is nothing to me," Douglass wrote to Sumner, "but as the President, the Republican President of the country, I am anxious . . . to hold him in all honor."[36] In 1872, Douglass and Sumner cast their votes against each other.

Douglass embraced Grant in 1872 and beyond for a reason similar to his more restrained endorsement of Lincoln in 1860—Grant was the candidate the South and the resurgent Democrats feared most. He had moved effectively to defeat the Klan. Douglass had long ago learned that, politically, what white Southerners feared and opposed, blacks ought to embrace. Hence he concluded his official endorsement of Grant in 1872 by stating, "Long ago we adopted the maxim 'never to occupy ground which our enemies desired us to occupy' if we could help it."[37] Such a maxim tells us much about why Douglass's loyalty to Republicans endured to the end of his days.

That loyalty was at times sorely tested. Douglass and Grant did work together on one important and complicated venture—American annexation of Santo Domingo. Ulysses Grant was an ardent expansionist. The prospect of drawing Santo Domingo (what became the Dominican Republic) into the United States was a major political crisis of his first term as president. The idea of Santo Domingo's annexation predated Grant's presidency. His motives and ethics, and especially those of some key aides, were mixed. Business and real estate interests as well as the acquisition of a major Caribbean naval base for the US navy fueled pro-annexation sentiment.

But Grant also saw Santo Domingo as a kind of safety-valve solution for the biggest problem of Reconstruction—Ku Klux violence and the fate of millions of freedpeople in the South. He imagined Santo Domingo as a site of new relocation schemes for blacks. Grant did not advocate any large-scale colonization, but he and many others envisioned Santo Domingo, like adjoining Haiti, as a black country, a place where African Americans could choose to make a new home.[38]

Grant's great nemesis on Santo Domingo was Sumner, who was chairman of the Senate Foreign Relations Committee. Unlike many fellow Republicans, including Douglass, who so greatly admired the Massachusetts abolitionist, Sumner rejected all humanitarian explanations for annexation anywhere in the Caribbean. He saw the effort as the ultimate destruction of a black nation, a fate that would also extend to Haiti. Sumner opposed annexation as blatant American imperialism and an abandonment of the domestic struggle to enforce Reconstruction racial policies in the South. In November 1869, Grant's representative, his old military aide from the war years Orville Babcock, went to the island nation and negotiated a treaty with the president of Santo Domingo, Buenaventura Báez, an insecure ruler who was threatened by internal rivals and external pirates. A majority of the US Senate favored the annexation agreement. But, especially under Sumner's powerful opposition, the measure never achieved the necessary two-thirds majority. The treaty was formally defeated in June 1870 and left a permanent, embittered rift between Grant and Sumner.[39]

The treaty's failure also left Douglass in a quandary, since from the beginning, the new Washington resident favored American expansion to such regions occupied and led by people of color. He had also supported the "free Cuba" movement in 1869, when rebels launched resistance to Spanish rule that would grow into the Ten Years' War. Douglass joined other abolitionists in believing that the new, antislavery, post–Thirteenth and Fourteenth Amendments United States ought now to export its victories over racial oppression. He was caught between the old abolitionist he honored most (Sumner) and the president to whom he had pledged loyalty.

A great deal of political prestige within the Republican Party was at stake in the Santo Domingo debate. Douglass played now for access, credibility, and status in high places. In every venture Douglass risked in the labyrinthine politics of Reconstruction, he had a package of values and assets to offer. Sometimes they led to success; often they did not. All of these values depended in the end on a swirling universe of patronage and clientage.

He did generally remain an old abolitionist man of principles, especially in the demands he made on the Republican Party. But Douglass's assets were essentially his story, his skill at the lectern, and, with his biting pen, his racial symbol, his emblematic place in a reborn America, and above all his dignity. Just how he could now balance firm beliefs and philosophies with old and new friendships, how he could achieve a place at the national table of power brokers and sustain his vaunted dignity, would be the central challenge of his public life.[40] No black man in America had ever quite done this and lived to tell it.

Grant revived the Santo Domingo initiative in December 1870 with explicit plans for the purchase of the Samaná region, the peninsula that juts out from the northeast coast of Hispaniola. Douglass took a special interest in the group of African Americans from Philadelphia who had emigrated in 1824 to Samaná. The immigrants had established an agricultural and religious community, and when Santo Domingo won its independence from Haiti in 1844, they had opposed an attempt at annexation into the proslavery United States. But by the late 1860s, with the new United States, born of emancipation and the promise of black equality, they were favorable to rejoining their former homeland. Sumner brutally counterattacked and delivered a speech in the Senate that accused Grant essentially of bullying his way into the Caribbean to forge an "imperial system" through a "dance of blood." Sumner likened the scheme to a betrayal of black liberty and rights. The attack on Grant seemed so vicious that Douglass wrote to Sumner, declaring himself "embarrassed" to openly disagree with his "honored" friend. Douglass had been in the gallery of the Senate on December 21 when Sumner spoke, an experience Douglass considered both thrilling and shocking. "Candidly," he judged his friend "bitterly severe" and wrong about the whole scheme of Santo Domingo expansion.[41]

Refusing to give up, Grant appointed a Commission of Inquiry to travel to Santo Domingo. The three commissioners were all prominent Republicans with solid antislavery credentials: former Ohio senator Benjamin Wade, social reformer Samuel Gridley Howe, and Cornell University president Andrew D. White. As a slap at Sumner and to reflect perhaps Grant's own interests in the island, he appointed Douglass and former Union army general Franz Sigel to serve as assistant secretaries for the commission, under the lead secretary, Allan A. Burton. Since Douglass was appointed in a subordinate role, some grumbling occurred publicly among blacks that the assignment was merely symbolic. In part, Grant was trying to neutralize

Sumner's power by appointing the senator's close friends Howe and especially Douglass, a longtime archenemy of colonization schemes. The commission's charge was to examine Santo Domingo's political and economic conditions; to investigate land acquisitions; and to accumulate testimony on whether the people of the island desired annexation. Douglass's role was especially to visit and report on the people of Samaná.[42]

For the large delegation with support staff and a dozen newspaper reporters, the eight-week mission to Santo Domingo aboard the navy warship USS *Tennessee* was a profound experience. Since the 1840s, Douglass had always possessed a growing international consciousness, although with much greater interest in Europe and the Caribbean than in Africa. He had expressed such a broadening outlook in August 1865 to a French editor, Melvil-Bloncourt, who had congratulated Douglass on the achievement of black freedom. "The cause of freedom and justice is as big as the world," Douglass wrote. "It is limited neither by countries nor by climate, nor by color. Whoever cooperates with a good deed . . . is no longer a stranger, but a compatriot, a man of the same family, an ally, a dear brother." [43] The old abolitionist accustomed to activism from outside the circles of power now became an insider assisting a scheme to take over another country justified by refurbished nationalism and claims of a new racial vision of equality.

The commission left New York on January 17, 1871. Douglass kept a sporadic diary that began on the day before departure as the delegation assembled at the fashionable Astor House hotel on Broadway between Vesey and Barclay Streets. Charles Douglass accompanied his father on the voyage in the official role of "messenger." In the elder Douglass's absence, Frederick Jr. reported himself in charge of the "business management" of the *New National Era,* and his brother Lewis served as editor. Ottilie Assing may have contributed articles as well during the two-month absence, and she vicariously imagined herself once again into the center of Douglass's public life. "I would have loved to join him, but *only* men were going, and so it was impossible," she wrote to her sister.[44] Such comments in private letters that only Ludmilla ever saw point to the sad naïveté at the heart of Ottilie's life with her beloved Douglass. At least she had her sister with whom to share her fantasy.

Charles became sick along with many others on the second day at sea, but after a week they reached the Bay of Samaná, where the commission was "received kindly by the people." Douglass was stunned at the beauty of this tropical-island universe, the deep ocean bay and the mountains by the interior. From January 24 to 29, he served as chief interrogator of the English-speaking residents. He also delivered a formal speech in front of a large gathering on January 28, depicted in a drawing in *Frank Leslie's Illustrated* in March. Douglass is shown on a high platform with his whitened hair; the blacks represented tend to be barefoot. The official report of the commission showed that Douglass questioned residents about the colony's population (nearly eight hundred), and basic economic and social conditions. At every stop the commission asked explicitly what residents thought of annexation. In Samaná, Douglass elicited that they were "tired of war" and political chaos. They were not afraid of any takeover from Haiti, but greatly feared a recurring strongman who puts himself "at the head of a revolution ... brings on war ... and plunders the people of their property." The resounding answer among the Samaná settlers seemed to be, yes, they needed the United States as "a strong government to lean against for protection." [45]

Predisposed toward annexation, the commission may have tended to hear what it wanted to hear; but it did encounter a great deal of pro-annexation sentiment. In his diary, Douglass recorded some passages that ended up in the official report. "Can't be worse off than they are," he wrote. On the last day in Samaná, Douglass spent considerable time walking along the beach with an old man, Mr. Dichmain, who had been a settler there for sixty years. He listened to the man's tales of Toussaint and Christophe, the Haitian Revolution, and the atrocities committed "under the first Nap" (Napoléon Bonaparte). In parting, Douglass took up a collection of $64 among the commissioners and journalists for the Samaná settlers to support repairs on their church. The *Tennessee* then steamed for two days around the east end of the island and arrived at the capital city, Santo Domingo, on January 31. For three weeks the commission made the capital its headquarters. Some excursions occurred to interview people in the interior, where the diarist reported "people ... everywhere raising the American flag." Given his limited role, Douglass had a great deal of time for sightseeing and study. He worked on learning Spanish and demonstrated a particular fascination with any place or relic associated with Christopher Columbus, including an old house said to be that of the mariner as well as the castle-prison where he was confined and died. Douglass liked the hot weather and wrote about numerous excursions to the beach, "bathing in the surf." One such outing turned dangerous when the fifty-three-year-old Douglass stepped out too far "among

Frederick Douglass on the deck of the USS Tennessee, *Key West,
Florida, January 17, 1871. Oliver B. Buell photographer.*

the rocks . . . was handled very roughly by a heavy wave," and found himself "much bruised and . . . near being swept off to the sharks."[46]

There were many "dull" days for the assistant secretary when all he
could record was that Charley was "winning golden opinions for his pen-
manship." But on a Sunday he reported seeing his first "cock fight," which
left a revolting and lasting impression. By the end of February, the commission was back aboard ship and steamed to Port-au-Prince, the capital
of Haiti. Douglass logged that the historic city looked beautiful and "cheerful" from the bay, but once they landed, up close it looked "sadder, houses
inferior, streets dirty, people depressed in spirit." Douglass recorded meeting the US minister to Haiti, the African American Ebenezer D. Bassett, but
then had nothing more to say about a full week in Haiti. Nor, frustratingly,
did he report anything in the diary about some five days the commission
spent in port at Kingston, Jamaica. The diary ends as Douglass observed
"the first breath of reviving N air" along the coast of slaveholding Cuba.[47]
The *Tennessee* went into port briefly in both Key West, Florida, and Charles-

ton, South Carolina, on its journey to Washington. At Charleston, the delegation boarded a train for the trip northward; Douglass left no written impression of his first view of the city of secession.

As the commission's highly publicized mission ended, Douglass experienced two acts of Jim Crow snubbing. When the delegation reached Aquia Creek, Virginia, they took a Potomac River steamer to Washington; as they gathered for an afternoon dinner on board, the ship captain refused to allow Douglass to be served with his colleagues. Howe, Wade, and White all protested and refused the captain's table. Soon after arrival in the capital, President Grant invited the commissioners to the White House for dinner; again, Douglass was not among the guests invited. The loyal Douglass remained largely silent in the ensuing months about these incidents. But as the political season heated up in 1872, Sumner repeatedly made an issue of the alleged ill treatment of Douglass by Grant. The commissioners themselves, particularly White, came to Grant's defense, stressing that in all the time aboard the *Tennessee* and in Santo Domingo, Douglass had frequently dined at the captain's table. Racial rejections of this kind cut Douglass to the bone, but he kept his sense of humor. A year later, as the issue remained controversial, he wrote to Gerrit Smith about the oddity of his new fame merely because he "was not invited to dine." He did admit that he wished Grant had personally issued a "reproof" for the "insult" on the Potomac by the steamer captain. Douglass was "so used to being snubbed, and receiving insults because of my color," though, that he gave Grant a pass, since he had not been "educated in the Gerrit Smith school."[48]

Jim Crow dining habits notwithstanding, Douglass went to his desk and out on the speaking circuit as a steadfast proponent of annexation. It is never easy to be a good imperialist, but the old abolitionist did his best. Douglass wrote to Secretary of State Hamilton Fish on April 3, 1871, declaring his work for the commission finished and, somewhat oddly, "regretting that my services . . . were inconsiderable and unimportant." But within a month, Douglass was on the rails lecturing on behalf of Santo Domingo statehood. Annexation failed again to get two-thirds support in the Senate, but not because Douglass did not do his part to sway public opinion. He advanced a refurbished Manifest Destiny for a new era, and he saw no reason to limit expansion to one part of Hispaniola. "The natural thing for Hayti, Cuba, and for all the islands of the Caribbean Sea," he wrote in May 1871, "is to come as soon as possible under the broad banner of the US, and conform themselves to the grand order of progress upon which this great Republic has now . . . earnestly entered."[49]

Douglass treated audiences to romantic descriptions of "intoxicating" sea air in the islands, and the "verdure of perpetual summer." Frequently, he invoked his memory of standing "where Columbus first stood" and breathing "the American air that Columbus first breathed." Santo Domingo was at heart a "civilization . . . so feeble," so materially "desolated," that it needed an American "restoring hand." It is too easy to merely dismiss Douglass's support of such an imperialist venture as mere opportunism; he did openly desire a presidential appointment. William Lloyd Garrison joined the chorus accusing Douglass of personal aggrandizement. "Of course, Frederick Douglass favors the measure, and already has his reward," Garrison wrote to Sumner. "It is not the first time his ambition and his selfishness have led him astray." But the contexts for his advocacy of annexation are much broader than individual ambition.[50]

At times Douglass could sound like a standard-issue imperialist for American superiority. Only "for the sake of . . . isolated" Santo Domingo should the United States bring the struggling country into the Union, said the editor. "We would make her the black sister of Massachusetts, and transplant within her tropical borders the glorious institutions which have lifted that grand old commonwealth to her present commanding elevation." Before 1865, Douglass could never have uttered such tranquil pieties about America. He insisted on a tattered faith in America's democratic promise even as he had earlier delivered some of the most ferocious denunciations of slaveholding hypocrisy. But the war and emancipation had crushed the first nation, and emancipation followed by the three constitutional amendments had given birth to the second. "Things have changed," Douglass announced in 1871 with Yankee superiority. "The Republic when smitten with contagious disease and death could not be confined within limits too narrow" he declared; "but now that she is healthy and life giving, she cannot extend too far. The whole continent is not too large for the full illustration of the ideas . . . with which it is her mission to bless the world." Douglass believed he had sailed to Santo Domingo aboard a ship flying "the flag . . . I could now call mine." Annexation was a clear ideological marker to him "between the old time and the new."[51]

Douglass saw Reconstruction's egalitarian promises—the end of slavery, equality before law, birthright citizenship, and the right to vote—as catalysts and justifications of American expansion. A new America—the new Jerusalem—presented itself to the world. It was now to be the living exper-

iment in racial equality and it ought to export the verdicts of Appomattox, the blood-won liberty of Fort Wagner, section one of the Fourteenth
Amendment, and abolitionism itself in a still slaveholding and oppressive world. He may have expressed these sentiments most hopefully in the
speech "Composite Nation," which was the template of his numerous editorials and many dozens of addresses about Santo Domingo from 1870 into
1873. A reborn America now embodied a romantic missionary nationalism
and offered a melting pot open to all. As a political liberal, Douglass made
his case for the second United States as the model for "human rights" above
all conceptions of racial or ethnic identities. The mission of his new nation,
he declared, was to provide the world a "composite . . . perfect illustration
of the unity and dignity of the human family." Since he saw the Fifteenth
Amendment as merely a beginning for a new political age, he hoped annexation of Santo Domingo would bring thousands of new black voters into
the United States.[52]

From April to June 1871 in the *New National Era*, Douglass wrote a series of seven pro-annexation essays. He expressed detailed interest in the
economic development of Santo Domingo, naming "timber, dye woods,
sugar, coffee, cotton, and indigo" as products worthy of American commerce. Douglass was, after all, becoming a real estate investor in Washington, and though he never said so explicitly, he may have entertained some
inclination to land speculation. He praised the fertility of the island: "The
land was rich but the people poor." They lacked the "comforts and conveniences of civilized life," and the United States could deliver them. As to
the anti-imperialist logic of the opposition, he asked why a country that
had annexed "Louisiana, Texas, California, and Alaska, and who are for annexing Mexico and Canada in good time," should be so reticent about the
Caribbean.[53]

Douglass blatantly rejected the arguments used by critics (including
Sumner) about black people belonging in southern climatic zones and
whites to the northern latitudes. Even more vehemently he denounced
the open racism of anti-annexation voices who simply did not want any
more black people in America. Douglass rather admired the mixed racial
people he had seen on the island, and he welcomed ways Santo Domingo
might darken the nation. Always under suspicion and criticism from other
black leaders, a proud Douglass pushed back at his "reverend friend" Henry
Highland Garnet, who openly accused Douglass of being President Grant's
lackey in the Santo Domingo commission. The editor considered Garnet
a leader among those who "may ever be expected to promptly take sides

against almost any subject or measure it is my fortune to advocate." Garnet even accused Douglass of viewing the Haitians as an "inferior race" to the Dominicans. With great resentment, Douglass denied the charge and declared his admiration equal to his accuser's for the "truly heroic struggles of Hayti for freedom and independence." He said Dominicans had asked for annexation and Haitians had not. In a public letter, Douglass drew a stark line: "Mr. Garnet shall not find me joining with all the negro-haters and murderers of the colored race in opposing the measure. Santo Domingo is opposed mainly, if not wholly, because her people are not white. If they were of the pure caucasion race all parties would jump at the acquisition." Such public spats only demonstrated that blacks could attack each other as well as white Democrats during Reconstruction.[54]

Douglass was not as tolerant or ecumenical about the religion he saw practiced among the Dominicans; the country suffered from too much "superstition and Catholic religion," he wrote, and needed more Protestant "sober monitions of reason." Douglass's anti-Catholicism could raise its head at any time, especially when abroad. He ended his series of essays with the encompassing moral claim that Americans should want Santo Domingo as a state because it would "enable us better to discourage slavery and promote the freedom of mankind." He seemed fully aware of the irony that on the largest point of contention—race—both sides of the debate agreed for completely different reasons.[55]

In 1874, Douglass risked yet one more venture that failed swiftly on his watch. No other experience left him with "a feeling of humiliation," he candidly admitted, as much as his ill-considered presidency of the Freedmen's Savings and Trust Company (known as Freedmen's Bank). On the same day as it created the Freedmen's Bureau, March 3, 1865, Congress chartered the bank. Rooted initially in an effort to help black soldiers save some of their wages, the bank quickly became a savings and loan institution primarily for freedmen and their families. Its primary founder, John Alvord, a Congregational minister, abolitionist, and first superintendent of education for the Freedmen's Bureau, assembled approximately twenty wealthy philanthropists in New York and launched what became for blacks and their allies one of the most popular initiatives of Reconstruction. The bank moved to Washington, DC, in 1867, seemed to flourish, and established branches in cities all over the South. By 1871, the Bank could boast thirty-seven branches in seventeen states and the District of Columbia.[56]

A board of trustees of some fifty mostly white men operated the bank, although by the early 1870s only a dozen or so who lived in Washington attended meetings or assessed the institution's loan portfolios. Douglass became a trustee soon after moving to the capital, but admitted that his function at meetings was merely "the pleasure of listening to rapid reports." The bank built a magnificent five-story building at 1507 Pennsylvania Avenue, within viewing distance of the White House. Douglass described the interior as beautifully "finished with black walnut and furnished with marble counters and all the modern improvements." Black freedom and wealth, the stunning brownstone seemed to announce, had come to stay at the heart of American power. Where thousands of refugee escaped slaves had gathered in the streets and in makeshift contraband camps during the war, they could now take their meager wages to the well-dressed black tellers with pencils behind their ears beneath the fancy light fixtures of the building named for them. The bank ultimately counted approximately $57 million in total deposits from nearly seventy thousand depositors. Those depositors hailed from all corners of the nation; some deposited from $1 to $5, some eventually much more. Douglass's sons were occasional depositors.[57]

With missionary zeal, the promotional literature of the bank portrayed the enterprise as a thoroughly national institution. Passbooks included images of Abraham Lincoln and broken shackles, William T. Sherman, and other Union generals. One pamphlet fervidly promised, "The whole institution is under the charter of Congress, and received the commendation and countenance of the sainted Abraham Lincoln." Depositors were told that their money was trusted to "some of the best men" in the land, and that legally and financially they were on the same footing with all other Americans. The federal government monetarily backed the bank, or so it seemed. But financially, the bank was private and not guaranteed by the Treasury Department, which was located across the street from the ornate headquarters. Under such misleading impressions, the bank flooded the freedpeople with advice literature exhorting, "No one of you need remain poor if you are careful and do not spend money for candy or whiskey or costly clothes." Freed *men* were especially urged to avoid tobacco and whiskey. The Bank calculated that abstinence from cigars and whiskey would garner each man "$31.20" in annual savings.[58]

But events and bad management overwhelmed the dream. In 1873 an economic depression hit the United States like no previous one. The mid-century railroad boom ground to a halt, the stock market crashed, and by late 1874, nearly half the iron furnaces in the nation had shut down. The

Panic of 1873 brought about the failure of some ten thousand businesses over the next four years. Widespread unemployment swept through all of America's industrializing cities, the price of all major agricultural products plummeted, and violent labor unrest exploded in countless places. The panic soon had profound implications for the fate of Reconstruction. In the winter and spring 1874, the Freedmen's Bank fell into deep trouble, although its leadership seemed only marginally aware of the danger. Over time the institution had issued an array of bad loans and made ill-advised investments that its board had hardly scrutinized. Many of its white trustees had long abandoned ship, and in some of the branches, such as in Atlanta, cashiers were caught up in embezzlement. A group of seven or eight active black trustees, led by Charles B. Purvis, the chief surgeon at Freedmen's Hospital and a professor of medicine at Howard University, and John Mercer Langston, the law professor, led an effort in March to depose Alvord as president. As a means of restoring confidence, they hoped, Purvis became first vice president and Langston chairman of the Finance Committee. Then the board, in a divided vote (Langston opposed), asked Douglass, because he was the most prestigious of all black Americans, to be the new president.[59]

Among all the younger, formally educated black leaders who tried to knock the king of the hill off his heights, Langston had been perhaps the most aggressive, their rivalry already many years old. Charles often sent his father Washington gossip about how Langston was "trying to build himself up in running you down." The professor would leave "no stone unturned to cripple ... your popularity." Dignity and duty prevailed over good sense; Douglass stepped into a poisoned situation in more ways than one. In March he found "himself seated in a comfortable arm chair, with gold spectacles on my nose," as president of the Freedmen's Bank. Douglass took the job, he admitted, over the stern objections of his daughter and, without her saying them publicly, of Ottilie Assing. She accused him of a naïveté, but also a certain spinelessness, since his adult children had, in her view, never learned "to stand on their own two feet" financially. Douglass obviously knew his role was to instill faith by his presence. Never had his well-starched dignity seemed so important as now. But never would his fame prove so useless, even damaging. During the 1870s Douglass wore white shirts with both *Douglass* in his own handwriting and an English script *D* in red specially monogrammed on the high collars. Coming close to self-satire in his remembrance of the bank episode, he could not resist mentioning the contrast of "the slave boy running about Col. Lloyd's with only a tow linen shirt" and now the "president" counting "assets by millions." He confessed that these "golden dreams" were painfully unreal.[60]

Soon after taking over the job, Douglass expressed all the necessary optimism required of him. He provided an object for symbolic veneration and the language of uplift and hope. But banking acumen, he freely admitted, he did not possess. He promised on March 30, 1874, to "look deeper than I have yet been able to do" into the bank's problems, and, above all, that he would operate with "absolute honesty" and in "no sympathy with Mr. Langston's idea that now is a good time to wind up the concern." But two months later he reported to his son-in-law, Nathan, that he felt himself "in a hard place in this Freedmen's Bank and shall consider myself fortunate if I get out of it as easily as I got into it." Douglass felt anxious to get back to his "literary work which I should have never abandoned." A comptroller's report in March indicated a huge deficit in the bank's holdings. Many branches were highly unprofitable, and the bank moved to close them, which in turn caused panic and wild runs on the local offices. The Democratic Party press viciously attacked the bank as part of the failure of Radical Reconstruction as well as a demonstration of African American incompetence. Some in the black press, such as the *Christian Recorder*, the national organ of the AME Church, tried to shore up faith by pointing to Douglass himself, who "superabounds in . . . well preserved character." But as the historian Benjamin Quarles aptly remarked, only fools "believed that the presence of Douglass at a glass top desk was superior to the working of economic law." [61]

Douglass loaned $10,000 of his own money to the bank as a show of confidence. But in late May he testified to the US Senate that he advised the closure of the institution in the hope that the government might help make good some percentage of the depositors' savings. He then curiously changed course in a last-ditch public circular on June 25, in which he argued for saving the bank exclusively for black depositors. The circular beamed with race pride, and an embittered declaration that "no people can well rise to a high degree of mental or even moral excellence without wealth." Blacks would continue to be "dependent and despised" unless they forged a "wealthy class." Four days later, though, with much public confusion, the bank's board voted 11–1 to close. Congressional committees continued to monitor the long process of attempted reimbursement of depositors for the next forty-five years. But when it closed doors in July, and Douglass stepped back into his life with lasting scars, the bank owed $2,993.79 on 61,144 accounts.[62]

The affair ranks as one of the great aspirations, but also genuine racial tragedies, of Reconstruction. The bank could likely have been rescued had the moral and political will existed in the Congress, especially among the freedmen's friends, to underwrite the debts and payments run up by bad management. But the Republican Party had already changed its bearings, and in the fall 1874 congressional elections it would be overthrown by the Democrats for the first time since before the Civil War. Douglass's $10,000 was eventually repaid, but most depositors never saw much more than sixty cents on their dollar.[63] The black farmers, washerwomen, ministers, draymen, and general jobbers who had opened their meager accounts and proudly carried passbooks had not made the hapless investments in badly managed construction firms, nor in the hopelessly corrupt Union Pacific or Northern Pacific Railroads. They were the ultimate victims of this debacle when capitalism and racism ground down a jewel of a good idea into dust.

In Douglass's assessment of his short and disastrous whirl with the bank, he both took responsibility and flung blame all around. The experience was a rude awakening for the man who had striven so hard to get to the center of American political life. "The truth is, I have neither taste or talent for the place [the bank]," he admitted in June, as he acknowledged the firm was not sound. But in his estimation he had inherited and not created the situation. In early 1875, Douglass wrote to Oliver O. Howard in agony and disgust, "I never was so imposed upon by any concern in my life. It is bad enough to plunder the rich. It is worse to plunder the poor . . . under the disguise of Christian philanthropy." In *Life and Times*, he wrote with both self-deprecation and anger. He confessed that three months at the bank made him reconsider his view of "human nature." Some of those nattily attired young black clerks, "adorned with pens and bouquets," he implied, had been stealing money. He blamed both the larger society's deep-seated racism as well as his fellow trustees, black and white, who pushed him to take the post. The bank had served, he told Gerrit Smith, as "the black man's cow, but the white man's milk." He knew he had been in over his head, but insisted that he "did not know what I should have been told" by the bank's governors. Douglass was criticized a great deal in the press and in investigations of the bank's failure. But "the fact is," he wrote, "and all investigation shows it, that I was married to a corpse."[64]

For Douglass and his family enterprises, 1874 was a terrible year. Hard on the heels of the failure of the bank, the *New National Era*, long losing subscribers, went under. In its last months, as in many earlier periods, Douglass had left its management to Lewis and Frederick Jr. On May 30, Douglass painfully informed Sprague, whose bulging family remained dependent on the father-in-law, that "the boys are struggling manfully to keep their paper afloat." He hoped they would not have to let *their* "paper fail, but I fear they will have to." By October, Douglass's last newspaper closed its doors, and his two sons were again looking for work. The elder Douglass estimated that he had lost approximately $10,000 on the enterprise. He had once again lost his personal literary mouthpiece. From as early as March 1874, Lewis and Frederick Jr. were in court repeatedly, sued by creditors, whom they sued in return over the finances of the paper. The Douglass brothers had established a firm called the Colored Citizen Publishing Company; several black Washingtonians sued for pay never received for services as associate editors. After numerous injunctions, a judge threw the cases out of court, leaving bad feelings aimed at the Douglass clan for years to come.[65]

In these sobering circumstances, Douglass found himself retreating to his house on A Street, a rather exhausted man wondering where next to turn. On September 1, 1874, on a fragment of paper, he penned a note of advice to an unnamed recipient, perhaps indeed to himself: "There is for men and women no happiness without venture."[66] He had ventured so much in the last several years, with considerable financial and political loss. His spirits in near collapse, Douglass would, as previously, forge a robust recovery; some of his greatest literary, political, and symbolic work lay ahead.

Chapter 25

WHAT WILL PEACE AMONG THE WHITES BRING?

The signs of the times are not all in our favor. There are, even in the Republican party, indications of a disposition to get rid of us.

—FREDERICK DOUGLASS, JULY 5, 1875

By 1875, Frederick Douglass felt adrift, frustrated, and angry. Personal losses and professional failures of recent years had left him floundering and searching for footing in the quicksand of Washington politics. Once again without a newspaper, a job, or other forms of livelihood apart from itinerant oratory, he observed with fear the unraveling of Reconstruction from under the feet of his people. Douglass's abiding loyalty to the Republican Party and a Grant administration fraught with corruption felt more unstable than ever. His daughter's family continued to grow as it needed his largesse. His three sons once more struggled for meaningful employment in the extended economic depression; Charles especially was helplessly in debt. Grandchildren, siblings, and various other adoptees to the extended family all needed his help. Anna's health was not stable as she entered her sixties. Across the South, all but four of the former Confederate states had been "redeemed" by the Democratic Party; white mob violence surged again, stalking and murdering the freedmen. The man of words fell back upon his old weapon, but with a contradictory anguish reminiscent of the late 1850s.

Throughout 1874–75, Douglass followed closely the Democratic Party's counterrevolution of white supremacy in the South as well as its takeover of the US Congress. He now lived in a capital with a scandal-ridden

Republican president and with Democrats, whom Douglass still identified with slavery, the Confederacy, and the Klan, running the House of Representatives. Grant-era corruption normally involved businesses making payments to public officials for favors, contracts, and vast amounts of railroad land. Cries for civil service "reform" coming from within the Republican ranks stemmed from both moral embarrassment and political fear. Indictments and acquittals, as well as the brazen corruption of congressmen, cabinet secretaries, or vice presidents, replaced the fate of Reconstruction in the headlines.[1]

With Americans deflected from Southern and racial questions by economic depression, the fall congressional elections of 1874 were a disaster for Republicans. Overnight, the House of Representatives went from a Republican majority of 110 to a Democratic majority of 60. "The Republican Party Struck by Lightning!" read a typical headline, even in that party's own papers. In thirty-five states holding elections, twenty-three were won by Democrats. Southern Democrats especially rejoiced; they now had a right to believe, as one Tennessee politician said, that this had not been an election at all, but "the country coming to a halt and changing front. . . . The whole scheme of reconstruction stands before the country today a naked, confessed, stupendous failure." Grant's secretary of state, Hamilton Fish, declared Republicans "so flat on our backs, that we can only be looking up." A worried Douglass took to the road wherever invited, warning desperately of a forgetful, money- and blood-drenched "peace" that seemed to be taking over the body politic. He demanded from a New Hampshire crowd in early 1875 "not a peace which rested on one man's standing on the neck of another, but a peace which arises out of equal justice and equal rights to all."[2] Just what kind of peace might unfold in America became for Douglass a central theme during the remainder of Reconstruction and beyond.

Douglass knew the fragility of his words and feared for the future of the cause of his life. He was left to watch more than fight, as the Fourteenth and Fifteenth Amendments crumbled to dust in the face of armed white resistance. He especially felt shocked at the reports of intimidation and terror perpetrated against blacks in elections in various Southern states. In August 1874, resurgent Democrats in Alabama used an array of coercion, targeted assassinations, and, in one instance in Eufaula in Barbour County, the murder of seven blacks and the wounding of some seventy more on Election

Day to defeat an already divided Republican interracial coalition. In Mobile, blacks were driven from polls by white mobs, and in other places ballot boxes were burned. In September 1874 in New Orleans, in the "Battle of Liberty Place," a throng of thirty-five hundred "White Leaguers," composed largely of Confederate veterans, drove black militiamen and Metropolitan Police away from official buildings and took over city hall, the statehouse, and an arsenal. Stunned by this uprising, President Grant, who had been reluctant to take such federal action in the states, ordered US troops to the city to restore order. But order and Republican rule did not last long in Louisiana either. Across the North, sentiment now ran against such federal interventions. A retreat from Reconstruction among white Northerners sent slow waves of fear through black communities. Indeed, assertions of states' rights, as well as the idea that the South should be left alone to solve its problems, poured forth now even from Republicans.[3]

Mississippi produced the worst violence of all. Municipal and county elections in and around Vicksburg in August–September 1874 pitted "White League Clubs" (Democrats) against a weakening Republican Party, led by the Northern-bred governor Adelbert Ames. Grant refused for too long to intervene in Mississippi, and by fall some three hundred blacks had been killed in political terror throughout the countryside. In 1875 statewide election campaigns white vigilante mobs attacked and shot people with impunity in broad daylight. The Democrats' "Mississippi Plan" used intimidation as well as murder to keep blacks from the polls in several key black belt counties. Grant's inaction left Ames's government on its own to face the crisis; Ames was forced to resign and leave the state in what amounted to a violent coup d'état. The one surviving black Republican from Mississippi in Congress, John Roy Lynch, said that the results of the armed white-supremacist revolt in his state meant that "the war was fought in vain." Ames called it a "revolution . . . by force of arms—and a race . . . disfranchised [and] returned to . . . an era of second slavery."[4]

Sickened, Douglass observed the bloodshed and political transformation somewhat helplessly from afar. National press coverage confirmed that Southern violence had won the day inasmuch as even Republican editors denounced further federal action in the South. The *New York Evening Post* held that "no political quack medicines such as federal interference or military protection" would do any good, since when troops were removed, mob violence would only begin again. The Washington *National Republican* offered only benign resignation: "Northern people have lost all interest in the welfare of colored Southern Republicans."[5]

Frederick Douglass, January 26, 1874.
John Howe Kent photographer.

Outraged, Douglass responded in early February 1875 with a public letter to the *National Republican.* Ten years after Appomattox he declared himself in favor of the "bonds of peace" and against fanning the flames of "sectional hostility." However, Douglass identified "two kinds of peace." One peace lived by a "just respect . . . for the rights of all." To describe the other peace, he returned to the old prison metaphors of his earliest auto- biography. That second kind of peace, said a furious Douglass, "arises out of the relation of slavery, a peace that may be seen and felt in a prison . . . a peace where the heels of one class are on the necks of another." The old rad- ical found his voice again. A group of black leaders in Washington had been accused of incendiary rhetoric by some newspapers for their resolutions protesting white Southern violence. "The serpent may hiss," wrote the old editor, "the crushed worm may turn, the wild beast may warn the hunter of dangerous pursuit, but you, colored man, must not say that there is even a possibility of danger to the midnight riders and murderers by whom you are slaughtered, lest our saying so will be considered as an invitation to a war of races." Douglass must have felt as though it were the late 1840s again, when he was accused of being a black demagogue denouncing his country. This time, though, his fame and friendships were so widespread that he gar- nered some admiration for his spirited protests. Some papers published a portrait of Douglass as the "first man of his race." The *Rochester Express* applauded the public letter, announcing, "Douglass was never more needed by his people than now" as their champion.[6]

In nearly a dozen speeches in New Hampshire in winter 1875, anticipating a congressional and gubernatorial election there in March, Douglass attacked the national retreat from Reconstruction. He used bloody-shirt language to draw audiences back to the war, to the "mourning, distress, and desolation" they had endured on home fronts and battlefronts. As Union soldier monuments had begun to appear on town greens, he gave patriotic New Englanders their due credit for answering the "hour of battle and danger." Huge crowds in Lancaster, Manchester, and Concord applauded him for such tributes. To the constitutional argument against "centralization" advanced by opponents of Reconstruction, Douglass had ready answers. Democrats had never shied away from using federal military power when the object was returning fugitive slaves, or handing over John Brown to be executed. He wondered why if the "American people could stand centralization for slavery," they could not also "stand centralization for liberty." As for the charges that the new Civil Rights Act pending in the Senate (eventually passed in honor of Charles Sumner) might advance "social equality" between whites and blacks, Douglass exploited the reality of racial mixture: "What is social equality? They had a great deal of it where I came from. A great deal of the social, but no equality." Two races arrived in North America in the early seventeenth century, said Douglass, one on the *Mayflower* at Plymouth, and the other on a "Dutch galliot . . . at Jamestown." At that time there were no "intermediate races," but now, two and a half centuries later, because of slavery and long-practiced "social inequality there had come a million and a half of intermediates." His roaring Yankee audiences loved the joke. As for the election, a vote for Republicans meant protection for blacks, and a vote for Democrats meant more "dripping blood of my people."[7]

Increasingly, Douglass found himself speaking at commemorative gatherings, probing the meaning of memory in this time of embittered national reconciliation. He was especially effective at calling his fellow abolitionists back to their story of greatness. In Philadelphia in April 1875, Douglass shared a platform with many old colleagues and rivals at the hundredth anniversary of America's oldest antislavery organization, the Pennsylvania Society for Promoting the Abolition of Slavery. He marveled at the uniqueness of a centennial celebration in such a young country, comparing the old abolitionists' modest gathering to the anticipated centennial of the United States to occur the following year. He claimed for his fellow reformers a "higher, broader, and more sacred" purpose. Because of the unraveling of Reconstruction, Douglass put cause above country: the "Centennial of Seventy-Six stands for patriotism; ours stands for philanthropy." The nation's anniversary was "transient," the abolitionists' crusade "permanent." Douglass insisted that he and his colleagues, black and white, survey a century of epic change in ending slavery and proudly tell the world that they had led "the noblest cause in modern history." Generations later historians would agree.[8]

Douglass could soar in these commemorative moments; he made audiences all but forget dire present circumstances and dream again. He refused to countenance "talk of the dead past." To him, "no part of the past is dead or indifferent." He took up the great nineteenth-century abstraction of human progress, asking whether such a thing really existed. To the naysayers, he offered with exclamation the abolitionists' story: "There is no more impressive contradiction than in the history of the antislavery cause. I know of no one period of the world's age for which I would be willing to exchange the present." To buttress the idea of progress, Douglass held aloft a nearly two-hundred-year-old book given him as a gift in England thirty years earlier. From the Anglican missionary Morgan Godwyn's *Negro's and Indians Advocate*, published in 1680, he took a reassuring lesson of change, since this work's "anti-slavery tendency" had advanced not abolition itself, but the idea that it was right in God's lights to "baptize a negro," which two centuries earlier had been seen as a "quite radical doctrine." With such a prop in hand, Douglass asked his audience, young and old, to fight on to a "second centennial." The American freedmen, he said, had been given "freedom and famine" at the same time. "Talk of having done enough for these people," Douglass insisted, "is absurd, cruel, and heartless." Above all they needed protection for the ballot. Their challenge, he told his fellow abolitionists, was to secure the results of the great moral change they had won.[9]

That summer of 1875 Douglass gave a Fourth of July address in Washington that was one of the most controversial and compelling efforts of his postwar life. In the Hillsdale section of Anacostia, formerly called Uniontown and where Douglass's sons had made their homes, a large crowd gathered outdoors in a grove for a picnic and speeches on July 5 (in black tradition the alternative date). Some 375 acres of what had formerly been the Barry Farm had been set aside by the Freedmen's Bureau in this section of the District; five hundred black families had settled there by 1870. Following a prayer and then a twenty-five-member children's choir singing patriotic songs, John Mercer Langston spoke, appealing vigorously for black self-help. Langston wanted blacks to manage their own institutions, singling out Howard University, where he was on the faculty and Douglass a trustee, for special criticism.[10]

In his turn before the holiday throng, Douglass delivered a remarkable address that was at once angry, historical, antiracist, and a confrontational appeal to black community self-reliance. In front of church ladies with fans, restless children, and male laborers with a day off, Douglass offered a history lesson. On this ninety-ninth anniversary of American independence, blacks must now face their "trial" as "citizens of this Republic," just as the white founders had done in their time. Both the Revolution and the Civil War's second revolution were the heritage of African Americans as well as whites. Americans collectively should be by "historic associations and achievements" all one people, he argued. Then in the form of a question, Douglass changed tone and gave the keynote not only to that day in the grove at Hillsdale, but to the concluding years of Reconstruction. He anticipated the impending US centennial the following year, when the nation would "lift to the sky its million voices in one grand Centennial hosanna of peace and good will to all the white race of this country—from gulf to lakes and from sea to sea." As black citizen and spokesman, he dreaded the day "when this great white race has renewed its vows of patriotism and flowed back into its accustomed channels." Proud but worried, with the promises of emancipation endangered, Douglass looked back upon fifteen years of revolutionary change and darkly queried, "If war among the whites brought peace and liberty to the blacks, what will peace among the whites bring?" Douglass warned that "justice" and "reconstruction" did not have a deep enough hold upon the nation.[11] From experience and with great solicitude, the orator envisioned a road to reunion paved only for white people.

A "peace among the whites" is a striking way of thinking about the waning of Radicalism and the end of Reconstruction. The Democrats' counterrevolution in the South was indeed a successful white-supremacist insurgency—a political war *by* whites to forge a peace *for* whites. Douglass aimed his speech in July 1875 directly at his own black community. He implored his people to fight back with the tools of peace. African Americans were a "divided people," he argued, and lacked great men in their own ranks to lead them out of their wilderness. Langston and a few other community leaders may have bristled at that comment. In an unveiled reference to his own recent woes, Douglass lamented that the race lacked its own "grand organ" (newspaper) to defend and advance its cause. "We are disparaged, vilified, slandered as a people," Douglass asserted, "but . . . we are dumb and have no press to answer and expose the injustice." Blacks lacked not only leadership, but basic self-worth. Two hundred years of slavery had taught his people to "respect white men and despise ourselves." [12]

As a scold, Douglass was not out to make friends that day in Hillsdale. Oddly, he demanded a reinvigorated self-reliance from the picnicking throng, condemning "the swarm of white beggars that sweep the country in the name of the colored race." He boldly recited a slightly revised version of the opening paragraphs of the Declaration of Independence, calling on his people to exercise the right of consent and revolution and to "alter or abolish" their ties to benevolent organizations. Blacks needed less charity and more "justice and fair play." Douglass mocked the "begging class," which he said was "composed of broken-down preachers without pulpits, lawyers without clients, professors without chairs . . . who fail in everything but managing money given for the benefit of the negro." The only aim of such a class, he caustically maintained, was "to slip into the money boxes of these associations." Douglass hid nothing of his own bitterness about the Freedmen's Bank failure as he listed the types of charitable organizations he rejected: "African educational societies, Lincoln and Howard Universities, and freedmen's banks." It was as if Douglass breathed real-life anger and contempt into one of the central themes—"the great Negro University Swindle"—of Mark Twain's 1873 novel, *The Gilded Age*. "They [the associations] keep the public mind constantly upon the poor, wretched negro," said Douglass, "and thus damn the whole race . . . in pity." In the Babel that was Congress in Twain's 1870s Washington, money flows toward any project with the word *Negro* attached. When Laura Hawkins, as deep in graft for her family's interests as any congressman, lines up votes for the black university in Tennessee on her ancestral land, she hides nothing: "Now, said she, these gentlemen are to vote and work for the bill out of love of the negro—and out of pure generosity I have put in a relative of each as a member of the University incorporation." [13] Douglass and Twain were on the same page, one with a withering jeremiad and the other with a raucous satire.

Few of Douglass's Reconstruction-era speeches garnered as much press attention as his Hillsdale Fifth of July address. Democratic Party papers seized on the appeal for black independence, thus using Douglass as a way of condemning the "Radical party" and remaining elements of Reconstruction policy. The *Washington Gazette* claimed that Douglass had urged blacks to abandon the Republicans, whereas the *New Orleans Louisianan* saw the speech the other way around. Another Washington paper acknowledged that the address had "been shot with more rapidity all over the country" than any other Fourth of July utterance. The *American Citizen* found some of the speech "enigmatical," wondering just what Douglass had intended. But it lampooned how Democratic papers were "indulging in hearty guffaw" and "hugging, embracing, and rolling over each other . . . at having at last received the long wished for views of the colored people's desertion of the Republican party." Such celebration, said the *Citizen*, was merely an "illusion." [14]

Because of so much conflicted public response, Douglass quickly released a revised edition of the text of the speech. He also published a letter in the *Washington Republican* explaining himself. Friends had written to Douglass worried that Democrats were making great political capital out of his chastisements of black leadership as well as charitable organizations. They especially wanted clarification of Douglass's views on whether blacks should desert the Republicans. He responded that he had been misunderstood because of "stray sentences torn from their connections." He tried to set the record straight: "There is no truth . . . to the story that I at Hillsdale, or anywhere else, advised colored men to abandon . . . the Republican party and set up for themselves." That day would come, he said, only when both parties were "equally good or equally bad." He characterized the address as "an appeal to the American people to substitute the simple rule of justice for the rule of invidious charity in their treatment of the negro—to give him his rights rather than alms." [15]

This is a prototypical case of a prominent black spokesman whose forthright statements about his people's behavior and self-criticisms were appropriated by racist forces. Douglass was a worried, ambivalent man in the mid-1870s, and feeling his sense of authority dissipating. A year after the Hillsdale speech, he still found himself defending it to the American Missionary Association. In a letter to that organization's journal, Douglass reasserted his desire for "justice . . . more than alms," even as he welcomed their aid. Above all, he did not want violent white-supremacist Democrats using his words to their ends any more than he could stomach the "sectarian and selfish purposes" of the "hungry class" out to lift the destitute Negro of their imaginations. We have watched this scene so many times in modern American politics: current Republicans, some of whom love to appropriate Douglass, lifting him out of context to use him in service to causes he would abhor. [16]

* * *

If the political scene offered only an unwelcome, dangerous peace, no economic peace took hold in the mid-1870s either. Economic strife fueled the American retreat from Reconstruction. Both before and after the Panic of 1873 widened its swath of ruin, Douglass engaged the great struggle between labor and capital. He was never fond of labor organizations and trade unions largely because of their discriminatory practices against black and Chinese workers. Douglass was a pro-tariff protectionist Republican. The high tariff on imports, he said in 1871, had "done more to promote the true interests of the workingmen of this country . . . than all the trade unions, eight hour leaguers, and other combinations to force up their wages and force down the hours of labor that will be organized to the end of time can ever accomplish." Before the panic, at least, he put full faith in the market, what he called "the great law of trade." Unions, Douglass believed, remembering his sons' struggles, had no right to prevent "others from working for less." Leaders of workingmen's associations, in his view, spent too much time "making war on capital" and advocating "communism." Douglass maintained that "real pauperism . . . can always be traced back to faulty political institutions." As a true adherent of political liberalism, he argued, sometimes vaguely, that extending the franchise did more for the poor than "all those who attempt to stir up hostility to wealth and encourage outrage and violence." Sometimes he simply retreated into conservative resignation on the labor issue. "The labor question . . . is one of the most difficult and perplexing," he wrote in February 1872. "Its satisfactory solution seems to be reserved for a distant future." [17]

But economic reality did not wait for human solutions to perplexity. Douglass's vision of Reconstruction often lacked thoroughgoing economic analysis, which hardly made him an exception, even among Radical Republicans. For this pragmatic, classical proponent of liberal democracy, a set of fundamental assumptions about economic life created several contradictions in his postemancipation thought: a fierce belief in the sanctity of private property while demanding land for the powerless freedpeople; what often appeared to be laissez-faire individualism and black self-reliance coupled with demands for federal aid to former slaves denied human capital for generations; and political liberty viewed as the source and stimulant of economic independence and civic equality. Moral and political phenomena had always dominated Douglass's mind; the meaning of liberty for a fugitive slave rising to fame as a reformer, repeatedly rewritten and preached by the self-made hero, had always been intensely individualistic. Despite many pesky facts in his amazing story, Douglass could never give up on the idea that he, like others, had *willed* his freedom, livelihood, and future. American individualism had few more potent voices than the postwar Douglass, who struggled for creative prescriptions for the improvement of America's recently enslaved peasantry in an age rapidly growing hostile to humanitarian reform.

In September 1873, Douglass was the keynote speaker in Nashville at the annual fair of the Tennessee Colored Agricultural and Mechanical Association. A huge procession escorted him to an amphitheater at the fairgrounds, where in bright sunlight he addressed some five thousand people, not all of whom, according to press reports, were fully attentive in the "holiday" festival atmosphere. Douglass offered a prolonged apology for a lack of genuine agricultural knowledge, but then delivered a good deal of farming advice, as well as brief commentaries on meteorology, insect infestation, the history of the plow, and the romance of rural life. Above all he administered what became for him a common, stern message about the work ethic. Douglass's prescriptions were as simple and practical as "be sure of your water and wood!" But they were ultimately moralistic and paternalistic. "Time is money," Douglass asserted, Ben Franklinesque, and he urged farmers to maintain family "peace at home." Above all he delivered a racial-historical plea to these black tillers of the soil to slough off slavery's influence, the "entrenched errors and habits of centuries." Douglass's speech in Tennessee was at once a celebration of modernity and its new technologies and an appeal to stay on the land, "the grand old earth," which harbored "no prejudices against race, color, or previous condition of servitude." [18]

In the postwar era, few black leaders delivered more resounding pleas for self-reliance than Douglass. To Douglass, black self-improvement had always meant adherence to the traditional values of thrift, sobriety, and work; as the years passed, he became a self-styled, unapologetic advocate of the Gospel of Wealth. At the Tennessee fair he declared that the great question left unanswered by the war was "whether the black man will prove a better master to himself than his white master was to him." Blacks must stake their own claim to civilization and create their own culture, Douglass asserted, otherwise they would continue "wearing the old clothes left by a bygone generation." They would have "no science nor philosophy of their own ... neither history nor poetry." [19] Such medicine about self-reliance may have been hard to take for some blacks struggling to feed their families.

In such settings Douglass exhibited a hidebound traditional conception of history and culture. He knew that William Wells Brown and William Cooper Nell had written histories; and he surely knew the poetry of

Phillis Wheatley and the numerous slave-narrative authors, among whom he was the most famous. Moreover, he was not the only black journalist in a tradition now decades old. His musings on a lack of black cultural creativity were not generous. But perhaps as a way of prodding the young in his audiences, he pronounced, "The books we read, the sermons we hear, the prayers we repeat, are all obtained from the white race. We have neither made books, sermons, prayers or hymns." One wonders if Douglass knew that such a statement was both false and painfully useful. He had, after all, sold thousands of his own books. But the forbidding scold could make the pill even more bitter to swallow with invidious ethnic comparisons. According to Douglass, blacks lacked the unity and peculiar skills of other American immigrant groups, images of which he fashioned in well-worn stereotypes. "We are not like the Irish, an organized political power, welded together by a common faith." His people also were "not shrewd like the Hebrew, capable of making fortunes by buying and selling old clothes." Further, they were no match for the Germans, "who can spend half their time in lager beer saloons and still get rich." Blacks, said schoolmaster Douglass, were a "laborious, joyous, thoughtless, improvident people," just released from slavery.[20]

As Douglass counseled the freedpeople to not migrate, to "accumulate property," and to create lives "founded on work," he sometimes revived his older notion that blacks should be left alone to work out their own destiny. He often couched this "let alone" or "do nothing" dictum in an equally vehement appeal for justice and fair play. But undoubtedly, in the midst of the political wars over Reconstruction policy, and this new age's constant strife over the meaning of activist government, Douglass's plea that the nation leave the freedmen alone sometimes puzzled his friends and armed his enemies. While his son Charles sent him volumes of documents from within the Freedmen's Bureau, detailing massive efforts for freedmen's education and land acquisition, Charles also reported that John Mercer Langston and director Oliver O. Howard both wanted clarification of what Douglass meant by "let alone." According to Charles, Langston had said, "I don't understand him," and hoped that the elder Douglass would "read this report and look over the statistics." More so, the son conveyed Howard's direct request: "Write to your father and give him the facts as to the condition of the freedmen in the South. . . . A great many old and infirm colored people . . . would perish if let alone."[21]

Douglass had staked out a moral position on self-reliance that no amount of data could dislodge, although he modified it with time and events. His position was a mixture of moral philosophy and political strategy. Too much had been done to blacks throughout the history of slavery; the idealist in the postemancipation Douglass wanted political democracy to be laid so deep in law and society that his people could simply rise each day, make their own livings, and pursue an education in peace. But the elusiveness, even impossibility, of such a peace became the reality of Reconstruction; Douglass understood this evolving truth deep in his bones even as he preached bootstrap sermons to his fellow former slaves. Confounding both friend and enemy, he developed canny ways to condemn sloth, indulgence, and indifference in one breath, while in the next demanding the highest forms of political and legal justice.

Douglass advanced his "let alone" philosophy throughout the Reconstruction years, but in New York in May 1869, at the meeting of the American Anti-Slavery Society, he had delivered one of its most forceful assertions. This audience of old abolitionists was especially pliant to the argument. They had met to push with confidence for ratification of the Fifteenth Amendment, what Douglass called the keystone of their cause. He entertained with mimicry and raucous humor about the many times he had been called "nigger" but still, by close associations or experience, had won over his adversaries. The great obstacle in front of the freedpeople was their poverty; they desperately needed aspiration and education. Douglass told of running into a black whitewasher one day recently. "We are great on white!" Douglass shouted to his laughing throng. Then he quoted the "colored man" with the brush: "As to this thing you call learning, book learning, I ain't much at that; but that thing you call laying whitewash on the wall, I am dar." What blacks most needed, the orator maintained, was "elbow room and enlarged opportunities."[22] Humor could assuage pain and make an audience listen.

So "let alone" was really a companion to its apparent opposites: protection, a social contract, government responsibility and enforcement. Douglass wanted land, jobs, and education. "My politics in regard to the negro is simply this," he announced in clear terms. "Give him fair play and let him alone, but be sure you give him fair play [as] a man before the law." Blacks needed money and a "class of men of wealth." They needed leisure to pursue intellect and the arts. If his auditors or readers were confused by his position, Douglass was not. He believed government must act as the arbiter of fairness. He gave his fellow white citizens, if they would listen, their marching orders. "If you see a negro wanting to purchase land, let him alone; let him purchase it. If you see him on the way to school, let him go; don't say he shall not go into the same school with other people. . . . If you see him on his way to the workshop, let him alone; let him work; don't say you will not work with him." [23]

In other words, "let alone" meant rule of law and social peace. It meant stop killing the freedmen and denying them access to civic life, make the revolution of emancipation real, enforce it by law, protect it in the courts, teach it in schools, keep the ballot box safe and free to defend that revolution, and reimagine government itself as the source and shield for a brave new economic world. "Let alone" and "fair play" demanded that whites open their minds and let blacks find their own place in equality before the law, announced in the Fourteenth Amendment. Douglass chose unfortunate passive words for a plan of social and political action. He knew this was a somewhat utopian vision. But he was in for the long haul, and he often prefaced any talk of his "let alone" theory with the sobering admission that slavery "did not die honestly." It had died in all-out war, from necessity, not from enlightenment and morality alone. It had been crushed in blood, not merely legislated out of existence. Its ideology and habits, its racial assumptions, lived on in virulent forms. When those were crushed too, then, said Douglass to friend and foe, "you shall have peace." [24]

One of Douglass's fullest expressions of the doctrine of self-reliance, though it is much more, was his famous speech "Self-Made Men," delivered dozens of times from 1859 to the early 1890s. The lecture reflected the culture and political economy of the Gilded Age; he appears to have carried it along with him on many of his speaking tours. For example, on the day after he addressed the Tennessee agricultural fair in 1873, he lectured on "Self-Made Men" to the black students at the new Fisk University in Nashville. The speech was very much a celebration of representative "great men" (borrowing from Emerson, whom Douglass warmly acknowledged) and a meditation on success, while offering an extended philosophical discussion of individualism. Emerson's notion that "all history resolves itself very easily into the biography of a few stout and earnest persons" echoes loudly in Douglass. "Mr. Emerson," said the orator, "has declared that it is natural to believe in great men. Whether this is a fact or not, we do believe in them and worship them." Before launching into his own litany of models for great men, Douglass was cautious, warning of how history so often produces the "false prophet." But like Emerson, who told of the "sot" who "now and then wakes up, exercises his reason and finds himself a true prince," Douglass cherished the underdog Lincoln, "the King of American self-made men," who "mastered his grammar" in a "log hut . . . by the steady glare of

*A freedwoman with seventeen children in front of their cabin, c. 1870. The
Civil War had wrought great change, but in much of the South, Douglass's
message of self-reliance confronted poverty, lack of education, and terror.*

a pine wood knot." [25] Whenever Douglass delivered those lines, he felt their
roots in his memory of the loft at the Aulds' house in Baltimore, the boy by
glare of a candle reading his *Columbian Orator.*

Douglass rejected the idea of "genius," abhorred the "accident or good
luck theory" of human achievement, and above all exalted hard work.
Winners and achievers in the race of life could be comprehended by "one
word, and that word is WORK! WORK!! WORK!!! WORK!!!!" "Chance"
could never explain greatness or even professional accomplishment; only
a sense of "order," trained "habit," and "systematic endeavor" could lead to
world-changing ideas. He had no patience either with those who looked to
divine favor to find good fortune. The "miracle working priest" was a mere
"pretender." In his elder years, Douglass certainly did not reject the Bible as
a source of wisdom, but he levied harsh criticisms at black ministers who
with emotional "fervor . . . prayed for knowledge . . . [yet] they who prayed
loudest seemed to get the least." Douglass much preferred to employ passages such as John 5:17, when Jesus is condemned to death because he broke
the law and labored on the Sabbath: "My father worketh, said the Savior,
and I also work." [26]

"Self-Made Men" was Douglass's ultimate commentary on human nature, a theme he first explored in his early two autobiographies. People were essentially "lazy," Douglass believed. "All men," he said with his well-honed Protestant ethic, "however industrious, are either lured or lashed through the world." The lecture is at times knitted together by lines that read like platitudes in a young man's advice manual. "A man never knows the strength of his grip till life and limb depend upon it. Something is likely to be done when something must be done." A laborer with "broad axe or hoe" needed "hard hands . . . for the blister is a primary condition to the needed hardness." For Douglass the greatest cause of human striving was the "sting" of "necessity." [27]

Like Emerson, Douglass's embrace of individualism called for finding motivation, truth, and one's own character from within one's own "soul." Douglass may have borrowed actual words as well as ideas from Emerson's classic essay "Self-Reliance." But Douglass's assertion of individualism was cautionary. Emerson beautifully urged us to listen to the "voices which we hear in solitude," but warned that they "grow faint and inaudible as we enter into the world. Society everywhere is a conspiracy against . . . every one of its members . . . a joint stock company, in which the members agree, for the better securing of his bread to each shareholder, to surrender the liberty and culture of the eater." Douglass, however, chose his metaphors from nature. Absolute "individual independence," he wrote, "of the past and present . . . can never exist." "I believe in individuality, but individuals are, to the mass, like waves to the ocean. The highest order of genius is as dependent as the lowest. It, like the loftiest waves of the sea, derives its power . . . from the grandeur and vastness of the ocean of which it forms a part. We differ as the waves, but are one as the sea." Douglass's striving self was forever dramatically leaping above the waves in rare moments of greatness after years of treading water. [28]

Amid bland comments about an alleged harmony between labor and capital, Douglass trumpeted his demand for fair play and justice for blacks. The speech also contained a remarkable critique of inequality and what might be done about it in the vicious materialism of the Gilded Age. African Americans, he insisted, began life at a very different starting line from whites. Some scholars have suggested that inside the "Self-Made Men" lecture was Douglass's theory of "reparations." Whether we should call these ideas by that term is debatable. But his judgments about the need for historical justice were unequivocal: "Should the American people put a schoolhouse in every valley of the South and a church on every hill side and supply the one with teachers and the other with preachers, for a hundred years to come, they would not then have given fair play to the negro." Lacking specifics, Douglass nevertheless called for a debt to be paid over time with action. "The nearest approach to justice to the negro for the past," said the orator, "is to do him justice in the present. Throw open to him the doors of the schools, the factories, the workshops, and all mechanical industries."[29] Americans were brutally unequal in their beginnings; so act now to repair the past, Douglass seemed to say to white Americans, for you can never really act enough.

Douglass especially celebrated those, such as himself, who rose from the depths to the heights of their fields. No one could miss the self-references as he honored those men especially "who owe little or nothing to birth . . . to wealth inherited or to early approved means of education." Particularly in America, the best self-made men were those "who are not brought up but are obliged to come up . . . but often in open and derisive defiance of all the efforts of society . . . to repress, retard and keep them down." One hears the repressed voice of Fred Bailey in these passages, and that of Frederick Douglass unleashed on the lecture circuit in the early 1840s. By the time Douglass achieved ever-growing fame by giving this special speech in so many places in the 1870s and 1880s, he had long stood as America's representative self-liberated slave, who with "derisive defiance" had remade himself. In America, he claimed, men were not judged by their "brilliant fathers," but merely on their own merits.[30] Four younger Douglasses—Rosetta, Lewis, Frederick Jr., and Charles—had so long wished that this piety were true.

The "Self-Made Men" address is an exaltation of at least the promise in American democracy. Douglass plied the depths of American mythology, sounding like the early Whitman: "We have as a people no past and very little present, but a boundless and glorious future." Douglass kept that line in the speech even as it did not fit his own emerging mood during the unraveling of Reconstruction. America was, he claimed, still "the social wonder of the world," tolerating no "fixed classes" as did the older Europe. Douglass celebrated the overwork of Americans. He offered a flawed prediction about the future of American capitalism: "To my mind, we have no reason to fear that either wealth, knowledge, or power will here be monopolized by the few as against the many."[31] To understand Douglass during the Gilded Age we have to comprehend why he could be so wrong with such a surmise, and why he needed to believe in it.

Although he invoked many passages from the Bible and Shakespeare as well as other poets and literary worthies throughout the speech, he borrowed as much as any from Robert Burns. "Scotia's matchless son of song," as Douglass called Burns, was a lifetime passion for the black writer. Burns's spirit of democracy, cultivated in Ayr on the west coast of Scotland during the maritime threat of the American Revolution, his rebellion against monarchy, aristocracy, and all manner of convention, and especially his literary probings of the idea of equality had always inspired Douglass. The American also felt a personal affinity with the legendary Scot because, as historian John Stauffer has said, "Both men had been born poor, were oppressed by elite whites and treated like brutes, and found in language a way to remake themselves and build a vision of humanity." In "Self-Made Men" Douglass used Burns to assert the majesty of work well done, and especially to show how the lowly can achieve greatness: "I see how folks live that hae riches, / But surely poor folks maun be wretches."[32]

In Douglass's pantheon of self-made men, Burns, like Lincoln and others, provided a model of self-education combined with a holy respect for learning. The orator's self-revelatory meditation on a life of the mind at the end of the speech is its most moving element. He took his jabs at America's most elite universities: "There is a small class of very small men who turn their backs upon anyone who presumes to be anybody, independent of Harvard, Yale, Princeton or other similar institutions of learning. . . . With them the diploma is more than the man." He lampooned the "haughty manner" of Yale boys, but never learning itself. "There never was a self-educated man who, with the same exertion, would not have been better educated by the aid of schools and colleges." How viscerally Fred Bailey had yearned for formal education. Douglass worshipped books, cherished contemplation and debate; he all but lived for his next well-crafted sentence. Words and ideas were the bread and wine of his life. But always, from the streets of Baltimore to an ancient hall in Edinburgh, under a New England church steeple, or in the shadows of the US Capitol, this self-made man had worried how he could measure up. "A man may know much about educating himself," Douglass said, "but little about the proper means of educating others." A self-made man, he well knew, would always be insecure and self-conscious. He "is liable to be full of contrarieties. He may be large, but at the same time awkward; swift but ungraceful; a man of power, but deficient in the polish and amiable proportions of the affluent and regularly educated man."[33] An almost magical fact of Douglass's life is how gracefully he hid such insecurity.

. . .

In the pivotal political year of 1876, Douglass worried less about his gracefulness than about his country, the fate of the freedmen, and especially that of his own burgeoning family. In the 1870s, Douglass carried on a deeply personal correspondence with Rosetta, especially when she moved back to Rochester with her brood of children. The "peace at home" that Douglass had urged upon black farmers was sadly missing for at least two of his own children. Little record exists of how or about which personal matters the old abolitionist talked to his wife in the couple's later years. But to his daughter Douglass frequently complained about aging, about his weariness and bad health, and about the rigors of the road. "I find my continuous working power, in some measure failing me," he admitted in late 1873, "and my health rather uncertain as I grow older." Two months later, the fifty-five-year-old confided that he had "little heart left for the field," and that only the "lash and sting of necessity" compelled him to get on the trains. Many of the behavioral prescriptions and ambitions he recommended for his thousands of auditors in "Self-Made Men" were all but killing him. So weary of travel, he told Rosetta, he often wished to stay home in the "chimney corner."[34]

Only a few days before delivering the Hillsdale Fifth of July speech in 1875, Douglass wrote to Rosetta of his desperation for the hearth. Such fatigue and desire for domestic peace were also exacerbated by financial anxiety. In Anna's much smaller garden at the A Street town house than the one she'd had in Rochester, Douglass had himself a little corner of his own to cultivate. He cherished it, he informed his daughter, as he also did his "horse and carriage, and my house duties." He considered the next lecture journey a "positive misfortune." Instead he yearned to "remain in the same place, dine at the same table, sleep in the same bed, bathe in the same tub, and do an hundred other same things." Douglass was tired and otherwise unemployed. He told Rosetta that a "thousand times" he had wished that he had never left Rochester. "I have been nearly ruined financially by coming here [Washington]." He looked forward to talking with his mature daughter because his affairs now made him "fear the worst. Age and want are an ill matched pair."[35]

Moreover, when one of Rosetta's daughters, Alice, died rather suddenly that same summer at age six, Douglass wrote with a mixture of grief, spiritual sterility, and fear. His devastated daughter might not have been much comforted by her father's philosophizing about death. First, he hoped that Rosetta would not suffer from the "superstitious terrors with which priest craft has surrounded the great and universal fact of death." Douglass, who would later lose many more grandchildren to early and infant death, urged calmness. "Death," he said, "is the common lot of all—and the strongest of us will soon be called away. It is well! Death is a friend, not an enemy." Its real "price . . . is with the living, not with the dead." These were hard but genuine lessons all nineteenth-century families learned; Allie's passing surely brought a rush of memories of Annie's death in 1860. As for after-life, Douglass counseled a sorrowful Rosetta to think rationally: "Whatever else it may be, it is nothing that our taking thought about it can alter or improve. The best any of us can do is to trust in the eternal powers which brought us into existence, and this I do, for myself and for all." The grand-father did not go to Rochester for Allie's burial in Mount Hope Cemetery. Anna apparently did, since Douglass told Rosetta that he did not want to leave the A Street house unoccupied. He expressed fear about arson and ter-ror, even in Washington: "We have been burnt out once and may be burnt out again, and if burnt out a second time I have no more strength to start life anew again. . . . We are not among friends here any more than in Roch-ester." The elder Douglass was wracked with self-pity at this juncture. "It is our misfortune to create envy wherever we go. The white people don't like us and the colored people envy us." A depressed Douglass seemed to lean on his grieving daughter as much as she could lean on him. His stated reason for not attending the funeral, however, may have been, in part, disingenu-ous; Ottilie Assing was in all likelihood staying at the Douglass house at that very time.[36]

A year later, Rosetta's life took worse turns yet, and she begged her father for comfort. She and Nathan were undergoing a marital separation, and she was desperate for help. "My breaking up has caused such a flitter among Nathan's creditors and I am being sued on every side," Rosetta lamented. One creditor pursued the thirty-seven-year-old mother of five surviving children with a note for $91.48. Rosetta refused to sign, and soon a consta-ble arrived to confiscate all manner of household goods—furniture, clocks, rugs, and even her piano. She was selling off "many of Charles's things" to make money, as a court was about to determine whether she was responsi-ble for Nathan's debts. "I am all torn up," she reported. "Dear father, I wish I could be with you tonight—and be out of this turmoil. I never knew so lit-tle what to think in my life."[37]

We do not have the father's response to his daughter's distress. But he likely helped financially. The three years after the bank and the newspaper failures were troublesome financial times for Douglass. Charles was once again mired in desperation over money and livelihood. After leaving the Treasury Department, Charles had moved back to Rochester, but his debts had pushed him into legal trouble and damaged the trust between father and son. In 1875 and 1876 some of Charles's creditors threatened legal action and adverse publicity against Douglass himself. Charles sought and received a new job in the foreign service (with the help of his father), as a man named Hollensworth pursued him for payments of obligations several years old. Charles wrote to his father in July 1875 saying that this creditor claimed that the elder Douglass had advised him (Hollensworth) to go to the State Department and prevent the younger Douglass from going to his appointment in Santo Domingo. "I am not running away," Charles pleaded to his father. "I am under obligations to you in a larger sum by five times than to all others together." Charles knew he had lost his father's faith; worse, his marriage to his wife, Libbie (Mary Elizabeth Murphy), was in trouble due to her claims about his infidelity. "I know how you feel towards me and would do anything to change that feeling," wrote son to father. Douglass immediately replied and apparently accused his youngest son of "dissipation," of squandering money on extravagance and parties. Charles shot right back, saying, "I have acknowledged my faults to you over and over again," but denied the frivolity and irresponsibility. His problems were due, he said, to "making bad investments," and he maintained that he had held only "two gatherings at my house" in eight years. He did admit to some unfortunate choices about "furniture."[38]

In early 1876, Charles's creditors continued to stalk his famous father, who everyone seemed to assume was wealthier than he was. A W. B. Shaw, a Union veteran amputee, wrote to Douglass and demanded payment of a $175 debt run up for services unpaid when Charles had served as treasurer of a county school board. Shaw heard that Charles was heading for Santo Domingo and told Douglass that he would suffer unwanted "publicity" if he did not pay up the "defrauded" money on behalf of his son. As in other situations, the father probably settled this mess out of court with quiet payments of cash. From Puerto Plata, Santo Domingo, in August 1876, a lonely Charles, feeling pathetic, wrote in a tone his father had heard all too many times. "Under the circumstances of the many failures in life," he declared, "I have felt my letters were not desired. . . . It seems that under any circumstances I am to fail in my undertakings, and my life is to be one series of blunders. I have been here nearly a year and I don't know how I have lived." Correspondence such as this from his children, riddled with despair, must have sent Douglass into hiding in his chimney corner. Charles's travail became worse when two years later his wife, Libbie, died and left a helpless husband seeking assistance from his extended family in raising his two children. The family was relatively silent on this horrible loss; the burial of "Mary Elizabeth Douglass, wife of Charles R. Douglass," on September 21, 1878, "in Cypress Hills Cemetery . . . next to a tree, near Corona, NY state," was recorded in the handwriting of one of the brothers in their scrapbooks.[39]

It was not only his children who so often pressed the peripatetic orator for money. The depression had hit the District of Columbia black community hard. Douglass's close Washington friend and occasional political collaborator George T. Downing asked him in early 1877 for a loan of $500 so he could keep his home. In these same years Douglass became a mentor and sometime benefactor for the young historian-minister George Washington Williams, paying for him a $14-per-month board during his first year in the capital. When Williams moved out to Cincinnati, he kept his older hero informed of his scholarly habits and endeavors. By 1879, Douglass sent a $1 contribution to Amy Post's ongoing efforts to financially support Sojourner Truth in her elderly years. He wished he could send $10, he said to Post, but "Washington has been a financial misfortune." He reminded his old Rochester neighbor that he had lost $10,000 on his newspaper, and tragedies within his family had created more dependents than ever. Moreover, he complained, "My position here exposes me to an unceasing stream of applications for help and I try to respond favorably to most of them."[40] It turned out that self-made men did not live lives of heroic contemplation and achievement alone.

During the 1870s, Ottilie Assing remained very much part of the universe of Douglass's family, as well as his personal life. Lewis and Charles, and perhaps Rosetta as well, took loans from her at times. Her retreat in Rochester no longer an option, she now spent parts of summers and some autumns in Washington, living at the A Street house, especially after a new wing was completed in 1874. Assing liked the political hustle and gossip of the capital. Her new hideaway, only a few blocks from the Douglass home, was the Library of Congress, where she could escape for whole days in books. Ottilie continued to nudge Douglass to make the European tour with her. In 1876, with the continued urgings of her German friends in the Hoboken circle, she finally planned her trip. In June she may even have extracted some kind of promise (she at least interpreted it this way) from Douglass that the following spring, after his winter lecture commitments, he would join her in Paris.[41]

Some of Assing's friends were concerned about her psychological state and pushed her to travel to Europe for health. It was "a huge decision to tear myself away from here," she wrote her sister in Italy, "and especially the long separation from Douglass and from my faithful green macaw [her bird] will almost kill me, so that I am already homesick while I am still here." Her annual ritual of such indecision finally ended because Douglass joined her for three special days in early June visiting the opening of the US Centennial Exposition in Philadelphia. Among the attractions was Rochester artist J. M. Mundy's bust of Douglass. But for Ottilie the days alone with her man were a rare kind of happiness. She called it her "experiment . . . so perfect in every respect." Whether Douglass actually promised to go to Europe the following year we do not know. He may have thoroughly enjoyed the dreamy conversations about Parisian delights with his friend on their days wandering the exhibitions; or he may also have, as Maria Diedrich speculates, "tired of her pleading" and just decided to assuage her any way possible. Ottilie departed on a steamer on July 13, and she and Douglass would not see each other again for more than a year.[42]

After twenty-three years away from her homeland, Assing conducted a journey full of spectacular excursions to art museums, the Alps, historic sites and ruins, and especially Rome, where she experienced intense loneliness and a horrible estrangement from her emotionally tyrannical sister. Ottilie and Frederick carried on a correspondence during her year in Europe; she all but punished him with long descriptions of beauty and a historical sense of place at every turn, as she somehow kept alive her hope of his joining her in spring 1877. Douglass continued to confide in Assing, as her letters show her well informed of some of the family dramas and financial debacles. Their rendezvous never occurred, and likely Douglass never intended it to. Assing worried endlessly about Douglass's health and well-being as she described the romance and layered character of Roman history. She cherished his occasional letters. As she told of her new and old friends, kept up with news of American politics, and painfully recounted the destruction of her relationship with Ludmilla, Douglass seems to have pulled back and begun to sever a deep connection in his life that he either no longer needed or could no longer manage with the logistical and emotional dexterity he had so long maintained.[43] A complete severing would take a few more years and come at a great price for the sad, devoted Ottilie.

· · ·

Even before Assing went to Europe in 1876, Douglass was engulfed in the new election season. As early as the fall of 1875 he toured, especially in New England, on behalf of Republicans. He spoke at a huge clambake in September in Old Orchard Beach, near Portland, Maine, at what a local paper called the largest rally ever held in that state. Some seventeen thousand to twenty thousand people arrived on special trains for this combination of late-summer state fair and political festival. Douglass did not disappoint. He told all who could hear him that everything was at stake in the next presidential contest. Blacks in the South faced "utter extinction" if Democrats won. "I beseech you, shelter us from the storm." At these rallies, and throughout the campaign the following year, Douglass made the case about what the nation, and therefore white people, owed blacks. Reconstruction had to be sustained. "Save us a few years more, until the old rebels die out," he pleaded, "and we have a chance to present ourselves to hands unstained by treason." Douglass asked his countrymen to enlist in repairing the past with their votes in the present. "I tell you all you can do for the next fifty years," he shouted, "will not atone for the wrong and oppression of two hundred years." At the end of his address, according to the *Portland Daily Press*, a huge throng "crowded about" Douglass congratulating him and wanting to shake his hand or touch his coat, as "women were moved to tears and men to righteous wrath." [44]

As the election neared in 1876, all knew that the last vestiges of Reconstruction policies and regimes were at stake in the remaining "unredeemed" Southern states. One was Louisiana, which for three years had experienced not only continued violence, but also labyrinthine politics that had produced a US senator, or at least aspirant, P. B. S. Pinchback, a black Republican of mixed race and a flamboyant past. Pinchback, who briefly served as Louisiana's governor, and Douglass became correspondents and friends. The Louisianan stayed at Douglass's house during some of his long visits to Washington awaiting congressional approval of the legitimacy of his seat. Perhaps no other electoral saga of Reconstruction is quite as Byzantine as Pinchback's. Everyone seemed to know about Pinchback's past as a riverboat gambler, a street fighter, and allegedly a dandy among women. Closely tied to former Louisiana governor Henry Clay Warmoth, Pinchback also had his hands in financial corruption and vote buying. But he was a staunch advocate of black civil and political rights as well as federal engagement and Republican rule in his state. Pinchback was first appointed by the Louisiana legislature to the US Senate in January 1873. But partisan warfare, as well as the man's taint of corruption, led to one delay or vote to block his seating after another.[45]

Douglass, as he tended to do with most accusations of Republican corruption, ignored Pinchback's background and embraced him as a pioneer black politician with a genuine right to his place in the Senate. Douglass had long ago learned that politics contained multiple rights and wrongs; in this case Reconstruction itself, and therefore the rights of black people, were at stake. In the *New National Era*, the editor had declared that slavery had been "so monstrous that the blackest charges and . . . rumor grow clean under its awful enormities. Some become great rowers in Harvard or Cambridge who would have been boatmen without the opportunities of an education, others gamble with cards because they are reduced by the laws" to other means in the "management of men." The escaped slave who led by language and symbol knew a useful boatman when he met one.[46]

Douglass did all in his power to support the black senator from Mississippi Blanche K. Bruce, as well as the handful of other black Southerners who were elected to the House of Representatives. They all represented a dream come true, Douglass believed, as long as the Republican Party survived to defend them. Most black Southern politicians came from different pasts than Douglass; some were former slaves, and even Union soldiers, while some also had been educated in the North, as had Bruce. Few had careers in the abolition movement or had achieved any literary fame like Douglass. They were all Republicans, but struggled mightily to sustain faith in the party as Reconstruction waned. In April 1875, Pinchback wrote to Douglass, complaining about the compromises of Louisiana Republicans, many of whom, he thought, were only interested in "unloading the Negro." He worried about "cowardly white Republicans" nationally who would ultimately betray black rights. Pinchback looked up to Douglass: "Oh God how I wish I had your knowledge and ability to grapple with the difficulties I see on every hand besetting us." Their people, he told Douglass, needed a "great mind to guide them in this crisis of our history."[47] Both men were vexed about solutions.

Pinchback went in and out of favor even with his fellow Republicans in the bizarre twists and turns that led to a final vote on his seating in March 1876. Seven cold-footed Republicans joined with Democrats to block Pinchback's entry to the Senate by a vote of 32–29. Bitter partisanship and questions about his character led to the final failure of Pinchback's appointment. On the night after the vote Douglass spoke at a rally on behalf of the

Louisianan in Washington, attended by more than four hundred, mostly black, supporters. It was easy to blame the racist Democrats, but primarily Douglass vented anger on the "mean and malignant prejudice of race" from the small group of recalcitrant Republicans. A great wrong had been done, but Douglass tried to rally the gathering. He still believed the Republicans were the "party of justice and freedom," and he trusted that American voters would not deliver the country later that fall "back into the hands of the party of rebellion and slavery." After the speeches, much of the crowd of supporters marched to Douglass's house on A Street, for one final rally.[48]

A month later, Douglass delivered his magnificent "Freedmen's Memorial Address" at the unveiling of the Lincoln monument in Washington, the speech assessed at length in the opening chapter of this book. In that remarkable oration, Douglass offered perhaps his most sophisticated warning on behalf of black people about the consequences of a failure of Reconstruction.[49] The fate of the era's transformations lay in the balance, Douglass firmly believed, in the election of 1876. The standing Lincoln and the kneeling slave were either gazing out at an egalitarian future rooted in black freedom and equality, or at their disastrous betrayal in a political culture stultified by racism and economic strife.

In this intensely hot political context Douglass attended in June the Republican National Convention in Cincinnati. Since Grant had decided not to run for a third term, something Douglass had openly advocated, the frontrunner for the Republican nomination was the former House Speaker James G. Blaine. But in April a story broke that Blaine had used his influence to garner land grants for one railroad and taken a personal "loan" from another that went unpaid; his candidacy steadily collapsed. Many Republicans concluded that they needed a candidate untainted by scandal. So the party chose the safe, unoffending, relatively little-known Union veteran and three-time governor of Ohio Rutherford B. Hayes as its standard-bearer. Hayes was sturdy, favored hard money over paper currency, possessed a Harvard law degree, seemed to have no obvious enemies, and was willing to soft-pedal on the "Southern question," which was always code language for black rights. The party's platform was rather tepid on further enforcement of Reconstruction policies, vague on women's suffrage, and promised to prosecute corruption. Hayes strove for an honest, if naïve, sectional "pacification," a new harmony between the races and the sections.[50]

Contrary to those who claim that Douglass "did not see what was happening" in the 1876 campaign, the orator was deeply engaged and profoundly worried. The Cincinnati convention included a significant number of black delegates, many of whom were serving congressmen. Following after the Reverend Henry Highland Garnet, Douglass was one of the black speakers welcomed to the rostrum. In a short but poignant address, Douglass provided a mixture of entertainment, bloody-shirt waving, abolitionist principles, and jeremiad. He garnered laughter by saying this was the first time he had ever enjoyed the "pleasure of looking the Republican party squarely in the face," and that they seemed "pretty good looking." He invoked the battlefields where their sons had "poured out their blood." [51]

Then Douglass directly challenged the white delegates on the vagueness of their platform and the weakness of their commitments. Reminiscent of the Fourth of July address of twenty-four years earlier, he flung the pronouns "you" and "your" down on his audience, as they ceased laughing. "You have emancipated us. I thank you for it," Douglass announced. "You have enfranchised us, and I thank you for it. But what is your emancipation . . . if the black man, after having been made free by the letter of the law, is unable to exercise that freedom; and after having been freed from the slaveholder's lash he is to be subject to the slaveholder's shotgun?" He reminded this political class that in Exodus the Israelites, when emancipated, "were told to go borrow of their neighbors . . . [to] load themselves down with the means of subsistence after they should go free in the land which the Lord God gave them." But now, more than a decade after the revolution, he bemoaned the situation: "You turned us loose to the sky, to the storm . . . and, worst of all, you turned us loose to the wrath of our infuriated masters." Douglass left the Republicans with a resounding question: "Do you mean to make good the promises in your Constitution? Talk not to me of finance. Talk not of mere reform in your administration . . . but tell me, if your hearts be as my heart, that the liberty which you have asserted for the black man in this country shall be maintained!" [52] This was hardly the rhetoric of a man merely seeking favor and office with the pliant Hayes.

Douglass's courage was both rewarded and attacked. He received mostly favorable press from Republican friends, but racist loathing and lampooning from Democrats. His enemies had noticed the speech. A Port Jervis, New York, paper reported that "Fred Douglass got off a lot of nonsense about Southern outrages" and Republican Party failures "to do its whole duty to the colored people in not giving each voter forty acres and a mule, and providing a file of soldiers to take him to the polls." The *New York Evening Post* "regretted that Frederick Douglass will not teach the colored people the lesson of self-dependence, instead of always demanding . . . fresh guarantees, by proclamation, by statute, and by bayonet, of the rights which they must largely maintain for themselves." The *Post*'s editors had missed the countless appeals the orator had made to black self-reliance. A Tuscaloosa, Alabama, paper complained that the Centennial Exposition opening in Philadelphia had allowed "a nigger" like Douglass any official status. Later that summer, Douglass campaigned vigorously for Hayes, especially in New England, his expenses paid by the Republican Party. For the busy orator, faith and fear marched together.[53]

What choice did he have? The Democrats ran as their presidential candidate Samuel J. Tilden, governor of New York, one of the richest men in America and the legal counsel to financial titans on Wall Street. A Democratic victory would plainly bring white supremacy forcefully back into federal power, endangering all the Reconstruction legislation. Hayes himself, who proffered a naïve goodwill and preferred ambiguous suggestions of "a hearty and generous recognition of the rights of all," and an end to the "distinction between North and South," nevertheless admitted openly that "the true issue in the minds of the masses is simply, shall the late Rebels have the Government."[54] Douglass could only hope that Hayes's particular combination of the bloody shirt and sectional reconciliation might serve the cause of black life and liberty, and not merely Republican power.

In 1876 the project of Reconstruction, and perhaps the United States itself, were like a huge battleship slowly turning around as it lost power; once turning, it could hardly be stopped, even if the same group of officers remained at the helm. That year the Supreme Court weakened the Reconstruction-era constitutional amendments by emasculating the enforcement clause of the Fourteenth Amendment and revealing deficiencies in the Fifteenth Amendment. In *US v. Cruikshank*, based on prosecutions for the horrible Colfax massacre of 1873, the Court overruled the conviction of Louisiana whites who had attacked a political meeting of blacks and conspired to deprive them of their rights. The justices ruled that the Fourteenth Amendment did not give the federal government power to uphold a conviction against the whites who had committed a mass murder of more than one hundred black Louisianans exercising political liberty. The duty of protecting citizens' equal rights, the Court said, "rests alone with the States." Such judicial conservatism and embrace of states' rights doctrine, practiced by the justices, all of whom had been appointed by Republican presidents Lincoln and Grant, left a resounding imprint on what remained of Reconstruction.[55]

In the disputed election of 1876, Tilden in all likelihood won the popular vote by more than two hundred thousand votes and 3 percent, but did not become president. When election returns poured in, it appeared that Hayes had failed, but the three "unredeemed" Southern states of Louisiana, Florida, and South Carolina were fiercely and violently contested. With 185 electoral votes needed for victory, without the three disputed states Tilden had 184 and Hayes 166. Both sides claimed they had won and accused their opponents of fraud in the disputed states, although most of the bloodshed and intimidation committed in those states had been against black Republican voters. To resolve this unprecedented situation, Congress established a fifteen-member electoral commission, balanced between Democrats and Republicans. Because Republicans held a majority in the overall Congress, they prevailed 8–7 on repeated attempts to "count" the confused returns. As the midwinter crisis dragged on in Washington, it appeared Hayes would become president. Democrats controlled the House and launched a filibuster to block action on the count.[56]

Many Americans worried that the nation would once again slip into civil war, as some Southerners vowed, "Tilden or fight!," and Hayes's managers refused any retreat from their claim to the 19 disputed electoral votes and therefore a victory of 185–184 in the Electoral College. This cliff-hanging constitutional crisis found an end in what became known as the Compromise of 1877, a deal struck in part in a smoke-filled room of a Washington hotel at the eleventh hour. Democrats acquiesced in the election of Hayes in exchange for promises to the South of government aid to railroads, internal improvements, federal patronage, possibly one cabinet position, and the removal of any remaining troops in the ex-Confederacy. Thus Hayes became president, inaugurated privately inside the White House to avoid any threat of violence. White Southern Democrats rejoiced in what they clearly saw as the end of Reconstruction, while African Americans had little choice but to grieve over what appeared as a betrayal of their hopes for equality.[57]

Douglass watched and worried about the disputed election of 1876 and its subsequent compromise. He saw grounds for hope in that the Republicans held the presidency, even as judicial and congressional intervention on behalf of black rights seemed in grave jeopardy. He dearly wanted to trust Hayes. Soon, the new president, continuing his remarkable dance between vague promises to enforce equal rights and actions that eroded or destroyed those rights, offered Douglass the salaried federal appointment, subject to Senate approval, that he had long coveted. Douglass was not silent or out of touch as some suggested during the 1876–77 crises, and he had bravely challenged his own party to live up to its promises.[58] But words had, for once, partly failed him at this turn in his career. Soon he was sworn in as marshal of the District of Columbia and could leave the speaking circuit to a degree. Above all, he had to serve and symbolically lead now in an America he had painfully predicted, one taken over by a "peace among the whites."

Chapter 26

AN IMPORTANT AND LUCRATIVE OFFICE

When the influence of office or any other influence shall soften my hatred of tyranny and violence do not spare me; let fall upon me the lash of your keenest and most withering censure.

—FREDERICK DOUGLASS, 1879

In mid-January 1877, a blizzard swept across western New York State. Frederick Douglass was once again out on the winter lecturing circuit. He found himself "snowbound fifteen miles from Corfu," a town between Buffalo and Rochester. He was unable to get east or west for two days, he told his friend Amy Post, who had long been an important confident. With the assistance of seven locomotives, he slowly reached Buffalo on tracks overlaid with snowdrifts. Almost unbelievably, his destination on this trip was first Detroit and then Traverse City, Michigan, far up in the northwest corner of that state's lower peninsula. "I am now about disgusted with my tour and wish myself back under your hospitable roof," he wrote to Mrs. Post, "but the idea of duty, which has hitherto commanded me is still my master and will compel me to go on." He persevered and did indeed reach Traverse City to lecture there on January 19. This grueling two-month tour of at least thirty-three hundred miles by rail, carriages, horseback, and perhaps even oxcart, delivering both political speeches and the "Self-Made Men" address in at least thirty-three towns and cities, took him from Pennsylvania through New York, to Michigan, Illinois, Wisconsin, Iowa, Missouri, Kansas, and back through Ohio to Pennsylvania again and home to Washington, DC. The tour included all the usual indignities, including yet another Jim Crow incident. In Springfield, Missouri, Douglass was "invited," as he put it, into the kitchen to get his breakfast at his hotel. He re-

*Amy Post, Douglass's old friend
and confidant in Rochester.*

jected the segregation and refused to eat. "The South is still the hell-black South," he remarked to a reporter, "and will remain so for a good while longer."[1] That "idea of duty" Douglass named was still the primary livelihood of the burgeoning extended family of Douglasses, Spragues, and others.

While passing through Columbus, Ohio, on February 17, Douglass conducted an interview with the presumptive president-elect, Rutherford B. Hayes, then still governor of that state. James Poindexter, the black minister of Second Baptist Church in Columbus, accompanied Douglass to the meeting. Even with the disputed election crisis in full fury, they may have discussed an appointment for Douglass in the federal government. Hayes recorded in his diary that Douglass gave him "many useful hints" about the "Southern question." The governor then described his position to Douglass: "My course is firm assertion and maintenance of the rights of the colored people of the South, according to the 13th, 14th, and 15th amendments—coupled with a readiness to recognize all Southern people, without regard to past political conduct, who will now go with me heartily and in good faith in support of these principles." These were the two opposed parts of Hayes's vision of the post-Reconstruction South. Douglass had both personal and ideological reasons to share in such hope. Within a week of his meeting with Douglass, the president-elect crafted three paragraphs to be used in pending speeches. Again, Hayes searched for a careful, if firm, middle ground. The three amendments were to be "sacredly observed and faithfully enforced," and a new policy enacted to "cause sectionalism to disappear, and that will tend to wipe out the color line."[2]

Douglass had long known that even forlorn hope that mocked historical experience was sometimes better than despair. A year and a half later in a newspaper interview, however, he recollected the Columbus session with Hayes in harsher political terms. In the meeting, Douglass had announced his "sense of alarm" at the new president's conciliation toward the South. For an hour, Douglass claimed, he gave Hayes a historical review of the last forty years of the "exactions and arrogance" of the Slave Power. He warned that white Southerners considered themselves above the law, and that they had the blood of thousands of blacks on their hands. Douglass insisted that a policy of "conciliation would be as pearls cast before swine," and that what white Southerners most needed "was to be taught that there is a God in Israel."[3] After inviting God's wrath down on the South, he and Hayes had parted, Douglass remembered, with mutual respect.

Shortly after the inauguration in early March, Hayes put Douglass's name forward for marshal of the District of Columbia. All of Douglass's family, as well as many friends, dearly hoped for such a position. Early that spring Ottilie Assing, for once speaking for all of them, said that the appointment might not only be "honorable and lucrative," but relieve the orator "of the necessity of undertaking each winter those dangerous, difficult, and unhealthy lecture tours." The appointment as marshal was the first time in American history that an African American was nominated for a position that required Senate approval. The job, which Douglass himself later called "important and lucrative," made him part of the federal criminal justice system. The marshal posted all bankruptcies in the District and remanded all prisoners back and forth between jail and the courts. In effect, he helped run the federal court that once adjudicated fugitive-slave cases. Hayes did, however, buckle under to prejudice by relieving Douglass of one traditional duty—introducing distinguished guests at White House receptions. The new marshal accepted the slight, although in his later autobiography he lampooned the reasons for it. The great apprehension at his appointment reflected not only fear that he would "Africanize the courts," he wrote, by hiring black clerks, but of the "dreadful" image of "a colored man at the Executive Mansion in white kid gloves, sparrow-tailed coat, patent-leather boots, and alabaster cravat, performing the ceremony—a very empty one—of introducing the aristocratic citizens." [4] Douglass might have enjoyed wearing the cravat and the fancy coat, but had no interest in being a high-placed butler.

Odd as it may seem to us today, the appointment caused both a storm of protest and a wave of celebration in the press. Opposition to Douglass's appointment came primarily from a group of white Washington lawyers, as well as a few black leaders and office seekers. "Everybody admits that he is a man of high culture," said the *Washington Star*, "and thoroughly educated, but they claim he is too theoretical." Some blacks supposedly complained that Douglass was "too high-toned" to represent the "mass of his people." Members of the bar association argued that the former slave possessed the "incapacity of a child for a position requiring tact, executive ability and a large knowledge of man." Other whites dismissed him for lacking "business capacity." Many newspapers covered Douglass's elevation to marshal with what the *New York Times* called "dramatic interest." The *Washington Sentinel* complimented Hayes's fervor for civil service reform as evidenced in the Douglass appointment. But *Forney's Sunday Chronicle* said the president should have given Douglass a position "less embarrassing." One paper could not resist the ironies of this former outlaw slave now so central to law enforcement. The *New York Evangelist* reported that an ex-constable in the city, when asked by a bailiff "if he was looking for Marshal Douglass," replied, "No, sir, not now; but there was a time, when he was a fugitive slave, when I tried hard to find him." [5]

Some journalists considered the marshal's job in the District second in importance only to cabinet secretaries, while others thought it largely symbolic. But the symbolism of a black man selected by the president carried broad significance. News of the appointment had "spread with astonishing rapidity among the negroes of the South," reported the *Chicago Evening Journal*. "Every surviving victim of the bull-dozing [violence and terror] sees therein assurance of protection." Such firsts were a big deal in the uncertain racial atmosphere of post-Reconstruction America. A New Jersey paper put wish fulfillment ahead of reality with the headline "Color Line Abolished." One New York paper gushed that Douglass was "the ablest negro produced in the United States . . . the negro longest in the public eye . . . nearly a Negro Washington, except in deeds of arms." A Michigan paper declared that a new day had arrived in the national capital: "An ex-slave is now marshal of that old Babylonian city. Verily Babylon has fallen!" Old abolitionist friends rejoiced in private letters, such as Theodore

Tilton in New York: "How the world wags! To me the spectacle of Frederick Douglass as marshal of the Capital . . . is a greater evidence of human progress than if I could see either Abraham, Isaac, or Jacob elected by a returning board as mayor of Jerusalem!"[6]

The *Washington Star*, which pruriently began to cover Douglass's family almost as a kind of black first family, reported within a week of the appointment that Lewis and Frederick Jr. were hard at work answering their father's letters of congratulations, many of which ended with pleas for jobs. Douglass now played the role of patron in more ways than one. Lewis was soon appointed as a deputy at the marshal's office; all of his siblings would in time work there as well, or in other appointed positions, under considerable controversy. And at least one African American commentator, Fanny M. Jackson, wrote as though Douglass were what a century later might be considered the first affirmative-action appointment. She thought Douglass more than qualified, "but the idea that this distinguished man has been honored on account of his color, and that we ought to be particularly jubilant over it, is not only great nonsense, but positively harmful to us." In language that would fit a similar debate today, she wished for transcendence of race: "If anything else but fitness has put him into this position, his appointment is simply a great . . . blunder. . . . It is just this sort of skin-deep qualification for superior advantages and honors that we have been fighting all our days."[7] As the author of some of the most searching analyses of race and racism in the nineteenth century, the new federal officeholder must have observed all these opinions with wry smiles.

One of the most trenchant responses to Douglass's elevation to marshal came from the pen of Sara Jane Lippincott (known by her pen name Grace Greenwood). A journalist who had cut a wide literary path since the early 1850s, when she was the copy editor of *Uncle Tom's Cabin* as it was serialized at the *National Era*, Greenwood later became the first woman on the staff of the *New York Times*, and one of the first to gain access to the press galleries of the US Capitol. Greenwood wrote with sarcasm and celebration about Douglass's appointment. She lampooned the opposition as cowardly "bitter society dogs" who could be seen "barking at the enemy around the corner," and who "yelped themselves hoarse and fell into spasms of color-phobia." After exhausting all their excuses for opposing Douglass, said Greenwood, the haughty lawyers were left only with their one "real objection"—he was not a white man. An admirer of Douglass's writing, Greenwood defended the former slave's peculiar education with a flourish of portraiture.[8]

Greenwood argued that living in racist America had provided Douglass's education. His adroitness at leadership had been forged in "Freedom's High School of politics." Douglass inspired these kinds of physical and aesthetic descriptions throughout his career. Greenwood fashioned one of the best, finding in his visage a "courtly grace" and a raw power that took her inevitably to *Othello*. "Not that he need say," wrote Greenwood, so she said it for him: "Haply, for I am black / And have not those soft parts of conversations / That chamberers have." Greenwood bitingly declared that Douglass's enemies managed only "envious vulgarity" and saw "in his genius and culture only opportunities to wound and insult him." She saw "Othello's visage in his mind" and captured three and a half decades of Douglass's encounter with white-American racial resentment.[9]

So Othello had found a good-paying job. For his part Douglass later remembered this episode with measured perspective, writing, "An appointment to any important and lucrative office brings . . . praise and congratulation on the one hand and much abuse and disparagement on the other." If only serving as marshal, though, had been as dramatic as becoming marshal. The marshalship gave Douglass a new kind of fame. In April,

WASHINGTON, D. C.—THE NEW ADMINISTRATION—COLORED CITIZENS PAYING THEIR RESPECTS TO MARSHAL FREDERICK DOUGLASS, IN HIS OFFICE AT THE CITY HALL.—SKETCHED BY OUR SPECIAL ARTIST.

"Colored Citizens Paying Respects," Frank Leslie's Illustrated Newspaper, *April 7, 1877, lithograph. It depicts Douglass in his new job as marshal of the District of Columbia.*

Frank Leslie's Illustrated Newspaper ran a lithograph depicting Douglass in his office greeting a line of both elderly and young black well-wishers. The stout and dignified Douglass is the epitome of respectability, while the picture is set off by a white aide behind him who cannot be bothered to stop reading his morning newspaper. Soon after taking the office, Douglass experienced yet another postslavery reunion. After forty-one years, the Harris brothers, John and Henry, with whom Fred Bailey had shared the life-altering escape plot and deep bond of friendship on the Freeland farm in 1836, discovered their old comrade. John, who had worked for years in a Baltimore shipyard, and accompanied by the son of another brother, William, followed the publicity about the famous marshal and came to Washington to see him. Henry apparently did not make the journey from the Eastern Shore. Douglass would have relished such a meeting with Henry, the one to whom he had been chained in their humiliating trek to jail in Easton.[10] We can imagine the strange pleasure and discomfort of this encounter of former slaves, one an unknown dockworker, the other a national political and literary celebrity.

Douglass's private life as well as his every public action more and more became newsworthy. As he found footing in official Washington, he began to embody a series of contradictions that both enriched and circumscribed his life. He was now the outsider who would be the insider, an anointed symbol and heroic icon of the past who still wanted to be the activist in the present. Would he grow old and lose his voice in appointed office or still be a voice of resistance and protest? Would his leadership slip into the merely emblematic or fiercely resist all forms of white supremacy? Entering his sixties, was he a figure of the past or still of the future? How would the country's most famous former slave balance vengeance with forgiveness in this era of increasing sectional reconciliation? How would Douglass help blacks and whites remember or forget the great epoch they had just endured? How could a bureaucrat remain a radical?

The philosopher Cornel West meditated on this question of whether Douglass fell "out of touch" in his later years as he became a Republican making some "vulgar compromises." The "freedom fighter" who shifted from "prudence to opportunism," argues West, ended up "defanged" as the insider in Washington. West wishes Douglass might have "sided with the populist movement," instead of embracing a political system that could "absorb him, incorporate him, diffuse his fire." These sentiments have some veracity; Douglass had to grow old in the Gilded Age, make a living for all those around him, while embodying a living symbol as few others ever have. But Othello needed new occupations and livelihoods. He forever remade himself, and such an imperative was no less the case in post-Reconstruction America than in his earlier heroic life. Many have wished upon the old orator a sterner economic analysis of inequality, or a less triumphal advocacy of self-reliance. But he lived his life in the nineteenth century as a consummate political liberal. It further does little good to ask, with West, "Where is the voice of the early Douglass . . . as Jim Crow is developing in the 1870s and 1880s?" That voice changed and emerged less aggressively perhaps; but it never died. He kept his fangs filed on issues of racism, violence, states' rights, and the nation's memory. He had been Jim-Crowed so many times he quit counting. He answered such humiliations with dignity, eloquence, disobedience, and intelligence. West does consider Douglass "deeply prophetic," a voice of wisdom beyond his time. And West acknowledges that Douglass understood that "you don't find truth in the middle of the road; you find truth beneath the superficial, mediocre, mainstream dialogue . . . buried . . . hidden . . . and when you connect with that truth, you have to take a stand."[11] Some freedom fighters wear starched shirts, cultivate their appearance, and battle evil with words.

From 1877 into the early 1880s, Douglass only rarely left the environs of Washington, Baltimore, and other parts of Maryland or Virginia to lecture; for a while, as he reached sixty years old, no more Midwest winter tours threatened his health. In May 1877, barely a month into his tenure as marshal, he delivered a speech in Baltimore, "Our National Capital," that caused a firestorm of reaction. He had now lived in Washington full-time for six years and knew its culture. In 1871, appointed by President Grant, Douglass had served a brief two months in the Legislative Council when the District of Columbia had territorial status. Because of his heavy speaking schedule, he resigned and his son Lewis served out the two years of the term. Douglass might have had little interest in the daily running of the District, but he became deeply concerned as Washington's mere three years as a territory came to an abrupt end when Democrats gained control of Congress in 1874.[12]

Given his official position, the directness of Douglass's statements about both the racism and the political skulduggery at the center of Gilded Age politics in 1877 was more than his enemies could bear. Initially, Douglass celebrated a transformed Washington, an urban landscape revitalized by the "vast and wonderful revolution . . . during the last dozen years." Emancipation, the saving and remaking of the Union, had given the city new life, and the Capitol grounds themselves had been reimagined by the genius of landscape architect Frederick Law Olmsted. Under the Republicans' territorial government, and especially the Board of Public Works, led by Alexander Shepherd, thoroughfares and parks had replaced the prewar squalor with beauty and promise. The board spent a great deal of money on urban improvements, including new housing and schools for a city that had become one-third black.[13]

The city was still awash too often in a "cant of patriotism," in Douglass's view. But a promising new brand of postwar nationalism reigned. With his hopeful hat on, Douglass declared that "men of all races, colors, and conditions . . . [were] thrilled with the sentiment of equal citizenship and common country." The costs and sorrows of the war still hung all over the city, but so did the new nation's "trophies and her monuments . . . her witnesses are a free country, a united country, and emancipated millions forever redeemed from the horror of slavery." Douglass announced his own sense of belonging, as he also delivered a full-throated embrace of the centralization of power in the federal government. He denounced the states' rights doctrines emanating from the Democratic Party and the federal courts as a path to "disorganization and disorder." Then he slipped his cynical hat on and spoke for the remaining two-thirds of the address about the differences between what "ought to be" and the historical "reality" of the federal city.[14]

Douglass identified "disgraceful and scandalous contradictions" all around. He made an argument for home rule for residents of the District of Columbia, observing that apart from women, they were the only Americans disenfranchised. Above all he fashioned a social analysis of the class divisions and prewar proslavery as well as postwar white supremacy in the capital's political culture. He argued that the national capital should never have been moved from Philadelphia, since Washington was and always had been too pro-Southern. He skewered all brands of "lobbyists" and "spoilsmen."[15]

With unabashed caricature he put his hatred of the slaveholding South on full satirical display. Although diminished in stature since the war, the "old slaveholding stock of Virginia and Maryland" were still visible in the capital in pursuit of "Uncle Sam's good things" with "leisurely indolence."

The Washingtonian of Southern background was "never in a hurry . . . his gait is slow . . . his arms dangle," since his "muscles have had little to do." Douglass warmed to his prey. The Southern man possessed the "sitting power of a Turk," always "toying with a cane . . . as a badge of authority." This living relic tilted his hat lower than most over his eyes since he could not abide a "manly openness of character." Most telling, the white Washingtonian of Southern influence had "something of the negro in his speech." Here Douglass anticipated by almost a century Ralph Ellison's observations about an "American language" that had always evolved as a "vernacular revolt . . . merging the sounds of many tongues." Whether acknowledged or not, said Ellison, "that language is derived from the timbre of the African voice and the listening habits of the African ear." "Slave speech" sounded beneath "Harvard accents, and if there is such a thing as a Yale accent, there is a Negro wail in it—doubtlessly introduced there by Old Yalie John C. Calhoun, who probably got it from his mammy." Douglass had reached the same position. "Born and reared among negro slaves," he said, "learning their first songs and stories from their lips, they [whites] have naturally enough adopted the negro's manner of using his vocal organs." Douglass relished the "consolation" that "if blacks are too low to learn from the whites, the whites are not too high to learn from the blacks." [16]

No one was safe from Douglass's acid satire, especially the "whirlpools of social driftwood" who floated into the capital as office seekers and thrived on the "buncombe" of political transactions. This included black "place hunters" who stalked Douglass and any other black men of prominence. "Get to Washington and find Douglass" was their battle cry. From white supplicants he had realized that there were "a great many more Underground Railroad Stations at the North than I ever dreamed of when I sorely needed one myself." He lampooned the District's large supply of "poor white trash," who before the war were "generally on hand when a refractory negro was to be beaten," and they "would follow the track of a negro as a dog will follow a bone, or a shark will follow a slave ship." Since the war, this class all but lived to "resent the emancipation" and tried to find occupations "by hunting, gunning, fishing, and huckstering." His evisceration of lobbyists and corruption all but did Mark Twain one better. Washington, according to Douglass, attracted more than its share of vice and crime, especially prostitution. Above all, the capital had simply never risen above its poisoned past of slavery and racism; every man of standing, black or white, seemed to require a "black boy" to do everything for the "boss," who wielded the whip on "the horse, the ox, the mule, or the boy." [17] Douglass's satirical voice had never been in better form.

This remarkable speech entertained his biracial Baltimore audience in May 1877, but as excerpts appeared in national papers, calls for Douglass's political head rang out. Petitions circulated in the capital (allegedly they reached a total of twenty thousand signatures) demanding that President Hayes remove Douglass from office. The *Washington Star* called his appointment as marshal a mistake. Some influential blacks, especially John Mercer Langston, disassociated themselves from Douglass's parodies of white Washingtonians. Under several days of headlines such as "An Insulted City," the *National Republican* ran many pages of commentary on Douglass's notorious speech, calling it a "gratuitous and stupid insult" to the city. The *Washington Chronicle* called for him to step down, and the *Gazette*, a Democratic paper, characterized Douglass as an "inspired liar," a "dirty befouler," and an ungrateful "pet lamb" of the Republicans. Another paper wrote that Douglass, the "blatant blatherskite," got away with his slanders only because he was black. [18]

Douglass responded as best he could to these condemnations. His office was in the District of Columbia City Hall, where on May 12 he was confronted by a reporter who asked him to confirm or deny parts of the speech. Douglass responded that he had been "misquoted," and that "all the good . . . words of commendation for the city and its residents" had not been reported. The defensive marshal wrote public letters in at least four newspapers, denying that he had slandered anyone while reinforcing his claim that white Washingtonians had absorbed "negro pronunciation" and "negro manner." Still, he felt astonished at the "tempest of rage," said he was "not ashamed of a single sentence," and especially lashed back at his black critics. [19] By June, the controversy had blown over, and the prurient press's favorite black celebrity left town on a special journey.

Douglass was a proud man—proud of his fame, his tailored suits, his books, his cultivated mastery of language, his physical image in photographs, his position in the government. In April 1877, *Harper's Weekly* ran a lithograph of a Douglass photograph, showing the bearded iconic face from a left profile. That same year he sat for a stunning Mathew Brady photograph in Washington. By 1883 he appeared famously on the cover of *Harper's*. But he never stopped searching to unravel the mystery behind his highly visible life: how a barefoot slave boy on the Wye plantation ever made it to lecture halls in London and Edinburgh, or how a wretched teenager in rags in the Talbot County courthouse jail ever made it to the White House to discuss emancipation with Lincoln. Douglass could never entirely believe his own myth even as he forged it; often he asked himself, How did I get here? In mid-June 1877 he decided for the first time in forty-one years to return to the Eastern Shore, to St. Michaels, and to meet with an aging and infirm Thomas Auld. Douglass had spent much of his public life seeking and explaining vengeance; but retribution alone was not enough. By the late 1870s he still desperately sought knowledge of his patrimony, his birthday, the meaning of his roots in what was once a place of pain and among relationships he would recall with "extremest abhorrence." He was a genius at fashioning his story of ascendance, but also forever in search of a lost past that might allow him a stable psychic peace.[20] For complex reasons he also needed to exercise some forgiveness. Public vengeance and distrust for the slaveholding South lived in Douglass alongside a solicitude for the people who had owned him. Only in immersing himself in that contradiction could he truly gain self-knowledge.

In Baltimore, at Fell's Point, Douglass boarded the steamer *Matilda* for an overnight trip down the Chesapeake Bay, the water highway that had car-

Frederick Douglass, Washington, DC, 1877. Matthew Brady photographer.

ried so many of his dreams. On board the two-hundred-foot stern-wheeler were approximately a hundred blacks, like Douglass on a brief holiday. The ship had no real accommodations, and Douglass reportedly found the behavior of his fellow passengers appalling. With banjos strumming, dancing ensued, liquor bottles were passed; revelers made loud noise all night and relieved themselves over the deck railings. With his sense of racial pride and class dignity insulted, the *Baltimore Sun* recorded Douglass complaining that "100 colored people aboard made as much noise as 500 whites would have done." In his speech made at a picnic ground in St. Michaels a day later, he preached to the blacks assembled, "We must not talk about equality until we can do what white people can do. As long as they can build vessels and we cannot, we are their inferiors. . . . As long as they can found governments and we cannot, we are their inferiors."[21] This harsh language flowed from Douglass when he felt embarrassed by some of his people. At this stage of life, his class status seemed easily offended. Such were the contradictions of his chosen path of leadership. The paragon of respectability found some of the fun-loving habits of the recently emancipated unsavory. Douglass much preferred violins to banjos.

When Douglass arrived in St. Michaels, he found a town where most blacks still lived in shacks and their economic conditions had not changed much since the end of slavery. A crowd of blacks and whites followed him as he strolled through streets. Many came up to shake his hand, and although his sister Eliza was not among them, a group of younger Mitchells (her extended family) and other kinfolk joined the impromptu parade. In this sleepy oyster-harvesting and boatbuilding town, Douglass must have appeared like some tall, leonine, white-haired African ruler returning in Western clothing. He later called this homecoming "strange enough in itself," but that he was about to meet his former master was "still more strange." A messenger brought word that Auld had agreed to see him at the home of the old man's daughter and son-in-law, Louisa and William H. Bruff. The gawking entourage followed him to the corner of Cherry Street and Locust Lane, where, as Dickson Preston, our best chronicler of Douglass's returns to the Eastern Shore, wrote, "It was the first time that a black man had ever entered a white home in St. Michaels by the front door, as an honored guest."[22]

Auld was sick, bedridden, his hands "palsied," as Douglass described him. The two men met for about twenty minutes in an emotional, humane encounter of past and present. Douglass thought he was witnessing Auld on his deathbed, although the former slaveowner would not die for two and a half more years. As autobiographer, Douglass re-created this drama with a customary vividness and irony. He entitled the chapter "Time Makes All Things Even"; he did not say time cures all ills, nor had he "begged" for Auld's "forgiveness," as the *Baltimore Sun*'s reporter claimed. But he may have revealed a deep yearning to heal his own soul, to find a purging of his scarred memory, to forgive in a way that helped *him* to finally declare publicly his survival and triumph. In much of Christian tradition—in which Douglass had learned to think and write—the forgiver often forgives for his own sake, not to excuse the oppressor. He forgives to strengthen his own heart, to work through grief, pain, loss, and hatred. Douglass had striven long and far and come to see that some self-understanding may rest at the end of the precept "Forgive, and ye shall be forgiven." [23] Former slave met former owner, but Douglass needed this meeting most.

In part, Douglass used the reunion to try to demonstrate a changed country as measured in his own life. Auld had "made property to my body and soul," wrote the memoirist, "reduced me to a chattel, hired me out to a noted slave-breaker to be worked like a beast and flogged into submission." In turn, Douglass had traveled the world, making his old master's "name and his deeds familiar . . . in four different languages" as the symbol of all that was evil in American slavery. For so many years Douglass had wreaked a prophetic vengeance on slavery, slaveholders, the Confederacy, their memory, and all they stood for. Now, in a bedroom of an old brick house in St. Michaels, Maryland, nearby where Auld had whipped Fred Bailey and rented him down the road to Edward Covey, it was as if the aging Douglass glimpsed his own mortality and his own frail humanity way down beneath all the brilliant antislavery rhetoric. Douglass irresistibly went to the sick man's bedside and suddenly found himself "holding his [Auld's] hand and in friendly conversation with him in a sort of final settlement of past differences preparatory to his stepping into his grave, where all distinctions are at an end, and where the great and the small, the slave and his master, are reduced to the same level." [24]

So Douglass went to St. Michaels to declare his equality, and in a way to practice a self-renewing forgiveness. *He* was the one dispensing the equality. With words, he was trying to bury slavery once and for all in the very soil of his birth. The entire nation's sins were still in desperate need of remission. "He was to me no longer a slaveholder either in fact or in spirit," wrote the famous black man of the obscure white man, "and I regarded him as I did myself, a victim of the circumstances of birth, education, law, and custom." Their mutual fates had been "determined for us, not by us." Douglass the avenger changed his tune as both men shed tears, one of them with hand trembling, and "ready to step into the eternal unknown." Douglass, the former war propagandist, recalled, "Even the constancy of hate breaks down . . . before the brightness of infinite light." He had long needed breaks from hating. The two men talked about the past. Auld called the younger man "Marshal Douglass," and the former slave called the older man "Captain Auld." But Douglass interrupted and insisted, "Not *Marshal*, but Frederick to you as formerly." The scene later caused a swirl of protest among younger blacks, since it was reported in papers as "just call me Fred." This made the former slave look as though he had kowtowed to the former slaveholder; a cartoon even appeared showing Douglass kneeling as he approached Auld.[25]

Douglass was keenly interested in what Auld thought of his running away, to which the old denizen of Methodist camp meetings answered, "Frederick, I always knew you were too smart to be a slave." Douglass assured Auld that he had not run away from "*you*, but from *slavery*; it was not that I loved Caesar less, but Rome more." Douglass apologized for his former charge that Auld had put his grandmother Betsy out to die. That had been, Douglass admitted, "a mistake in my narrative." Finally, the former Fred Bailey of mysterious patrimony even asked Auld if he could determine his [Douglass's] birth year, to which the old master replied, 1818, making his guest a year younger than he had realized. That "destitution" of never knowing his birthday was now at least partially assuaged. Just why and how Auld knew the year so readily remains part of the mystery.[26]

Douglass took such care with this account in *Life and Times*, he maintained, because his ever-ready critics—the "heartless triflers"—had made mischief out of his return to St. Michaels. He tried to set the record straight. But he also needed to know if the shabby surroundings of the Eastern Shore could quiet the noise in his soul, help him to discover just who he was now that he had transcended Covey's farm for Washington's City Hall. Douglass visited the palsied Auld to see whether a qualified forgiveness for one slaveowner could still his rage against all of them. This search for self-knowledge, however, did not in the least diminish his embrace of self-help doctrines. In his outdoor speech that afternoon, he declared himself a lover of Maryland, a proud "Eastern Shoreman," and above all, he urged the poorer black folk to "get money and keep it" and thereby demand self-respect.[27] As the visit to the Eastern Shore demonstrated, the famous Douglass now lived a life of constant conflict between public and private imperatives. He needed the beatitudes for his own quiet reasons.

A year and a half later, in the late fall of 1878, Douglass returned a second time to the Eastern Shore. Invited by the local Republican Party for a paid lecture, he went to speak at the Talbot County Courthouse, where he had been jailed for plotting to escape in 1836, as well as at the Bethel and Asbury AME Churches. This time he journeyed aboard an overnight steamer, *Highland Light*, on which he broke a color line by staying in a stateroom. The visit to Easton became a kind of celebrity's welcome. Breaking yet another color barrier, Douglass stayed at the Brick Hotel, the town's finest, and took meals at Lowe's Tavern, just across the street from where he and the Harris brothers had been jailed in chains, and where forty-five years earlier he had witnessed tobacco-chewing, gazing slave traders groping and sizing up their prey. The former slave relished all these ironies; the old prison metaphors of the *Narrative* gave way in *Life and Times* to new rushes of memory: "There stood the old jail, with its white-washed walls and iron gratings, as when in my youth I heard its heavy locks and bolts clank behind me." The nearly eighty-year old Joseph Graham, former sheriff of Talbot County and the man who had locked Douglass in that jail so long ago, attended the lecture in the courthouse, welcoming the former inmate and shaking his hand.[28]

High-altitude aerial view of Bay Hundred with Kent Island and Poplar Island and Western Shore, c. 1930. The expanse of Chesapeake Bay is in the distance.

All eyes in Easton were on the tall, sixty-year-old man with the large crop of gray hair, as he strolled the streets that had been so forbidden in his youth. An *Easton Gazette* reporter seemed to follow Douglass everywhere, describing a "large man of full habit, but not obese . . . his color that of a bright mulatto . . . his features not at all those of a Negro, except that there is a slight depression of the nose and spreading of the nostrils." The two black congregations of Bethel and Asbury gathered to hear the returning hero on the Sunday afternoon, November 24. On Monday, to a racially mixed audience crowded into the courthouse, Douglass gave a modified version of "Self-Made Men." His speech, according to the one account, came with two stern messages—prescriptions for self-help and hard work for blacks, and for whites his old plea to give the freedman "fair play" and then "let him alone." To the whites he further demanded that they "not form your Ku Klux Klan and your rifle clubs to drive him [the Negro] from the polls." The *Gazette* reporter thought the lecture had "thrilled every bosom." [29]

Perhaps the most poignant moment in that evening's speech came when Douglass described his daytime journey in a hired rig out to Tappers Corner, and the walk through fields of the farm once owned by Aaron Anthony, to the horseshoe bend in the Tuckahoe River, searching for the exact location of his birth. Louis Freeman, a local former slave who had once lived on that same farm, accompanied Douglass. The two of them studied the landscape and found a long gulley leading up from the river; here was what Douglass had once remembered as the "ravine." Grandma Betsy's cabin was long gone, as was the old well. Douglass trudged into the briars and brush looking for an old cedar tree. There it was, grown much larger than in his boyhood; he believed he had found the spot. Douglass knelt in solitude and reverence and with bare hands scooped up handfuls of soil to take back with him to his Washington home. [30]

That night in the lecture, he told the assembled that he had obtained "some of the very soil on which I first trod." With some of Talbot County's dirt, Douglass now had a sacred talisman—to observe or touch, or perhaps even smell—when he needed to reflect on the meaning of his double life on both sides of the Chesapeake. Through his senses, it might have given him a way to pay homage to his mother and grandmother, to the blood and toil they had left in that soil. In the *Narrative* Douglass told us he had no recollection of seeing his "mother by the light of day." In *Bondage and Freedom*, his more lengthy attempt to remember his mother could end only with "her grave is, as the grave of the dead at sea, unmarked, and without stone or stake." [31] Bowing down on the ground where his life began, his hands shoving aside the late-November leaves, and pushing down into the cold soil, may have been for Douglass a profoundly private way of recognizing how unsettling, unfinished, and even unattainable the story of his life truly remained. That soil provided, though, one kind of fact he had come to the Eastern Shore to find. Harriet Bailey was there somewhere; and so was he.

Before leaving the Eastern Shore, Douglass paid a visit to Charleston, to the south in Dorchester County, the area where Harriet Tubman had hailed from. He reconnected once again with his brother Perry, now old and infirm. Douglass took Perry back to Washington with him, and until Perry died less than two years later, he lived with the Douglasses among the growing household clan. Pointing to this touching fact, an *Easton Gazette* reporter struggled to capture the remarkable contrasts of Douglass's visit. Calling the story "wonderful," the *Gazette* fashioned a memory of it to fit both reality and mythology: "He left our county under compulsion. . . . He comes back by invitation . . . not to ask pardon of those whom he had disobeyed, but to extend pardon to those by whom he had been wronged. He left as a fugitive. . . . He comes back our equal before law." As if white Marylanders could now claim Douglass in the present by erasing his past, the paper concluded, "He left us a 'nigger,' he returns a gentleman." [32] With a bag full of soil and his older brother, the marshal hurried back to the District of Columbia.

By the end of the 1870s, Douglass thrived, at least symbolically, at the center of American political life. He continued in the mundane tasks of the marshal's office, but what he dealt with daily were the vicissitudes of fame, constant criticism, and controversy. Douglass is a distinctive example of the nature of fame in nineteenth-century America. His was a fame of achievement, the celebrated American self-made variety. This fame was enmeshed with the country's most compelling story of slavery, its destruction, and new visions of freedom about which he was a prominent author. But his was also, as the historian Leo Braudy writes, a "visible . . . modern fame" that emerged in the age of "the rapid growth of newspapers and magazines, the development of the railroad and the telegraph, along with the rapid sophistication of photography." [33] Douglass was a lover and student of photography, which he cultivated as a means of spreading his influence through his image.

Over more than fifty years, 1841–1894, Douglass sat for approximately 160 photographs and wrote some four essays or addresses that were in part about the craft and meaning of pictures. In engravings and lithographs his image graced the pages or cover of all major illustrated papers in England and the United States. His picture was captured in all major forms of photography, from the daguerreotype to stereographs and wet-plate albumen prints. Photographers, some famous and some not, all across the country sought out Douglass for his image. As the historians of his image have shown, the orator performed for the camera. He especially presented himself without props, his own stunning person representing African American "masculinity and citizenship." He helped to choose the frontispieces for his autobiographies, which carried his photograph, and he especially sought to create for a wide audience successive images of the intelligent, dignified black man, and statesmanlike elite, at the same time he understood that photography had evolved into a "democratic art," allowing almost anyone to leave an image for posterity.[34] Visually, by the 1870s and 1880s, Douglass was one of the most recognizable Americans; the dissemination of photographs of him became, therefore, a richly political act. Loved and hated, along with the living Grant and the mythic Lincoln, he *was* the American story, and he put a face on it.

Douglass instinctively loved politics and debate and never lacked for opinions. He continued to preach unapologetically to blacks about self-reliance. In February 1878, at an unveiling of a print of Francis Bicknell Carpenter's famous painting, *First Reading of the Emancipation Proclamation*, at Howard University, where Douglass served as a trustee, and in the presence of President Hayes and other dignitaries, Douglass stressed the necessity of blacks learning to "build ships [and] domes," as the path to social respect. These kinds of remarks brought steady chastisement from some quarters. By early 1879 an Elmira, New York, paper accused Douglass of believing "nothing can be done" in the face of the collapse of Hayes's policy of conciliation and the South's increased violence and discrimination against blacks. The editorialist claimed Douglass had "settled down in his old age" in a comfortable federal office, counseling his people to "suffer and wait. . . . This is not the tone of his olden speech. . . . It is sad to see such a transformation." Douglass had become pathetic, said his former allies, a mere "small voice for peace."[35] They got the old radical's attention.

Douglass wrote an angry letter to the *Elmira Advertiser*. "I never said nothing can be done," he roared, calling for "moral indignation" and investigations of Southern conditions. They had wounded him. "When the influence of office or any other influence shall soften my hatred of tyranny and violence do not spare me; let fall upon me the lash of your keenest and most withering censure." He received plenty of censure, even from old comrades such as Samuel Porter in Rochester, who cautioned him about losing his moral bearings as a political insider. Douglass responded with this metaphoric assurance of his integrity: "Thanks for your gentle warning. . . . The perils are abundant in every part of the voyage of life—and are as abundant when nearing the shore as when in mid ocean. I can only promise to keep a man at the 'mast head' and a sharp look out and a firm hand on the helm."[36]

Despite all these challenges, Douglass continued to carry the "Self-Made Men" lecture all over the American map. A typical example is a trip he made out to Staunton, Virginia, in the Shenandoah Valley in April 1879. As so often happened with these events, a brass band and large delegation met Douglass at the depot and escorted him first to a hotel, where local worthies called upon him, and then to Augusta Street Methodist Church. The sanctuary was filled to the rafters, reported the *Valley Virginian*, to see the "bright mulatto" orator. The middle pews were reserved for some two hundred white people, with the City Council sitting up front. Blacks sat around the sides and in a balcony. A black "Jubilee Choir" sang, and then Douglass held forth for two and a half hours, performing, according to the local reporter, routines and arguments intended to entertain and please the whites.[37] He allowed the white town fathers to feel proud of their Christian paternalism, as long as they exercised it with benevolence.

Anticipating in style and substance some of what Booker T. Washington would later make legendary, Douglass prescribed self-reliance for the balcony and peace and economic cooperation for the middle pews. "These negroes are among you and will remain with you," declared Douglass to the Virginians. Then came the Indian analogy, devoid of any attention to the murder and mass displacement of Native peoples under way at that very moment. "You need not expect them to die out like the Indians. They are too fond of civilizing influences. . . . An Indian is contented with a blanket, while a negro's ambition is a swallow-tailed coat; the Indians don't like churches and steeples, while the negro thinks the higher the steeple the nearer they are to heaven." Douglass urged the Staunton whites to embrace their sturdy black neighbors in economic and political harmony. "They [blacks] are essentially imitative, and if by their efforts they seek to raise themselves from poverty and attain to the excellence of good citizenship, give them a chance. Don't place unnecessary obstacles in their way; let them alone, and if they die out let them die. . . . Sell them lands and let them practice your economy and thrift."[38] Such rhetoric may have worked in making the middle pews in a Southern church feel a social peace on a spring afternoon. But out in the larger society at that very moment a different, desperate movement had taken hold.

In the spring and through the summer of 1879, Kansas fever, an "exodus" impulse, spread over the desperately poor tenant farming blacks of the states of Tennessee, Mississippi, Louisiana, and Texas. The urge to migrate to better conditions, with the dream of land ownership and economic independence, had risen and fallen in parts of the South ever since emancipation. But by the spring of 1879, a perfect storm of causes and inducements coalesced to prompt approximately six thousand freedpeople and their children to head for the banks of the Mississippi River in search of steamboats. They were driven by a combination of tenant-farming debt and economic despair since the depression of 1873. Most worked on "shares" of their cotton in a cash-poor economy, faced extortion practiced by landowners and furnishing merchants, and a resurgence of "bulldozing," the night-riding violence against black communities. They further set hopeful eyes on Kansas because of some political promises of federal financial assistance made by their remaining Republican allies in the US Congress. And for many desperate people, a millenarian religious impulse pushed them to the horizons seeking a new dispensation from God on their Kansas Exodus to a promised land—not of milk and honey, but of property ownership and flourishing schools in their own black-run towns a long way from pharaoh's night riders.[39]

The Kansas Exodus received enormous press attention around the country and was fiercely debated among black leaders and their allies, even as some white Southerners lowered rents on their tenants, frightened that they might lose their laborers. Should agricultural black Southerners leave the homes and lands they had always known and worked? Fed up with betrayal, political exclusion, and terror, many black leaders urged on the Exodus, raised money, and demanded the government help finance and protect the migration. President Hayes's policy of conciliation toward the South in return for promises of reform, peace, and protection of black rights from Southern Democrats had failed disastrously; indeed, Democrats took control of both houses of Congress in the elections of 1878, and the Republican Party was a dying institution in the former Confederacy. Hayes put faith in the long-term effects of education and urged blacks to learn "industry, self-reliance, self control, economy and thrift." To a black educator in Florida considering migration to the Midwest in July 1879, Hayes urged, "Stay where you are. . . . You are natives of the South and you are entitled to remain there. I know you are assaulted and bulldozed, but stick. Time and the

North will set you right." In such pathetic terms, Hayes had given up on any real federal protection for the freedmen.[40] On the Exodus, with different reasoning, Douglass essentially agreed with the president.

The Exodus inspired an extremely divisive debate. "I never found myself more . . . painfully at variance with leading colored men of the country," Douglass wrote just two years later, "than when I opposed the effort to set in motion a wholesale exodus of colored people." In 1878 he reiterated that he had always, abstractly, seen such schemes of emigration as "a delusion and a scam. The white race is everywhere on the face of the globe and we could not get away from them if we would." Especially agonizing for Douglass were claims made by fellow blacks that he "had deserted to the old master class" and become "a traitor to my race." At a mass meeting about the Exodus in New York in late April 1879, attended by an array of black and white former abolitionists, Douglass was loudly hissed when he was announced to speak in opposition to the Kansas movement. He responded in speeches and with letters to his critics in the press. He angrily wrote to the *People's Advocate* of Washington after that paper accused him of "turning a deaf ear to the sufferings" of the Exodusters: "You could hardly make a more grievous charge against me, and let me therefore ask you for the evidence upon which it is based. . . . The reputation of colored public men built up by long years of public service should not be wantonly thrown away." But this debate functioned less on evidence than on racial solidarity and despair at Reconstruction's failure. Blacks everywhere fiercely disputed whether the South had become an irredeemable Egypt or a promised land still worth fighting for. Douglass was especially wounded by critics who called him a "fawning sycophant" who abandoned his people.[41]

A target now for many disappointments among black leadership in the Gilded Age, Douglass tried to fight back. With few exceptions, such as Blanche K. Bruce and P. B. S. Pinchback, black Southern politicians who opposed mass immigration from Louisiana or Mississippi, Douglass stood virtually alone as the major opponent of the Exodus. His celebrity brought perhaps inordinate attention to his opinions. Black Southern politicians favored the Exodus in varying ways. So did the legendary Sojourner Truth, who went to Kansas herself and lent moral support to the migrants. Northern black leaders who had long been either friends or rivals of Douglass's, such as George T. Downing, Richard T. Greener, and John Mercer Langston, all became vocal advocates of the Exodus. Douglass held open public debates with Langston and Greener. Douglass further came under censure in state-level black conventions, such as one in Nashville, Tennessee, in May 1879, where the Kentucky-born Ohio State legislator Robert J. Harlan (a half brother of Supreme Court justice John M. Harlan) argued in a widely reprinted speech that the South had collapsed into "another Egypt" and that emigration westward was the freedpeople's only remedy.[42]

Douglass fired some angry salvos in a speech in Baltimore in May 1879, where he vigorously rejected the equivalencies drawn by some Exodus advocates between prewar chattel slavery and the current plight of the freedpeople. He renewed his long-practiced loathing of "schemes of colonization and emigration," which he believed had historically hurt black people. Moreover, in a piece in the *National View*, Douglass laid out ten reasons why he was opposed to this exodus. His arguments boiled down to the idea that blacks, however poor or scorned, should never give up on the revolution of emancipation, not offer an "untimely concession" to white racism, and never surrender on the achievement of equality. By November, Douglass was still devoting enormous time to point-by-point attempts in newspapers to refute Langston or others.[43]

Douglass wrote a lengthy paper on the Exodus in September 1879 at the invitation of the American Social Science Association. He was to appear in a point-counterpoint debate with Richard T. Greener, Harvard's first black graduate, dean of the Howard University law school, and a cantankerous intellectual nemesis of Douglass's. At the last minute Douglass did not travel to Saratoga Springs, New York, in September to the association's annual meeting; the address was read for him by Francis Wayland III, professor and dean of the Yale Law School. In this carefully crafted essay, later published with Greener's rejoinder, Douglass first demonstrated a sympathetic understanding of the economic plight of black Southerners and why they would feel entitled to their right to emigrate. He delivered a robust, if somewhat naïve, analysis of the South's dependence on black labor: black brawn and skill had always been the "admitted author of whatever prosperity, beauty and civilization . . . possessed by the South . . . the arbiter of her destiny." The freedman, Douglass argued, in defiance of much evidence, had a "monopoly on the labor market" and with "no competitors . . . he can demand living prices with the certainty that the demand will be complied with." How dearly so many desperate sharecroppers wished they had some control over such a bargain. Naïvely, Douglass sustained his faith in the triumph of free labor and universal manhood suffrage. It was as though the busy marshal-orator had thrown up a psychological wall of denial in his mind about the reality of racial oppression in the South. He believed all successful people and cultures must have a "native land." A "wandering" people, in his view, only garnered collective disrespect.[44]

But at its heart the Saratoga address was a plea against what the Washington insider deemed a "surrender, a premature, disheartening surrender" of the great causes of the Civil War era: abolitionism, emancipation, the Reconstruction amendments, equal rights, independence and self-reliance, and the US government's responsibility of protection and enforcement. In Douglass's logic, the Exodus was an abandonment of all worthy principles; it was victory turned into "a miserable compromise" or, worse, into slow defeat of the second American republic. Leaving the South meant that in the long run the Confederacy had won. Douglass demanded that blacks stay and fight, with their labor and especially their votes. The "possibility of power," he argued, existed only where blacks could sustain large populations, breed their own officeholders, and prevail at the ballot box. It was as if Douglass counseled a million desperate tenant farmers who had watched some of their kinfolk brutalized or murdered trying to vote to bide their time and stay and fight for the dream of political liberalism. Douglass had always hated the arguments at the base of colonization schemes. The Exodus was to him, therefore, an "apostleship of despair" that the old orator in the Oberlin tent in 1848, from Corinthian Hall's stage in 1852, or on the altar of Tremont Temple in 1863 and a thousand other venues just could not abide.[45] But a tide of history had swept over his cherished principles and left them in tatters.

No matter the depth of their misery, humiliation, or hopelessness, Douglass urged black Southerners to stay put and keep fighting. In effect, he asked poor farmers who despaired of their future to take a long view and to carry the weight of *his* version of the nation's memory and history. At stake was the very integrity of his own story and that of Union victory. The animating center of a series of twelve resolutions against the Exodus that he prepared for a public gathering in Hillsdale, District of Columbia, in the summer of 1879 was his claim that mass migration now meant "the late rebellion will have triumphed . . . the rebel South will have been exalted."[46] So Douglass stood his ground, flailed away at bitter reality, and insisted that history, against the odds, stay on course. Those poor farmers caught up in migration fever, however, were not playing for history; they needed safety, their own land, an escape from the furnishing merchant, and hope.

Douglass was not merely "blind" and out of touch, as some biographers have contended.[47] He found himself in a position, a decade and a half after emancipation, not unlike many leaders of the modern civil rights movement. They have to fight to protect political and constitutional triumphs, as well as a new national historical memory, while they also face a deepening crisis of structural repression and inequality. Douglass's story, when he was heroically right as well as disappointingly wrong, was a rehearsal for the long haul of postemancipation and post–civil rights black and progressive leadership who have encountered foes as virulent as the Democratic Party's Southern Redeemers of the 1870s and much of the Republican Party in the late twentieth and early twenty-first centuries.

With a $6,000 loan in 1878 from a black friend and former abolitionist Robert Purvis, Douglass purchased Cedar Hill, a house on a fifteen-acre estate on the heights in Anacostia in the southeast part of the District of Columbia. He and Anna, and parts of the extended family, moved permanently to the estate in 1878. Some forty yards or so out behind the big house, beyond the lawn where friends and family played croquet, Douglass constructed his "growlery," a small single-room stone structure complete with a writing desk and a chaise longue. At times the desk may have been that of Charles Sumner, a keepsake the black leader had received upon the senator's death in 1874. He borrowed the name for his writer's retreat from Charles Dickens's *Bleak House*. In the novel, Mr. Jarndyce established such a "little library of books and papers" as the "refuge" in which he hid when "out of humor," the place "I come and growl." When besieged by his large extended family of adult children, growing numbers of grandchildren, siblings real and fictive, his increasingly sickly wife, and assorted others, Douglass escaped to his growlery.[48] Major parts of the first edition of *Life and Times*, published in 1881, were likely written there. His effort to order and control time in his final memoir masks the hidden pressures and dilemmas of his personal life. In that realm, about which he wrote so little, Douglass experienced plenty of pain and frustration about which to growl.

As 1880 arrived, Douglass's personal life at Cedar Hill remained a roiling hub of family joy, domestic comfort, and turmoil. The continuing financial and career struggles of his sons and his daughter, as they began to reach early middle age with growing families, is the subtext for Douglass's steadfast views on black self-reliance, migration, property, the work ethic, and other values. All around him at every turn he saw necessity, striving, failure, dependence, contradiction, and more than twenty grandchildren, whom he hoped would live into the next century in a modern, more en-

lightened America. The personal and the public were thoroughly intertwined in every day of the aging Douglass's life. In speeches, such as the
one he gave at a black agricultural exposition in Raleigh, North Carolina, in
October 1880, one hears echoes of his family's travails: the "greatest want"
of blacks is "regular and lucrative employments"; they should acquire property and save money. The "want of money," Douglass repeatedly declared
to black workers and farmers, "is the root of very many evils." It may seem
harsh to us today, but in this period of racial subjugation, he maintained
that blacks were despised more for their "poverty" than for their "color."[49]

New life constantly flowed in and out of the universe of Cedar Hill and
the Douglass clan, as Anna Murray Douglass became sometimes debilitated
by illness. Douglass reported to Amy Post in April 1879 that his financial
situation had nearly "touched bottom." He had "three families to support," including three of "Rosa's children . . . part of Charley's whose wife is
dead, and my old sick brother Perry and his daughter." Death began to visit
with regularity, sometimes in natural course and sometimes with shocking alarm. Charles, who was once again unemployed, with his two children,
Freddie and Joseph, eleven and nine years old, moved in with his brother
Frederick Jr. in November. The situation must have been tense and difficult;
Frederick Jr. reported in handwritten notes in the scrapbooks he assembled
that the two children "were taken away by their father" on January 3, 1881,
after Charles secured a job with the US Census Bureau. Moreover, on August 18, 1880, Douglass's half brother Perry Downs died at Cedar Hill at age
sixty-seven and was buried the following day in the Hillsdale cemetery.[50]
Many more funerals would soon be performed and planned from Cedar
Hill.

Into the early 1880s Ottilie Assing remained occasionally in Douglass's
life, and often in his correspondence. With keen desire she awaited her less
regular "orders," as she put it, to come to Washington for extended visits.
Some stays in Washington, she told her correspondents, were truncated or
burdened by the constant flow of cousins, grandchildren, and other "parasites" pursuing her beloved Douglass. She unabashedly complained that son
Charles was still "on the dole" in 1878 and that the family whirlwind around
Cedar Hill was "uncivilized." She never seems to have commented on the
sheer challenge of all the grandchildren for Anna, only for Assing's admired
male host. By the end of 1880, she reported a new tally of Eastern Shore kin
who had arrived at Cedar Hill, including another half sister named Kitty,
and her son and his wife, who were living in a cottage by the garden. And an
eight-year-old boy had just arrived, grandchild of another half sister; Ottilie

thought him a "bright boy" who could read and write and might, therefore, bring Douglass "some joy."[51]

Assing loved the expansive mansion house and the grounds of nearly fifteen acres. The house had been built in 1855–59 for an architect, John Welsh Van Hook. Douglass purchased the property with nine acres; over the next sixteen years he acquired six more adjoining acres and expanded the structure from fourteen to twenty-one rooms, adding a large new kitchen wing and remodeling the attic into new bedrooms. On her first visit in October 1878, Assing called it "one of the most beautiful places" in America, high "on top of a hill, with magnificent old trees." The view included the Capitol itself across the bridge over the Anacostia River. The grounds and stables included horses and cows, and Ottilie especially enjoyed sitting on the grass and playing with a calf. But she never wrote to her friend Sylvester Koehler about her time at Cedar Hill without swipes at the domestic situation. The grandchildren included at one point a "completely uncivilized" girl of six years, "so backward" that even "Mrs. Douglass" could not provide "educational influence." A one-year-old boy, she observed, was a "miserable, weakly child," about whom she thought it a "veritable crime" to have brought him into the world. Once again, Anna, as well as Rosetta, who was frequently in and out of the house with her own six children, somehow coexisted with Assing, if not with her attitudes. In an 1878 letter to Douglass, Ottilie left a revealing self-description: "I am so entirely unlike the majority of men that I cannot well consider myself at all a standard by which to measure the feelings and sensations of others. A queer and unfortunate mixture of earthly and unearthly matter!"[52] Did Douglass sigh with pain or laughter or both? He was losing patience.

By the late 1870s Assing sometimes grumbled about "not receiving my weekly allowance" (a letter from Douglass). He rarely visited her and her friends in Hoboken anymore, since that group had begun to disperse and she found her life there increasingly lonely and, as she wrote in late 1878, "quieter and more boring every year." Assing frequently referred to her Hoboken circle of friends with the German word *Bande*, which denotes close emotional, almost kinshiplike, ties. Her *Bande* had been dissolving and she was adrift.[53]

The relationship with Douglass was in its last stage as Ottilie quarreled mightily with her sister over their estate, fell into depressions, and once again, indecisively, planned a trip to Europe. In late summer 1878, Douglass expressed "apprehensions" about her potential visit, and apparently about their friendship itself, although we do not know precisely what he said. Some kind of "experiment" had been proposed, possibly about her staying away. "My *feelings* for you can never change," she wrote painfully, "but if all this, after all, is nothing to *you*, or if *you* anticipate for yourself more pain than pleasure, you know that you can shake me off whenever you please. Border State [Anna] is my smallest trouble. I think I have shown my diplomatic tact by getting along with her nearly twenty years without any serious trouble." Douglass and Assing were undergoing a slow, if affectionate, breakup. There would be further visits to Washington until Assing sailed for Germany for the final time in August 1881. From a subordinate position, Assing continued to judge and try to micromanage her friend's ideas, actions, and financial decisions. She forever insisted on her absolutist approach to the "monster" of religion, and on one remarkable evening in late 1880, the two of them paid a visit to the home of a famous agnostic, Robert Ingersoll. The two had enriched, if complicated, each other's life in countless ways, and Douglass did not give up easily on this long-term relationship rooted in intellectual power. She still bought him cigars, and he rejoiced that he could "yet write without spectacles." Her letter to him with the profoundly sad offer that he could "shake" her when he pleased, ended with Ottilie's sudden, mundane spouselike question "Are you sufficiently insured?" [54]

From as early as late 1878, Assing became aware that Douglass's huge family was not her only competition as the much-younger forty-year-old Helen Pitts entered Douglass's circle of friends. Born in Honeoye, New York, of parents with strong abolitionist and feminist backgrounds, well educated at Mount Holyoke College and a former teacher in freedmen's schools during the Civil War, Pitts first visited her uncle Hiram Pitts in Washington in the summer of 1878. Smart, outgoing, a lover of music, and adroit with her strong views on women's rights, Helen met the marshal and later got a job in his office. She also became involved with the journal *Alpha*, a publication of the Moral Education Society. [55]

Assing detested, as she was also threatened by, Helen Pitts. After meeting her and participating in conversations, Ottilie wrote to Douglass with a venomous pen. Discussing press coverage about the orator's reputation, she remarked, "I anticipated nothing better on the part of the Pitts set and those connected with them. Mrs. Pitts [Helen was not married] is a crafty plotting woman." Ottilie seemed convinced that Helen was trying to extract money for some scheme from Douglass and offered strong unsolicited advice. "The falling off in Mrs. Pitts' visits I should however consider a gain at any rate. There is a distressing lack of genuineness about her, which I imagine even to notice in her face." Assing's scorn utterly transparent, she spared Douglass none of her bitter emotions. She hated *Alpha*, calling it "infamous," and claiming that "no good and pure-minded woman can advocate those monstrous doctrines . . . [of] obscene stuff hidden under religious cant." The magazine promoted combinations of religious faith, feminism, and women's education and equal rights. Only someone, Assing held, who was "incurably and irredeemably stupid" could support such a journal.[56] Such early denunciations of Helen came as Anna, ignored by the absolutist Ottilie, was still very much alive. There was only one future Mrs. Douglass, and Ottilie Assing struggled hopelessly against the knowledge that it was not her.

Chapter 27

JOYS AND SORROWS AT CEDAR HILL

My joys have far exceeded my sorrows and my friends have brought me far more than my enemies have taken from me.

—FREDERICK DOUGLASS, 1881

The Douglasses were blessed with some twenty-one grandchildren, and at any given time many of them were either living at or visiting Cedar Hill. According to one of them, Fredericka Sprague Perry, the fifth of Rosetta's seven children, who wrote an extraordinary memoir about her grandfather in 1941, Frederick Douglass was "the best play fellow" a child could ever want. When at home, the patriarch daily observed "two distinct periods . . . his Work-time and his Play-time." When at work behind his "closed study door," remembered Fredericka, who was born in 1872, the children knew that their grandfather would be "greatly displeased by our noise." They would "tip-toe down the hall" in anticipation. When the door "swung back on its hinges, we knew we were in for fun!"[1]

Douglass stood with his legs braced apart, his large stout frame ready for the onslaught. Taking the smallest child up on his shoulder, and with several others hanging on to arms, legs, and coattail, he would, "singing and shouting, march down the hall" toward the kitchen, where Grandma Anna stood amused and distressed, "supervising preparation for the evening meal." In this idealized domestic remembrance, perfected by time, the grandpa in his sixties would often go to all fours and play horse. As the children clamored on his broad back, Fredericka recalled that the "prize seat was nearest the head—nearly on his neck so that his long hair might serve as reins and away we would gallop." The girls especially loved to run their hands in Douglass's ample head of hair ("thick but not kinky"), and he loved having the oldest among them comb and braid it. In quiet evening moments, the grand old man with "closed eyes" would sit an hour at a time as two girls brushed and tied the "silvery locks" into "tight braids . . . independently stiff" and touched off on the ends with "various colored ribbons." Douglass loved having his hair so treated, as it left him in a "peaceful countenance." No one but the family ever saw this image, which occasioned much-needed laughter and shared bliss for Frederick and Anna. One time, Fredericka reported, this reverie was interrupted by the doorbell and an important formal visitor. Douglass rushed to his bedroom, Anna and Rosetta in tow, to "restore the head to its normal style of hair dress" to greet the guest, as giggly girls scampered to other corners of the house.[2]

Douglass's favorite outdoor game was croquet; the backyard of the A Street house, and especially the more spacious grounds at Cedar Hill, saw many such family competitions for young and old. Ottilie Assing wrote of playing croquet with a group of Douglasses in the hilltop space between the house and the growlery in summer weather. Once it was playtime, the children enjoyed "carefree, unrestrained freedom" around their grandfather, Fredericka reported. The extended family caused his financial burdens and numerous adult conflicts, but Douglass loved to entertain the children and let himself go. In the ceiling of the front porch of Cedar Hill, Douglass attached two "rubber-covered spring rods," about twenty inches long. Each had a ring, and the adventurous could elevate and hang or do chin-ups from the handles. With his large body swinging in air, Douglass would dangle from these rings, the young children dancing and squealing at his feet as he kicked and shoved them about. This is hardly the textbook image of the noble, serious Douglass we have from his photographs, but the large, burly man pulling himself up and down, with "flying feet," is how Fredericka and her mates could remember him. They adored their "big playmate," their "mischievous tease," and their "idolized teacher," who, Fredericka claimed, instructed them about the "beauty of generosity." What child would not thrill to have her grandfather transform into a human tree, "stand perfectly erect, feet in bracing position, shoulders squared . . . and arms extended straight out even with the shoulders," bidding each child to clasp one of his arms and "swing her body from the ground." The "grandpa . . . full of life and energy" wrested a coveted joy from this endless swarm of love and ado-

Cedar Hill, c. 1891. Douglass is standing at left, and likely his wife,
Helen Pitts Douglass, with her sister Jennie at right on the porch.

ration.[3] It must have left all concerned with memories of Anna smiling and laughing, although no one ever wrote about her quite that way. Joy and sorrow lived together at Cedar Hill.

In the presidential election of 1880, Douglass campaigned for candidate James A. Garfield wherever Republicans allowed him to go. In this first post-Reconstruction presidential contest, Douglass's voice and symbolic service were less important to his party than in the Grant and Hayes administrations. For a while the old abolitionist's star faded, eclipsed to a degree by the sheer sordidness and fury of Gilded Age politics, in which he was a practicing insider, and by a new generation of black leaders eager to shove the "Grand Old Man" from his pedestal. In February of that year Douglass's reputation suffered as he endured two days of testifying in the Capitol before Congress's Select Committee to Investigate the Freedmen's Savings and Trust Company. In the hearings he told the story of the demise of the bank on his watch six years earlier, and of his $10,000 investment, which he did recoup. He admitted under oath that he "knew nothing about banking; my life had been a theoretical one rather than a practical one—on the stump— and I hesitated about it until I was persuaded that as the colored people of the country generally had confidence in me." In this public testimony, Douglass halfheartedly took responsibility, but laid greater blame for the bank's failure on other managers who made sure that he as president had been "kept ignorant" of the institution's real condition until it was too late. It was not Douglass's finest hour; he was treated fairly, since his good friend Senator Blanche Bruce chaired the committee.[4]

Garfield, the former Civil War general, nine-term congressman from Ohio, and Hayes loyalist with whom Douglass enjoyed only a distant and formal relationship, was the unlikely dark-horse standard-bearer of the Republicans in the raucous election of 1880. Deep fissures ran through American party politics that year. The Democrats controlled a relatively solid South and staked their future nationally on white supremacy. Republicans were divided into two broad ideological camps, both of which devoted decreasing attention to black rights. The Stalwart faction, led by Senator Roscoe Conkling, the extraordinarily corrupt and arrogant boss politician of New York City, originally took its name from staunch opposition to Hayes's "let alone" policy toward the South during Reconstruction. By 1880, however, this class of elected officeholders managed a vast patronage system, especially fee-based federal and state bureaucracies, that opposed civil service reform and fought to sustain the spoils system of appointments for the party faithful. Stalwarts still gave lip service to support of freedmen's rights but offered little in the way of action.

The second bloc among Republicans, known as the Half-Breeds, emerged around James G. Blaine, the senator from Maine. Blaine, a tall, natural politician, champion debater, and personal rival of Garfield's since the two entered Congress in 1863, had led occasional opposition to Grant from within the Republican Party, especially in response to the scandals of the general's second term. *Half-Breed* was at first an epithet against this group, but as Grant-era corruption tainted the party at the end of Reconstruction, the term became a positive moniker. Half-Breeds tended to be more open to civil service reform and, generally, more fiscally conservative.[5]

Some vestiges of the Civil War–era Republican "party of Lincoln" still limped along, alive but crippled. The center of gravity in American politics had shifted decidedly to the Midwest, although it did not contain the nation's primary centers of patronage and wealth. The Republican Party had now largely become a vessel of big business, of corporate enterprise, of sound money backed by specie, and antilabor, especially since the violent nationwide Great Railroad Strike of 1877, when Hayes had used the US army to crush union militants. Many conservative moral and social reform organizations of the era also drew thousands of adherents. The Christian lobby and groups such as the Women's Christian Temperance Union worked for laws against polygamy, obscenity, and alcohol. Intellectual liberal reformers, led by William Dean Howells, worried endlessly about what they deemed "dangerous tendencies in American life," such as hostility to property, the "excesses" of universal suffrage, the masses of immigrants gaining access to the printing press and the ballot. Older Protestant, educated elites feared Eastern European immigrants, labor unions and anti-monopolism, lawless mobs, and socialism. Some third parties emerged as well, particularly the Greenback Party, made up of workers, farmers, and some socialists who advocated the paper money printed so successfully during the Civil War. The Greenback insurgency was a threat to Republicans in some localities, but in 1880 it garnered just over three hundred thousand votes.[6] The abolitionists' heyday of holy crusades against the evil of slavery were long gone.

In such a rapidly shifting social landscape, the divided Republicans met for their nominating convention in Chicago in June. Feeling less welcome, Douglass, still marshal in the District of Columbia, did not attend. Although he tilted to and fro on some issues, Douglass remained a Stalwart and supported a third run by Grant. Indeed, he later admitted that "Mr. Garfield, though a good man, was not my man for the presidency . . . even defeat with Grant was better than success with a temporizer." In pre-campaign speeches Douglass had firmly stated his disappointment with Hayes's Southern policy, creating distance from his benefactor. Another candidacy at the convention, seen as an alternative, was that of John Sherman, another Ohioan and secretary of the treasury under Hayes, and brother of the famous general William T. Sherman. James Garfield, the bookish, studious reader of economics and spreadsheets, former soldier and Ohio farm boy turned intellectual as well as experienced congressional-committee chairman, openly supported Sherman and claimed not to be interested in the presidency. But a less than secret campaign elevated him to the top of the ticket as a way out of the morass in which the party found itself. The deadlocked convention broke open on the thirty-sixth ballot of a tempestuous gathering of eight hundred delegates and fifteen thousand spectators and nominated Garfield for president. As his running mate, and as a sop to Conkling and the patronage-drunk Stalwarts, Garfield chose Chester A. Arthur, a handsome man-about-town New Yorker who had never held elective office but had occupied the lucrative position of collector of the Port of New York.[7]

For their part Democrats nominated a more famous Civil War general,

Winfield Scott Hancock, the Pennsylvanian who had held the center of the Union line at the battle of Gettysburg. Hancock had no political record to defend, rarely appeared in any capacity in civilian life, and held a quiet army administrative post on Governors Island in New York harbor. He did not cut a dashing military figure anymore; since the war a sedentary life had made him a rotund and relatively immobile three hundred pounds. Hancock was willing to don the mantles of both white supremacy and re-form while the Democrats ran a scurrilously negative campaign against the alleged corruption of Garfield's and Conkling's minions. Neither side had a corner on hypocrisy or mischief in this election, and both proved why American politics in the Gilded Age was such rich terrain for satirists. In Henry Adams's novel *Democracy*, anonymously published in 1880, the am-bitious widow Madeleine Lightfoot Lee marvels at the corruption she ob-serves in Washington. "What deeper abyss could have opened under the nation's feet," she wonders, as she asks the most powerful man in the Senate his view. "The pleasure of politics lay in the possession of power," answers Silas Ratcliffe. "Here I am and here I mean to stay."[8]

Much was at stake nevertheless in an election that turned out 9 mil-lion voters and which Garfield only narrowly won by a plurality of fewer than ten thousand votes. That the Republicans nearly lost to such a weak and uninspiring Democrat demonstrates how vulnerable they were in 1880. Garfield ran a vague campaign; he favored such good generalities as free and unintimidated voting rights, civil service reform by Congress, popular education, high tariffs, and improved navigation on the Mississippi River, while opposing the doctrine of state sovereignty, sectarian (meaning Cath-olic) schools, "doubtful financial experiments" such as greenbacks, and any increase in Chinese immigration. Garfield steered clear of labor rights, a proposed graduated income tax, or any regulation of large corporations. Douglass joined the canvass as a proudly loyal party man, especially in up-state New York and on one long speaking excursion to Indiana. Undoubt-edly, the orator hoped for a second federal appointment out of the new Republican president; despite lacking passion for the nominee of the party, he knew where the interests of African Americans lay. He had no problem with Republican antilabor positions; he too opposed unions, especially if segregated, and he enjoyed stressing that Garfield was a genuine self-made man.[9] Given the bold-faced white supremacy of the Democrats, Douglass still saw the Republicans as his only political home.

Campaign rhetoric elicited from Douglass a storehouse of wit and sar-casm. He enjoyed few things more in his older years than strapping the

Democratic Party to a metaphorical stake and lashing it with an old anti-slavery whip. He was a master of the bloody shirt and the perfect partisan on the stump. As historian Sean Wilentz has argued, Americans have for more than two centuries distrusted political parties and, in a dreamlike, ahistorical fashion, wished for a politics above partisanship. Not Douglass. By experience—from learning through the crises of the Civil War to filter his radicalism through a hard-earned pragmatism, to seeing emancipation and Radical Reconstruction emerge from a party's aggressive action—Douglass understood that great historical change came when a party decided to step out amid the currents of history and lead. Although it always required some compromise of personal moral belief, there was no more loyal party man in 1880 than the Republican Douglass; if only he could now persuade his party to stand up to the resurgent white South and not treat it with, as he feared, a "sickly conciliation."[10]

In Elmira, New York, on August 3, 1880, at a West Indian Emancipation Day celebration, Douglass delivered a typical campaign address. The large outdoor audience in Hoffman's Grove included hundreds of blacks. The orator spoke for two hours from a prepared manuscript, a formality he employed more and more in his older years. He reminded the audience that at this hour the "fourteenth and fifteenth amendments . . . are practically of no force or effect" in the South. The canvass, he maintained, was not about personalities; it was about the "merits of parties." Trust the Republican Party and its history, he especially urged the black voters, whatever they thought of the candidates. He did honor Garfield as a man of intellect, "devoted to art and science." Douglass made distinctions between the soldier Hancock, who was the product of West Point, and Garfield, who was a patriotic volunteer during the war. Douglass spoke of history—of the war—as a past his listeners must summon. Democrats were the party, said Douglass, of slavery, secession, treason, and rebellion. Their history was "hoary with years and gory with crime." They had dragged the nation through war and opposed the abolition of slavery and the enfranchisement of the freedmen in peace. With his black audience he drew upon biblical sanction: "The sins of the fathers descend to the children even unto the third and fourth generation." And lest they entertain any doubts, Douglass declared that each black voter must remember his sacred obligation laid down in his version of Psalm 137: "May my hand forget its cunning and my tongue cleave to the roof of my mouth if ever I raise my voice or give my vote for the nominees of the Democratic party."[11]

In September and October, Douglass barnstormed across upstate New York and especially in Indiana, which proved in one election after another to be a crucial swing state for the Republicans. At every stop he presented the election as "the same old question of the war." It was "national supremacy against state supremacy," the "civilization of the South or the civilization of the North." He recycled his old mythos about the "free spirit" and principles that had built the Republican Party arriving on the *Mayflower* in New England, while a "cargo of twenty slaves" with the "bull-whip, the chain, the fetters" of the South had arrived on the James River in Virginia. Douglass was brilliant at the politics of memory.[12]

In some cities in Indiana, such as at the fairgrounds in Indianapolis, he would deliver as many as three outdoor speeches in one day. On September 5, another crowd of four thousand had to be turned away since Douglass had lost his voice. Two days later, he mustered voice enough to speak to three thousand in Pendleton, Indiana, on the very site where he had been mobbed and injured in 1843; some attendees in 1880 had been there thirty-seven years earlier. The press reported Douglass taking breaks in the middle of addresses and speaking in a "calm, deliberate manner." To a Kokomo audience he told of a Quaker woman named Miss Minnie Trueblood who had helped save him from the anti-abolition mob of yesteryear. At many other stops, Douglass waved the bloody shirt on behalf of the party as much as for Garfield.[13] He was greeted as an iconic celebrity from the abolitionist past appearing like a risen spirit in the present.

"Mr. Douglass arose . . . and at the sight of his old gray head," said the *Madison Daily Evening Star*, "the cheer that went up nearly lifted the crowd off its feet. It was like the roar of the hurricane through the pines, like the rushing of the mighty waters." Douglass thrived on the cheers and soaked in the roar. But his voice had mostly failed again and he announced awkwardly that he could not speak in the open. So the old lion said he would adjourn to the courthouse and address as many of the throng there as could occupy the space. "He placed his fingers to his mouth and blew a loud shrill whistle which stopped and startled the crowd," a reporter wrote. Then Douglass led the procession to the indoor venue. He was so prominent in the Indiana campaign that his image, with flying white hair, appeared up front in a September 29 cartoon in *Puck*, showing an almost infinite array of people, from politicians to farm wives with babes in their arms, all standing on stumps over the caption "Great Political Excitement in Indiana: The Whole State on the Stump."[14]

"Great Political Excitement in Indiana," Puck, September 29, 1880. Douglass especially campaigned for the Republican presidential candidate each election year in Indiana.

As an autobiographer, Douglass dwelt at length on Garfield's inauguration in March 1881, on his shocking assassination later that summer by the deranged Stalwart Republican office seeker Charles Guiteau, and especially on Douglass's own place in these dramas. As marshal, Douglass had the privilege of marching next to the outgoing and incoming presidents, ushering their procession from the Senate chamber through the Capitol rotunda to the back portico for the swearing in and inaugural address. He placed himself, and thereby black people, at the center of this presidential story. On the "day of glory" (inauguration), Douglass stressed that he, in his symbolic role, "was treading the high places of the land," and because of him, "the colored man could occupy this height" as well. As before, he reminded his readers that here was Fred Bailey, the "unlettered slave," escorting presidents through the US Capitol.[15] These images are almost that of the butler performing his careful duties at the ceremonies of the highborn and the powerful. But he never stopped playing the representative man, which he considered a duty.

Although always wishing to be the creature of his own heroic making, he admitted that he, "like many others," had been "tossed by the late war to the surface." When he turned to the assassin and the issue of patronage at the root of the tragic crime, Douglass left a trenchant, if ironic, characterization of Gilded Age office seeking. Much of the pomp and enthusiasm at a presidential inauguration, he argued, was both false and purposeful: "To the office-seeker the whole is gone through with as a mere hollow, dumb show. It is not uncommon to hear men boast of how much they did for the victorious party. . . . The madness of Guiteau was but the exaggerated madness of other men." [16] Douglass lived in the midst of this world of glad hands, gleaming smiles, and scheming eyes in pursuit of money and place. And he understood what happened when the cheering stopped.

Garfield's brief presidency turned into a macabre spectacle; Douglass could not let it go without a prolonged reminiscence of his meeting with the president only three weeks before the shooting, when they discussed the chief executive's desire to appoint some black men to foreign-service posts. Most important, Douglass made the best of what was for him a demotion from marshal to the recorder of deeds for the District. All those speeches, the backbreaking travel, the sore throats in Indiana, had resulted in what Douglass lamely claimed was a position less onerous, with no social obligations, and more time for writing and speaking. Douglass had likely allowed himself to hope for something much higher, perhaps a cabinet post. No less than Mark Twain had written to Garfield on Douglass's behalf suggesting such a position. The famed writer had been moved, he said, by the former slave's "history." [17] But the recorder swallowed the insult, rejoiced that no black man had ever held this office either, and did his duty. As ever, with the extended family pressing down on his resources, he needed the money, and he did have writing to do.

In the summer of 1881, during the drama of the assassination of Garfield and the president's prolonged and highly publicized deathbed watch, Douglass finished and published his *Life and Times*. Sometime in 1879 or 1880 he had begun work on this third, long autobiography. The book garnered considerable publicity and fanfare even as its sales were disappointing. Ottilie Assing had offered occasional advice as he planned to write about his life from where *Bondage and Freedom* had left off in the 1850s. She reminded him of the great men and events in his epic life, urging him to reach for literary fame one more time by writing the "sequel" of his life's story. [18]

For Douglass, the return to telling his narrative a third time was as renewing as it was risky and difficult. *Life and Times* would be an aging man's summing up of his tale, a journey into and out of his memory. That constant quest in writing to grasp and explain his personal past may tell us much about why Douglass clung so fiercely to his views on black self-reliance, on faith in voting and political solutions, and on forging an abolitionist memory of the Civil War epoch. The memory was both retrievable and not; it was bracing, startling, and had to somehow be harnessed in the service of a narrative about increasing fame and achievement. This search for himself again in the storybook of his life was never as easy to achieve as he wished. In *Life and Times* he ceases his description of experience at one point and reflects, "When one has advanced far in the journey of life . . . and has had many and strange experiences of shadow and sunshine, when long distances of time and space have come between him and his point of departure, it is natural that his thoughts should return to the place of his beginning . . . to revisit scenes of his early recollection, and live over in memory the incidents of his childhood." It was as though he hoped that telling his story once again, and constantly revising it, might bring symmetry to his life in the present.[19] But great change would soon once again sweep over Douglass's affairs, public and private; during his remaining fourteen years he robustly lived looking ahead in real time, while he also lived, as a writer, inside the inscrutable, if magical, power of memory.

Life and Times, both the first and the revised and updated edition of 1892, has always been at least two remarkable, if confounding, things: first, an indispensable source for at least the last forty years of Douglass's life; and second, a repeatedly revised, sometimes exhilarating, and sometimes torpid memoir about the accomplishments of a Gilded Age gentleman who conquered some if not all racial boundaries, and who rose from radical outsider to insecure insider. On most of the 620 pages Douglass sought a unity for the theory of the American self-made man. He hoped to make his own life a kind of monument, an edifice so strong that no surge of racism, no embittered rivalry, no lynch mob, no conservative Supreme Court decision, no Lost Cause romance, nor even the ravages of time could tear down. *Life and Times* is memoir as a living museum designed to repudiate the unpredictable fates of America's racial history. Whatever might occur in the future, whatever forms white supremacy might take, Douglass wanted to be sitting there for us to gaze at, his story there as bold refutation.

Douglass believed that the United States had undergone apocalyptic regeneration in the Civil War; so too, as the autobiographer kept trying to demonstrate, had he. Hence, almost by definition, after the revolution and the constitutional remaking of the nation, Douglass could not sustain a revolutionary voice. The quest for freedom had inspired a heroic literary style; the achievement of freedom flattened out the story's trajectory, even the prose. In the self-made hero's autobiographical life, the story of becoming free had always been more dramatic than being free. Or, as the critic Darryl Pinckney put it in assessing black autobiography generally, "hell has more and better details."[20]

On the next-to-last page of the 1881 edition of *Life and Times*, Douglass announced that he had "lived several lives in one: first the life of slavery; secondly, the life of a fugitive from slavery; thirdly, the life of comparative freedom; fourthly, the life of conflict and battle; and fifthly, the life of victory, if not complete, at least assured."[21] He had suffered and overcome, he instructs his reader. He had persevered through hopelessness, led his people through the fiery trial, and reached a personal triumph. His story was no longer merely the ascension from slavery to freedom, but elevation to citizenship, to self-worth. In Douglass's five stages for his life, we see his self-image as the lost fugitive risen to racial and national leader, the person and the nation regenerated and redeemed together. These passages are revealing of both the public persona he so wished to portray, the famous man looking at himself as he let others see him, and the private man who believed desperately that he had to live out and embody the image he had created.

To some of his readers at the time, and certainly to some critics today, this tale about the "fruits of victory" can seem strange and out of place. But *Life and Times* fit into as it led the genre of black autobiography during the Gilded Age. William Wells Brown, John Mercer Langston, and many others wrote of their lives in a similar "up from slavery" mode. In varying ways, they all contributed, wittingly or not, to the Horatio Alger mythology of their time. They were and had to be success stories wrested from the depths of obscurity and repression. Langston even gave his autobiography the subtitle *Self-Reliance, the Secret of Success.* This age of Progress required a writer with Douglass's story to be a kind of missionary for success, and therefore to distance himself from his roots and from the Southern black folk around whom he found a beginning.[22] In this sense, Douglass built his own monument.

But the story he fashioned in his writing spaces at Cedar Hill was a highly revised version of the one he had given the world in *Bondage and Freedom* a quarter century earlier. The great indictment of slavery and the abolitionist manifesto of *Bondage* got softened in *Life and Times*. He tempered his words now, trying to put a positive face on his slave experience when possible. He changed some chapter titles and subheadings as he line-edited himself. "A Chapter of Horrors" in *Bondage* became "Characteristics of Overseers" in *Life and Times.* He significantly softened his portrayal of Thomas Auld. In another instance, he changed "oppressors and tyrants" to "our masters." Moreover, he erased the voices of some other slaves in *Life and Times*, thus reducing access to the interior psychology of slave life, which was one brilliant feature of the first two autobiographies. And he wrote unflatteringly about the habits of the freedpeople. Perhaps Douglass was in his own way, as some critics have suggested, using his autobiography to serve the cause of official national reconciliation and progress after the Civil War. He still mustered an old millennial rhetoric in some of his speeches about memory, refuting the ideology of the Lost Cause at every turn; but as Zoe Trodd has argued, Douglass's voice in *Life and Times* often sounds like that of "the complacent grandfather . . . of his earlier self." [23]

The richly political text of 1855 survived to a degree in the 1881 book, until he wrote about the postwar years, which became more a catalog of episodes with Douglass ascending the stairway of national affairs. He praised his allies and comrades and tried to settle some scores with his critics. But he really searched for coherence, both with small revisions of prose and with his big themes. At the beginning of the second part's chapter 15, "Weighed in the Balance," he spoke with remarkable confidence: "Whatever of good or ill the future may have in store for me . . . I am impressed with a sense of completeness—a sort of rounding up of the arch to the point where the keystone may be inserted, the scaffolding removed, and the work, with all its imperfections and faults, left to speak for itself." Age, fame, and circumstance had mellowed him. But it is stunning that Douglass, in a life full of such turmoil and fateful turns that might have left him discredited, exiled, or dead, could also write in the last chapter in 1881, "My day has been a pleasant one. My joys have far exceeded my sorrows and my friends have brought me far more than my enemies have taken from me." [24] He left such passages from 1881 in the 1892 edition, despite experiences that contradicted these sentiments. He needed the symmetry and completeness more than he needed bitter truths.

In at least two further ways Douglass made the third telling of his life very different from the first two—the intriguing choices of illustrations, and the selection of George L. Ruffin to introduce the book. In 1881 he included eighteen pictures, seven of which depicted his life as a slave or as a runaway slave. Six others are either portraits of himself (the frontispiece) or the famous abolitionists and statesmen he had known. The remainder include an image of his house at Cedar Hill, his role as marshal at the inauguration of Garfield, his visit back to the Wye plantation on the Eastern Shore, a group image of the commissioners to Santo Domingo, and a single illustration of him fighting a mob in Indiana as an abolitionist. But for the 1892 edition Douglass reduced the number of images to eleven, and six of the seven deletions are representations of his slave experience. The only one that survived is "The Last Time He Saw His Mother."[25] The illustrations in the later edition thus, like some of the writing, deemphasized slavery in favor of the ascendant great man.

The choice of George Ruffin to introduce his new book may seem puzzling to us today, but clearly it was not to Douglass. Ruffin had been born free in Richmond, Virginia, in 1834 and moved north to Boston. He was active in abolitionism and the recruiting of black soldiers during the war; as a Gilded Age man of merit he became a prominent pillar of black Boston society. He was a "first" of several kinds, which no doubt Douglass found intriguing—first African American to graduate from Harvard Law School (in 1869), to serve in the Massachusetts state legislature (1869–71), to serve on the Boston City Council (1876–78), and to be appointed a district judge (1884). He even unsuccessfully ran for attorney general in Massachusetts. Here was a symbol of social rectitude, racial progress, and, indeed, like James McCune Smith, who had introduced *Bondage*, the high education Douglass never enjoyed. An exchange of letters between the two men in May and June 1881 demonstrates that the author courted the civil servant. Ruffin at first demurred and worried that he could never match the brilliance of McCune Smith's effort in 1855, that he was "disposed to shrink" from the honor, but that he would assume the "duty" for its "historical sense."[26]

In Ruffin's introduction, it was as though he read Douglass's "Self-Made Men" speech with great care and distinctly avoided McCune Smith's lyrical 1855 essay on the author's meaning to the slavery crisis. Ruffin gave the reader the black Horatio Alger with no hyperbole spared. Douglass was a "sui generis" historical figure, and an American original that could never be matched. He had risen from ignorance and slavery through "toil and industry" to the status of "cultivated gentleman." Douglass belonged on a pedestal, said Ruffin, the gentlemen's club president in Boston, and Douglass had a "halo of peace about him." Following Douglass's lead, Ruffin declared the victory won, the "culmination of his life . . . the object . . . Emancipation . . . accomplished." Douglass now deserved "serenity" and "repose." Here was the psychic order Douglass had claimed for himself. In Ruffin's portrayal, the hero need only stand and take applause. But Ruffin could not stop there. Ruffin even bizarrely provided some old plantation-days imagery for white readers conditioned by the stock popular literature about the Old South and the patriarchal peculiar institution. Colonel Lloyd's plantation was the scene of "the great house and the cabins, the old Aunties, and patriarchal Uncles, little picanninies and picanninies not so little, of every shade and complexion, from ebony black to whiteness of the master race; mules, overseers, and broken down fences. . . . Here was slave breeding and slave-selling, whipping, torturing, and beating to death." [27] We do not know whether Douglass smiled or cringed when he read the draft of the introduction. But he chose to include it in both editions.

Nothing in *Life and Times* may have led Ruffin to his sentimental vision of Douglass's rise in social status quite like the author's descriptions of his third return to the Eastern Shore in June 1881. Douglass had long sought a chance to return to the Wye plantation, still owned by the Lloyds, and on June 12–13 he seized an opportunity. He went at the invitation of fellow Republican and friend John L. Thomas, the customs collector at the port of Baltimore. On the US revenue cutter *Guthrie*, they took a four-hour cruise down the Chesapeake and anchored in the Wye River, just off the Lloyd estate, where Douglass reported that he could see for the first time since 1825 "the stately chimneys of the grand old mansion." [28]

Colonel Edward Lloyd V, the master of the Wye plantation, former governor of Maryland, whom Douglass had known as a child, was long gone. The estate was now run by Edward Lloyd VII, who had been alerted that the former slave intended to visit. The Lloyds had long been steeped in proslavery and then postwar Democratic politics, but were also adept at aristocratic manners. Lloyd had hosted Jefferson Davis in 1867, shortly after the Confederate president had been released from prison in Virginia, and two famous Confederate officers, Admiral Franklin Buchanan and General Charles S. Winder, were buried in the Wye graveyard. Each of them had married a Lloyd daughter. To this bastion of the Old South, Douglass in effect invited himself. When a note was sent ashore to announce the *Guthrie*'s arrival, the senior Lloyd was conveniently gone to Easton on business; his sons, eighteen-year-old Howard and eight-year-old DeCourcy, met the visitors and escorted them on an extraordinary and, for Douglass, nostalgic tour of the "Great House Farm." Gone now in Douglass's observations was what he had described in 1845 as the place of "atrocities which would make your blood to boil." Wye plantation was no longer the place of totalizing fear where Colonel Lloyd would make every slave "stand, listen, and tremble," and tell old Barney, who ran the stable, to kneel on the ground and bare his back to the savage whips of Lloyd's three sons.[29]

Instead, Douglass took a stroll into memory and was "deeply moved." Curiously, he claimed to recall the "form and features" of the Colonel Lloyd he had known fifty-six years earlier, and he admiringly saw the same "aristocratic descent" in the faces of the two great-grandsons conducting his tour. A careful reader of *Life and Times* might fairly wonder if Douglass was not declaring his own lineage in and returning home to this family of aristocrats. He was agreeably surprised by how little had changed around the place. Almost nothing seemed "missing except the squads of little black children which were once seen in all directions, and the great number of slaves in its fields." Most of the old buildings were still there for him to remember. Aaron Anthony's house still stood with the window beneath which he used to sing for Miss Lucretia when hungry. Passages from his autobiographies floated in his head as he saw the old shoemaker's and blacksmith's shops, or the ground outside Aunt Katy's kitchen, "where I last saw my mother." Lyrically, he looked into the "old barn . . . a place of wonderful interest to me in my childhood, for there I often repaired to listen to the chatter and watch the flight of the swallows among its lofty beams." Douglass replaced the pain and loneliness of boyhood trauma now with poetry. The famous man dissolved the choked agony of a slave boy with beautiful, detailed reminiscence: "Time had wrought some changes in the trees and foliage. The Lombardy poplars, in the branches of which the redwinged blackbirds used to congregate and sing, and whose music awakened in my young heart sensations and aspirations deep and undefinable, were gone; but the oaks and elms, where young Daniel . . . used to divide with me his cakes and biscuits, were there as . . . beautiful as ever."[30]

Young Howard Lloyd and his little brother may have been in awe of Douglass, a reversal the elder statesman may have relished. While strolling through the family burial ground, a place of "unusual solemnity," Howard "gathered for me," said Douglass, "a bouquet of flowers and evergreens . . . which I carefully brought to my home for preservation." After walking through the still-magnificent Wye garden, Douglass and his small party were invited onto the veranda and then into the dining room of the great house. Sipping wine and sitting in wickers on the veranda, "hedged . . . and adorned with fruit trees and flowers of almost every variety," Douglass was moved to write a very personal description of the scene that was at once about memory, nature, and power: "A more tranquil and tranquilizing scene I have seldom met in this or any other country." [31]

This tranquilized state of memory was in part what Douglass sought in his richly symbolic returns to the Eastern Shore. He still harbored vestiges of that old rage that needed expending; and mysteries yet floated in his psyche about how Fred Bailey became Frederick Douglass. He craved the Lloyds' recognition and respect; in his estimation, at least, he got it. On his walk back to the boat, a group of black workers on the plantation gathered around. Many were the children of people Douglass had known as a boy, and he called out some of the names of "old servants." The author had almost never used the word *servant* for *slave* in earlier writings. He spent a little time with these people and then bade them all farewell, with special thanks to the young Lloyds. [32]

The honor Douglass came to seize that day could only be extended by white people named Lloyd. His steamer next took him to the Miles River estate called the Rest, where he paid a cordial and welcomed visit to Mrs. Franklin Buchanan, the former Ann Catherine Lloyd, one of the surviving daughters of Colonel Lloyd. Proudly, Douglass reported how Mrs. Buchanan invited him to sit close by her side, introducing her grandchildren. She treated him as though he "was an old acquaintance and occupied an equal station with the most aristocratic of the Caucasion race." Again, he observed "the features of her father" in her visage. After an hour's conversation, a little granddaughter presented Douglass another bouquet of June flowers, which the autobiographer soon converted into an awkward declaration of a "new dispensation of justice, kindness, and human brotherhood" between North and South. Douglass knew better, but these reunions and nostalgic visits to his past caused in him gushes of personal reconciliation that he could feel better than explain. Oddly, he went so far as to state that his pleasant time at the Wye and the Rest showed that the "war and the slavery that caused the war were things of the past." [33]

On many public platforms in these years, however, Douglass argued exactly the opposite. Indeed, he had done so only two weeks before his visit to the Wye plantation in a remarkable Memorial Day address on John Brown at Harpers Ferry. In that speech, as elsewhere, he laid down a detailed historical and mythic image of Brown and of the Harpers Ferry raid, as "not a story to please but to pain." Brown was a martyr and a victor, but also a classically tragic hero never to be forgotten, a symbol always to trouble and spur the American conscience. Douglass used Brown as a call to action in the memory war with the South's Lost Cause ideology and with the nation's susceptibility to a sectional reconciliation based on white supremacy. "When John Brown stretched forth his arm the sky was cleared," Douglass had declared on May 30, 1881. "The time for compromise was gone—the armed hosts of freedom stood face to face over the chasm of a broken Union—and the clash of arms was at hand. The South ... drew the sword of rebellion and thus made her own, and not Brown's, the lost cause of the century."[34] It remained to be seen just who would win this struggle over memory. So powerful, though, was his own story—at least to him— that Douglass seemed to wish against all odds and reality that personal memory might yet defeat the political hold of the past on American society. Douglass took his Eastern Shore flowers from the Lloyds back to Cedar Hill, where they would be no use in fighting the battles that lay ahead.

Douglass's conspicuous fame drew enemies and critics at every turn in the 1880s. Upon his return to Washington from the Eastern Shore, he soon found himself embroiled in another press controversy, this time about his alleged practice of nepotism in hiring for the Recorder of Deeds Office. Washington, DC, had several black newspapers by the 1880s, at least one of which operated as a scandal sheet. In June and July 1881, the *New South*'s editor complained that Garfield had made only two appointments of blacks to federal offices, and "one is the veteran placehunter, the indefatigable and obsequious Fred. Douglass." The other was former senator Blanche K. Bruce. Some black leaders (implying Douglass), argued the *New South*, were too ready "to forgive betrayal and ingratitude." Worse, the paper blasted the recorder for hiring in his office his two sons Charles and Lewis, his daughter Rosetta ("Miss Sprigg"), another young black woman from New York named Miss Blanche Washington, the niece of Charles Purvis of Philadelphia, and a man named Campbell "from the West Indies" who was not a citizen. The *New South* tallied "four Douglasses, two female non-residents, and a foreigner, all ... in one month. Fred Jr. is downstairs in the marshal's office—making five of a family in one building. Great God!"[35]

Another paper, the *People's Advocate*, defended Douglass and his brood, claiming that only two of the employees were on fixed salaries, Lewis and a Mr. Schayer, and the rest were paid according to how much work each did. Charles had been dismissed from the Census Office, losing yet another post. According even to the *People's Advocate*, Charles was "temporary" in the Recorder's Office, but he really needed a job. "Members of Mr. Douglass's family," declared the journal in a lame defense of nepotism, "have families of their own to support." This paper at least tried to shield the Douglass family, and especially the patriarch himself, from attacks. "Frederick Douglass is our most illustrious American Negro," it announced on July 25. "He stands preeminently our foremost man, towering above all others . . . his character as fixed as the Alleghenies or the Rocky Mountains. Of better educated men we have scores. Of men more cultured, more harmonious . . . in their proportions, there may have been . . . but there has been, and there can be but ONE Frederick Douglass."[36] Many other black men, especially of two generations, would dispute that claim the rest of Douglass's life.

By any measure, the charge of nepotism was amply true. Douglass's *Account Book* for 1881–83, a daily tabulation of all receipts and payments to the recorder's staff, verifies that during virtually every week of this two-year period, all the names mentioned in the press, and especially the names of "Charley" or "Chs. Douglass," "Lewis Douglass," "Fredk. Douglass, Jr.," "Mrs. Sprague" (Rosetta), and by 1882 "Miss Pitts" (Helen), appear on the payroll. Lewis was paid in large lump sums of $25 or $40 and sometimes more. The other Douglass relatives, working as clerks, were paid by the amount of deeds or other paperwork processed in smaller amounts, carefully recorded as $2 or $12.12 or $6.45. Often the primary breadwinner for her six children in the absence of her estranged husband, Nathan, Rosetta had some good weeks and bad weeks at the office. She took home $16.65 on June 23, 1881, $17.80 on July 2, but only $4.89 on July 11. Charles may have only been part-time, but on July 9 that summer he took home $14.90 and had many other days just as gainful. Frederick Jr. was not on salary, but somehow he garnered $800 for his services on July 20, 1881. This record makes clear that the entire Douglass extended family lived on the considerable sums made in the collective operation of the Recorder's Office, all having received their appointments from the boss upstairs.[37] This kind of Gilded Age corruption was apparently standard operating procedure, although it tarnished the reputation of the black first family. The Recorder's Office was a Douglass-family cash cow.

The recorder's duties, as well as the demands of the extended family, now kept the Sage of Cedar Hill closer to home. So did Anna's health. Anna was finally free from Assing's summer intrusions by 1881, when Assing sailed for Europe, never to return. But by 1882 Anna suffered increasingly from neuralgia and rheumatoid arthritis. The housekeeping at the Cedar Hill mansion fell increasingly to Rosetta and her sister-in-law Louisa Sprague, who had been living with the Douglasses since the late 1860s and had become a close companion to Anna. By the early 1880s Frederick and Anna had watched and mourned the deaths of no fewer than four of their grandchildren by various illnesses, a harrowing fact of nineteenth-century life. But now the mother figure of this turbulent but enriching extended family of kin and adopted kin fell disabled.[38]

A handwritten note by Frederick Jr. in one of the family scrapbooks recorded a simple statement: "Mother Douglass was stricken with paralysis on the morning of July 7 between six and seven am, 1882." Frederick Sr. was at home the morning the stroke occurred, and close by during Anna's final month of bedridden debilitation. Anna's room was on the second floor at Cedar Hill, across the hall from her husband's. As Lewis, Rosetta's daughters, and the older children of Frederick Jr. and Charles gathered about in a daily vigil, Anna still tried to give directions for household duties. Rosetta remembered that "altho' perfectly helpless," her mother "insisted from her sickbed to direct her home affairs. The orders were given with precision and they were obeyed with alacrity." Unconscious for the final ten days, Anna Murray Douglass, a freeborn American black woman who grew up on the east bank of the Tuckahoe River in Denton, Caroline County, Maryland, the gardener, baker, cook, household manager, keeper of financial balances, shoe binder, seamstress, zealous if quiet participant in women's antislavery fairs, protector and provider for fugitive slaves, and the unsung heroine who forged the domestic worlds of the great man she married, died on the morning of August 4, 1882.[39] She was either sixty-eight or sixty-nine years old.

The passing made headlines, especially for those who saw Anna Douglass as the paragon of a deeply traditional vision of womanhood and motherhood, and who would use her death to cast an even greater light on the celebrity of her husband. The *New York Globe* rigidly laid down the gender line, portraying Anna as a heroine of the house. Douglass had "spent most of his time in the campaign battling for the emancipation of the race," while his mate made certain that "the utmost diligence had been bestowed upon every branch of his domestic affairs." The *Globe* even quoted Anna from an alleged earlier interview: "My husband is battling with the minions of oppression, why not I endure hardship that my race may be free? I will do my duty as a wife toward him and our children; they shall look neat and spruce on the street, in the house, in the schoolroom." As though the paper were copying from a manual of true womanhood, Anna was honored for her "women's wit," for always "uttering words of cheer to her struggling he-

Anna Murray Douglass, c. 1863.

roic husband."[40] In such earnest drivel, the black and white public learned about a woman so few knew.

Douglass had time to face the loss of Anna, and he managed to carry on some normal aspects of his work and political life. During the two weeks or so after the funeral he engaged in a fierce personal exchange with George T. Downing by letters in the *New York Globe* over whether blacks should remain devoted to the Republican Party or engage in "independence" or "revolt." Douglass gave as he took, as usual, demanding that the race not "make the mistake of jumping out of the frying pan into the fire, of flinging away the substance and grasping at the shadow." Moreover, he managed a sense of humor on August 21 in responding to a letter from S. W. Cowles (a collector?) requesting that the famous ex-slave send or sell him a "pair of handcuffs and slave shackles." Douglass wrote back saying that Cowles would be more likely to find such items among former slaveholders: "I have been better known for getting rid, than getting possession of such emblems of our civilization."[41]

But for some time during and after the period of Anna's death, Douglass seems to have fallen apart. He saw a "dawn of hope," as he wrote to old friend Amy Post by mid-July, since Anna had temporarily regained the ability to speak. But to old abolitionist comrade Parker Pillsbury, he wrote four days later that Anna was "pressing near the gates of death." As the older granddaughters nursed Anna toward the end and helped other women prepare the body for the burial ceremony in the front parlor at Cedar Hill,

Douglass clutched his daughter. "Ah! Rosa," he pleaded one day while hugging Rosetta, "if she could have only lived a few years longer." The forty-three-year-old Rosetta observed that her weeping father "seemed to feel that she [Anna] was a protection to him in many ways." Protector, guardian, helpmate, the embodiment of *home* indeed she had been for forty-four years. Fredericka Sprague Perry, at that time one of the younger granddaughters, remembered that at one point in the funeral preparation she and other female sisters and cousins gathered about their grandfather, "still as mice . . . wiping our tears away because grandpa wiped his." He moaned openly in front of the children, said Fredericka, declaring, "Mother was dead! Your grandma has gone away—you have no grandma now! He did not want us to forget grandma."[42]

The funeral was an extraordinarily public affair; according to many press reports three thousand people attended, with dignitaries riding in some one hundred carriages to the Graceland Cemetery, a prominent biracial burial ground on the edge of Washington. The pallbearers composed a small who's who of prominent Washington, DC, black leaders, including former senator Blanche K. Bruce, the famous entrepreneur and hotel owner James Wormley, and the former chairman of the District's Republican Party, John F. Cook. Many of Douglass's aspiring black rivals attended, but were not asked to serve as pallbearers. The funeral sermon, delivered by AME bishop T. M. D. Ward, was a tribute to Douglass and his abolitionist compatriots, virtually all dead, including Benjamin Lundy, Nat Turner, Denmark Vesey, Richard Allen, John Brown, William Lloyd Garrison, Charles Sumner, Gerrit Smith, Henry Highland Garnet, and even two presidents, Lincoln and Garfield. It was as though the bishop anticipated the future eulogies of Douglass while acknowledging the death of his wife. As in life, Anna's husband's fame hovered over, even smothered, her identity at her death. Rosetta later admitted, "It is difficult to say anything of mother without mention of father, her life was so enveloped in his."[43] We have no record of how much Rosetta or her brothers might have wished they could have replaced the good bishop at the lectern that day and reversed the narrative from their father to their publicly unknown mother. Perhaps they let well enough alone as she might wish.

Such a eulogy could be done only in private and then later find public expression in Rosetta's remarkable memoir about Anna Douglass, "My Mother as I Recall Her," delivered as a speech to the Anna Murray Douglass Union of the Women's Christian Temperance Union in Washington, DC, on May 10, 1900. Rosetta's daughter, Fredericka, set the tone in a preface with a poem, "Mother of Cedar Hill":

> *God thought to give the sweetest thing*
> *In his almighty power*
> *To earth; and deeply pondering*
> *What it should be, one hour,*
> *In fondest joy and love of heart*
> *Out weighing every other,*
> *He moved the gates of heaven apart*
> *And gave to earth—You—mother!*

From Rosetta's reminiscence, we learn that Anna had learned her trade, "household management," while first working as a teenage servant in the houses of white people in Baltimore, two of which the daughter actually went to that city sometime in the late 1890s to visit, observing the furnishings and "appointments so frequently spoken of by my mother." Rosetta also recalled that her father had taken her back to New Bedford in 1890 to visit the two-room apartment on Elm Street, her birthplace in 1839, where she could appreciate and imagine the "daily toil, the wife at the washboard, the husband with saw, buck, and axe." The "economical habits" of the Douglass household, sustained over the years, argued Rosetta, were a "characteristic of my mother." Rosetta remembered distinctive details that allow us a fair knowledge of the woman so few really understood. In the early years in freedom, near poverty despite all their industry, Rosetta said her father often commented on how Anna would create a "nicely prepared" supper on a "neatly set table with its snowy white cloth—coarse tho' it was." During the "days of anxious worry" while Douglass was in England in 1845–47, Anna fed her children with money she made shoe binding in a Lynn factory. Anna had considerable "executive ability," said Rosetta. Upon the worldly father's return from the British Isles to their cottage, he worried aloud about all the bills that must be due. One day, "mother arose and quietly going to the bureau drawer produced a Bank book with sums deposited just in the proportion father had sent, the book also containing deposits of her own earnings—and not a debt had been contracted during his absence." [44] Anna may have remained largely illiterate, but she understood arithmetic and budgets. Anna's domesticity had meant her family's survival.

Rosetta saw her mother perhaps as Rosetta saw herself, as a quiet heroine of her gender. While Rosetta was well educated, her devotion to her disastrous marriage had led to her delivering seven babies between the ages of twenty-five and thirty-eight. In Rochester, Anna had been "called up at all hours of the night" to feed hungry fugitive slaves running toward Canada. She set her supper table with extra food for the family on "publication day," the time each week when *Frederick Douglass' Paper* came off the presses at the print shop two miles down the hill in the center of Rochester. Rosetta portrayed her mother with an "acrid" wit and a sense of "grim humor," but also intolerant of alcohol and frivolity among the former slave population in Washington. Anna was a "strict disciplinarian—her *no* meant *no* and *yes, yes*, but more frequently the *no*'s had it." Anna did not like social occasions and almost never traveled with her husband. But Rosetta did recall one moving "tableau" that reveals much. At the spacious house of Samuel J. May in Boston, a major Garrisonian, Anna sat in the parlor when the three giants of the American Anti-Slavery Society, Wendell Phillips, William Lloyd Garrison, and Sydney Howard Gay, gathered around and engaged her in polite chat, "as refreshments were served on trays."[45] Anna was usually the one serving the trays in her house. Such a scene in the early or mid-1840s was one Anna likely made sure she never had to repeat.

Above all, we can see even in this sentimental tribute that Anna took her role as Douglass's personal shield and gatekeeper seriously. Loyal to her mother's memory, Rosetta had to be thinking, though, of the contradictions in her statement about Anna's "gracious" hospitality. Rosetta had to sigh about Ottilie Assing when she wrote, "There were a few who presumed on the hospitality of the home and officiously insinuated themselves and their advice in a manner that was particularly disagreeable to her." A better description of Anna's struggle over the years with Frederick's friendship with the German lady could hardly have been written. Charles Douglass also, in his 1917 reminiscence about his parents, portrayed his mother as a woman of unfailing loyalty and "sacrifice," the person who "toiled side by side with my father from the day he escaped from bondage until the day of her death in 1882."[46]

In the second edition of *Life and Times*, Douglass declared, "It is far easier to write about others than about one's self." He said he had been "morally forced" to craft so much autobiography, to bear "witness . . . for a people . . . not allowed to speak for themselves." But in that 620-page re-creation of his public life, Anna was one of the others who received exactly one mention, not by name but as "my intended wife" and a "free woman" who joined him in New York to be married after his escape from slavery. The mother figure at the heart of his home for forty-four years, and whose death set him emotionally adrift in summer and fall 1882, remained forever a subject about whom he could not write public words. Privately, Douglass mourned deeply. The weekend after the funeral, he, Rosetta, and his oldest grandchild, the almost eighteen-year-old Annie Sprague, escaped the heat of Washington and took the train to Rochester to be with the dearest of old friends, the Posts. It had been ten years since the house fire, and perhaps he and these special women took a stroll out to the hill to walk over whatever remained of Anna's garden. By October, back at Cedar Hill and at work in the Recorder's Office, he wrote to a friend that Anna's death had caused him "a lesson of thought, silence, humility and resignation." His initial feeling, he said, was to "break up my home and possibly go to Europe—but upon reflection—I felt it too late in life to . . . become a wanderer." [47] Had he done so, he might have had to encounter that estranged wanderer Ottilie Assing.

In responses to condolence letters, Douglass kept seeking the language for his loss. In those letters he expressed a dark, eloquent truth. "Mother was the post in the center of my house," he said to Sarah Loguen, "and held us together . . . the main pillar of my house has fallen," and "life cannot hold much for me, now that she has gone." [48] Ever since his grandmother Betsy plopped him down at the Wye plantation alone as a child, since the last moment he ever saw his mysterious mother, Harriet Bailey, since Sophia Auld rejected him as both reader and surrogate son, when he could no longer sing for food and affection at Lucretia Auld's window, since he lost Julia Griffiths from the daily labor and emotional sustenance of his home and print shop, and since the long intellectual affair of the heart with Ottilie Assing had soured and ended, Douglass had long desperately needed women to provide the pillars and posts in his life. He had needed none more than Anna Douglass, even as he would not allow her frustrating, indispensable, loving-yet-unseen presence to intrude on the epic tale of the self-made genius.

On New Year's Day, January 1, 1883, in Washington, DC, a large American flag hung at one end of a banquet room at Freund's Restaurant on Ninth Street; a sumptuous feast for more than fifty African American men filled a long table bedecked with flowers and lit by candles. It was the twentieth anniversary of the Emancipation Proclamation. They gathered to mark the special date by honoring Frederick Douglass, the one among them around whom a cluster of divergent race leaders might coalesce in celebration of black freedom. Douglass's closest friends and supporters in the group may also have arranged the fete to help assuage his loneliness and dislocation in the wake of Anna's death. Blanche Bruce called the banquet together. The *Washington Bee* remarked, "Never before in the history of the American negro has there ever been such an assemblage of leading colored men."[49] The elaborate dinner lifted up Douglass as the principal symbol of a people's journey from slavery to liberation.

The guests comprised a who's who of two generations of black politicians, civil servants, journalists, writers, professors, ministers, and soldiers. Prominent among them were the Pan-Africanist scholar Edward Blyden; the former emigrationist, soldier, politician, and Douglass's coeditor back at the beginning of the *North Star*, Martin Delany; the heroic wartime boat pilot and later congressman from South Carolina, Robert Smalls. Richard T. Greener and James M. Gregory of Howard University (where Douglass was a trustee) were among a group of academics. The young historian George Washington Williams highlighted the contingent of writers. The Reverend Benjamin T. Tanner, editor of the AME Church's influential *Christian Recorder*, and the bold, young editor of the *New York Globe*, T. Thomas Fortune, headlined the ranks of newspapermen. The War Department clerk and Congressional Medal of Honor winner, Christian A. Fleetwood, appeared and was addressed as "Captain." Douglass's sons Lewis and Charles, veterans of the famed Fifty-Fourth Massachusetts regiment, conspicuously attended the tribute to their father. Along with their brother, Frederick Jr., they needed affirmation in their own careers, which had never blossomed as they had hoped. Among the revelers were congressmen, including John R. Lynch of Mississippi, and members of state legislatures from South and North, men who owned their own businesses, and ministers of prominent churches. Many among them had fiercely disagreed with one another about issues and strategies for best advancing the race, some with Douglass himself, which the guest of honor freely acknowledged.[50] Rivalries were left at the door—especially Douglass's bitter feuds with Greener and others over loyalty to the Republican Party—and the generational divide was put aside for at least one evening. They gathered to contemplate and to declare their place in national memory.

As the gentlemen settled in for a long evening (they did not adjourn until 3:00 a.m.), some forty-one toasts were offered to virtually every aspect of black life and aspiration, as well as to heroes of the antislavery cause, living and dead. At this men's-only banquet (no women writers or leaders were invited), one toast was offered to "the ladies." Douglass was the final speaker, responding to Bruce's long personal tribute and to a toast to the day; he reached for the lodestar of recent American history. To hear Douglass on these occasions when he spoke about historical memory must have been to feel one's inheritance, to almost see history flowing as a procession in time. Who were black people in America at this moment of remembrance in 1883? According to the orator they were a people reborn with emancipation, and a new nation had been born with them. After several minutes of wit and humor about how he had "no talent" for "after-dinner speeches," and that he had never succeeded at brevity, Douglass found his theme. "This high festival of ours is coupled with a day which we do well to hold in sacred and everlasting honor," he announced, "a day . . . which may well count for a thousand years." [51]

T. Thomas Fortune later recollected the evening as a transcendent experience. Normally, said the New York editor, he found Washington, DC, "depressing" and "nauseating" in its political cynicism. "But the Douglass banquet, a spontaneous tribute of love, respect, honor, and veneration bridged over many a sigh. . . . Indeed, the Douglass banquet was an event in the history of the race." Fortune forgot for the moment his own harsh criticism of Douglass's symbolic politics and acknowledged the event as one for the transmission of memory, where "tender youth" was instructed by "mature age." Douglass, said Fortune, "bent low his majestic head of snowy whiteness and received with pleasurable emotions the homage" of the throng of leaders, "the majority of whom were unborn or in their infancy when he was thundering against the iniquity of the slave power." What unified the disparate gathering of professions and egos, Fortune argued, was the "cause of the race," and gratitude and love for the great Douglass. [52] A talented writer and thinker, Fortune would become much better at history and activism than he was at homage to his elders.

Douglass made their hearts pump and their throats choke. He filled the room with Civil War memory well past midnight and gave the occasion an incantatory refrain, which he used some sixteen times in a breathless expression of the nation's rebirth. *"Until this day,"* he proclaimed, "slavery, the sum of all villainies, like a vulture, was gnawing at the heart of the Republic; until this day there stretched away behind us an awful chasm of darkness and despair of more than two centuries; until this day the American slave, bound in chains, tossed his fettered arms on high and groaned for freedom's gift in vain." Even those who readily saw Douglass as a rival and were jealous of his fame probably could not resist the rhetorical power of this litany of images from memory. "Until this day," continued the speaker at the head of the table, "the colored people of the United States lived in the shadow of death . . . and had no visible future. . . . Until this day it was doubtful whether liberty or union would triumph, or slavery and barbarism. Until this day victory had largely followed the arms of the Confederate army. . . . Until this day . . . ," Douglass sang on.[53]

In these visions, Douglass lent more than sermonic flourish to this occasion of commemoration. He took the central idea of Lincoln's Gettysburg Address as well as his own "Mission of the War" address of 1863–64—national rebirth and redefinition—and rendered it palpable and inspirational in the present. The public Douglass as orator was very much back. Some press coverage described a prolonged evening of tributes. A *Cleveland Herald* reporter said that the assembled "listened as they had not before. . . . He speaks as he did twenty years ago. . . . His eyes flashed, his long silvery hair seemed to stand on end and his voice was as the sound of many waters."[54]

But the same reporter then indicated that disputes broke out late after Douglass's main speech, with Greener and Fortune calling for blacks to seek independence from political parties and to strive more to free themselves rather than relying on white allies. Douglass rose again with ire, said the journalist, denounced the "croakers," and yanked his audience back to the heart of the war. "When the recruiting officers," shouted Douglass, "were going up and down the street begging for men to enlist, when the cause of the Union hung in the balance, when foreign powers were ready to recognize the South, the negro with arms of iron and fingers of steel, grasped the Union cause and held it together!" Then the orator "became calmer" and said, "Young men . . . let me say as did John, when speaking to the multitude of Christ, 'You must increase, but I decrease.' " The evening ended with all standing and declaring "three cheers for Old Man Eloquent."[55] Douglass, however, did not intend to pass any batons to the next generation.

Chapter 28

WATCHMAN, WHAT OF THE NIGHT?

I am not at all surprised when some of those for whom I have lived and labored lift their heels against me. Since the days of Moses such has been the fate of all men earnestly endeavouring to serve the oppressed and unfortunate.

—FREDERICK DOUGLASS, MAY 1883

In July 1883, an African American member of the US legation in Monrovia, Liberia, wrote to Douglass after reading the orator's April speech commemorating emancipation in the District of Columbia. The foreign-service worker had also apparently read *Life and Times*. He was impressed that the aging Douglass could still write and perform with such "vigor, brilliancy, and . . . power after . . . nearly a half century in the cause of our oppressed people." The American abroad felt "reminded" of the "frequently repeated" concern among Douglass's admirers: Now that "slavery . . . had been practically abolished . . . 'Mr. Douglass's occupation is gone!' What would he talk about now?" [1] From his reading of the April address, the correspondent felt reassured that Othello still had much to say.

Following a long parade earlier in the day through the streets of the city, on April 16, 1883, the twenty-first anniversary of emancipation in the District of Columbia, Douglass was orator of the evening at the packed First Congregational Church. The Young Men's Citizens Club of the District presented him with flowers, a show of respect by the next generation who awaited a passing of the baton. Many difficult issues had arisen throughout the day's festivities and for months in the newspapers: racial discrimination, the denial of black voting rights in the District, disappointment with the Republican Party, recurring violence against freedpeople in the South, and emerging fears that the great changes wrought by the Reconstruction amendments were under dire threat. Douglass delivered his classic medicine of hope and progress wrested from vivid illustrations of despair. It was vintage Douglass, a speech full of memory and appeals for faith made through awareness of how the "sky of the Negro is dark, but not rayless." He demanded an abiding sense of history braced by tragic sensibility. "Men are prepared by preceding events for those which are to come. We neither know the evil nor the good which may be in store for us." He embraced the honor paid him by the "promising young colored men of Washington." "I represent the past, they the present . . . their mission begins where my mission ends." Douglass borrowed from Isaiah to illustrate the challenge: "As an old watchman on the walls of liberty, eagerly scanning the social and political horizon, you naturally ask of me, What of the Night?" [2] Then he lectured the young and the old about the lessons of the past. The night was dark, but he anticipated the dawn, still ready to be their watchman.

In an oration sizzling with black patriotism, appeals for self-reliance, a fierce faith in free speech, the right to vote, and the new Reconstruction Constitution, Douglass demanded hope. But only after naming the evils of racism: "While a slave there was a mountain of gold on his [the Negro's] breast to keep him down, now that he is free there is a mountain of prejudice to keep him down." But as long as blacks could assert their place before law and speak through a free press, their cause would never die. "There is no modern Joshua," Douglass insisted, "who can command this resplendent orb of popular discussion to stand still." [3] But *discussion* made for a tenuous political platform for a people divided and distressed.

Douglass received a large correspondence about his speech, which he mailed far and wide as a pamphlet. The US consul in Manchester, England, wrote to assure the orator he had not lost any of "the force and fire of earlier years." A black railroad steward in Rhode Island read the emancipation day speech and declared "amen to every sentiment you uttered." Many still wrote to him in 1883 from as far away as Michigan to say they had just read *Life and Times* and were inspired. Some friends wrote to say they were covering Douglass's back in conversations where people used "denunciatory" language about him. And he must have been heartened when his old friend Julia Griffiths Crofts wrote from England. She was moved by the April oration: "It brought the old days nobly to my . . . head & those 4th of July and 1st of August addresses of the past." [4] Douglass could still count on friends, as he encountered critics at every turn.

• • •

For Douglass, during the mid-1880s, this ebb and flow of hope and despair was both a public and a private matter. By the spring of 1883, a new season of bitter rivalries had broken out between the recorder and other black leaders, especially George Washington Williams, John Mercer Langston, and Richard T. Greener. Douglass engaged in public arguments about black identity and destiny, contending against those who, in frustration over American racism, considered themselves "not Americans but Africans." Douglass had no sympathy for the latest surge of emigrationism. With anger, he argued that neither slavery nor prejudice nor vicious mobs could change one's nationality and human worth: "We are born on American soil, and are of American soil. . . . Every muscle and fiber of our bodies have been taken from it. . . . What right then has any man to call us Africans?" Since an initial interest in American abolitionists' creation of the Mendi Mission in Sierra Leone in the 1840s, Douglass had taken little interest in African history or in the continent's descent into colonialism. He viewed any effort by American blacks to seek either "return" or new cultural and national identities based on African lineage as mere distraction from their Anglo-American heritage. Moreover, he accused the young historian Williams of "deliberate falsehoods" in his portrayal of the older leader's views on the Exodus. With the lawyer and ambitious politician Langston, Douglass continued a prolonged, personal feud—one that would explode in the ensuing years—over whether blacks should stay loyal to the Republicans, over personal family matters, and even over who deserved the honor of speaking for the race.[5]

Many younger men were pounding away at the base of Old Man Eloquent's pedestal. Hypersensitive about these constant attacks, Douglass remained fully aware that black leaders, whether preachers, editors, or itinerant orators, had few institutions and public mechanisms through which to process their disagreements and political divisions. Lacking a normal politics embedded in legitimate rival parties, they slashed at each other in an all too receptive press and fought for position, reputation, and tenuous leadership perches in the recurring but inchoate convention movement.

In 1883 Douglass locked horns with Richard Greener over how and whether blacks ought to assemble a major convention to present their grievances to the nation. But their clash became as personal as it was strategic. Born in 1844 in Philadelphia to free parents, Greener grew up mostly in

Boston. The same generation as Douglass's children, Greener was an intellectual prodigy who first studied at a Cambridge, Massachusetts, school and later at Andover Academy. During the Civil War, Greener spent two years in preparatory school at Oberlin College and in 1865 entered Harvard, where he became the first African American graduate in 1870. He worked as a staff writer briefly for the Douglasses on the *New National Era*, and in 1873 he moved to Reconstruction South Carolina, where he taught philosophy and studied for his law degree by 1876 from the state university in Columbia. When white-supremacist Democrats took control of South Carolina in 1877 and drove blacks out of the university, Greener returned to Washington, DC, where for a short time he served as dean of the Howard University law school. Greener convened nearly a hundred delegates, many from the South, for a black convention in May 1883 advocating for a broader collective voice on black rights and against a national convention in the fall that Douglass endorsed. From spring through the summer, the two Washington-based leaders conducted ugly exchanges in the press. Douglass accused Greener of being behind an attack on him, signed by "L," whom the patriarch of Cedar Hill identified as "Liar." The piece, said Douglass, was an attack "upon my integrity as a Republican, and charging me with the purpose of trading off the colored vote of the country for office." The Republican functionary declared himself fed up with "anonymous falsifiers" driven by "ambition and jealousy."[6]

Lewis Douglass took to the press as well, defending his father, chastising Greener, and calling for a national convention. Greener shot back in more than one outlet with an unveiled denigration of Douglass's sons, whom he implied were men "deluded with the chimera of their immense political influence and army record; parasites that crawl into sunlight and notoriety by the permission of defunct greatness [and] know well when to cash a note or obtain a mortgage by obsequious flattery and subservient toadying." But Greener, a wordsmith in his own right, saved the worst for the elder Douglass. There had long been "two Douglasses," Greener maintained, "the one velvety, deprecatory, apologetic—the other insinuating, suggestive, damning with a shrug, a raised eyebrow, or a look of caution." He called Douglass's responses in the press "platitudinous" and claimed that without a convention to lead the old editor's "trilogy would be incomplete, the banquet, the emancipation celebration, the convention!"[7]

The ugliness of such press exchanges led the *New York Globe*, edited by T. Thomas Fortune, to call Greener's attacks "shameful." "Has Frederick Douglass lived too long," asked a correspondent to the *Globe* who

Richard T. Greener, c. 1870.

might have been Lewis Douglass, "that Mr. Greener and his followers desire to exterminate him?" Moreover, the *Christian Recorder* urged Douglass
and Greener to "bottle up their wrath" and especially demanded that the
younger man know his place in the pantheon of leaders, fall in line to "ven-
erate" the famed orator, and stop trying "to silence these old guns yet loaded
to the very breech."[8]

Greener's contempt for all the Douglasses reflected a cluster of educational assumptions and status resentments. Douglass's sons monitored all of
their father's critics and performed as, in effect, managers of their father's
political war room. Lewis often warned his father about the young men in
Washington waiting for their chance "to claim reward for what they suppose
to be service to you." Their only motive, Lewis maintained, was to use Douglass "as a ladder upon which they may climb to importance." Frederick Jr. expressed even more invective about the ingratitude of blacks generally toward
his famous father's career and churlishly insisted that he and his siblings had
to feel the pain as well. "I feel that we children have shared in a measure your
sacrifices for the good of the Cause in years past & hence, I feel the slurs and
smears pointed at you." He told his father that summer not to worry about
the "youngsters." "With truth on our side," Frederick Jr. said with familial
vanity, "Lew, Charley and I will be able to keep the flies off." One irony festering beneath all this bad blood was that at this very moment Greener, whose
marriage had broken up and who was estranged from his six children, was
renting an apartment in property owned by Frederick Douglass Jr.[9]

By July 1883, Douglass fell ill or likely experienced some kind of emotional breakdown. Not quite a year since Anna had died, feeling political and verbal attacks from all sides, and with a physician's encouragement, he went by himself up to Maine for respite and recovery. He stayed for most of a month in Poland Spring, either boarding at the new lodge constructed in 1876 or possibly with a local farmer. Various parts of the black press monitored Douglass's getaway; the *Christian Recorder* announced that he was seeking rest from recurring "nervous troubles." [10]

From there, Douglass carried on a vigorous correspondence with Lewis, Frederick Jr., Rosetta, her daughter Annie, and Louisa Sprague, Rosetta's sister-in-law. The three women were holding down the household at Cedar Hill, and all four Douglass children kept their father abreast of the personnel dramas at the Recorder Office, and about the status of new real estate deals. They all "rejoiced to know that you are improving," as Rosetta said, although she openly wished her father would not attend any convention that required long travel, especially into the South, where she worried for his safety. Lewis and Frederick Jr. kept assuring Douglass that his friends outnumbered the "assailants" and "sharks" awaiting his return. Some employees at the Recorder's Office were not competent, but they were all getting to know "Miss Pitts," who was by all accounts very efficient. [11] That autumn, or perhaps even earlier, Douglass made some secret plans with Helen Pitts, the well-educated forty-five-year-old suffragist whom he had hired the previous year.

But first there was the big convention, originally planned for Washington but now in deference to black Southerners booked for Louisville, Kentucky, in September. Douglass returned from the cool breezes and magnificent views of the White Mountains in mid-August. Before leaving for Louisville he gave an interview to the *New York World.* At Cedar Hill, Douglass received the reporter, who upon entry noticed the large picture of Lincoln in a place of honor in the main parlor, set off by many other images of abolitionists and women's rights leaders. Asked what the Louisville convention would be all about, Douglass sat in a chair, "brushing back the long white hair from his forehead" as he "looked steadily for a full minute at the pictures on the wall." The delegates could not ignore politics, said the Lion of Anacostia, but what he hoped for most was a collective "growl" for enforcement of existing laws, especially in the South. He further hoped they would get the nation's attention about violence and protection for the right to vote as well as for "better educational privileges." As for the coming 1884 presidential contest, Douglass hoped the Republicans would anoint Robert Lincoln, son of the martyred hero. He laughed off the controversy about his alleged motives for a convention that would personally serve his connections to President Arthur. Douglass expected a gathering with "a loud cry for more offices" for blacks because "there is trouble in our kitchen and Oliver Twist wants more." On the walls of Douglass's impressive home, the heroes of many victories were looking down—Toussaint Louverture, John Brown, William Lloyd Garrison, Cinqué, Charles Sumner, Wendell Phillips, and many more.[12] Now, if only those victories could be preserved in American racial memory and reality.

Nearly three hundred delegates from twenty-six states assembled in Louisville on September 24–25. A number of prominent black leaders boycotted the convention, some believing that the day of separate black conventions had passed and some in revolt against the Republican Party. The gathering first faced a long struggle over choosing its chairman, with Douglass finally winning by a vote of 201–57. His critics included those convinced that he was too cozy with the Republicans. In its resolutions the convention refused to endorse Chester Arthur. It did appeal to the memory of the Lincoln-era Republicans, expressing gratitude for the "miraculous emancipation." But the bulk of the eleven resolutions in effect pronounced the Fourteenth Amendment and the civil rights legislation of Reconstruction "nothing more than dead letters."[13]

Douglass delivered a formal keynote address on the twenty-fifth to more than two thousand people in Liederkranz Hall. After a troupe of New Orleans Jubilee Singers chanted the Lord's Prayer, Douglass rose to the lectern and spoke to every theme the convention had announced, and in so doing made them his own. In a familiar move, he opened by addressing the nation and white people explicitly, insisting that blacks were "in every sense Americans," completely part of "your country," "your pride," and equally invested in "this stupendous revolution in our national history" (emancipation). He boldly chastised those black naysayers, the "betrayers and informers," even the "traitors among us" who in seeking status would exalt themselves over the good of the whole. After such shots at his intraracial enemies, Douglass got down to the business of analyzing the grievances of his people.[14]

Such conventions, said Douglass, were much preferable to "violence, dynamite, and all sorts of revolutionary action." The constitutional amendments and civil rights laws of Reconstruction had given the nation a new legal regime, but at every level of polity enforcement was the question. In a favorite argument, Douglass reminded the country that black freedom had not emerged from "the sober dictates of wisdom," but "of battle and of blood . . . from the hell of war." He delivered a detailed analysis of the color line, of mob violence in the South reinforced by "lynch law [and] lynch courts," of the dead-end conditions of black laborers in American agriculture, and of the failure of black education. Douglass minced no words, calling the infinite manifestations of racism a "National faith." Well before Jim Crow laws dominated Southern statute books, Douglass described the "color madness" that infected social and economic life in the former Confederate states. Behind the pernicious color line, he argued, the lynch mob's "rope . . . in . . . darkness," as well as the cowardly, silent pulpit and press, played the enforcer of a terror regime. Thus the color line, Douglass declared, "hunts us at midnight, it denies us accommodation in hotels and justice in the courts, excludes our children from schools, refuses our sons the right to learn trades and compels us to pursue only such labor that will bring the least reward." Douglass's critique of the relationship of labor and capital, of the "slavery of wages" faced by powerless farmworkers and sharecroppers, was a departure for him. His faith in political solutions seemed shaken. Twenty years out from emancipation and the dream of land ownership, the vast bulk of freedmen toiled with little hope and no clout, crushed by debt and white landowners' "power of life and death held over labor." [15] Rarely had Douglass employed a class analysis so directly and darkly.

Anger, outrage, and the intellectual demands of such a keynote address had seemingly revived Douglass from his emotional breakdown of the previous summer. He ultimately directed this jeremiad at Republicans and at the federal government: "If the Republican party cannot stand a demand for justice and fair play, it ought to go down." He pleaded for further federal enforcement of voting rights against the Democrats' violent suppression in the South and even demanded a federal compulsory-school-attendance law as well as federal aid to schools in the states. Otherwise, Douglass contended, blacks could only conclude that "they have been abandoned by the Government and left to the laws of nature. So far as they are concerned, there is no Government or Constitution of the United States." With such eloquent complaint, wondering whether Americans still lived in the land of the Fourteenth Amendment, Douglass reached back more than thirty years into his well of old abolitionist radicalism. His ending reworked both Jefferson and Lincoln: "We hold it to be self-evident that no class or color should be the exclusive rulers of this country. If there is such a ruling class, there must of course be a subject class, and when this condition is once established this Government of the people, by the people and for the people, will have perished from the earth." [16]

The delegates from the Louisville convention had hardly returned home when the US Supreme Court landed a bombshell in their laps. A group of civil rights cases based on seven incidents had been pending before the Court throughout the year. All involved the denial of access for blacks to facilities, including hotel accommodations in Kansas and Missouri, seats at a theater in San Francisco and at the opera in New York, and of a woman trying to ride in the ladies' car on the Memphis and Charleston Railroad. This cluster of cases demonstrated that racial discrimination was not solely a Southern problem. The 8–1 ruling in *United States v. Stanley* (known as the Civil Rights Cases) held that the equal-protection clause of the Fourteenth Amendment applied only to states and not to individual acts of discrimination by a person or a business establishment. The decision meant, therefore, that discriminatory acts by private persons or entities were beyond the safeguards of the Fourteenth Amendment or federal jurisdiction; a person wronged had redress only to state courts. The Court further declared unconstitutional the Civil Rights Act of 1875, which only eight years earlier had explicitly guaranteed all citizens "the full and equal enjoyment of accommodations, facilities, and privileges of inns, public conveyances on land and water, theaters and other places of public amusement." [17] All that Douglass, the black press, and the Louisville convention had demanded about federal enforcement of black rights seemed suddenly dissolved in this bitter betrayal. Soon Jim Crow could march through an open door; night had fallen.

The Supreme Court had just eviscerated one of the greatest achievements of Reconstruction. From the *Slaughter-House Cases* of 1873, to *United States v. Cruikshank* in 1876, and on down to *Plessy v. Ferguson* in 1896, Fourteenth Amendment jurisprudence consistently embraced a states' rights interpretation of equal protection of the law. A conservative conception of federalism, a reluctance to sanction federal enforcement of civil and political rights, much less intervention, *in the states* gave racial equality a tenuous and ultimately disastrous trajectory in American courts. Today it can seem astonishing that a war and a reimagined Constitution expanding equal rights to all citizens could be won by extraordinary uses of federal military and legal power, and through enormous bloodshed, yet for generations to follow those achievements could be protected only by local authority in the states. But such was the hold of states' rights doctrines on legal thinking that it led to what the constitutional historian Akhil Amar has called "these stingy Reconstruction decisions." The Republicans who wrote the Fourteenth and Fifteenth Amendments tragically retreated from their own creation with a stultified constitutional imagination.[18]

On October 22, one week after the Civil Rights Cases decision, a standing-room-only mass protest meeting was held in Washington. Two thousand people crammed into Lincoln Hall as Lewis Douglass read eight resolutions demanding enforcement of civil rights. Frederick Douglass delivered the keynote speech, in which he announced that the issues were so crucial that he wrote out his words. He announced that black folk and their allies had been "grievously wounded, wounded in the house of our friends." He invoked the *Dred Scott* case, Bleeding Kansas, the Fugitive Slave Act, to give weight to the moment's anxiety. The Court's action "makes us feel," he declared, "as if someone were stamping on the graves of our mothers, or desecrating our sacred temples of worship." After so many years of struggle, blood, defeat, and then triumph, the moment, Douglass intoned, felt like a "moral cyclone" blowing through history.[19]

Douglass devoted much of the speech to the Fourteenth Amendment, quoting verbatim section one. The language of that amendment was likely much more common coin in American awareness then than it is now a century and a half later. He blasted the logic of states' rights, so reinforced in the Court decision: "It gives to a South Carolina, or a Mississippi railroad conductor, more power than it gives to the National Government." And "it gives a hotel-keeper" with "prejudice born of the rebellion" the authority to expel black men and women as he so wished. Douglass further delivered a lawyerly argument about "intention" in law and the Constitution. During more than seventy years of slavery times, he said, the notion of original intention had been constantly invoked in support of every kind of proslavery interest. Now, he asked, why could not the intention of the Fourteenth Amendment—citizenship rights for all Americans—be the new guide to jurisprudence? Poignantly Douglass demanded, "O for a Supreme Court of the United States which shall be as true to the claims of humanity, as the Supreme Court formerly was to the demands of slavery!"[20]

Moreover, as he did now in so many public utterances, Douglass interpreted the Court's decision of 1883 as a failure of historical memory and national commitment to the fruits of Union victory. So important was the Civil Rights Cases to Douglass that he devoted a chapter to it in the revised version of *Life and Times*, the bulk of which was a reprinting of his Washington speech. As he introduced it, he contended that "the future historian will turn to the year 1883 to find the most flagrant example of this national deterioration." White racism, he remarked, seemed to grow in proportion to the "increasing distance from the time of the war." Douglass blamed not only the passing of time, but, more important, the spirit of reconciliation between North and South. Justice and liberty for blacks, he maintained, had lost ground from "the hour that the loyal North . . . began to shake hands over the bloody chasm." Douglass saw the Supreme Court decision as part of a pattern of the corruption of historical memory. Thus he believed blacks could see the Court's judgment only as a "bewildering surprise," and an act of "absurdity and injustice." "The surrender of the national capital to Jefferson Davis in time of war," he asserted, "could hardly have caused a greater shock." [21]

Douglass's reactions echoed widely across the black press. The *Christian Recorder* counseled defiance, calling the Court decision "humiliating" and "maddening," and urging blacks to prepare to live in a segregated society. The anniversary year that began in the commemorative spirit about emancipation gave way to a deepening sense of fear and betrayal. The *New York Globe* said the decision had made blacks feel "as if they had been baptized in ice water." The *Boston Hub* thought the ruling "worthy of the Republic fifty years ago." And the *Detroit Plaindealer* joined the chorus, likening the decision to "an avalanche, carrying our fondest hopes down the hill of despair." [22]

By November, Douglass had carefully read the famous lone dissent of Justice John Marshall Harlan and wrote him a letter of admiration and gratitude. With "boundless satisfaction," Douglass consumed the dissent and its forceful claim that the "recent amendments to the Constitution have been sacrificed by a subtle and ingenious verbal criticism." Douglass felt so moved that he wished the dissent could "be scattered like the leaves of autumn over the whole country . . . and be read by every citizen." He felt heartened by Harlan's condemnation of both racial discrimination and the tortured claims of states' rights doctrine. Harlan had helped Douglass find voice to condemn the justice's "Brothers on the Supreme Bench," and to find access to "how they could at this day and in view of the past commit themselves and the country to such a surrender of national dignity and duty." Douglass stood angry and baffled at the majority's states' rights vision, which he deemed "superficial . . . smooth and logical within the narrow circumference beyond which they do not venture." Such was the stranglehold of states' rights on Fourteenth Amendment jurisprudence in the late nineteenth century; the orator wanted the dissenter to know that black Americans had his back. If Harlan felt "alone on the bench," Douglass assured the justice, "you are not alone in the country." [23]

In his personal life, Douglass too had chosen not to be alone. On January 24, 1884, he and Helen Pitts put in nearly a full workday at the Recorder's Office, where Helen was one of the copyists. She would have worked closely that day, like others, with Lewis and Rosetta. Sometime earlier that day, Douglass had paid a short visit to the city clerk's office to purchase a $1 marriage license. According to a prurient reporter for the *National Republican*, the famous man seemed "hurried and flurried" as he took the chief clerk aside for a "whispered conversation," then "sheepishly . . . walked out." By early evening, both Douglass and his new bride had gone home, he to Cedar Hill and she to her apartment on E Street, to change into more formal clothing, Helen appearing for her wedding in a "garnet velvet and silk" dress, and her beau in a new black suit. By 6:00 p.m. a carriage delivered them to the parsonage of the Reverend Francis J. Grimké, the young minister and activist who had been born in South Carolina in 1850 to a liaison between a white planter and a biracial slave mother, at the Fifteenth Street Presbyterian Church, 1608 R Street. With former senator Blanche Bruce and his wife, Josephine, and Grimké's wife, Charlotte Forten Grimké, the abo-

Blanche K. Bruce, senator from Mississippi, c. 1880.

litionist and author of a multivolume autobiography, as the only witnesses or guests, the almost sixty-six-year-old Douglass and the forty-six-year-old Pitts were secretly married.[24] Quickly the secret exploded.

Douglass had not told any of his children, with whom he worked daily, and other than Grimké, it does not appear that Douglass told many other associates or friends. Helen too had kept the plans largely secret from her family, most of whom soon condemned her. According to press notices, Rosetta learned of the wedding from a reporter who informed her before she left the Recorder's Office, leaving her stunned and "visibly affected." Reporters stalked the newlyweds back to Helen's residence, where Douglass was compelled to address them from a porch, where he supposedly "smiled," but declared the questions "rather cheeky."[25] Just why Frederick and Helen had kept their intentions so quiet says much about his struggles with the perils of fame and a scandalous press; it also demonstrates just how shocking their racially transgressive act would be to both blacks and whites. If they had announced even a brief engagement period, they might have faced scurrilous attacks and pressure to desist. So they simply married as quietly as possible and let the storm blow after the fact. Not telling Rosetta, Lewis, Frederick Jr., or Charles and their families may be a measure of just how much the patriarch understood the volatile complexities of his extended domestic circle in Washington.

The Douglass children swallowed much of their surprise and disappointment—perhaps less at Helen's whiteness than at not being consulted—as they kept their demeanor in talking to the solicitous press. Lewis told a reporter, "Father had a right to marry whom he pleased, and that is the way we regard it." Rosetta too kept the stiff upper lip, but admitted publicly, "I would have preferred at his age he should not have married again." Rosetta's sister-in-law Louisa had been running Cedar Hill since Anna's death, but now that Helen moved in immediately, Louisa left the big house, leading her brother, Nathan, to actions that would soon cause an uglier scandal. Rosetta also brought her adult daughter, Annie, away from Cedar Hill, believing her coexistence with Helen as the new mistress of the house would be untenable. Douglass may have encouraged these departures for Helen's sake.[26] Feelings ran raw.

For a month and beyond the national press had a field day with this racial, sexual, and family drama. Headlines screamed, "A Black Man's Bride"; "The Venerable Colored Orator Takes a White Wife"; "His Queer Choice." In various newspapers Helen's age was continually lowered from her forties to her thirties—in one report "a red head white girl 33 years old"—while

Douglass in some reports greatly aged, becoming as old as seventy-five as he pursued this much younger woman. At forty-four and forty-six, Rosetta and Helen were nearly the same age. Helen was sometimes portrayed as "low" born or "common." Douglass underwent a public shaming by many black critics. Editorial writers thought the marriage was ruining the great man "politically and socially," that it had "dethroned him" from racial leadership, and that the Sage of Cedar Hill had made "the fatal error of his life." A Petersburg, Virginia, paper announced the "Negro Idol has fallen," and from Little Rock, Arkansas, he was accused of branding blacks "by his own act as inferior to the white race, which reverses the labors of his life." The *Washington (DC) Grit* called the marriage "a national calamity." And in Pittsburgh a correspondent worried about the fate of "black blood" and denounced Douglass: "We have no further use for him as a leader. His picture hangs in our parlor, we will hang it in the stable." [27]

Hyperbole aside, this was the nineteenth century, and there had never been such an open interracial marriage by such a famous and important black man. No people, moreover, understood better than African Americans how white men had for so long exploited black women for desire and power, and at a time when their communities' safety and basic liberties were under violent attack and legal subordination, racial pride easily felt wounded. For some, Douglass's wedding seemed like a collective loss or even disgrace. Occasionally a black pundit reached for psychological explanations to grasp the great man's blunder. In Springfield, Ohio, a writer worried that Douglass's mind was "succumbing to the influences of a second childhood." [28]

But Douglass was still in his right mind and he had his defenders. Blanche Bruce, old friend Robert Purvis, Howard University professor James M. Gregory, and the New York editor T. Thomas Fortune all honored the old abolitionist's right to marry whom he pleased. Purvis likened the controversy to "making a mountain out of a mole hill," Bruce said it was "not the public's business," and Gregory admired the leader's desire to "thoroughly Americanize his race." The resentful nemesis Richard Greener, however, snidely called the marriage "inconsistent," accusing Douglass of preferring his own race when engaged in "office-getting and giving," but going white in his wife selection. Douglass did receive personal comfort from abroad. He had not alerted his old companion Julia Griffiths Crofts of his marital intentions. But by mid-February from England came Julia's letter indicating that Rochester friends had sent her a press clipping about the wedding. "I, as one of your truest and warmest friends," wrote the aging

Julia, "hasten to send you (and Mrs. Douglass) my most sincere congrat-ulations." She hoped that the union would give him "true happiness in the evening of your days," and she was eager to hear from Douglass's "own hand a few particulars regarding the lady." [29]

In the swirl of scandalmongering press coverage, with sighs of disdain, Douglass felt the need to defend himself and his basic rights. He had long been a very public figure, and he had sought such distinction, but nothing about his personal life had ever received this much attention. On the day after the marriage, he allowed a *Washington Post* reporter to interview him at Cedar Hill. Douglass refused to be baited by sensationalism. But the en-counter in his parlor illustrates the late nineteenth century's version of what we have come to know in late-twentieth- and early-twenty-first-century politics and media as the blurred line between the public and the private. Why was Douglass's marriage to a white woman, whatever her age or back-ground, anyone's business but his own? In his case, the answer is partly fame, but mostly race.

To the *Post* reporter, Douglass simply declared his marriage "not an event of public moment." His action was a family matter, and he owed no one any explanation or apology. His labors for justice, he continued, had never been solely "because I am a negro, but because I am a man." Then Douglass tried, as he had so many times before, to puncture the logic of racial thinking; he insisted that he did not think with his race, but with his heart and head. Helen Pitts was only a "few shades lighter than my-self," he declared, and he pushed his interlocutor to face the ultimate absur-dity about "complexions." Douglass drew indirectly from Acts 17 as he left the reporter with some instructions. "God Almighty made but one race," said the old prophetic orator. "I adopt the theory that in time the variet-ies of races will be blended into one. . . . You may say that Frederick Doug-lass considers himself a member of the one race that exists." J. M. Dalzell, an Ohio politician with whom Douglass had worked on the Garfield cam-paign, wrote in the same week with concern about what the marriage would do to the black leader's "greatness." Tongue in cheek, in a widely reprinted public response, Douglass said he would say "farewell to all my greatness" and demanded that Dalzell stumble out of his racist assumptions. A mil-lion Americans were of mixed blood, said Douglass, due to the historical exploitation of black women by white men. "It would seem that what the American people object to is not the mixture of the races, but honorable marriage between them." Douglass had learned that if "God . . . hath made of one blood all nations of men," he also "giveth to all life, and breath, and all things." Among all those things—natural rights—was the right to marry whom one pleased.[30]

No matter how much Douglass tried to protect her, Helen became en-snarled in the controversy as well. She took significant social risks in marrying Douglass; members of her immediate family, including her father, Gideon, and her uncle Hiram, with whom she lived in Washington, ostracized her and never reconciled. Her mother, Jane Wells Pitts, and her two sisters eventually, if slowly, accepted the union and came to visit at Cedar Hill. Descendant Katy O'dell, whose great-grandmother was Helen's first cousin in western New York, where the Pittses were prosperous farmers, remembers the lore of the scandalous marriage to Douglass, as it was passed down in her family. Helen endured a vicious press, including all manner of falsehoods and rumors that her family sought to have the marriage annulled.[31]

Helen was well educated and possessed a remarkable history of activism in women's rights, temperance, and antislavery. She had long ago taken personal risks. Raised in a strong abolitionist home influenced by the rise of the Liberty Party in the 1840s and 1850s, she had first met Douglass when she was fourteen, in 1852, when he visited the family farm on a lecture tour. Few blacks were in or around the town of Honeoye, with its two thousand residents, and none in the Union church. One of her sisters took a master's degree at Cornell University, and Helen and her other sister, Jennie, spent three years at Genesee Seminary in Lima, New York. From there she went to

Frederick Douglass with Helen Pitts Douglass, seated, and her sister Jennie Pitts, Washington, DC, c. 1885. In Helen's family, only her sister, and later to an extent, her mother, supported the marriage.

Mount Holyoke College for women in South Hadley, Massachusetts, where she graduated in 1859.[32]

A patriotic supporter of the Union war effort and especially emancipation, by April 1863, Helen Pitts secured a position as a teacher for the American Missionary Association in Norfolk, Virginia. Occupied by Union forces since 1862, Norfolk became a major center for freedmen's education as well as the recruitment of black Union soldiers. This was baptism in activism under great stress; Douglass did not see or visit a contraband camp himself until the end of the war. For nearly a year Helen taught former slaves of all ages who passionately desired education. At first she was one of only four teachers for a growing throng of hundreds of pupils, and the labor in this crossroads of war-born disease seriously threatened her health. She caught malaria among other ailments. The debilitated twenty-six-year-old stayed into 1864, but was forced to take leave and go home to the healthier western New York. Her supervisors found Helen courageous and "indispensable." She worked closely with many black soldiers and collected their petitions about army abuses of their own health and rights. Helen hoped to return to the war front, but she could not recover from illness for what appears to have been some years. What is certain is that Helen's experiences of emancipation and war were not in any way the abstractions they might have been for other Northern reformers.[33]

For most of Reconstruction Helen lived in western New York with her parents. But in 1877 she came to Washington, taking up a room with her uncle Hiram, an immediate neighbor of the Douglasses'. She did some teaching, but by September 1881 she took a patronage job from the recorder of deeds, who was happy to hire his neighbor's niece. In many ways Helen was overqualified, but did her job as copyist processing deeds with zeal. Only one person ever suggested rumors of a courtship between Helen and her boss after Anna's death, and that was her aunt Frances Pitts, Hiram's wife. Douglass objected about such "hints, innuendos or implications" in a letter to Frances, and the matter fell silent until the sudden wedding. However much Frederick and Helen secretly shared a desire to test America's obsession with race, what they did clearly find in common was affection, experience, companionship, and a growing love.[34] The public furor over their marriage was not for the fainthearted; Douglass seems to have known that this spiritual, smart, confident veteran of the freedmen's schools and hospitals could take it and endure. What's more, she was perfectly willing to assume the role of Mrs. Douglass, fellow traveler and fellow reader.

• • •

From inside Douglass's conflicted family, the newlyweds had no peace for some time. Nathan Sprague had come to despise the hand that fed him, and he wanted revenge. Louisa, Nathan's sister, had lived and worked in the Douglass home for more than ten years. Frederick and Anna had taken her in as a daughter, even as she labored at many household chores. In the middle of the marriage controversy, and from an array of motives—extortion, resentment of Helen, embittered hostility to his father-in-law, and perhaps even self-loathing—Nathan engaged Thomas J. Mackey, an attorney and former judge, as well as a former Confederate and Democrat with no love for black leaders, to bring a lawsuit against Douglass. The *Washington Star* and other newspapers were more than happy to fan the flames of this ugly family drama. It is not clear how much Rosetta encouraged this scurrilous public humiliation of her father, but she did not stop her husband's action. Before it was over Nathan, Douglass himself, his sons Lewis and Charles, and even Louisa weighed in all too publicly with accusations and denunciations. Lewis told reporters that he did not believe Louisa had pushed the matter at all, but that Nathan wanted to injure Douglass. Charles pointed to all of Nathan's employment and business failures, accused him of blatant ingratitude and of a "malicious conspiracy" to ruin Douglass.[35] As February dragged on, the Sage of Cedar Hill must have wondered how he could escape and hide from public view.

Unmistakably, Nathan wanted money, but he also sought to politically ruin his wife's famous father. Nathan originally asked for $2,640 in back pay for his sister's service, accusing Douglass in effect of treating her like a servile laborer. On the day the formal writ was filed and delivered to Douglass, February 16, the total read $2,025, with over $600 subtracted for clothing provided over the years. The nefarious Nathan had fed all manner of shady information to the press. He addressed Douglass directly via reporters. "You place yourself on a lofty pedestal and flaunt your assumed dignity before the public," said the unemployed father of Rosetta's six children. "I have viewed your marriage more in sorrow than in anger, and as to that have accorded to you the charity of my silence. . . . I sincerely trust that your white wife will experience more justice and consideration at your hands than you ever gave your worthy colored wife." Nathan claimed his suit was entirely about money, and that Douglass had reneged on a "contract" for certain monthly wages. In the next breath he stated that Louisa did not dislike Helen "because she was white or because she married Mr. Douglass. Louisa disliked her long before that."[36] We can only begin to fathom the class and racial resentments at the root of these sentiments. Douglass did the only thing he could: he struck back in the same newspapers.

The father-in-law accused Sprague of blackmail and "taking advantage of the supposed unpopularity of his recent marriage." In a formal letter released to the press, Douglass said he had never hired Louisa at any time, but that he would "submit to fair arbitration." The money demanded for housework and as seamstress "is higher than I should have paid her had I offered to hire her." Douglass accused Sprague of extortion; Douglass dove into the sordid details and gave almost as much as he took: "I knew nothing of Louisa as a seamstress, except in making and mending her own clothes and the clothes of your own children while she and they were being fed at my table and sheltered under my roof." Douglass maintained that he had several times tried to pay Louisa but she declined. He further told Sprague that he was "not favorably impressed with the extraordinary manner" in which the younger man had gone about this "cowardly" affair, especially "the monstrous story that I am worth $200,000 and much other stuff and nonsense."[37]

Louisa was the one most caught in a terrible bind; she was a single black woman in need of work and never set foot again at Cedar Hill. Douglass settled out of court; he paid Louisa $645, and she and her opportunistic brother dropped the case. She and Rosetta likely forced Sprague to go silent to get this family disaster out of the papers. Before Washington papers moved on to other sensations, however, the Douglasses had to endure one more awful, if painfully true, joke. The aptly named *Washington Grit* said that P. T. Barnum "could make a mint of money out of this couple [Helen and Frederick] if they would consent to go on exhibition."[38]

In the midst of the controversy over his marriage and the Sprague lawsuit, Douglass exchanged letters with Ottilie Assing. Since the fall of 1881, Assing had made Florence her base in Europe in her frustrating, hopeless struggle to make claims on the will of her deceased sister, Ludmilla. Assing had also encountered many pages of Ludmilla's diaries that only deepened the hatred Ottilie felt for her sister even in death. Alone and as usual fiercely independent, the indefatigable traveler went on tour through southern Italy, much of Germany, Switzerland, Austria, and then to Paris by 1884. Ottilie carried on a correspondence with Douglass, and especially with the Koehlers and others in her old "gang." A long silence seems to have ensued between Frederick and Ottilie during 1882, and for a long time after Anna's death. He received a condolence letter from Sylvester Koehler, but, so far as we know, none from Assing, who had spent more than twenty years despising and wishing Anna out of her husband's life. Neither Anna's death nor Douglass's emotional travail in summer 1883 are anywhere mentioned in an extant Assing letter. Douglass himself vanished from any of her extant letters to other friends during the final two years of her life, which were spent as the intrepid, and at times joyous if lonely, wanderer through the Alps and many European capitals. In Munich she even found a new outlet as a writer in a radical socialist journal.[39] It is hardly likely that Douglass would have informed Assing of his marriage to Helen Pitts beforehand, since he kept it a secret from his own family.

Sometime during 1884 Assing became aware of cancerous tumors in her breast. She had found many friends with whom to stay for weeks at a time during her travels, but in what her biographer considers a wise judgment, she likely did not want to impose the "indignity, humiliation of sickness and dying" on any of them. She was fundamentally homeless, as Maria Diedrich has shown. But to interpret her demise through the German Romantic literary tradition, the idealization of suicide shaped so much by Goethe's *Werther*, can be only one among other speculative explanations. Surely it is one important context, and an outlook influenced by however she had become aware of Douglass's marriage to Helen Pitts. But despair of Assing's kind is born of myriad roots, of many years of psychological turmoil and depression, and certainly now including the terrible determinism of breast cancer. On August 21, 1884, on a sunny afternoon, Ottilie Assing walked from the Hôtel d'Espagne to the Bois de Boulogne, the huge bucolic park in the Sixteenth Arrondissement in Paris. She sat on a bench alone and swallowed a vial of potassium cyanide. When found, her elegantly dressed body was taken to the Paris morgue, where two weeks ensued before a German friend identified her. With assistance from the American consul in Paris, Assing was interred in the Cimetière de la Morgue in Ivry on September 13.[40]

Exactly when and how Douglass learned of Ottilie's suicide we do not know. But on November 4, 1884, he wrote a revealing letter to his old Rhode Island friend Martha Greene. He had just returned from stumping across the Midwest for James G. Blaine and the Republican ticket that fall. He felt "irrepressibly sad" at receiving confirmed news "of the death of my dear friend Miss Assing—who is supposed to have committed suicide on account of what she considered her incurable cancer on her left breast." When he learned of the illness, wrote Douglass, "I felt and have felt afraid that she would do precisely as she is reported to have done."[41] A mourning Douglass controlled his words, but in death he wrote more openly, so far as the record shows, than he ever before had about Assing.

"She has always maintained her right in case of being afflicted with an incurable disease to save herself the pain of a lingering death and her friends the trouble of caring for her," offered Douglass. These kinds of informed sentiments may have stemmed from letters, or from long-remembered conversations. Douglass made no mention of Assing's staunch atheism. But she had shared deeply personal trusts and pledges with Douglass. "I have lost a precious friend," he told Martha, and had "never had one more sincere." When Assing "parted with me for Europe four years ago, she told me that in case she should die abroad she had made her will and left a fund of ten thousand dollars for my benefit." Douglass did not seem to betray any guilt or remorse about the bequest of such money. He simply reported that it was left in the care of a Henry Bergh, the head of an organization against animal cruelty, a keen interest of Assing's. Douglass further said he had always thought he would die before Ottilie, since he was two years older. He also reported that Assing had left him her books. Finally, he mentioned his knowledge of the cancer: "Her last letters to me spoke of incurable cancer but said nothing of her intention to shorten her days." In some ways, though, that Douglass could not quite face, Assing's last letters to him may have in effect been her suicide notes. For his part, he simply repeated that the death in Paris was "a distressing stroke to me."[42] He offered no public or private tribute to Assing's remarkable life and career as a voice in American reform.

Back in 1871 Assing had drawn up a will, making Henry Bergh, president of the American Society for the Prevention of Cruelty to Animals, her executor. At that time she bequeathed a sum of $13,000 to "the Hon. Frederick Douglass, to pay over the net interest and income therefrom by equal semi-annual payments . . . during the term of his natural life, in recognition of his noble labors in the antislavery cause." He was also to receive Assing's gold pens and books. The year 1871 had been a particularly difficult time financially for Douglass, with the *New National Era* struggling to survive, his sons in and out of employments, and the pending move to Washington. Ottilie had also left a substantial sum to a niece, who by 1883 had died. Thus, the European traveler had made revisions in the will. She also included some of her Hoboken friends, especially the Koehlers. Bergh informed Douglass of the death and these arrangements in an early–October 1884 letter; Douglass may also have learned details in a published conversation with Bergh in the *New York Tribune* late that month. He received a copy of the will by January 1885, but as Bergh declined to be executor, Douglass and Sylvester Koehler enlisted a young former student of Assing's and attorney, Hermann C. Kudlich, to handle the affairs.[43]

As Assing's obituaries appeared in American papers in 1885, due to the processing of the will, most of them highlighted her suicide but especially that she left money, variously reported at either $18,000 or $20,000, to Douglass. The *Washington Critic* even ran a brief notice under the headline "Fred Douglass's Fortune." One significant stipulation in the will garnered no public comment, but gained Douglass's keen interest: "All the letters which will be found in my possession are to be destroyed immediately." By the summer of 1885, Kudlich informed Douglass that he had done the painful duty. "I . . . destroyed a large number of carefully preserved packages of letters arranged according to date from the year 1830. They constituted a treasure in themselves and bore the signatures of eminent men and women and I was reluctant to permit these precious documents to disappear in smoke." Was Assing protecting or, as Diedrich has argued, "haunting" Douglass with these acts?[44] What were Douglass's most personal views of this erasure of memory and evidence? His virtual silence about "Miss Assing" had always been his only stance. The man who wrote so much to try to shape his life and legacy supported the destruction of this valuable historical record. Moving ahead with his personal life at this crossroads meant a good deal of private forgetting and public control. He had lost a dear friend and left it at that.

In the presidential election of 1884, Grover Cleveland and the Democrats narrowly won back the White House for the first time since 1861. The campaign was raucous and full of ugly mudslinging. If the Reconstruction-era elections were the most racist, this may have been the dirtiest in American history to that date. The Republicans ran the former secretary of state James G. Blaine of Maine. Blaine was popular with the Irish but somewhat notorious for financial shenanigans. Cleveland, the one-term governor of New York, an anti–Tammany Hall worthy, and bachelor, got mired in a paternity matter, an out-of-wedlock child from previous years. Cleveland won by only a razor-thin margin of under twenty-five thousand votes out of almost 10 million cast. He took the electoral college 218–182, with an extremely close win in New York and by carrying the Democratic "solid South" as well as all the border states. Blaine may have blundered into the close loss in

New York; while attending a sermon by a Protestant minister who attacked the Democrats as the party of "rum, Romanism, and rebellion," he failed to react, losing some support with immigrant Catholics.[45]

Douglass took to the stump for Blaine, especially again where the Republican Party most desired his voice, the swing state of Indiana. But he started campaigning in August in New England and across New York, and this time he traveled with Helen. They stayed quite visibly at the Parker House in Boston; in Rhode Island Douglass spoke to a gathering of black Union veterans. The orator judged the earlier part of this tour, a kind of extended honeymoon at two thousand miles, and observed that he had "not been subjected to a single instance of indignity." They vacationed at Niagara Falls, went up the St. Lawrence River, and visited the Thousand Islands area, as well as other parts of Canada. Such experiences told Douglass that the country did not need more laws; it needed to enforce existing ones. In Indianapolis he spoke to four thousand in a baseball park after a torchlight parade. The Republican Party was for blacks the good "helmsman," the "capable pilot," Douglass maintained, who could chart the way through the troubled waters of the 1880s. He assured the throng, a racially and ethnically mixed audience, that despite his gray head and "voice less powerful," he would always remain a Republican "battling in your interest." Republicans would keep "memory" and "truth" alive, he insisted, while Democrats would make the nation forget the past.[46]

In Syracuse in early October, at an anniversary of the Jerry Rescue (a fugitive slave) of 1851, Douglass delivered an extraordinary speech about memory: "It is not well to forget the past. Memory was given to man for some wise purpose." He was worried about sectional reconciliation and its costs for blacks, especially in this election year. Douglass summoned remembrance of the vast transformation of the Civil War era; it could make one "almost realize the feeling of John," he said, "when he saw in the apocalyptic vision a new heaven and a new earth." But Americans were "far more likely to forget too soon, than remember too long, the history of the great American conflict with slavery." Douglass reminisced about all the deceased abolitionists in the New York region, then turned his attention to current race relations. Mobs and lynchings were escalating. "This color hate is so universal and so intense." Douglass especially analyzed the social implications of whites' racist expectations of blacks. "Everybody is ready to help him [a black man] on his downward way," he observed. "But if he aspires to be a man, and his course is upward, his way will be disputed at every turn."[47]

The black man was the universal subject on everyone's mind in the

Gilded Age. "He is pictured on our street corners, heard in our songs, seen and talked of in all our market places." Douglass insisted that nothing less than "the wheels of the world's moral progress must be reversed." It was as if Gilded Age white supremacy had become a soul-killing hydra worse than slavery itself. He still put his faith in an ultimate jubilee rooted in faith ("the steady light of stars"), in ideas and laws. Ever the moralist and the believer in politics, he breathed a hope that in these darkening days, the cause of justice, "like the ghost of the murdered Hamlet, will appear and reappear." Even more poignantly, the old abolitionist reached deep into his spiritual and rhetorical well. Paraphrasing John 11:11, he demanded hope. "The assumption that the cause of the negro is a dead issue is an utter illusion. For the moment he may be buried under the dust and rubbish of endless discussion concerning civil service, tariff, and free trade, labor and capital . . . but our Lazarus is not dead. He only sleeps."[48] Douglass often drew upon this biblical story of miraculous rebirth, on its anguished but affirming fusion of life with death.

This kind of faith in historical and moral rebirth was much in need after the Republican defeat that fall. After twenty-four years, what Douglass called in a postelection interview "the old exploded slave power" was back in charge. A political force "opposed to negro citizenship, negro equality before law, negro education, and negro progress," and its constitutionalism defined by "the doctrine of state sovereignty," threatened to reduce black people "to semi-slavery." Press reports from across the country, especially emanating from Democratic regions, confirmed the case for fear. Under headlines in the *New York Tribune* such as "Dixie, Victorious, at Last Exults" came stories of celebration in the South of a return to the "white man's country," rule by the "proud Anglo-Saxon race, whose courage, genius and energy rescued this country from barbarism." "Africa has been vanquished, and it is settled forever," announced a Lynchburg, Virginia, paper. In some Southern towns election celebrations involved joyous displays of Confederate flags, uniforms, and other symbols, including mock slave auctions.[49]

In late 1884 and into 1885, Douglass came under stinging criticism from some blacks for not resigning his recorder's post in the Cleveland administration. As early as November 29 a black editor, Howard S. Smith, attacked Douglass and Blanche Bruce as "renegades," claiming they had come to support Cleveland and that the two Washington functionaries "live solely for themselves and not for the race." The Sage of Anacostia tried to ignore this kind of ugly harping, but as usual he could not. He saved his fullest defense for the second edition of *Life and Times*, where he pointed out that the recorder's position was not a federal job, but a thoroughly local matter. He had been employed by the District of Columbia, his salary the result of a fee-based system determined by the work done by himself and his employees. But his defense rested primarily on an image of Cleveland, despite his party's evils, as an advocate of civil service reform, of keeping professional government workers in office based on performance and not on party spoils. Cleveland did keep Douglass in the job for well over a year, which was so important to Rosetta, Lewis, Frederick Jr., Charles, and their families. The elder Douglass based his strongest case against resigning, though, on the lack of home rule in the District of Columbia. The District was under congressional control, its citizens a "disfranchised people," struggling under "plenty of taxation, but no representation." The issue of District home rule is still mired in a partisan morass today. Douglass also admitted that despite all his bitter political differences with Cleveland, this president had invited him and Helen to numerous White House receptions, unfazed by the interracial marriage. Douglass thought these social gestures remarkable at a time when "false friends of both races were loading me with reproaches."[50]

From 1884 to 1886, Douglass tried to find a new equilibrium between his private peace and happiness with Helen, and the despairing and dangerous public-political climate. He frequently had to face the impression among younger black leaders that he had become irrelevant. He and Helen appeared frequently in many public venues, including front pews in major churches in Washington, where white congregants were sometimes outraged at their presence, as at the prominent First Presbyterian Church in 1885. With such incidences so often splashed in the press, Douglass had to deny publicly that he had tried to rent a pew close to the president's pew. Douglass always tried humor in these instances, suggesting that the "critics must be people who want his job as Recorder," now that a Democrat was president. He and Helen occasionally caused a great stir by attending a session of Congress and sitting in the "ladies gallery," whereupon all business stopped during the "craning of necks in all parts of the House," and "opera glasses" flashing in the hands of members on the floor. The couple's life was more public than they may have wished, but Helen also now took over and hosted receptions for invited guests at Cedar Hill, a practice never done while Anna was alive. Unfortunately, funerals still visited regularly at the mansion on the heights. On February 9, 1886, Frederick Aaron Douglass, son of Frederick Jr. and Virginia Douglass, died at age fifteen. He was a successful student at the Howard Normal School. Douglass almost never commented on these recurring deaths of his grandchildren, many more of which would darken his household in the coming year.[51]

During the mid and late eighties, one of the sons, as well as Nathan Sprague, occasionally fell into more legal trouble either in lawsuits or in scrapes with the police. Douglass himself continued to carry on open disputes with some of his black rivals. Beginning in the 1884 election year, John Mercer Langston and the recorder sparred, often viciously, with their scraps always becoming brutally personal, over the usefulness of conventions and Republican loyalty. Langston believed blacks ought to "divide up between the parties" with their votes. Langston accused Douglass of convening black conventions to achieve a cabinet position in a Republican administration. Personal vitriol seemed to know no limit for Langston in judging his rival's ambitions and character. Langston charged Douglass with the "climax" of "marrying a white woman and announcing that there is not a drop of black blood in his veins." Worse, he aimed at Douglass's alleged greed. "We have been pouring money into his pockets for years because he is a colored man. . . . It is enough to make a man sick to hear him prate about his Caucasion blood." Langston further ground in the knife about the old issue of the failure of the Freedmen's Bank, which he attributed to the former slave's "insane itching desire for prominence."[52]

This meltdown between two titans only got worse in the coming two to three years. Langston's son was indicted for murder in the District of Columbia, and by early 1886 the lawyer accused the recorder of trying to get the son convicted. Douglass had no choice but to fire back more than once, accusing Langston of a "murderous assault on my reputation," and with being a "heartless maligner." The *Washington Bee* claimed its reporter overheard a chance encounter between the two men in January 1886, at which Langston reportedly said to Douglass, "I hate you, sir! I hate the ground upon which you walk!" Some black readers of the press coverage of this kind of ugly personal warfare were likely entertained, and others sickened.[53]

In March 1886, President Cleveland did finally decide to replace Douglass as recorder, appointing a black lawyer from Albany, New York, James C. Matthews. The two men exchanged letters and had a smooth transition, with some of Douglass's children staying on as employees. When asked by reporters about his future plans, Douglass said he was considering taking a trip to Europe, and that he might now spend the "remainder of my days in peaceful retirement." The *Brooklyn Eagle* declared a kind of official "Retirement of Frederick Douglass," in a bold headline, as it also claimed the great

John Mercer Langston,
professor of law at Howard
University, 1870s.

man had "made and saved a fortune" from public money.[54] In such reports, the trip to Europe survived as the only secure fact.

Douglass knew the Lazarus story well. He knew that Jesus had been stoned for blasphemy before and after his raising Lazarus from the dead. Deep in its tragic heart the story was about faith. Douglass hardly knew what to do about miracles, although something akin to that is what he sometimes wished for in history and in his own life. Above all, from the Lazarus tale and from his long experience, personal and public, he came to understand the utterly intertwined nature of light and darkness, love and hatred, life and death. "Except a corn of wheat fall into the ground and die," God said to his doubters, "it abides alone; but if it die, it bringeth forth much fruit."[55] Without a job at sixty-eight years old, some of Douglass had died even as he chose new life.

Chapter 29

BORN TRAVELER

Man is by nature a migratory animal . . . a born traveler.

—FREDERICK DOUGLASS, 1886

I n April 1886, in the burgeoning black community of Washington, DC, considerable controversy arose over the anniversary of emancipation in the capital. Two rival celebrations took place, one organized by the editor of the *Washington Bee*, Calvin Chase, and a faction that had grown around him. This year they planned a more decorous parade than ever. A second faction emerged around a saloonkeeper named Perry Carson. Both factions conducted parades on April 16, with the Carson group, calling themselves the "people's procession," managing the larger performance, culminating in Lincoln Park. The Chase group held evening speeches at the Israel Bethel Colored Methodist Church, with Douglass delivering the keynote. The old orator found the competitive parades "mortifying" but cautioned that the "best of men will sometimes differ." Such rivalries and controversies continued for years over the anniversary.[1]

Douglass delivered a full-throated jeremiad against the depressing state of American race relations, and especially at the federal government's refusal to enforce law and protect black people. In an address infused with biblical passages and storytelling, the orator placed American emancipation in a tradition dating back to when Moses "smote the Red Sea and the Hebrews passed safely over from Egyptian bondage." His aggressive attacks got him accused of waving the bloody shirt by Democrats. Indeed he did; in the face of all the political violence in the South, Douglass wondered why the nation did not let forth a collective scream of pain. Drawing from Genesis, he declared, "How can I, how can you, how can any man with a heart . . . do otherwise when, louder than the blood of Abel, the blood of his fellow man cries from the ground."[2]

Douglass accused both political parties of immoral inaction, although he charged the Democrats with outright complicity in murder. His people had been abandoned in the South, he maintained, and the nation had abdicated its responsibilities. He pointed specifically to the recent massacre of a dozen or more blacks at the Carrollton, Mississippi, courthouse. An attempt by a mob to lynch three black men accused of crimes exploded into a mass murder, about which the Mississippi authorities refused even to hold an inquest. Douglass vividly captured a tragic national mood that later generations of Americans know all too well: "The sad thing is that in the average American mind, horrors of this character have become so frequent since the slaveholding rebellion, that they excite neither shame nor surprise; neither pity for the slain, nor indignation for the slayers." He used a verse from Alexander Pope, a line of which captured how inured American society had become to domestic terror as a part of politics: "We first endure, then pity, then embrace."[3]

Douglass ended on what he called a "moderate" hope in that springtime of anguish. He took some solace from the belief that "the white people of this country are asleep, but not dead." He could also still trust that "both the constitution of 1789 and the constitution with the fourteenth and fifteenth amendments" might still become "the law of the land for all the people."[4] In speaking engagements that summer Douglass continued to try to fashion hope from despair. But mostly, he planned with Helen a long and cherished trip to Europe. It was time to leave for a while the America of turmoil and conflict and seek joy, spirit, and new knowledge in travel abroad.

In forty-five years, since he first took to the platform as a Garrisonian itinerant in 1841, Douglass had logged well in excess of one hundred thousand miles on land and water in pursuit of both the cause of human freedom and equality as well as his own livelihood. More than perhaps any other American of the nineteenth century, Douglass had been traveling all of his adult life. But never like this—a private citizen on a grand European and classical Mediterranean tour intended as a vacation.

Douglass had many reasons to escape the country and his life as he knew it in 1886. The Douglasses had planned for an earlier departure, but several matters kept them at Cedar Hill through the summer. The old editor continued to endure all manner of criticism in the press, with one black Chicago paper even attacking him for the "courtesy" of his resignation letter from the position of recorder to President Cleveland. The Senate, moreover, lagged on the approval of his successor at the Recorder's Office. In late

April he wrote to his friend Francis Grimké that the dire state of violence and deteriorating race relations was so "pressing as to claim nearly all my time and attention." Then he quipped, "You will observe by the papers that I have almost as much trouble to get out of office as some men do to get into office." He wrote to one solicitous editor who was trying to get Douglass to produce an article that the sheer multitude of "requests for contributions from my pen and pocket stagger me."[5]

And then, journalists just showed up at Cedar Hill without appointments requesting interviews. He suffered through one of them in late May with a reporter from the *Washington Star* who subsequently wrote a rather exotic piece on Frederick and Helen. The writer misjudged the sixty-eight-year-old Douglass as seventy-six! He said the sage "looked like the King of Madagascar, or some land we have dimly heard of." Then came detailed descriptions of facial and bodily features, his "chin and jaws," the white mane of hair, of course, even the shape of his "nostrils." Although identifying Douglass as mixed race, the reporter thought the "colored portion of him . . . probably the most vigorous element." The intrusive guest acknowledged Douglass's great intelligence and felt assured that "after visiting him white men who came away find nothing to criticize in either taste or talk." Mrs. Douglass was "neither stout nor thin" and reminded this reporter of "the matron or superintendent of some philanthropic institution in which charity plays the principal part." He further admired her demonstrated "subordination . . . to her husband."[6] Reading such reports surely made Frederick and Helen relish sailing away to faraway lands.

With a Baedeker guidebook in hand, the Douglasses departed New York harbor on September 15 for an eight-day passage to Liverpool on the *City of Rome*, a 560-foot-long steamer, launched in 1881 and considered one of the largest and most beautiful ships afloat. It was Douglass's third Atlantic crossing from America, and Helen's first. Both Douglasses wrote diaries during the eleven-month journey, Frederick intermittently throughout their travels, but Helen only for the first three weeks. On the evening before the morning sail, they received a visit from Gustav Frauenstein, one of Ottilie Assing's closest friends in her old gang. Helen recorded a "pleasant visit" for the three of them. "We talked of Miss Assing," said Helen, "& as the genial Dr left he threw his arms around Frederick's neck in a good old fashioned hug & kissed him, kissed me, and ran off the steamer."[7] Perhaps Frauenstein conveyed some further knowledge of Assing's tragic demise, or of the estate, a portion of which Douglass may have used to pay for this long tour. But Douglass left no remarks in his diary about the conversation.

Both Frederick and Helen commented during the crossing on the majesty of the sea. Both read books about England in preparation for the first part of their tour, she a work by Richard Grant White, *England Without and Within*, and he Ralph Waldo Emerson's widely acclaimed *English Traits*. The couple shared many literary tastes and conversations and by all indications were remarkably compatible. Douglass hoped for solitude and to go unrecognized on the voyage. But that was not to be. Passengers asked him to deliver a speech, which he considered an "infliction." With Douglass dreading another lecture while he imagined a vacation, Helen considered his discomfort to be "nonsense." She described his shipboard "little address" as "over before anyone was ready for him to stop."[8]

The *City of Rome* docked in Liverpool on September 22. During a full week in Liverpool, Frederick and Helen walked the streets and visited art galleries, libraries, and churches. They both commented on the multitude of poor, barefoot children and women with "babe in arms . . . singing in mournful . . . heart breaking strains." Douglass, however, honored what he observed as the "immense energy" of the English working people. In a visit to the town of Chester, the Douglasses toured the cathedral, and Frederick made his first of many comments on the nature of "Romanism" and its influence on European culture. Over and again as their tour moved to the Continent and southward to Italy, Douglass released in his diary a level of anti-Catholicism that he had seldom expressed in public speeches. Helen wrote mostly with joy and awe. She observed the magnificence of the statuary in and around St. George's Hall in Liverpool. She insisted that they attend worship services most Sundays at Protestant churches. She also laced her diary with observations about how the public treated or viewed Douglass. "People will look at Frederick wherever we go," Helen wrote, "but they wear no unpleasant expression. Many have a decided appearance of interest." Sometimes she noted when an American recognized the famed orator and "accosted" him.[9]

Douglass had vainly hoped to see many old abolitionist comrades in England, only to realize that most were already dead. In *Life and Times*, he later trudged through a "melancholy enumeration" of the English notables of antislavery fame, demonstrating his deep connections to them. He reconnected with Anna and Ellen Richardson, the Quaker sisters, both now in their eighties, who had led the effort forty years earlier to purchase his freedom. Most important, the Douglasses spent a full week in October staying with Julia Griffiths Crofts in her small town of St. Neots, just west of Cambridge. Elderly and widowed, Julia hosted them with charm and joy.

Interestingly, Helen referred to their little group as "the trio." Douglass wrote nothing in his diary about the week with Julia; he had not seen her in twenty-six years. Helen honored Julia for accepting them with open arms and marveled at experiencing her "first night in a real English home." She loved the flat beautiful country roads of Cambridgeshire. They attended a Methodist church with Julia and took tea every day somewhere special. And the "trio" made an excursion to see "all the glories of Cambridge," including attending Evensong at the famed King's Chapel. Helen called it a time to be "treasured in memory forever." [10] What this all meant to Douglass to spend such time of solemnity and beauty with these two women from different times in his life he did not tell us.

Before leaving England, Douglass was imposed on to speak at least once in Bridgport. He also did an extensive interview with the *London Daily News*. The reporter noted Douglass's "features . . . of the negro type," although he "nevertheless" seemed a "man born for distinction" and a "name all England is familiar with." In the 1880s, though, Douglass's fame still had to be couched in the racialized claim that he represented "the one, and apparently only one, exception to the general laziness and ignorance of the black population in the midst of which he was born." Decades after emancipation, parts of the British press still marveled at how such a "cultured gentleman could have ever been a slave." [11] How old and tortured such notions must have seemed to the famous tourist.

Soon the touring couple crossed the Channel for the Continent and arrived in Paris on October 20. They appear to have spent the rest of the fall in or around Paris, staying at least two and a half months. Douglass ceased writing the diary when in Paris, although numerous press reports back in the United States had titles such as "Frederick Douglass in Paris." In January 1887, Douglass wrote a long piece about his observations on Parisian life, labor, and politics. The curious essay is full of his admiration as well as disdain for French society. It was sixteen years since the disaster of the Franco-Prussian War and the bloody Paris Commune. Douglass had little to say on that recent history, but he admired and cheered for the "possible permanency" of the French Republic. He greatly praised the dignity of labor, for men and women, among the busy and industrious Parisians: "All labor is here held in honor, all useful callings are respectable." This would have been news to many of Paris's working poor and to the growing anarchist groups. Douglass was later fond of describing how warmly he was received when he visited the French Senate, but he did not deliver well-informed observations on the country's politics. He liked the ways the city's people conserved fuel in winter. But he was less enamored with their "street manners" and their "Sabbath customs" as they conducted many business enterprises on Sundays. And he was intrigued to "notice much drinking, but little drunkenness." [12]

Douglass was an honest, if parochial, American in Paris. He knew enough of the city's bloody and volatile history to be wary of a "deep shadow of a terrible disaster" that might at any time explode, and he saw an alarming level of "divergence of classes." In later speeches he did stress how this city of beauty, fashion, and art had also "withstood the destructive shocks of twelve revolutions in a single century." But like almost any other visitor to the city of light, he marveled that no other place had done so much to "gratify the esthetic taste" of humanity. He was awed by the "miles of corridors" and the art at the Louvre. Douglass acknowledged the guidance around the city by Theodore Stanton, the son of Elizabeth Cady Stanton. He especially glowed with joy over meeting the eighty-two-year-old Victor Schoelcher, French senator and abolitionist who had led the effort for French slave emancipation in 1848. He was invited to Schoelcher's home for an extensive interview and, stunningly, found himself in the reformer's study "surrounded by broken fetters and other cast-off paraphernalia of the slave system." [13] Back at Cedar Hill, Douglass had already made his own parlors into a kind of museum of American abolitionism; he may have gained a few more ideas in Schoelcher's den.

By the time the couple left Paris to go south in early January, Douglass resumed brief entries about various French towns and landmarks. "I am keeping a diary," he wrote to his son Lewis in February, "and shall I live to get home be able to talk to you of my journeys." A little later that month he said that he had "little time to write. . . . I am not writing anything for publication" (which was untrue). The towns of Dejun, Lyon, Avignon, Marseille, and Nice all garnered special attention, as the Douglasses reached the Mediterranean. In Lyon, Douglass searched carefully and in vain for the grave of his old African American friend Henry O. Wagoner's son, who he knew had died in that town. At Marseilles, Frederick "took Helen into a small boat and was rowed out to the old Chateau D'If made famous by the story of Monte Cristo by Alex. Dumas." He loved Avignon, the "quaintest, crookedest, and queerest" place they had seen, with its narrow streets and alleys. But Avignon was also the city of "popes," and here Douglass let loose his contempt for the "dogmas of the Romish faith." "What a horrible lie that Romish Church has palmed off upon the people of this and other countries pretending that its Pope is the vice gerant of God. . . . How strange it is that millions of sane men have believed this stupendous and most arrogant lie." [14] When he encountered the vast physical remnants of feudalism and the historical power of Catholicism, Douglass was no cultural pluralist on a learning expedition.

By mid-January, the Douglasses had traversed the southern French coast and arrived in Genoa in Italy. Strikingly, as Douglass moved southward in Europe, he remembered seeing more "black hair, black eyes, full lips and dark complexions." He also observed that the "style of dress" with "gay colors" increased. He attributed all of this to the "wisdom of Africa and the social disposition of Africans imitated." By far, he was most taken in Genoa by Paganini's violin, "treasured in a glass case" in a museum. Douglass loved the violin and was proud of his own modest ability to play it. In *Life and Times*, he would spend two pages capturing how moved he was by this one "sacred" object, this "old violin of wood, horsehair and catgut" that had "delighted thousands" with its musical magic. [15]

After a stop in Pisa, the city of Galileo, about whom Douglass mused while visiting the Leaning Tower, the couple arrived in Rome on January 19. Douglass called the moment the "day of days," and soon he felt enveloped in the Eternal City's magnificence. Douglass's sense of history had never before been stirred quite like this. At every turn the "scenes and sounds" carried his "mind back over vast periods of history." Standing in the dome of St. Peter's Basilica, "no words at my command," wrote Douglass, could "fitly describe" his feelings of awe. Yet, "in looking at its splendor," he recorded, "one could not help being deeply impressed by its gorgeousness and perfection despite of its utter contradiction to the life and lessons of Jesus." But the more he saw of the Vatican's "treasures . . . of costly vestments ornamented with gold, silver . . . and all manner of precious stones," the more this son of Protestant America became the foreigner and religious critic. "The sight of these things," he wrote, "only increased my sense of the hollowness of the vast structure of the Romish Church and my conviction that Science must in the end do for that church what time has done for the vast structures of kingly pride and power." [16]

But when Douglass walked through the "ancient greatness" of the Roman Forum, he could only gush that he had "seen nothing more impressive and solemn, nothing that tells so eloquently the story that all who live must die and at last, not only for man, but for all his best endeavors it is dust to dust and ashes to ashes." Douglass relished, intellectually and spiritually, imagining "two thousand years" of the Roman ruins. In his narrative about Rome crafted after returning to America, he admitted to being "much more interested in the Rome of the past than in the Rome of the present," by which he meant the city-state ruled by the Vatican. He wanted to know more of the "preaching of Paul eighteen hundred years ago than of the preaching of the priests and popes of today." He wanted to find the location of Paul's house, and to walk "on the Appian Way where he walked." To Douglass, surrounded and awed by all the splendor of Rome, the origin story he most sought was that of his hero Paul, "the first great preacher of Christianity."[17]

Before leaving Rome for Naples, the Douglasses engaged in social visits with old friends, especially the African American sculptor Edmonia Lewis. The six-hour train ride to Naples offered glorious views of the "blue Mediterranean" and left Douglass "breathless" at a clear sighting of Mount Vesuvius. He could hardly contain himself in writing of a visit to the ruins of Pompeii, and to the Greek temple of Neptune at Paestum. But what especially impressed Douglass was "the landing place of Paul." He was well aware of Paul's epistles, but now he could see a landscape from which they emerged. In southern Italy, what interested him most, wrote Douglass, "was the fact that I was looking upon the country seen eighteen hundred years ago by the Prisoner apostle on his way to Rome to answer for his religion. It somehow gave me a more vivid impression of the heroism of the man as I looked upon the grand ruins of the religion against which Paul dared to preach." Arrested by the Romans in Jerusalem, Paul journeyed to Rome where he spent two years in house arrest, living with a chain. Douglass felt an affinity with Paul, perhaps seeing his own enslavement of twenty years in Paul's story of arrest and persecution.[18]

In Naples, Douglass lectured on the martyrdom of John Brown at the United Presbyterian Church. Sometime in February the Douglasses decided to extend their tour to Egypt and Greece. In the diary, Douglass declared his anticipation of seeing the "land of Joseph and his brethren, and from which Moses led the children of Abraham out of the house of bondage." Frederick marveled at his own fate, "born as I was a slave marked for a life under the lash in a corn field," and now to be "plowing this classic sea and on my way to the land of Moses and the Pharaohs." Aboard the steamer while passing Crete, Douglass again remembered the prisoner apostle: "I suppose there was no light there when Paul sailed along its coast."[19] The old orator may have envisioned himself the exiled prophet, this time as a world tourist.

On February 16 the Douglasses arrived at Port Said, the entrance to the Suez Canal. Going ashore at Ismailia, they took a train to Cairo. Douglass now had yet a new encounter with religion. He was at first much taken with

Islam. He commended the Muslim faith because it did "not make color the criterion of fellowship," and he liked the mosques because they displayed no "images or pictures of saints or God." But the Egyptian crowds in the streets and bazaars wore on him. The bulk of the people were desperately poor, and the "most painful feature" of life was the "veiled women" and the "men who own them as slaves."[20] Douglass spared few elements of Egyptian culture from judgment even as he felt enthralled by it.

On February 22, Douglass climbed the Great Pyramid of Cheops at Giza. For the sixty-nine-year-old the effort was all but overwhelming. He and Helen had their photograph taken at its base. The more than four-hundred-foot "ascent is both difficult and dangerous," the diarist recorded, "and I would not undertake it again for any consideration." After resting for a day or so to write letters, the Douglasses visited a Coptic Christian church and a Jewish synagogue in Cairo. Most strikingly, they also witnessed a group he called "Howling Dervishes," who reminded him of a Methodist camp meeting. He scolded the mystics. This rationalist student of the King James language could not resist rejecting so much of the religiosity he encountered in foreign lands. After a morning visit to an Islamic college, the best he could say about the devotion he witnessed among the students reading the Koran was that "if sincerity is any proof of the truth of their creed, they certainly give that proof—but alas! Sincerity is no proof." Douglass did admit to real enjoyment on a six-mile donkey ride among throngs of Egyptians, and especially on a five-day trip up the Nile River.[21]

By mid-March the Douglasses took passage on a steamer to Athens. When Douglass first saw the Acropolis and the Parthenon, he could hardly contain his romantic joy. They were "so beautiful in their ruin." He was utterly enchanted by the "power of the ancient people of this famous city." Just before departing Athens, Douglass went back up to the Acropolis, ascended a nearby hill known as Areopagus, and either read or listened to a reading of "Paul's famous address to the Athenians 18 hundred years ago." According to Acts 17:19, Paul had addressed an assemblage of Greek philosophers from that very hill, challenging what he considered their idolatry, and preaching about Jesus and the resurrection. It was also in that address that Paul declared all peoples the "offspring" of God and spoke the famous passage used over the ages by advocates of human unity: God "hath made of one blood all nations of men for to dwell on all the face of the earth."[22] It is fascinating that Douglass the tourist, the old abolitionist, chose to remember these biblical texts on his final day amid the temples of the Greek gods. Released from the ever-grinding American obsessions with race, the

The Acropolis as seen from the Areopagus Rock. Douglass went
up to Areopagus to read Saint Paul's letter to the Athenians and
commemorate the apostle's speech to the Greek skeptics.

former slave sought ways in his imagination, and in returning to Paul's heroism, to recollect his own quest for self-creation and universal recognition. Douglass never sought to be a martyr, although he spent a lifetime admiring them.

By April the Douglasses sailed back to Italy. After a second stay in Rome, the couple traveled north in mid-May and stopped in Florence and Venice before traversing the Alps and returning to Paris. In Florence, Douglass located the grave of the American abolitionist Theodore Parker and also inquired about and searched unsuccessfully for the home of Ludmilla Assing, "the sister of my friend of many years Miss Ottilie Assing." In Venice, Douglass found himself in touch with favorite scenes in Shakespeare. He was thrilled to find the "house where Desdemona resided when wooed by Othello." By early June, back in London, Douglass ceased writing in his leatherbound diary. On June 10, he wrote a telling letter to his old Rochester friend Amy Post in which he mused on old age and travel: "When I consider my starting point in life, it is marvelous that I have accomplished so much, but I feel that it has all come too late in life. I should have traveled thus when I was younger, and when my ambition for achievement was more vigorous."[23] After a short visit back to Dublin, Ireland, the couple returned to

*Frederick Douglass, Dublin, Ireland, at the end of the European
tour with Helen, July 1887. Alice M. Shackelton photographer.*

America by early August; but ambition was not yet played out for the weary
traveler.

Douglass's return to America and to Washington was news; some of the
press was quite fascinated by the interracial couple's long tour, and the Sage
of Cedar Hill cultivated their interest. By late August, the celebrity would
hold court some afternoons with reporters and talk at length about his European journey. He told the *National Republican* that everywhere he went
he was treated with equality. He had encountered not a "single gesture" of
disapproval about his "color or the kink in my hair." Walking the grounds
of Cedar Hill, Douglass entertained *Washington Post* writers with stories of
Egypt. He assured them that Negroes were not the descendants of pharaohs.
Recollecting the climbing of the pyramid, he told of carrying his "seventy
years and 230 pounds," but joked that he "had four Arabs to help me." He
also received a good deal of correspondence from friends and acquaintances
who were reassured to have him back home, desired favors, or invited him

to lecture. Soon, at Metropolitan AME Church and elsewhere, Douglass began to deliver formal speeches detailing his tour.[24]

The first of these lectures occurred on September 22, at which the orator dwelled largely on the question of Irish home rule versus "coercion" from England. He thought that the "spirit of the age" favored unification and larger nationalities, reflecting no doubt his own American experience. But he sided nonetheless with Ireland's independence as a matter of justice. At the end of the address, the host pastor, Theophilus Stewart, to loud applause, called for a Republican ticket in 1888 of Robert Todd Lincoln for president and Douglass as vice president.[25]

In December, again at Metropolitan AME, Douglass delivered a more formal speech about his European tour. This celebrity tourist had clearly taken to the idea of travel as a philosophical as well as a narrative challenge. The whole species followed a kind of destiny. "Man is by nature," said Douglass, "a migratory animal. It does not appear that he was intended to dwell in any one locality. He is a born traveler." Douglass even predicted air travel. "When lightning shall take the place of steam, he imagined, as it will do, just as steam has taken the place of wind, when men shall navigate the air just as freely as they now navigate the sea, travel will cease to be the exclusive privilege and luxury of the few and the wealthy." [26] But Douglass had now become one of the privileged.

On this December night Douglass talked into late hours and only got through the tour of England and to Paris. A text survives of an even longer address he wrote carrying the story all the way to Egypt and Greece. These public lectures were laced with more hostile reactions to the "religious shows" of Rome and elsewhere, but also wonderful anecdotes. Douglass remembered going in Paris to the Bibliothèque Nationale, "the largest library in the world," where he took a seat in the vast reading room and quietly inquired whether they might have any of his writings. In only minutes a librarian appeared at his desk with a copy of *My Bondage and My Freedom*, as well as a copy of a public letter Douglass had published in 1846.[27] The unschooled author was clearly moved; he had just done what most writers do in seeking a kind of immortality in the stacks of libraries.

Douglass maintained that his object in Egypt was ethnological research. He said he had intended to test the theory whether the darker races had indeed achieved the highest of civilization in ancient times. Were the people who built the pyramids black or white? he had asked. Among modern Egyptians answering this question, Douglass found only ambiguity about race. But he felt quite certain that he had transcendently experienced some of the lands of the Old Testament and its greatest stories. He felt an "infinite presence" of religious ideas from the deserts and mountaintops. "Moses learned more of the laws of God in the mountains than down among the people." The "Hebrew prophets," Douglass mused, "frequented dens and caves and desert places." His lifetime of reading and expropriating biblical narratives no longer solely occurred on an imagined physical landscape. His greatest "thrill of satisfaction" from visiting Egypt came when "viewing the scenes of one of the most affecting stories ever written—the story of Jacob." [28]

Douglass knew his Genesis, and he felt in its presence. Joseph, one of the sons of Jacob, who was himself a son of the patriarch, Abraham, was sold into slavery in Egypt by his own brothers. They then lied to their father, saying Joseph was dead. But Joseph had special powers to interpret dreams, and while imprisoned, he interpreted one of Pharaoh's nightmares. Joseph was freed and made, in effect, the second most powerful man in Egypt. Then a terrible famine ravaged all the lands surrounding Egypt, which became the only place left producing corn. Jacob and his many sons came down to Egypt from Canaan for survival, and Joseph arranged an audience for his father with Pharaoh. As a result, these earliest Israelites (Jacob's other name was Israel) were allowed to settle in the fertile land of Goshen. Joseph, the formerly enslaved and betrayed one, now redeemed and provided bread for his father, for all his brothers, and for the people of Egypt. [29] Thus all the descendants of Jacob's twelve sons were the founding Israelites who were eventually brutally enslaved, necessitating the ultimate "Exodus."

Here were the origins of the essential biblical story Douglass had adapted to himself, to his people, and to America itself for most of his life. It is a tale of "how the slave boy Joseph gained favor in the eyes of Pharaoh," said Douglass, and prophetically saved the people and the land. It is to the Judeo-Christian world the oldest story of betrayal, suffering, famine, and internecine family warfare, but then also of forgiveness, generosity, liberation, and redemption. It is the story of a people destined for destruction, yet who are ultimately renewed and reborn. "Than this simple tale nothing has been written," Douglass declared in his public addresses, "nothing can be found in modern literature more pathetic and touching." He marveled that he had set foot "here in the land of Goshen, with fields yet green, its camels still grazing and its corn still growing as when Jacob and his sons with their flocks and herds were settled here three thousand years ago." [30] To the extent Douglass had seen himself over the years as the slave boy who would confront and tell tales to American pharaohs, then become the shepherd-prophet, he had stood on the soil that gave that idea birth. He had seen the landscape that had given the world the Exodus story. He had seen the ancient roots of his own story. He could feel some mystical sense of being an American Joseph.

During these first months back in Washington after the foreign tour, and beneath these high moments of public storytelling, tragedy struck Douglass's extended family again. During a two-week period in November, five more of Douglass's grandchildren died, all apparently in a typhoid-fever epidemic. On November 2, Charles Frederick Douglass, oldest son of Charles and Libbie, died at twenty-one years old. The next day, Julia Ada Douglass, daughter of Charles, died at age fourteen. By the middle of the month, Charles and Libbie lost two more children, Edward and Anne Elizabeth. And on November 14, Gertrude Pearl Douglass, daughter of Frederick Jr. and his wife, Virginia, died at only four years old. This marked the deaths of six grandchildren over just a year and a half. All were given funerals from Cedar Hill and buried in Graceland Cemetery.[31]

In large families death could seem omnipresent in the nineteenth century. During his lifetime, Douglass saw ten of his grandchildren die of disease. For Frederick Jr. and Charles, these personal losses were devastating. By late summer of 1887 Frederick Jr. had lost his job at the Recorder's Office and was taking loans from his father and his brothers. His financial story was nearly as tragic as his family's loss by death. In December 1890, Frederick Jr.'s wife, Virginia Hewlett Douglass, died at age forty-one of what obituaries called "consumption." At her death, Virginia's brother, Emanuel Molyneaux Hewlett, took custody of the couple's two remaining children, Charles Paul and Robert Smalls Douglass.[32] How Douglass himself coped with all these personal losses that autumn, or during the final two decades of his life, he did not tell us. Having Helen always at his side had to be crucial and bracing, however tepid her relationships with the adult Douglass children. These family tragedies may partly explain why the old orator took so assiduously to the lecture circuit and to the political stump.

In 1888, in a new political season, Douglass, the traveling man, soon reentered the fray, in the press and on the road. Before their father arrived back in Washington in 1887, Lewis and Frederick Douglass Jr. both took to public platforms to condemn blacks who would change parties and support Democrats. By October and November, the elder Douglass resumed bitter press exchanges with his critics, especially those who advocated that blacks divide their loyalties between the two political parties for leverage. To

Douglass this scheme was "absurd," even "madness." He engaged in a particularly nasty exchange throughout November in the *New York Age* with T. McCants Stewart, an AME minister and lawyer, thirty-five years younger than Douglass, who had spent two years teaching in Liberia, and who advocated that the race consider joining the Democrats. Douglass would have none of it: "It is far better that all our ventures should be in a sound ship than to have any part of them in a ship that is unseaworthy." Even more directly, he pulled out the old bloody shirts. "I find that every shotgun aimed at the breast of a Negro at the South today is leveled by the hand of a Democrat; that every Negro strung up at the crossroads without judge or jury is so strung up by a Democratic mob; that every effort to defeat and annul the 14th and 15th Amendments . . . is made by Democrats." Douglass even wrote bloody-shirt letters to Republican state leaders in New York.[33]

On February 28, 1888, at Metropolitan AME in Washington, which became a kind of home church and public pulpit for Douglass, a huge gathering, including some congressmen, celebrated what they assumed was the famous man's seventy-first birthday. The guest of honor embraced the occasion, although in his speech he reminded the audience that he "had never had a birthday." Douglass told listeners, "We [slaves] were born at times—harvest times, watermelon times, and generally hard times." For Douglass, the occasion was about the power of the past, a chance to embrace living memory, and to make slavery that story never forgotten for the many children attending. "They used to tell me up in New England not to refer to the stripes on my back. But when I remembered that such a great man as Paul had told of the stripes he had received, I thought why should a little fellow like me be ashamed to acknowledge that I had been flogged." In this shared sense of suffering lay Douglass's personal affinity with the Prisoner Apostle. Douglass insisted on remembrance before any action: "Perhaps there is too much past. But remember that all the present rests on all the past. Remember is as good a word as forget."[34]

The next day he hit the rails for a speaking tour of South Carolina and Georgia. In the late 1880s a journey into the Deep South for such a conspicuous African American man was not without danger. Douglass went to lecture, but also to see firsthand the conditions of the freedpeople after almost a quarter century of freedom and its denial.

In the cradle of the Confederacy, Charleston, the storied city of secession and the entrepôt of so many African Americans and their ancestors as slaves into the United States, Douglass gave two lectures at the Mount Zion Church. Often called the daughter church of Mother Emanuel AME,

Mount Zion was opened for worship in 1883; its first minister, the Reverend Norman B. Sterrett, was a former Union soldier. Douglass delivered versions of "Self-Made Men" and of the "European Travels" addresses. He was given a carriage ride around the old city of Charleston, much of it still being rebuilt since the war, and was met by a black militia unit calling itself the Douglass Light Infantry. Just what Douglass thought of the charms and haunts of Charleston he did not tell us. One press report indicated that the large audience may have wanted to hear more from the great orator on the racial conditions in the South than about his pursuit of the racial character of Egyptians. Douglass found that the Egyptian "if . . . not a negro . . . could pass for one in the United States. He was of a color between that of a new saddle and that of an old one. He was of a mixed race, very much like some seen all around us." [35]

Douglass moved on to speak to large black audiences in Augusta, Georgia, where a local, embittered Lost Cause advocate lampooned him. "When it comes to degrading and debasing myself at the feet of a thick-lipped nigger demagogue," wrote "Indes," "a sense of decency . . . compels me to say to the white people of this community, leave my part of the freedom of the city when the keys are handed over to the Hon. Fred Douglass." Here was the irreconcilable divide in the South since the war, embodied in the presence of the country's most famous black man. Douglass was no mere carpetbagger; he was to the local Augustan the "political firebrand" thrown "into our midst." As in the old abolitionist tours of the 1840s in the North, Douglass relished this role of the hated outsider speaking truth to power, as long as he was not killed in the effort; that year an estimated 137 lynchings occurred across the country, most in the Deep South.[36]

Among the places Douglass spoke in Augusta was the Ware high school for blacks; the setting was decked out in flowers and a big sign in golden letters: WELCOME. Beneath on an easel were pictures of Ulysses Grant, Abraham Lincoln, Blanche Bruce, and Douglass. A program with students reading excerpts from Life and Times, according to local press, left the guest of honor conspicuously listening as "tears glistened in his eyes." Douglass traveled back into South Carolina, lecturing in Orangeburg, where he was verbally attacked for discussing equality of the races. He returned northward by mid-March, full of impressions of the South, which he soon examined in public speeches. En route, he was Jim-Crowed in Weldon, North Carolina, as the train stopped and he was not allowed to eat in a local restaurant.[37]

In Washington, on April 16, the annual anniversary celebration of DC

emancipation once again occurred amid controversy. Whether to have raucous parades and just where black political allegiances best lay led to two
separate keynote addresses, one by Douglass at the Fourth Baptist Church,
and one by his rival John Mercer Langston at the Asbury Methodist Episcopal Church. Douglass rode in a carriage at the front of a long procession of
militia units, floats, and bands. In his speech, Douglass addressed the conditions and violence in the lives of the freedmen. What he'd learned in South
Carolina and Georgia was "not favorable to my hopes for the race." He acknowledged that anniversaries are often devoted to "prophecy" of "smooth
things," the "joyful and glad." But on this occasion he told a dark story,
whether people found it tasteful or not. "There are times when neither hope
nor fear should be allowed to control our speech," he declared, and sought
tone and justification in Isaiah: "Cry aloud and spare not." [38]

Douglass was back to playing his old antebellum role of the Jeremiah.
Above all, his address in April 1888 was a diatribe against the Democratic
Party as a new kind of Slave Power conspiracy intending to seize "the powers of the federal government" to sustain white supremacy and crush the
liberties of blacks. He portrayed the nation's condition as a struggle over
memory. "Well may it be said that Americans have no memories. We look
over the House of Representatives and see the solid South enthroned there.
We listen with calmness to eulogies . . . of traitors, and forget Andersonville.
We look over the Senate and see the senator from South Carolina, and we
forget Hamburg" (a massacre of blacks in 1876). African Americans, Douglass maintained, had a special responsibility to make the nation remember
the deepest meanings of the Civil War and emancipation. "Well the nation
may forget; it may shut its eyes to the past, but the colored people of this
country are bound to keep fresh a memory of the past till justice shall be
done them in the present." [39] However difficult, Douglass asked his people
to shoulder this long-term burden.

The victim of a "cunningly devised swindle" (the sharecropping system), the "plantation negro" in the South was worse off than when a slave,
Douglass maintained. Freedmen farmers were in the orator's view systematically cheated out of fair wages and of land. They were "like a man in a
morass, the more he struggles the deeper he sinks." This "Satanic arrangement," as Douglass termed the Southern agricultural system and its new labor relations, especially through landlord and tenant laws, had buried the
freedmen in a dead end of debt and tenancy. Some in the press attacked
Douglass for his harsh rhetoric in this speech. The *Washington Bee* thought
the address a mere "scarecrow" to cover up more positive realities. But other

papers, such as the *Boston Morning Journal*, considered the speech a "staggering blow to the pleasing fiction of a new regenerated South."[40]

To all those twenty-first-century Republicans, desperate to find African American heroes and adherents in their long-ago past, Douglass left this statement of his real views on the nature of government: "I know it is said that the general government is a government of limited powers. It was also once said that the national government could not coerce a state. . . . But whenever an administration has had the will to do anything, it has generally found constitutional power to do it." Douglass drew on sacred memory and experience rooted in the federal power exercised to free the slaves in war and deliver them rights in a new Constitution. "If the general government had the power to make black men citizens," he sternly declared, "it has the power to protect them in that citizenship. If it had the right to make them voters it has the right to protect them in the exercise of the elective franchise." As Douglass condemned Democrats, he also challenged his own party to embody a "new departure" in which it would remember its storied past and use federal power to stem the "bloody tide" in the South and to win new victories in 1888 at the ballot box. "Enough of shaking hands over the bloody chasm," Douglass shouted, "enough of conciliation, enough of laudation of the bravery of our southern brethren." There was no honor to be found among ex-Confederates. Douglass demanded of Republicans a politics of confrontation before it was too late.[41] The old lion had found a new roar and was ready to take it out on the stump.

Douglass attended the Republican National Convention in Chicago in June, not as a delegate, but essentially as the celebrity symbol he had become for his party. Tall and conspicuous standing at the rear of the stage at the Chicago Armory on the convention's first day, he was, as usual, called on to speak by a swelling chorus from the thousands attending. "Douglass! Douglass!" the old familiar appeal rolled over the room. Douglass later admitted that he preferred Senator John Sherman of Ohio as the presidential candidate, but acquiesced in the nomination of Benjamin Harrison of Indiana. With a reputation as a moderate, Harrison had nevertheless supported Radical Reconstruction. He had also risen from lieutenant to brigade commander in a distinguished record as a soldier during the war. So the orator played off that story in his brief, one that he claimed was not "to tickle men's ears or to flatter party pride." He appealed to Republicans to act on their commitment to black rights and security because when "Abraham Lincoln called upon the Negro" in the crisis of war, he [the black man] reached "forth with his iron arm" and caught "with his steel fingers your faltering flag, and he came, he came full two hundred thousand strong." The partisan throng loved it. Now those same men in the South were "compelled to wade to the ballot box through blood." In these images of flag, blood sacrifice, and military glory, Douglass demanded that his party live up to its historic promises. As he ended, the crowd of delegates cheered wildly and shouted, "Douglass! Douglass!" So taken was the *Chicago Tribune* with Douglass's appearance at the convention that it printed two drawings of him, one speaking and the other holding the gavel.[42]

By August, Douglass resumed his ugly rivalry with John Mercer Langston, who was running for Congress from the heavily black Fourth District of Virginia. Douglass opposed Langston's candidacy on the grounds that he was insufficiently loyal to the Republican Party. The Sage of Cedar Hill exposed his insider status in the party by sidestepping this historic chance to see a black congressman from a state such as Virginia. Instead, he supported William Mahone, a former Confederate, although much changed, and now the Republicans' veritable party boss. Mahone would not step aside, forcing Langston to run as an independent. Douglass's public and personal disavowal of Langston brought a wave of criticism, even from old friends. T. Thomas Fortune in the *New York Age* accused Douglass of a "vain sacrifice of race to the fetish of party and personal pique." The *Washington Bee* claimed the dispute was pure "personal animosity" on Douglass's part and that the old leader "dislikes to see others succeed." It got worse, with some papers calling on Mrs. Douglass to step in and bring the old man to his senses. The family found itself dragged into the mud. Charles went to the press with a public letter defending his father and attacking Langston, even as Nathan Sprague condemned his father-in-law for not supporting the black candidate. Feuds occurred within feuds.[43]

Douglass wrote a long letter of defense that someone should have told him to scrap. It rather lamely made the old case for the Republican Party as the "sheet anchor" for black political hopes. He trotted out long quotations demonstrating the white-supremacist desires of Democrats to eliminate blacks from American life. He further claimed that Langston's candidacy was staked solely on color and not principle. Color, in this instance, Douglass argued, carried no "moral or political quality." The solidity of the Republican Party was at stake. He even attacked Langston, who had served seven years as US minister to Haiti, personally for past political sins, especially his advocacy that blacks divide their votes between the parties. Langston lost a close election, but after a two-year legal challenge to the fraud practiced by the Democrats in Virginia to win the election, he was seated by Congress in 1890 and served the last three months of the term. This entire affair embarrassed Douglass; a supreme irony of such a bitter relationship is that the two men agreed on many crucial issues such as federal supervision of voting in the South, integrated education, and enforcement of civil rights based on the Fourteenth Amendment.[44] Douglass simply was not good at forgetting.

In the fall campaign, reluctant as he was about Harrison, Douglass took the stump in at least five states: Connecticut, New York, New Jersey, Michigan, and Indiana. There comes a time, he wrote in *Life and Times*, when in every election "the judgment of factions must yield to the judgment of the majority." How agonizingly he had learned this lesson over and again at least since 1856. In 1888 the Democrats ran incumbent Grover Cleveland, this time on a platform of free trade and denunciation of the longtime protective-tariff policies of the Republicans. Harrison and the Republicans tried to focus their campaign squarely on the tariff; "protection" became all but a moral claim to saving American profits and workers at the same time. Neither party much addressed the race and violence question in the South. Douglass admitted that he felt almost too old for the daily speaking demands of an election tour. But he also stressed, as he did in New Haven, Connecticut, in October, that he did not want the Republican effort "confined to a single issue, though that be a grand economical question."[45]

In his stump speeches for Harrison, Douglass made his halfhearted arguments for the national tariff, but demanded more from the idea of protection. The parties, declared Douglass to a packed house in the Hyperion Theater, near Yale University, represented two opposite ideas. Ideological political warfare had formerly been a matter of "bullets" versus the "ballot." But now the two great ideas were one "born of slavery, of class dominion," and the other "born of liberty, of the respectability of labor." Democrats were afraid of the past, Douglass asserted; Republicans should embrace and use it. He offered a new party slogan few if any adopted: "I am for protection because I am for civilization."[46]

In an extremely close election, Cleveland won the popular vote by about 100,000 votes (5,540,309 to 5,439,853), but lost in the electoral college, 233–168. Harrison carried virtually all of New England, all of the Midwest, the Great Plains, and the far-western states. Cleveland's states, exclusively the "solid South," were insufficient to win a general election at this point in the Gilded Age. A Republican was going back to the White House with a geographically expanded Yankee vote. In early January 1889, Douglass gave a newspaper interview at Cedar Hill. When the journalist arrived, the host was practicing on his violin. The two had a wide-ranging conversation about the scale of suppression of the black vote in the recent election, but also about Douglass's excitement about a Republican return to power. He expressed the sunny faith that now the "American people . . . are to have one country, one law, one liberty, and a common destiny." As the interview ended, Douglass took up his violin, saying good-bye by playing "The Star-Spangled Banner" for his guest.[47]

As a surrogate who had labored hard for the Republican ticket, Douglass would be given a significant reward by President Harrison, if he chose to take it. But before that happened, in the winter and spring of 1889 Douglass made a second speaking tour of the Deep South.

On February 4, 1889, just as he arrived in Little Rock, Arkansas, Douglass sent a postcard to Helen: "All right. I am among . . . friends. Shall speak here tomorrow eve. . . . Somewhat worn by two days and two nights travel." After two weeks of lectures in at least three Arkansas cities, and then several in Kansas, Douglass rode the cars back home to Washington.[48] He was still making these trips and delivering "Self-Made Men" and other speeches for money; people flocked to see Old Man Eloquent, especially in places where he had never before appeared. Douglass was an icon of a kind in American civil religion, both a ghostlike figure of the bygone era of slavery and the war, as well as the living voice about the ever-dominant race question in the present.

In the first week of April, Douglass took the trains south again. In March, newspapers reported that the traveling man had committed to be the guest of honor at the Jacksonville, Florida, "Sub-Tropical Exposition." When his train stopped in Savannah, Georgia, a crowd of blacks, led by a black military company, gathered to see and greet the famous leader. "The train stayed only about half an hour," reported a local paper. But it was time enough for Old Man Eloquent to come out and greet the gathering. He begged off from making a speech, but reviewed the militia unit. The train rolled out of the depot amid loud cheering.[49] Within a stone's throw of one of the largest cotton-trading centers in the South, and in a city with thousands of black freedmen struggling to survive and live meaningful lives amid hostile white supremacy festering around each of its beautiful squares, the locals had only glimpsed their mysterious hero.

Douglass's extraordinary arrival amid huge crowds in Jacksonville was news even in the North. Excursion trains full of black folk from southern

Georgia and all over northern and central Florida filled Jacksonville with an estimated twenty thousand visitors. Two trains organized in Bainbridge, Georgia, charged $3 per person for the two days' journey. Some arrived by foot and some riding mules. A procession said to be over a mile long led Douglass, riding in a carriage, into the exposition grounds. Perhaps no other such assemblage of black people had ever occurred so openly in the Deep South. The *Florida Times Union* called Douglass "the most historic character" in the "checkered history" of black Americans. The white reporter was astonished at how "the colored people had the right of way" in the streets, dressed in all manner of gay clothing, and filling the thoroughfares as "a moving mass of picturesque humanity." The journalist seemed both fearful and impressed with such "turbulent exuberance of a tropical race." A band played at the station and at every stop Douglass made.[50]

It was April; flowers were everywhere. Douglass's reception was almost that of a visiting head of state. At the main exposition building, a double line of people "escorted him down a central aisle with the band blaring. He stepped up onto a "pedestal . . . richly decorated by magnolia leaves and choice flowers, the floor being carpeted by cut flowers." Douglass sat on a chair and received a line of local dignitaries who came to shake his hand. A line of "light-complexioned" teenage black girls, all dressed in white, also presented themselves, each representing one of the American states. After a couple hours of rest for the orator of the day, the crowds gathered at a grandstand to hear the "patriarch's speech," as the reporter called it. According to a young black man who helped with the introduction of Douglass, the old orator had arrived in the top rank of the American pantheon. "We have always learned in our schools," said Joseph E. Lee, "that the one who gave liberty to our country was George Washington. The one who will always be known as the savior of his country is Ulysses S. Grant. But we have one of our own race who . . . is as great as the greatest—one who carved his way from darkness into light. This man is Hon. Frederick Douglass!"[51]

After more pomp and introductions, one by the distinguished AME bishop Daniel Alexander Payne, Douglass finally took the lectern, smiling amid "deafening applause." He used some of his old self-effacing jokes: he feared he could only offer his "poor job-trot eloquence" compared to the good bishop's. Douglass's address, only one among several he was asked to give at the exposition, was a vintage combination of postemancipation hope and progress with jeremiadic warnings about the fragile nature of black freedom. Sometimes speaking in a Southern black dialect, he wrapped his message in occasional self-deprecating humor, as well as laughs gained at the expense of the old masters. Douglass stressed the "vast and wonderful change" since the 1860s. He marveled that he could "live to see the day when I could with safety to my person, to my liberty, tread the soil of Florida, of South Carolina, of Georgia." For so long the very names of those states "sent a shudder through me." But now, Douglass declared via Isaiah, "We see . . . a new heaven and a new earth." Many whites were in the audience that day as well, and the guest orator drew them in. "Even the old masters shall rejoice that they are liberated in our deliverance."[52]

But Douglass urged the freedmen and their sons and daughters to not overrate their progress. He urged remembrance of the blood and terror in the crucible of emancipation; they had not been "emancipated by moral convictions," but "in the tempest and whirlwind of civil rebellion." Then in a refrain, he argued that blacks had not been freed so much as "turned loose to the open sky." "Turned loose!" Douglass roared to the rear of the huge crowd. But he left this celebratory crowd laughing. He told of how the old masters desperately needed their black laborers and begged them to come back after 1865. "They found they had sent away the hands and left the mouths; they had sent away the muscle and had left the stomachs." He chided any old slaveholders present about their naming habits for their slaves. "Come back, Pompey, and come back, Caesar!" Douglass shouted in mimicry of the former master class. How honored blacks should have been, he said mockingly, that slaveholders "never called us by any other than those great names of the Greeks." He further ridiculed the old idea that with freedom blacks would begin to die out as a race. "If slavery could not kill us, liberty will not," he announced to great laughter and cheering. Douglass broke into dialect to proclaim how blacks and whites must learn to live with one another. Speaking to whites, he said, "Bre'dren, I has been wid you, and is still wid you, and mean to be wid you to de end." But as entertainer he was not finished. To show how blacks should be "measured from the depths from which we came," Douglass gave the howling audience almost a piece of minstrelsy (at least as portrayed by a reporter). "Did you ever think of a man like myself, who has grown up to weigh 235 pounds, that I have had to fight with a dog named Nep under my master's table for crumbs of bread? Well, I did. I had to skirmish with old Nep for a share of the Johnny-cakes. I used to fight for them; and now my friends, see how fat I am!"[53]

The following day Douglass spoke again, this time a speech called "The Lessons of the Hour," in which he condemned all talk of a "Negro problem." As he had so often before, he declared such a problem the nation's dilemma with racism and not with his race. On that second day, Douglass met a seventy-nine-year-old former slave who approached him to say that they had been companions in bondage near St. Michaels on the Eastern Shore. But the most remarkable member of Douglass's audiences in Jacksonville was the future poet, novelist, songwriter, and civil rights leader James Weldon Johnson. The seventeen-year-old native of the town, in his later autobiography, *Along This Way*, remembered seeing and hearing Douglass with great reverence. For a teenager who would later leave such an enduring mark on African American letters and leadership, this encounter with the great Douglass was transcendent.[54]

Johnson had not only heard a great deal about Douglass while growing up; as a child at the Stanton Grammar School he had won a book as a prize, *The Life and Times of Frederick Douglass*. Johnson said he read the autobiography with "feverish intensity," and that he looked forward to the former slave's coming to Jacksonville with "more than the glamorous curiosity with which" he had "looked forward to the coming of General Grant." He wanted to hear him speak and "catch his words." But, like all others, Johnson never forgot *seeing* Douglass. "No one could ever forget the first sight of Frederick Douglass," Johnson lyrically wrote. "A tall, straight, magnifi-

James Weldon Johnson, c. 1900.
Grace Nail photographer.

cent man with a lion-like head covered with a glistening white mane, who instantly called forth in one form or another Napoléon's exclamation when he first saw Goethe, 'Behold a man!' " Johnson's tribute left no doubt about a long-term inspiration that many in the Floridian's generation felt for their intellectual ancestor. "As I watched and listened to him," Johnson said, "for a half century the unafraid champion of freedom and equality for his race, I was filled with a feeling of worshipful awe." He did catch some of Douglass's memorable words. In particular he recalled the sage's response to a question about his second marriage, a statement Johnson claimed no one in his own time of the 1930s would "dare to make." He recollected Douglass saying that in his first marriage he "paid . . . compliments" to his mother's race, and in his second marriage to the race of his father. For the man who would write the complex and haunting novel *Autobiography of an Ex-Colored Man*, in which racial passing plays a powerful, ironic role, and who would work so long with the NAACP for a racially integrated vision of America, those words no doubt had staying power.[55]

After the festival in Jacksonville, on his journey north, Douglass stopped to speak to freedmen in Thomasville, Georgia. There, he again delivered stern advice about self-reliance to an audience of freedmen and had some exchanges in dialect. One black farmer kept interrupting the speaker with "Dat's so!" Before leaving Thomasville, Douglass went to a local bank and had his host convert the honorarium check from $150 down to $125 because the night's proceeds did not cover the full fee. A local paper expressed astonishment at the famous man's generosity. The wandering lecturer arrived back in Washington to deliver his usual annual address on April 16, DC Emancipation Day. In that effort, fraught with controversy again and much attacked by some black papers, Douglass used his recent Southern tour to argue forcefully that blacks in the former Confederacy were in dire danger for their rights and their lives. He also sought to banish the idea of a "negro problem." To Douglass this question was always and everywhere the "great national problem."[56]

Douglass could still command fees for lecturing and invitations poured in. But he was once again looking for a steady job. Back on March 7, between his two Southern tours, he wrote a carefully worded letter of application to the newly inaugurated President Harrison, seeking his old office as recorder of deeds. That would not work out. But another, perhaps more glamorous and dramatic appointment, one he had already explored for some time, appeared on the foreign horizon. Some in the black press attacked Douglass again as an office seeker out for his own fame and fortune. By late June, Harrison named the seventy-one-year-old Douglass US minister to Haiti.[57] Soon, he traveled on a steamer yet again on the deep blue sea, this time into a diplomatic quagmire.

Chapter 30

HAITI: SERVANT BETWEEN TWO MASTERS

A man must defend himself, if only to demonstrate his fitness to defend anything else.

—FREDERICK DOUGLASS, 1891

ouglass had been part of numerous racial firsts in his life, but this was not one of them. The position as minister and consul general to Haiti had been treated as a designated black assignment in the foreign service since the Grant administration. Douglass's old friend Ebenezer Bassett and Douglass's archrival John Mercer Langston had both served long terms in the post. Langston served with distinction from 1877 to 1885. Douglass and Bassett had first met in the younger man's hometown of New Haven, Connecticut, in 1855. Bassett had been primarily a career diplomat; his stint as US minister in Haiti (1869–77) ended less than successfully as he landed on the wrong side of a Haitian civil conflict. Bassett and Douglass communicated frequently in the months leading up to the old abolitionist's appointment as minister. They had reconnected during the 1888 campaign as Douglass spoke in New Haven. The two men also shared family connections and memories; Bassett and his wife, Eliza, had named a son Frederick Douglass Bassett, who died in his youth in Port-au-Prince.[1] The Sage of Cedar Hill would have preferred to stay home and resume his old job as recorder of deeds. But President Harrison and his secretary of state, James G. Blaine, had other plans for the most famous black Republican.

In 1889, Haiti was emerging from yet another civil war in its turbulent history; the appointment was therefore fraught with controversy over the character of US interests in the Caribbean, and of particular concern to New York merchants with keen eyes on Haiti's resources and steamship lines. From the beginning of his appointment to the Haiti position until well after it ended, Douglass served as a diplomatic spokesman (sometimes for both countries, explaining one to the other) as well as with ever-escalating self-justification. His Haitian sojourn, a difficult and exhausting interlude in an aging and unhealthy man's life, was anything but a diplomatic success; but it led Douglass to a new level of international and Atlantic consciousness, and to some degree even racial consciousness.[2]

Douglass's appointment as minister and consul general to Haiti in the summer of 1889 received both rave and critical reviews in the press, initiating the roller coaster of controversy to follow. The *New York Tribune* admired the appointment, although reminded readers that the "venerable" and yet "active and vigorous" Douglass was seventy-two years old. Initially the *New York Herald* thought Douglass's appointment would bring "universal satisfaction" because of his stature and because he was "above suspicion" regarding the influence of wealthy American merchants. The *New York Press* believed Douglass, because of "race kinship" with the Haitians, would make a "permanent pacificator . . . of that perturbed republic." Many black papers celebrated this elevation once again for "the Lion of the Colored People." The *New York World* overmatched all other hyperbole, although possibly tongue in cheek: "The Haytians will doubtless quit fighting when they hear that Mr. Douglass is coming to live among them."[3] Some of this rhetoric showed only how little most Americans knew about Haiti.

Somewhat more informed, the *Washington Post* nevertheless belittled the appointment, suggesting that Douglass had favored coercion and annexation of Santo Domingo when serving the 1871 commission under Grant. Douglass responded with a vigorous defense of himself and of Haiti. Harrison's appointment likely was not a "thoughtless reward" to a party loyalist, as a previous biographer suggested. But the new minister stood ready to protect his own honor as well as Haiti's history. Like many other African American intellectuals of the nineteenth century, Douglass had long admired the transcendent Haitian revolutionary leader Toussaint Louverture. Douglass and his sons had contributed to Toussaint's mythic place among black Americans by purchasing hundreds of pictures of the former slave general to use for publicity during the final two years (1873–74) of publication of the *New National Era.* By 1889, Douglass maintained a significant distinction between "coercion" and "annexation"; there had been a good argument (export of American abolitionist ideals to a desperate Caribbean country), he said, for annexing Santo Domingo without military force during Reconstruction. He especially claimed for Haiti an important place in the "future of the colored man on this continent." He believed Haiti was unfairly maligned as evidence that black people could not govern themselves. Haiti's recurring revolutions represented "the process of evolution, not of decay or retrogression." He urged *Post* readers to bury their racism and remember that France had experienced twelve revolutions in a century, and that the United States had only recently risen from a "tempest and whirlwind" of civil war "as wild, persistent and turbulent" as anything Haiti had experienced.[4]

Such bold words soon ran headlong into the silencing strictures of diplomatic office. But first Douglass had to endure the usual slamming from his black enemies at the *Washington Bee* and the *New York Sun.* Harrison had rewarded Old Man Eloquent whether, according to the *Sun,* the "chronic officeholder" needed employment or not. Worse, the *Sun* editor accused Douglass once again of nepotism in seeking federal appointments for his soon-to-be grandson-in-law, Charles S. Morris, who was still a college student. Annie Sprague, Rosetta's twenty-four-year-old daughter, married Morris, who did not get a foreign-service position and moved to Ann Arbor, Michigan, to attend college. The *Cleveland Gazette* wished that Douglass had stepped aside for the "more deserving, and more intelligent young men of the race." A younger Republican, the paper contended, was "not a blind follower of Fred. Douglass."[5] The critics were ever awaiting any misstep.

By late August, with Douglass's departure postponed because of the uncertain military situation on the island, the *New York Herald* changed its tune and urged the US State Department to send a white man to such a sensitive post, since "if there is anything the average Haytian loathes it is a mulatto"; and worse, Douglass was a "pronounced mulatto" married to a white woman. By September and October, when Frederick and Helen did depart, the *New York Times* and the *Herald* ran stories with rumors that Douglass's appointment was to be scuttled. These reports were likely the machinations of New York merchants who desired a different US envoy, one who might accommodate their interests. An elaborate ceremony at Metropolitan AME Church in Washington at which Douglass was presented with the departure gift of a special Bible likely assuaged some of the negative press coverage.

HON. FREDERICK DOUGLASS OFF FOR HAYTI.

"Hon. Frederick Douglass Off for Hayti," Indianapolis Freeman,
October 5, 1889. Henry Jackson Lewis illustrator.

The pastor honored the new minister's acceptance of the appointment in his "old age," comparing him to Moses and Joshua, who were said to be over eighty. After news that certain naval officers refused to sail with the interracial couple on board, the Douglasses finally embarked for Port-au-Prince on October 12 aboard the famous Civil War battleship the *Kearsarge*.[6] The former slave from the Tuckahoe had again managed, through thick and thin, to climb another historical height. He would soon find out whether he wanted to be there at all.

Rumors flew that Douglass had been assigned to Haiti with instructions to negotiate annexation of the country, and especially to secure a US naval station at Môle Saint-Nicolas, with its splendid harbor on the island's northwest coast. At least the second rumor was true, although it took time to evolve as a diplomatic strategy. Helen willingly accompanied her husband on this new journey to the tropics, although their interracial marriage was not easy to negotiate in the diplomatic social environment of Port-au-Prince. The flowers would be beautiful, the climate rough.[7]

Joining Douglass also was Ebenezer Bassett, who had in professional desperation begged the new minister to take him along as his personal secretary. Bassett spoke French, which Douglass did not, and the former minister had valuable knowledge of Haiti's labyrinthine political landscape. "I know them [Haitians]," Bassett wrote to Douglass, "their language and their inspirations, just as you know the people of the District of Columbia." Douglass needed Bassett as well to prepare him for the apparent transition of power, after bloody insurrection and war, from François Légitime's regime to that of the new ruler, General Florvil Hyppolite. The situation was fluid and violent in Haiti; as Douglass's departure was officially delayed, he relied on Bassett's experience and advice. On the idea of an American coaling station at Môle Saint-Nicolas, Bassett urged great caution. "Haytians generally are very sensitive to this matter of losing their autonomy," Bassett instructed in one of his letters, which he always labeled "Confidential." "It is one subject in which they all agree." The American scheme of gaining a naval station and greater commerce on Haitian soil would be relentless, Bassett warned. But he believed the two of them as a team could "face the music and . . . hold our own in the diplomatic dance around the Haytian plum when once we are on the scene."[8]

The scene in Port-au-Prince was hot, slow moving, and politically delicate. Upon his arrival in Haiti on October 15 and for some weeks afterward, Douglass wrote to Secretary of State Blaine about the "order and tranquility" in the capital, about how Hyppolite had just been "unanimously elected" by the Constituent Assembly and inaugurated amid "demonstrations of popular confidence." Every Haitian he met, said Douglass, had "had enough of war and is willing now to acquiesce in a condition of peace." But he was anxious to get his letter of credence to present to the new president; otherwise, he seems to have felt like a diplomat without portfolio or a functioning legation.[9]

With Bassett's assistance and from his own reading and correspondence, Douglass slowly became aware of the deeper context for his immediate challenge. As a scholar of Haiti has suggested, Harrison's appointment of Douglass had been carefully managed to put a distinguished black American in the role of negotiating deals already long in the making. Harrison and especially Blaine were advocates of a foreign policy of Pan-Americanism, the idea of ever-expanding commercial networks of trade, supported by US naval power, throughout the Western Hemisphere. Rhetorically, as Blaine expressed it at an international conference in Washington in October 1889, just as Douglass arrived in Haiti, such a policy was friendly and unthreatening. Blaine termed the policy "enlightened and enlarged intercourse of all."[10] This open trade, though, and especially the American desire to enforce its control over the Caribbean, required naval coaling stations. Neighborly and acquisitive at the same time, such policies embodied the contradictions of an emerging empire.

Hyppolite had overthrown Légitime's regime and come to power in a military insurgency supported in part by US weapons, including seventeen Gatling guns provided by an American merchant. A key figure in Hyppolite's new regime was Anténor Firmin, a lawyer and former schoolteacher from Le Cap in the north of Haiti, an intellectual who had lived and studied in Paris as an expatriate and written an important work of anthropology, *The Equality of the Human Races.* Firmin became Hyppolite's minister of foreign affairs and a key player for the next year and a half of negotiations about the US desire to possess Môle Saint-Nicolas.[11]

After an awkward wait of some three weeks, Douglass finally got his audience with President Hyppolite on November 14. Douglass wrote officially to Blaine that as Douglass's carriage approached the National Palace in Port-au-Prince, "long lines of soldiers . . . saluted" as he passed, their officers in "brilliant uniforms imparting to the scene quite a gay military aspect." Inside the grounds of the palace a band played "The Star-Spangled Banner" with "skill and effect." Douglass met Hyppolite, surrounded by his cabinet and trusted generals. Firmin formally presented Douglass, who delivered a short address. In his description of the scene for his boss back in Washington, Douglass offered a character sketch of the new leader. Hyppolite, wrote the minister, was a man of "medium height, of dark brown complexion and gray hair. He has a well balanced head, a clear steady eye, a calm temper and high intelligence." He was "evidently a man not to be trifled with."[12] The writer in Douglass could not be completely contained within the formality of diplomatic prose.

In his address Douglass said all the appropriate words about cordial relations and historical friendship. Then he moved quickly to stress modernity. "Art, science, discovery and invention" had advanced with such speed as to "transcend our ability to keep pace." "Steam, electricity, and enterprise" could now link the nations of the world in "universal brotherhood" and interdependence. Growing commerce would mean the "enlargement of human sympathies." Before closing, Douglass begged to speak a personal word about the symbolic meaning of his presence: "Mine has been a long and eventful life, identified with the maintenance of principles illustrated in the example of Haiti." The former slave from a backwater in a corner of the upper South did not have to put a name to slavery in front of men who had lived the history of Haiti. In his response, Hyppolite too pointed to a common fate for "all peoples of the civilized world." But he also trained that steady eye on Douglass and reminded him, as representative of the giant to the north that coveted coaling stations, that "every nation has therefore the right to be proud of its autonomy." Hyppolite ended, however, by acknowledging that Douglass himself was the "incarnation of the idea which Haiti is following—the moral and intellectual development of men of the African race by personal effort and mental culture."[13] For now, both men could walk away from this formal meeting with pride.

In the fall of 1889 the Douglasses looked with difficulty for suitable housing in Port-au-Prince. First they stayed in a hotel, then looked at various rentals, then took a temporary cottage up in the hills above the city. Eventually they settled into the Lucie Villa, which pleased Helen because of its beautiful gardens. They stayed there until Douglass took a leave back in the United States beginning in July 1890. In December, when they returned to Haiti after several months, the Douglasses, with more local knowledge, found an even nicer residence called Tivoli. Helen again described with near rapture the beauty of the place: "Many and many a night Mr. Douglass would arise, & while others slept, stand beneath the open sky & commune with the stars." Helen was more than equally inspired by the natural surroundings. Eloquently she declared, "Here I learned the mystery of the dawn & saw the night flee away—Down the mountain it would come audibly—the great banana leaves would begin to stir—& the air would be filled with the sense of life—and lo! Great diverging rays of rose & blue, perfect in their symmetry, would fill the east from horizon to zenith."[14]

The beauty of Haiti also inspired Frederick. He later characterized the island as "wonderfully beautiful, grand and impressive. Clothed in its blue and balmy atmosphere it rises from the surrounding sea in surpassing splendor." Douglass also admired Haiti's resources and therefore commercial potential. He thought it a land "of perpetual fertility. Its tropical heat and insular moisture keep its vegetation fresh, green and vigorous all the year round. . . . Its mountains are still covered with woods of great variety and of great value. Its climate . . . like that of California." He thought the Bay of Port-au-Prince almost as beautiful as the Bay of Naples, and Môle Saint-Nicolas the Gibraltar of the Caribbean.[15] Inspired by this extraordinary beauty, Douglass nevertheless arose every day to face the complex issues of word-twisting diplomacy.

In Haiti, Douglass found himself snared in policies he half believed in but could not fully embrace. He tried to imagine American expansion as humane and ultimately beneficial to Haitians. Especially on the issue of the coaling station at Môle Saint-Nicolas, but also on the overall relationship of the two nations, Douglass aimed for what the historian of Haiti Laurent Dubois called "happy globalization." The benevolent, emerging naval giant, presumably still advancing its egalitarian transformations from the Civil War and Reconstruction, would gain its exclusive port in one of Haiti's best harbors; the latest regime in Port-au-Prince would gain stability, prestige, protection, and especially growing commercial ties for its lucrative coffee, sugarcane, and logwood products. In the late twentieth and early twenty-first centuries, such an approach to foreign affairs became known as soft power, the use of persuasion, not coercion, negotiations and not military action, in the conduct of relations between nations. An early if unwitting visionary of "soft power," Douglass hoped that words would win over warships.[16]

In Anténor Firmin, the Haitian foreign minister, Douglass almost had a like-minded partner in this dual quest. But by December 1889, Firmin asked him to explain why an American warship, *Yantic*, ostensibly doing scientific work for the laying of a French cable between Haiti and Cuba, was so visible a presence at Môle Saint-Nicolas. The US minister conducted a good deal of correspondence, some of it awkward, with both Firmin and the captain of the *Yantic*, Commander C. H. Rockwell. On December 9, Douglass wrote to Blaine with what was, in diplomatic speak, a firm warning. Since so many articles had appeared in the American press, Douglass argued, "relative to an alleged purpose of the United States to gain some sort of foothold at the Môle, and in view also of what appears to me to be an extreme sensitiveness of the Haitian people generally on the subject of any possible alienation of their territory, it is but natural that the presence of the 'Yantic' and our naval officers at the Môle should occasion some comment in Haitian circles." Douglass even suggested that this issue could endanger the stability of the Hyppolite government; opponents already accused the president of a plan to "sell the country to the Americans."[17] Here began a year and a half of engagement with the central policy contention between the United States and Haiti. For now, the minister did his duty, and he and Helen enjoyed life among the diplomatic corps in Port-au-Prince.

On New Year's Eve 1889, the Douglasses attended a gala event at the National Palace; so did some well-dressed American naval officers, led by Rear Admiral Bancroft Gherardi, now Blaine's primary emissary, and soon the US minister's internal adversary in conducting diplomacy in Port-au-Prince.

Admiral Gherardi, a Civil War veteran of the Battle of Mobile Bay, had been commissioned by the Navy and State Departments to conduct a thorough study of all possible coaling stations in the West Indies. But during these winter months, financial matters preoccupied Douglass—the condition of the Haitian currency, rumors that European powers would be sending naval expeditions to Haiti to collect debts, and especially a debt of $60,000, dating from 1887, owed to an American citizen, Charles Adrian Van Bokkelen. Under Firmin's pleading, Douglass requested a delay by Blaine and the State Department; by summer 1890 Douglass successfully arranged for payment on installments over six years.[18]

These kinds of matters seemed at times to consume Douglass, who was no novice about money and persuasion. He frequently referred in his official letters to Washington to the interests of the "merchants and capitalists" on both sides. But he also reported often on the problems of social order and violence in Haiti. On January 17, 1890, Douglass described the Haitian legislative elections under way as "extremely cumbersome and complicated," with voting conducted over fifteen days. He acknowledged "considerable disorder and violence in some quarters, but not more than occur in some parts of our own country at elections." He was looking for silver linings in an election process where whatever party was in power, he admitted, was accused of "improper and undue influences." The presence of soldiers had intimidated some voters, he recognized. But trying to find a diplomatic middle ground, he declared the election "in the main . . . fair." In February, however, he reported violent unrest simmering in Port-au-Prince. A "possible danger to public peace" and to Hyppolite's government seemed a daily threat. At this very time, Admiral Gherardi produced his report about the strategic value of Haiti to the United States because of the "millions which American citizens are investing in the Nicaragua Canal," and "our fixed determination to allow no one to gain a foothold" on the island. Bassett had warned Douglass of the American desire to build a "white man's canal" across the isthmus of Central America.[19] Just how to represent that "fixed determination" of American expansion became the central challenge of the rest of Douglass's tenure in Haiti.

In late January 1890, Douglass made an official two-week visit to Santo Domingo, the capital of the Dominican Republic, to the east of Haiti. He went by sea aboard the US Navy ship *Dolphin*, to the Spanish-speaking city he had visited nearly twenty years earlier. But amid the tensions and adventures of his minister's duties, tragic news arrived from back home in Washington. Relentlessly, death continued to visit the extended Douglass family.

The Douglasses got the news before Christmas; Virginia Hewlett Douglass, for twenty years the wife of Frederick Jr., died after an extended illness. In handwritten notes preserved in scrapbooks Frederick Jr. recorded that his wife was "taken with hemorrhage" on October 18. At Virginia's death their four-year-old son, Robert Smalls Douglass, was sent to live with Hattie Sprague (where he remained for more than a year and a half), the twenty-three-year-old second daughter of Rosetta. Four of Frederick Jr.'s six children had already died young; he was now once again in dire straits as well as mourning for his forty-one-year-old wife. In that same December he ceased keeping his detailed personal account book. That fall Frederick Jr. had received yet three more loans totaling $130 from his father.[20]

Frederick, Jr., not in good health himself now at the age of forty-nine, seemed to process his confusion and grief in numbing, if settling, mathematical detail of his account books and in his notes about Virginia's death. "We were married 20 years, 6 months and 10 days," he wrote in careful words on December 21, 1889. "She was 40 years, 6 months and 13 days old at the time of her death. She was married 4 months and 10 days longer than she remained single." In Port-au-Prince that winter, Douglass may have stopped counting these deaths in his family as he felt the grief all over again for his son and his children. In less than three months came yet more bad news: Mary Louise Douglass, the sixteen-year-old only surviving daughter of Charles, died in early March. This made four of Charles's five children who had died in their youth. In a letter from Haiti, Douglass wrote to his son about death: "The blow is a sad one to us all, but we must suffer and be strong. I feel deeply for you because yours has been a most bitter experience. Few families have been made to suffer as yours has in the loss of dear ones but your experience should make you strong. You are still young ... and have I hope much of life and usefulness before you. It is not for you to despair."[21]

Charles had heard this form of fatherly advice and anguish before. Like his brother's, Charles's grief was compounded by his long-term indebtedness to his father. Just as Douglass received his appointment to go to Haiti, Charles had written a deeply despondent letter to his father about being in arrears on his rent in a house for which the elder had staked his son the money. Charles's only surviving son, twenty-year-old Joseph, a skilled violinist, was in Boston studying music at costs Charles could no longer afford and for which he also reached to his father for help. For ten years, Charles lamented, he had "tried to make ends meet" and "pay everybody something." He was once again without a steady job and hoped to find one through "connections to the Grand Army," the Union veterans' organization. "I shall pay you father, and it is not from dishonesty that I am behind."[22] The great voice of emancipationist Civil War memory, and of Union veterans' respect, must at times have felt anguish at the chasm between this national cause and the plight of his own sons. Only Lewis, who had no children due to his war wounds, seems to have developed a genuinely independent life.

By June, to avoid the repressive tropical heat, Douglass requested a leave to return home for the duration of the summer. He was fully aware now that he was at the center of an internal struggle in the Harrison administration, involving navy officers and merchants as well, over the American quest for foreign expansion in an age of empire. He still believed, against the tide, that Haiti was a place where those impulses could be tamed or restrained and made into a force for freedom. Douglass sailed for home with Helen on July 20, 1890, with rumors already at large about his possible resignation from the position as minister.[23]

As he and Helen waited at the New York train station for their journey to Washington, a *New York Tribune* reporter cornered Douglass to query him about his experience in Haiti. The minister tried to decline political questions, but pressed by the reporter, he came to Haiti's defense. The Hyppolite regime sat "as firmly seated as at any former time." Douglass strongly cautioned against the assumption that Haiti was always on the verge of chaos and incapable of self-government. "There is one thing in which the people of the United States could help the Haytians—by telling the truth about them, and not having them constantly paraded before the world as 'on the eve of revolution.'" He denounced the notion that he had been ostracized as a colored man in Port-au-Prince. Indiscreetly, Douglass warned of the impression in the island nation that the "United States is very anxious to get possession of Haiti." He claimed that "some of our papers" had created the impression, but he also knew that acquiring at least the Môle Saint-Nicolas harbor *was* the intention at the highest levels of American government and business.[24]

Douglass knew of what he spoke about American attitudes toward Haiti. He had endured an ugly piece of doggerel about himself back in March by an unknown poet published in the *New York Herald*:

Will you come back to us, Douglass, Douglass
  Douglass, Douglass, tender and true?
Is it a hated isle of Hayti,
  Is it true they'll have none of you . . . ?
Can't we get that Mole St. Nicolas, Douglass,
  Frederick Douglass, "tender and true?"
As there are cannibals still in Hayti.
  Aren't you afraid that they may eat you?
"Tender" hearts have been known to beat well
  Under a sable skin, as a buff—
Ministers have been known to eat well;
  Look out, Douglass, tender or tough?

Far more respectful, the black paper *New York Age* sent a reporter to interview Douglass immediately after his return to Cedar Hill. The *Age* called him the "venerable Moses of his race" and pointed to his concern about what Haiti might have done to his health. "Time is telling on me," said the tired Douglass, only hours off the train, "and the ten months in Hayti have made my step less firm." Again, he defended Haiti's "eighty-seven years" of revolutionary heritage in a world of hostility.[25]

Douglass's leave of two months turned into four, in large part because of a struggle within the administration. Blaine, Secretary of the Navy and former Civil War general Benjamin F. Tracy, and an American businessman with ravenous interests in Haiti, William P. Clyde, all either opposed or were at least suspicious of Douglass's return as minister. They did not trust the old abolitionist's dedication to expansion, especially the quest for Môle Saint-Nicolas. Still roiling among them was their desire for a white ambassador for their schemes. President Harrison seems to have played the key role in not only sustaining Douglass, but in moderating the imperialism of his chief aides and their clients. Harrison did, however, appoint Admiral Gherardi "to cooperate as special commissioner" with Douglass in the looming negotiations with the Haitian government, setting up an ultimately untenable arrangement. In the president's official instructions to Gherardi, Harrison made it clear that he sought "to acquire a coaling station for the United States in West India waters," but that it should be accomplished by a lease rather than by seizure of land. The idea of a lease on the Môle served as a vain American hope of circumventing Haitian sovereignty.[26]

Douglass had no intention of resigning his position during this leave period. At a large gathering at the black Methodist camp Wayman's Grove, outside Baltimore, he denounced those urging his resignation: "At them I fling the old adage: 'Few die and none resign.' . . . I am going back." He and Helen returned to Haiti under these diplomatic challenges on December 13, 1890; as they arrived in the harbor at Port-au-Prince, President Hyppolite sent two officers to meet them and drive them in his personal carriage to their residence. Douglass reported "good order" in the capital and progress in conditions, especially the "erection of numerous buildings for stores and dwellings." He also expressed great optimism about the imminent completion of the telegraph cable from Môle Saint-Nicolas to "all the great centers of modern civilization." [27] Both he and Helen were glad to be back among the flowering winter hibiscus.

But soon the coaling station negotiations began to run into trouble, despite Douglass's good relationship with Haitian foreign minister Firmin. On New Year's Day 1891, Firmin paid a visit to Douglass's home. The two had a frank exchange, with Firmin condemning a report in a New York paper claiming that Hyppolite had made a promise to allow the United States possession of Môle Saint-Nicolas. "With some feeling," Douglass reported, Firmin denied any such promise. The US minister did his best to support his counterpart's disdain for the scurrilous and jingoistic American press,

Frederick Douglass at his desk in Port-au-Prince, as US minister to Haiti, c. 1890.

something they shared. But he also told Firmin that his country was "very willing to acquire by any proper means, by lease, rent, purchase or any other way" the coveted coaling station. Douglass also reported, however, that he left this meeting "not sanguine of receiving any immediate encouragement" in negotiating for the Môle.[28] Admiral Gherardi was about to arrive and all but subvert the minister's best intentions. And Douglass had lost Firmin's trust.

Among Douglass's nemeses now in the troubled diplomatic relationship was William Clyde, the steamship line owner who tried to negotiate his own elaborate deal with Hyppolite's government, offering arms and ships for a monopoly on Haitian trade. Clyde attacked Douglass as soft and an obstacle to enterprise. The magnate pressed Douglass to help him seal the deal and get the Haitians to pay him for his "time and money" expended in establishing the trade line. But the minister, dropping any diplomatic pose, told the businessman no, while plunging a dagger into his integrity: "Then sir, as they will not allow you to put a hot poker down their backs, you mean to make them pay you for heating it!" Douglass later wrote that Clyde had viewed him as "more a Haitian than an American." Douglass described himself as "both surprised . . . and amused" by Clyde's greed and bad manners. Douglass admitted that he actually supported the idea of a steamship line, but had "nothing but disgust for the method by which this scheme was pressed upon Haiti."[29] Events and Douglass's own attempts to find middle paths to agreements that were out of reach painted him into a corner.

Admiral Gherardi's warship, the *Philadelphia*, anchored in Port-au-Prince harbor on January 25, 1891. The next day Douglass met with the admiral on board and read Blaine's, and therefore President Harrison's, instructions to seek and obtain the Môle as a coaling station. Douglass, Gherardi, and an interpreter met at the palace with Hyppolite and Firmin two days later. Since it had been made clear to Douglass that Gherardi was to be his "superior" in this negotiation, he unfortunately let the admiral dominate the exchanges over the "lease." Gherardi sowed the seeds of ultimate failure by stressing the "promises" made by Hyppolite's original provisional government to pay back the United States in some way for the arms and assistance given it as he took over Haiti in 1889. Firmin respectfully disagreed that there were any such promises, although the Haitian foreign minister did acknowledge that the request for the coaling station was "a simple application from one friendly power to another." Unwittingly, Gherardi may have doomed his cause when he claimed to Firmin and Hyppolite that "it was the destiny of the Môle to belong to the United States. No other power would be allowed to occupy it even though the Government of Haiti should cede it." That word "destiny" surely clanged in the ears of the Haitians as it was translated. The Americans left the meeting thinking they might have a deal.[30]

Any hope of the deal, however, collapsed within two months. A negotiation had quickly become a demand by an admiral backed up by warships arriving in Haitian ports. In later public writings Douglass distanced himself from Gherardi as he also condemned Clyde. Douglass felt trapped, or as he put it, "a servant between two masters." Negotiations faltered when Hyppolite left Port-au-Prince at the end of February for nearly two months to quell a rebellion in Jacmel in the south of the island. Moreover, in March some New York newspapers began to attack Douglass for the apparent failure of American interests in Haiti. "The remedy [for any further revolution]," said the *New York Herald*, "is clear. Let the United States send to Hayti a Minister of recognized force, ability, and above all, honesty. . . . He must be able to speak the French language. To gain any influence in the island he must be white" because Haitians "look upon a colored man as one of themselves, whereas they unwittingly recognize the superiority of the white race." Douglass was caught in contradictions of his own making, as well as in historical contexts over which he had little control. What he had learned, as he later wrote, was that Haitians would not tolerate "alienation of a single rod of their territory to a foreign power."[31] He also knew he faced a growing cadre of enemies in the rear at home.

By mid-April the US naval presence reached seven warships, which caused considerable alarm among Haitians. But the show of force did not work. Gherardi favored use of force to obtain the Môle. Douglass, however, broke with his conegotiator. In a message to Blaine he denied "in terms as explicit as usages of diplomatic correspondence will permit" that he in any way favored seizure, as Gherardi had implied. By April 21, Douglass reported to the State Department that "the presence in this harbor . . . of our war vessels . . . has created a feeling of apprehension, anxiety . . . beyond anything of the kind that I have ever before personally known to exist here." Rumors of war and an American military takeover flew around Haiti. On that same day Douglass, with Bassett as his translator, and Gherardi met with Firmin to make one more official appeal for the lease of the Môle. Firmin's written reply on the next day deftly captured the reality. The American request included a clause that, so long as the United States remained the lessee of Môle Saint-Nicolas, Haiti could not "dispose of any port or harbor or other territory in its dominions, or grant any special privileges or

rights of use therein, to any other power, state, or government." This offending language, Firmin argued, was "an outrage on the national sovereignty of
the Republic, and a flagrant violation of Article I of our Constitution; for in
renouncing the right to dispose of its territory, it would tacitly consent to
the alienation of it." [32]

Douglass thus saw to the crux of the failure. As he later wrote, the US demand to exclusive rights to Haitian ports was "a denial to all others of that
which we claimed for ourselves." He chastised his fellow American policy-
makers for their refusal to grasp Haitian history. Her fierce territorial sensitivities originated, he wrote, "very naturally, in the circumstance in which
Haiti began her national existence. . . . She, by her bravery and her blood,
was free." With warships in the harbor, the negotiation became impossible. "We appeared before the Haitians," Douglass said later, when out of office, "and before the world, with the pen in one hand and the sword in the
other." In Haiti's entire national history it had been menaced by imperial
powers. Now the United States acted like one of those powers. On April 23,
Douglass sent a telegram to Blaine with the simple statement "Hayti has declined lease of Mole." Douglass made his case even in formal dispatches to
his boss in Washington. On May 3, he wrote to Blaine about "passionate"
Haitian press accounts calling for resistance to the presence of US ships in
the island's harbors. He told Blaine and official Washington what they did
not want to hear: the United States had bullied its way to this diplomatic
debacle. [33] Slowly but surely, Douglass became a defender of Haiti more than
an advocate for his own country's policy, a contradiction he could only sustain for a short while longer.

By May 1891, Frederick and Helen Douglass witnessed a bloody Haitian
riot and rebellion against the Hyppolite regime. As early as May 7, Douglass warned the State Department of "signs of incipient revolution" and a
conspiracy to overthrow Hyppolite. On May 28, during the Feast of Corpus
Christi, a major Catholic holiday, as Haitians packed churches and President Hyppolite and his ministers attended a service in a cathedral, a band
of some seventy armed rebels stormed down from mountains above the
city, attacked the jail, and released more than a hundred prisoners. Then the
rebels dashed to attack the arsenal, but were repulsed. The initial uprising
lasted just over a half hour, but "the whole city was thrown into an uproar,"
the minister reported to Washington.

Like everyone else in Port-au-Prince, the Douglasses were initially terrified by the violence. They dragged furniture to block their doors and heard "stray bullets that were flying past." Douglass described hearing a "sharp" street fight and reported that Hyppolite himself took to the streets on horseback to lead the reprisals, ordering and participating in the killings. Bassett and Douglass did not find each other until evening at a hotel veranda, whereupon they fled to safety after hearing the firing of a Gatling gun. The killings that day by government troops were rather indiscriminate. Helen Douglass wrote, "The air was rent by the wailings, from various cottages, of women bereft of those they loved." In the wake of the uprising there were many accounts of summary executions as well as of the torture and killing of prisoners in custody.[34] For a time the scent of gunpowder replaced the fragrance of Haitian flowers.

Some have suggested that in his reporting on the violence Douglass demonstrated an undue coziness with Hyppolite's regime, to which he needed a relationship, and that he was just too naïve about the prospects of a black-led government. Hyppolite's "court," as it was called in the American press, shimmered with the trappings of pomp and circumstance that Douglass may have admired. When the president went into public for official matters, according to an engineer on Gherardi's ship, he surrounded himself with a detail of nearly thirty sharply uniformed military aides. Douglass's "failure," as it became widely viewed, in leading the Môle Saint-Nicolas strategy in Haiti was not due merely to naïveté. It was rooted in fundamental contradictions that he both embraced and ultimately rejected. But it may also have been simply one episode among many in the United States' approach to Haiti in the late nineteenth century. According to historian Michel-Rolph Trouillot, American foreign-policy leaders in Washington, and even the members of the black elite such as Douglass, never fully integrated themselves into the social and cultural practices, including how color determined status, within the island nation. German and French merchants and diplomats, Trouillot asserts, developed deeper personal and economic ties than the Americans by marrying Haitian women and engaging in the life of provincial towns.[35] The American racial symbolism Douglass represented was never the most significant element of such a relationship to the Haitians.

Douglass often described just what he saw. In his long dispatches to Blaine, he called Hyppolite's reactions to the attempted coup d'état "severe repressive measures." Very much against the actions and positions of the Haitian regime, he made a strong case for the principle of diplomatic asylum as the bloodshed resulted "in filling the legations and consulates with refugees." By his count, twenty-one refugees sought safety at the US legation and in Douglass's own house. They embarked on a French steamer to safety in Kingston, Jamaica. Without equivocation, the minister offered an earnest American judgment about Haitian political violence. "The real remedy will be found," he wrote on June 17, "when this people shall have worked their way out of the habit of irregular and violent changes of government, and shall come to a full respect for the independence and impartiality of their courts of justice."[36] Douglass criticized Haitian politics, all the while performing as a kind of protector of its history. This became a balancing act he could not sustain.

Increasingly the Douglasses were eager to leave Haiti. Douglass planned to resign his position, but on his own terms and by his own timing, not under the assault of American newspapers, many of which blamed him even for the May rebellion. As early as February 7, 1891, the *Washington Bee* claimed Douglass was about to resign under pressure. The minister had to remain largely mum about such matters publicly. But in letters to his sons he opened up with blunt honesty, providing templates for his more formal self-defenses written later. He was, as always, worried about the health and finances of the extended family. In a late-February letter to Charles he expressed hope that Frederick Jr. was about to get work. He would not yet give the *Bee*'s editor the satisfaction of Douglass's leaving his post. "I shall take my own time for resigning," wrote Douglass confidentially. "The aspirants for the place must wait a little longer." In April, he told Charles at length about his deep consternation with Gherardi and Clyde over the coaling station, the steamship line, and its attendant bribes, with which he would not associate. He complained of the racism among those who wished him out of their way. Somewhat petulantly, he also maintained he had been "selected to bear the blame" for failure of American policy.[37]

And in March to his oldest son, Lewis, Douglass especially wrote of family distress. He was particularly anxious about "how Fredk made out in obtaining the situation." Douglass recounted how Helen was sick with rheumatic fever. His own health too suffered in the Haitian climate. He felt weak, worn-out, and too far from home. Douglass probably already suffered symptoms of heart disease, whether he knew it or not. "My absence from home has been marked by so many changes," wrote the patriarch, "and some of them so distressing that I feel quite easily alarmed when I am told of ailments in our circle." His first wife, most of his old abolitionist friends, so many grandchildren, and one daughter-in-law had already died. More tragedies were yet to come. It was time once again to try retirement if he could. On June 27, 1891, Frederick and Helen took the steamer *Prince Willem III* to New York. Three days later from Cedar Hill, Douglass wrote a brief, formal resignation letter to President Harrison.[38] Douglass's Haitian sojourn was over, but not his defense of it nor his relationship to the island nation.

Upon his return to the United States and after his resignation, Douglass gave numerous interviews. One of the longest was with an unidentified black reporter for the *New York World* on July 12. The reporter arrived at Cedar Hill while parts of Douglass's family were playing croquet in the backyard. The two men sat on a bench in the summer heat before the host took him indoors. In this and other interviews and essays, Douglass made a forceful self-defense of his work in Haiti, blaming the failure of the coaling station policy especially on Gherardi and Clyde's quest for money and monopoly. But he especially counterattacked against the New York press that had held him personally responsible. He portrayed himself as the victim of outrageous attacks full of innuendo. "There are certain convenient forms under which a thousand lies may lurk in safety," he said, "such as 'It is said,' 'It is rumored,' 'It is generally believed to be true,' 'It is an open secret.' . . . They are all convenient formulas under which to hide a slander." Such language had been used against him and against Haiti. He defended Hyppolite as perhaps "unwise," but justly protecting his regime from violent disorder. Douglass called it "nonsense" that he or Bassett might have done anything to prevent the rebellion and bloodshed on May 28. In a *Washington Post* interview Douglass argued that he had worked assiduously to obtain Môle Saint-Nicolas, but that for "political reasons" Haitian leaders simply could not relinquish land or harbors to foreign powers.[39]

His most forceful self-defense came in two remarkable articles in September and October in the *North American Review*. Freed from diplomatic restraint, Douglass fought back for his reputation especially against the "grosser errors" of what he deemed a racist press and their commercial and political allies determined to blame him for the debacle of US policy in Haiti. He made no apologies for defending himself, and at this stage of his life he was particularly sensitive to preserving his historical legacy. He had a "duty" to respond forcefully, he said, because the "charges vitally affect one's standing with the people and the government of one's country."[40]

The two articles vented pent-up anger. "In such a case a man must defend himself," Douglass wrote, "if only to demonstrate his fitness to defend anything else." The great autobiographer and symbol of his race had much at stake. He had been accused of slothfulness, indifference, excessive sympathy for Haiti, all but disloyalty to the United States, and a general incompetence that some papers were all too willing to attribute to his race. The proud Douglass did as he had always done—he took to his pen and wrote a personal manifesto. He delivered point-by-point rebuttals of specific charges about moments in the negotiations. But most important, he counterattacked about race. Too many reporters, safely behind desks and the comfort of consensus white racial prejudice, openly stated that "my failure is my color." He had heard all of this a thousand times before, but the hyperpublic nature of this episode required the kind of irony and reversal at which Douglass excelled. Many in power in press and government "thought it monstrous to compel black Haiti to receive a minister as black as herself." Racism "sets all logic at defiance," Douglass wrote from experience. If the United States had sent a distinguished white diplomat, "would his American contempt for the colored race at home fit him to win the respect and good-will of colored people abroad? Or would he play the hypocrite and pretend to love negroes in Haiti when he is known to hate negroes in the United States?"[41] Douglass did not always paint whites with such a broad brush, but he did with fervor in this case.

With a subtlety that hardly made his enemies blink, Douglass argued that as long as white supremacy lay at the root of American foreign affairs, the country could never achieve noble aims abroad. The racial assumption that a white minister could woo the Haitians flew in the face of "plain facts" (Gherardi and Clyde had both spectacularly failed), but also showed only contempt for the Haitians. "Is the weakness of a nation a reason for robbing it?" Douglass asked. "Are we to wring from it by dread of our power what we cannot obtain by appeals to its justice and reason?"[42] This was not the voice of diplomatic dispatches nor of formal interviews. It was the old declarative abolitionist fire; Douglass knew he was not living back in the land of the Fourteenth Amendment anymore, and that he could not fully trust his own country.

But the former diplomat also vehemently defended his support of expansion. Many reporters attacking him "were in their petticoats," he claimed, when he advocated the acquisition of Samaná Bay in Santo Domingo in the early 1870s. He delivered a firm statement of his own brand of idealistic imperialism. "While slavery existed, I was opposed to all schemes of the extension of American power and influence. But since its abolition I have gone with him who goes farthest for such extension."[43] He placed himself in the long tradition of faith that American foreign policy could represent the enlightened values of the Civil War amendments, of the human-rights tradition, of respect for equality before law. If Douglass's approach to American foreign policy had an ideological core, this was it. He understood realpolitik, but preferred enlightened self-interest and the export of antislavery values. He had made the case to Firmin and the Haitians that an American presence at the Môle and as a commercial partner was in their best interests. This made him hardly the first American diplomat to fail at trying to advance a set of self-aware contradictions in a volatile foreign land. He had willfully lived by these contradictions, and his ministry died by them as well. He was a servant serving at least two masters, each of them at war within himself.

Douglass further came clean with his contempt for Gherardi, whom he accused of all manner of racial slights as well as bungling behavior. "Acting like a good soldier," as the admiral's subordinate, Douglass admitted that he found his position in the negotiations "galling." He reflected that he might have resigned out of "honor" in midwinter 1891, but that he "did not propose to be pushed out of office in this way." Accused of too much "sympathy for Haiti," he wrote, "I am not ashamed of that charge." But he steadfastly believed he did his "honorable duty" to his own country. A year later, when Douglass sat down to update *Life and Times*, bringing his story up-to-date with thirteen new chapters, three of them covered his experience in Haiti. He believed he could not improve on his two articles in the *North American Review* and reprinted them almost verbatim as chapters. The Haitian sojourn forms the ending of this final edition of *Life and Times*. In the book Douglass summed up his life as both "dark and stormy" and full of "sunshine and joy." He made a painful list of the obstacles overcome: "Servitude, persecution, false friends, desertion, and depreciation have not robbed my life of happiness or made it a burden." Haiti hangs uneasily in the balance of that statement. The two most "crowning" honors, he concluded, were President Harrison's appointment of him as minister to Haiti, and now just recently an invitation from President Hyppolite to "represent Haiti among all the civilized nations of the globe at the World's Columbian Exposition" in Chicago.[44] Douglass lived by many of the best elements of ambition and honor. Sometimes it brought out of him a nearly self-destructive hypersensitivity, and sometimes it prompted his best work.

· · ·

In a newspaper interview in August 1891, Douglass was asked about his plans for the future. He answered, "I have labored many years for the advancement of the colored race and I shall again take up the work. I can talk and I can write. I shall use both of these methods of usefulness until I am summoned hence." Late that summer and through the fall, he lectured many times in Washington and Baltimore, especially in black Methodist and Baptist churches. In another interview in early September in Baltimore, Douglass remarked that at the age of seventy-four he had a right to retire but was "unwilling to be an idler." He would devote his remaining time to literary work, "preparing for publication reminiscences . . . as a duty I owe to my children and grandchildren . . . that I may leave it as a monumental record of my life." Such familial motivations were surely true, but the engine of autobiography, updating as well as now defending his famous story, had been the driving force of his literary life for fifty years. Douglass could no more stop crafting his life's narrative than he could cease being the sibylline black man of words. In a ceremonial address at the Asbury Methodist Church in Washington on August 31, in honor of its minister, the Reverend John W. E. Bowen, Douglass paid a tribute unmistakably self-referential. He announced that he was himself not finished. "Great is the power of human speech," Douglass declared, "by it nations are enlightened and reformed; by it the cause of justice and liberty is defended." Then he invoked his favorite apostle. "The words of Paul still rock the world, though spoken two thousand years ago." Addressing the Reverend Bowen, he pronounced, "Your vocation is to speak the word; there is none higher."[45] With pen and voice, echoing the final sentence of *My Bondage and My Freedom*, the aged reformer still sought to change the world.

But the America of the 1890s was a wholly different world of troubles from the 1850s. That fall and into the winter of 1892 Douglass wrote the more than one hundred new pages for *Life and Times*. He was painfully aware that his memoir now landed in a society riven by escalated and violent racial strife. Had the stories of emancipation and legal equality that he had narrated through his own epic life been eclipsed or destroyed by a new white supremacy as potent as slavery ever was? Was the power of the word, the weapon of language, any longer enough to combat the growing horror of lynching? Could the Sage of Cedar Hill remain a relevant spokesman of his people as he defended himself? Were the specter of Jim Crow laws just a new challenge, or a resounding defeat of the revolutions of 1863 and 1868?

In February 1892, Douglass wrote to an old abolitionist friend, Marshall Pierce, about the struggles of old age, of losing their antislavery comrades who were like "trees falling all round us." He also reflected on the daunt-ing task of the new revision of *Life and Times*: "When I laid down my pen a dozen years ago I thought . . . I had reached the end, not of life, but of autobiographic writing. . . . I have always found it easier to speak than to write. These ten or twelve years have not been cheerful." Those lines con-tain multitudes—the passing of Anna, the death of grandchildren and of other kinfolk, the loss of Ottilie Assing, the social and familial turbulence over his marriage to Helen Pitts, the many events in the nation's retreat from Reconstruction, the ambivalence of his place as insider functionary in official Washington. "They have been years of reaction and darkness," Douglass went on. "The air has been filled with reconciliations between those who fought for freedom and those who fought for slavery. We have been . . . morally obscuring the difference between right and wrong. The Ship of State has been swinging back to its ancient moorings." Here Doug-lass showed how his private and public rhetoric about memory flowed into each other and informed his worldview. And he worried about his health and stamina to fight on: "Though my eyes are failing and my hand is not as nimble as it once was," he concluded, "I hope to do some service in writing [of] this period."[46]

With the kind of irony he had always thrived on, the nation of Haiti, as well as the increasing atrocities committed by lynch mobs in America, which he was forced to confront after touring the South, provided the el-derly Douglass one last opportunity to rock the world.

Chapter 31

IF AMERICAN CONSCIENCE WERE ONLY HALF-ALIVE

When it is asked why we [blacks] are excluded from the World's Columbian Exposition, the answer is Slavery.

—FREDERICK DOUGLASS, 1893

Writing in 1901, the great critic William Dean Howells compared Frederick Douglass and Booker T. Washington favorably as great, if different, black men of their times. Howells thought both men had exhibited "cool patience" for the challenges of their respective eras, but that the "temper" of Washington's mind was conservative, while Douglass's was "essentially militant." Washington led by "mild might," and Douglass was "a fighter."[1] These images folded a great deal of historical complexity into typologies of leadership. By 1892 the seventy-four-year-old Douglass and the thirty-six-year-old Washington were surely aware of each other. The two generational, transformative leaders were finally about to meet.

The famous "normal school" at Tuskegee, Alabama, was already ten years old when its founder came to Washington, DC, to speak in November of 1891. Because of ill health Douglass sent Washington a note of regret that he could not attend. The Sage of Anacostia wished the young institution builder the best with "your lecture and your vocation."[2] By the next spring, Douglass planned a lecture tour in Tennessee, Georgia, and Alabama as the Wizard of Tuskegee worked to get Old Man Eloquent to give the commencement address at his institute.

The two former slaves met in Washington on April 27, 1892, on one of Washington's many fund-raising and networking trips. Two days later on his return to Tuskegee the principal wrote a black organizer in Montgomery, Alabama, informing him that a plan to have Douglass speak in that city the day before the school's commencement was not acceptable. Ever attentive to the reputation and the funding of Tuskegee, Washington complained that arranging Douglass's visit was "a matter of business" with a "great amount of expense." Washington further groused that he had "to pay a man to accompany him [Douglass] on this trip." The principal was frustrated but determined. "It has taken me nearly six months to arrange this trip and [I] have had to bring pressure to bear from a very large number of sources in order to get Mr. Douglass to come." The famed abolitionist was still getting $100 to $150 for his speeches in most venues plus his travel expenses. Washington wrote to Douglass on April 29 to finalize the plan and make sure in no uncertain terms that the orator would not speak anywhere else in Alabama before the commencement.[3]

Washington wanted Douglass's imprimatur at Tuskegee without any competing publicity. The evolution of the old abolitionist's visit to Tuskegee demonstrates the wide difference between the leadership styles and purposes of the two leaders. Washington was ever the marketer of his institution, its security and interests. Douglass was at this late stage in life the celebrity courted to appear and speak, sometimes through elaborate planning. Both men would always be remembered as *national* black leaders, but in different nations in different eras. Washington built the remarkable Tuskegee, the Negro Business League, and other institutions. Douglass was in some ways his own Tuskegee.

Douglass's spring 1892 speaking tour began first with lectures in New York, Boston, and Asbury Park, New Jersey, in March. Then in May he took the train south to Tennessee, where he spoke in Knoxville, Nashville, and Chattanooga, May 18–21. On May 23 he spoke at a church in Atlanta as well as to the black graduates at the Atlanta University commencement. Three days later, and 130 miles southwest by rail, he was in Tuskegee as Washington's special guest. Nine men and six women with an average age of twenty-one graduated that day. The men went forth, according to a press report, into farming, sawmill work, carpentry, wheelwrighting, and printing, while the women had prepared for sewing, cooking, and housekeeping. As part of the day's ceremonies, the cornerstone was laid for a new "Bible training school." The scene, recorded another reporter, was "most picturesque," with a crowd of at least five thousand people arriving "in wagons, in carts, in

Frederick Douglass in the pavilion at Tuskegee Institute, Tuskegee,
Alabama, commencement day, May 26, 1892.

ox-teams, on horse-back, on mule-back, and on foot." As the throng filled
the school grounds, Douglass delivered a version of the "Self-Made Men"
speech. A journalist called the address "calm and dispassionate," as Douglass preached a customary cluster of "economy, thrift, and common sense."
Douglass once again urged the larger white society to "let us alone, and give
us a fair chance. But be sure you do give us a fair chance." A stunning photograph survives of the orator standing on a stage in the round, flanked by
a tightly packed audience, American flags aplenty throughout the pavilion.[4]

Douglass had taken the decades-old "let alone" dictum and his doctrine
of self-reliance to the new mecca, Booker Washington's industrial school in
the heart of cotton-belt Alabama. Just what Douglass thought of this extraordinary experience at Tuskegee he did not publicly record. But thousands
of Southern blacks in the heart of the old Confederacy had now seen and
heard Douglass, the living legend whose life and words had long provided a
mythic backdrop to the shamanism of the Tuskegee founder.

The next day the traveling orator was in Montgomery, Alabama, speaking to yet another black audience. Then he boarded another train for the
long ride back north to Rochester, where on Memorial Day, May 30, he
joined President Benjamin Harrison to dedicate a Civil War Soldiers' Mon-

ument in his old hometown. He and Harrison returned to Washington, DC, on an overnight train, where on the 31st Douglass gave an interview at Cedar Hill to an Indianapolis reporter about the impending 1892 Republican National Convention. He fully supported Harrison for renomination, stressing that this president had vigorously supported the Federal Elections Bill of 1890, which narrowly failed in Congress at creating renewed action to protect black voters in the South. The reporter could not resist physical descriptions of the venerable Douglass, "the old white-haired colored patriot," who when "the breezes . . . of Maryland blew about his shoulders, his long white fluffy locks" made him appear "the embodiment of all that could be pure and wise in man." Douglass returned the flight of rhetoric, declaring Harrison "the best president since Lincoln."[5]

With barely enough time to repack a bag, Douglass was off again on the long journey to Minneapolis for the Republican convention, where he performed not as a delegate but as a symbolic presence. During his tour of the South, Douglass could not have yet known that 1892 would suffer the most recorded lynchings (230 total, 161 blacks, 69 whites) of any year over the more than half century that the Tuskegee Institute archives kept its famous records. What he did soon know is that in March a white mob had destroyed the offices of the *Memphis Free Speech*, leading to the lynchings of three black businessmen, and the rapid emergence of a young antilynching and civil rights activist named Ida B. Wells.[6] Douglass soon met this extraordinary woman, who in her own way reinvigorated the aging leader's career as she also challenged him.

At the 1892 Republican convention in June, President Harrison was renominated, and Douglass joined other stalwarts in keeping his shoulder loyally to the stone of party unity. He saw no alternative to Harrison at the raucous convention and, as always, pledged to stump wherever Republicans would send him. But that spring and summer, an increasingly exhausted Douglass was deluged at times with requests to lecture as well as write for journals. He also heard frequently from old friends and from people he did not know with complaints and advice. Old comrade Martha Greene sewed Douglass a dressing gown and urged him upon his return from the Minneapolis convention to take a vacation and hoped he was not "wholly used up."[7]

All of these matters were normal in old age. But some must have deeply affected him. Elizabeth Cady Stanton wrote in early 1892 about how her movement for women's suffrage had made some progress, but that it felt like a horrible "tax on human patience to be forty years going through this moral wilderness with . . . no pillar of light to lead the way." She wished for a "golden calf whose ears and tails and legs . . . could provide us the means of war." Julia Crofts wrote in June, wishing the busy Frederick would write to her more often. She described her ill health and dwindling income. Her husband had died some time ago and she was lonely. "Think of me always as your old true friend," she begged, and urged Douglass to persist "til our work is done." His old friend and once employer of two of Douglass's sons, H. O. Wagoner, in Denver, wrote to say he had suffered blindness, but still had someone to read to him an essay the old abolitionist had written. Ellen Richardson from England, who had led the campaign to purchase Douglass's freedom, wrote to urge him to bear down on revising *Life and Times* because it was "fitting employment in old age."[8]

But Douglass, despite fatigue and likely the beginning of arterial heart disease, now had at least three jobs—as professional Republican; as commissioner for Haiti to the Chicago Exhibition, including planning and funding of the Haitian Pavilion; and still as patriarch and provider for his troubled extended family. In June, after returning from the Republican convention, he wrote to a friend that even after four days he had "not yet gotten over the strain put upon my nerves" by the political event. He felt in constant demand, and inadequate to the challenge. He complained that now he could "not stand the excitement of the crowd" as he once had. He further had to suffer hearing himself "referred to as an 'old man.'" But there was "still much work to do in the time I have"; he planned to spend up to six months in Chicago at the Exposition the following year. And famous friends kept prodding him to keep up the fight.[9] Douglass still had to be Douglass, as best he could.

The demands of fame and influence constantly beckoned. A "colored boy 18 years of age" from Natchitoches, Louisiana, named Edward Wright wrote in 1892 asking Douglass for advice on where he might "secure a splendid Educatchion north or south and where he can get his Legal Rights." He wanted the great man to help him "make a man of myself." In a long letter, a seventeen-year-old black girl from Omaha, Nebraska, Augusta Johnson, begged Douglass to financially support her effort to go to Tennessee Central College in Nashville. She currently had to work for her ill sister and family and did not want to be a servant anymore. "I have broader ideas than that," Miss Johnson asserted with confidence. She and her sister had read *Life and Times* and yearned for attention from the author. "Girls have to be so particular about where they are and what they do," wrote this child of Recon-

Frederick Douglass, on the grounds of Cedar Hill, c. 1892.

struction. Sometimes groups in the Deep South, such as one in Louisiana in June 1892, wrote to inform Douglass, the "hero" of the race, of the depths of oppression they faced. Their ballots suppressed, with no one representing them, in desperate need of physical protection, they beseeched the old leader to try to influence Congress. Naming only their parish, Terrebonne, they declared themselves "afraid to sign their names." [10] In the face of these requests and more, Douglass felt essentially helpless. His correspondence could be both heartening and heartbreaking.

But the wave of lynchings prompted him to take up the pen. In July 1892 he published "Lynch Law in the South" in the *North American Review*. Douglass tried to maintain composure as he developed an analysis of why lynching mobs seemed so shockingly ubiquitous across the South. But outrage and despair crept out of his words. Controversially, he suggested that even if some black men, like men of other races, had committed a rape, lynching provided merely "an effort to neutralize one poison by the employment of another." A "howling mob" ritually executing a man in public "without judge or jury," he wrote, is the real "crime," and the destruction of law and order. The alleged act of sexual outrage, Douglass maintained, was a mere "excuse" for violence against blacks. He still claimed a hope in good white people in the South, but acknowledged that too many in the mobs "have eyes, but see not, ears but hear not, and they rush to their work of death as pitilessly as the tiger rushes upon his prey." [11] The beast in the dark recesses of the human psyche was in the mob, not in the victim of ritual violence.

Douglass reminded his readers that the crime of rape had for more than two hundred years been committed by white men against black women with no redress. Protecting the "purity of white women" only provided yet another excuse to hide real causes. Douglass believed lynching occurred because blacks had made so much "progress" and were becoming "prosperous": "The negro meets no resistance when on a downward course." But "when he shakes off his rags and wretchedness and presumes to be a man . . . he contradicts this popular standard and becomes an offence to his surroundings." Douglass also asserted that during the Civil War, with white men gone to the battlefronts, many blacks were left on plantations with white women and no such sexual attacks occurred. So evolved Douglass's argument, made more fully in the coming two years, that lynching was a murderous, lawless, anarchic form of racial and social control justified by racist canards. He offered "two answers, one of hope and one of fear." The hope, expressed somewhat lamely, was in the law, the courts, and the good men and women of the South who might rise up and stop such horrors. The fear, however, stated in the old abolitionist line that "oppression can make a wise man mad," smoldered in the prospect of black retaliatory violence. Those who "sow the wind" will "reap the whirlwind," Douglass warned with a trusted Old Testament maxim. [12] He reached into his well of 1850s hope from the slavery crisis—faith placed in the best of human nature, in progress, in the Constitution, in evil that sows good through tragedy—but not much hope emerged from the lynching crisis of the 1890s.

Despair of another kind visited Douglass and his family in late July 1892. After his wife, Virginia, died in 1889, Frederick Douglass Jr.'s life spiraled downward. He had always struggled financially; now his health collapsed. In September of the previous year Frederick Jr. had checked into Freedmen's Hospital at Howard University for surgery. He suffered with respiratory disease, and now on July 26 he died at age fifty of what the era called consumption, or what the twentieth century knew as pulmonary tuberculosis. A funeral took place on the twenty-eighth at Frederick Jr.'s home in Hillsdale, District of Columbia, where on the same property for some years he had operated a grocery. According to a press report, the elder Douglass requested the ceremonies be kept brief and simple. Many friends gathered around a casket in the parlor, a quartet from an AME Church sang "Rock of Ages," and the Reverend Francis Jesse Peck officiated. The elder Douglass did not speak. A carriage transported the deceased to Graceland Cemetery, where he was buried next to Anna Murray Douglass, his mother.[13]

Although comforted by Helen and his other three children, this death of a son, in the wake of so many lost grandchildren, tested Douglass's emotional condition as few events had before. His sons had for so long been a source of pride and personal travail. Virtually nothing survives in his words of what this loss meant to him. Duty beckoned all around as he quietly mourned. Douglass received numerous condolence letters from friends and acquaintances, but some came as "sympathy" couched in demands on his time, and invitations to lecture, including details of train schedules. Some seemed to genuinely care about the father's grief, while others could not hide their desire for the orator's performance. And the begging letters still arrived as well. Two young black men in dire circumstances, one a "poor man without any parents," wrote in September, asking Douglass to help them get into Howard University. Douglass had trained his sons as printers, but they never enrolled at Howard.

> Rock of ages, cleft for me,
> Let me hide myself in thee:
> Could my tears forever flow,
> Could my zeal no languor know.[14]

Douglass could not hide, nor did he intend to; his rock had broken apart many times before. He had to be a rock—for family and for the race. By August and September he was off on speaking tours for the election campaign and in frequent correspondence and planning for the Haitian Pavilion at the Chicago World's Fair. Sometime that summer of 1892 he finally met Ida B. Wells, striking up an activist friendship that would animate his remaining years. Douglass was well aware of this extraordinary, but young and vulnerable, radical woman. He took on a fatherly mentor role toward her from the beginning, and she welcomed his support. From their first encounter, she saw Douglass as a heroic model, but one she felt safe in criticizing as well as adoring. Wells, who had fled Memphis and her native Mississippi for safety after writing bitter diatribes about lynchers and their acts, contemplated a tour of England to spread her cause. Douglass counseled her to take to the speaking and journalistic-writing circuit with all the courage and energy she could muster. He had told his people's story as no other; now she would be that person on the searing cause of antilynching. For two years they made a historic, if sometimes volatile, team. Wells considered herself, nevertheless, only a "mouthpiece" about the lynching story, whereas Douglass she considered the true "orator." [15]

Douglass wrote a public letter in October that Wells employed as an imprimatur in both of her famous books, *Southern Horrors* and *The Red Record*, each first published in 1892 and 1895 respectively; she also invoked Douglass's recommendation in sensitive situations where her veracity and gender equality were challenged. He in turn thanked Wells for her exposure of the "lynch abomination." Nowhere in journalism, Douglass said, had there been any "word equal to it in convincing power." "Brave woman!" he declared, "you have done your people and mine a service. . . . If American conscience were only half alive, if the church and clergy were only half Christianized, if American moral sensibility were not hardened . . . a scream of horror, shame, and indignation would rise to Heaven wherever your pamphlet shall be read." The letter was both a public appeal and a statement of spiritual and moral solidarity. It often felt, he wrote, that "we are deserted by earth and Heaven—yet we must still think, speak and work, and trust in the power of a merciful God for final deliverance." This was a newly impassioned and inspired Douglass. In her preface to *Southern Horrors*, Wells wrote that she offered no "shield" or "defense for the poor blind Afro-American Samsons who suffer themselves to be betrayed by white Delilahs." Instead, in a tradition Douglass and the abolitionists had forged, she presented the "truth, an array of facts" by which she hoped through "this great American Republic . . . justice be done though the heavens fall." [16] With help from political power and armies, truth and facts had brought down slavery; might that be true someday of the horror of lynching?

At the same time Douglass joined the antilynching crusade, he stumped for Harrison's reelection and felt the pain of the second presidential defeat for Republicans since the war. Harrison had been elected in 1888 without winning the popular vote, and Republicans had taken both houses of Congress. But the party had now evolved more as the agent of big business, of Andrew Carnegie's notion of wealth that would enable entrepreneurs to foster some trickle down to the masses. Above all the Republicans became the

Ida B. Wells, c. 1893, Mary Garrity photographer.

proponents of high tariffs. The Harrison administration wielded patronage without scruples, and its corporate identity made it vulnerable to populist insurgency. Between 1877 and 1890, 6.3 million immigrants had arrived in America, flooding labor markets and prompting industries to pay lower wages, thus fueling an ever-intense and violent conflict between labor and capital. Between 1880 and 1900 some 6.5 million workers participated in approximately twenty-three thousand strikes. Republicans became more and more antilabor, and the farmers' alliances, especially in the West, organized against them. The party of tariffs seemed to have abandoned workers by 1892, and of even greater importance to Douglass, it all but avoided talking about race or the party's egalitarian legacies from the Civil War and Reconstruction. Douglass went on the stump as usual, but the election was a disaster for the Republicans. The Democrat, Grover Cleveland, won the popular vote by nearly half a million votes, and the electoral college in a landslide. His party took back both houses of Congress; the entire federal government rested suddenly in Democratic hands for the first time since before the Civil War.[17]

The Republican Party was not quite in a death spiral, but it teetered in political shock. Economic collapse in 1893 would give it new opportunities to regain power. But the 1892 debacle would be the last presidential canvass for Douglass. He received so many requests to give his views on the lost election that he wrote an essay, distributed widely in printed form. In "Douglass on the Late Election," he tried to soft-pedal the defeat, predicting "no disastrous assault" upon the "welfare of the country," as well as "no marked and visible difference . . . in the condition of the colored people North or South." Incongruently, he seemed to speak as an official within government (though he now was not) trying to hold together a center and some institutional confidence in the midst of fear and turmoil. Douglass maintained that the Democrats' ideas about free trade were "more easily managed on the stump than in Congress." He urged calm and argued against the evidence that "mere party, as such, has upon the masses a weaker hold than at any time during the last thirty years."[18] A partisan to the end, this prophet of self-reliance misread once again the fervor of economic and labor populism.

Douglass admitted to both "fears and hopes" for blacks, despite racial violence and disfranchisement. He delivered, though, a harsh critique of his own party. He warned that for the short term, matters could be frightful. Contradicting himself, he suggested that blacks might "feel that the old slave power is again safely and securely in the national saddle." He warned that Democrats exhibited "contempt for human rights." But he somehow believed the Democratic insurgency would be only temporary. Republicans had too often backed off, refusing to counter the slanders of their opponents. He chastised his party for not aggressively defending blacks' right to vote. Republicans, he said, offered "not a single idea to touch the conscience. . . . All is as cold as dollars and dimes." But Douglass somehow extracted hope from defeat—the old wartime idea of necessary losses leading to ultimate victories. Straining for hope, he remarked, "I am convinced that as in the Bull Run disaster during the war, it [the election] will prove a blessing in disguise." He even put faith in Cleveland himself, a man who, he contended, would not tolerate lawless violence (a terrible prediction). Above all, Douglass would not abandon the Republican Party. "No party could have behind it a grander record," he asserted. "It has only to resume its old time character."[19] But the crises of the 1890s required much more than nostalgia for the days of Radical Republicanism.

• • •

In the spring of 1892, Douglass visited Chicago to see the sites for the fair-grounds and examine construction of the Columbian Exposition. In February he had been appointed "Full Commissioner of the Republic of Haiti" and later that summer learned that he would be paid $50 per month through May 1893 for his services. He worked for most of a year in close association with Charles Preston, the Port-au-Prince–born former head of the Haitian legation in Washington. Douglass became involved in selection of the site of the pavilion, its costs and fund-raising, the transport of exhibition contents from the island, and even in questions of whether the pavilion would be open on the Sabbath, which he strongly favored, denouncing opposition as "bigotry and superstition." By June he wrote to Preston about his apprehensions over whether the pavilion would be completed on time, and especially over whether the government in Haiti would fully fund the project. Despite family affairs and his declining health, Douglass made his representation of Haiti the central commitment of his life over the next year.[20]

The Columbian Exposition was so vast and ambitious that it could not be completed and opened until 1893, a year later than planned. The fair had been many years in the planning by the business titans of Chicago, as well as by state and federal governments. The "White City," as the exposition became known, ultimately displayed a neoclassical and Romanesque architectural achievement like no other. The great theme of the fair was "progress" and the onward march of civilization, categorized and displayed in racial and ethnic hierarchies, as well as machines and technology. Visitors were invited to come and dream of new utopian futures. Spectacular expectation and boosterism led to a total attendance of 27,529,400 people at the fair in its six months of operation in 1893. The fair drew people to the idea of immensity, to artistic beauty, to a vision of the United States as gleaming and unified a mere twenty-eight years after its Civil War, to the experience of collective play in a circus atmosphere, and to the fascination with categories of racial types as well as inferior and superior cultures. The fair trumpeted the forces of nationalism, imperialism, and consumerism as verities of the age. Moreover, the exposition, writes one of its best historians, rested on a "dual foundation": one, the Midway Plaisance, a "honky-tonk sector" over a mile long and six hundred feet wide, characterized by the giant 280-foot-high Ferris wheel; and two, the theory of "evolution," rooted in ethnological or racial performances by groups from all corners of the world.[21]

Architecturally, the mixtures of images and scale inspired awe. The grand Court of Honor, with its long lagoon, gondolas afloat, and Daniel Chester French's huge *Statue of the Republic* in its midst stopped anyone in his or her tracks to gaze in wonder. The horizontal magnificence of the Machinery Hall, or the towers and glow of the Electricity Building, or the Golden Door on the Transportation Building, or the United States Government Building with its stunning blue dome, looking like some combination of an English palace and the US Capitol, as well as many other edifices gave visitors all manner of illusions of an imperial Venice on Lake Michigan. Most of the structures were built to be temporary, with steel skeletons covered over with a mixture of jute and plaster, designed to provide an alabaster gleam. But the fair was about people, about which civilizations, cultures, or races had prevailed in the world. The superiority of Anglo-Saxon thought and arts, of an America run by a white ruling class forging progress, unmistakably dominated the Exhibition.[22]

African Americans and Native Americans were conspicuous at the fair either by their absence or by their vivid denigration. Along the Midway the fair organizers placed a variety of "ethnological villages," depicting the cultures of many nonwhite groups. As the manager of such exhibits the fair appointed the Harvard anthropologist Frederic Ward Putnam. Exoticism became a commodity as people paid admission to see a village of the Inuit tribes—Native peoples from Alaska and Canada, commonly called Eskimos in the United States. The Inuit set up camps on the edge of the fair in the fall of 1892, and their physical conditions worsened over the winter and into the spring of 1893. They were asked to don their fur garments and hoods and perform dances as though in the Artic during a Chicago summer.[23]

In early planning, several Native American leaders petitioned the fair organizers to create their own exhibits "in the hands of capable men of our own blood." They asked to be part of the central purpose of the grand show: "Give us . . . some reason to be glad with you that [America] was so discovered." Fair authorities were all too happy to have Indians as part of the ethnological Midway, but not on Indian terms. They were instead exploited for entertainment as concessions were awarded to white showmen who specialized in degrading exhibitions of premodern Indian culture. They staged a "Sitting Bull's Cabin," a large tepee lived in by nine Sioux in crowded conditions. Moreover, out beyond the boundaries of the fair Buffalo Bill Cody's "Wild West Show" competed with the grand Midway. Native Americans were paid for their humiliations in a complicated mixture of commerce and racism.[24]

Despite the hopes of Douglass and other black leaders, exposition officials treated African Americans at the fair with a combination of neglect, paternalism, and tokenism. Frederick and Helen journeyed to Chicago for the October 12, 1892, dedication of the exposition. They stayed first at the Palmer House hotel, and later, during the long months of 1893, the Haitian commissioner boarded with Fannie Barrier Williams and S. Laing Williams, a prominent Chicago clubwoman and her husband, a lawyer. The event would not actually open for some seven more months, but over one hundred thousand people turned out for parades and for prolonged celebrations of the "progress of civilization." Douglass attended receptions in his role as Haitian commissioner, often receiving formal applause. Other than symbolism, he had no role in representing black Americans. Francis J. Bellamy, editor of *Youth's Companion*, composed the Pledge of Allegiance for the occasion, and on a well-organized cue, millions of children across the country recited the pledge to "one nation indivisible, with liberty and justice for all." African American proposals and exhibits were rejected by the fair's organizing committees. The black press condemned the exposition's racial exclusion. In the wake of the dedication day, Douglass delivered a restrained rebuke. He found the inauguration ceremonies "glorious," he said, but "one thing . . . dimmed their glory." He admired the talk of "human brotherhood," yet he detected "an intentional slight to that part of the American population with which I am identified." [25] The problems had only begun.

Back home in November for a while, Douglass became preoccupied with the belated and disappointing publication of the final edition of *Life and Times*. He did not like DeWolfe and Fiske's layout, the paper quality, and their long delays. But it was out, the final installment in all of its sometimes overwritten, often rigidly protective, name-dropping, but also richly detail-laden glory. The great autobiographer had completed this part of his literary journey, begun on his small desk in Lynn, Massachusetts. More than seventy years of memory had been plowed into one of the greatest autobiographical performances in American history. In the same month, Douglass exchanged letters with Julia Crofts. She was ill and lonely and worried about money. But she also observed her friend's "weakened handwriting" and warned him to take care of his ever-present cough. She reminisced about the forty years since they had first met and looked ahead to meeting in "the blessed place where farewells are . . . unknown—where the wicked cease from troubling & and the weary are at rest." [26] A weary and unhealthy Douglass rested up before his return to the fray on the Chicago Midway.

By comparison to some of the grand structures, the Haitian Pavilion emerged as a small but significant feature of the Columbian Exposition. Completed ahead of schedule and on budget, the structure was ready for its commissioner to take possession by January 1893. The combination colonial- and Grecian-style building stood in a corner lot next to the much larger German pavilion, Das Deutsche Haus, as well as the national edifices of Spain and Canada. Forty-nine nations in all participated in the exposition. One hundred fifty by one hundred feet and fifty feet high at the top of its central dome, the all-wood Haitian Pavilion spread its footprint with twelve-foot-wide verandas on three sides. The front portico displayed the coat of arms of the island nation and the words RÉPUBLIQUE HAITIENNE in gold letters along with three dates—1492, 1804, and 1892. The building had the look of one built for the tropical islands, where any breezes could be captured on the verandas. Inside, a kitchen served Haitian coffee at ten cents per cup. Assorted other relics and special objects included a bust of Toussaint Louverture, and allegedly one of Columbus's anchors. The left wing of the building contained offices; here Douglass moved into the largest one, set aside for the commissioner.[27] The former diplomat now presided over a symbolic representation of Haiti, a black nation born in one of the most violent slave rebellions in history, placed in a gigantic world's fair in the middle of the great White City in the dead of a Chicago winter.

Back in Chicago for the building's completion ceremony, Douglass delivered two speeches on January 2, the first to a hastily gathered small audience at the pavilion. In this short address, he heaped great praise on President Hyppolite for his "diligence . . . sagacity and his patriotism" in providing the money and material to build the pavilion. Douglass garnered applause in placing Haiti securely by this act in "possession of our nineteenth century's civilization." Douglass spoke not as an American, but as an honorary Haitian. But he honored the fair's directors for giving "us" one of "the very best sites," and not relegating Haiti to an obscure corner of the grounds. "It is not a candle put under a bush," he gushed, "but a city set upon a hill." Douglass believed Haiti had added its piece to the fair's "magic to dazzle and astonish the world."[28]

Then the orator shifted to a full-throated celebration of Haitian independence and a somewhat purple narrative of the military victory of the black forces against the inhumane French. The Haitian rebels, said Douglass, with their slave heritage and lack of training, nevertheless fought "deception with deception, arms with arms . . . blood with blood," and they never gave up. Above all, Haitians had in ninety years "never surrendered"

The Haitian Pavilion, Columbian Exposition, Chicago, summer 1893.

their precious independence. Their victory had been more "herculean," fought through more "terribleness," than the Americans had endured in their revolution against the British. Douglass left his afternoon audience contemplating Bonaparte and the "bones of his unfortunate soldiers whitened upon a soil made rich with patriot blood." Progress needed some transformative history in order to seem real.[29]

In the evening of January 2, at the Quinn Chapel, the oldest black church (AME) in the city, founded by former slaves, and now in a brand-new neo-Gothic structure on Wabash Avenue in a growing black neighborhood known as Bronzeville, Douglass delivered a much longer speech to a crowd of fifteen hundred prominent Chicagoans. In the United States, Haiti, its natural beauty and its history, had never been celebrated quite like this. He announced his big theme as Haiti's "history . . . her probable destiny." It was particularly an address about the meaning of Haiti in the nineteenth century for *black* people. A revolution and the making of a republic by Africans and their descendants drove his narrative. "We have not yet forgiven Haiti for being black, or forgiven the Almighty for making her black." The oration simmered throughout with the tense politics of race in Douglass's own country. A Haitian, he claimed, could travel anywhere in the world with respect, except within the United States.[30] Douglass thus made Haiti a grand metaphor for human freedom won in blood.

The orator wove natural beauty into politics at nearly every rhetorical turn, warning his American audience that the Unites States' quest to obtain the magnificent Môle Saint-Nicolas would fail because of Haiti's "repugnance to losing control over a single inch of her territory." Douglass warned off the American "sharks, pirates, and Shylocks" who would exploit Haiti. Having known and worked with President Hyppolite, he vigorously defended the dictator, even comparing him to Lincoln in defending his nation against treason and rebellion.[31]

After some awkward defenses of Haitian society against accusations about its poverty (children "running nude in the streets"), its strange practices of voodoo, its "snake worship," or its alleged lazy cultural habits, Douglass honored the country for its world-historical mission. Haiti had "taught the world the danger of slavery and the value of liberty. In this respect she has been the greatest of all our modern teachers." "Until Haiti spoke," he declared in a refrain used many times, the world had not comprehended a path to the abolition of slavery. Douglass celebrated the slaughter of the French army on Haitian soil as a triumph of black people, sanctioned by ancient biblical roots. In blood sacrifice are nations and peoples born, Douglass asserted. "Pharaoh and his hosts" met their just fate at the hands of "Negro manhood, Negro bravery, Negro military genius and skill."[32] On a cold night in Chicago, the most famous black American warmly embraced the bloodiest nation-building story in the history of the Americas. In a United States where lynchings were now constantly in the news and Jim Crow laws emerged from Southern legislatures, Douglass stood as the spokesman of the once dreaded legacy of the Haitian Revolution. At Chicago in 1893 this American patriot, sickened once again at the power of white supremacy, needed an alternative nation to celebrate.

Douglass returned home to Cedar Hill for much of the winter of 1892–93. The fair's official opening did not take place until May. But the man from the Tuckahoe still wore many hats. Despite the embrace of his honorary Haitian identity and a kind of Pan-Africanism in the Chicago speech, he was still a professional Republican in this season of the party's defeat. On February 13, at the Union League Club of Brooklyn, New York, Douglass delivered an hour-long tribute to Abraham Lincoln. At this annual birthday commemoration of Lincoln, three hundred Republicans gathered for an elaborate banquet amid "bunting, flags and flowers, and a fine oil painting of the martyred President," as reported in the press.[33]

Introduced to a prolonged ovation, Douglass served up his share of Lincoln legend. But he never spoke publicly about the sixteenth president without a political purpose that served the cause of black freedom or civil rights. In this atmosphere of mystic hero worship Douglass called Lincoln "godlike" and the greatest American who "ever stood or walked upon the continent." Douglass placed Lincoln in the line of classic heroes, those who had been tested in crisis and led nations through their "darkest hours." Douglass had this audience of Gilded Age New Yorkers in the palm of his hand: "The time to see a great captain is not when the wind is fair and the sea is smooth, and the man in the cross-trees . . . can safely sing out, 'All is well.' At such a time a pigmy may seem a giant. . . . You must see him when the sky is dark . . . see him in the hour of danger . . . when his ship is in distress." Because he had taken the country through its worst storm, Lincoln was "such a captain" and a "hero worthy of your highest worship."[34] How dearly in the 1890s, the orator implied, the nation needed such a captain now.

The image of the savior Lincoln characterized much Lincoln oratory. But Douglass put it to his own ends: "I had the good fortune to know Abraham Lincoln personally and peculiarly." The "peculiar" element was the black man welcomed without racist pretension at the White House. Douglass thus brought attention to his own prominence, relishing the tales of his meetings with Lincoln and his pride of place in history, which is what almost every Yankee did who knew Lincoln. But it was also a commentary on the racism deep in so many human relationships all over America. Douglass was fond of using Lincoln's ability to "make me at ease" as a metaphor for the possibility of equality in race relations. Gone in this speech were any "stepchildren" metaphors, used so brilliantly in 1876; gone also were any identifications with Pan-Africanism or refrains about "when Haiti spoke." Instead, he returned to the idea of a composite America: "I have seen both sides of this great world. I have seen men of all conditions . . . high and low, rich and poor, slave and free, white and black." Douglass used Lincoln to appeal to human unity. "I feel it more to be a man and a member of the great human family," he announced, "than to be a member of any one of the many varieties of the human race, whether Anglo-Saxon, Anglo-African, or any other."[35] In this his last public Lincoln eulogy, it was as if Douglass imagined that the pernicious exhibition of human types about to be displayed on the Chicago Midway could be refuted by a vision of human unity forged through the prairie politician who overcame his roots and saved the Union.

The Chicago Haiti speech and the Brooklyn Lincoln speech, though they seem so different, were not opposite stories for Douglass. Even if stretching the threads of history a bit, they were a way of linking Toussaint and Lincoln as different kinds of liberators, different providential actors in an apocalyptic historical trajectory; portraits of both figures hung in prominent places in Douglass's parlor at Cedar Hill. Nation making needed blood sacrifice and even martyrdom. If the times demanded the model of Haiti as a black republic, they needed even more the legacy of a reinvented American republic and the life and death of Lincoln in whose blood symbolically a new country was born. In national memory, blacks now needed Lincoln as he now needed them. But the symbolic Lincoln could do nothing about a collapsing economy. A mere three weeks before Grover Cleveland's second inauguration, three major American railroads went under, and before long some five hundred banks and fifteen thousand companies would fail in the devastating Panic of 1893.[36]

With his Brooklyn audience Douglass remembered walking in the mud of Pennsylvania Avenue behind Lincoln's carriage on the day of his second inauguration, a deep "foreboding" in Douglass's mind about plots to murder the president. Then deftly, Douglass quoted the strongest antislavery lines from the Second Inaugural Address: "Every drop of blood drawn by the lash shall be paid by another drawn by the sword." Such inspiring language, Douglass claimed, he had never otherwise witnessed. "There seemed at the time to be in the man's soul the united souls of all the Hebrew prophets." This was no mere hyperbole by one who had so carefully read those prophets and adopted their stories of destruction and rebirth. Moreover, Douglass instructed these staunch advocates of tariffs and sound money that Lincoln's assassination was the "natural outcome of a war for slavery." Lincoln the emancipator loomed large not only for a party that had lost its conscience, but in an era when the federal government would exercise "no power . . . to protect the lives and liberties of American citizens in any of our Southern states from barbarous, inhuman, and lawless violence."[37] Ever the ironist, and modeling his favorite prophets, even as the after-banquet speaker in the club of his friends, Douglass enlisted Lincoln in the fight against lynching.

• • •

With Douglass's strong support, on April 5, 1893, Ida Wells embarked on a speaking tour of England. Two of Douglass's friends, Isabella Fyvie Mayo, a well-connected Scottish reformer, and Catherine Impey, a wealthy English Quaker activist and editor, invited Wells to make the journey and spread the cause of antilynching. Impey in particular corresponded with Douglass, often looking for black activists who might come to England and help her promote her own journal, *Anti-Caste*, and its various causes. "I was a guest in Mr. Douglass's home when the letter [from Impey] came," Wells remembered in her autobiography. "It said that they knew Mr. Douglass was too old to come. . . . I gave him the letter to read and . . . he said, 'You go my child, you are the one to go, for you have the story to tell.' " The frustrated young activist was elated: "It seemed like an open door in a stone wall." [38]

At first Wells's tour succeeded gloriously, especially in Scotland, with Mrs. Mayo and Miss Impey organizing the engagements and introducing Wells to reform leadership. Just as Douglass had done forty-six years earlier with the abolitionist cause, Wells now stood before large audiences (one thousand five hundred men in Aberdeen), she later wrote, "telling of conditions in the South since the Civil War, Jim Crow laws, ballot-box intimidation . . . laws against inter-marriage . . . , cruel physical atrocities vented upon my race." Wells was a sensation; a new era with new issues had a new voice. She collected piles of clippings about her performances from the British press, carried them home, and later filled her autobiography with extensive excerpts. A feud and scandal erupted, however, over Impey's open sexual relationship with the "darker" George Ferdinands, a dentist and house guest of Mayo's who was from Ceylon. Wells defended Impey and her right to any interracial relationship. Mayo condemned and shunned both women. Wells had also openly defended Douglass's marriage to Helen Pitts, whom she warmly befriended. Mayo had financed the young American's travels; after five weeks Wells returned to America, worried for her own reputation but inspired by her experience abroad. [39] Soon she was in Chicago planning and working with Douglass at the Haitian Pavilion.

Even before her British tour, Wells had discussed with Douglass and two other men, Ferdinand Barnett, a Chicago lawyer and her future husband, and I. Garland Penn, an educator, the prospect of producing a pamphlet that would expose the discrimination against blacks at the Columbian Exposition. But the project needed money, and though Douglass took the lead in fund-raising among his friends, he initially failed in the face of the deepening Panic of 1893. It took many months and much controversy before *The Reason Why the Colored American Is Not in the World's Columbian Ex-*

position was published. Douglass enlisted Frederick J. Loudin, a shoe man-ufacturer and manager of the Fisk Jubilee Singers, to join him in issuing a fund-raising appeal, "To the Friends of Equal Rights." Douglass and Lou-din each put up $50 of their own money, but the appeal failed with blacks, much less with whites.[40]

The Chicago fair was a spectacle that all wanted to see; but for blacks and other nonwhite groups it was both irresistible and appalling. It offered all manner of intellectual and scientific "congresses," as well as an anthro-pological freak show. The exposition leadership planned a Colored Peo-ple's Day on August 25. Wells vehemently opposed such a segregated day, while Douglass decided that such a "Jubilee Day" could be used to show and tell the story of African American progress. The old pragmatist thought he could still reach open minds. He had not come to Chicago for the entire summer merely to provide an object for gawkers. Douglass would use the day to challenge the White City. Wells worried that to participate in such a day would imply black contentment with their lot. Some black newspapers, especially the *Indianapolis Freeman*, attacked the idea as well as the pro-posed pamphlet. "No 'Nigger Day' " and "No 'Nigger Pamphlet'!" screamed its headlines. While Wells was still in England, Douglass fought back. "Why may we not tell of our persecution and murder in this country because of our race and color?" he demanded in a letter to the paper. "Shall our voices be mute and our tongues paralyzed because our words may pain the ears of our oppressors? . . . No brother Freeman, we must not be silent. We have but one weapon unimpaired and that is the weapon of speech, and not to use it . . . is treason to the oppressed." Douglass almost gave up on the pam-phlet, but when Wells returned to Chicago, the two allies raised $500 from black women's organizations, and the book moved ahead. It was not pub-lished in four languages as hoped (including French, Spanish, and German) but only in English with prefaces in the other three.[41]

Privately, however, in midsummer Douglass admitted to his daughter Rosetta a deep frustration. Complaining of his failing eyesight and feeling that he was "going downhill," he also revealed that he had loaned the Hai-tian government $1,400 to keep the pavilion open. Worse, he felt discour-aged at the fate of blacks amid all the wonders of the fair: "We cut no great figure at this fair. We do not seem to be a part of it. . . . It seems like hop-ing against hope." As Colored People's Day neared, many blacks planned to boycott the event. Wells agreed to disagree with her hero. August 25 became a day of anguish for many and inspiration for some. For many weeks, the large Midwestern R. T. Davis Milling Company had maintained a booth at the fair, featuring Nancy Green, a fifty-nine-year-old former slave and long-time servant for a prominent white Chicagoan, as "Aunt Jemima." The stereotypical plantation "mammy" Green flipped pancakes while wearing a red bandanna, smiling and talking in Southern country dialect. The booth, in the shape of a huge flower barrel, became a must-see at the fair. But worse, on Jubilee Day as people arrived in the morning, they were met with watermelon stands placed throughout the grounds. Douglass joined many of his race in bitter disappointment when he saw this affront and nearly called off the events he had planned for Festival Hall, a large venue at the exposition. More than a thousand people attended on a hot day, most of them black. Wells stayed home in disgust and left the old man to preside over what could have been one of the greatest embarrassments of his life.[42]

The best eyewitness account of what happened is that of the twenty-one-year-old poet Paul Laurence Dunbar. Dunbar had recently relocated to Chicago and published his first book of poems, *Oak and Ivy*. Dunbar found a job working for meager wages as a "washroom caretaker" at the fair. He also made good friends with the young poet-artist James Weldon Johnson, who with a group of college classmates came up from Atlanta for the summer to work as "chair boys," driving carts carrying people around the fair. Johnson too witnessed Douglass's Colored People's Day address. Dunbar, unlike Johnson, had met Douglass, at a social event; the Sage had read some of the young man's poems and all but adopted him on the spot. A music teacher introduced Dunbar to Joseph Douglass, the violinist grandson, who was to play at the festivities. When he met the elder statesman, Dunbar remembered the scene: "The old man was just finishing dinner. He got up and came tottering into the room. 'And this is Paul Dunbar,' he said, shaking hands and patting me on the shoulder." The artist was awed and quoted Douglass as saying, "Paul, how do you do? I've been knowing you for some time and you're one of my boys." Then Douglass asked Dunbar to read his "Ode to Ethiopia" to the gathered social group, after which Old Man Eloquent took up the young man's book and himself read "The Ol' Tunes." Douglass further invited Dunbar to come to Washington and live with him for a while after the fair. He said he would take care of the struggling artist. "I have got one fiddler" (the grandson), Douglass remarked, "and now I want a poet." After this extraordinary meeting Douglass made sure that Dunbar had a place on the program for August 25 and gave him a position at the Haitian Pavilion as

Paul Laurence Dunbar, c. 1893.

well at $5 per week out of the commissioner's own pocket.[43] He took care of the young artist.

At the ceremony Douglass walked to the stage with Isabella Beecher-Hooker, sister of Harriet Beecher Stowe. Then he took the podium and introduced numerous black ministers, including the AME bishop Henry McNeal Turner. As keynoter, Douglass delivered a version of his speech "The Race Problem in America." As the Sage began reading the typewritten address, hecklers around the rim of the hall shouted catcalls, recorded Dunbar. Douglass became unnerved; his hand holding the text began shaking and his "voice faltered." But suddenly he threw the pages down on the lectern, pulled off his spectacles, and tossed them down on the text. With "fire in his eyes," the Lion showed the "battle that had flamed on so many abolition platforms." Dunbar recited his stunning memory: Douglass "tossed back his head, ran his fingers through the lion-like mane of hair," and spoke in "sonorous tones, compelling attention, drowning out catcalls as an organ would a penny whistle." The hecklers, recalled Dunbar, went silent.[44]

In what became a precursor for the last great speech of the orator's life, "The Lessons of the Hour," first delivered in the fall of 1893 and then many times in 1894, Douglass found the old voice and preached an old creed. He forthrightly faced the lynching issue on this supposed day of celebration:

"Men talk of the Negro problem. There is no Negro problem. The problem is whether the American people have honesty enough, loyalty enough, honor enough, patriotism enough to live up to their Constitution." Too many whites had branded the Negro a "moral monster," against all reasonable evidence. In too many places "mobs have taken the place of law. . . . They hang, shoot, burn men of the race without justice and without right." An embittered Douglass declared the United States a tyranny, a nation of corrupted memory, abandoning its victories in favor of power, greed, racial fear, and pride. "We only ask to be treated as well as you treat the late enemies of your national life." These were stirring strokes about how the Civil War now felt nearly lost. But he also acknowledged the ugly theme of the exposition. He asked the audience to observe black progress since slavery: Do not "measure the Negro" by the "standard of the splendid civilization of the Caucasian. . . . Measure him by the depths out of which he has risen." When Ida Wells heard about Douglass's performance, she hurried down to the fair and "begged his pardon," she recalled, "for presuming in my youth and inexperience to criticize him for an effort which had done more to bring our cause to the attention of the American people than anything else which had happened during the fair." [45]

Five days later ten thousand copies of *The Reason Why the Colored American Is Not in the World's Columbian Exposition* were published, and Douglass, Wells, and Dunbar handed it out in the central hall of the Haitian Pavilion every day for the remaining two months of the exposition. According to Wells, Douglass had reported for duty daily at the pavilion all summer, where he "held high court." Most days, she said, the black celebrity was "swamped by white persons who wanted to shake his hand, tell of some former time when they had heard him speak." She even complained that while walking around the fairgrounds with Douglass, she never managed any conversation because he attracted constant fans and onlookers. These images prompted one Douglass biographer to call his presence in Chicago that of "the antique abolitionist . . . as much a relic as any on display" over on the Midway.[46] Hordes of white and foreign visitors did gaze at a symbol of a vanished slavery, and of a bloody old conflict now, in their view, overcome. The large, stocky, elderly black man with stunning white hair might have stimulated both pride and perversity in the throngs of people who came to "see Douglass." But Douglass was no caged exhibit; he brought his pen and voice and they were not yet worn-out. No relic, he was a living, talking monument with much left to say, even if his voice could not unseat the powerful. Nowhere in the United States had a humane memorial yet been erected to the endurance and life-affirming survival of American slaves, much less to the black soldiers who had fought and died for freedom. But in Chicago for six months in 1893 slavery had both an embodiment and a refutation.

Douglass wrote the introduction for *The Reason Why*, and anyone who read it could not miss the author's central point: slavery—its moral tentacles, its spirit, its revived ideology, its history—still infested the fabric of American society. Douglass delivered an indictment of his country and its failure to live up to the promises of 1863 to 1868. "So," he wrote directly, "when it is asked why we are excluded from the World's Columbian Exposition, the answer is Slavery."[47]

Douglass plunged his reader into a past that would not die. Many good things awaited saying, he wrote, about "our country and countrymen, of which we would be glad to tell . . . if we could do so, and at the same time tell the truth." Then followed perhaps the longest sentence Douglass ever wrote (a page and a half), identifying more than twenty "things" he wished were true: "that American law is now the shield alike of black and white; that the spirit of slavery and class domination has no longer any lurking place in any part of this country; . . . that here Negroes are not tortured, shot, hanged or burned to death, merely on suspicion of crime and without seeing a judge." The litany of dispossession, horror, and betrayal finally ended with "that to the colored people of America, morally speaking, the World's Fair now in progress is not a whited sepulcher." This was Douglass the orator of old, the master of repetition and metaphor. To read it closely was to hear Jeremiah updated to 1893. He may have stunned readers into despair. Too many white Americans gave no value to black life, he argued fifty-one years after his Fourth of July speech. The murder of a black man, said Douglass, no longer mattered "in point of economy" as it had during slavery. And the central motive of lynching? he asked. Political "disfranchisement"—the elimination of black votes.[48] History, he demanded, was never over, whether at moments of high triumph or horrible defeat.

The truth was terrifying; the "whited sepulcher" needed some kind of redemptive meaning. Like the Douglass of old, he provided an ending of strained hope. All the violent reaction to black progress was proof of the race's advancement: "A ship rotting at anchor meets with no resistance, but when she sets sail on the sea, she has to buffet opposing billows." Keep "faith in the power of truth," he urged, "faith in work and faith in . . . manly character." He even suggested a "cheerful spirit" and that readers exercise patience. Lamely he counseled, "Next to victory is the glory and happiness of manfully contending for it. Therefore, contend! contend!"[49] A sad, if not defeated, man had written those words. If only metaphors could stop lynch mobs.

Douglass stayed in the Midwest most of the fall of 1893, closing out his duties for Haiti and reworking a lecture he took on the road. But more anguished news soon arrived from the family. Rosetta's oldest daughter, Annie, married to Charles S. Morris, sometimes Douglass's young traveling companion, and a student at the University of Michigan who tried to finance his education as a bootblack, had taken ill. She had been living at Cedar Hill, apart from her husband. In October, Douglass reluctantly loaned $300 to Charles to move Annie, who was now pregnant, out to Ann Arbor, Michigan. On November 11, Rosetta wrote in shock to her father, who was off lecturing, "I received the heartbreaking news of my dear Annie's death. . . . I am utterly dazed and crushed." Two weeks later, Rosetta wrote again in grief; Annie had died just before her twenty-ninth birthday. "If only she hadn't gone to Ann Arbor she would have been living today." The doctor had said she was "not equal to such travel."[50] Douglass may have lost count of how many grandchildren had passed on, and by late fall he had not seen any of them in many months. Rosetta and Nathan had now lost two of their seven children. Through motherhood, joy and loss had long been Rosetta's fate. Out on the lonely lecture circuit, a grandfather wept. He had now lost an Anna and two Annies.

The Columbian Exposition concluded at the end of October after 184 days. Lynchings continued throughout the country; the economic depression deepened as labor unrest exploded. Among the many "congresses" held during the fair was one on labor late in the summer. On September 2, Douglass presided at an extraordinary session, "Negro Labor." The speakers included Booker T. Washington, Ida B. Wells, and Henry Demarest Lloyd, the muckraking progressive journalist and labor activist who organized the session. Labor leaders and reformers from around the world attended the congress. In his remarks, the still relatively little-known Washington criticized the crop lien system in the South and the endless debt it forced blacks to suffer. He emphasized Southern blacks' desire for manual labor, and to receive a "fair chance," as he touted the successes of Tuskegee Institute in its short history. If fairness and conciliation prevailed, "friction between the races is to pass away," and a solution could be found to the race problem, said Washington.

Wells and Douglass expressed starkly different views. Wells challenged the idea that good race relations lay ahead, since whites desperately needed black workers and purposely kept them in poverty and debt. For his part, Douglass acknowledged the necessity of self-reliance, since he had so often preached it himself. But he countered Washington, arguing that blacks in the South were denied property ownership, money, and savings. They were victims of the "mortgage system" and the "script system." Blacks, said Douglass, faced a vicious economic structure. "The man who in slavery days said to the Negro, 'You shall be a slave or die,' now added, 'You shall work for me at the wages I propose or starve.'"[51] The panel had laid bare the fault lines in economic and social thought among black leadership for a generation to come.

On September 22, Emancipation Day, Douglass spoke in Springfield, Illinois, and visited Lincoln's tomb. Struggling now with his strength and health, he nevertheless stayed on the road, and in Detroit on October 5 at a theater he delivered what was likely the first full version of "The Lessons of the Hour," a speech that sometimes also went under the titles "Why the Negro Is Lynched" and "The Negro Problem." On October 7, he wrote a telling letter to his son Charles. Douglass's hand no longer worked effectively while writing, and he complained about dictation. Worn-out and homesick, he reported that he was "still suffering from my cough and am tempted to break away and come home. . . . I shall try however to pull through to the end of the fair." He told Charles that his son Joseph was "playing finely," but he (the grandfather) still urged him "on to perfection." Douglass worried about his apples and pears going to waste in the Cedar Hill orchards. He hoped someone back home could make sure he "could have a little apple sauce in the coming winter." He had frequently written about his ill health, complaining to Charles earlier in the summer of "a cough and la grippe" (diarrhea).

Charles "shuddered" at the reports of his father's recurring bad health, begging that "if you ever intend to relax your efforts, it seems to me that now is full the time." Exhausted and lonely, the elder Douglass oddly sought recognition and respect from his sons. He yearned so much to "plant my feet on Cedar Hill" again, but admitted he should be satisfied. "I am certainly doing . . . good in the life I am living," wrote Douglass, feeling old but in a tender moment. "I am holding up the standard for my people—you would be proud to see the respect and esteem I am everywhere commanding for my race as well as for myself."[52] In such personal tones, Douglass seemed to need to convince himself of the public relevance of his storied career, and that he could still forge on.

Having started life around brutal violence on the Wye plantation, having been pummeled by thugs on the Baltimore docks and beaten to his knees by Edward Covey, and having argued righteously for the blood of slaveholders as a war propagandist during the war, Douglass had at least one more fight in him. Black votes were endangered, but he still owned his pen and his voice. So he purloined hope and despair through an analysis of the times. Douglass delivered "Lessons" in many cities and venues in 1894. One of the most telling was in Metropolitan AME Church on January 9 in front of a packed house. He had long rehearsed many of the oration's arguments, even in brief inscriptions in his books. On January 22, 1893, in the flyleaf of a copy of *Life and Times* signed to a De Witt Miller, Douglass wrote, "Not a Negro Problem, not a race problem, but a national problem; whether the American people will ultimately administer equal justice to all the varieties of the human race in this Republic." [53]

In a careful explication of the origins of lynching emerged the final cause of his life. It was an ugly irony. Douglass grabbed his audience's attention by describing the lawless terror practiced at lynchings: "mob law" had taken on "frantic rage and savage extravagance." Evil had been unleashed in the human spirit. Using Psalm 91, he declared, "When the poison of anarchy is once in the air, like the pestilence that walketh in the darkness, the winds of heaven will take it up and favor its diffusion." Douglass acknowledged that the "mis-called negro problem" belonged to the "whole country." The shock of the news came nearly every day now: "Not a breeze comes to us from the late rebellious states that is not tainted and freighted with negro blood." Mobs had replaced constables and police. America had descended into racial chaos, and apologists for the "mobocratic murderers" had too much sway over public opinion. Facts and truth seemed hardly to matter anymore. Douglass first demanded that his auditors see and listen, before analyzing a lynching: "It is commonly thought that only the lowest and most disgusting birds and beasts, such as buzzards, vultures and hyenas, will gloat over and prey upon dead bodies. But the southern mob in its rage feeds its vengeance by shooting, stabbing and burning when their victims are dead." [54]

Douglass contended that antilynching activists faced a virulent misinformation campaign. Blacks had to be defended as a group against the charge of "rape." Though it is difficult to "prove a negative," he asserted that the long-standing character of black Southerners, as well as the character of their accusers, were both grounds for denial. "The mob . . . brings this charge," Douglass declared, and "it is the mob that the country has accepted as its witness." He offered an argument that has resonated right into the twenty-first century. The accusers as well as those who committed the atrocities were "men who justify themselves in cheating the Negro out of his constitutional right to vote." No one should believe those who surround "the ballot box with obstacles and sinuosities . . . intended to . . . defeat . . . the elective franchise." At the bottom of lynchings lay lodes of "vulgar popular prejudice."[55] But so did bold political motives of greed and power. A colossal lie in the service of political and social control drove the terror. A disfranchiser today might be a lyncher tomorrow. Killing blacks killed their votes.

Douglass offered some history, and thereby a kind of lawyerly devastation of lynching's defenses. Three "distinct periods of persecution" against blacks, and therefore three sets of "excuses," provided the hideous mythology that fueled the lynching epidemic. All of the excuses began with the idea that if charges of rape by black men of white women were true, why did authorities not stop mobs and demand adjudication in courts? The "modesty" of white women had always been a central concern of courts. But Douglass gave the story a long view. In the prolonged night of slavery, violence always lurked ready to respond to the excuse of "insurrection." Rumor of rebellion, much less actual revolts, had led to many a terrified slave's death. During Reconstruction, the fear of "negro supremacy" (the second excuse) became the battle cry of white supremacists, who used murder to destroy their potential political adversaries. And now, in a third era in which social order seemed desperately at stake and blacks demanded their promised citizenship rights, the alleged "assault upon defenseless women" provided the third and most lethal excuse for ritualistic murder of black men. When old excuses wore out their use, white Southerners found "sterner and stronger" reasons to destroy the African American quest for dignity and life.[56]

The "new charge," rape, Douglass maintained, had tainted everything about race relations across the land. He especially argued that alleged sexual assault and the violence exacted against blacks meant "paving the way for our [blacks'] entire disfranchisement." Slavery had always been a "system of legalized outrage" upon black women by white men, and "no white man was ever shot, burned, or hanged for availing himself of all the power that slavery gave him." The perceived loss of that power drove men now to lynch mobs and ritual killings. Too many white Southerners still lived by a slaveholding mentality: "Their institutions have taught them no respect for human life, and especially the life of the negro." A Black Lives Matter counterargument to the extralegal killing of black people is more than a century old. It leaped from the text of Douglass's "Lessons" speech. On the day of Douglass's speech in Washington, January 9, 1894, a black man named Samuel Smith was lynched in Greenville, Madison County, Florida. He had been accused of murder.[57]

Douglass's speech on lynching oozed pain and despair. He believed that lynchings constituted the political silencing of black people. Such a big goal needed a big "lie" as justification: "Yet, while any lie may be safely told against the negro . . . this lie will find eloquent mouths bold enough to tell it, and pride themselves upon their superior wisdom in denouncing the ignorant negro voter." Lynching, therefore, was fundamentally a problem of politics, morality, economy, and memory. Looming behind sharecropping and the desire of landholders to keep blacks "fastened to the land as by hooks of steel" were their threats of violence. Whites, North and South, could twist language and contend that disfranchisement was a moderate reform to contain black lust and aggression. Moreover, the struggle over the memory of the Civil War and Reconstruction had been hijacked and corrupted by the lynching narrative. "Principles which we all thought to have been firmly and permanently settled by the late war have been boldly assaulted and overthrown by the defeated party." Douglass had nearly lost hope. "Rebel rule is nearly complete in many states," he declared nearly three decades after Appomattox, "and it is gradually capturing the nation's Congress. The cause lost in the war, is the cause regained in peace, and the cause gained in war, is the cause lost in peace." This was about as bad a fate as Douglass might ever have imagined for the cause at the heart of his life. Some hostile white newspapers, such as one in Alexandria, Virginia, found the speech "incendiary" and "dangerous," even fearing it would only instill "nihilistic ideas" in his audiences.[58]

In Metropolitan AME's pulpit that night in January 1894, Douglass tried to awaken the slumbering conscience of the country with a renewed fire and indignation, to drive a dagger into the political heart of the nation that betrayed its own rebirth. The fate of the republic was at stake in this crisis of violence. Stop violating the Constitutional amendments, he demanded. "Cultivate kindness and humanity" instead of hatred. Cease degrading one group to elevate another. And to white people, he admonished, "Conquer your prejudices." As a great and abiding nineteenth-century liberal he asked the nation to go back to the "glorious truths" in its creeds, to hear the best voices of its history as the "trump of an arch angel, summoning hoary forms of oppression and time honored tyranny to judgment." Never forget, he pleaded, that America's mission still stood as "the redemption of the world from the bondage of ages." [59] The best instincts of moral suasion were never out-of-date, but in this moment they were as much a prayer as an analysis.

The crowd in the pews were on their feet cheering as Douglass reached these crescendos. Then the exhausted old orator folded his text to sit down. A reporter for the *Evening Star* recorded, "Thus spoke Frederick Douglass . . . with uplifted eyes and arms, as if to invoke heaven to bear witness, and the echoes of his words were drowned in a tumultuous storm of applause." Douglass remained "slightly bent" during the address, wrote the journalist, but performed with "voice unshaken." Just as he had begun his career fifty-four years earlier, he fought with his only real weapon—the infinity, majesty, and power of words. Douglass concluded, "Based upon the eternal principles of truth, justice and humanity . . . your Republic will stand and flourish forever." [60] Then he dropped his arms and bowed.

THEN DOUGLASS PASSED

Oh, Douglass, thou hast passed beyond the shore,
  But still thy voice is ringing o'er the gale!
Thou'st taught thy race how high her hopes may soar,
  And bade her seek the heights, nor faint, nor fail.
She will not fail, she heeds thy stirring cry,
She knows thy guardian spirit will be nigh,
And, rising from beneath the chast'ning rod,
She stretches out her bleeding hands to God!

—PAUL LAURENCE DUNBAR,
"FREDERICK DOUGLASS," 1895

Amid weariness and inconsistent health, Douglass remained astonishingly active and engaged in the last months of life. In February 1894 he wrote to old comrade Julia Crofts, "I am still alive and in active service." Given the violence and racism that now "assailed" blacks, he fell back upon a sense of Providence around which he and Julia had long ago found common cause: "As things are, we can only labor and wait in the belief that God reigns in Eternity and that all things work together for good." Nearly a year later, he wrote to J. E. Rankin, of Howard University, banishing any rumors that he would be interested in taking on the presidency of that institution: "I have been a long time in this world and a long time acquainted with myself, and I know . . . just what I am fit for." On February 6, 1895, he rejected an invitation to speak on February 21 (which would be the day after his death) with the disclaimer: "I have more work on my hands than I know how to accomplish and cannot well take any more on or give promises to any more."[1] It was a time for taking stock of past and present, but Douglass never retired his pen or his voice.

Until his dying day Old Man Eloquent received an unending array of invitations to lecture, many of which he accepted. He continued to deliver the "Lessons" lecture in various forms. The extended Douglass family still provided him with joy, especially the surviving grandchildren, as well as financial and emotional travail. With son Lewis taking the lead, Douglass invested further in real estate in Washington, near Annapolis, and in Baltimore. Fame remained a serious problem; he performed repeatedly as the race's representative man, enduring the usual slings and arrows that role entailed. His health seemed to rise and fall, and he disliked the perception that he was now an old man.[2] Moreover, Douglass never stopped trying to ascertain the identity of his father and his own birthday. It gnawed at him like a hunger that could never be fulfilled.

After trying to rest at Cedar Hill through the winter following the eight-month Chicago sojourn, by March 1894, Douglass resumed his never-ending pursuit of just who he was amid all the mysteries of the Eastern Shore. While his heart still beat, the lynching crisis and the nation's fate might wait for a moment. Douglass wrote to Benjamin F. Auld, a son of Hugh Auld, Douglass's former owner, asking for information less about the paternity than about his accurate age. He reminisced of going to Baltimore in 1825 to be the companion of Benjamin's brother, Thomas, and believed himself to have been eight years old then. Douglass wondered if Auld could help him "get some idea of my exact age." He remembered amusingly that he had been "big enough to bring a good sized bucket of water from the pump on Washington Street to our house." The search continued to the very end. "I have always been troubled by the thought of having no birthday." He reckoned that he was "about 77 years old," as usual one year in error. But in his assiduous search among possible kinfolk Douglass assured Benjamin how "happy" he had been to be sent back to Baltimore, to his "good home" with Benjamin's "good mother," Sophia Auld, after the Anthony slaves were divided.[3] Douglass had to feel secure at least in his waning years to thus alter older versions of these traumas in his youth; the Aulds now appeared in memory in soft tones. The appeal turned up no new evidence. His process of always giving shape and meaning to his life's story remained frustrated by his being unable to give it a fully factual beginning.

Frederick Douglass, in his library at Cedar Hill, c. 1893.

Over his final year Douglass gave the "Lessons" speech about lynching many times, and he received a great deal of heartening response. So concerned was the orator about the substance of this lecture, and for his delivery style now as an elderly man, that just before first giving the address in Washington, Douglass invited a friend, William Tunnell, up to Cedar Hill to listen to a dry run. Tunnell worked as a kind of press agent for the speech, visiting the *Washington Post* and other papers, drumming up "sympathy and interest" as well as "influential circulation." Since his first days on the *North Star* in the 1840s, Douglass's career had been in some form a marketing operation. Ida Wells also tried to sell copies of the "Lessons" speech during her second tour of England. The day after the performance in Washington at Metropolitan AME in January 1894, a worker at the Record and Pensions Bureau of the War Department, Alfred Anderson, wrote to say that it was "all the topic of conversation" around his office. He believed he had just read the "great Negro Gladstone of America." Patients gathered in the District of Columbia Homeopathic Hospital to read the speech and begged Douglass to come visit them. Some people wrote just to tell Douglass that their entire families were discussing the speech, including their children. His granddaughter Estelle Sprague wrote to tell Douglass that at the school in which she taught in Virginia the entire student body gathered on a Sunday to listen to the young teacher read aloud her famous grandfather's speech.[4] Could an old man still living by his voice ever receive better affirmations?

Gratified, Douglass had produced for the violent and depression-ridden 1890s one of his best efforts, and it led to endless invitations from churches, clubs, schools, and colleges to speak all across the nation. He had named the problem brilliantly and laid a dagger once again into the nation's moral heart. The disruptive, disturbing prophet of justice was back on his game. In 1893, blacks in Kansas wanted Douglass to come on Emancipation Day, September 22, and a civic club in Nebraska wanted him for a similar event on January 1, 1894. Some all but demanded that he come support their schools or communities, such as a black church in Baltimore that audaciously asked, "Will not he who has reached transcendent eminence remember the rock from which he was hewn?" His friends kept warning him about all the "self-seeking" in the world that weighed him down, but the unknown and intimately known kept beseeching him to go speak, including Susan B. Anthony and his daughter Rosetta. As the "venerable chieftain of the race," so called by the leaders of a Baptist church in West Virginia, Douglass took in the cascade of invitations. He accepted too many. "Though I am no longer young and begin to feel the touch of time and toil," he admitted to a friend in May 1894, "I spend much of my time in traveling and speaking." He rejoiced in reporting that he had just addressed an audience of two thousand in Boston about lynching.[5]

Fame further meant that Douglass remained the target of never-ending requests for money. Begging letters poured into Cedar Hill from unknown people, friends, and family members. The family was constantly a draw on the patriarch's bank accounts and emotions. The handsome grandson-in-law Charles Morris became a wanderer after his wife's death, as well as a frequent correspondent in need of money. Douglass's generosity was remarkable, but sometimes he expressed anger at how some kinfolk squandered his largess. He considered the $200 advanced to Charles to pay for his wife's funeral "as so much taken out of my pocket for which no note or written acknowledgement was given." Douglass chastised his grandson-in-law, who had apparently lost the money: "There is nothing that separates people more widely than the failure to pay honest debts." On the more positive side of the ledger, the grandfather lovingly supported Joseph, Charles's son and the violin prodigy, in his musical education and tours.[6]

Four granddaughters, all Rosetta's children, worked or taught at black schools or in a federal agency: Annie in Harpers Ferry, West Virginia, Hattie at the Florida Baptist Academy, Estelle at the Gloucester County School in Virginia, and Fredericka at the Recorder of Deeds Office in Washington. Hattie wrote in March 1894 thanking her grandfather profusely for the $15 that had just arrived. She would have borrowed it from Uncle Lewis, she said, but "both Estelle and Fredericka had borrowed same from him." Trying to step out independently into the work world, these young women surely had their mother's moral support, but could not rely upon their father, Nathan Sprague, who was still a personal and financial embarrassment to the elder Douglass. In January 1894, a coal dealer wrote to Douglass complaining of a debt owed him by Nathan. After many excuses and being rejected at the Spragues' doorstep, the coal provider wrote to Cedar Hill, "For forty years I have known and honored Mr. Douglass and I regret that I am compelled to think less of a member of his family."[7] As always, Douglass mostly suppressed his anger and absorbed these woes stoically.

To some extent, Douglass had joined a donor class. He gave money to various black schools, colleges, and churches, including to Tuskegee Institute, where he helped Booker Washington by enlisting old abolitionist friends to donate as well. He donated more than his speaking fee to Metropolitan AME Church shortly after he delivered the "Lessons" address there in January 1894. He sometimes answered money requests from ordinary people with checks for small amounts. A young black portrait artist in Illinois enlisted a friend to write to the "great chieftain among the Negroes," asking to paint his portrait for a fee. A twelve-year-old boy in North Carolina did the same in sending his crayon drawing of the famous man. Douglass sent a $15 payment to a carpenter in South Carolina who made him a cane and then promptly asked for more money for personal support. An "orphan boy" who was "born free" in Georgia had three more terms in school and demanded, "Oh! kind sir, please do not deny me. Help me all you can." Moreover, good friends, old and young, begged Douglass for support. Ebenezer Bassett, down on his luck in the depression of 1894 and looking for work, was "far from giving up on the race of life," but deeply stressed at the debts he already owed Douglass. The desperate young poet Paul Laurence Dunbar, who could not find work in Ohio, reported himself "well in body but not in mind"; he needed help sustaining his reputation and begged for "rescue." Douglass's collaborator on the Chicago World's

Fair book I. Garland Penn, his situation "urgent," appealed openly for funds.[8] Hard times caused awkward letters, strained friendships, and endless decisions on whom or what to support.

All was not stress and strain, however, in Douglass's life during his final year. From May through October 1894 in at least three cities—Boston and New Bedford, Massachusetts, and Flemington, New Jersey—he sat for some endearing photographs. They included beautiful pictures of the patriarch with grandson Joseph (violin in hand), and with his grandson-in-law Charles Morris, standing with a hand on the old man's shoulder. They also include the splendid images of a sitting, and portly, Douglass, and two exquisite views of the great wise face, crowned with white mane, and in one of them, smiling. In one image from May, by Denis Bourdon of Boston, the eyes almost gleam with an old fire and he seems about to utter an oracle. In a second, from October, by Phineas Headley Jr. and James Reed of New Bedford, Douglass seems about to grin his way into an amusing story. For nearly fifty years he had been photographed more than any other American of the nineteenth century. The old radical was going out with a gentle smile.[9]

Moreover, Douglass enjoyed the deep love and companionship of his wife, Helen; no amount of public hostility ever seems to have damaged

Frederick Douglass, New Bedford, Massachusetts, October 31, 1894. Phineas C. Headley Jr. and James E. Reed photographers.

their genuine mutual affection. Near the end of his long stay in Chicago, she wrote to him confessing that she felt "awfully lonesome" without him. Their mutual tenderness flowered in letters. "If I could take your cold and your perplexities I would do so," Helen confided. "May God in heaven keep you and bring you safely home, and may your spoken word be like winged arrows." Helen also wrote of her husband to other prominent people, demonstrating not only her unconditional devotion, but a certain savvy ability in promoting his image. To a New York minister who had just delivered a sermon on Douglass, Helen wrote in January 1895 describing the orator as a "witness against a nation . . . the shining angel of truth by whose side I believe he was born, and by whose side he unflinchingly walked through life." Helen's perception of her husband became deeply religious, prophetic by any measure of the era. In March 1895, just after returning from Douglass's funeral in Rochester, she would write to Francis Grimké, the friend who had married them and who had written an extraordinary eulogy-essay. Helen wrote revealingly, "I used to tell Mr. Douglass that nothing in his later life was to me more wonderful than his character as a child, and it does seem as if the flaming sword of an archangel had been about him from his birth to his death."[10] Like few others, Helen had taken on the role of custodian of the legacy. In domestic terms, Douglass was a lucky man; with Helen he had found a stable intellectual and spiritual partner.

The old radical also became somewhat of an art patron. In spring 1894 he combined with a wealthier friend to buy the painter Henry Ossawa Tanner's *The Bagpipe Lesson* for the library at Hampton Institute in Virginia. Douglass loved not only music and art, but also modern technologies. In that last spring of his life, one evening he visited a friend, "Mr. Anderson," at his home to listen for the first time to a phonograph. Douglass's fascination with modernity never abated. He declared himself "amazed and wonderstruck" as he "heard coming out of that trumpet the voice and clear cut sentences of my friend Isaiah Wear" (probably Isaiah C. Wears, prominent black orator from Philadelphia). Douglass wrote a letter of gratitude and profound delight: "The phonograph brought me nearest to a sense of divine creative power than anything I ever witnessed before. It raises the question as to the boundary of the human soul, the dividing line between the finite and the infinite." Douglass's reaction to this machine revealed much about himself. He found "something solemn in the thought that though being dead and turned to dust a man's voice may yet live and speak." His reaction was genuinely spiritual: "I feel somewhat over this instrument in your hand as a man feels when he embraces religion." The "faces and forms of our departed" were important; but "this thing makes us hear their voices." [11] We have no evidence that Douglass was ever recorded on a phonograph. But he desired nothing more than that his spoken and written voice would survive infinitely for humankind. Survive it did by other means.

On February 20, 1895, a destitute African American named Lucius Harrod wrote to the Sage of Anacostia from just down the road in Hillsdale. Harrod was feeble, in ill health, and had not worked since 1888. He had no coal for heating fuel in the winter. "I am poor and needy, yet the Lord thinketh upon me," he wrote, directly quoting Psalm 40:17 to the great man up on the hill. "If you can do me any good in whatever way." The letter included at bottom a PS: "Often read 32nd ch. Isaiah, 2nd v of your 1862 July." Harrod may have remembered a Douglass speech he had read that included the Isaiah passage, but on this day of all days, to reference Isaiah, which Douglass had done so many times himself, gives a special poignancy to the moment: "And a man shall be as a hiding place from the wind, and a covert from the tempest; as rivers of water in a dry place, as the shadow of a great rock in a weary land." [12] Harrod had no idea he had suggested an apt epitaph for the man whose aid he sought.

At approximately 7:00 p.m. that evening, at age seventy-seven, Douglass fell to the floor in the front hallway of Cedar Hill, dead from an apparent heart attack. He first fell slowly to his knees, then spread out on the floor. Helen Douglass was at his side, alone. She went to the front door and cried for help. In a short while a doctor, J. Stewart Harrison, was at the stricken man's side and pronounced him dead. The man of millions of words had gone cold and silent. He was scheduled to give a lecture that evening in a local black church in Hillsdale, and the carriage arrived just as he fell dead. Lucius Harrod never received a reply as he searched for a covert that winter from his travail. [13] Douglass's joyous and turbulent tempest was over.

That morning, February 20, Frederick and Helen had taken a carriage down into the middle of Washington. Helen went to the Library of Congress while Douglass attended for most of the day the meeting of the National Council of Women at Metzerott Hall on Pennsylvania Avenue (at the location of today's FBI Building). May Wright Sewall presided, and Douglass sat on the platform next to his old friend Susan B. Anthony. Douglass seemed in good health through the day among the fifty delegates, although one woman later reported that he continually rubbed his left hand as though it were "benumbed." He did not make an address. He returned home to Cedar Hill around 5:00 p.m. The news of his death spread rapidly through Washington that evening and across the country. At the Women's Council meeting that evening Sewall announced that Douglass had died. Anthony, in agony, could not continue. The next day, with bitter opposition from Southern members, the US Senate passed a resolution, 32–25, to adjourn out of respect for Douglass.[14]

Within four days funeral preparations had been completed. On February 25, the memorial for Douglass was primarily a black-Washington solemn tribute to its most famous resident. After a small family service at Cedar Hill a hearse-carriage transported the oak casket down into the city to Metropolitan AME Church, where Douglass not only had been a member but had delivered so many memorable addresses. A huge mixed-race crowd gathered at the church early in the morning. Between 9:30 a.m. and 1:30 p.m. that day throngs of people processed by the casket, in one side of the edifice and out the other. "Quiet and orderly," reported the *Washington Post*, the young and old, black and white, passed around the funeral bier. Lewis and Charles were conspicuous in organizing the procession. The church groaned to capacity, and during the nearly four-hour service to follow, "thousands" more waited and milled around outside. Five hundred seats inside were reserved, and a "wild rush" occurred for the rest of the pews when the signal came. Actress, lecturer, and journalist Kate Field attended the service. She marveled at the mixture at Douglass's funeral of the famous and the ordinary, even if the speeches were much too long. She watched "the Moses of the black race" honored in death.[15]

Four members of the black Sons of Veterans stood, two at either end of the coffin, as honor guards throughout the ceremony. The actual pallbearers consisted of twelve men in uniform from the "colored letter carriers" of the City of Washington. Among the honorary pallbearers were a who's who of black Washington, including former senator Blanche Bruce, former congressman John Lynch, hotel entrepreneur W. H. A. Wormley, and Douglass's old friend Charles Purvis. Senator John Sherman as well as Supreme Court justice John Marshall Harlan also attended the service. A Boston singer, Moses Hodges, sang Mendelssohn's "O Rest in the Lord," and John Hutchinson, a survivor of the famous abolitionist Hutchinson Family Singers, who had many times appeared with Douglass, sang and chanted "Dirge for a Soldier": "Lay him low, lay him low / Under the grasses or under the snow; / What cares he? He cannot know. / Lay him low, lay him low."[16]

Among the many sermons and eulogies was one biblical tribute by the white president of Howard University, the Reverend J. E. Rankin. Rankin knew his audience. He preached on Psalm 105:17–19: "He sent a man before them. He was sold for a servant. His feet they hurt with fetters. He was laid in chains of iron. Until the time when his word came to pass, the word of the Lord tried him." Rankin likened the youthful Douglass to the Dante of the *Inferno*, a man who had been to hell to find righteousness. Like other eulogists Rankin stressed the "wonderful contrasts and antitheses" of the deceased's life. He also pointed to the theme of forgiveness in how Douglass had searched to know his slaveholding kinfolk. Those close to the altar would have noticed that among the flower displays was one from the Auld family. But Rankin framed his sermon with the story of young Douglass's many sessions with the Baltimore preacher "Uncle Lawson." Helen likely approved of Rankin's theme of how the old preacher had showed the teenager "how God was girding him for that day when he was to go town to town, from state to state, a flaming herald of righteousness; to cross oceans . . . lifting up the great clarion voice, which no one who ever heard can forget." This was funeral rhetoric, but who could resist the story of the orphan slave who would be king of abolitionism?[17]

The casket was taken through the streets of Washington, guarded by a contingent of 150 black Grand Army of the Republic veterans, to the train station, where it departed at 7:00 p.m. for New York City. From Grand Central Terminal the casket was taken downtown to City Hall early in the morning of the twenty-sixth. There the next morning in City Hall, where both Lincoln and Ulysses Grant had lain in state, Douglass too received such an honor for two hours. From 8:00 to 10:00 a.m. a long winding line of New Yorkers viewed Douglass's remains in the hall's vestibule. Promptly the New York stop ended, and soon the casket and family were on the train again across New York State to Rochester.[18]

All business and upper grades of schools were suspended in Rochester on the day of Douglass's burial, February 27. Huge crowds gathered around City Hall, draped in black bunting and American flags, as the body arrived, escorted by the leaders of a local "Douglass League." At Central Church, the largest in the city, eulogies were offered by the Reverends H. H. Stebbins and W. R. Taylor. A male quartet sang "Hide Thou Me," and the organist struck up the old spiritual "Swing Low, Sweet Chariot." A "surging mass of people," said the *New York Tribune*, surrounded the church and the streets during the three hours of public viewing. Accompanying Douglass's body to Rochester were Helen, sons Lewis and Charles, Rosetta and two of her daughters, Estelle and Harriet, and the grandson Joseph. Nathan Sprague apparently did not attend. After the church service in the afternoon, dozens of carriages followed the hearse out to Mount Hope Cemetery, and on a gentle hillside Douglass was laid to rest in the winter landscape. A year later, Lewis and Charles had their mother, Anna Douglass, reinterred from Graceland Cemetery in Washington, DC, to Rochester; she is buried between Frederick and their daughter Annie. The three living children had many years of memories associated with Rochester, some cherished and some anguished. It had never been Helen's home. In a short time Lewis, perhaps with some help from Charles, would paste dozens of newspaper obituaries and eulogies about their father into a scrapbook. Among them was one from a California gathering at which Ida Wells gave the eulogy, and a newspaper report claiming that each son had received a $50,000 inheritance. The battle over Douglass's estate, his will, and for Cedar Hill itself had only begun.[19] On this day, though, a nation and even other parts of the world thought of inheritances of other kinds from the man who had left so much to contemplate with his voice, his pen, and his vote.

In countless speeches and in the autobiographies, Douglass had imposed himself on so many who would attempt his eulogy. As early as the very next day, long obituaries and tributes appeared in newspapers across the country. He was the "self-made" American who had conquered the greatest odds, the man of mixed race but in some ways of no race, the "serf" who had risen to the unrivaled "intellectual standard" of his people, the stunning physical presence—one of the most recognizable persons in the nation. Many eulogies drew deeply from the memoirs and recited actual scenes from Douglass's life. The story was ready and waiting, and Americans in the age of Horatio Alger loved the tale, or perhaps especially needed it in a time when fiends with lynching ropes and torches stalked black men of lesser fame, as well as a time when banks failed everywhere, savings accounts vanished, and economic failure hounded millions. "His history has often been told," said the *Brooklyn Eagle*, as it also declared Douglass "thrice an American . . . in his veins ran the blood of three races . . . the Indian, the white man, and the Negro." Other eulogies played out this fascination with the orator's race. The *New York Times* announced with certainty that Douglass's "white blood" explained his "remarkable energy" and "superior intelligence." A paper in Rome, New York, characterized him as the "most picturesque" of Americans, and his rare ability it attributed to that he "was almost a white man."[20]

But at the center of most eulogies stood the slave who had conquered chattel bondage, this most notorious of American fates. "Sweet are the uses of adversity," rhapsodized the *Eagle*. "It is the north wind that toughens the oak, not the caressing breezes of the south." And the *New York Tribune* instructed its readers that Douglass "became the representative man of his race . . . by virtue of self-help . . . [and] self-education." Douglass's death inspired lofty language, North and South. The "world's greatest Negro" had died, said a Springfield, Illinois, paper, and in a Norfolk, Virginia, journal the "greatest man of African descent this century has seen" passed on. The *Washington Star* declared the passing era the "Douglassian age" and compared the deceased as symbol to the Statue of Liberty in New York Harbor. Exuberant eulogists compared the fallen statesman and man of letters to Gladstone and Bismarck, Goethe and Schiller, Emerson and Victor Hugo.[21]

Eulogies also took on odd, mixed forms. Some papers competed with claims of possessing the last letter Douglass wrote. Some groups, such as a gathering of black Methodist preachers in Richmond, decided it would be too time-consuming to conduct a major memorial for Douglass, who had appeared in so many of their pulpits, since three to four such "men of genius" now came along every year. Some papers reprinted from other sources the claim, without evidence, that Douglass was worth $300,000 at his death. Many press reports from the white South were anything but mournful. The Wilmington, North Carolina, *Messenger* mocked blacks for being "anxious that Congress should prostitute itself like the Radical Legislature—by allowing the remains of Fred Douglass 'to lie in state' in the national capital. Why . . . what has he done to merit such attentions?" This paper dismissed the deceased as a "stirrer up of bad blood and a very diligent Government teat holder and sucker, and enemy of the South." The North Carolinian editor cultivated common public racism by urging "white faced fellows" never to "feel that they are no better than Sambo and Cuffee." An Oshkosh, Wisconsin, account, otherwise laudatory, could not resist pointing out that Douglass had caused "serious detraction" for his reputation by the "unnatural step" of marrying a white woman. But a Milwaukee paper quickly pointed out that Frederick Bailey's owner had taken a black woman as his "consort" to give birth to the man in question. The *New Orleans Picayune* tried to acknowledge Douglass as the "most eminent" man of his race, but since he was a "half-breed," he could never be the group's exemplar.[22] In Douglass, living and dead, Americans found a persona around which to exhibit some of their worst prejudices. But it is equally stunning how much of the country seemed to know his story.

All kinds of reminiscences flowed from articles and public memorials by people who had heard Douglass speak. Someone in every town seemed to claim that distinction. Douglass could be a man for all tastes and seasons. A Washington, DC, account admired how his "intellectuality" grew from an early "fanaticism" to more "conservative" positions. A journalist named Charles T. Congdon remembered hearing Douglass engage a hostile audience from an abolitionist platform in New Bedford. As an anti-abolitionist heckler "hissed," the young orator pointed at the offender and launched into a paraphrase of Genesis 3:14—"I told you so. Upon thy belly shalt thou go, dust shalt thou eat, and hiss all the days of thy life." In these tellings the hecklers always shut up in the face of Douglass's moral and verbal power. Some reminiscences relished stories of the great man's grace and humor. The *Boston Transcript* repeated the oft told tale of how Douglass so often ended up sitting alone on railcars, since no one would take the seat next to the black man. " 'You are occupying an entire seat,' complained a patron. 'I know that,' said Mr. Douglass. 'Well, what right have you to it?' exclaimed the man. 'Because I am a nigger,' returned Douglass. 'That don't give you a right to two seats,' said the man—and Mr. Douglass made room for him." Douglass thus received credit for laughing at and changing racial habits.[23]

Above all, blacks in communities all across the land, in the South and the far West, as well as the North, held meetings of tribute to Douglass, often passing local resolutions of honor and gratitude. The Assembly Club of San Francisco sent a list of typed resolutions to Lewis Douglass and the family. Within a week and a half of the death a gathering in Sumter County, Georgia, produced ten such resolutions. One large meeting in Atlanta rocked with "protests" against racism and violence, while another in Tuskegee came off with propriety and good order. At the Atlanta gathering, Charles Morris, the grandson-in-law, delivered a eulogy devoted to the crisis of Jim Crow railway cars and got carried away, comparing Douglass to Jesus Christ. The black *Cleveland Gazette* announced a simple truth exhibited during the months of Douglass commemorations: "His life and work has been public property almost since the day of his birth. . . . The race will miss him more than it can at this time realize."[24]

But Douglass was not gone; he was merely dead. New geniuses were, indeed, coming along, and two of them would utter important speeches, albeit one famous and the other obscure, that very year. Booker Washington later that fall delivered his pivotal public address, often called the "Atlanta Compromise," at the Cotton States Exhibition. In it he called for accommodation by blacks with certain elements of white supremacy and Jim Crow in exchange for industrial education and social security. Washington would to

a degree trade disfranchisement and segregation for racial peace and economic opportunity.[25] Although never sharing Washington's acquiescence
with Jim Crow or any diminution of the right to vote, Douglass had long
prefigured the Wizard of Tuskegee on the philosophy of self-reliance.

On March 9 in Wilberforce, Ohio, W. E. B. Du Bois, a twenty-seven-year-
old professor at the black college, just returned the previous year from his
extraordinary educational sojourn in Germany, gave a short, remarkable
speech, "Douglass as a Statesman." In his eulogy the Massachusetts-born
and Harvard-educated Du Bois urged students and faculty not to cry out
in "half triumphant sadness" at the death of their leader, but to engage in
"careful conscientious emulation." Du Bois remembered Douglass's leadership in abolitionism, in the recruiting of black soldiers in the war, in the
achievement of black male suffrage, and in civil rights. As a leader Douglass had reached for goals considered "dangerous" and all but "impossible."
He was not afraid of the American "experiment in citizenship." Douglass
had proven himself a "builder of the state" largely from outside traditional
power. "Our Douglass," asserted the young intellectual, was the man of the
race, but he had also "stood outside mere race lines . . . upon the broad
basis of humanity." It had been Du Bois's manner of thought and ambition to say whenever possible that history should make way now for a humane, learned race man much like himself.[26] He seemed to understand and
admire Douglass's work and persona enough to make the model in part
his own.

At the end of his speech, Du Bois offered a brief but remarkable anecdote: "The first and last time I saw Douglass, he lectured on Hayti and the
Haytians and here again he took a position worthy of his life and reputation." Du Bois honored Douglass for choosing principle over diplomacy in
regard to seizure of Haitian territory when he had served as US minister.
Du Bois pushed hard on the irony: "To steal a book is theft, but to steal an
island is missionary enterprise." Du Bois the graduate student was in Berlin
all of 1893 and therefore did not witness the Chicago Haiti speeches. It is
likely, then, that Du Bois heard Douglass speak in Boston at Tremont Temple on March 16, 1892, before the younger man departed for Germany. According to the Boston press, Douglass did indeed speak that night on Haiti
and the Haitians to a full house. Du Bois needed to claim Douglass, to own
the mantle, to join the national chorus of those older than him who *saw*
Douglass. The old abolitionist had fought the "preliminaries . . . for us,"
said the brilliant new voice, "but the main battle he has left for us." We cannot know whether the fresh-faced Du Bois had felt in awe of what a Boston

reporter called Douglass's "manly bearing" on the Tremont Temple stage with his "thick whitening hair brushed back from his forehead, and his eye as keen and brain as clear as ever." But Du Bois no doubt joined the "rounds of applause" when the venerable orator announced himself "a friend to Haiti. . . . I say I am a friend to any people who have known the yoke of slavery as I have."[27] Few people ever awed Du Bois; but Douglass may have been one of them.

Du Bois knew *his* Douglass well enough that only a few years later as he crafted the lyrical history in his masterpiece, *The Souls of Black Folk*, a reader can feel and almost hear Douglass's words informing the text. In his chapter on Booker T. Washington, Du Bois pays an homage to Douglass, saying that the former abolitionist, "in his old age, still bravely stood for the ideals of his early manhood" and had "passed away in his prime." In the famous second chapter of *Souls*, "Of the Dawn of Freedom," a vivid, polemical account of Reconstruction, the author offered what many scholars have come to consider a "Du Boisian" form of history. His biographer David Levering Lewis calls this Du Bois's "signature," the compression of huge pieces of history and human aspiration into single paragraphs, images, or metaphors.[28]

The brooding ending of "Dawn of Freedom" argues that for America to find its soul, it had to free the slaves and now continue freeing the slaves' "children's children." "I have seen a land right merry with the sun. . . ." Du Bois wrote, "and there in the King's Highway . . . sits a figure veiled and bowed, by which the traveller's footsteps hasten as they go. On the tainted air broods fear. Three centuries' thought has been the raising and unveiling of that bowed human heart, and now behold a century new for the duty and the deed. The problem of the Twentieth Century is the problem of the color line." Significantly this tragic ending is placed between two chapters in *Souls* that end with ringing appeals to the first principles of the Declaration of Independence. Du Bois's history is a prophetic demand upon the creeds of a forgetful country. In the nineteenth century, no one had laid down that prophetic demand quite like Douglass, and Du Bois knew it.[29] Du Boisian history was first Douglassonian history: the problem of the nineteenth century had been the problem of slavery, revealed and written in thousands of pages and spoken from countless platforms by the fugitive from the Tuckahoe. Douglass had seen to it that his story had always provided a "raising and an unveiling"—by prophetic witness, through scars, pain, anger, unforgettable metaphors, and patriotic triumphs.

Douglass had long offered himself as Du Bois's "figure veiled and bowed" along the highway, yet one who stood up to preach a "sacrilegious irony" about the crimes of the nation, as he put it in the Fourth of July speech. In Douglass's great orations of the 1850s, the air also hung tainted with a fear perhaps even greater than Du Bois imagined for the turn of the twentieth century. Just after placing his people in the midst of the ancient Hebrews' Bablylonian Captivity, Douglass announced the essential theme of his life: "My subject, then, fellow-citizens, is AMERICAN SLAVERY." And so it always was. The abolitionist filled the tainted air with jeremiadic words and sounds. He heard the "mournful wail of millions! whose chains" clanked "heavy and grievous." Throughout his fifty years of oratory and writing, Douglass had employed all manner of blood metaphors for the nature of African American history, none more often than the line used yet again in his Haiti speeches, which Du Bois heard: the history of black people "might be traced, like a wounded man through a crowd, by the blood." Douglass had been the man bowed by the roadside, with a trail of blood, but then the risen slave, the free man and voice, telling the nation a history it did not wish to hear. He told it all over again in the lynching crisis of the 1890s. "My language . . . is less bitter than my experience," he announced in an 1853 address. "I am alike familiar with the whip and the chain of slavery, and the lash and the sting of public neglect and scorn." Speaking for the bowed figure, he argued that slavery had always "shot its leprous distilment through the life-blood of the nation." It had always "intended to put thorns under feet already bleeding, to crush a people already bowed down." [30] Hundreds of thousands of people across the nineteenth century had witnessed or read Douglass's story of the risen figure from the side of the road. He had striven to be both a prophet of doom and of redemption.

When Douglass died, Du Bois wrote a private poem he called "The Passing of Douglass." He etched the date, "20 February, 1895," and the place, "Wilberforce, Green Co., Ohio," beneath and above his title.

> Then Douglass passed—his massive form
> Still quivering at unrightful wrong;
> His soul aflame, and on his lips
> A tale and prophecy of waiting work.

Personal, heroic, elegiac, Du Bois tried to take up a standard for the next generation.

> Not as the sickening dying flame,
> That fading glows into the night

Passed our mightiest—nay, but as the watch-
Warning and sending in common glory,
Suddenly flocks to the Mountain, and leaves
A grim and horrid blackness in the world.

But amid the feeling of darkness, Du Bois made Douglass his own.

Live, warm and wondrous memory, my Douglass
Live, all men do love thee. . . .
Rest, dark and tired soul, my Douglass,
   Thy God receive thee.
   Amen![31]

For decades countless Americans had looked at and listened to Douglass; they had admired and hated him, loved, followed, envied, denounced, and tried to destroy him. Many had tried to make him their own, to control his trajectory, even his words. He had been gawked at, photographed, and studied; he had won many arguments and lost many others. People had for decades named their children for him. Eulogies reflected this range of reactions over the decades. Similar to Lincoln, Douglass offered an original American to those who sought such images; he was the sui generis former slave who found books, the boy beaten into a benumbed field hand who fought back and mastered language and wielded a King James–inspired prose at the world's oppressions with a genius to behold. He was spiritual and secular, consummately political and deeply moralistic, romantic and pragmatic, a philosopher of democracy and natural rights and a preacher of a firm doctrine of self-reliance. Douglass provided a living symbol by his physical presence and skill that refuted all manner of racist notions and reinforced others for the ignorant and the fearful. He rose from nowhere to the centers of power, or so it had seemed. He loved power but found he could wield it only with limits and often softly. He had made vanity and pride often into weapons alongside his words; he outlasted most of his enemies, except the ideology of white supremacy, which only seemed to transmogrify into more virulent forms in his old age. Underneath Douglass's grand dignity, deep in his soul, ran a lode of humility born of experience and a long view of history, but embedded in that soul as well was his fierce, sometimes insecure, but often magnificent quest for respect, to compete, and to conquer his foes. Embedded there as well were an insatiable intellectual curiosity and a spirituality that sustained him through many trials. And so Douglass passed, but the words, and much more, endure.

In the frightening racial climate of the mid-1890s some in the next generation of black artists and thinkers saw Douglass's death with dark foreboding. Douglass's young protégé Paul Dunbar viewed blacks in the 1890s as a kind of crucified people, and his mentor as their "guardian" prophet, the voice forever "nigh" and sounding forth over "the gale" of racism and violence. In his 1895 poem, Dunbar also imagined Douglass as both a warrior and a resurrected Christ figure for the race. Whatever a prophet really is, in his grief at Douglass's death, Dunbar believed blacks had lost theirs.[32]

One of the most remarkable eulogies of Douglass was delivered on March 10, 1895, in Washington by his close younger friend the Reverend Francis Grimké, the Presbyterian minister who had married Frederick and Helen. Grimké especially defended his friend against all claims about his "selfishness," that the Sage of Cedar Hill had always looked out for himself and his pocketbook. No one had ever given or sacrificed more for the race than Douglass, argued Grimké. But placed in that long address is a short, compelling anecdote about Douglass's humanity, and especially his love of music. Three weeks before Douglass died, Grimké had been at Cedar Hill for dinner. As the meal ended, "all repaired to the sitting room," and the old orator demanded they all sing. Grandson Joseph took the lead on the violin, and someone else played the piano. Grimké remembered poignantly, "In the singing he [Douglass] took the lead." The guest left this unforgettable image of the host: "Standing in the doorway between the sitting room and the hall, with violin in hand, he struck up . . . 'In Thy cleft, O Rock of Ages,' and sang it through to the very end with a pathos that moved us all. . . . It seemed to take hold of him so." Grimké witnessed Douglass's spirituality in full force. "I can almost hear now the deep mellow tones of his voice and feel the solemnity that pervaded the room as he sang the words:

> *In the sight of Jordan's billow,*
> *Let Thy bosom be my pillow;*
> *Hide me, O Thou Rock of Ages,*
>   *Safe in Thee."*

Grimké felt a "kind of presentiment that the end was near, that he [Douglass] was already standing on the very brink of that Jordan over which he was soon to pass."[33]

. . .

If slavery and race were the centerpieces of American history through the nineteenth century's rise, fall, and then resurrection of the republic, no one represented that saga quite like Douglass. As the modern poet Robert Hayden so beautifully put it:

> *When it is finally ours, this freedom, this beautiful*
> *and needful thing, needful to man as air, usable as earth;*
> > *when it belongs at last*
> > *to all . . . when it is finally won . . .*
> *this man, this Douglass, this former slave, this Negro*
> *beaten to his knees, exiled, visioning a world*
> *where none is hunted, alien,*
> *this man, superb in love and logic, this man*
> *shall be remembered.*
> *Oh, not with statues' rhetoric,*
> *Not with legends and poems and wreaths of bronze alone,*

Frederick Douglass seated with grandson Joseph Douglass, who was a concert violinist, New Bedford, Massachusetts, October 31, 1894. Phineas C. Headley Jr. and James E. Reed photographers.

But with the lives grown out of his life, the lives
Fleshing his dream of the beautiful, needful thing.[34]

Douglass was the prose poet of America's and perhaps of a universal body politic; he searched for the human soul, envisioned through slavery and freedom in all their meanings. There had been no other voice quite like Douglass's; he inspired adoration and rivalry, love and loathing. His work and his words still wear well. What shall we make of "our Douglass" in our own time? The problem of the twenty-first century is still some agonizingly enduring combination of legacies bleeding forward from slavery and color lines. Freedom in its infinite meanings remains humanity's most universal aspiration. Douglass's life, and especially his words, may forever serve as our watch-warnings in our unending search for the beautiful, needful thing.

ACKNOWLEDGMENTS

This book reflects nearly a decade of research, conversations, and writing. But since my first book in 1989 was also on Frederick Douglass, this work is in some ways the product of nearly my entire professional career.

My gratitude goes to more people and institutions than I can express. I had no intention of writing a full life of Douglass until I went to Savannah, Georgia, to deliver a lecture to local teachers on Douglass's *Narrative*. While there my hosts, the Georgia Historical Society, introduced me to Walter Evans, a collector extraordinaire of African American art, rare books, and manuscripts. Walter's remarkable collection of Douglass materials is the reason I wrote this book. I have spent countless days and weeks doing research on the dining room table—at "my chair"—at the Evans house on Jones Street. To Walter and Linda Evans I have, in part, dedicated this book. I owe them this opportunity and am forever grateful for the special private access to the scrapbooks and other documents, but most of all for their abiding friendship and confidence in me. I give a special thanks as well to Stan Deaton, Todd Groce, and the staff at the Georgia Historical Society for their many kindnesses during my Savannah sojourns.

Over the years I have benefited enormously from conversations, critiques, and readings from many scholars of Douglass and other subjects. William S. McFeely helped and mentored me when I really needed it, and his biography and prose are still an inspiration. The late James Horton was as good a friend as I ever had telling the world our stories. I owe a great deal to Lonnie Bunch, who sees and creates worlds while the rest of us try to help as mates on the ship. Caryl Phillips is a confidant and writer like no other; he knows Douglass and should still write the script. Peter Almond and I have shared perhaps more hours of Douglass discussion and imagination than anyone. Richard Rabinowitz is an intellectual companion, fellow traveler, and theological and life adviser; I wish I knew as much about anything as Richard does about everything. Joyce Seltzer is a legendary editor, and I count myself fortunate to have worked with her. Marsha Andrews endured and supported the writing of this book for many years, from Savannah to Cambridge and the Eastern Shore.

For reading chapters and sending me critiques I am deeply indebted to Henry Louis Gates Jr., Lois Horton, Richard Blackett, Leigh Fought, Richard Rabinowitz, John Stauffer, Zoe Trodd, Peter Almond, and Jane Coppock. All took more time with my writing than I deserved. Jane gave me the failsafe eye of a former editor. To Leigh I am grateful for many shared documents and collaborations. Thanks to Skip for his deep knowledge of Mr. D, detailed notes, and Sunday-morning emails. Lois got my attention about gender many times. Zoe's and John's legendary knowledge of the photographs was invaluable. No one knows transatlantic abolitionists like Blackett. David Brion Davis's inspiration flows through this book. Four great deceased Douglass scholars have been with me from the beginning: Benjamin Quarles, Philip S. Foner, Dickson J. Preston, and Nathan I. Huggins.

All of the following had important professional and personal influence in helping me think about and write this book: A. J. Aiséirithe, Steve Alderman, Shawn Alexander, James Basker, Ira Berlin, Celeste-Marie Bernier, W. Fitzhugh Brundage, Nicholas Buccola, Randall Burkett, Jeannine DeLombard, Maria Diedrich, Douglas Egerton, Eric Foner, Leslie Frost, Annette Gordon-Reed, James Grossman, Christopher Hager, Lesley Herrmann, Nzadi Keita, Peter Kunhardt, Rudy Langlais, Michael LeMahieu, Michael McManus, Uday Mehta, James Miller, Fred Morsell, Hannah-Rose Murray, Richard Newman, James Oakes, Peter Onuf, Gunther Peck, John Pepper, James B. Stewart, Jean Strouse, James Trotman, Paul Webb, and Sean Wilentz.

Karin Beckett has listened and read for many years about Douglass and my travails in pursuing him; I am forever grateful. I am thrilled that Perry Beckett loves history. My brother and sister-in-law, James Blight and Janet Lang, remain my closest kin and my heroes. Richard Sewell taught me how to write when I first tackled Douglass.

For particularly helpful theological advice on Douglass as a biblical reader and storyteller, I am grateful to Reverend Donald Shriver, Rabbi James Ponet and Elana Ponet, the late Reverend Eugene Winkler, Reverend Ally Brundige, and the Reverend Doug Tanner. Many of my former graduate students have endured and contributed to this book in ways they know. Among them are Alice Baumgartner, Christopher Bonner, Sarah Bowman,

Blake Gilpin, Tiffany Hale, Andrew Horowitz, Brian Jordan, Carolee Klimchock, Jake Lundberg, Katherine Mooney, Nichole Nelson, Benjamin Parten, Steven Prince, Justin Randolph, Samuel Schaffer, James Shinn, Caitlin Verboon, Connor Williams, and Owen Williams. Katherine, thanks once again for the detour down the Robert Penn Warren road.

Several former students have provided crucial research assistance. They include: Ilan Ben-Meir, Griffin Black, Bianca Dang, Shoshana Davidoff-Gore, and Isabel Singer. Griffin has found original Douglass sources and his readings of my notes are superhuman. A very special thanks to Katharina Schmidt, lawyer and historian, who so expertly translated the Ottilie Assing letters for me from the old German to English. Her interpretations of Assing, in both writing and many conversations, have been crucial to my own analysis of this complex woman.

Among my supportive colleagues at Yale on the long journey of this book are Elizabeth Alexander, Beverly Gage, Glenda Gilmore, Jacqueline Goldsby, Jonathan Holloway, Matthew Jacobson, Naomi Lamoreaux, Edward Rugemer, Caleb Smith, Robert Stepto, Laura Wexler, and John Witt. I am grateful to Tony Kronman, Robert Post, and Akhil Amar for many conversations. Jay Winter, teaching comrade and ultimate memory man, led me to a book title. I am further thankful to a series of deans, two provosts, and two Yale presidents for their support. At Yale University Press I give thanks to John Donatich, Sarah Miller, and Heather Gold for pulling me in to edit Douglass's second autobiography at just the time I needed to do it.

In the Yale libraries I am grateful to many curators and archivists, especially Nancy Kuhl, Melissa Barton, George Miles, David Gary, and William Landis. Thanks especially to George for helping me use all the "missing issues" of Douglass's newspaper. Many other institutions helped me with research. They include: the University of Rochester Library; the American Philosophical Society; the Historical Society of Pennsylvania; the Gilder Lehrman Collection at the New-York Historical Society (especially Sandra Trenholm); the New York Public Library; the Moorland-Spingarn Collection at Howard University; the infinite depths of the Library of Congress; the Smithsonian American Art Museum; the Maryland Historical Society in Baltimore; the Boston Public Library; the Syracuse University Library; the University Library, Cambridge University, United Kingdom; the Whaling Museum, New Bedford, Massachusetts; the New Bedford Free Public Library; the Mitchell Library, Glasgow, Scotland; Talbot County Archives, Easton, Maryland; the American Antiquarian Society, Worcester, Massachusetts.

To Jack McKivigan and Robin Condon at the Frederick Douglass Papers in Indianapolis, Indiana, I owe many thanks. Jack's headnotes, and those of his many assistants over the years, in the volumes of speeches and correspondence are a gold mine of information. The National Park Service in New Bedford, Massachusetts, was graciously helpful. And the National Park Service curators at Cedar Hill, the Frederick Douglass National Historic Site in Washington, DC, have been special partners on this book. I am deeply thankful to Ka'Mal McClarin for the research aid, special after-hours tours, and many photographs. Without Pembroke Herbert of Picture Research Consultants, I would never have assembled the images in this book. Her work was beyond crucial; Pembroke is the best in the business.

My numerous visits to the Eastern Shore of Maryland have been supported by the good people of Washington College, particularly Adam Goodheart, and especially by Harriette and Eric Lowery of the Frederick Douglass Honor Society, Priscilla Morris, and Tenny Sener. A special thanks to Richard and Beverly Tilghman, owners of the Wye House plantation. The Tilghmans' hospitality, knowledge, photographs, and grace in their embrace of Douglass are truly special. Priscilla has been my angel of the Shore for local knowledge and research. The boat rides out to the Wye House and especially up the Tuckahoe on that misty morning are unforgettable. I am thankful to a Douglass descendant on the Eastern Shore, Tarence Bailey, for a new friendship. Robert Benz of the Frederick Douglass Family Foundation is a longtime confidant and collaborator. And a heartfelt thanks to the Douglass descendants Nettie Washington Douglass and her son, Ken Morris, whose work on behalf of their famous ancestor's legacy is exemplary. I owe Ken a great deal for his friendship and collaborations out on the Douglass trails.

Three fellowships helped support the conception and writing of this book. I am grateful to Jean Strouse and the Cullman Center for Scholars and Writers at the New York Public Library for the Performing Arts; Roy Ritchie and the many brilliant curators at the Huntington Library, especially Jenny Watts; and to my wonderful colleagues at Cambridge University in England for hosting me as the Pitt Professor. Sarah Pearsall, Andrew Preston, Sarah Meer, and Tony Badger were perfect companions. The late Michael O'Brien, as good a historian of American ideas and the South as ever lived, was my principal host. He still inspires me by his sublime writing and for introducing me to the Tottenham Spurs.

At Yale I could not function in my multiple tasks without the team at the Gilder Lehrman Center for the Study of Slavery, Resistance, and Abolition, of which I am director. Dana Schaffer and David Spatz have served as associate directors, and they know how much they mean to me. Michelle Zacks currently holds that position and has aided and advised me on numerous aspects of finishing this book. She was by my side for support on the day I hit the send button. Tom Thurston has been a partner in taking the history of slavery to the world for thirteen wonderful years. Daniel Vieira took a photograph in this book and gives us youthful media savvy. And I cannot thank Melissa McGrath enough for all her work at the GLC, for her joyous deep intelligence, and for making me family. The GLC team has lived the life of this book. On York Street in New Haven, Connecticut, I robustly thank two generations of baristas at Blue State Coffee, especially Cody Whetstone.

At Simon & Schuster I have been a very lucky author to work with the consummate professional editor, Bob Bender. His two astute line-edits of the manuscript astonished me for their friendly toughness. And I also give warm thanks to Johanna Li, Elizabeth Gay, and Jonathan Karp for their persistent help and confidence.

My agent, Wendy Strothman, is a magnificent professional, a great friend, and my enduring source of advice and confidence.

At the copyediting stage of this book I lost the best friend I ever had, and my tribute to Jeff Ferguson appears on the dedication page. I will forever try to read, think, and embrace friendship like Jeff.

David W. Blight
New Haven, Connecticut
June 2018

NOTES

Introduction

1 http://time.com/4506800/barack-obama-african-american-history-museum-transcript/.

2 John Stauffer, Zoe Trodd, and Celeste-Marie Bernier, *Picturing Frederick Douglass: An Illustrated Biography of the Nineteenth Century's Most Photographed American* (New York: Liverlight, 2015).

3 James Baldwin, "Smaller than Life," review of *There Once Was a Slave: The Heroic Story of Frederick Douglass*, by Shirley Graham, *Nation*, July 19, 1947, in *James Baldwin, Collected Essays* (New York: Library of America, 1998), 578; Michael Lind, *The Next American Nation: The New Nationalism and the Fourth American Revolution* (New York: Free Press, 1995), 379. The statue was unveiled June 19, 2013, https://www.washingtonpost.com/local /dc-politics/frederick-douglass-statue-unveiled-in-the-capitol/2013/06/19/a64916cc-d906 -11e2-a9f2-42ee3912ae0e_story.html?utm_term=.3cbf70ac4859.

4 Abraham J. Heschel, *The Prophets* (1955; repr., New York: Jewish Publication Society of America, 1962), 10.

5 Frederick Douglass, *My Bondage and My Freedom* (1855; repr., New Haven, CT: Yale University Press, 2014), 325.

Chapter 1: First Things

1 *Inaugural Ceremonies of the Freedmen's Memorial Monument to Abraham Lincoln. Washington City, April 14, 1876* (St. Louis: Levison & Blythe, 1876), 3 (copy in Huntington Library, San Marino, CA).

2 Ibid., 3–4.

3 Ibid., 4–5; and see Kirk Savage, *Standing Soldiers, Kneeling Slaves: Race, War, and Monument in Nineteenth-Century America* (Princeton, NJ: Princeton University Press, 1997), 114.

4 *Inaugural Ceremonies*, 5.

5 Ibid., 5–7.

6 Ibid., 8–9.

7 Ibid., 10–15.

8 Douglass, in *Anglo-African*, September 3 and November 4, 1886; and Savage, *Standing Soldiers, Kneeling Slaves*, 90–94, 103–4.

9 "Oration in Memory of Abraham Lincoln, Delivered at the Unveiling of the Freedmen's Monument . . . in Lincoln Park, Washington, DC, April 14, 1876," in *Life and Writings of Frederick Douglass*, 5 vols., ed. Philip S. Foner (New York: International Publishers, 1952), 4:311.

10 Ibid., 4:309–10.

11 Ibid., 4:310–11.

12 Ibid., 4:312.

13 Ibid.

14 Ibid., 4:312–13.

15 Ibid., 4:314–15.

16 Ibid., 4:316.

17 See George C. Rable, *But There Was No Peace: The Role of Violence in the Politics of Reconstruction* (Athens: University of Georgia Press, 1984), 144–85.

18 "Oration in Memory of Abraham Lincoln," 4:317–19.

19 *Narrative of the Life of Frederick Douglass, an American Slave* (1845; repr., Boston: Bedford Books, 1993), 44; *Bondage*, 30–33; Talbot Land Commission Records, 1818–30, Courthouse, Easton, MD, 307–21, in Dickson J. Preston, *Young Frederick Douglass: The Maryland Years* (Baltimore: Johns Hopkins University Press, 1980), 27, 31–34. On Dorsch's birth, see "List of Slaves of Aaron Anthony, 1830," Maryland Historical Society, Baltimore, MD. The line reads "Frederick Augustus, son of Harriet, Feby 1818."

20 *Bondage*, 29–30, 37–39. For my knowledge of the landscapes, the back roads and waterways, of Tuckahoe and all of Talbot County, I wish to thank two local resident experts, Priscilla Morris of Easton, Maryland, and Dale Green, a professor of religion and history at Morgan State University in Baltimore. They also provided me with extraordinary maps, both nineteenth century and current. On June 18–20, 2011, Priscilla took me all over Talbot and Caroline Counties, as well as out on the Wye and Tuckahoe Rivers. My notes are crucial to writing Douglass's early life.

21 *Bondage*, 39–40; Preston, *Young Frederick Douglass*, 6.

22 *Bondage*, 42. In the year or two before finishing *My Bondage and My Freedom* (1855), Douglass had been reading a great deal of "natural history" and ethnography for his major address "The Claims of the Negro Ethnologically Considered," delivered at Western Reserve College, July 12, 1854. Prichard's work was not published until 1855, but Douglass must have been reading it as he wrote *Bondage*. He found the picture of Ramses in the chapter "Of the Egyptian Race," and in the text the features of the figure are described as "calm and dignified; the forehead is somewhat flat; the eyes are widely separated from each other; the nose is elevated, but with spreading nostrils; the ears are high; the lips large, broad, and turned out, with sharp edges; in which points there is a deviation from the European countenance." Douglass denounced the racism at the core of most natural-history writing in those years, yet in the autobiography he attributed his skill with words "*not* to my admitted Anglo-Saxon paternity," but to his black (and vaguely Egyptian) mother. See James Cowles Prichard, *The Natural History of Man: Inquiries into the Modifying Influence of Physical and Moral Agencies on the Different Tribes of the Human Family* (London: H. Baillieer, 1855), 143. At the top of the following page are three images, "painted in fresco," that appear to be particularly attractive Egyptian women; it is possible this affected Douglass's use of the images together to remember his mother.

23 Preston, *Young Frederick Douglass*, 62–64; *Bondage*, 44–45.

24 *Bondage*, 45–46.

25 *Narrative*, 42; *Bondage*, 42, 46; Frederick Douglass, *Life and Times of Frederick Douglass* (1881; repr., New York: Collier, 1962), 29. See Preston, *Young Frederick Douglass*, 23. Douglass does not tell us the "reason" he doubted Anthony as his father.

26 *Bondage*, 41, 61–63.

27 Preston, *Young Frederick Douglass*, 22–30. On Anthony's land holdings, I am grateful for Priscilla Morris's research in Talbot County property records. Email, Morris to author,

June 28, 2011, includes among other valuable information an 1866 land deed from John P. Anthony, Aaron's grandson.

28 *Narrative*, 44–46; *Bondage*, 65–67.

29 *Bondage*, 66–67.

30 Ibid., 47.

31 Ibid., 46–47.

32 Ibid., 46.

33 Ibid., 47.

34 Ibid., 31–35.

35 Ibid., 34.

36 Ibid., 35.

Chapter 2: A Childhood of Extremes

1 *Bondage*, 40; Preston, *Young Frederick Douglass*, 38–39.

2 *Bondage*, 38.

3 Ibid., 39–40.

4 Ibid., 50–52. Today the Wye House is still a private home, lived in by the Richard and Beverly Tilghman family, the direct descendants of the original Lloyds. I was the grateful beneficiary of a wonderful three-hour tour of the house and grounds by the Tilghmans on June 19, 2011. And in May 2017 I stayed overnight in the remodeled old "kitchen house" on the grounds. Tilghman is a lawyer and has taken a deep interest in Frederick Douglass's connections to his family's property, financing a major archaeological dig on-site to uncover the nature of slave life at Wye.

5 Ira Berlin, *Generations of Captivity: A History of African American Slaves* (Cambridge, MA: Harvard University Press, 2003), 8–10; Douglass, "An Appeal to the British People," reception speech at Finsbury Chapel, Moorsfield, England, May 2, 1846, in Foner, *Life and Writings*, 1:155.

6 *Bondage*, 53, 56.

7 Ibid., 59; Preston, *Young Frederick Douglass*, 54–56; tour with Richard Tilghman, June 19, 2011.

8 Samuel Alexander Harrison, *History of Talbot County, Maryland, 1661–1861* (Baltimore: Williams & Wilkins, 1915), 184–210; Dickson J. Preston, *Talbot County: A History* (Centreville, MD: Tidewater Publishers, 1983), 86, 89–91; *Narrative*, 53.

9 *Bondage*, 60, 82–83.

10 Ibid., 78–79, 83–85, 99, 101.

11 Saint Augustine, *Confessions*, trans. Edward Bouverie Pusey (New York: Book-of-the-Month Club, 1996), 240; Jerome Bruner, "Self-Making Narratives," in *Autobiographical Memory and the Construction of a Narrative Self: Developmental and Cultural Perspectives*, ed. Robyn Fivush and Catherine A. Haden (Mahwah, NJ: Lawrence Erlbaum Associates, 2003), 211.

12 *Bondage*, 80.

13 Ibid., 55–56.

14 Ibid., 70–73. On Sevier's identity, see Preston, *Young Frederick Douglass*, 70–71. In the *Narrative*, Douglass actually spelled the name *Severe*.

15 *Bondage*, 72.

16 Ibid., 90–93; Preston, *Young Frederick Douglass*, 72–74. Preston demonstrates with some keen research that Denby did die in 1824, before Frederick Bailey had moved to the Wye plantation.

17 *Bondage*, 92.

18 Ibid., 84–85.

19 Ibid., 75–76. On the opposites in Douglass's writing, see Henry Louis Gates Jr., "Binary Oppositions in Chapter One of *Narrative of the Life of Frederick Douglass, an American Slave, Written by Himself*," in *Figures in Black: Words, Signs, and the 'Racial' Self"* (New York: Oxford University Press, 1987), 80–97.

20 *Bondage*, 101, 68–69.

21 Ibid., 69.

22 Ibid., 100.

23 *Narrative*, 59.

24 *Bondage*, 99–100.

25 Ibid., 98.

26 *Narrative*, 49–50; *Bondage*, 74–75.

27 *Narrative*, 51; *Bondage*, 75.

28 *Bondage*, 76.

29 Jeremiah 8:22. On the quest for a degree of "certainty" in slave songs, see Lawrence W. Levine, *Black Culture and Black Consciousness: Afro-American Folk Thought from Slavery to Freedom* (New York: Oxford University Press, 1977), 30–55.

30 *Bondage*, 74–75. For the impact of slave songs, especially the spirituals, on children, see Wilma King, *Stolen Childhood: Slave Youth in Nineteenth Century America* (Bloomington: Indiana University Press, 1995), 83–88.

31 *Bondage*, 203–4; *Life and Times*, 159–60.

Chapter 3: The Silver Trump of Knowledge

1 *Bondage*, 100–101; Preston, *Young Frederick Douglass*, 81–82.

2 *Narrative*, 60–61; *Bondage*, 101–102. And see Preston, *Young Frederick Douglass*, 82.

3 *Narrative*, 61; *Bondage*, 103. Numerous paintings and lithographs depict Baltimore harbor bustling with dozens of ships from the 1820s to the 1850s. The clipper ships were schooner-rigged vessels with two masts and a hull designed for speed. They became the fastest sailing craft afloat and were built in the neighborhood where Douglass lived. See Francis F. Beirne, *Baltimore: A Picture History, 1858–1958* (New York: Hastings House, 1957), 16, 26–27; and Howard Irving Chapelle, *The Baltimore Clipper: Its Origins and Development* (Salem, MA: Maine Research Society, 1930). On the B&O, see Barbara Jeanne Fields, *Slavery and Freedom on the Middle Ground: Maryland during the Nineteenth Century* (New Haven, CT: Yale University Press, 1985), 44. For detailed maps of Fell's Point, Baltimore, see Thomas G. Bradford and S. G. Goodrich, eds., *A General Atlas of the World* (Boston: C. Strong, 1841), cartweb.geography.ua.edu. On Despeaux and the Haitian slaves, see Madison Smartt Bell, *Charm City: A Walk through Baltimore* (New York: Crown Publishers, 2007), 95–96.

4 *Narrative*, 61; Christopher Phillips, *Freedom's Port: The African American Community of Baltimore, 1790–1860* (Urbana: University of Illinois Press, 1997), 14–15; Beirne, *Baltimore*, 13, 21; George W. Howard, *The Monumental City: Its Past History and Present Resources* (Baltimore: J. D. Ehlers, 1873), 68–70.

5 *Bondage*, 105; Fields, *Slavery and Freedom*, 40–49, 62; Phillips, *Freedom's Port*, 57–82.

6 *Bondage*, 103.

7 *Narrative*, 63; *Bondage*, 106–8.

8 *Narrative*, 63; Douglass, "The Bible Opposes Oppression, Fraud, and Wrong: An Address Delivered in Belfast, Ireland," January 6, 1846, in John W. Blassingame et al., eds., *Frederick Douglass Papers*, ser. 1, vol. 1 (New Haven, CT: Yale University Press, 1979), 127–28.

9 Job 3:11, 23; 6:25–26; 7:11.

10 *Bondage*, 108–9.

11 Ibid., 109.

12 G. W. F. Hegel, *The Phenomenology of Mind*, 2nd ed., trans. J. B. Baillie (New York: Harper & Row, 1964), 239–40. On Hegel and slavery, see David Brion Davis, *The Problem of Slavery in the Age of Revolution, 1770–1828* (Ithaca, NY: Cornell University Press, 1975), 558–64.

13 *Narrative*, 65–66; *Bondage*, 112–14.

14 *Bondage*, 114.

15 Ibid., 115.

16 Ibid., 115–16; *Life and Times*, 83.

17 *Bondage*, 116–17; Caleb Bingham, *The Columbian Orator: Containing a Variety of Original and Selected Pieces Together with Rules Calculated to Improve Youth and Others in the Ornamental and Useful Art of Eloquence* (1797; repr., Boston: Manning and Loring, 1897). Subsequent references are to this third Boston edition. But also see David W. Blight, ed., *The Columbian Orator*, 200th anniversary ed. (New York: New York University Press, 1998), especially the introduction, "The Peculiar Dialogue between Caleb Bingham and Frederick Douglass," xiii–xxix.

18 Born in 1757 in Salisbury, Connecticut, Caleb Bingham went to Dartmouth College during the American Revolution. Moving to Boston, he became an important school reformer and the author and compiler of several bestselling school textbooks until his death in 1817. Books such as *A Child's Companion* (a spelling book) and *The American Preceptor* (designed to teach moral values to children) eventually graced shelves next to the Bible and an almanac in hundreds of thousands of American homes. See William B. Fowle, "Memoir of Caleb Bingham," *American Journal of Education* 5 (1858): 325–26; Paul Eugen Camp, "Caleb Bingham," *Dictionary of Literary Biography* 42 (1985): 88; and Lillian O. Rosenfield, "Caleb Bingham, 1757–1817" (unpublished paper written at the Library Science School, Simmons College, January 1954), 18, copy in American Antiquarian Society, Worcester, MA. On Lincoln, see Fred Kaplan, *Lincoln: Biography of a Writer* (New York: HarperCollins, 2008), 50–59; and Kenneth Cmiel, *Democratic Eloquence: The Fight over Popular Speech in Nineteenth Century America* (New York: William Morrow, 1990), 59. Testimony to the antislavery character of the *Columbian Orator* appeared at the height of the sectional crisis, in *De Bow's Review* 10 (January 1856): 69. *De Bow's* included the book on a list of abolitionist books found in Southern schools.

19 Bingham, *Columbian Orator* (1998), xx–xxi.

20 Bingham, *Columbian Orator* (1797), 50–54, 72–73, 189–94, 242.

21 *Bondage*, 116–17.

22 Bingham, *Columbian Orator* (1797), 104; and see William S. McFeely, *Frederick Douglass* (New York: Norton, 1991), 35–36.

23 Bingham, *Columbian Orator* (1797), 7–8, 12–19.

24 *Bondage*, 118–19; *Narrative*, 68–69.

Chapter 4: Baltimore Dreams

1 *Bondage*, 109–10, 112, 115, 134.

2 Ibid., 128; *Narrative*, 71–72.

3 *Bondage*, 129; Preston, *Young Frederick Douglass*, 88–91.

4 *Bondage*, 128–29. For the concept of "social death," see Orlando Patterson, *Slavery and Social Death: A Comparative Study* (Cambridge, MA: Harvard University Press, 1982).

5 *Bondage*, 130; Preston, *Young Frederick Douglass*, 91. On Andrew Anthony's intemperance,

Preston reports (n. 10, p. 224) that Harriet Lucretia Anthony (Andrew's granddaughter) wrote in the margins of her copy of Douglass's *Bondage*, "As my grandfather, Andrew Skinner Anthony, died a young man I know nothing of his cruelty, but I fear Fred is right about his intemperate habits."

6 *Bondage*, 119–20.

7 Ibid., 120–21.

8 Ibid., 122. On the rapid and widespread news of the Nat Turner rebellion, and its impact on surrounding states, see Scot French, *The Rebellious Slave: Nat Turner in American Memory* (Boston: Houghton Mifflin, 2004), 33–86; Henry Irving Tragle, *The Southampton Slave Revolt: A Compilation of Source Material* (Amherst: University of Massachusetts Press, 1971), 27–170, 370–88. In her slave narrative, Harriet Jacobs prominently discussed the impact of the Turner rebellion in her native section of North Carolina. See Harriet Jacobs, *Incidents in the Life of a Slave Girl, Written by Herself* (Cambridge, MA: Harvard University Press, 1987), 63–68.

9 Bingham, *Columbian Orator*, 27.

10 *Bondage*, 122–23; Galatians 3:26–28; 2 Corinthians 8:14.

11 *Bondage*, 122–23.

12 Ibid., 123; Preston, *Young Frederick Douglass*, 97–98; Romans 2:15. For the biblical and philosophical origins and full meanings of the natural-rights tradition, especially as a "moral heritage," see Paul K. Conkin, *Self-Evident Truths: Being a Discourse on the Origins & Development of the First Principles of American Government* (Bloomington: Indiana University Press, 1974), 75–101.

13 *Bondage*, 124, 134–35; Daniel 10:2, 11–12.

14 *Bondage*, 125–26.

15 Ibid., 133–37.

16 Ibid., 134.

17 Ibid., 138–40; Preston, *Young Frederick Douglass*, 107–8.

18 *Narrative*, 76–77; *Bondage and Freedom*, 140–41.

19 *Bondage*, 142–44; "General Camp Meeting for Talbot County," *Easton Gazette*, July 20, 1833. This article announces the camp meeting, beginning August 19 at "Haddaway's Woods on the Bay Side," and stresses good access to water and ferries. Douglass's depictions of the Eastern Shore camp meeting conform to many in histories of the Methodist camp-meeting revival movements of the nineteenth century. See for example, Dickson D. Bruce Jr., *And They All Sang Hallelujah: Plain-Folk Camp Meeting Religion, 1800–1845* (Knoxville: University of Tennessee Press, 1974), 61–95; and John H. Wigger, *Taking Heaven by Storm: Methodism and the Rise of Popular Christianity in America* (New York: Oxford University Press, 1998), 80–103.

20 *Bondage*, 143–44.

21 Ibid., 146–47.

22 Ibid., 147–49.

23 Ibid., 150; *Narrative*, 83.

24 *Bondage*, 152, 158, 169; Preston, *Young Frederick Douglass*, 117–19.

25 *Bondage*, 152–54.

26 Ibid., 157–60. There are many literary analyses of Douglass's portrayal of Covey's violence, and then of his own in self-defense. See in particular Eric J. Sundquist, "Frederick Douglass: Literacy and Paternalism," and Thad Ziolkowski, "Antitheses: The Dialectic of Violence and Literacy in Frederick Douglass's *Narrative* of 1845," both in *Critical Essays on Frederick Douglass*, ed. William L. Andrews (Boston: G. K. Hall, 1991), 120–32, 148–65.

27 *Narrative*, 83.

28 Ibid., 83–84.

29 Ibid., 84.

30 *Bondage*, 164–66.

31 Ibid., 167–72.

32 Ibid., 173–74.

33 Ibid., 175.

34 Ibid., 176–80.

35 John Stauffer, "Frederick Douglass and the Aesthetics of Freedom," *Raritan*, 2005, 114–15; Preston, *Young Frederick Douglass*, 127; *Bondage*, 180–82.

Chapter 5: Now for Mischief!

1 *Bondage*, 184–87.

2 "Temperance Viewed in Connection with Slavery: An Address Delivered in Glasgow, Scotland," February 18, 1846, in *Douglass Papers*, ser. 1, 1:166; *Bondage*, 192–93, 205; Preston, *Young Frederick Douglass*, 129–30; 1 Corinthians 15:46.

3 *Bondage*, 193, 197.

4 Ibid., 192–93, 195, 201.

5 Ibid., 195–97, 205; *Narrative*, 94.

6 *Bondage*, 199–200.

7 Ibid., 201–3, 208–9.

8 Ibid., 207, 211. On the plight of the runaway contemplating escape in the slave narratives more broadly, see William L. Andrews, *To Tell a Free Story: The First Century of Afro-American Autobiography, 1760–1865* (Urbana: University of Illinois Press, 1986), 1–32, 199–204. The escape became, as Andrews shows, a "rite of passage" of various kinds for slave-narrative authors. Also see Fergus M. Bordewich, *The Underground Railroad and the War for the Soul of America* (New York: HarperCollins, 2005), parts 3 and 4. And for another classic example of the "preparation for escape" in the narratives, see Harriet A. Jacobs, *Incidents in the Life of a Slave Girl, Written by Herself* (1861; repr., Cambridge, MA: Harvard University Press, 1987), 148–55.

9 *Bondage*, 203–5.

10 *Narrative*, 96–97; *Bondage*, 207.

11 *Bondage*, 211–14; Preston, *Young Frederick Douglass*, 136–37.

12 *Bondage*, 215–17. For help in understanding the exact location of Freeland's farm and the Hambleton home farm, the access to the Bay of Hambleton's wharf and boats, as well as the route and distances of the forced march to Easton of Douglass and his fellow prisoners, I am indebted to a tour led by Priscilla Morris in June 2011 and to many emails, especially that of June 12, 2012.

13 Preston, *Young Frederick Douglass*, 138–39; McFeely, *Frederick Douglass*, 54–56; *Bondage*, 215–19.

14 *Bondage*, 220–21; Preston, *Young Frederick Douglass*, 139–40.

15 See McFeely, *Frederick Douglass*, 56–57; and Preston, *Young Frederick Douglass*, 140–41. McFeely may overestimate how much Douglass "had loved" Auld during these years. In the *Narrative* in 1845, Douglass did not acknowledge Auld's leniency on his possible punishments, but he did so in *Bondage*, 223–24.

16 Phillips, *Freedom's Port*, 15; *Bondage*, 224.

17 *Bondage*, 224–26; Preston, *Young Frederick Douglass*, 142–43.

18 *Bondage*, 228–29.

19 Ibid., 230–31.

20 Ibid., 226–27, 232. Also see McFeely, *Frederick Douglass*, 62–63.

21 Amitav Ghosh, *Sea of Poppies* (New York: Picador, 2008), 10–14, 49–51.

22 *Bondage*, 232–33; Preston, *Young Frederick Douglass*, 148–49; William E. Lloyd to Douglass, June 13, 1870, FD Papers (LC). Lloyd wrote to Douglass to invite him back to Baltimore to speak and help raise money for a local church. Lloyd also expressed a great eagerness to once again see Anna Douglass. On the free black community of Baltimore, see Seth Rockman, *Scraping By: Wage Labor, Slavery, and Survival in Early Baltimore* (Baltmore: Johns Hopkins University Press, 2009), 33–36, 41–42, 49–50, 166–69, 184–88, 238–40.

23 Caroline County Court records, certificates of freedom, 1827–51, Anna Murray (CM866), Maryland State Archives (MSA SC 5496-051245), http://www.msa.md.gov; Rosetta Douglass Sprague, "Anna Murray Douglass: My Mother as I Recall Her," 1900, FD Papers (LC), 6–8. On the location and circumstances of Anna's birth and the manumission of her parents, I am indebted to email correspondence, Priscilla Morris to author, June 28, 2011.

24 Rockman, *Scraping By*, 247.

25 *Bondage*, 233, 237–39.

26 Ibid., 240–41.

27 *Bondage*, 242–43; *Life and Times*, 198–99; Rockman, *Scraping By*, 258; Douglass Sprague, "My Mother as I Recall Her," 10; McFeely, *Frederick Douglass*, 69–73. For an 1841 map of Baltimore, see http://cartweb.geography.ua.edu (file name Maryland1841b.sid).

28 *Life and Times*, 198–99. To protect any living people who may have helped him, Douglass did not tell all of the details of his escape until writing this, the third of his autobiographies.

29 Ibid., 199–201.

30 Ibid., 201; *Bondage*, 247.

31 *Bondage*, 248.

32 Ibid., 248–51; *Narrative*, 112. For two speeches in the 1840s where Douglass told of the plight of the fugitive slaves, often reciting long lists of actual runaway advertisements from newspapers, see "Slavery Corrupts American Society and Religion: An Address Delivered in Cork, Ireland, October 17, 1845"; and "The Horrors of Slavery and England's Duty to Free the Bondsman: An Address Delivered in Taunton, England, September 1, 1846," in *Douglass Papers*, ser. 1, 1:51–52, 377–78.

33 Graham Hodges, *David Ruggles: A Radical Black Abolitionist and the Underground Railroad in New York City* (Chapel Hill: University of North Carolina Press, 2010), 1–2, 103–41. For Frederick's presence at Ruggles's court testimony, *New York Times*, March 11, 1870. On Ruggles and Douglass's escape, see Eric Foner, *Gateway to Freedom: The Hidden History of the Underground Railroad* (New York: Norton, 2015), 1–7, 63–68, 71–77.

34 *Bondage*, 251; Douglass Sprague, "My Mother as I Recall Her," 9.

35 *Narrative*, 114; Richard Blackett, "James W. C. Pennington: A Life of Christian Zeal," in *Beating Against the Barriers: Biographical Essays in Nineteenth Century Afro-American History* (Baton Rouge: Louisiana State University Press, 1986), 1–15.

36 *Life and Times*, 205–6; *Bondage*, 251.

Chapter 6: Living a New Life

1 *Narrative*, 107, 114. In his poignant claim about the Underground Railroad, Douglass wrote, "I have never approved of the very public manner in which some of our western friends have conducted what they call the *underground railroad*, but which, I think, by their open declarations, has been made most emphatically the *upper-ground railroad*." On the fugitive slave experience, see R. J. M. Blackett, *Fugitive Slaves, The 1850 Fugitive Slave Law, and the Politics of Slavery* (Cambridge, UK: Cambridge University Press, 2018).

2 Ibid., 115; *Bondage*, 252; Henry H. Crapo, comp., *New Bedford Directory, Containing the Names of the Inhabitants, Their Occupations, Places of Business and Dwelling Houses* (New Bedford, MA: Benjamin Lindsey, 1839), 91–92, New Bedford Free Public Library. On Douglass's years and associations in New Bedford, see Griffin Black, "Lion at the Lectern: Frederick Douglass Becomes an Orator 1838–1845," senior thesis, Yale University, 2018.

3 *Bondage*, 252–53; Robert Stepto, "Introduction: Frederick Douglass Writes His Story," *Narrative of the Life of Frederick Douglass, an American Slave, Written by Himself* (Cambridge, MA: Harvard University Press, 2009), xiv–xv; *Lady of the Lake*, in *The Poetical Works of Sir Walter Scott* (Paris: A. & W. Galignani, 1851), 169–70. On *Lady of the Lake* as a bestseller in 1810 and for years afterward, and on Scott's popularity and the forging of not only a Scottish nationalism but also a wave of Scott tourism to the Highlands, see Stuart Kelly, *Scotland: The Man Who Invented a Nation* (Edinburgh: Polygon, 2010), 79–81, 95–98.

4 Everett S. Allen, *Children of the Light: The Rise and Fall of New Bedford Whaling and the Death of the Arctic Fleet* (Boston: Little, Brown, 1973), 82–83; Daniel Ricketson, *The History of New Bedford, Bristol County, Massachusetts* (New Bedford, MA: by the author, 1858), 372–73; Andrew Delbanco, *Melville: His World and Work* (New York: Knopf, 2005), 40. On the free-black and fugitive-slave community of New Bedford, see Kathryn Grover, *The Fugitive's Gibraltar: Escaping Slaves and Abolitionism in New Bedford, Massachusetts* (Amherst: University of Massachusetts Press, 2001), 1–66. The identities and numbers of fugitive slaves are difficult to determine. Town directories and censuses recorded blacks, but rarely determined whether they were fugitives. Grover cites white abolitionists who put the total of fugitives in New Bedford at 300–700 between 1845 and 1863. Grover found the names or locations of some 170 in her study. Because fugitives tended to dominate the black population, it was predominantly male. The 12,354 residents in New Bedford in 1839 included 709 black males and 342 black females. See Crapo, *New Bedford Directory* (1841), 28.

5 Herman Melville, *Moby-Dick* (1851; repr., London: New World Classics, 2011), 49–50.

6 Delbanco, *Melville*, 38.

7 Robert K. Wallace, *Douglass and Melville: Anchored Together in Neighborly Style* (New Bedford, MA: Spinner Publications, 2005), 3–21; Robert S. Levine and Samuel Otter, eds., *Frederick Douglass and Herman Melville: Essays in Relation* (Chapel Hill: University of North Carolina Press, 2008), 3; McFeely, *Frederick Douglass*, 80–81; *Bondage*, 253–54; Grover, *Fugitive's Gibraltar*, 118–43.

8 *Bondage*, 254–55; Melville, *Moby-Dick*, 29–42.

9 *Life and Times*, 210, 212–13; *Bondage*, 257; Grover, *Fugitive's Gibraltar*, 146; William M. Emory, "A New England Romance That Touched New Bedford: The Story of Ephraim and Mary Jane Peabody, Told by Their Sons—Courtship of an Early Minister of the Unitarian Church," *New Bedford Morning Mercury*, February 22, 1924, Box 21, Sub-Group 1, series H, folder 1, The First Unitarian Church Records, New Bedford Whaling Museum Archives. I am grateful to Griffin Black for this discovery.

10 *Bondage*, 256–57; Crapo, *New Bedford Directory* (1839), 69; Crapo, *New Bedford Directory* (1841), 65; Wallace, *Douglass and Melville*, 15.

11 *Bondage*, 58–60.

12 Frederick Douglass to James W. Wood, December 17, 1894, reprinted in Lenwood G. Davis, "Frederick Douglass as a Preacher, and One of His Last Most Significant Letters," *Journal of Negro History* 66, no. 2 (Summer 1981): 141; *Life of Rev. Thomas James, by Himself* (Rochester, NY: Post Express Printing, 1886), 8–9; *Bondage*, 260; William L. Andrews, "Frederick Douglass, Preacher," *American Literature* 54 (December 1982): 592–96; Crapo, *New Bedford Directory* (1841), 65. Testimony to Douglass's formal associations with the AMEZ Church is also found in David Henry Bradley Jr., *A History of the AME Zion Church, 1796–*

1872, 2 vols. (Nashville, TN: Parthenon Press, 1956), 1:111–12. On Douglass as Sunday school superintendent, see Gregory P. Lampe, *Frederick Douglass: Freedom's Voice, 1818–1845* (East Lansing: Michigan State University Press, 1998), 38–39.

13 Ellis Gray Loring to Hiram Wilson, August 20, 1840, marked "confidential," Loring Papers, Letter Press Book, 1837–41, Schlesinger Library, Harvard University. I am grateful to historian Kate Masur for informing me of this letter. And see Black, "Lion at the Lectern," especially on the influence of the *Liberator* on the young fugitive, 17–30.

14 Henry H. Crapo, comp., *Taxes for 1840*, Town of New Bedford, "Frederic Douglas" is listed "paid," "Feby. 17, 1841"; *Taxes for 1841*, Town of New Bedford, "Frederick Douglass," "paid," "March 18, 1842," New Bedford Free Public Library, manuscripts and archives. Also see Grover, *Fugitive's Gibraltar*, 148–49. *List of Voters in the Town of New Bedford* (New Bedford, MA: Benjamin Lindsey, 1839), New Bedford Free Public Library.

15 *Bondage*, 60–61. On Douglass, moral suasion, and oratory, see Lampe, *Frederick Douglass*, 44–45.

16 *Liberator*, January 18, February 15, March 8 and 15, 1839.

17 Ibid., March 1 and 8, April 4, May 3, 1839. See Black, "Lion at the Lectern."

18 Ibid., March 15, April 12, 1839. I am grateful to Griffin Black for pointing me to these citations.

19 *Bondage*, 261; *Life and Times*, 213–14; Henry Mayer, *All on Fire: William Lloyd Garrison and the Abolition of Slavery* (New York: St. Martin's Press, 1998), 248.

20 *Bondage*, 262.

21 See Lampe, *Frederick Douglass*, 40–42; Arthaniel Edgar Harris Sr., "Worship in the A.M.E. Zion Church," *AME Zion Quarterly Review* 97 (July 1986): 34–35; William J. Walls, *The African American Episcopal Zion Church: Reality of the Black Church* (Charlotte, NC: A.M.E. Zion Publishing House, 1974), 148–50.

22 *Liberator*, March 29, 1839. In Lampe, *Frederick Douglass*, 46, 55 (nn. 48, 49, 50, 51), the author mistakenly cites several times the *Liberator* for March 12, 1839. There is no such issue. March 12 is the date of the abolition meeting. In a subsequent note (n. 52) he cites March 29, which is the correct date. For Douglass's fond remembrance of the Garnet speech, see "Colored People Must Command Respect: An Address Delivered in Rochester, New York, March 13, 1848," *Douglass Papers*, ser. 1, 2:113–15.

23 *Bondage*, 263; Grover, *Fugitive's Gibraltar*, 148, 169; *New Bedford Register*, July 7, 1841. At one anticolonization meeting, Douglass led in condemning specifically the right of Maryland slaveholders to send blacks to Africa, indicating likely the significant numbers of fugitive slaves from that state in New Bedford.

24 *Liberator*, August 20, 1841; *New Bedford Register*, August 10, 1841; Parker Pillsbury, *Acts of the Antislavery Apostles* (Concord, NH: Clague, Wegman, Schlight, 1883), 324–25. Also see Lampe, *Frederick Douglass*, 58–59.

25 Pillsbury, *Acts of the Antislavery Apostles*, 325; Foner, *Life and Writings*, 1:26; *National Anti-Slavery Standard*, August 26, 1841.

26 Minutes of the Nantucket convention, *Liberator*, August 20, 1841.

27 Samuel J. May, *Some Recollections of the Antislavery Conflict* (1869; repr., New York: Arno Press, 1968), 293–94; Pillsbury, *Acts of the Antislavery Apostles*, 326; *National Anti-Slavery Standard*, August 26, 1841. Just before adjournment on the night of August 12, Douglass was called upon again to speak; he did so briefly, with yet again a response from Garrison. See Lampe, *Frederick Douglass*, 62.

28 William Lloyd Garrison, "Preface," May 1, 1845, *Narrative*, 31–32. The most extensive account of Douglass's role at the Nantucket convention is in Lampe, *Frederick Douglass*, 59–

62. For a well-written account, but with some inaccuracies of the Nantucket convention, see McFeely, *Frederick Douglass*, 86–90. The author has the convention taking place, under threat of a mob attack, on August 16 at a large square building on the edge of town called the Big Shop. McFeely seems to have relied in part on personal correspondence with and a book by Robert F. Mooney and Andre R. Sigourney, *The Nantucket Way: Untold Legend and Lore of America's Most Intriguing Island* (Garden City, NY: Doubleday, 1980), and on twentieth-century articles and reminiscences in the Nantucket local newspaper, *Inquirer and Mirror.*

29 *Bondage*, 263–64; *Narrative*, 119; Garrison, "Preface," *Narrative*, 32.

30 *Bondage*, 264–65.

31 Melville, *Moby-Dick*, 58.

Chapter 7: This Douglass!

1 Douglass, "My Slave Experience in Maryland," an address delivered in New York, May 6, 1845, in *Douglass Papers*, ser. 1, 1:9. The epigraph comes from a typescript, two-page fragment of a speech by Douglass, "Mass Meeting, Faneuil Hall, Feb. 4, 1842," Walter O. Evans Collection, Savannah, GA, "Assorted Material" box.

2 "From the *Herald of Freedom*, Frederick Douglass in Concord, N.H.," in *Liberator*, February 23, 1844.

3 Ibid.

4 On Douglass's physical appearance, see John Stauffer, *Giants: The Parallel Lives of Frederick Douglass and Abraham Lincoln* (New York: Twelve, 2008), 5–6; and Stauffer, "Frederick Douglass and the Aesthetics of Freedom," 114–36. On Douglass as symbol, there are many commentators, but a good place to start is John Blassingame's introduction, *Douglass Papers*, 1:xxix, lv.

5 *Life and Times*, 17. For the idea of an era of "Bible politics," and for two quotations, see James B. Stewart, "God, Garrison, and the Coming of the Civil War," in *William Lloyd Garrison at Two Hundred*, ed. James B. Stewart (New Haven, CT: Yale University Press, 2008), 46–47, 94–95; Higginson, quoted in Mayer, *All on Fire*, 326. For an overstatement of the argument that the abolitionists in the United States were essentially "united," see Manisha Sinha, *The Slave's Cause: A History of Abolition* (New Haven, CT: Yale University Press, 2016), 5, 256–65, and throughout.

6 For a succinct outline of the major tenets of Garrisonianism, see David W. Blight, "William Lloyd Garrison at Two Hundred: His Radicalism and His Legacy for Our Time," in Stewart, *Garrison at Two Hundred*, 6–7. And see James B. Stewart, *William Lloyd Garrison and the Challenge of Emancipation* (Arlington Heights, IL: Harlan Davidson, 1992), chs. 3–6; and Aileen S. Kraditor, *Means and Ends in American Abolitionism: Garrison and His Critics on Strategy and Tactics, 1834–1850* (New York: Random House, 1967), chs. 3–5.

7 William Lloyd Garrison to Elizabeth Pease, September 16, 1841, in *No Union with the Slaveholders, 1841–1849: The Letters of William Lloyd Garrison*, vol. 3, ed. Walter M. Merrill (Cambridge, MA: Harvard University Press, 1973), 29–30. Garrison drew here from Job 5:13.

8 Matthew 5:48. And see James B. Stewart, *Holy Warriors: The Abolitionists and American Slavery* (New York: Hill & Wang, 1996), 88–91.

9 Stewart, *Holy Warriors*, 92–94. On the origins of the Liberty Party, see Richard H. Sewell, *Ballots for Freedom: Antislavery Politics in the United States, 1837–1860* (New York: Norton, 1976), 43–79.

10 On the schism and the developing ideological "war" between "old organization" and "new organization" activists, especially its implications for black abolitionists, see Stephen Kantrowitz, *More than Freedom: Fighting for Black Citizenship in a White Republic, 1829–1889* (New York: Penguin, 2012), 99–121.

11 *Bondage*, 264–65; Oliver Johnson, quoted in Lampe, *Frederick Douglass*, 63.

12 *Liberator*, August 27, 1841.

13 *Life and Times*, 223–24.

14 *National Anti-Slavery Standard*, September 2, 1841; *Liberator*, September 3, 10, and 24, 1841; and see Lampe, *Frederick Douglass*, 64. Address delivered in Lynn, Massachusetts, early October, from *Pennsylvania Freeman*, October 20, 1841, in *Douglass Papers*, ser. 1, 1:3.

15 Address in Lynn, in *Douglass Papers*, ser. 1, 1:3–5.

16 John A. Collins to Garrison, October 4, 1841, in *Liberator*, October 15, 1841; *Life and Times*, 224.

17 Collins to Garrison, *Liberator*, October 4, 1841. Blacks forced into the Jim Crow car on the same Eastern Railroad were an all-too-common occurrence in 1841. The staunch Garrisonian and future historian William Cooper Nell experienced the same in August while traveling with Wendell Phillips. See *Liberator*, September 3, 1841.

18 Collins to Garrison, *Liberator*, October 4, 1841; *Life and Times*, 24–25.

19 Collins to Garrison, *Liberator*, October 4, 1841; Mayer, *All on Fire*, 306–7; McFeely, *Frederick Douglass*, 92–93. By the spring of 1842, as the railroads published their schedules, Garrison began printing a weekly column called "travelers' directory," with commentaries and rankings on the degree to which the eight companies serving Boston treated the "human rights" of their passengers. See *Liberator*, April 8, 1842.

20 Douglass Sprague, "My Mother as I Recall Her," 10–12; Charles R. Douglass, "Some Incidents of the Home Life of Frederick Douglass," 2–3, an address delivered at Lincoln Memorial Church, Rochester, February 1917, handwritten MS, Evans Collection, "Assorted Material" box. Charles pays special tribute to Anna for her adaptability as mother and wife, and her skill as a shoe binder.

21 Frederick Douglass Jr., a brief autobiographical sketch, Evans Collection, "Douglass Family Papers" file. Frederick Jr. here records that he was born in New Bedford; Charles Douglass, "Some Incidents," 3; Lampe, *Frederick Douglass*, app. 3, 295.

22 *Life and Times*, 222.

23 Alonzo Lewis, *The History of Lynn, Including Nahant* (Boston: Samuel N. Dickinson, 1844), 2nd ed., 20, 249–52, 255, 258–64; Scott Gac, *Singing for Freedom: The Hutchinson Family Singers and the Nineteenth Century Culture Reform* (New Haven, CT: Yale University Press, 2007), 131–32.

24 Edmund Quincy to Caroline Weston, October 21, 1841, Weston Family Papers, Boston Public Library (BPL); Proceedings of the Plymouth Co. Antislavery Society at Hingham, reported by the editor of the *Hingham Patriot*, in *Liberator*, December 3, 1841.

25 David N. Johnson, *Sketches of Lynn: Changes of Fifty Years* (Lynn, MA: Thomas P. Nichols, 1880), 230–31. Raleigh Register (NC), repr. in *Charleston Courier* (SC), August 9, 1845; *New Orleans Picayune* (LA), September 26, 1843; and see Black, "Lion at the Lectern," 42–43.

26 Letter by Stanton, in *In Memoriam: Frederick Douglass*, ed. Helen Pitts Douglass (Philadelphia: John C. Yorston, 1897), reprint, 44. On the setting in Faneuil Hall, January 28, 1842, see Lampe, *Frederick Douglass*, 107–9. To date, this gathering of four thousand was the largest audience Douglass had ever addressed. See *Liberator*, February 4, 1842; and *Douglass Papers*, serv. 1, 1:15.

27 A. W. Weston to D. Weston, April 1, 1842, Weston Family Papers, BPL.

28 "American Prejudice and Southern Religion: An Address Delivered in Hingham, Massachusetts, Nov. 4, 1841," in *Douglass Papers*, ser. 1, 1:10–11.

29 "The Southern Style of Preaching to Slaves: An Address Delivered in Boston, Massachusetts, Jan. 28, 1842," in *Douglass Papers*, ser. 1, 44.

30 "I Am Here to Spread Light on American Slavery: An Address Delivered in Cork, Ireland, Oct. 14, 1845," *Douglass Papers*, ser. 1, 44; in 1:16–17, 44; Garrison to George W. Benson, January 29, 1842, Merrill, *Letters of Garrison*, 48. On Douglass's use of contrasts and antithesis, see Lampe, *Frederick Douglass*, 80.

Chapter 8: Garrisonian in Mind and Body

1 *Liberator*, April 1, 8, and 22, and May 13, 1842; *National Anti-Slavery Standard*, May 19, 1842. For the speaking itinerary, see Lampe, *Frederick Douglass*, 295–97. Smith eventually wrote columns in Douglass's newspapers as well as the introduction for *My Bondage and My Freedom*.

2 *Douglass Papers*, ser. 3, 1:9n7; John Stauffer, ed., *The Works of James McCune Smith: Black Intellectual and Abolitionist* (New York: Oxford University Press, 2006), xiii–xl; and David W. Blight, "In Search of Learning, Liberty, and Self-Definition: James McCune Smith and the Ordeal of the Antebellum Black Intellectual," *Afro-Americans in New York Life and History* 9, no. 2 (July 1995): 7–26.

3 *Liberator*, July 1, 1842.

4 Ibid., July 8, 1842.

5 Ibid., July 15, 1842.

6 Ibid., Douglass, "I Am Here to Spread Light"; "Slavery Corrupts American Society and Religion," address delivered in Cork, Ireland, October 17, 1845, in *Douglass Papers*, ser. 1, 1:42, 42–51; Theodore Dwight Weld, *American Slavery As It Is: Testimony of a Thousand Witnesses* (New York: American Anti-Slavery Society, 1839), 62–63, 73, 144. And see Lampe, *Frederick Douglass*, 120.

7 *Liberator*, September 2, 1842.

8 *Herald of Freedom*, August 26, 1842, in Lampe, *Frederick Douglass*, 126.

9 Dorothy Sterling, *Ahead of Her Time: Abby Kelley and the Politics of Antislavery* (New York: Norton, 1991), 1–5, 107–28; Mayer, *All on Fire*, 265–67.

10 *Liberator*, August 1842; Lampe, *Frederick Douglass*, 136–38, 144.

11 Erasmus D. Hudson, "Journal," August 26–27, 1842, 51–52, Hudson Family Papers, box 2, folder 37, Special Collections and Archives, University of Massachusetts, Amherst Library; Matthew 23:27, 23:16. Also see Isaiah 5:20.

12 On the Erie Canal and its impact, see Carol Sheriff, *Artificial River: The Erie Canal and the Paradox of Progress, 1817–1862* (New York: Hill & Wang, 1996); and Daniel Walker Howe, *What Hath God Wrought: The Transformation of America, 1815–1845* (New York: Oxford University Press, 2007), 216–20. On the emerging new middle class of New York State, see Mary Ryan, *Cradle of the Middle Class: The Family in Oneida County, New York, 1790–1865* (Cambridge, UK: Cambridge University Press, 1981).

13 Hudson, "Journal," September 1–2, 8, 11–12, 14, and 16–29, 18–42, 55–57, 59–62, 65–67; *National Anti-Slavery Standard*, October 13, 1842. See Lampe, *Frederick Douglass*, 143. Isaiah 53:3, 5, 11.

14 Robert Barclay, *Agricultural Tour in the United States and Upper Canada* (London, 1842), quoted in Oliver W. Holmes and Peter T. Rohrbach, *Stagecoach East: Stagecoach Days in the East from the Colonial Period to the Civil War* (Washington, DC: Smithsonian Press, 1983),

47; Charles Dickens, *American Notes for General Circulation* (1842; repr., New York: Penguin, 2000), 207–9, 213–14.

15 Harriet Martineau, *Society in America*, vol. 2 (New York: Saunders & Otley, 1837), 13–15, 19, 23–24, 106–36, 214; Dickens, *American Notes*, 72.

16 *Liberator*, October 28 and November 25, 1842; *Latimer Journal and North Star*, November 18 and 23, 1842. On Latimer case, see Kantrowitz, *More than Freedom*, 70–74.

17 *Liberator*, November 4, 1842; *National Anti-Slavery Standard*, November 10, 1842; Douglass to Garrison, Lynn, November 8, 1842, in *Liberator*, November 18, 1842; and see Lampe, *Frederick Douglass*, 146.

18 Douglass to Garrison, Lynn, November 8, 1842, in *Liberator*, November 18, 1842; and see Kantrowitz, *More than Freedom*, 73–74. On Garrisonian ideology and theology, see John R. McKivigan, *The War against Proslavery Religion: Abolitionism and the Northern Churches, 1830–1865* (Ithaca, NY: Cornell University Press, 1984), chs. 1–8; Lewis Perry, *Racial Abolitionism: Anarchy and the Government of God in Antislavery Thought* (Ithaca, NY: Cornell University Press, 1974), chs. 1–7; and W. Caleb McDaniel, *The Problem of Democracy in the Age of Slavery: Garrisonian Abolitionists and Transatlantic Reform* (Baton Rouge: Louisiana State University Press, 2013), esp. 1–87.

19 Antislavery meeting, Princeton, MA, February 1–2, 1843, *Liberator*, March 10, 1843.

20 A. W. Weston to Maria Weston Chapman, extract of letter, Boston, March 6, 1843, Weston Family Papers, BPL; antislavery meeting, Lowell, MA, April 25, 1843, *Liberator*, May 12, 1843.

21 "The Anti-Slavery Movement, the Slave's Only Earthly Hope," speech, New York, May 9, 1843, *Douglass Papers*, ser. 1, 1:21–23; Garrison's letter about the New York convention, May 9, 1843, in Merrill, *Letters of William Lloyd Garrison*, 3:64; *National Anti-Slavery Standard* (hereafter *NASS*), June 8, 1843; *Liberator*, May 26, 1843. See Lampe, *Frederick Douglass*, 156–62.

22 *Liberator*, June 16, 1843; for schedules of conventions, see *Liberator*, July 14 and October 13, 1843; *Life and Times*, 226; Douglass to Abby Kelley, June 19, 1843, *Douglass Papers*, ser. 3, 1:8–9.

23 *Life and Times*, 227.

24 Ibid., 228; Douglass to Maria Weston Chapman, September 10, 1843, *Douglass Papers*, ser. 3, 1:12.

25 John Collins to Chapman, August 23, 1843; Mrs. E. M. Collins to Chapman, August 15, 1843, Weston Family Papers, BPL; Douglass to Chapman, September 10, 1843, *Douglass Papers*, ser. 3, 1:10–13. See Lampe, *Frederick Douglass*, 176–79.

26 *Liberator*, August 25, 1843; *Life and Times*, 229.

27 *Life and Times*, 229; Lampe, *Frederick Douglass*, 180.

28 Holley's daughter quoted in Frederick May Holland, *Frederick Douglass: The Colored Orator* (New York: Haskell House, 1891), 93–94; Ephesians 6:5; Luke 12:47.

29 Howard Holman Bell, ed., *Minutes of the Proceedings of the National Negro Conventions, 1830–1864* (New York: Arno Press, 1969), Buffalo Convention, 4–5; Benjamin Quarles, *Black Abolitionists* (New York: Oxford University Press, 1969), 184–85, 226–27.

30 Martin B. Pasternak, *Rise Now and Fly to Arms: The Life of Henry Highland Garnet* (New York: Garland, 1995), 3–15; Reverend Henry Highland Garnet, *A Memorial Discourse, Delivered in the Hall of the House of Representatives, Washington, DC, Feb. 12, 1865*, introduction by James McCune Smith (Philadelphia: Joseph M. Wilson, 1865), 17–36. Smith's biographical sketch of Garnet's life is the best place to begin. Also see Joel Schor, *Henry Highland Garnet: A Voice of Black Radicalism in the Nineteenth Century* (Westport, CT: Greenwood Press, 1977).

31 Quarles, *Black Abolitionists*, 226–27; Stanley Harrold, *The Rise of Aggressive Abolitionism:*

Addresses to the Slaves (Lexington: University of Kentucky Press, 2004), "An Address to the Slaves of the United States," 180–88.

32 Bell, *Minutes*, 12–13, 15, 18–19, 23–24; Maria Weston Chapman, in *Liberator*, September 22, 1843. And see Sinha, *Slave's Cause*, 418–19.

33 *Liberator*, September 22 and October 13, 1843; *Life and Times*, 230; *National Anti-Slavery Standard*, October 19, 1843.

34 William A. White to "Dear friend," *Liberator*, October 13, 1843; *NASS*, October 19, 1843; *Life and Times*, 231. White's detailed account of the Pendleton mob scene is crucial for its descriptive character. But also see McFeely, *Frederick Douglass*, 108–12, who points to the deep class prejudices in White's account, as well as in the understandings of the Boston Garrisonians.

35 Douglass to William A. White, Scotland, July 30, 1846, FD Papers (LC), reel 1; Joseph Borome, ed., "Two Letters of Frederick Douglass," *Journal of Negro History* 33 (October 1948): 470–71; and Lampe, *Frederick Douglass*, 186–89.

36 *Liberator*, October 20, 1843; Abraham Brooke to Maria Weston Chapman, October 5 and October 10, 1843, Weston Family Papers, BPL. See McFeely, *Frederick Douglass*, 112–13; and Lampe, *Frederick Douglass*, 190–91.

37 *Cincinnati Philanthropist* and *New Lisbon Advocate*, in *Liberator*, November 17 and December 8, 1843; Bradburn to John Collins, November 22, 1843, quoted in Benjamin Quarles, *Frederick Douglass* (1948, repr., New York: Atheneum, 1968), 33.

38 Milo A. Townsend to Garrison, New Brighton, Beaver County, PA, November 10, 1843, in *Liberator*, December 8, 1843; *Pittsburgh Spirit of Liberty*, in *Liberator*, December 1, 1843.

39 *Philadelphia Weekly Cultivator*, in *Liberator*, December 22, 1843; itineraries, in Lampe, *Frederick Douglass*, 301–302.

40 Douglass to Wendell Phillips, February 10, 1844, quoted in Lampe, *Frederick Douglass*, 208–09; Douglass to Garrison, in *Liberator*, March 15, 1944. Money was very much an issue now for the AASS and its agents. See Abby Kelley to E. D. Hudson, Durham, NH, July 23, 1844, Hudson Family Papers, box 2, folder 53. "Let us remember we have not an individual person to give us a cent or to ask others to give us a cent," Kelley wrote. The AASS was "in great need of funds."

41 Douglass to Garrison, in *Liberator*, November 1, 1844. See itineraries, Lampe, *Frederick Douglass*, 302–5.

42 *Narrative*, 62. The book was published in late May 1845 at the Antislavery Office, 25 Cornhill Street, Boston, Massachusetts.

Chapter 9: The Thought of Writing for a Book!

1 Frederick Douglass, "The Folly of Our Opponents," *Liberty Bell* (Boston: Antislavery Office, 1845), 166–72, in Foner, *Life and Writings*, 1:113.

2 *Liberator*, May 9, 1845. Garrison's endorsement of the book is a genuine preface, while Phillips's imprimatur is a letter written to Douglass, April 22, 1845. See *Narrative*, 31–40.

3 Charles T. Davis and Henry Louis Gates Jr., eds., *The Slave's Narrative* (New York: Oxford University Press, 1985), xvi; Andrews, *To Tell a Free Story*, 97–98; *Douglass Papers*, 1:59n11; and Charles H. Nichols, "Who Read the Slave Narratives?," *Phylon* 20 (Summer 1959): 149–62; *Liberator*, August 29, 1845.

4 *Liberator*, August 22, 1845. On Buffum, see *Douglass Papers*, 1:50–51n5. Buffum may have been instrumental in financially helping Anna and the family. Douglass always recollected Buffum warmly as "my friend." See *Life and Times*, 232, 246, 467.

5 www.norwayheritage.com/p_ship.asp; Dale Cockrell, ed., *Excelsior: Journals of the Hutchin-*

son *Family Singers, 1842–1846* (Stuyvesant, NY: Pendragon, 1989), 315–16, 319; Scott Gac, *Singing for Freedom: The Hutchinson Family Singers and the Nineteenth Century Culture of Antebellum Reform* (New Haven, CT: Yale University Press, 2007), 208–10; Simon Schama, "Sail Away," *New Yorker*, May 31, 2004.

6 *Life and Times*, 233.

7 Douglass to Garrison, Dublin, September 1, 1845, in *Liberator*, September 26, 1845; Delbanco, *Melville*, 145. By "Governor Hammond's Letters," Douglass refers to James Henry Hammond's *Two Letters on Slavery in the United States, Addressed to Thomas Clarkson, Esq.*, published in 1845. Hammond had been elected governor of South Carolina in 1842 and owned a ten-thousand-acre plantation and 147 slaves. His proslavery writings were among the most influential of the antebellum era (the "Letters" were actually extended essays). See Drew Gilpin Faust, *The Ideology of Slavery: Proslavery Thought in the Antebellum South, 1830–1860* (Baton Rouge: Louisiana State University Press, 1981), 168–205.

8 Douglass to Garrison, September 1, 1845, in *Liberator*, September 26, 1845; *Bondage*, 270–71.

9 *Bondage*, 280.

10 Cockrell, *Excelsior*, 320; Douglass to Garrison, Dublin, September 1 and 16, 1845, in *Liberator*, September 26 and October 10, 1845; Tom Chaffin, *Giant's Causeway: Frederick Douglass's Irish Odyssey and the Making of an American Visionary* (Charlottesville: University of Virginia Press, 2014), 35–47.

11 Richard Webb to Maria Weston Chapman, May 16, 1846, Antislavery Collection, BPL.

12 Douglass to Garrison, in *Liberator*, October 24, 1845.

13 McFeely, *Frederick Douglass*, 119–20; Jane Jennings to Maria Weston Chapman, Cork, November 26, 1845, Weston Family Papers, BPL.

14 Isabel Jennings to Maria Weston Chapman, Cork, October 15, 1845, and Isabel Jennings to Chapman, 1845 (n.d.), Weston Family Papers, BPL.

15 *Cork Examiner*, October 15, 1845, report of "My Experience and My Mission to Great Britain," delivered in Cork, Ireland, October 14, 1845, *Douglass Papers*, ser. 1, 1:37. For Douglass's response to such characterizations, see Lee Jenkins, "Beyond the Pale: Frederick Douglass in Cork," *Irish Review* 24 (1999): 90–91. On Douglass in Ireland, there is a growing literature. See Tom Chaffin, "Frederick Douglass's Irish Liberty," *New York Times*, Opinionator column, February 25, 2011; and Chaffin, *Giant's Causeway*, 70–79.

16 *Cork Southern Reporter*, October 16, 1845, and *Cork Examiner*, October 15, 1845, quoted in *Douglass Papers*, ser. 1, 1:39; Belfast quotation in Jenkins, "Beyond the Pale," 91.

17 James Buffum to Caroline Weston, Perth, Scotland, June 25, 1846; James Buffum to M. W. Chapman, Perth, Scotland, June 26, 1846; and Richard D. Webb to M. W. Chapman, Dublin, May 16, 1846; Weston Family Papers, BPL.

18 Douglass to Richard D. Webb, Belfast, December 6, 1845; Douglass to Webb, Limerick, Ireland, November 10, 1845; Douglass to Webb, Limerick, December 5 and 6, 1845; and Richard D. Webb to M. W. Chapman, Dublin, May 16, 1846; Weston Family Papers, BPL.

19 Douglass to Maria Weston Chapman, Kilmarnock, Scotland, March 29, 1846; and Douglass to Webb, Belfast, December 6, 1845; Weston Family Papers, BPL.

20 Douglass to Webb, Belfast, March 29, 1846, Weston Family Papers, BPL.

21 "Intemperance and Slavery," address delivered in Cork, Ireland, October 20, 1845; "American Prejudice against Color," address at Imperial Hotel, Cork, Ireland, October 23, 1845; "The Annexation of Texas," address at the Independent Chapel, Cork, Ireland, November 3, 1845; and "Slavery and America's Bastard Republicanism," address delivered at Belford Row Independent Chapel, Limerick, Ireland, November 10, 1845; in *Douglass Papers*, ser. 1, 1:55–87. And see Chaffin, *Giant's Causeway*, 84–93.

22 "The Cambria Riot, My Slave Experience, and My Irish Mission," speech delivered in Belfast, December 5, 1845; and "The Slanderous Charge of Negro Inferiority," Belfast, December 11, 1845; *Douglass Papers*, ser. 1, 1:93–97, 98–100; "Slavery and the Slave Power," Rochester, December 1, 1850, *Douglass Papers*, ser. 1, 2:258; Jenkins, "Beyond the Pale," 83–84; Chaffin, *Giant's Causeway*, 94–101.

23 "Baptists, Congregationalists, the Free Church and Slavery," Belfast, December 23, 1845, *Douglass Papers*, ser. 1, 1:105–6; Mary Ireland to Maria Weston Chapman, January 24, 1846, Weston Family Papers, BPL.

24 Mary Ireland to Maria Weston Chapman, January 24, 1846, Belfast, Weston Family Papers, BPL. Many were "offended," according to Mary Ireland, because of Douglass's "uncompromising tone." "Baptists, Congregationalists, the Free Church and Slavery," 103, 105, 108–9, 113–18; Matthew 23:15; Luke 10:30–35; Daniel 6:12–23.

25 Christine Kinealy, *The Great Irish Famine: Impact, Ideology, and Rebellion* (New York: Palgrave, 2002), 17–19; Lawrence M. Geary, "What People Died of during the Famine," in *Famine 150: Commemorative Lecture Series*, ed. Cormac O'Grada (Dublin: Teagasc, 1997), 95. An excellent introduction to the Irish famine as history and memory is James S. Donnelly Jr., *The Great Irish Potato Famine* (Gloucestershire, UK: Sutton, 2001), 1–40. Donnelly is especially interesting on historiography and on whether Ireland was sliding "toward the abyss" of agricultural catastrophe well before 1845. On emigration and population decline, see John Keating, *Irish Famine Facts* (Dublin: Teagasc, 1996), 67–76.

26 Colm Tóibín and Diarmaid Ferriter, *The Irish Famine: A Documentary* (London: London Review of Books, 2002), 40; Douglass to William Lloyd Garrison, Montrose, Scotland, February 26, 1846, in *Liberator*, March 27, 1846.

27 Douglass to Garrison, February 26, 1846; Kinealy, *Great Irish Famine*, 29.

28 Douglass to Garrison, February 26, 1846. On Douglass's response to the famine, both during his visit to Ireland and in years afterward, see Patricia Ferreira, " 'All but a Black Skin and Wooly Hair': Frederick Douglass's Witness of the Irish Famine," *American Studies International* 37 (June 1999): 69–83; and Douglass, "Thoughts and Recollections of a Tour of Ireland," *AME Church Review* 3 (1886): 138–44.

29 Ibid.; Tóibín and Ferriter, *Irish Famine*, 39–40. The worst of the evictions and effects of the Poor Laws did not take place until 1847, after Douglass had left Ireland. See Kinealy, *Great Irish Famine*, 29–46, 141–42.

30 *Bondage*, 74. "The Green Fields of Americay" is a traditional Irish folk song about emigration to America. See http://www.clarelibrary.ie/eolas/coclare/songs/cmc/the_green_fields_of_america_jlyons.htm.

31 Douglass to Garrison, Victoria Hotel, Belfast, January 1, 1846, in Foner, *Life and Writings*, 1:125–27.

32 Ibid., 126–29.

33 Frederick Douglass, *Narrative of the Life of Frederick Douglass, an American Slave, Written by Himself* (Dublin: Webb and Chapman, 1846), the second Dublin edition, copy in Beinecke Library, Yale University, iii–iv, cxxxii. On the Irish editions, see Fionnghuala Sweeney, *Frederick Douglass and the Atlantic World* (Liverpool: Liverpool University Press, 2007), 13–36.

Chapter 10: Send Back the Money!

1 Isaiah 1:5, 15, recited by Douglass in "The Free Church of Scotland and American Slavery," delivered in Dundee, Scotland, January 30, 1846, in *Douglass Papers*, ser. 1, 1:146–47.

2 C. Duncan Rice, *The Scots Abolitionists, 1833–1861* (Baton Rouge: Louisiana State Uni-

versity Press, 1981), 116–30; George Shepperson, "The Free Church and American Slavery," *Scottish Historical Review* 30 (October 1951): 126–43; George Shepperson, "Frederick Douglass and Scotland," *Journal of Negro History* 38 (July 1953): 307–21; Alisdair Pettinger, "Send Back the Money: Douglass and the Free Church of Scotland," in *Liberating Sojourn: Frederick Douglass and Transatlantic Reform*, ed. Alan J. Rice and Martin Crawford (Athens: University of Georgia Press, 1999), 31–49; Paul Giles, "Douglass's Black Atlantic: Britain, Europe, and Egypt," in *The Cambridge Companion to Frederick Douglass*, ed. Maurice S. Lee (Cambridge, UK: Cambridge University Press, 2009), 132–36.

3 Douglass, "An Account of American Slavery," delivered at City Hall, Glasgow, Scotland, January 15, 1846, *Douglass Papers*, ser. 1, 1:133, 138–42.

4 Isaiah 1:4, 10, 15. On the jeremiad, see Perry Miller, *The New England Mind: From Colony to Province* (Boston: Beacon Press, 1961), 27–39; Sacvan Bercovitch, *The American Jeremiad* (Madison: University of Wisconsin Press, 1978), 148–210; David W. Blight, *Frederick Douglass' Civil War: Keeping Faith in Jubilee* (Baton Rouge: Louisiana State University Press, 1989), 101–5, 117–20; and David Howard-Pitney, *The African American Jeremiad: Appeals for Justice in America* (Philadelphia: Temple University Press, 2005). On the Hebrew prophets, see Abraham Heschel, *The Prophets* (New York: Harper, 1962). And on Douglass's use of biblical narrative to engage the "Free Church" debate in Scotland, see D. H. Dilheck, *Frederick Douglass: America's Prophet* (Chapel Hill, NC: University of North Carolina Press, 2018), 63–74.

5 *Bondage*, 281.

6 Douglass, "Charges and Defense of the Free Church," delivered in Dundee, Scotland, March 10, 1846, *Douglass Papers*, ser. 1, 1:178–79.

7 Ibid., 180–82; Philemon 1:10–11; Colossians 4:9. Paul, while in a Roman prison, sends the slave (servant), Onesimus, to Philemon likely for manumission and for the furthering of faith.

8 Anonymous to Thomas Chalmers, April 2, 1846, Thomas Chalmers Papers, New College Library, Edinburgh, quoted in Pettinger, "Send Back the Money," in Rice and Crawford, *Liberating Sojourn*, 42.

9 Douglass to Richard D. Webb, Dundee, Scotland, February 10, 1846; Douglass to Garrison, Glasgow, April 16, 1846; Douglass to Amy Post, Edinburgh, April 28, 1846; *Douglass Papers*, ser. 3, 1:92–93, 109, 122; *Bondage*, 283; Rice, *Scots Abolitionists*, 144–45.

10 Vernon Loggins, "Writings of the Leading Negro Antislavery Agents, 1840–1865" (1931), in Andrews, *Critical Essays*, 45. On the sheer scale of Douglass's popularity in Scotland and England, see R. J. M. Blackett, *Building an Antislavery Wall: Black Americans and the Atlantic Abolitionist Movement, 1830–1860* (Baton Rouge: Louisiana State University Press, 1983), 89–90, 106–12.

11 *Bondage*, 280; Douglass to Garrison, Perth, Scotland, January 27, 1846, *Douglass Papers*, ser. 1, 1:81–83, 86 n1. Thompson's full name was the improbable Absalom Christopher Columbus Americus Vespucious Thompson. He was born in 1822, and his father owned a farm near St. Michaels, Maryland, and therefore in proximity to Auld's home and store in the town. Douglass had baited Thompson sufficiently enough by his response, as had the *Albany Patriot* editor, that Thompson further sought to discredit Douglass's veracity. The Albany letter is reprinted in *Liberator*, February 27, 1846.

12 Douglass to Garrison, January 27, 1846, *Douglass Papers*, ser. 3, 1:84–85.

13 Douglass, *Narrative of the Life of Frederick Douglass, an American Slave, Written by Himself* (Dublin: Webb and Chapman, G. T. Brunswick Street, 1846), preface, February 6, 1846, vi, cxxiii–cxxviii. On the Irish edition and the Thompson exchange, see Patricia J. Ferreira, "Frederick Douglass in Ireland: The Dublin Edition of his Narrative," *New Hibernian Review* 5, no. 1 (Spring 2001): 60–67.

14 See Blackett, *Building an Antislavery Wall*, 85; and Louisa Cheves Stoney, ed., *Thomas Smyth: Autobiographical Notes, Letters, and Reflections* (Charleston, SC, 1914), 362–75. Blackett discovered this story, and his judgment that the episode was "transparent and tasteless" seems accurate, even if gracefully understated. It was one among other uses of racial-sexual stereotypes to discredit Douglass during his early career.

15 Douglass to Horace Greeley, Glasgow, April 15, 1846, in *New York Tribune*, May 20, 1846, *Douglass Papers*, ser. 3, 1:103–6, and nn. 6–7, 107; Matthew 12:20; *Othello*, act 1, sc. 3, lines 80–81. The attacks on Douglass appeared in the *New York Herald*, September 27, October 6, and December 1, 1845, and the *New York Express* attack was reprinted in *National Anti-Slavery Standard*, February 12, 1846.

16 Douglass to Garrison, Glasgow, Scotland, April 16, 1846; Douglass to William A. White, Edinburgh, July 30, 1846; *Douglass Papers*, ser. 3, 1:108, 147–50.

17 Leigh Fought, "Frederick Douglass's Lost 'Sister': Harriet Bailey/Ruth Cox Adams," manuscript essay provided by the author. *Douglass Papers*, ser. 3, 1:125–26n1. The editors of the *Douglass Papers* have mistakenly dated Cox's escape as 1842 and her meeting with Douglass as 1843. Fought's research has clarified these details. Also see McFeely, *Frederick Douglass*, 98–99, 103, 136–38. McFeely first exposed this story and, understandably, portrayed Harriet Bailey and Ruth Cox as two separate women who claimed to be Douglass's sisters.

18 Douglass to Ruth Cox, May 16, 1846, *Douglass Papers*, ser. 3, 1:124.

19 Ibid., 125. Editors of *Douglass Papers* suggest the song "Camels a Coming" was a Scottish jig, "The Campbells Are Coming," adapted by Robert Burns. But there is little reason for Douglass to assume Harriet would know that tune. It just as easily could have been some variation on the biblical story Genesis 24:60–63. "And they blessed Rebekah, and said unto her, Thou art our sister, be thou the mother of thousands of millions, and let thy seed possess the gate of those which hate them. / And Rebekah arose, and her damsels, and they rode upon the camels, and followed the man: and the servant took Rebekah, and went his way. / And Isaac came from the way of the well La-hai-roi; for he dwelt in the south country. / And Isaac went out to meditate in the field at the eventide: and he lifted up his eyes, and saw, and, behold, the camels were coming." Also see John Stauffer, *The Black Hearts of Men: Radical Abolitionists and the Transformation of Race* (Cambridge, MA: Harvard University Press, 2002), 159–60. Stauffer says the song was an old favorite from Douglass's slave days.

20 Douglass to Ruth Cox, London, August 18, 1846, *Douglass Papers*, ser. 3, 1:156–57.

21 Fought, "Frederick Douglass's Lost 'Sister,'" 3–11.

22 Douglass to Francis Jackson, Dundee, Scotland, January 29, 1846, *Douglass Papers*, ser. 3, 1:89–90. Jackson was part of Garrison's close-knit "Boston clique" of funders and supporters. See Stewart, *William Lloyd Garrison*, 128–30.

23 Douglass to Abigail Mott, Ayr, Scotland, April 23, 1846, *Douglass Papers*, ser. 3, 1:111–13; Robert Crawford, *The Bard: Robert Burns, a Biography* (Princeton, NJ: Princeton University Press, 2009), 4–6. On Douglass and Burns, and the American's fondness for quoting from the poem "A man's a man for a' that," see Pettinger, "Send Back the Money," in Rice and Crawford, *Liberating Sojourn*, 44–46, 49.

24 William Lloyd Garrison to Helen E. Garrison, "At Sea," July 26 and 31, 1846, in Merrill, *Letters of Garrison*, 3:354–57; *Bondage*, 275; *Life and Times*, 241.

25 Douglass to R. D. Webb, Glasgow, Scotland, April 16, 20, and 26, 1846, Garrison MSS., BPL; R. D. Webb to M. W. Chapman, September 1 and October 31, 1846, Weston Family Papers, BPL; Douglass to Maria Weston Chapman, London, August 18, 1846, Garrison MSS., BPL. On these disputes with Webb and Chapman, see Blackett, *Building an Antislavery Wall*, 109–12; and McFeely, *Frederick Douglass*, 136.

26 Douglass to Isabel Jennings, Edinburgh, July 30, 1846, *Douglass Papers*, ser. 3, 1:152–53; Garrison to Helen Garrison, London, September 17, 1846, in Merrill, *Letters of Garrison*, 3:415.

27 Douglass to Ruth Cox, Belfast, July 17, 1846, *Douglass Papers*, ser. 3, 1:144; McFeely, *Frederick Douglass*, 136–38.

28 Douglass to Garrison, London, May 23, 1846, *Douglass Papers*, ser. 3, 1:131–32. On the matter of the Aulds' alleged desire to find and re-enslave Douglass, see Preston, *Young Frederick Douglass*, 173–74. Preston aptly points out that Auld needed the money more than he needed Douglass.

29 Alfred M. Duster, ed., *Crusade for Justice: The Autobiography of Ida B. Wells* (Chicago: University of Chicago Press, 1970), 161–63.

30 Douglass to Anna Richardson, London, August 19, 1846, in private hands, sold at auction by Seth Kaller, Inc., copy provided the author by Leigh Fought in email, October 7, 2013; Douglass to James Wilson, Belfast, July 23, 1846, *Douglass Papers*, ser. 3, 1:145–46; Garrison to Helen E. Garrison, London, September 17, 1846, in Merrill, *Letters of Garrison*, 3:415.

31 Douglass to Isabel Jennings, Glasgow, September 22, 1846, *Douglass Papers*, ser. 3, 1:166.

32 Anna Richardson to Hugh Auld, Newcastle-upon-Tyne, August 17, 1846; and Hugh Auld to Mrs. Anna Richardson, Baltimore, October 6, 1846, in Preston, *Young Frederick Douglass*, 174. Douglass reprinted the sale and manumission documents in *Life and Times*, 256–57. Many in the press called the deal a "ransom," but so did Douglass himself. See Douglass to John Hardinge Veitch, Coventry, January 22, 1847; and for further details on the purchase, Henry C. Wright to Douglass, Doncaster, December 12, 1846, *Douglass Papers*, ser. 3, 1:182–83, n. 1, 198. On the purchase of Douglass's freedom, and the role of the lawyers, see McFeely, *Frederick Douglass*, 143–45. One of the major contributors to the fund to purchase Douglass's freedom was John Bright, the distinguished Quaker and radical British statesman, who gave £50.

33 Douglass to Henry C. Wright, Manchester, December 22, 1846, *Douglass Papers*, ser. 3, 1:196–99. Henry C. Wright to Douglass, December 12, 1846; Douglass to Veitch, January 22, 1847; *Douglass Papers*, ser. 3, 1:179–82, 183–89; *Ohio Antislavery Bugle*, n.d., and Garrison's response of approval of the "ransom," in *Liberator*, February 12, 1847. To his credit, Garrison defended the entire purchase effort.

34 McDaniel, *Problem of Democracy*, 143–44; Richard Bradbury, "Frederick Douglass and the Chartists," in Rice and Crawford, *Liberating Sojourn*, 169–72; Garrison to Helen Garrison, London, August 13, 1846, in Merrill, *Letters of Garrison*, 368–69. On Chartism as a movement, also see Malcolm Chase, *Chartism: A New History* (Manchester, UK: Manchester University Press, 2007).

35 Garrison to Edmund Quincy, London, August 14, 1846; Garrison to Richard D. Webb, Birmingham, September 4, 1846; in Merrill, *Letters of Garrison*, 3:372–73, 396; Douglass to Garrison, London, May 23, 1846, *Douglass Papers*, ser. 3, 1:129. On Douglass and his ambivalent relationship to Chartism, see McFeely, *Frederick Douglass*, 138–42.

36 William Lovett, *The Life and Struggles of William Lovett* (London: Bell, 1920), 328–29, quoted in Bradbury, "Douglass and the Chartists," 178.

37 Douglass, "Slavery as It Now Exists in the United States," address in Bristol, England, August 25, 1846; and Douglass, "American Slavery and Britain's Rebuke of Manstealers," address in Bridgewater, England, August 31, 1846; *Douglass Papers*, ser. 1, 1:343–44, 365–66. On the wage-slavery/black-slavery tension, and Douglass's own struggle over it, see McDaniel, *Problem of Democracy*, 144–48.

38 Douglass, "American Slavery Is America's Disgrace," address in Sheffield, England, March 25, 1847, *Douglass Papers*, ser. 1, 2:11.

39 Hannah Rose Murray compiled Douglass's speeches, http://site/frederickdouglassinbrit-ain/frederick-douglass-s-mission-to-britain/map-of-speaking-locations. On the crowd es-timations, see *Douglass Papers*, ser. 1, 1:269, 459, 466; and "electric speed," in Douglass, "Farewell Address to the British People, London," March 30, 1847, Foner, *Life and Writings*, 1:230.

40 *Douglass Papers*, ser. 1, 2:20; Douglass, "Farewell Address," 1:208–9, 213.

41 Douglass, "Farewell Address," 1:209, 212–13, 216.

42 Ibid., 1:214, 224–25, 232; *London Morning Chronicle*, March 31, 1847, in *Douglass Papers*, ser. 1, 2:20.

43 *Sheffield Mercury*, September 11, 1846, in *Douglass Papers*, ser. 1, 1:398. The price of pas-sage and discrimination on the *Cambria* in *Life and Times*, 258; and especially Douglass to John Thadeus Delane, editor of the *London Times*, Liverpool, April 3, 1847, *Douglass Pa-pers*, ser. 3, 1:201–2; and enormous press coverage reprinted in *Liberator*, May 14, 1847. On Douglass's return to America also see Stauffer, *Giants*, 93–95; and McFeely, *Frederick Doug-lass*, 145.

44 Douglass to Anna Richardson, Lynn, April 29, 1847, *Douglass Papers*, ser. 3, 1:208–9. The verse is from the Burns poem "Tam O'Shanter, a Tale."

Chapter 11: Demagogue in Black

1 Douglass to William and Robert Smeal, Lynn, April 29, 1847, *Douglass Papers*, ser. 3, 1:205–6. His son Lewis was five and a half years old and Charles was two and a half.

2 Ibid., 206–7; letter reprinted in *NASS*, July 8, 1847; Wendell Phillips to Sidney H. Gay, Bos-ton, April 23, 1847, Sidney Howard Gay Papers, Columbia University. Douglass detailed his *Cambria* experience in a letter, *NASS*, May 6, 1847.

3 *Douglass Papers*, ser. 1, 2:57–58, headnote; *NASS*, May 13, 1847; Garrison to *Liberator*, May 11, 1847, in Merrill, *Letters of Garrison*, 3:478–79. Rosetta was seven years old in the spring of 1847.

4 Douglass, "The Right to Criticize American Institutions," in Foner, *Life and Writings*, 1:235–36. An original typescript of this special speech is in the Evans Collection, Savannah, GA, "Assorted Material" box.

5 Ibid., 237. Jack R. Lundbom, *The Hebrew Prophets: An Introduction* (Minneapolis: Fortress Press, 2010), 88–100; John Bright, ed. and trans., *Jeremiah* (New York: Doubleday, 1965), 9–18, 60–74; Jeremiah 4:5–31, 5:1–31, 6:1–30, 7:1–34, 8:1–3, 9:1–21.

6 "Right to Criticize American Institutions," 237–43. From his British sojourn Douglass raised for special chastisement the Reverends Samuel H. Cox, who had publicly attacked Douglass's insistence on bringing the subject of slavery into the World's Temperance Con-vention in London in 1846, and Thomas Smyth, the South Carolina Presbyterian who demanded sympathy for slaveholders' dilemmas at the London Evangelical Alliance; Jere-miah 6:14.

7 Letter in *Liberator*, June 4, 1847; *New York Sun*, May 13, 1847; Whittier, *National Era*, May 20, 1847, quoted in *Douglass Papers*, ser. 1, 2:58, and ser. 3, 1:219.

8 Douglass to Thomas Van Rensselaer, Lynn, May 18, 1847, *Douglass Papers*, ser. 3, 1:210–12, reprinted in *Liberator*, June 4, 1847.

9 Douglass to Garrison, Lynn, June 7, 1847, *Douglass Papers*, ser. 3, 1:214–18; Elias Smith to Sidney Howard Gay, New York, May 29, 1847, Gay Papers, Columbia University. Smith wrote to Gay, worried about this "serious charge" against Douglass, suggesting that Miss Mott had traveled with him to help him work on his speech, and the claim that they were "caught in bed together" was "false in toto."

10 Douglass to Garrison, Lynn, June 7, 1847, *Douglass Papers*, ser. 3, 1:215–16.

11 Ibid., 214; Samuel May Jr. to John B. Estlin, July 1, 1847, quoted in *Douglass Papers*, ser. 3, 1:219n1; Douglass to *Boston Daily Whig*, Lynn, June 27, 1847, in Foner, *Life and Writings*, 1:252–53; *Liberator*, July 9 and 16, 1847.

12 Douglass to Garrison, Lynn, July 18, 1847, *Douglass Papers*, ser. 3, 1:223.

13 Douglass, "Pioneers in a Holy Cause," address in Canandaigua, NY, August 2, 1847, *Douglass Papers*, ser. 1, 2:71–83.

14 See Garrison to Henry C. Wright, Boston, July 16, 1847, in Merrill, *Letters of Garrison*, 3:202.

15 On the prospects for the Ohio tour, see Mayer, *All on Fire*, 363–66.

16 On comeouterism, see Kraditor, *Means and Ends in American Abolitionism*, 105, 115; Mayer, *All on Fire*, 300–304. On disunion, see Stewart, *William Lloyd Garrison*, 124–38, Douglass, "The Material and Moral Requirements of Antislavery Work," Norristown, PA, August 5, 1847, *Douglass Papers*, ser. 1, 2:84, 86. Though there were many speakers at this gathering, Garrison admitted that Douglass was "the lion of the occasion."

17 Douglass, "Brethren, Rouse the Church," Philadelphia, August 6, 1847, *Douglass Papers*, ser. 1, 2:91–93.

18 Douglass to Sydney H. Gay, Harrisburg, PA, August 8, 1847, *Douglass Papers*, ser. 3, 1:223–26; Garrison to Helen Garrison, Harrisburg, PA, August 9, 1847, *Letters of WLG*, 3:506–7. Douglass wrote several letters to Gay during the tour that were meant for publication in the *NASS*, and Garrison wrote many to his wife, some of which were published in the *Liberator*.

19 Douglass to Readers of the *Ram's Horn*, New Brighton, PA, August 13–14, 1847, *Douglass Papers*, ser. 3, 1:228–31.

20 Douglass to Gay, Austinburg, OH, August 31, 1847; and Douglass to Gay, Cleveland, September 17, 1847; *Douglass Papers*, ser. 3, 1:239–42, 244–45; Garrison to *Liberator*, Richfield, OH, August 25, 1847, *Letters of WLG*, 3:518–19. Garrison described the "wonderful spectacle" of these gatherings and reported that "one colored man rode three hundred miles on horseback to be at the meeting."

21 Douglass to Gay, Austinburg, OH, August 31, 1847; and Douglass to Gay, Cleveland, September 17, 1847; *Douglass Papers*, ser. 3, 1:239–41, 244–48; Samuel May to Gay, October 5, 1847, quoted in *Douglass Papers*, ser. 1, 2:94n2. On the Oberlin Tent, see Mayer, *All on Fire*, 367–69. It was created by the Tappan brothers in 1836.

22 Garrison to Helen Garrison, Youngstown, OH, August 16, 1847; Garrison to Helen Garrison, New Lyme, OH, August 20, 1847; *Letters of WLG*, 3:512, 516; Douglass to Gay, Winfield, OH, September 26, 1847, *Douglass Papers*, ser. 3, 1:250–53.

23 Douglass to Gay, West Winfield, NY, September 26, 1847, *Douglass Papers*, ser. 3, 1:250–53; Garrison to Helen Garrison, Cleveland, October 19 and 20, 1847, *Letters of WLG*, 3:531–33. Douglass included in his letter to Gay a detailed account of all he knew about Garrison's dire illness. On the beginnings of the split between the two men, see Mayer, *All on Fire*, 371–75.

24 Howard Holman Bell, ed., "1847—Troy: Proceedings of the National Convention of Colored People, and Their Friends," in *Minutes of the Proceedings*, 1–32. See Douglass to Gay, Albany, October 4, 1847, *Douglass Papers*, ser. 3, 1:256–59.

25 See McFeely, *Frederick Douglass*, 147–48. Letters to Chapman, see for example Mary Estlin to Chapman, October 18, 1847; Mary Brady to Chapman, n.d., but has to be summer at least of 1847; Lucy Browne to Chapman, April 14, 1847; and Isabel Jennings to Chapman, August 2, 1847, Weston Family Papers, BPL.

26 Douglass to Julia Griffiths, Lynn, October 13, 1847, *Douglass Papers*, ser. 3, 1:262; Janet Douglas, "A Cherished Friendship: Julia Griffiths Crofts and Frederick Douglass," *Slavery and Abolition*, June 2012, 265–66. Douglass's letter to Griffiths was reprinted in *NASS*, January 13, 1848.

27 Douglass to Amy Post, Boston, October 28, 1847; Douglass to Jonathan D. Carr, Lynn, November 1, 1847; Douglass to Martin R. Delany, Rochester, January 19, 1848, *Douglass Papers*, ser. 3, 1:266–67, 282–83, 283n6; *North Star*, December 3, 1847. On how early Douglass began to embrace political antislavery, see Blight, *Frederick Douglass' Civil War*, 28–30; and James Oakes, *The Radical and the Republican: Frederick Douglass, Abraham Lincoln, and the Triumph of Antislavery Politics* (New York: Norton, 2007), 14–17. Also see Stauffer, *Giants*, 133–35; McFeely, *Frederick Douglass*, 149–50; Quarles, *Frederick Douglass*, 80–83.

28 *North Star*, December 3, 1847.

29 *Douglass Papers*, ser. 3, 1:268n7; McFeely, *Frederick Douglass*, 152–53; Gerrit Smith to Douglass, Peterboro, NY, December 8, 1847; David Ruggles to Douglass and Delany, Northampton, MA, January 1, 1848; and Henry O. Wagoner to Douglass, Chicago, January 27, 1848; *Douglass Papers*, ser. 3, 1:276–77, 281–82, 286–88.

30 Douglass to Delany, Rochester, January 12 and 19, 1847, FD Papers (LC); *North Star*, January 28, 1848; Robert S. Levine, *Martin Delany, Frederick Douglass, and the Politics of Representative Identity* (Chapel Hill: University of North Carolina Press, 1997), 18–22.

31 Levine, *Delany, Douglass*, 32–48; Delany to Douglass, *North Star*, January 28, March 27, April 15 and 28, and June 7 and 18, 1848; Douglass, "What Are the Colored People Doing for Themselves?," *North Star*, July 14, 1848, in Foner, *Life and Writings*, 1:314–20.

32 Delany to Douglass, *North Star*, April 15, May 20, and June 9, 1848. See Douglass, "The War with Mexico" and "Northern Whigs and Democrats," *North Star*, January 21 and July 7, 1848.

33 Douglass to Isaac Post, Rochester, February 3, 1848; Douglass to Abigail and Lydia Mott, Rochester, February 21, 1848; *Douglass Papers*, ser. 3, 1:290–91, 297–98.

34 McFeely, *Frederick Douglass*, 153–55; Stauffer, *Giants*, 135–36; Jane Marsh Parker, "Reminiscences of Frederick Douglass," *Outlook* 51 (April 6, 1895): 552; Charles R. Douglass, "Some Incidents in the Home Life of Frederick Douglass," February 17, 1917, an address delivered at the hundredth anniversary of his father's birth, Evans Collection, "Assorted Materials" box.

35 Douglass to Julia Griffiths, Rochester, April 28, 1848, *Douglass Papers*, ser. 3, 1:302–3.

36 *Bondage*, 291; *North Star*, December 3, 1847; *Life and Times*, 264. See Blight, *Frederick Douglass' Civil War*, 18.

37 Lori D. Ginzberg, *Elizabeth Cady Stanton: An American Life* (New York: Hill & Wang, 2009), 56–62; Philip S. Foner, ed., *Frederick Douglass on Women's Rights* (New York: DaCapo Press, 1992), 4–24; Stauffer, *Black Hearts of Men*, 224–26; Waldo Martin, *The Mind of Frederick Douglass* (Chapel Hill: University of North Carolina Press, 1984), 145–50; McFeely, *Frederick Douglass*, 155–56.

38 "The Rights of Women," *North Star*, July 28, 1848; *Life and Times*, 472–74.

39 McFeely, *Frederick Douglass*, 152; Stauffer, *Giants*, 33.

40 Douglass, "A Day, a Deed, an Event, Glorious in the Annals of Philanthropy," address delivered in Rochester, NY, August 1, 1848, *Douglass Papers*, ser. 1, 2:135, 142.

41 Ibid., 141; Douglass, "The Slave's Right to Revolt," address in Boston, May 30, 1848, *Douglass Papers*, ser. 1, 2:131–33. Also see "The North and the Presidency," "Northern Whigs and Democrats," *North Star*, March 17 and July 7, 1848.

42 Douglass to Thomas Auld, Rochester, September 3, 1848, in Foner, *Life and Writings*, 1:336–43. The letter was reprinted widely in the antislavery press and even in Southern

newspapers. See *NASS*, September 14, 1848; *Liberator*, September 22, 1848. As "Letter to his old Master," the document was also reprinted as part of the appendix of *My Bondage and My Freedom* in 1855.

43 McFeely, *Frederick Douglass*, 158; Douglass to Auld, September 3, 1848, 337, 343. See John Jacobus Flournoy to Douglass, Athens, GA, November 10, 1848, *Douglass Papers*, ser. 3, 1:336–39.

44 Douglass to Auld, September 3, 1848, 338–39, 341. On Douglass's claims to self-ownership and natural rights in this letter, see Nicholas Buccola, *The Political Thought of Frederick Douglass* (New York: NYU Press, 2012), 30–32.

45 Douglass to Auld, September 3, 1848, 341–42.

46 Ibid., 342–43. "The Blood of the Slave on the Skirts of the Northern People," *North Star*, November 17, 1848. And see Martin, *Mind of Frederick Douglass*, 136–56.

47 "Blood of the Slave on the Skirts."

48 Ibid.

Chapter 12: My Faithful Friend Julia

1 "Men and Brothers," May 7, 1950, address delivered in New York, AASS Annual Meeting, *Douglass Papers*, ser. 1, 2:238.

2 Garrison to Helen Garrison, New York, May 7, 1850, *Letters of WLG*, 4:7; Kevin Kenny, ed., *New Directions in Irish American History* (Madison: University of Wisconsin Press, 2003), 113–15; *Douglass Papers*, ser. 1, 2:237n1; Tyler Anbinder, "Isaiah Rynders and the Ironies of Popular Democracy in Antebellum New York," in *Contested Democracy: Freedom, Race and Power in American History*, ed. Marisha Sinha and Penny von Eschew (New York: Columbia University Press, 2007), 3–53.

3 *Douglass Papers*, ser. 1, 2:238–39.

4 Ibid., 239–43; Garrison to editor of the *New York Tribune*, Boston, May 13, 1850, *Letters of WLG*, 4:12–13.

5 Rynders in *New York Times*, January 14, 1885, in Anbinder, "Isaiah Rynders," 40.

6 *Douglass Papers*, ser. 1, 2:513n4; Maria Diedrich, *Love Across Color Lines: Ottilie Assing & Frederick Douglass* (New York: Hill & Wang, 1999), 181; McFeely, *Frederick Douglass*, 162–71.

7 *London Times*, June 10 and 11, 1850; "At Home Again," *North Star*, May 30, 1850.

8 "At Home Again."

9 "Prejudice against Color," *North Star*, June 13, 1850; Douglass to editor of the *London Times*, Rochester, June 29, 1850, in Foner, *Life and Writings*, 2:131.

10 Sarah Meer, "Public and Personal Letters: Julia Griffiths and Frederick Douglass' *Paper*," *Slavery and Abolition*, June 2012, 253; Janet Douglas, "A Cherished Friendship: Julia Griffiths Crofts and Frederick Douglass," *Slavery and Abolition*, June 2012, 266. The song was published in *New Monthly Belle Assemblee* 26 (1847): 125. McFeely, *Frederick Douglass*, 145. For Griffiths's Literary Notices, and her own literary flare, see *Frederick Douglass' Paper* (hereafter *FDP*), October 15 and November 2, 1852, and many other issues.

11 Post and May quotes in Douglas, "Cherished Friendship," 267; Thompson quote in Clare Taylor, *British and American Abolitionists: An Episode in Transatlantic Understanding* (Edinburgh: Edinburgh University Press, 1974), 376.

12 Erwin Palmer, "A Partnership in the Abolition Movement," *University of Rochester Library Bulletin* 26 (1970–71): 1–5; *Douglass Papers*, ser. 3, 1:385n5, 398n2.

13 Julia Griffiths to Gerrit Smith, 1850, n.d., Gerrit Smith Papers (hereafter GS Papers), University of Syracuse Library.

14 Stauffer, *Black Hearts of Men*, 71–82, 102–104, 98–108; Lawrence J. Friedman, "The Gerrit Smith Circle: Abolitionism in the Burned-Over District," *Civil War History* 26 (March 1980): 18–38.

15 Gerrit Smith to Douglass, March 16 and March 30, 1849, *Douglass Papers*, ser. 1, 2:371–72, 377–78; Douglass to Gerrit Smith, March 18 and March 30, 1849, GS Papers.

16 Howard W. Coles, *The Cradle of Freedom: A History of the Negro in Rochester, Western New York and Canada*, vol. 1 (Rochester: Oxford Publishers, 1941), 129–30, 158.

17 Griffiths to Smith, two letters, 1850, n.d., GS Papers.

18 Smith to Griffiths, July 25, 1851, GS Papers; *FDP*, July 17 and 24, 1851. On Douglass and his photographs, see Stauffer, *Black Hearts of Men*, 45–56; and especially John Stauffer, Zoe Trodd, and Celeste Bernier, *Picturing Frederick Douglass* (New York: Liveright, 2015), intro.

19 Griffiths to Smith, July 23, 1851, August 26, 1851, GS Papers. Further examples of Julia's appeals for money are Griffiths to Smith, February 22 and 28, 1851, July 19, 1851, GS Papers.

20 Douglass to Smith, September 3, 1851; Griffiths to Smith, October 26, 1852, GS Papers; *FDP*, July 24, 1851; Michael S. Kimmel, "The Birth of the Self-Made Man," in *Manhood in America: A Cultural History* (New York: Oxford University Press, 2006), 11–20.

21 Griffiths to Smith, November 24, 1851, GS Papers. Robert Burns, "The Cotter's Saturday Night," http://www.robertburns.org.uk/Assets/Poems_Songs/cotters_saturday_night.htm. On Douglass's shared veneration for Burns, see Meer, "Public and Personal Letters," 260–61. *FDP*, December 4, 11, and 18, 1851.

22 Coles, *Cradle of Freedom*, 156–57; Douglass Sprague, "My Mother as I Recall Her," 6.

23 Douglass to Smith, May 21, June 10, and May 1, 1851, GS Papers. On the idea of "companionate marriage," and how some radical abolitionists tried to forge such equality in matrimony, see Chris Dixon, *Perfecting the Family: Antislavery Marriages in Nineteenth Century America* (Amherst: University of Massachusetts Press, 1997), 7–20, 157–233.

24 For Smith pleading with Douglass on constitutionalism, see Smith to Douglass, February 9, 1849, *Douglass Papers*, ser. 3, 1:356–57; Luther R. Marsh, ed., *Writings and Speeches of Alvan Stewart on Slavery* (New York, 1860); William Goodell, *Views of American Constitutional Law, in Its Bearing upon American Slavery* (n.p., 1844); Lysander Spooner, *The Unconstitutionality of Slavery*, 2nd ed. (1845; repr., New York, 1965); John R. McKivigan, "The Frederick Douglass–Gerrit Smith Friendship and Political Abolitionism in the 1850s," in *Frederick Douglass: New Literary and Historical Essays*, ed. Eric J. Sundquist (Cambridge, UK: Cambridge University Press, 1990), 205–32; Richard H. Sewell, *Ballots for Freedom: Antislavery Politics in the United States, 1837–1860* (New York: Norton, 1976), 94–95; Blight, *Frederick Douglass' Civil War*, 26–34.

25 On Chase's view, see Eric Foner, *Free Soil, Free Labor, Free Men: The Ideology of the Republican Party before the Civil War* (New York: Oxford University Press, 1970), 73–77, 83–87; and Salmon Chase to Douglass, January 23, 1849; Douglass to Salmon Chase, February 2, 1849; in Foner, *Life and Writings*, 1:352–53.

26 Douglass to C. H. Chase, February 9, 1849, *Douglass Papers*, ser. 3, 1:355; Douglass to Salmon Chase, *North Star*, February 8, 1849. C. H. Chase, no relation to Salmon, is Charles Chase of Brighton, New York, who had challenged Douglass to debate the constitutionality of slavery. On Douglass's political philosophy, see Buccola, *Political Thought of Frederick Douglass*, 1–14, 142–43; and David E. Schrader, "Natural Law in the Constitutional Thought of Frederick Douglass," in *Frederick Douglass: A Critical Reader*, ed. Bill E. Lawson and Frank M. Kirkland (Malden, MA: Blackwell, 1999), 85–99. On Douglass's shift toward Smith's legal views, see Stauffer, *Black Hearts of Men*, 160, 162–66.

27 *North Star*, April 5, 1850; Oakes, *Radical and the Republican*, 92.

28 Douglass to Smith, January 31, 1851, GS Papers.

29 Smith to Douglass, June 9, 1851, *Douglass Papers*, ser. 3, 1:452–53.

30 *North Star*, May 15, 1851; *Liberator*, May 23, 1851.

31 Douglass to Smith, May 21 and June 10, 1851, GS Papers. Also see Douglass to Smith, May 1, May 15, May 28, May 29, June 4, June 10, and June 18, 1851, GS Papers.

32 Isabel Jennings to Mary Estlin, Cork, Ireland, May 24, 1851; Abby Kelley Foster to Garrison, March 30, 1852; WLG Papers, BPL; Anne Weston to Maria Weston Chapman, June 5, 1849, Weston Family Papers, BPL. And see McFeely, *Frederick Douglass*, 170.

33 "The Annual Meeting of the American Antislavery Society," *FDP*, May 20, 1852; Douglass to Gerrit Smith, May 15, 1852, GS Papers. Accounts of the Garrison-Douglass breakup are in Foner, *Life and Writings*, 53–60; and Quarles, *Frederick Douglass*, 70–79.

34 *FDP*, May 20, 1852. Douglass to Gerrit Smith, April 15, 1852, GS Papers. The alleged contribution to Douglass's paper was by Benjamin Coates, of Philadelphia, just before the AASS convention in Rochester. *FDP*, March 11 and May 20, 1852.

35 *FDP*, June 24, 1852. On the changing times, AASS, and the Garrison-Douglass dispute, see Stewart, *William Lloyd Garrison*, 133–41; and Mayer, *All on Fire*, 128–33. Mayer's account is sympathetic to Garrison. On Stowe's book, see David S. Reynolds, *Mightier than the Sword: Uncle Tom's Cabin and the Battle for America* (New York: Norton, 2011).

36 Walt Whitman, "Song of Myself," *Leaves of Grass*, in *The Portable Walt Whitman* (New York: Penguin, 1945), 95–96.

37 *FDP*, May 20, 1852; Douglass to Gerrit Smith, May 15, 1852, GS Papers. See Heschel, *Prophets*, 103–39, 145–58.

38 *FDP*, May 20, 1852; Douglass to Gerrit Smith, May 15, 1852, GS Papers; *Othello*, act 3, sc. 3.

39 Douglass to Gerrit Smith, July 14, 1852, GS Papers.

40 Anna Douglass quoted in Susan B. Anthony to Garrison, December 13, 1853, quoted in Mayer, *All on Fire*, 431; Douglass to Samuel D. Porter, January 12, 1852 (likely misdated, this should be 1853), *Douglass Papers*, ser. 3, 1:512–13; Leigh Fought, *The Women in the World of Frederick Douglass* (Oxford: Oxford University Press, 2017), 133–41.

41 *FDP*, May 27 and August 19, 1853. Also see Douglas, "Cherished Friendship," 267–68; McFeely, *Frederick Douglass*, 171, 175.

42 *FDP*, August 19 and December 9, 1853; *Liberator*, September 16, 1853; Douglass to Gerrit Smith, August 18, 1853, GS Papers.

43 *FDP*, March 2 and 16, 1855; *FDP*, January 7, 1859. On Douglass's disputes with Brown, see Ezra Greenspan, *William Wells Brown: An African American Life* (New York: Norton, 2014), 317–20.

44 *Liberator*, September 16 and 23, and November 18, 1853; reprinted in *FDP*, December 9, 1853.

45 From *Liberator*, November 18, 1853, reprinted in *FDP*, December 9, 1853; *NASS*, September 24, 1853; Oliver Johnson to Garrison, December 10, 1853, quoted in Foner, *Life and Writings*, 2:59.

46 *Liberator*, December 16, 1853; *FDP*, January 7, 1853, and December 9, 1853. The book sold for seventy-five cents. Julia Griffiths, ed., *Autographs for Freedom* (Boston: Jewett and Company, 1853); Julia Griffiths, ed., *Autographs for Freedom* (Rochester: Wanzer, Beardsley, and Company, 1854), copies in Beinecke Library, Yale University. The array of writers in the two volumes included, among others, William H. Seward, Harriet Beecher Stowe, John Greenleaf Whittier, Charles Sumner, Horace Greeley, James Birney, Joshua Giddings, Theodore Parker, and, in volume 2, none other than Ralph Waldo Emerson, weighing in with a poem, "Freedom." On Douglass's pride in Julia's role in the Ladies' Anti-Slavery Society of Rochester, see Douglass to Gerrit Smith, September 3, 1851, GS Papers.

47 Robert Purvis to Garrison, *Liberator*, September 16, 1853; William Cooper Nell to Amy Post, August or September, n.d., 1853; August 12, 1853; December 10, 1853; December 20, 1853; January 20, 1854; Post Family Papers, Rare Books and Special Collections, University of Rochester Library.

48 *FDP*, December 9, 1853.

49 Ibid.

50 Ibid.

51 Ibid.

52 Garrison to Harriet Beecher Stowe, November 30, 1853, in *Letters of WLG*, 4:280–86; Stowe to Garrison, December 19, 1853, in *Life and Letters of Harriet Beecher Stowe*, ed. Annie Fields (London: Sampson Low, Marston and Company, 1898), 214–15, copy in Rare Book Room, Cambridge University Library, UK. On the Stowe meetings, see McFeely, *Frederick Douglass*, 178.

Chapter 13: By the Rivers of Babylon

1 Douglass, "What to the Slave Is the Fourth of July," speech delivered July 5, 1852, Rochester, NY, *Douglass Papers*, ser. 1, 2:368; Robert P. Carroll, *Jeremiah: A Commentary* (London: SCM Press, 1986), 33–35, 497–508; R. N. Whybray, *The Second Isaiah* (London: T & T Clark International, 1988), 8–12, 20–41. In 587 BC the kingdom of Judah, the surviving part of the once-larger kingdom of Israel, fell disastrously to the military power of the Neo-Babylonian Empire. As Jeremiah and Ezekiel had predicted, their capital, Jerusalem, and its great temple were laid waste. The survivors were deported to Babylonia, in ancient Mesopotamia between the Tigris and Euphrates Rivers. See Christine Hayes, *Introduction to the Bible* (New Haven, CT: Yale University Press, 2012), 1–14, 298–314.

2 Robert Alter, *The Art of Biblical Narrative* (1981; repr., New York: Basic Books, 2011), 25–54; Heschel, *Prophets*, 12; Whybray, *Second Isaiah*, 20; Isaiah 38:1; Jeremiah 2:2, 1:9. On black Jeremiahs and uses of the Jeremiadic tradition by Douglass, see David Howard-Pitney, *The African American Jeremiad: Appeals for Justice in America* (Philadelphia: Temple University Press, 2005), 1–52; and Wilson J. Moses, *Black Messiahs and Uncle Toms: Social and Literary Manipulations of a Religious Myth* (University Park: Penn State University Press, 1982), 30–66.

3 Douglass to Mrs. S. D. Porter, president, Ladies' Anti-Slavery Society of Rochester, March 27, 1852, in Foner, *Life and Writings*, 2:175–76; *FDP*, January 19, 1855 (this announcement included Theodore Parker, Ralph Waldo Emerson, and Henry Ward Beecher); Douglass to Gerrit Smith, July 7, 1852, GS Papers; *FDP*, July 1, 9, and 16, 1852. For the Fifth of July tradition, see Mitch Kachun, *Festivals of Freedom: Memory and Meaning in African American Emancipation Celebrations, 1808–1915* (Amherst: University of Massachusetts Press, 2003), 42–53.

4 *FDP*, July 1 and 9, 1852. On eyewitness accounts of Douglass's nervousness and trembling hands when beginning a speech, see *Douglass Papers*, ser. 1, vol. 1, intro., xxx.

5 "What to the Slave Is the Fourth of July," 2:359–60.

6 "Do Not Send Back the Fugitive," address in Boston, October 14, 1850, *Douglass Papers*, ser. 1, 2:247; *FDP*, June 17 and 24, 1852.

7 "What to the Slave Is the Fourth of July," 2:360–64; and see James A. Colaiaco, *Frederick Douglass and the Fourth of July* (New York: Palgrave, 2006), 33–43.

8 "What to the Slave Is the Fourth of July," 2:365–66.

9 Ibid., 2:366–67.

10 Ibid., 2:366–68; Psalm 137:1–6; and see Jeremiah 9:19: "For a voice of wailing is heard out

of Zion. How are we spoiled!" On Douglass's use of Hebrew prophets in this speech, see Dilbeck, *Frederick Douglass*, 85–89.

11 "What to the Slave Is the Fourth of July," 2:369–71. On Douglass's approach in this moment of the speech and his advocacy of natural rights more broadly, see Peter C. Myers, *Frederick Douglass: Race and the Rebirth of American Liberalism* (Lawrence: University of Kansas Press, 2008), 49–56.

12 "What to the Slave Is the Fourth of July," 2:371–74.

13 Ibid., 2:375–78; Matthew 23:23.

14 Isaiah 1:13–17.

15 "What to the Slave Is the Fourth of July," 2:387–88.

16 Ibid., 2:383–87; and see Colaiaco, *Douglass and the Fourth of July*, 57–71; Isaiah 59:1. The full text reads, "Behold, the Lord's hand is not shortened, that it cannot save; neither his ear heavy, that it cannot hear." On Douglass's embrace of the antislavery interpretation of the Constitution in the context of this speech, see Colaiaco, *Frederick Douglass and the Fourth of July*, 73–107; and Dilbeck, *Frederick Douglass*, 76–80.

17 Psalm 68:31; Garrison, "The Triumph of Freedom," *Liberator*, January 10, 1845; *FDP*, July 9, 1852.

18 August Meier, introduction to Benjamin Quarles, *Black Mosaic: Essays in Afro-American History and Historiography* (Amherst: University of Massachusetts Press, 1988), 4–6; also see Myers, *Frederick Douglass*, 47–49; and Blight, *Frederick Douglass' Civil War*, 1–25.

19 Jeremiah 20:9; James Darsey, *The Prophetic Tradition and Radical Rhetoric in America* (New York: NYU Press, 1997), 16–18, 20–22, 27–28; Heschel, *Prophets*, 16, 22. Darsey makes the case that American abolitionists especially fit these patterns and forms; see 61–84. Also see Claus Westermann, *Basic Forms of Prophetic Speech*, trans. Hugh Clayton White (Philadelphia: Westminster Press, 1967); and Lundbom, *Hebrew Prophets*, 7–36.

20 Bercovitch, *American Jeremiad*, 141–42; Jeremiah 8:22, 31:17; Michael Walzer, *Exodus and Revolution* (New York: Basic Books, 1985), 17.

21 Douglass to Gerrit Smith, January 21, 1851, GS Papers; "Slavery and the Slave Power," address in Rochester, December 1, 1850, *Douglass Papers*, ser. 1, 2:249–50.

22 Douglass's first encounter with colonization in print was "Great Anti-Colonization Meeting in New York," *Liberator*, February 1, 1839, one of the first issues of that paper he read. "Persecution on Account of Faith, Persecution on Account of Color," speech in Corinthian Hall, Rochester, January 26, 1851; "Henry Clay and Colonization Cant, Sophistry, and Falsehood," speech in Corinthian Hall, February 2, 1851; *Douglass Papers*, ser. 1, 2:301, 310–13, 318; "Horace Greeley and Colonization," *FDP*, February 26, 1852; "The Present Condition and Future Prospect of the Negro People," speech at the annual meeting of American and Foreign Anti-Slavery Society, New York, May 1853, in Foner, *Life and Writings*, 2:250; "Horace Greeley and the People of Color," *FDP*, January 29, 1852. For Satan turning into an "angel of light," Douglass drew from 2 Corinthians 11:14.

23 "Henry Clay and Colonization Cant," 2:314. For Douglass's assertion that he was mustering "evidence," see 319–20. See Exodus 1:10–13.

24 "Persecution on Account of Faith," 2:307–10.

25 *Life and Times*, 279–80; "Do Not Send Back the Fugitive," speech in Boston, October 14, 1850, *Douglass Papers*, ser. 1, 2:246–48.

26 "Resistance to Blood-Houndism," address at a New York State anti–Fugitive Slave Bill convention, January 8, 1851; and "Slavery's Northern Bulwarks," speech in Rochester, January 12, 1851; *Douglass Papers*, ser. 1, 2:275–77, 280–82.

27 Isaiah 2:4; Jeremiah 51:7. And see Heschel, *Prophets*, 159–68.

28 "Henry Clay and Colonization Cant," 2:315–17; *FDP*, October 2, 1851. And see Jane H.

Pease and William H. Pease, *They Who Would Be Free: Blacks' Search for Freedom, 1830–1861* (New York: Atheneum, 1974), 206–16.

29 *Liberator*, October 10, 1851; *FDP*, April 8, 1852 and February 4, 1853; and see Pease and Pease, *They Who Would be Free*, 219–25.

30 Thomas P. Slaughter, *Bloody Dawn: The Christiana Riot and Racial Violence in the Antebellum North* (New York: Oxford University Press, 1991), 43–93; *FDP*, September 25, 1851. And see the memoir by William Parker, "The Freedman's Story," *Atlantic Monthly* 18 (February–March 1866): 154–57, 160–66.

31 Douglass to Samuel D. Porter, Rochester, September 1851, *Douglass Papers*, ser. 3, 1:489; Julia Griffiths to Gerrit Smith, September 24, 1851, GS Papers; *Life and Times*, 280–82; and also see Coles, *Cradle of Freedom*, 140–42, 161. Coles embellishes the story with hyperdramatic prose and a claim that Douglass had dressed the fugitives as women.

32 Parker, "Freedman's Story," 290–92; and see Slaughter, *Bloody Dawn*, 78–79.

33 *FDP*, September 25, 1851.

34 Ibid. Douglass continued to follow and comment on the indictments and the trial for the Christiana case, as well as to monitor the fate of Parker and his comrades in Canada. See *FDP*, October 23, and November 13, 1851, and June 24, 1852.

35 "The Fugitive Slave Law," speech at the National Free Soil Convention, Pittsburgh, August 11, 1852, in Foner, *Life and Writings*, 2:206–7; *FDP*, February 26, 1852.

36 "Is It Right and Wise to Kill a Kidnapper?," *FDP*, June 2, 1854. On Douglass's changing views on violence within his conception of reform, see Martin, *Mind of Frederick Douglass*, 166–68.

37 Martin, *Mind of Frederick Douglass*, 166–68. I have drawn on the discussion of Douglass's philosophical quandary on violence in Frank M. Kirkland, "Enslavement, Moral Suasion, and Struggles for Recognition: Frederick Douglass's Answer to the Question—'What Is Enlightenment?,'" in Lawson and Kirkland, *Frederick Douglass*, 279–94.

38 Isaiah 57:20–21, and also 48:22. "No Peace for the Slaveholder," address in New York, May 11, 1853; and "God's Law Outlawed," speech in Manchester, NH, January 24, 1854; *Douglass Papers*, ser. 1, 2:421–23, 435, 457. And on the redemptive power of violence, see Frantz Fanon, *The Wretched of the Earth*, trans. Richard Philcox (1961; repr., New York: Grove Press, 2004).

39 *FDP*, March 4, 1853.

40 *FDP*, March 11, 1853; Celeste-Marie Bernier, "Dusky Powder Magazines: The Creole Revolt (1841) in Nineteenth Century American Literature" (PhD diss., University of Nottingham, UK, 2002), 1–33; Robert B. Stepto, "Storytelling in Early Afro-American Fiction: Frederick Douglass's 'The Heroic Slave,'" in Andrews, *Critical Essays*, 108–10. On the six speeches in which Douglass addressed Madison Washington's story, see Bernier, "Dusky Powder Magazines," ch. 2, 34–81; Douglass, "Slavery: The Slumbering Volcano," address in New York, April 23, 1849, *Douglass Papers*, ser. 1, 2:154–58.

41 Shelley Fisher Fishkin and Carla L. Peterson, "'We Hold These Truths to Be Self-Evident': The Rhetoric of Frederick Douglass's Journalism," in Sundquist, *Frederick Douglass*, 198–99; Stepto, "Storytelling in Early Afro-American Fiction," 110–11. On Douglass giving Washington a "voice," see William L. Andrews, "The Heroic Slave," headnote to reprint of the novella, in *The Oxford Frederick Douglass Reader*, ed. William L. Andrews (New York: Oxford University Press, 1996), 131.

42 Levine, *Delany, Douglass*, 83–85. Douglass's ambivalence about *Uncle Tom's Cabin* especially aimed at Stowe's use of ideas about mulatto temperament, colonization, and Christian pacifism.

43 Eric J. Sundquist, *To Wake the Nations: Race in the Making of American Literature* (Cambridge, MA: Harvard University Press, 1993), 105; and see Stepto, "Storytelling in Early Afro-American Fiction, 111–12.

44 "The Heroic Slave," 133–35. On Listwell, see Fisher Fishkin and Peterson, " 'We Hold These Truths to be Self-Evident,' " 199–200.

45 "The Heroic Slave," 142–53, 157–63. On Douglass and masculinity in the story, see Richard Yarborough, "Race, Violence and Manhood: The Masculine Ideal in Frederick Douglass's 'The Heroic Slave,' " in Sundquist, *Frederick Douglass*, 168–70.

Chapter 14: My Voice, My Pen, or My Vote

1 Douglass to Gerrit Smith, November 6, 1852, GS Papers.

2 "The Anti-Slavery Movement," lecture, Rochester, January 1855, in Foner, *Life and Writings*, 2:333, 351–52. On Douglass's emerging politics see Blight, *Frederick Douglass' Civil War*, 26–58; and Oakes, *Radical and the Republican*, 3–38, 87–132. On the Liberty Party, see Bruce Laurie, *Beyond Garrison: Antislavery and Social Reform* (Cambridge, UK: Cambridge University Press, 2005, 10–11, 57–59, 65–74, 135–40.

3 The first three chapter titles of *Bondage and Freedom* begin with "The Author. . . ." On sales, see C. Peter Ripley, "The Autobiographical Writings of Frederick Douglass," *Southern Studies: An Interdisciplinary Journal of the South* 24 (Spring 1985): 17. For the anecdote about Douglass's son selling the book at lectures, see John David Smith, introduction, *My Bondage and My Freedom* (New York: Penguin, 2003), xlv; *FDP*, August 17, 1855.

4 The prefatory letter is dated July 2, 1855, *Bondage and Freedom*, 6–7.

5 See Robert S. Levine, "Identity in the Autobiographies," in Lee, *Cambridge Companion to Frederick Douglass*, 36–39; Levine, *Delany, Douglass*, 99–102, 112–20; and Andrews, *To Tell a Free Story*, 214–39.

6 Stauffer, *Works of James McCune Smith*, xix–xxi.

7 Ibid., xxi–xxxiii; *FDP*, January 12 and February 9, 1855; Pease and Pease, *They Who Would be Free*, 140–42, 153–55; Stauffer, *Black Hearts of Men*, 160–61.

8 Blight, "In Search of Learning," 7–26; Stauffer, *Black Hearts of Men*, 186; Stauffer, *Works of James McCune Smith*, xxviii–xxxiv, 187–89; *FDP*, May 27, 1853.

9 *FDP*, June 3 and November 18, 1853; McCune Smith to Gerrit Smith, July 20, 1848, in Stauffer, *Works of James McCune Smith*, 312. On the dedication, see Douglass to Gerrit Smith, August 14, 1855, GS Papers. Douglass responds to Smith's grateful acknowledgment of the dedication, and yet another draft of $50, by saying that he wished "to couple my poor name with the name I love and honor."

10 *Bondage and Freedom*, 10–11.

11 Ibid., 18–19, 21, 25.

12 Ibid., 10–13.

13 Ibid., 20–22.

14 Ibid., 20–24. Robert Alter, *Pen of Iron: American Prose and the King James Bible* (Princeton, NJ: Princeton University Press, 2010), 2, 4, 19, 40–41. And see Mark A. Noll, "The United States as a Biblical Nation," in *The Bible in America*, ed. Nathan O. Hatch and Mark A. Noll (New York: Oxford University Press, 1982), 45; and George P. Landow, *Elegant Jeremiahs: The Sage from Carlyle to Mailer* (Ithaca, NY: Cornell University Press, 1986), 17–40. On the "Americanization" of Christian theology, see Mark A. Noll, *America's God: From Jonathan Edwards to Abraham Lincoln* (New York: Oxford, 2002), 227–364.

15 *Bondage and Freedom*, 84; Jeremiah 49:23; Isaiah 57:20.

16 *Bondage and Freedom*, 22, 24. On autobiography and loss, see James Olney, *Metaphors of Self: The Meaning of Autobiography* (Princeton, NJ: Princeton University Press, 1972); James Olney, ed., *Autobiography: Essays Theoretical and Critical* (Princeton, NJ: Princeton University Press, 1980); and David W. Blight, "Several Lives in One: Frederick Douglass's

Autobiographical Art," in *Beyond the Battlefield: Race, Memory, and the American Civil War* (Amherst: University of Massachusetts Press, 2002), 11–27.

17 *Bondage and Freedom*, 14; *New York Tribune* in *FDP*, March 31, 1854; *FDP*, October 27 and November 3, 1854; *Congressional Globe*, 36th Cong., 1st sess., 1859–60, 29, pt. 1, 239–40. I am grateful to Josh Lynn for these references to the two Douglasses, and to his unpublished paper, "The Black Douglass and the White Douglas: Frederick, Stephen, and the Embodiment of Racial Citizenship."

18 *Bondage and Freedom*, 146–47; *Narrative*, 78–79. See the remarkably sympathetic letter from John Mannoss to Douglass, Hillsdale, Michigan, January 14, 1856, FD Papers (LC).

19 *Narrative*, 79–89; *Bondage and Freedom*, 165–69; Matthew 23:4, 13–15.

20 *Bondage and Freedom*, 150–51, 154–55, 162–63, 179.

21 Ibid., 177–80, 215. See Levine, "Identity in the Autobiographies," 38–39; and "Is It Right and Wise to Kill a Kidnapper?," *FDP*, June 2, 1854.

22 "Poets to Come," in *The Portable Walt Whitman* (New York: Penguin, 1945), 182; *Bondage and Freedom*, 266.

23 *Bondage and Freedom*, 277–86, 292.

24 Ibid., 291, 298.

25 *Life and Times*, 329.

26 "Notes by the Way," *FDP*, March 30, 1855.

27 Douglass to Gerrit Smith, May 23, 1856, GS Papers.

28 Griffiths to Gerrit Smith, September 9 (no year), GS Papers.

29 Griffiths, "Letters from the Old World," no. 1, *FDP*, August 10, 1855; no. 22, *FDP*, July 4, 1856. See Meer, "Public and Personal Letters," 251–64.

30 Diedrich, *Love across Color Lines*, 131–42; Christoph Lohmann, ed., *Radical Passion: Ottilie Assing's Reports from America and Letters to Frederick Douglass* (New York: Peter Lang, 1999), xii–xx; McFeely, *Frederick Douglass*, 183–85; Stauffer, *Black Hearts of Men*, 230–31. The full title of the German journal was *Morgenblatt für Gebildete Leser* (Morning Journal for Educated Readers), edited by Johann Friedrich Cotta. The German edition of *Bondage and Freedom* was *Sklaverei und Freiheit: Autobiographie von Frederick Douglass* (Hamburg: Hoffman and Campe, 1860).

31 Douglass to Mrs. Lydia Dennett, April 17, 1857, in Foner, *Frederick Douglass on Women's Rights*, 21–22; and see Diedrich, *Love Across Color Lines*, 176–85. On Douglass's need for a sense of "home," see Andrews, *To Tell a Free Story*, 218–20, 230–35.

32 "The Fugitive Slave Law," speech delivered at the National Free Soil Convention, Pittsburgh, August 11, 1852, in Foner, *Life and Writings*, 2:206–9; Sewell, *Ballots for Freedom*, 245–47.

33 *FDP*, July 30, August 13, September 10, and October 1, 1852.

34 *FDP*, September 3 and 17, and October 1 and 29, 1852.

35 *FDP*, September 17, and October 15 and 22, 1852; Proverbs 14:34; 14:8, 18; 11:23; 13:16.

36 *FDP*, September 10, 1852.

37 Douglass to Gerrit Smith, November 6, 1852, GS Papers; *FDP*, May 26, 1854. For the reactions of political abolitionists to the Kansas-Nebraska Act, see Sewell, *Ballots for Freedom*, 254–66; Foner, *Free Soil, Free Labor*, 93–95; and William E. Gienapp, *The Origins of the Republican Party, 1852–1856* (New York: Oxford, 1987), 72–87.

38 *FDP*, November 16, 1855. On Seward's "Irrepressible Conflict" speech of 1858, see Foner, *Free Soil, Free Labor*, 69–70; and for Republicans' ideas about the inevitability of slavery's demise, see James Oakes, *Freedom National: The Destruction of Slavery in the United States, 1861–1865* (New York: Norton, 2013), 29–34.

39 "Present Condition and Future Prospect"; "The Kansas-Nebraska Bill," speech in Metro-

politan Hall, Chicago, October 30, 1854; both in Foner, *Life and Writings*, 2:245–48, 323. On the Slave Power concept, see Leonard L. Richards, *The Slave Power: The Free North and Southern Domination, 1780–1860* (Baton Rouge: LSU Press, 2000), 1–27; Sewell, *Ballots for Freedom*, 86–89, 102–6, 257–60.

40　"Present Condition and Future Prospect," 2:247; *FDP*, February 24, 1854; "Slavery Rules Everything," *FDP*, August 24, 1855.

41　*Life and Times*, 292–302. See Richards, *Slave Power*, 16–27.

42　*FDP*, April 5, 1856; *FDP*, September 28, 1855. Douglass got Greeley's attention; see exchange, *FDP*, October 5 and 12, 1855.

43　*FDP*, July 27, 1855.

44　*FDP*, August 24 and December 7, 1855. On the "cordon" concept, see Oakes, *Freedom National*, 256–300.

45　*FDP*, April 25, 1856.

46　"Kansas-Nebraska Bill," 320; *FDP*, September 15, 1854. On free-labor ideology, see Foner, *Free Soil, Free Labor*, 9–39.

47　*FDP*, April 25, June 20, and August 15, 1856.

48　*FDP*, August 15 and September 12, 1856.

49　Douglass to Gerrit Smith, August 31, 1856, GS Papers; *FDP*, November 13, 1857.

50　https://supreme.justia.com/cases/federal/us/60/393/case.html, *Dred Scott v. Sandford*; the court clerk misspelled the owner's name, Sanford. See Richard H. Sewell, *A House Divided: Sectionalism and the Civil War, 1848–1865* (Baltimore: Johns Hopkins University Press, 1988), 56–59.

51　See Sewell, *Ballots for Freedom*, 299–300.

52　"The Dred Scott Decision," address delivered at the Anniversary of the American Abolition Society, New York, May 14, 1857, mss., FD Papers (LC).

53　Ibid.

54　Ibid. On Douglass and millennialism, see Blight, *Frederick Douglass' Civil War*, 8–12, 73–78, 102–3; and Maurice O. Wallace, "Violence, Manhood, and War in Douglass," in Lee, *Cambridge Companion to Frederick Douglass*, 73–86.

55　"Dred Scott Decision"; the complete poem, with twenty-nine stanzas, appears in *FDP*, January 16, 1857. On "The Tyrant's Jubilee," see William Gleason, "Volcanoes and Meteors: Douglass, Melville, and the Poetics of Insurrection," in Levine and Otter, *Frederick Douglass and Herman Melville*, 110–33. On Brown in Rochester, see *Life and Times*, 314–16.

Chapter 15: John Brown Could Die for the Slave

1　*Life and Times*, 271. The exact timing of this first meeting remains ambiguous. Brown biographers contain slightly different accounts. Given the evidence from Douglass's own reporting, they met in either late 1847 or early 1848 the first time, and they definitely met again in Springfield in October or November of 1848. *North Star*, February 11, November 17, November 24, and December 8, 1848. See Oswald Garrison Villard, *John Brown, 1800–1859, a Biography Fifty Years After* (Boston: Houghton Mifflin, 1910), 57–58; David S. Reynolds, *John Brown, Abolitionist: The Man Who Killed Slavery, Sparked the Civil War, and Seeded Civil Rights* (New York: Knopf, 2005), 103–104; Stauffer, *Black Hearts of Men*, 172–73; Quarles, *Frederick Douglass*, 170–71; Tony Horwitz, *Midnight Rising: John Brown and the Raid That Sparked the Civil War* (New York: Henry Holt, 2011), 30–31.

2　*Springfield Republican*, quoted in *North Star*, February 11 and 18, 1848.

3　*Life and Times*, 271–73. On the interpretations of Brown over time, including Brown's own self-fashioning, see R. Blakeslee Gilpin, *John Brown Lives! America's Long Reckoning with*

Violence, Equality, and Change (Chapel Hill: University of North Carolina Press, 2011), 12, 17–31; Bertram Wyatt-Brown, " 'A Volcano beneath a Mountain of Snow': John Brown and the Problem of Interpretation," in *His Soul Goes Marching On: Responses to John Brown and the Harpers Ferry Raid,* ed. Paul Finkelman (Charlottesville: University of Virginia Press, 1995), 10–38; and Louis A. DeCaro, "The John Browns of History," in *John Brown: The Man Who Lived, Essays in Honor of the Harpers Ferry Raid Sesquicentennial 1859–2009* (New York: Lulu, 2009), 3–30.

4 Horwitz, *Midnight Rising,* 9–19; John Brown to Simon Perkins, August 15, 1849, in *A John Brown Reader, the Making of a Revolutionary: The Story of John Brown in His Own Words and in the Words of Those Who Knew Him,* ed. Louis Ruchames (1969; repr., New York: Grosset & Dunlap, 1975), 68–69. Brown, $13,000 in debt at the time, took passage to England in August 1849 to revive his woolens enterprise. See Stauffer, *Black Hearts of Men,* 172.

5 *Life and Times,* 273–75.

6 Ibid., 275; Brown to Mary Brown (wife), Boston, December 22, 1851; Brown to Douglass, Akron, OH, January 9, 1854; in Ruchames, *John Brown Reader,* 78–79, 84.

7 Brown to Douglass, January 9, 1854, 84–85; Deuteronomy 23:15; Matthew 7:12; Nehemiah 13:11, 17, 25, 30–31. See Robert E. McGlone, *John Brown's War Against Slavery* (Cambridge, UK: Cambridge University Press, 2009), 7–10, 80–82, 309–28.

8 *Life and Times,* 272. On millennialism, see James H. Moorhead, *American Apocalypse: Yankee Protestants and the Civil War, 1860–1869* (New Haven, CT: Yale University Press, 1978), 1–128; James H. Moorhead, "Between Progress and Apocalypse: A Reassessment of Millennialism in American Religious Thought, 1800–1880," *Journal of American History* 71 (December 1984), 524–42; Ernest Lee Tuveson, *Redeemer Nation: The Idea of America's Millennial Role* (Chicago: University of Chicago Press, 1968), 1–90, 187–214; and Edmund Wilson, *Patriotic Gore: Studies in the Literature of the American Civil War* (1962; repr., Boston: Northeastern University Press, 1984), 91–106.

9 Salmon Brown, "Reminiscences," 1913, in *Meteor of War: The John Brown Story,* ed. Zoe Trodd and John Stauffer (Maplecrest, NY: Brandywine Press, 2004), 68. On Brown's religious faith and how it changed toward perfectionist, millennial Calvinism, see Stauffer, *Black Hearts of Men,* 120–23.

10 Brown to "Dear children," Troy, NY, January 23, 1852; Brown to John Jr., Akron, OH, August 26, 1853; in Ruchames, *John Brown Reader,* 79–80, 82–83; Joshua 24:15; Deuteronomy 29:18; Judges 2:19; Samuel 15:22. On John Jr. and his mental instability, see Horwitz, *Midnight Rising,* 56, 205.

11 Charles R. Douglass to Douglass, March 20, 1860, FD Papers (LC).

12 "West Indian Emancipation," speech delivered at Canandaigua, NY, August 4, 1857, *Douglass Papers,* ser. 1, 3:204; McCune Smith, introduction, *Bondage and Freedom,* 18–19.

13 "The Final Struggle," *FDP,* November 16, 1855, in Foner, *Life and Writings,* 2:377–78.

14 "West Indian Emancipation," 190, and headnote, 183, for more than one thousand attendance.

15 Douglass to secretary of the Edinburgh New Antislavery Society, July 9, 1857, FD Papers (LC). Italics added by author.

16 "West Indian Emancipation," 194–96; Isaiah 58:1–7.

17 McCune Smith in *FDP,* August 8, 1856; "West Indian Emancipation," 200–201, 204–8; *Childe Harold's Pilgrimage,* canto 2, in *Lord Byron's Selected Poems,* ed. Susan J. Wolfson (New York: Penguin, 1996), 120–21.

18 Typical of such sentiments at the time of Brown's execution was that expressed by Charles Langston of Ohio, a black abolitionist who had been a leader of the Oberlin-Wellington

rescue of fugitive slaves a year earlier. "I never thought that I should ever join in doing honor to or mourning for any American *white* man," wrote Langston on December 2, 1859, the day of Brown's hanging. In Brown the dead hero he found "a lover of mankind—not of any particular class or color, but of all men." See Charles Langston, "Speech in Cleveland," December 2, 1859, in *The Tribunal: Responses to John Brown and the Harpers Ferry Raid*, ed. John Stauffer and Zoe Trodd (Cambridge, MA: Harvard University Press, 2012), 131–32.

19 John Brown, "Sambo's Mistakes," 1848, in Stauffer and Trodd, *Tribunal*, 3–6. And see Stauffer, *Black Hearts of Men*, 172–73. The *Ram's Horn* editor was Willis Hodges, a friend of Brown's and later a neighbor in the settlements at Timbucto.

20 Lecture "West Indian Emancipation," Canandaigua, NY, August 3, 1857, *Douglass Papers*, ser. 1, 3:200–201; Smith as "Communipaw," *FDP*, September 21, 1855; Benjamin Quarles, *Allies for Freedom: Blacks on John Brown* (New York: Da Capo Press, 1974), 22–25; Horwitz, *Midnight Rising*, 32–34. On "Gerrit Smith's Land" in the North Elba region, see Douglass's report as well as John Brown's survey, in *North Star*, December 8, 1848.

21 "Self-Elevation," *FDP*, April 13, 1855; "West Indian Emancipation," 201.

22 "These Questions Cannot Be Answered by the White Race," address in New York, May 11, 1855, *Douglass Papers*, ser. 1, 3:86–89.

23 Ibid., 90. Charles Lenox Remond spoke after Douglass with a decidedly Garrisonian dissenting opinion.

24 "Citizenship and the Spirit of Caste," address in New York, May 11, 1858, in *Douglass Papers*, ser. 1, 3:209–12.

25 Diedrich, *Love across Color Lines*, 125–29; Lohmann, *Radical Passion*, xvii–xix. Diedrich portrays Assing as constantly in quest of a black literary "protagonist" for the new narrative of America she sought to discover and write. In Douglass, Diedrich argues, she found such an ideal.

26 Assing, preface to the German translation of *Bondage and Freedom*, in Lohmann, *Radical Passion*, 68–69. And see McFeely, *Frederick Douglass*, 183–85; and Diedrich, *Love across Color Lines*, 131–36. Diedrich invents a fictional dialogue between Assing and Douglass as a scene-setting way of narrating the first meeting.

27 Assing, preface, in Lohmann, *Radical Passion*, 69. Douglass gave his approval to the German edition of *Bondage and Freedom*.

28 Stauffer, *Black Hearts of Men*, 8–11; John Brown to John Jr., August 21, 1854, in Trodd and Stauffer, *Meteor of War*, 80; John Jr. to John Brown, May 20, 1855, quoted in Horwitz, *Midnight Rising*, 41.

29 *FDP*, July 6, 1855.

30 *FDP*, July 6 and July 20, 1855.

31 Horwitz, *Midnight Rising*, 43–45; Villard, *John Brown*, 87–90.

32 Horwitz, *Midnight Rising*, 47–55; McGlone, *John Brown's War Against Slavery*, 114–42. For the context of violence in Kansas, see Reynolds, *John Brown, Abolitionist*, 140–78. Reynolds finds Brown's crimes at Pottawatomie "explainable" by use of Doris Lessing's notion of "good terrorism," by which is meant "terrorism justified by obvious social injustice." Reynolds's spacious definition allows that Brown modeled insurrectionary slaves, justified in killing their oppressive masters.

33 Quarles, *Allies for Freedom*, 38; Reynolds, *John Brown, Abolitionist*, 9, 100–101, 105–9; *Life and Times*, 302–3.

34 Quarles, *Allies for Freedom*, 38–39; "Old Brown's Farewell to the Plymouth Rocks, Bunker Hill Monuments, Charter Oaks, and Uncle Thoms Cabbins," April 1857; and "To the Friends of Freedom," March 1857, in *New York Tribune*, March 4, 1857; in Ruchames, *John*

Brown Reader, 102, 106. On "Secret Six," see Jeffrey Rossbach, *Ambivalent Conspirators: John Brown, the Secret Six, and a Theory of Slave Violence* (Philadelphia: University of Pennsylvania Press, 1982), 1–120.

35 *Life and Times*, 314–15; Brown to "My Dear Wife and Children, Every One," January 30, 1858; and Brown to Higginson, February 12, 1858; in Ruchames, *John Brown Reader*, 109–11. On the at least four meetings between Douglass and Brown in Rochester, see *Douglass Papers*, ser. 2, vol. 3, Historical Annotations for *Life and Times*, 824–25.

36 "Provisional Constitution and Ordinances of the People of the United States, May 8, 1858," in Trodd and Stauffer, *Meteor of War*, 109–20; Horwitz, *Midnight Rising*, 80–84.

37 *Life and Times*, 315–16; Quarles, *Frederick Douglass*, 173; Brown to John Jr., February 4, 1858, quoted in Quarles, *Allies for Freedom*, 39.

38 Quarles, *Allies for Freedom*, 39–40; Horwitz, *Midnight Rising*, 66–69.

39 Quarles, *Allies for Freedom*, 41; Brown to "My Dear Wife and Children, Every One," January 30, 1858, in Ruchames, *John Brown Reader*, 110.

40 Quarles, *Frederick Douglass*, 174–76; *Life and Times*, 316–17; Quarles, *Allies for Freedom*, 52. On Forbes, see Horwitz, *Midnight Rising*, 70–72.

41 On the Forbes postponement, especially the crucial involvement of the Secret Six in demanding it, see Rossbach, *Ambivalent Conspirators*, 160–81; John Brown to *New York Tribune*, Trading Post, Kansas, January 1859, in Ruchames, *John Brown Reader*, 114–15. On Brown back in Kansas in 1858–59 and the Missouri rescue, see Quarles, *Allies for Freedom*, 53–59; Horwitz, *Midnight Rising*, 88–90; and Reynolds, *John Brown, Abolitionist*, 277–84.

42 Luke 2:29–30; Quarles, *Allies for Freedom*, 60.

43 Quarles, *Allies for Freedom*, 60–61; Rosetta Douglass to Douglass, February 2, 1859, FD Papers (LC); *FDP*, April 15, 1859.

44 John Brown Jr. to John Kagi, August 11, 1859, in Quarles, *Frederick Douglass*, 176–77; *Life and Times*, 317–18.

45 *Life and Times*, 318–19.

46 Ibid., 319–20; Horwitz, *Midnight Rising*, 264–66.

47 "Our Recent Western Tour," *Douglass' Monthly* (hereafter *DM*), April 1859; "1859: The New Year," *DM*, February 1859. For speaking itineraries, see *Douglass Papers*, ser. 1, 3:xxix–xxx. For McCune Smith's editorship, *DM*, March 1859. For appeals for payment from subscribers, see *FDP*, December 4, 1857; October 29 and December 31, 1858.

48 *FDP*, January 7, 1859.

49 *FDP*, January 7 and 14, 1859; on Haiti, see *FDP*, March 11, April 29, and May 6, 1859.

50 "African Civilization Society," *FDP*, February 1859; *FDP*, March 25, 1859; "The True Test," *DM*, July 1859; "Progress of Slavery," *DM*, August 1859; "Non-Extension vs. Abolition of Slavery," *DM*, October 1859.

51 "The Ballot and the Bullet," *DM*, October 1859. On Douglass and the ambivalence between rhetorical and actual violence, see John H. Cook, "Fighting with Breath, Not Blows: Frederick Douglass and Antislavery Violence," in *Antislavery Violence: Sectional, Racial, and Cultural Conflict in Antebellum America*, ed. John R. McKivigan and Stanley Harrold (Knoxville: University of Tennessee Press, 1999), 138–63.

52 Horwitz, *Midnight Rising*, 291–92; *New York Herald*, October 18, 1859; *Frank Leslie's Illustrated Newspaper*, October 29, 1859; *Cincinnati Enquirer*, October 20, 1859; *Life and Times*, 307.

53 For Hurn interview, see James M. Gregory, *Frederick Douglass the Orator: Containing an Account of His Life; His Eminent Public Services . . .* (Springfield, MA: Willey & Co., 1893), 46–48; *Life and Times*, 308–9; Stauffer, Trodd, and Bernier, *Picturing Frederick Douglass*, 19.

54 Diedrich, *Love Across Color Lines*, 217–18. In McFeely, *Frederick Douglass*, 197–98, the au-

thor mistakenly adds one more piece of drama to Douglass's presence in Philadelphia. In *Life and Times*, Douglass (much later in the book than his coverage of the Harpers Ferry revelations) describes receiving a note following a speech at National Hall in Philadelphia, informing him that a Mrs. Amanda Auld Sears had been in the audience. She was the daughter of Douglass's former owners, Thomas and Lucretia Auld. Amanda and Frederick had not seen each other since childhood, and Douglass tells of their emotional reunion a full day after his speech, and of how Amanda had forgiven any harsh elements of the author's representations of her father. McFeely portrays Douglass as staying nearly two extra days in the city before fleeing for his life northward. Maria Diedrich, in *Love across Color Lines*, 216–17, picked up the story from McFeely and made it part of her narrative as well. Douglass spoke at National Hall, Philadelphia, at least two other times, January 14, 1862, and July 6, 1863. This first reunion with Amanda Sears could not have occurred in October of 1859, given how hurriedly Douglass fled the city. See *Life and Times*, 392–95; and *Douglass Papers*, ser. 2, vol. 3, Historical Annotations, 905–6.

55 *Life and Times*, 309–10. See letter, Henry A. Wise to "His Excellency James Buchanan, President of the United States, and to the Honorable Postmaster General of the United States," Richmond, November 13, 1859.

56 Douglass to Amy Post, October 27, 1859, Post Family Papers. The black leader John Sella Martin accused Douglass of failure to make good on his promises at Harpers Ferry in *Weekly Anglo-African*, October 29, 1859; and see Quarles, *Allies for Freedom*, 114–15.

57 Douglass to the *Rochester Democrat and American*, October 31, 1859, in Foner, *Life and Writings*, 2:460–63, also reprinted in *Toronto Daily Globe*, November 4, 1859; *Frank Leslie's Illustrated Newspaper*, November 12, 1859.

58 Douglass to the *Rochester Democrat and American*, October 31, 1859, 2:462–63.

59 "Capt. John Brown Not Insane," *FDP*, November 11, 1859; Brown to Franklin Sanborn, February 24, 1858, quoted in Horwitz, *Midnight Rising*, 239. Another of Brown's biblical self-identifications was with the apostle Paul and his imprisonment and death at the hands of the Romans. See McGlone, *John Brown's War against Slavery*, 323–24. For the "creative vocation" of martyrdom, see Wyatt-Brown, "Volcano beneath a Mountain of Snow," 33. For an effective treatment of how Brown had a kind of "second plan" to orchestrate his own symbolic death at Harpers Ferry, or by execution afterward, see Horwitz, *Midnight Rising*, 239–43. On the outpouring of poetry, song, and melodramatic plays in the wake of Brown's execution, see Reynolds, *John Brown, Abolitionist*, 436–77. On martyrdom, also see Charles Joyner, " 'Guilty of Holiest Crime': The Passion of John Brown," in Finkelman, *His Soul Goes Marching On*, 296–334.

60 "Capt. John Brown Not Insane."

61 *Life and Times*, 321–22; *Toronto Daily Globe*, November 9, 1859; letter aboard ship, in *FDP*, December 16, 1859.

Chapter 16: Secession: Taught by Events

1 Douglass to Samuel J. May, August 30, 1861, in Foner, *Life and Writings*, 3:159; *Life and Times*, 336. On Douglass and the idea of the "logic of events," see Blight, *Frederick Douglass' Civil War*, 107–9.

2 "1859—the New Year," *DM*, February 1859; for faith and sight expression, he drew from 2 Corinthians 5:7.

3 *New York Times*, December 19, 1859; Douglass, "The Present Condition of Slavery," address delivered in Bradford, England, January 6, 1860, *Douglass Papers*, ser. 1, 3:302–9.

4 "John Brown and the Slaveholders' Insurrection," address delivered in Edinburgh, Scot-

land, January 30, 1860, *Douglass Papers*, ser. 1, 3:316–17; "Reception Soiree to Mr. Frederick Douglass," *Glasgow Herald*, February 1, 1860, Mitchell Public Library, Glasgow, Scotland.

5 "To My American Readers and Friends," *DM*, November 1859.

6 Douglass to Amy Post, May 25, 1860, Post Family Papers, Rochester; *DM*, March and May, 1859; Pillsbury to Samuel J. May, quoted in Douglas, "Cherished Friendship," 269; and on H. O. Crofts, see *Report of the American Board of Commissioners for Foreign Missions*, annual meeting, Rochester, NY, September 1843 (Boston: Crocker & Brewster, 1843), 15. Crofts is reported that year living in Montreal.

7 *DM*, February 1859; Douglass quoted and membership statistics in Douglas, "Cherished Friendship," 270–71; Griffiths to Ladies' Anti-Slavery Society of Rochester, March 9, 1860, in *DM*, April 1860.

8 DeCaro, *John Brown: The Cost of Freedom* (New York: International Publishers, 2007), 64–69, 169n103; McFeely, *Frederick Douglass*, 195–96; Kagi letter, June 23, 1859, quoted in McGlone, *John Brown's War against Slavery*, 228–29; Katherine Mayo interview with Mrs. Russell, in Ruchames, *John Brown Reader*, 239. Anne Brown Adams (daughter) especially spread the rumor over time about Shields Green as a "substitute."

9 DeCaro, *John Brown: Cost of Freedom*, 67–68; Brown to "Brother Jeremiah," November 12, 1859, in Stauffer and Trodd, *Tribunal*, 61; Brown to wife, Mary, November 10, 1859, in Villard, *John Brown*, 540–41. On the song, see John Stauffer and Benjamin Soskis, *The Battle Hymn of the Republic: A Biography of the Song That Marches On* (New York: Oxford University Press, 2013), 3–72.

10 *Report of the Select Committee of the Senate Appointed to Inquire into the Late Invasion and Seizure of the Public Property at Harpers Ferry*, Committee no. 278, 36th Cong., 1st sess. (Washington, DC, 1860); Villard, *John Brown*, 580–83; Stephen B. Oates, *To Purge This Land with Blood: A Biography of John Brown* (New York: Harper & Row, 1970), 359–60.

11 *Report of the Select Committee*, 2–10, 21–25; McGlone, *John Brown's War against Slavery*, 237–39. On December 8, 1859, in the US Senate, Davis called Seward a "traitor" for his moral and personal support of Brown. See Trodd and Stauffer, *Meteor of War*, 260–61.

12 Douglass to Maria Webb, Halifax, England, November 30, 1859, Gilder Lehrman Collection, New-York Historical Society.

13 "John Brown and the Slaveowners' Insurrection," 3:322, 324.

14 "Progress and Divisions of Anti-Slavery," address delivered in Glasgow, Scotland, February 14, 1860, *Douglass Papers*, ser. 1, 3:326–30.

15 Glasgow Emancipation Society Minute Books, April 3, 1869, Smeal Collection, Mitchell Library, Glasgow, reel 1. Douglass borrowed from the American divine George Cheever. "British Racial Attitudes and Slavery," address delivered in Newcastle upon Tyne, England, February 23, 1860; "The American Constitution and the Slave," address delivered in Glasgow, Scotland, March 26, 1860; in *Douglass Papers*, ser. 1, 3:334–40, 351–65.

16 *Newcastle Daily Express*, February 21, 1860, in *DM*, April 1860; R. J. M. Blackett, "Cracks in the Antislavery Wall: Frederick Douglass's Second Visit to England (1859–1860) and the Coming of the Civil War," in Rice and Martin, *Liberating Sojourn*, 188–90, 192–93, 200–203.

17 *Life and Times*, 322–23; Diedrich, *Love across Color Lines*, 222–24.

18 Diedrich, *Love across Color Lines*, 220–23; Assing, "The Aftermath of John Brown's Trial" and "John Brown's Execution and Its Consequences," in Lohmann, *Radical Passion*, 170–80. On Douglass's efforts to secure a passport to go to France, see *Douglass Papers*, ser. 2, vol. 3, Historical Annotations, 842–43. The French consul at Newcastle did indeed issue Douglass a passport, as reported in the *Newcastle Courant*, February 3, 1860, but he did not use the opportunity.

19 Annie Douglass to Douglass, December 7, 1859; Rosetta Douglass to Douglass, December 6, 1859, FD Papers (LC); Rosetta Douglass to Aunt Harriet, April 20, 1860, Douglass Papers, unpublished mss., Indianapolis, quoted in McFeely, *Frederick Douglass*, 207; "Death of Little Annie Douglass," *DM*, April 1860.

20 Rosetta Douglass to Aunt Harriet, April 20, 1860; "To My British Anti-Slavery Friends," May 26, 1860, in *DM*, June 1860; Charles R. Douglass, "Some Incidents of the Home Life of Frederick Douglass," February 1917, Evans Collection.

21 "To My British Anti-Slavery Friends."

22 Diedrich, *Love across Color Lines*, 226–30; "Going to England Given Up," *DM*, September 1860; "Political Abolition Convention in Worcester," *DM*, November 1860.

23 Douglass to Elizabeth Cady Stanton, August 25, 1860, in Foner, *Life and Writings*, 2:497–98; "Seventh Annual Clam Bake," *DM*, December 1860.

24 "To My British Anti-Slavery Friends." On the issue of "politics and principles" regarding the Republican Party and the election of 1860, see Sewell, *Ballots for Freedom*, 343–65.

25 "The Chicago Nominations," *DM*, June 1860.

26 Douglass to Gerrit Smith, July 2, 1860, GS Papers; "The Republican Party," *DM*, August 1860; Sewell, *Ballots for Freedom*, 338.

27 Oakes, *Radical and the Republican*, 92; "The Presidential Campaign of 1860," speech at celebration of West Indian emancipation, August 1, 1860, Foner, *Life and Writings*, 2:506–7; "The Speech of Senator Sumner," *DM*, July 1860; *DM*, August 1860.

28 "Chicago Nominations." On denationalization and the Republicans, see Sewell, *Ballots for Freedom*, 304, 308–15; Oakes, *Freedom National*, xx–xxx.

29 "Republican Party." On nativists in the Republican Party, see Gienapp, *Origins of the Republican Party*, xx–xxx; and Sewell, *Ballots for Freedom*, 266–75.

30 "The Democratic Party" and "The Prospect in the Future," *DM*, August 1860.

31 "Prospect in the Future"; Genesis 4:3–34.

32 "Prospect in the Future."

33 "Presidential Campaign of 1860," 2:514–15. See Blight, *Frederick Douglass' Civil War*, 52–58.

34 On Myers and the suffrage campaign, see C. Peter Ripley et al., eds., *Black Abolitionist Papers* (Chapel Hill, NC: University of North Carolina Press, 1993), 4:326–30; Stauffer, *Works of James McCune Smith*, 182–83; Blight, *Frederick Douglass' Civil War*, 60–61; Quarles, *Frederick Douglass*, 166–67. And see Phyllis F. Field, *The Politics of Race in New York: The Struggle for Black Suffrage in the Civil War Era* (Ithaca, NY: Cornell University Press, 1982), 114–46.

35 "Republican Opposition to the Right of Suffrage," *DM*, October 1860.

36 "Equal Suffrage Defeated," *DM*, December 1860.

37 "The Late Election," *DM*, December 1860.

38 Ibid.; "Southern Thunder—Spirit of the Press," *DM*, December 1860. On Georgia's debate and divided vote in its secession convention, and the impulse among its Unionists toward "resistances short of secession," see William W. Freehling and Craig M. Simpson, eds., *Secession Debated: Georgia's Showdown in 1860* (New York: Oxford University Press, 1992), xviii–xxi.

39 On mob violence against abolitionists, see James M. McPherson, *Struggle for Equality: Abolitionists and the Negro in the Civil War and Reconstruction* (Princeton, NJ: Princeton University Press, 1964), 40–45.

40 "Legacy of John Brown," *Douglass Papers*, ser. 1, vol. 3, headnote, and 387–97. The editors recorded this event and the commentary from various newspapers, including *Boston Post*, December 4, 1860; *Boston Semi-Weekly Courier*, December 6, 1860; *Boston Daily Evening*

Transcript, December 3, 1860; *New York Tribune*, December 4 and 7, 1860; *Liberator*, December 7, 1860; *NASS*, December 8, 1860; and *DM*, January 1861.

41 "Legacy of John Brown," 3:399–400.

42 Ibid., 400–401, 405, 407; Exodus 31:18.

43 "Speech on John Brown," Boston, December 3, 1860, in Foner, *Life and Writings*, 2:533–37; *Douglass Papers*, ser. 1, vol. 3, headnote, 412–13.

44 "Dissolution of the American Union," *DM*, January 1861. On the early part of the secession winter and the "street festival" atmosphere of Charleston in South Carolina, see William L. Barney, "Rush to Disaster: Secession and the Slaves' Revenge," in Robert J. Cook, William L. Barney, and Elizabeth R. Varon, *Secession Winter: When the Union Fell Apart* (Baltimore: Johns Hopkins University Press, 2013), 30–31; and Steven A. Channing, *Crisis of Fear: Secession in South Carolina* (New York: Simon & Schuster, 1970), chs. 1–2.

45 "Dissolution of the American Union." An excellent and concise treatment of the nature and causes of secession is Charles B. Dew, *Apostles of Disunion: Southern Secession Commissioners and the Causes of the Civil War* (Charlottesville: University Press of Virginia, 2001), 1–21.

46 "The Union and How to Save It," *DM*, February 1860. For "drink the wine cup of wrath and fire," Douglass could be drawing from Luke 22:39–46, Psalm 75:8, or Matthew 26:39.

47 "Union and How to Save It"; Kenneth M. Stampp, *And the War Came: The North and the Secession Crisis, 1860–1861* (Baton Rouge: Louisiana State University Press, 1960), 13–14; David M. Potter, *The Impending Crisis, 1848–1861* (New York: Knopf, 1976), 524–28. And see Daniel W. Crofts, *Reluctant Confederates: Upper South Unionists in the Secession Crisis* (Chapel Hill: University of North Carolina Press, 1989); William W. Freehling, *The Road to Disunion*, vol. 2: *Secessionists Triumphant, 1854–1861* (New York: Oxford University Press, 2007); and Stephanie McCurry, *Confederate Reckoning: Power and Politics in the Civil War South* (Cambridge, MA: Harvard University Press, 2010).

48 Stampp, *And the War Came*, 21, 129–31.

49 Ibid., 130–47; Potter, *Impending Crisis*, 529–35.

50 "Proslavery Mobs and Proslavery Ministry," *DM*, March 1861. Douglass was the primary speaker at the Spring Street Church weekly meetings, but it also attracted other abolitionists and reformers such as Lucy Colman, Susan B. Anthony, Parker Pillsbury, and Jermain Loguen. See *Douglass Papers*, ser. 1, 3:424.

51 "Union and How to Save It."

52 "The New President," *DM*, March 1861; "Future of the Abolition Cause," *DM*, April 1861.

53 "Hope and Despair in These Cowardly Times," address delivered in Rochester, Spring Street AME Zion Church, April 28, 1861, *Douglass Papers*, ser. 1, 3:424; and see Blake McKelvey, *Rochester: The Flower City, 1855–1890* (Cambridge, MA: Harvard University Press, 1949), 62–64.

Chapter 17: The Kindling Spirit of His Battle Cry

1 "New President," *DM*, May 1861; Paul Laurence Dunbar, "Douglass," in *Lyrics of Love and Laughter* (New York: Dodd, Mead, 1913), 128–29.

2 "The President-Elect," *DM*, March 1861; "The Inaugural Address," *DM*, April 1861; David Herbert Donald, *Lincoln* (New York: Simon & Schuster, 1995), 273–75; Stauffer, *Giants*, 219–20. On the tension and "paralysis" of Northern communities during the secession winter, covered virtually week by week or even day by day, see Russell McClintock, *Lincoln and the Decision for War: The Northern Response to Secession* (Chapel Hill: University of North Carolina Press, 2008).

3 "Inaugural Address", Abraham Lincoln, "First Inaugural Address," in *Abraham Lincoln, Slavery, and the Civil War*, ed. Michael P. Johnson (Boston: Bedford Books, 2001), 109–10, 112–13.

4 "Emigration to Hayti," *DM*, January 1861. Redpath was the general agent of the Haitian Bureau of Emigration. See Foner, *Life and Writings*, 2:556n24. Blake McKelvey, "Lights and Shadows in Local Negro History," in *Rochester History* 21 (October 1959), 11. Douglass wishes "safe and speedy voyage" to twenty-six adults and twelve children, mostly from Rochester, heading to Haiti to take up life growing cotton.

5 "Haitian Emigration" and "Proslavery Mobs and Proslavery Ministry," *DM*, March 1861; "Emigration to Hayti." Douglass used both spellings of *Haiti*.

6 "A Trip to Haiti," *DM*, May 1861; "Outbreak of Hostilities—Martial Spirit," *Morganblatt*, May 1861, in Lohmann, *Radical Passion*, 207; Diedrich, *Love across Color Lines*, 234–35, 237.

7 "Trip to Haiti."

8 Ibid., "Outbreak of Hostilities," 207–9; Diedrich, *Love across Color Lines*, 237–39.

9 *Bondage and Freedom*, 184.

10 "The Victors Conquered by the Vanquished," *DM*, March 1861.

11 "Nemesis," *DM*, May 1861; Isaiah 58:6.

12 "Who Killed the American Eagle?," *DM*, April 1861.

13 Ibid. On how Douglass fit into the biblical traditions of millennialism and apocalypticism and their role in the coming of the Civil War, see Moorhead, *American Apocalypse*, 42–81; Tuveson, *Redeemer Nation*, 137–86; Blight, *Frederick Douglass' Civil War*, esp. ch. 5.

14 "Revolutions Never Go Backward," speech in Rochester, May 5, 1861, *Douglass Papers*, ser. 1, 3:427–29; Exodus 7:10–12; *DM*, June 1861.

15 "Hope and Despair in These Cowardly Times," speech in Rochester, April 29, 1861, *Douglass Papers*, ser. 1, 3:424–25.

16 "Antislavery in Rochester," *DM*, June 1861; "The American Apocalypse," speech in Rochester, June 16, 1861; "Revolutions Never Go Backward," *Douglass Papers*, ser. 1, 3:434, 442; Griffiths Crofts to Douglass, Sherwood, England, February 12, 1861, *DM*, April 1861.

17 "The Reign of Ruffianism—the Brutal Oppression and Blood-Stained South—Life in the Land of Chivalry," *DM*, May 1861; "Black Regiments Proposed," *DM*, May 1861; "Revolutions Never Go Backward," 3:431, 434–35.

18 "American Apocalypse," 3:444; "Position of the Government toward Slavery," *DM*, June 1861.

19 "American Apocalypse," 3:437–38; Revelation 12:7–9.

20 On Douglass and violence, see Ronald T. Takaki, *Violence in the Black Imagination: Essays and Documents* (New York: Putnam, 1972), 17–35; Leslie F. Goldstein, "Violence as an Instrument for Social Change: The Views of Frederick Douglass," *Journal of Negro History* 61 (1976): 61–72; Martin, *Mind of Frederick Douglass*, 24, 167–68; Blight, *Frederick Douglass' Civil War*, 91–97.

21 Barbara Ehrenreich, *Blood Rites: The Origins and History of the Passions of War* (New York: Granta, 1997), 132; "American Apocalypse," 3:437. On the dangers and misuse of biological metaphors to understand war, and the notion that beliefs and ideology prompt men to war, see Jeffrey H. Goldstein, "Beliefs About Human Aggression," and Jay Winter, "Causes of War," both in *Aggression and War: Their Biological and Social Bases*, ed. Jo Groebel and Robert A. Hinde (Cambridge, UK: Cambridge University Press, 1989), 10–19, 194–201.

22 See Peter Walker, *Moral Choices: Memory, Desire, and Imagination in Nineteenth Century American Abolition* (Baton Rouge: Louisiana State University Press, 1978), 225, 236, 247. And see the work of psychologist Allison Davis, *Leadership, Love and Aggression* (San Diego: Harcourt Brace, 1983), 20–23, 29, 35–37, 41, 52–53, 58, 74, 79. Davis agrees that

Douglass carried out of slavery a genuine hatred for slaveholders, but that it was "healed" or resolved essentially by 1860. Davis does not follow the issue of vengeance into the war years.

23 "Sudden Revolution in Northern Sentiment" and "The Past and the Present," *DM*, May 1861. See Walt Whitman, "Beat! Beat! Drums!," in *Portable Walt Whitman*, 216–17. On the dehumanization of enemies or victims, see Herbert C. Kelman, "Violence without Moral Restraint: Reflections on the Dehumanization of Victims and Victimizers," in *Varieties of Psychohistory*, ed. George M. Kren and Leon H. Rappaport (New York: Springer, 1976), 282–314.

24 "The Future of the Abolition Cause," *DM*, April 1861.

25 "American Apocalypse," 3:440–42.

26 "Revolutions Never Go Backward," 3:432; "American Apocalypse," 3:439.

27 "Shall Slavery Survive the War?," *DM*, September 1861; "The War and Slavery," *DM*, August 1861. On the reactions of Northern conservatives to the First Battle of Bull Run, see George M. Frederickson, *The Inner Civil War: Northern Intellectuals and the Crisis of the Union* (New York: Oxford University Press, 1965), 73–76.

28 "The Rebels, the Government, and the Difference Between Them," *DM*, August 1861.

29 "The Duty of Abolitionists in the Present State of the Country," *DM*, October 1861; "Signs of the Times," *DM*, November 1861, a response to a letter from S. Dutton, Meredith, NY, October 14, 1861.

30 "Signs of Barbarism," *DM*, December 1861. Douglass cited as his source the *Norfolk (VA) Day Book*. "The Slaveholders' Rebellion," speech delivered at Himrods Corners, NY, July 4, 1862, *DM*, August 1862, in Foner, *Life and Writings*, 3:242, 244.

31 See Noll, *America's God*, 424–26; Moorhead, *American Apocalypse*, 1–128. On the doctrine of Providence and millennial worldviews, see Nicholas Guyatt, *Providence and the Invention of the United States, 1607–1876* (Cambridge, UK: Cambridge University Press, 2007), 249–52, 259–326.

32 "Notes on the War," *DM*, July 1861; "Rebels, the Government"; and see James M. McPherson, *Battle Cry of Freedom: The Civil War Era* (New York: Oxford University Press, 1988), 345–49.

33 Julia G. Crofts to Douglass, Edinburgh and Leeds, England, August 5 and 21, 1861, in *DM*, October 1861.

34 "The Contraband Goods and Fortress Monroe," *DM*, July 1861; and see Eric Foner, *The Fiery Trial: Abraham Lincoln and American Slavery* (New York: Norton, 2010), 169–71.

35 "War and Slavery"; Kate Masur, "A Rare Phenomenon of Philological Vegetation: The Word 'Contraband' and the Meanings of Emancipation in the United States," *Journal of American History* 93 (March 2007): 1054–59; Louis P. Masur, *Lincoln's Hundred Days: The Emancipation Proclamation and the War for the Union* (Cambridge, MA: Harvard University Press, 2012), 42–65, 81–97.

36 "War and Slavery."

37 *Chicago Tribune*, June 16, 1861, quoted in Foner, *Fiery Trial*, 170; "War and Slavery."

38 "How to End the War," *DM*, May 1861; "War and Slavery"; Foner, *Fiery Trial*, 176–79; Oakes, *Radical and the Republican*, 159–65, 169–70.

39 "Cast Off the Millstone," *DM*, September 1861; "General Fremont's Proclamation to the Rebels of Missouri," *DM*, October 1861.

40 Reminiscence of Lincoln, from Don E. Fehrenbacher and Virginia Fehrenbacher, comp. and eds., *Recollected Words of Abraham Lincoln* (Stanford, CA: Stanford University Press), 433, quoted in Oakes, *Radical and the Republican*, 168; "Fremont and His Proclamation," *DM*, December 1861.

41 On the First Confiscation Act, see Foner, *Fiery Trial*, 174–75.

42 Lincoln, "Annual Message to Congress," December 3, 1861, in Johnson, *Abraham Lincoln*, 141–44; John H. Bryant to Lyman Trumbull, December 6, 1861, quoted in Foner, *Fiery Trial*, 187; Douglass to S. Dutton, *DM*, November 1861.

Chapter 18: The Anthem of the Redeemed

1 "The Day of Jubilee Comes," address at Spring Street AME Zion Church, Rochester, December 28, 1862, *Douglass Papers*, ser. 1, 3:543.

2 Ibid., 543–44. Douglass here plays on the language in Lincoln's Preliminary Emancipation Proclamation ("henceforth and forever free"); John Wesley's image of the slave trade as "that execrable sum of all villainies"; and Chief Justice Taney's use of the statement in *Dred Scott v. Sandford* that black people "had no rights which the white man was bound to respect."

3 "Free Speech Maintained in Syracuse" and "The Would-Be Mobocrats in Syracuse," *DM*, December 1861.

4 On Civil War casualties, see J. David Hacker, "A Census-Based Count of the Civil War Dead," *Civil War History*, December 2011, 306–47; *New York Times*, April 2, 2012; and Historynet.com/Civil War death statistics; "Of the War," *DM*, May 1862; "Dealings with Slavery and Contrabands," *DM*, December 1861. On the freedpeople, contraband camps, and disease, see Jim Downs, *Sick from Freedom: African American Illness and Suffering during the Civil War and Reconstruction* (New York: Oxford University Press, 2012), chs. 1–3.

5 Douglass to Smith, December 22, 1861, GS Papers; Smith to Douglass, December 25, 1861, FD Papers (LC).

6 McPherson, *Battle Cry of Freedom*, 389–91.

7 Julia Griffiths Crofts to Douglass, Leeds, England, December 6, 1861, FD Papers (LC); "War with England," *DM*, January 1862.

8 As Paul Fussell wrote of World War I, the experience had its way of causing a "strict division" between "Time Before and Time After." See Paul Fussell, *The Great War in Modern Memory* (London: Oxford University Press, 1975), 80; "The Slave Power at Washington," *DM*, January 1862. For a month-by-month account of the significance of 1862, and Lincoln's role in events, see David Von Drehle, *Rise to Greatness: Abraham Lincoln and America's Most Perilous Year* (New York: Henry Holt, 2012).

9 Julia G. Crofts to Douglass, September 24, 1861, reprinted in *DM*, January 1862; "The State of the War," *DM*, February 1862.

10 "The Reasons for Our Troubles," speech delivered in National Hall, Philadelphia, January 14, 1862, in Foner, *Life and Writings*, 3:197–99; *Hamlet*, act 3, sc. 1; Mathew 10:16; Isaiah 1:5.

11 "Reasons for Our Troubles," 196, 205.

12 Ibid., 196, 207; Douglass, "Love of God, Love of Man, Love of Country," speech delivered in Syracuse, NY, September 24, 1847, *Douglass Papers*, ser. 1, 2:103; Donald W. Shriver Jr., *Honest Patriots: Loving a Country Enough to Remember Its Misdeeds* (New York: Oxford University Press, 2005), 3–13, 127–205. Also see Reinhold Niebuhr, *The Irony of American History* (New York: Charles Scribner's Sons, 1952).

13 "The Future of the Negro People of the Slave States," speech delivered in Tremont Temple, Boston, February 12, 1862, in Foner, *Life and Writings*, 3:214–15, 221.

14 Ibid., 213.

15 "Service of Colored Men," *DM*, July 1861; Charles Dickens, *Martin Chuzzlewit* (1844, repr., New York and London: Wordsworth Classics, 1997), 246, 272.

16 Dickens, *Martin Chuzzlewit*, 246, 272, 278, 282; Douglass, "What to the Slave Is the Fourth of July?," 2:370–71.

17 Foner, *Fiery Trial*, 18–19, 34–62, 168.

18 "Message to Congress," March 6, 1862, in *The Collected Works of Abraham Lincoln*, ed. Roy P. Basler (New Brunswick, NJ: Rutgers University Press, 1953), 5:144–46.

19 Phillips quoted in Foner, *Fiery Trial*, 196; "The War and How to End It," *DM*, April 1862; "The War and How to End It," speech delivered in Corinthian Hall, Rochester, March 25, 1862, *Douglass Papers*, ser. 1, 3:518.

20 See Foner, *Fiery Trial*, 123–28; Masur, *Lincoln's Hundred Days*, 46–51.

21 Foner, *Fiery Trial*, 197–201; Douglass to Charles Sumner, April 8, 1862, in Foner, *Life and Writings*, 3:233–34.

22 Foner, *Fiery Trial*, 200–201, 212–13.

23 "Future of the Negro People of the Slave States," 3:216. On idea of "military necessity," see Masur, *Lincoln's Hundred Days*, 26, 28, 36, 74–75.

24 *Springfield Republican*, quoted in Foner, *Fiery Trial*, 215. On content of the Second Confiscation Act, see Silvana R. Siddali, *From Property to Person: Slavery and the Confiscation Acts, 1861–1862* (Baton Rouge: Louisiana State University Press, 2005); Foner, *Fiery Trial*, 215–16.

25 "The Situation of the War" and "The Popular Heart," *DM*, March 1862; McPherson, *Battle Cry of Freedom*, 405–13.

26 *DM*, August 1862; "Appeal to Border State Representatives to Favor Compensated Emancipation," July 12, 1862, in Basler, *Collected Works*, 5:317–19.

27 Julia G. Crofts to Douglass, June 18, 1862, London, in *DM*, August 1862.

28 "Meeting at Himrods Corners" and "The Fourth at Himrods," *DM*, August 1862.

29 "The Slaveholders' Rebellion," in Foner, *Life and Writings*, 3:242–58.

30 Ibid., 243; and see Blight, *Frederick Douglass' Civil War*, 76–77.

31 "The Proclamation and the Negro Army," speech at Cooper Union, New York, February 1863, *DM*, March 1863.

32 "Anti-Slavery Progress," *DM*, September 1862. The lyrics appeared on the cover, *Atlantic Monthly*, February 1862; and see Stauffer and Soskis, *Battle Hymn of the Republic*.

33 Nicholas Guyatt, " 'The Outskirts of Our Happiness': Race and the Lure of Colonization in the Early Republic," *Journal of American History* 95, no. 4 (March 2009): 986–1011; David Brion Davis, *The Problem of Slavery in the Age of Emancipation* (New York: Knopf, 2014), 83–104, 126–31. Guyatt shows that colonization's more "idealistic" roots and motives, while complex and real, declined in the face of harsher forms of racism and proslavery ideology after 1840.

34 "Dr. M. R. Delany," *DM*, August 1862; "Colonization," *North Star*, January 26, 1849; Douglass to Benjamin Coates, April 17, 1856, in Foner, *Life and Writings*, 2:387–88; speech at Shiloh Church, New York City, April 30, 1863, *DM*, June 1863; "The Present and Future of the Colored Race in America," speech at Church of the Puritans, New York City, May 1863, in Foner, *Life and Writings*, 3:350.

35 On Crosby instructions, see Walter A. Payne, "Lincoln's Caribbean Colonization Plan," *Pacific Historian* 7 (May 1963): 67–68. On Chiriqui initiative, see Paul J. Sheips, "Lincoln and the Chiriqui Colonization Project," *Journal of Negro History* 37 (October 1952): 419–21. On Lincoln's early colonizationist thought, see Basler, *Collected Works*, 2:132, 255, 298–99, 409–10.

36 Sheips, "Lincoln and the Chiriqui Colonization Project," 424–27. For West Indian initiatives, see "Correspondence Respecting the Emigration of Free Negroes from the United States to the West Indies," CO 884/2, June 19, 1863, Confidential Print, Public Record Of-

fice, London, England. On the British West Indian connection, see Tom W. Shick, *Behold the Promised Land: A History of Afro-American Settler Society in Nineteenth Century Liberia* (Baltimore: Johns Hopkins University Press, 1977), 124–29; Foner, *Fiery Trial*, 222–23; and Michael Burlingame, *Lincoln: A Life*, vol. 2 (Baltimore: Johns Hopkins University Press, 2008), 394–95.

37 The other four clergymen were John F. Cook, John T. Costin, Cornelius Clark, and Benjamin McCoy. Allen C. Guelzo, *Lincoln's Emancipation Proclamation: The End of Slavery in America* (New York: Simon & Schuster, 2004), 142; "Address on Colonization to a Deputation of Negroes," Basler, *Collected Works*, 5:370–71.

38 "Address on Colonization," Basler, *Collected Works*, 5:371.

39 Ibid., 372–73.

40 Ibid., 374–75; and see Burlingame, *Lincoln*, 387–89.

41 "The President and His Speeches," *DM*, September 1862.

42 Ibid.

43 The New York and Philadelphia resolutions are in Herbert Aptheker, ed., *A Documentary History of the Negro People in the United States* (New York: Citadel Press, 1968), 1:472–74; Smith letter in *DM*, October 1862; *Liberator*, August 22, 1862; Beriah Green to Gerrit Smith, September 12, 1862, GS Papers; and also see Burlingame, *Lincoln*, 389–91.

44 On Pomeroy and black interest, see S. C. Pomeroy to James R. Doolittle, October 20, 1862, Doolittle Papers, State Historical Society of Wisconsin, Madison, WI; and Benjamin Quarles, *Lincoln and the Negro* (New York: Oxford University Press, 1962), 122–23. Douglass reported that a group of blacks in Washington, DC, had petitioned the government to be colonized in Africa, *DM*, May 1862. He also received letters from a W. W. Tate, who challenged the editor's position on colonization and argued that it was the best option for blacks; and from a John W. Menard of Washington, DC, who argued that the idea of a "white nationality" could never be overcome in America; *DM*, July 1862 and April 1863. On Pomeroy and Douglass's sons, see Douglass to Montgomery Blair, September 16, 1862, in *DM*, October 1862.

45 Ronald C. White, *A. Lincoln* (New York: Random House, 2009), 511; Oakes, *Radical and the Republican*, 119–32, 191–95; Guelzo, *Lincoln's Emancipation Proclamation*, 144; Burlingame, *Lincoln*, 384; David Herbert Donald, *Lincoln* (New York: Simon & Schuster, 1995), 352–53; Gabor S. Boritt, "The Voyage to the Colony of Linconia: The Sixteenth President, Black Colonization, and the Defense Mechanism of Avoidance," *Historian* 37 (August 1975), 619–33; Foner, *Fiery Trial*, 127, 184–86, 198–200, 221–29; and Masur, *Lincoln's Hundred Days*, 88–90.

46 "President and His Speeches."

47 "The Spirit of Colonization," *DM*, September 1862.

48 Ibid. "The Claims of the Negro Ethnologically Considered," address delivered at Western Reserve College, July 12, 1854, in Foner, *Life and Writings*, 2:295. For this formal address at a college commencement, Douglass immersed himself in the ethnological-origins debates about "races."

49 The letter to Pomeroy does not survive. Embedded in the protest to Pomeroy was Douglass's letter of recommendation for his oldest son, Lewis. Montgomery Blair to Douglass, September 11, 1862, in Foner, *Life and Writings*, 3:281–83.

50 Douglass to Montgomery Blair, September 16, 1862, in Foner, *Life and Writings*, 3:283–85. On white supremacy in the nineteenth century, see George M. Fredrickson, *The Black Image in the White Mind: The Debate on Afro-American Character and Destiny, 1817–1914* (New York: Harper & Row, 1971), 130–64.

51 Douglass to Montgomery Blair, September 16, 1862, 3:286.

52 Ibid., 288–90; Foner, *Fiery Trial*, 231–32; Burlingame, *Lincoln*, 407–11.

53 Lincoln to George B. McClellan, September 15, 1862; "Reply to Emancipation Memorial Presented by Chicago Christians of All Denominations," September 13, 1862; in Basler, *Collected Works*, 5:426, 420–25; Donald, *Lincoln*, 358–60.

54 "Preliminary Emancipation Proclamation," in Basler, *Collected Works*, 5:433–35; and see introduction by Harold Holzer at www.nysl.nysed.gov/ep/.

55 "Preliminary Emancipation Proclamation," 434–35.

56 Harrisburg (PA) *Weekly Patriot and Union*, quoted in *Liberator*, October 3, 1862; *New York Express*, n.d.; *New York Herald*, n.d.; Albert G. Browne, *Sketch of the Official Life of John A. Andrew* (New York: Hurd & Houghton, 1868), 74; all in Masur, *Lincoln's Hundred Days*, 106, 110, 114–15; Donald, *Lincoln*, 369.

57 "Emancipation Proclaimed," *DM*, October 1862.

58 Donald, *Lincoln*, 368; Democrats quoted in Foner, *Fiery Trial*, 233–34.

59 "The Expedition to Chiriqui" and "Central American Scheme of Colonization," *DM*, November 1862.

60 "The Slave Democracy Again in the Field," *DM*, November 1862.

61 H. Oscar to Douglass, Cairo, IL, September 25, 1862, in *DM*, November 1862.

62 "Address to Our Friends in Great Britain and Ireland" and "Already Bearing Fruit," *DM*, November 1862. On Douglass's fund-raising with British friends, see especially Maria Webb to Douglass, Dublin, March 15, 1862; John Smith to Douglass, Glasgow, May 16, 1862; unsigned to Douglass, Westmoreland Terrace, England, August 21, 1862; Julia G. Crofts to Douglass, September 1 and December 5, 1862; Henry Richardson to Douglass, Newcastle, December 4, 1862; Mary Carpenter to Douglass, Halifax, December 5, 1862; and Alexander Imes to Douglass, Liverpool, December 23, 1862; in FD Papers (LC).

63 Lincoln, "Annual Message to Congress," December 1, 1862, in Basler, *Collected Works*, 5:534; *Liberator*, January 9, 1863; and see Benjamin Quarles, *The Negro in the Civil War* (1953, repr., New York, Da Capo Press, 1989), 170–71.

64 *Liberator*, January 16, 1863; Quarles, *Negro in the Civil War*, 171–72; Mayer, *All on Fire*, 545–47; Blight, *Frederick Douglass' Civil War*, 106.

65 *Life and Times*, 352–53.

66 Ibid., 353–54; Quarles, *Negro in the Civil War*, 173–74.

Chapter 19: Men of Color to Arms!

1 "Men of Color to Arms!," a broadside, Rochester, March 21, 1863, in Foner, *Life and Writings*, 3:317–18; Douglass to Gerrit Smith, March 6, 1863, GS Papers.

2 See letters, Lewis to Amelia Loguen, first fiancée and later wife, from 1860 to circa 1907, Evans Collection, Savannah, GA, "Assorted Material" box.

3 Rosetta Douglass to Douglass, Philadelphia, April 4, 1862; Rosetta to Douglass, Salem, NY, August 31, September 24, and October 9, 1862, FD Papers (LC). On Rosetta's moves and teaching jobs, also see Julia Crofts to Douglass, Leeds, December 5, 1862, FD Papers (LC). Julia expressed concern that a "Rochester Society" had not "appointed Rosetta," and that she may also have sought a position in Washington, DC. On Rosetta, see McFeely, *Frederick Douglass*, 218–23.

4 Rosetta Douglass to Douglass, October 9 and December 28, 1862, FD Papers (LC). Business card for Lewis and Frederick Jr., Evans Collection, scrapbook 1. According to Charles Douglass's later reminiscence, Lewis was also teaching school in Salem up until enlistment in the late winter of 1863. See Charles Douglass, "Some Incidents of the Home Life."

5 Diedrich, *Love across Color Lines*, 171–88; Assing to Douglass, August 21, 1878, in

Lohmann, *Radical Passion*, 340, and see xx–xxi; Fought, *Women in the World of Frederick Douglass*, 149–51.

6 Douglass Sprague, "My Mother as I Recall Her."

7 "The Proclamation and the Negro Army," speech delivered at Cooper Institute, in Foner, *Life and Writings*, 3:321; "January First, 1863," *DM*, January 1863.

8 "Proclamation and the Negro Army," 3:321–22. Douglass gave variations on this speech perhaps two dozen times; for example in Chicago, Metropolitan Hall, January 19, 1863, see *Douglass Papers*, ser. 1, 3:620–21.

9 Michael Walzer, *Exodus and Revolution* (New York: Basic Books, 1985), 17, 21–22; "Proclamation and the Negro Army," 3:325–26; Heschel, *Prophets*, 16, 22.

10 "Proclamation and the Negro Army," 3:323–24, 326–27; James Baldwin, "As Much Truth as One Can Bear," *New York Times*, January 14, 1962.

11 "Proclamation and the Negro Army," 3:333–36.

12 "Massachusetts" and "Movers," *DM*, April 1863; Douglass to Gerrit Smith, March 6, 1863, GS Papers; Gerrit Smith to Douglass, March 10, 1863, FD Papers (LC). On Stearns and organization of the Fifty-Fourth Regiment, see McPherson, *Struggle for Equality*, 202–6.

13 Edwin S. Redkey, "Brave Black Volunteers: A Profile of the Fifty-Fourth Massachusetts Regiment," in *Hope and Glory: Essays on the Legacy of the Fifty-Fourth Massachusetts Regiment*, ed. Martin H. Blatt, Thomas J. Brown, and Donald Yacovone (Amherst: University of Massachusetts Press, 2001), 22–25; Russell Duncan, *Where Death and Glory Meet: Colonel Robert Gould Shaw and the 54th Massachusetts Infantry* (Athens: University of Georgia Press, 1999), 66–68.

14 George L. Stearns to Douglass, Buffalo, March 24, 1863, FD Papers (LC); Charles Douglass, "Some Incidents in the Home Life"; Lewis Douglass to Amelia Loguen, Camp Meigs, March 31, 1863, Evans Collection, "Assorted Material" box. Amelia, nineteen years old in 1863, was the daughter of Jermain Loguen, former fugitive slave and abolitionist in Syracuse.

15 *DM*, April 1863; "Men of Color to Arms!," 3:318; original sheet music for "John Brown" song, in Stauffer and Soskis, *Battle Hymn of the Republic*, after p. 151; Douglass to Gerrit Smith, March 10, 1863, GS Papers; and on Syracuse and Elmira recruits, see Milton C. Sernett, *North Star Country: Upstate New York and the Crusade for African American Freedom* (Syracuse, NY: Syracuse University Press, 2002), 240–42.

16 "Another Word to Colored Men," *DM*, April 1863; "Men of Color to Arms! To Arms!," original broadside in Gilder Lehrman Collection, New-York Historical Society; Elizur Wright, "To the Men of Color," February 15, 1863, Antislavery Collections, Boston Public Library. The angel Gabriel has many appearances and purposes in the Bible, especially that of blowing the horn that will announce God's coming; see Daniel 8:12; Luke 1:19. William Shakespeare, *Henry V.*

17 "Men of Color to Arms!," 3:318–19.

18 "Why Should the Colored Man Enlist?," *DM*, April 1863; "Great Meeting at Shiloh Church," *DM*, July 1863. The meeting took place on April 27 and was presided over by the Reverend Henry Highland Garnet.

19 "Another Word to Colored Men," *DM*, April 1863; "Address for the Promotion of Colored Enlistments," speech in Philadelphia, July 6, 1863, in Foner, *Life and Writings*, 3:365.

20 Lewis Douglass to Amelia Loguen, Camp Meigs, May 9 and 20, 1863, Evans Collection; Charles R. Douglass to Douglass, Readville, July 6, 1863, FD Papers (LC).

21 Lewis Douglass to Amelia Loguen, Camp Meigs, April 15, May 9, and May 20, 1863, Evans Collection; Douglass visited the camp on May 16–17, while staying with Lewis Hayden in Boston, see *DM*, August 1863.

22 Luis F. Emilio, *A Brave Black Regiment: History of the Fifty-Fourth Regiment Massachu-*

setts Volunteer Infantry, 1863–1865 (Boston: Boston Book Co., 1891), 3–7, 19–23; Peter Burchard, *One Gallant Rush: Robert Gould Shaw and His Brave Black Regiment* (New York: St. Martin's, 1965), 4–21, 74–92; Joan Waugh, " 'It Was a Sacrifice We Owed': The Shaw Family and the 54th Massachusetts Regiment," in Blatt, Brown, and Yacovone, *Hope and Glory*, 52–55, 63–66; Duncan, *Where Death and Glory Meet*, 11–34; Shaw to father, Maryland Heights, September 21, 1862, in *Blue-Eyed Child of Fortune: The Civil War Letters of Colonel Robert Gould Shaw*, ed. Russell Duncan (Athens: University of Georgia Press, 1992), 241.

23 Burchard, *One Gallant Rush*, 91–92; Emilio, *Brave Black Regiment*, 24–30; Lewis Douglass to Amelia Loguen, May 27, 1863, Evans Collection. The regiment received four flags from Andrew in the ceremony. See Shaw's letters to his mother, May 17 and 18, 1863, in Duncan, *Blue-Eyed Child of Fortune*, 332–33.

24 Emilio, *Brave Black Regiment*, 31–33; Duncan, *Where Death and Glory Meet*, 85–86.

25 Emilio, *Brave Black Regiment*, 33; Duncan, *Where Death and Glory Meet*, 87–88.

26 Lewis Douglass to Amelia Loguen, St. Simon's Island, June 18, 1863, Evans Collection; Burchard, *One Gallant Rush*, 96–111; *Savannah News*, quoted in Duncan, *Where Death and Glory Meet*, 95.

27 Duncan, *Where Death and Glory Meet*, 103–8; Emilio, *Brave Black Regiment*, 199–216.

28 Burchard, *One Gallant Rush*, 130–37.

29 Ibid., 137–41; casualty report, and General Q. A. Gillmore's report from the field, July 21, 1863, *The War of the Rebellion: A Compilation of the Official Records of the Union and Confederate Armies*, ser. 1, vol. 28 (Washington, DC: Government Printing Office, 1890), 201–202, 210.

30 Lewis Douglass to Amelia Loguen, July 20, 1863, quoted in Duncan, *Where Death and Glory Meet*, 114; Lewis Douglass to father and mother, Morris Island, July 20, 1863, in *DM*, August 1863.

31 Douglass reprinted General Rufus Saxton's official account of Shaw's death, addressed to "colored soldiers and freedmen," July 27, 1863, *DM*, August 1863. And see David W. Blight, "The Shaw Memorial in the Landscape of Civil War Memory," in Blatt, Brown, and Yacovone, *Hope and Glory*, 79–93.

32 For early doubts and warnings about unequal pay, before and as recruiting began, see *Christian Recorder*, July 26, 1862, and February 14, 1863. On the unequal pay struggle, see Ira Berlin et al., eds, *Freedom: A Documentary History of Emancipation, 1861–1867* (Cambridge, UK: Cambridge University Press, 1985), ser. 2, vol. 1, 17–21, 362–68; and Dudley T. Cornish, *The Sable Arm: Negro Troops in the Union Army, 1861–1865* (New York: Longman's Green, 1956), 181–96.

33 Gooding letter in Berlin et al., *Freedom*, ser. 2, 386; George Stephens to editor, Morris Island, SC, August 7, 1863, and August 1, 1864, in *A Voice of Thunder: The Civil War Letters of George E. Stephens*, ed. Donald Yacovone (Urbana: University of Illinois Press, 1997), 252–54, 320. On mutinies, see Donald Yacovone, "The Fifty-Fourth Massachusetts Regiment, the Pay Crisis, and the 'Lincoln Despotism,' " in Blatt, Brown, and Yacovone, *Hope and Glory*, 38–49.

34 Wicker letter in Berlin et al., *Freedom*, ser. 2, 402; *Life and Times*, 343; *DM*, August 1863.

35 "Condition of the Country," *DM*, February 1863; "Another Law against Common Sense," *DM*, March 1863.

36 Stearns quoted in McPherson, *Struggle for Equality*, 203; "Great Meeting at Shiloh Church," New York, *DM*, June 1863; "Address for the Promotion of Colored Enlistments," delivered at National Hall, Philadelphia, July 6, 1863, in Foner, *Life and Writings*, 3:362. On "double battle," see Blight, *Frederick Douglass' Civil War*, 163–67.

37 *Life and Times*, 356.

38 "The Commander-in-Chief and His Black Soldiers," *DM*, August 1863. Douglass reprinted Lincoln's order in the August issue of his paper. On the retaliation issue, see Quarles, *Lincoln and the Negro*, 173–76. Lincoln ordered his cabinet to investigate ways to protect black troops as early as February 1863.

39 Douglass to Stearns, August 1, 1863, in Foner, *Life and Writings*, 3:367–69; Martha Greene to Douglass, July 7, 1863, FD Papers (LC).

40 Stauffer, *Giants*, 3–6; *Life and Times*, 346–47; and see McFeely, *Frederick Douglass*, 228–30.

41 Douglass to Stearns, Philadelphia, August 12, 1863, Abraham Barker Papers, Historical Society of Pennsylvania; *Life and Times*, 349. Stanton wanted Douglass to go to Vicksburg, Mississippi.

42 This extraordinary "To whom it may concern" letter/pass is in FD Papers (LC); and see Stauffer, *Giants*, 11–12.

43 "Our Work Is Not Done," speech delivered at the annual meeting of the American Anti-Slavery Society, Philadelphia, December 3–4, 1863, in Foner, *Life and Writings*, 3:383–84.

44 *Life and Times*, 347; "Our Work Is Not Done," 384.

45 Douglass to Stearns, August 12, 1863; and see Oakes, *Radical and the Republican*, 210–17.

46 *Life and Times*, 348; Douglass to Stearns, August 12, 1863; Stauffer, *Giants*, 22; "To whom it may concern" pass.

47 Douglass to Stearns, August 12, 1863; "Valedictory," August 16, 1863, *DM*, August 1863; C. W. Foster to Douglass, August 13 and August 21, 1863; C. W. Foster to Brigadier General Daniel H. Rucker, August 13, 1863, authorizing Douglass's transportation; and Stearns to Douglass, August 29, 1863; all in FD Papers (LC). Foster was Stanton's secretary. As late as August 29, Stearns believed Douglass was still going to Mississippi. See Stearns to Douglass, August 29, 1863, FD Papers (LC).

48 H. Ford Douglas to Douglass, Collinsville, TN, January 8, 1863, and Douglass's response, *DM*, February 1863.

49 *Life and Times*, 350; Douglass to Thomas Webster, August 19, 1863, in Foner, *Life and Writings*, 3:377.

50 Douglass to *Anglo-African*, Rochester, July 27, 1863, *DM*, August 1863, in Foner, *Life and Writings*, 3:360–61.

51 Charles R. Douglass to Douglass, Boston, September 8, September 18, and December 20, 1863, FD Papers (LC).

52 Lewis Douglass to Amelia Loguen, August 15 and August 27, 1863, Morris Island, SC, Evans Collection; Henry Gooding to editors, September 9, 1863, in *On the Altar of Freedom: A Black Soldier's Civil War Letters from the Front*, ed. Virginia Matzke Adams (Amherst: University of Massachusetts Press, 1991), 56–58. On the siege of Charleston and the relentless shelling of Forts Wagner and Gregory and the long-term efforts to take Fort Sumter, see Joseph Kelly, *America's Longest Siege: Charleston, Slavery, and the Slow March Toward Civil War* (New York: Overlook Press, 2013), 301–12; and E. B. Long, *The Civil War Day by Day: An Almanac, 1861–1865* (New York: Doubleday, 1971), covering August 8 to September 7, 395–406.

53 George E. Stephens to editor, September 1863, in Yacovone, *Voice of Thunder*, 269; Douglass to Gerrit Smith, October 10, 1863, GS Papers. The hospital may have been McDougall Hospital, Fort Schuyler, at Throggs Neck, where the East River meets Long Island Sound. Lewis Douglass, "Regimental Descriptive Book," National Archives, http://www.archives.gov/education/lessons/blacks-civil-war/douglass-sons.html; certification by Dr. James McCune Smith, October 6, 1863, in "Compiled Military Service Records of Volunteer Union Soldiers," US Colored Troops, 54th Mass. Infantry, reel 5, National Archives; and see Doug-

las R. Egerton, *The Wars of Reconstruction: The Brief Violent History of America's Most Progressive Era* (New York: Bloomsbury, 2013), 37–41, 370–81; and Diedrich, *Love Across Color Lines*, 354–55.

54 Julia Griffiths Crofts to Douglass, September 1, 1862, April 3, 1863, and December 10, 1863, all in FD Papers (LC). For the continued flow of British funds to Douglass's support, professional and personal, see Julia Griffiths Crofts to Douglass, Leeds, February 5 and April 15, 1864; an unsigned letter to Douglass, March 5, 1864, telling of a children's musical concert planned to raise money for Douglass's cause; Mary Carpenter to Douglass, Halifax, February 19, 1864, and August 5, 1864; and numerous letters from an admirer, Ame Draz, to Douglass, July 12, August 17, and December 15, 1863, and March 24 and October 15, 1864, all in FD Papers (LC).

55 "Address delivered at the Dedication of the Cemetery at Gettysburg," November 19, 1863, Basler, *Collected Works*, 7:22–23; Douglas L. Wilson, *Lincoln's Sword: The Presidency and the Power of Words* (New York: Knopf, 2006), 201, 206–37; and see Garry Wills, *Lincoln at Gettysburg: The Words That Remade America* (New York: Simon & Schuster, 1992), 38, 40.

56 "Annual Message to Congress," December 8, 1863, in Basler, *Collected Works*, 7:49–51, 53; "The Mission of the War," delivered at Cooper Institute, New York, February 13, 1864, in Foner, *Life and Writings*, 3:401.

Chapter 20: Abolition War, Abolition Peace

1 "Our Work Is Not Done," 3:378–83.

2 Thomas H. C. Hinton, *Christian Recorder*, December 26, 1863.

3 Ibid.; Lincoln, "Annual Message to Congress," 7:49, 51, 53. While in Washington, Douglass visited the burgeoning contraband camp, known as Freedmen's Village, in Arlington, across the Potomac River.

4 Kate Masur, *An Example for All the Land: Emancipation and the Struggle over Equality in Washington, DC* (Chapel Hill: University of North Carolina Press, 2010), ch. 1; Ernest B. Furgurson, *Freedom Rising: Washington in the Civil War* (New York: Knopf, 2004), 197–98, 256–57; Constance McLaughlin Green, *The Secret City: A History of Race Relations in the Nation's Capital* (Princeton, NJ: Princeton University Press, 1967), 62–64.

5 Harriet Jacobs, "Life Among the Contrabands," *Liberator*, September 5, 1862; Jean Fagan Yellin, *Harriet Jacobs: A Life* (New York: Basic Books, 2004), 159, 164–67; Amy Post to Isaac Post, Washington, DC, December 11, 1863, Post Family Papers, University of Rochester.

6 Julia Crofts to Douglass, Leeds, England, February 5, 1864, FD Papers (LC). Douglass's letter to Julia, which does not survive, had been dated January 9. Assing, "Anniversary of the Antislavery Society," *Morgenblatt*, January 1864; and Assing, "A Negro Regiment—Radical Germans," *Morgenblatt*, March 1864; in Lohmann, *Radical Passion*, 275, 280.

7 Martha Greene to Douglass, July 7, 1864; Julia Crofts to Douglass, April 15, 1864; and Mary Carpenter to Douglass, February 19, 1864; FD Papers (LC).

8 "The Mission of the War," address delivered in New York, January 13, 1864, *Douglass Papers*, ser. 1, 4:3–5, 7, 23.

9 Ibid., 8–9, 13.

10 Ibid., 16.

11 Ibid., 19, 24; Isaiah 48:18. In his ending of the "Dream" speech, King used the words in Amos 5:24: "Let justice run down like waters, and righteousness like a mighty stream." Whether King was aware of Douglass's speech, delivered a hundred years earlier, is not clear. See Drew D. Hansen, *The Dream: Martin Luther King, Jr., and the Speech That Inspired a Nation* (New York: Ecco, HarperCollins, 2003), 104.

12 "Genealogy and Descendants of Frederick Douglass," prepared for author by Christine McKay, 2013; McFeely, *Frederick Douglass*, 222–23; Egerton, *Wars of Reconstruction*, 41; and Julia Crofts to Douglass, December 10, 1863 and February 5, 1864, FD Papers (LC). Rosetta and Nathan Sprague lived with her parents at the beginning of their marriage, but eventually moved to a house owned by the elder Douglass on Hamilton Place in Rochester. See http://rochester.twcnews.com/content/news/492838/frederick-douglass—forgotten-home-now-a-landmark/?ap=1&MP4/.

13 Lewis Douglass to Douglass, August 22, 1864, FD Papers (LC); Lewis Douglass, "Regimental Descriptive Book," National Archives.

14 Charles Douglass to Douglass, City Point, VA, near Bermuda Hundred, May 31, 1864, FD Papers (LC); *War of the Rebellion*, vol. 36, pt. 1, 258, and vol. 51, pt. 1, 251.

15 Charles Douglass to Douglass, May 31, 1864.

16 Charles Douglass, "Regimental Descriptive Book"; Douglass to Abraham Lincoln, undated, and Lincoln endorsement, September 1, 1864, service record of Charles R. Douglass, National Archives; Charles Douglass to Father and Mother, Point Lookout, September 15, 1864, FD Papers (LC).

17 McKay, "Genealogy and Descendants of Frederick Douglass."

18 "Mission of the War," 4:4, 13.

19 "The Work of the Future," *DM*, November 1862, in Foner, *Life and Writings*, 3:290–92.

20 "What Shall Be Done with the Slaves if Emancipated," *DM*, January 1862, in Foner, *Life and Writings*, 3:188. And see "Arms Not Alms for the Contrabands," *DM*, May 1862. See Clarence Thomas's dissent in *Grutter v. Bollinger* 539 US 206 (2003). Thomas quoted at length from Douglass's 1862 speech to justify his opposition to affirmative action programs at the University of Michigan and elsewhere. On Thomas's misunderstandings of Douglass, see Buccola, *Political Thought of Frederick Douglass*, 162–67. For a critique of Thomas and other misuses of Douglass by the American right wing, see Jack Turner, "Douglass and Political Judgment: The Post-Reconstruction Years," copy of MS provided to the author. Also see Sean Coons, "Frederick Douglass: New Tea Party Hero?," *Salon*, July 3, 2013.

21 On British friends and their money (for Douglass's own work and travel as well as for freedmen's relief) during wartime, see Julia Crofts to Douglass, February 5, April 15, August 19, and November 23, 1864; Mary T. Cropper to Douglass, July 12, 1864; Mary Carpenter to Douglass, August 5, 1864; Thomas Coates to Douglass, February 25, 1865; Ame Draz to Douglass, February 26, 1865; all in FD Papers (LC).

22 "The Future of the Negro People of the Slave States," Boston, February 12, 1862, in Foner, *Life and Writings*, 3:211; "What Shall Be Done with the Slaves," 3:190–91; and see Martin, *Mind of Frederick Douglass*, 67–70.

23 "What Shall Be Done With the Slaves," 3:190.

24 "Future of the Negro People of the Slave States," 3:222.

25 Ibid., 3:218.

26 Douglass to an English correspondent, June 1864, in Foner, *Life and Writings*, 3:404; "A Day for Poetry and Song," remarks at Zion Church, December 28, 1862, Foner, *Life and Writings*, 3, 312.

27 "What the Black Man Wants," speech delivered in Boston, April 1865, in Foner, *Life and Writings*, 4:158–60.

28 Montgomery Blair, *Comments on the Policy Inaugurated by the President, in a Letter and Two Speeches* (New York: Hall, Clayton, & Medole, 1863), 10, 17–19; Lincoln to Zachariah Chandler, November 20, 1863, in Basler, *Collected Works*, 7:24; and see Foner, *Fiery Trial*, 268–75.

29 See reminiscences and quotations in Burlingame, *Lincoln*, 2:609–16. On Lincoln's Ten Per-

Cent plan as "gradualism" and as a means of making "emancipation and reunion palatable," see Foner, *Fiery Trial*, 269–70; and Stauffer, *Giants*, 278–79.

30 Phillips quoted in Burlingame, *Lincoln*, 2:637, and see 632–35; and on Frémont third-party movement, also see Michael Vorenberg, *Final Freedom: The Civil War, the Abolition of Slavery, and the Thirteenth Amendment* (Cambridge, UK: Cambridge University Press, 2001), 116–21. Garrison in *Liberator*, March 18, 1864. Also see Blight, *Frederick Douglass' Civil War*, 183–84. On the Phillips-Garrison split, see McPherson, *Struggle for Equality*, 260–67.

31 Lincoln to Nathaniel P. Banks, November 5, 1863, in Boston, *Collected Works*, 7:1; *War of the Rebellion*, ser. 1, 15:666–67, vol. 34, pt. 2, 227–31; McPherson, *Struggle for Equality*, 243–45, 289–90.

32 *Liberator*, March 11, 1864; McPherson, *Struggle for Equality*, 289–90; Douglass to E. Gilbert, Esq., Rochester, May 23, 1864, in Foner, *Life and Writings*, 3:405.

33 Douglass to an English correspondent, June 1864, in *Liberator*, September 16, 1864; and Foner, *Life and Writings*, 3:404.

34 Gay to Elizabeth Gay, August 8, 1864, quoted in McPherson, *Struggle for Equality*, 280; Blight, *Frederick Douglass' Civil War*, 183.

35 White, *A. Lincoln*, 612–13; Blight, *Frederick Douglass' Civil War*, ch. 5; Lincoln, "A House Divided," speech in Springfield, IL, June 16, 1858, in Johnson, ed., *Abraham Lincoln, Slavery and the Civil War: Selected Writings and Speeches* (Boston: Bedford Books, 2001), 63; Douglass, "What to the Slave Is the Fourth of July," 2:361, 368, 387; Lincoln, "Annual Message," December 1, 1862, in Boston, *Collected Works*, 5:537; Douglass, "Antislavery Progress," *DM*, September 1862. Lincoln drew from 1 Peter 4:12 and Douglass from 1 Corinthians 3:15.

36 Richard J. Carwardine, *Lincoln* (London: Pearson, Longman, 2003), 220–25; Lincoln, "Meditation on the Divine Will," in Boston, *Collected Works*, 5:403–4. For the most sustained analyses of this document, see Wilson, *Lincoln's Sword*, 253–63; and White, *A. Lincoln*, 612–15. Wilson makes a compelling case for dating the "Meditation" in 1864 (see pp. 329–30).

37 See Blight, *Frederick Douglass' Civil War*, 106–8; "Nemesis," *DM*, May 1861; and Isaiah 10:27. Another favorite scriptural text for Douglass, which he used in many ways, was Isaiah 1:4–5.

38 John Eaton, *Grant, Lincoln, and the Freedmen: Reminiscences of the Civil War* (New York: Longman's, Green, 1907), 168–69. On Eaton and the contraband camps, see Ira Berlin et al., eds., *Free at Last: A Documentary History of Slavery, Freedom, and the Civil War* (New York: New Press, 1992), 185–200. As for Lincoln's famous public letters that could have influenced Douglass, I have in mind especially Lincoln to James C. Conkling, August 26, 1863, and Lincoln to Albert G. Hodges, April 4, 1864, in Johnson, *Abraham Lincoln*, 255–58, 285–86.

39 Eaton, *Grant, Lincoln, and the Freedmen*, 173–75; Stauffer, *Giants*, 282–85.

40 "Interview with Alexander W. Randall and Joseph T. Mills," in Basler, *Collected Works*, 7:508.

41 "Mission of the War," in Foner, *Life and Writings*, 3:394; *Life and Times*, 359.

42 *Life and Times*, 358. Many prominent Republicans, as well as some of Lincoln's closest advisers in his cabinet, believed as late as August that he would not win reelection. See Vorenberg, *Final Freedom*, 150–52.

43 *Life and Times*, 359; Eaton, *Grant, Lincoln, and the Freedmen*, 175–76; Stauffer, *Giants*, 290.

44 Julia Crofts to Douglass, Hawley, Staffordshire, England, August 19, 1864, FD Papers (LC); Douglass to Abraham Lincoln, August 29, 1864, in Foner, *Life and Writings*, 3:405–6; *Life and Times*, 358.

45 McPherson, *Battle Cry of Freedom*, 771–74; William T. Sherman to Henry W. Halleck, south of Atlanta, September 3, 1864, in *Sherman's Civil War: Selected Correspondence of William T. Sherman*, ed. Brooks D. Simpson and Jean V. Berlin (Chapel Hill: University of North Carolina Press, 1999), 695–96; Allan Nevins and Milton Halsey Thomas, eds., *Diary of George Templeton Strong* (New York: MacMillan, 1952), 480–81.

46 Douglass to Theodore Tilton, October 15, 1864, in Foner, *Life and Writings*, 3:423–24. On abolitionists stumping for Lincoln in 1864, see McPherson, *Struggle for Equality*, 383–84.

47 Job 1:21.

Chapter 21: Sacred Efforts

1 *Proceedings of the National Convention of Colored Men, Held in the City of Syracuse, NY, October 4–7, 1864* (Boston: Rand & Avery, 1864), 3–4, copy in Sterling Library, Yale University. McCune Smith died a year later in November 1865. Also see Vorenberg, *Final Freedom*, 158–59.

2 *Proceedings of the National Convention of Colored Men*, 4–7.

3 Ibid., 8–9, 12–13, 15. The black regiment was also known as the First Louisiana Native Guards.

4 "Address of the Colored National Convention, to the People of the United States," Syracuse, NY, October 4–7, 1864, in Foner, *Life and Writings*, 3:409–10.

5 Ibid., 410–13.

6 Ibid., 412, 416.

7 Ibid., 418–21. On Douglass and political liberalism, see Myers, *Frederick Douglass*, 1–16, 127–37; and Buccola, *Political Thought of Frederick Douglass*, 65–75.

8 Lincoln, "To Whom It May Concern," July 18, 1864, in Basler, *Collected Works*, 7:451; Vorenberg, *Final Freedom*, 146–49; *Cincinnati Enquirer*, July 25, 1864, in Vorenberg, *Final Freedom*, 149.

9 Vorenberg, *Final Freedom*, 155–56; "Address of the Colored National Convention," 3:414–15.

10 *Miscegenation: The Theory of the Blending of the Races, Applied to the American Man and Negro* (New York: H. Dexter, Hamilton, 1864); Vorenberg, *Final Freedom*, 101; Forrest G. Wood, *Black Scare: The Racist Response to Emancipation and Reconstruction* (Berkeley: University of California Press, 1968), 53–79; Paul D. Escott, *Lincoln's Dilemma: Blair, Sumner, and the Republican Struggle over Racism and Equality in the Civil War Era* (Charlottesville: University Press of Virginia, 2014), 174–76.

11 *New York World*, September 23, 1864; miscegenation passages all quoted in Vorenberg, *Final Freedom*, 160–62.

12 W. Dean Burnham, *Presidential Ballots, 1836–1892* (Baltimore: Johns Hopkins University Press, 1955), 247, 888; McPherson, *Battle Cry of Freedom*, 803–5; "Diary" of Christian Fleetwood, Christian Abraham Fleetwood Papers, Library of Congress manuscript division; citation for Medal of Honor, http://amhistory.si.edu/militaryhistory/collection/object.asp?ID=417.

13 *Rochester Democrat and Chronicle*, June 2, 1882, Evans Collection, Savannah, scrapbook 2. The letter to the editor was by a person who had just seen Douglass deliver a Decoration Day address in Rochester, May 30, 1882.

14 "The Final Test of Self-Government," address in Rochester, Spring Street AME Zion Church, November 13, 1864, *Douglass Papers*, ser. 1, 4:31–32; Genesis 8:11–13. For understanding of Noah's ark and the flood, and Genesis generally, see Walter Brueggemann,

Genesis: A Bible Commentary for Teaching and Preaching (Atlanta: John Knox Press, 1982), 11–88.

15 "Final Test of Self-Government," 4:33–34, 36–37.

16 Vorenberg, *Final Freedom*, 172–74; Preston, *Young Frederick Douglass*, 163–64; Douglass to a friend in England, *New York Independent*, March 2, 1865; "A Friendly Word to Maryland," address delivered in Baltimore, November 17, 1864, *Douglass Papers*, ser. 1, 3:38–39.

17 "Friendly Word to Maryland," 3:41–42; *Liberator*, November 25 and December 2, 1864; *NASS*, November 26, 1864.

18 "Friendly Word to Maryland," 3:39–40, 43–44; *Narrative*, 84.

19 "Friendly Word to Maryland," 3:45–46, 49.

20 Ibid., 3:47–48.

21 Ibid., 3:50.

22 Lewis Douglass to Douglass, June 9, 1865, Douglass Collection, Moorland-Spingarn Center, Howard University, Washington, DC; and see Preston, *Young Frederick Douglass*, 164–65.

23 Benjamin F. Auld to Douglass, September 11, 1891, FD Papers (LC); *Douglass Papers*, ser. 1, vol. 3, partial speaking itinerary, 1864–80, xix–xx; and see Preston, *Young Frederick Douglass*, 165–67.

24 *Liberator*, December 30, 1864, and January 20, 1865; *Douglass Papers*, ser. 1, vol. 3, speaking itinerary, xx.

25 Douglass Sprague, "My Mother as I Recall Her."

26 Frederick Douglass Jr., "F. Douglass, Jr. in Brief from 1842 to 1890," handwritten personal narrative, n.d., Evans Collection, Assorted Material box; Charles R. Douglass to Douglass, Freedmen's Hospital, Washington, DC, February 19, 1865, FD Papers (LC). On the Fifty-Fifth Massachusetts and the Battle of Honey Hill, see Luis F. Emilio, *A Brave Black Regiment: History of the Fifty-Fourth Regiment Massachusetts Volunteer Infantry, 1863–1865* (Boston: Boston Book Co., 1891), 236–53.

27 Lewis Douglass to Amelia Loguen, Mitchellville, Maryland, September 28, 1864; and Lewis to Amelia, Rochester, March 26, 1865; Evans Collection, family letters. In Mitchellville, which is on the Western Shore, at a federal hospital, Lewis may have been engaged in another part of his convalescence.

28 Diedrich, *Love across Color Lines*, 255–58.

29 Assing to Ludmilla Assing, Hoboken, NJ, April 3, 1868, and Rochester, NY, August 24, 1868, Karl August Varnhagen von Ense Papers, Jagiellonian Library, Jagiellonian University, Krakow, Poland, with assistance of Leigh Fought, translated by Katharina Schmidt.

30 Ottilie Assing, "The Presidential Election," *Morgenblatt*, September 1864; "The Presidential Election," November 1864, in Lohmann, *Radical Passion*, 283–92.

31 Assing, "Presidential Election," *Morgenblatt*, November 1864; "Christmas and New Year's—Slavery—Everett—a New German Book," *Morgenblatt*, January 1865; in Lohmann, *Radical Passion*, 288, 295.

32 Assing to Ludmilla Assing, Hoboken, NJ, February 3, 1865, Varnhagen von Ense Papers. And see Vorenberg, *Final Freedom*, 197–204.

33 Charles Douglass to Douglass, February 9, 1865, FD Papers (LC); *Douglass Papers*, ser. 1, vol. 3, itineraries, xx; Vorenberg, *Final Freedom*, 205–10.

34 "Black Freedom Is the Prerequisite for Victory," address at Cooper Institute, New York, January 13, 1865, *Douglass Papers*, ser. 1, 4:51, 58.

35 "What the Black Man Wants," address delivered in Boston, January 26, 1865, *Douglass Papers*, ser. 1, 4:61–64, 66.

36 "Black Freedom Is the Prerequisite to Victory" and "What the Black man Wants," 4:57–59, 66.

37 "What the Black Man Wants," 4:58.

38 Luke 16:19–31. "Rock My Soul" was popularized by Peter Paul & Mary as well as Elvis Presley in the 1960s. The story of Lazarus and the rich man has been used through the ages as a mirror for inequality, for how the last shall be first.

39 "Black Freedom Is the Prerequisite for Victory" and "The Fall of Richmond," address delivered in Faneuil Hall, Boston, April 4, 1865, both in *Douglass Papers*, ser. 1, 4:55–56, 73–74.

40 Ronald C. White, *Lincoln's Greatest Speech: The Second Inaugural* (New York: Simon & Schuster, 2002), 24–29; Stauffer, *Giants*, 292–95; and see Masur, *Example for All the Land*, 22–28, 30–32, 54–55; Ferguson, *Freedom Rising*, 197–98, 256–57; and Green, *Secret City*, 62–64.

41 *Life and Times*, 361–62.

42 Ibid., 364–65; White, *Lincoln's Greatest Speech*, 37–39; and see John Muller, *Frederick Douglass in Washington, D.C., the Lion of Anacostia* (Charleston, SC: History Press, 2012), 31–33.

43 *Life and Times*, 364; Lincoln, "Second Inaugural," in Basler, *Collected Works*, 8:56–57; "Abraham Lincoln: Great Man of Our Century," address delivered in Brooklyn, NY, February 13, 1893, *Douglass Papers*, ser. 1, 5:535–37.

44 *Life and Times*, 365.

45 Ibid., 365–66.

46 Ibid., 366; and see David W. Blight, "Abraham Lincoln and Frederick Douglass: A Relationship in Language, Politics and Memory," in Blight, *Beyond the Battlefield*, 78–79, 87. Henry C. Warmoth, an army officer from Illinois and later Reconstruction governor of Louisiana, was an eyewitness to this exchange at the White House, confirming the president's appeal to Douglass about the speech. See Henry Clay Warmoth Diary, March 4, 1865, Henry Clay Warmoth Papers, Southern Historical Collection, University of North Carolina, Chapel Hill; and see Foner, *Fiery Trial*, 405n10.

47 Douglass, "Abraham Lincoln, a Speech," FD Papers (LC), hdl.loc.gov/loc.mss/mfd.22015; Martha Hodes, *Mourning Lincoln* (New Haven, CT: Yale University Press, 2015), 11; and see Richard Wightman Fox, *Lincoln's Body: A Cultural History* (New York: Norton, 2015), 24–46.

48 *Life and Times*, 371; "Our Martyred President," speech delivered at City Hall, Rochester, April 15, 1865, *Douglass Papers*, ser. 1, 4:74–76. I also relied on a handwritten manuscript version of this speech, in which the language, if not the spirit, of the published text changes. Speech on Lincoln's death, Rochester, handwritten MS, Evans Collection, Savannah, scrapbook 4.

49 "Our Martyred President," 4:76–78; speech on Lincoln's death, Evans Collection, scrapbook 4.

50 "Our Martyred President," 4:77–78.

51 *Life and Times*, 372; and see Blight, *Frederick Douglass' Civil War*, 188.

Chapter 22: Othello's Occupation Was Gone

1 *Life and Times*, 373.

2 *Shakespeare's Tragedy of Othello: The Moor of Venice*, as produced by Edwin Booth, intro. by Henry L. Hinton (New York: Henry L. Hinton, 1870), 86–93; and http://www.shakespeare-navigators.com/othello/S33.html#exitdesdemona.

3 Tilden G. Edelstein, "Othello in America: The Drama of Racial Intermarriage," in *Region, Race and Reconstruction: Essays in Honor of C. Vann Woodward*, ed. J. Morgan Kousser and James M. McPherson (New York: Oxford University Press, 1982), 179–85; Adams quota-

tion, 185. And see Marjorie Garber, *Shakespeare and Modern Culture* (New York: Pantheon Books, 2008), 154–77.

4 Ottilie Assing to Ludmilla Assing, May 23, 1869, Varnhagen von Ense Papers; *Shakespeare's Tragedy of Othello*, intro., iii–ix; Edelstein, "Othello in America," 186–91; Arthur W. Bloom, *Edwin Booth: A Biography and Performance History* (Jefferson, NC: McFarland, 2013), ch. 13.

5 *Shakespeare's Tragedy of Othello*, 61–62; and for the ways Shakespeare helped shape American speech and his sheer popularity, see Lawrence W. Levine, *Highbrow/Lowbrow: The Emergence of Cultural Hierarchy in America* (Cambridge, MA: Harvard University Press, 1988), 37–38, 48–52, 57–60.

6 Phebe Dean to Amy Post, February 27, 1868, Post Family Papers; Chase invitation and Douglass response in McFeely, *Frederick Douglass*, 254; the desire to meet Auld, Douglass to Lydia Maria Child, July 30, 1865, Post Family Papers; on possible farming, see *Life and Times*, 374; and see Diedrich, *Love across Color Lines*, 258, 261–62.

7 Julia Crofts to Douglass, April 28 and May 19, 1865, FD Papers (LC). With the May letter Griffiths sent £27, including her own and that of three other ladies' associations. Extract from *Augusta (GA) Constitutionalist*, n.d., Evans Collection, scrapbook 1.

8 Exodus 14:13; "In What New Skin Will the Old Snake Come Forth?," address delivered in New York, Church of the Puritans, May 10, 1865, *Douglass Papers*, ser. 1, 4:79–85; *Liberator*, May 26, 1865.

9 J. Thomas Scharf, *The Chronicles of Baltimore, Being a Complete History of Baltimore Town and Baltimore City from the Earliest Period to the Present Time* (Baltimore: Turnbull Brothers, 1874), 661; and see from Maryland State Archives, http://msa.maryland.gov/msa/stagser/s1259/121/6050/html/douginst.html.

10 "The Douglass Institute," address in Baltimore, September 29, 1865, *Douglass Papers*, ser. 1, 4:86–89.

11 Ibid., 91–96. Near the end of the speech, Douglass deftly quoted, unannounced and slightly altered, a verse from Whittier's poem "Pennsylvania Hall." See Horace E. Scudder, ed., *The Complete Poetical Works of John Greenleaf Whittier*, Cambridge ed. (New York: Houghton Mifflin, 1894), 280. Whittier had delivered the poem at the dedication of Pennsylvania Hall, an antislavery edifice, on May 15, 1838.

12 *Life and Times*, 374–76.

13 "Reconstruction," *Atlantic Monthly*, December 1866, in Foner, *Life and Writings*, 4:198–99, 202.

14 Ibid., 199–201; Herman Melville, *Battle Pieces and Aspects of the War* (New York: Harper & Brothers, 1866), 272. Melville's "Supplement," a kind of epilogue, was itself an essay on the nature and meaning of Reconstruction.

15 Hans Trefousse, *Andrew Johnson: A Biography* (New York: Norton, 1989), 69–254; Eric L. McKitrick, *Andrew Johnson and Reconstruction* (Chicago: University of Chicago Press, 1960), 85–92, 158–74, 253–59.

16 John Hope Franklin, *Reconstruction after the Civil War* (Chicago: University of Chicago Press, 1961), 54–58; Eric Foner, *Reconstruction: America's Unfinished Revolution, 1863–1877* (New York: Harper & Row, 1988), 199–201; "In What Skin Will the Old Snake Come Forth?" and "Douglass Institute," 4:82, 91.

17 Foner, *Reconstruction*, 246–47, 252–61; Franklin, *Reconstruction after the Civil War*, 57–58.

18 *Report of the Joint Committee on Reconstruction*, 1st sess., 39th Cong. (Washington, DC: Government Printing Office, 1866), 224–29, 112–13; Benjamin B. Kendrick, *The Journal of the Joint Committee of Fifteen on Reconstruction* (New York: Columbia University, 1914), 264–67; Foner, *Reconstruction*, 246–47; Franklin, *Reconstruction after the Civil War*, 58–59.

19 George T. Downing to Douglass, January 18, 1866, FD Papers (LC). Henry Highland Garnet to Lewis Douglass, January 17, 1866; Lewis Douglass to General Oliver O. Howard, January 22, 1866; George T. Downing, Frederick Douglass, Lewis Douglass, and six others to Charles Sumner, n.d., but is January 1866; Evans Collection, scrapbook unnumbered. "The Claims of Our Race," interview with President Andrew Johnson, Washington, DC, February 7, 1866, *Douglass Papers*, ser. 1, 4:96–99; Egerton, *Wars of Reconstruction*, 192–93.

20 "Claims of Our Race," 4:99–100; *Life and Times*, 382.

21 "Claims of Our Race," 4:101–5.

22 Ibid., 97, 104–5. Philip Ripley was the correspondent of the *New York World*. The stenographer was James O. Clephane of the *Washington Evening Star*. See *Evening Star*, February 7, 1866. Quotes in Trefousse, *Andrew Johnson*, 242. And see Quarles, *Frederick Douglass*, 226–28.

23 "Reply of the Colored Delegation to the President," February 7, 1866, in Foner, *Life and Writings*, 4:191–93.

24 *Life and Times*, 378; "Sources of Danger to the Republic," speech delivered in St. Louis, MO, February 8, 1867, *Douglass Papers*, ser. 1, 4:149, 159–60, 167.

25 "In What New Skin Will the Old Snake Come Forth?," 4:83; Patrick W. Riddleberger, *1866: The Critical Year Revisited* (Carbondale: Southern Illinois University Press, 1979); Howard K. Beale, *The Critical Year: A Study of Andrew Johnson and Reconstruction* (New York: Harcourt Brace, 1930); Douglass to Charles Sumner, October 19, 1866, in Foner, *Life and Writings*, 4:198.

26 Charles Douglass to Douglass, December 14, 1866, and February 10 and 24, 1867; Rosetta Sprague to Douglass, April 24, 1867; FD Papers (LC); see itineraries, *Douglass Papers*, ser. 1, 4:xxi–xxii.

27 William L. Hodge to Johnson, February 8, 1866; James H. Embry to Johnson, February 9, 1866; Ralph Phinney to Johnson, February 15, 1866; Administration Friend to Johnson, March 10, 1866; James B. Bingham to Johnson, May 17, 1866; in Paul H. Bergeron, ed., *The Papers of Andrew Johnson*, vol. 10 (Knoxville: University of Tennessee Press, 1992), 60–63, 102, 232, 513–14.

28 Foner, *Reconstruction*, 243–46; Trumbull quote, 243.

29 "Veto of Civil Rights Bill," Washington, DC, March 27, 1866, in Bergeron, *Papers of Andrew Johnson*, 10:313–14, 318–20; and see Trefousse, *Andrew Johnson*, 245–49.

30 Bingham, in *Congressional Globe*, 37th Cong., 2nd sess. (1862), 1639; Stevens, "The Pending Canvass! Speech of the Honorable Thaddeus Stevens," Bedford, PA, September 4, 1866, both quoted in William E. Nelson, *The Fourteenth Amendment: From Political Principle to Judicial Doctrine* (Cambridge, MA: Harvard University Press, 1988), 72. And see Gerard N. Magliocca, *American Founding Son: John Bingham and the Invention of the Fourteenth Amendment* (New York: NYU Press, 2013).

31 John Bingham, "Speech: The Amendment of the Constitution," January 25, 1866 (Washington, DC: Congressional Globe Office, 1866), 2, 4, Huntington Library, San Marino, CA.

32 "Majority and Minority Reports of the Joint Committee on Reconstruction," June 18, 1866, in Edward McPherson, *The Political History of the United States of America during the Period of Reconstruction, April 15, 1865–July 15, 1870* (1871; repr., New York: Da Capo Press, 1972), 92–93; Howard N. Meyer, *XIV: The Amendment That Refused to Die* (Boston: Beacon, 1973), 39–68; John Bingham, "One Country, One Constitution, One People," February 28, 1866 (Washington, DC: Congressional Globe Office, 1866), 1–3, 6, Huntington Library, San Marino, CA. On Bingham's role in the Fourteenth Amendment, see Garrett Epps, *Democracy Reborn: The Fourteenth Amendment and the Fight for Equal Rights in Post–Civil War America* (New York: Henry Holt, 2006), 95–99, 164–72, 225–27.

33 Epps, *Democracy Reborn*, 224–39, 247–50; Nelson, *Fourteenth Amendment*, 40–90; and Harold M. Hymen, *A More Perfect Union: The Impact of the Civil War and Reconstruction on the Constitution* (Boston: Houghton Mifflin, 1975), 446–71.

34 For full text and vote counts, see McPherson, *Political History of the United States*, 102–6.

35 Ibid., 102.

36 "The Assassination and Its Lessons," speech delivered in Washington, DC, at First Presbyterian Church, February 13, 1866, *Douglass Papers*, ser. 1, 4:106; see headnote, 108–10, 115–16.

37 Genesis 18:16–19:29; Brueggemann, *Genesis*, 162–76.

38 "The Issues of the Day," address in Washington, DC, March 10, 1866, *Douglass Papers*, ser. 1, 4:118–23; for broadside, see Administration Friend to Johnson, March 10, 1866, 10:234.

39 *NASS*, July 7, 1866; see Hans Trefousse, *Thaddeus Stevens: Nineteenth Century Egalitarian* (Chapel Hill: University of North Carolina Press, 1997).

40 Foner, *Reconstruction*, 261–63; Ted Tunnell, *Crucible of Reconstruction: War, Radicalism, and Race in Louisiana, 1862–1877* (Baton Rouge: Louisiana State University Press, 1984), 103–7.

41 McPherson, *Struggle for Equality*, 360–62; Blight, *Frederick Douglass' Civil War*, 192; Foner, *Reconstruction*, 264; Douglass to John Van Voorhis, August 30, 1866, *Rochester Union and Advertiser*, September 1, 1866; McFeely, *Frederick Douglass*, 250–51.

42 *Life and Times*, 387–89.

43 Ibid., 390–92. See McFeely, *Frederick Douglass*, 250–52.

44 Stevens to William D. Kelley, September 6, 1866, quoted in Trefousse, *Thaddeus Stevens*, 198.

45 "We Are Here and Want the Ballot Box," address in Philadelphia, September 4, 1866; "The Altered State of the Negro," address in Philadelphia, September 5, 1866, in *Douglass Papers*, ser. 1, 4:123–38.

46 "We Are Here and Want the Ballot Box," 4:129–30; Frederick E. Hoxie, *The Final Promise: The Campaign to Assimilate the Indians, 1888–1920* (Lincoln: University of Nebraska Press, 1984); David Wallace Adams, *Education for Extinction: American Indians and the Boarding School Experience* (Lawrence: University of Kansas Press, 1995); Robert F. Berkhofer Jr., *The White Man's Indian: Images of the American Indian from Columbus to the Present* (New York: Random House, 1978), 166–75; Colin G. Calloway, *First Peoples: A Documentary Survey of American Indian History* (Boston: Bedford St. Martin's, 2004), 335–51.

47 "We Are Here and Want the Ballot Box," 4:127, 129, 131; "Altered State of the Negro," 4:134, 137; "Govern with Magnanimity and Courage," address in Philadelphia, September 6, 1866, *Douglass Papers*, ser. 1, 4:145.

48 *Life and Times*, 396; "Govern with Magnanimity and Courage," 4:137; Quarles, *Frederick Douglass*, 232–34; McPherson, *Struggle for Equality*, 128–32; Anna Dickinson to Douglass, September 12, 1866, FD Papers (LC).

49 *Life and Times*, 390; *New Orleans Daily Picayune*, September 14, 1866; *Harrisburg Weekly Patriot and Union*, October 4, 1866; both quoted in Egerton, *Wars of Reconstruction*, 204.

50 Douglass to Elizabeth Cady Stanton, February 16, 1866, quoted in McFeely, *Frederick Douglass*, 249.

51 *NASS*, November 10 and 17, 1866; "Let No One Be Excluded from the Ballot Box," address delivered in Tweedle Hall, Albany, NY, *Douglass Papers*, ser. 1, 4:146–47.

52 Lori D. Ginzberg, *Elizabeth Cady Stanton: An American Life* (New York: Hill & Wang, 2009), 116–21; Susan B. Anthony to Douglass, December 15, 1866, FD Papers (LC); Stanton to Douglass, January 8, 1867, in *The Selected Papers of Elizabeth Cady Stanton and*

Susan B. Anthony, Ann D. Gordon, ed. (New Brunswick, NJ: Rutgers University Press, 2000), 2:10–11.

53 A strong defense of Stanton is Ann D. Gordon, "Stanton and the Right to Vote: On Account of Race or Sex," in *Elizabeth Cady Stanton, Feminist as Thinker: A Reader*, ed. Ellen Carol DuBois and Richard Candida Smith (New York: NYU Press, 2007), 111–27. On Stanton as "absolutist," see Ginzberg, *Elizabeth Cady Stanton*, 120–21, 124–28; Stanton, "Manhood Suffrage," December 24, 1868, in Gordon, *Selected Papers of Stanton and Anthony*, 2:194–95.

54 "Manhood Suffrage," 2:196; Ginzberg, *Elizabeth Cady Stanton*, 123; Faye E. Dudden, *Fighting Chance: The Struggle over Woman Suffrage and Black Suffrage in Reconstruction America* (New York: Oxford University Press, 2011), 136–39; Fought, *Women in the World of Frederick Douglass*, 197.

55 Anthony, Remarks at the American Equal Rights Association meeting, New York, May 12, 1869, in Gordon, *Selected Papers of Stanton and Anthony*, 2:239–40.

56 Addresses on Fifteenth Amendment, New York, May 12–13, *Douglass Papers*, ser. 1, 4:216–17. And see Dudden, *Fighting Chance*, 178–79.

57 Stanton quoted in Dudden, *Fighting Chance*, 169–70, 177; Ginzberg, *Elizabeth Cady Stanton*, 120, 134. And see McFeely, *Frederick Douglass*, 265–69.

58 On Douglass's calm and civility, see Dudden, *Fighting Chance*, 177–78; "Women and Negroes Must Work Together," address in Providence, RI, December 11, 1868, *Douglass Papers*, ser. 1 4:185.

59 Stanton, editorial correspondence, Galena, IL, March 3, 1869, in Gordon, *Selected Papers of Stanton and Anthony*, 2:224.

60 *New National Era*, October 20 and 27, 1870, in Foner, *Frederick Douglass on Women's Rights*, 90–95; and see Fought, *Women in the World of Frederick Douglass*, 202–3.

61 Charles Douglass to Douglass, February 26, 1870; Julia G. Crofts to Douglass, July 16 and October 18, 1866, FD Papers (LC); Assing to Ludmilla, July 16, 1868, Varnhagen von Ense Papers.

Chapter 23: All the Leeches That Feed on You

1 Perry Downs to Douglass, February 1867, Douglass Collection, Moorland-Spingarn Research Center, Howard University, Washington, DC; Douglass to J. J. Spelman, July 11, 1867, in *New York Independent*, July 25, 1867; and Preston, *Young Frederick Douglass*, 21, 175–76.

2 Douglass to Theodore Tilton, *New York Independent*, September 12, 1867, in Foner, *Life and Writings*, 4:205–6; itineraries, *Douglass Papers*, ser. 1, 4:xxiii.

3 Clipping in Evans Collection, Savannah, scrapbook 1. Tilton used the letter and story to give a tribute to Douglass. Tilton called this "brotherly" action "deeply affecting . . . another proof that truth is stranger than fiction . . . poetic justice rewarding hope deferred." Charles Douglass to Douglass, August 16, 1867; Rosetta Sprague to Douglass, February 4, 1868; FD Papers (LC).

4 Charles Douglass to Douglass, August 18 and 19, 1865, FD Papers (LC). Charles told his father that on the fifteenth he had sent "the boy" (Strothers) by train to Rochester. Mary Carpenter to Douglass, January 26, 1868; Douglass to Rosine Ame Draz, May 6, 1868; FD Papers (LC).

5 Lewis Douglass to Douglass, October 29, 1866; H. O. Wagoner to Douglass, August 27, 1866; FD Papers (LC).

6 Charles Douglass to Douglass, February 24, 1867; Nathan Sprague to Douglass, March 26,

1867; Rosetta Sprague to Douglass, April 11 and 24, 1867, FD Papers (LC). McKay, "Genealogy and Descendants of Frederick Douglass."

7 Rosetta Sprague to Douglass, April 11 and 24, 1867, FD Papers (LC). On these family problems over time and Anna's health, see Diedrich, *Love across Color Lines*, 272–82.

8 Charles Douglass to Douglass, April 20, May 9, May 17, May 25, and June 24, 1867, FD Papers (LC); itineraries, Douglass Papers, 4:xxiii. The request for an $1,800 loan was on May 9, but on May 24, Charles followed up with gratitude for his father's "advice" and declared, "I shall wait until I am able to do it with my own earnings." He did not wait, but continued the requests.

9 Mary Carpenter to Douglass, January 26, 1868, FD Papers (LC).

10 Charles Douglass to Douglass, November 6, 1867; Nathan Sprague to Douglass, March 10, 1868; FD Papers (LC).

11 Rosetta Sprague to Douglass, February 4, 1868, FD Papers (LC).

12 Rosetta Sprague to Douglass, February 18, 1869, FD Papers (LC).

13 Rosetta Sprague to Douglass, March 10, 1869, FD Papers (LC).

14 Ibid. Some of what Rosetta says in this letter conforms with her much later reminiscence, "My Mother as I Recall Her."

15 Ibid.

16 Scrapbooks, Evans Collection, Savannah. On the cover of scrapbook 1, Lewis inscribed, "This scrapbook I wish to have taken care of and which I give to my nephew, Haley G. Douglass. It contains the history of my doings in the government printing office and several other matters. This book will be given on my death to Haley G. Douglass. August 2, 1907, Washington, DC." And see Ellen Gruber Garvey, *Writing with Scissors: American Scrapbooks from the Civil War to the Harlem Renaissance* (New York: Oxford University Press, 2013), 131–34, 174.

17 "Meeting of Colored Citizens," clipping, newspaper unknown, Evans Collection, Savannah, scrapbook 1; Lewis Douglass to Amelia, December 5, 1870, Evans Collection, Savannah.

18 Lewis Douglass to Amelia Loguen, February 10, 1868, Evans Collection, Savannah.

19 Lewis Douglass, "Black Loyalty," *Colorado Tribune* (Denver), October 17, 1867; Frederick Douglass Jr. to Simon Wolf, May 21, 1869, newspaper title illegible, both in Evans Collection, Savannah, scrapbook 1.

20 Clipping, "The Case of the Colored Printer, Douglass," *Gazette* (Colorado), January 1, 1870, Evans Collection, Savannah, scrapbook 1; "My Son, Lewis Douglass," *New York Times*, August 8, 1869, in Foner, *Life and Writings*, 4:218–20.

21 Charles Douglass to Douglass, April 24 and 29, September 2, 7, 11, and 22, and October 27, 1868, FD Papers (LC).

22 Charles Douglass to Douglass, September 11 and 18, 1868, FD Papers (LC).

23 Charles Douglass to Douglass, February 26, March 21, and April 20, 1869, FD Papers (LC); "Progress of Negro Domination," *Washington Patriot*, June 12, 1871, Evans Collection, Savannah, scrapbook 1.

24 Charles Douglass to Douglass, February 26, 1870, FD Papers (LC); itineraries, *Douglass Papers*, 4:xxviii.

25 Charles Douglass to Douglass, August 10, 1867, FD Papers (LC); Ryan A. Swanson, *When Baseball Went White: Reconstruction, Reconciliation, and Dreams of a National Pastime* (Lincoln: University of Nebraska Press, 2014), 3–12, 117–21; box score and article, "Baseball—Excelsior of Rochester vs. National of Oswego," unidentified paper, 1865, Evans Collection, Savannah, scrapbook 1. Even Charles's letters that focused on the joy of playing baseball were also laced with troubles about money, possessions, and debts.

26 Swanson, *When Baseball Went White*, 114–17, 184–90; *New National Era*, April 17 and October 23, 1873.

27 Charles Douglass to Douglass, May 6, 1870, FD Papers (LC).

28 Charles Douglass to Douglass, May 10 and June 9 and 16, 1870, FD Papers (LC).

29 M. Nzadi Keita, *Brief Evidence of Heaven: Poems from the Life of Anna Murray Douglass* (Camden, NJ: Whirlwind Press, 2014), 96; Fought, *Women in the World of Frederick Douglass*, 206–8, 213–19.

30 Ottilie Assing to Sylvester Koehler, August 29, 1867, September 4, 1868, and May 20, 1870, Sylvester Rosa Koehler Papers, Archives of American Art, Washington, DC; Assing to Douglass, December 2, 1878, in Lohmann, *Radical Passion*, 345. Maria Diedrich incorrectly states that Assing "never mentioned" Perry Downs and his family in her correspondence. See Diedrich, *Love across Color Lines*, 278.

31 On Assing's dependency, see Diedrich, *Love across Color Lines*, 274; Assing to Douglass, December 2, 1878.

32 Assing to Ludmilla Assing, December 21, 1873, and January 29 and March 26, 1874, Varnhagen von Ense Papers. My translator, Katharina Schmidt, indicates that the word *Ungetüm* can be translated as "monster" or "beast." She also concludes that Assing's use of the word *Fatalität* (fate) in this case means hard or bitter outcome. See Wolfgang von Goethe, *Die Wahlverwandtschaften* (1809).

33 Assing to Ludmilla Assing, October 15, 1869, February 16 and June 5, 1870, and April 30 and June 11, 1876, Varnhagen von Ense Papers; Assing to Douglass, February 11, 1877, FD Papers (LC); Fought, *Women in the World of Frederick Douglass*, 148–50, 218–19.

34 Douglass to Rosetta Douglass, November 4, 1872, Post Family Papers, Rochester; Charles Douglass to Douglass, June 25, 1868, FD Papers (LC); Assing to Douglass, March 19, 1879, in Lohmann, *Radical Passion*, 345. In the mere three mentions of Ottilie Assing in the third autobiography, all associated with her role in his escape during the John Brown events of 1859, she is referred to once as "Miss Ottilie Assing" and twice as "Miss Assing." That is two more than the one reference to Anna Murray Douglass, mentioned only as the woman he married upon his escape from slavery, and not by name. See *Life and Times*, 204–5, 308–9, 317. And see Diedrich, *Love across Colors Lines*, 274, 287.

35 Charles Douglass to Douglass, June 25, 1868, FD Papers (LC); Assing to Ludmilla Assing, July 16, 1868, Varnhagen von Ense Papers; see McFeely, *Frederick Douglass*, 262.

36 Assing to Frau Koehler, November 3, 1874; Assing to S. Koehler, October 21, 1868; Koehler Papers; Assing to Douglass, January 5, 1877, in Lohman, *Radical Passion*, 333.

37 Assing to Ludmilla Assing, June 22 and August 10, 1869, and December 3, 1870, Varnhagen von Ense Papers; Assing to Douglass, April 14, 1870, in Lohmann, *Radical Passion*, 329.

38 Assing to Feuerbach, New York, May 15, 1871, in Diedrich, *Love across Color Lines*, 227, 259–60; Ludwig Feuerbach, *The Essence of Christianity* (1841; repr., Amherst, NY: Prometheus Books, 1989).

39 Feuerbach, *Essence of Christianity*, 3–6, 12.

40 Diedrich, *Love Across Color Lines*, 228–30; "What to the Slave Is the Fourth of July," 2:376–81; James 1:27; Isaiah 1:13–17.

41 Assing to Ludmilla Assing, May 23, 1869, and January 8, 1871, Varnhagen von Ense Papers. For the circle of friends from Hoboken to Boston, see Diedrich, *Love across Color Lines*, 261, 275, 280–82. On Douglass's need for recognition, see McFeely, *Frederick Douglass*, 254.

42 Douglass to Koehler, June 9, no year indicated, but must predate 1872, quoted in Diedrich, *Love across Color Lines*, 63.

43 *Bondage and Freedom*, 40, 42–43, 47; see Maggie Scarf, *Intimate Partners: Patterns in Love and Marriage* (New York: Random House, 1987), 40–58, 74–77, 176–77.

44 I am indebted to Leigh Fought, Lois Horton, Sarah Pearsall, and Carolyn Webb for sources, conversations, and correspondence on these questions.

45 "History," in Keita, *Brief Evidence of Heaven*, 140–41.

46 Douglass Sprague, "My Mother as I Recall Her."

Chapter 24: Ventures

 1 Bibliography, the Douglass Book Collection, National Park Service, Museum Resource Center, Landover, MD; *Rochester Democrat and Chronicle*, June 3, 1872. See McFeely, *Frederick Douglass*, 274–75; and Victoria Sandwick Schmitt, "Rochester's Frederick Douglass," *Rochester History* 4 (Fall 2005): 15–16.

 2 *Rochester Democrat and Chronicle*, June 3, 1872; *New York Times*, June 6, 1872, from *Rochester Express*, June 3, 1872, in Schmitt, "Rochester's Frederick Douglass," 16–17.

 3 *New National Era* (hereafter *NNE*), June 13, 1872; *Rochester Union and Advertiser*, June 17, 1872.

 4 *Rochester Union and Advertiser*, June 17, 1872. Eventually Douglass did redeem the money. See Douglass to Amy Post, July 18, 1872, Post Family Papers, University of Rochester.

 5 Assing to Ludmilla Assing, June 11, 1872, Varnhagen von Ense Papers.

 6 *NNE*, June 13, 1872; *Rochester Union and Advertiser*, June 17, 1872.

 7 Allen W. Trelease, *White Terror: The Ku Klux Klan Conspiracy and Southern Reconstruction* (New York: Harper and Row, 1971), 3–10, 49–64, 261–73; Foner, *Reconstruction*, 425–31; David W. Blight, *Race and Reunion: The Civil War in American Memory* (Cambridge, MA: Harvard University Press, 2001), 108–17; George C. Rable, *But There Was No Peace: The Role of Violence in the Politics of Reconstruction* (Athens: University of Georgia Press, 1984), 15–96.

 8 *NNE*, April 6 and November 2, 1871, and May 23, 1872. For Douglass's steady coverage of Klan violence and the federal government's response, see *NNE*, January 16, February 2, March 2, 9, 16, 23, and 30, and April 6, 1871.

 9 Douglass to Samuel D. Porter, June 18, 1873, FD Papers (LC); Douglass to Horatio Gates Warner, June 18 and July 2, 1973, Douglass Papers, University of Rochester.

10 *Life and Times*, 398, 409–10.

11 McFeely, *Frederick Douglass*, 260; Douglass to William Slade, August 12, 1867, in Foner, *Life and Writings*, 4:204–5.

12 J. Sella Martin to Douglass, August 24, 1868, and March 29, 1869, FD Papers (LC); Douglass to J. Sella Martin, April 5, 1869, in Foner, *Life and Writings*, 4:213–15; Diedrich, *Love across Color Lines*, 294; McFeely, *Frederick Douglass*, 271–72. On creation of *New National Era*, see Muller, *Frederick Douglass in Washington*, 47–61.

13 Charles Douglass to Douglass, January 16, 1873, FD Papers (LC); Assing to Koehler, July 4, 1874, Koehler Papers.

14 "A Reform Absolutely Complete," address in New York, April 9, 1870, *Douglass Papers*, ser. 1, 4:260. On abolitionists and the Fifteenth Amendment, see McPherson, *Struggle for Equality*, 424–30.

15 *NNE*, May 26, 1870. See Quarles, *Frederick Douglass*, 249–51.

16 *NNE*, October 6, 1870.

17 See itineraries, *Douglass Papers*, ser. 1, 4:xxiv–xxix.

18 "Frederick Douglass Interviewed, on the Rail," *Milwaukee Sentinel*, January 20, 1872; Douglass to Rosetta Douglass, November 4, 1872, Samuel Porter Papers, Rochester.

19 Douglass to Gerrit Smith, August 24, 1868, in Foner, *Life and Writings*, 4:210–11; Douglass to James Redpath, July 29, 1871, quoted in *Douglass Papers*, ser. 1, vol. 4, headnote, 186;

John Lothrop Motley, *The Rise of the Dutch Republic, a History*, 3 vols. (New York: Harper, 1858–62), 1:v–vi, 91. There were many editions of Motley, and Douglass owned all three volumes, Douglass Book Collection. Douglass to Amy Post, March 17, 1873, Post Family Papers.

20 "William the Silent," address in Cincinnati, OH, February 8, 1869, *Douglass Papers*, ser. 1, 4:187–88; *Gettysburg Star and Sentinel*, January 29, 1869; *Gettysburg Compiler*, January 29, 1869. Thanks to Codie Eash of the Gettysburg Seminary Ridge Museum for providing me these two clippings.

21 "William the Silent," and headnote, 187, 190–94; letter from S. Bower, pastor of St. Joseph Catholic Church, Fremont, OH, to editor, *Fremont Weekly Journal*, April 9, 1869; in *Douglass Papers*, ser. 1, vol. 4, appendices, 615–16.

22 "William the Silent," 195–98; Assing to Koehler, December 12, 1868, Koehler Papers.

23 Assing to Koehler, May 20, 1870, Koehler Papers; Assing to Ludmilla Assing, August 15, 1872, Varnhagen von Ense Papers.

24 *NNE*, November 24 and September 15, 1870. On Douglass and the memory of the war, see David W. Blight, " 'For Something beyond the Battlefield': Frederick Douglass and the Struggle for the Memory of the Civil War," *Journal of American History*, March 1989, 1156–78; and Blight, *Beyond the Battlefield*, 76–210.

25 *NNE*, November 10, 1870, and January 19, 1871.

26 "Speech at the Thirty-Third Anniversary of the Jerry Rescue," Syracuse, NY, 1884, FD Papers (LC). The literature on historical memory is vast. As a place to begin, see Pascal Boyer, "What Are Memories For? Functions of Recall in Cognition and Culture"; Daniel L. Schacter, Angela H. Gutchess, and Elizabeth A. Kensinger, "Specificity of Memory: Implications for Individual and Collective Remembering"; James W. Wertsch, "Collective Memory"; and David W. Blight, "The Memory Boom: Why and Why Now?," in *Memory in Mind and Culture*, ed. Pascal Boyer and James V. Wertsch (Cambridge, UK: Cambridge University Press, 2009), 3–32, 83–116, 117–37, 238–51.

27 *The Golden Age*, quoted in *NNE*, August 8, 1872; "Address at the Grave of the Unknown Dead," Arlington, VA, May 30, 1871, FD Papers (LC). Typescript copy of the same speech, in Evans Collection, "Assorted Materials" box, includes information about eleven hundred Union dead. Douglass reprinted the speech as "Decoration Day," *NNE*, June 1, 1871. He also reprinted an article from the *Grand Army Journal* with favorable treatment of his speech; see "Forget the War and Who Fought It? Never!," *NNE*, June 15, 1871. See Psalm 137:5–6; and Walter Brueggemann, *Out of Babylon* (Nashville: Abingdon Press, 2010).

28 *NNE*, December 1, 1870, January 3, May 11, and November 30, 1871, and August 1, 1872.

29 *NNE*, November 3, 1870, and April 6, 1871.

30 *NNE*, Douglass to "son" (Lewis or Frederick Jr.), August 29 and November 7, 1872.

31 *NNE*, September 8, 1870, and November 2, 1871.

32 *NNE*, September 8, 1870; "I Am a Republican," speech at Rochester City Hall, November 4, 1870, *Douglass Papers*, ser. 1, 4:276–80; "A Word on Mr. Downing's Letter," *NNE*, June 8, 1871.

33 *NNE*, September 26 and May 30, 1872. On the Liberal Republican movement, see William Gillette, *Retreat from Reconstruction, 1869–1879* (Baton Rouge: Louisiana State University Press, 1979), 56–72; Richard A. Gerber, "The Liberal Republicans of 1872 in Historiographical Perspective," *Journal of American History*, June 1975, 40–73; James M. McPherson, "Grant or Greeley? The Abolitionist Dilemma in the Election of 1872," *American Historical Review* (October 1965), 43–61.

34 *NNE*, April 4, March 21, and April 25, 1872. The exchange with the *Tribune* is in *NNE*, September 19, 1872; the *Times* is in *NNE*, October 3, 1872.

35 Douglass to Gerrit Smith, September 24, 1874, GS Papers; Julia Foster Sagendorf to Douglass, July 13, 1873, FD Papers (LC); *NNE*, March 14, 1872.

36 Douglass to C. M. Clay, July 26, 1871, FD Papers (LC); Douglass to Sumner, January 6, 1871, in Foner, *Life and Writings*, 4:240.

37 "U.S. Grant, 1872," *NNE*, November 2, 1871. On Grant's political skills, see William S. McFeely, *Grant: A Biography* (New York: Norton, 1981), 380–99.

38 McFeely, *Grant*, 337–45; Merline Pitre, "Frederick Douglass and the Annexation of Santo Domingo," *Journal of Negro History*, October 1977, 390–91; Charles C. Tansill, *The United States and Santo Domingo, 1798–1873: A Chapter in Caribbean Diplomacy* (Baltimore: Johns Hopkins University Press, 1938), 338–99.

39 McFeely, *Grant*, 340–46; David Herbert Donald, *Charles Sumner and the Rights of Man* (New York: Knopf, 1970), 435–36.

40 On Douglass's "emblematic leadership," see Martin, *Mind of Frederick Douglass*, 55–56.

41 Christopher Wilkins, " 'They Had Heard of Emancipation and the Enfranchisement of Their Race': The African American Colonists of Samaná, Reconstruction, and the State of Santo Domingo," in *The Civil War as Global Conflict: Transnational Meanings of the American Civil War*, ed. David T. Gleason and Simon Lewis (Columbia: University of South Carolina Press, 2014), 211–18; *Congressional Globe*, 41st Cong., 3rd sess., prt. 1, 227–30, December 21, 1870; McFeely, *Frederick Douglass*, 351–52; Douglass to Sumner, December 12, 1870, and January 6, 1871, in Foner, *Life and Writings*, 4:239–40.

42 Allan A. Burton, memorandum to Douglass, January 26, 1871, FD Papers (LC). The instruction reads, "Resolved: that Frederick Douglass be requested to report to the commission about the condition of the English speaking peoples in the town of Samana."

43 Nicholas Guyatt, "America's Conservatory: Race, Reconstruction, and the Santo Domingo Debate," *Journal of American History*, March 2011, 989–90; Douglass to Mr. Melvil-Bloncourt, in *New Orleans Tribune*, August 18, 1865. I am grateful to Rebecca Scott for providing this letter in translation. On Douglass's lack of interest in Africa, see Daniel Kilbride, "What Did Africa Mean to Frederick Douglass?," *Slavery and Abolition*, March 2015, 40–62; Martin, *Mind of Frederick Douglass*, 202–10.

44 Frederick Douglass Jr. to Amy Post, January 20, 1871, Post Family Papers; Assing to Ludmilla Assing, March 3, 1871, Varnhagen von Ense Papers; Douglass, diary of visit to Santo Domingo, 1871, FD Papers (LC), transcription provided by Ka'Mal McClarin and A. J. Aiseirthe, Washington, DC.

45 Diary of visit to Santo Domingo; drawing by James E. Taylor, *Frank Leslie's Illustrated Newspaper*, March 11, 1871; *Report of the Commission of Inquiry to Santo Domingo* (Washington, DC: Government Printing Office, 1871), 231–32, copy in Sterling Library, Yale University; Guyatt, "America's Conservatory," 990–92.

46 Diary of visit to Santo Domingo; *New York World*, February 21, 1871; and see Wilkins, "They Had Heard of Emancipation," 223n102, 233. Douglass was carried away with romance about Columbus, who did not die in Santo Domingo but in Valladolid, Spain, May 20, 1506.

47 Diary of visit to Santo Domingo. And see Christopher Teal, *Hero of Hispaniola: America's First Black Diplomat, Ebenezer D. Bassett* (Westport, CT: Praeger, 2008), 70.

48 *New York Times*, August 6 and 10, and September 17, 1872; Douglass to Gerrit Smith, August 15 and September 11, 1872, in Foner, *Life and Writings*, 4:297; Pitre, "Frederick Douglass and the Annexation," 393–94; Quarles, *Frederick Douglass*, 257–58.

49 Douglass to Secretary of State Hamilton Fish, April 3, 1871, FD Papers (LC); *NNE*, May 11 and 16, 1871.

50 "Santo Domingo," speech delivered in St. Louis, MO, January 13, 1873, *Douglass Papers*,

ser. 1, 4:342, 345–53. For this interpretation of Douglass's motives as "ambition," see McFeely, *Frederick Douglass*, 276–77; Diedrich, *Love across Color Lines*, 298; and Levine, *Delany, Douglass*, 227–28. For the desire to run for Congress mentioned explicitly, see *NNE*, April 6, 1871. Garrison to Sumner, April 24, 1871, quoted in Guyatt, "America's Conservatory," 982.

51 *NNE*, January 12, 1871; *Life and Times*, 410.

52 "Composite Nation," speech delivered many times, 1867 into 1870s, given in Boston, 1867, typescript, FD Papers (LC). The speech was a staple of more than one winter lecture season: see Douglass to Theodore Tilton, December 2, 1869, Post Family Papers. See Pitre, "Frederick Douglass and the Annexation," 394–98; Sarah Luria, "Santo Domingo, or the Ambiguities: Frederick Douglass, Black Imperialism, and the Ku Klux War" (unpublished paper), 2–4; Wilkins, "They Had Heard of Emancipation," 220–23.

53 *NNE*, April 6, 13, 20, and 27, and May 18, 1871. See Guyatt, "America's Conservatory," 981–88.

54 *NNE*, April 6 and 13, and May 18, 1871; Douglass to Henry Highland Garnet, public letter, *Charleston Daily Republican* (Massachusetts?), n.d., 1871, clipping, Evans Collection, scrapbook 2; and see Luria, "Santo Domingo, or the Ambiguities," 5–8.

55 *NNE*, April 13 and May 18, 1871; see Wilkins, "They Had Heard of Emancipation," 226.

56 *Life and Times*, 400; Carl R. Osthaus, *Freedmen, Philanthropy, and Fraud: A History of the Freedmen's Savings Bank* (Urbana: University of Illinois Press, 1976), 1–2, 12–13; *Registers of Signatures of Depositors in Branches of the Freedmen's Savings and Trust Company, 1865–1874* (Washington, DC: National Archives and Records Service, 1970), 3–6; and see a special "Prologue" for genealogists, http://www.archives.gov/publications/prologue/1997/http://www.archives.gov/publications/prologue/1997/summer/freedmans-savings-and-trust.html.

57 *Life and Times*, 401; McFeely, *Frederick Douglass*, 280–81; and on depositors, see Osthaus, *Freedmen, Philanthrophy, and Fraud*, 82–95.

58 *National Savings Bank, Freedmen's Savings and Trust Company* (pamphlet), (Washington, DC: Government Printing Office, 1869), digital copy, Sterling Library, Yale University.

59 Foner, *Reconstruction*, 512–15; Osthaus, *Freedmen, Philanthropy, and Fraud*, 183–86.

60 Charles Douglass to Douglass, January 20, 1872; Douglass to "My Dear Sir," March 30, 1874; Assing to Douglass, May 1, 1874; FD Papers (LC); *Life and Times*, 402; Assing to Mrs. Koehler, September 18, 1874; Assing to Koehler, November 3, 1874; Koehler Papers. Assing was in Washington helping Douglass. She described him as "deceived in the most shameful of ways," but also "guileless" since he knew the bank was "built on sandy ground." On shirts, guided by Ka'Mal McClarin, I saw one preserved at the National Park Service, Museum Resource Center, Landover, MD.

61 Douglass to S. L. Harris, and Douglass to "My Dear Sir," March 30, 1874; Douglass to Sprague, May 30, 1874; FD Papers (LC); Osthaus, *Freedmen, Philanthropy, and Fraud*, 187–91, 202; *Christian Recorder*, in *NNE*, May 7, 1874; Quarles, *Frederick Douglass*, 270.

62 Circular, reprinted in *NNE*, June 25, 1874; Osthaus, *Freedmen, Philanthropy, and Fraud*, 195–99. For many years House and Senate committees held hearings and issued reports resulting from investigations. See especially the 409-page *United States Congress Senate Select Committee on the Freedman's Savings and Trust Company* (Washington, DC, 1880), electronic copy in Sterling Library, Yale University. Douglass testified at this 1880 hearing.

63 Osthaus, *Freedmen, Philanthropy, and Fraud*, 203–5; *Life and Times*, 404.

64 Douglass to unnamed, n.d., June 1874, FD Papers (LC); Douglass to Oliver O. Howard, February 18, 1875, Oliver O. Howard Papers, Bowdoin College Archives, New Brunswick, ME; *Life and Times*, 404–5; Douglass to Gerrit Smith, July 3, 1874, GS Papers. And see

McFeely, *Frederick Douglass*, 281–86, the best overall treatment by a historian of Douglass's role in the bank controversy.

65 Douglass to Sprague, May 30, 1874, FD Papers (LC); Douglass to Amy Post, April 19, 1879, Post Family Papers; and on demise of *NNE, Washington Star*, March 5, 7, 10, and 12, 1874, in Evans Collection, scrapbook 2. See Muller, *Frederick Douglass in Washington*, 58–61.

66 Advice fragment, September 1, 1874, Douglass Papers, Rochester.

Chapter 25: What Will Peace Among the Whites Bring?

1 Foner, *Reconstruction*, 465–68, 486–87, 565–66.

2 *Buffalo Commercial Advertiser*, November 4, 1874; Hamilton Fish to Adam Badeau, November 15, 1874, quoted in Gillette, *Retreat from Reconstruction*, 245–49; "New Hampshire for the Republicans," address in Concord, NH, February 26, 1875, *Douglass Papers*, ser. 1, 4:404.

3 See Foner, *Reconstruction*, 551–53; Rable, *But There Was No Peace*, 113–21.

4 For Ames, Lynch, and the Mississippi Plan generally, see Foner, *Reconstruction*, 253–63; and see Gillette, *Retreat from Reconstruction*, 150–55.

5 *New York Evening Post*, December 17, 1874; *Washington National Republican*, December 12, 1874; both quoted in Gillette, *Retreat from Reconstruction*, 152.

6 The portrait in *New York Weekly Witness*, October 10, 1874; "Douglass Aroused! Trumpet Notes from the Great Orator," *Rochester Express*, February 10, 1875; both in Evans Collection, scrapbook 1.

7 "New Hampshire for the Republicans," 4:403–5; on Civil Rights Act of 1875, see Foner, *Reconstruction*, 553–56. The bill was designed to protect voting rights and quickly became a major political liability for Republicans in the the mid-1870s.

8 "Celebrating the Past, Anticipating the Future," address in Philadelphia, April 14, 1875, *Douglass Papers*, ser. 1, 4:407–9. A lengthy report of this gathering appeared in *Philadelphia Press*, April 15, 1875, in Evans Collection, scrapbook 1. Douglass was introduced by the vice president of the United States, Henry Wilson. See Seymour Drescher, *The Mighty Experiment: Free Labor Versus Slavery in British Emancipation* (New York: Oxford University Press, 2002), 3–18; and as David Brion Davis has written, the ending of New World slavery over a century was "both astonishing and believable." See Davis, *Problem of Slavery*, 336.

9 "Celebrating the Past, Anticipating the Future," 4:410–13; Morgan Godwyn, *The Negro's & Indian's Advocate, Suing for Admission into the Church* (London: printed for the author, 1680), copy in Beinecke Library, Yale University. Godwyn was a Presbyterian minister who had spent time in Virginia.

10 Muller, *Frederick Douglass in Washington*, 95–98; on Hillsdale, see https://thelionofanacos tia.wordpress.com/tag/hillsdale/. The farm along the Anacostia River was purchased from James D. Barry in 1867 and set off in lots over a large expanse of land adjacent to the Government Hospital for the Insane.

11 "The Color Question," speech at Hillsdale, Washington, DC, July 5, 1875, FD Papers (LC), 1–4. Same version is reprinted in *Douglass Papers*, ser. 1, 4:414–22.

12 Ibid., 5.

13 Ibid., 5–8; Mark Twain and Charles Dudley Warner, *The Gilded Age* (1873; repr., New York: Oxford University Press, 1996), 386, 394.

14 *Washington Republican*, July 10, 1875; *Washington Gazette*, July 11, 1875; *New Orleans Louisianan*, July 17, 1875; *American Citizen*, July 17, 1875; all in Evans Collection, scrapbook 1.

15 J. A. Emerson to Douglass, July 28, 1875; F. G. Barbadoes to Douglass, July 25, 1875; and

Douglass's reply, *National Republican*, n.d. indicated on clipping, Evans Collection, scrapbook 1.

16 Douglass reply, *National Republican*, n.d., Evans Collection, scrapbook 1; Douglass to Rev. M. E. Strieby, July 8, 1876, in *American Missionary* 20 (September 1876): 208. Many websites and organizations appropriate Douglass to the ends of Republican and black conservative political agendas. He is the patron saint of small groups of modern black conservatives and libertarians. See, for example, http://frederickdouglassrepublican.com/; http://www.nationalblackrepublicans.com/index.cfm?fuseaction=pages.blackgop; http://www.newrepublic.com/article/91574/frederick-douglass-clarence-thomas.

17 *NNE*, October 26, November 16, and April 20, 1871, and February 29, 1872.

18 "Agriculture and Black Progress," address delivered in Nashville, TN, September 18, 1873, *Douglass Papers*, ser. 1, 4:375–86, 389, 393.

19 Ibid., 392–93. See *NNE*, January 27 and September 22, 1870. On Douglass and self-reliance, see Martin, *Mind of Frederick Douglass*, 67–72, 254–55; Buccola, *Political Thought of Frederick Douglass*, 6, 114–16; and Myers, *Race and Rebirth of American Liberalism*, 113–19.

20 "Agriculture and Black Progress," 4:392, 386.

21 Ibid., 393–94; Charles Douglass to Douglass, April 28 and August 12, 1868, FD Papers (LC).

22 "Let the Negro Alone," address delivered in New York, May 11, 1869, *Douglass Papers*, ser. 1, 4:199, 201, 203, 208–10.

23 Ibid., 202–3. See Myers, *Race and Rebirth of American Liberalism*, 110–13. For a discussion of how Douglass balanced "let alone" with "fair play," see Buccola, *Political Thought of Frederick Douglass*, 165–69. For a less favorable take on Douglass and self-reliance, see McFeely, *Frederick Douglass*, 242, 292–303. McFeely accuses Douglass of "callousness," "myopia," and holding views that supported the "white redeemers."

24 "Let the Negro Alone," 4:211.

25 Ralph Waldo Emerson, "Self-Reliance," in *Selected Essays, Ralph Waldo Emerson* (New York: Penguin, 1982), 185–86; "Self-Made Men," address delivered in Carlisle, PA, March 1893, and many other locations earlier, *Douglass Papers*, ser. 1, 5:547–48, 566; Tennessee speech, *Douglass Papers*, ser. 1, 4:376; John 5:17.

26 "Self-Made Men," 5:552–53, 555–56, 562–63.

27 Ibid., 558–59.

28 Emerson, "Self-Reliance," 178; "Self-Made Men," 5:549. On Douglass and Emerson, see Henry Louis Gates Jr., "Frederick Douglass's Camera Obscura: Representing the Anti-Slave 'Clothed and in Their Own Form,'" *Critical Inquiry*, Fall 2015; and Len Gougeon, "Militant Abolitionism: Douglass, Emerson, and the Anti-Slave," *New England Quarterly* 85, no. 4 (December 2012): 622–57. I am grateful to Gates for conversation about Douglass and Emerson.

29 "Self-Made Men," 5:557–58. On Douglass and "reparations," see Myers, *Race and Rebirth of American Liberalism*, 143–45.

30 "Self-Made Men," 5:570–72.

31 Ibid., 5:572.

32 Ibid., 5:551, 565; Crawford, *The Bard, Robert Burns*, 145–49, 219, 373; Stauffer, *Giants*, 125. A counting in "Self-Made Men" of literary references (actual quotations primarily, but also mentions), and relying on the editors of the *Douglass Papers*, produces the following tally: Bible—8; Shakespeare—6; Burns—5; Emerson—2; Harriet Beecher Stowe—2; and one each for Abraham Lincoln, Alexander Pope, Paul Laurence Dunbar, William Makepeace Thackeray, William Ellery Channing, Benjamin Banneker, Wendell Phillips, William Wordsworth, Thomas Jefferson, Louis Kossuth, Hugh Miller, Elihu Burritt, and Robert

Nicoll. Other self-made men are invoked, such as Toussaint Louverture and William Dietz, but not for literary purposes.

33 "Self-Made Men," 5:573–74.

34 Douglass to Rosetta Sprague, August 28 and October 16, 1873, and May 25, 1878, FD Papers (LC).

35 Douglass to Rosetta Sprague, June 30, 1875, FD Papers (LC).

36 Douglass to Rosetta Sprague, June 3, 1875, FD Papers (LC). Douglass did visit Rochester later in the summer. See Douglass to Rosetta Sprague, August 23, 1875, FD Papers (LC). Diedrich, *Love across Color Lines*, 318–20.

37 Rosetta Sprague to Douglass, September 17, 1876, FD Papers (LC).

38 Charles Douglass to Douglass, July 28 and August 3, 1875, FD Papers (LC). Charles and Elizabeth had married in September 1866, and had two sons, Charles Frederick, known as Freddie, born June 21, 1867, and Joseph Henry, born July 3, 1869. When Charles went off to Santo Domingo in early 1876, he said he would leave "three months provisions" for his family. "Descendants of Frederick Douglass," genealogy prepared for author by Christine McKay.

39 W. B. Shaw to Douglass, February 7, 1876; Charles Douglass to Douglass, August 5, 1876; FD Papers (LC); Evans Collection, handwritten lines in scrapbook 1.

40 George T. Downing to Douglass, February 28, 1877; George W. Williams to Douglass, July 14, 1875, and May 3, 1876; FD Papers (LC); Douglass to Amy Post, April 19, 1879, Post Family Papers. And see John Hope Franklin, *George Washington Williams: A Biography* (Chicago: University of Chicago Press, 1985), 28–34.

41 Diedrich, *Love across Color Lines*, 319–22.

42 Ibid., 322; Assing to Ludmilla Assing, June 11, 1876, Varnhagen von Ense Papers.

43 Assing to Douglass, Rome, January 5, 1877; Rome, February 11, 1877; Munich, July 12, 1877; in Lohmann, *Radical Passion*, 333–39.

44 *Portland Daily Press*, September 3, 1875, clipping provided the author by Tom Desjardin.

45 See Philip Dray, *Capitol Men: The Epic Story of Reconstruction through the Lives of the First Black Congressmen* (Boston: Houghton Mifflin, 2008), 222–25.

46 *NNE*, January 15, 1874.

47 P. B. S. Pinchback to Douglass, April 20, 1875, FD Papers (LC).

48 Dray, *Capitol Men*, 225–28; "The Country Has Not Heard the Last of P. B. S. Pinchback," address in Washington, DC, at Clarke's Hall, March 13, 1876, *Douglass Papers*, ser. 1, 4:422–27. On black politicians, see Eric Foner, *Freedom's Lawmakers: A Directory of Black Officeholders during Reconstruction* (Baton Rouge: Louisiana State University Press, 1993).

49 "Oration in Memory of Abraham Lincoln," 4:312–14; and see chapter 1, this volume, 1–13.

50 Brooks D. Simpson, *The Reconstruction Presidents* (Lawrence: University of Kansas Press, 1998), 199–212; Foner, *Reconstruction*, 566–67; Charles W. Calhoun, *From Bloody Shirt to Full Dinner Pail: The Transformation of Politics and Governance in the Gilded Age* (New York: Hill & Wang, 2010), 49–55.

51 McFeely, *Frederick Douglass*, 289; "Looking the Republican Party Squarely in the Face," address delivered at the Republican National Convention, June 14, 1876, Cincinnati, OH, *Douglass Papers*, ser. 1, 4:440–41.

52 "Looking the Republican Party Squarely," 4:441–42; Exodus 12:34–36.

53 *Port Jervis (NY) Gazette*, June 15, 1876; New York Times, June 15, 1876; *New York Evening Post*, June 15, 1876, all quoted in Gillette, *Retreat from Reconstruction*, 304; *Tuskaloosa Gazette*, n.d., in *New York Times*, June 1, 1876, and numerous other clippings from 1876, in Evans Collection, scrapbook 1.

54 Zachary Chandler to Douglass, August 11, 1876, FD Papers (LC); Chandler was chairman of the Hayes campaign. Hayes quotes in Simpson, *Reconstruction Presidents*, 202.

55 Foner, *Reconstruction*, 530–31; Michael Les Benedict, "Preserving Federalism: Reconstruction and the Waite Court," *Supreme Court Review*, 1978, 55–57, 69–73.

56 Gillette, *Retreat from Reconstruction*, 303–34; Foner, *Reconstruction*, 566–80.

57 Simpson, *Reconstruction Presidents*, 203–9; C. Vann Woodward, *Reunion and Reaction: The Compromise of 1877 and the End of Reconstruction* (New York: Doubleday, 1951), 201–76.

58 As Douglass settled into his role as a Republican insider in Washington, he would often be accused of falling out of touch. See for example the *Elmira (NY) Daily Advertiser*, January 15, 1879, clipping in Evans Collection, scrapbook 2.

Chapter 26: An Important and Lucrative Office

1 Douglass to Amy Post, January 15, 1877, Post Family Papers; itineraries, *Douglass Papers*, ser. 1, 4:xxxv–xxxvi; *New York Tribune*, February 6, 1877, in Evans Collection, scrapbook 1.

2 Charles R. Williams, ed., *Diary and Letters of Rutherford Birchard Hayes* (Columbus: Ohio State Archaeological and Historical Society, 1924), 3:417, 421; T. Harry Williams, ed., *Hayes: The Diary of a President, 1875–1881* (New York: David McKay, 1964), 83, March 16, 1877, entry in which Hayes calls Douglass the "most distinguished and able colored man in the nation." And see Simpson, *Reconstruction Presidents*, 205–6. As much as any policy, Hayes sought a "union of hearts" between North and South.

3 Interview, *Washington Evening Star*, November 13, 1878, in *Douglass Papers*, ser. 1, 4:493–95. The interview was widely reprinted in papers across the country. 1 Samuel 17:46.

4 Assing to Ludmilla Assing, March 26, 1877, Varnhagen von Ense Papers; *Life and Times*, 419–20; Muller, *Frederick Douglass in Washington*, 64–65. On the appointment and Senate vote, see Michael A. Bellesiles, *1877: America's Year of Living Violently* (New York: New Press, 2010), 48–49.

5 *Washington Star*, March 15–16, 1877; *Washington Republican*, March 17, 1877; *New York Times*, March 16, 1877; *Washington Sentinel*, March 17, 1877; and *Forney's Sunday Chronicle*, March 18, 1877; clippings in Evans Collection, scrapbook 1. *New York Evangelist*, April 19, 1877, quoted in Muller, *Frederick Douglass in Washington*, 63.

6 *Washington Sentinel*, March 17, 1877; *Chicago Evening Journal*, March 19, 1877; *Orange (NJ) Journal*, March 24, 1877; *New York Graphic*, March 16, 1877; *Muskegon (MI) Chronicle*, March 23, 1877; clippings in Evans Collection, scrapbook 1; Theodore Tilton to Douglass, March 16, 1877, FD Papers (LC).

7 *Washington Star*, March 22, 1877; *People's Advocate* (Washington, DC), March 24, 1877; in Evans Collection, scrapbook 1.

8 Greenwood, in *New York Times*, March 24, 1877, in John Ernest, ed., *Douglass in His Own Time: A Biographical Chronicle of His Life, Drawn from Recollections, Interviews, and Memoirs by Family, Friends, and Associates* (Iowa City: University of Iowa Press, 2014), 133–34.

9 Ibid., 135–36; *Othello*, act 3, sc. 3.

10 *Life and Times*, 419; *Washington Republican*, May 1, 1877, Evans Collection, scrapbook 1. On the bond between Douglass and the Harris brothers, see McFeely, *Frederick Douglass*, 49–55. *Frank Leslie's Illustrated*, April 7, 1877.

11 Cornel West, *Black Prophetic Fire: In Dialogue with and Edited by Christa Buschendorf* (Boston: Beacon Press, 2014), 13, 15–16, 28, 33, 36. For two other trenchant analyses of Douglass's intellectual legacy from both early and late stages of his life, see Michael Lind, *The Next American Nation: The New Nationalism and the Fourth American Revolution* (New York: Free Press, 1995), 378–83; and Gregory Stephens, *On Racial Frontiers: The New Cul-*

ture of Frederick Douglass, Ralph Ellison, and Bob Marley (Cambridge, UK: Cambridge University Press, 1999), 54–113.

12 Muller, *Frederick Douglass in Washington*, 44–46; *Life and Times*, 412; Masur, *Example for All the Land*, 207–56; Green, *Secret City*, 104–5.

13 "Our National Capital," speech delivered at Douglass Hall, Baltimore, May 8, 1877, *Douglass Papers*, ser. 1, 4:443–48; Masur, *Example for All the Land*, 214–21; Dray, *Capitol Men*, 64. Alexander Shepherd was known as "boss Shepherd"; under his reign Washington, DC, planted thousands of trees, installed thousands of streetlamps, and paved 365 miles of sidewalks and streets.

14 "Our National Capital," 4:449–53.

15 Ibid., 4:458, 461–62.

16 Ibid., 4:458–59; Ralph Ellison, "What Would America Be Like Without Blacks" (1970), in *Going to the Territory* (New York: Vintage, 1986), 108–9.

17 "Our National Capital," 4:462–68.

18 *Washington National Republican*, May 11–13, 1877; *Washington Star*, May 12, 1877; *Washington Chronicle*, May 13, 1877; *Washington Gazette*, May 13, 1877; Press, May 19, 1877; all in Evans Collection, scrapbook 2. On what Douglass termed the "violent hostility" to his speech, see *Life and Times*, 424–27.

19 *National Republican*, May 13, 1877; *Washington Plain Dealer*, May 19, 1877; *Christian Recorder*, May 17, 1877; Evans Collection, scrapbook 2. "Popular feeling was so violent" over this speech, Douglass said in his third autobiography, that he crafted a three-and-a-half-page "explanatory letter" to the *Washington Star*. For full reprint see *Life and Times*, 421–24.

20 Stauffer, Trodd, and Bernier, *Picturing Frederick Douglass*, 45, 51; *Life and Times*, 440; and see Walker, *Moral Choices*, 211, 225, 363.

21 *Baltimore Sun*, June 19, 1877, in *Douglass Papers*, ser. 1, 4:479. This report was widely reprinted around the country. See *New York Times*, June 20, 1877. And see Preston, *Young Frederick Douglass*, 182–83.

22 *Life and Times*, 440; Preston, *Young Frederick Douglass*, 183–84.

23 Preston, *Young Frederick Douglass*, 231; *Life and Times*, 440; *Baltimore Sun*, June 19, 1877. Douglass said his return to see Auld had a "peculiar poetic force, and might well enough be dramatized for the stage." Mark 2:4–11; Luke 6:37.

24 *Life and Times*, 440–41.

25 Ibid., 441–44.

26 Ibid., 443; *Bondage and Freedom*, 30. So far as one can know, Douglass did not ask Auld if he was his father; if Douglass had, it is likely that he would have revealed the fact.

27 *Life and Times*, 442; *Baltimore Sun*, June 19, 1877.

28 *Easton Gazette*, November 30, 1878; *Life and Times*, 444; Preston, *Young Frederick Douglass*, 189. I am grateful to Priscilla Morris, resident of Easton, for providing me with a full text of one of the *Gazette* articles, as well as her incomparable knowledge of Talbot County landscapes.

29 *Easton Gazette*, November 30, 1878; "Easement" for Bethel AME Church, Easton, MD, http://msa.maryland.gov/megafile/msa/stagsere/se1/se5/027000/027700/027726/pdf/msa_se5_27726.pdf. The Bethel AME had just been rebuilt the previous year, 1877.

30 *Easton Gazette*, November 30, 1878; Preston, *Young Frederick Douglass*, 190n15, 232.

31 *Narrative*, 43; *Bondage and Freedom*, 50.

32 *Easton Gazette*, November 30, 1878, in Evans Collection, scrapbook 2.

33 Leo Braudy, *The Frenzy of Renown: Fame and Its History* (New York: Oxford University Press, 1986), 450–51, 506–14.

34 Stauffer, Trodd, and Bernier, *Picturing Frederick Douglass*, ix, xv–xxviii.

35 *Washington National Union*, February 15, 1878.

36 *Elmira (NY) Daily Advertiser*, January 15, 1879, Evans Collection, scrapbook 2; Douglass to Samuel D. Porter, June 30, 1879, Porter Family Papers, University of Rochester Library. And see Diedrich, *Love across Color Lines*, 417n44.

37 *Valley Virginian* (Staunton, VA), April 17, 1879, Evans Collection, scrapbook 2.

38 Ibid.

39 Nell Irvin Painter, *Exodusters: Black Migration to Kansas after Reconstruction* (New York: Knopf, 1977), 3–5, 54–68, 146–59, 175–78, 184–202.

40 Ibid., 228–29; Williams, *Hayes*, May 19, 1878; Hayes, July 1879, quoted in Simpson, *Reconstruction Presidents*, 224–25.

41 *Life and Times*, 428. *Washington Star*, January 13, 1878; *New York Times*, April 24, 1879; *People's Advocate*, April 26 and May 5, 1879; all in Evans Collection, scrapbook 2.

42 Painter, *Exodusters*, 243–47; Robert J. Harlan, "Migration Is the Only Remedy for Our Wrongs," address delivered in Nashville, May 8, 1897, in *Proceedings of the National Conference of Colored Men of the United States, Held in the State Capitol at Nashville, Tennessee, May 6–9, 1879* (Washington, DC, 1879), 30–32; and see Rhondda Robinson Thomas, *Claiming Exodus: A Cultural History of Afro-Atlantic Identity, 1774–1903* (Waco, TX: Baylor University Press, 2013), 127–29.

43 *New York Herald*, September 13, 1879; *Washington Star*, September 30, 1879; "The Condition and Relations of the Colored People," speech at the Centennial Colored M. E. Church, *Baltimore Morning Herald*, May 5, 1879; *National View*, May 3, 1879; *Progressive American* (New York), November 6, 1879; all in Evans Collection, scrapbook 2.

44 "The Exodus from the Gulf States," paper read in Saratoga, New York, September 12, 1879, *Douglass Papers*, ser. 1, 4:510–15, 518, 527–28, 531; same essay also published in *Journal of Social Science*, May 1880, 1–21.

45 "Exodus from the Gulf States," 4:521, 525–29.

46 "Frederick Douglass on the Exodus," a series of resolutions submitted by Douglass to a meeting in Hillsdale, DC, 1879, at which he debated Richard T. Greener, FD Papers (LC).

47 On Douglass, the Exodus, and the Saratoga address, see McFeely, *Frederick Douglass*, 300–304. McFeely unrelentingly condemns Douglass's views on the migration, calling him "blind," lacking in "systematic intellectual analysis," and "perverse," and calling the Social Science Association address an "appalling paper." Condemnation does not get us to the root, though, of why Douglass so loathed all notions of colonization or emigration. This episode does demonstrate, however, that Douglass was left as always with words and little in the way of real political power with which to act.

48 Notes, conversations with Ka'Mal McClarin, museum curator, Frederick Douglass National Historic Site, National Park Service, September 28, 2014; Charles Dickens, *Bleak House* (1853, repr., New York, Penguin, 2003), 117.

49 "Oration at the Second Annual Exposition of the Colored People of North Carolina," October 1, 1880, Raleigh, NC, FD Papers (LC).

50 Douglass to Amy Post, April 19, 1879, Post Family Papers; handwritten notes by Frederick Douglass Jr., Evans Collection, scrapbook 2. On the death of Libbie and the "burden" on the Douglasses of caring for Charles's children, see Assing to Koehler, October 2, 1878; and on Charles's job at the Census Bureau, see Assing to Koehler, November 13, 1880, Koehler Papers.

51 Assing to Douglass, September 26, 1878; Assing to Douglass, March 19, 1879; in Lohmann, *Radical Passion*, 342, 358–59.

52 On Cedar Hill, see http://www.nps.gov/frdo/learn/historyculture/places.htm; Assing to

Koehler, October 6 and November 12, 1878, Koehler Papers; Assing to Douglass, September 6, 1878, in Lohmann, *Radical Passion*, 340.

53 Assing to Douglass, August 21, 1878, in Lohmann, *Radical Passion*, 339–40; Katharina Isabel Schmidt, "Strategically Navigating the Publicist Sphere: Ottilie Assing and America's German Intellectual Communities, 1865–1884" (unpublished manuscript, provided to the author).

54 Assing to Douglass, September 14, 1878; Assing to Douglass, December 2, 1878; Assing to Douglass, December 10, 1878; in Lohmann, *Radical Passion*, 340–41, 346, 348; Assing to Koehler, October 2, 1878; Assing to Koehler, November 13, 1880; Koehler Papers.

55 Diedrich, *Love across Color Lines*, 350–51; Fought, *Women in the World of Frederick Douglass*, 238–42.

56 Assing to Douglass, December 10, 1878, in Lohmann, *Radical Passion*, 347.

Chapter 27: Joys and Sorrows at Cedar Hill

1 Fredericka Douglass Perry, "Recollections of Her Grandfather," holograph, typed, October 6, 1941, 7–8, Frederick Douglass Collection, Moorland-Spingarn Research Center, Manuscripts Division, Howard University. Thanks to Leigh Fought for leading me to this document. Fredericka was born in August 1872 in Rochester, a short time after the burning of the South Avenue house. She grew up largely in Washington and married in 1913 to a John Edward Perry, a medical doctor, and moved to Kansas City, where she lived until she died in 1943. She was a teacher and a women's rights reformer and had no children. "Descendants of Frederick Douglass," family tree prepared for the author by Christine McKay.

2 Perry, "Recollections of Her Grandfather," 9–12.

3 Ibid., 2–3, 13, 15, 17.

4 Increasingly in press coverage Douglass was referred to as "Old Man Eloquent" or the "Grand Old Man," sometimes endearingly and sometimes not. See "The Grand Old Man Talks Eloquently to and for His People," *Topeka Daily Capital*, December 11, 1883, Evans Collection, scrapbook 4. Testimony before Congressional Select Committee to Investigate the Freedmen's Savings and Trust Company, February 14 and 19, 1880, *Douglass Papers*, ser. 1, 4:546–62.

5 See Ira Rutkow, *James A. Garfield* (New York: Times Books, 2006), 31–32, 48–56; Kenneth D. Ackerman, *Dark Horse: The Surprise Election and Political Murder of President James A. Garfield* (New York: Carroll & Graf, 2003), 141–228; and Richard White, *The Republic for Which It Stands: The United States in Reconstruction and the Gilded Age, 1865–1896* (New York: Oxford University Press, 2016), 609–11.

6 Heather Cox Richardson, *To Make Men Free: A History of the Republican Party* (New York: Basic Books, 2014), 109–18; White, *Vanished Twin*, 585–607; Mark A. Lause, *The Civil War's Last Campaign: James B. Weaver, the Greenback-Labor Party and the Politics of Race and Section* (New York: University Press of America, 2001), 3–38, 105–46, 207–28.

7 Rutkow, *Garfield*, 53–59; White, *Republic for Which It Stands*, 573–77; Ackerman, *Dark Horse*, 141–84; *Life and Times*, 523–24.

8 Rutkow, *Garfield*, 59–63; Henry Adams, *Democracy: An American Novel* (1880; repr., New York: Penguin, 1983), 53–54. On Adams's *Democracy*, see White, *Vanished Twin*, 569–73.

9 On Douglass's views on the labor question and unions, see Buccola, *Political Thought of Frederick Douglass*, 53–54, 135–36.

10 Sean Wilentz, *The Politicians and the Egalitarians: The Hidden History of American Politics* (New York: Norton, 2016), xii–xvi; *Life and Times*, 524.

11 "The Lessons of Emancipation to the New Generation," address in Elmira, NY, August 3, 1880, *Douglass Papers*, ser. 1, 4:262–63, 568–71, 573–76, 578–81; Psalm 22:1; Psalm 137:5–6.

12 Vincent P. De Dantis, "The Republican Party Revisited, 1877–1897," in *The Gilded Age: A Reappraisal*, ed. H. Wayne Morgan (Syracuse, NY: Syracuse University Press, 1963), 93; *Binghamton Daily Republican*, October 19 and 20, 1879; and *Peru (IN) Republican*, September 17, 1880; Evans Collection, scrapbook 3.

13 *Indianapolis Journal*, September 5 and 7, 1880; and *Peru Republican*, September 17, 1880; Evans Collection, scrapbook 3.

14 *Madison Daily Evening Star*, September 10 and 11, 1880, Evans Collection, scrapbook 3; Frederick Burr Opper, "Great Political Excitement in Indiana: The Whole State on the Stump," *Puck*, September 29, 1880, in Stauffer, Trodd, and Bernier, *Picturing Frederick Douglass*, 89.

15 *Life and Times*, 517–18; McFeely, *Frederick Douglass*, 305–6. On the assassination, see James C. Clark, *The Murder of James A. Garfield: The President's Last Days and the Trial and Execution of His Assassin* (Jefferson, NC: McFarland, 1993).

16 *Life and Times*, 519–20.

17 Ibid., 520–24; Samuel L. Clemens to James A. Garfield, January 22, 1881, James A. Garfield Papers (LC); McFeely, *Frederick Douglass*, 305.

18 In letters as early as November 1878, Assing urged Douglass to "employ" his "leisure hours in writing the sequel of your autobiography." See Assing to Douglass, November 18 and 28, 1878, Lohmann, *Radical Passion*, 343–45. On publicity for *Life and Times*, see numerous clippings and a poster for a British edition, introduction by John Bright, MP, Evans Collection, scrapbook 2. On sales, which likely never exceeded five thousand copies for both editions, see Robert S. Levine, *The Lives of Frederick Douglass* (Cambridge, MA: Harvard University Press, 2016), 10.

19 *Life and Times*, 444–45; and on the perpetual revision or the "seriality" of the autobiographies, see Levine, *Lives of Frederick Douglass*, 1–30.

20 Darryl Pinckney, "Promissory Notes," *New York Review of Books*, April 6, 1995, 5; Stauffer, "Frederick Douglass and the Aesthetics," 117.

21 *Life and Times*, 479.

22 Ibid.; see William Wells Brown, *My Southern Home; or the South and Its People* (Boston: A. G. Brown, 1880); and John Mercer Langston, *From the Virginia Plantation to the National Capitol, or the First and Only Negro Representative in Congress from the Old Dominion: Self-Reliance, the Secret of Success* (Hartford, CT: American Publishing Co., 1894). And see Kenneth W. Warren, "Frederick Douglass's *Life and Times*: Progressive Rhetoric and the Problem of Constituency," in Sundquist, *Frederick Douglass*, 253–56; and Pinckney, "Promissory Notes," 1–2.

23 See Zoe Trodd, "A Hid Event, Twice Lived: The Post-War Narrative Sub-Versions of Douglass and Melville," *Leviathan* (Melville Society), 2008, 61–68; and Stauffer, "Douglass and the Aesthetics," 130–36. On the revisions in *Life and Times*, see Levine, *Lives of Frederick Douglass*, 1–4, 236–38, 245–46.

24 *Life and Times*, 407, 478.

25 I used two original editions, both at Beinecke Library, Yale University. *Life and Times of Frederick Douglass* (Hartford, CT: Park Publishing, 1882); and *Life and Times of Frederick Douglass*, new rev. ed. (Boston: De Wolfe, 1893).

26 George L. Ruffin to Douglass, May 24 and June 1, 1881, FD Papers (LC). On Ruffin, see William J. Simmons, *Men of Mark: Eminent, Progressive and Rising* (Cleveland: George M. Rewell, 1887), 740–43.

27 *Life and Times* (1882), Ruffin, introduction, 17–22.

28 Ibid., 445; Preston, *Young Frederick Douglass*, 192–93; *Washington Critic*, June 16, 1881, Evans Collection, scrapbook 2.

29 *Narrative*, 53; "My Slave Experience in Maryland," speech delivered in New York City, May 6, 1845, *Douglass Papers*, ser. 1, 1:27–34; Preston, *Young Frederick Douglass*, 192–93; *Life and Times*, 446.

30 *Life and Times*, 446–48. On Douglass's trip to the Wye plantation, see *Washington Critic*, June 16, 1881; and *New South*, June 18, 1881, Evans Collection, scrapbook 3. *New South* lampooned Douglass for trying to visit Thomas Auld, whom the paper falsely claimed had rejected the visitor.

31 *Life and Times*, 448–49.

32 Ibid., 449.

33 Ibid., 450. Ann Catherine Lloyd had married Admiral Franklin Buchanan, the Confederate naval officer. Preston, *Young Frederick Douglass*, 192, 232n20.

34 "Did John Brown Fail?," address in Harpers Ferry, WV, May 30, 1881, delivered at commencement ceremonies at Storer College, *Douglass Papers*, ser. 1, 5:7, 9–10, 35. And see Blight, *Frederick Douglass' Civil War*, 225–35. Especially by the 1880s, Douglass employed a "never forget" rhetorical strategy against the Lost Cause ideology.

35 *New South*, June 25 and July 16, 1881, Evans Collection, scrapbook 3.

36 *People's Advocate*, July 25, 1881. On Garfield's appointment of blacks, or lack thereof, see *New York Times*, April 9, 1881; *National Republican*, April 9, 1881, all in Evans Collection, scrapbook 3.

37 *Account Book, 1881–1883*, Recorder of Deeds Office, FD Papers (LC). It is hard to believe that Douglass himself kept these daily accounts; the more likely person keeping the accounts was Frederick Jr.

38 Assing to Koehler, August 22, 1881, Koehler Papers. All who knew her acknowledged Anna's role as "mother," or "altogether so motherly," as one condolence letter related. Douglass himself referred to Anna as "mother" in years of correspondence to his children. See Rosetta Douglass Sprague, "My Mother as I Recall Her," a published version in *Journal of Negro History* 8, no. 1 (January 1923), 100–101. The four grandchildren who died were Alice Louise Sprague, Rosetta's third daughter, at age six; and Frederick Jr. and wife Virginia's second, third, and fourth children, Jean Hewlett, Lewis Henry, and Maud Ardelle, all of whom died in infancy in the 1870s. "Descendants of Frederick Douglass," compiled for author by Christine McKay.

39 Evans Collection, scrapbook 2; Sprague, "My Mother as I Recall Her," 96, 100; and see Fought, *Women in the World of Frederick Douglass*, 225–28.

40 *New York Globe*, August 12, 1882, Evans Collection, scrapbook 2.

41 Exchange of letters between Douglass and George T. Downing, *New York Globe*, August 14, 19, and 22, 1882, Evans Collection, scrapbook 2; Douglass to S. W. Cowles, August 21, 1882, Harriet Beecher Stowe Center Archive, Hartford, CT. One irony of the letter about the slave shackles is that the cords tying back the draperies over the entrance to the main parlor at Cedar Hill during the last years of Douglass's residence were specially made balls and chains.

42 Douglass to Amy Post, July 14, 1882, Post Family Papers; Douglass to Parker Pillsbury, July 18, 1882, FD Papers (LC); Rosetta Douglass Sprague to Susan B. Anthony, January 27, 1896, Frederick Douglass Collection, Moorland-Spingarn Collection, manuscript division, Howard University; Perry, "Recollections of Her Grandfather," 24.

43 *New York Globe*, August 12, 1882; *People's Advocate*, August 12, 1882, Evans Collection, scrapbook 2; Muller, *Frederick Douglass in Washington*, 132–33; Sprague, "My Mother as I Recall Her," 101; and see Fought, *Women in the World of Frederick Douglass*, ch. 8.

44 Rosetta Douglass Sprague, "My Mother as I Recall Her," address delivered to the Anna Murray Douglass Union, WCTU, Washington, DC, May 10, 1900, reprinted as pamphlet, 1923. For quotations see "My Mother as I Recall Her," *Journal of Negro History* version, 93–101.

45 Ibid., 97–99; see Fought, *Women in the World of Frederick Douglass*, ch. 8.

46 Sprague, "My Mother as I Recall Her," 99–100; Charles Douglass, "Some Incidents in the Home Life."

47 *Life and Times*, 204–5; Douglass to Grace Greenwood, October 9, 1882, FD Papers (LC); and see McFeely, *Frederick Douglass*, 312–13.

48 Douglass to Sarah M. Loguen, August 12, 1882, Moorland-Spingarn Collection, Howard University, and quoted in Foner, *Frederick Douglass on Women's Rights*, 22. Letters with similar language were published in the press. See Douglass to Alfred J. Anderson, *Cincinnati Commercial*, August 27, 1882, Evans Collection, scrapbook 2.

49 *Washington Bee*, January 6, 1883; see Blight, *Race and Reunion*, 301–303.

50 *People's Advocate*, January 6, 1883, clipping originally found in Leon Gardiner Collection, Pennsylvania Historical Society, Philadelphia, PA; *Washington Bee*, January 6, 1883.

51 "Freedom Has Brought Duties," address delivered in Washington, DC, January 1, 1883, *Douglass Papers*, ser. 1, 5:52–56; *Washington Bee*, January 6, 1883.

52 *New York Globe*, January 6, 1883.

53 "Freedom Has Brought Duties," 5:57–58.

54 *Cleveland Herald*, January 8, 1883, Evans Collection, scrapbook 3.

55 Ibid.; *Washington Post*, January 2, 1883, Evans Collection, scrapbook 3; John 3:30.

Chapter 28: Watchman, What of the Night?

1 Illegible name to Douglass, Legation of the United States, Monrovia, Liberia, July 25, 1883, FD Papers (LC).

2 "Our Destiny Is Largely in Our Own Hands," address in Washington, DC, April 16, 1883, *Douglass Papers*, ser. 1, 5:59–61, 66, 79; Isaiah 21:11; *Washington People's Advocate*, April 21, 1883.

3 "Our Destiny Is Largely in Our Own Hands," 5:62–75.

4 Albert Shaw to Douglass, US Consul, Manchester, UK, May 3, 1883; George A. Rice to Douglass, April 21, 1883; Charles Burns to Douglass, February 26, 1883; E. S. Shaner to Douglass, January 29, 1883; H. C. Mears to Douglass, April 28, 1883; Julia Crofts to Douglass, May 4, 1883; FD Papers (LC). Douglass had sent the pamphlet personally to Crofts, as well as other friends.

5 "Are American Colored People Americans?," *Christian Recorder*, February 1, 1883; *Washington Bee*, May 5, 1883; *Cleveland Herald*, May 5 and 9, 1884; Evans Collection, scrapbook 2; and see Daniel Kilbride, "What Did Africa Mean to Frederick Douglass?," *Slavery and Abolition* 36, no. 1 (March 2015): 40–62. Douglass did not lack an intellectual interest in Africa, but he steadfastly opposed all colonization or emigration movements. Douglass met George Thompson, one of the intrepid founders of the Mendi Mission, in the early 1850s. Joseph Yannielli has provided me numerous clippings about Douglass's interest in the Mendi, especially *North Star*, May 1851, and undated articles from the *Colonization Herald*, the *Pennsylvania Freeman*, and the *New York Colonization Journal*.

6 "For Good Government and Urban Politics: The Career of R. T. Greener '70," *Harvard Alumni Bulletin*, December 12, 1964, 266–68; *National Republican*, May 21, 1883, Evans Collection, scrapbook 4.

7 Lewis Douglass in *People's Advocate*, May 19, 1883; Greener in *National Republican*, May 22, 1883; Evans Collection, scrapbook 4.

8 *New York Globe*, May 26, 1883, Evans Collection, scrapbook 4; *Christian Recorder*, May 31, 1883.

9 Lewis Douglass to Douglass, July 25, 1883; Frederick Douglass Jr. to Douglass, July 26, 1883; FD Papers (LC); Frederick Douglass Jr. Account Book, Evans Collection, in separate box.

10 *Christian Recorder*, July 26, 1883.

11 G. Radke to Douglass, July 9, 1883; Rosetta Sprague to Douglass, July 19, 26, and 28, 1883; Lewis Douglass to Douglass, July 19 and 25, 1883; Frederick Douglass Jr. to Douglass, July 21, 1883; Louisa Sprague to Douglass, July 15 and 19, 1883; Annie Sprague to Douglass, July 15, 1883; Martha Greene to Douglass, June 25, 1883; FD Papers (LC). Radke advised Douglass about accommodations in Maine.

12 Interview in Washington, DC, *New York World*, September 12, 1883, *Douglass Papers*, ser. 1, 5:80–84. On my tour of Cedar Hill, along with the curator, in September 2014, I recorded the name and image of each person in the dozens of pictures on the walls in several rooms. Today's restoration and presentation of Douglass's collection conforms in great part with the reporter's observations from 1883. Douglass made his home into at least a visual museum of the antislavery movement. The original call for the convention came out in May and was signed by both Douglass and Greener among twenty-five other men. See *Christian Recorder*, May 23, 1883.

13 *Christian Recorder*, October 4, 1883; Blight, *Race and Reunion*, 307–9.

14 "Address to the People of the United States," speech delivered at convention, Louisville, KY, September 24, 1883, *Douglass Papers*, ser. 1, 5:85–90.

15 Ibid., 5:90–94, 96–100.

16 Ibid., 5:95, 102–104, 108–10.

17 Rayford Logan, *The Betrayal of the Negro: From Rutherford B. Hayes to Woodrow Wilson* (New York: Collier, 1965), 114–18.

18 Akhil Reed Amar, *America's Constitution: A Biography* (New York: Random House, 2006), 283–84; William E. Nelson, *The Fourteenth Amendment: From Political Principle to Judicial Doctrine* (Cambridge, MA: Harvard University Press, 1988), 193–200.

19 "This Decision Has Humbled the Nation," speech delivered at mass meeting, Washington, DC, October 22, 1883, *Douglass Papers*, ser. 1, 5:111–13.

20 Ibid., 5:113–14, 116, 118–20.

21 *Life and Times*, 539–40.

22 All reprinted in *Christian Recorder*, October 25, 1883.

23 Douglass to John Marshall Harlan, November 27, 1883, https://brandeisandharlanwatch .wordpress.com. I am grateful to Katherine Mooney for alerting me to this letter.

24 *National Republican*, January 25, 1884; *Washington Critic*, January 25, 1883; both in Evans Collection, scrapbook 4; Francis J. Grimké, "The Second Marriage of Frederick Douglass," *Journal of Negro History* 19 (July 1934): 324–25; Fought, *Women in the World of Frederick Douglass*, 229–30. On the marriage, see McFeely, *Frederick Douglass*, 318–21; and Stauffer, *Giants*, 313–14. On Francis and Charlotte Forten Grimké, see Henry Louis Gates Jr. and Evelyn Brooks Higginbotham, eds., *African American Lives* (New York: Oxford University Press, 2014), 362–64.

25 *National Republican*, January 25, 1884, Evans Collection, scrapbook 4.

26 *Washington Star*, February 7–9, 1884, Evans Collection, scrapbook 4; and see Fought, *Women in the World of Frederick Douglass*, ch. 9, 22.

27 See Fought, *Women in the World of Frederick Douglass*, 229–46; *Washington Star*, January 25, 1884; *National Republican*, January 25, 1884; *Huntsville (AL) Gazette*; all in *New*

York Globe, February 9, 1884, Evans Collection, scrapbook 4. *Birmingham (AL) Pilot*; *Petersburg (VA) Southern Tribune*; *Little Rock (AR) Mansion*; *Pittsburgh Weekly News*; *Washington (DC) Grit*; all in *New York Globe*, February 9, 1884, Evans Collection, scrapbook 4.

28 *Springfield (OH) Weekly Review*, in *New York Globe*, February 9, 1884, Evans Collection, scrapbook 4.

29 Greener, Gregory, Bruce, and Purvis in *Washington Post*, January 26, 1884; Fortune quoted *Philadelphia Record*, January 28, 1884; all in Evans Collection, scrapbook 4; Julia Crofts to Douglass, February 11, 1884, FD Papers (LC). *Christian Recorder*, January 26, 1884, also openly supported Douglass's choice in his marriage.

30 Interview, *Washington Post*, January 26, 1884, in *Douglass Papers*, ser. 1, 5:145–47; Douglass to J. M. Dalzell, February 1, 1884, in *Washington Star*, February 9, 1884, Evans Collection, scrapbook 4. Acts 17:25–26.

31 Interview of direct Pitts descendant Katy O'dell, with author, Saratoga Springs, NY, July 2014; *New York Evening Star*, January 26, 1884, Evans Collection, scrapbook 4. See Fought, *Women in the World of Frederick Douglass*, 241–54.

32 Fought, *Women in the World of Frederick Douglass*, 234–38.

33 Ibid., 238–42.

34 Douglass to Francis Pitts, undated, but c. 1882–83, FD Papers (LC). As a way of seeing the relationship on the level of love and affection, see the poem "Love Letters of Helen Pitts Douglass," in Michael S. Harper, *Songlines in Michaeltree: New and Collected Poems* (Urbana: University of Illinois Press, 2000), 295–96. Harper imagines a gentle eroticism in the relationship, she enjoying running her "fingers in that mane" of his, and her feeling the "cusp of his palms on my shoulder blades." Why, asks Harper in effect, do we ever deny the love in this controversial marriage?

35 *Washington Star*, February 9, 1884; *Philadelphia Press*, February 7, 1884; Evans Collection, scrapbook 4; Charles Douglass to Douglass, February 17, 1884, FD Papers (LC); Fought, *Women in the World of Frederick Douglass*, ch. 9, 23–24.

36 *Washington Star*, 9, 14, and 16, 1884, Evans Collection, scrapbook 4; Fought, *Women in the World of Frederick Douglass*, ch. 9, 27.

37 *Washington Star*, February 12, 1882, Evans Collection, scrapbook 4.

38 *Washington Grit*, February 16, 1884, in Fought, *Women in the World of Frederick Douglass*, ch. 9, 28.

39 Douglass to Mrs. Marks, February 13, 1884, Evans Collection, scrapbook 5; Diedrich, *Love across Color Lines*, 361–70.

40 Ibid., 371–74.

41 Douglass to Martha Greene, November 4, 1884, FD Papers (LC).

42 Ibid.

43 Ottilie Assing, "Last Will and Testament," November 9, 1871, Surrogate's Office, County of Hudson, NJ, FD Papers (LC); Ottilie Assing, revision of "Last Will and Testament," April 7, 1883, FD Papers (LC); *New York Tribune*, October 27, 1884, under "Local Miscellany"; Henry Bergh to Douglass, October 5, 1884, and January 26, 1885, FD Papers (LC). See Diedrich, *Love across Color Lines*, 379–81.

44 Obituaries in *Jackson (MI) Daily Citizen*, January 28, 1885; *Chicago Tribune*, January 29, 1885; *Marion (OH) Star*, January 30, 1885; *Trenton (NJ) Evening Times*, January 28, 1885; *Arkansas Gazette*, January 30, 1885; *New York Tribune*, May 20, 1885; *Washington Critic*, May 23, 1885; *National Tribune* (Washington, DC), May 28, 1885. The Marion, Ohio, notice is the only one I found that mentions Assing's "literary work" and "translations." Douglass's fame and the substantial amount of money involved may have been the sole

reason Assing's obituary appeared so widely. Hermann C. Kudlich to Douglass, July 18, 1885, FD Papers (LC); Diedrich, *Love across Color Lines*, 380.

45 See Mark Wahlgren Summers, *Rum, Romanism and Rebellion: The Making of a President, 1884* (Chapel Hill: University of North Carolina Press, 2003).

46 *Boston Globe*, August 15, 1884; *Indianapolis Journal*, October 18, 1884; Evans Collection, scrapbook 4.

47 "Speech at the Thirty-Third Anniversary of the Jerry Rescue," Syracuse, NY, n.d., but on or near October 1, 1884, FD Papers (LC); John 11:11–14.

48 "Speech at the Thirty-Third Anniversary"; John 11:14.

49 Interview in *National Republican*, November 18, 1884; *New York Tribune*, November 17, 20, and 24, 1884; Evans Collection, scrapbook 5.

50 *National Leader*, November 29, 1884, Evans Collection, scrapbook 5; *Life and Times*, 532–35.

51 *Meigs County (OH) Republican*, May 7, 1884; *Washington Critic*, May 18, 1885; *Toledo (OH) Bee*, May 1, 1884; Evans Collection, scrapbook 4; Fought, *Women in the World of Frederick Douglass*, 29–30; handwritten note, likely by Frederick Jr., which reads, "FAD, son of F & Virginia Douglass Jr. died February 9, 1886 at 1:40 pm. Surrounding his death bed in his final moments: His father, mother, sister & brother, his grand father & wife, his aunt Amelia," Evans Collection, scrapbook 2.

52 *National Republican*, August 7, 1884; *Washington Star*, August 11 and 13, 1884; Evans Collection, scrapbook 4. Frederick Jr. and his brother-in-law E. M. Hewlett got into a nasty conflict over a fence put up by a neighbor in Uniontown, DC. Frederick Jr. was charged with assault, but the case was dismissed in court. Frederick Jr. may have dismantled the fence with an ax. On this stage of the Langston conflict, see *Cleveland Herald*, May 5 and 9, 1884; *Rochester Democrat and Chronicle*, May 11, 1884.

53 *Washington Bee*, January 23, 1886; *New York Enterprise*, February 17, 1886; *Cleveland Gazette*, February 6, 1886; Evans Collection, scrapbook 2. On Langston, see Kenneth W. Mack, *Representing the Race: The Creation of the Civil Rights Lawyer* (Cambridge, MA: Harvard University Press, 2012), 13–26; Gates and Higginbotham, *African American Lives*, 512–14. Langston had a distinguished career as a lawyer, law professor (he founded the law department at Howard University in 1869), federal government appointee, and especially as US minister and consul general to Haiti, 1877–85.

54 *National Republican*, March 5, 1886; *Brooklyn Eagle*, March 1886; *Washington Star*, August 10, 1886; Evans Collection, scrapbook 6.

55 John 12:24–25. These verses include the famous, ironic, seemingly paradoxical passage "He that loveth his life shall lose it; and he that hateth his life in this world shall keep it until life eternal."

Chapter 29: Born Traveler

1 "Speech delivered in Washington, DC," April 16, 1886, headnote, Douglass Papers, ser. 1, 5:212–13, 216; *Washington Bee*, March 10 and 17, and April 24, 1886; *Washington Post*, April 17, 1886; and see "Political Speech (fragment)," FD Papers (LC).

2 "Speech in Washington, DC," 5:215–16, 228; Exodus 14:21–30; Genesis 4:10.

3 "Speech in Washington, DC," 5:226–27, 237–38.

4 Ibid., 238.

5 *Chicago Conservator*, March 27, 1886, Evans Collection, scrapbook 6. Douglass to Francis J. Grimké, April 24, 1886; Douglass to W. H. Thomas, July 16, 1886; in Foner, *Life and Writings*, 4:442–44.

6 *Washington Star*, May 22, 1886, Evans Collection, scrapbook 6.

7 Both diaries are reprinted from the Douglass Papers (LC) in Mark G. Emerson, "Scholarly Edition of the Grand Tour Diaries of Frederick Douglass and Helen Pitts Douglass" (master's thesis, Indiana University, Department of History, 2003), copy provided to author by Leigh Fought. "Travel Diary of Helen Pitts Douglass," 136. On the four, see Fought, *Women in the World of Frederick Douglass*, 554–63. On Helen Pitts, Fought's work is the best ever written.

8 Douglass Diary, 38–39; Pitts Douglass Diary, 141–42, 146, 152.

9 Douglass Diary, 42–43, 46; Pitts Douglass Diary, 156, 160–62, 165–66.

10 *Life and Times*, 557–61; Pitts Douglass Diary, 171–76; and see McFeely, *Frederick Douglass*, 326.

11 *London Daily News*, October 19 and 21, 1886, Evans Collection, scrapbook 6. And see Hannah Murray's website of Douglass in Britain, http://www.frederickdouglassinbritain.com/. She finds only the two indications for 1886 of a speech in Bridgeport and the interview with the London paper.

12 "Correspondence: Frederick Douglass in Paris," January 28, 1887, newspaper not indicated; "Fred Douglass Abroad," *New York Star*, February 14, 1887; *Detroit Plaindealer*, May 13, 1887; Evans Collection, scrapbook 6; John Merriman, *The Dynamite Club: How a Bombing in Fin-de-Siècle Paris Ignited the Age of Modern Terror* (New Haven, CT: Yale University Press, 2009), 51–68.

13 "Correspondence: Frederick Douglass in Paris." Douglass was especially intrigued by Schoelcher's current effort to write a biography of Toussaint Louverture. "My Foreign Travels," speech delivered in Washington, DC, December 15, 1887, *Douglass Papers*, ser. 1, 5:294–97.

14 Douglass to Lewis Douglass, February 11 and 20, 1887, FD Papers (LC); Douglass Diary, 48–54.

15 Douglass Diary, 55; "My Foreign Travels," 5:308; *Life and Times*, 570–71.

16 Douglass Diary, 56–61.

17 Ibid., 58–59; *Life and Times*, 576–77.

18 Douglass Diary, 63–68, 73–74; Acts 28:13–31.

19 Douglass Diary, 72–73, 81–84.

20 Ibid., 90–93. On the long visit to Egypt, also see McFeely, *Frederick Douglass*, 330–32.

21 Douglass Diary, 98–104, 108–11.

22 Acts 17:16–34; the passage "one blood all nations" is Acts 17:26. Douglass employed this passage and its metaphors many times. See "What to the Slave Is the Fourth of July," 2:383.

23 Douglass Diary, 112–26; Douglass to Amy Post, June 10, 1887, Post Family Papers.

24 *National Republican*, August 13, 1887; *Washington Post*, August 14 and 22, 1887; *Washington Star*, September 23, 1887; Evans Collection, scrapbook 6. Douglass to H. C. Smith, August 24, 1887; John A. Brooks to Douglass, August 30, 1887; and H. J. Gamble to Douglass, September 11, 1887; FD Papers (LC). Brooks wrote of how wonderful it was to have the "incomparable Douglass" back in the midst of his people, "to speak for us and protect our interests."

25 "Sentimental Visit to England," speech at Metropolitan AME Church, September 22, 1887, *Douglass Papers*, ser. 1, 5:263–73.

26 "My Foreign Travels," 5:279–83.

27 Ibid., 5:301.

28 Ibid., 5:305–6, 329–30.

29 Ibid., 5:334–35.

30 Genesis 37–50. "My Foreign Travels," 5:335; especially Genesis 47.

31 *Washington Post*, November 5, 1888; *Washington Star*, November 3, 1888; *Washington Bee*, November 19, 1888; Evans Collection, scrapbook 2.

32 Account Books, from 1871 to 1890, kept and recorded largely by Frederick Douglass Jr., Evans Collection, scrapbook 5; "Douglass Family Genealogy," prepared for author by Christine McKay. Handwritten notes and narrative, recorded in scrapbooks by Frederick Jr., December 21, 1889. He recorded his wife, Virginia, experiencing "Hemorages" on October 18, 1889, Evans Collection, scrapbook 2.

33 *Boston Herald*, August 3, 1887; *State Capital* (Springfield, IL), August 6, 1887; *New York Tribune*, October 26, 1887; *Washington Bee*, October 29, 1887; *New York Age*, November 12, 19, and 26, 1887; Evans Collection, scrapbook 6. Douglass to C. M. Bliss, October 5, 1887, FD Papers (LC).

34 *Washington Republican*, February 29, 1888; *Washington Post*, February 29, 1888; Evans Collection, scrapbook 6, "Old Men Can Be as Bashful as Young Men," speech at birthday celebration, Washington, DC, *Douglass Papers*, ser. 1, 5:344–45, 347–48. On Paul's sufferings and beatings, see 2 Corinthians 23–30.

35 *Washington Republican*, March 5, 1888; *Charleston News and Courier*, March 7, 1888; Evans Collection, scrapbook 6; *Charleston Post and Courier*, December 19, 2015.

36 *Charleston News and Courier*, March 7, 1888, Evans Collection, scrapbook 6; http://racial injustice.eji.org/timeline/1880s/.

37 *Augusta (GA) Chronicle*, March 11, 1888; *Columbia (SC) Register*, March 9, 1888; Evans Collection, scrapbook 6.

38 "In Law Free, in Fact a Slave," address delivered in Washington, DC, April 16, 1888, *Douglass Papers*, ser. 1, 5:357–59; *Washington Bee*, March 21 and 28, 1888; *Washington National Republican*, March 3, 27, and 29, and April 16, 1888. Isaiah 58:1. The entire chapter 58 of Isaiah is one of the great biblical passages about social justice drawn from obedience to God's commands.

39 "In Law Free, in Fact a Slave," 5:361–62. And see Blight, *Frederick Douglass' Civil War*, ch. 10.

40 "In Law Free, in Fact a Slave," 5:362–66. *Washington Bee*, March 21, 1888; *Boston Morning Journal*, April 20, 1888, Evans Collection, scrapbook 6.

41 "In Law Free, in Fact a Slave," 5:358, 369–72.

42 *Life and Times*, 591–92. *New York Tribune*, June 20, 1888; *Chicago Tribune*, June 20 and 23, 1888; Evans Collection, scrapbook 6. "Continue to Wave the Bloody Shirt," speech at Republican National Convention, Chicago, *Douglass Papers*, ser. 1, 5:388–90.

43 William Cheek and Aimee Lee Cheek, "John Mercer Langston: Principle and Politics," in *Black Leaders of the Nineteenth Century*, ed. Leon Litwack and August Meier (Urbana: University of Illinois Press, 1988), 121–24. *New York Age*, August 25, 1888; *Washington Bee*, August 25 and September 1, 1888; *Petersburg (VA) Herald*, n.d., *People's Advocate*, August 25, 1888; Evans Collection, scrapbook 4.

44 *New York Age*, August 25, 1888; *Washington Post*, August 21, 1888; Evans Collection, scrapbook 4; Cheek and Cheek, "John Mercer Langston," 123–24; William Cheek, "A Negro Runs for Congress: John Mercer Langston and the Virginia Campaign of 1888," *Journal of Negro History* 52 (January 1967).

45 *Life and Times*, 591; "Parties Are to Be Judged by Their Fruits," speech in New Haven, CT, October 25, 1888, *Douglass Papers*, ser. 1, 5:590–92; interview in Washington, DC, January 1889, *Douglass Papers*, ser. 1, 5:398–403.

46 "Parties Are to Be Judged by Their Fruits," 5:391, 396–97. In autobiographical memory a few years later, Douglass took the idea of "protection" even further: "No colored man can consistently base his support of any party upon any other principle than that which looks to the protection of men and women from lynch law and murder"; *Life and Times*, 595.

47 http://millercenter.org/president/biography/bharrison-campaigns-and-elections. This was only the second time in American history when the winner of the popular vote did not become president; the other was the Hayes-Tilden election in 1876.

48 Postcard, Douglass to Helen Douglass, February 4, 1889, FD Papers (LC).

49 *Florida Sentinel*, March 22, 1889; *Savannah Tribune*, April 6, 1889; Evans Collection, scrapbook 6.

50 *Florida Times Union*, April 5, 1889; *New York World*, April 6, 1889; Evans Collection, scrapbook 6. *Bainbridge (GA) Democrat*, April 4, 1889 (thanks to Jon Butler for providing this clipping).

51 *Florida Times Union*, April 5, 1889.

52 Ibid. Isaiah 65:17; Revelation 21:1.

53 *Florida Times Union*, April 5, 1889, Evans Collection, scrapbook 6.

54 *Florida Times Union*, April 6, 1889, Evans Collection, scrapbook 6; James Weldon Johnson, *Along This Way: The Autobiography of James Weldon Johnson* (New York: Viking, 1933), 60–61.

55 Johnson, *Along This Way*, 60–61.

56 *Washington Post*, April 12, 1889, Evans Collection, scrapbook 6; *Thomasville (GA) Times*, April 13, 1889; "The Nation's Problem," address at Metropolitan AME Church, April 16, 1889, *Douglass Papers*, ser. 1, 5:403–404, 406, 409, 416–26.

57 Douglass to President Benjamin Harrison, March 7, 1889, FD Papers (LC). Douglass drafted at least four different versions of this handwritten letter. *Chicago Conservator*, May 4, 1889; *New York Tribune*, June 29, 1889; *Washington Post*, July 3, 1889; Evans Collection, scrapbook 6.

Chapter 30: Haiti: Servant Between Two Masters

1 See Christopher Teal, *Hero of Hispaniola: America's First Black Diplomat, Ebenezer D. Bassett* (Westport, CT: Praeger, 2008), 147–61; Cheek and Cheek, "John Mercer Langston," 122.

2 *Life and Times*, 599.

3 *New York Tribune*, June 29, 1889; *New York Herald*, June 30, 1889; *New York Press*, n.d., and *New York World*, n.d., in *Leader* (Washington, DC), July 11, 1889. *Parkersburg (WV) State Journal*, July 4, 1889, in Evans Collection, scrapbook 5.

4 McFeely, *Frederick Douglass*, 335; *Washington Post*, July 3 and 4, 1889; Account Books, 1873–74, kept by Frederick Douglass Jr., Evans Collection, scrapbook 5. On Douglass's solid knowledge of Haitian history, see Laurent Dubois, *Haiti: The Aftershocks of History* (New York: Metropolitan Books, 2012), 190.

5 *New York Sun*, n.d., and *Cleveland Gazette*, n.d., in *Washington Bee*, July 13, 1889.

6 *New York Herald*, August 26, September 29, and October 3, 1889; *New York Times*, August 26, 1889; *Chicago Tribune*, October 18, 1889; *Christian Recorder*, September 26, 1889; McFeely, *Frederick Douglass*, 334.

7 Helen Pitts Douglass to "Dear Ones," FD Papers (LC), unpub., Indianapolis, quoted in McFeely, *Frederick Douglass*, 334. *New York Herald*, December 21, 1889, and *Washington Bee*, June 28, 1890, reported "ostracism" of Helen Douglass "socially," although the *Bee* was never a friend of Douglass for "having married outside his color."

8 Rayford W. Logan, *The Diplomatic Relations of the United States with Haiti, 1776–1891* (Chapel Hill: University of North Carolina Press, 1941), 427–30. Ebenezer Bassett to Douglass, June 27, July 11 and 25, and September 9, 1889, FD Papers (LC).

9 Douglass to James G. Blaine, October 15 and 26, 1889, from Port-au-Prince, in Foner, *Life and Writings*, 4:455–57.

10 Dubois, *Haiti*, 186–88; Millery Polyne, *From Douglass to Duvalier: U.S. African Americans, Haiti, and Pan Americanism, 1870–1964* (Gainesville: University Press of Florida, 2010), 30, 46–47.

11 Dubois, *Haiti*, 186–90. Anténor Firmin, *The Equality of the Human Races*, trans. Asselin Charles (1895; repr., New York: Garland, 2000).

12 Douglass to Blaine, November 18, 1889; Douglass to Anténor Firmin, November 1, 1889; Firmin to Douglass, November 11, 1889; in Norma Brown, ed., *A Black Diplomat in Haiti: The Diplomatic Correspondence of U.S. Minister Frederick Douglass from Haiti, 1889–91*, 2 vols. (Salisbury, NC: Documentary Publication, 1977), 1:33–36.

13 Douglass, address to President Hyppolite, November 14, 1889; and Hyppolite, response to Douglass, November 14, 1889; in Brown, *Black Diplomat in Haiti*, 1:40–46.

14 Pitts Douglass to "Dear Ones," 339.

15 "Haiti and the Haitian People," address in Chicago, January 2, 1893, *Douglass Papers*, ser. 1, 5:512–13.

16 Dubois, *Haiti*, 189–90. See Joseph S. Nye, *Bound to Lead: The Changing Nature of American Power* (New York: Basic Books, 1990); Joseph S. Nye, *Soft Power: The Means to Success in World Politics* (New York: Public Affairs, 2004).

17 Douglass to Blaine, December 9, 1889; Douglass to C. H. Rockwell, November 19 and December 2, 1889; Rockwell to Douglass, November 19, 1889; Firmin to Douglass, November 30, 1889; Rockwell to General in Command, Môle Saint-Nicolas, November 21, 1889; Douglass to Firmin, December 2 and 7, 1889; all in Brown, *Black Diplomat in Haiti*, 1:58, 60–70.

18 On finances and debts, especially the Van Bokkelen matter, see two letters, Douglass to Blaine, January 6 and May 21, 1890, with many enclosures of other correspondence; and numerous enclosures of correspondence between Douglass and Firmin; all in Brown, *Black Diplomat in Haiti*, 1:95–129, 175–92. For the Van Bokkelen protocol, see Douglass to Blaine, July 16, 1890; Douglass to Firmin, July 14, 1890; in Brown, *Black Diplomat in Haiti*, 2:25–28, 32–33. See Logan, *Diplomatic Relations*, 413–14, 433.

19 Douglass to Blaine, January 17 and February 20, 1890, in Brown, *Black Diplomat in Haiti*, 1:130–32, 140–44; Gherardi's report, quoted in Logan, *Diplomatic Relations*, 432–33; Bassett to Douglass, September 2, 1889, FD Paper (LC).

20 Douglass to Blaine, February 6, 1890, in Brown, *Black Diplomat in Haiti*, 1:136–37. Handwritten notes and commentary by Frederick Douglass Jr., Account Books, 1880–90, kept by Frederick Jr., Evans Collection, scrapbooks 5 and 6.

21 Frederick Jr., handwritten notes; Douglass to Charles Douglass, April 1891, Evans Collection, scrapbook 5.

22 Charles Douglass to Douglass, May 27, 1889, FD Papers (LC); see Blight, "For Something Beyond the Battlefield," 1156–78.

23 For request for leave, see Douglass to Blaine, May 31, 1890, in Brown, *Black Diplomat in Haiti*, 1:210; "Will Mr. Douglass Resign," *New York Age*, August 2, 1890; McFeely, *Frederick Douglass*, 344.

24 *New York Tribune*, July 26, 1890.

25 *New York Herald*, March 16, 1890; *New York Age*, August 2, 1890.

26 On Tracy, Clyde, and this entire transition of Douglass's leave back to Haiti, see Logan, *Diplomatic Relations*, 414–15, 436–39. Harrison's instructions to Gherardi, quoted on 439. And see McFeely, *Frederick Douglass*, 347.

27 Two separate letters, Douglass to Blaine, December 18, 1890, in Brown, *Black Diplomat in Haiti*, 2:40–43; *Christian Recorder*, September 18, 1890.

28 Douglass to Blaine, January 5, 1891, in Logan, *Diplomatic Relations*, 438–39. Also see Dubois, *Haiti*, 190–91.

29 Frederick Douglass, "Haiti and the United States: Inside History of the Negotiations for the Môle St. Nicolas, II," *North American Review* 153 (October 1891): 456–58; and see Dubois, *Haiti*, 191; Logan, *Diplomatic Relations*, 446–47.

30 Douglass to Blaine, January 29 and February 18, 1891, in Brown, *Black Diplomat in Haiti*, 2:57–65; Gherardi to Blaine, January 31, 1891, in Logan, *Diplomatic Relations*, 442.

31 Douglass to Blaine, February 18 and 28, 1891, in Brown, *Black Diplomat in Haiti*, 2:71–80; *New York Herald*, March 23, 1891. The *Herald* was an occasional mouthpiece for Clyde and his minions.

32 Douglass to Blaine, April 20 and 21, 1891; Firmin to Douglass and Gherardi, April 22, 1891; in Brown, *Black Diplomat in Haiti*, 2:93–98, 113–14; and see Logan, *Diplomatic Relations*, 448–50; Dubois, *Haiti*, 193–95. The four new warships were the *Boston*, the *Atlanta*, the *Chicago*, and the *Yorktown*.

33 Douglass, "Haiti and the United States. II," 453–54. Telegram, US Legation to State Department, April 23, 1891; Douglass to Blaine, May 3, 1891; in Brown, *Black Diplomat in Haiti*, 2:106, 130–32; and see Robert Debs Heinl Jr. and Nancy Gordon Heinl, *Written in Blood: The Story of the Haitian People, 1492–1995* (Lanham, MD: University Press of America, 1996), 296.

34 Douglass to Blaine, May 7 and 30, 1891, in Brown, *Black Diplomat in Haiti*, 2:141–44, 149–53; interviews with Douglass, *New York Sun*, July 4, 8, and 10, 1891; Helen Pitts Douglass, "Haiti," FD Papers (LC); and see McFeely, *Frederick Douglass*, 352.

35 McFeely, *Frederick Douglass*, 353–54; L. Diane Barnes, *Frederick Douglass: Reformer and Statesman* (New York: Routledge, 2013), 131–32; the Gherardi engineer quoted in Heinl and Heinl, *Written in Blood*, 297; Michel-Rolph Trouillot, *Haiti, State against Nation: The Origins and Legacy of Duvalierism* (New York: Monthly Review Press, 1990), 53–55, 110–13.

36 Douglass to Blaine, two letters, June 19, 1891, in Brown, *Black Diplomat in Haiti*, 2:204–23.

37 *Washington Bee*, February 7, 1891; and *New York Herald*, June 5, 1891, also speculated that Douglass had resigned. Douglass to Charles Douglass, February 25 and April, n.d., 1891, Evans Collection, box of family letters.

38 Douglass to Lewis Douglass, March 7, 1891, Evans Collection, box of family letters. Douglass to Blaine, June 27, 1891; Douglass to President Harrison, July 30, 1891; in Brown, *Black Diplomat in Haiti*, 226, 245–46.

39 Interview, *New York World*, July 13, 1891; interview, *Washington Post*, August 10, 1891; both in *Douglass Papers*, ser. 1, 5:456–69, 470–74.

40 Frederick Douglass, "Haiti and the United States: Inside History of the Negotiations for the Môle St. Nicolas I," *North American Review* 153 (September 1891): 337–38. For an example of further attacks on Douglass, see *New York Times*, August 24, 1891; and for two further interviews, see *New York Herald*, July 10, 1891; *New York Age*, July 11, 1891.

41 Douglass, "Haiti and the United States. I," 338–39. On the *North American Review* essays, see McFeely, *Frederick Douglass*, 356–58.

42 Douglass, "Haiti and the United States. I," 339–41. For ways in which Douglass was placed in a "marginal role" by his own superiors in Washington while he was in Haiti, see Polyne, *From Douglass to Duvalier*, 50–53.

43 Douglass, "Haiti and the United States. I," 340.

44 Ibid., 340–45; *Life and Times*, 595–619, and final quotations, 619–20.

45 Interview, *Washington Post*, August 10, 1891; interview, *Baltimore American*, September 6,

1891; address delivered at Asbury Methodist Church, Washington, DC, August 31, 1891, all in *Douglass Papers*, ser. 1, 5:473, 476–78.

46 Douglass to Marshall Pierce, February 18, 1892, FD Papers (LC).

Chapter 31: If American Conscience Were Only Half-Alive

1 William Dean Howells, "An Exemplary Citizen," book review, *North American Review* 173 (August 1901): 280–88, in *The Booker T. Washington Papers* (hereafter *BTW Papers*), ed. Louis R. Harlan and Raymond W. Smock (Urbana: University of Illinois Press, 1977), 6:191–200.

2 Douglass to Washington, November 20, 1891, in *BTW Papers*, 3:183.

3 Washington to Alex C. Bradford, April 29, 1892; Washington to Douglass, April 29, 1892; *BTW Papers*, 223–25.

4 *Christian Union*, May 28, 1892; W. W. Blake, "An Account of the Tuskegee Institute Commencement," *Southern Workman* 21 (July 1892): 122; an albumen print, taken by unknown photographer, Tuskegee, AL, May 26, 1892, in Stauffer, Trodd, and Bernier, *Picturing Frederick Douglass*, 66.

5 "Renominate Benjamin Harrison: An Interview," Washington, DC, May 31, 1892, *Indianapolis Journal*, June 1, 1892, in *Douglass Papers*, ser. 1, 5:486–88.

6 Tuskegee University Archives, "Lynching, Whites & Negroes, 1882–1968," comp. Monroe Work, http://192.203.127.197/archive/bitstream/handle/123456789/511/Lynching%201882%201968.pdf?sequence=1&isAllowed=y.

7 Martha Greene to Douglass, January 25 and July 3, 1892; J. S. Wood to Douglass, March 11, 1892; Harper Ward to Douglass, May 17, 1892; all in FD Papers (LC). Wood asked Douglass to come out to Illinois to give a series of lectures, and Ward, editor of the *Independent*, invited Douglass to write a piece on what Christopher Columbus had done for the Negro, "blessing or curse?" Neither request was fulfilled.

8 Elizabeth Cady Stanton to Douglass, January 29, 1892; Julia Crofts to Douglass, June 10, 1892; H. O. Wagoner to Douglass, April 10 and July 24, 1892; Ellen Richardson to Douglass, February 16, 1892; all in FD Papers (LC).

9 Douglass to Mrs. Walters, June 21, 1892; Albion Tourgee to Douglass, June 8, 1892; both in FD Papers (LC).

10 Edward S. Wright to Douglass, January 10, 1892; Augusta Johnson to Douglass, April 16, 1892; State of Louisiana, County of Terrebonne to Douglass, June 14, 1892; all in FD Papers (LC).

11 Frederick Douglass, "Lynch Law in the South," *North American Review* 155, no. 428 (July 1892): 17–19.

12 Ibid., 19–24; Hosea 8:7.

13 *Washington Evening Star*, July 28, 1892; and obituary notices, *Washington Bee*, July 28, 1892; and *Washington Post*, July 28, 1892. The Freedmen's Hospital had been founded in 1863, came under the Interior Department of the Federal Government in 1872, and became the teaching hospital for Howard University. See W. Montague Cobb, "A Short History of Freedmen's Hospital," *Journal of the National Medical Association* 54, no. 3 (May 1962): 272–87.

14 W. E. Chandler to Douglass, July 27, 1892; John Cook to Douglass, July 28, 1892; H. O. Wagoner to Douglass, August 9, 1892; James H. A. Johnson to Douglass, August 20, 1892; Cicero Saxon to Douglass, September 6, 1892; S. W. Watkins to Douglass, September 14, 1892; all in FD Papers (LC).

15 On the first meeting of Douglass and Wells, see McFeely, *Frederick Douglass*, 361–62, who

suggests it occurred in New York; Patricia A. Schechter, *Ida B. Wells-Barnett and American Reform, 1880–1930* (Chapel Hill: University of North Carolina Press, 2001), 21, who relies on Ida Wells-Barnett, *Crusade for Justice*, 86, and reports that they met in Washington after giving lectures. See Mia Bay, *To Tell the Truth Freely: The Life of Ida B. Wells* (New York: Hill & Wang, 2009), 5–6.

16 Douglass to Ida B. Wells, October 25, 1892; and Ida B. Wells, preface, *Southern Horror*, in *Southern Horrors and Other Writings: The Anti-Lynching Campaign of Ida B. Wells, 1892–1900*, ed. Jacqueline Jones Royster (1892: repr., Boston: Bedford Books, 1997), 50–51.

17 Richardson, *To Make Men Free*, 123–31.

18 "Douglass on the Late Election," November 10, 1892, FD Papers (LC).

19 Ibid.

20 Haitian Secretary of State, unnamed, to Douglass, February 11, 1892; Charles S. Preston to Douglass, July 22, 1892; Douglass to William E. Curtis, May 3, 1892; Douglass to Mr. Buttersworth, January 20, 1892; Douglass to Preston, June 18, 1892; all in FD Papers (LC).

21 Robert W. Rydell, *All the World's a Fair* (Chicago: University of Chicago Press, 1984), 39–45; David F. Burg, *Chicago's White City of 1893* (Lexington: University of Kentucky Press, 1976), 75–113.

22 Neil Harris, Wim de Wit, James Gilbert, and Robert W. Rydell, *Grand Illusions: Chicago's World's Fair of 1893* (Chicago: Chicago Historical Society, 1893), 4–73; Rydell, *All the World's a Fair*, 55–60; Richard White, *The Republic for Which It Stands: The United States During Reconstruction and the Gilded Age* (New York: Oxford University Press, 2017), MSS, 1190–93.

23 Harris et al., *Grand Illusions*, 157–61.

24 Ibid., 160; White, *Republic for Which It Stands*, 1197–99.

25 McFeely, *Frederick Douglass*, 366; Rydell, *All the World's a Fair*, 46; Douglass quoted in Burg, *Chicago's White City*, 109.

26 Preston to Douglass, October 5 and December 21, 1892, FD Papers (LC). In these letters Preston sent Douglass "small photos" and "lithographic views," as well as a "general account" of finances for the pavilion. Douglass to DeWolfe and Fiske, November 18, 1892; Julia Crofts to Douglass, December 8, 1892; both in FD Papers (LC).

27 *A Week at the Fair: Illustrating the Exhibits and Wonders of the World's Columbian Exposition* (Chicago: Rand, McNally, 1893), map of fairgrounds, opposite 12, and 190–91.

28 "Haiti among the Foremost Civilized Nations of the Earth," address in Chicago, January 2, 1893, *Douglass Papers*, ser. 1, 5:501–5.

29 Ibid., 5:506–9. Douglass's Haiti speeches in Chicago received favorable coverage in Haiti. See Preston to Douglass, February 6, 1893; Douglass to Hyppolite, January 25, 1893; both in FD Papers (LC).

30 "Haiti and the Haitian People," address delivered in Quinn Chapel, Chicago, IL, January 2, 1893, *Douglass Papers*, ser. 1, 5:509–11.

31 Ibid., 5:512–19.

32 Ibid., 5:522–34. See Connor Williams, "'Until Haiti Spoke': Discourse of Diaspora, Self-Sovereignty, and Equality in Frederick Douglass's 1893 Columbian Exposition Speeches," unpub. essay, Yale University, author's possession.

33 *New York Sun*, February 14–15, 1893; *New York Times*, February 14, 1893.

34 "Abraham Lincoln: The Great Man of Our Century," speech delivered in Brooklyn, NY, February 13, 1893, *Douglass Papers*, ser. 1, 5:536–37.

35 Ibid., 5:536, 539; and see David W. Blight, "Abraham Lincoln and Frederick Douglass: A Relationship in Language, Politics, and Memory," in Blight, *Beyond the Battlefield*, 86–88;

and Merrill D. Peterson, *Lincoln in American Memory* (New York: Oxford University Press, 1994), 155–74.

36 Notes from author's tour of Cedar Hill, September 2014.

37 "Abraham Lincoln: Great Man of the Century," 5:543–45.

38 Catherine Impey to Douglass, September 4, 1889; July 4, 1887; March 12, 1890; all in FD Papers (LC); Wells-Barnett, *Crusade for Justice*, 85–86.

39 Wells-Barnett, *Crusade for Justice*, 87–105; Schechter, *Ida B. Wells-Barnett*, 91–94.

40 Robert W. Rydell, ed., *The Reason Why the Colored American Is Not in the World's Columbian Exposition*, by Ida B. Wells, Frederick Douglass, Irvine Garland Penn, and Ferdinand L. Barnett (1893; repr., Urbana: University of Illinois Press, 1999), introduction, xxiv–xxvi.

41 Ibid., xxvi–xxx; Wells-Barnett, *Crusade for Justice*, 116–17; *Indianapolis Freeman*, February 25 and April 8, 1893.

42 Douglass to Rosa (Rosetta Sprague), June 20, 1893, FD Papers (LC); Rydell, *Reason Why*, introduction, xxxi–xxxiii.

43 Virginia Cunningham, *Paul Laurence Dunbar and His Song* (New York: Dodd, Mead, 1947), 96–100; Eugene Levy, *James Weldon Johnson: Black Leader, Black Voice* (Chicago: University of Chicago Press, 1973), 37–41.

44 Cunningham, *Paul Laurence Dunbar*, 102–104; and see McFeely, *Frederick Douglass*, 370–71.

45 Quotations in Rydell, ed., *Reason Why*, xxxii; Wells-Barnett, *Crusade for Justice*, 118–19.

46 Wells-Barnett, *Crusade for Justice*, 116; McFeely, *Frederick Douglass*, 369.

47 Douglass, "Introduction," in Rydell, *Reason Why*, 10.

48 Ibid., 7–9, 12.

49 Ibid., 14–15.

50 Charles Morris to Douglass, October 3, 1893; Rosetta Sprague to Douglass, November 11 and 27, 1893; all in FD Papers (LC). And see McFeely, *Frederick Douglass*, 372–73.

51 Booker T. Washington, "An Account of a Speech before the Labor Congress," September 2, 1893, *BTW Papers*, 3:364–66; *Chicago Inter-Ocean*, September 3, 1893; Rydell, *Reason Why*, xxxiii–xxxvii.

52 *Douglass Papers*, ser. 1, 5:575–76, headnote; Douglass to Charles Douglass, October 7, 1893, Evans Collection, box of family letters; Charles Douglass to Douglass, May 15, 1893, FD Papers (LC).

53 Douglass to De Witt Miller, January 22, 1893, in Foner, *Life and Writings*, 4:477.

54 "Lessons of the Hour," address delivered at Metropolitan AME Church, Washington, DC, January 9, 1894, *Douglass Papers*, ser. 1, 5:576–77; Psalm 91:5.

55 "Lessons of the Hour," 5:582–83.

56 Ibid., 5:585–88.

57 Ibid., 5:588–90; *Thirty Years of Lynching in the United States, 1889–1918* (New York: National Association for the Advancement of Colored People, 1919), 54.

58 "Lessons of the Hour," 5:594–96, 600; *Alexandria (VA) Gazette*, January 10, 1894.

59 "Lessons of the Hour," 5:604–6.

60 Ibid., 5:607; *Washington Evening Star*, January 10, 1894.

Epilogue: Then Douglass Passed

1 Douglass to unnamed, but clearly Julia Griffiths Crofts, February 4, 1894; Douglass to "Doctor Rankin" (J. E. Rankin), January 4, 1895; Douglass to "Dear Sir," February 6, 1895; all in FD Papers (LC). On Douglass's many references to bad health, see Fought, *Women in the World of Frederick Douglass*, 264.

2 Douglass to Mrs. Helen P. Bright Clark, July 19, 1894, FD Papers (LC). Douglass discusses his old age in many other letters also.

3 Douglass to B. F. Auld, March 24, 1894, Gilder Lehrman Collection, New-York Historical Society.

4 William V. Tunnell to Douglass, December 20 and 21, 1893; Ida B. Wells to Douglass, June 3, 1894; Alfred J. Anderson to Douglass, January 10, 1894; George M. Drake to Douglass, January 11, 1894; Estelle Sprague to "Grandpa," February 14, 1894; all in FD Papers (LC).

5 John Roberts to Douglass, August 9, 1893; Colonel A. A. Jones to Douglass, November 1, 1893; President P. A. Cool to Douglass, George R. Smith College, November 16, 1893; Thurman Hall to Douglass, Waugh Methodist Episcopal Church, Baltimore, January 12, 1894; Martha Greene to Douglass, March 1, 1894; Rosetta Sprague to Douglass, October 4, 1894; Susan B. Anthony to Douglass, June 25, 1893; A. J. Smith to Douglass, First Baptist Church, Montgomery, WV, September 29, 1894; Douglass to R. A. Armstrong, May 22, 1894; all in FD Papers (LC). See Carolyn J. Sharp, *Old Testament Prophets for Today* (Louisville, KY: Westminster John Knox Press, 2009), 8–10, 16.

6 Douglass to Rosetta Sprague, June 20, 1893; C. Haeutjens to Douglass, December 8, 1893; Douglass to C. Haeutjens, December 12, 1893; Douglass to Charles S. Morris, July 24, 1894; Joseph Douglass to Douglass, January 15 and February 7, 1894; all in FD Papers (LC). The Haiti government loan was eventually repaid.

7 Estelle Sprague to Douglass, January 3, 1894; Hattie Sprague to Douglass, February 27 and March 4, 1894; Fredericka Sprague to C. H. J. Taylor, Recorder of Deeds, June 29, 1894; John S. Poler, coal dealer, to Douglass, January 5, 1894; all in FD Papers (LC).

8 Booker T. Washington to Douglass, April 2, 1894; P. A. Goins, secretary of Metropolitan AME, to Douglass, January 23, 1894; W. B. Weaver, principal of Gloucester Agricultural and Industrial School, to Douglass, February 1, 1894; James E. Giveau, on behalf of Fannie R. Hicks, to Douglass, December 3, 1893; Willie Penn to Douglass, December 13, 1894; R. Devane, carpenter who made cane, to Douglass, January 28, 1894; Joseph P. Brown, Thomasville, GA, to Douglass, August 23, 1894; E. D. Bassett to Douglass, January 18, 1894; Paul Laurence Dunbar to Douglass, December 30, 1893, and September 7, 1894; I. Garland Penn to Douglass, May 15, 1894; all in FD Papers (LC).

9 Stauffer, Trodd, and Bernier, *Picturing Frederick Douglass*, 70, 74, 195–96.

10 Helen Douglass to Douglass, November 18 and 27, 1893; Helen Douglass to the Reverend Wallace Radcliffe, January 10, 1895; all in FD Papers (LC); Helen Douglass to Francis J. Grimké, March 11, 1895, in *The Works of Francis J. Grimké*, ed. Carter G. Woodson (Washington, DC: Associated Publishers, 1942), 4:36. See Fought, *Women in the World of Frederick Douglass*, 241–62.

11 Henry O. Tanner to Douglass, May 7, 1894; Douglass to Henry O. Tanner, May 14, 1894; the other patron was a "Mr. Wanamaker"; Douglass to Mr. Anderson, March 26, 1894; all in FD Papers (LC).

12 Douglass to Frank Hacker and Henry Haigh, president and secretary of the Michigan Club, February 19, 1895; L. Harrod to Douglass, February 20, 1895, Hillsdale, DC; all in FD Papers (LC); Isaiah 32:2.

13 *New York Times*, February 20, 1895; *New York Tribune*, February 21, 1895; see Muller, *Frederick Douglass in Washington*, 165–67. Muller's research in the Washington, DC, City Directory for 1896 found Harrod's survival, employment as a pastor, and first name.

14 *New York Times*, February 20, 1895; *New York Tribune*, February 21, 1895; *Daily Gazette for Middlesbrough* (England), February 22, 1895; and reprinted in many other foreign papers.

15 *Washington Post*, February 26, 1895; Kate Field, in *Kate Field's Washington*, n.d., Evans Collection, scrapbook 1.

16 *Washington Post*, February 26, 1895; Kate Field, in *Kate Field's Washington*, n.d., Evans Collection, scrapbook 1.

17 *Washington Post*, February 26, 1895; J. E. Rankin, "Frederick Douglass's Character and Career," February 25, 1895, in Ernest, ed., *Douglass in His Own Time*, 168–75; and as reported in the *Gloucester Letter* (Cappahosic, VA), March 1895, Evans Collection, scrapbook 1.

18 *Washington Post*, February 26, 1895; *New York Tribune*, February 24, 1895; *Chicago Daily Tribune*, February 24, 1895. *New York Exchange*, February 26, 1895, Evans Collection, scrapbook 1.

19 *New York Tribune*, February 27, 1895; *New York Times*, February 27, 1895. *San Francisco (CA) Budget*, March 9, 1895, Evans Collection, scrapbook 1. Fought, *Women in the World of Frederick Douglass*, 291–94, 303.

20 *Brooklyn Eagle*, February 21, 1895; *New York Times*, February 27, 1895. *Rome (NY) Daily Sentinel*, March 7, 1895, Evans Collection, Douglass Family scrapbook.

21 *Brooklyn Eagle*, February 21, 1895; *New York Tribune*, February 22, 1895. *Springfield (IL) State Capitol*, n.d.; *Norfolk (VA) Recorder*, n.d.; *Washington Star*, March 18, 1895; Evans Collection, Douglass Family scrapbook.

22 Last letter claims: clipping from Butte, Montana, unnamed paper, and *Philadelphia Press*, February 22, 1895, a letter by Douglass to a Mrs. George Morris Phillips, about black music compared to Irish music; *New York Sun*, March 8, 1895; *Cincinnati Gazette*, February 21, 1895; *Wilmington (NC) Messenger*, February 26, 1895; *Oshkosh (WI) Northwestern*, n.d., in *Milwaukee Evening Wisconsin*, February 22, 1895; *New Orleans Picayune*, February 21, 1895; all in Evans Collection, scrapbook 1.

23 *Washington News*, February 21, 1895; *Boston Transcript*, February 26, 1895; *Baltimore News*, March 4, 1895; all in Evans Collection, scrapbook 1.

24 San Francisco resolutions; *Americus (GA) Messenger*, March 2, 1895; *Birmingham (AL) Age-Herald*, March 3, 1895; *Waco (TX) Searchlight*, March 30, 1895; all in Evans Collection, scrapbook 1; Atlanta meeting and Morris reported in *Baltimore Sun*, February 27, 1895.

25 Booker T. Washington, "Atlanta Exposition Address," *BTW Papers*, 3:583–87.

26 A program from the Wilberforce memorial event, Evans Collection, scrapbook 1; W. E. B. Du Bois, "Douglass as a Statesman," Wilberforce, Ohio, March 9, 1895, https://www.google .com/#q=Du+Bois%2C+%22Douglass+as+a+statesman%22; and Herbert Aptheker, ed., *Writing of W. E. B. Du Bois in Non-Periodical Literature, Edited by Others* (Millwood, NY: Kraus-Thomson, 1982), 1:29–40. On his twenty-fifth birthday in Berlin, Du Bois wrote and performed a remarkable ritual. He celebrated himself by himself with wine, music, and his own testament: W. E. B. Du Bois Papers, University of Massachusetts, Amherst, archives; and David Levering Lewis, *W. E. B. Du Bois: Biography of a Race, 1868–1919* (New York: Henry Holt, 1993), 134–35.

27 Du Bois, "Douglass as a Statesman"; *Boston Globe*, March 17, 1892; *Boston Daily Advertiser*, March 17, 1892. Both papers record the title and subject of Douglass's address. Herbert Aptheker reprinted the speech "Douglass as a Statesman" for perhaps the first time, in which he erroneously stated that Du Bois would have witnessed Douglass speak on Haiti in Chicago in January 1893. That did not happen; but he could surely have been in Tremont Temple, March 9, 1892. See "Du Bois on Douglass: 1895," *Journal of Negro History* 49 (October 1964): 264–68.

28 W. E. B. Du Bois, *The Souls of Black Folk*, ed. David W. Blight and Robert Gooding-Williams (1903; repr., Boston: Bedford Books, 1997), 66–67; Lewis, *W. E. B. Du Bois*, 280.

29 Du Bois, *Souls of Black Folk*, 55, 61.

30 "What to the Slave Is the Fourth of July," 2:368; "Haiti and the Haitian People," 5:527; "Present Condition and Future Prospect," 2:245, 248.

31 W. E. B. Du Bois, "The Passing of Douglass," handwritten MS, Du Bois Papers.

32 "Frederick Douglass," in *The Collected Poetry of Paul Laurence Dunbar*, ed. Joanne M. Braxton (1913; repr., Charlottesville: University of Virginia Press, 1993), 6–7.

33 Francis Grimké, "Frederick Douglass," address delivered March 10, 1895, Washington, DC, in Woodson, *Works of Francis Grimké*, 1:52–53.

34 Robert Hayden, "Frederick Douglass," in *The Poetry of the Negro, 1746–1970*, ed. Langston Hughes and Arna Bontemps, rev. ed. (Garden City, NY: Doubleday, 1970), 296.

ILLUSTRATION CREDITS

p. 3 Library of Congress, Prints and Photographs Division

p. 10 Library of Congress, Geography and Maps Division

p. 21 Courtesy of Richard and Beverly Tilghman family collection

p. 30 Courtesy of Richard and Beverly Tilghman family collection

p. 43 Frederick Douglass National Historic Park, National Park Service

p. 56 Maryland Historical Society, Baltimore, MD

p. 69 H. Robins Hollyday Collection, Talbot County Historical Society

p. 74 Easton National Bank Collection, Courtesy of the Talbot County Historical Society, Easton, Maryland

p. 85 National Portrait Gallery, Smithsonian Institution

p. 90 New Bedford Whaling Museum

p. 96 Courtesy Picture Research Consultants and Archives, Topsfield, MA

p. 108 Collection of Greg French

p. 117 New-York Historical Society

p. 122 American Antiquarian Society, Worcester, MA

p. 132 Portrait collection, Schomburg Center for Research in Black Culture, Photographs and Prints Division

p. 148 Boston Public Library, Print Department

p. 160 akg-images

p. 164 Adams, Douglass, Vanderzee, & McWilliams collection, Nebraska State Historical Society

p. 168 Parker Collection, Thomas Crane Public Library, Digital Commonwealth, Massachusetts Collections Online

p. 184 Albert Cook Myers Collection, Chester County Historical Society, PA

p. 189 National Portrait Gallery, Smithsonian Institution

p. 193 U. S. Military History Institute, Carlisle, PA

p. 210 Art Institute of Chicago

p. 216 Randolph Linsly Simpson African American Collection, James Weldon Johnson Memorial Collection, Beinecke Rare Book and Manuscript Library

p. 220 Boston Public Library, Print Department

p. 230 Rochester Public Library, Local History Division

p. 241 Randolph Linsly Simpson African American Collection, James Weldon Johnson Memorial Collection, Beinecke Rare Book and Manuscript Library

p. 248 Library of Congress Prints and Photographs Division

p. 255 Collection of David W. Blight

p. 262 Nelson Atkins Museum of Art, Kansas City, MO

p. 266 John B. Cade Library, Southern University and A & M College, Baton Rouge, LA

p. 688 Randolph Linsly Simpson African American Collection, James Weldon Johnson Memorial Collection, Beinecke Rare Book and Manuscript Library

p. 694 No Credit

p. 703 Frederick Douglass National Historic Site, National Park Service

p. 716 Library of Congress, Prints and Photographs Division

p. 719 Archives of American Art, Washington, D.C.

p. 723 National Portrait Gallery, Smithsonian Institution

p. 729 Chicago Historical Society

p. 736 Randolph Linsly Simpson African American Collection, James Weldon Johnson Memorial Collection, Beinecke Rare Book and Manuscript Library

p. 747 Frederick Douglass National Historic Site, National Park Service

p. 750 New Bedford Whaling Museum

p. 763 Randolph Linsly Simpson African American Collection, James Weldon Johnson Memorial Collection, Beinecke Rare Book and Manuscript Library

Front endpaper: Special Collections, Lavery Library, St. John Fisher College

Rear endpaper: Randolph Linsly Simpson African American Collection, James Weldon Johnson Memorial Collection, Beinecke Rare Book and Manuscript Library

INDEX

Page numbers in *italics* refer to illustrations.

AASS. *See* American Anti-Slavery Society

Abel, 226, 324

abolitionists, abolitionism, 4, 51–52, 84, 190–92, 208, 213, 226–27, 236, 246–47, 251, 252–53, 260, 264, 270–72, 293–94, 323–24
  African American support for, 193–94, 220–21, 240, 280, 288–89
  ascendancy of, 104
  attacks on, 119–20, 121–22, 123, 128
  British, 168–69, 171, 173, 183–84, 189–90, 196, 248–49, 286, 312–17, 320, 359
  characteristics of, 95–96
  and Congress, 95
  disagreements/schisms within, 104–5, 106, 117–18, 128, 130, 135
  FD and, xii, 190–92, 208, 213, 226–27, 236, 246–47, 251, 252–53, 260, 264, 270–72, 293–94, 323–24, 351–52, 358, 417, 420, 421, 424, 428, 443, 555–56, 626–27, 757
  FD as speaker for, 100–101, 102–4, 106–10, 112–15
  and FD belief in Garrisonianism, 116–36, 137
  FD initial enthusiasm for, 94–101
  FD relationship with, 177
  funding for, 139
  Frémont's order praised by, 352
  Garrison views about, 105
  and immediatism, 106
  Garrisonianism in, 162, 172, 175, 180, 189, 201, 207, 208, 213–19, 221–27, 229, 245, 249, 252–53, 255, 263, 285, 304–5, 313, 316–17, 320–21, 330
  Lincoln's criticism of, 353
  and Lincoln's emancipation plan, 363–64
  and manumission of slaves, 93, 172
  and middle class, 123
  Nantucket meeeting of, 98–100
  as outraged at Lincoln's Reconstruction plan, 431
  political, 190–92, 208, 213, 226–27, 236, 246–47, 251, 252–53, 260, 264, 270–72, 293–94, 323–24
  as political threat, 123
  and Quakers, 121
  and religion, 96–97, 123
  spread of, 94–95, 155
  and women, 95
  See also Garrisonians; Tappanites; *specific person or organization*

Abraham, 159, 165, 226, 232, 482

Adams, Henry, 615

Adams, Perry Frank, 166

Adams, Ruth Cox (Harriet Bailey, FD's adopted sister), 163–66, *164*, 170, 319

"An Address to the Slaves of the United States" (Garnet), 131–33

Aesop's fables, 139

African Americans:
  abolition supported by, 193–94, 220–21, 240, 280, 288–89
  churches of, 185–86, 193, 229, 291, 301–2, 329–30
  citizenship for, 264, 277–79
  colonization and, *see* African colonization movement
  at Columbian Exposition, 714, 725–27, 733–39
  communities of, 186, 191–94, 229, 231, 242, 244, 256–57, 277–78, 288–89, 293
  education of, 260, 288
  and enlistment in military, 351, 354, 359, 361, 388, 390–91, 392–96, 401, 402–4, *405*, 407, 410–11, 414, 424, 470
  Freedmen's Memorial and, 5
  identity of, 88
  leadership of, 131–33, 225–27, 254–55, 303, 307
  literacy of, 258
  mixed race, 260

African Americans (*cont.*)
  nationalism for, 289
  pay of soldiers of, 402–3
  power of, 273
  as prisoners of war, killing of, 405–6
  racism endured by, 181–83, 188, 189, 190,
    193, 202–5, 218, 238–39, 289–90, 304,
    317, 318, 326
  resistance of, 131–33
  rights of, 94, 95, 113–14, 131
  segregation of, 177, 178–79, 188, 269, 290, 303
  self-improvement of, 192–94, 211, 240, 254,
    288–89
  self-respect of, 246–47
  vigilance committees of, 242, 300
  voting rights of, *see* black suffrage
  women, 186, 199–200, 203
  see also specific person or topic
African colonization movement,95, 97–98, 218,
    238–40, 256, 275, 278, 303–4, 369–79,
    380, 387, 428
  denounced at Syracuse convention, 440
  Johnson's embrace of, 474, 476
African Free School, 131
African Free School no. 2, 255
African Methodist Episcopal Zion Church
    (New Bedford), FD as speaker at, 93–94,
    97, 98
Agassiz, Louis, 376
agricultural activism, 289
Albany, N.Y., 122, 179, 181, 188–89
Aldridge, Ira, 466
Alert Base Ball Club, 507
Alexander, Archer, 3
Alger, Horatio, 621, 623
Allegheny Mountains, 282, 330
Along This Way (Johnson), 688
Alter, Robert, 229, 258–59
Alvord, John, 545
Amanda (sloop), 56
Amar, Akhil, 647
AME Zion Church, 93–94, 97, 98
American and Foreign Anti-Slavery Society,
    106, 131
American Anti-Slavery Society (AASS), 171,
    179–81, 184, 189, 202–4, 216, 217–19,
    221–22, 224, 291, 320–21, 416–17, 468–69
  and Buffum-FD relationship, 145
  conventions/annual meetings of, 106, 116–17,
    127
  disputes within, 104–5, 129
  FD as speaker for, 100–101, 102–4, 106–10,
    112–15, 116–36, 137
  and FD financial affairs, 111, 129

  FD's lectures to, 525, 563–64
  FD traveling circuit for, 100–101, 102–4,
    106–10, 112–15
  funding for, 105
  and Garrison, 105, 106
  and Garrisonian doctrines, 106
  Massachusetts Hundred Conventions tour
    of, 136–37
  One Hundred Conventions tour of, 128–36
  and Tappanites, 106
  and women's equality, 106
  See also specific person
American Colonization Society, 97, 238–40
American Missionary Association, 559
American Revolution, 244, 309, 395
American Slavery as It Is (Weld), 119
American Social Science Association, 603
Ames, Adelbert, 553
Amistad mutiny (1839), 287
Anderson, Alfred, 747
Anderson, Mr., 751
Andersonville prison, 392
Andover, Mass., 247
Andrew, John, 315, 379, 398
  black troops mobilized by, 391, 403
Anglo-African, 321, 403, 411
Anglo-African Institute for the
    Encouragement of Industry and Art, 371
Annapolis, Md., 36
Anthony, Aaron, 9–10, 13–14, 19, 22–23, 25,
    35, 56, 597, 625
Anthony, Andrew, 13, 48–49
Anthony, Ann Catherine Skinner, 14
Anthony, Richard, 13, 48
Anthony, Susan B., 488–91, 492–93, 748, 752,
    753
Anti-Caste (journal), 733
anti-Catholicism, of FD, 528–29, 545, 670–71
Antietam, Battle of, 357, 376, 397
Anti-Slavery League, 175
"Appeal to Free Colored People of the United
    States, The," 373
aristocracy, 174–75
Arthur, Chester A., 614, 644
ashcake, 23, 24
Assembly Club, 757
Assing, Ludmilla, 451
Assing, Ottilie, xvii, 268, 290–92, 299, 306,
    317–19, *318,* 320, 338–39, 404, 413, 419,
    493–94, 509, 512–13, 518, 519
  and Anna Douglass, 387, 388, 451, 511–12,
    514, 521–22, 608, 657
  in attempt to convert FD to atheism, 514–15
  on Cedar Hill family times, 611

in desire to go to Europe, 452
as disgusted with Perry's family, 510–11
and Douglass house fire, 521–22
on election of 1864, 452–53
and FD's District of Columbia marshal
    position, 583
and FD's family difficulties, 570
and FD's move south, 414
FD's relationship with, 521–22, 529, 570,
    572–73
on FD's speeches, 525, 529
FD taught by, 516–17
and financial issues, 521–22
and *Life and Times of Frederick Douglass,* 619
and *New National Era,* 525, 529–30, 539
Othello watched by, 466–67
separation from FD of, 606–9, 656–57
suicide of, 657–59
Atheneum, 100
Atlanta, Ga., 436–37
Atlanta University, 715
Atlantic Monthly, 369, 471
Augustine, Saint, 24
Auld, Benjamin, 449, 746
Auld, Hugh, 35, 36, 38, 39, 40, 49, 51, 55–56,
    75–76, 78, 80–81, 103, 134, 153, 163,
    170–73, 176, 240, 565, 746
    FD as "given" to, 159, 176
    FD comments about, 170, 176
    and manumission of FD, 170, 171–73
Auld, Lucretia, 23, 30–31, 35, 48, 55, 485
Auld, Rowena Hamilton, 55, 57, 75
Auld, Sophia, 36, 38–39, 40, 41–42, 48–49, 50–51,
    52, 56, 76, 103, 449, 565, 746
Auld, Thomas, 23, 31, 48, 49, 55–56, 57–59,
    63, 73, 74–75, 80, 83, 109, 115, 134, 150,
    153, 158–59, 161, 163, 171, 176, 198–200,
    260–61, 449, 468, 485, 746
    emotional breakdown of, 58
    FD's 1877 encounter with, 592–95
Auld, Tommy (Hugh's son), 35, 38, 48, 75
Aunt Katy (Arnold family cook), 11–12, 22, 24
Autobiography of an Ex-Colored Man
    (Johnson), 689
Autographs for Freedom (Griffiths, ed.), 224,
    225, 227, 249
Ayr, Scotland, 167

Babcock, Orville, 537
Babylonian Captivity, 228
Babylon, 228, 237, 242, 251
Báez, Buenaventura, 537
Bagpipe Lesson, The (painting), 751
Bailey, Augustus, 11

Bailey, Betsy, xii, 9, 11, 13, 14, 17, 49, 198, 502,
    517
Bailey, Eliza, 20, 49, 56–57, 163
Bailey, Frederick, and FD slave name, 14, 152,
    161, 164, 171–73, 756
Bailey, Harriet (FD's adopted sister) *see*
    Adams, Ruth Cox
Bailey, Harriet (FD's mother), xii, 11–12, 16,
    88, 163, 258, 495, 502
    and FD's post-Reconstruction Eastern
        Shore visits, 597–98
    FD's relationship with, xii, 517–18
Bailey, Henny, 55–56, 59
Bailey, Hester, 14–15, 24
Bailey, Isaac, 9, 11
Bailey, Joseph, 42
Bailey, Perry, 20, 49
Bailey, Priscilla, 56
Bailey, Sarah, 20, 49
Bailey, Tom, 75
Baldwin, James, xiii, 389–90
Ball, Thomas, 2–3
"Ballot and the Bullet, The" (Douglass), 304–5
Baltimore American, 51
Baltimore, Md., 34, 35–47, 48–66, *56,* 166, 181,
    190, 199, 222, 261, 268
    African American religious community of, 53
    European immigration to, 37
    FD flight from, 140
    FD in, 89, 103, 157
    FD's plan to move to, 468
    free blacks in, 37, 75, 78
    Methodist Episcopal Church Conference
        in, 95
    poverty in, 90
Baltimore and Ohio Railroad (B&O), 36
Banks, Nathaniel P., 430, 431
"Banks o' Doon, The" (Burns), 167
Baptists:
    and AASS tour of New York State, 123
    and One Hundred Conventions campaign,
        130, 133–34
Barnett, Ferdinand, 733
Barnstable, Mass., FD speeches at, 118
baseball, 507–8
Bassett, Ebenezer D., 541, 691, 694–95, 749
Batchelder, James, 245–46
"Battle Hymn of the Republic" (Howe), 369
"Battle of Liberty Place" (New Orleans, 1874),
    553
Bay Side, Md., 58
Beecher-Hooker, Isabella, 736
Beggs, Mrs., 167
Belfast, Ireland, 38, 145, 149, 150, 153–54, 162

Belknap Street Church, 222

Bellamy, Francis J., 727

Berlin, Ira, 20

Bethel AME Church (Fell's Point), 446

Bible, xi, xv-xvi, 156, 157, 165, 167, 190, 197,
    222, 226, 228–38, 258–59, 261, 263–70,
    272, 283–85, 287, 293–94, 316, 324

  of Burns (Robert), 167

  and FD's Europe trip (1886), 677–78

  and FD as orator, 122, 131, 150, 157–58

  and FD religious faith, 92, 94

  and FD's self-reliance philosophy, 565

  and FD "Slaveholder's Sermon," 114

  and Garrisonian campaign of "Bible"
    politics, 104

  and Garrisonism, 96, 126

  see also specific books

Bill of Rights, 181, 479

Bingham, Caleb, 43, 44

Bingham, John, 479–80

Birney, James, 311

Blackall, B. F., 306

black codes, 472

"black laws," 188

Black Lives Matter, 743

black preachers, 53

black suffrage, 213, 214, 217, 264, 273, 288–89,
    304–5, 324–25, 416–17, 426, 427, 428,
    429, 431–32, 442, 444, 454–55, 469, 475,
    480–81, 483, 487, 503

  FD on, 597

  Fifteenth Amendment, 525–27, 552

  and violence against African Americans,
    552–53, 578, 579

Blaine, James G., 576, 613, 659–60

  and Haiti, 691, 695–96, 699

Blair, Montgomery, 407, 408, 428

  colonization supported by, 376–77, 379,
    387, 428, 429

  racial amalgamation warned against by, 429

"blood" metaphor, 176

"Bleeding Kansas," 264, 272, 274–75, 285, 293,
    294–96, 297, 299, 300

Blyden, Edward, 635

Bondage and Freedom (Douglass), 24, 28–29,
    77, 88, 153, 340, 449, 517

Bonney, Isaac, 92, 114

Booth, Edwin, 466–67

Booth, John Wilkes, 460, 461

"border ruffians," 294–95

border states, 351, 353, 354, 363, 366

Boston, Mass., 114, 124–25, 177, 197–98, 222,
    242–43, 246, 328–30, 454, 455

  See also Faneuil Hall

"Boston Board," 183

Boston Transcript, 757

Bourdon, Denis, 750

Boutwell, George, 2

Bradburn, George, 98, 117–18, 128, 130, 133,
    134, 135

Bradford, England, 311

Brady, Mathew, 591

Braudy, Leo, 598

Brazil, 370

Breckinridge, John C., 321

Bridgwater, England, 174

Bristol County Anti-Slavery Society, 98

Bristol, England, FD in, 174

Britain-Ireland tour:

  in England, 168–77

  and FD as homesick, 163–64, 165, 169–70, 171

  FD farewell speech for, 175–77

  and FD-Garrisonians relationships, 145–49

  FD on, 140–55, 156–77

  and FD return to U.S., 171, 177

  in Ireland, 139, 142–55

  and media, 142, 144–45

  reasons for, 154–55

  in Scotland, 156–63, *160*, 166–68

British and Foreign Anti-Slavery Society, 148,
    169

British Anti-Slavery League, 175

"British Racial Attitudes" (Douglass), 317

British West Indies, 370

Broadbent, Samuel S., *220*

Broadway Tabernacle, 179–81, 202–5

Brooke, Abraham, 135

Brooklyn Eagle, 755, 756

Brown, Anne, 313

Brown, Jeremiah, 314

Brown, John, 280–320, *297*, 328, 329, 337, 390,
    395, 435, 437

  FD on, 626–27

  FD's differences with, 336

Brown, John, Jr., 285, 293, 298, 301, 313, 315, 330

Brown, John M., 2

Brown, Mary, 299, 313, 314

Brown, Oliver, 294

Brown, Owen, 281–82

Brown, Ruth, 300, 313

Brown, Salmon, 284, 313

Brown, William Wells, 223, 382, 383, 391, 440,
    561, 621

  at second annual celebration of
    Emancipation Proclamation, 449

Bruce, Blanche K., 2, *649*, 753

  and Anna Douglass's death, 631

  and Cleveland, 661

and election of 1876, 575
and emancipation anniversary celebrations
  (1883), 635
and FD's second marriage, 649, 651
and Freedmen's Bank testimony, 613
and Kansas Exodus, 602
and nepotism accusations, 627
Bruce, Josephine, 649
Brueggemann, Walter, 482
Bruff, Louisa, 593
Bruner, Jerome, 24
Buchanan, Ann Lloyd, 626
Buchanan, James, 276, 277, 306, 340
Buckinham, William, 436
Buffalo, N.Y., 122, 269
  and One Hundred Conventions campaign,
    129–31
Buffum, James, 110, 139, 140, 141, 143, 145–46,
  147, 149, 158
Bugle, 184
Bull Run, First Battle of, 345, 348, 349, 350
Bunker Hill, Battle of, 309
Burch, J. Henri, 2
Burns, Anthony, 245–46
Burns, Robert, 166, 167–68, *168*, 177, 212, 247,
  567–68
Burns Monument, 167
Burton, Allan A., 538
Butler, Benjamin, 351
Byron, George Gordon, Lord, 273, 287

Cain, 226, 324
Caldwell, Handy, 68
Caldwell, James, 392
Calhoun, John C., 135, 185, 249, 290
Calvinism, 281
Cambria, 140–42, 147, 157, 177, 178–79, 263,
  282
Camden, N.J., 306
Cameron, Simon, 351
Camp Barker, 418
Camp Meigs, 396, 397
Camp William Penn, 404
Canada, 190, 231, 240, 242, 243, 244, 250, 281,
  293, 294, 297, 300, 306–10, 312, 315
Canandaigua, N.Y., 183, 286
Cape Cod, FD-Garrison tour on, 117, 119
Capitol, US, 479–80
  statue of FD in, xiv
"Capt. John Brown Not Insane" (Douglass),
  308–9
Carnegie, Andrew, 722
Caroline (slave), 262
Carpenter, Mary, 419, 497

Carr, Jonathan D., 190
Carson, Perry, 665
Carwardine, Richard, 433
Cayuga Lake, 269
Cedar Mountain, Battle of, 357
Central America, 370, 372, 374, 380
Central Church, 754
Chaffin's Farm, Battle of, 445
Chalmers, Thomas, 156, 158, 160
Chambers, James, 49
Chapman, Maria Weston, 127, 129, 135, 142,
  144, 145, 146–47, 148–49, *148*, 169, 189
Charleston, S.C., 399–402
Charles Town, Va., 308
Chartist movement, 173–75
Chase, Calvin, 665
Chase, Salmon P., 214, 323, 429–30, 457, 458, 476
Chatham, Ontario, 297
Chesapeake Bay, 36, 62, 70
Chester, William, 78
Chicago, Ill., 508
Chicago Tribune, 351
Childe Harold's Pilgrimage (Byron), 287
Choptank River, 10
Christiana Riot (1851), 243–45, 262–63, 287
Christianity, 187, 235, 236–38, 244, 281–82,
  316, 320
Christian Recorder, 417
Church of England, 144
Church of Scotland, 156
churches:
  FD views about, 103, 126, 127, 149
  Garnet views about, 132
  and Garrisonian doctrine, 105
  hypocrisy of, 96–97, 103, 115, 126, 132, 149,
    158–59, 175
  Jim Crow in, 110, 114–15
  and One Hundred Conventions campaign,
    130
  in Scotland, 156–57
  See also clergy; religion; *specific person,*
    church, or denomination
Cincinnati Enquirer, 443
Cinqué, Joseph, 132, 287
citizenship, 478–79
City Point, 422–23
civil liberties, 391, 442
civil rights, xii, 426, 428, 440
Civil Rights Act (1865), 473, 477, 478
Civil Rights Act (1866), 478–79
Civil Rights Act (1875), 555, 646
Civil Rights Cases (*United States v. Stanley*),
  646, 647–49
civil rights movement, 605

Civil War, US, xiii, 1, 252, 264, 274, 305, 310,
    327–34
  casualties of, 357, 471
  FD on meaning of, 359–61
  FD's frustration with, 350, 353–54
  FD's welcoming of, xii, 335–36, 339–42,
    343–45, 357
  as "holy war," 341
  Lost Cause ideology, 530–32, 533, 535, 627,
    680
  Peninsula Campaign in, 365
  savagery of, 348–49
  start of, 339
Civil War Soldiers' Monument, 716–17
Clarkson, Thomas, 168–69, 183
Clay, Henry, 135, 190–91, 238–40, 249, 290, 363
clergy:
  and Britain-Ireland tour, 141, 155
  Burns views about, 167
  FD views about, 118, 126, 127
  and Garrisonian doctrine, 104
  Garrisonian hostility to, 96, 103, 104
  hypocrisy of, 95, 96, 114, 126
  in Scotland, 156
  See also churches; religion; *specific person*
Cleveland, Grover, 659, 723
  in election of 1888, 684
  and FD's Recorder of Deeds position, 661–62,
    663, 666
Cleveland, Ohio, 188
Cleveland Gazette, 757
Clifton, Ontario, 307, 308
clipper ships, 36
Clough, William, 191
Clyde, William P., 702, 704, 705
Cochrane, John, 430
Cody, Buffalo Bill, 726
Cold Harbor, Battle of, 423
Coles, Howard, 208
Colfax massacre (1873), 578
Collamer, Jacob, 314
Collins, John A., 98, 100–101, 106–7, 109–11,
    120, 121, 128, 129
"Colonization Cant" (Douglass), 239
Colored Citizen Publishing Company, 550
Colored Methodist Church, 186
Colored Convention of Black Leaders (Buffalo,
    1843), 131–33
Colored Vigilance Committee, 300
color line, *see* Jim Crow
Columbian Exposition:
  African Americans and Native Americans
    at, 714, 725–27, 733–39
  conclusion of, 739

Deutsche Haus at, 728
  ethnological villages at, 725–26
  Haitian Pavilion at, 718, 721, 727–28, *729*,
    733, 735, 737
  Midway Plaisance at, 725, 726, 732, 737
  "Negro Labor" session at, 739–40
  planning and building of, 725–26
  "Sitting Bull's Cabin" at, 726
Columbian Orator (Bingham), 43–46, *43*, 52,
    68, 85, 94, 97, 102
Columbia Typographical Union, 505
"comeoutism," 185
"Composite Nation" (Douglass), 528, 544
Compromise of 1850, 202, 332
Compromise of 1877, 579–80
Concert Hall (Liverpool), 175
Concord, Mass., 136–37
Concord, N.H., 102–4, 128
Confederacy:
  death penalty for black soldiers ordered by,
    404–5
  diplomacy of, 358
  FD's criticism of, 420
  FD's desire for remaking of, 471
  and negotiated peace settlement, 441
Confiscation Acts, 478
Congdon, Charles T., 757
Congregational Church, 129
Congress, US, 22, 95, 214, 238–40, 252, 260,
    270, 313, 332–33
Conkling, Roscoe, 613, 614
Constitution, US, xiii, 8, 102, 104, 105, 131, 176,
    180, 198, 200–201, 208, 213, 214–15, 233–34,
    236, 253, 275, 293, 316–17, 323, 515
contraband camps, 381
Conway, T. W., 495
Cook, John, 307
Cook, John F., 631
Cooper Institute, 389, 419, 453, 454
Cooperstown, N.Y., 124
Copeland, John A., 395
Copper, Isaac, 24
Copperheads, 452, 453
Corinthian Hall, 229–36, *230*, 238, 333
Cork, Ireland, 143–45, 149
Cork Ladies Anti-Slavery Society, 144
corruption, political, 197
Cosdry, William, 42
"Cotter's Saturday Night, The" (Burns), 212
cotton, 49
Cotton States Exhibition, 757
Couch, Darius N., 484
Covey, Edward, 59–66, 67, 68, 115, 134, 153,
    161, 222, 261–62, 447, 741

Cox, Ebby, 163
Crampton's Gap, 377
Crédit Mobilier scandal, 535
Creole, 248–51, 287
Crittenden, John J., 332
Crittenden Compromise, 332–33
Crofts, Henry O., 311, 312, 319
Crofts, Julia Griffiths, xvii, 170–71, 189–90,
    195, 201, 202–8, 243–44, 249, 251, 253,
    265–69, 286, 311, 312–13, 317, 319, 320,
    350, 358, 359, 367, 381, 512, 518, 718,
    727, 745
  English network informed about Douglass's
    family by, 497
  FD given money by, 501
  FD's 1886 visit to, 668–69
  and FD's plan to move to Baltimore, 468
  and FD's second marriage, 651–52
  on FD's trip to Arlington Heights, 418–19
  FD warned about South by, 414, 438
Croly, David, 444
Crosby, Elisha Oscar, 370
Crown and Anchor Tavern, 173
Cuba, 141, 142, 537
Currier & Ives, *241*
Cyrus (fugitive slave), 289

Dallas, George, 318
Dalzell, J. M., 652
Daniel (Bible), 150
Daniels, Jim, 300
Daniels, John Brown, 300
Dante Alighieri, 754
Darg, John P., 84
Darsey, James, 237
Davis, Henry Winter, 429
Davis, Jefferson, 314, 315, 339, 381, 456
Davis, Samuel, 131
"Day and Night in 'Uncle Tom's Cabin,' A"
    (Douglass), 247–48
Dead Rabbits, 203
DeBaptiste, George, 300
Declaration of Independence, xiii, 98, 132, 196,
    230, 232, 233, 234–35, 368, 515
"Declaration of Sentiments," 196–97
Delany, Martin R., 186–87, 188, 191–95, *193*,
    222–23, 239, 255, 285, 297, 370, 371, 391,
    635
Delaware, 364, 454
Delaware Republican, 161
Delbanco, Andrew, 141
Democracy (Adams), 615
"Democrat carriage," 244
Democratic Convention of 1864, 439

Democratic Party, 8, 202, 245, 260, 269, 274,
    276, 314, 315, 324, 326, 333
  in election of 1862, 380–81
  in election of 1864, 441–42, 452
  in election of 1872, 534–35
  in election of 1874, 549, 551–52
  in election of 1876, 577–78
  in election of 1880, 613, 614–15, 616
  in election of 1884, 659
  FD on, 529, 530, 532, 533, 558–59, 681
  and Freedmen's Bank, 548
  Lincoln criticized by, 443–44
  and negotiated peace settlement, 441–42
  Peace, 443, 453
  in post-Reconstruction years, 601
  racism of, 416
De Molay, 399
"denationalization," 323
Denby, Bill, 26
denominational dissenters, 185
Denton, 10
Despeaux, Joseph, 36
Detroit River, 300, 313
"Dialogue Between a Master and a Slave"
    (Everett), 45
Dick, John, 188, 204
Dickens, Charles, 123–24, 175, 362
Dickinson, Anna, 487
Diedrich, Maria, 317–18, 573
Dilworth, William H., *10*
District of Columbia, 95
District of Columbia Homeopathic Hospital, 747
Divine Providence, 235
doctrines, Garrisonian, 104–5, 147
    See also specific doctrine
Doolittle, James R., 314
Dorgan, Gustav, 42
Dorsey, Thomas J., 458, 459
Douglas, H. Ford, 411
Douglas, Stephen A., 260, 321
Douglass, Amelia Loguen, 392, 397, 402, 411,
    450, 504
Douglass, Anna Murray, xvii, 79–80, 81–82, 84,
    163, 164, 165–66, 169, 171, 172, 177, 179,
    181, 190, 194–95, 206–10, 212, 213, 221–22,
    224, 265, 267–68, *268,* 296, 298, 306–7, 320,
    401, 424, 509, 518–19, *630,* 721, 755
  and birth of children, 92, 112, 137
  Assing and, 387, 388, 451, 511–12, 514,
    521–22, 608, 628
  and children's service in Civil War, 385–86
  concerns about safety of FD of, 101, 140
  Cox (Ruth) relationship with, 164, 165, 166,
    170

Douglass, Anna Murray (*cont.*)
  death of, 629–34, 657
  and Douglass house fire, 520, 521
  and family dispute, 500
  and FD as family man, 166
  and FD as traveler, 126, 164, 165, 170, 171
  FD's first meeting with, 446
  FD relationship with, 98–99, 112, 125, 126,
      137, 140, 164, 165, 169, 171
  and FD tour of Britain and Ireland, 140,
      163, 165, 170, 171
  and financial affairs, 112, 129, 140, 147, 171
  health problems of, 499, 551, 606, 628
  household run by, 387–88, 449, 452, 502,
      508, 519
  in Lynn, 125, 126, 137
  and manumission of FD, 171, 172
  and move South, 414
  and move to Lynn, 111
  Nantucket trip of, 98–99
  in New Bedford, 87, 88, 92, 94, 101, 109, 112
  in post-Reconstruction family times, 610, 612
  as shoe binder, 112
Douglass, Annie, *266*, 318–20, 755
  death of, 519
Douglass, Charles Frederick, 111, 194–95, 285,
      296, 320, 477, 483, 499, 504, 506, 513,
      740–41, 753, 754, 755
  baseball played by, 507–8
  birth/childhood of, 137, 140, 165, 166
  and black leadership conflicts, 683
  in Civil War, 385, 386, 392, 396, 412, *412*,
      422–23, 424, 450, 519
  colonization considered by, 373
  and emancipation anniversary celebrations,
      635
  and family deaths, 700
  in family disputes, 497–98, 500, 504–7, 509
  FD relationship with, 140
  and FD's Freedmen's Bank presidency, 547
  and FD tour of Britain and Ireland, 140,
      163, 170
  financial difficulties of, 571–72, 606, 700–701
  Freedmen's Bureau job of, 499, 507
  and nepotism accusations, 627, 628
  and passage of Thirteenth Amendment,
      454
  and Santo Domingo annexation project, 539
  and Sprague lawsuit, 655
Douglass, Eliza, 163–64, 207
Douglass, Frederick, vii, 1
  abolitionism and, xii, 102–4, 106–10,
      112–15, 190–92, 208, 213, 226–27, 236,
      246–47, 251, 252–53, 260, 264, 270–72,

  293–94, 323–24, 351–52, 358, 417, 420,
      421, 424, 428, 443, 555–56, 626–27, 757
  aborted 1861 Haiti trip of, 338–39
  ambition of, 186–90, 195, 260, 267
  Andrew Anthony's death and, 48–49
  anger of, 179–81, 198–200, 213, 222, 267,
      289–90
  and Anna's death, 629–34
  Anna's relationship with, 98–99, 112, 125,
      126, 137, 140, 164, 165, 169, 171
  anti-Catholicism of, 528–29, 545, 670–71
  anti-Garrisonian views of, 189, 201, 208,
      213–14, 215, 216–19, 223–27, 229, 252–53,
      255, 263, 285, 304–5, 313, 316–17, 320–21,
      330
  arrest warrant for, 306–7
  as art patron, 751
  Assing's relationship with, 387, 451, 493–94
  and Assing's suicide, 657–59
  attachment to grandmother of, 517
  audiences for, 229–36
  Auld as former master of, 158–59, 161, 163,
      171, 176, 198–200, 260–61
  in Baltimore, 48–66, 89
  Baltimore speech of, 446–48
  and Battle of Fort Wagner, 401
  beatings endured by, 260–61
  Bible of, *360*
  biographies of, 167–68, 197, 198
  birth of, xii, 9–10
  black education demanded by, 469–70, 472
  black enlistment in military desired by, 351,
      359, 361, 390–91, 392–96, 401, 403–4,
      405, 407, 410–11, 414, 424, 470
  and black leadership conflicts, 544–45,
      602–3, 637, 640–42, 663, 678–79
  black rivals of, 186–87, 188, 191–95, 222–23
  breakdown of (July 1883), 643
  Brown's differences with, 336
  in Canada, 297, 306–10
  Cedar Hill estate of, 605, 607, 610–12, *612*,
      719, 747
  in Chambersburg, Penn., 301–3, 308, 314
  childhood of, 10–12, 17–18, 19–34, 48–66,
      253, 258
  civil liberties demanded by, 391, 442
  and Civil Rights Cases, 646–49
  Civil War recruiting by, 385
  Civil War trip to DC of, 406–8
  Civil War welcomed by, xii, 335–36, 339–42,
      343–45, 357
  colonization opposed by, 95, 97–98, 370,
      372–73, 374, 375, 376–77, 379, 380, 387
  at Columbian Exposition, 714, 733–40

combativeness of, 222–23
commemorative speeches by, 555–56
compared to Lincoln, 761
correspondence of, 165, 167, 189–90, 194, 199, 206, 208, 213, 217, 283, 301, 315–16, 322
at Covey's farm, 222, 261–62
criticism of, 162–63, 171–72, 180, 181, 197, 218–27, 276–77, 307–8
criticized for failing to fight, 411–12
Daniel Lloyd's friendship with, 21–22
death and burial of, 752–55
as "demagogue in black," 181, 197
District of Columbia marshal position of, 583–88, *586*
disunionism as viewed by, 104, 108, 114, 126, 136, 147, 185, 200–201, 214, 252, 316, 327, 330, 333
divorce as option for, 267–68
Dunbar's eulogy for, 335
editorials of, 215, 222, 223, 246, 271, 274, 304–5, 321, 323, 326, 327
education of, 22, 50, 97, 103, 104, 260
at Edward Covey's farmstead, 59–66
1886 European trip of, 666–78, *674*, *675*
and election of 1864, 439, 445–46
and election of 1872, 533, 534–35, 542
and election of 1876, 574–78, 579–80
and election of 1880, 612, 613–17, *618*
and election of 1884, 659–61
and election of 1888, 682–85
and emancipation anniversary celebrations, 634–37, 638–39, 665–66, 680–82
emancipation cheered by, xii, 365–66
Emancipation Proclamation praised by, 355–57, 379–80, 382–84, 388, 389
emigration considered by, 170, 337–38, 464
English exile of, 309–20
English tour of (1846–47), 162–77, 178, 179, 180, 190, 223, 254, 263, 282
escape from slavery by, 182–83, 198, 242
escape plan of, 81–86
eulogies for, 755–64
and family deaths, 570–71, 699–700
and family financial difficulties, 571–72
as father, 92, 94, 101, 126, 140, 147, 163, 166, 171, 177, 178, 190, 199, 206, 207, 209–10, 265, 267, 285, 292, 298, 306–7
father's identity sought by, 13–16, 746
fiction written by, 224, 248–51
in fight with Covey, 65–66, 67, 68
finances of, 101, 105, 111, 129, 136, 140, 146, 147, 148, 149, 154, 169, 171, 177, 183, 184, 190, 195, 207, 209, 210–11, 213, 221, 253, 265, 282, 320, 513

financial aid sought from, 748–50, 752
first escape plot of, 69–74
food scrounged by, 57
as former slave, 160–64, 171–73, 182–83, 198–99, 222, 240, 242, 258–62
Fourteenth Amendment supported by, 481, 483
Fourth of July speech of (1852), 229–36, 516
Frederick Bailey as original name of, 152, 161, 164, 171–73, 199
Frederick Jr.'s death and, 720–21
Freedmen's Bank presidency of, 545–49, 558, 612–13, 663
Freedmen's Bank testimony of, 612–13
Freedmen's Bureau position rejected by, 524
Freedmen's Memorial address of, 4–9
Frémont convention in 1864 supported by, 430, 431
friendships of, 21–22, 170–71, 177, 191, 196, 205–6, 208–12, 220, 223, 224, 251, 254–60, 265–67, 317–19, 721–22
as frustrated with Civil War, 350, 353–54
fugitive slaves as concern of, 351
at Gardiner's shipyard, 75–77
German translator of, 267, 290–92, 317–19
in Haiti, *see* Haiti, FD as US minister to
on Haiti and Haitians, 728–30, 758–59, 760
Harpers Ferry raid involvement of, 280, 301–8, *308*, 314, 329
heat stroke of, 63
Hillsdale Fourth of July speech of (1875), 556–59
house fire and, 520–23
Howells's comparison of B. T. Washington to, 714
humor and irony of, 157, 176, 203, 228, 231, 233–34, 236, 316
illnesses of, 125, 126, 134, 183, 187–88, 209–12, 229, 708
on Indians, 486
influences on, 97, 104, 153–54
intelligence of, 23–24
Irish jokes of, 389–90, 417, 453, 455, 487
jeremiads of, 156–58, 179–80, 228–37, 254, 263, 368, 434, 458, 515, 558, 577, 645, 665, 681, 686, 738, 760
Jim Crow experiences of, 109–11, 141, 177, 581–82
Johnson criticized by, 476, 477, 482–83, 487
Johnson's meeting with, 474–75, 477, 482
in journey from outsider to political insider, xvi
and Kansas Exodus, 601–5
and killing of black prisoners, 405–6

Douglass, Frederick (*cont.*)
  language as used by, xv, xvi, xvii, 13, 263; *see also* jeremiads of *above,* as orator *below*
  learning from Assing, 516–17
  lectures and speeches of, 157, 174, 179–88, 197–98, 202–5, 212, 229–36, 239, 241–42, 248–49, 252–53, 267–72, 278–79, 289–90, 295–96, 301–5, 311–17, 323, 328–30, 332, 333–34
  letter on black rights from, 473–74
  letter to Blair from, 376–77, 387
  Lewis's scrapbook on, 503–4
  on Lincoln, 5–8
  Lincoln administration accused of treason by, 359
  on Lincoln assassination, 460, 461, 462–63
  and Lincoln's emancipation plan, 363–64, 366–67, 378–79
  Lincoln's first inaugural criticized by, 336–37
  Lincoln's first meeting with, 408–10
  Lincoln's meeting on Reconstruction with, 436–37
  Lincoln's "negro hatred" criticized by, 373, 374
  Lincoln's procession to inaugural witnessed by, 336
  and Lincoln's revocation of Frémont's emancipation edict, 352–54
  at Lincoln's second inauguration, 457–60, 461–62
  in Lincoln tribute at Union League Club, 730–33
  literacy of, 38–42, 54–55, 64–65, 68
  loneliness/homesickness of, 21, 163–64, 165, 169–70, 171
  Lucretia Auld and, 30–31
  Lynn home of, 111–12, 164–65, 166, 172, 177, 178, 179, 183, 184, 188, 190, 194
  manumission papers for, 93, 170, 171–73, 240
  marriage of Helen and, 643, 649–54, 655–56, 667, 750–51
  marriages of, *see* Douglass, Anna Murray; Douglass, Helen Pitts
  on meaning of Civil War, 359–61
  memory of, 257–59
  millennialism of, 349–50, 389, 419, 432, 433–34, 471
  mob violence against, 101, 107, 109–10, 120, 126, 127–28, 133–34, 139, 142, 162, 163, 186, 189, 193, 202–4, 218, 243, 328–30, 333
  moral convictions of, 270, 279, 282, 285–86, 295, 333–34
  and moral suasion, 157, 162–63, 173, 174, 175
  mother of, *see* Bailey, Harriet
  mother's relationship with, 517–18
  in movement to get Lincoln off Republican ticket, 429
  in move to Baltimore, 35–47
  in move to Washington, 523
  in move to Wye plantation, 19–34
  music enjoyed by, 130, 165, 174
  name change of, 84
  and National Convention of Colored Men, 640, 643–46
  at National Union Convention, 484–87
  newspaper plans of, 177, 183, 186–87
  newspapers edited by, *see Douglass' Monthly; Frederick Douglass' Paper; New Era; New National Era; North Star*
  new technology and, xii, 751–52
  New York arrival of, 82–83
  non-slaveholding whites criticized by, 347
  northern hatred of slaveholders fanned by, 348–50
  as orator, xii, 100–101, 102–4, 108–9, 113, 114, 126–27, 130–31, 147, 149, 157, 176, 191, 197–98, 229–36, 237, 241, 271–73, 274; *see also above* jeremiads of
  Othello watched by, 466–67
  "Our National Capital" speech of, 588–91
  passport of, 318
  on patriotism, 361–63, 486
  patrons of, 168–74, 189–90, 211–16, 221
  pen and inkwell of, *347*
  Perry Downs's reunion with, 495–96
  personality of, 143, 144, 147, 176–77, 210–12, 222–27, 236–38, 254, 263, 264–65
  as philanthropist, 749
  philosophical outlook of, xvii, 254–60; *see also* self-reliance, FD's doctrine of
  photographs and images of, xi, xii, *241, 184, 209, 210, 255, 262, 266, 292, 305–7, 308, 332, 356, 390, 434, 489, 534, 541, 554, 591, 592, 598–99, 653, 675, 703, 719, 747, 750*
  physical description of, 102, 113, 145, 147, 291–92
  plan for emancipation of, 425–28
  in plan to infiltrate South, 437–38
  in plan to move to Baltimore, 468
  as political activist, 717, 722–23, 724
  political strategy of, 177, 184–85, 194, 195–98, 208, 214–16, 220, 225–26, 236, 238, 246–47, 251, 258–59, 260, 264, 268–70, 321–27
  post-raid exile of, 305–10
  post-Reconstruction Eastern Shore visits by, 592–98, 624–27
  postwar plans of, 468–69

pragmatism of, xiii, xvi, 133, 196, 252, 270, 273–74, 275, 325, 362–63, 404, 409–10, 433, 483, 492, 515, 523–24, 534, 560, 616

press coverage of, 177, 180, 181–82, 203–4, 218, *241*, 260, 305, 307, *308*, 311

at Price's shipyard, 77–81

problems of Reconstruction faced by, 424–28, 430, 431–32, 435–37, 454, 470–71, 473, 476–77, 479–80, 481, 503

on progress, 389–91

public letters issued by, 182–83, 198, 307, 320

public speaking begun by, 68–69

racial identity of, 203

racial stereotypes opposed by, 455–56

racist criticism of, 478, 487–88

radicalism of, xiv, xvi, 196, 216, 252, 257, 260, 273, 275–76, 282–83, 325, 409–10, 433, 492, 523, 616

Recorder of Deeds position of, 619, 627–28, 661–62, 663–64

religious awakening of, 51–55

religious views of, 320, 387, 389, 432–34, 514–16

reputation of, 108–9, 120, 135, 136, 137, 138, 144–45, 146, 158, 160–61, 177, 186, 187–88, 204–6, 208–9, 218–19, 221–24, 229, 242, 253–54, 260, 290–92

in returns to US, 168, 177, 310

in return to Baltimore, 75–78

Rochester homes of, 190, 194–98, 204–8, 213, 217–19, 229–36, *230*, 243, 253, 264–65, 268, 270, 272, 279, 291, 292, 295, 296–99, 301, 306–7, 313, 319, 320, 324, 326, 333–34

Rosetta loaned money by, 498–99

Sabbath school taught by, 68–69, 101

in St. Michaels, Md., 161, 260, 261

and Santo Domingo annexation project, 536–37, 538–45, 692

in Scotland, 156–63, 178, 266–67, 286, 311–12, 313, 316

self-perception of, 88, 138, 147, 165

"selling" of young, 159

and send-off of Fifty-Fourth Massachusetts regiment, 398, 399

in separation from Assing, 606–9, 656–57

sexual rumors about, 181–83, 221–25, 229

sisters of, 163–64, 199, 207

on slave music, 32–34

softening of ire toward Lincoln by, 435

Sophia Auld's falling-out with, 50–51

Southern trip planned by, 407–8, 410

speaking tours of, 527–28, 679–80, 685–89

Sprague lawsuit and, 655–56

and squabbles among family, 483–84, 497–98, 500–503, 505–6, 508–9, 513

subscription list of, 213, 218, 268–69

Sunday lectures of, 238–39

as symbol of slavery, 104, 109, 118, 119, 125, 127, 137, 175–76

Syracuse convention held by, 440–44

teaching by, 68–69

on Thomas Auld, 57–58

Thomas Auld's beating of, 59

threats to, 357

on *Trent* Affair, 358–59

Tuskegee Institute and, 714–16, *716*, 739, 749

Union as conceived by, 341–42

violin playing of, 165

Virginia visited by, 418–19

voice of, 209, 232

voting by, 94

voting rights demanded by, 416–17, 426, 427, 431–32, 442, 454–55, 469, 475, 503

war propoganda of, 345–48

Webster compared with, 113

Wells's friendship with, 721–22

White as saving, 134, 163

women's adoration of, 144, 169

and women's voting rights, 488–93

see also specific person, speeches and writings, tour, or topic

Douglass, Frederick, Jr., 177, *498*, 504, 506, 509, 720–21

birth of, 111–12

and black leadership conflicts, 642

in Civil War, 385, 386, 411, 422, 424, 450, 519

and Cox, 165, 166

and family difficulties, 606, 700

in family disputes, 497, 500, 504–6

and FD Britain-Ireland tour, 163, 170, 177

and FD's District of Columbia marshal position, 585

financial difficulties of, 550, 678, 700

and mother's death, 629

and nepotism accusations, 628

and *New National Era*, 525, 539, 550

Douglass, Frederick Aaron, 662–63

Douglass, Helen Pitts, xvii, 643, 649–54, *653*, 655–56, 667, *675*, 727, 750–51, 752, 754

and Assing, 608–9

background of, 608, 653–54

and election of 1884, 660

in Haiti, 694, 697

and nepotism accusations, 628

in post-Reconstruction years, 666–75

Douglass, Joseph, 700, 735, 740, 750, 754, 762, *763*

Douglass, Lewis, 177, 306, 448, 497, 509, 746, 753, 754, 755, 757
  Assing's criticism of, 513
  birth of, 92
  and black leadership conflicts, 641, 642
  business pursued by, 386–87, 450–51
  childhood/youth of, 94, 101, 109, 112, 140
  on Civil Rights Cases, 647
  in Civil War, 385, 386, 392, 394, 396, 397, 399, 400, 402, *402*, 412–13, 422, 424, 519
  colonization considered by, 373
  and Cox, 165, 166
  and emancipation anniversary celebrations, 635
  FD relationship with, 140
  FD scrapbook kept by, 503–4
  and FD's District of Columbia marshal position, 585
  and FD's second marriage, 650
  and FD tour of Britain and Ireland, 140, 163, 170, 177
  financial difficulties of, 550
  letter on black rights from, 473–74
  marriage of, 450
  and meeting with Johnson, 474, 476
  and mother's death, 629
  and nepotism accusations, 627, 628
  in New Bedford, 92, 94, 101, 109, 112
  and *New Era,* 524
  and *New National Era,* 525, 529, 539, 550
  and Sprague lawsuit, 655
Douglass, Mary Elizabeth Murphy "Libbie," 498, 499, 513, 571, 572
Douglass, Rosetta, *see* Sprague, Rosetta Douglas
Douglass, Virginia Hewlett, 678, 700, 720
Douglass Institute, 469–70
Douglass' Monthly, 303, 319, 320, 322, 327
  Assing's writing modeled on, 339
  final issue of, 410, 411, 419, 465
  funding for, 381
  Haitian trip announced in, 338
  Lewis's letter in, 401
  "Men of Color to Arms!" in, 393–95
  Rosetta's reading of, 387
"Douglass on the Late Election," 724
Douglass Union, 186
Downing, George T., 440, 474, 524, 572, 602, 630
Downs, Maria, 495
Downs, Perry, 495–96, 510–11, 598, 606
Dred Scott v. Sanford (1857), 223, 277–79, 282, 286, 290, 304, 316, 332, 356, 481
Drew, Thomas, 155
Dublin, Ireland, 152

Dubois, Laurent, 698
Du Bois, W. E. B., 758–61
due process, 214
Dunbar, Paul Laurence, 335, 735–36, *736,* 745, 749, 762
Dundee, Scotland, 157–58
Durgin and Bailey Shipyard, 42, 48, 55

Ealton, John, Jr., 435
East Baltimore Mental Health Society, 78–79
Eastern Railroad, 109–11, 112
Easton, Md., 199
Eaton, John, Jr., 435, 437, 438
Edinburgh, 157, 160–61, *160,* 163, 166–67, 168, 175, 311, 313, 319
Edinburgh Ladies New Anti-Slavery Association, 313
education, 426, 469–70, 472
  and self-reliance, 568
Edward White Gallery, *184*
Egypt, 469, 470
Ehrenreich, Barbara, 345
Eighty-Eighth Pennsylvania Regiment, *405*
elections, US:
  of 1840, 311
  of 1848, 197, 200, 276
  of 1852, 252, 268–70, 273, 276
  of 1856, 430, 274, 276–77
  of 1860, 314, 315, 320, 321–27
  of 1862, 380–81
  of 1864, 428, 429–30, 431, 432, 437, 438, 439, 441–43, 444–46, 452–53, 472
  of 1868, 524
  of 1872, 533, 534–35, 542
  of 1876, 574–78, 579–80
  of 1880, 612, 613–17, *618*
  of 1884, 659–61
  of 1888, 682–85
Eliot, George, 515
Ellison, Ralph, 590
emancipation, xxii, 279, 282, 285–87
  considered as military necessity, 351–52, 365
  in DC, 364–65
  FD's plan for, 425–28
  Lincoln's movement to, 354
  Lincoln's plan for, 363–64, 366–67, 377–78
Elm Street Methodist Church (New Bedford), 92
Emancipation Act of the State of New York (1827), 254
Emancipation Day, 740, 748
Emancipation Proclamation, 4, 7, 374, 378–80
  as dependent on election of 1864, 437
  1883 anniversary celebrations of, 634–37

FD's praise for, 355–57, 379–80, 382–84, 388, 389
issuing of final, 382–84, 388, 397
second anniversary of, 449
Embry, James H., 478
Emerson, Ralph Waldo, 382, 564, 668
emigration, 337–38
enabling clause, 214
England:
Britain-Ireland tour in, 168–77
FD in, 162, 164, 165–66, 168–77
Garrison fundraising in, 107
Garrisonians in, 107
media in, 142
suffrage in, 173
workers in, 173–75
See also Chartist movement; Great Britain
Enlightenment, 228, 238
Ephesians, 131
equal rights, xii, 191, 205, 216, 226, 254, 257, 273, 288–89, 291, 323, 324–25, 326
Equal Rights Association, 488, 490
Erie, Lake, 269
Erie Canal, 189, 190
Erie Railroad, 306
Eskimos, 726
Essence of Christianity, The (Feuerbach), 515
Ethiopia, 470
Evangelical Alliance, 175–76
evangelicals, 105
Evans, Walter O., xvii
Everett, David, 44–45
Excelsior Club, 507
exclusion laws, 303
Exodus, Book of, 229, 232, 238, 239, 265–66, 329, 369, 389, 469, 515
"Extract from an Orator on Eloquence Pronounced at Harvard University, on Commencement Day, 1794, An" (Perkins), 52
Ezekiel, 104, 228

Faneuil Hall, 102, 114, 115, 125, 187, 197–98
"Farewell Address to the British People" (Douglass), 175–77, 179
"Farewell to Frederick Douglass" (Griffiths), 206
Farity, Charles, 42
Fasset, Samuel Montegue, *434*
Fay, Richard S., 328–29
Federal Elections Bill (1890), 717
federalism, 471
Fell's Point, 36, 37, 48
Ferdinands, George, 733
Ferris, Jacob, 128

Feuerbach, Ludwig, 514–15
Field, Kate, 753
field hands, 23
Fifteenth Amendment, 487, 491, 492, 525–27, 552, 563, 578, 647
Fifth Amendment, 214
Fifty-Fourth Massachusetts Regiment, 385, 391–92, 397–402, *402*, 403, *412*, 422, 424, 450
Fillmore, Millard, 276
Finsbury Chapel, 175
Firmin, Anténor, 696, 698, 703–4, 705–6
First Confiscation Act, 354
First Louisiana Colored Troops, 441
Fish, Hamilton, 552
Fishkin, Shelley Fisher, 249
Fisk, Clinton B., 473
Fisk Jubilee Singers, 734
Fisk University, 564
Fitch, G. N., 314
Fleetwood, Christian A., 444–45, 635
Florida, 8, 370, 440
Foner, Eric, 374
Forbes, Hugh, 298–300
"Forbes postponement," 300
Fort Donelson, 357, 366
Fort Gregg, 413
Fort Henry, 366
Fort Lee, N.J., 321
Fortress Monroe, 351
Fort Sumter, 339, 340, 352, 400, 422
Fortune, T. Thomas, 635, 636, 637, 641–42, 651, 683
Fort Wagner, 399–402, 405, 412, 413, 505
Foster, Abby Kelley, *see* Kelley, Abby
Foster, Stephen, 108, 120, 121, 184, 218, 221–22
Fought, Leigh, 166, 387
Fourteenth Amendment, 477, 479, 480–81, 552, 564, 578, 646–47, 648–49
opposition to, 481, 483, 488–89
Fourth US Colored Troops, 444
Fox (cat), 452
Framingham, Mass., 222
France, 318, 512
Frank Leslie's Illustrated Newspaper, 305, 307, 308
Franklin, John Hope, 472
Frauenstein, Gustav, 516, 667
Frederick Douglass' Paper, 213, 217, 265, 266, 285, 286, 289, 294, 301
Fredericksburg, Battle of, 357
free blacks, 161, 186, 188, 190, 238–39, 257, 260, 271–72, 275, 301
Free Church of Scotland, 156–60, 162

Free Democracy, 269
Freedmen's Bank, 545–49, 558, 612–13, 663
Freedmen's Bureau, 427, 444, 472, 473, 482, 484, 524
    Charles Douglass's job at, 499, 507
    and FD's self-reliance philosophy, 562
Freedmen's Bureau bill, 473, 478
Freedmen's Memorial, dedication of, 1–9, *3*
"Freedmen's Memorial Address" (Douglass), 4–9, 576
freedmen's relief efforts, 425
Freedmen's Savings and Trust Company, *see* Freedmen's Bank
"Freedom's Battle at Christiana" (Douglass), 244
free-labor movement, 187, 275
Freeland, Betsy, 72–73
Freeland, William, 67–68, 69–70, 72, 74
Freeland Farm, *69*, 94, 101, 340
Freeman, Louis, 597
Freemason, 193
Free Soil Party, 200, 214, 218, 245, 268, 269, 270, 274, 276, 293–94, 303
free speech, right of, 128
free trade, 724
Free Trade Hall, 175
Frémont, John C., 275, 276, 352–54
    and election of 1864, 430, 431, 432, 439, 453
French, Daniel Chester, 725
Fugitive Blacksmith, The (Pennington), 291
Fugitive Slave Act (1850), 202, 214, 231, 234, 238, 240–45, *241*, 268, 270, 273, 282, 289, 316, 323, 327
Fugitive Slave Law (1793), 125

Gardiner, William, 75–77
Gardiner's shipyard, 78
Garfield, James A.:
    assassination of, 618–19
    in election of 1880, 612, 613, 614, 615
    inauguration of, 618
Garibaldi, Giuseppe, 298, 330
Garner, Margaret, 287
Garnet, Henry Highland, 131–33, *132*, 183, 222–23, 298, 303–4, 371, 391, 440, 441, 544–45, 577
Garrison, William Lloyd, 59, 168, 169, 171, 173–74, 178, 179, 182, 183, 184, 185–88, *189*, 191, 197, 201, 202–3, 213–14, 215, 216, 218, 224–27, 236, *241*, 285, 321, 361, 382, 469, 543
    and AASS, 105, 106
    attacks on, 120
    and attempts to control FD, 146
    and "Bible politics" campaign, 104

and characteristics of abolitionists, 95–96
    and Chartist movement, 173–74
    Civil War supported by, 397–98
    criticisms of, 95
    and disputes among abolitionists, 104, 105
    doctrines of, 104–6
    on emancipation, 416
    endorsement of FD by, 99–100
    enemies of, 104
    and evangelicals, 105
    Faneuil Hall speech of, 125
    and FD as homesick, 163, 170, 171
    and FD Britain-Ireland tour, 141, 151–52, 153–54, 163, 168, 170, 171, 173–74
    FD early tours with, 117
    and FD *Narrative*, 138–39
    and FD on AASS travel circuit, 108
    FD public letters to, 125–26, 141, 151–52, 153–54, 170, 174
    FD relationship with, 104, 106, 117, 118–19, 125–26, 137, 168, 169, 171
    Garnet break with, 131
    influence on FD of, 94–97, 104
    and Kelley, 121
    as *Liberator* founder, 104
    Lincoln supported by, 430
    in Nantucket, 99–100
    and perfectionism, 105–6
    at second annual celebration of Emancipation Proclamation, 449
    self-image of, 105
    and slaveholding as sin, 94–95
    style of, 104
    and Tappanites, 106
    See also Liberator
Garrisonians, 162, 172, 175, 180, 189, 201, 207, 208, 213–19, 221–27, 229, 245, 249, 252–53, 255, 263, 285, 304–5, 313, 316–17, 320–21, 330
    attacks on religious hypocrisy by, 103
    attempts to control FD by, 145–49, 169
    and "Bible politics" campaign, 104
    and Chartist movement, 173
    and clergy, 96, 103
    Collins's defense of, 107
    and colonization movement, 95, 97–98
    disunity among, 162
    doctrine of, 104–6
    in England, 107
    essentials of, 96
    FD belief in, 116–36, 137
    FD relationship with, 145–49
    goals of, 126
    and Jim Crow, 111

and Liberty Party, 128
and manumission of slaves, 172
One Hundred Conventions campaign of, 128–36
as religious-social crusade, 114
reputation of, 105–6
self-destruction of, 127
See also American Anti-Slavery Society; *specific person*
Garrity, Mary, 723
Gay, Sydney, 128, 432
Genesis, Book of, 165, 232, 324, 440, 445, 447, 482
Georgia, 198, 242–43, 432, 443, 444
German Americans, 453
Gettysburg Address, 414–15
Gherardi, Bancroft, 698–99, 702, 704–5
Ghosh, Amitav, 78
Giddings, Joshua, 315
Gilded Age, xii, xvii, 564, 566, 587–89, 612, 615, 619, 628, 661
The Gilded Age (Twain), 558
Gillmore, Quincy A., 399–400
Glasgow, Scotland, 157–60, 162–63, 311–12, 316–17, 318, 319
Glasgow City Hall, 157
Glasgow Emancipation Society, 316–17
Glocester, James, 301
Godwyn, Morgan, 556
Goethe, Johann Wolfgang von, 512, 514
Goodell, William, 214
Gooding, James H., 392, 403, 413
Gore, Orson, 25, 26, 27
Golden Rule, 115
good and evil, FD views about, 167
Gorsuch, Edward, 243–45
Gospel of Wealth, 561
Grafton, Massachusetts, 107
Graham, Joseph, 596
Grand Army of the Republic, 754
Grant, Ulysses S., xii, 2, 3, 5, 6, 8, 456, 461, 480, 754
and corruption, 535–36, 551–52, 613
Eaton appointed superintendent of freedmen by, 435
in election of 1868, 524
in election of 1872, 533, 542
and election of 1880, 614
Ku Klux Klan suppressed by, 522, 536
and Lost Cause ideology, 531
and Santo Domingo annexation project, 536–37, 538–45, 692
and violence against African Americans, 553
Gray, James, 125

Great Britain:
attitudes toward Ireland in, 151
and FD "Farewell Address to the British People," 176–77
as proposed home for FD family, 163, 170
slavery in, 174–75
and *Trent* Affair, 358–59
workers in, 173–75
See also Britain-Ireland tour; England; Ireland; Scotland
Great Irish Famine, 150–51
Great Railroad Strike (1877), 613
Greeley, Horace, 162–63, 239, 273, 299, 443, 517, 534, 535
Green, Beriah, 373
Green, Nancy, 735
Green, Shields, 301, 302–3, 314, 395
"The Green Fields of Americay," 153
Greenback Party, 614
Greene, Martha, 406, 717
Greener, Richard T., 602, 603, 635, 637, 640–42, *642*, 651
Greenwood, Grace, 585–86
Gregory, James M., 635, 651
Griffiths, Eliza, 190
Griffiths, Julia, *see* Crofts, Julia Griffiths
Griffiths, Thomas, 190
Grimké, Charlotte Forten, 649–50
Grimké, Francis J., 649, 751, 762
Grinnell, Iowa, 300
Groton, Mass., 136
Guatemala, 370
guerrilla warfare, 282, 293, 300
Guiteau, Charles, 618, 619
Guthrie, Woody, 154

habeas corpus, 214, 380
Hahn, Michael, 435
Haiti, 7, 36, 304, 337, 338, 470, 541, 545, 728–30, 758–59, 760
FD's aborted 1861 visit to, 338–39
Haiti, FD as US minister to, 689–711, *703*
appointment, 689–90
and Bassett, 694–95, 699
and 1891 rebellion, 706–8
FD's articles on, 709–11
and financial matters, 699
and housing, 697
and Môle Saint-Nicolas coaling station, 694, 695, 696, 698, 702, 703–6, 709
and Pan-Americanism, 695–96
presentation address of, 696–97
press coverage of, 692–94, *694*, 701–2, 705, 707, 708, 709

Haiti, FD as US minister to (*cont.*)
  resignation of, 708–9
  and US expansionism, 697–98, 699, 701, 702
Hale, Edward Everett, 382
Hale, John P., 268, 270
Halifax, England, 311, 312–13, 319
Hambleton, William, 70, 72, 74, 75
Hamilton, William, 55
Hamilton College, 207
Hammond, James Henry, 141–42
Hampton Institute, 751
Hancock, Winfield Scott, 615
Hanson, Rev., 52–53
Hardy, Neal, 134
Harlan, John Marshall, 648–49, 753
Harlan, Robert J., 603
Harpers Ferry, 376
Harpers Ferry raid (1859), 280, 288–320, *308*, 322, 329, 390
Harris, George, 249
Harris, Henry, 68, 72, 73, 587
Harris, John, 68, 72, 73, 587
Harrisburg, Penn., 186
Harrison, Benjamin, 682–83, 684, 685, 716–17, 722–23
  FD appointed minister to Haiti by, 689–90, 691, 702
Harrison, J. Stewart, 752
Harrod, Lucius, 752
Hartford, Conn., 127–28
Havana, 358
Havre de Grace, Md., 82
Hawes, Josiah John, *189*
Hayden, Robert, 763
Hayes, Rutherford B.:
  in election of 1876, 576, 577, 578, 579
  and FD's District of Columbia marshal position, 583
  FD's interview with, 582–83
  and Kansas Exodus, 601–2
  and labor movement, 613
  Southern conciliation policy of, 583, 599, 601, 614
Hays, Ned, 76
Hazzard, Mr., and *Cambria* voyage, 142
Headley, Phineas Jr., 750, 763
"Heads of the Colored People" (Smith), 256
Hebrew prophets, xv–xvi, 228–38, 242, 247, 251, 254, 258–59, 263, 283–84
Hebrews, Book of, 293
Hegel, Georg, 40
Heinzen, Karl, 516
Henry, Jerry, 243

Henry, Patrick, 72, 100, 132
Henry V (Shakespeare), 394
Henry VIII (Shakespeare), 240
Herodotus, 385
"Heroic Slave, The" (Douglass), 224, 248–51
Heschel, Abraham, xvi, 229, 237, 389
Higginson, Thomas Wentworth, 104, 296
Highgate, Edmonia, 441
Hillsboro, 10
Himrods Corners, N.Y., 367–68
Hingham, Mass., 113
"History" (Keita), 518
History, The (Herodotus), 385
Hoboken, N.J., 306, 513, 514
Hodes, Martha, 460
Hodge, William L., 478
Hodges, Moses, 753
Holley, Myron, 130
Holme Hill Farm, 10, 49
Holmes, Oliver Wendell, 382
Honduras, 370
Honey Hill, Battle of, 450
Hopkins, James, 25
house of ill repute, FD at, 162
House of Representatives, US, 2
  Fourteenth Amendment in, 480
  Thirteenth Amendment in, 443, 453–54
Howard, Oliver O., 482, 499, 562
Howard University, 1, 557, 720, 721, 745, 753
Howe, Julia Ward, 369
Howe, Samuel Gridley, 296, 315, 538, 539, 542
Howells, William Dean, 614, 714
Hubbardston, Mass., 111–12
Hudson, Erasmus D., 121–22, 123
Hughs, Thomas, 84
Hughes, Langston, 154
human rights, 471
Humboldt, Alexander von, 291
Humphreys, Tom, 76
Hundred Conventions tour, 146
Hurn, John, 305–6
Hutchinson, John, 753
Hutchinson Family Singers, 112, 136, 139, 140, 141, 359, 753
Hutchinson, John, 112, 139, 141
Hyannis, Mass., 119
Hyatt, Thaddeus, 315
hypocrisy:
  of churches/clergy, 95, 96–97, 114, 115, 126, 132, 149, 158–59, 175
  and FD as orator, 158–59
  FD views about, 149, 158–59, 175
  of government, 105, 126
  and manumission of slaves, 172, 173

of political parties, 126
of religion, 95, 96–97, 103, 114–15, 119,
    121–22, 149
and slavery, 95, 96–97, 103, 114–15, 126,
    132, 149, 158–59, 175
Hyppolite, Florvil, 695, 696, 699, 701, 703, 704,
    706, 707–8, 728, 730

Illinois, 507
"I'll Never Get Drunk Again," 290
immediatism, 94–95, 104, 106
immigrants and immigration, 188, 203, 723
Impey, Catherine, 733
Independent, 471
Indiana, 128, 133–35, 507, 512
Indiana State Anti-Slavery Society, 134–35
Indianapolis Freeman, 734
individualism, 560–61, 566
Inferno (Dante), 754
Inuit, 726
Iowa, 507
Ireland, 139, 142–55, 162, 173, 174, 203
    famine in, 150–51, 153
    influence on FD of, 153–54
    Jim Crow in, 154
    slavery compared with poverty in, 149–50,
        151, 152, 173
    See also Great Britain
Irish Americans, 203, 396, 417, 453, 455,
    487
"irrepressible conflict," 271
Isaac, 165, 226
Isaiah, Book of, xvi, 122, 123, 156, 157–58,
    190, 219, 228, 229, 235, 237, 242, 247,
    259, 272, 287, 311–12, 360, 421, 434, 515,
    516, 639, 681, 687, 752
"Is It Right and Wise to Kill a Kidnapper?"
    (Douglass), 246
Israel, 232, 237, 239, 284, 285
Ithaca, N.Y., 123, 269

Jackson, Francis, 166
Jackson, Stonewall, 376, 381
Jacob, 237, 287
Jacobs, Harriet, 418
James, Thomas, 93, 97
Jefferson, Thomas, 376
Jefferson, Thomas (free black), 289
Jenkins, Sandy, 64–65, 68, 72
Jennings, Charlotte, 144
Jennings, Helen, 144
Jennings, Isabel, 144, 169–70, 171, 217
Jennings, Jane, 144
Jennings, Thomas and Anna, 143–44

Jeremiah, Book of, xi, xvi, 33, 157–58, 179, 180,
    197, 200, 219, 228, 229, 237, 242, 259,
    434, 515
Jersey City, N.J., 256
Jerusalem, 228, 229, 284
Jesus Christ, 53, 150, 207, 261, 284, 314, 316,
    637, 757
Jim Crow:
    and Britain-Ireland tour, 141, 149, 154
    on *Cambria,* 141, 177
    in churches, 110, 114–15
    FD on, xii–xiii, 645
    FD's experiences of, 109–11, 542, 581–82
    and FD's self-reliance philosophy, 588
    in Ireland, 154
    in New Bedford, 92–93, 114–15
    and One Hundred Conventions campaign, 136
    on railroads, 109–11
    and religion, 92–93
    Supreme Court support for, 646–47
Jim Crow laws, 269, 303, 730, 757–58
Job, Book of, 39
"John Brown's Body," 309, 393
Johnson, Abraham, 243–45
Johnson, Andrew, 458, 471, 472
    anti-coercive policy of, 480
    Civil Rights Act vetoed by, 479
    FD's criticism of, 476, 477, 482–83, 487
    FD's meeting with, 474–75, 477, 482
    Freedmen's Bureau position offered to FD
        by, 524
Johnson, Augusta, 718
Johnson, Charles, 53
Johnson, David N., 113
Johnson, James Weldon, 688–89, *688,* 735
Johnson, Mary, 87
Johnson, Nathan, 87, 88, 90–91
Johnson, Oliver, 218, 224
John W. Richard (steamer), 85
Joiner, Charles, 190
Joint Committee on Reconstruction, 473, 480
Joshua, Book of, 285
"Jubilee doctrine," 293–94
Judah, 237
Judas, 314
Judkins, Charles, 141
Julian, George, 268

Kagi, John, 301–2, 313–14
Kansas, 264, 272, 274–75, 285, 293, 294–96,
    297, 299, 300
Kansas Exodus (1879), 601–5
Kansas-Nebraska Act (1854), 260, 264, 270,
    274–75, 283, 293

Keita, M. Nzadi, 510, 518
Kellem, Nelly, 25
Kelley, Abby, 106, 108, 120–21, *122*, 123, 124, 128, 129, 136, 184, 187, 217, 218, 285
Kelley, William D., 482, 487
Kennedy farm, 301, 305
Kentucky, 351, 352, 364, 473
Kerr, John Leeds, 163
Kimmel, Michael, 211
Kinealy, Christine, 151, 152
King, Martin Luther, Jr., 421
Knight, Nathaniel, 43
Know-Nothing Party, 287, 323
Koehler, Sylvester Rosa, 451, 510, 516, 517
Ku Klux Klan, 504
    FD on, 522–23, 532
    Grant's suppression of, 522, 536

labor movement, 560
Ladies' Anti-Slavery Society of Rochester, 224, 227, 229–36, 252
Lady of the Lake (Scott), 88
laissez-faire, 425
Lancaster County, Pa., 243–45
Lange, Johannes, 516
Langston, John Mercer, 1, 2, 3, 4, 391, 440, 441, *664*
    and election of 1888, 683–84
    and emancipation anniversary celebrations, 681
    FD's conflicts with, 640, 663, 683, 684
    and Freedmen's Bank, 547, 548
    Hillsdale Fourth of July speech of (1875), 556–57
    and Kansas Exodus, 602
    on "Our National Capital" speech, 591
    on self-reliance, 562
    and slave narrative genre, 621
    as US minister to Haiti, 691
Latimer, George, 124–26, 127
Latimer, Rebecca, 125
Lawrence, Kan., 294
Lawson, Charles, 53–54, 57, 70, 92, 157, 754
Lazarus, 456–57
Lee, Joseph E., 686
Lee, Robert E., 369, 377, 381, 418, 456, 461, 473, 480, 530
Lee's Mill, 11
Légitime, François, 695, 696
Leonard, William, 49
"Lessons of the Hour" (Douglass), 687–88, 736, 740, 741, 743, 746, 747, 749
"Letters from the Old World" (Griffiths), 266–67
Levine, Robert, 249

Lewis, David Levering, 759
Lewis, Edmonia, 672
Lewis, George, 158–59
Lewis, Joseph, 78
Lexington and Concord, Battles of, 244, 309
Liberal Republicans, 534–36
Liberator, 94–97, *96,* 100, 104, 107, 125, 133, 138, 161, 183, 188, 189, 191, 223, 224, 225, 226
Liberia, 370
Liberty Party, 106, 114, 128, 130, 131, 133, 136, 148, 213, 217, 218, 241, 243, 252–53, 268, 270, 274, 276, 311, 322
    See also specific person
Life and Times of Frederick Douglass (Douglass), 13, 42, 96, 112, 244, 264, 272, 280, 281, 284, 295, 306, 310, 384, 411, 462, 465, 485, 619–24, 718, 727, 741
    on Anna Murray Douglass, 633–34
    on Civil Rights Cases, 647–48
    on Eastern Shore visits, 595, 596, 624–27
    on election of 1888, 684
    on Europe trip (1886), 668, 671
    on Freedmen's Bank, 549
    illustrations in, 622–23
    and James Weldon Johnson, 688
    on post-Reconstruction years, 661–62
    publication of, 619
    on Reconstruction Washington, 524
    revision of, 713
    Ruffin's introduction for, 623–24
    self-image in, 620–21
    on slavery, 621–22
    writing of, 605, 619–20, 712
Limerick, Ireland, 149
Lincoln, Abraham, 1, 4, 5–6, 40, 44, 239, 321–27, 333–34, *462,* 754
    assassination of, 9, 438, 460–61, *462*–63, 479
    colonization plans of, 370–73, 374–75, 379, 380, 382
    as constitutionalists, 363
    in election of 1864, 428, 429–30, 431, 432, 437, 438, 439, 443, 444–46, 452, 453, 472
    emancipation plan of, 363–64, 366–67, 377–78
    Emancipation Proclamation issued by, 357, 374, 378–79, 383, 397
    FD compared to, 761
    FD's Brooklyn tribute speech on, 730–32
    FD's first meeting with, 408–10
    FD's meeting on Reconstruction with, 436–37
    and FD's self-reliance philosophy, 564–65
    FD's softening of ire toward, 435
    first inaugural of, 336–37

Frémont's emancipation edict revoked by, 352–54
Gettysburg Address of, 414–15
habeas corpus suspended by, 380
and killing of black prisoners, 405–6
millennialism of, 432–34
and movement to drop from Republican ticket, 429–30
and Niagara peace conference, 443
party unity desired by, 429
and pay of black soldiers, 403
Reconstruction as envisioned by, 430–31, 435–37
Second Inaugural Address of, 433, 458–60, 461–62
second inauguration of, 457–59
slavery opposed by, 363
Ten-Percent Plan of, 431
and *Trent* Affair, 358–59
Lincoln (Ray), 4
Lincoln, Robert, 644
Lind, Michael, xiii–xiv
Lippincott, Sara Jane, *see* Greenwood, Grace
literacy, of slaves, 340
"Literary Notices" (Griffiths), 206
Liverpool, England, 140, 142, 175, 177, 282, 309, 319
Lloyd, Daniel, 21–22, 30
Lloyd, Edward, V, 14, 22, 23, 26, 27, 32, 36, 161, 624
Lloyd, Edward, VII, 624
Lloyd, Henry Demarest, 739
Lloyd, William E., 78
Lloyd family, 20, 22, 35
   see also Wye Plantation
Loggins, Vernon, 160
Loguen, Amelia, *see* Douglass, Amelia Loguen
Loguen, Jermain, 299, 440
London, 168–69, 173, 175–77, 204
London Tavern, 175–77
London Committee. *See* British and Foreign Anti-Slavery Society
London Working Men's Association, 173
Longfellow, Henry Wadsworth, 232, 382
Loring, Ellis Gray, 93, 171
Lost Cause ideology, 530–32, 533, 535, 627, 680
Lot's wife, 481–82
Loudin, Frederick Jr.., 734
Louisiana, 8, 431
Lovett, William, 173–74
Lowell, Mass., 127
Lowenthal, E. J., 516
Lowrie, Walter, 171
Luke, Gospel of, 131

Lynch, John Roy, 553, 635, 753
lynchings, xii–xiii, 680, 719–20, 722, 730, 732, 741–44
   1892 statistics for, 717
   see also "Lessons of the Hour" (Douglass)
Lynn, Mass., 30, 62–63, 177
   description of, 112
   farewell to FD in, 139–40
   FD home in, 111–12, 120, 124, 125, 126, 128, 136, 137, 164, 166, 171
   FD speeches in, 108–9, 120
   Jim Crow in, 109–11
   Quakers in, 112
Lynn Record (newspaper), 111

McCann, Colum, 138
McClellan, George B., 359, 362, 368, 377, 379
   in election of 1864, 432, 436, 444
   in Peninsula Campaign, 365
McClintock, Elizabeth, 196
McClintock, Mary Ann, 196
McCune Smith, James, 623
McGowan (ship's captain), 82
Mackey, Thomas J., 655
Magna Carta, 316
Maine, 137
Mahone, William, 683
Malvern Hill, Battle of, 357
"The Man and the Lion" (Aesop fable), 139
Manassas Junction, 357
Manchester, England, 162, 175
Manchester, N.H., 247
Manifest Destiny, 185
manumission of slaves, 171–73
Marks, Mrs., 306
marriage, FD views about, 165–66
"Marseillaise, La," 174
Martin Chuzzlewit (Dickens), 362
Martin, John Sella, 524, 525
Martineau, Harriet, 123, 124
Maryland, 26, 158, 164, 166, 190, 198, 260, 301, 313, 364, 378, 444–45, 446–47, 449, 454
   free Constitution of, 446
Mason, James, 314, 358
Mason Committee, 314–15
Massachusetts, 107, 116, 126, 137, 242–43, 245, 366, 454
   black enlistment in, 391
   See also specific town
Massachusetts Anti-Slavery Society, 100–101
Matthew, Gospel of, 122, 150, 283
Matthews, James C., 663
May, Samuel J., 99, 100, 108

Mayflower, 316
May, Samuel J., 187, 206, 218
Mayo, Isabella Fyvie, 733
Mayo, Katherine, 314
"Meditation on the Divine Will" (Lincoln), 433
Meier, August, 236
media:
  and Britain-Ireland tour, 142, 144–45, 161, 177
  criticisms of FD in, 162–63
  in England, 142
  and FD as orator, 130
  and FD in Scotland, 161
  and FD reputation, 177
  and manumission of FD, 172
  and One Hundred Conventions campaign, 130
  See also specific organization
Melville, Herman, 87, 89, 90, 91, 101, 141, 471
memory, xvii, 24, 30
Memphis, Tenn., race riot in, 483–84, 488
Memphis Free Speech, 717
Mendelssohn, Felix, 753
"Men of Color to Arms!" (Douglass), 385, 392, 393–96, *394*
Messenger, 756
messianic tradition, 236–38
Methodists, 92, 95, 161, 198, 260
Metropolitan AME Church (Washington), 679, 693, 741–44, 749, 753
Mexican-American War, 171, 184–85, 200, 268, 332
Mexico, 271
Michigan, 507
middle class, 123, 256
Middlebury, Vt., 128
Millbury, Mass., 108
millennialism, 207, 236–38, 284–86, 349–50, 389, 419, 432–34, 471
Miller, De Witt, 741
Miller, Orton and Mulligan, 253
Miller, Samuel T., *210*
Miller, William, 207
Mills, Joseph T., 436, 437
Mingo, James, 78
Minkins, Shadrack, 242, 243
Minnesota, 277
minstrels, 317
Mirror of Liberty, 84
miscegenation, 444, 482
Miscegenation: The Theory of the Blending of the Races (Croly and Wakeman), 444
"Mission of the War, The" (Douglass), 415, 416–17, 419–21, 424, 435, 436, 449, 637

Mississippi, 440, 444
Missouri, 270, 277, 294–95, 300, 301, 352–53, 364, 440
Missouri Compromise (1820), 270, 277
Mitchell, Eliza Bailey, 446, 448
Mitchell, James, 59
Mitchell, Mary Douglass, 446
Mitchell, Peter, 57
Mobile Bay, 444
Moby-Dick (Melville), 87, 89, 141
Môle Saint-Nicolas coaling station, 694, 695, 696, 698, 702, 703–6, 709, 730
Monroe, James, 128
Moore, Daniel, 461
moral suasionism, 157, 162–63, 173–75, 207, 214, 249, 252, 304–5
  and Chartist movement, 173, 174, 175
  definition of, 94
  FD speeches/views about, 94, 108, 114, 119, 135, 137, 157, 162–63, 173, 174, 175
  Garnet break with, 131
  as Garrisonian doctrine, 104, 105, 121, 128
  and schisms among AASS/abolitionists, 105, 117–18
morality, and Garrison influence on FD, 96
"Morals of Slavery" (Martineau), 124
Morgenblatt, 267, 338, 387, 419, 452, 511
Morris, Anna Rosine Sprague, 424, 693, 739, 749
  and Douglass house fire, 520
  and FD's second marriage, 650
Morris, Charles S., 693, 739, 748, 750, 757
Morris Island, 400–402, 412, 422
Morton, Oliver P., 2, 485
Moses, 94, 285, 300
Mother Bethel AME Church (Philadelphia), 185–86
"Mother of Cedar Hill" (Perry), 632
Motley, John Lothrop, 528
Mott, Abigail, 167, 179, 181–83, 194
Mott, Lucretia, 187, 196
Mott, Lydia, 179, 181–83, 194
Mount Vernon (Washington estate), 513
Mount Zion Church (Charleston), 679–80
mulattos, 222
Mundy, J. M., 573
Murray, Anna, *see* Douglass, Anna Murray
Murray, Bambarra, 79
Murray, Charlotte, 79
Murray, Elizabeth "Lizzy," 79, 386
Murray, Mary, 79
Murray, Perry, 386
Murray, Philip, 79
music, 31–34, 165, 174
Mutual Base Ball Club, 507

"My American Readers and Friends"
(Douglass), 312
My Bondage and My Freedom (Douglass), xviii,
53, 67–68, 251, 253–54, *255*, 257–64, 265,
267, 290–92, 294, 317–19
and FD's Europe trip (1886), 676
on FD's mother, 517–18, 597
on slavery, 621–22
Smith's introduction for, 623
Myers, Stephen A., 325
"My Mother as I Recall Her" (Sprague), 631–33
Mystery, 191

Nantucket, FD speeches in, 98–100, 119–20
*Narrative of the Life of Frederick Douglass, an
American Slave* (Douglass), xiv, 13, 24,
32, 47, 53, 63, 85, 137, 158, 161–62, 169,
251, 253, 261, 447
appendix in, 155
and Britain-Ireland tour, 142, 143, 145,
146–47, 155, 158, 160, 161–62, 169
Drew comments about, 155
and fame of FD, 138
on FD's mother, 517, 597
and FD as orator, 149
and FD financial affairs, 169
and FD paternity, 176
financial gains from, 146, 148, 149, 154
and Fred Bailey story, 161
and Garrison endorsement of FD, 99–100
Garrison preface for, 138–39
Irish editions of, 143, 146–47, 148, 154,
161–62
Nelson comments about, 155
Phillips endorsement of, 138–39
prison metaphors in, 596
and "Send Back the Money" campaign, 160
Thompson challenge to veracity of, 161–62
Nassau, 248–49
National Anti-Slavery Standard, 189, 225, 256,
432, 483
National Colored Convention, 188–89
National Convention of Colored Men (1883),
640, 643–46
National Council of Women, 752, 753
National Hall, 305
National League, 508
National Museum of African American
History and Culture, xi
National Republican, FD's 1875 letter to, 554–55
National Union Convention, 484–87
Native Americans, 486, 726
nativists, 274, 276
Natural History of Man (Prichard), 11

natural rights, xiii, xvii, 26, 53, 57, 97, 132, 180,
198–99, 215, 233–34, 245, 254, 262
Negro's and Indians Advocate (Godwyn), 556
Nehemiah, Book of, 283
Nell, William Cooper, 188, 191, 222, 224–25,
382, 561
Nelson, Isaac, 155
New Bedford, Mass., 85, 166, 171, 225
abolitionist conventions in, 119
black community in, 87–88
FD as preacher in, 93–94
FD as resident of, 87, 89–101, 109, 111–12, 166
FD autobiographical writing about, 89, 90–91
FD farewell to, 139
FD jobs in, 91–92
FD religious life in, 92–94
FD speeches in, 97–98, 115
fugitive slaves in, 89
Garrison in, 96, 98
Jim Crow in, 92–93, 114–15
Latimer meetings in, 125–26
modern conveniences in, 91
population of, 89
Quakers in, 91
religion in, 92–94
whaling industry in, 89–90, *90,* 91
Newcastle, England, 170–71, 317
New England, 295–96, 299, 390
New England Convention, 171
New Era, 524–25
New Hampshire:
FD tours in, 107, 137
See also specific town
New Jersey, 333, 366
New National Era, 521, 522, 525, 529–33, 539,
544–45, 549–50
New Orleans, La.:
"Battle of Liberty Place" in, 553
1866 riot in, 483, 484, 488
New Orleans Picayune, 756
New York, 120, 121–24, 128, 182, 188, 254, 269,
324–26, 366, 392
New York Central Railway, 123
New York, N.Y., 83–84, 116–17, 127, 179–81,
202–5, 254–55, 272–73, 306, 324, 508
New York Express, 162
New York Globe, 204–5
New York Herald, 162–63, 202, 305
New York Independent, 485
New York Post, 349
New York State Assembly, 182
New York State Suffrage Association, 325–26
New York Sun, 181
New York Times, 311, 755

New York Tribune, 162, 239, 260, 273, 299, 754, 756
New York Vigilance Committee, 83–84
New York World, 326, 444, 475
Newcastle, England, FD in, 170–71
Noah, 447, 482
Noah's Ark, 445, 447, 462, 488
nonresistance (pacifism):
    and Britain-Ireland tour, 147
    Colored Convention debate about, 131–33
    and FD on AASS travel circuit, 108
    FD views about, 118, 119, 134, 167
    Garnet views about, 132
    and Garrison-FD relationship, 119
    as Garrisonian doctrine, 104, 118, 121
    and One Hundred Conventions campaign, 134
North, Edward, 76
North American Review, 471, 719
North Carolina, 440
North Elba, N.Y., 288–89, 293, 299
North Star, 178, 188–200, 204, 206–8, 210, 213, 216–17, 221, 229, 257, 268, 280, 291, 747
Norton, Charles Eliot, 382
Nova Scotia, 309

Oak and Ivy (Dunbar), 735
Oakes, James, 215, 322, 352
Obama, Barack, xi–xii, 5
Oberlin Tent, 187
O'Connell, Daniel, 143
Odd Fellows, 193, 331
O'dell, Katy, 653
Ohio, 187–88, 192, 268, 269, 281, 507, 512
    and One Hundred Conventions campaign, 128, 133, 135
Old Barney (slave), 23, 27
Old Congregational Meeting House (New Bedford), Garrison speech at, 96
Old Testament, xv–xvi, 157, 165, 197, 228–38, 239, 258–59, 263, 265–66, 283–85, 316
    see also specific books
Olmsted, Frederick Law, 589
One Hundred Conventions, 128–36, 186
Oneida, N.Y., 207
Orr, James L., 484
Oscar, H., 381
Othello (Shakespeare), 162, 220, 465–67, *466*
Ottman, S., 230
"Our National Capital" (Douglass), 588–91
overseers, 23, 24–26

pacifism, 77
    See also nonresistance
Paine, Thomas, 231

Palmerston, Henry John Temple, 358
Pan-Africanism, 730, 731
Panama, 370, 373, 380
Pan-Americanism, 695–96
panic of 1819, 207
panic of 1857, 295–96
Panic of 1873, 546–47, 552, 560
Panic of 1893, 732, 733
Parker, Theodore, 296
Parker, Warren S., *168*
Parker, William, 243–45, 287
Parkman, Francis, 382
Parliament, British, 173
Passover, 231
patriotism, definition of, 162
Paterson, N.J., 306
Paul, St., 281
Payne, Daniel Alexander, 686
Peabody family, 91–92
Peace Democrats, 443, 453
Peck, Francis Jesse, 721
Pendleton, Ind., 163
    attack on FD in, 133–34, 163
    One Hundred Conventions campaign in, 133–34
Penn, I. Garland, 733, 750
Pennington, James W. C., 84–85, *85,* 291
Pennsylvania, 128, 135–36, 137, 163, 70, 499
Pennsylvania Freeman, 225
Pennsylvania Society for Promoting the Abolition of Slavery, 555–56
"People's Charter" (1838), 173
perfectionism, 105–6, 121
Perkins, William, 52
Perry, Fredericka Sprague, 610–12, 631
personal liberty law, Massachusetts, 126
Peterboro, N.Y., 208, 211
Petersburg, Siege of, 422
Peterson, Carla, 249
Philadelphia, Pa., 136, 184–86, 204, 305–6, 313–14, 373, 404, 508
Philadelphia Pythons, 507
philanthropists, FD views about, 152
Phillips, Wendell, 108, 136, 178, 179, 218, 222, 285, 291, 330, 363, 397, 398, 430
    endorsement of FD *Narrative* by, 138–39
    Faneuil Hall speech of, 125
    Fourteenth Amendment opposed by, 483
    made head of Anti-Slavery Society, 469
phrenology, 256
Pierce, Franklin, 245
"pig's foot" joke, 158
Pillsbury, Parker, 98, 100, 136, 221–22, 312–13

Pinchback, P. B. S., 574–75, 602
Pinckney, Alexander, 243–45
Pinckney, Darryl, 621
Pitts, Frances, 654
Pitts, Helen, *see* Douglass, Helen Pitts
Pitts, Jane Wells, 653
Pitts, Jennie, *653*
Pittsburgh, Pa, 186, 191, 268
Pledge of Allegiance, 727
Plessy v. Ferguson, 646
Plug Uglies, 203
Plumbly, Rush, 225
"Poets to Come" (Whitman), 263
Poindexter, James, 582
Point Lookout, 422
politics:
    abolitionists as threat to, 123
    and Britain-Ireland tour, 141
    and FD on AASS travel circuit, 108
    FD views about, 135–36
    and Garrisonian doctrine, 104, 121
    and hypocrisy of political parties, 126
    and schisms within AASS, 117–18
    in Scotland, 156
poll tax, 94
Pomeroy, Samuel, 373–74, 376, 380, 407, 408
Poor Laws, British, 173
"popular sovereignty," 293
Port Byron, N.Y., AASS speakers in, 123
Porter, John, 521
Porter, John and Mary, 221, 265
Porter, Maria G., 229
Porter, Mary, 521
Porter, Samuel, 600
Porter, Samuel D., 221, 243, 306
Port Hudson, Battle of, 441
Post, Amy, 121, 130, 188, 190, 196, 306, 307,
    418, 468, *582*
    and Anna Douglass's death, 634
    and Douglass house fire, 521
    and Sojourner Truth, 572
Post, Isaac, 121, 130, 188, 194, 206, 306
    and Anna Douglass's death, 634
    and Douglass house fire, 521
Pottawatomie Creek massacre (1856), 294–95
poverty:
    FD views about, 90–91
    of Irish, 149–51, 152, 153, 173
"Practical Illustration of the Fugitive Slave
    Law," *241*
prayer, FD views about, 120
Preliminary Emancipation Proclamation,
    378–79, 380, 381
Presbyterians, 121, 156–57, 162, 284

press:
    on Anna Murray Douglass's death, 629–30
    on Assing's suicide, 659
    on black leadership conflicts, 641–42, 663,
      683
    on Civil Rights Cases, 648
    on Douglass house fire, 520
    on election of 1872, 535
    on election of 1876, 577–78
    on election of 1880, 617, *618*
    on election of 1884, 661
    on election of 1888, 683, 684–85
    on emancipation anniversary celebrations,
      635, 637
    on FD's commemorative speeches, 556
    on FD's District of Columbia marshal
      position, 584–86, *586*
    on FD's Eastern Shore visits, 593, 594, 597,
      598
    on FD's emancipation anniversary
      celebration address (1888), 681–82
    on FD's Europe trip (1886), 669, 675
    on FD's Hillsdale Fourth of July speech,
      558–59
    on FD's retirement, 663–64, 666
    on FD's second marriage, 650–51, 652, 653,
      667
    on FD's Southern speaking tours, 686
    on FD's speaking style, 527
    on Freedmen's Bank, 548
    on Haiti, 692–94, *694*, 701–2, 705, 707, 708
    on nepotism accusations, 627–28
    on "Our National Capital" speech, 591
    on Sprague lawsuit, 655, 656
    on violence against African Americans, 553,
      554–55
Preston, Charles, 725
Preston, Dickson, 593
Price's shipyard, 77
Prince (slave), 184
private property, Collins views about, 129
"Proclamation of Amnesty and
    Reconstruction," 430
progress, 389–91
propaganda, 198, 205, 244
property requirements, 325–26
Protestants, 281, 284
Proverbs, Book of, 269–70
Providence, R.I., 212
"Provisional Constitution," 296–98
Psalm 91, 420
Psalm 137, 233
"Psalm of Life, A" (Longfellow), 232
Psalms, 100, 157

Puritans, 157, 229

Purvis, Charles B., 547, 753

Purvis, Robert, 218, 220–21, 222, 224, 605
    and FD's second marriage, 651

Putnam, Frederic Ward, 726

Quakers, 91, 112, 121, 130, 131, 134, 164, 170,
        178, 196, 203
    See also specific person

Quarles, Benjamin, 548

Queens, N.Y., 373

Queen Street Hall, 311

Quincy, Edmund, 98, 108, 113

Quinn Chapel, 729

racism:
    and FD as orator, 157
    FD views about, 118, 120, 154
    and Garrisonian doctrine, 104

Radical Abolition Party, 275–76, 293–94, 322

Radical Republicans, 429–30, 472, 478
    Reconstruction plan of, 431, 471, 477

railroads, 109–11, 123, 124
    See also specific railroad

Ramses, king of Egypt, 11

Ram's Horn, 181, 288

Rankin, J. E., 745, 753–54

rape, 200
    of black women during slavery, 742
    of white women by blacks, as excuse for
        lynchings, 719–20, 741–42

Ray, Cordelia, 4

Raymond, Robert R., 230

*Reason Why the Colored American Is Not in the
        World's Columbian Exposition*, 733–34, 737

Rebekah, 165

Reconstruction, xii, xiii, 4, 8, 416, 454, 508
    "Battle of Liberty Place" in, 553
    counterrevolution against, 8–9
    and election of 1868, 524
    and election of 1872, 533, 534–35, 542
    and election of 1874, 549, 551–52
    and election of 1876, 574–78, 579–80
    ex-Confedereates and, 472–73
    FD on problems of, 424–28, 430, 431–32,
        435–37, 454, 470–71, 473, 476–77, 479–80,
        481, 503
    and FD's self-reliance philosophy, 560–68,
        578
    and Freedmen's Bank, 545–46, 548, 549, 558
    Lincoln's vision of, 430–31, 435–37
    and Panic of 1873, 546–47, 552
    Radical plan for, 431, 471, 477
    and Republican Party, 532–34, 549, 553
    retreat from, 578, 579–80, 582–83, 599
    violence against African Americans during,
        522–23, 532, 537, 551, 552–55, 570, 578,
        579

Redeemers, 477

Redpath, James, 315, 328, 337

Reed, James E., 750, 763

Refuge of Oppression (Douglass column), 223

religion:
    and abolitionism, 96–97, 123
    and Britain-Ireland tour, 141, 149, 150,
        152–53, 155
    and FD as preacher in New Bedford, 93–94
    FD views about, 149, 150, 152–53, 154, 155
    and Garrisonian doctrine, 105
    hypocrisy of, 95, 96–97, 103, 114–15, 119,
        121–22, 149
    and Jim Crow, 92–93
    in New Bedford, 92–94
    role in FD life of, 92–94
    in Scotland, 156–59
    See also Bible; churches; clergy; *specific
        person, church, or denomination*

Remond, Charles Lenox, 178, 183, 218, 220–21,
        220, 285, 382, 391
    and Collins-FD dispute, 129
    and Colored Convention of Black Leaders
        (Buffalo, 1843), 131
    and disagreements among abolitionists, 135
    Faneuil Hall speech of, 123
    and FD on AASS travel circuit, 108
    in Ireland, 145
    and One Hundred Conventions campaign,
        128, 129–30, 131, 133, 135

Republican National Convention (1892), 717

Republican Party, 214, 252–53, 260, 264, 265, 271,
        274, 275, 276–77, 301, 303, 304, 314–15,
        316–17, 321–27, 332, 333, 722–24
    and black leadership conflicts, 635, 663
    and corruption, 535–36, 551–52, 613, 615
    in election of 1868, 524
    in election of 1872, 533, 534–36
    in election of 1874, 549, 552
    in election of 1876, 574–77
    in election of 1880, 613–14, 615
    in election of 1884, 660
    in election of 1888, 682–83
    Liberal faction of, 534–35
    and National Convention of Colored Men,
        644
    in post-Reconstruction years, 601
    and Reconstruction, 532–34, 549, 553
    and Santo Domingo annexation project, 537
    Stalwart faction of, 613, 614

"Resistance to Blood-Houndism" (Douglass), 241–42
Revelation, Book of, 183, 185
Revels, Hiram, 507
Revolution, 490
revolutions of 1848, 197, 240
Rhode Island, 107, 126, 137
    See also specific town
Richardson, Anna, 170–71, 172, 177, 668
Richardson, Ellen, 170, 171, 668, 718
Richetson's candle works, 91
Richmond, Va., 367, 508
Richmond's brass foundry, 91
Right and Wrong Among the Abolitionists (Collins), 107
rights:
    of African Americans, 131
    of working men, 134
    See also natural rights; voting rights
Riotte, C. N., 516
Rise of the Dutch Republic (Motley), 528
Roberts, Ned, 15
Robinson, Ezekiel, 461
Rochester, N.Y., 121–22, 129–30
    FD's homes in, 121, 130, 190, 194–98, 204–8, 213, 217–19, 229–36, *230,* 243, 253, 264–65, 268, 270, 272, 279, 291, 292, 295, 296–99, 301, 306–7, 313, 319, 320, 324, 326, 333–34
    and Lincoln assassination, 460–61, 462–63
Rockman, Seth, 80
Rockwell, C. H., 698
Rogers, Nathaniel, 102, 103, 120
Rolles, Henry, 78
Rolles, Isaac, 81
Root, Samuel, *489*
R. T. Davis Milling Company, 735
Ruffin, George, 623–24
Ruggles, David, 83–84, 85–86, 87, 242
Russell, Mrs., 314
Rynders, Isaiah, 202–5

Sabbath schools, 101, 260
"sailing ships" metaphor, FD, 139
"sailor's protection," 81
St. Catharines, Ontario, 299
St. Croix, 370
Saint Domingue, *see* Haiti
St. Michaels, Md., 55–56, 59, 90
Sally Lloyd (sloop), 35, 36
Sam (slave), 131
Samaná peninsula, 538, 539–40
"Sambo's Mistakes" (Brown), 288, 289
Samson, 309

Sanborn, Franklin B., 296, 313–14, 315, 328
Sanderson, Jeremiah Burke, 170
Santo Domingo annexation project, 536–37, 538–45, *541,* 692
Satan, 316
scarlet fever, 183
Schoelcher, Victor, 670
Schouler, William, 399
Schurz, Carl, 453
scientific racism, 376
Scotland:
    and Britain-Ireland tour, 156–63, *160,* 166–68
    FD in, 146, 152, 154–55, 156–63, *160,* 166–68
    fund-raising for, 156–57, 158
    media in, 161
    religion in, 156–59
    "Send Back the Money" campaign in, 158, 159–60
    See also Great Britain
Scott, Charlotte, 2
Scott, Walter, *160,* 167, 267
script system, 730
Sea of Poppies (Ghosh), 78
Sears, Amanda, 485
secession crisis, 310–11, 326–34
Second Coming, 284
Second Confiscation Act, 365, 366
Second Street AME Zion Church (New Bedford), 97, 98
"secret six," 296, 315
Seddon, James A., 404
segregation. *See* Jim Crow
"Self-Made Men" (Douglass), 470–71, 528, 564–68, 597, 600–601, 623, 680, 716
self-protection societies, 243–45
self-reliance, FD's doctrine of, xiii, xiv, 560–68, 716, 724, 740, 757, 758, 761
    American Anti-Slavery Society speech on, 563–64
    and Burns, 567–68
    criticisms of, 599–600
    and election of 1876, 578
    Hillsdale Fourth of July speech on, 557–58
    and individualism, 560–61, 566
    and Ruffin, 623
    "Self-Made Men" on, 528, 564–68, 597, 600–601, 623, 680
    and slave narrative genre, 561–62, 621
    Tennessee Colored Agricultural and Mechanical Association address on, 561
    West on, 588
Senate, US, 313, 314–15, 319–20
    Fourteenth Amendment passed in, 480
    Thirteenth Amendment passed in, 443

"Send Back the Money" campaign, 158, 159–60
Seneca County Courier, 196
Seneca Falls convention (1848), 196–97, 488
Sermon on the Mount, 96
Serrington, William, 93, 97
Seven Days, Battle of the, 365
Seven Pines, Battle of, 357
"Seventh Annual Clam Bake" (1860), 321
Sevier, William, 25
Sewall, May Wright, 752, 753
Seward, William H., 271, 314–15, 321, 409, 443
Sewell, Richard, 322
Shakespeare, William, xi, 162, 220, 240, 247,
    465–67
Sharp Street AME Church (Baltimore), 79
Shaw, Francis George, 397
Shaw, Lemuel, 125
Shaw, Robert Gould, 397–98, 401, 402
Shaw, Sarah Blake, 397
Sheffield, England, 175
Shenandoah Valley, 444
Shepherd, Alexander, 589
Sherman, John, 2, 614, 682, 753
Sherman, William, 436–37, 456
Shiloh, Battle of, 357, 366
Shiloh Presbyterian Church, 248, 289–90, 291
Shriver, Donald W., Jr., 361
Sigel, Franz, 538
Sims, Thomas, 242–43
sin, slavery/slaveholding as, 94–95, 126
"Sitting Bull's Cabin" (Columbian Exposition),
    726
"Situation of the War, The" (Douglass), 366
Sixth Avenue Railroad, 290
Slade, William, 524
Slaughter-House Cases, 646
slave breakers, 59–66
slave catchers, 83, 240–42, 245–47, 251, 282, 290
"slave churches," 158
slaveholders, 141, 161–62, 190–91, 198–99,
    241–47, 251, 253, 259, 260–63, 272–73,
    277–79, 300, 307, 327, 329
    mentality of, 67–68
    as slavery as sin, 94–95
    wealth of, 157
"Slaveholder's Rebellion, The" (Douglass),
    367–68
"Slaveholder's Sermon" (Douglass), 114–15,
    126–27, 130, 135, 137, 149, 162, 184, 212
slave narratives, 158, 161–62, 169, 176, 250,
    251, 253, 261, 561–62, 621
    see also specific works
slave rebellions, 197–98, 243–45, 248–51,
    260–63, 282, 287–88

slavery, 6, 176, 231, 264, 279, 330
    black progress since, 737
    British workers compared with, 174–75
    compromise in, 185, 197–98, 215, 270, 273,
        323, 332–34
    divine law as opposed to, 235, 237, 278–79,
        283–87, 294, 323, 324
    expansion of, 185, 194, 200, 214, 264, 271,
        273, 275–76, 277, 294–96, 323
    FD as symbol of, 104, 109, 118, 119, 125,
        127, 137, 175–76
    FD views about, 149, 176
    Frederick Douglass's introduction to the
        realities of, 19–20
    freedom from, 171–73, 226, 264, 271, 280,
        289–90, 333–34
    Haiti and dangers of, 730
    history of, 183–84, 272, 324
    hypocrisy about, 95, 96–97, 103, 114–15,
        126, 132, 149, 158–59, 175
    immorality of, 215, 221–23, 242, 246, 264,
        272, 274, 278–79, 283, 316
    "impudence" as crime in, 25
    Irish compared with, 149–50, 151, 152, 173
    legality of, 233–34
    Lincoln's assassination and, 732
    and manumission of slaves, 171–73
    as piracy, 242, 270
    property rights in, 172, 179–80, 244–45,
        248–49, 261, 277–79, 282
    religious hypocrisy of, 58–59, 60, 157, 175,
        185, 198, 200, 212, 226, 234–35, 316
    resistance to, 238–39, 242, 283, 284–86, 300,
        323–24, 330–32
    sexual exploitation of women in, 345, 742
    as sin, 94–95, 126
    "societies with slaves" vs. "slave societies"
        in, 20
    as theme of FD's life, 759–60
    Thirteenth Amendment and, 443, 453–54,
        474, 478
    violence in, 14–17, 23, 24–27
    violent opposition to, 240–50, 254, 262, 271,
        274, 279, 281, 282–83, 289–90, 304–5,
        328–30, 334
    westward expansion of, 49
    white supremacy in, 238–40
    white workers alliance with, 173–74
    See also specific person, organization, or
        topic
slaves:
    auctions of, 159, 198–99, 229
    baptism of, 390
    Columbian Exposition and, 714, 737–38

escape into Union lines of, 350–51, 355–56, 379, 381, 422

escape network for (Underground Railroad), 243–45, 250, 294, 296, 298, 302

fugitive, 71–72, 88, 89, 161–62, 186, 190, 202, 214, 223, 231, 234, 240–45, 249–51, 255, 262–63, 268, 270, 273, 277–79, 282, 286, 289, 290, 298, 300, 302, 304, 312, 316, 323, 327, 332

literacy of, 340

murder of, 26

music of, 31–34

sales of, 159, 163–64, 198–99, 229, 240

whites as fathers of, 13–14

See also specific person

Slaves in Barbary: A Drama in Two Acts (Everett), 45

slave trade, 7, 51, 73–74, 183–84, 234, 240, 250, 327

slavocracy, 183–84, 198–200, 272–74, 323

Slidell, John, 358

Smalls, Robert, 399, 635

Smith, A. P., 373

Smith, Gerrit, 191, 202, 207, 209, 211, 213, 215–16, *216*, 219, 221, 222, 236, 238, 243–44, 252, 257, 265, 267, 268, 270, 275, 276, 285, 288–89, 296, 322, 358, 385, 393, 413, 430

FD given money by, 501

Fourteenth Amendment opposed by, 483

Smith, Howard S., 661

Smith, James McCune, 95, 116–17, *117*, 252, 254–60, 267, 285, 286, 287, 288, 289, 293–94, 303, 325, 413, 440

Smith, Peter, 207

Smith, Samuel, 743

Smith, Stephen, 298

Smith, Wealtha, 208

Smyth, Thomas, 162

Social Darwinism, 425

Society in America (Martineau), 124

Somerset case (1772), 184

"Song of Myself" (Whitman), 219

Sons of Veterans, 753

Souls of Black Folk, The (Du Bois), 759

sound money, 732

"Sources of Danger to the Republic" (Douglass), 476

South America, 271, 330–31

South Carolina, 8, 327

Southern Horrors (Wells), 722

South Mountain, 377

Southworth, Albert Sands, *189*

Spelman, J. J., 495

Sperry, James, 230

Spooner, Lysander, 214

Spotsylvania, Battle of, 422

Sprague, Alice:
  death of, 569–70
  and Douglass house fire, 520

Sprague, Anna Rosine, *see* Morris, Anna Rosine Sprague

Sprague, Estelle, 748, 749, 754

Sprague, Fredericka, 749

Sprague, Harriet "Hattie," 749, 754
  and Douglass house fire, 520

Sprague, Louisa, 628–29, 650, 655–56

Sprague, Nathan, 421–22, 423–24, *506*, 739, 749, 754
  Assing's criticism of, 513–14
  and black leadership conflicts, 683
  Charles's dispute with, 50, 497–98, 500, 505–7, 508
  and Douglass house fire, 520, 521
  FD's loan to, 498–99
  financial difficulties, 570
  lawsuit against FD, 655–56
  in marital separations, 500–502
  and *New National Era,* 550

Sprague, Rosetta Douglass, 84, 166, 179, 181, 194, 212, 301, 319, *338*, 386–87, 424, 450, 477, 519, 734, 739, 748
  birth of, 92
  Cedar Hill housekeeping duties of, 628–29
  childhood/youth of, 94, 101, 109, 112, 140
  and Douglass house fire, 520
  education of, 167
  FD relationship with, 140
  in family disputes, 497–98, 500–503, 505, 508–9
  FD's correspondence with, 569–70
  and FD's Freedmen's Bank presidency, 547
  FD's loan to, 498–99
  and FD's second marriage, 650
  and FD tour of Britain and Ireland, 140, 163, 170
  financial difficulties of, 570
  Haiti trip planned by, 338–39
  in Lynn, 111
  in marital separations, 500–502
  marriage of, 421–22
  and mother's death, 629, 631–33
  and nepotism accusations, 627, 628
  in New Bedford, 92, 94, 101, 109, 112
  and Sprague lawsuit, 656

Sprague, Stella, and Douglass house fire, 520

Sprigg, Samuel, 421

Springfield, Mass., 280–82

Springfield Republican, 365
Spring Street AME Zion Church (Rochester),
  333–34, 342, 345, 347, 355, 445, 446
Stanley (black sailor), 81, 82
Stanton, Edwin, 391, 403, 407, 410
Stanton, Elizabeth Cady, 113–14, 196, 488–91,
  492–93, *492,* 717–18
Stanton, Theodore, 670
states' rights, 331
Statue of the Republic, 725–26
Stauffer, John, 568
Stearns, George Luther, 296, 315, 391, 404,
  406, 410
Stebbins, H. H., 754
Stephens, Alexander, 473
Stephens, George F., 403, 413
Stepto, Robert, 88, 249
Stevens, Thaddeus, 479, 483, 484, 485–86
Stewart, Alvan, 128, 214
Stewart, Bill, 76
Stewart, T. McCants, 679
Still, William, 298
Stone, Lucy, 488
Stowe, Harriet Beecher, 218, 226–27, 231,
  247–48, *248,* 249, 270, 382, 736
Strong, George Templeton, 439
Strothers, Henry, 497
Subterranean, 181–83
suffrage:
  and Chartist movement, 173
  in England, 173
  FD views about, 174
  Stanton-FD debate about, 113–14
  universal male, 173
*Suffrage Question in Relation to Colored Voters
  in the State of New York, The,* 325
Sumner, Charles, 322, 384, 429, 473, 476, 477,
  536, 537, 538–39, 542, 555, 605
sunstroke, 261
Supreme Court, US, 2, 277–79
  US, black citizenship decisions of, 117
"Sweet Highland Mary" (Burns), 167
Switch, 181–83
Switzerland, 512
Syracuse, N.Y., 122, 128–29, 241–42, 243,
  293–94
Syracuse convention, 440–44

Tabor, Iowa, 298
Talbot County, Md., xii, 10–11, *10,* 91, 164–65,
  166
Talbot County courthouse, 73, *74*
Talman Building, 190
Tammany Hall, 202

"Tam O'Shanter" (Burns), 167
Taney, Roger B., 277, 278, 356, 481
Tanner, Benjamin T., 635
Tanner, Henry Ossawa, 751
Tappan, Arthur, 106
Tappan, Lewis, 106
Tappanites, 106
tariffs, 723, 732
taxation, 324
Taylor, W. R., 754
Taylor, Zachary, 200
temperance, 143, 153, 175
Ten Commandments, 284
Tennessee, 444, 473
Tennessee Colored Agricultural and
  Mechanical Association, 561
Ten-Percent Plan, 431
Texas, annexation of, 149
Thirteenth Amendment, 443, 453–54, 474, 478
Thirteenth New York Volunteers, 342
Thomas, Clarence, 425
Thomas, Edward M., 371, 372
Thomas, John (FD's assistant), 268
Thomas, John L., 624
Thomas, Lorenzo, 407, 410
Thompson, A. C. C., 161–62
Thompson, George, 158, 168, 171, 173, 174,
  206–7, 316
Thompson, Henry, 294
three-fifths clause, 480
Tilden, Samuel J., 578, 579
Tilton, Theodore, 439, 485, 486, 487, 584–85
  and FD's reunion with Perry, 495, 496
Timbucto settlements, 289
Times (London), 204
Tocqueville, Alexis de, 124
Tóibín, Colm, 151, 153
Tompkins County, N.Y., 269
Toussaint-Louverture, François-Dominique,
  692–93, 728
Tracy, Benjamin F., 702
Train, George Francis, 490
treason, 245
Treasury Department, US, 507
Tremont Temple, 328–29, 382–83, 758–59
Trent Affair, 358–59
"Triumph of Freedom, The" (Garrison), 236
Trodd, Zoe, 622
Trouillot, Michel-Rolph, 707
Troy, N.Y., 188–89, 454
Trumansburg, N.Y., 123
Trumbull, Lyman, 354, 478–79
Truth, Sojourner, 392, 572, 602
Tubman, Harriet, 299, 412

Tuckahoe Neck, Md., 14, 79
Tuckahoe River, 9, 14
Tunnell, William, 747
Turner, Henry McNeal, 736
Turner, Nat, 51–52, 59, 132, 197–98, 201,
    260–61, 287, 395
Tuskegee Institute, 714–16, 739, 749
Twain, Mark, xii, 558, 619
Twelfth Baptist Church (Boston), 383–84
tyranny, 261–62
"Tyrant's Jubilee, The" (Douglass), 279

Uncle Tom's Cabin (Stowe), 218, 226, 231, 247–48,
    249, 270
Underground Railroad, 71, 243–45, 250, 294,
    296, 298, 302
Union Baseball Club, 507
Union League Club, 730
unions, *see* labor movement
Uniontown, 506
United States:
    as corrupt, 176
    democracy in, 248–49
    FD views about, 154, 162, 175–77
    federal government of, 238, 277–79, 294,
        330–31
    founding fathers of, 214, 215
    and Haiti, 70–71, 697–98, 699, 702
    hypocrisy of, 105, 126
    legal system of, 214, 216
    as republic, 228, 235, 262–63, 283
    and Santo Domingo annexation project,
        536–37, 538–45, 692
    territories of, 185, 264, 271, 273
    as theme of FD as orator, 176
United States Colored Troops, 422
United States v. Cruikshank, 578, 646
United States v. Stanley (Civil Rights Cases),
    646, 647–49
universal suffrage, 173
Usher, John, 407, 443
Utica, N.Y., 122, 128

Van Bokkelen, Charles Adrian, 699
Van Buren, Martin, 200
Van Rensselaer, Thomas, 181
Vashon, John, 186
Vermont, 128
Vesey, Denmark, 132, 287, 395
Vicksburg, Miss., 410, 414, 422
Vienna, N.Y., 123
Vierra, Daniel, *255*
Villard, Oswald Garrison, 314
Vincent, Henry, 173

violence:
    Garnet-FD views about, 131–33
    See also specific event
Virginia, 242, 245, 282, 295, 296, 306, 307, 308,
    311, 315, 378, 432, 440, 443, 444
    rumors of slave insurrections in, 381–82
Vogelsang, Peter, 392
voting rights:
    of African Americans, 94, 95, 113–14, 416–17,
        426, 427, 428, 429, 431–32, 442, 444, 454–55,
        469, 475, 480–81, 483, 487, 503
    of FD, 94
    and Garrisonian doctrine, 104
    and poll tax, 94
    Stanton-FD debate about, 113–14
    of women, 113–14, 480, 488–93, 717–18

Wade, Benjamin, 538, 542
Wade-Davis Bill, 431
wages, 426, 427
Wagoner, H. O., 497, 718
Wahlverwandtshaften, Die (Goethe), 512
Waite, Morrison, 5
Wakeman, George, 444
Walzer, Michael, 237–38, 389
Ward, Samuel Ringgold, 183
Ward, T. M. D., 631
War Department, US, 381, 402, 411
    Record and Pensions Bureau of, 747
Warner, Horatio Gates, 523
Washington, Booker T., 600
    "Atlanta Compromise" speech of, 757–58
    FD and Tuskegee Institute, 714–15, 749
    Howells compares with FD, 714
    as speaker at Columbian Exposition, 739
Washington, DC, 214, 323, 418, 508
    1876 parade in, 1–2
    emancipation anniversary celebrations in,
        638–39, 665–66, 680–82
    emancipation in, 364–65
    FD's marshal position in, 583–88, *586*
    home rule issue in, 662
    "Our National Capital" on, 588–91
Washington, George, 232
Washington, Madison, 132, 248–51, 287
Washington Mall, 2
Washington Monument (Baltimore), 37
Washington Nationals, 508
Washington Post, 747, 753
Washington Star, 756
Waugh, Beverly, 52
"Way in Which Frederick Douglass Fights
    Wise of Virginia, The," *308*
Wayland, Francis, III, 603

Wears, Isaiah C., 751
Webb, Hannah, 142
Webb, James A., 142
Webb, Maria, 315–16
Webb, Richard D. 142, 143, 146–47, 160, 162, 169
Webster, Daniel, 110, 113, 135, 249, 290
Weld, Theodore, 119
Wells, Ida B., 170, *723*
   at Columbian Exposition, 733–35, 737, 739–40
   emergence as activist, 717
   eulogy for FD, 755
   and FD's "Lessons of the Hour" speech and, 747
   friendship with FD, 721–22
   speaking tours in England, 733, 747
Wells family, 79–80
Wesleyan Methodist Chapel, 196
West, Cornel, 587, 588
West Africa, 337
Western Reserve, 187, 281
Western Sanitary Commission, 2, 3
West Indies, 197, 221, 286, 287, 323, 390
Weston, Anne, 127
Weston, Maria. *See* Chapman, Maria Weston
West Virginia, 499
Weymouth, Mass., FD speech in, 114
whaling industry, 89–90, *90*, 91
"What the Black Man Wants" (Douglass), 428
Wheatley, Phillis, 562
Whig Party, 190, 239, 269, 274
whips, 23
White, Andrew D., 538, 542
White, Richard Grant, 668
White, Ronald, 432
White, William, 128, 133, 134, 136, 163, 169, 170, 171
White House, 2
"white slaves," 174
white supremacy, 8, 364, 367, 372–73, 376
Whitman, Walt, 154, 219, 263, 346, 567
Whittier, John Greenleaf, 181, 382
Wilberforce, William, 183, 322
Wildcat (schooner), 48
Wilderness, Battle of, 422
"Wild West Show," 726
Wilentz, Sean, 616
Wilk Street Methodist Church, 52
Williams, Fannie Barrier, 727
Williams, George Washington, 572, 635, 640
Williams, Peter A., 321
Williams, S. Laing, 727

"William the Silent" (Douglass), 528–29
Wilmington, Del., 82
Wilmot Proviso, 185
Wilson, Douglas, 414
Wilson, Henry, 315
Wilson, Hiram, 93
Windsor, Ontario, 300
Wise, Henry, 306, 307, *308*, 329
witches, 390
Wolf, Simon, 504
women:
   and AASS, 106, 121
   and abolitionism, 95
   adoration for FD from, 144, 146, 169
   black, 186, 199–200, 203
   equality of, 121
   FD views about, 121
   and Garrisonian doctrine, 104
   rights of, xii, 113–114, 196–97, 211, 221, 480, 488–93, 717–18
   Stanton-FD debate about, 113–14
   and Tappanites, 106
   white, 189, 204–6, 208–12, 221–24, 268
Women's Christian Temperance Union, 614
Women's Loyal League, 419
women's suffrage, 480, 488–93, 717–18
Worcester, Mass., 295–96
Worcester County Anti-Slavery Society, FD speech before, 127
workers:
   slave alliance with white, 173–74
   See also Chartist movement
workers' rights, 134, 173–75, 323
working class, 173–75, 323, 328
Wormley, James, 631
Wormley, W. H. A., 753
Wright, Edward, 718
Wright, Henry C., 158, 172, 174, 221–22
Wye plantation, 10, 11, 14, 17, 20–21, *21*, 22–23, 27, *30*, 35, 36, 259, 624–26
   Denby's murder on, 26
   house servants of, 23
   music on, 31–34
   overseers on, 25

Yale Divinity School, 85
Yates, Richard, 492
Yeatman, James E., 2–3
Young Barney (slave), 23
Youngstown, Ohio, 188
Youth's Companion, 727